STAFFING ORGANIZATIONS
Sixth Edition

Herbert G. Heneman III
University of Wisconsin–Madison

Timothy A. Judge
University of Florida

Mendota House
Middleton, WI

McGraw-Hill
Irwin

Boston   Burr Ridge, IL   Dubuque, IA   New York   San Francisco   St. Louis
Bangkok   Bogotá   Caracas   Kuala Lumpur   Lisbon   London   Madrid   Mexico City
Milan   Montreal   New Delhi   Santiago   Seoul   Singapore   Sydney   Taipei   Toronto

Dedication
To Susan and Jill

McGraw-Hill
Irwin

STAFFING ORGANIZATIONS

Published by Mendota House, Inc., 5621 Mendota Drive, Middleton, WI, 53562, in collaboration with McGraw-Hill/Irwin, a business unit of The McGraw-Hill Companies, Inc., 1221 Avenue of the Americas, New York, NY, 10020. Copyright © 2009, 2006, 2003, 2000, 1997, and 1994 by Mendota House, Inc. All rights reserved. No part of this publication may be reproduced or distributed in any form or by any means, or stored in a database or retrieval system, without the prior written consent of the publisher, including, but not limited to, in any network or other electronic storage or transmission, or broadcast for distance learning.

Some ancillaries, including electronic and print components, may not be available to customers outside the United States.

This book is printed on acid-free paper.

This publication is designed to provide accurate and authoritative information in regard to the subject matter covered. It is sold with the understanding that the publisher is not engaged in rendering legal, accounting, or other professional services. If legal advice or other expert assistance is required, the services of a competent professional should be sought. (FROM A DECLARATION OF PRINCIPLES JOINTLY ADOPTED BY A COMMITTEE OF THE AMERICAN BAR ASSOCIATION AND A COMMITTEE OF PUBLISHERS.)

2 3 4 5 6 7 8 9 0 DOC/DOC 12 11 10 09

ISBN 978-0-07-353027-7
MHID 0-07-353027-1

Publisher: *Paul Ducham*
Managing developmental editor: *Laura Hurst Spell*
Editorial assistant: *Jane Beck*
Executive marketing manager: *Rhonda Seelinger*
Senior project manager: *Susanne Riedell*
Lead production supervisor: *Michael R. McCormick*
Design coordinator: *Joanne Mennemeier*
Lead media project manager: *Cathy L. Tepper*
Cover design: *Matthew Baldwin*
Typeface: *11/12.5 Times Roman*
Compositor: *Kinetic Publishing Services, LLC*
Printer: *R. R. Donnelley*

> # Note to the Instructor:
> Mendota House and McGraw-Hill/Irwin have combined their respective skills to bring *Staffing Organizations* to your classroom. This text is marketed and distributed by McGraw-Hill/Irwin. For assistance in obtaining information or supplementary material, please contact your McGraw-Hill/Irwin sales representative or the customer services division of McGraw-Hill/Irwin at 800-338-3987.

Address orders and customer service questions to:
McGraw-Hill Higher Education
1333 Burr Ridge Parkway
Burr Ridge, IL 60527
1-800-338-3987

Address editorial correspondence to:
Herbert G. Heneman III, President
Mendota House, Inc.
5621 Mendota Drive
Middleton, WI 53562
hheneman@bus.wisc.edu

Library of Congress Cataloging-in-Publication Data

Heneman, Herbert Gerhard, 1944-
    Staffing organizations / Herbert G. Heneman III, Timothy A. Judge—6th ed.
      p. cm.
    Includes index.
    ISBN-13: 978-0-07-353027-7 (alk. paper)
    ISBN-10: 0-07-353027-1 (alk. paper)
    1. Employees—Recruiting. 2. Employee selection. I. Judge, Tim. II. Title.
HF5549.5.R44H46 2009
658.3'11—dc22

                        2008013238

AUTHOR PROFILES

Herbert G. Heneman III is the Dickson-Bascom Professor Emeritus in the Management and Human Resources Department, School of Business, at the University of Wisconsin–Madison. He also serves as a senior researcher in the Wisconsin Center for Educational Research. Herb has been a visiting faculty member at the University of Washington and the University of Florida, and he was the University Distinguished Visiting Professor at the Ohio State University. His research is in the areas of staffing, performance management, compensation, and work motivation. He is currently investigating the design and effectiveness of teacher performance management and compensation systems. Herb is on the board of directors of the Society for Human Resource Management Foundation and serves as its director of research. He is the senior author of three prior textbooks in human resource management. Herb is a Fellow of the Society for Industrial and Organizational Psychology, the American Psychological Association, and the Academy of Management. He is also the recipient of the career achievement award from the Human Resources Division of the Academy of Management.

Timothy A. Judge is the Matherly-McKethan Eminent Scholar, Department of Management, Warrington College of Business, University of Florida. Prior to receiving his PhD at the University of Illinois, Tim was a manager for Kohl's department stores. Tim has also served on the faculties of Cornell University and the University of Iowa. Tim's teaching and research interests are in the areas of personality, leadership and influence behaviors, staffing, and job attitudes. He serves on the editorial review boards of *Journal of Applied Psychology, Personnel Psychology, Human Resource Management Review,* and *International Journal of Selection and Assessment.* Tim is a former program chair for the Society for Industrial and Organizational Psychology and past chair of the Human Resources Division of the Academy of Management. Tim is a Fellow of the American Psychological Association, the Society for Industrial and Organizational Psychology, the American Psychological Society, and the Academy of Management. In 1995 he received the Ernest J. McCormick Award for Distinguished Early Career Contributions from the Society for Industrial and Organizational Psychology. In 2001 he received the Cummings Scholar Award for the Academy of Management.

PREFACE

The sixth edition of *Staffing Organizations* contains many updates and additions that reflect the rapidly evolving terrain of strategic, technological, practical, and legal issues confronting organizations and their staffing systems. As always, we provide considerable updating of our references, found as chapter endnotes. Relative to other editions, we have made more structural changes in the chapters themselves. In Chapter 3, we have added coverage regarding the prevalence of outsourcing, both domestically and internationally. In Chapter 4, we have revamped the introductory section to reflect the changing nature of jobs. To reflect the continuing push for accountability in human resources, both Chapter 5 and Chapter 6 now include tables illustrating metrics for recruiting, and in Chapter 7, we have added a new section on staffing metrics and benchmarks. Three recent trends in initial selection practice have been a heightened focus on résumé fraud and distortion, the appearance of new licensing and certification requirements for many jobs, and heightened attention to background checks. Accordingly, in Chapter 8 we devote considerably more attention to these topics. In Chapter 9, to reflect a rapidly expanding research base, we devote new sections to situational judgment tests and emotional intelligence. In Chapter 12, to reflect some current controversies, we present expanded material on hiring bonuses, reneging on accepted job offers, and enforcement of non-compete agreements. Chapter 13 has been extensively revised to reflect the nearly universal acceptance of human resource information systems in organizations of all sizes.

While we have made many changes and made some significant additions, we have held the length of the book by trimming those areas that have waned in interest or importance (e.g., graphology, accomplishment records, customized skills inventories).

New to the last edition was a section on staffing ethics in the first chapter, a set of staffing ethics guidelines, and, at the end of each chapter, two ethical issues to ponder, discuss, and resolve. We hope you will gain a greater appreciation for the existence of many ethical issues confronting those responsible for staffing in organizations and gain some practice in trying to "do the right thing" in conducting staffing, even though the ethical dilemmas do not have easy or necessarily correct solutions.

We have also made improvements to the case that runs throughout the book, known as the Tanglewood Stores case. The case was developed by Professor John Kammeyer-Mueller at the University of Florida, and we thank him for this great contribution to the book. Tanglewood is depicted as an up-and-coming retailing organization concentrated in the northwest United States. It has expansion plans that will allow it to challenge the many national retail chains. Tanglewood emphasizes an outdoor, Western theme in its merchandise and stores. While most of its staffing policies and practices have been decentralized to the regional or store level, Tanglewood is in the process of centralizing the human resources function, including staffing, in order to promote consistency in practices and presentation of the Tanglewood brand. At the end of chapters 1, 3, 5, 7, 9, 11, and 14 you will encounter a brief description of the specific case relevant to that chapter, along with specific tasks required of you to analyze the case material by applying material directly from the chapter. The full text of the case and your assignment are located online at the Web site *www.mhhe.com/heneman6e*.

Listed below is the chapter structure for the sixth edition, along with additional updates to each chapter.

Chapter One: Staffing Models and Strategy

- New section on short-term (critical skills shortages) vs. long-term (talent management) focus in staffing
- Revamped and updated section on the changing nature of jobs
- New section on outsourcing as a staffing strategy
- Expanded material on the effects of globalization on staffing strategies
- New material on how to select for work engagement

Chapter Two: Legal Compliance

- New material on retaliation
- Revised material on disparate impact, employment advertising, and policies favoring older workers under the Age Discrimination in Employment Act (ADEA)
- New material on favoring older workers
- Updated information on pregnancy discrimination
- Updates on definition of a disability and on reasonable accommodation under the Americans With Disabilities Act (ADA)
- Updates on latest Equal Employment Opportunity Commission (EEOC) initiatives
- New material on Uniformed Services Employment and Reemployment Rights Act (USERRA)
- New material on immigration law (temporary visas)

Chapter Three: Planning

- New section on outsourcing
- Updated information on economic conditions
- Updated discussion of changes in the workforce
- New section on technological changes and their impact on HR planning
- New material on trend analyses
- Updated material on succession planning
- Updated material on legality of affirmative action plans; diversity programs

Chapter Four: Job Analysis and Rewards

- New section on job analysis for teams
- New material on changing nature of jobs and work
- Increased and updated coverage of the Position Analysis Questionnaire (PAQ)
- Updated material on competencies

Chapter Five: External Recruitment

- New table contrasting features of open vs. targeted approaches to recruitment
- More discussion of Internet-based advertising techniques
- Revamped and updated section on electronic databases
- New section on external recruiting metrics
- New summary figure on recruiting metrics across sources
- New material on advertisements
- Updated material on Organizational Web site
- Added discussions on applicant tracking technology
- Added legal coverage of definition of an Internet job applicant; electronic recruitment—visually impaired; video résumés

Chapter Six: Internal Recruitment

- New section on talent management systems
- New section on career development services
- New section on internal recruiting metrics
- New summary figure on internal recruiting metrics
- Updated material on mobility paths
- More discussion of "sequences of development experiences"
- Updated material on mobility policies
- Revised material on requisitions and coordination
- Updated material on closed and open internal recruitment systems

- Revised targeted system of internal recruitment
- Updated material on communication message and medium

Chapter Seven: Measurement

- New section on benchmarks and staffing metrics
- Revised material on validity generalization

Chapter Eight: External Selection I

- Completely revamped, updated, and expanded section on résumés, with a particular focus on résumé fabrications and distortions and tips for applicants to get a résumé noticed
- New and expanded section on licensing and certification requirements
- New material on background checks
- New material on legal issues with disclaimers
- New material on legality of criminal background checks

Chapter Nine: External Selection II

- New section on emotional intelligence
- New section on situational judgment tests
- New section on assessment for team environments
- Extensively updated material on personality tests, including new material on faking, narrow traits, and evaluation of personality tests
- Updated example of cognitive ability testing in the NFL, and on diversity issues in ability testing
- Updates to integrity tests, including reasons for use and objections
- Updated material on structured interviews
- Extensive updates to drug testing, including new exhibit on positive samples

Chapter Ten: Internal Selection

- New material on when logic of prediction breaks down (title inflation)
- Updated material on skills inventory
- Updated material on self-assessments
- Updated material on informal discussions and recommendations
- Revised material on assessment centers, including on typical exercises used
- New material on the glass ceiling

Chapter Eleven: Decision Making

- Extensive updates to compensatory model section
- New material on role of adverse impact in decision making

- Updated and expanded material on how to maximize diversity in weighting selection measures
- New legal material on how to emphasize diversity while avoiding "reverse discrimination"

Chapter Twelve: Final Match

- Extensively revised material on orientation
- New material on special hiring inducements
- New material on restrictions of employees ("clawbacks")
- New material on reneging, including new exhibit
- Updates on socialization
- New material on authorization to work

Chapter Thirteen: Staffing System Management

- Updated material on organizational arrangements
- Updates to jobs in staffing section
- Revised material regarding organizational justice and its impact on policies and procedures
- Updated and expanded material on technology
- Updated material and new exhibit on outsourcing
- Update on staffing process results
- New exhibit on staffing costs
- Update to applicant tracking systems
- New EEO-1 report

Chapter Fourteen: Retention Management

- Updated information on nature of the turnover problem
- Updated discussion of measuring turnover
- Increased coverage of diversity issues and turnover
- Expanded and updated material on what organizations do to prevent turnover
- New discussion of the use of work/life balance programs to improve retention
- Updated guidelines for increasing job satisfaction and retention
- Updated discussion of staffing levels and quality

In preparing this edition we have benefited greatly from the critiques and suggestions of numerous people whose assistance was invaluable. They helped us identify new topics, as well as clarify, rearrange, and delete material. We extend our many thanks to the following individuals:

- Karen Bilda, Cardinal Stritch University
- James Brakefield, Western Illinois University

- Dennis Cockrell, Washington State University
- Randy Dunham, University of Wisconsin–Madison
- Fred Eck, Miami University, Ohio
- Lynda Hartenian, University of Wisconsin–Oshkosh
- Anthony Milanowski, University of Wisconsin–Madison
- Lori Muse, Western Michigan University
- Cynthia Ruzkowski, Illinois State University

We wish to extend a special note of thanks to John Kammeyer-Mueller at the University of Florida for development of the Tanglewood Stores case, revision of several chapters, and preparation of the instructor's manual. We also thank the McGraw-Hill/Irwin publishing team—in particular, John Weimeister, Laura Spell, and Susanne Riedell—for their hard work and continued support of the #1 staffing textbook in the market. Thanks also to John Ferguson and Ruth Ames at Kinetic Publishing Services for their dedicated work in this collaborative undertaking. Finally, we wish to thank you—the students and faculty who use the book. If there is anything we can do to improve your experience with *Staffing Organizations*, please contact us. We would be happy to hear from you.

CONTENTS

STAFFING
ORGANIZATIONS
Sixth Edition

The Staffing Organizations Model

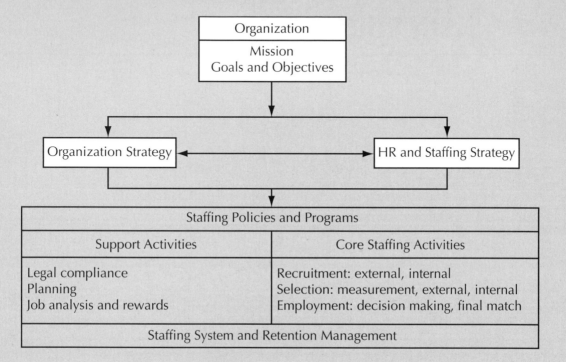

PART ONE

The Nature of Staffing

CHAPTER ONE
Staffing Models and Strategy

CHAPTER ONE

Staffing Models and Strategy

The Nature of Staffing
   The Big Picture
   Definition of Staffing
   Implications of Definition
   Staffing System Examples

Staffing Models
   Staffing Quantity: Levels
   Staffing Quality: Person/Job Match
   Staffing Quality: Person/Organization Match
   Staffing System Components
   Staffing Organizations

Staffing Strategy
   Staffing Levels
   Staffing Quality

Staffing Ethics

Plan for the Book

Summary

Discussion Questions

Ethical Issues

Applications

Tanglewood Stores Case

Staffing is a critical organizational function concerned with the acquisition, deployment, and retention of the organization's workforce. This chapter begins with a look at the nature of staffing. This includes a view of the "big picture" of staffing, followed by a formal definition of staffing and the implications of that definition. Examples of staffing systems for airport security screeners, pharmaceutical industry managers, and direct sales representatives are given.

Five models are then presented to elaborate on and illustrate various facets of staffing. The first model shows how projected workforce head-count requirements and availabilities are compared to determine the appropriate staffing level for the organization. The next two models illustrate staffing quality, which refers to matching a person's qualifications with the requirements of the job or organization. The person/job match model is the foundation of all staffing activities; the person/organization match model shows how person/job matching could extend to how well the person will also fit with the organization. The core staffing components model identifies recruitment, selection, and employment as the three key staffing activities, and it shows that both the organization and the job applicant interact in these activities. The final model, staffing organizations, provides the entire framework for staffing and the structure of this book. It shows that organizations, human resources (HR), and staffing strategy interact to guide the conduct of staffing support activities (legal compliance, planning, job analysis) and core staffing activities (recruitment, selection, employment); employee retention and staffing system management are shown to cut across both types of activities.

Staffing strategy is then explored in detail by identifying and describing a set of 13 strategic staffing decisions that any organization is confronted with. Several of the decisions pertain to staffing levels, and the remainder to staffing quality.

Staffing ethics, which involves moral principles and guidelines for acceptable practice, is discussed next. Several pointers that can serve as guides to ethical staffing conduct are indicated, as are some of the common pressures to ignore these pointers and compromise one's ethical standards. Suggestions for how to handle these pressures are also made.

Finally, the plan for the remainder of the book is presented. The overall structure of the book is shown, along with key features of each chapter.

THE NATURE OF STAFFING

The Big Picture

Organizations are combinations of physical, financial, and human capital. Human capital refers to the knowledge, skill, and ability of people and their motivation to use them successfully on the job. The term "workforce quality" is a way of referring to an organization's human capital. The organization's workforce is thus a stock of human capital it acquires, deploys, and retains in pursuit of organizational outcomes such as profitability, market share, customer satisfaction, and environmental sustainability. Staffing is the organizational function used to build the organization's workforce through such systems as staffing strategy, HR planning, recruitment, selection, employment, and retention.

At the national level, the collective workforces of organizations total over 137 million employees spread across over almost 8 million work sites. The work sites vary considerably in size, with 55% of employees in work sites of fewer than 100 employees, 37% in work sites between 100 and 1,000 employees, and 12% in work sites over 1,000 employees.[1] Each of these work sites used some form of a staffing process to acquire each of these employees. It is estimated that nationally there are more than 4 million new hire transactions each month, or over 50 million annually. This figure does not include the hiring of temporary employees, or internal transfers and promotions, so the total number of staffing transactions is much greater than the 50 million figure.[2] Volumewise, staffing is thus big business for both organizations and job seekers.

For most organizations a workforce is also an expensive proposition and cost of doing business. It is estimated that an average organization's employee cost (wages or salaries and benefits) is over 25% of its total revenue.[3] The percentage is much greater for organizations in labor-intensive industries—the service-providing as opposed to goods-producing industries—such as retail trade, information, financial services, professional and business services, education, health care, and leisure and hospitality. Since service-providing industries now dominate our economy, matters of employee cost and whether the organization is acquiring a high-quality workforce loom large for many organizations.

A shift from viewing employees as just a cost of doing business to valuing employees as human capital that creates competitive advantage for the organization is gradually occurring. Organizations that can deliver superior customer service, for example, much of which is driven by highly knowledgeable employees with fine-tuned customer service skills, have a definite and hopefully long-term "leg up" on their competitors. The competitive advantage derived from such human capital has important financial implications.

Organizations are increasingly recognizing the value creation that can occur through staffing. Quotes from several organization leaders attest to this, as shown in Exhibit 1.1.

Definition of Staffing

The following definition of staffing is offered and will be used throughout this book:

> Staffing is the process of acquiring, deploying, and retaining a workforce of sufficient quantity and quality to create positive impacts on the organization's effectiveness.

EXHIBIT 1.1 **The Importance of Staffing to Organizational Leaders**

"Staffing is absolutely critical to the success of every company. To be competitive in today's economy, companies need the best people to create ideas and execute them for the organization. Without a competent and talented workforce, organizations will stagnate and eventually perish. The right employees are the most important resources of companies today."[4]

Gail Hyland-Savage, chief operating officer
Michaelson, Connor & Bowl—real estate and marketing

"The new economy, very much the Internet and the entrepreneurial opportunities it created, intensified the competition for outstanding people. And we started to grow to a size and scope where it was important for us not only to get outstanding people but also to get them in significant numbers. So the emphasis shifted towards making to people value propositions that were the absolute best they could be."[5]

Rajat Gupta, managing director
McKinsey & Company—consulting

"I think about this in hiring, because our business all comes down to people. . . . In fact, when I'm interviewing a senior job candidate, my biggest worry is how good they are at hiring. I spend at least half the interview on that."[6]

Jeff Bezos, chief executive officer
Amazon.com—Internet merchandising

"The time and money spent on finding good employees at GEMA are considerable, but so is the payoff in terms of workforce creativity. The amount of time from problem to solution is shorter than I have ever seen it in my 17 years at Chrysler."[7]

Mark Dunning, senior manager of human resources
Global Engine Manufacturing Alliance,
Chrysler—automotive manufacturing

"GE's 100-year-plus track record is simply about having the very best people at every single position. That is its No. 1 core competency. No one has better people. No one else's bench strength comes even close. It's that obsession with people that requires all GE leaders to spend a huge amount of their time on human resources processes—recruiting, reviewing, tracking, training, mentoring, succession planning. When I was at GE, I spent over half of my time on people-related issues. When you get the best people, you don't have to worry as much about execution, because they make it happen."[8]

Larry Johnston, chief executive officer
Albertson's—retail grocery

This straightforward definition contains several implications, which are identified and explained next.

Implications of Definition

Acquire, Deploy, Retain

Any organization must have staffing systems that guide the acquisition, deployment, and retention of its workforce. Acquisition activities involve external staffing systems that govern the initial intake of applicants into the organization. It involves planning for the numbers and types of people needed, establishing job requirements in the form of the qualifications or KSAOs (knowledge, skill, ability, and other characteristics) needed to perform the job effectively, establishing the types of rewards the job will provide, conducting external recruitment campaigns, using selection tools to evaluate the KSAOs that applicants possess, deciding which applicants are the most qualified and will receive job offers, and putting together job offers that applicants will hopefully accept.

Deployment refers to the placement of new hires on the actual job they will hold, something that may not be entirely clear at the time of hire, such as the specific work unit or geographic location. Deployment also encompasses guiding the movement of current employees throughout the organization through internal staffing systems that handle promotions, transfers, and new project assignments for employees. Internal staffing systems mimic external staffing systems in many respects, such as planning for promotion and transfer vacancies, establishing job requirements and job rewards, recruiting employees for promotion or transfer opportunities, evaluating employees' qualifications, and making them job offers for the new position.

Retention systems seek to manage the inevitable flow of employees out of the organization. Sometimes these outflows are involuntary on the part of the employee, such as through layoffs or the sale of a business unit to another organization. Other outflows are voluntary in that they are initiated by the employee, such as leaving the organization to take another job (a potentially avoidable turnover by the organization) or leaving the organization to follow one's spouse or partner to a new geographic location (a potentially unavoidable turnover by the organization). Of course, no organization can or should seek to completely eliminate employee outflows, but the organization should try to minimize the types of turnover in which valued employees leave for "greener pastures" elsewhere—namely, voluntary-avoidable turnover. Such turnover can be very costly to the organization. So can turnover due to employee discharges and downsizing. Through various retention strategies and tactics, the organization can combat these types of turnover, seeking to retain those employees it thinks it cannot afford to lose.

Staffing as a Process or System

Staffing is not an event, such as "we hired two people today." Rather, staffing is a process that establishes and governs the flow of people into the organization, within the organization, and out of the organization. There are multiple interconnected systems that organizations use to manage the people flows. These include planning, recruitment, selection, decision making, job offer, and retention systems. Occurrences or actions in one system inevitably affect other systems. If planning activities show a forecasted increase in vacancies relative to historical standards, for example, the recruitment system will need to gear up for generating more applicants than previously, the selection system will have to handle the increased volume of applicants needing to be evaluated in terms of their KSAOs, decisions about job offer receivers may have to be speeded up, and the job offer packages may have to be "sweetened" in order to entice the necessary numbers of needed new hires. Further, steps will have to be taken to try to retain the new hires in order to avoid having to repeat the above experiences in the next staffing cycle.

Quantity and Quality

Staffing the organization requires attention to both the numbers (quantity) and the types (quality) of people brought into, moved within, and retained by the organization. The quantity element refers to having enough head count to conduct business, and the quality element entails having people with the requisite KSAOs so that jobs are performed effectively. It is important to recognize that it is the combination of sufficient quantity and quality of labor that creates a maximally effective staffing system.

Organization Effectiveness

Staffing systems exist, and should be used, to contribute to the attainment of organizational goals such as survival, profitability, and growth. A macro view of staffing like this is often lost or ignored because most of the day-to-day operations of staffing systems involve micro activities that are procedural, transactional, and routine in nature. While these micro activities are essential for staffing systems, they must be viewed within the broader macro context of the positive impacts staffing can have on organization effectiveness. There are many indications of this critical role of staffing.

Leadership talent is at a premium, with very large stakes associated with the new leader acquisition. Sometimes new leadership talent is bought and brought from the outside to hopefully execute a reversal of fortunes for the organization or a business unit within it. Other organizations acquire new leaders to start new business units or ventures that will feed organization growth. The flip side of leadership acquisition is leadership retention. A looming fear for organizations is the unexpected loss of a key leader, particularly to a competitor. The exiting leader carries a wealth of knowledge and skill out of the organization and leaves a hole that may be hard to fill, especially with someone of equal or higher leadership stature. The leader may also take other key employees along, thus increasing the exit impact.

Organizations also recognize that talent hunts and loading up on talent are ways to expand organization value and provide protection from competitors. Such a strategy is particularly effective if the talent is unique and rare in the marketplace, valuable in the anticipated contributions to be made (such as new product creations or design innovations), and difficult for competitors to imitate (such as through training current employees). Talent of this sort can serve as a source of competitive advantage for the organization, hopefully for an extended time period.[9]

Talent acquisition is essential for growth even when it does not have such competitive advantage characteristics. Information technology companies, for example, cannot thrive without talent infusions via staffing. An Internet start-up called edocs, inc., sold Internet bill presentment and payment software. It doubled its employee ranks to over 100 in five months and sought to double that number in another five months. The CEO said this was necessary or "we won't have the resources we need to keep up the growth and go public. You grow fast or you die."[10] Quantity or quality labor shortages can mean lost business opportunities, scaled-back expansion plans, inability to provide critical consumer goods and services, and even threats to organization survival.

Finally, for individual managers, having sufficient numbers and types of employees on board is necessary for the smooth, efficient operation of their work unit. Employee shortages often require disruptive adjustments, such as job reassignments or overtime for current employees. Underqualified employees present special challenges to the manager, such as a need for close supervision and training. Failure of the underqualified to achieve acceptable performance may require termination of employees, a difficult decision to make and implement.

In short, organizations experience and respond to staffing forces and recognize how critical these forces can be to organizational effectiveness. The forces manifest themselves in numerous ways: acquisition of new leaders to change the organization's direction and effectiveness; prevention of key leader losses; use of talent as a source of growth and competitive advantage; shortages of labor—both quantity and quality—that threaten growth and even survival; and the ability of individual managers to effectively run their work units.

Staffing System Examples

Airport Security Screeners

After the terrorist attacks on September 11, 2001, the airline industry was in a state of disarray and possible collapse. Restoration of safe travel was an overriding objective for the industry. In response, Congress created the Transportation Security Agency (TSA). One of its key tasks was to develop from scratch a valid selection system for airport security screeners, and then recruit, hire, and train more than 50,000 new personnel by November 2002 for the country's 429 commercial airports. Special development teams identified the critical work behaviors and associated knowledges and skills for the new job; these included language skills (English), stress tolerance, customer service skills, information and communication technical skills, use of specific equipment and tools, and physical and medical requirements. Assessment methods for gauging knowledge and skills were developed and then put in place. In the selection process, applicants were first prescreened for meeting the minimum qualifications (e.g., U.S. citizen); those who passed attended a daylong assessment process of three sequential phases, each of which the applicant had to pass. In phase one, applicants took a computerized test battery for numerous skills (e.g., customer service, English proficiency, and screener technical aptitudes such as visual observation of X-ray images). In phase two, applicants underwent a structured interview, a physical abilities test, and a medical evaluation. In phase three, applicants underwent a security check (fingerprints, background investigation) and received a hiring offer and job orientation. Recruitment for the job was conducted nationally; job fairs were held in 84 cities. By November 2002 the TSA had processed 1.8 million applicants, tested 340,000 of them, and hired 50,000 screeners. In line with workforce diversity objectives, the resulting workforce was 38% women and 44% ethnic minorities. Subsequent workforce planning led to the redeployment of at least 100 screeners to each of the six busiest airports. In the first year and a half of operation, the screener workforce seized 3.5 million knives, 63,000 box cutters, and 1,700 firearms. Customers gave the screeners an 86% approval rating.

The TSA also contracted with a consulting firm (CPS) to establish and operate 20 local hiring centers, and three mobile hiring teams, in proximity to the nation's largest airports. This permits a close working relationship between the hiring centers and the airport security directors.[11]

Pharmaceutical Industry Managers

Though Pfizer has been recognized by other pharmaceutical companies as a leader in selecting and developing its employees, it recently realized it needed to dramatically overhaul its approach to staffing. Despite the previous success of its selection efforts, "Pfizer was not focused on managing the external environment," said Pfizer executive Chris Altizer. In the past, according to Altizer, Pfizer would project what kind of talent it would need in the next 10 years and then select employees whose skills matched the talent needs. Pfizer now believes that that plan no longer works because there is increased global competition, especially from smaller start-up pharmaceutical firms that can rush products quickly to market. That puts a premium on adaptability.

To address changing market conditions, Pfizer now focuses on hiring employees who can jump from one position to another. In hiring, that means that Pfizer focuses less on job descriptions (i.e., hiring for skills that fit a specific job) and more on general competencies that will translate from job to job. According to

Altizer, Pfizer needs "a person who can switch from working on a heart disease product to one that helps people stop smoking"—in other words, rather than relying on past experience with one product (say, heart disease medications), Pfizer is looking for competencies that will allow the employee to quickly and proficiently move from one venture to the next.[12]

Direct Sales Representatives

Avon Products, Inc., uses multilevel direct selling of its many cosmetic products to its customers. Avon has 25,000 sales representatives who are part of a sales force Avon calls Leadership. The Leadership program was undertaken to reenergize the sales force and boost sales. The sales representatives are independent contractors, not employees. During the selling process and customer exchanges, the representatives use the opportunity to recruit the customers themselves to become sales representatives. The sales representative receives two biweekly checks: one is for sales commissions, and the other is a commission for recruiting and training new sales representatives. The program has helped increase the number of sales representatives by 3%, sales have grown by 4%, and profits have increased 20%. Because the sales representatives are increasing the number of recruits they train and manage, Avon has been able to reduce the number of district managers of the sales representatives. A remaining problem is turnover among the sales representatives, which runs more than 50% annually. To improve retention, Avon began investing $20 million in a series of programs (e.g., training) to help sales representatives increase their sales and thus their desire to remain with Avon.[13]

STAFFING MODELS

Several models depict various elements of staffing. Each of these is presented and described to more fully convey the nature and richness of staffing the organization.

Staffing Quantity: Levels

The quantity or head-count portion of the staffing definition means organizations must be concerned about staffing levels and their adequacy. Exhibit 1.2 shows the basic model. The organization as a whole, as well as each of its units, forecasts workforce quantity requirements (the needed head count) and then compares these to forecasted workforce availabilities (the likely employee head count) to determine its likely staffing level position. If head-count requirements match availabilities, the projection is that the organization will be fully staffed. If requirements exceed availabilities, the organization will be understaffed, and if availabilities exceed requirements, the organization will be overstaffed.

EXHIBIT 1.2 **Staffing Quantity**

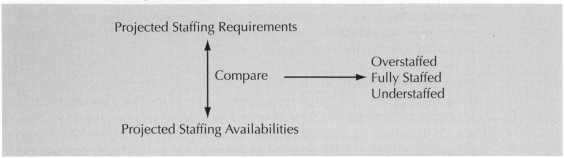

Making such forecasts to determine appropriate staffing levels and then developing specific plans on how to cope with them are the essence of planning. Being understaffed means the organization will have to gear up its staffing efforts, starting with accelerated recruitment and carrying on through the rest of the staffing system. It may also require development of retention programs that will slow the outflow of people, thus avoiding costly "turnstile" or "revolving door" staffing. Overstaffing projections signal the need to slow down or even halt recruitment, as well as to take steps that will actually reduce head count, such as reduced workweeks, early retirement plans, or layoffs.

Staffing Quality: Person/Job Match

The person/job match seeks to align characteristics of individuals and jobs in ways that will result in desired HR outcomes. Casual comments made about applicants often reflect awareness of the importance of the person/job match. "Clark just doesn't have the interpersonal skills that it takes to be a good customer service representative." "Mary has exactly the kinds of budgeting experience this job calls for; if we hire her, there won't be any downtime while she learns our systems." "Gary says he was attracted to apply for this job because of its sales commission plan; he says he likes jobs where his pay depends on how well he performs." "Diane was impressed by the amount of challenge and autonomy she will have." "Jack turned down our offer; we gave him our best shot, but he just didn't feel he could handle the long hours and amount of travel the job calls for."

Comments like these raise four important points about the person/job match. First, jobs are characterized by their requirements (e.g., interpersonal skills, previous budgeting experience) and embedded rewards (e.g., commission sales plan, challenge and autonomy). Second, individuals are characterized by their level of qualification (e.g., few interpersonal skills, extensive budgeting experience) and motivation (e.g., need for pay to depend on performance, need for challenge and autonomy). Third, in each of the previous examples the issue was the likely degree of fit or match between the characteristics of the job and the person. Fourth, there are implied consequences for every match. For example, Clark may not perform very well in his interactions with customers; retention might quickly become an issue with Jack.

These points and concepts are shown more formally through the person/job match model in Exhibit 1.3. In this model, the job has certain requirements and rewards associated with it. The person has certain qualifications, referred to as KSAOs, and motivations. There is a need for a match between the person and the job. To the extent that the match is good, it will likely have a positive impact on HR outcomes, particularly attraction of job applicants, job performance, retention, attendance, and satisfaction.

There is actually a need for a dual match to occur: job requirements to KSAOs, and job rewards to individual motivation. In and through staffing activities, there are attempts to ensure both of these. Such attempts collectively involve what will be referred to throughout this book as the matching process.

Several points pertaining to staffing need to be made about the person/job match model. First, the concepts shown in the model are not new.[14] They have been used

EXHIBIT 1.3   Person/Job Match

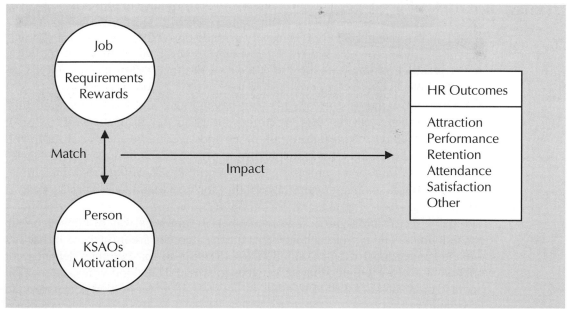

for decades as the dominant way of thinking about how individuals successfully adapt to their work environments. The view is that the positive interaction of individual and job characteristics creates the most successful matches. Thus, a person with a given "package" of KSAOs is not equally suited to all jobs, because jobs vary in the KSAOs required. Likewise, an individual with a given set of needs or motivations will not be satisfied with all jobs, because jobs differ in the rewards they offer. Thus, in staffing, each individual must be assessed relative to the requirements and rewards of the job being filled.

Second, the model emphasizes that the matching process involves a dual match of KSAOs to requirements and motivation to rewards. Both matches require attention in staffing. For example, a staffing system may be designed to focus on the KSAOs/requirements match by carefully identifying job requirements and then thoroughly assessing applicants relative to these requirements. While such a staffing system may be one that will accurately identify the probable high performers, problems may arise with it. By ignoring or downplaying the motivation/rewards portion of the match, the organization may have difficulty getting people to accept job offers (an attraction outcome) or having new hires remain with the organization for any length of time (a retention outcome). It does little good to be able to identify the likely high performers if they cannot be induced to accept job offers or to remain with the organization.

Third, job requirements should usually be expressed in terms of both the tasks involved and the KSAOs thought necessary for performance of those tasks. Most of the time, it is difficult to establish meaningful KSAOs for a job without having first identified the job's tasks. KSAOs usually must be derived or inferred from knowledge of the tasks. An exception to this involves very basic or generic KSAOs, such as literacy and oral communication skills, that are reasonably deemed necessary for most jobs.

Fourth, job requirements often extend beyond task and KSAO requirements. For example, the job may have requirements about reporting to work on time, attendance, safety toward fellow employees and customers, and needs for travel. With such requirements, the matching of the person to them must also be considered when staffing the organization. Travel requirements of the job, for example, may involve assessing applicants' availability for, and willingness to accept, travel assignments.

Finally, the matching process can yield only so much by way of impacts on the HR outcomes. The reason for this is that these outcomes are influenced by factors outside the realm of the person/job match. Retention, for example, depends not only on how close a match there is between job rewards and individual motivation but also on the availability of suitable job opportunities in other organizations and labor markets.

Staffing Quality: Person/Organization Match

Often the organization seeks to determine how well the person fits or matches not only the job but also the organization. Likewise, applicants often assess how well they think they might fit into the organization, in addition to how well they match the specific job's requirements and rewards. For both the organization and the applicant, therefore, there may be a concern with a person/organization match.[15]

Exhibit 1.4 shows this expanded view of the match. The focal point of staffing is the person/job match, and the job is like the bull's-eye of the matching target. Four other matching concerns involving the broader organization also arise in staffing. These concerns involve organizational values, new job duties, multiple jobs, and future jobs.

EXHIBIT 1.4   Person/Organization Match

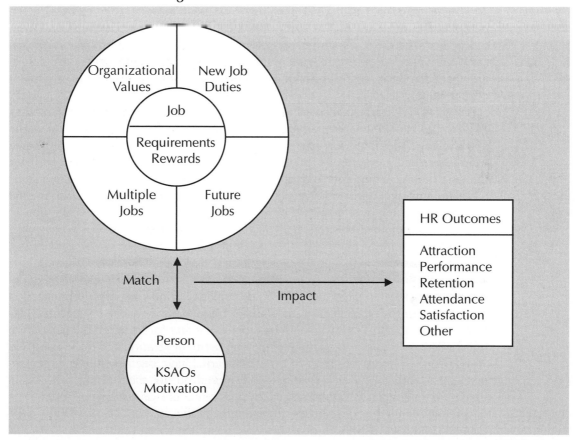

Organizational values are norms of desirable attitudes and behaviors for the organization's employees. Examples include honesty and integrity, achievement and hard work, and concern for fellow employees and customers. Though such values may never appear in writing, such as in a job description, the likely match of the applicant to them is judged during staffing.

New job duties represent tasks that may be added to the target job over time. Organizations desire new hires who will be able to successfully perform these new duties as they are added. In recognition of this, job descriptions often contain the catchall phrase "and other duties as assigned." These other duties are usually vague at the time of hire, and they may never materialize. Nonetheless, the organization would like to hire persons it thinks could perform these new duties. Having such people will provide the organization a degree of flexibility in getting new tasks done without having to hire additional employees to do them.

Flexibility concerns also enter into the staffing picture in terms of hiring persons who could perform multiple jobs. Small businesses, for example, often desire new hires who can wear multiple hats, functioning as jacks-of-all-trades; or, organizations experiencing rapid growth may require new employees who can handle several different job assignments, splitting their time between them on an as-needed basis. Such expectations obviously require assessments of person/ organization fit.

Future jobs represent forward thinking by the organization and the person as to what job assignments the person might assume beyond the initial job. Here the applicant and the organization are thinking of long-term matches over the course of transfers and promotions as the employee becomes increasingly "seasoned" for the long run. As technology and globalization cause jobs to change at a rapid pace, more organizations are engaging in "opportunistic hiring," where an individual is hired into a newly created job or a job that is an amalgamation of previously distributed tasks. In such cases, person/organization match is more important than person/job match.[16]

In each of the above four cases, the matching process is expanded to include consideration of requirements and rewards beyond those of the target job as it currently exists. Though the dividing line between person/job and person/organization matching is fuzzy, both types of matches are frequently of concern in staffing. Ideally, the organization's staffing systems focus first and foremost on the person/job match. This will allow the nature of the employment relationship to be specified and agreed to in concrete terms. Once these terms have been established, person/ organization match possibilities can be explored during the staffing process. In this book for simplicity's sake we will use the term "person/job match" broadly to encompass both types of matches, though most of the time the usage will be in the context of the actual person/job match.

Staffing System Components

As noted, staffing encompasses managing the flows of people into and within the organization, as well as retaining them. The core staffing process has several components that represent steps and activities that occur over the course of these flows. Exhibit 1.5 shows these components and the general sequence in which they occur.

As shown in the exhibit, staffing begins with a joint interaction between the applicant and the organization. The applicant seeks the organization and job opportunities within it, and the organization seeks applicants for job vacancies it has or anticipates having. Both the applicant and the organization are thus involved as "players" in the staffing process from the very beginning, and they remain joint participants throughout the process.

At times, the organization may be the dominant player, such as in aggressive and targeted recruiting for certain types of applicants. At other times, the applicant may be the aggressor, such as when the applicant desperately seeks employment with a particular organization and will go to almost any length to land a job with it. Most of the time, staffing involves a more balanced and natural interplay between the applicant and the organization, which occurs over the course of the staffing process.

EXHIBIT 1.5   Staffing System Components

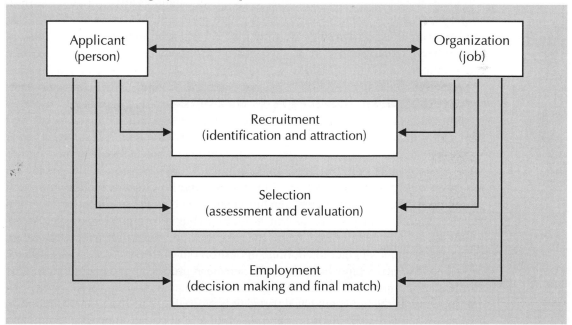

The initial stage in staffing is recruitment, which involves identification and attraction activities by both the organization and the applicant. The organization seeks to identify and attract individuals so that they become job applicants. Activities such as advertising, job fairs, use of recruiters, preparation and distribution of informational brochures, and "putting out the word" about vacancies among its own employees are undertaken. The applicant attempts to identify organizations with job opportunities through activities such as reading advertisements, contacting an employment agency, mass mailing résumés to employers, and so forth. These activities are accompanied by attempts to make one's qualifications (KSAOs and motivation) attractive to organizations, such as by applying in person for a job or preparing a carefully constructed résumé that highlights significant skills and experiences.

Gradually, recruitment activities phase into the selection stage and its accompanying activities. Now, the emphasis is on assessment and evaluation. For the organization, this means the use of various selection techniques (interviews, application blanks, and so on) to assess applicant KSAOs and motivation. Data from these assessments are then evaluated against job requirements to determine the likely degree of person/job match. At the same time, the applicant is assessing and evaluating the job and organization. The applicant's assessment and evaluation are based on information gathered from organizational representatives (e.g., recruiter, manager with the vacancy, other employees); written information (e.g., brochures, employee handbook); informal sources (e.g., friends and relatives who are current employees); and visual inspection (e.g., a video presentation, a work site tour). This information, along with a self-assessment of KSAOs and motivation, is evaluated against the applicant's understanding of job requirements and rewards to determine if a good person/job match is likely.

The next core component of staffing is employment, which involves decision making and final match activities by the organization and the applicant. The organization must decide which applicants to reject from further consideration and which to allow to continue in the process. This may involve multiple decisions over successive selection steps or hurdles. Some applicants ultimately become finalists for the job. At that point, the organization must decide to whom it will make the job offer, what the content of the offer will be, and how it will be drawn up and presented to the applicant. Upon the applicant's acceptance of the offer, the final match is complete, and the employment relationship is formally established.

For the applicant, the employment stage involves self-selection, a term that refers to decisions about whether to continue in or drop out of the staffing process. These decisions may occur anywhere along the selection process, up to and including the moment of the job offer. If the applicant continues as part of the process through the final match, the applicant has decided to be a finalist. The individual's attention now turns to a possible job offer, possible input and negotiation on its content, and making a final decision about the offer. The applicant's final decision is based on overall judgment about the likely suitability of the person/job match.

It should be noted that the above staffing components apply to both external and internal staffing. Though this may seem obvious in the case of external staffing, a brief elaboration may be necessary for internal staffing. In internal staffing, the applicant is a current employee, and the organization is the current employer. Job opportunities (vacancies) exist within the organization and are filled through the activities of the internal labor market. Those activities involve recruitment, selection, and employment, with the employer and employee as joint participants. For example, at the investment banking firm Goldman Sachs, candidates for promotion to partner are identified through a multistep process.[17] They are "recruited" by division heads identifying prospective candidates for promotion (as in many internal staffing decisions, it is assumed that all employees are interested in promotion). Candidates are then vetted based on input from senior managers in the company and are evaluated from a dossier that contains the candidate's photograph, credentials, and accomplishments. After this six-month process, candidates are recommended for partner to the CEO, who then makes the final decision and offers partnership to those lucky enough to be selected (partners average $7 million a year, plus perks). When candidates accept the offer of partnership, the final match has occurred, and a new employment relationship has been established.

Staffing Organizations

The overall staffing organizations model, which forms the framework for this book, is shown in Exhibit 1.6. It depicts that the organization's mission and goals and objectives drive both organization strategy and HR and staffing strategy, which interact with each other when they are being formulated. Staffing policies and programs result from such interaction and serve as an overlay to both support activities and core staffing activities. Employee retention and staffing system management concerns cut across these support and core staffing activities. Finally, though not shown in the model, it should be remembered that staffing levels and staffing quality are the key focal points of staffing strategy, policy, and programs. A more thorough examination of the model follows next.

Organization, HR, and Staffing Strategy

Organizations formulate strategy to express an overall purpose or mission and to establish broad goals and objectives that will guide the organization toward fulfillment of its mission. For example, a newly formed software development organization may have a mission to "help individuals and families manage all of their personal finances and records through electronic means." Based on this mission statement, the organization might then develop goals and objectives pertaining to product development, sales growth, and competitive differentiation through superior product quality and customer service.

Underlying these objectives are certain assumptions about the size and types of workforces that will need to be acquired, trained, managed, rewarded, and retained.

EXHIBIT 1.6   Staffing Organizations Model

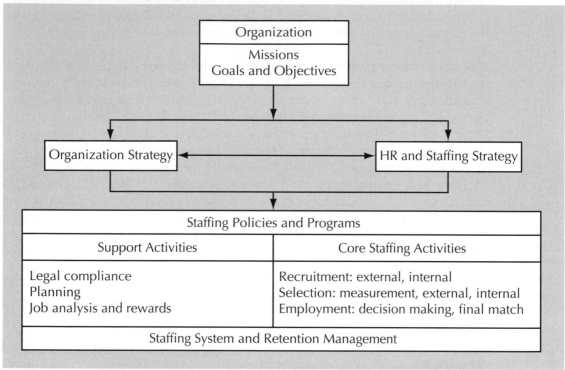

HR strategy represents the key decisions about how these workforce assumptions will be handled. Such HR strategy may not only flow from the organization strategy but also may actually contribute directly to the formulation of the organization's strategy.

Consider again the software development organization and its objective pertaining to new product development. Being able to develop new products assumes that sufficient qualified product-development team members are available internally and externally, and assurances from the HR department about availability may have been critical in helping the organization decide on its product development goals. From this general assumption, HR strategy may suggest (1) obtaining new, experienced employees from other software companies rather than going after newly minted college and graduate school graduates; (2) building a new facility for software development employees in a geographic area that will be an attractive place to work, raise families, and pursue leisure activities; (3) developing relocation assistance packages and family-friendly benefits; (4) offering wages and salaries above the market average, plus using hiring bonuses to help lure new employees away from their current employers; (5) creating special training budgets for each employee to use at his or her own discretion for skills enhancement; and (6) putting in place a promotion system that is fast-track and allows employees to rise upward in either their professional specialty or the managerial ranks. In all of these ways, HR strategy seeks to align acquisition and management of the workforce with organization strategy.

Staffing strategy is an outgrowth of the interplay between organization strategy and HR strategy, described above. It deals directly with key decisions regarding the acquisition, deployment, and retention of the organization's workforces. Such decisions guide the development of recruitment, selection, and employment programs. In the software development example discussed above, the strategic decision to acquire new employees from the ranks of experienced people at other organizations may lead the organization to develop very active, personalized, and secret recruiting activities for luring these people away. It may also lead to the development of special selection techniques for assessing job experiences and accomplishments. In such ways, strategic staffing decisions shape the staffing process.

Support Activities

Support activities serve as the foundation and necessary ingredients for the conduct of core staffing activities. Legal compliance represents knowledge of the myriad laws and regulations, especially equal employment opportunity and affirmative action (EEO/AA), and incorporation of their requirements into all phases of the core staffing activities. Planning serves as a tool for first becoming aware of key external influences on staffing, particularly economic conditions, labor markets, and labor unions. Such awareness shapes the formulation of staffing levels—both requirements and availabilities—the results of which drive staffing planning for the core staffing activities. Job analysis represents the key mechanism by which the organization identifies and establishes the KSAO requirements for jobs, as well as the rewards jobs will provide, both first steps toward seeking to begin filling projected vacancies through core staffing activities.

Returning to the software development organization, if it meets various size thresholds for coverage (usually 15 or more employees), it must ensure that the staffing systems to be developed comply with all applicable federal, state, and local laws and regulations. Planning activities will revolve around first determining the major types of jobs that will be necessary for the new product development venture, such as computer programmers, Internet specialists, and project managers. For each job, a forecast must be made about the number of employees that will be needed and the likely availability of individuals both externally and internally for the job. Results of such forecasts serve as the key input to the development of detailed staffing plans for the core staffing activities. Finally, job analysis will be needed to specify for each job exactly what KSAOs and rewards will be necessary for these sought-after new employees. Once all of these support activities are in place, the core staffing activities can begin.

Core Staffing Activities

Core staffing activities focus on recruitment, selection, and employment of the workforce. Since staffing levels have already been established as part of staffing planning, emphasis shifts to staffing quality to ensure that successful person/job and person/organization matches will be made. Accomplishment of this end result will require multiple plans, decisions, and activities, ranging from recruitment methods to use, communication with potential applicants with a special recruitment message, recruitment media, types of selection tools, deciding which applicants will receive job offers, and job offer packages. Both staffing experts and the hiring manager will be involved in these core staffing activities. Moreover, it is likely that the activities will have to be developed and tailor made for each type of job.

Consider the job of computer programmer in our software development example. It will be necessary to decide and develop specific plans for such issues as: Will we recruit only online, or will we use other methods such as newspaper ads or job fairs (recruitment methods)? What exactly will we tell applicants about the job and our company (recruitment message), and how will we deliver the message, such as on our Web site or in a recruitment brochure (recruitment media)? What specific selection tools, such as interviews, assessments of experience, work samples, and background checks, will we use to assess and evaluate the applicants' KSAOs (selection techniques)? How will we combine and evaluate all of the information we gather on applicants with these selection tools and then decide which applicants will receive job offers (decision making)? What exactly will we put in the job offer, and will we be willing to negotiate on the offer (employment)?

Staffing and Retention System Management

The various support and core staffing activities are quite complex, and they must be guided, coordinated, controlled, and evaluated. Such is the role of staffing system management. In our new product development example, what will be the role of the HR department, and what types of people will it need to develop and manage the new staffing systems (administration of staffing systems)? How will we evaluate the results of these systems—will we collect and look at cost-per-hire and time-to-hire data (evaluation of staffing systems)? Data such as these are key effective indicators that both general and staffing managers are attuned to.

Finally, voluntary employee departure from the organization is usually costly and disruptive, and it can involve the loss of critical talent that is difficult to replace. Discharges too can be disruptive. Unless the organization is downsizing, however, replacements must be found in order to maintain desired staffing levels. The burden for such replacement staffing can be substantial, particularly when the turnover was unanticipated and unplanned. Other things being equal, greater employee retention means less staffing, so that effective retention programs complement staffing programs.

In our software development organization example, the primary focus will likely be on "staffing up" in order to keep producing existing products and developing new ones. Unless attention is also paid to employee retention, however, maintaining adequate staffing levels and quality may become problematic. Hence, the organization will need to monitor the amount and quality of employees who are leaving and the reasons they are leaving in order to learn how much of the turnover is voluntary and avoidable; monitoring discharges will also be necessary. Based on these data, specific and tailor-made retention strategies and programs to better meet employees' needs can be developed. If these are effective, strains on the staffing system will be lessened.

The remainder of the book is structured around and built on the staffing organizations model shown in Exhibit 1.6.

STAFFING STRATEGY

As noted, staffing strategy requires making key decisions about the acquisition, deployment, and retention of the organization's workforce. Thirteen such decisions are identified and discussed below. Some decisions pertain primarily to staffing levels and others primarily to staffing quality. A summary of the decisions is shown in Exhibit 1.7. While each decision is shown as an either-or, each is more appropriately thought of as lying on a continuum anchored at either end by these

---

EXHIBIT 1.7   Strategic Staffing Decisions

Staffing Levels
- Acquire or Develop Talent
- Hire Yourself or Outsource
- External or Internal Hiring
- Core or Flexible Workforce
- Hire or Retain
- National or Global
- Attract or Relocate
- Overstaff or Understaff
- Short- or Long-Term Focus

Staffing Quality
- Person/Job or Person/Organization Match
- Specific or General KSAOs
- Exceptional or Acceptable Workforce Quality
- Active or Passive Diversity

either-or extremes. When discussing the decisions, continued reference is made to the software development organization involved in developing personal finances software.

Staffing Levels

Acquire or Develop Talent

To fulfill its staffing needs, a pure acquisition staffing strategy would have an organization concentrate on acquiring new employees who can "hit the ground running" and be at peak performance the moment they arrive. These employees would bring their talents with them to the job, with little or no need for training or development. A pure development strategy would lead to acquisition of just about anyone, as long as he or she was willing and able to learn the KSAOs required by the job. Staffing strategy must position the organization appropriately along this "buy or make your talent" continuum. For critical positions and newly created ones, such as might occur in the software company example, the emphasis would likely be on acquiring talent because of the urgency of developing new products. There may be no time to train, nor may qualified internal candidates be available.

Hire Yourself or Outsource

Increasingly, organizations are outsourcing their hiring activities, meaning they use outside organizations to recruit and select employees. Although there are variations of staffing outsourcing (we'll have more to say about it in Chapter 3), in some cases, an organization wholly cedes decision-making authority to the vendor. Why might an organization do this? First, it may believe that the vendor can do a better job of identifying candidates than the organization itself can do. This is particularly true for small and midsized companies that lack a professional HR function. Second, in labor shortages, an organization may not be able to recruit enough employees on its own, so it may supplement its recruiting or selection efforts with those of a vendor that specializes in staffing. Finally, outsourcing may also have advantages for legal compliance, as many vendors maintain their own procedures for tracking compliance with equal-opportunity laws.

External or Internal Hiring

When job vacancies occur or new jobs are created, should the organization seek to fill them from the external or internal labor market? While some mixture of external and internal hiring will be necessary in most situations, the relative blend could vary substantially. To the extent that the organization wants to cultivate a stable, committed workforce, it will probably need to emphasize internal hiring. This will allow employees to use the internal labor market as a springboard for launching long-term careers within the organization. External hiring might then be restricted to specific entry-level jobs, as well as newly created ones for which there are no acceptable internal applicants. External hiring might also be necessary when there is rapid organization growth, such that the number of new jobs created outstrips internal supply.

Core or Flexible Workforce

The organization's core workforce is made up of individuals who are viewed (and view themselves) as regular employees of the organization, either full time or part time. They are central to the core goods and services delivered by the organization.

The flexible workforce is composed of more peripheral workers who are used on an as-needed, just-in-time basis. They are not viewed (nor do they view themselves) as "regular," and legally, most of them are not even employees of the organization. Rather, they are employees of an alternative organization, such as a staffing firm (temporary help agency) or independent contractor that provides these workers to the organization. Strategically, the organization must decide whether it wishes to use both core and flexible workforces, what the mixture of core versus flexible workers will be, and in what jobs and units of the organization these mixtures will be deployed. Within the software development organization, programmers might be considered as part of its core workforce, but ancillary workers (e.g., clerical) may be part of the flexible workforce, particularly since the need for them will depend on the speed and success of new product development.

Hire or Retain

There are trade-offs between hiring and retention strategies for staffing. At one extreme the organization can accept whatever level of turnover occurs and simply hire replacements to fill the vacancies. Alternatively, the organization can seek to minimize turnover so that the need for replacement staffing is held to a minimum. Since both strategies have costs and benefits associated with them, the organization could conduct an analysis to determine these and then strive for an optimal mix of hiring and retention. In this way the organization could control its inflow needs (replacement staffing) by controlling its outflow (retention).

National or Global

As we noted earlier, one form of outsourcing is when organizations outsource staffing activities. Of course, many organizations outsource more than staffing activities—technical support, database management, customer service, and manufacturing are common examples. For example, a growing number of computer-chip makers, such as IBM, Intel, and Motorola, contract with outside vendors to manufacture their chips; often these companies are overseas. Offshoring is related to, but distinct from, outsourcing. Whereas outsourcing is moving a business process (service or manufacturing) to another vendor (whether that vendor is inside or outside the organization's home country), offshoring is the organization setting up its own operations in another country (the organization is not contracting with an outside vendor; rather, it is establishing its own operations in another country). In the above computer-chip example, outsourcing would be if the company, say, IBM, contracted with an outside vendor to manufacture the chips. Offshoring would be if IBM set up its own plant in another country to manufacture the chips.

Increasingly, U.S. organizations are engaged in both overseas outsourcing and offshoring, a trend spurred by three forces. First, most nations have lowered trading and immigration barriers, which has facilitated offshoring and overseas outsourcing. Second, particularly in the United States and Western Europe, organizations find that by outsourcing or offshoring, they can manufacture goods or provide services more cheaply than they can in their own country. Third, some organizations find they cannot locate sufficient talent in their host countries, so they have to look elsewhere. Many high-tech companies in the United States and Western Europe are facing severe talent shortages. Siemens, the German engineering giant, has 2,500 positions for engineers open in Germany alone. These shortages have required many companies like Siemens to outsource overseas, to offshore, or to do both.[18]

Attract or Relocate

Typical staffing strategy is based on the premise that the organization can induce sufficient numbers of qualified people to come to it for employment. Another version of this premise is that it is better (and cheaper) to bring labor to the organization than to bring the organization to labor. Some organizations, both established and new ones, challenge this premise and decide to go to locations where there are ample labor supplies. The shift of lumber mills and automobile manufacturing plants to the southern United States reflects such a strategy. Likewise, the growth of high technology pockets such as Silicon Valley reflects establishment or movement of organizations to geographic areas where there is ready access to highly skilled labor and where employees would like to live, usually locations with research universities nearby to provide the needed graduates for jobs. The software development organization might find locating in such an area very desirable.

Overstaff or Understaff

While most organizations seek to be reasonably fully staffed, some opt for or are forced away from this posture to being over- or understaffed. Overstaffing may occur when there are dips in demand for the organization's products or services that the organization chooses to "ride out." Organizations may also overstaff in order to stockpile talent, recognizing that the staffing spigot cannot be easily turned on or off. Understaffing may occur when the organization is confronted with chronic labor shortages, such as is the case for nurses in health care facilities. Also, prediction of an economic downturn may lead the organization to understaff in order to avoid future layoffs. Finally, the organization may decide to understaff and adjust staffing level demand spikes by increasing employee overtime or using flexible staffing arrangements such as temporary employees. The software development organization might choose to overstaff in order to retain key employees and to be poised to meet the hopeful surges in demand as its new products are released.

Short- or Long-Term Focus

Although any organization would want to have its staffing needs fully anticipated for both the short term and the long term, optimizing both goals is difficult, so trade-offs are often required. In this case, it often means balancing addressing short-term labor shortages with the identification and development of talent for the long term. Bringing to mind John Maynard Keynes's comment, "In the long run we are all dead," when forced to choose, organizations focus on their short-term needs. This is understandable because labor shortages can be debilitating. Take the example of prison guards. As the number of inmates in U.S. prisons grows (currently numbering more than 1.5 million), the number of prison guards has shrunk, such that it's not uncommon for 17 or 18 prison guards to be responsible for 1,000 inmates. It is difficult to recruit prison guards because the pay is relatively low and the working conditions obviously difficult. The head of Florida's Department of Corrections says the guard shortages are "one of the central challenges of the department." In response, the department spent $400,000 on an advertising campaign to recruit more corrections officers.[19]

Labor shortages are hardly limited to prison guards. Although labor shortages in some high-end industries (e.g., technology) and entry-level industries (e.g., fast food) are legendary, a labor shortage can happen in any industry. For example, when business leaders in the trucking industry were asked to identify their top business concerns, 86% of executives listed the unavailability of drivers as one of their top three concerns.[20] Labor shortages happen in nearly all industries, and when they do, companies are often in a crisis management mode to deal with them because they represent an imminent threat to the organization.

Balanced against this short-term "crisis management" focus are long-term concerns. Organizations with a longer view of their staffing needs have put in place talent management programs. In some cases, this means thinking about the strategic talent, or future skill, needs for the entire organization. Other organizations focus their talent management programs only on key contributors, such as managers and professional-technical employees.

One factor in talent management programs is the change in demographics. Whereas the workforce is projected to grow by 12% by 2012, the baby boom generation will start to retire in record numbers. A survey by the Society for Human Resource Management (SHRM) revealed that most organizations are either just becoming aware of the upcoming potential shortages (38%) or just beginning to examine staffing policies and practices to deal with the shortages (39%).[21]

Most talent management programs, while focusing on long-term needs, are relatively informal. A survey of organizations revealed that only 16% had formal talent management programs in place, whereas another survey showed that half of company leaders believe their organization is ineffective at talent management.[22] These may be related—by failing to have a person in charge of talent management, it does not acquire the priority it should, and managers instead spend their time moving from one short-term skill shortage to another.

Staffing Quality

Person/Job or Person/Organization Match

When acquiring and deploying people, should the organization opt for a person/job or person/organization match? This is a complex decision. In part a person/job match will have to be assessed any time a person is being hired to perform a finite set of tasks. In our software development example, programmers might be hired to do programming in a specific language such as Java, and most certainly the organization would want to assess whether applicants meet this specific job requirement. On the other hand, jobs may be poorly defined and fluid, making a person/job match infeasible and requiring a person/organization match instead. Such jobs are often found in technology and software development organizations.

Specific or General KSAOs

Should the organization acquire people with specific KSAOs or more general ones? The former means focusing on job-specific competencies, often of the job knowledge and technical skill variety. The latter requires a focus on KSAOs that will be applicable across a variety of jobs, both current and future. Examples of such KSAOs include flexibility and adaptability, ability to learn, written and oral communication skills, and algebra/statistics skills. An organization expecting rapid changes in job content and new job creation, such as in the software development example, might position itself closer to the general competencies end of the continuum.

Exceptional or Acceptable Workforce Quality

Strategically, the organization could seek to acquire a workforce that was preeminent KSAO-wise (exceptional quality) or one that was a more "ballpark" variety KSAO-wise (acceptable quality). Pursuit of the exceptional strategy would allow the organization to stock up on the "best and the brightest" with the hope that this exceptional talent pool would deliver truly superior performance. The acceptable strategy means pursuit of a less high-powered workforce and probably a less expensive one as well. For the software development organization, if it is trying to create clearly innovative and superior products, it will likely opt for the exceptional workforce quality end of the continuum.

Active or Passive Diversity

The labor force is becoming increasingly diverse in terms of demographics, values, and languages. Does the organization want to actively pursue this diversity in the labor market so that its own workforce mirrors it, or does the organization want to more passively let diversity of its workforce happen? Advocates of an active diversity strategy argue that it is legally and morally appropriate and that a diverse workforce allows the organization to be more attuned to the diverse needs of the customers it serves. Those favoring a more passive strategy suggest that diversification of the workforce takes time because it requires substantial planning and assimilation activity. In the software development illustration, an active diversity strategy might be pursued as a way of acquiring workers who can help identify a diverse array of software products that might be received favorably by various segments of the marketplace.

STAFFING ETHICS

Staffing the organization involves a multitude of individuals—hiring managers, staffing professionals, potential coworkers, legal advisors, and job applicants. During the staffing process all of these individuals may be involved in recruitment, selection, and employment activities, as well as staffing decision making. Are there, or should there be, boundaries on these individuals' actions and decisions? The answer is yes, for without boundaries potentially negative outcomes and harmful effects may occur. For example, many times staffing is a hurried process, driven by tight deadlines and calls for expediency (e.g., the hiring manager who says to the staffing professional, "Just get me someone now—I'll worry about how good they are later on."). Such calls may lead to negative consequences, including hiring someone quickly without proper assessment and having him or her subsequently perform poorly, ignoring many applicants who would have been successful performers, failing to advance the organization's workforce diversity initiatives and possible legal obligations, and making an exceedingly generous job offer that provides the highest salary in the work unit, causing dissatisfaction and possible turnover among other work unit members. Such actions and outcomes raise staffing ethics issues.

Ethics involves determining moral principles and guidelines for acceptable practice. Within the realm of the workplace, ethics emphasizes "knowing organizational codes and guidelines and behaving within these boundaries when faced with dilemmas in business or professional work."[23] More specifically, organizational ethics seeks to do the following:

- Raise ethical expectations
- Legitimize dialogue about ethical issues
- Encourage ethical decision making
- Prevent misconduct and provide a basis for enforcement

While organizations are increasingly developing general codes of conduct, it is unknown whether these codes contain specific staffing provisions. Even the general code will likely have some pertinence to staffing through provisions on such issues as legal compliance, confidentiality and disclosure of information, and use of organizational property and assets. Individuals involved in staffing should know and follow their organization's code of ethics. As pertains to staffing specifically, there are several points that can serve as a person's guide to ethical conduct. These points are shown in Exhibit 1.8 and elaborated on below.

EXHIBIT 1.8 Suggestions for Ethical Staffing Practice

1. Represent the organization's interests.
2. Beware of conflicts of interest.
3. Remember the job applicant.
4. Follow staffing policies and procedures.
5. Know and follow the law.
6. Consult professional codes of conduct.
7. Shape effective practice with research results.
8. Seek ethics advice.

The first point is that the person is serving as an agent of the organization and is duty bound to represent the organization first and foremost. That duty is to bring into being effective person/job and person/organization matches. The second point indicates that the agent must avoid placing his or her own interest, or that of a third party (such as an applicant or friend), above that of the organization. Point three suggests that even though the HR professional represents the organization, he or she should remember that the applicant is a participant in the staffing process. The type of treatment he or she provides applicants may well lead to reactions by them that are favorable to the organization and further its interests, let alone those of applicants. Point four reminds the HR professional to know the organization's staffing policies and procedures and adhere to them. The fifth point indicates a need to be knowledgeable of the myriad laws and regulations governing staffing, to follow them, and to seek needed assistance in their interpretation and application. Point six guides the HR professional toward professional codes of conduct pertaining to staffing and human resources. The SHRM has a formal code of ethics (*www.shrm.org/ethics*). The Society for Industrial and Organizational Psychology follows the ethics code of the American Psychological Association and has issued a set of professional principles to guide appropriate use of employee selection procedures (*www.siop.org*). The seventh point means that there is considerable useful research-based knowledge about the design and effectiveness of staffing systems and techniques that should guide staffing practice. Much of that research is summarized in usable formats in this book. The final point suggests that when confronted with ethical issues, it is appropriate to seek ethical advice from others. Handling troubling ethical issues alone is unwise.

It should be recognized that many pressure points on HR professionals may cause them to compromise the ethical standards discussed above. Research suggests that the principal causes of this pressure are the felt need to follow a boss's directive, meet overly aggressive business objectives, help the organization survive, meet scheduling pressures, be a team player, save jobs, and advance the boss's career.[24]

The suggestions for ethical staffing practice in Exhibit 1.8 are guides to one's own behavior. Being aware of and consciously attempting to follow these constitutes a professional and ethical responsibility. But what about situations in which ethical lapses are suspected or observed in others?

One response to the situation is to do nothing—not report or attempt to change the misconduct. Research suggests a small proportion (about 20%) choose to ignore and not report misconduct.[25] Major reasons for this response include a belief that no action would be taken, a fear of retaliation from one's boss or senior management, not trusting promises of confidentiality, and a fear of not being seen as a team player. Against such reasons for inaction must be weighed the harm that has, or could, come to the employer, employee, or job applicant. Moreover, failure to report the misconduct may well increase the chances that it will be repeated, with continuing harmful consequences. Not reporting misconduct may also conflict with one's personal values and create remorse for not having done the "right thing." Finally, a failure to report misconduct may bring penalties to oneself if that failure subsequently becomes known to one's boss or senior management. In short, "looking the other way" should not be viewed as a safe, wise, or ethical choice.

A different way to handle unethical staffing practices by others is to seek advice from one's boss, senior management, coworkers, legal counsel, ethics officer or ombudsperson, or an outside friend or family member. The guidelines in Exhibit 1.8 could serve as a helpful starting point to frame the discussion and make a decision about what to do.

At times, the appropriate response to others' misconduct is to step in directly to try to prevent or rectify the misconduct. This would be especially appropriate with employees that one supervises or with coworkers. Before taking such an action, it would be wise to consider whether one has the authority and resources to do so, along with the likely support of those other employees or coworkers.

PLAN FOR THE BOOK

The book is divided into six parts:

1. The Nature of Staffing
2. Support Activities
3. Staffing Activities: Recruitment
4. Staffing Activities: Selection
5. Staffing Activities: Employment
6. Staffing System and Retention Management

Each chapter in these six parts begins with a brief topical outline to help the reader quickly discern its general contents. The "meat" of the chapter comes next. A chapter summary then reviews and highlights points from the chapter. A set of discussion questions, ethical issues to discuss, applications (cases and exercises), the Tanglewood Stores case (in some chapters), and detailed endnotes complete the chapter.

The importance of laws and regulations is such that they are considered first in Chapter 2 (Legal Compliance). The laws and regulations, in particular, have become so pervasive that they require special treatment. To do this, Chapter 2 reviews the basic laws affecting staffing, with an emphasis on the major federal laws and regulations pertaining to EEO/AA matters generally. Specific provisions relevant to staffing are covered in depth. Each subsequent chapter then has a separate section at its end labeled "Legal Issues" in which specific legal topics relevant to the chapter's content are discussed. This allows for a more focused discussion of legal issues while not diverting attention from the major thrust of the book.

The endnotes at the end of each chapter are quite extensive. They are drawn from academic, practitioner, and legal sources with the goal of providing a balanced selection of references from each of these sources. Emphasis is on inclusion of recent references of high quality and easy accessibility. Too lengthy a list of references to each specific topic is avoided; instead, a sampling of only the best available is included.

The applications at the end of each chapter are of two varieties. First are cases that describe a particular situation and require analysis and response. The response may be written or oral (such as in class discussion or a group presentation). Second are exercises that entail small projects and require active practice of a particular task. Through these cases and exercises the reader becomes an active participant in the learning process and is able to apply the concepts provided in each chapter.

Interspersed throughout the book at the end of some chapters are instructions for completing assignments for the Tanglewood Stores case. The full case and assignments are located on the following Web site: *www.mhhe.com/heneman6e.* You will see that Tanglewood Stores is an up-and-coming retailing organization in the Pacific Northwest. Tanglewood is in an expansion mode, seeking to aggressively grow beyond the current 243 stores. As Tanglewood pursues expansion, numerous staffing issues arise that require analysis, decisions, and recommendations from you. You will receive assignments in the areas of staffing strategy (Chapter 1), planning (Chapter 3), external recruitment (Chapter 5), measurement (Chapter 7), external selection (Chapter 9), decision making (Chapter 11), and retention (Chapter 14).

SUMMARY

At the national level, staffing involves a huge number of hiring transactions each year, is a major cost of doing business, especially for service-providing industries, and can lead to substantial revenue and market value growth for the organization. Staffing is defined as "the process of acquiring, deploying, and retaining a workforce of sufficient quantity and quality to create positive impacts on the organization's effectiveness." The definition emphasizes that both staffing levels and labor quality contribute to an organization's effectiveness, and that a concerted set of labor acquisition, deployment, and retention actions guides the flow of people into, within, and out of the organization. Descriptions of three staffing systems help highlight the definition of staffing.

Several models illustrate various elements of staffing. The staffing level model shows how projected labor requirements and availabilities are compared to derive staffing levels that represent being overstaffed, fully staffed, or understaffed. The next two models illustrate staffing quality via the person/job and person/organization match. The former indicates there is a need to match (1) the person's KSAOs to job requirements and (2) the person's motivation to the job's rewards. In the person/organization match, the person's characteristics are matched to additional factors beyond the target job, namely, organizational values, new job duties for the target job, multiple jobs, and future jobs. Managing the matching process effectively results in positive impacts on HR outcomes such as attraction, performance, and retention. The core staffing components model shows that there are three basic activities in staffing. Those activities and their fundamental purposes are recruitment (identification and attraction of applicants), selection (assessment and evaluation of applicants), and employment (decision making and final match). The staffing organizations model shows that organization, HR, and staffing strategies are formulated and shape staffing policies and programs. In turn, these meld into a set of staffing support activities (legal compliance, planning, and job analysis), as well as the core activities (recruitment, selection, and employment). Retention and staffing system management activities cut across both support and core activities.

Staffing strategy is both an outgrowth of and a contributor to HR and organization strategy. Thirteen important strategic staffing decisions loom for any organization. Some pertain to staffing level choices, and others deal with staffing quality choices.

Staffing ethics involves determining moral principles and guidelines for practice. Numerous suggestions were made for ethical conduct in staffing, and many pressure points for sidestepping such conduct are in operation. There are some appropriate ways for handling such pressures.

The staffing organizations model serves as the structural framework for the book. The first part treats staffing models and strategy. The second part treats the support activities of legal compliance, planning, and job analysis. The next three parts treat the core staffing activities of recruitment, selection, and employment. The last section addresses staffing systems and employee retention management. Each chapter has a separate section labeled "Legal Issues," as well as discussion questions, ethical issues questions, applications, the Tanglewood Stores case (in some chapters), and endnotes (references).

DISCUSSION QUESTIONS

1. What would be potential problems with having a staffing process in which vacancies were filled (1) on a lottery basis from among job applicants, or (2) on a first come–first hired basis among job applicants?
2. Why is it important for the organization to view all components of staffing (recruitment, selection, employment) from the perspective of the job applicant?
3. Would it be desirable to hire people only according to the person/organization match, ignoring the person/job match?
4. What are examples of how staffing activities are influenced by training activities? Compensation activities?
5. Are some of the 13 strategic staffing decisions more important than others? Which ones? Why?

ETHICAL ISSUES

1. As a staffing professional in the department or as the hiring manager of a work unit, explain why it is so important to represent the organization's interests (see Exhibit 1.8). What are some possible consequences of not doing so?
2. One of the strategic staffing choices is whether to pursue workforce diversity actively or passively. First suggest some ethical reasons for active pursuit of diversity, and then suggest some ethical reasons for a more passive approach. Assume that the type of diversity in question is increasing workforce representation of women and ethnic minorities.

APPLICATIONS

Staffing for Your Own Job

Instructions

Consider a job you previously held or your current job. Use the staffing components model to help you think through and describe the staffing process that led to your getting hired for the job. Trace and describe the process (1) from your own perspective as a job applicant and (2) from the organization's perspective. Listed below are some questions to jog your memory. Write your responses to these questions and be prepared to discuss them.

Applicant Perspective
Recruitment:

1. Why did you identify and seek out the job with this organization?
2. How did you try to make yourself attractive to the organization?

Selection:

1. How did you gather information about the job's requirements and rewards?
2. How did you judge your own KSAOs and needs relative to these requirements and rewards?

Employment:

1. Why did you decide to continue on in the staffing process, rather than drop out of it?
2. Why did you decide to accept the job offer? What were the pluses and minuses of the job?

Organization Perspective
Even if you do not know, or are unsure of, the answers to these questions, try to answer them or guess at them.
Recruitment:

1. How did the organization identify you as a job applicant?
2. How did the organization make the job attractive to you?

Selection:

1. What techniques (application blank, interview, etc.) did the organization use to gather KSAO information about you?
2. How did the organization evaluate this information? What did it see as your strong and weak points, KSAO-wise?

Employment:

1. Why did the organization decide to continue pursuing you as an applicant, rather than reject you from further consideration?
2. What was the job offer process like? Did you receive a verbal or written (or both) offer? Who gave you the offer? What was the content of the offer?

Reactions to the Staffing Process
Now that you have described the staffing process, what are your reactions to it?

1. What were the strong points or positive features of the process?
2. What were the weak points and negative features of the process?
3. What changes would you like to see made in the process, and why?

Staffing Strategy for a New Plant

Household Consumer Enterprises, Inc. (HCE) has its corporate headquarters in downtown Chicago, with manufacturing and warehouse/distribution facilities throughout the north-central region of the United States. It specializes in the design and production of nondisposable household products such as brooms, brushes, rakes, kitchen utensils, and garden tools. The company has recently changed its mission from "providing households with safe and sturdy utensils" to "providing households with visually appealing utensils that are safe and sturdy." The new emphasis on "visually appealing" will necessitate new strategies for designing and producing new products that have design flair and imagination built into them. One strategy under consideration is to target various demographic groups with different utensil designs. One group is 25–40-year-old professional and managerial people, who it is thought would want such utensils for both their visual and conversation-piece appeal.

A tentative strategy is to build and staff a new plant that will have free rein in the design and production of utensils for this 25–40 age group. To start, the plant will focus on producing a set of closely related (designwise) plastic products: dishwashing pans, outdoor wastebaskets, outdoor plant holders, and watering cans. These items can be produced without too large a capital and facilities investment, can be marketed as a group, and can be on stores' shelves and on HCE's store Web site in time for Christmas sales.

The facility's design and engineering team has initially decided that each of the four products will be produced on a separate assembly line, though the lines will share common technology and require roughly similar assembly jobs. Based on advice from the HR vice president, Jarimir Zwitski, it is decided the key jobs in the plant for staffing purposes will be plant manager, product designer (computer-assisted design), assemblers, and packers/warehouse workers. The initial staffing level for the plant will be 150 employees. Because of the riskiness of the venture and the low margins that are planned initially on the four products due to high start-up costs, the plant will be run on a continuous basis six days per week (i.e., a 24/6 schedule), with the remaining day reserved for cleaning and maintenance. It is planned for pay levels to be at the low end of the market, except for product designers, who will be paid above market. There will be limited benefits for all employees, namely, health insurance with a 30% employee copay after one year of continuous employment, no pension plan, and an earned time-off bank (for holidays, sickness, and vacation) of 160 hours per year.

The head of the design team, Maria Dos Santos, and Mr. Zwitski wish to come to you, the corporate manager of staffing, to share their preliminary thinking with you and ask you some questions, knowing that staffing issues loom large for this new venture. They ask you to discuss the following questions with them, and they send them to you in advance so you can prepare for the meeting. Your task is to write out a tentative response to each question that will be the basis for your discussion at the meeting. The questions are:

1. What geographic location might be best for the plant in terms of attracting sufficient quantity and quality of labor, especially for the key jobs?
2. Should the plant manager come from inside the current managerial ranks or be sought from the outside?
3. Should staffing be based on just the person/job match or also the person/organization match?
4. Would it make sense to staff the plant initially with a flexible workforce by using temporary employees and then shift over to a core workforce if it looks like the plant will be successful?
5. In the early stages, should the plant be fully staffed, understaffed, or overstaffed?
6. Will employee retention likely be a problem, and if so, how would this affect the viability of the new plant?

TANGLEWOOD STORES CASE

In this chapter you read about the relationship between organizational strategy and organizational staffing practices. The introductory section of the casebook will give you an opportunity to see how these principles are put into practice. The goal of this section is to help you learn more about how competition, strategy, and culture jointly inform the effective development of staffing strategy.

The Situation

The case involves a series of staffing exercises related to the Tanglewood Department Stores. You will act as an external consultant for the organization's staffing services department. Tanglewood Department Stores is a chain of general retail stores with an "outdoors" theme, including a large camping and outdoor living section in every store. The organization's culture is based on a set of core values that includes employee participation and a commitment to being a positive place to work. The context section provides additional details regarding Tanglewood's industry, core jobs, market niche, and other strategic concerns.

Your Tasks

For each of the issues related to strategic staffing levels and staffing quality in Exhibit 1.7, make a statement regarding where Tanglewood should position itself. For example, the first decision is to develop or acquire talent. To what extent should Tanglewood follow either strategy and why? Repeat this process for each of the staffing level and staffing quality dimensions. The background information for this case, and your specific assignment, can be found at *www.mhhe.com/heneman6e.*

ENDNOTES

1. *Monthly Labor Review,* Feb. 2003, p. 78.

2. *Monthly Labor Review,* Aug. 2004, p. 84.

3. Saratoga Institute, *2000 Human Capital Benchmarking Report* (Santa Clara, CA: author, 2000), p. 73.

4. G. Hyland-Savage, "General Management Perspective on Staffing; The Staffing Commandments," in N. C. Burkholder, P. J. Edwards, Jr., and L. Sartain (eds.), *On Staffing* (Hoboken, NJ: Wiley, 2004), p. 280.

5. J. V. Singh, "McKinsey's Managing Director Rajat Gupta on Leading a Knowledge-Based Global Consulting Organization," *Academy of Management Executive,* 2001, 15(2), p. 35.

6. G. Anders, "Taming the Out-of-Control In-Box," *Wall Street Journal,* Feb. 4, 2000, p. 81.

7. J. Marquez, "Engine of Change," *Workforce Management,* July 17, 2006, p. 27.

8. "America's Most Admired: GE," *Fortune,* Mar. 6, 2006, p. 104.

9. J. B. Barney and P. M.Wright, "On Becoming a Strategic Partner: The Role of Human Resources in Gaining Competitive Advantage," *Human Resource Management,* 1998, 37(1), pp. 31–46; C. G. Brush, P. G. Greene, and M. M. Hart, "From Initial Idea to Unique Advantage: The Entrepreneurial Challenge of Constructing a Resource Base," *Academy of Management Executive,* 2001, 15(1), pp. 64–80.

10. J. S. Lublin, "An E-Company CEO Is Also Recruiter-in-Chief," *Wall Street Journal,* Nov. 9, 1999, p. B1.

11. M. Adams and C. Woodyard, "Screeners Shifted to Cover Busier Airports," *USA Today,* May 27, 2004, p. 113; A. Fox, "TSA: From 0 to 55,000 in One Year Flat," June 1, 2004 (*www.shrm.org/hr/news*); CPS Human Resource Services, "CPS Opens 20 Offices Across the Country," *HR Practitioner Newsletter,* Fall 2004, p. 1; E. Kolmstetter, "I-O's Making an Impact: TSA Transportation Screener Skill Standards, Selection System, and Hiring Process," *The Industrial-Organizational Psychologist,* Apr. 2003, pp. 39–46.

12. J. Marquez, "A Talent Strategy Overhaul at Pfizer," *Workforce Management,* Feb. 12, 2007, pp. 1, 3.

13. N. Byrnes, "Avon Calling—Lots of Reps," *Business Week,* June 2, 2003, pp. 53–54.

14. D. F. Caldwell and C. A. O'Reilly III, "Measuring Person-Job Fit With a Profile-Comparison Process," *Journal of Applied Psychology,* 1990, 75, pp. 648–657; R. V. Dawis, "Person-Environment Fit and Job Satisfaction," in C. J. Cranny, P. C. Smith, and E. F. Stone, *Job Satisfaction* (New York: Lexington, 1992), pp. 69–88; R. V. Dawis, L. H. Lofquist, and D. J.Weiss, *A Theory of Work Adjustment (A Revision)* (Minneapolis: Industrial Relations Center, University of Minnesota, 1968).

15. D. E. Bowen, G. E. Ledford, Jr., and B. R. Nathan, "Hiring for the Organization and Not the Job," *Academy of Management Executive,* 1991, 5(4), pp. 35–51; T. A. Judge and R. D. Bretz, Jr., "Effects of Work Values on Job Choice Decisions," *Journal of Applied Psychology,* 1992, 77, pp. 1–11; C. A. O'Reilly III, J. Chatman, and D. F. Caldwell, "People and Organizational Culture: A Profile Comparison Approach to Assessing Person-Organization Fit," *Academy of Management Journal,* 1991, 34, pp. 487–516; A. L. Kristof, "Person-Organization Fit: An Intergrative Review of Its Conceptualizations, Measurement, and Implications," *Personnel Psychology,* 1996, 49, pp. 1–50.

16. L. L. Levesque, "Opportunistic Hiring and Employee Fit," *Human Resource Management,* 2005, 44, pp. 301–317.

17. S. Craig, "Inside Goldman's Secret Rite: The Race to Become Partner," *Wall Street Journal,* Oct. 13, 2006, pp. A1, A11.

18. M. Kessler, "More Chipmakers Outsource Manufacturing," *USA Today,* Nov. 16, 2006, p. B1; C. Dougherty, "Labor Shortage Becoming Acute in Technology," *New York Times,* Mar. 10, 2007, pp. 1, 4.

19. G. Fields, "Bulging Jails and Tight Budgets Make Job of Guard Even Tougher," *Wall Street Journal,* Nov. 2, 2005, pp. A1, A9; K. Voyles, "Florida Seeking to Recruit and Retain Prison Employees," *Gainesville Sun,* Jan. 25, 2007, p. 5B.

20. S. Wisnefski, "Truckers' Worries: Fuel, Driver Shortfall," *Wall Street Journal,* Oct. 25, 2006, p. B3A.

21. J. Collison, *Future of the U.S. Labor Pool* (Alexandria, VA: Society for Human Resource Management, 2005).

22. F. Hansen, "What Is 'Talent'?" *Workforce Management,* Jan. 15, 2007, p. 12.

23. *www.shrm.org/kc.*

24. J. Joseph and E. Esen, *2003 Business Ethics Survey* (Alexandria, VA: Society for Human Resource Management, 2003), pp. 1–10.

25. Joseph and Esen, *2003 Business Ethics Survey,* pp. 10–11.

The Staffing Organizations Model

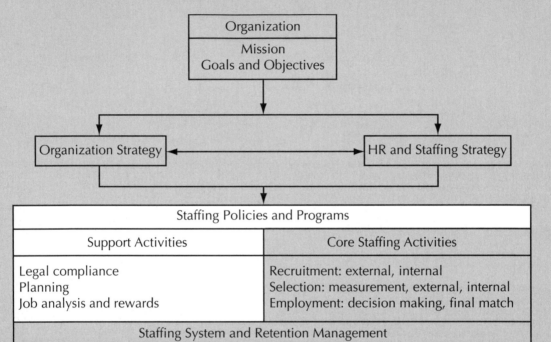

PART TWO

Support Activities

CHAPTER TWO

Legal Compliance

The Employment Relationship
    Employer–Employee
    Independent Contractors
    Temporary Employees

Laws and Regulations
    Need for Laws and Regulations
    Sources of Laws and Regulations

EEO/AA Laws: General Provisions and Enforcement
    General Provisions
    Enforcement: EEOC
    Enforcement: OFCCP

EEO/AA Laws: Specific Staffing Provisions
    Civil Rights Acts (1964, 1991)
    Age Discrimination in Employment Act (1967)
    Americans With Disabilities Act (1990)
    Rehabilitation Act (1973)
    Executive Order 11246 (1965)

EEO/AA: Information and Initiatives
    Information Sources
    Initiatives

Other Staffing Laws
    Federal Laws
    State and Local Laws
    Civil Service Laws and Regulations

Legal Issues in Remainder of Book

Summary

Discussion Questions

Ethical Issues

Applications

Laws and regulations have assumed an importance of major proportions in the process of staffing organizations. Virtually all aspects of staffing are subject to their influence. No organization can or should ignore provisions of the law; in this case, ignorance truly is not bliss.

This chapter begins by discussing the formation of the employment relationships from a legal perspective. It first defines what an employer is, along with the rights and obligations of being an employer. The employer may acquire people to work for it in the form of employees, independent contractors, and temporary employees. Legal meanings and implications for each of these terms are provided.

For many reasons, the employment relationship has become increasingly regulated. Reasons for the myriad laws and regulations affecting the employment relationship are suggested. Then, the major sources of the laws and regulations controlling the employment relationship are indicated.

Equal employment opportunity and affirmative action (EEO/AA) laws and regulations have become paramount in the eyes of many who are concerned with staffing organizations. The general provisions of five major EEO/AA laws are summarized, along with indications of how these laws are administered and enforced. While voluntary compliance is preferred by the enforcement agencies, if it fails, litigation may follow. Litigation is based on the key concepts of disparate treatment and disparate impact.

For these same five laws, their specific (and numerous) provisions regarding staffing are then presented in detail. Within this presentation the true scope, complexity, and impact of the laws regarding staffing become known.

Numerous information sources about EEO/AA laws and regulations are then presented. Also described are several compliance and outreach initiatives by the Equal Employment Opportunity Commission (EEOC).

Attention then turns to other staffing laws and regulations. These involve myriad federal laws, state and local laws, and civil service laws and regulations. These laws, like federal EEO/AA laws, have major impacts on staffing activities.

Finally, the chapter concludes with an indication that each of the following chapters has a separate section, "Legal Issues," at the end of it. In these sections, specific topics and applications of the law are presented. Their intent is to provide guidance and examples (not legal advice per se) regarding staffing practices that are permissible, impermissible, and required.

THE EMPLOYMENT RELATIONSHIP

From a legal perspective the term "staffing" refers to formation of the employment relationship. That relationship involves several different types of arrangements between the organization and those who provide work for it. These arrangements have special and reasonably separate legal meanings. This section explores those arrangements: employer–employee, independent contractor, and temporary employee.[1]

Employer–Employee

By far the most prevalent form of the employment relationship is that of employer–employee. This arrangement is the result of the organization's usual staffing activities—a culmination of the person/job matching process. As shown in Exhibit 2.1, the employer and employee negotiate and agree on the terms and conditions that will define and govern their relationship. The formal agreement represents an employment contract, the terms and conditions of which represent the promises and expectations of the parties (job requirements and rewards, and KSAOs [knowledge, skill, ability, and other characteristics] and motivation). Over time, the initial contract may be modified due to changes in requirements or rewards of the current job, or employee transfer or promotion. The contract may also be terminated by either party, thus ending the employment relationship.

Employment contracts come in a variety of styles. They may be written or oral (both types are legally enforceable), and their specificity may vary from extensive to bare bones. In some instances, where the contract is written, terms and conditions are described in great detail. Examples of such contracts are collective

---

EXHIBIT 2.1   Matching Process, Employment Contract, and Employment Relationship

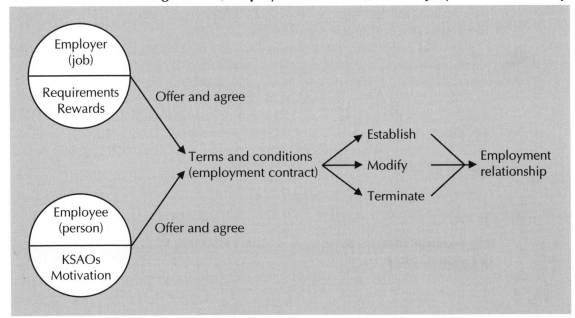

bargaining agreements and contracts for professional athletes, entertainers, and upper-level executives. At the other extreme, the contract may be little more than some simple oral promises about the job, such as promises about wages and hours, agreed to on the basis of a handshake.

From a legal perspective, an employer is an entity that employs others (employees or independent contractors) to do its work or work in its behalf. When these "others" are employees, the employer has the right to specify both the work output (results) expected and the work methods to be followed. In exchange for this right to control employees, the employer incurs certain legal responsibilities and liabilities. Specifically, the employer becomes (1) required to withhold employee payroll taxes (income, Social Security), (2) required to pay taxes (unemployment compensation, employer's share of Social Security and Medicare), (3) covered under the myriad laws and regulations governing the employment relationship, and (4) liable for the acts of its employees during employment.

When and how the employment relationship may end is a matter of great importance to the employer and the employee. For the employer, it bears on the degree of staffing flexibility possible to quickly terminate employees without constraint. For employees, the issue is the degree of continued employment and job security that will be expected. Under the common-law principle of employment-at-will, in the absence of any contract language to the contrary, the employment relationship is strictly an at-will one, meaning that either the employer or the employee may terminate the employment relationship at any time, for any reason, without prior notification. Restrictions on the employment-at-will right are usually established as part of the employment contract (such as termination for "just cause" only); other restrictions come about from federal, state, and local laws (such as nondiscrimination in termination).[2]

Independent Contractors

The employer may also hire independent contractors.[3] An independent contractor is not legally considered an employee, however; because of this the rights and responsibilities the employer has toward the independent contractor are different from those for its employees. Classifying and using a person as an independent contractor frees the employer of the tax withholding and tax payment obligations it has for employees. It may also reduce employer exposure under laws and regulations governing the employment relationship. For example, nondiscrimination laws (e.g., Civil Rights Act) apply to the employer and its employees, but not to its independent contractors.

In exchange for these advantages of using independent contractors, the employer substantially loses the right to control the contractor. In particular, while the employer can still control expected results, the employer cannot dictate where, when, or how work is to be done. Thus, the employer loses control over the means (work processes, tools, equipment, work schedules, and so forth) by which the work is performed.

Beyond this crucial distinction, the line of demarcation between what constitutes an employee and what constitutes an independent contractor is often fuzzy. Numerous other factors come into play. For example, a person is more likely to be considered an independent contractor than an employee in the following situations:

- Working in a distinct occupation or business
- Working without supervision or oversight from the employer
- Paying one's own business and travel expenses
- Setting one's own hours of work
- Possessing a high degree of skill
- Using one's own tools, materials, office
- Working on a project with a definite completion date
- Working on relatively short projects
- Being paid by the project or commission rather than by the time spent

The above examples are based on common-law interpretations and on a list of 11 criteria used by the Internal Revenue Service to determine the appropriate classification of people as employees or independent contractors. Misclassification of people as independent contractors can result in substantial tax liabilities and fines for the employer.

Temporary Employees

Temporary employees do not have special legal stature. They are considered employees of the temporary help agency (staffing firm) that obtained them through its own staffing process. Temporary employees are then given job assignments with other employers (clients) by the staffing firm. During these assignments the temporary employee remains on the payroll of the staffing firm, and the client employer simply reimburses the staffing firm for its wage and other costs. The client employer must recognize that it has a severely limited right to control temporary employees that it utilizes, because they are not its employees but employees of the staffing firm.

Use of temporary employees often raises issues of coemployment, in which the client employer and the staffing firm share the traditional role of employer.[4] Because both function as employers to an extent, there is a need to sort out their obligations and liabilities under various laws. Depending on the specific issue and law involved, both the client employer and the staffing firm may be legally considered the employer. Employment discrimination laws such as the Civil Rights Act, for example, apply to both the client employer and the staffing firm. Thus, usage of temporary employees by a client employer should be preceded by a thorough review of the coemployment legal ramifications.

The demarcation between an employee and a temporary employee becomes increasingly blurred when an employer uses a set of temporary employees from a staffing firm on a long-term basis, resulting in so-called permatemps. Nationally,

29% of such employees work for the same client employer for a year or more, so they appear more like employees of the client than of the staffing firm. Which are they, and what factors might determine this? Several court cases suggest that these individuals are in fact employees of the client employer rather than of the staffing firm, particularly because of the strong degree of control the client employer typically exercises over those people. Hence, to help ensure that per-matemps will not be legally considered the client's employees, the client must give up, or never exercise, direct control over these people and treat them as truly separate from regular employees. This may require, for example, not training or supervising them, not listing them in the phone directory, and not allowing them to use the organization's stationery. Clearly, therefore, organizations must examine all policies and practices regarding the acquisition and management of temporary employees to ensure that they are being appropriately treated and classified as such.[5]

LAWS AND REGULATIONS

Establishment and maintenance of the employment relationship involves exercising discretion on the part of both the employer and the employee. Broadly speaking, laws affecting the employment relationship spring from a need to define the scope of permissible discretion and place limits on it. Specific factors contributing to the need for laws and regulations and the sources of laws and regulations are explored below.

Need for Laws and Regulations

Balance of Power

Entering into and maintaining the employment relationship involve negotiating issues of power.[6] The employer has something desirable to offer the employee (a job with certain requirements and rewards), and the employee has something to offer the employer (KSAOs and motivation). Usually, the employer has the upper hand in this power relationship because the employer has more to offer, and more control over what to offer, than does the employee. It is the employer who controls the creation of jobs, the definition of jobs in terms of requirements and rewards, access to those jobs via staffing systems, movement of employees among jobs over time, and, ultimately, the retention or termination of employees. While employees participate in these processes and decisions to varying degrees, it is seldom as an equal or a partner of the employer. Employment laws and regulations thus exist, in part, to reduce or limit the employer's power in the employment relationship. Laws pertaining to wages, hours, equal employment opportunity, and so forth, all seek to limit employer discretion in the establishment of the terms and conditions of employment.

Protection of Employees

Laws and regulations seek to provide specific protections to employees that they could conceivably, though improbably, acquire individually in an employment contract.[7] These protections pertain to employment standards, individual workplace rights, and consistency of treatment. Employment standards usually represent minimum acceptable terms and conditions of employment. Examples include minimum wage, nondiscrimination, overtime pay, and safety and health standards. Laws and regulations also provide employees with individual rights that they could not acquire alone in a contract with their employers. Examples of these are organizing and collective bargaining rights, civil rights protections, and constraints that place limits on the right of the employer to unilaterally terminate the employment relationship. Finally, laws and regulations, in effect, provide guarantees of consistency of treatment among employees. They constitute a constraint on the employer to treat employees differently from one another in terms and conditions of employment and afford employees some measure of procedural justice, or fairness in the process whereby decisions are made about them. Hiring and promotion decisions, for example, cannot be made on the basis of protected employee characteristics (e.g., race, sex).

Protection of Employers

Employers also gain protections from laws and regulations. First, they provide guidance to employers as to what are permissible practices as well as impermissible practices. The Civil Rights Act, for example, not only forbids certain types of discrimination on the basis of race, color, religion, sex, and national origin but also specifically mentions employment practices that are permitted. One of those practices is the use of professionally developed ability tests, a practice that has major implications for external and internal selection. Second, questions about the meaning of the law are clarified through many avenues—court decisions, policy statements from government agencies, informal guidance from enforcement officials, and networking with other employers. The result is increasing convergence on what is required to comply with the laws. This allows the employer to implement needed changes, which then become standard operating procedure in staffing systems. In this manner, for example, affirmative action programs have developed and been incorporated into the staffing mainstream for many employers.

Sources of Laws and Regulations

There are numerous sources of laws and regulations that govern the employment relationship. Exhibit 2.2 provides examples of these as they pertain to staffing. Each of these is commented on next.

Common Law

Common law, which has its origins in England, is court-made law, as opposed to law from other sources, such as the state. It consists of the case-by-case decisions of the court, which determine over time permissible and impermissible practices, as well as their remedies. There is a heavy reliance on common law in the precedence established in previous court decisions. Each state develops and administers its own common law. Employment-at-will and workplace tort cases, for example, are treated at the state level. As noted, employment-at-will involves the rights of the employer and the employee to terminate the employment relationship at will. A tort is a civil wrong that occurs when the employer violates a duty owed to its employees or customers that leads to harm or damages suffered by them. Staffing tort examples include negligent hiring of unsafe or dangerous employees, fraud and misrepresentation regarding employment terms and conditions, defamation of former employees, and invasion of privacy.[8]

EXHIBIT 2.2   Sources of Laws and Regulations

SOURCE	EXAMPLES
Common law	Employment-at-will Workplace torts
Constitutional law	Fifth Amendment Fourteenth Amendment
Statutory law	Civil Rights Act Age Discrimination in Employment Act Americans With Disabilities Act Rehabilitation Act Immigration Reform and Control Act Fair Credit Reporting Act Employee Polygraph Protection Act Uniformed Services Employment and Reemployment Rights Act State and local laws Civil service laws
Executive order Agencies	11246 (nondiscrimination under federal contracts) Equal Employment Opportunity Commission (EEOC) Department of Labor (DOL) Office of Federal Contract Compliance Programs (OFCCP) Department of Homeland Security State Fair Employment Practice (FEP) agencies

Constitutional Law

Constitutional law is derived from the U.S. Constitution and its amendments. It supersedes any other source of law or regulation. Its major application is in the area of the rights of public employees, particularly their due process rights.

Statutory Law

Statutory law is derived from written statutes that are passed by legislative bodies. These bodies are federal (Congress), state (legislatures and assemblies), and local (municipal boards and councils). Legislative bodies may create, amend, and eliminate laws and regulations. They may also create agencies to administer and enforce the law.

Agencies

Agencies exist at the federal, state, and local level. Their basic charge is to interpret, administer, and enforce the law. At the federal level, the two major agencies of concern to staffing are the Department of Labor (DOL) and the Equal Employment Opportunity Commission (EEOC). Housed within the DOL are several separate units for administration of employment law, notably the Office of Federal Contract Compliance Programs (OFCCP). The Department of Homeland Security handles issues regarding foreign workers and immigration in its agency the U.S. Citizenship and Immigration Services.

Agencies rely heavily on written documents in performing their functions. These documents are variously referred to as rules, regulations, guidelines, and policy statements. Rules, regulations, and guidelines are published in the *Federal Register*, as well as incorporated into the Code of Federal Regulations (CFR), and they have the weight of law. Policy statements are somewhat more benign in that they do not have the force of law. They do, however, represent the agency's official position on a point or question.

EEO/AA LAWS: GENERAL PROVISIONS AND ENFORCEMENT

In this section, the major federal EEO/AA laws are summarized in terms of their general provisions. Mechanisms for enforcement of the laws are also discussed.[9] More details may be found online (*www.eeoc.gov; www.dol.gov/esa*).

General Provisions

The major federal EEO/AA laws are the following:

1. Title VII of the Civil Rights Acts (1964, 1991)
2. Age Discrimination in Employment Act (1967)
3. Americans With Disabilities Act (1990)

4. Rehabilitation Act (1973)
5. Executive Order 11246 (1965)

Exhibit 2.3 contains a summary of the basic provisions of these laws, pertaining to coverage, prohibited discrimination, enforcement agency, and important rules, regulations, and guidelines. Inspection of Exhibit 2.3 suggests that these laws are appropriately labeled "major" for several reasons. First, the laws are very broad in their coverage of employers. Second, they specifically prohibit discrimination on the basis of several individual characteristics (race, color, religion, sex, national origin, age, disability, handicap). Third, separate agencies have been created for their administration and enforcement. Finally, these agencies have issued numerous rules, regulations, and guidelines to assist in interpreting, implementing, and enforcing the law. Three sets of regulations that are of particular importance to staffing are the Uniform Guidelines on Employee Selection Procedures (*www. eeoc.gov*), Affirmative Action Programs regulations (*www.dol.gov/esa*), and the Employment Regulations for the Americans With Disabilities Act (*www.eeoc.gov*). The specifics of these regulations will be discussed in subsequent chapters.

For the Civil Rights Act, Age Discrimination in Employment Act (ADEA), and Americans With Disabilities Act (ADA), Exhibit 2.3 shows that whether the organization is covered depends on its number of employees. To count employees, the EEOC has issued guidance indicating that the organization should include any employee with whom the organization had an "employment relationship" in each of 20 or more calendar weeks during the current or preceding year. In essence, this means that full-time and part-time employees—and possibly temporary employees if there is true coemployment—should be included in the employee count.[10]

Individuals who oppose unlawful practices, participate in proceedings, or request accommodations are protected from retaliation under the laws shown in Exhibit 2.3. The term "retaliation" is broadly interpreted by the courts and the EEOC to include refusal to hire, denial of promotion, termination, other actions affecting employment (e.g., threats, unjustified negative evaluations), and actions that deter reasonable people from pursuing their rights (e.g., assault, unfounded civil or criminal charges) (*www.eeoc.gov*). The EEOC has issued specific guidance on what constitutes evidence of retaliation, as well as special remedies for retaliatory actions by the employer.[11]

Three other general features of the EEO laws, as interpreted by the EEOC and the courts, should be noted.[12] First, state (but not local) government employers are immune from lawsuits by employees who allege violation of the ADA or the ADEA. State employees must thus pursue age and disability discrimination claims under applicable state laws. Second, company officials and individual managers cannot be held personally liable for discrimination under the Civil Rights Act, the ADA, or the ADEA. They might be liable, however, under state law. Third, the ADA, the Civil Rights Act, and the ADEA extend to U.S. citizens employed overseas by American employers. Also, a foreign company that is owned or controlled

EXHIBIT 2.3   Major Federal EEO/AA Laws: General Provisions

Law or Executive Order	Coverage	Prohibited Discrimination	Enforcement Agency	Important Rules, Regulations, and Guidelines
Civil Rights Act (1964, 1991)	Private employers with 15 or more employees Federal, state, and local governments Educational institutions Employment agencies Labor unions	Race, color, religion, national origin, sex	EEOC	Uniform Guidelines on Employee Selection Procedures Sex Discrimination Guidelines Religious Discrimination Guidelines National Origin Discrimination Guidelines
Age Discrimination in Employment Act (1967)	Private employers with 20 or more employees Federal, state, and local governments Employment agencies Labor unions	Age (40 and over)	EEOC	Interpretations of the Age Discrimination in Employment Act
Americans With Disabilities Act (1990)	Private employers with 15 or more employees Federal, state, and local governments	Qualified individual with a disability	EEOC	ADA–Employment Regulations Definition of the Term Disability Pre-Employment Disability-Related Questions and Medical Examinations
Rehabilitation Act (1973)	Federal contractors with contracts in excess of $2,500	Individual with a handicap	DOL (OFCCP)	Affirmative Action Regulations on Handicapped Workers
Executive Order 11246 (1965)	Federal contractors with contracts in excess of $10,000	Race, color, religion, national origin, sex	DOL (OFCCP)	Sex Discrimination Guidelines Affirmative Action Programs regulations

NOTE: Full text of the laws and Executive Order, as well as the important rules, regulations, and guidelines, may be found in the Bureau of National Affairs *Labor and Employment Law Library* (*www.bna.com*).

by an American employer and is doing business overseas generally must also comply with the Civil Rights Act, the ADA, and the ADEA.

Not shown in Exhibit 2.3 is the broadsweeping nature of the specific employment practices affected by the federal EEO/AA laws. An overview of those practices is shown in Exhibit 2.4.

EXHIBIT 2.4   Illegal Employment Discrimination Under Federal Law

Under Title VII of the Civil Rights Act of 1964, the Americans With Disabilities Act (ADA), and the Age Discrimination in Employment Act (ADEA), it is illegal to discriminate in any aspect of employment, including:

- Hiring and firing
- Compensation, assignment, or classification of employees
- Job advertisements
- Recruitment
- Testing
- Use of company facilities
- Training and apprenticeship programs
- Fringe benefits
- Pay, retirement plans, and disability leave
- Other terms and conditions of employment

Discriminatory practices under these laws also include:

- Harassment on the basis of race, color, religion, sex, national origin, disability, or age
- Retaliation against an individual for filing a charge of discrimination, participating in an investigation, or opposing discriminatory practices
- Employment decisions based on stereotypes or assumptions about the abilities, traits, or performance of individuals of a certain sex, race, age, religion, or ethnic group, or individuals with disabilities, and
- Denying employment opportunities to a person because of marriage to, or association with, an individual of a particular race, religion, national origin, or an individual with a disability. Title VII also prohibits discrimination because of participation in schools or places of worship associated with a particular racial, ethnic, or religious group

Employers are required to post notices to all employees advising them of their rights under the laws EEOC enforces and their right to be free from retaliation. Such notices must be accessible, as needed, to persons with visual or other disabilities that affect reading.

Note: Many states and municipalities also have enacted protections against discrimination and harassment based on sexual orientation, status as a parent, marital status and political affiliation. For information, please contact the EEOC District Office nearest you.

SOURCE: Equal Employment Opportunity Commission, Nov. 2004 (*www.eeoc.gov*).

Enforcement: EEOC

As shown in Exhibit 2.3, the EEOC is responsible for enforcing the Civil Rights Act, the ADEA, and the ADA. Though each law requires separate enforcement mechanisms, some generalizations about their collective enforcement are possible.[13]

Disparate Treatment and Disparate Impact

Claims of discrimination in staffing ultimately require evidence and proof, particularly as these charges pertain to the staffing system itself and its specific characteristics as it has operated in practice. Toward this end, there are two different avenues or paths to follow—disparate treatment and disparate impact.[14] Both paths may be followed for Title VII of the Civil Rights Act, ADA, and ADEA claims.

Disparate Treatment. Claims of disparate treatment involve allegations of intentional discrimination where it is alleged that the employer knowingly and deliberately discriminated against people on the basis of specific characteristics such as race or sex. Evidence for such claims may be of several sorts.

First, the evidence may be direct. It might, for example, involve reference to an explicit, written policy of the organization such as one stating that "women are not to be hired for the following jobs."

The situation may not involve such blatant action, however, but may consist of what is referred to as a mixed motive. Here, both a prohibited characteristic (e.g., sex) and a legitimate reason (e.g., job qualifications) are mixed together to contribute to a negative decision about a person, such as a failure to hire or promote. If an unlawful motive, such as sex, plays any part in the decision, it is illegal, despite the presence of a lawful motive as well.

Finally, the discrimination may be such that evidence of a failure to hire or promote because of a protected characteristic must be inferred from several situational factors. Here, the evidence involves four factors:

1. The person belongs to a protected class.
2. The person applied for, and was qualified for, a job the employer was trying to fill.
3. The person was rejected despite being qualified.
4. The position remained open and the employer continued to seek applicants as qualified as the person rejected.

Most disparate treatment cases involve and require the use of these four factors to initially prove a charge of discrimination.

Disparate Impact. Disparate impact is also known as adverse impact and focuses on the effect of employment practices, rather than on the motive or intent underlying them. Accordingly, the emphasis here is on the need for direct evidence that, as a result of a protected characteristic, people are being adversely affected by a practice. Statistical evidence must be presented to support a claim of adverse impact.[15] Three types of statistical evidence may be used, and these are shown in Exhibit 2.5.

Shown first in the exhibit are applicant flow statistics, which look at differences in selection rates (proportion of applicants hired) among different groups for a particular job. If the differences are large enough, this suggests that the effect of the selection system is discriminatory. In the example, the selection rate for men is .50 (or 50%) and for women it is .11 (or 11%), suggesting the possibility of discrimination.

A second type of statistical evidence, shown next in the exhibit, involves the use of stock statistics. Here, the percentage of women or minorities actually employed in a job category is compared with their availability in the relevant population. Relevant is defined in terms of such things as "qualified," "interested," or "geographic." In the example shown, there is a disparity in the percentage of minorities employed (10%) compared with their availability (30%), which suggests their underutilization.

EXHIBIT 2.5   Types of Disparate Impact Statistics

A. FLOW STATISTICS

Definition:

Significant differences in selection rates between groups

Example

Job Category: Customer Service Representative

No. of Applicants		No. Hired		Selection Rate (%)	
Men	**Women**	**Men**	**Women**	**Men**	**Women**
50	45	25	5	50%	11%

B. STOCK STATISTICS

Definition:

Underutilization of women or minorities relative to their availability in the relevant population

Example

Job Category: Management Trainee

Current Trainees (%)		Availability (%)	
Nonminority	**Minority**	**Nonminority**	**Minority**
90%	10%	70%	30%

C. CONCENTRATION STATISTICS

Definition:

Concentration of women or minorities in certain job categories

Example

	Job Category			
	Clerical	**Production**	**Sales**	**Managers**
% Men	3%	85%	45%	95%
% Women	97%	15%	55%	5%

The third type of evidence involves use of concentration statistics. Here, the percentages of women or minorities in various job categories are compared to see if women are concentrated in certain workforce categories. In the example shown, there is a concentration of women in clerical jobs (97%), a concentration of men in production (85%) and managerial (95%) jobs, and roughly equal concentrations of men and women in sales jobs (45% and 55%, respectively).

Initial Charge and Conciliation

Enforcement proceedings begin when a charge is filed by an employee or job applicant (the EEOC itself may also file a charge). In states where there is an EEOC-approved fair enforcement practice (FEP) law, the charge is initially deferred to the state. An investigation of the charge occurs to determine if there is "reasonable cause" to assume discrimination has occurred. If reasonable cause is not found, the charge is dropped. If reasonable cause is found, however, the EEOC attempts conciliation of the charge. Conciliation is a voluntary settlement process that seeks agreement by the employer to stop the practice(s) in question and abide by proposed remedies. This is the EEOC's preferred method of settlement. Whenever the EEOC decides not to pursue a claim further, it will issue a "right to sue" letter to the complaining party, allowing a private suit to be started against the employer.

Complementing conciliation is the use of mediation. With mediation, a neutral third party mediates the dispute between the employer and the EEOC and obtains an agreement between them that resolves the dispute. Participation in mediation is voluntary, and either party may opt out of it for any reason. Mediation proceedings are confidential. Any agreement reached between the parties is legally enforceable. More than 70% of complaints that go to mediation are resolved, and 96% of employers who use the EEOC mediation program say they would do so again.[16] In short, the EEOC prefers settlement to litigation. An example of a settlement is shown in Exhibit 2.6.

Litigation and Remedies

Should conciliation fail, suit is filed in federal court. The ensuing litigation process under Title VII is shown in Exhibit 2.7. As can be seen, the charge of the plaintiff (charging party) will follow either a disparate treatment or a disparate impact route.[17] In either event, the plaintiff has the initial burden of proof. Such a burden requires the plaintiff to establish a prima facie case that demonstrates reasonable cause to assume discrimination has occurred. Assuming this case is successfully presented, the defendant must rebut the charge and accompanying evidence.

In disparate treatment cases, the defendant must provide nondiscriminatory reasons during rebuttal for the practice(s) in question. In disparate impact cases, the employer must demonstrate that the practices in question are job related and consistent with business necessity.

EXHIBIT 2.6   Example of a Settlement Agreement With the EEOC

DENVER—The U.S. Equal Employment Opportunity Commission (EEOC) announced today that it has reached agreement with Seattle-based window manufacturer, Milgard Manufacturing, Inc. (Milgard) to resolve a lawsuit alleging that Milgard engaged in racially discriminatory hiring practices at its Colorado facility and retaliated against a human resource assistant, Leigh Ann Ornelas (Ornelas), who complained about the unlawful practices. Ms. Ornelas, who was also named plaintiff in the lawsuit, was represented by Tom Arckey of the law firm Arckey & Reha, LLC.

While Milgard has denied engaging in any wrongful conduct, the company has agreed to pay a total of $3.1 million to resolve the lawsuit, plus up to $270,000 in expenses for administering the costs of the settlement. From the settlement, a fund will be established to provide payments to African Americans or other black individuals who have applied for work at Milgard since 1997 and were not offered jobs. The EEOC anticipates that the settlement fund will be ready to accept claims by July 1, 2004. In the meantime, individuals who believe they are entitled to receive payment from the settlement fund may contact the EEOC at (303) 866-1346.

In addition to the monetary settlement, Milgard has agreed to undertake a comprehensive review of its policies and procedures to ensure compliance with federal antidiscrimination laws; to provide increased training to its Colorado employees and managers regarding workplace discrimination issues; and to engage in recruitment and outreach programs to increase the proportion of African Americans and blacks in its applicant pool. Milgard has also agreed that its current operation in Colorado, and any future operations that might be opened in Colorado, will be under continued monitoring by the EEOC for a period of three years.

The lawsuit arose out of events in 1998, when Leigh Ann Ornelas was the person responsible for conducting initial interviews of job applicants at Milgard Windows' plant, then located in the Montebello area of Denver. The EEOC and Ms. Ornelas maintained that the then–plant manager of the Montebello facility told Ms. Ornelas not to hire or refer black applicants for certain positions in the plant. Ms. Ornelas and the EEOC also have alleged that when Ms. Ornelas complained to various managers concerning these instructions, no action was taken against the plant manager and Ms. Ornelas was subjected to retaliatory harassment and eventually forced to resign. The EEOC also asserted that a statistical analysis of the job applications submitted to Milgard's Colorado facility since 1997 shows that Milgard hired significantly fewer African Americans and blacks than would be predicted based on the demographics of the areas where applicants lived.

Joseph H. Mitchell, regional attorney for the EEOC's Denver District Office, said, "We are pleased to resolve this case and commend Milgard for acknowledging the importance of preventing discriminatory hiring practices and the importance of not retaliating against employees like Leigh Ann Ornelas, who risked her job to champion the rights of the black applicants who were being denied jobs."

SOURCE: Equal Employment Opportunity Commission, May 26, 2004 (*www.eeoc.gov*).

EXHIBIT 2.7   Basic Litigation Process Under Title VII: EEOC

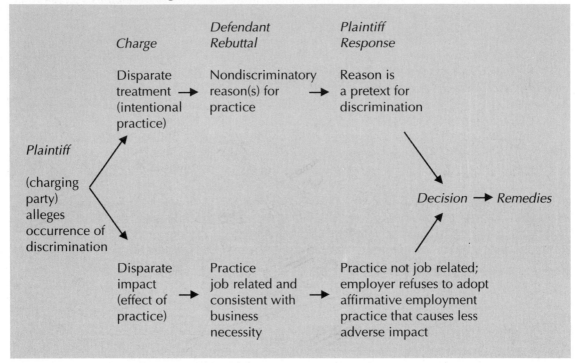

Following rebuttal, the plaintiff may respond to the defense provided by the defendant. In disparate treatment cases, that response hinges on a demonstration that the defendant's reasons for a practice are a pretext, or smoke screen, for the practice. In disparate impact cases, the plaintiff's response will focus on showing that the defendant has not shown its practices to be job related and/or that the employer refuses to adopt a practice that causes less adverse impact.

Disparate impact litigation involving age discrimination charges is somewhat different. After the disparate impact claim (supported by disparate impact statistics) is made, the defendant rebuttal will involve an attempt to prove that the challenged practice is supported by a reasonable factor other than age, and the plaintiff response will attempt to prove that the factor cited is unreasonable and not the true reason for the practice.

Who bears the final, or ultimate, burden of proof? In disparate treatment cases, the plaintiff must ultimately prove that the defendant's practices are discriminatory. For disparate impact cases, on the other hand, the burden is on the defendant. That is, it is the defendant who must prove that its practices are not discriminatory.

The plaintiff and the defendant have an opportunity to end their dispute through a consent decree. This is a voluntary, court-approved agreement between the two parties. The consent decree may contain not only an agreement to halt certain practices but also an agreement to implement certain remedies, such as various forms of monetary relief and AA programs. An example of a consent decree is shown in Exhibit 2.8.

EXHIBIT 2.8   Example of a Consent Decree

LOS ANGELES—The U.S. Equal Employment Opportunity Commission (EEOC) and private plaintiffs today announced their mutual resolution of the lawsuit entitled *EEOC v. Abercrombie & Fitch Stores, Inc.*, Case No. CV-04-4731 SI, which was filed on November 10, 2004, in the United States District Court for the Northern District of California in San Francisco. The lawsuit alleged that Abercrombie & Fitch, which operates a nationwide chain of retail stores, violated Title VII of the Civil Rights Act of 1964 by maintaining recruiting and hiring practices that excluded minorities and women and adopting a restrictive marketing image, and other policies, which limited minority and female employment.

The lawsuit was amicably resolved by entry of a Consent Decree in the U.S. District Court, which provides that Abercrombie & Fitch will pay $50 million to resolve the EEOC lawsuit along with two private class actions filed against Abercrombie & Fitch: *Gonzalez et al. v. Abercrombie et al.* and *West v. Abercrombie et al.*

The Consent Decree enjoins Abercrombie & Fitch from:
a. Discriminating against applicants based upon race, color, national origin which includes African Americans, Asian Americans, and Latinos;
b. Discriminating against women due to their sex, and,
c. Denying promotional opportunities to women and minorities

Abercrombie & Fitch has also agreed to develop and implement hiring and recruiting procedures to ensure compliance under the Decree. Abercrombie & Fitch agreed to ensure that minorities and women are promoted into manager-in-training and manager positions without discrimination. A Monitor will be hired to ensure Abercrombie's compliance with the terms of the Consent Decree, including reporting. Abercrombie & Fitch will hire a vice president of diversity and employ up to 25 diversity recruiters. Abercrombie & Fitch will devise new protocols for each of these areas. Abercrombie & Fitch will post a notice on an internal Web site and at all stores which will be periodically distributed to employees. Additionally, Abercrombie & Fitch will provide training to all of its managers. Most importantly, Abercrombie & Fitch also agreed to ensure that its marketing materials will reflect diversity.

EEOC's General Counsel Eric Dreiband stated, "The retail industry and other industries need to know that businesses cannot discriminate against individuals under the auspice of a marketing strategy or a particular 'look.' Race and sex discrimination in employment are unlawful, and the EEOC will continue to aggressively pursue employers who choose to engage in such practices."

SOURCE: Equal Employment Opportunity Commission, Nov. 18, 2004 (*www.eeoc.gov*).

In the absence of a consent decree, the court will fashion its own remedies from those permitted under the law. There are several remedies available. First, the court may enjoin certain practices, which means requiring the defendant to halt the practices. Second, the court may order the hiring or reinstatement of individuals. Third, the court may fashion various forms of monetary relief, such as back pay, front pay, attorney's fees, and compensatory and punitive damages. Compensatory and punitive damages may be applied only in cases involving disparate treatment, and there is a cap of $300,000; front pay and back pay are excluded from the cap. Finally, under the Civil Rights Act and the ADA, the court may order "such affirmative action as may be appropriate," as well as "any other equitable relief" that the court deems appropriate. Through these provisions, the court has considerable latitude in the remedies it imposes. Note that this court's prerogative includes imposition of AA plans.

Enforcement: OFCCP

Enforcement mechanisms used by the OFCCP are very different from those used by the EEOC.[18] Most covered employers are required to develop and implement written AA plans for women and minorities. Specific AA plan requirements for employers under Executive Order 11246 are spelled out in Affirmative Action Programs regulations.

To enforce these requirements, the OFCCP conducts off-site desk audits and reviews of employers' records and AA plans and on-site visits and compliance reviews of employers' AA plans. It also investigates complaints charging noncompliance. Employers found to be in noncompliance are urged to change their practices through a conciliation process. Should conciliation not be successful, employers are subject to various penalties that affect their status as a federal contractor. These include cancellation of contracts and debarment from bidding on future contracts.

EEO/AA LAWS: SPECIFIC STAFFING PROVISIONS

Each of the major laws covered in the previous section contains specific provisions pertaining to staffing practices by organizations. This section summarizes those specific provisions, including agencies' and courts' interpretations of them. Phrases in quotation marks are direct quotations from the laws themselves. Applications of these provisions to staffing policies, practices, and actions occur throughout the remainder of the book.

Civil Rights Acts (1964, 1991)

The provisions of the Civil Rights Acts of 1964 and 1991 are combined for discussion purposes here. The 1991 law is basically a series of amendments to the 1964 law, though it does contain some provisions unique to it.

Unlawful Employment Practices

This section of the law contains a comprehensive statement regarding unlawful employment practices. Specifically, it is unlawful for an employer

1. "to fail or refuse to hire or to discharge any individual, or otherwise discriminate against any individual with respect to his compensation, terms, conditions, or privileges of employment, because of such individual's race, color, religion, sex, or national origin"; or
2. "to limit, segregate, or classify his employees or applicants for employment in any way which would deprive or tend to deprive any individual of employment opportunities or otherwise adversely affect his status as an employee because of such individual's race, color, religion, sex, or national origin."

These two statements are the foundation of civil rights law. They are very broad and inclusive, applying to virtually all staffing practices by an organization. There are also separate statements for employment agencies and labor unions.

Establishment of Disparate Impact

As discussed previously, a claim of discrimination may be pursued via a disparate impact or disparate treatment approach. The law makes several points regarding the former approach.

First, staffing practices that may seem unfair, outrageous, or of dubious value to the employer, but do not cause adverse impact are not illegal (assuming, of course, that no intention to discriminate underlies them). Thus, they are a matter of legal concern only if their usage causes disparate impact.

Second, staffing practices that the plaintiff initially alleges to have caused adverse impact are unlawful unless the employer can successfully rebut the charges. To do this, the employer must show that the practices are "job related for the position in question and consistent with business necessity." Practices that fail to meet this standard are unlawful.

Third, the plaintiff must show adverse impact for each specific staffing practice or component. For example, if an employer has a simple selection system in which applicants first take a written test and those who pass it are interviewed, the plaintiff must show adverse impact separately for the test and the interview, rather than for the two components combined.

Disparate Treatment

Intentional discrimination with staffing practices is prohibited, and the employer may not use a claim of business necessity to justify intentional use of a discriminatory practice.

Mixed Motives

An employer may not defend an action by claiming that while a prohibited factor, such as sex, entered into a staffing decision, other factors, such as job qualifications, did also. Such "mixed motive" defenses are not permitted. A plaintiff may pursue a mixed motive claim with either circumstantial or direct evidence of discrimination.

Bona Fide Occupational Qualification (BFOQ)

An employer may attempt to justify use of a protected characteristic, such as national origin, as being a bona fide occupational qualification, or BFOQ. The law permits such claims, but only for sex, religion, and national origin—not race or color. The employer must be able to demonstrate that such discrimination is "a bona fide occupational qualification reasonably necessary to the normal operation of that particular business or enterprise." Thus, a maximum security prison with mostly male inmates might hire only male prison guards on the grounds that by doing so it ensures the safety, security, and privacy of inmates. However, it must be able to show that doing so is a business necessity.

Testing

The law explicitly permits the use of tests in staffing. The employer may "give and act upon the results of any professionally developed ability test, provided that such test, its administration, or action upon the basis of results is not designed, intended, or used to discriminate because of race, color, religion, sex, or national origin."

Interpretation of this provision has been difficult. What exactly is a "professionally developed ability test"? How does an employer use a test to discriminate? Not discriminate? The need for answers to such questions gave rise to the Uniform Guidelines on Employee Selection Procedures (UGESP).

Test Score Adjustments

Test scores are not to be altered or changed to somehow make them more fair; test scores should speak for themselves. Specifically, it is an unlawful employment practice "to adjust the scores of, use different cutoff scores for, or otherwise alter the results of employment-related tests on the basis of race, color, religion, sex, or national origin." This provision bans so-called race norming, in which people's scores are compared only to those of members of their own racial group and separate cutoff or passing scores are set for each group.

Seniority or Merit Systems

The law explicitly permits the use of seniority and merit systems as a basis for applying different terms and conditions to employees. However, the seniority or merit system must be "bona fide," and it may not be the result of an intention to discriminate.

This provision has particular relevance to internal staffing systems. It in essence allows the employer to take into account seniority (experience) and merit (e.g., KSAOs, promotion potential assessments) when making internal staffing decisions.

Employment Advertising

Discrimination in employment advertising is prohibited. Specifically, the employer may not indicate "any preference, limitation, specification, or discrimination based on race, color, religion, sex, or national origin." An exception to this is if sex, religion, or national origin is a BFOQ.

Pregnancy

The Pregnancy Discrimination Act (PDA) is an amendment to Title VII. Under the PDA, an employer cannot refuse to hire a pregnant woman because of her pregnancy, because of a pregnancy-related condition, or because of the prejudices of coworkers, clients, or customers. There are also many provisions regarding pregnancy and maternity leave.

Preferential Treatment and Quotas

The law does not require preferential treatment or quotas. Thus, the employer is not required to have a balanced workforce, meaning one whose demographic composition matches or mirrors the demographic makeup of the surrounding population from which it draws its employees.

Note that the law does not prohibit preferential treatment, AA, and quotas. It merely says they are not required. Thus, they may be used in certain instances, such as a voluntary AA plan or a court-imposed remedy.

Age Discrimination in Employment Act (1967)

Prohibited Age Discrimination

The law explicitly and inclusively prohibits discrimination against those age 40 and older. It is unlawful for an employer

1. "to fail or refuse to hire or to discharge any individual or otherwise discriminate against any individual with respect to his compensation, terms, conditions or privileges of employment, because of such individual's age"; and
2. "to limit, segregate, or classify his employees in any way which would deprive or tend to deprive any individual of employment opportunities or otherwise adversely affect his status as an employee, because of such individual's age."

These provisions are interpreted to mean that "favoring an older individual over a younger individual because of age is not unlawful . . . even if the individual is at least 40 years of age" (*www.eeoc.gov*). Thus, discrimination based on relatively older age, not on age generally, is prohibited.

Bona Fide Occupational Qualification (BFOQ)

Like the Civil Rights Act, this law contains a BFOQ provision. Thus, it is not unlawful for an employer to differentiate among applicants or employees on the basis of their age "where age is a bona fide occupational qualification reasonably necessary to the normal operation of the particular business."

Reasonable Factors Other Than Age

The employer may use "reasonable factors other than age" in making employment decisions. Such factors must be applied equally to all applicants, cannot include age in any way, must be job related, and cannot result in discrimination on the basis of age. Factors that are correlated with age, such as job experience, may be used.

Seniority Systems

The law permits the use of seniority systems (merit systems are not mentioned). Thus, the employer is permitted "to observe the terms of a bona fide seniority system that is not intended to evade the purposes" of the act.

Employment Advertising

Employment advertising may not contain terms that limit or deter the employment of older individuals. It is permissible, however, to use terms or phrases that express a preference for older workers, such as "over age 60," "retirees," or "supplement your pension."

Americans With Disabilities Act (1990)

The ADA's basic purpose is to prohibit discrimination against qualified individuals with disabilities and to require the employer to make reasonable accommodation for such individuals unless that would cause undue hardship for the employer.

Prohibited Discrimination

The law contains a broad prohibition against disability discrimination. It specifically says that an employer may not "discriminate against an individual with a disability because of the disability of such individual in regard to job application procedures, the hiring, advancement or discharge of employees, employee compensation, job training, and other terms, conditions, and privileges of employment." Also prohibited is discrimination based on an applicant's or employee's association with a person with a disability.

The law does not apply to all disabled people, only those who are "otherwise qualified." To determine if a person is covered under the ADA, it must be determined if the person has a disability, and if so, is otherwise qualified for the job.

Definition of Disability

Disability refers to both physical and mental impairments that substantially limit a major life activity of the person (e.g., breathing, walking, working). It also refers to persons who have a record of such impairment in the past or are regarded by others as having such an impairment. Determination of whether a person has a disability should take into account measures that mitigate or correct the impairment, such as eyeglasses or medication, so that the impairment is assessed in its mitigated or corrected state.[19]

Disability refers not only to obvious impairments, such as blindness, but also to many others—for example, cancer, AIDS, and many mental illnesses. Current users of illegal drugs are excluded from coverage. Recovering former drug users, though, are covered, as are both practicing and recovering alcoholics.

The EEOC has provided written clarification of the meaning of the term "disability." First, the EEOC defines an impairment as "a physiological disorder affecting one or more of a number of body systems or a mental or psychological disorder." Excluded from this definition are (1) environmental, cultural, and economic disadvantages, (2) homosexuality and bisexuality, (3) pregnancy, (4) physical characteristics, (5) common personality traits, (6) normal deviations in height, weight, or strength, and (7) compulsive gambling. Second, the EEOC expanded major life activities to include "sitting, standing, lifting, and mental and emotional processes such as thinking, concentrating, and interacting with others." Third, whether an impairment is substantially limiting depends on its nature and severity, duration or expected duration, and its permanency or long-term impact. For example, a broken arm or leg would generally not be considered a disability. Fourth, to be substantially limiting, the impairment must prevent or significantly restrict the individual from performing a class of jobs or a broad range of jobs in various classes. For example, an impairment that prevented an individual from performing only a single job likely would not be considered a disability,[20] nor would an impairment that kept an individual from performing just certain tasks on a particular job.

Additional guidance from the EEOC pertains to persons with psychiatric disabilities as mental impairments (*www.eeoc.gov*). A mental impairment includes mental or emotional illness, examples of which are major depression, bipolar disorder, anxiety disorders (including panic disorder, obsessive-compulsive disorder, and post-traumatic stress disorder), schizophrenia, and personality disorders. To count as a disability, the mental impairment must substantially limit one or more of the major life activities as defined above.

Additional guidance from the EEOC is provided in question-and-answer documents targeted to specific disabilities: deafness and hearing impairments, blindness and vision impairments, diabetes, epilepsy, intellectual disabilities, and cancer.

The documents explain when each of these will count as a disability, address what questions may (or may not) be asked of job applicants, provide reasonable accommodation examples, and tell how to handle safety and harassment concerns (*www. eeoc.gov*). Finally, the EEOC and the courts are exploring if, and when, obese individuals might be considered disabled under the ADA.[21]

Qualified Individual With a Disability

A qualified individual with a disability is "an individual with a disability who, with or without reasonable accommodation, can perform the essential functions of the employment position that such individual holds or desires."

Essential Job Functions

The law provides little guidance as to what are essential job functions. It would seem that they are the major, nontrivial tasks required of an employee. The employer has great discretion in such a determination. Specifically, "consideration shall be given to the employer's judgment as to what functions of a job are essential, and if an employer has prepared a written description before advertising or interviewing applicants for the job, this description shall be considered evidence of the essential functions of the job." Subsequent regulations amplify on what are essential job functions; these are explored in Chapter 4.

Reasonable Accommodation and Undue Hardship

Unless it would pose an "undue hardship" on the employer, the employer must make "reasonable accommodation" to the "known physical or mental impairments of an otherwise qualified, disabled job applicant or employee." The law provides actual examples of such accommodation. They include changes in facilities (e.g., installing wheelchair ramps); job restructuring; telework; changes in work schedules; employee reassignment to a vacant position; purchase of adaptive devices; provision of qualified readers and interpreters; and adjustments in testing and training material. For mental impairment and psychiatric disabilities, EEOC guidance indicates several types of reasonable accommodations: leaves of absence and other work schedule changes, physical changes in the workplace, modifications to company policy, adjusting supervisory methods, medication monitoring, and reassignment to a vacant position (*www.eeoc.gov*). In general, only accommodations that would require significant difficulty or expense are considered to create an undue hardship.

A suggested four-step problem-solving approach for handling a reasonable accommodation request from an applicant or employee is as follows.[22] First, conduct job analysis to determine the job's essential functions. Second, identify performance barriers that would hinder the person from doing the job. Third, work with the person to identify potential accommodations. Fourth, assess each accommodation and choose the most reasonable one that would not be an undue hardship.

Selection of Employees

The law deals directly with discrimination in the selection of employees. Prohibited discrimination includes

1. "using qualification standards, employment tests or other selection criteria that screen out or tend to screen out an individual with a disability or a class of individuals with disabilities unless the standard, test, or other selection criteria, as used by the covered entity, is shown to be job related for the position in question and is consistent with business necessity"; and
2. "failing to select and administer tests concerning employment in the most effective manner to ensure that, when such a test is administered to a job applicant or employee who has a disability that impairs sensory, manual, or speaking skills, such results accurately reflect the skills, aptitude or whatever other factor of such applicant or employee that such test purports to measure, rather than reflecting the impaired sensory, manual, or speaking skills of such employee or applicant (except where such skills are the factors that the test purports to measure)."

These provisions seem to make two basic requirements of staffing systems. First, if selection procedures cause disparate impact against people with disabilities, the employer must show that the procedures are job related and consistent with business necessity. The requirement is similar to that for selection procedures under the Civil Rights Act. Second, the employer must ensure that employment tests are accurate indicators of the KSAOs they attempt to measure.

Medical Exams for Job Applicants and Employees

Prior to making a job offer, the employer may not conduct medical exams of job applicants, inquire whether or how severely a person is disabled, or inquire whether the applicant has received treatment for a mental or emotional condition. Specific inquiries about a person's ability to perform essential job functions, however, are permitted.

After a job offer has been made, the employer may require the applicant to take a medical exam, including a psychiatric exam. The job offer may be contingent on the applicant successfully passing the exam. Care should be taken to ensure that all applicants are required to take and pass the same exam. Medical records should be confidential and maintained in a separate file.

For employees, medical exams must be job related and consistent with business necessity. Exam results are confidential.

Direct Threat

The employer may refuse to hire an individual who poses a direct threat to the health and safety of others, or themselves.

Affirmative Action

There are no affirmative action requirements for employers.

Rehabilitation Act (1973)

The Rehabilitation Act has many similarities to the ADA. Indeed, the ADA draws heavily on it and complements it in providing similar coverage to employers who are not federal contractors. Hence, its provisions are mentioned only briefly.

Prohibited Discrimination

According to the law, "no otherwise qualified individual with handicaps . . . shall, solely by reason of his handicaps, be excluded from participation in, or denied the benefits of, or be subjected to discrimination under any program or activity receiving federal assistance." The term "handicaps" is used in a similar fashion and with similar meaning to the term "disability" under the ADA. There are other similarities between the two laws as well. Both, for example, use the terms "otherwise qualified," "essential job functions," and "reasonable accommodation."

Affirmative Action

The law explicitly requires employers to undertake affirmative action. It says that the federal contractor "shall take affirmative action to employ and advance in employment qualified individuals with handicaps."

Executive Order 11246 (1965)

Prohibited Discrimination

The federal contractor is prohibited from discrimination on the basis of race, color, religion, sex, and national origin. (A similar prohibition against age discrimination by federal contractors is contained in Executive Order 11141.)

Affirmative Action

The order plainly requires affirmative action. It says specifically that "the contractor will take affirmative action to ensure that applicants are employed, and that employees are treated during employment, without regard to their race, color, religion, sex, or national origin. Such actions shall include, but not be limited to the following: employment, upgrading, demotion, or transfer; recruitment or recruitment advertising; layoff or termination; rates of pay or other forms of compensation; and selection for training, including apprenticeship." (Executive Order 11141 does not require affirmative action.) Regulations for these affirmative action requirements are discussed below.

EEO/AA: INFORMATION AND INITIATIVES

Information Sources

The sheer volume and complexity of EEO/AA laws and regulations is staggering. Several key information sources are available that collect, categorize, and summarize the information in very understandable, user-friendly ways. Each of these sources is described next, and the reader is well advised to become familiar with these sources and consult them for assistance.

Enforcement Agencies

The enforcement agencies have considerable online information available, including text of laws, compliance manuals, regulations, and policy guidance. Consult the EEOC (*www.eeoc.gov*), the DOL (*www.dol.gov*), and the OFCCP (*www.dol.gov/esa/ofccp*) Web sites.

Information Services

Two major fee-based information services organizations are the Bureau of National Affairs (BNA) and the Commerce Clearing House (CCH). The BNA (*www.bna.com*) offers numerous products in print, on CD-ROM, and on the Web. These include a policy and practice series on fair employment practices; official government compliance manuals for EEO/AA, and disability compliance; fair employment practice cases; individual employment rights cases; EEOC litigation and charge resolution; and an employment discrimination report. The CCH (*www.cch.com*) likewise offers several products in print, on CD-ROM, and in online format. Finally, Findlaw (*www.findlaw.com*) provides considerable free employment law information, including the full text of major laws.

Reference Books

There are many books that summarize EEO/AA laws, regulations, compliance, and permissible and impermissible practices. Examples are *Employment Relationships: Law and Practice, Equal Employment Law Update,* and *The Employer's Legal Handbook.*[23]

Professional Associations and Web Sites

Most professional associations provide informational services to their members. For example, the Society for Human Resource Management publishes *HR Magazine,* a monthly journal frequently containing staffing and EEO/AA articles (*www.shrm.org*). The society also puts out a monthly newsletter and a quarterly legal report, which often contain EEO/AA material. Likewise, the International Public Management Association for Human Resources publishes *Public Personnel Management* and a monthly newsletter, both containing EEO/AA material (*www.ipma-hr.org*). Two employment law Web sites are the employment law practice center (*www.law.com*) and hr compliance (*www.hrcompliance.ceridian.com*).

Initiatives

The EEOC is responsible for not only enforcement and litigation but also outreach and education. It is continually developing and undertaking new initiatives that will help it better fulfill these multiple responsibilities. For example, the EEOC will highlight "best practices" of companies that have taken proactive steps to correct past discrimination or have otherwise been progressive in promoting EEO in their organizations. Fuller descriptions and content are on the EEOC Web site (*www.eeoc.gov*).

E-Race
The Eradicating Racism and Colorism from Employment (E-Race) initiative addresses rising problems of race and color discrimination as the workforce becomes more diverse. A section on race and color discrimination is now in the EEOC Compliance Manual.

Caregivers
Caregiving responsibilities for working parents and others are increasing. The EEOC has developed guidance to deal with possible unlawful disparate treatment of a caregiver based on sex and/or race.

Systemic Discrimination
Systemic discrimination is a pattern or practice, policy and/or class of cases where alleged discrimination has a broad impact on an industry, profession, company, or geographic location. The EEOC implemented a nationwide systemic antibias program. Of particular concern are hiring and promotion practices affecting entry into top management and people of color.

Mediation
With its preference to settle cases rather than litigate them, the EEOC's mediation program is emphasized. Thousands of cases are successfully resolved through mediation each year.

People With Disabilities
The EEOC's New Freedom Initiative seeks to expand employment opportunities for people with disabilities. Free workshops, outreach speakers, corporate leadership conferences, a state's best practices project, a question-and-answer series about various disabilities, and information for small businesses are used. The EEOC's LEAD (Leadership for the Employment of Americans With Disabilities) initiative seeks to increase the employment of people with severe disabilities in the federal government workforce.

Youth @ Work
The Youth @ Work initiative is designed to educate young workers about their workplace rights and responsibilities. A Web site (*www.youth.eeoc.gov*) explains different types of discrimination young workers might experience and suggests strategies for responding to or preventing the occurrences. Outreach activities and partnerships with business leaders and associations are also undertaken.

OTHER STAFFING LAWS

In addition to the EEO/AA laws, there are a variety of other laws and regulations affecting staffing. At the federal level are the Immigration Reform and Control Act (IRCA), the Employee Polygraph Protection Act, and the Fair Credit Reporting Act. At the state and local level are a wide array of laws pertaining to EEO, as well as a host of other areas. Finally, there are civil service laws and regulations that pertain to staffing practices for federal, state, and local government employers.

Federal Laws

Immigration Reform and Control Act (1986)

The purpose of the IRCA and its amendments is to prohibit the employment of unauthorized aliens and to provide civil and criminal penalties for violations of this law. The law covers all employers regardless of size.

Prohibited Practices.   The law prohibits the initial or continuing employment of unauthorized aliens. Specifically,

1. "it is unlawful for a person or other entity to have, or to recruit or refer for a fee, for employment in the United States an alien knowing the alien is an unauthorized alien with respect to such employment"; and
2. "it is unlawful for a person or other entity, after hiring an alien for employment . . . to continue to employ the alien in the United States knowing the alien is (or has become) an unauthorized alien with respect to such employment." (This does not apply to the continuing employment of aliens hired before November 6, 1986.)

The law also prohibits employment discrimination on the basis of national origin or citizenship status. The purpose of this provision is to discourage employers from attempting to comply with the prohibition against hiring unauthorized aliens by simply refusing to hire applicants who are foreign-looking in appearance or have foreign-sounding accents.

Employment Verification System.   The employer must verify that the individual is not an unauthorized alien and is legally eligible for employment. To do this, the individual seeking employment must offer proof of identity and eligibility for work. Documents that will establish proof are shown on the back of the I-9 form, which must be signed by the employer and the employee. To prevent illegal discrimination, the organization should not ask for these documents until after the individual is actually hired. The new employee is entitled to three days to produce the documents. Only documents shown on the I-9 form may be requested. The I-9 information should be kept separate from the employee's personnel file. More information on verification is in Chapter 13.

Temporary Visas. The employer may apply for temporary visas for up to six years for foreign workers under two major visa categories (there are other, minor categories not covered here). The major category is H-1B visa. An H-1B non-immigrant must have a bachelor's degree (or equivalent) or higher in a specific specialty. These workers are typically employed in occupations such as architect, engineer, computer programmer, accountant, doctor, and professor. The employer must pay the person the prevailing wage for employees working in a similar position for the employer and attest that the employee will not displace any other U.S. employee. Congress sets an annual cap on the number of visas issued, which is 65,000. H-1B nonimmigrants employed by universities and nonprofit (including government) organizations are exempt from the annual cap. There is also an exception (with a 20,000 annual cap) for workers with a master's degree or higher from a U.S. university. H-1B visa holders may change jobs as soon as their employer files an approval petition, and they are not restricted to their current geographic area.

The H-2B visa category is for employers with peak load, seasonal, or intermittent needs to augment their regular workforce. Examples of such employers are construction, health care, resort/hospitality services, lumber, and manufacturing. There is an annual cap of 65,000 workers.

Enforcement. The law is enforced by the U.S. Citizenship and Immigration Services (*www.uscis.gov*) within the Department of Homeland Security. Noncompliance may result in fines of up to $10,000 for each unauthorized alien employed, as well as imprisonment for up to six months for a pattern or practice of violations. Federal contractors may be barred from federal contracts for one year.

Employee Polygraph Protection Act (1988)

The purpose of the Employee Polygraph Protection Act is to prevent most private employers from using the polygraph or lie detector on job applicants or employees. The law does not apply to other types of "honesty tests," such as paper-and-pencil ones.

Prohibited Practices. The law prohibits most private employers (public employers are exempted) from (1) requiring applicants or employees to take a polygraph test, (2) using the results of a polygraph test for employment decisions, and (3) discharging or disciplining individuals for refusal to take a polygraph test.

There are three explicit instances in which the polygraph may be used. First, it may be used by employers that manufacture, distribute, or dispense controlled substances, such as drugs. Second, the polygraph may be used by private security firms that provide services to businesses affecting public safety or security, such as nuclear power plants or armored vehicles. Third, the polygraph may be used in an investigation of theft, embezzlement, or sabotage that causes economic loss to the employer.

Enforcement.   The law is enforced by the DOL. Penalties for noncompliance are fines of up to $10,000 per individual violation. Also, individuals may sue the employer, seeking employment, reinstatement, promotion, and back pay.

Fair Credit Reporting Act (1970)

The Fair Credit Reporting Act, as amended, regulates the organization's acquisition and use of consumer reports on job applicants. A consumer report is virtually any information on an applicant that is compiled from a database by a consumer reporting agency and provided to the organization. The information may be not only credit characteristics but also employment history, income, driving record, arrests and convictions, and lifestyle; medical information may not be sought or provided without prior approval of the applicant. Specific requirements for gathering and using the information are provided in Chapter 8.

A second type of consumer report is investigative. It is prepared on the basis of personal interviews with other individuals, rather than a search through a database. There are separate compliance steps for this type of report.

Enforcement.   The law is enforced by the Federal Trade Commission (*www.ftc.gov*). Penalties for willful or negligent noncompliance go up to $1,000.

Uniformed Services Employment and Reemployment Rights Act (1994)

The purpose of the Uniformed Services Employment and Reemployment Rights Act (USERRA) is to prohibit discrimination against members of the uniformed services and to extend reinstatement, benefit, and job security rights to returning service members.

Coverage.   All employers, both private and public, regardless of size, are covered. All people who perform or have performed service in the uniformed services have USERRA rights, but only a person who was employed, is an applicant, or who is currently employed can invoke these rights.

Requirements.   Employers may not take negative job actions (e.g., firing, demoting, transferring, refusing to hire) against members (and applicants for membership) in the uniformed services. The employer must reinstate (within two weeks of application for reinstatement) employees who have taken up to five total years of leave from their position in order to serve. These employees are entitled to be returned to the position they would have held if they had been continuously employed (this is called an "escalator" position). If the employee is not qualified for the escalator position, the employer must make a reasonable effort to help the employee qualify. Those employees are also entitled to promotions, raises, and other seniority-based benefits they would have received. There are many exceptions to both the five-year service limit and the reinstatement rights. Certain benefits must be made available to those who take leave for service, and benefits must be restored to those who return. An employee may not be fired, except for cause, for up to one year after returning from service.

Enforcement.   The law is enforced by the Veterans Employment and Training Service (VETS) within the DOL (*www.dol.gov/vets*). There are also regulations for employer compliance.

State and Local Laws

The emphasis in this book is on federal laws and regulations. It should be remembered, however, that an organization is subject to law at the state and local level as well. This greatly increases the array of applicable laws to which the organization must attend.

EEO/AA Laws

EEO/AA laws are often patterned after federal law. Their basic provisions, however, vary substantially from state to state. Compliance with federal EEO/AA law does not ensure compliance with state and local EEO/AA law, and vice versa. Thus, it is the responsibility of the organization to be explicitly knowledgeable of the laws and regulations that apply to it.

Of special note is the fact that state and local EEO/AA laws and regulations often provide protections beyond those contained in the federal laws and regulations. State laws, for example, may apply to employers with fewer than 15 employees, which is the cutoff for coverage under the Civil Rights Act. State laws may also prohibit certain kinds of discrimination not prohibited under federal law, for example, sexual orientation and gender identity or expression. The law for the District of Columbia prohibits 13 kinds of discrimination, including sexual orientation, physical appearance, matriculation, and political affiliation. Finally, state law may deviate from federal law with regard to enforcement mechanisms and penalties for noncompliance.

Other State Laws

Earlier reference was made to employment-at-will and workplace torts as matters of common law, which, in turn, are governed at the level of state law. Statutory state laws applicable to staffing, in addition to EEO/AA laws, are also plentiful. Examples of areas covered in addition to EEO/AA include criminal record inquiries by the employer, polygraph and "honesty testing," drug testing, AIDS testing, and employee access to personnel records.

Civil Service Laws and Regulations

Federal, state, and local government employers are governed by special statutory laws and regulations collectively referred to as civil service. Civil service is guided by so-called merit principles that serve as the guide to staffing practices. Following these merit principles results in notable differences between public and private employers in their staffing practices.

Merit Principles and Staffing Practices

The essence of merit principles relevant to staffing is fourfold:

1. To recruit, select, and promote employees on the basis of their KSAOs
2. To provide for fair treatment of applicants and employees without regard to political affiliation, race, color, national origin, sex, religion, age, or handicap
3. To protect the privacy and constitutional rights of applicants and employees as citizens
4. To protect employees against coercion for partisan political purposes[24]

Merit principles are codified in civil service laws and regulations.

Comparisons With Private Sector

The merit principles and civil service laws and regulations combine to shape the nature of staffing practices in the public sector. This leads to some notable differences between the public and private sectors. Examples of public sector staffing practices are:

1. Open announcement of all vacancies, along with the content of the selection process that will be followed
2. Very large numbers of applicants due to applications being open to all persons
3. Legal mandate to test applicants only for KSAOs that are directly job related
4. Limits on discretion in the final hiring process, such as number of finalists, ordering of finalists, and affirmative action considerations
5. Rights of applicants to appeal the hiring decision, testing process, or actual test content and method[25]

These examples are unlikely to be encountered in the private sector. Moreover, they are only illustrative of the many differences in staffing practices and context between the private and public sectors.

LEGAL ISSUES IN REMAINDER OF BOOK

The laws and regulations applicable to staffing practices by organizations are multiple in number and complexity. The emphasis in this chapter has been on an understanding of the need for law, the sources of law, general provisions of the law, and a detailed presentation of specific provisions that pertain to staffing activities. Little has been said about practical implications and applications.

In the remaining chapters of the book, the focus shifts to the practical, with guidance and suggestions on how to align staffing practices with legal requirements. The last section of each remaining chapter, "Legal Issues," discusses major issues from a compliance perspective. The issues so addressed, and the chapter in which they occur, are shown in Exhibit 2.9. Inspection of the exhibit should reinforce the importance accorded laws and regulations as an external influence on staffing activities.

It should be emphasized that there is a selective presentation of the issues in Exhibit 2.9. Only certain issues have been chosen for inclusion, and only a summary of their compliance implications is presented. It should also be emphasized that the discussion of these issues does not constitute professional legal advice.

SUMMARY

Staffing involves the formation of the employment relationship. That relationship involves the employer acquiring individuals to perform work for it as employees, independent contractors, and temporary employees. The specific legal meanings and obligations associated with these various arrangements were provided.

Myriad laws and regulations have come forth from several sources to place constraints on the contractual relationship between employer and employee. These constraints seek to ensure a balance of power in the relationship, as well as provide protections to both the employee and the employer.

Statutory federal laws pertaining to EEO/AA prohibit discrimination on the basis of race, color, religion, sex, national origin, age, and disability. This prohibition applies to staffing practices intentionally used to discriminate (disparate treatment), as well as to staffing practices that have a discriminatory effect (disparate or adverse impact). The EEO/AA laws also contain specific provisions pertaining to staffing, which specify both prohibited and permissible practices. In both instances, the emphasis is on use of staffing practices that are job related and focus on the person/job match.

A variety of information sources are available to help organizations design and conduct staffing practices that are in compliance with EEO/AA laws and regulations. The EEOC also undertakes many specific initiatives to further its compliance and outreach responsibilities.

Other laws and regulations also affect staffing practices. At the federal level, there is a prohibition on the employment of unauthorized aliens and on the use of the polygraph (lie detector), constraints on the use of credit reports on job applicants, and specification of the employment rights of those in the uniformed services. State and local EEO/AA laws supplement those found at the federal level.

EXHIBIT 2.9   Legal Issues Covered in Other Chapters

Chapter Title and Number	Topic
Planning (3)	Affirmative action plans and diversity programs
	Legality of affirmative action plans (AAPs)
	Diversity programs
	EEO and temporary employment agencies
Job Analysis (4)	Job-relatedness and court cases
	Job analysis and selection
	Essential job functions
External Recruitment (5)	Definition of job applicant
	Targeted recruitment
	Electronic recruitment
	Job advertisements
	Fraud and misrepresentation
Internal Recruitment (6)	Affirmative action programs regulations
	Bona fide seniority system
	Glass ceiling
Measurement (7)	Disparate impact statistics
	Standardization and validation
External Selection I (8)	Disclaimers
	Reference and background checks
	Preemployment inquiries
	Bona fide occupational qualifications (BFOQs)
External Selection II (9)	Uniform Guidelines on Employee Selection Procedures (UGESP)
	Selection under the ADA
	Drug testing
Internal Selection (10)	UGESP
	Glass ceiling
Decision Making (11)	UGESP
	Diversity and hiring decisions
Final Match (12)	Authorization to work
	Negligent hiring
	Employment-at-will
Staffing System Management (13)	Record keeping and privacy
	EEO-I Report
	Audits
	Training for managers and employees
	Alternative dispute resolution
Retention Management (14)	Separation laws and regulations
	Performance appraisal

Many other staffing practices are also addressed by state and local law. Finally, civil service laws and regulations govern staffing practices in the public sector. Their provisions create marked differences in certain staffing practices between public and private employers.

Legal issues will continue to be addressed throughout the remainder of this book. The emphasis will be on explanation and application of the laws' provisions to staffing practices. The issues will be discussed at the end of each chapter, beginning with the next one.

DISCUSSION QUESTIONS

1. Do you agree that "the employer usually has the upper hand" when it comes to establishing the employment relationship? When might the employee have maximum power over the employer?
2. What are the limitations of disparate impact statistics as indicators of potential staffing discrimination?
3. Why is each of the four situational factors necessary to establishing a claim of disparate treatment?
4. What factors would lead an organization to enter into a consent agreement rather than continue pursuing a suit in court?
5. What are the differences between staffing in the private and public sectors? Why would private employers probably resist adopting many of the characteristics of public staffing systems?

ETHICAL ISSUES

1. Assume that you're the staffing manager in an organization that informally, but strongly, discourages you and other managers from hiring people with disabilities. The organization's rationale is that people with disabilities are unlikely to be high performers or long-term employees, and are costly to train, insure, and integrate into the work unit. What is your ethical assessment of the organization's stance? Do you have any ethical obligations to try to change the stance, and if so, how might you go about that?
2. Assume the organization you work for practices strict adherence to the law in its relationships with its employees and job applicants. The organization calls it "staffing by the book." But beyond that it seems that "anything goes" in terms of tolerated staffing practices. What is your assessment of this approach?

APPLICATIONS

Age Discrimination in a Promotion?

The Best Protection Insurance Company (BPIC) handled a massive volume of claims each year in the corporate claims function, as well as in its four regional claims centers. Corporate claims was headed by the senior vice president of corporate claims (SVPCC); reporting to the SVPCC were two managers of corporate claims (MCC-Life and MCC-Residential) and a highly skilled corporate claims specialist (CCS). Each regional office was headed by a regional center manager (RCM); the RCM was responsible for both supervisors and claims specialists within the regional office. The RCMs reported to the vice president of regional claims (VPRC). Here is the structure before reorganization:

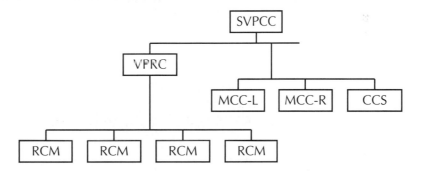

BPIC decided to reorganize its claims function by eliminating the four regional offices (and the RCM position) and establishing numerous small field offices throughout the country. The other part of the reorganization involved creating five new CCS positions. The CCS job itself was to be redesigned and upgraded in terms of knowledge and skill requirements. It was planned to staff these new CCS positions through internal promotions from within the claims function.

The plaintiff in the case was Gus Tavus, a 52-year-old RCM. Since his job was being eliminated, Gus was asked by the SVPCC to apply for one of the new CCS positions, as were the other RCMs, all of whom were over 40 years of age. Neither Gus nor the other RCMs were promoted to the CCS positions. Other candidates were also bypassed, and some of them were also over 40. The promotions went to five claims specialists and supervisors from within the former regional offices, all of whom were under age 40. Two of these newly promoted employees had worked for, and reported to, Gus as RCM.

Upon learning of his failure to be promoted, Gus sought to determine why he was not promoted. What he learned (described below) led him to feel he had been discriminated against because of his age. He then retained legal counsel, attorney Bruce Davis. Bruce met informally with the SVPCC to try to determine what had happened in the promotion process and why his client Gus had not been promoted. He was told that there were a large number of candidates who were better qualified than Gus and that Gus lacked adequate technical and communication skills for the new job of CCS. The SVPCC refused to reconsider Gus for the job and said that all decisions were "etched in stone." Gus and Bruce then filed suit in federal district court, claiming a violation of the Age Discrimination in Employment Act. They also subpoenaed numerous BPIC documents, including the personnel files of all applicants for the CCS positions.

Based on these documents, and discussions with Gus, the following information emerged about the promotion process actually used by BPIC. The SVPCC and the two MCCs conducted the total process; they received no input from the VPRC or the HR department. There was no formal, written job description for the new CCS position, nor was there a formal internal job posting as required by company policy. The SVPCC and the MCCs developed a list of employees they thought might be interested in the job, including Gus, and then met to consider the list of candidates. At that meeting, the personnel files and previous performance appraisals of the candidates were not consulted. After deciding on the five candidates who would be offered the promotion (all five accepted), the SVPCC and MCCs did scan the personnel files and appraisals of these five (only) to check for any disconfirming information about the employees. None was found. Inspection of all the files by Bruce Davis revealed no written comments suggesting age bias in past performance appraisals for any of the candidates, including Gus. Also, there was no indication that Gus lacked technical and communication skills. All of Gus's previous appraisal ratings were above average, and there was no evidence of decline in the favorability of the ratings recently. Finally, an interview with the VPRC (Gus's boss) revealed that he had not been consulted at all during the promotion process, that he was "shocked beyond belief" that Gus had not been promoted, and that there was "no question" but that Gus was qualified in all respects for the CCS job.

1. Based on the above facts, prepare a written report that presents a convincing disparate treatment claim that Gus had been intentionally discriminated against on the basis of his age. Do not address the claim as a disparate impact one.
2. Present a convincing rebuttal, from the viewpoint of BPIC, to this disparate treatment claim.

Disparate Impact: What Do the Statistics Mean?

Claims of discrimination can be pursued under an allegation of disparate impact. According to this approach, the effect or impact of staffing practices can be discriminatory and thus in violation of the Civil Rights Act. Such an impact could occur even though there may be no underlying intention to discriminate against members of a protected group or class (e.g., women or minorities). Pursuit of a disparate impact claim requires the use of various statistics to show that, in effect, women or minorities are being treated differently than men or nonminorities under the law.

Exhibit 2.5 shows three types of disparate impact statistics: flow statistics, stock statistics, and concentration statistics. Also shown is a statistical example of disparate impact for each type. For each of these three types of statistics, prepare a report in which you discuss the following:

1. How could an organization go about collecting and reporting these statistics in the form shown in Exhibit 2.5?

2. What "rule of thumb" or guidelines would you recommend for deciding whether statistical differences between men and women, or nonminorities and minorities, reflect discrimination occurring through an organization's staffing system?

3. What types of staffing activities (recruitment, selection, employment) might be causing the statistical differences? For example, in Exhibit 2.5 the selection rate for men is 50% and for women is 11%. How would the organization collect the data necessary to compute these selection rates, how would you decide if the difference in selection rates (50% vs. 11%) is big enough to indicate possible discrimination, and what sorts of practices might be causing the difference in selection rates?

ENDNOTES

1. M. W. Bennett, D. J. Polden, and H. J. Rubin, *Employment Relationships: Law and Practice* (Frederick, MD: Aspen, 2004), pp. 1-1 to 3-50; D. J. Walsh, *Employment Law for Human Resource Practice,* second ed. (Mason, OH: Thompson Higher Education, 2007), pp. 33–60.

2. C. J. Muhl, "The Employment-at-Will Doctrine: Three Major Exceptions," *Monthly Labor Review,* Jan. 2001, pp. 3–11.

3. S. Bates, "A Tough Target: Employee or Independent Contractor?" *HR Magazine,* July 2001, pp. 69–74; Bennett, Polden, and Rubin, *Employment Relationships: Law and Practice,* pp. 1-4 to 1-7; K. D. Meade, J. W. Pegano, I. M. Saxe, and J. A. Moskowitz, "Revisit Independent Contractor Classifications," *Legal Report,* Society for Human Resource Management, Oct./Nov. 2007, pp. 7–8.

4. D. C. Feldman and B. S. Klaas, "Temporary Workers: Employee Rights and Employer Responsibilities," *Employee Rights and Responsibilities Journal,* 1996, 9(1), pp. 1–21; B. Lanza and M. R. Maryn, "Legal Status of Contingent Workers," *Compensation and Benefits Review,* July/Aug. 2003, pp. 47–60.

5. R. J. Bohner, Jr., and E. R. Salasko, "Beware the Legal Risks of Hiring Temps," *Workforce,* Oct. 2003, pp. 50–57; D. J. Walsh, *Employment Law for Human Resource Practice,* pp. 42–43.

6. A. G. Feliu, *Primer on Individual Employee Rights,* second ed. (Washington, DC: Bureau of National Affairs, 1996), pp. 1–5.

7. Feliu, *Primer on Individual Employee Rights,* pp. 1–5.

8. P. Salvatore and A. M. Gutterman, "The Risk of Intentional Torts," *HR Magazine,* Aug. 2003, pp. 109–114.

9. L. Guerin and A. DelPo, *The Essential Guide to Federal Employment Laws* (Berkeley, CA: Nolo, 2006).

10. Equal Employment Opportunity Commission, *EEOC Enforcement Guidance on How to Count Employees When Determining Coverage Under Title VII, the ADA, and the ADEA* (Washington, DC: author, 1997).

11. Equal Employment Opportunity Commission, *EEOC Guidance on Investigating, Analyzing Retaliation Claims* (*www.eeoc.gov*).

12. W. Bliss, "The Wheel of Misfortune," *HR Magazine,* May 2000, pp. 207–218; W. A. Carmell, "Application of U.S. Antidiscrimination Laws to Multinational Employers," *Legal Report,* Society for Human Resource Management, May/June 2001; S. Lash, "Supreme Court Disables State Employees," *HR News,* Apr. 2001, p. 6.

13. Bennett, Polden, and Rubin, *Employment Relationships: Law and Practice,* pp. 4-75 to 4-82.

14. Bennett, Polden, and Rubin, *Employment Relationships: Law and Practice,* pp. 4-75 to 4-82.

15. R. D. Arvey and R. H. Faley, *Fairness in Selecting Employees,* second ed. (Reading, MA: Addison-Wesley, 1988), pp. 73–80; J. Cook, "Preparing for Statistical Battles Under the Civil Rights Act," *HR Focus,* May 1992, pp. 12–13; W. M. Howard, "The Decline and Fall of Statistical Evidence as Proof of Employment Discrimination," *Labor Law Journal,* 1994, 45, pp. 208–220.

16. K. Tyler, "Mediating a Better Outcome," *HR Magazine,* Nov. 2007, pp. 63–66.

17. Bennett, Polden, and Rubin, *Employment Relationships: Law and Practice,* pp. 4-75 to 4-82; T. S. Bland, "Anatomy of an Employment Lawsuit," *HR Magazine,* Mar. 2001, pp. 145–151.

18. Bureau of National Affairs, *Fair Employment Practices,* Vol. 1, pp. 431:55–64, 481–490.

19. D. Massengill, "How Much Better Are You? Impairments, Mitigating Measures and the Determination of Disability," *Public Personnel Management,* 2004, 33, pp. 181–199.

20. Equal Employment Opportunity Commission, "Definition of the Term Disability," *Compliance Manual Section 902* (Washington, DC: author, 1995).

21. J. Staman, "Obesity Discrimination and the Americans With Disabilities Act," Congressional Research Service, Library of Congress, 2007.

22. J. R. Mook, "Accommodation Paradigm Shifts," *HR Magazine,* Jan. 2007, pp. 115–120.

23. Bennett, Polden, and Rubin, *Employment Relationships: Law and Practice*; R. T. Seymour and J. F. Aslin, *Equal Employment Law Update* (Washington, DC: Bureau of National Affairs, 2004); F. S. Steingold, *The Employer's Legal Handbook,* sixth ed. (Berkeley, CA: Nolo Press, 2004); D. J. Walsh, *Employment Law for Human Resource Practice.*

24. J. P. Wiesen, N. Abrams, and S. A. McAttee, *Employment Testing: A Public Sector Viewpoint* (Alexandria, VA: International Personnel Management Association Assessment Council, 1990), pp. 2–3.

25. Wiesen, Abrams, and McAttee, *Employment Testing: A Public Sector Viewpoint,* pp. 3–7.

CHAPTER THREE

Planning

External Influences
Economic Conditions
Labor Markets
Technology
Labor Unions

Human Resource Planning
Process and Example
Initial Decisions
Forecasting HR Requirements
Forecasting HR Availabilities
Reconciliation and Gaps
Action Planning

Staffing Planning
Staffing Planning Process
Core Workforce
Flexible Workforce
Outsourcing

Legal Issues
Affirmative Action Plans (AAPs)
Legality of AAPs
Diversity Programs
EEO and Temporary Workers

Summary

Discussion Questions

Ethical Issues

Applications

Tanglewood Stores Case

Human resource (HR) planning is the process of forecasting the organization's future employment needs and then developing action staffing plans and programs for fulfilling these needs in ways that are in alignment with the strategy. It is important to recognize and consider the impact of external influences on HR planning and the resultant staffing planning. Four major external influences are economic conditions, labor markets, technology, and labor unions. The nature and examples of these forces are described first. Attention then turns to HR planning, staffing planning, and legal issues.

The HR planning process involves several components, simplified examples of which are presented for the sales and customer service unit of an organization. Then, each of these components is described in detail. These components consist of making initial planning decisions, forecasting HR requirements, forecasting HR availabilities, determining employee shortages and surpluses, and developing action plans. For each of these components, specific examples are provided, drawing from the initial example of the sales and customer service unit.

Staffing planning is shown to be a logical outgrowth of HR planning. Guided by staffing strategy, one of the key staffing planning areas involves planning for the core workforce (regular employees) and the flexible workforce (temporary employees and independent contractors). The unique nature and requirements for planning each type of workforce are indicated. Organizations also need to decide whether to outsource certain functions.

The major legal issue for HR staffing planning is that of affirmative action plans (AAPs). The basic components of an AAP are provided, along with the AAP requirements for federal contractors. A summary of the legality of AAPs is then presented. Diversity programs represent a natural extension of AAPs. They seek to prepare organizational members for a diverse workforce and to develop HR programs that will foster successfully acquiring, managing, and retaining a diverse workforce. A different legal issue, that of equal employment opportunity (EEO) coverage for temporary employees and their agencies, is also discussed.

EXTERNAL INFLUENCES

There are four major sources of external influence on HR and staffing planning, namely, economic conditions, labor markets, technology, and labor unions. Exhibit 3.1 provides specific examples of these influences, which are discussed next.

Economic Conditions

Numerous macro forces operate to determine the overall economic climate in which the organization functions. These include product and labor market competition (both national and global), inflation, interest rates, currency exchange rates, and government fiscal and monetary policy. Resulting from such forces is the degree of overall economic expansion or contraction.

EXHIBIT 3.1   Examples of External Influences on Staffing

ECONOMIC CONDITIONS
- Economic expansion and contraction
- Job growth and job opportunities
- Internal labor market mobility
- Turnover rates

LABOR MARKETS
- Labor demand: employment patterns, KSAOs sought
- Labor supply: labor force, demographic trends, KSAOs available
- Labor shortages and surpluses
- Employment arrangements

TECHNOLOGY
- Elimination of jobs
- Creation of jobs
- Changes in skill requirements

LABOR UNIONS
- Negotiations
- Labor contracts: staffing levels, staffing quality, internal movement
- Grievance systems

A direct derivative of expansion and contraction forces is the amount of job creation and growth, both positive and negative. Positive job growth means expanding job opportunities for individuals, while slowdowns or contractions in job growth yield dwindling job opportunities. Organizations move people into (new hires), within (internal labor markets), and out of (turnover) the organization in varying rates, depending on the amount of job growth. Job growth thus functions like a spigot governing the movement of people.

Consider the case of job expansion. When new jobs are created, new hire rates begin to increase for both entry-level and higher-level jobs. These new hires are either new entrants into the labor force (e.g., recent college graduates) or current members of the labor force, both unemployed and employed. There will also be increased movement within organizations' internal labor markets through the operation of their promotion and transfer systems. This movement will be necessitated by a combination of new jobs being created that will be filled internally and the exit of current employees from the organization. Most likely, the departure of employees will be due to their leaving the organization to take new jobs at other organizations. Some, however, may be temporarily unemployed (while they look for new job opportunities), and others may leave the labor force entirely.

With lesser rates of job growth or actual job contraction, the movement flows are lessened. Organizations will be hiring fewer people, and job seekers will have longer job searches and fewer job opportunities to choose from. Promotion and transfer opportunities for current employees will dry up, voluntary turnover rates will decrease, and many employees may even experience termination through involuntary layoff or a voluntary early retirement program.

Labor Markets

In and through labor markets, organizations express specific labor preferences and requirements (labor demand), and persons express their own job preferences and requirements (labor supply). Ultimately, person/job matches occur from the interaction of the demand and supply forces. Both labor demand and supply contain quantity and quality components, as described below. Labor shortages and surpluses, and a variety of possible employment arrangements are also discussed.

Labor Demand: Employment Patterns

Labor demand is a derived demand, meaning it is a result of consumer demands for the organization's products and services. The organization acquires and deploys its workforce in ways that will allow it to be responsive to consumer demand in a competitive manner.

To learn about labor demand, national employment statistics are collected and analyzed. They provide data about employment patterns and projections for industries, occupations, and organization size.

Projections to year 2014 indicate that most job growth will occur in the services sector, led by the education and health services industries, followed by business and professional services. Manufacturing and federal government employment will remain steady, and declines will occur in mining and agriculture.[1]

Employment growth to 2014 will vary across occupations, with most of the growth concentrated in health care and information technology, and most of the losses concentrated in clerical and manufacturing. Examples of growth "winners" include biomedical engineers (34%), medical assistants (52%), computer software engineers (48%), home health aides (56%), and post-secondary teachers (32%). Examples of growth "losers" include word processors and typists (–15%), telephone operators (–36%), textile machine operators (–36%), and computer operators (–33%).[2]

Labor Demand: KSAOs Sought

Knowledge, skill, ability, and other characteristics (KSAO) requirements or preferences of employers are not widely measured, except for education requirements. Data collected by the Bureau of Labor Statistics suggest a continued increase in demand for individuals with college degrees or more. Occupations requiring only a high school degree or less are expected to make up 45.9% of all jobs, occupations requiring a high school degree plus some specialized training (including vocational degrees and associates' degrees) will make up 28.4% of all jobs, and those requiring a bachelor's degree or more will make up 25.7% of all jobs.[3] The increasing demand for education most likely reflects advances in technology that have made many jobs more complex and technically demanding.[4]

A very thorough and systematic source of information about KSAOs needed for jobs is the Occupational Outlook Handbook (available at *www.bls.gov*). It does not indicate KSAO deficiencies. Rather, it provides detailed information about the nature of work and the training and KSAOs required for the entire spectrum of occupations in the United States. At the managerial level, an interesting attempt was made to have experts forecast the most critical skills that managers will need for the future. The six identified skills are rapid response, sharp focus, stress busting, strategic empowerment, juggling, and team building.[5]

Survey results show that employers have multiple general KSAO requirements that accompany their quantitative labor requirements. Naturally, the more specific requirements vary according to type of employer and type of job. It also appears that employers have identified general future KSAO needs for their workforces on the basis of skill gaps in their current workforces and, in the case of managers, what their projected critical KSAO requirements will be.

Labor Supply: The Labor Force and Its Trends

Quantity of labor supplied is measured and reported periodically by the Bureau of Labor Statistics in the U.S. Department of Labor. An example of basic results for September 2003 through 2007 is given in Exhibit 3.2. It shows that the labor force reached about 153 million individuals (employed + unemployed) and that unemployment ranged from 5.7% to 4.4%.

Data reveal several labor force trends that have particular relevance for staffing organizations. Labor force growth is slowing, going from an annual growth rate of around 2% in the early 1990s to a projected rate of 1.0% by the year 2014. There are increasingly fewer new entrants to the labor force. This trend, coupled with the severe KSAO deficiencies that many of the new entrants will have, creates major adaptation problems for organizations.

Demographically, the labor force has become more diverse, and this trend will continue. Data starting in the 1980s and projected through 2014 show a slow trend toward nearly equal labor force participation for men and women, a slight decrease in the proportion of whites in the workforce, and large proportional growth in the representation of Hispanics and Asians. There will also be a dramatic shift toward fewer younger workers and more workers over the age of 55.

Other, more subtle labor force trends are also under way. There has been a slight upward movement overall in the average number of hours that people work and a strong rise in the proportion of employees who work very long hours in certain occupations, such as managers and professionals. Relatedly, there is an increase in multiple job holding, with 6.2% of employed people holding more

EXHIBIT 3.2   Labor Force Statistics

	2003	2004	2005	2006	2007
Civilian noninstitutional population (in millions)	221.8	223.9	226.7	229.4	232.5
Civilian labor force (in millions)	146.1	147.1	149.9	151.6	153.4
Employed (in millions)	137.7	139.6	142.6	145.0	146.4
Unemployed (in millions)	8.4	7.5	7.3	6.6	7.0
Not in labor force (in millions)	75.7	76.8	76.8	77.8	79.1
Labor force participation rate (%)	65.9	65.7	66.1	66.1	66.0
Unemployment rate (%)	5.7	5.1	4.9	4.4	4.6

SOURCE: U.S. Department of Labor, "The Employment Situation," *News*, Nov. 2, 2007.

than one job. There are a growing number of immigrants in the population; nearly 1 in 10 people is foreign born, the highest rate in more than 50 years. New federal and state policies are increasingly pushing welfare recipients into the labor force, and they are mostly employed in low-wage jobs with low educational requirements. People historically out of the labor force mainstream—such as those with disabilities and the growing number of retirees—may assume a greater presence in the labor force.[6]

Labor Supply: KSAOs Available

Data on KSAOs available in the labor force are very sparse. A labor force survey showed that about 32% of the population age 25 and older had attained a college degree or higher, whereas 10% had less than a high school diploma; the remainder had education attainment levels within this band.[7]

A survey of 431 HR professionals found that 40% of employers indicated that high school graduates lacked basic skills in reading comprehension, writing, and math required for entry-level jobs, and 70% of employers said high school graduates are deficient in work habits such as professionalism, critical thinking, personal accountability, and time management.[8] Most respondents believed that college graduates were somewhat better prepared for work, but 44% of applicants with college degrees were still rated as having poor writing skills. Economists and sociologists are quick to note that these skills shortages are being reported despite consistent gains in standardized test scores and educational attainment in the labor force since the 1960s.[9] Thus, it appears that the problem is that demand for advanced skills is increasing, as we noted earlier, and not that the supply of skilled workers is decreasing. This idea is reinforced by another survey of 726 HR professionals that found 98% of respondents reported that the competition for talented workers has increased in recent years.[10] Data such as these reinforce the serious KSAO deficiencies reported by employers in at least some portions of the labor force.

Labor Shortages and Surpluses

When labor demand exceeds labor supply for a given pay rate, the labor market is said to be "tight" and labor shortages are experienced by the organization. Shortages tend to be job or occupation specific. Low unemployment rates, surges in labor demand in certain occupations, and skill deficiencies all fuel both labor quantity and labor quality shortages for many organizations. The shortages cause numerous responses:

- Increased pay and benefit packages
- Hiring bonuses and stock options
- Alternative work arrangements to attract and retain older workers
- Use of temporary employees
- Recruitment of immigrants
- Lower hiring standards
- Partnerships with high schools, technical schools, and colleges
- Increased mandatory overtime work
- Increased hours of operation

These types of responses are lessened or reversed when the labor market is "loose," meaning there are labor surpluses relative to labor demand.

Employment Arrangements

Though labor market forces bring organizations and job seekers together, the specific nature of the employment arrangement can assume many forms. One form is whether the person will be employed on a full-time or a part-time basis. Data show that about 83% of people work full time and 17% work part time.[11] Although many people prefer part-time work, approximately 23% of part-time workers are seeking full-time employment.

A second arrangement involves the issue of flexible scheduling and shift work. The proportion of the workforce covered by flexible shifts has steadily grown from 12.4% of the workforce in 1985 to 27.5% in 2004. Many of these workers are covered by formal flextime programs. Work hours are often put into shifts, and about 15% of full-time employed adults work evening, night, or rotating shifts.[12]

Two other types of arrangements, often considered in combination, are (1) various alternative arrangements to the traditional employer–employee relationship, and (2) the use of contingent employees. Alternative arrangements include the organization filling its staffing needs through use of independent contractors, on-call workers and day laborers, temporary help agency employees, and employees provided by a contract firm that provides a specific service (e.g., accounting). Contingent employees do not have an explicit or implicit contract for long-term employment; they expect their employment to be temporary rather than long term. Contingent employees may occur in combination with any of the four alternatives given above.

National data on the use of alternative employment arrangements and contingent employees are shown in Exhibit 3.3. It can be seen that 89.3% of surveyed individuals worked in a traditional employer–employee arrangement, and the vast majority of these (97.1%) considered themselves noncontingent. The most prevalent alternative was to work as an independent contractor (7.5%), followed by on-call employees and day laborers (1.7%), temporary help agency employees (.9%), and employees provided by a contract firm (.6%). The percentage of contingent employees in these alternative arrangements ranged from 3.4% (independent contractors) to 60.7% (temporary help employees).

Exhibit 3.4 shows several other workforce trends that were identified by a survey of 1,232 HR professionals.

Technology

Changes in technology can influence the staffing planning process significantly. In some cases, technology can serve as a substitute for labor by either eliminating or dramatically reducing the need for certain types of workers. As we noted earlier, the economy as a whole has shown decreased demand for positions like clerical workers, telephone operators, and many manufacturing operators as technology has replaced labor as an input to production. Ironically, changes in software that have made computers easier to use for nonspecialists have even eliminated many jobs in computer programming.

At the same time, technology can serve to create new jobs as new business opportunities emerge. In place of the jobs that are eliminated, demand for technical occupations like robotics engineers, systems and database analysts, and software engineers has increased. Increasing productivity as a result of technological change can also spur increased firm performance, and this will, in turn,

---

EXHIBIT 3.3   Usage of Alternative Employment Arrangements and Contingent Workers

Arrangement	Total (millions)	Percent	Percent Contingent	Percent Noncontingent
Alternative Arrangements				
Independent contractor	10.3	7.5	3.4	96.6
On-call workers and day laborers	2.4	1.7	24.6	75.4
Temporary help agency workers	1.2	.9	60.7	39.3
Workers provided by contract firm	.8	.6	19.5	80.5
Traditional Arrangements	122.8	89.3	2.9	97.1
	137.5	100		

Source: U.S. Department of Labor, Bureau of Labor Statistics, *Contingent and Alternative Employment Arrangements,* Feb. 2005.

EXHIBIT 3.4   Major Workforce Trends

- Increasing number of workers over the age of 55 will mean higher health care costs for employers
- Aging of the workforce, and attendant increase in retirement, will lead to shortage of skilled workers in some fields
- Changing attitudes toward retirement, especially an increased tendency for retirees to remain in the workforce to some extent
- Changes in technology will lead to changes in skills demanded by employers
- Increased internationalization of the labor pool, including increased outsourcing, immigration, and international corporations
- Increased costs of health care for employers due to increased employee demand for insurance programs and increased premiums from insurance companies
- Employees are seeking more accommodation for work/life balance programs and flexible scheduling
- Greater concerns about identity theft and data security for organizational records
- Increased focus on productivity and demonstrated results for investments in human capital

SOURCE: J. Schramm, *Workplace Forecast, 2005–2006* (Alexandria, VA: Society for Human Resource Management, 2006).

create more jobs. Often these new jobs will require a completely different set of KSAOs than previous jobs, meaning that increased staffing resources will have to be devoted to either retraining or replacing the current workforce. Research conducted in both the United States and Germany shows that computerization has led to an increase in the demand for highly educated specialists, leading overall to an increased market demand for skills in science and mathematics, which in turn has led to dramatic increases in wages for individuals with these skills.[13] Employers that adopt new technology for any aspect of their operations will also have to consider what changes will need to be made to tap into labor markets that have these new skills.

Labor Unions

Labor unions are legally protected entities that organize employees and bargain with management to establish terms and conditions of employment via a labor contract. About 12% of the labor force is unionized, with 7.4% unionization in the private sector and 36% in the public sector.[14]

Labor and management are required to bargain in good faith to try to reach agreement on the contract. Many staffing issues may be bargained, including staffing levels, location of facilities, overtime and work schedules, job description and

classifications, seniority provisions, promotions and transfers, layoffs and terminations, hiring pools, KSAO requirements, grievance procedures, alternative dispute
resolution procedures, employment discrimination protections, and, very important, pay and benefits. Virtually all aspects of the staffing process are thus affected
by negotiations and the resultant labor agreement.

Once a contract is agreed to, it standardizes the terms and conditions of employment, making them uniform for all covered employees. The contract cannot be
replaced or supplemented by individual agreements with employees, as would be
the case in a nonunion setting. Moreover, the terms in the contract are binding
and cannot be unilaterally changed by management, thus "locking in" everything
agreed to.

Labor unions thus have direct and powerful impacts on staffing and other HR
systems. Even in nonunion situations the union influence can be felt through "spill-
over effects" in which management tries to emulate the pay and benefits, as well as
staffing practices, found in unionized settings.

HUMAN RESOURCE PLANNING

Human resource planning (HRP) is a process and set of activities undertaken to
forecast an organization's labor demand (requirements) and internal labor supply
(availabilities), to compare these projections to determine employment gaps, and
to develop action plans for addressing these gaps. Action plans include staffing
planning to arrive at desired staffing levels and staffing quality.

A general model depicting the process of HRP is presented first, followed by
an operational example of HRP. Detailed discussions of the major components of
HRP are then given.[15]

Process and Example

The basic elements of virtually any organization's HRP are shown in Exhibit 3.5.
As can be seen, the HRP process involves four sequential steps:

1. Determine future HR requirements.
2. Determine future HR availabilities.
3. Reconcile requirements and availabilities—that is, determine gaps (shortages
   and surpluses) between the two.
4. Develop action plans to close the projected gaps.

An example of HRP, including results from forecasting requirements and availabilities, is shown in Exhibit 3.6. The exhibit shows a partial HRP being conducted
by an organization for a specific unit (sales and customer service). It involves only
two job categories (A or sales, and B or customer service) and two hierarchical

EXHIBIT 3.5   The Basic Elements of Human Resource Planning

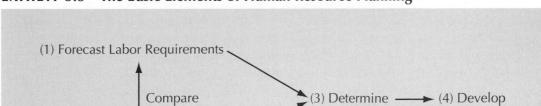

(1) Forecast Labor Requirements

Compare

(2) Forecast Labor Availabilities

(3) Determine
Gaps

(4) Develop
Action
Plans

levels for each category (1 or entry level, and 2 or manager level). All of the HRP steps are confined to this particular organizational unit and its job categories/levels, as shown.

The current workforce size (number of employees) is given for each job category/level. Requirements and availabilities are forecast for a one-year time frame, and the results are shown in the relevant columns. After the reconciliation process, final gap figures are agreed on and entered into the gap column. It can be seen that in total there is an estimated shortage of 145 employees. This overall shortage is very unevenly distributed across the four job categories/levels. In three of these, there are shortages projected (39, 110, and 3), and in the remaining one, there is a projected surplus (7).

These gap data serve as the basic input to action planning. Because the gaps show both shortages and a surplus, and because the gaps vary in severity relative to the current workforce, a specific action plan will probably have to be developed and implemented for each job category/level. The resultant four staffing (and other) plans hopefully will bring staffing into an orderly balance of requirements and availabilities over the course of the planning period.

The above process and example identify and illustrate the rudiments of HRP. Within them are several distinct HRP components that require elaboration. We turn now to these components, emphasizing that each component represents a factor that must be considered in HRP and that there are specific choices to be made regarding the operational details for each component.

Initial Decisions

Before HRP per se can be undertaken, there are several critical decisions that must be made. These decisions will shape the nature of the resultant HRP process, and they will influence the output of the process, namely, the gap estimates. The quality

EXHIBIT 3.6 Operational Format and Example for Human Resource Planning

Organizational Unit: Sales and Customer Service

Job Category and Level	Current Workforce	Forecast for Workforce— One Year		Reconciliation and Gaps	Action Planning
		Requirements	Availabilities		
A1 (Sales)	100	110	71	−39 (shortage)	Recruitment Selection
A2 (Sales manager)	20	15	22	+7 (surplus)	Employment Retention
B1 (Customer service representative)	200	250	140	−110 (shortage)	Compensation Training and development
B2 (Customer service manager)	15	25	22	−3 (shortage)	
	335	400	255	−145 (shortage)	

and potential effectiveness of the action plans developed from the gap estimates are thus at stake when these initial decisions are confronted and made.

Strategic Planning

Often, HRP takes place as an integral part of an organization's strategic planning process; this is referred to as plan-based HRP. This is a logical approach because most organizations do strategic planning, and these plans almost always have HR implications. It is always a good idea to have a close, reciprocal linkage between business and HR plans. Managers engaged in HRP should be aware of environmental contingencies and strategic goals that will affect the size of various business units. Changes in technology and strategy will also impact the KSAOs that will be needed in the future.

However, not all important business developments are captured in formal business plans, particularly if they occur rapidly or unexpectedly. Sudden changes in consumer preferences or legal requirements, for example, can wreak havoc on business plans. Organizational responses to these changes often occur in the form of special projects, rather than in changes in the total business plan. Part of each response requires consideration of HR implications, however, resulting in what is called project-based HRP. This type of planning helps ensure that the necessary creation of new jobs, changes in requirements and rewards for existing jobs, and employee job changes are undertaken systematically and without undue interruption.

In addition, many organizations do HRP outside the formal planning cycle for critical groups of employees on a regular basis. This often occurs for jobs in which there are perennial shortages of employees, both externally and internally. Examples here include nurses in health care organizations, faculty in certain specialized areas at colleges and universities, and teachers in elementary and secondary schools. Planning focused on a specific employee group is referred to as population-based HRP.

Also important is a firm grasp of an organization's internal environment. Thus, planners must be out and about in their organizations, taking advantage of opportunities to learn what is going on. Informal discussions with key managers can help, as can employee attitude surveys, special surveys, and the monitoring of key indicators such as employee performance, absenteeism, turnover, and accident rates. Of special interest is the identification of nagging personnel problems, as well as prevailing managerial attitudes concerning HR.

Nagging personnel problems refer to recurring difficulties that threaten to interfere with the attainment of future business plans or other important organizational goals. High turnover in a sales organization, for example, is likely to threaten the viability of a business plan that calls for increased sales quotas or the rapid introduction of several new products.

The values and attitudes of managers, especially top managers, toward HR are also important to HRP. Trouble brews when these are inconsistent with the organization's business plans. For example, a midsized accounting firm may have formulated a business plan calling for very rapid growth through aggressive marketing and selected acquisitions of smaller firms, but existing management talent may be inadequate to the task of operating a larger, more complex organization. Moreover, there may be a prevailing attitude among the top management against investing much money in management development and against bringing in talent from outside the firm. This attitude conflicts with the business plan, requiring a change in either the business plan or attitudes.

Planning Time Frame

Since planning involves looking into the future, the logical question for an organization to ask is, How far into the future should our planning extend? Typically, plans are divided into long term (three years and more), intermediate (one to three years), and short term (one year or less). Organizations vary in their planning time frame, often depending on which of the three types of HRP is being undertaken.

For plan-based HRP, the time frame will be the same as that of the business plan. In most organizations, this is between three and five years for so-called strategic planning and something less than three years for operational planning. Planning horizons for project-based HRP vary depending on the nature of the projects involved. Solving a temporary shortage of, say, salespeople for the introduction of a new product might involve planning for only a few months, whereas planning for the start-up of a new facility could involve a lead time of two or more years. Population-based HRP will have varying time frames, depending on the time necessary for labor supply (internal as well as external) to become available. As an example, for top-level executives in an organization, the planning time frame will be lengthy.

Job Categories and Levels

The unit of HRP and analysis is composed of job categories and hierarchical levels among jobs. These job category/level combinations, and the types and paths of employee movement among them, form the structure of an internal labor market. Management must choose which job categories and which hierarchical levels to use for HRP. In Exhibit 3.6, for example, the choice involves two jobs (sales and customer service) and two levels (entry and manager) for a particular organizational unit.

Job categories are created and used on the basis of the unit of analysis for which projected shortages and surpluses are being investigated. Hierarchical levels should be chosen so that they are consistent with or identical to the formal organizational hierarchy. The reason for this is that these formal levels define employee promotions (up levels), transfers (across levels), and demotions (down levels). Having gap information by level facilitates planning of internal movement programs within the internal labor market. For example, it is difficult to have a systematic promotion-from-within program without knowing probable numbers of vacancies and gaps at various organizational levels.

Head Count (Current Workforce)

Exactly how does an organization count or tally the number of people in its current workforce for forecasting and planning purposes? Simply counting the number of employees on the payroll at the beginning of the planning period may be adequate for intended purposes. It ignores two important distinctions, however.

First, it ignores the amount of scheduled time worked by each employee relative to a full workweek. For example, it treats full-time employees as synonymous with part-time employees. To rectify this, an employee head count may be made and stated in terms of full-time equivalents, or FTEs. To do this, simply define what constitutes full-time work in terms of hours per week (or other time unit), and count each employee in terms of scheduled hours worked relative to a full workweek. If full time is defined as 40 hours per week, a person who normally works 20 hours per week is counted as a .50 FTE, a person normally working 30 hours per week is a .75 FTE, and so on.

A second problem with current payroll head count is that it ignores vacancies that exist at the time of the count. Since most of such vacancies are probably so-called authorized ones, derived from previous HRP, they are better added into any head-count tallies for the current workforce.

Roles and Responsibilities

Both line managers and staff specialists (usually from the HR department) become involved in HRP, so the roles and responsibilities of each must be determined as part of HRP. Most organizations take the position that line managers are ultimately responsible for the completion and quality of HRP. But the usual practice is to have HR staff assist with the process.

Initially, the HR staff take the lead in proposing which types of HRP will be undertaken and when, and in making suggestions with regard to comprehensiveness, planning time frame, job categories and levels, and head counts. Final decisions on these matters are usually the prerogative of line management. Once an approach has been decided on, task forces of both line managers and HR staff people are assembled to design an appropriate forecasting and action planning process and to do any other preliminary work.

Once these processes are in place, the HR staff typically assumes responsibility for collecting, manipulating, and presenting the necessary data to line management and for laying out alternative action plans (including staffing plans). Action planning usually becomes a joint venture between line managers and HR staff, particularly as they gain experience with, and trust for, one another.

Forecasting HR Requirements

Forecasting HR requirements is a direct derivative of business and organizational planning. As such, it becomes a reflection of projections about a variety of factors, such as sales, production, technological change, productivity improvement, and the regulatory environment. Many specific techniques may be used to forecast HR requirements; these are either statistical or judgmental in nature, and they are usually tailor-made by the organization.

Statistical Techniques

A wide array of statistical techniques are available for use in HR forecasting. Prominent among these are regression analysis, ratio analysis, trend analysis, time series analysis, and stochastic analysis. Brief descriptions of three of these techniques are given in Exhibit 3.7.

The use of integrated workforce planning software, which can be combined with data from other organizational databases, means that it is becoming easier to use these statistical techniques than it was in the past. As we noted earlier, HR practitioners are also increasingly expected to back up their proposals and plans with hard data. The three techniques shown in Exhibit 3.7 have different strengths and weaknesses. Ratio analysis, which uses data from prior sales figures or other operational data to predict expected head count, is useful as a method to integrate HR plans with other departments. However, this model cannot directly account for any changes in technology or skill sets that might change these ratios. The regression analysis technique can be used with historical predictors and can make more statistically precise estimates of future expectations by taking several factors into account simultaneously; however, collecting enough data to make good estimates can be time consuming and does require judgment calls. Trend analysis is useful when organizations have data mostly on historical staffing levels with less detailed information on specific predictors. The decomposition of data into specific time periods of demand is also often used in health care or retail settings, where staffing levels vary greatly over the course of a year or even at different times of the day. Unfortunately, trend analysis does not directly take into account external factors that might change trends. In light of the problems with each of these methods, managers should only take these statistical estimates as a starting point, which may need to be modified based on ongoing strategic and environmental changes.

Judgmental Techniques

Judgmental techniques represent human decision-making models that are used for forecasting HR requirements. Unlike statistical techniques, judgmental techniques use a decision maker who collects and weighs the information subjectively and then turns it into forecasts of HR requirements. The decision maker's forecasts may or may not agree very closely with those derived from statistical techniques.

Implementation of judgmental forecasting can proceed from either a "top-down" or "bottom-up" approach. In the former case, top managers of the organization, organizational units, or functions rely on their knowledge of business and organizational plans to make predictions about what future head counts will be. At times, these projections may, in fact, be dictates rather than estimates, necessitated by strict

---

EXHIBIT 3.7   Examples of Statistical Techniques to Forecast HR Requirements

(A)   Ratio Analysis

1. Examine historical ratios involving workforce size.

Example: $\dfrac{\$ \text{ sales}}{1.0 \text{ FTE}} = ?$ $\dfrac{\text{No. of new customers}}{1.0 \text{ FTE}} = ?$

2. Assume ratio will be true in future.
3. Use ratio to predict future HR requirements.

Example: (a) $\dfrac{\$40{,}000 \text{ sales}}{1.0 \text{ FTE}}$ is past ratio
   (b) Sales forecast is $4,000,000
   (c) HR requirements = 100 FTEs

(B)   Regression Analysis

1. Statistically identify historical predictors of workforce size.

Example: FTEs = $a + b_1$ sales + b_2 new customers

2. Only use equations with predictors found to be statistically significant.
3. Predict future HR requirements, using equation.

Example: (a) FTEs = 7 + .0004 sales + .02 new customers
   (b) Projected sales = $1,000,000
       Projected new customers = 300
   (c) HR requirements = 7 + 400 + 6 = 413

(C)   Trend Analysis

1. Gather data on staffing levels over time and arrange in a spreadsheet with one column for employment levels and another column for time.
2. Predict trend in employee demand by fitting a line to trends in historical staffing levels over time (this can be done by using regression or graphical methods in most spreadsheet programs).
3. Calculate period demand index by dividing each period's demand by the average annual demand.

   Example: January demand index = Avg. January FTE/Avg. annual FTE

4. Multiply the previous year's FTEs by the trend figure, then multiply this figure by the period's demand index.

   Example: A retail store finds that the average number of employees over the past five years has been 142, 146, 150, 155, and 160. This represents a consistent 3% increase per year; to predict the next year's average demand, multiply 160 by 1.03 to show a 3% expected increase. Over this same time period, it averaged 150 FTEs per month, with an average of 200 FTEs in December. This means the December demand index is 200/150 = 1.33, so their estimate for next year's December FTE demand will be (160 × 1.03) × 1.3 = 219 FTEs.

adherence to the business plan. Such dictates are common in organizations undergoing significant change, such as restructuring, mergers, and cost-cutting actions.

In the bottom-up approach, lower-level managers make initial estimates for their unit (e.g., department, office, or plant) based on what they have been told or presume are the business and organizational plans. These estimates are then consolidated and aggregated upward through successively higher levels of management. Then, top management establishes the HR requirements in terms of numbers.

Forecasting HR Availabilities

In Exhibit 3.6 head-count data are given for the current workforce and their availability as forecast in each job category/level. These forecast figures take into account movement into each job category/level, movement out of each job category/level, and exit from the organizational unit or the organization. Described below are three different approaches to forecasting availabilities: manager judgment, Markov Analysis, and replacement and succession planning.

Manager Judgment
Individual managers may use their judgment to make availability forecasts for their work units. This is especially appropriate in smaller organizations or in ones that lack centralized workforce internal mobility data and statistical forecasting capabilities. Continuing the example from Exhibit 3.6, assume the manager is asked to make an availability forecast for the entry sales job category A1. The template to follow for making the forecast and the results of the forecast are shown in Exhibit 3.8. To the current staffing level in A1 (100) is added likely inflows to A1 (10), and then likely outflows from A1 (37) are subtracted to yield the forecasted staffing availability (73). Determining the inflow and outflow numbers requires judgmental estimates as to the numbers of promotions, transfers, demotions, and exits. As shown at the bottom of Exhibit 3.8, promotions involve an upward change of job level within or between

---

EXHIBIT 3.8   Manager Forecast of Future HR Availabilities

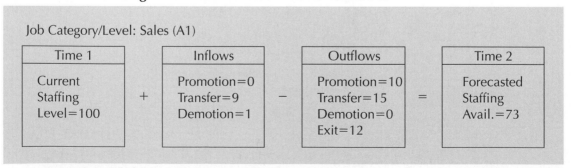

Job Category/Level: Sales (A1)

Time 1		Inflows		Outflows		Time 2
Current Staffing Level=100	+	Promotion=0 Transfer=9 Demotion=1	−	Promotion=10 Transfer=15 Demotion=0 Exit=12	=	Forecasted Staffing Avail.=73

NOTE: Promotion is A1 to A2, A1 to B2, B1 to B2, or B1 to A2; transfer is A1 to B1, A2 to B2, B1 to A1, or B2 to A2; is A2 to A1, A2 to B1, B2 to B1, or B2 to A1.

job categories; transfers are lateral moves at the same job level across job categories; demotions are downward changes of job level within or between job categories. Separate forecasts may be done for the other job category/levels (A2, B1, and B2).

To provide reliable estimates, the manager must be very knowledgeable about both organizational business plans and individual employee plans or preferences for staying in their current job versus moving to another job. Knowledge of business plans will be helpful in judging the likely internal mobility opportunities for employees. Business expansion, for example, will likely mean expanding internal mobility opportunities. Knowledge of employee plans or preferences will help pinpoint which employees are likely to change jobs or leave the work unit or organization.

The estimated staffing availability (n = 73) in Exhibit 3.8 coincides closely with the availability estimate (n = 71) derived from forecasting based on Markov Analysis results, discussed below. This is intentional. Markov Analysis uses historical mobility data and probabilities to forecast future availabilities, while managers' judgment uses current knowledge of business and employees' plans to forecast employee movements person by person. Results from the two different approaches to availability forecasts will not necessarily coincide, but they can be quite close if the manager is knowledgeable about past mobility patterns, employee mobility intentions, and mobility opportunities.

A major problem with using manager judgment to forecast availabilities is that the manager may lack the necessary business plan and employee intention information to provide solid estimates, as opposed to casual "guesstimates." In addition, if there are large numbers of employees and job category/levels in the work unit, the sheer complexity of the forecasting task may overwhelm the manager. Markov Analysis presents a way out of this dilemma, since it substitutes historical data about internal mobility and exit rates for the manager's judgment as a basis for making availability forecasts, and it simultaneously considers all types of possible employee movement in the forecasts.

Markov Analysis

Markov Analysis is used to predict availabilities on the basis of historical patterns of job stability and movement among employees. Consider again the four job category/levels: A1, A2, B1, B2 in the sales and customer service unit (Exhibit 3.6). Note that between any two time periods, the following possibilities exist for each employee in the internal labor market:

1. Job stability (remain in A1, A2, B1, B2)
2. Promotion (move to a higher level: A1 to A2, A1 to B2, B1 to B2, B1 to A2)
3. Transfer (move at the same level: A1 to B1, B1 to A1, A2 to B2, B2 to A2)
4. Demotion (move to a lower level: A2 to A1, A2 to B1, B2 to B1, B2 to A1)
5. Exit (move to another organizational unit or leave the organization)

These possibilities may be thought of in terms of flows and rates of flow or movement rates. Past flows and rates may be measured and then used to forecast the future availability of current employees, based on assumptions about the extent to which past rates will continue unchanged in the future. For example, if it is known that the historical promotion rate from A1 to A2 is .10 (10% of A1 employees are promoted to A2), we might predict that A1 will experience a 10% loss of employees due to promotion to A2 over the relevant time period. To conduct Markov Analysis we must know all of the job stability, promotion, transfer, demotion, and exit rates for an internal labor market before we can forecast future availabilities.

The elements of Markov Analysis are shown in Exhibit 3.9 for the organizational unit originally presented in Exhibit 3.6. Refer first to part A of Exhibit 3.9. There are four job category/level combinations for which movement rates are calculated between two time periods (T and T+1). This is accomplished as follows. For each job category/level, take the number of employees who were in it at T, and use that number as the denominator for calculating job stability and movement rates. Then, for each of those employees determine which job category/level they were employed in at T+1. Then, sum up the number of employees in each job category/ level at T+1, and use these as the numerators for calculating stability and movement rates. Finally, divide each numerator separately by the denominator. The result is the stability and movement rates expressed as proportions, also known as transition probabilities. The rates for any row (job category/ level) must add up to 1.0.

For example, consider job category/level A1. Assume that at time T in the past there were a total of 400 people in it. Further assume that at T+1, 240 of these employees were still in A1, 40 had been promoted to A2, 80 had been transferred to B1, 0 had been promoted to B2, and 40 had exited the organizational unit or the organization. The resulting transition probabilities, shown in the row for A1, are .60, .10, .20, .00, and .10. Note that these rates sum to 1.00.

By referring to these figures, and the remainder of the transition probabilities in the matrix, an organization can begin to understand the workings of the unit's internal labor market. For example, it becomes clear that 60–80% of employees experienced job stability and that exit rates varied considerably, ranging from 10% to 35%. Promotions occurred only within job categories (A1 to A2, B1 to B2), not between job categories (A1 to B2, B1 to A2). Transfers were confined to the lower of the two levels (A1 to B1, B1 to A1). Only occasionally did demotions occur, and only within a job category (A2 to A1). Presumably, these stability and movement rates are a reflection of specific staffing policies and procedures that were in place between T and T+1.

With these historical transitional probabilities, it becomes possible to forecast the future availability of the current workforce over the same time interval, T and T + 1, assuming that the historical rates will be repeated over the time interval and that staffing policies and procedures will not change. Refer now to part B of Exhibit 3.9. To forecast availabilities, simply take the current workforce column

EXHIBIT 3.9   Use of Markov Analysis to Forecast Availabilities

A. Transition Probability Matrix Job Category and Level		A1	A2	T + 1 B1	B2	Exit
	A1	.60	.10	.20	.00	.10
	A2	.05	.60	.00	.00	.35
T	B1	.05	.00	.60	.05	.30
	B2	.00	.00	.00	.80	.20

B. Forecast of Availabilities	Current Workforce				
A1	100	60	10	20	0
A2	20	1	12	0	0
B1	200	10	0	120	10
B2	15	0	0	0	12
		71	22	140	22

and multiply it by the transition probability matrix shown in part A. The resulting availability figures (note these are the same as those shown in Exhibit 3.6) appear at the bottom of the columns: A1 = 71, A2 = 22, B1 = 140, B2 = 22. The remainder of the current workforce (80) is forecast to exit and will not be available at T+1.

Limitations of Markov Analysis.   Markov Analysis is an extremely useful way to capture the underlying workings of an internal labor market and then use the results to forecast future HR availabilities. Markov Analysis, however, is subject to some limitations that must be kept in mind.[16]

The first and most fundamental limitation is that of sample size, or the number of current workforce employees in each job category/level. As a rule, it is desirable to have 20 or more employees in each job category/level. Since this number serves as the denominator in the calculation of transition probabilities, with small sample sizes there can be substantial differences in the values of transition probabilities, even though the numerators used in their calculation are not that different (e.g., 2/10 = .20 and 4/10 = .40). Thus, transition probabilities based on small samples yield unstable estimates of future availabilities.

A second limitation of Markov Analysis is that it does not detect multiple moves by employees between T and T+1; it only classifies employees and counts their movement according to their beginning (T) and ending (T+1) job category/level, ignoring any intermittent moves. To minimize the number of undetected multiple moves, therefore, it is necessary to keep the time interval relatively short, probably no more than two years.

A third limitation pertains to the job category/level combinations created to serve as the unit of analysis. These must be meaningful to the organization for the HRP purposes of both forecasting and action planning. Thus, extremely broad categories (e.g., managers, clericals) and categories without any level designations should be avoided. It should be noted that this recommendation may conflict somewhat with HRP for affirmative action purposes, as discussed later.

Finally, the transition probabilities reflect only gross, average employee movement and not the underlying causes of the movement. Stated differently, all employees in a job category/level are assumed to have an equal probability of movement. This is unrealistic because organizations take many factors into account (e.g., seniority, performance appraisal results, and KSAOs) when making movement decisions about employees. Because of these factors, the probabilities of movement may vary among specific employees.

Replacement and Succession Planning

Replacement and succession planning focus on the identification of individual employees who will be considered promotion candidates, along with thorough assessment of their current capabilities and deficiencies, coupled with training and development plans to erase any deficiencies. The focus is thus on both the quantity and the quality of HR availability. Through replacement and succession planning the organization constructs internal talent pipelines that ensure steady and known flows of qualified employees to higher levels of responsibility and impact. Replacement planning precedes succession planning, and the organization may choose to stop at just replacement planning rather than proceeding into the more complex succession planning.[17]

Replacement and succession planning can occur at any and all levels of the organization. It is most widely used at the management level, starting with the chief executive officer and extending downward to the other officers or top managers. But it can be used throughout the entire management team, including the identification and preparation of individuals for promotion into the entry management level. It may also be used for linchpin positions—ones that are critical to organization effectiveness (such as senior scientists in the research and development function of a technology-driven organization) but not necessarily housed within the management structure.

Replacement Planning.   Results of replacement planning are shown on a replacement chart, an example of which is in Exhibit 3.10. The chart is based on the previous sales–customer service unit in Exhibit 3.6. The focus of attention is replacement planning for sales managers (A2) from the ranks of sales associates (A1), as part of the organization's "grow your own," promotion-from-within HR strategy. The top part of the chart indicates the organization unit and jobs covered by replacement planning, as well as the minimum promotion eligibility criteria. The next part shows the actual replacement chart information for the

EXHIBIT 3.10   Replacement Chart Example

Organizational Unit: Merchandising—Soft Goods
Replacement for: Department Sales Manager (A2)
Pipelines for Replacement: Department Sales (A1)—preferred; External Hire—last resort
Minimum Eligibility Requirements: Two years full-time sales experience, overall performance rates of "exceeds expectation"; promotability rating of "ready now" or "ready in < 1 yr"

Department: Menswear
Store: Cloverdale

Incumbent Manager	Years in Job	Overall Performance Rating		
7 Seng Woo	7	X Exceeds expectations	___ Meets expectations	___ Below expectations
Promote to		**Promotability Rating**		
Group Sales Manager		X Ready now	___ Ready in < 1 yr.	___ Ready in 1–2 yrs. ___ Not promotable

Replacement	Years in Job	Overall Performance Rating		
Shantara Williams	8	X Exceeds expectations	___ Meets expectations	___ Below expectations
Promote to		**Promotability Rating**		
Sales Manager		X Ready now	___ Ready in < 1 yr.	___ Ready in 1–2 yrs. ___ Not promotable

Replacement	Years in Job	Overall Performance Rating		
Lars Stemke	2	X Exceeds expectations	___ Meets expectations	___ Below expectations
Promote to		**Promotability Rating**		
Sales Manager		___ Ready now	X Ready in < 1 yr.	___ Ready in 1–2 yrs. ___ Not promotable

incumbent department manager (Woo) and the two eligible sales associates (Williams, Stemke) in the menswear department at the Cloverdale store. The key data are length of service, overall performance rating, and the promotability rating. When the incumbent sales manager (Woo) is promoted to group sales manager, both sales associates will be in the promotion pool. Williams will likely get the position because of her "ready now" promotability rating. Given his relatively short length of service and readiness for promotion in less than one year, Stemke is probably considered a "star" or a "fast tracker" whom the organization will want to promote rapidly. Similar replacement charts could be developed for all departments in the store, and for all hierarchical levels, up to and including store manager. Replacement chart data could then be aggregated across stores to provide a corporate composite of talent availability.

The process of replacement planning has been greatly accelerated by human resources information systems. Many human resource information systems (HRISs) systems make it possible to keep data on KSAOs for each employee based on job history, training, and outside education. Software also allows organizations to create lists of employees who are ready to move into specific positions and to assess potential risks that managers or leaders will leave the company. The ability to keep track of employees across the organization by standardized inventories of skill sets means that staffing managers will be able to compare a variety of individuals for new job assignments quickly and consistently. A large database of candidates also makes it possible to seek out passive internal job candidates who aren't actively looking for job changes but who might be willing to take new positions if offered. Many organizations that use integrated database systems that track candidates across a variety of locations report that they are able to consider a larger pool of candidates than they would with a paper-based system. Some HRISs also send automatic alerts to human resources when key positions come open, so the process of finding a replacement can get under way quickly. The development of comprehensive replacement planning software is typically quite expensive, with expenses reaching hundreds of thousands of dollars, meaning that they are probably most useful for large organizations that will be able to capitalize on the costs of a large system. However, smaller organizations may find it possible to create their own simpler databases of skills within the organization as a means of facilitating the internal replacement process.[18]

Succession Planning. Succession plans build upon replacement plans and directly tie into leadership development. The intent is to ensure that candidates for promotion will have the specific KSAOs and general competencies required for success on the new job. The key to succession planning is assessing each promotable employee for KSAO or competency gaps, and where there are gaps, creating employee training and development plans that will close the gap.

Continuing the example from replacement planning, Exhibit 3.11 shows a succession plan example for the two promotable sales associates. The company has

---

EXHIBIT 3.11 Succession Plan Example

Organizational Unit: Merchandising–Soft Goods
Department: Menswear
Position to Be Filled: Sales Manager (A2)
Leadership Competencies Required
- Plan work unit activities
- Budget preparation and monitoring
- Performance management of sales associates

Eligible Replacements	Promotability Ratings	Competency Gaps	Development Plans
S. Williams	Ready now	Budget prep	Now completing in-house training course
L. Stemke	Ready in < 1 year	Plan work	Shadowing sales manager
		Budget prep	Starting in-house training course
		Perf. mgt.	Serving as sales manager 10 hours per week
			Taking course on performance management at university extension

developed a set of general leadership competencies for all managers, and for each management position (such as sales manager) it indicates which of those competencies are required for promotion, in addition to the minimum eligibility requirements. It is the focus on these competencies, and the development plans to instill them in promotion candidates lacking them, that differentiates replacement and succession planning.

It can be seen that Williams, who is "ready now," has no leadership competency gaps, with the possible exception of an in-house training course on budget preparation and monitoring, which she is currently completing. Stemke, while having "star" potential, must undertake development work. When he completes that work successfully, he will be promoted to sales manager as soon as possible. Alternatively, he might be placed in the organization's "acceleration pool." This pool contains hotshots like Stemke from within the organization who are being groomed for management positions generally, and for rapid acceleration upward, rather than progressing through the normal promotion paths.

It should be noted that replacement and succession planning require managers' time and expertise to conduct, both of which the organization must be willing to provide to those managers. Replacement and succession planning software might be helpful in this regard. Moreover, there must be effective performance appraisal and training and development systems in place to support replacement and succession planning. For example, overall performance and promotability ratings, plus assessment of competency gaps and spelling out development plans, could occur annually as part of the performance appraisal process conducted by management. Finally, making promotability and development assessments requires managers to make tough and honest decisions. A study of successful succession management in several Fortune 500 organizations concluded that "succession management is possible only in an organizational culture that encourages candor and risk taking at the executive level. It depends on a willingness to differentiate individual performance and a corporate culture in which the truth is valued more than politeness."[19]

An example of successful succession planning is the system used by Wellpoint Health Network in California, which has 16,500 employees and 50 million members throughout many subsidiaries such as Blue Cross of California.[20] The plan covers 600 managers in the top five levels of management, which Wellpoint thought was necessary to handle the multiple job shifts set in motion by filling a high-level vacancy. An HRP system was used to catalog detailed information about managers—including performance and promotability ratings, major accomplishments, and career goals. The system allows for organization-wide identification of eligible candidates for each management position. A unique feature is "challenge sessions," in which managers review one another's staffs, looking for hidden candidates who might have been overlooked by the immediate supervisor. Succession planning and performance appraisal are combined into one annual process, where the manager rates the person's performance, core competencies, and promotability. These data are placed in an online (secure Internet Web site) résumé, along with other KSAO information such as education, language skills, and past experiences. Special training programs are undertaken when serious competency gaps are discovered. Use of the succession planning system had good results. When a very senior manager left the organization, filling his position and the four other vacancies that occurred through musical chairs was done internally, filling all the positions quickly and saving about $1 million on what an executive search firm would have cost to conduct external searches. More generally, the system allowed for 86% of management vacancies to be filled from within, saved $21 million in external recruitment and new hire training, and reduced the time to fill management vacancies from 60 to 35 days.

Reconciliation and Gaps

The reconciliation and gap determination process is best examined by means of an example. Exhibit 3.12 presents intact the example in Exhibit 3.6. Attention is now directed to the reconciliation and gaps column. It represents the results of bringing

EXHIBIT 3.12   Operational Format and Example for Human Resource Planning

Organizational Unit: Sales and Customer Service

Job Category and Level	Current Workforce	Forecast for Workforce— One Year		Reconciliation and Gaps	Action Planning
		Requirements	Availabilities		
A1 (Sales)	100	110	71	−39 (shortage)	Recruitment Selection
A2 (Sales manager)	20	15	22	+7 (surplus)	Employment Retention
B1 (Customer service representative)	200	250	140	−110 (shortage)	Compensation Training and development
B2 (Customer service manager)	15	25	22	−3 (shortage)	
	335	400	255	−145 (shortage)	

together requirements and availability forecasts with the results of external and internal environmental scanning. Gap figures must be decided on and entered into the column, and the likely reasons for the gaps need to be identified.

Consider first job category/level A1. A relatively large shortage is projected due to a mild expansion in requirements coupled with a substantial drop in availabilities. This drop is not due to an excessive exit rate but to losses through promotions and job transfers (refer back to the availability forecast in Exhibit 3.9).

For A2, decreased requirements coupled with increased availabilities lead to a projected surplus. Clearly, changes in current staffing policies and procedures will have to be made to stem the availability tide, such as a slowdown in the promotion rate into A2 from A1 or an acceleration in the exit rate, such as through an early retirement program.

Turning to B1, note that a huge shortage is forecast. This is due to a major surge in requirements and a substantial reduction in availabilities. To meet the shortage, the organization could increase the transfer of employees from A1. While this would worsen the already projected shortage in A1, it might be cost effective to do this and would beef up the external staffing for A1 to cover the exacerbated shortage. Alternately, a massive external staffing program could be developed and undertaken for B1 alone. Or, a combination of internal transfers and external staffing for both A1 and B1 could be attempted. To the extent that external staffing becomes a candidate for consideration, this will naturally spill over into other HR activities, such as establishing starting pay levels for A1 and B1. Finally, a very different strategy would be to develop and implement a major retention program for employees in customer service.

For B2 there is a small projected shortage. This gap is so small, however, that for all practical purposes it can be ignored. The HRP process is too imprecise to warrant concern over such small gap figures.

In short, the reconciliation and gap phase of HRP involves coming to grips with projected gaps and likely reasons for them. Quite naturally, thoughts about future implications begin to creep into the process. Even in the simple example shown, it can be seen that considerable action will have to be contemplated and undertaken to respond to the forecasting results for the organizational unit. That will involve mixtures of external and internal staffing, with compensation as another likely HR ingredient. Through action planning these possibilities become real.

Action Planning

Action planning involves four basic sequential steps: set objectives, generate alternative activities, assess alternative activities, and choose alternative activities. Movement through these steps is a logical outgrowth of HRP and is greatly enhanced by its occurrence. Indeed, without HRP the organization rarely has the luxury of doing action planning. Instead, reaction becomes the mode of operation, leading to crash or crisis activities and programs.

These general statements apply to virtually all HR activities that are in any way dependent on the existence of employment gaps and the need to close them. The focus in this chapter is on staffing planning as a specific form of action planning.

STAFFING PLANNING

The four stages of action planning translate directly into a general staffing planning process. After the general process is discussed, staffing planning is divided into planning for the core and flexible workforces.

Staffing Planning Process

Staffing Objectives

Staffing objectives are derived from identified gaps between requirements and availabilities. Thus, they involve objectives responding to both shortages and surpluses. They may require the establishment of quantitative and qualitative targets.

Quantitative targets should be expressed in head count or FTE form for each job category/level and will be very close in magnitude to the identified gaps. Indeed, to the extent that the organization believes in the gaps as forecast, the objectives will be identical to the gap figures. A forecast shortage of 39 employees in A1, for example, should be transformed into a staffing objective of 39 accessions (or something close to it) to be achieved by the end of the forecasting time interval. Exhibit 3.13 provides an illustration of these points regarding quantitative staffing objectives. For each cell, enter a positive number for head-count additions and a negative number for head-count subtractions.

Qualitative staffing objectives refer to the types or qualities of people in KSAO-type terms. For external staffing objectives, these may be stated in terms of averages, such as average education level for new hires and average scores on ability tests. Internal staffing objectives of a qualitative nature may also be established. These may reflect desired KSAOs in terms of seniority, performance appraisal record over a period of years, types of on- and off-the-job training, and so forth.

Results of replacement and succession planning, or something similar to that, will be very useful to have.

Generating Alternative Staffing Activities

With quantitative and, possibly, qualitative objectives established, it is necessary to begin identifying possible ways of achieving them. At the beginning stages of generating alternatives, it is wise to not prematurely close the door on any alternatives. Exhibit 3.14 provides an excellent list of the full range of options available for initial consideration in dealing with employee shortages and surpluses.

EXHIBIT 3.13   Setting Numerical Staffing Objectives

Job Category and Level	Gap	Objectives					Total
		New Hires	Promotions	Transfers	Demotions	Exits	
A1	−39	52	−6	−3	0	−4	+39
A2	+7	0	+2	−8	0	−1	−7
B1	−110	+140	−5	−3	−2	−20	+110
B2	−3	+2	+4	−1	0	−2	+3
Total							

NOTE: Assumes objective is to close each gap exactly.

As shown in Exhibit 3.14, both short- and long-term options for shortages, involving a combination of staffing and workload management, are possible. Short-term options include better utilization of current employees (through more over-time, productivity increases, buybacks of vacation and holidays), outsourcing work to other organizations (subcontracts, transfer work out), and acquiring additional employees on a short-term basis (temporary hires and assignments). Long-term options include staffing up with additional employees (recall former employees, transfer in employees from other work units, new permanent hires), skill enhancement (retrain), and pushing work on to other organizations (transfer work out).

Assessing and Choosing Alternatives

As should be apparent, there is a veritable smorgasbord of alternative staffing activities available to address staffing gaps. Each of these alternatives needs to be assessed systematically to help decision makers choose from among them.

The goal of such assessment is to identify one or more preferred activities. A preferred activity is one offering the highest likelihood of attaining the staffing objective, within the time limit established, at the least cost or tolerable cost, and with the fewest negative side effects. There are a wide variety of metrics available to assess potential activities. First, a common set of assessment criteria (e.g., time for completion, cost, probability of success) should be identified and agreed on. Second, each alternative should be assessed according to each of these criteria. In this way, all alternatives will receive equal treatment, and tendencies to jump at an initial alternative will be minimized.

All of these alternatives must be considered within the broader context of how the organization creates and structures its workforce. This involves the key strategic issue of core versus flexible workforce usage. Many of the staffing activity alternatives are more applicable to one type of workforce than another.

EXHIBIT 3.14   **Staffing Alternatives to Deal With Employee Shortages and Surpluses**

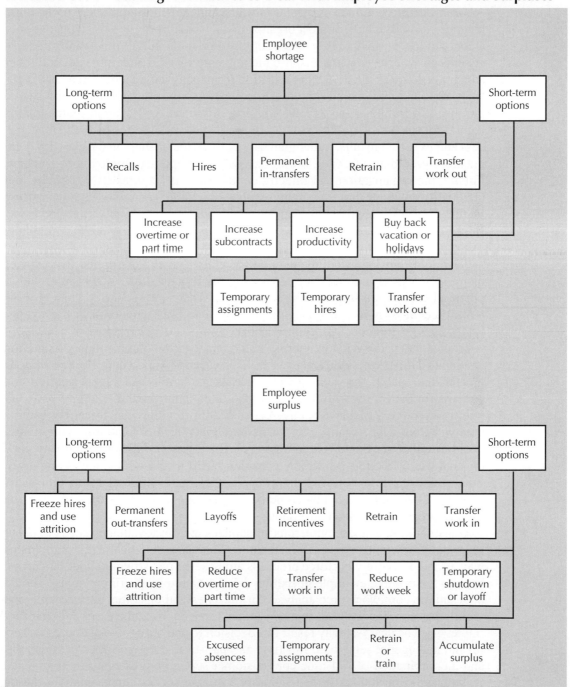

Core Workforce

A core workforce, defined as regular full-time and part-time employees of the organization, forms the bulk of most organizations' workforces. The key advantages of a core workforce are stability, continuity, and predictability. The organization can depend on its core workforce and build strategic plans based on it. Several other advantages also accrue to the organization from using a core workforce. The regularity of the employment relationship fosters a sense of commitment and shared purpose toward the organization's mission. Also, the organization maintains the legal right to control employees working in its behalf, in terms of both work process and expected results, rather than having to divide or share that right with organizations providing a flexible workforce, such as temporary employment agencies. Finally, the organization can directly control how it acquires its workforce and the qualifications of those it employs through the management of its own staffing systems. By doing so, the organization may build not only a highly qualified workforce but also one more likely to be retained, thus lessening pressure to continually restaff the organization.

Several disadvantages of a core workforce also exist. The implied permanence of the employment relationship "locks in" the organization's workforce, with a potential loss of staffing flexibility to rapidly increase, reduce, or redeploy its workforce in response to changing market conditions and project life cycles. Reductions of the core workforce, in particular, can be very costly in terms of severance pay packages, low morale, and damage to the organization's reputation as a good employer. Additionally, the labor costs of the core workforce may be greater than that of the flexible workforce due to (1) higher wages, salaries, and benefits for the core workforce, and (2) the fixed nature of these labor costs, relative to the more variable costs associated with a flexible workforce. By using a core workforce, the organization incurs numerous legal obligations—particularly taxation and employment law compliance—that could be fully or partially avoided through use of flexible workforce providers, who would be the actual employer. Finally, use of a core workforce may deprive the organization of new technical and administrative knowledge that could be infused into it by use of flexible workers such as programmers and consultants.

Consideration of these numerous advantages and disadvantages needs to occur separately for various jobs and organizational units covered by the HR plan. In this way, usage of a core workforce proceeds along selective, strategic lines. Referring back to the original example in Exhibit 3.6, for example, staffing planners should do a unique core workforce analysis for the sales and customer service unit, and within that unit, for both sales and customer service jobs at the entry and managerial levels. The analysis may result in a decision to use only full-time core workers for the managerial jobs, both full-time and part-time core workers for sales jobs, and a combination of full-time core customer service representatives augmented by both full-time and part-time temporary customer service representatives during peak sales periods. Once the job and work unit locations of the core workers have been determined, specific staffing planning for effective acquisition must occur. This involves planning of recruitment, selection, and employment activities; these topics will be covered in subsequent chapters. However, one overarching issue needs to be addressed very early on because of its pervasive implications for all of these staffing activities. The issue is staffing philosophy.

Staffing Philosophy

In conjunction with the staffing planning process, the organization's staffing philosophy should be reviewed. Weighed in conjunction with the organization's staffing strategies, results of this review help shape the direction and character of the specific staffing systems implemented. The review should focus on the following issues: internal versus external staffing, EEO/AA practices, and applicant reactions.

The relative importance to the organization of external or internal staffing is a critical matter because it directly shapes the nature of the staffing system, as well as sends signals to applicants and employees alike about the organization as an employer. Exhibit 3.15 highlights the advantages and disadvantages of external and internal staffing. Clearly there are trade-offs to consider in deciding the optimal internal-external staffing mix. The point regarding time to reach full productivity warrants special comment. Any new hire, either internal or external, will require time to learn the new job and reach a full productivity level. It is suggested that internal new hires have the advantage here. This reflects an assumption that internal new hires will require relatively little orientation time and may have received special training and development to prepare them for the new job. This specific advantage for internal new hires, however, needs to be weighed in tandem with the other advantages and disadvantages of each type of new hire.

In terms of EEO/AA, the organization must be sure to consider or develop a sense of importance attached to being an EEO/AA-conscious employer and the commitment it is willing to make in incorporating EEO/AA elements into all phases of the staffing system. Attitudes toward EEO/AA can range all the way from outright hostility and disregard to benign neglect to aggressive commitment and support. As should be obvious, the stance that the organization adopts will have major effects on its operational staffing system, as well as on job applicants and employees.

As a final point about staffing philosophy, planners must continue to bear in mind that staffing is an interaction involving both the organization and job applicants as participants. Just as organizations recruit and select applicants, so, too, do applicants recruit and select organizations (and job offers). Through their job search strategies and activities, applicants exert major influence on their own staffing destinies. Once the applicant has decided to opt into the organization's staffing process, the applicant is confronted with numerous decisions about whether to continue on or withdraw from further consideration. This process of self-selection is inherent to any staffing

EXHIBIT 3.15   **Staffing Philosophy: Internal Versus External Staffing**

	Advantages	Disadvantages
Internal	• Positive employee reactions to promotion from within • Quick method to identify job applicants • Less expensive • Less time required to reach full productivity	• No new KSAOs into the organization • May perpetuate current underrepresentation of minorities and women • Small labor market to recruit from • Employees may require more training time
External	• Brings employees in with new KSAOs • Larger number of minorities and women to draw from • Large labor market to draw from • Employees may require less training time	• Negative reaction by internal applicants • Time consuming to identify applicants • Expensive to search external labor market • More time required to reach full productivity

system. During staffing planning, those within the organization must constantly consider how the applicant will react to the staffing system and its components, and whether they want to encourage or discourage applicant self-selection.

Flexible Workforce

The two major components of the flexible workforce are temporary employees provided by a staffing firm and independent contractors. Planning for usage of the flexible workforce must occur in tandem with core workforce planning; hence, it should begin with a review of the advantages and disadvantages of a flexible workforce.[21] The key advantage is staffing flexibility. The flexible workforce may be used for adjusting staffing levels quickly in response to changing technological or consumer demand conditions and to ebbs and flows of orders for products and services. Other flexibility advantages are the ability to quickly staff new areas or projects and the ability to fill in for core workers absent due to illness, vacations, and holidays. Relative to the core workforce, the flexible workforce may also present labor cost advantages in the form of lower pay and benefits, more variable labor costs, and reduced training costs. It should be noted, however, that the temporary workforce provider shoulders many of these costs and simply passes them on to the organization through the fees it charges for its services. Another advantage is possibly being relieved of many tax and employment law obligations, since flexible workers are often not considered employees of the organization. For temporary employees, however, the organization may be considered a coemployer subject to some legal obligations, especially pertaining to EEO. An emerging advantage is that the flexible workforce, especially in the professional and technical ranks, may be an important source of new knowledge about organizational best practices and new skills not present in the core workforce, especially "hot skills" in high market demand. In a related vein, organizations use temporary or interim top executives to fill in until a permanent hire is found and on board, to spur change, and to launch special projects requiring their expertise.[22] Finally, usage of a flexible workforce relieves the organization of the need to design and manage its own staffing systems, since this is done by the flexible workforce provider. An added advantage here is that the organization might use flexible workers on a "tryout" basis, much like a probationary period, and then hire into its core workforce those who turn out to be a solid person/job match. Many temporary workers, for example, are "temp-to-perm," meaning that the organization will hire them permanently if they perform successfully in the temporary role. Such an arrangement is usually negotiated up front with the staffing services company.

These numerous advantages must be weighed against several potential disadvantages. Most important is the legal loss of control over flexible workers because they are not employees of the organization. Thus, although the organization has great flexibility in initial job assignments for flexible workers, it is very limited in the amount of supervision and performance management it can conduct for them. Exacerbating the situation is that frictions between core and flexible workers may also arise. Core workers, for example, may feel that flexible workers lack knowledge and experience, are just "putting in time," receive the easy job assignments, and do not act like committed "team players." Also, flexible workers may lack familiarity with equipment, policies, procedures, and important customers; such deficiencies may be compounded by a lack of training in specific job requirements. Finally, it should be remembered that the quality of the flexible workforce will depend heavily on the quality of the staffing and training systems used by the provider of the flexible workers. The organization may end up with flexible but poorly qualified workers.

If the review of advantages and disadvantages of flexible workers confirms the strategic choice to use them in staffing, plans must be developed for the organization units and jobs in which they will be used, and for how they will be acquired. Acquisition plans normally involve the use of staffing firms and independent contractors, both of which perform the traditional staffing activities for the organization. Hence, in contrast to the substantial and sustained staff planning that must occur for the core workforce, planning for the flexible workforce is primarily a matter of becoming knowledgeable about these potential sources and "lining them up" in advance of when they are actually needed.

Staffing Firms

Recall that staffing firms (also called temporary help agencies) are the legal employers of the workers being supplied, though there may also be matters of coemployment that may arise. Hence, the staffing firm conducts recruitment, selection, training, compensation, performance appraisal, and retention activities for the flexible workers. The firm is also responsible for their on-site supervision and management, as well as all payrolling and the payment of legally required insurance premiums. For such services the firm charges the organization a general fee for its labor costs (wages and benefits) plus a "markup" percentage of labor costs (usually 40–50%) to cover these services' costs plus provide a profit. There may be additional charges for specially provided services, such as extra testing or background checks, or skill training. Temp-to-perm workers may be hired away from the firm (with its permission and for a special fee) by the organization to become regular employees in the core workforce. For larger clients the firm may provide an on-site manager to help the organization plan its specific staffing needs, supervise and appraise the performance of the temporary workers, handle discipline and complaints, and facilitate firm–organization relations. With such additional staffing services, the firm functions increasingly like a staffing partner rather than just a staffing supplier.

Use of a staffing firm requires advance planning, rather than a panicky phone call to a firm at the moment of staffing need. In addition to becoming aware of firms that might be accessed, it is wise to become familiar with their characteristics and services. Shown in Exhibit 3.16 are descriptions of the various factors and issues to become knowledgeable about for any firm.

When a firm is actually chosen for use, a formal written agreement should be entered into by both parties. That agreement should cover such matters as specific services to be provided, costs, steps to ensure that the flexible workers are employees of the firm (such as having an on-site manager for them), and the process for terminating the firm–organization relationship. It is best to have the agreement prepared/reviewed by legal counsel.

Occasionally the organization may decide to establish its own in-house staffing firm. When this is done, the employees of the firm may even be employees of the organization. Managers thus have readily available flexible workers to whom they can turn, without having to go through all the planning steps mentioned above.

EXHIBIT 3.16 Factors to Consider When Choosing a Staffing Firm

Factor	Issues
Agency and Its Reputation	How long in business; location; references from clients available.
Types of Workers Provided	What occupation and KSAO levels; how many available.
Planning and Lead Time	Does agency help client plan staffing levels and needs; how quickly can workers be provided.
Services Provided	
Recruitment	What methods are used; how targeted and truthful is recruitment process.
Selection	What selection techniques are used to assess KSAOs.
Training	What types of training, if any, provided before workers placed with client.
Wages and Benefits	How are wages determined; what benefits are provided.
Orientation	How does the agency prepare workers for assignment with client; does agency have an employee handbook for its workers.
Supervision	How does agency supervise its workers on site of client; does agency provide on-site manager.
Temp-to-Perm	Does agency allow client to hire its temporary workers as permanent employees.
Client Satisfaction	How does agency attempt to gauge client satisfaction with services, workers, costs.
Worker Effectiveness	
Punctuality and Attendance	Does the agency monitor these; what is its record with previous clients.
Job Performance	Is it evaluated; how are the results used.
Retention	How long do workers remain on an assignment voluntarily; how are workers discharged by the agency.
Cost	
Markup	What is the percentage over base wage charged to client (often it is 50% to cover benefits, overhead, profit margin).
For Special Services	What services cost extra beyond the markup (e.g., temp to-perm), and what are those costs.

Independent Contractors

An independent contractor (IC) provides specific task and project assistance to the organization, such as maintenance, bookkeeping, advertising, programming, and consulting. The IC can be a single individual (self-employed, freelancer) or an employer with its own employees. Neither the IC nor its employees are intended to be employees of the organization utilizing the IC's services, and care should be taken to ensure that the IC is not treated as an employee (see Chapter 2).[23]

As with staffing firms, the organization must take the initiative to identify and check out ICs for possible use in advance of when they are actually needed. It is desirable to solicit and examine references from past or current clients of the IC. Also, as much as possible the organization should seek to determine how the IC staffs, trains, and compensates its employees. This could occur during a preliminary get-together meeting with the IC. In these ways, the organization will have cultivated and screened ICs prior to when they are actually needed.

It is recommended that the IC and the organization prepare and enter into a written agreement between them. In general, the agreement should clarify the nature and scope of the project and contain language that reinforces the intent to have the IC function as such, rather than as an employee. For example, the agreement should refer to the parties as "firm" and "contractor," describe the specific work to be completed, specify that payment will be for completion of the project (rather than time worked), make the IC responsible for providing all equipment and supplies, exclude the IC from any of the organization's benefits, and ensure that the IC is responsible for paying all legally required taxes. Preparation of such an agreement might require the assistance of legal counsel.

Outsourcing

Outsourcing of work functions can be defined as the transfer of a business process to an external organization. This is a more drastic step than simply using ICs or temporary employees. The primary difference is that when processes are outsourced, the organization expects to receive a completely finished product from the external source. This means the organization does not hire, direct, or control the way in which work is performed; rather, it only receives the end result of the work. Within the HR department, it has become the norm for organizations to completely outsource payroll tasks, meaning that data from the organization is sent to a third-party vendor that will assess taxes and withholdings and take care of either directly depositing or sending out paychecks for employees.[24]

Organizations outsource for a variety of reasons. An obvious reason for outsourcing of manufacturing and routine information-processing tasks is the availability of less expensive labor on the global market. Often, specialized vendors can achieve economies of scale for routine tasks that are performed across a variety of organizations. Organizations will also outsource functions that have highly cyclical demand, so that they do not have to make major capital outlays and go through the cost of hiring and training permanent workers to perform tasks that may not be needed in the future. Sometimes organizations will also outsource functions that require specific expertise that cannot be economically generated in-house. Smaller organizations that require legal services, for example, often choose to hire an external law firm rather than establishing their own pool of legal specialists. As we have noted, many organizations also outsource routine business functions, such as having payroll or benefits administration tasks completed by third-party vendors.

One variant of outsourcing is termed "offshoring," which means that products or services are provided by an external source outside the country where the organization's core operations take place.[25] The outsourcing of manufacturing to lower-wage countries has a long history, and this practice looks likely to continue unabated. For example, in the computer industry it is common for large companies to have many subcomponent electronic parts manufactured by third-party vendors overseas, with final assembly of products performed domestically. Many companies have also outsourced routine computer programming and telephone help services to third-party providers in India because of the availability of a highly skilled labor force that typically draws only a fraction of the wages paid in North America. Offshoring is no longer limited to just blue- and pink-collar jobs. There has been a dramatic increase in offshoring white-collar technical and professional work in the initial years of the twenty first century, fueled by improvements in global education, an increasingly positive climate for business in China and India, and increased demand for products and services in multinational organizations.

The decision to outsource is likely to be very controversial.[26] Outsourcing is usually done for activities that have low added value for the organizations. Normal transactional or procedural work that could be easily replicated has a high likelihood of being outsourced. High value-added operations that are core to the organization's business strategy almost certainly should not be outsourced. Although most managers are certainly aware that it is unwise to outsource work that is fundamental to a business's core operations, there are still many cases where organizations have discovered, too late, that they have outsourced work that should have been done internally. Additionally, offshoring has been the focus of media and political scrutiny. Extremely low wages and dangerous working conditions provided by external partners in foreign countries have created a backlash against certain companies that have offshored manufacturing jobs. Negative press about poor working conditions in overseas "sweatshops" has been especially prominent in the clothing industry. The import of children's toys tainted with lead made by outsourced manufacturing labor in overseas factories has been a major financial and media debacle for several American toy makers. When outsourcing, an organization needs to make certain that it is not losing too much control over its major work processes. Just because a business process has been outsourced does not mean that the organization has lost the responsibility (and this sometimes includes legal liability) for the actions of external partners.

LEGAL ISSUES

The major legal issue in HR and staffing planning is that of AAPs. AAPs originate from many different sources—voluntary employer efforts, court-imposed remedies for discriminatory practices, conciliation or consent agreement, and requirements as a federal contractor. Regardless of source, all AAPs seek to rectify the effects of past employment discrimination by increasing the representation of certain groups (minorities, women, disabled) in the organization's workforce. This is to be achieved through establishing and actively pursuing hiring and promotion goals for these groups.

This section describes the general content of AAPs, discusses the affirmative action requirements for federal contractors under Affirmative Action Programs regulations, and provides some general indications as to the legality of AAPs. Also, brief presentations are made of diversity programs and of Equal Employment Opportunity Commission (EEOC) guidance on use of temporary workers.

Affirmative Action Plans (AAPs)

AAPs are organization-specific plans that, as noted above, have a legal origin and basis. They preceded diversity programs, which organizations have voluntarily undertaken for strategic business reasons, rather than legal ones. Often, however, the structure and content of AAPs and diversity programs are very similar. Diversity programs are discussed separately below. While AAPs are organization specific, they all share a common architecture composed of three major components—availability analysis of women and minorities, placement (hiring and promotion) goals derived from comparing availability to incumbency (percentages of women and minority employees), and action-oriented programs for meeting the placement goals. These components, and accompanying details, are spelled out in the federal regulations put forth and enforced by the Office of Federal Contract Compliance Programs (OFCCP).

Affirmative Action Programs Regulations

All but very small federal contractors must develop and implement AAPs according to the OFCCP's affirmative action regulations (*www.dol.gov/esa/ofccp*). Described below is a summary of those regulations. A very useful sample of an AAP for small employers is on the OFCCP Web site shown above. The contractor must develop a separate AAP for each of its establishments with more than 50 employees. With advance approval from the OFCCP, the contractor may sidestep separate establishment plans by developing a functional plan that covers employees in discrete functional or business units, even though in different locations. All employees must be included in either AAP. The description that follows is for an establishment plan. The description is based on the EEO-1 form previously required. The currently required EEO-1 form is shown in Chapter 13. The OFCCP has not yet provided guidance on how to use the new EEO-1 form for AAP.

Organization Profile.   An organization profile is a depiction of the staffing pattern within an establishment. It provides a profile of the workforce at the establishment, and it assists in identifying units in which women or minorities are underrepresented. The profile may be done through either an organizational display or a workforce analysis. The latter requires a showing of job titles, which the former does not. Key elements in both approaches are a showing of organizational structure of lines of progression (promotion) among jobs, or organization units, the total number of job incumbents, the total number of male and female incumbents, and the total number of male and female minority incumbents in each of the following groups: Blacks, Hispanics, Asians/Pacific Islanders, and American Indians/Alaskan Natives.

Job Group Analysis.   Jobs with similar content, wage rates, and opportunities (e.g., promotion, training) must be combined into job groups; each group must include a list of job titles. Small establishments (fewer than 150 employees) may use as job groups the nine categories on the EEO-1 form: officials and managers, professionals, technicians, sales, office and clerical, craft workers (skilled), operatives (semiskilled), laborers (unskilled), and service workers. The percentage of minorities and the percentage of women (determined in the previous step) employed in each job group must be indicated.

Availability Determination.   The availability of women and of minorities must be determined separately for each job group. At least the following two factors should be considered when determining availability:

1. The percentage of minorities or women with requisite skills in the reasonable recruitment area
2. The percentage of minorities or women among those promotable, transferable, and training with the organization

Current census data (2000), job service data, or other data should be consulted to determine availability. When there are multiple job titles in a job group, with different availability rates, a composite availability figure for the group must be calculated. This requires summing weighted availability estimates for the job titles.

Exhibit 3.17 shows an example of availability determination for a single job group (officials and managers) based on the EEO-1 form. Listed on the left are the two availability factors that must be considered. Shown next are the raw statistic availability estimates for females and minorities (summed across the four minority groups) for each of the two availability factors (refer to the source of statistics column to see the sources of data for these estimates). Next, the value weights represent an estimate of the percentages of the total females and minorities available according to each availability factor (50% for each group). The weighted statistics represent the raw statistics multiplied by the value weight (e.g., $41.8\% \times .50 = 20.9\%$). A summing of the weighted statistics yields the total availability estimate percentages (47.6% for female; 18.1% for minority).

EXHIBIT 3.17   Determining Availability of Minorities and Women

| Job Group: 1 | Raw Statistics | | Value Weight | Weighted Statistics | | Sources of Statistics | Reason for Weighting |
	Female	Minority		Female	Minority		
1. Percentage of minorities or women with requisite skills in the reasonable recruitment area	41.8%	9.4%	50.0%	20.9%	4.7%	2000 Census Data The reasonable recruitment area for this job group is the St. Louis, MO–IL metropolitan statistical area (MSA).	50% of placement into this job group are made from external hires.
2. Percentage of minorities or women among those promotable, transferable, and trainable within the contractor's organization	53.3%	26.7%	50.0%	26.7%	13.4%	The group of promotable employees in job group 2	50% of placement into this job group are made from internal promotions.
Totals:			100%	47.6%	18.1%	<Final Factor	

SOURCE: Sample Affirmative Action Program for Small Employers, 2004, *www.dol.gov/esa.*

Comparison of Incumbency to Availability.   For each job group, the percentages of women and minority incumbents must be compared to their availability. When the percentage employed is less than would reasonably be expected by the availability percentage, a placement goal must be established.

Exhibit 3.18 shows the comparisons of incumbency to availability for eight job groups including the officials and managers group (job group 1). The comparisons are shown separately for females and minorities. Where incumbency is less than availability, it may be decided to establish a placement goal. In job group 1, it was concluded that the differences between availability and incumbency percentages for both females and minorities were sufficient to warrant placement goals (47.6% for females and 18.1% for minorities). Note also that an incumbency percentage less than an availability percentage does not automatically trigger a placement goal (e.g., females in job group 5).

How does the organization decide whether to set a placement goal for females or minorities in a job group? The OFCCP permits some latitude. One possibility is to set a placement goal whenever incumbency is less than availability, on the theory that any differences between availability and incumbency represent underutilization of females and minorities. A second possibility is based on the theory that some differences in percentages are due to chance, so some amount of tolerance of differences is permissible. The rule of thumb is 80% tolerance. This means that if the ratio of incumbency percentage to availability percentage is greater than 80%, no placement goal is needed. If the ratio is less than 80%, then a placement goal must be set. The 80% rule was followed in Exhibit 3.18. Though the incumbency percentage for females was less than the availability percentage in both job groups 1 and 5, the difference was less than 80% in only job group 1, triggering a placement goal just for that group.

Placement Goals.   If called for, an annual placement goal at least equal to the availability percentage for women or minorities must be established for the job group. Placement goals may not be rigid or inflexible quotas; quotas are expressly forbidden. Placement goals do not require hiring a person who lacks the qualifications to perform the job successfully, or hiring a less-qualified person in preference to a more-qualified one.

Designation of Responsibility.   An official of the organization must be designated as responsible for the implementation of the affirmative action program.

EXHIBIT 3.18   Determining Affirmative Action Goals: Comparing Incumbency to Availability and Annual Placement Goals

Job Group	Female Incumbency %	Female Availability %	Establish Goal? Yes/No	If Yes, Goal for Females	Minority Incumbency %	Minority Availability %	Establish Goal? Yes/No	If Yes, Goal for Minorities
1	0.0%	47.6%	Yes	47.6%	11.1%	18.1%	Yes	18.1%
2	45.5%	43.8%	No		18.2%	8.2%	No	
4	20.0%	34.5%	Yes	34.5%	0.0%	12.4%	Yes	12.4%
5	83.3%	87.7%	No		43.3%	27.6%	No	
6	9.3%	5.5%	No		34.9%	23.2%	No	
7	10.0%	6.3%	No		30.0%	37.5%	No	
8	6.3%	19.1%	Yes	19.1%	37.5%	26.3%	No	

NOTE: The 80% rule of thumb was followed in declaring underutilization and establishing goals when the actual employment of minorities or females is less than 80% of their availability. If the female/minority incumbency percent (%) is less than the female/minority availability percent (%) and the ratio of incumbency to availability is less than 80%, a placement goal should be included in the appropriate "If Yes" column.

SOURCE: Sample Affirmative Action Program for Small Employers, 2004, www.dol.gov/esa.

Identification of Problem Areas. The organization must evaluate the following:

1. If there are problems of minority or female utilization or distribution in each job group
2. Personnel activity (applicant flow, hires, terminations, promotions) and other personnel actions for possible selection disparities
3. Compensation systems for possible gender-, race-, ethnicity-based disparities
4. Selection, recruitment, referral, and other procedures to see if they result in disparities in employment or advancement of minorities or women

Action-Oriented Programs. Where problem areas have been identified, the organization must develop and execute action-oriented programs to correct problem areas and attain placement goals. (No specific guidance as to the nature of these programs is provided—suggestions are provided in Chapters 5, 6, 8, 9, and 10.) A good-faith effort to do this must be demonstrated.

Internal Audit and Reporting. An auditing system must be developed that periodically measures the effectiveness of the total affirmative action program.

It should be apparent that required affirmative action plans are complex undertakings that must be an integral part of overall staffing planning. Also, it should be remembered that the OFCCP monitors organizations for compliance with the Affirmative Action Programs regulations. Research by the OFCCP indicates several specific reasons why contractors may have their compliance status questioned. These are (1) lack of commitment and EEO/AA accountability by top management; (2) failure to conduct self-audits; (3) absence of consistent personnel policies; (4) faulty job application procedures; (5) lack of proactive recruitment, mentoring, and race and sexual harassment programs; (6) lack of participation of an EEO knowledgeable person in selection decisions; and (7) failure to develop and listen to internal support groups.[27]

Legality of AAPs

AAPs have been controversial since their inception, and there have been many challenges to their legality. Questions of legality involve complex issues of constitutionality, statutory interpretations, differences in the structure of the AAPs being challenged in the courts, claims that affirmative action goals represent hiring quotas, and, very importantly, differences in the amount of weight actually being placed on race or gender in the ultimate selection decisions being made about job applicants. The initial impetus for AAPs historically was for organizations to use them as a tool for overcoming the effects of previous employment discrimination that had been practiced. That purpose still remains, but has been augmented by the rationale that AAPs are necessary to increase the diversity of the organization's workforce regardless of previous discrimination in order to enhance organizational effectiveness.

Despite these problems, it is possible to provide several conclusions and recommendations regarding affirmative action. AAPs in general are legal in the eyes of the Supreme Court. However, to be acceptable, an AAP should be based on the following guidelines:[28]

1. The plan should have as its purpose the remedying of specific and identifiable effects of past discrimination.
2. There should be definite underutilization of women and/or minorities currently in the organization.
3. Regarding nonminority and male employees, the plan should not unsettle their legitimate expectations, not result in their discharge and replacement with minority or women employees, and not create an absolute bar to their promotion.
4. The plan should be temporary and should be eliminated once affirmative action goals have been achieved (this occurred, for example, to the AAP for firefighters in the city of Boston).[29]
5. All candidates for positions should be qualified for those positions.
6. The plan should include organizational enforcement mechanisms, as well as a grievance procedure.

Recent court rulings on the constitutionality of federal and state government AAPs suggest that even more strict guidelines than those above may be necessary. Insofar as these programs are concerned, racial preferences are subject to strict constitutional scrutiny. They may be used only when there has been specific evidence of identified discrimination, when the remedy has been narrowly tailored to only the identified discrimination, when only those who have suffered discrimination may benefit from the remedy, and when other individuals will not carry an undue burden, such as job displacement, from the remedy. Lesser scrutiny standards may apply for gender preferences.[30] Some states have even banned the use of AAPs by government employers, contractors, and educational institutions.[31]

The most recent court rulings have involved the question of whether an applicant's race may enter into a final selection decision, and if so, exactly how it should be factored into the decision. It has been held that use of race is permissible as part of a narrowly tailored diversity plan for admissions into a university program, but only if race is considered along with other factors on a case-by-case basis, rather than as part of a formula that rigidly allocates a set number of points for race.[32] It is unclear whether this will extend to private sector employers. A further discussion of the permissible role of race in choosing among finalists for the job is contained in the "Legal Issues" section of Chapter 11.

AAPs are not separate staffing systems but integral parts of general staffing systems. As such, AAPs should be incorporated into more general HR and staffing planning. In this way, there is a single, unified staffing system to serve both broad organizational goals and more specific affirmative action goals.

Diversity Programs

Much of staffing focuses on the initial acquisition of people and creation of the initial person/job match. AAPs and, to an extent, organization diversity programs likewise share this emphasis. Once the initial match has occurred, however, the organization must be concerned about employee adaptation to the job, upward job mobility, and maintenance of the employment relationship over time.

Diversity programs arise out of a recognition that the labor force, and thus the organization's workforce, is becoming more demographically and culturally diverse. Another major focus of diversity programs is on the assimilation and adaptation of a diverse workforce once it has been acquired. Diversity programs thus may be viewed as a logical continuation of AAPs.

Diversity programs lack the legal basis and imperative given to AAPs. Instead, they rest on a foundation of a presumed strategic business imperative. The following illustrates that imperative: "The big topic these days is integrating diversity into the business. . . . This means recognizing that diversity is not just a recruitment, retention, and employee development issue, but that the benefits of diversity can extend to marketing, expanding market share, and improving customer loyalty. Companies have been pretty good about recruiting diverse talent, but now, once they get that talent in the door, they are looking for ways to really leverage that diversity. Diversity today has to be a comprehensive strategy. It has to include communication, education, recruitment, and vendor/supplier relationships; all of these need to be coordinated from the top. That comes from having a business sense that diversity is about business performance enhancement."[33]

Specific examples of how the diversity imperative might affect business performance are expanded talent pools associated with recruitment from among all demographic groups, a diverse workforce that better understands the needs of a diverse customer base, diversity enhancing the creativity and problem-solving effectiveness of work teams, diversity leading to the fostering of long-term relationships with suppliers, and diversity boosting job satisfaction, thus reducing costly absenteeism and turnover.

To foster workforce diversity and to help strengthen the diversity–organizational effectiveness link, organizations have designed and implemented a wide variety of diversity initiatives and programs. Many of these initiatives involve staffing, since a diverse workforce does not generally just happen but must be actively identified, acquired, deployed, and retained. Most organizations supplement the staffing component of their diversity initiatives with many other programs, including diversity training for managers and employees to heighten awareness and acceptance of diversity, mentoring relationships, work/life balance actions such as flexible work schedules, team building, and special career- and credential-building job assignments.[34]

Research shows that diversity-oriented practices, including targeted recruitment, inclusion of women and African Americans on the top management team, work family accommodations, the creation of AAPs, and diversity councils, can increase the racial and gender diversity of the organization's entire managerial workforce. Effects of such practices on the composition of the nonmanagerial workforce is not known. Research is mixed on whether workforce diversity and diversity practices improve organizational performance. It should be remembered that myriad staffing laws and regulations also apply to diversity initiatives, so the legal ramifications of any diversity-oriented policies and procedures should be considered.[35]

EEO and Temporary Workers

The EEOC has provided guidance on coverage and responsibility requirements for temporary employment agencies (and other types of staffing firms) and their client organizations.[36] When both the agency and the client exercise control over the temporary employee and both have the requisite number of employees, they are considered employers and jointly liable under the Civil Rights Act, Age Discrimination in Employment Act (ADEA), Americans With Disabilities Act (ADA), and the Equal Pay Act. It should be noted that these laws also apply to individuals placed with organizations through welfare-to-work programs. The agency is obligated to make referrals and job assignments in a nondiscriminating manner, and the client may not set discriminatory job referral and job assignment criteria. The client must treat the temporary employees in a nondiscriminatory manner; if the agency knows this is not happening, the agency must take any corrective actions within its control. There are substantial penalties for noncompliance (e.g., back pay, front pay, compensatory damages) that may be obtained from either the agency or the client, or both. There is special guidance for ADA-related issues.

SUMMARY

External forces shape the conduct and outcomes of HRP. The key forces and trends that emerge from them are economic conditions, labor markets, technology, and labor unions.

HRP is described as a process and set of activities undertaken to forecast future HR requirements and availabilities, resulting in the identification of likely employment gaps (shortages and surpluses). Action plans are then developed for addressing the gaps. Before HRP begins, initial decisions must be made about its comprehensiveness, planning time frame, job categories and levels to be included, how to "count heads," and the roles and responsibilities of line and staff (including HR) managers.

A variety of statistical and judgmental techniques may be used in forecasting. Those used in forecasting requirements are typically used in conjunction with business and organization planning. For forecasting availabilities, techniques must be used that take into account the movements of people into, within, and out of the organization, on a job-by-job basis. Here, manager judgment, Markov Analysis, and replacement and succession planning are suggested as particularly useful techniques.

Staffing planning is a form of action planning. It is shown to generally require setting staffing objectives, generating alternative staffing activities, and assessing and choosing from among those alternatives. A fundamental alternative involves use of core or flexible workforces, as identified in staffing strategy. Plans must be developed for acquiring both types of workforces. Advantages and disadvantages of each type are provided; these should first be reviewed to reaffirm strategic choices about their use. Following that, planning can begin. For the core workforce, this first involves matters of staffing philosophy that will guide the planning of recruitment, selection, and employment activities. For the flexible workforce, the organization should establish early contact with the providers of the flexible workers (i.e., staffing firms and independent contractors). Organizational leaders should also consider the advantages and disadvantages of outsourcing some jobs at this point.

AAPs are an extension and application of general HR and staffing planning. AAPs have several components. The Affirmative Action Programs regulations, which apply to federal contractors, specify requirements for these components. The legality of AAPs has been clearly established, but the courts have fashioned limits to their content and scope. Diversity programs are organizational initiatives to help effectively manage a diverse workforce. Such programs have the potential for successfully working in tandem with AAPs by contributing to the attraction and retention of AAP-targeted people. To clarify how EEO laws apply to temporary employees and agencies, the EEOC has issued specific guidance.

DISCUSSION QUESTIONS

1. What are ways that the organization can ensure that KSAO deficiencies do not occur in its workforce?

2. What are the types of experiences, especially staffing-related ones, that an organization will be likely to have if it does not engage in HR and staffing planning?

3. Why are decisions about job categories and levels so critical to the conduct and results of HRP?

4. What are the advantages and disadvantages of doing succession planning for all levels of management, instead of just top management?

5. What is meant by reconciliation, and why can it be useful as an input to staffing planning?

6. What criteria would you suggest using for assessing the staffing alternatives shown in Exhibit 3.14?

7. What problems might an organization encounter in creating an AAP that it might not encounter in regular staffing planning?

ETHICAL ISSUES

1. Does an organization have any ethical responsibility to share with all of its employees the results of its forecasting of HR requirements and availabilities? Does it have any ethical responsibility to not do this?
2. Identify examples of ethical dilemmas an organization might confront when developing an AAP.

APPLICATIONS

Markov Analysis and Forecasting

The Doortodoor Sports Equipment Company sells sports clothing and equipment for amateur, light sport (running, tennis, walking, swimming, badminton, golf) enthusiasts. It is the only company in the nation that does this on a door-to-door basis, seeking to bypass the retail sporting goods store and sell directly to the customer. Its salespeople have sales kits that include both sample products and a full-line catalog they can use to show and discuss with customers. The sales function is composed of full-time and part-time salespeople (level 1), assistant sales managers (level 2), and regional sales managers (level 3).

The company has decided to study the internal movement patterns of people in the sales function, as well as to forecast their likely availabilities in future time periods. Results will be used to help identify staffing gaps (surpluses and shortages) and to develop staffing strategy and plans for future growth.

To do this, the HR department first collected data for 2005 and 2006 to construct a transition probability matrix, as well as the number of employees for 2007 in each job category. It then wanted to use the matrix to forecast availabilities for 2008. The following data were gathered:

Job Category	Level	Transition Probabilities (2005–06)					Current (2007) No. Employees
		SF	SP	ASM	RSM	Exit	
Sales, Full-time (SF)	1	.50	.10	.05	.00	.35	500
Sales, Part-time (SP)	1	.05	.60	.10	.00	.25	150
Ass't. Sales Mgr. (ASM)	2	.05	.00	.80	.10	.05	50
Region. Sales Mgr. (RSM)	3	.00	.00	.00	.70	.30	30

Based on the above data:

1. Describe the internal labor market of the company in terms of job stability (staying in same job), promotion paths and rates, transfer paths and rates, demotion paths and rates, and turnover (exit) rates.

2. Forecast the numbers available in each job category in 2008.

3. Indicate potential limitations to your forecasts.

Deciding Whether to Use Flexible Staffing

The Kaiser Manufacturing Company (KMC) has been in existence for over 50 years. Its main products are specialty implements for use in both the crop and dairy herd sides of the agricultural business. Products include special attachments to tractors, combines, discers, and so on, and add-on devices for milking and feeding equipment that enhance the performance and safety of the equipment.

KMC has a small corporate office plus four manufacturing plants (two in the midwest and two in the south). It has a core workforce of 725 production workers, 30 clericals, 32 professional and engineering workers, and 41 managers. All employees are full time, and KMC has never used either part-time or temporary workers. It feels very strongly that its staffing strategy of using only a core workforce has paid big dividends over the years in attracting and retaining a committed and highly productive workforce.

Sales have been virtually flat at $175 million annually since 2002. At the same time KMC has begun to experience more erratic placement of orders for its products, making sales less predictable. This appears to be a reflection of more turbulent weather patterns, large swings in interest rates, new entrants into the specialty markets, and general uncertainty about the future direction and growth in the agricultural industry. Increased unpredictability in sales has been accompanied by steadily rising labor costs. This is due to KMC's increasingly older workforce, as well as shortages of all types of workers (particularly production workers) in the immediate labor markets surrounding the plants.

Assume you are the HR manager responsible for staffing and training at KMC. You have just been contacted by a representative of the Flexible Staffing Services (FSS) Company, Mr. Tom Jacoby. Mr. Jacoby has proposed meeting with you and the president of KMC, Mr. Herman Kaiser, to talk about FSS and how it might be of service to KMC. You and Mr. Kaiser agree to meet with Mr. Jacoby. At that meeting, Mr. Jacoby makes a formal presentation to you in which he describes the services, operation, and fees of FSS and highlights the advantages of using a more flexible workforce. During that meeting, you learn the following from Mr. Jacoby.

FSS is a recent entrant into what is called the staffing industry. Its general purpose is to furnish qualified employees to companies (customers) on an as-needed basis, thus helping the customer implement a flexible staffing strategy. It furnishes employees in four major groups: production, clerical, technical, and professional/managerial. Both full-time and part-time employees are available in each of these groups. Employees may be furnished to the customer on a strictly temporary basis ("temps") or on a "temp-to-perm" basis in which the employees convert from being temporary employees of FSS to being permanent employees of the customer after a 90-day probationary period.

For both the temp and temp-to-perm arrangements, FSS offers the following services. In each of the four employee groups it will recruit, select, and hire people to work for FSS, which will in turn lease them to the customer. FSS performs all recruitment, selection, and employment activities. It has a standard selection system used for all applicants, composed of an application blank, reference checks, drug testing, and a medical exam (given after making a job offer). It also offers customized selection plans in which the customer chooses from among a set of special skill tests, a personality test, an honesty test, and background investigations. Based on the standard and/or custom assessments, FSS refers to the customer what it views as the top candidates. FSS tries to furnish two people for every vacancy, and the customer chooses from between the two.

New hires at FSS receive a base wage that is similar to the market wage, as well as close to the wage of the customer's employees with whom they will be directly working. In addition, new hires receive a paid vacation (one week for every six months of employment, up to four weeks), health insurance (with a 25% employee co-pay), and optional participation in a 401(k) plan. FSS performs and pays for all payroll functions and deductions. It also pays the premiums for workers' compensation and unemployment compensation.

The fees charged by FSS to the customer are as follows. There is a standard fee per employee furnished of 1.55 × base wage × hours worked per week. The 1.55 is labeled "markup"; it covers all of FSS's costs (staffing, insurance, benefits, administration) plus a profit margin. On top of the standard fee is an additional fee for customized selection services. This fee ranges from .50 to .90 × base wage × hours worked per week. Finally, there is a special one-time fee for temp-to-perm employees (a one-month pay finder's fee) payable after the employee has successfully completed the 90-day probationary period and transferred to being an employee of the customer.

Mr. Jacoby concludes his presentation by stressing three advantages of flexible staffing as provided by FSS. First, use of FSS employees on an as-needed basis will give KMC greater flexibility in its staffing to match fluctuating product demand, as well as movement from completely fixed labor costs to more variable labor costs. Second, FSS provides considerable administrative convenience, relieving KMC of most of the burden of recruitment, selection, and payrolling. Finally, KMC will experience considerable freedom from litigation (workers' comp, EEO, torts) since FSS and not KMC will be the employer.

After Mr. Jacoby's presentation, Mr. Kaiser tells you he is favorably impressed, but that the organization clearly needs to do some more thinking before it embarks on the path of flexible staffing and the use of FSS as its provider. He asks you to prepare a brief, preliminary report including the following:

1. A summary of the possible advantages and disadvantages of flexible staffing
2. A summary of the advantages and disadvantages of using FSS as a service provider
3. A summary of the type of additional information you recommend gathering and using as part of the decision-making process

TANGLEWOOD STORES CASE

The planning chapter explained how organizations can integrate their strategic goals and administrative data to determine staffing needs. The planning case will illustrate how these activities are implemented by Tanglewood.

The Situation

The process of planning involves a combination of forecasting labor needs, comparing these needs to labor availabilities, and determining where gaps exist. Data from Tanglewood's historical hiring practices are provided to assist you in developing these estimates. Beyond developing objectives for the number of individuals to be hired, you will need to take the demographic composition of the workforce into consideration to ensure that the company's commitment to diversity is maintained. This is an extension of the affirmative action discussion in the textbook.

Your Tasks

You will first complete a forecast of HR availabilities. Due to the strong emphasis on corporate culture at Tanglewood, you will also consider whether it should move toward the use of a flexible workforce strategy. You will also estimate the representation of women and minorities in several job categories as part of affirmative action planning. The background information for this case, and your specific assignment, can be found at *www.mhhe.com/heneman6e*.

ENDNOTES

1. D. E. Hecker, "Occupational Employment Projection to 2014," *Monthly Labor Review,* 2005, 128(11), pp. 45–69.
2. Hecker, "Ocupational Employment Projection to 2014," pp. 45–69.
3. Hecker, "Occupational Employment Projection to 2014."
4. A. Spitz-Oener, "Technical Change, Job Tasks, and Rising Educational Demands: Looking Outside the Wage Structure," *Journal of Labor Economics,* 2006, 24, pp. 235–270.
5. Society for Human Resource Management, "Management Skills for the Future," *Issues in HR,* Mar./Apr. 1995, p. 5.

6. M. Toossi, "Labor Force Projections to 2014; Retiring Boomers," *Monthly Labor Review,* 2005, 128(11), pp. 25–44; P. L. Rones, R. E. Ilg, and J. M. Garner, "Trends in Hours of Work Since the Mid-1970s," *Monthly Labor Review,* 1997, 120(4), pp. 3–14; J. Schramm, *SHRM Workplace Forcast* (Alexandria, VA: Society for Human Resource Management, 2006); P. J. Kiger, "With Baby Boomers Graying, Employers Are Urged to Act Now to Avoid Skills Shortages," *Workforce Management,* 2005, 84(13), pp. 52–54; J. F. Stinson, Jr., "New Data on Multiple Job Holding Available From the CPS," *Monthly Labor Review,* 1997, 120(3), pp. 3–8; Manpower Ind., *Employment Outlook Survey: United States* (Milwaukee, WI: author, 2007).

7. Hecker, "Occupational Employment Projections to 2014."

8. T. Minton-Eversole and K. Gurchiek, "New Workers Not Ready for Prime Time," *HR Magazine,* Dec. 2006, pp. 28–34.

9. M. J. Handel, "Skills Mismatch in the Labor Market," *Annual Review of Sociology,* 2003, 29, pp. 135–165.

10. BMP Forum and Success Factors, *Performance and Talent Management Trend Survey 2007* (San Mateo, CA: author, 2007).

11. Bureau of Labor Statistics, "Employed and Unemployed Full- and Part-Time Workers by Age, Race, Sex and Hispanic or Latino Ethnicity," Dec. 2007 (*www.bls.gov/public/special.requests/lf/aat8.txt*).

12. U.S. Department of Labor, "Workers on Flexible and Shift Schedules in May 2004," *News,* July 1, 2005.

13. T. Dunne, L. Foster, J. Haltiwanger, and K. R. Troske, "Wage and Productivity Dispersion in United States Manufacturing: The Role of Computer Investment," *Journal of Labor Economics,* 2004, 22, pp. 397–429; A. Spitz-Oener, "Technical Change, Job Tasks, and Rising Educational Demands: Looking Outside the Wage Structure," *Journal of Labor Economics,* 2006, 24, pp. 235–270.

14. U.S. Department of Labor, "Union Members in 2006," *News,* Jan. 25, 2007.

15. C. R. Greer, *Strategic Human Resource Management,* second ed. (Upper Saddle River, NJ: Prentice Hall, 2001); International Personnel Management Association, *Workforce Planning Guide for Public Sector Human Resource Professionals* (Alexandria, VA: author, 2002); D. W. Jarrell, *Human Resource Planning* (Englewood Cliffs, NJ: Prentice-Hall, 1993); J. W. Walker, *Human Resource Strategy* (New York: McGraw-Hill, 1992).

16. H. G. Heneman III and M. H. Sandver, "Markov Analysis in Human Resource Administration: Applications and Limitations," *Academy of Management Review,* 1977, 2, pp. 535–542.

17. J. A. Conger and R. M. Fuller, "Developing Your Leadership Pipeline," *Harvard Business Review,* Dec. 2003, pp. 76–84; International Public Management Association–Human Resources, *Succession Planning* (Alexandria, VA: author, 2003); S. J. Wells, "Who's Next?" *HR Magazine,* Nov. 2003, pp. 45–50.

18. E. Frauenheim, "Software Products Aim to Streamline Succession Planning," *Workforce Management,* Jan. 2006 (*www.workforce.com/archive/feature/24/24/94/242496.php?*).

19. Conger and Fuller, "Developing Your Leadership Pipeline," p. 84.

20. P. J. Kiger, "Succession Planning Keeps WellPoint Competitive," *Workforce,* Apr. 2002, pp. 50–55.

21. S. F. Matusik and C. W. L. Hill, "The Utilization of Contingent Work, Knowledge Creation, and Competitive Advantage," *Academy of Management Review,* 1998, 23, pp. 680–697; Society for Human Resource Management, *Alternative Staffing Survey* (Alexandria, VA: author, 2000); C. V. von Hippel, S. L. Mangum, D. B. Greenberger, R. L. Heneman, and J. D. Skoglind, "Temporary Employment: Can Organizations and Employees Both Win?" *Academy of Management Executive,* 1997, 11, pp. 93–104.

22. G. Weber, "Temps at the Top," *Workforce,* Aug. 2004, pp. 27–31; M. Frase-Blunt, "Short Term Executives," *HR Magazine,* June 2004, pp. 110–114.

23. J. Brown, "Contingent Workers: Employing Nontraditional Workers Requires Strategy," *IPMA-HR News,* June 2004, pp. 9–11; A. Davis-Blake and P. P. Hui, "Contracting for Knowledge-Based Competition," in S. E. Jackson, M. A. Hitt, and A. S. DeNisi (eds.), *Managing Knowledge for Sustained Competitive Advantage* (San Francisco: Jossey-Bass, 2003) pp. 178–206.

24. D. Arthur, *Recruiting, Interviewing, Selecting, and Orienting New Employees,* fourth ed. (New York: Arthur Associates Management Consultants Limited, 2006); E. Esen, *Human Resource Outsourcing Survey Report* (Alexandria, VA: Society for Human Resource Management, 2004); J. Schramm, *Workplace Forecast, 2005–2006* (Alexandria, VA: Society for Human Resource Management, 2006).

25. P. Babcock, "America's Newest Export: White-Collar Jobs," Apr. 2004, *HR Magazine,* pp. 50–57; B. Tai and N. R. Lockwood, *Outsourcing and Offshoring HR Series Part I* (Alexandria, VA: Society for Human Resource Management, 2006).

26. M. Belcourt, "Outsourcing—The Benefits and the Risks," *Human Resource Management Review,* 2006, 16, pp. 269–279; B. M. Testa, "Tales of Backshoring," *Workforce Management,* Dec. 2007 (*www.workforce.com/section/09/feature/25/27/70/index.html*); A. Meisler, "Think Globally, Act Rationally," *Workforce Management,* Jan. 2004, pp. 40–45.

27. Bureau of National Affairs, "Regional OFCCP Directors Describe Top Ten Reasons Contractors Get in Trouble," *Daily Labor Report,* Aug. 21, 1998, p. C-2.

28. D. D. Bennett-Alexander and L. B. Pincus, *Employment Law for Business,* second ed. (Burr-Ridge, IL: Irwin McGraw-Hill, 1998), p. 139; C. R. Gullett, "Reverse Discrimination and Remedial Affirmative Action in Employment," *Public Personnel Management,* 2000, 29(1), pp. 107–118; T. Johnson, "Affirmative Action as a Title VII Remedy: Recent U.S. Supreme Court Decisions, Racial Quotas and Preferences," *Labor Law Journal,* 1987, 38, pp. 574–581; T. Johnson, "The Legal Use of Racial Quotas and Gender Preferences by Public and Private Employers," *Labor Law Journal,* 1989, 40, pp. 419–425; D. J. Walsh, *Employment Law for Human Resource Practice*, second ed. (Mason, OH: Thompson Higher Education, 2007).

29. A. R. Mc Ilvaine, "Court: Boston Must Hire White Firefighters," *Human Resource Executive,* Feb. 2004, p. 13.

30. R. T. Seymour and B. B. Brown, *Equal Employment Law Update* (Washington, DC: Bureau of National Affairs, 1997), pp. 23-553 to 23-558.

31. M. P. Crockett and J. B. Thelen, "Michigan's Proposal 2: Affirmative Action Law Shifts at the State Level," Legal Report, *Society for Human Resource Management,* July–Aug. 2007, pp. 5–8.

32. A. Gutman, "On the Legal Front: The Grutter, Gratz, and Costa Rulings," *The Industrial-Organizational Psychologist,* Oct. 2003, pp. 117–127; A. Gutman, "On the Legal Front: Grutter goes to Work," *The Industrial-Organizational Psychologist,* Apr. 2004, pp. 71–77; A. Gutman and E. Dunleavy, "The Supreme Court Ruling in Parents v. Seattle School District: Sending Grutter and Gratz Back to School." *The Industrial/Organizational Psychologist*, Oct. 2007, pp. 41–49.

33. "Winning With Diversity" (no author). Special Advertising Supplement to the *New York Times Magazine,* Mar. 28, 2004, p. 66.

34. T. Kochan, K. Bezrukova, R. Ely, S. Jackson, A. Jishi, K. Jehn, L. Leonard, D. Levine, and D. Thomas, "The Effects of Diversity on Business Performance: Report of the Diversity Research Network," *Human Resource Management,* 2003, 42, pp. 3–21.

35. M. E. A. Jayne and R. Dipboye, "Leveraging Diversity to Improve Business Performance: Research Findings and Recommendations for Organizations," *Human Resource Management,* 2004, 43, pp. 409-424; Kochan et al. "The Effects of Diverstiy on Business Performance: Report

of the Diversity Research Network"; A. Kalev, F. Dobins, and E. Kelley, "Best Practices or Best Guesses? Assessing the Efficacy of Corporate Affirmative Action and Diversity Policies," *American Sociological Review,* 2006, 71, pp. 589–617; N. R. Lockwood and J. Victor, *Recruiting for Workplace Diversity: A Business Strategy* (Alexandria, VA: Society for Human Resource Management, 2007).

36. Equal Employment Opportunity Commission, *EEOC Policy Guidance on Temporary Workers* (Washington, DC: author, 1997); Equal Employment Opportunity Commission, *Enforcement Guidance: Application of the ADA to Contingent Workers Placed by Temporary Agencies and Other Staffing Firms* (Washington, DC: author, 2000).

CHAPTER FOUR

Job Analysis and Rewards

This chapter begins with a description of the changing nature of jobs. Though continually evolving, all jobs may be analyzed and described in terms of specific job requirements (tasks, KSAOs [knowledge, skill, ability, and other characteristics], job context) and competency requirements (general and job-spanning KSAOs). Job analysis is the general process of studying and describing these requirements. Separate approaches are needed for job requirements and competency requirements.

Job requirements job analysis is discussed first. It is guided by the job requirements matrix, which contains the three basic components (tasks, KSAOs, job context) that must be considered during the job analysis. Detailed descriptions of each component are provided. Also described are job analysis methods, sources, and processes for collecting the job requirements information.

Competency-based job analysis is described next. It is very new on the job requirements scene. It seeks to identify more general KSAO requirements, such as KSAOs necessary for all jobs to meet the organization's mission and goals and KSAOs that cut across interdependent jobs, such as with work teams. These competencies are presumed to provide a foundation for more flexible staffing in initial job assignments for new hires and in job and project assignments for current employees.

Attention then turns to job rewards. Discussed first are the multitude of extrinsic and intrinsic rewards jobs may provide to employees; the totality of these rewards form the employee value proposition (EVP). Special challenges in creating the EVP are providing rewards of the right magnitude, mix, and distinctiveness. It is suggested that job rewards information be collected within, and from outside, the organization. The focus should be on learning about employee reward preferences, and various ways to accomplish this are discussed. More and more work is being done in teams. Jobs that are team based need to be analyzed differently in some key areas.

Finally, two legal issues pertaining to job analysis are treated. Both issues involve the job requirements approach to job analysis as it applies to equal employment opportunity and affirmative action (EEO/AA) under the Civil Rights Act and the Americans With Disabilities Act (ADA).

CHANGING NATURE OF JOBS

Jobs are the building blocks of an organization, in terms of both job content and the hierarchical relationships that emerge among them. They are explicitly designed and aligned in ways that enhance the production of the organization's goods and services. Job analysis thus must be considered within the broader framework of the design of jobs, for it is through their design that jobs acquire their requirements and rewards.

Jobs are constantly evolving—they are born out of organizational need, grow in scope and responsibilities as the needs grow, and, sometimes, die when the needs change. For example, at one time all airlines had the job of flight engineer, whose job was to monitor air-to-ground communications and to watch and control certain aircraft systems during flight. Cockpits were designed so that the flight engineer sat at a panel behind the pilot and copilot. However, as computer technology advanced, the job of flight engineer became obsolete and virtually disappeared from commercial aviation. Such is the case with a surprising number of jobs. Scores of jobs are created, while an equal number of others are eliminated every year. This is one of the reasons for the growth in competency-based job analysis, which is seen as a more flexible alternative to traditional job analysis.

Before describing approaches to job analysis, let us describe in a bit more detail the traditional way jobs are designed in organizations and how contemporary trends are shaping how jobs are designed and analyzed.

The traditional way of designing a job is to identify and define its elements and tasks precisely and then incorporate them into a job description. This task core includes virtually all tasks associated with the job, and from it a fairly inclusive list of KSAOs will flow. Thus defined, there are clear lines of demarcation between jobs in terms of both tasks and KSAOs, and there is little overlap between jobs on either basis. Each job also has its own set of extrinsic and intrinsic rewards. Such job design is marked by formal organization charts, clear and precise job descriptions and specifications, and well-defined relationships between jobs in terms of mobility (promotion and transfer) paths. Also, traditional jobs are very static, with little or no change occurring in tasks or KSAOs.

Certain terms are used frequently in discussions of traditional jobs. Definitions of some of the key terms, and examples of them, are provided in Exhibit 4.1. Note that the terms are presented in a logically descending hierarchy, starting with job category or family, and proceeding downward through job, position, task dimension, task, and element.

One challenge to this traditional perspective is that jobs are constantly evolving. Generally, these changes are not so radical that a job ceases to exist (like the job of flight engineer), and they are often due to technological or workload changes. An excellent example of such an evolving job is that of secretary. Traditional or core tasks associated with the job include typing, filing, taking dictation, and answering phones. However, in nearly all organizations the job has evolved to include new tasks such as word processing, managing multiple projects, creating spreadsheets, purchasing supplies and office technology, and gathering information on the Internet. These task changes led to new KSAO requirements such as planning and coordination skills and knowledge of spreadsheet software. Accompanying these changes is a change in job title to that of "administrative assistant." It should be noted that jobs may evolve due to changing organization and technology requirements, as well as employee-initiated changes through a process of job crafting.

EXHIBIT 4.1 **Terminology Commonly Used in Describing Jobs**

TERM	DEFINITION
Job family	A grouping of jobs, usually according to function (e.g., production, finance, human resources, marketing)
Job category	A grouping of jobs according to generic job title or occupation (e.g., managerial, sales, clerical, maintenance), within or across job families
Job	A grouping of positions that are similar in their tasks and task dimensions
Position	A grouping of tasks/dimensions that constitute the total work assignment of a single employee; there are as many positions as there are employees
Task dimension	A grouping of similar types of tasks, sometimes called "duty," "area of responsibility," or "key results area"
Task	A grouping of elements to form an identifiable work activity that is a logical and necessary step in the performance of a job
Element	The smallest unit into which work can be divided without analyzing separate motions, movements, and mental processes

Another challenge to the traditional view is the need for flexibility. Flexible jobs have frequently changing task and KSAO requirements. Sometimes these changes are initiated by the job incumbent who constantly adds and drops (or passes off) new assignments or projects in order to work toward moving targets of opportunity. Other times the task changes may be dictated by changes in production schedules, client demands, or technology. Many small-business owners, general managers of start-up strategic business units, and top management members perform such flexible jobs.

A third factor that has changed the traditional view of job design and analysis is the need for new, general skills or competencies. Two important new skills or competencies are teamwork and engagement. We discuss team-based job analysis toward the end of the chapter. As for engagement, job analysis typically focuses on skills and abilities to a greater degree than motivational factors. As more and more organizations emphasize employee engagement—or the degree to which an employee identifies with and has enthusiasm for his or her work—our analysis of jobs needs to take motivational factors into account. As Jack Welch stated, "[no] company, small or large, can win over the long run without energized employees who believe in the [firm's] mission and understand how to achieve it." A large-scale study of 7,939 business units supports Welch's assertion that organizations whose employees reported above-average levels of engagement performed significantly better (63% of such organizations had above-average levels of performance) than those whose employees were below average on engagement (37% of such organizations had above-average levels of performance).

Measures of engagement reflect innate psychological characteristics that are usually not subjects of job analysis. For example, Dell assesses employee engagement with items such as, "Considering everything, Dell is the right place for me." Intuit measures engagement with statements like "I am proud to work for Intuit." Because engagement is inherently one of the KSAO "other" characteristics, there is very little work into how engagement can be factored into job analysis. One way to incorporate engagement into job analysis is to consider it a general competency in competency-based job analysis, a method we cover later in the chapter. As one reviewer of the engagement literature suggests, "Identify those candidates who are best-suited to the job and your organization's culture."[1]

JOB REQUIREMENTS JOB ANALYSIS

Overview

Job analysis may be defined as the process of studying jobs in order to gather, analyze, synthesize, and report information about job requirements. Note in this definition that job analysis is an overall process as opposed to a specific method or technique. A job requirements job analysis seeks to identify and describe the specific tasks, KSAOs, and job context for a particular job. This type of job analysis is the most thoroughly developed and commonly used by organizations. A second type of job analysis, competency-based, attempts to identify and describe job requirements in the form of general KSAOs required across a range of jobs; task and work context requirements are of little concern. Interpersonal skills, for example, might be identified as a competency for sales and customer service jobs; leadership is a likely competency requirement for managerial jobs. Competency-based job analysis is more recent in origin, though it has some similarities to job requirements job analysis. It is discussed separately later in this chapter.

Job requirements job analysis yields information helpful in the recruitment, selection, and employment domains in such activities as communicating job requirements to job applicants, developing selection plans for KSAOs to focus on when staffing a job, identifying appropriate assessment methods to gauge applicants' KSAOs, establishing hiring qualifications, and complying with relevant laws and regulations. Competency-based job analysis results will be helpful primarily in identifying a common set of general KSAOs in which all applicants must be proficient, regardless of the specific job for which they are applying.

Effective staffing definitely requires job requirements information, and possibly competency information, for each of the types of jobs described above. Traditional and evolving jobs readily lend themselves to this. Their requirements are generally well known and unlikely to change except gradually. For idiosyncratic, flexible, team-based, and telework jobs, job analysis is more difficult and problematic. The requirements for these jobs may frequently be changing, difficult to pinpoint, and even unknown because they depend heavily on how the job incumbent defines them. Due to the often ambiguous and fluid nature of these jobs, the organization may focus on analyzing and defining them in terms of competencies rather than specific tasks and KSAOs.

Job analysis and the information it provides thus serve as basic input to the totality of staffing activities for an organization. In this sense, job analysis is a support activity to the various functional staffing activities. Indeed, without thorough and accurate information about job requirements and/or competencies, the organization is greatly hampered in its attempts to acquire a workforce that will be effective in terms of human resource (HR) outcomes such as performance, satisfaction, and retention. Job analysis thus is the foundation upon which successful staffing systems are constructed.

A framework depicting job requirements job analysis is shown in Exhibit 4.2. As can be seen, the job analysis begins by identifying the specific tasks and the job context for a particular job.[2] After these have been identified, the KSAOs necessary for performing these tasks within the work context are inferred. For example, after identifying for a sales manager's job the task of "developing and writing monthly sales and marketing plans," the job analysis would proceed by inferring what specific KSAOs are necessary for performance of this task. The task might require knowledge of intended customers, arithmetic skills, creative ability, and willingness and availability to travel frequently to various organizational units. No particular job context factors, such as physical demands, may be relevant to performance of this task or to its required KSAOs. The task and job context information are recorded in a job description, whereas the KSAO requirements are placed into a job specification. In practice, these are often contained within a single document.

Job Requirements Matrix

The job requirements matrix shows the key components of job requirements job analysis, each of which must be explicitly considered for inclusion in any job requirements job analysis. Completion of the cell entries in the matrix represents the information that must be gathered, analyzed, synthesized, and expressed in usable written form.

A completed job requirements matrix, a portion of which is shown in Exhibit 4.3 for the job of administrative assistant, serves as the basic informational source or document for any job in terms of its job requirements. The resultant information serves as a basic input and guide to all subsequent staffing activities.

Referring to Exhibit 4.3, five specific tasks identified via job analysis are listed. Note that only a portion of the total tasks for the job is shown. In turn, these have been categorized into two general task dimensions—supervision and word processing. An indication of their importance to the overall job is the percent time spent on each, specifically 30% and 20%, respectively. For each task dimension and its specific tasks, several KSAOs have been inferred to be necessary for

EXHIBIT 4.2   Job Requirements Approach to Job Analysis

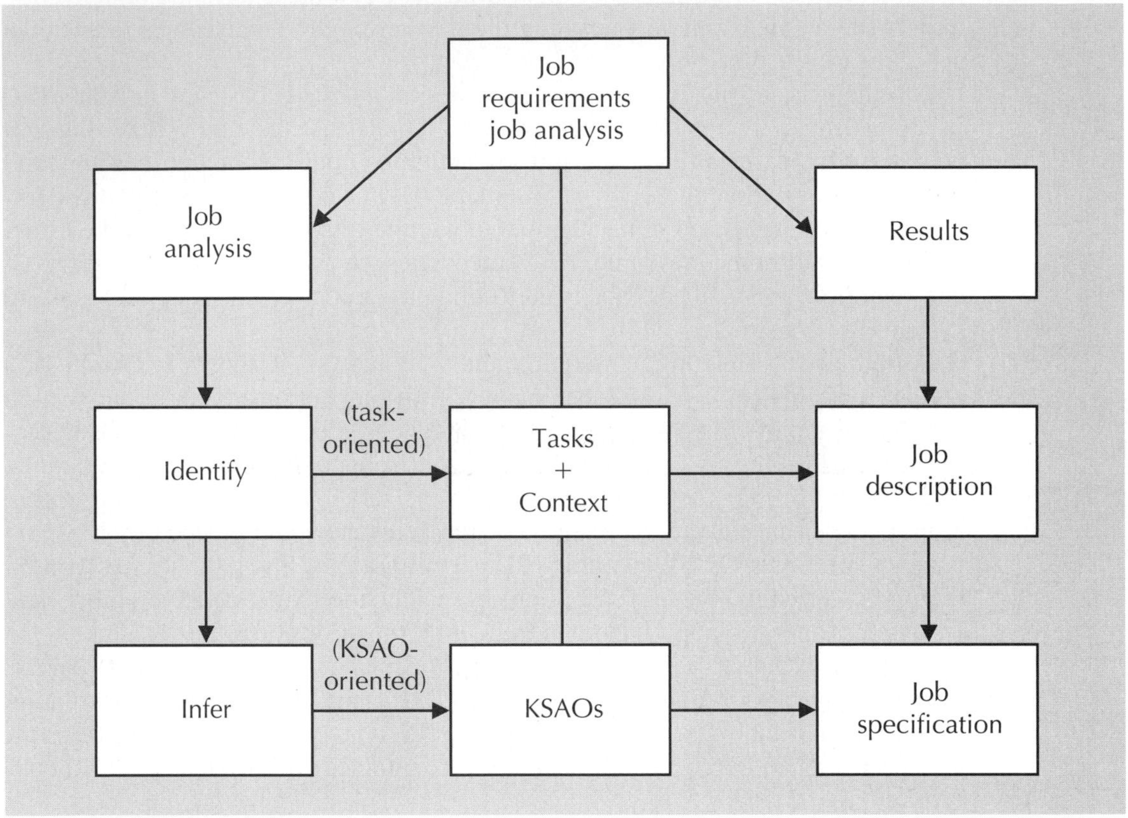

performance. The nature of these KSAOs is presented, along with a rating (1–5 scale) of how important each KSAO is for performance of the task dimension. At the bottom of the matrix are indications of job context factors pertaining to work setting (indoors), privacy of work area (cubicle), attire (business clothes), body positioning (mostly sitting and standing), and physical work conditions (no environmental or job hazards).

We now turn to a thorough discussion of each of the components of the job requirements matrix: tasks, task dimensions and their importance, KSAOs and their importance, and job context. Discussed are specific definitions, techniques, and taxonomies useful for successfully gathering and recording the information needed in a job requirements matrix. After that, the actual process of collecting job information and conducting the job analysis is discussed.

Task Statements

Job analysis begins with the development of task statements, whose objective is to identify and record a set of tasks that includes all of the job's major tasks and

EXHIBIT 4.3   Portion of Job Requirements Matrix for Job of Administrative Assistant

	Tasks		KSAOs	
Specific Tasks	Task Dimensions	Importance (% time spent)	Nature	Importance to Tasks (1–5 rating)
1. Arrange schedules with office assistant/volunteers to ensure that office will be staffed during prescribed hours	A. Supervision	30%	1. Knowledge of office operations and policies	4.9
2. Assign office tasks to office assistant/volunteers to ensure coordination of activities	A. Supervision		2. Ability to match people to tasks according to their skills and hours of availability	4.6
			3. Skill in interaction with diverse people	2.9
			4. Skill in determining types and priorities of tasks	4.0
3. Type/transcribe letters, memos, and reports from handwritten material or dictated copy to produce final copy, using word processor	B. Word processing	20%	1. Knowledge of typing formats	3.1
			2. Knowledge of spelling and punctuation	5.0
4. Prepare graphs and other visual material to supplement reports, using word processor	B. Word processing		3. Knowledge of graphics display software	2.0
			4. Ability to proofread and correct work	5.0
5. Proofread typed copy and correct spelling, punctuation, and typographical errors in order to produce high-quality materials	B. Word processing		5. Skill in use of WordPerfect (most current version)	4.3
			6. Skill in creating visually appealing and understandable graphs	3.4

Job Context: Indoors, cubicle, business clothes, mostly sitting and standing no environmental or job hazards.

excludes nonrelevant or trivial tasks. The resultant task statements serve as the building blocks for the remainder of the job requirements job analysis.

Identification and recording of tasks begins with the construction of task statements. These statements are objectively written descriptions of the behaviors or work activities engaged in by employees in order to perform the job. The statements are made in simple declarative sentences.

Ideally, each task statement will show several things:

1. What the employee does, using a specific action verb at the start of the task statement
2. To whom or what the employee does what he or she does, stating the object of the verb
3. What is produced, indicating the expected output of the verb
4. What equipment, materials, tools, or procedures, are used

Use of the sentence analysis technique is very helpful for writing task statements that conform to these four requirements. An example of the technique is shown in Exhibit 4.4 for several tasks from very different jobs.

In addition to meeting the preceding four requirements, there are several other suggestions for effectively writing task statements. First, use specific action verbs that have only one meaning. Examples of verbs that do not conform to this suggestion include "supports," "assists," and "handles."

Second, focus on recording tasks, as opposed to specific elements that compose a task. This requires use of considerable judgment because the distinction between a task and an element is relative and often fuzzy. A useful rule to keep in mind here is that most jobs can be adequately described within a range of 15–25 task statements. A task statement list exceeding this range is a warning that it may be too narrow in terms of activities defined.

Third, do not include minor or trivial activities in task statements; focus only on major tasks and activities. An exception to this recommendation occurs when a so-called minor task is judged to have great importance to the job (see the following discussion).

Fourth, take steps to ensure that the list of task statements is reliable.[3] The basic way to conform to this suggestion is to have two or more people ("analysts") independently evaluate the task statement list in terms of both inclusiveness and clarity. Close agreement between people signifies high reliability. Should disagreements between people be discovered, the nature of the disagreements can be discussed and appropriate modifications to the task statements made.

Fifth, have at least the manager and a job incumbent serve as the analysts providing the reliability checks. It is important to have the manager participate in this process in order to verify that the task statements are inclusive and accurate. For the job incumbent, the concern is not only that of verification but also acceptance of the task statements as adequate representations that will guide incumbents'

EXHIBIT 4.4 **Use of the Sentence Analysis Technique for Task Statements**

Sentence Analysis Technique			
What does the worker do?		Why does the worker do it? What gets done?	What is the final result or technological objective?
Worker action		Purpose of the worker actions	Materials, products, subject matter, and/or services
(Worker function)	(Work devices, people, or information)	(Work field)	(MPSMS)
Verb	Direct object	Infinitive phrase	
		Infinitive	Object of the infinitive
Sets up *(setting up)*	various types of metal-working machines *(work device)*	to machine *(machining)*	metal aircraft parts. *(material)*
Persuades *(persuading)*	customers *(people)*	to buy *(merchandising)*	automobiles. *(product)*
Interviews *(analyzing)*	clients *(people)*	to assess *(advising– counseling)*	skills and abilities. *(subject matter)*
Drives *(driving– operating)*	bus *(work device)*	to transport *(transporting)*	passengers. *(service)*

SOURCE: Vocational Rehabilitation Institute, *A Guide to Job Analysis* (Menomonie, WI: University of Wisconsin-Stout, 1982), p. 8.

performance of the job. Ideally, there should be multiple managers and job incumbents, along with a representative of the HR department, serving as analysts. This would expand the scope of input and allow for more precise reliability checks.

Finally, recognize that the accuracy or validity of task statements cannot be evaluated against any external criterion, because there is no external criterion available for use. Task descriptions are accurate and meaningful only to the extent that people agree on them. Because of this, the preceding recommendation regarding checks on content validity and reliability takes on added importance.

Task Dimensions

Task statement lists may be maintained in list form and subsequently incorporated into the job description. Often, however, it is useful to group sets of task statements into task dimensions, and then attach a name to each such dimension. Other terms for task dimensions are "duties," "accountability areas," "responsibilities," and "performance dimensions."

A useful way to facilitate the grouping process is to create a task dimension matrix. Each column in the matrix represents a potential task dimension, and a label is tentatively attached to it. Each row in the matrix represents a particular task statement. Cell entries in the matrix represent the assignment of task statements to task dimensions (the grouping of tasks). The goal is to have each task statement assigned to only one task dimension. The process is complicated by the fact that the dimensions and labels must be created prior to grouping; the dimensions and labels may have to be changed or rearranged to make task statements fit as one progresses through the assignment of task statements to dimensions.

Several things should be kept in mind about task dimensions. First, their creation is optional and should occur only if they will be useful. Second, there are many different grouping procedures, ranging from straightforward judgmental ones to highly sophisticated statistical ones.[4] For most purposes, a simple judgmental process is sufficient, such as having the people who participated in the creation of the task statements also create the groupings as part of the same exercise. As a rule, there should be four to eight dimensions, depending on the number of task statements, regardless of the specific grouping procedure used. Third, it is important that the grouping procedure yield a reliable set of task dimensions acceptable to managers, job incumbents, and other organizational members. Finally, as with task statements, it is not possible to empirically validate task dimensions against some external criterion; for both task statements and dimensions, their validity is in the eyes of the definers and beholders.

Importance of Tasks/Dimensions

Rarely are all tasks/dimensions of a job thought to be of equal weight or importance. In some general sense, it is thus felt that these differences must be captured, expressed, and incorporated into job information, especially the job description.

Normally, assessments of importance are made just for task dimensions, though it is certainly possible to make them for individual tasks as well.

Before actual weighting can occur, two decisions must be made. First, the specific attribute to be assessed in terms of importance must be decided (e.g., time spent on the task/dimension). Second, a decision is required regarding whether the attribute will be measured in categorical terms (e.g., essential or nonessential) or continuous terms (e.g., percent of time spent, 1–5 rating of importance). Exhibit 4.5 shows examples of the results of these two decisions in terms of commonly used importance attributes and their measurement.

Once these decisions are made, it is possible to proceed with the actual process of assessing or weighting the tasks/dimensions in terms of importance. It should be

---

EXHIBIT 4.5   Examples of Ways to Assess Task/Dimension Importance

A. **Relative Time Spent**

For each task/dimension, rate the amount of time you spend on it, relative to all other tasks/dimensions of your job.

1	2	3	4	5
Very small amount		Average amount		Very large amount

B. **Percentage (%) Time Spent**

For each task/dimension, indicate the percentage (%) of time you spend on it (percentages must total to 100%).

Dimension _____   % Time spent _____

C. **Importance to Overall Performance**

For each task/dimension, rate its importance to your overall job performance.

1	2	3	4	5
Minor importance		Average importance		Major importance

D. **Need for New Employee Training**

Do new employees receive a standard, planned course of training for performance of this task, other than a customary job orientation?

_____ Yes

_____ No

noted here that if the tasks/dimensions are not explicitly assessed in such a manner, all tasks/dimensions end up being weighted equally by default.

If possible, it is desirable for the assessments to be done initially by independent analysts (e.g., incumbents and managers). In this way, it will be possible to check for the degree of reliability among raters. Where differences are found, they can be discussed and resolved. Just as it is desirable to have high reliability in the identification of tasks and dimensions, it is desirable to have high reliability in judgments of their importance.[5]

KSAOs

KSAOs are inferred or derived from knowledge of the tasks and task dimensions themselves. The inference process requires that the analysts explicitly think in specific cause-and-effect terms. For each task or dimension, the analyst must in essence ask, "Exactly what KSAOs do I think will be necessary for (will cause) performance on this task or dimension?" Then the analyst should ask, "Why do I think this?" in order to think through the soundness of the inferential logic. Discussions among analysts about these questions are encouraged.

When asking and answering these questions, it is useful to keep in mind what is meant by the terms "knowledge," "skill," "ability," and "other characteristics." It is also very helpful to refer to research results that help us better understand the nature and complexity of these concepts. As described below, these results have been synthesized to create the Occupational Information Network, or O*NET (see *www.onetcenter.org*).

Knowledge.   Knowledge is a body of information (conceptual, factual, procedural) that can be applied directly to the performance of tasks. It tends to be quite focused or specific in terms of job, organization, or occupation. Assistance to the analyst in identifying and writing statements of knowledge requirements is available from O*NET. It provides definitions of 33 knowledges that might generally be necessary, in varying levels, in occupations. Exhibit 4.6 provides a listing of those knowledges. Definitions of the knowledges are also provided by O*NET, in print and online. For example, "sales and marketing" knowledge is defined as "knowledge of principles and methods involved in showing, promoting, and selling products or services; this includes marketing strategies and tactics, product demonstration and sales techniques, and sales control systems."[6] Use of O*NET knowledges and their definitions is a helpful starting point in preparing knowledge statements. As the knowledges are intended for general occupations, they will probably have to be supplemented with more job-specific statements crafted by the job analyst. When doing so, analysts should be particularly wary of using global or shorthand terms such as "knowledge of accounting principles." Here, it would be better to indicate which accounting principles are being utilized and why each is necessary for task performance.

EXHIBIT 4.6   Knowledges Contained in O*NET

Knowledge Areas

- Business and management
  - Administration and management
  - Clerical
  - Economics and accounting
  - Sales and marketing
  - Customer and personal service
  - Personnel and human resources
- Manufacturing and production
  - Production and processing
  - Food production
- Engineering and technology
  - Computers and electronics
  - Engineering and technology
  - Design
  - Building and construction
  - Mechanical
- Mathematics and science
  - Mathematics
  - Physics
  - Chemistry
  - Biology
  - Psychology
  - Sociology and anthropology
  - Geography
- Health services
  - Medicine and dentistry
  - Therapy and counseling
- Education and training
  - Education and training
- Arts and humanities
  - English language
  - Foreign language
  - Fine arts
  - History and archaeology
  - Philosophy and theology
- Law and public safety
  - Public safety and security
  - Law, government, and jurisprudence
- Communications
  - Telecommunications
  - Communications and media
- Transportation
  - Transportation

SOURCE: Adapted from N. G. Peterson, M. D. Mumford, W. C. Borman, P. R. Jeanneret, E. A. Fleishman, and K. Y. Levin, *O*NET Final Technical Report, Vol. 1* (Salt Lake City: Utah Department of Workforce Services, 1997), pp. 4-1 to 4-26. ©Utah Department of Workforce Services on behalf of U.S. Department of Labor.

Skill.   Skill refers to an observable competence for working with or applying knowledge to perform a particular task or a closely related set of tasks. A skill is not an enduring characteristic of the person; it depends on experience and practice. Skill requirements are directly inferred from observation or knowledge of tasks performed.

Considerable research has been devoted to identifying particular job-related skills and to organizing them into taxonomies. Job analysts should begin the skills inference process by referring to the results of this research.

An excellent example of such useful research is found in O*NET.[7] O*NET identifies and defines 46 skills applicable across the occupational spectrum. The first 10 of these are basic skills involving acquiring and conveying information; the remaining 36 are cross-functional skills used to facilitate task performance. Exhibit 4.7 provides a listing of all these skills. Definitions are also provided by O*NET, in print and online. For example, the basic skill "reading comprehension" is defined as "understanding written sentences and paragraphs in work-related documents"; the cross-functional skill "negotiation" is defined as "bringing others

EXHIBIT 4.7 Skills Contained in O*NET

Basic Skills

- Content
    - Reading comprehension
    - Active listening
    - Writing
    - Speaking
    - Mathematics
    - Science
- Process
    - Critical thinking
    - Active learning
    - Learning strategies
    - Monitoring

Cross-Functional Skills

- Social skills
    - Social perceptiveness
    - Coordination
    - Persuasion
    - Negotiation
    - Instructing
    - Service orientation
- Complex problem-solving skills
    - Problem identification
    - Information gathering
    - Information organization
    - Synthesis/reorganization
    - Idea generation
    - Idea evaluation
    - Implementation planning
    - Solution appraisal
- Resource management skills
    - Time management
    - Management of financial resources
    - Management of material resources
    - Management of personnel resources
- Technical skills
    - Operations analysis
    - Technology design
    - Equipment selection
    - Installation
    - Programming
    - Equipment maintenance
    - Troubleshooting
    - Repairing
    - Testing
    - Operation monitoring
    - Operation and control
    - Product inspection
- Systems skills
    - Visioning
    - Systems perception
    - Identification of downstream consequences
    - Identification of key causes
    - Judgment and decision making
    - Systems evaluation

SOURCE: Adapted from N. G. Peterson, M. D. Mumford, W. C. Borman, P. R. Jeanneret, E. A. Fleishman, and K. Y. Levin, *O*NET Final Technical Report, Vol. 1* (Salt Lake City: Utah Department of Workforce Services, 1997), pp. 3-1 to 3-36. ©Utah Department of Workforce Services on behalf of U.S. Department of Labor.

together and trying to reconcile differences." Reference to these 46 skills is a good starting point for the job analyst. More specific skills may need to be identified and described for the particular job being analyzed. An excellent example in this regard is computer-related skills such as use of spreadsheets and databases, use of software such as MS Word, and various types of programming.

Ability. An ability is an underlying, enduring trait of the person that is useful for performing a range of different tasks. It differs from a skill in that it is less likely to change over time and is applicable across a wide set of tasks encountered in many different jobs. Four general categories of abilities are commonly recognized: cognitive, psychomotor, physical, and sensory. O*NET contains a complete taxonomy of these four categories; they are shown in Exhibit 4.8. Definitions (not shown) accompany the abilities in print and online. The ability "oral expression," for example, is defined as "the ability to communicate information and ideas in speaking so others will understand." As another example, "dynamic flexibility" is "the ability to quickly and repeatedly bend, stretch, twist, or reach out with the body, arms and/or legs."[8]

Other Characteristics. This is a catchall category for factors that do not fit neatly into the K, S, and A categories. Despite the catchall nature of these requirements, they are very important for even being able to enter the employment relationship (legal requirements), being present to perform the job (availability requirements), and having values consistent with organizational culture and values (character requirements). Numerous examples of these factors are shown in Exhibit 4.9. Care should be taken to ensure that these factors truly are job requirements, as opposed to whimsical and ill-defined preferences of the organization.

KSAO Importance

As suggested in the job requirements matrix, the KSAOs of a job may differ in their weight or contribution to task performance. Hence, their relative importance must be explicitly considered, defined, and indicated. Failure to do so means that all KSAOs will be assumed to be of equal importance by default.

As with task importance, deriving KSAO importance requires two decisions. First, what will be the specific attribute(s) on which importance is judged? Second, will the measurement of each attribute be categorical (e.g., required-preferred) or continuous (e.g., 1–5 rating scale)? Examples of formats for indicating KSAO importance are shown in Exhibit 4.10. O*NET uses a 1–5 rating scale format and also provides actual importance ratings for many jobs.

Job Context

As shown in the job requirements matrix, tasks and KSAOs occur within a broader job context. A job requirements job analysis should include consideration of the

---

EXHIBIT 4.8　Abilities Contained in O*NET

Cognitive Abilities
- Verbal abilities
  - Oral comprehension
  - Written comprehension
  - Oral expression
  - Written expression
- Idea generation and reasoning abilities
  - Fluency of ideas
  - Originality
  - Problem sensitivity
  - Deductive reasoning
  - Inductive reasoning
  - Information ordering
  - Category flexibility
- Quantitative abilities
  - Mathematical reasoning
  - Number facility
- Memory
  - Memorization
- Perceptual abilities
  - Speed of closure
  - Flexibility of closure
  - Perceptual speed
- Spatial abilities
  - Spatial organization
  - Visualization
- Attentiveness
  - Selective attention
  - Time sharing

Psychomotor Abilities
- Fine manipulative abilities
  - Arm-hand steadiness
  - Manual dexterity
  - Finger dexterity
- Control movement abilities
  - Control precision
  - Multilimb coordination
  - Response orientation
  - Rate control

- Reaction time and speed abilities
  - Reaction time
  - Wrist-finger dexterity
  - Speed of limb movement

Physical Abilities
- Physical strength abilities
  - Static strength
  - Explosive strength
  - Dynamic strength
  - Trunk strength
- Endurance
  - Stamina
- Flexibility, balance, and coordination
  - Extent flexibility
  - Dynamic flexibility
  - Gross body coordination
  - Gross body equilibrium

Sensory Abilities
- Visual abilities
  - Near vision
  - Far vision
  - Visual color discrimination
  - Night vision
  - Peripheral vision
  - Depth perception
  - Glare sensitivity
- Auditory and speech abilities
  - Hearing sensitivity
  - Auditory attention
  - Sound localization
  - Speech recognition
  - Speech clarity

Source: Adapted from N. G. Peterson, M. D. Mumford, W. C. Borman, P. R. Jeanneret, E. A. Fleishman, and K. Y. Levin, *O*NET Final Technical Report, Vol. 2* (Salt Lake City: Utah Department of Workforce Services, 1997), pp. 9-1 to 9-26. ©Utah Department of Workforce Services on behalf of U.S. Department of Labor.

EXHIBIT 4.9   Examples of Other Job Requirements

Legal Requirements
   Possession of license (occupational, driver's, etc.)
   Citizen or legal alien?
   Geographic residency (e.g., within city limits for public employees)
   Security clearance

Availability Requirements
   Starting date
   Work site locations
   Hours and days of week
   Travel
   Attendance and tardiness

Character Requirements
   Moral
   Work ethic
   Background
   Conscientiousness
   Honesty and integrity

job context and the factors that are important in defining it. Such consideration is necessary because these factors may have an influence on tasks and KSAOs; further, information about the factors may be used in the recruitment and selection of job applicants. For example, the information may be given to job applicants to provide them a realistic job preview during recruitment, and consideration of job context factors may be helpful in assessing likely person/organization fit during selection.

O*NET contains a wide array of job and work context factors useful for characterizing occupations.[9] Consider the O*NET classification of physical work conditions: setting, attire, body positioning, environmental conditions, and job hazards. Within each of these categories are numerous specific facets; these are shown in Exhibit 4.11. The job analyst should use a listing such as this to identify the relevant job context factors and include them in the job requirements matrix.

O*NET also contains work context factors pertaining to interpersonal relationships (communication, types of role relationships, responsibility for others, and conflictual contact with others) and to structural job characteristics (criticality of position, routine versus challenging work, pace and scheduling). These factors might also be considered in the job analysis.

EXHIBIT 4.10   Examples of Ways to Assess KSAO Importance

A.   **Importance to (acceptable) (superior) task performance**
1 = minimal importance
2 = some importance
3 = average importance
4 = considerable importance
5 = extensive importance

B.   **Should the KSAO be assessed during recruitment/selection?**
☐ Yes
☐ No

C.   **Is the KSAO required, preferred, or not required for recruitment/selection?**
☐ Required
☐ Preferred
☐ Not required (obtain on job and/or in training)

Job Descriptions and Job Specifications

As previously noted, it is common practice to express the results of job requirements job analysis in written job descriptions and job specifications. Referring back to the job requirements matrix, note that its sections pertaining to tasks and job context are similar to a job description, and the section dealing with KSAOs is similar to a job specification.

There are no standard formats or other requirements for either job descriptions or job specifications. In terms of content, however, a job description should usually include the following: job family, job title, job summary, task statements and dimensions, importance indicators, job context indicators, and date job analysis conducted. A job specification should usually include job family, job title, job summary, KSAOs (separate section for each), importance indicators, and date conducted. An example of a combined job description/specification is shown in Exhibit 4.12.

Collecting Job Requirements Information

Job analysis involves consideration of not only the types of information (tasks, KSAOs, and job context) to be collected but also the methods, sources, and processes to be used for such collection. These issues are discussed next, and as will be seen, there are many alternatives to choose from for purposes of developing an overall job analysis system for any particular situation. Potential inaccuracies and other limitations of the alternatives will also be pointed out.[10]

EXHIBIT 4.11 Job Context (Physical Work Conditions) Contained in O*NET

Work Setting
- How frequently does this job require the worker to work:
  Indoors, environmentally controlled
  Indoors, not environmentally controlled
  Outdoors, exposed to all weather conditions
  Outdoors, under cover
  In an open vehicle or operating open equipment
  In an enclosed vehicle or operating enclosed equipment
- Privacy of work area
- Physical proximity

Work Attire
- How often does the worker wear:
  Business clothes
  A special uniform
  Work clothing
  Common protective or safety attire
  Specialized protective or safety attire

Body Positioning
- How much time in a usual work period does the worker spend:
  Sitting
  Standing
  Climbing ladders, scaffolds, poles, and so on
  Walking or running
  Kneeling, stooping, crouching, or crawling
  Keeping or regaining balance
  Using hands to handle, control, or feel objects, tools, or controls
  Bending or twisting the body
  Making repetitive motions

Environmental Conditions
- How often during a usual work period is the worker exposed to the following conditions:
  Sounds and noise levels that are distracting and uncomfortable
  Very hot or very cold temperatures
  Extremely bright or inadequate lighting conditions
  Contaminants
  Cramped work space that requires getting into awkward positions
  Whole body vibration

Job Hazards
- How often does this job require the worker to be exposed to the following hazards:
  Radiation
  Diseases/infections
  High places
  Hazardous conditions
  Hazardous equipment
  Hazardous situation involving likely cuts, bites, stings, or minor burns

Source: Adapted from N. G. Peterson, M. D. Mumford, W. C. Borman, P. R. Jeanneret, E. A. Fleishman, and K. Y. Levin, *O*NET Final Technical Report, Vol. 2* (Salt Lake City: Utah Department of Workforce Services, 1997), pp. 7-1 to 7-35. ©Utah Department of Workforce Services on behalf of U.S. Department of Labor.

EXHIBIT 4.12   Example of Combined Job Description/Specification

FUNCTIONAL UNIT: CHILDREN'S REHABILITATION
JOB TITLE: REHABILITATION SPECIALIST
DATE: 12/5/04

JOB SUMMARY

Works with disabled small children and their families to identify developmental strengths and weaknesses, develop rehabilitation plans, deliver and coordinate rehabilitation activities, and evaluate effectiveness of those plans and activities.

PERFORMANCE DIMENSIONS AND TASKS   **Time Spent (%)**

1. Assessment   **10%**

Administer formal and informal motor screening and evaluation instruments to conduct assessments. Perform assessments to identify areas of strengths and need.

2. Planning   **25%**

Collaborate with parents and other providers to directly develop the individualized family service plan. Use direct and consultative models of service in developing plans.

3. Delivery   **50%**

Carry out individual and small group motor development activities with children and families. Provide service coordination to designated families. Work with family care and child care providers to provide total services. Collaborate with other staff members and professionals from community agencies to obtain resources and specialized assistance.

4. Evaluation   **15%**

Observe, interpret, and report on client to monitor individual progress. Assist in collecting and reporting intervention data in order to prepare formal program evaluation reports. Write evaluation reports to assist in developing new treatment strategies and programs.

JOB SPECIFICATIONS

1. License: License to practice physical therapy in the state

2. Education: B.S. in physical or occupational therapy required; M.S. preferred

3. Experience: Prefer (not required) one year experience working with children with disabilities and their families

4. Skills: Listening to and interacting with others (children, family members, coworkers)
Developing treatment plans
Organizing and writing reports using Microsoft Word

JOB CONTEXT: Indoors, office, business clothes, no environmental or job hazards.

Methods

Job analysis methods represent procedures or techniques for collecting job information. There have been many specific techniques and systems developed and named (e.g., Functional Job Analysis, Position Analysis Questionnaire [PAQ]). Rather than discuss each of the many techniques separately, we will concentrate on the major generic methods that underlie all specific techniques and applications. There are many excellent descriptions and discussions of the specific techniques available.[11]

Prior Information.   For any job, there is usually some prior information available that could and should be consulted. Indeed, this information should routinely be searched for and used as a starting point for a job analysis.

There are many possible organizational sources of job information available, including current job descriptions and specifications, job-specific policies and procedures, training manuals, and performance appraisals. Externally, job information may be available from other employers, as well as trade and professional associations. Both the Society for Human Resource Management (SHRM) (*www.shrm.org*) and the International Public Management Association for Human Resources (IPMA-HR) (*www.ipma-hr.org*) provide sample job descriptions online. Also, job information is available commercially on the Web (e.g., *www.jobdescription.com*).

Finally there is O*NET (*www.onetcenter.org*). O*NET contains extensive research-based taxonomies in several categories: occupational tasks, knowledges, skills, abilities, education and experience/training, work context, organizational context, occupational interests and values, and work styles.[12] Additionally, O*NET contains ratings of the specific factors within each category for many occupations; ratings for additional occupations are constantly being added. For example, occupational and importance ratings of the specific knowledges, skills, and abilities shown in Exhibits 4.6, 4.7, and 4.8 are provided. The job analyst could use these ratings as benchmarks against which to compare specific importance ratings the analyst determines for a specific job. For example, if the analyst was developing importance ratings for these knowledges, skills, and abilities for the job of registered nurse in a particular hospital, the compiled ratings could be compared with the ratings in O*NET for the same occupation. Reasonable similarity between the two sets of ratings would serve as a source of confirmation of the analyst's accuracy.

Obvious advantages of O*NET are its flexibility (it can be applied to many different types of jobs) and, in particular, its ease of use.[13] The ready availability of prior job information needs to be balanced with some possible limitations. First, there is the general issue of completeness. Usually, prior information will be deficient in some important areas of job requirements, as in evolving or nontraditional types of jobs. Sole reliance on prior information thus should be avoided. A second limitation is that there will be little indication of exactly how the information was collected and, relatedly, how accurate it is. These limitations suggest that while prior information should be the starting point for job analysis, it should not be the stopping point.

Observation.   Simply observing job incumbents performing the job is obviously an excellent way to learn about tasks, KSAOs, and context. It provides a thoroughness and richness of information unmatched by any other method. It is also the most direct form of gathering information because it does not rely on intermediary information sources, as would be the case with other methods (e.g., interviewing job incumbents and supervisors).

The following potential limitations to observation should be kept in mind. First, it is most appropriate for jobs with physical (as opposed to mental) components and ones with relatively short job cycles (i.e., amount of time required to complete job tasks before repeating them). Second, the method may involve substantial time and cost. Third, the ability of the observer to do a thorough and accurate analysis is open to question; it may be necessary to train observers prior to the job analysis. Fourth, the method will require coordination with, and approval from, many people (e.g., supervisors and incumbents). Finally, the incumbents being observed may distort their behavior during observation in self-serving ways, such as making tasks appear more difficult or time consuming than they really are.

Interviews.   Interviewing job incumbents and others, such as their managers, has many potential advantages. It respects the interviewee's vast source of information about the job. The interview format also allows the interviewer to explain the purpose of the job analysis and how the results will be used, thus enhancing likely acceptance of the process by the interviewees. It can be structured in format to ensure standardization of collected information.

As with any job analysis method, the interview is not without potential limitations. It is time consuming and costly, and this may cause the organization to skimp on it in ways that jeopardize the reliability and content validity of the information gathered. The interview, not providing anonymity, may lead to suspicion and distrust on the part of interviewees. The quality of the information obtained, as well as interviewee acceptance, depends on the skill of the interviewer. Careful selection and possible training of interviewers should definitely be considered when the interview is the method chosen for collecting job information. Finally, the success of the interview also depends on the skill and abilities of the interviewee, such as verbal communication skills and the ability to recall tasks performed.

Task Questionnaire.   A typical task questionnaire contains a lengthy list of task statements that cut across many different job titles and is administered to incumbents (all or samples of them) in these job titles. For each task statement, the respondent is asked to indicate (1) whether the task applies to the respondent's job (respondents should always be given a DNA—does not apply—option) and (2) task importance (e.g., a 1–5 scale rating difficulty or time spent).

A questionnaire-based job analysis tool—the PAQ—is perhaps the single most popular specific job analysis method. The PAQ consists of 300 items completed by job incumbents. These items are sorted into six major divisions: (1) *information input* (e.g., use of written materials), (2) *mental processes* (e.g., use of reasoning and problem solving), (3) *work output* (e.g., use of keyboard devices), (4) *interpersonal activities* (e.g., serving/catering), (5) *work situation and job context* (e.g., working in low temperatures), and (6) *miscellaneous aspects* (e.g., irregular hours). Once the employees evaluate how well each of the 300 items applies to their jobs, the completed questionnaires are scored by computer, and a report is generated that provides scores for the divisions (and more finely grained subdivisions).[14]

The advantages of task questionnaires are numerous. They are standardized in content and format, thus yielding a standardized method of information gathering. They can obtain considerable information from large numbers of people. They are economical to administer and score, and the availability of scores creates the opportunity for subsequent statistical analysis. Finally, task questionnaires are (and should be) completed anonymously, thus enhancing respondent participation, honesty, and acceptance.

A task questionnaire is potentially limited in certain ways. The most important limitation pertains to task statement content. Care must be taken to ensure that the questionnaire contains task statements of sufficient content relevance, representativeness, and specificity. This suggests that if a tailor-made questionnaire is to be used, considerable time and resources must be devoted to its development to ensure accurate inclusion of task statements. If a preexisting questionnaire (e.g., the PAQ) is considered, its task statement content should be assessed relative to the task content of the jobs to be analyzed prior to any decision to use the questionnaire.

A second limitation of task questionnaires pertains to potential respondent reactions. Respondents may react negatively if they feel the questionnaire does not contain task statements covering important aspects of their jobs. Respondents may also find completion of the questionnaire to be tedious and boring; this may cause them to commit rating errors. Interpretation and understanding of the task statements may be problematic for respondents who have reading and comprehension skill deficiencies.

A third limitation is that questionnaires such as the PAQ assume that the incumbent is reasonably intelligent, experienced in the job, and sufficiently educated to evaluate the items. To the extent incumbents are less intelligent, lack experience, or have little education, the familiar dictum "garbage in, garbage out" may apply.

Finally, it should be remembered that a typical task questionnaire focuses on tasks. Other job requirement components, particularly KSAOs and those related to job context, may be ignored or downplayed if the task questionnaire is relied on as the method of job information collection.

Committee or Task Force.   Job analysis is often guided by an ad hoc committee or task force. Members of the committee or task force will typically include job experts—both managers and employees—as well as a representative from the HR staff. These members may conduct a number of activities, including (1) reviewing existing information and gathering sample job descriptions, (2) interviewing job incumbents and managers, (3) overseeing the administration of job analysis surveys and analyzing the results, (4) writing task statements, grouping them into task dimensions, and rating the importance of the task dimensions, and (5) identifying KSAOs and rating their importance. Use of a committee or task force brings considerable job analysis expertise to the process, facilitates reliability of judgment through conversation and consensus building, and enhances acceptance of the final results.

Combined Methods.   Only in rare instances does a job analysis involve use of only a single method. Much more likely is a hybrid, eclectic approach using multiple methods. This makes job analysis a more complicated process to design and administer than implied by a description of each of the methods alone.

Criteria for Choice of Methods.   Some explicit choices regarding methods of job analysis need to be made. One set of choices involves decisions to use or not use a particular method of information collection. An organization must decide, for example, whether to use an off-the-shelf method or its own particular method that is suited to its own needs and circumstances. A second set of choices involves how to blend together a set of methods that will all be used, in varying ways and degrees, in the actual job analysis. Some criteria for guidance in such decisions are shown in Exhibit 4.13.

EXHIBIT 4.13   Criteria for Guiding Choice of Job Analysis Methods

1. Degree of suitability/versatility for use across different types of jobs
2. Degree of standardization in the process and in the reporting of results
3. Acceptability of process and results to those who will serve as sources and/or users
4. Degree to which method is operational and may be used "off the shelf" without modification, as opposed to method requiring tailor-made development and application
5. Amount of training required for sources and users of job information
6. Costs of the job analysis, in terms of both direct administrative costs and opportunity costs of time involvement by people
7. Quality of resultant information in terms of reliability and content validity
8. Usability of results in recruitment, selection, and employment activities

SOURCE: Adapted from E. L. Levine, R. A. Ash, H. Hall, and F. Sistrunk, "Evaluation of Job Analysis Methods by Experienced Job Analysts," *Academy of Management Journal,* 1983, 26, pp. 339–348.

Sources to Be Used

Choosing sources of information involves considering who will be used to provide the information sought. While this matter is not entirely independent of job analysis methods (e.g., use of a task questionnaire normally requires use of job incumbents as the source), it is treated as such in the sections that follow.

Job Analyst.   A job analyst is someone who, by virtue of job title and training, is available and suited to conduct job analyses and to guide the job analysis process. The job analyst is also "out of the loop," being neither manager nor incumbent of the jobs analyzed. Thus, the job analyst brings a combination of expertise and neutrality to the work.

Despite such advantages and appeals, reliance on a job analyst as the job information source is not without potential limitations. First, the analyst may be perceived as an outsider by incumbents and supervisors, a perception that may result in questioning the analyst's job knowledge and expertise, as well as trustworthiness. Second, the job analyst may, in fact, lack detailed knowledge of the jobs to be analyzed, especially in an organization with many different job titles. Lack of knowledge may cause the analyst to bring inaccurate job stereotypes to the analysis process. Finally, having specially designated job analysts (either employees or outside consultants) tends to be expensive.

Job Incumbents.   Job incumbents seem like a natural source of information to be used in job analysis, and indeed they are relied on in most job analysis systems. The major advantage to working with incumbents is their familiarity with tasks, KSAOs, and job context. In addition, job incumbents may become more accepting of the job analysis process and its results through their participation in it.

Some skepticism should be maintained about job incumbents as a source of workplace data, as is true for any source. They may lack the knowledge or insights necessary to provide inclusive information, especially if they are probationary or part-time employees. Some employees may also have difficulty in describing the tasks involved in their job or in being able to infer and articulate the underlying KSAOs necessary for the job. Another potential limitation of job incumbents as an information source pertains to their motivation to be a willing and accurate source. Feelings of distrust and suspicion may greatly hamper employees' willingness to function capably as sources. For example, incumbents may intentionally fail to report certain tasks as part of their job so that those tasks are not incorporated into the formal job description. Or, incumbents may deliberately inflate the importance ratings of tasks in order to make the job appear more difficult than it actually is.

Supervisors.   Supervisors could and should be considered excellent sources for use in job analysis. They not only supervise employees performing the job to be analyzed but also have played a major role in defining it and later in adding/deleting job tasks (as in evolving and flexible jobs). Moreover, supervisors ultimately have to accept the resulting descriptions and specifications for jobs they supervise; inclusion of them as a source seems a way to ensure such acceptance.

Subject Matter Experts.   Often, the sources previously mentioned are called subject matter experts, or SMEs. Individuals other than those mentioned may also be used as SMEs. These people bring particular expertise to the job analysis process, an expertise not thought to be available through standard sources. Though the exact qualifications for being designated an SME are far from clear, examples of sources so designated are available. These include previous jobholders (e.g., recently promoted employees), private consultants, customer/clients, and citizens-at-large for some public sector jobs, such as superintendent of schools for a school district. Whatever the sources of SMEs, a common requirement is that they have recent, firsthand knowledge of the job being analyzed.[15]

Combined Sources.   Combinations of sources, like combinations of methods, are most likely to be used in a typical job analysis. This is not only likely but also desirable. As noted previously, each source has some potentially unique insight to contribute to job analysis, as well as some limitations. Through a pooling of such sources and the information they provide, an accurate and acceptable job analysis is most likely to result.

Job Analysis Process

Collecting job information through job analysis requires development and use of an overall process. Unfortunately, there is no set or best process to be followed; the process has to be tailor made to suit the specifics of the situation in which it occurs. There are, however, many key issues to be dealt with in the construction and operation of the process.[16] Each of these is briefly commented on next.

Purpose.   The purpose(s) of job analysis should be clearly identified and agreed on. Since job analysis is a process designed to yield job information, the organization should ask exactly what job information is desired and why. Here, it is useful to refer back to the job requirements matrix to review the types of information that can be sought and obtained in a job requirements job analysis. Management must decide exactly what types of information are desired (task statements, task dimensions, and so forth) and in what format. Once the desired output and the results of job analysis have been determined, the organization can then plan a process that will yield the desired results.

Scope.   The issue of scope involves which job(s) to include in the job analysis. Decisions about actual scope should be based on consideration of (1) the importance of the job to the functioning of the organization, (2) the number of job applicants and incumbents, (3) whether the job is entry level and thus subject to constant staffing activity, (4) the frequency with which job requirements (both tasks and KSAOs) change, and (5) the amount of time lapsed since the previous job analysis.

Internal Staff or Consultant.   The organization may conduct the job analysis using its own staff, or it may procure external consultants. This is a difficult decision because it involves not only the obvious consideration of cost but also many other considerations. Exhibit 4.14 highlights some of these concerns and the trade-offs involved.

EXHIBIT 4.14   **Factors to Consider in Choosing Between Internal Staff or Consultants for Job Analysis**

Internal Staff	Consultant
Cost of technical or procedural failure is low	Cost of technical or procedural failure is high
Project scope is limited	Project scope is comprehensive and/or large
Need for job data ongoing	Need for job data is a one-time, isolated event
There is a desire to develop internal staff skills in job analysis	There is a need for assured availability of each type and level of job analysis skill
Strong management controls are in place to control project costs	Predictability of project cost can depend on adhering to work plan
Knowledge of organization's norms, "culture," and jargon are critical	Technical innovativeness and quality are critical
Technical credibility of internal staff is high	Leverage of external "expert" status is needed to execute project
Process and products of the project are unlikely to be challenged	Process and products of the project are likely to be legally, technically, or politically scrutinized
Rational or narrative job analysis methods are desired	Commercial or proprietary job analysis methods are desired
Data collected are qualitative	Data collection methods are structured, standardized, and/or quantitative

Organization and Coordination.   Any job analysis project, whether conducted by internal staff or external consultants, requires careful organization and coordination. There are two key steps to take to help ensure that this is achieved. First, an organizational member should be appointed to function as a project manager for the total process (if consultants are used, they should report to this project manager). The project manager should be assigned overall responsibility for the total project, including its organization and control. Second, the roles and relationships for the various people involved in the project—HR staff, project staff, line managers, and job incumbents—must be clearly established.

Communication.   Clear and open communication with all concerned facilitates the job analysis process. Job analysis will be thought of by some employees as analogous to an invasive, exploratory surgical procedure, which, in turn, naturally raises questions in their minds about its purpose, process, and results. These questions and concerns need to be anticipated and addressed forthrightly.

Work Flow and Time Frame.   Job analysis involves a mixture of people and paper in a process in which they can become entangled very quickly. The project manager should develop and adhere to a work flowchart that shows the sequential ordering of steps to be followed in the conduct of the job analysis. This should be accompanied by a time frame showing critical completion dates for project phases, as well as a final deadline.

Analysis, Synthesis, and Documentation.   Once collected, job information must be analyzed and synthesized through use of various procedural and statistical means. These should be planned in advance and incorporated into the work-flow and time-frame requirements. Likewise, provisions need to be made for preparation of written documents, especially job descriptions and job specifications, and their incorporation into relevant policy and procedure manuals.

Maintenance of the System.   Job analysis does not end with completion of the project. Rather, mechanisms must be developed and put into place to maintain the job analysis and information system over time. This is critical because the system will be exposed to numerous influences requiring response and adaptation. Examples of these influences include (1) changes in job tasks and KSAOs—additions, deletions, and modifications; (2) job redesign, restructuring, and realignment; and (3) creation of new jobs. In short, job analysis must be thought of and administered as an ongoing organizational process.

Example of Job Analysis Process.   Because of the many factors involved, there is no best or required job analysis process. Rather, the process must be designed to fit each particular situation. Exhibit 4.15 shows an example of the job analysis

EXHIBIT 4.15 Example of Job Requirements Job Analysis

1. Meet with manager of the job, discuss project → 2. Gather existing job information from O*NET, current job description, observation of incumbents → 3. Prepare tentative set of task statements →

4. Review task statements with incumbents and managers; add, delete, rewrite statements → 5. Finalize task statements, get approval from incumbents and managers → 6. Formulate task dimensions, assign tasks to dimension, determine % time spent (importance) for each dimension →

7. Infer necessary KSAOs, develop tentative list → 8. Review KSAOs with incumbents and managers; add, delete, and rewrite KSAOs → 9. Finalize KSAOs, get approval from incumbents and manager →

10. Develop job requirements matrix and/or job description in usable format →11. Provide matrix or job description to parties (e.g., incumbents, manager, HR department) →12. Use matrix or job description in staffing activities, such as communicating with recruits and recruiters, developing the selection plan →

process with a narrow scope, namely, for a single job—that of administrative assistant (secretary). This is a specially conducted job analysis that uses multiple methods (prior information, observation, interviews) and multiple sources (job analyst, job incumbents, supervisors). It was conducted by a previous holder of the job (SME), and it took the person about 20 hours over a 30-day period to conduct and prepare a written job description as the output of the process.

COMPETENCY-BASED JOB ANALYSIS

A recently emerging view of job requirements comes from the concepts of competency and competency models. These concepts are closely akin to KSAOs in some respects and are a substantial extension of KSAOs in other respects. They are an innovative and potentially fruitful approach to the identification, definition, and establishment of job requirements. Discussed below are the nature of competencies and the collection of competency information.

Nature of Competencies

A competency is an underlying characteristic of an individual that contributes to job or role performance and to organizational success.[17] Competencies specific to a particular job are the familiar KSAO requirements established through job requirements job analysis. Competency requirements may extend beyond job-specific ones to those of multiple jobs, general job categories, or the entire organization. These competencies are much more general or generic KSAOs, such as "technical expertise" or "adaptability." A competency model is a combination of the several competencies deemed necessary for a particular job or role. Usage of competencies and competency models in staffing reflects a desire to (1) connote job requirements in ways that extend beyond the specific job itself; (2) describe and measure the organization's workforce in more general competency terms; and (3) design and implement staffing programs focused around competencies (rather than just specific jobs) as a way of increasing staffing flexibility in job assignments.

Despite the strong similarities between competencies and KSAOs, there are two notable differences. First, competencies may be job spanning, meaning that they contribute to success on multiple jobs. Members of a work team, for example, may each hold specific jobs within the team but may be subject to job-spanning competency requirements, such as adaptability and teamwork orientation. Such requirements ensure that team members will interact successfully with one another and will even perform portions of others' jobs if necessary. As another example, competency requirements may span jobs within the same category, such as sales jobs or managerial jobs. All sales jobs may have as a competency requirement "product knowledge," and all managerial jobs may require "planning and results orientation." Such requirements allow for greater flexibility in job placements and job assignments within the category.

Second, competencies can contribute not only to job performance but also to organizational success. These are very general competencies applicable to, and required for, all jobs. They serve to align requirements for all jobs with the mission and goals of the organization. A restaurant, for example, may have "customer focus" as a competency requirement for all jobs as a way of indicating that servicing the needs of its customers is a key component of all jobs.

Competency Example

An illustration of the competency approach to job requirements is shown in Exhibit 4.16. The Green Care Corporation produces several lawn maintenance products: gas and electric lawn mowers, gas and electric "weed whackers," manual lawn edgers, and electric hedge trimmers. The company is in a highly competitive industry. To survive and grow, the company's core mission is product innovation and product reliability; its goals are to achieve annual 10% growth in revenues and 2% growth in market share. To help fulfill its mission and goals the company has established four general (strategic) workforce competencies—creativity/innovation, technical expertise, customer focus, and results orientation. These requirements are part of every job in the company. At the business unit (gas lawn mowers) level, the company has also established job-specific and job-spanning requirements. Some jobs, such as design engineer, are traditional or slowly evolving jobs and, as such, have only job-specific KSAO or competency requirements. Because the products are assembled via team assembly processes, jobs within the assembly team (such as engine assembler, final assembler) have both job-specific and job-spanning competency requirements. The job-spanning competencies—team orientation, adaptability, communication—are general and behavioral. They are necessary because of task interdependence between engine and final assembly jobs and because employees may be shifted between the two jobs in order to cover sudden employee shortages due to unscheduled absences and to maintain smooth production flows. Each job in the business unit thus has four general competency requirements, multiple job-specific competency requirements, and, where appropriate, job-spanning competency requirements.

Organization Usage

Organizations are beginning to experiment with the development of competencies and competency models and to use them as the underpinnings of several HR applications.[18] Research indicates that the experimentation is occurring in organizations of all sizes, but especially in large ones. The three key strategic HR reasons for doing competency modeling are to (1) create awareness and understanding of the need for change in business, (2) enhance the skill levels in the workforce, and (3) improve

---

EXHIBIT 4.16 **Examples of Competencies**

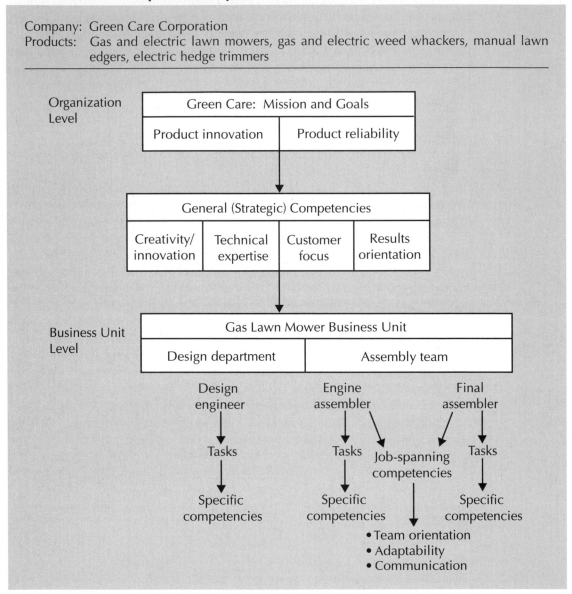

Company: Green Care Corporation
Products: Gas and electric lawn mowers, gas and electric weed whackers, manual lawn edgers, electric hedge trimmers

Organization Level

Green Care: Mission and Goals

| Product innovation | Product reliability |

General (Strategic) Competencies

| Creativity/innovation | Technical expertise | Customer focus | Results orientation |

Business Unit Level

Gas Lawn Mower Business Unit

| Design department | Assembly team |

Design engineer → Tasks → Specific competencies

Engine assembler → Tasks → Specific competencies

Final assembler → Tasks → Specific competencies

Job-spanning competencies
- Team orientation
- Adaptability
- Communication

---

teamwork and coordination. Most of the emphasis has been on establishing general competencies, as illustrated by the "Great Eight" competencies used in one framework:[19]

- Leading (initiates action, gives direction)
- Supporting (shows respect, puts people first)

- Presenting (communicates and networks effectively)
- Analyzing (thinks clearly, applies expertise)
- Creating (thinks broadly, handles situations creatively)
- Organizing (plans ahead, follows rules)
- Adapting (responds to change, copes with setbacks)
- Performing (focuses on results, shows understanding of organization)

Competency models are being used for many HR applications, especially staffing, career development, performance management, and compensation. Pertaining to staffing, one important application is in HR and staffing planning. Here, workforce requirements are specified in competency terms and compared to current workforce competency levels to identify competency gaps. Such comparisons may be particularly appropriate in replacement and succession planning. Another important staffing application is in external and internal selection, where applicants are assessed not only for job-specific competencies but also for general competencies. For external hiring, competency-based interviews with applicants are conducted to gauge general competencies as a key factor in selection decisions and then in job placement decisions for those hired. For promotion decisions, competency-based interviews are used in conjunction with supervisory assessments of promotability.[20]

Despite their many potential applications to various staffing activities, adoption of competency models should be undertaken cautiously since research has identified many potential barriers to success in their usage. Prominent among these barriers are (1) a lack of buy-in from top management, who may be unwilling to apply the competency model to themselves or see its usefulness, (2) the readiness of employees generally to accept the competency model and learn the new competency behaviors required by the model, (3) conflicts as to whether there should be separate models for separate units of the organization and the relative emphases to be placed on general, job-spanning, and job-specific competencies, and (4) the time and resources needed to implement the competency model, train employees in its usage, and maintain and update the model. On the positive side, research does indicate that when raters are trained in how to use a competency approach and are given detailed information upon which to base their ratings, competency-based approaches can be valid and accurate.[21]

Collecting Competency Information

Techniques and processes for collecting competency information are still in their infancy.[22] An exception, of course, is job requirements job analysis for job-specific competencies. For more general competencies, much less is known about the best ways to identify and define competencies. General competencies at the organization (strategic) level are likely to be established by top management, with guidance from strategic HR managers. At a minimum, effective establishment of general competency requirements would seem to demand the following. First, it is crucial that the organization establish its mission and goals prior to determination of competency requirements; this will help ensure that general competencies are derived from knowledge of mission and goals, much as job-specific competencies are derived from previously identified job tasks. Second, the general competencies should be truly important at all job levels, so that usage of the competencies as job requirements will focus and align all jobs with the organization's mission and goals. This principle also holds in the case where, instead of general competency requirements at the organization level, there are general competency requirements at the strategic business unit or subunit level. Third, all general competencies should have specific behavioral definitions, not just labels. These definitions provide substance, meaning, and guidance to all concerned.

For job-spanning competencies, these definitions will necessarily be more task specific. To ensure effective identification and definition, several tasks should be undertaken. First, it is crucial to know the major tasks for which the competencies are to be established, meaning that some form of job analysis should occur first. For now, that process will have to be crafted by the organization since we lack prototypes or best practice examples as guidance. Second, SMEs familiar with all the jobs or roles to which the competencies will apply should be part of the process. Third, careful definition of the competencies will be necessary. Acquiring definitions from other organizations, consultants, or O*NET will be useful steps here.

A final cautionary note is that the collection and usage of competencies beyond job-specific ones will occur in uncharted legal waters. Recalling the legal standard of job-relatedness for staffing practices that cause adverse impact, will staffing practices and decisions based on general competencies be construed as job related? Will it be a defensible argument to say that although a particular competency requirement may not have a strong contribution to job success, it is necessary for organizational success? Such questions will inevitably arise; to address them, the organization should conduct a thorough process for establishing competency requirements using the suggestions above as a starting point.

JOB REWARDS

In the person/job match model, jobs are composed of requirements and rewards. The focus so far in this chapter has been on job requirements vis-à-vis the discussion of job analysis. Attention now turns to job rewards. Providing and using rewards is a key staffing strategy for motivating several HR outcomes—applicant attraction, employee performance, and employee retention in particular. Successfully matching rewards provided with rewards desired will be critical in attaining the HR outcomes. Doing so first of all requires specification of the types of rewards potentially available and desired.

Types of Rewards

Organizations and jobs provide a wide variety of rewards. It is common to classify each reward as either extrinsic or intrinsic in nature. Extrinsic rewards are tangible factors external to the job itself that are explicitly designed and granted to employees by representatives of the organization (e.g., pay, benefits, work schedule, advancement, job security). Intrinsic rewards are the "intangibles" that are more internal to the job itself and experienced by the employee as an outgrowth of actually doing the job and being a member of the organization (e.g., variety in work duties, autonomy, feedback, coworker and supervisor relations).[23]

Employee Value Proposition

The totality of rewards, both extrinsic and intrinsic, associated with the job constitutes the EVP.[24] The EVP is akin to the "package" or "bundle" of rewards provided to employees and to which employees respond by joining, performing, and remaining with the organization. It is the "deal" or "bargain" struck between the organization and the employee, first as a promise to the prospective employee, later as a reality to the actual new employee, and later still as a new deal as the EVP changes due to reward improvements and/or internal job changes by the employee. The EVP thus functions like a glue that binds the employee and the organization, with the employee providing certain behaviors (attraction, performance, retention, and so forth) in exchange for the EVP.

The challenge to the organization is to create EVPs for various employee groups that, on average, are both attractive and affordable (how to create an individual EVP in the form of a formal job offer to a prospective employee is considered in Chapter 12). No reward, extrinsic or intrinsic, is costless, so the organization must figure out what it can afford as it creates its EVPs. Regardless of cost, however, the rewards must also be attractive to those for whom they are intended, so attraction and cost must be considered jointly when developing EVPs. The dual affordable-attractive requirements for EVPs may create some potential problems: wrong magnitude, wrong mix, or not distinctive.[25]

Wrong magnitude refers to a package of rewards that is either too small or too great monetarily. To the prospective or current employee, too small a package may be viewed as simply inadequate, noncompetitive, or an insult, none of which are desirable perceptions to be creating. Such perceptions may arise very early in the applicant's job search, before the organization is even aware of the applicant, due to word-of-mouth information from others (e.g., former applicants or employees) or information obtained about the organization, such as through its print or electronic recruitment information. Alternatively, too small a package may not become an issue until fairly late in the job search process, as additional bits of reward package information become known to the applicant. Regardless of when the too-small perceptions emerge, they can be deal killers that lead to self-selection out of consideration for the job, job offer turndowns, or decisions to quit. While too-small packages may be unattractive, they often have the virtue of being affordable for the organization.

Too large a package creates affordability problems for the organization. Those problems may not surface immediately, but long term they can threaten the organization's financial viability and possibly even its survival. Affordability problems may be particularly acute in service-providing organizations, where employee compensation costs are a substantial percentage of total operating costs.

Wrong mix refers to a situation in which the composition of the rewards package is out of sync with the preferences of prospective or current employees. A package that provides excellent retirement benefits and long-term performance incentives to a relatively young and mobile workforce, for example, is most likely a wrong mix. Its attraction and retention power in all likelihood is minimal. It might also be relatively expensive to provide.

Not distinctive refers to individual rewards packages that are viewed as ho-hum in nature. They have no uniqueness or special appeal that would either win or retain employees. They do not signal anything distinctive about the organization or give the job seeker or employee any special reason to think the "deal" is one that simply cannot be passed up or given up.

In short, creating successful EVPs is a challenge, and the results can have important implications for workforce attraction, retention, and cost. To help create successful EVPs, the organization should seek to systematically collect job rewards information in order to learn about rewards that are important or unimportant to employees.

Collecting Job Rewards Information

Unlike job analysis as a mechanism for collecting job requirements information, mechanisms for collecting job rewards information are more fragmentary. Nonetheless, there are several things that can be done, all of which seek to provide data about the importance of rewards to employees—which rewards they most and least prefer. Armed with knowledge about employee preferences, the organization can begin to build EVPs that are of the right magnitude, mix, and distinctiveness. One approach for collecting job rewards information is to gauge the preferences of the organization's own employees. A different approach is to learn about employee preferences, and actual rewards provided, in other organizations.

Within the Organization

To learn about employee reward preferences within the organization, interviews with employees, or more formal surveys of them, might be used.

Interviews With Employees. The interview approach requires decisions about who will guide the process, interview content, sampling confidentiality, data recording and analysis, and reporting of the results. The following are a few suggestions to guide each of those decisions. First, a person with special expertise in the employee interview process should guide the total process. This could be a person within the HR department, a person outside of HR with the expertise (such as in marketing research), or an outside consultant. The person guiding the process may be the only interviewer; if not, he or she should carefully select and train those who will do the interviews, including supervising a "dry run" of the interview.

Second, the interviews should be structured and guided. The major content areas, and specific questions, should be decided in advance, tested on a small sample of employees as to their clarity and wording, and then placed in a formal interview protocol to be used by the interviewer. An example of potential questions is shown in Exhibit 4.17. Note that the major content areas covered in the interview are rewards offered, reward magnitude, reward mix, and reward distinctiveness.

Third, employees from throughout the organization should be part of the sample. In small organizations, it might be possible to include all employees; in larger organizations, random samples of employees will be necessary. When sampling, it is important to include sample employees from all job categories, organizational units, and organizational levels.

EXHIBIT 4.17   Examples of Reward Preferences Interview Questions

Rewards to Offer
- Are there any rewards you wish the organization would provide now?
- Looking ahead, are there any rewards you hope the organization will provide?

Reward Magnitude
- Overall, do you think the level of pay and benefits is too much, too little, or about right compared to other jobs like yours?
- Overall, do you think the reward intangibles are too much, too little, or about right compared to other jobs like yours?
- Would you be willing to pay the cost of certain rewards to ensure the organization continues to provide them?

Reward Mix
- Would you prefer the mix of pay and benefits shift more toward pay, benefits, or stay the same?
- What are the two most important rewards to you?
- What rewards are irrelevant to you?

Rewards Distinctiveness
- Which rewards that you receive are you most likely to tell others about?
- Which of our rewards really stand out to you? To job applicants?
- What rewards could we start offering that would be unique?

Fourth, it is strongly recommended that the interviews be treated as confidential, and that the responses of individuals be seen only by those recording and analyzing the data. At the same time, it would be useful to gather (with their permission) interviewees' demographic information (e.g., age, gender) and organizational information (e.g., job title, organizational unit) since this will permit breakouts of responses during data analysis. Such breakouts will be very useful in decisions about whether to create separate EVPs for separate employee groups or organizational units.

Fifth, interviewees' responses should be recorded rather than trusted to the memory of the interviewer. The preferred way to record responses is for the interviewer to take notes. Verbatim electronic recording of responses will likely threaten the interviewees' sense of confidentiality, plus require subsequent costly transcription. The response data will need to be analyzed with an eye toward capturing major "themes" in the data, such as the most and least important rewards and the rewards that the employees could do without. These findings can then be incorporated into a report that will be presented to organizational representatives.

Surveys of Employees.   A survey of employees should proceed along the same lines, following many of the same recommendations, as for an employee interview process. The biggest difference will be the mechanism for gathering the data—namely, a written set of questions with response scales rather than a verbally administered set of questions with open-ended responses. To construct the survey, a listing of the rewards to be included on the survey must be developed. These could be chosen from a listing of the organization's current extrinsic rewards, plus some questions about intrinsic rewards. For response scales, it is common to use a 1 (very unimportant) to 5 (very important) rating format. An example of a partial employee reward preferences survey is shown in Exhibit 4.18.

As with interviews, it is recommended that a person with special expertise guide the project, that the survey content be specially constructed (rather than canned), that sampling include employees throughout the organization, that employees be assured of confidentiality, that thorough analysis of results be undertaken, and that reports of findings be prepared for organizational representatives.

Which to Use?   Should the organization opt for use of interviews, surveys, or both? The advantages of an interview are that it is of a personal nature; employees are allowed to respond in their own words; it is possible to create questions that probe preferences about reward magnitude, mix, and distinctiveness; and a very rich set of data is obtained that provides insights beyond mere rating scale responses. On the downside, interviews are costly to schedule and conduct, data analysis is messy and time consuming, and statistical summaries and analysis of the data are difficult. Surveys are easier to administer (especially online), and they permit statistical summaries and analyses that are very helpful in interpreting responses. The biggest downsides to surveys are the lack of richness of data and

EXHIBIT 4.18   **Examples of Reward Preferences Survey Questions**

	Very Unimportant		Neither Important nor Unimportant		Very Important
Extrinsic Rewards					
Base pay	1	2	3	4	5
Incentive pay	1	2	3	4	5
Overtime pay	1	2	3	4	5
Health insurance	1	2	3	4	5
Promotion opportunities	1	2	3	4	5
Job security	1	2	3	4	5
Intrinsic Rewards					
Using my skills	1	2	3	4	5
Doing significant tasks	1	2	3	4	5
Deciding how to do my job	1	2	3	4	5
Getting feedback from job	1	2	3	4	5
Trust in management	1	2	3	4	5
Communications from management	1	2	3	4	5

the difficulty in constructing questions that tap into employees' preferences about reward magnitude, mix, and distinctiveness.

Assuming adequate resources and expertise, a combined interview and survey approach would be best. This would allow the organization to capitalize on the unique strengths of each approach, as well as offset some of the weaknesses of each.

A final cautionary note is that both interviews and surveys of current employees miss out on two other groups from whom reward preference information would be useful. The first group is departing or departed employees, who may have left due to dissatisfaction with the EVP. In Chapter 14 we discuss the exit interview as a procedure for learning about this group. The second group is job applicants. Presumably the organization could conduct interviews and surveys with this group, but that could be administratively challenging (especially with Internet applicants). Also applicants might feel they are "tipping their hand" to the organization in terms of what they desire or would accept in a job offer. The more common way to learn about applicant reward preferences is from surveys of employees outside the organization, who might be representative of the types of applicants the organization will encounter.

Outside the Organization

Other Employees.   Data on the reward preferences of employees outside the organization are available from surveys of employees in other organizations. To the extent these employees are similar to the organization's own applicants and employees, the data will likely provide a useful barometer of preferences. An example is the Job Satisfaction survey conducted by the SHRM. It administered an online survey to a national random sample of n = 604 employees. The employees rated the importance of 21 extrinsic and intrinsic "rewards" to their overall satisfaction on a 1–5 (very unimportant to very important) scale. The percentage of employees rating each reward as "very important" is shown in Exhibit 4.19. The data for 2004 are shown along with data from a similar survey in 2002.

It can be seen that extrinsic rewards, especially "benefits" and "pay," topped the reward preferences, followed by "feeling safe in the work environment," "job security," and "flexible to balance work/life issues." For the most part, reward importance was very similar in the two time periods. An exception to this was a large increase in the importance of feeling safe in the work environment.

Not shown in Exhibit 4.19 were two other important findings. First, a sample of HR professionals was asked to predict the importance that employees attached to the rewards, and the HR professionals' predictions did not correspond all that closely to the actual employee ratings. For example, the two top rewards predicted by the HR professionals were "relationship with immediate supervisor" and "management recognition of employee job performance." And "feeling safe in the work environment" was the 13th most important reward as predicted by the HR professionals. A second finding was that there were some differences in reward importance as a function of employee age, tenure, gender, and industry; these differences, however, were relatively small.

Organizational Practices.   A less direct way to assess the importance of rewards to employees is to examine the actual rewards that other organizations provide their employees. The assumption here is that these other organizations are attuned to their employees' preferences and try to provide rewards that are consistent with them. Since pay and benefits loom large in most employees' reward preferences, it is particularly important to become knowledgeable of other organizations' pay and benefit practices to assist in the development of the EVP.

The best single source of pay and benefit information comes from the National Compensation Survey, conducted by the Bureau of Labor Statistics within the Department of Labor (*www.bls.gov*). The pay part of the survey reports average pay for employees, broken out by occupation, private-public sector, organization size, and geographic area. Another feature of the pay part is occupational leveling, in which pay rates for jobs with dissimilar occupation and job titles may be compared with one another because they share common job content. The benefits part of the survey presents detailed data about the percentage of employees who have access to

EXHIBIT 4.19   "Very Important" Aspects of Employee Job Satisfaction (Employees)

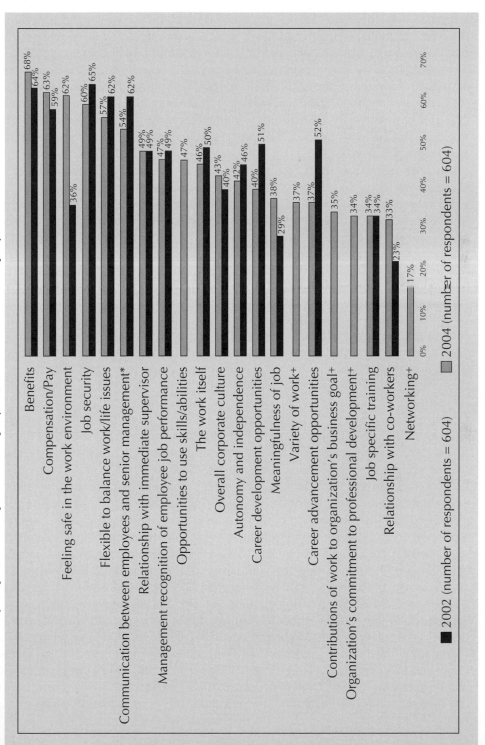

NOTE: Aspects are in order of importance by 2004 data.

*This question was modified in 2004 by specifying communication with "senior management" instead of "management."

+This aspect was added in 2004. Therefore, no comparable data exist for 2002.

Source: E. Essen, *Job Satisfaction Series* (Alexandria, VA: Society for Human Resource Management, 2004), p. 156. Used with permission.

a benefit or the average benefit provision. Data about the following benefits are provided: retirement, health care coverage (medical, dental, vision) and required employee contributions, short- and long-term disability, paid holidays, paid vacation, paid jury duty leave, paid military leave, assistance for child care, adoption assistance, long term care insurance, flexible workplace, employer-provided PC for home use, and subsidized commuting. The data are broken out by white collar, blue collar, and service occupations, full time–part time, union–nonunion, average wage greater or less than $15/hour, organization size, goods-service producing, and geographic area.

Another important source of information about benefits is the Society for Human Resource Management Annual Benefits Survey (*www.shrm.org*). It provides very detailed information about specific benefits provided in each of the following areas: family friendliness, housing and relocation, health care and wellness, personal services, financial, business travel, leave, and other benefits. The data are broken out by organization size.

JOB ANALYSIS FOR TEAMS

More and more work is being done in work teams. A work team is an interdependent collection of employees who share responsibility for achieving a specific goal. Examples of such goals include developing a product, delivering a service, winning a game, conducting a process, developing a plan, or making a joint decision.

Teams, and thus team-based jobs, occur in multiple forms. Teams are often formed around projects, such as to develop or launch a new product or manage an existing project or brand, or as part of a task force to address some critical issue or crisis. Other teams are designed to absorb management functions so that the teams themselves manage and supervise the work to be done.

No matter its form and function, every team is composed of two or more employees, and there is an identifiable collection of tasks that the team is to perform. Usually, these tasks will be grouped into specific clusters, and each cluster constitutes a position or job. A project management team, for example, may have separate jobs and job titles for budget specialists, technical specialists, coordinators, and field staff. Each of these jobs may be traditional, evolving, flexible, or idiosyncratic.

An example of a project team is the team that developed Motorola's Razr phone, which was the first flat-profile cell phone on the market (and led competitors to scramble to follow suit). Work on the Razr was done with a specially formed team that comprised employees from Motorola's downtown Chicago innovation lab (known as "Moto City") and from its Libertyville, Illinois, research and development facility. Other companies such as Fisher-Price, Procter & Gamble, and Boeing (which used teams to develop its 787 Dreamliner) have made considerable use of project teams and innovation labs to create new products and bring them to market quickly.[26]

Another type of team, one that encompasses elements of all the above team types, is the global virtual team.[27] Such a team is composed of members who are geographically dispersed, are from multiple cultures, and are working in collaboration electronically. These teams are often assigned temporary, critical tasks such as globally developing new products, setting up and overseeing offshore facilities, conducting global audits, and managing brands.

While teams differ in many respects, two differences are very important in terms of their job analysis and staffing implications. Many team members perform multiple jobs (rather than a single job). In such cases, staffing must emphasize recruitment and selection for both job-specific KSAOs and job-spanning KSAOs. Another term used to connote job-spanning KSAOs is "competencies." Many of these job-spanning KSAOs will involve flexibility, adaptability, and rapid learning skills that will facilitate performing, and switching between, multiple jobs.[28]

As examples of the above points, a product development team may include mechanical engineers, computer-assisted design specialists, product safety experts, and marketing specialists. Each team member will likely perform only one of these jobs, and thus staffing these jobs will be targeted toward job-specific KSAOs. As a different example, a team responsible for assembly of lawn mower engines may require different members to perform different jobs at any particular moment, but it may also require each member to be (or become) proficient in all phases of engine assembly. Staffing this team will require acquisition of team members who have both job-specific and job-spanning KSAOs.

The second important difference between teams regarding staffing is the degree of task interdependence among team members. The greater the task interdependence, the greater the importance of KSAOs pertaining to interpersonal qualities (e.g., communicating, collaborating, and resolving conflicts) and team self-management qualities (e.g., setting group goals, inspecting each other's work). Thus, task interdependence brings behaviorally oriented KSAOs to the forefront of job requirements for team-based jobs.

LEGAL ISSUES

This chapter has emphasized the crucial role that job analysis plays in establishing the foundations for staffing activities. That crucial role continues from a legal perspective. Job analysis becomes intimately involved in court cases involving the job relatedness of staffing activities. It also occupies a prominent position in the UGESP. Finally, the ADA requires that the organization determine the essential functions of each job, and job analysis can play a pivotal role in that process. As these issues are discussed in the following sections, note the direct relevance of the job requirements matrix and its development to them.

Job Relatedness and Court Cases

In EEO/AA court cases, the organization is confronted with the need to justify its challenged staffing practices as being job related. Common sense suggests that this requires first and foremost that the organization conduct some type of job analysis to identify job requirements. If the case involves an organization's defense of its selection procedures, the UGESP require the conduct of job analysis. In addition, specific features or characteristics of the job analysis make a difference in the organization's defense. Specifically, an examination of court cases indicates that for purposes of legal defensibility the organization should conform to the following recommendations:

1. "Job analysis must be performed and must be for the job for which the selection instrument is to be utilized.
2. Analysis of the job should be in writing.
3. Job analysts should describe in detail the procedure used.
4. Job data should be collected from a variety of current sources by knowledgeable job analysts.
5. Sample size should be large and representative of the jobs for which the selection instrument is used.
6. Tasks, duties, and activities should be included in the analysis.
7. The most important tasks should be represented in the selection device.
8. Competency levels of job performance for entry-level jobs should be specified.
9. Knowledge, skills, and abilities should be specified, particularly if a content validation model is followed."[29]

These recommendations are very consistent with our more general discussion of job analysis as an important tool and basic foundation for staffing activities. Moreover, even though these recommendations were made several years ago, there is little reason to doubt or modify any of them on the basis of more recent court cases.

Essential Job Functions

Recall that under the ADA, the organization must not discriminate against a qualified individual with a disability who can perform the "essential functions" of the job, with or without reasonable accommodation. This requirement raises three questions: What are essential functions? What is evidence of essential functions? What is the role of job analysis?

What Are Essential Functions?

The ADA employment regulations provide the following statements about essential functions:

1. "The term essential functions refers to the fundamental job duties of the employment position the individual with a disability holds or desires. The term essential function does not include the marginal functions of the position; and

2. A job function may be considered essential for any of several reasons, including but not limited to the following:

   - The function may be essential because the reason the position exists is to perform the function;
   - The function may be essential because of the limited number of employees available among whom the performance of that job function can be distributed; and/or
   - The function may be highly specialized so that the incumbent in the position is hired for his or her expertise or ability to perform the particular function."

Evidence of Essential Functions

The employment regulations go on to indicate what constitutes evidence that any particular function is in fact an essential one. That evidence includes, but is not limited to, the following:

1. The employer's judgment as to which functions are essential
2. Written job descriptions, prepared before advertising or interviewing applicants for the job
3. The amount of time spent on the job performing the function
4. The consequences of not requiring the incumbent to perform the function
5. The terms of a collective bargaining agreement
6. The work experience of past incumbents in the job
7. The current work experience of incumbents in similar jobs

Role of Job Analysis

What role(s) might job analysis play in identifying essential functions and establishing evidence of their being essential? The employment regulations are silent on this question. However, the Equal Employment Opportunity Commission (EEOC) has provided substantial and detailed assistance to organizations to deal with this and many other issues under the ADA.[30] The specific statements regarding job analysis and essential functions of the job are shown in Exhibit 4.20.

Examination of the statements in Exhibit 4.20 suggests the following. First, while job analysis is not required by law as a means of establishing the essential functions of a job, it is strongly recommended. Second, the job analysis should focus on tasks associated with the job. Where KSAOs are studied or specified,

EXHIBIT 4.20 Job Analysis and Essential Functions of the Job

Job Analysis and the Essential Functions of a Job

The ADA does not require that an employer conduct a job analysis or any particular form of job analysis to identify the essential functions of a job. The information provided by a job analysis may or may not be helpful in properly identifying essential job functions, depending on how it is conducted.

The term "job analysis" generally is used to describe a formal process in which information about a specific job or occupation is collected and analyzed. Formal job analysis may be conducted by a number of different methods. These methods obtain different kinds of information that is used for different purposes. Some of these methods will not provide information sufficient to determine if an individual with a disability is qualified to perform "essential" job functions.

For example: One kind of formal job analysis looks at specific job tasks and classifies jobs according to how these tasks deal with data, people, and objects. This type of job analysis is used to set wage rates for various jobs; however, it may not be adequate to identify the essential functions of a *particular* job, as required by the ADA. Another kind of job analysis looks at the kinds of knowledge, skills, and abilities that are necessary to perform a job. This type of job analysis is used to develop selection criteria for various jobs. The information from this type of analysis sometimes helps to measure the importance of certain skills, knowledge and abilities, but it does not take into account the fact that people with disabilities often can perform essential functions using other skills and abilities.

Some job analysis methods ask current employees and their supervisors to rate the importance of general characteristics necessary to perform a job, such as "strength," "endurance," or "intelligence," without linking these characteristics to *specific* job functions or specific tasks that are part of a function. Such general information may not identify, for example, whether upper body or lower body strength is required, or whether muscular endurance or cardiovascular endurance is needed to perform a particular job function. Such information, by itself, would not be sufficient to determine whether an individual who has particular limitations can perform an essential function with or without an accommodation.

As already stated, the ADA does not require a formal job analysis or any particular method of analysis to identify the essential functions of a job. A small employer may wish to conduct an informal analysis by observing and consulting with people who perform the job, or have previously performed it, and their supervisors. If possible, it is advisable to observe and consult with several workers under a range of conditions, to get a better idea of all job functions and the different ways they may be performed. Production records and workloads also may be relevant factors to consider.

(continued)

EXHIBIT 4.20   Continued

To identify essential job functions under the ADA, a job analysis should focus on the purpose of the job and the importance of actual job functions in achieving this purpose. Evaluating importance may include consideration of the frequency with which a function is performed, the amount of time spent on the function, and the consequences if the function is not performed. The analysis may include information on the work environment (such as unusual heat, cold, humidity, dust, toxic substances, or stress factors). The job analysis may contain information on the manner in which a job currently is performed, but should not conclude that ability to perform the job in that manner is an essential function, unless there is no other way to perform the function without causing undue hardship. A job analysis will be most helpful for purposes of the ADA if it focuses on the results or outcome of a function, not solely on the way it customarily is performed.

For example:
- An essential function of a computer programmer job might be described as "ability to develop programs that accomplish necessary objectives," rather than "ability to manually write programs." Although a person currently performing the job may write these programs by hand, that is not the essential function, because programs can be developed directly on the computer.
- If a job requires mastery of information contained in technical manuals, this essential function would be "ability to learn technical material," rather than "ability to read technical manuals." People with visual and other reading impairments could perform this function using other means, such as audiotapes.
- A job that requires objects to be moved from one place to another should state this essential function. The analysis may note that the person in the job "lifts 50-pound cartons to a height of 3 or 4 feet and loads them into truck-trailers 5 hours daily," but should not identify the "ability to manually lift and load 50-pound cartons" as an essential function unless this is the only method by which the function can be performed without causing an undue hardship.

A job analysis that is focused on outcomes or results also will be helpful in establishing appropriate qualification standards, developing job descriptions, conducting interviews, and selecting people in accordance with ADA requirements. It will be particularly helpful in identifying accommodations that will enable an individual with specific functional abilities and limitations to perform the job.

SOURCE: Equal Employment Opportunity Commission, *Technical Assistance Manual for the Employment Provisions (Title I) of the Americans With Disabilities Act* (Washington, DC: author, 1992), pp. II-18 to II-20.

they should be derived from an explicit consideration of their probable links to the essential tasks. Third, with regard to tasks, the focus should be on the tasks themselves and the outcome or results of the tasks, rather than the methods by which they are performed. Finally, the job analysis should be useful in identifying potential reasonable accommodations.[31]

SUMMARY

Organizations design and use various types of jobs—as jobs change and evolve, new design approaches are sometimes needed. All design approaches result in job content in the form of job requirements and rewards. Job analysis is described as the process used to gather, analyze, synthesize, and report information about job content. The job requirements approach to job analysis focuses on job-specific tasks, KSAOs, and job context. Competency-based job analysis seeks to identify more general KSAOs that apply across jobs and roles.

The job requirements approach is guided by the job requirements matrix. The matrix calls for information about tasks and task dimensions, as well as their importance. In a parallel fashion, it requires information about KSAOs required for the tasks, plus indications about the importance of those KSAOs. The final component of the matrix deals with numerous elements of the job context.

When gathering the information called for by the job requirements matrix, the organization is confronted with a multitude of choices. Those choices are shown to revolve around various job analysis methods, sources, and processes. The organization must pick and choose from among these; all have advantages and disadvantages associated with them. The choices should be guided by a concern for the accuracy and acceptability of the information that is being gathered.

A very new approach to identifying job requirements is competency-based job analysis. This form of job analysis seeks to identify general competencies (KSAOs) necessary for all jobs because the competencies support the organization's mission and goals. Within work units, other general competencies (job-spanning KSAOs) may also be established that cut across multiple jobs. Potential techniques and processes for collecting competency information are suggested.

Jobs offer a variety of rewards, both extrinsic and intrinsic. The totality or package of these rewards constitutes the EVP. To help form EVPs, it is necessary to collect job rewards information about employee reward preferences and rewards given to employees at other organizations. Numerous techniques for doing this are available.

As team-based jobs continue to expand, our approaches to job analysis need to expand too. In particular, both job-specific and job-spanning KSAOs need to be emphasized, as does the focus on interpersonal qualities.

From a legal perspective, job analysis is shown to assume major importance in creating staffing systems and practices that are in compliance with EEO/AA laws and regulations. The employer must ensure (or be able to show) that its practices are job related. This requires not only conducting a job requirements job analysis but also using a process that itself has defensible characteristics. Under the ADA, the organization must identify the essential functions of the job. Though this does not require a job analysis, the organization should strongly consider it as one of the tools to be used. Over time, we will learn more about how job analysis is treated under the ADA.

DISCUSSION QUESTIONS

1. Identify a team-based job situation. What are examples of job-spanning KSAOs required in that situation?
2. How should task statements be written, and what sorts of problems might you encounter in asking a job incumbent to write these statements?
3. Would it be better to first identify task dimensions and then create specific task statements for each dimension, or should task statements be identified first and then used to create task dimensions?
4. What would you consider when trying to decide what criteria (e.g., percent time spent) to use for gathering indications about task importance?
5. What are the advantages and disadvantages of using multiple methods of job analysis for a particular job? Multiple sources?
6. What are the advantages and disadvantages of identifying and using general competencies to guide staffing activities?
7. Why do you think HR professionals were not able to very accurately predict the importance of many rewards to employees? What are the implications for creating the EVP?

ETHICAL ISSUES

1. It has been suggested that "ethical conduct" be formally incorporated as a general competency requirement for any job within the organization. Discuss the pros and cons of this suggestion.
2. Assume you are assisting in the conduct of job analysis as an HR department representative. You have encountered several managers who want to delete certain tasks and KSAOs from the formal job description that have to do with employee safety, even though they clearly are job requirements. How should you handle this situation?

APPLICATIONS

Conducting a Job Requirements or Job Rewards Job Analysis

Job analysis is defined as "the process of studying jobs in order to gather, synthesize, and report information about job content." Based on the person/job match model, job content consists of job requirements (tasks and KSAOs) and job rewards (extrinsic and intrinsic). The goal of a job requirements job analysis is to produce the job requirements matrix.

Your assignment is to conduct either a job requirements or job rewards job analysis. In this assignment you will choose a job you want to study, conduct either a job requirements or job rewards job analysis of that job, and prepare a written report of your project.

Your report should include the following sections:

1. The Job—What job (job title) did you choose to study and why?
2. The Methods Used—What methods did you use (prior information, observation, interviews, task questionnaires, committee, combinations of these), and exactly how did you use them?
3. The Sources Used—What sources did you use (job analyst, job incumbent, supervisor, SMEs, combinations of these), and exactly how did you use them?
4. The Process Used—How did you go about gathering, synthesizing, and reporting the information? Refer back to Exhibit 4.15 for an example.
5. The Matrix—Present the actual job requirements matrix.

Maintaining Job Descriptions

The InAndOut, Inc., company provides warehousing and fulfillment services (order receiving and filling) to small publishers of books with small print runs (number of copies of a book printed). After the books are printed and bound at a printing facility, they are shipped to InAndOut for handling. Books are received initially by handlers, who unload the books off trucks, place them on pallets, and move them via forklifts and conveyors to their assigned storage space in the warehouse. The handlers also retrieve books and bring them to the shipping area when orders are received. The books are then packaged, placed in cartons, and loaded onto delivery trucks (to take to air or ground transportation providers) by shippers. Book orders are taken by customer service representatives via written, phone, or electronic (e-mail, fax) forms. New accounts are generated by marketing representatives, who also service existing accounts. Order clerks handle all the internal paperwork. All of these employees report to either the supervisor–operations or the supervisor–customer service, who in turn reports to the general manager.

The owner and president of InAndOut, Inc., Alta Fossom, is independently wealthy and delegates all day-to-day management matters to the general manager,

Marvin Olson. Alta requires, however, that Marvin clear any new ideas or initiatives with her prior to taking action. The company is growing and changing rapidly. Many new accounts, often larger than the past norm, are opening. Publishers are demanding more services and faster order fulfillment. Information technology is constantly being upgraded, and new machinery (forklifts, computer-assisted conveyor system) is being utilized. And the workforce is growing in size to meet the business growth. There are now 37 employees, and Marvin expects to hire another 15–20 new employees within the next year.

Job descriptions for the company were originally written by a consultant about eight years ago. They have never been revised and are hopelessly outdated. For the job of marketing representative there is no job description at all, because the job was created only five years ago. As general manager, Marvin is responsible for all HR management matters, but he has little time to devote to them. To help him get a better grip on his HR responsibilities, Marvin has hired you as a part-time HR intern. He has a "gut feeling" that the job descriptions need to be updated or written for the first time and has assigned you that project. Since Marvin has to clear new projects with Alta, he wants you to prepare a brief proposal that he can use to approach her for seeking approval. In that proposal he wants to be able to suggest the following to Alta:

1. Reasons why it is important to update and write new job descriptions
2. An outline of a process that might be followed for doing this that will yield a set of thorough, current job descriptions
3. A process to be used in the future for periodically reviewing and updating these new job descriptions

Marvin wants to meet with you and discuss each of these points. He wants very specific suggestions and ideas from you that he can use to prepare his proposal. What exactly would you suggest to Marvin?

ENDNOTES

1. R. J. Vance, *Employee Engagement and Commitment* (Alexandria, VA: Society for Human Resource Management, 2006), pp. 1, 13; J. K. Harter, F. L. Schmidt, and T. L. Hayes, "Business-Unit-Level Relationship Between Employee Satisfaction, Employee Engagement, and Business Outcomes: A Meta-Analysis," *Journal of Applied Psychology,* 2002, 87, pp. 268–279.
2. For excellent overviews and reviews, see M. T. Brannick and E. L. Levine, *Job Analysis* (Thousand Oaks, CA: Sage, 2002); S. Gael (ed.), *The Job Analysis Handbook for Business, Industry and Government,* Vols. 1 and 2 (New York: Wiley, 1988); R. D. Gatewood and H. S. Feild, *Human Resource Selection,* fifth ed. (Orlando, FL: Harcourt, 2001), pp. 267–363; J. V. Ghorpade, *Job Analysis* (Englewood Cliffs, NJ: 1988); R. J. Harvey, "Job Analysis," in M. D. Dunnette and L. M. Hough (eds.), *Handbook of Industrial and Organizational Psychology,* Vol. 2 (Palo Alto, CA: Consulting Psychologists Press, 1991), pp. 71–163.

3. E. T. Cornelius III, "Practical Findings From Job Analysis Research," in Gael, *The Job Analysis Handbook for Business, Industry and Government,* Vol. 1, pp. 48–70.

4. C. J. Cranny and M. E. Doherty, "Importance Ratings in Job Analysis: Note on the Misinterpretation of Factor Analysis," *Journal of Applied Psychology,* 1988, 73, pp. 320–322.

5. Gatewood and Feild, *Human Resource Selection,* pp. 295–298; Harvey, "Job Analysis," in Dunnette and Hough, pp. 75–79; M. A. Wilson, "The Validity of Task Coverage Ratings by Incumbents and Supervisors: Bad News," *Journal of Business and Psychology,* 1997, 12, pp. 85–95.

6. D. P. Costanza, E. A. Fleishman, and J. C. Marshall-Mies, "Knowledges: Evidence for the Reliability and Validity of the Measures," in N. G. Peterson, M. D. Mumford, W. C. Borman, P. R. Jeannerert, E. A. Fleishman, and K. Y. Levin, *O*NET Final Technical Report, Vol. 1* (Salt Lake City: Utah Department of Workforce Services, 1997), pp. 4-1 to 4-26.

7. M. D. Mumford, N. G. Peterson, and R. A. Childs, "Basic and Cross-Functional Skills: Evidence for Reliability and Validity of the Measures," in Peterson et al., *O*NET Final Technical Report Vol. 1,* pp. 3-1 to 3-36.

8. E. A. Fleishman, D. P. Costanza, and J. C. Marshall-Mies, "Abilities: Evidence for the Reliability and Validity of the Measures," in Peterson et al., *O*NET Final Technical Report, Vol. 2,* pp. 9-1 to 9-26.

9. M. H. Strong, P. R. Jeanneret, S. M. McPhail, and B. R. Blakley, "Work Context: Evidence for the Reliability and Validity of the Measures," in Peterson et al., *O*NET Final Technical Report Vol. 2,* pp. 7-1 to 7-35.

10. F. P. Morgeson, K. Delaney-Klinger, M. S. Mayfield, P. Ferrara, and M. A. Campion, "Self-Presentations Processes in Job Analysis: A Field Experiment Investigating Inflation in Abilities, Tasks, and Competencies," *Journal of Applied Psychology,* 2004, 89, pp. 674–686.

11. For detailed treatments, see Brannick and Levine, *Job Analysis*; Gael, *The Job Analysis Handbook for Business, Industry and Government,* pp. 315–468; Gatewood and Feild, *Human Resource Selection,* pp. 267–363; Harvey, "Job Analysis," in Dunnette and Hough, *Handbook of Industrial and Organizational Psychology*; M. Mader-Clark, *The Job Description Handbook* (Berkeley, CA: Nolo, 2006).

12. Peterson et al., *O*NET Final Technical Report, Vols. 1, 2, 3*; N. G. Peterson, M. D. Mumford, W. C. Borman, P. R. Jeanneret, E. A. Fleishman, K. Y. Levin, M. A. Campion, M. S. Mayfield, F. S. Morgeson, K. Pearlman, M. K. Gowing, A. R. Lancaster, M. B. Silver, and D. M. Dye, "Understanding Work Using the Occupational Information Network: Implications for Research and Practice," *Personnel Psychology,* 2001, 54, pp. 451–492.

13. R. Reiter-Palmon, M. Brown, D. L. Sandall, C. B. Buboltz, and T. Nimps, "Development of an O*Net Web-Based Job Analysis and Its Implementation in the U.S. Navy," *Human Resource Management Review,* 2006, 16, pp. 294–309.

14. M. T. Brannick, E. L. Levine, and F. P. Morgeson, *Job and Work Analysis* (Thousand Oaks, CA: Sage Publications, 2007).

15. R. G. Jones, J. I. Sanchez, G. Parameswaran, J. Phelps, C. Shop-taugh, M. Williams, and S. White, "Selection or Training? A Two-fold Test of the Validity of Job-Analytic Ratings of Trainability," *Journal of Business and Psychology,* 2001, 15, pp. 363–389; F. J. Landy and J. Vasey, "Job Analysis: The Composition of SME Samples," *Personnel Psychology,* 1991, 44, pp. 27–50; D. M. Truxillo, M. E. Paronto, M. Collins, and J. L. Sulzer, "Effects of Subject Matter Expert Viewpoint on Job Analysis Results," *Public Personnel Management,* 2004, 33(1), pp. 33–46.

16. See Brannick and Levine, *Job Analysis,* pp. 265–294; Gael, *The Job Analysis Handbook for Business, Industry and Government,* pp. 315–390; Gatewood and Feild, *Human Resource Selection,* pp. 267–363.

17. American Compensation Association, *Raising the Bar: Using Competencies to Enhance Employee Performance* (Scottsdale, AZ: author, 1996); M. Harris, "Competency Modeling: Viagraized Job Analysis or Impotent Imposter?" *The Industrial-Organizational Psychologist,* 1998, 36(2), pp. 37–41; R. L. Heneman and G. E. Ledford, Jr., "Competency Pay for Professionals and Managers in Business: A Review and Implications for Teachers," *Journal of Personnel Evaluation in Education,* 1998, 12, pp. 103–122; J. S. Shipman, R. A. Ash, M. Battista, L. Carr, L. D. Eyde, B. Hesketh, J. Kehoe, K. Pearlman, E. P. Prien, and J. I. Sanchez, "The Practice of Competency Modeling," *Personnel Psychology,* 2000, 53, pp. 703–740; L. M. Spenser and S. M. Spencer, *Competence at Work* (New York: Wiley, 1993).

18. American Compensation Association, *Raising the Bar: Using Competencies to Enhance Employee Performance,* pp. 7–15.

19. D. Bartram, "The Great Eight Competencies: A Criterion-Centric Approach to Validation," *Journal of Applied Psychology,* 2007, 90, pp. 1185–1203.

20. American Compensation Association, *Raising the Bar: Using Competencies to Enhance Employee Performance,* pp. 35–36.

21. D. Rahbar-Daniels, M. L. Erickson, and A. Dalik, "Here to Stay: Taking Competencies to the Next Level," *WorldatWork Journal,* 2001, First Quarter, pp. 70–77.

22. Shipman et al., "The Practice of Competency Modeling."

23. F. H. Borgen, "Occupational Reinforcer Patterns," in Gael, *The Job Analysis Handbook for Business, Industry and Government,* Vol. 2, pp. 902–916; R. V. Dawis, "Person-Environment Fit and Job Satisfaction," in C. J. Cranny, P. C. Smith, and E. F. Stone (eds.), *Job Satisfaction* (New York: Lexington, 1992); C. T. Kulik and G. R. Oldham, "Job Diagnostic Survey," in Gael, *Handbook for Analyzing Jobs in Business, Industry and Government,* Vol. 2, pp. 936–959; G. Ledford, P. Mulvey, and P. LeBlanc, *The Rewards of Work* (Scottsdale, AZ: WorldatWork/Sibson, 2000).

24. E. E. Ledford and M. I. Lucy, *The Rewards of Work* (Los Angeles, CA: Sibson Consulting, 2003).

25. Ledford and Lucy, *The Rewards of Work,* p. 12.

26. "'Mosh Pits' of Creativity," *Business Week,* Nov. 7, 2005, pp. 98–100.

27. M. Harvey, M. M. Novicevic, and G. Garrison, "Challenges to Staffing Global Virtual Teams," *Human Resource Management Review,* 2004, 14, pp. 275–294.

28. Brannick et al., *Job and Work Analysis.*

29. D. E. Thompson and T. A. Thompson, "Court Standards for Job Analysis in Test Validation," *Personnel Psychology,* 1982, 35, pp. 865–874.

30. Equal Employment Opportunity Commission, *Technical Assistance Manual on the Employment Provisions (Title 1) of the Americans With Disabilities Act* (Washington, DC: author, 1992), pp. II-19 to II-21.

31. K. E. Mitchell, G. M. Alliger, and R. Morgfopoulos, "Toward an ADA-Appropriate Job Analysis," *Human Resource Management Review,* 1997, 7, pp. 5–26; F. Lievens, J. I. Sanchez, and W. De Corte, "Easing the Inferential Leap in Competency Modelling: The Effects of Task-Related Information and Subject Matter Expertise," *Personnel Psychology,* 2001, 57, pp. 847–879; F. Lievens and J. I. Sanchez, "Can Training Improve the Quality of Inferences Made by Raters in Competency Modeling: A Quasi-Experiment," *Journal of Applied Psychology,* 2007, 92, pp. 812–819.

The Staffing Organizations Model

PART THREE

Staffing Activities: Recruitment

CHAPTER FIVE

External Recruitment

The objective of the external recruitment process is to identify and attract job applicants from outside the organization. In external recruiting, the organization is trying to sell itself to potential applicants, so many principles from marketing are applied improve recruiting yields. From among these applicants hiring decisions are to be made.

The recruitment process begins with a planning phase during which both organizational and administrative issues, as well as those pertaining to recruiters, are addressed. Organizational issues include in-house versus external recruitment locations, individual versus cooperative recruitment alliances, and centralized versus decentralized recruitment functions. Administrative issues include requisitions, timing, number, and types of contracts; the recruitment budget; and development of a recruitment guide. Finally, the selection and training of recruiters must be planned.

Next, a recruitment strategy is formed in order to know where, and how, to look for qualified applicants. Knowing where to look requires an understanding of open and targeted recruitment strategies. Knowing how to look requires an understanding of recruitment sources and deciding which ones to use.

Following the formation of strategy, the message to be communicated to job applicants is established, and it is decided which medium should be used to convey the message. The message may be realistic, branded, or targeted. It may be communicated with recruitment brochures or videos, advertisements, voice messages, videoconferencing, online, radio, or e-mail.

Special consideration must be given to applicant reactions to recruiters and the recruitment process in undertaking each of these phases of the external recruitment process. Close attention must also be given to legal issues. This includes consideration of the definition of job applicant, disclaimers, targeted recruitment, electronic recruitment, job advertisements, and fraud and misrepresentation.

RECRUITMENT PLANNING

Before actually identifying and attracting applicants to the organization, two issues must be resolved. First, organizational plans must be made to coordinate the identification and attraction of applicants. Second, administrative issues, such as the number of contacts to be made, recruiters to be used, and the budget to be spent, need to be considered to ensure that there are adequate resources to conduct a successful recruitment campaign.

Organizational Issues

The recruitment process in an organization can be organized in a variety of ways. It can be coordinated in-house or by an external recruitment agency. An organization can do its own recruiting or cooperate with other organizations in a recruitment alliance. Authority to recruit may be centralized or decentralized in the organization.

In-House Versus External Recruitment Agency

Most organizational recruiting is done in-house. Smaller organizations may rely on external recruitment agencies rather than an in-house function to coordinate their recruitment efforts, as smaller organizations may not have the staff or budget to run their own recruitment functions. Organizations with low turnover rates may also prefer to use external recruitment agencies because they recruit so infrequently that it would not make sense to have a recruitment function of their own.

External recruitment agencies are growing in number. Some agencies, such as Elaine R. Shepherd Company, provide full-scale recruitment services ranging from identifying recruitment needs to advertising for applicants and checking references. Others, such as American Classified Services, Inc., simply perform one recruitment activity. Although these services are expensive, the costs may be justified for organizations without a recruitment function or for employers with infrequent vacancies.

Large organizations and ones with frequent recruitment needs should have their own in-house recruitment function. An in-house function is needed to ensure that recruitment costs are minimized, recruitment searches are consistent from opening to closing, and the specific needs of the organization are being met.

Individual Versus Cooperative Recruitment Alliances

Most organizations, especially ones that compete with one another in the same product and labor markets, do not cooperate with one another when recruiting, because one organization's gain (a well-qualified hire) is another organization's loss (loss of a well-qualified candidate). Instead, they conduct their own recruitment programs to maintain a competitive advantage.

There are times, however, when even competitors may enter into cooperative recruitment alliances where arrangements are made to share recruitment resources. Smaller organizations may gain from cooperating with one another in order to minimize recruitment costs. If there is an abundance of applicants in the labor market, with enough good applicants to go around, it may also make sense to cooperate. For example, a group called Hospital Personnel Exchange in Melbourne, Florida, temporarily transferred personnel among hospitals to eliminate the problems of seasonal over- and understaffing for hospitals.

Recruitment alliances take many forms. One major form is government–employer partnership. Such partnerships can involve states or local communities. At the state level, Nebraska discovered that its residents were fleeing to California more than to any other state. In response, Nebraska ran ads at football games, on television, and in print, extolling the state's low cost of living and quality of life. Other states (Michigan, Maryland) have formed similar economic development initiatives to help employers lure qualified applicants to their locations. Even school districts have formed partnerships with local companies to facilitate the hiring of district high school graduates. Another form of partnership involves organizational alliances. The Atlanta Chamber of Commerce, for example, has developed a campaign to lure high-tech talent to the metro area. Syracuse, New York, employers formed a partnership to promote the area as a place to live and work. The goal is to transform Syracuse's permafrost image to a vibrant high-tech center.[1]

Even in a tight market it may make sense to cooperate when it comes to the spouses of job applicants. For example, the Personnel Association of Central Ohio (PACO) has a "trailing spouse network," where employers have a common pool of résumés from spouses following their partner's career move to central Ohio. All PACO members take from and contribute to the résumé pool. By doing so, they are able to hire those job applicants who are unable to relocate unless their spouses find a job in the same area.

Centralized Versus Decentralized Recruitment

The recruitment of external job applicants can be centralized or decentralized by an organization. In a centralized recruitment function, recruitment activities are coordinated by a central group, usually human resources (HR) professionals in the corporate offices. In a decentralized recruitment system, recruitment activities are coordinated by individual business units or individual managers. In most larger organizations, the recruitment function is centralized. Although the ultimate hiring decision resides in the business unit, most organizations centralize the administrative activities associated with recruiting and screening applicants.

One advantage to a centralized recruitment function is that duplications of effort are eliminated. For example, when recruiting at a school, only one advertisement is placed rather than multiple ads for multiple business units. Another advantage to a centralized approach is that it ensures that policy is being interpreted consistently across business units. For example, GM centralized its recruiting system to transmit a consistent message to applicants.[2] Along the same lines, a centralized function helps ensure compliance with relevant laws and regulations. Another factor that facilitates centralized recruiting is the growth in staffing software (see Chapter 13).

Some organizations do have decentralized recruitment functions. One advantage to decentralized recruitment is that recruitment efforts may be undertaken in a more timely manner when there are fewer people to recruit than when a centralized approach is used. Also, the recruitment search may be more responsive to the business unit's specific needs because those involved with recruitment may be closer to the day-to-day operations of the business unit than are their corporate counterparts.

Administrative Issues

In the planning stage of recruitment, attention must be given to administrative issues as well as organizational issues. Human resources information systems (HRISs) are used by many organizations to integrate the filing of requisitions, to develop recruitment budgets, and to process flows.

Requisitions

A requisition is a formal document that authorizes the filling of a job opening, indicated by the signatures of top management. Supervisors are not given discretion to authorize the filling of job openings. Top managers, rather than supervisors, are more likely to be familiar with staffing planning information for the entire organization, and their approval is needed instead to ensure that recruitment activities are coordinated with staffing planning activities.

An example of a requisition is shown in Exhibit 5.1. A well-developed requisition will clearly specify both the quantity and the quality (knowledge, skill, ability and other characteristics [KSAOs]) of labor to be hired. Hence, each requisition will list the number of openings per job and the minimum qualifications an applicant must have. Qualifications should be based on the job requirements matrix.

Many smaller organizations do not have requisitions. They should, however, for two reasons. First, the procedure ensures that staffing activities are consistent with the business plan of the organization. Second, it ensures that the qualifications of the job are clearly detailed so that a good person/job match is made.

Timing

Two factors that drive the decision of when to look for job applicants are lead time concerns and time sequence concerns. As staffing managers have been increasingly called upon to show concrete results for their work, the importance of documenting the time to fill requisitions has grown.

Lead Time Concerns.   Although managers would like to have each position filled immediately on approval of requisitions, this goal is not possible, as recruiters handle a large number of vacancies at any one time. It is possible, however, to minimize the delay in filling vacancies by planning for openings well in advance of their actual occurrence. Effective planning requires that top management prioritize job openings so that they can be filled in the order that best meets the needs of the business. It also requires that recruiters be fully prepared to conduct the search. To do so, recruiters must be knowledgeable about print deadlines for the placement of ads in appropriate periodicals. Also, recruiters should be knowledgeable about the availability of labor in the marketplace. With the growth of Internet recruiting, much hiring is now continuous.[3] For example, log on to Starbucks Web site (*www.starbucks.com*) where a list of job openings is continuously displayed.

Time Sequence Concerns.   In a successful recruitment program, the steps involved in the process are clearly defined and sequenced in a logical order. A staffing flowchart should be used to organize all components of the recruitment process. The sequence of recruitment activities has a large bearing on the time that will be required to fill job vacancies.

A very useful set of indicators for time sequence concerns is known as time-lapse statistics. These statistics provide data on the average length of time that

EXHIBIT 5.1   Personnel Requisition

Position title	Division	Department	Department #
Salary/grade level	Work hours	Location	Reports to

Position eligible for the following incentive programs ☐ Sales commission ☐ Key contributor ☐ Production incentive ☐ Other (specify) ☐ Management incentive ☐ _____	Budgeted ☐ Replacement for: _____ ☐ Yes Transfer/term date_____ ☐ No ☐ Addition to staff

POSITION OVERVIEW

Instructions: (1) Complete Parts I, II, and III. (2) Attach position description questionnaire (if available) or complete reverse side.

I. POSITION PURPOSE: Briefly state in one or two sentences the primary purpose of this position.

II. POSITION QUALIFICATIONS: List the *minimum* education, formal training, and experience required to perform this position.

III. SPECIAL SKILLS: List the specialized clerical, administrative, technical, or managerial skills needed to perform this position.

Do current or previous incumbents possess these qualifications and skills? If no, please describe the reason for these requirements when hiring for this position.

APPROVALS	**FOR HUMAN RESOURCES USE ONLY**
Party responsible for conducting second interview	Posting date_____ Advertising date _____
	Req number _____ Job number _____
Hiring supervisor/manager Date	
	Acceptance date _____Start date _____
Next approval level Date	
	New employee_____
	Source _____
Human resources approval Date	

SOURCE: Reprinted with permission from United Health Care Corporation.

expires between various phases in the recruitment process. Organizations should routinely collect these data in order to assist managers in planning when vacancies are to be filled (see Chapter 13).

Number of Contacts

The pool of applicants to be selected almost always needs to be larger than the number of applicants that eventually will be hired. Some applicants who are contacted may not be interested in the position, and others may not be qualified.

It is very difficult to identify the exact number of contacts needed to fill a particular vacant position. However, historical data are very useful in establishing the targeted number of contacts. If careful records are kept, then yield ratios can be calculated to summarize the historical data and guide decisions about the number of contacts to make. A yield ratio expresses the relationship of applicant inputs to outputs at various decision points. For example, if 90 people were contacted (as identified by the number of résumés submitted) to fill one position, then the yield ratio would be 90:1. To fill two identical positions, it would be necessary to contact 180 applicants, based on the historical yield ratio of 90:1.

Types of Contacts

The types of contacts to be made depend on two factors. First, it is essential that the qualifications needed to perform the job are clearly established. This is done through the process of job analysis, which results in the job requirements matrix. The more clearly these requirements are specified, the smaller the number of applicants who must be contacted to yield a successful candidate, and the narrower the recruitment search can be.

Second, consideration must be given to the job search and the choice process used by applicants. That is, the organization must be aware of where likely applicants search for employment opportunities and what it will take to attract them to the organization. One consistent finding in the research is that job seekers are more likely to find out about jobs through friends and family than they are through employment agencies. Another consistent finding in the research is that job seekers rely heavily on advertisements.

How proactive the organization should be in soliciting applicants is a policy issue that arises when deciding on the types of contacts the organization will make. Some organizations spend very few resources identifying contacts and actively soliciting applicants from these sources. For example, many times grocery stores simply post a job opening in their store window to fill a vacancy. Other organizations, however, are very proactive in making their presence known in the community. Many organizations are becoming involved with educational institutions through scholarships, adopt-a-school programs, mentorships, equipment grants, internships, and career planning services. NASA has programs to help educate teachers, students, and administrators on the application of science and math.[4]

These approaches are likely to build goodwill toward an organization in the community and, as a result, foster greater informal contacts with job applicants.

Research has shown that greater employer involvement with prospective applicants is likely to improve the image of the organization. In turn, a better image of the organization is likely to result in prospective applicants pursuing contact with the organization.[5]

Recruitment Budget

The recruitment process is a very expensive component of organizational staffing. The average cost per hire is $8,924 for exempt employees and $865 for nonexempt employees. As a result of these high costs, many organizations are currently using cost containment programs in their recruitment efforts. Examples include the elimination of display advertising, greater reliance on state employment agencies, and the reduction of on-campus visits for college recruitment.[6] An example of a recruitment budget is shown in Exhibit 5.2.

The high costs of recruitment also point to the importance of establishing a well-developed recruitment budget. Two issues need to be addressed in establish-

---

EXHIBIT 5.2 Example of a Recruitment Budget for 500 New Hires

Administrative Expenses

Staff	32,000
Supplies	45,000
Equipment	10,000
	$87,000

Recruiter Expenses

Salaries	240,000
Benefits	96,000
Expenses	150,000
	$486,000

Candidate Expenses

Travel	320,000
Lodging	295,000
Fees	50,000
Relocation	150,000
	$815,000

Total Recruitment Expenses

87,000 + 486,000 + 815,000 = $1,388,000

Total Cost per Hire

$1,388,000/500 new hires = $2,776

ing a recruitment budget. First, a top-down or bottom-up procedure can be used to gather the information needed to formulate the budget. With a top-down approach, the budget for recruitment activities is set by top management on the basis of the business plan for the organization and on the basis of projected revenues. With a bottom-up approach, the budget for recruitment activities is set up on the basis of the specific needs of each business unit. The former approach works well when the emphasis is on controlling costs. The latter approach works better when commitment to the budget by business unit heads is the goal. A cumbersome, yet useful, method is to combine these two approaches into program-oriented budgeting in which there is heavy involvement in the budgeting process by both top management and business unit leaders.

A second issue that needs to be addressed in establishing a well-developed recruitment budget is to decide whether to charge recruitment costs to business unit users. That is, should recruitment expenses be charged to HR or to the business unit using HR services? Most organizations charge the HR department for the costs of recruitment rather than the business unit users of recruitment activities. Perhaps this is done to encourage each business unit to use the recruitment services of the HR group. However, it should be recognized that this practice of not charging the business unit may result in the business unit users not being concerned about minimizing recruitment costs.

Development of a Recruitment Guide

A recruitment guide is a formal document that details the process to be followed to attract applicants to a job. It should be based on the organization's staffing flowcharts, if available. Included in the guide are details such as the time, money, and staff required to fill the job as well as the steps to be taken to do so. An example of a recruitment guide is shown in Exhibit 5.3.

Although a recruitment guide takes time to produce—time that may be difficult to find in the face of an urgent requisition to be filled—it is an essential document. It clarifies expectations for both the recruiter and the requesting department as to what will be accomplished, what the costs will be, and who will be held accountable for the results. It also clarifies the steps that need to be taken to ensure that they are all followed in a consistent fashion and in accordance with organization policy as well as relevant laws and regulations. In short, a recruitment guide safeguards the interests of the employer, applicant, and recruiter.

Process Flow and Record Keeping

Prior to deciding where and how to look for applicants, it is essential that the organization prepare for the high volume of data that accompanies the filling of vacancies. This high volume of data results from the use of multiple sources to identify candidates (e.g., advertisements, walk-ins, employment agencies), the need to circulate the applicant's credentials to multiple parties (e.g., hiring managers, human resources), and the need to communicate with candidates regarding the status of

---

EXHIBIT 5.3 Recruitment Guide for Director of Claims

Position: Director, Claims Processing

Reports to: Senior Director, Claims Processing

Qualifications: 4-year degree in business;
8 years experience in health care, including 5 in claims, 3 of which should be in management

Relevant labor market: Regional Midwest

Timeline: week of 1/17: Conduct interviews with qualified applicants
2/1/05: Targeted hire date

Activities to undertake to source well-qualified candidates:

Regional newspaper advertising

Post job opening on company Web site

Request employee referrals

Contact regional health and life insurance associations

Call HR departments of regional health and life insurance companies to see if any are outplacing any middle managers

Contact, if necessary, executive recruiter to further source candidates

Staff members involved:

HR Recruiting Manager
Sr. Director, Claims Processing
V.P. Human Resources
Potential peers and direct reports

Budget:

$3,000–$5,000

---

their application. If process flow and record-keeping issues are not addressed before the recruitment search, the organization may become overwhelmed with correspondence that is not dealt with in a timely and professional manner; in turn, the organization may lose well-qualified applicants.

To manage the process flow and record-keeping requirements, an information system must be created for recruitment efforts. An effective information system for recruitment purposes allows the candidate, the hiring manager, and HR representatives to know the status of a candidate's application file at any point in time. The information system tracks the status of the applicant's file as it flows through the recruitment process in the organization. The information system can also periodically issue reports on the timeliness and accuracy with which applicant information is being processed.

The process of managing data and records has been transformed by online applications. Indeed, one might characterize it as a double-edged sword. On the one hand, data entry and record maintenance are facilitated in that applications are immediately transferred into a standardized database, which eliminates data entry and keeps everything in a standard form and a searchable database. On the other hand, using online applications generates much more data, including many applications from individuals who are poorly motivated to join the organization or obviously unqualified for the position, so there is much more data to wade through. To facilitate combing through all of this information, many Web-based recruiting systems have integrated screening tools to eliminate completely unqualified applicants early in the process.

As the applicant progresses through the hiring process, additional record keeping is required. Information needs to be kept as to who has reviewed the file, how long each individual has had the file to be reviewed, what decision has been reached (e.g., reject, invite for a visit, conduct a second interview), and what step needs to be taken next (e.g., arrange for a flight and accommodations, schedule an interview). Throughout the process, communications with the applicant must also be tracked to ensure that applicants know when and if their credentials will receive further review and also to know what other steps, if any, they need to take to secure employment.

Even when an applicant is rejected for a position, there are record-keeping responsibilities. The applicant's file should be stored in the event that another search arises that requires someone with the applicant's qualifications. Such storage should be for a maximum of one year (see "Legal Issues," at the end of the chapter).

Recruiters

Selecting Recruiters

Many studies have been conducted to assess desirable characteristics of recruiters. Reviews of these studies indicate that an ideal recruiter would possess the following characteristics:[7] strong interpersonal skills; knowledge about the organization, jobs, and career-related issues; technology skills (e.g., knowing how to mine databases, Internet recruiting); and enthusiasm about the organization and job candidates. These characteristics represent a start on developing a set of KSAOs to select recruiters.

Actual recruiters used by organizations come from a variety of sources, including HR professionals, line managers, and employees. Each of these sources generally has some distinct advantages and disadvantages relative to the list of desirable characteristics for recruiters. HR professionals may be very knowledgeable about career development issues and enthusiastic about the organization, but lack detailed knowledge regarding specific job responsibilities. Line managers may have detailed knowledge about the company and jobs that they supervise, but not be particularly knowledgeable about career development opportunities. Similarly, employees may have an in-depth understanding of their own jobs, but not have much knowledge of the larger organization. As a result of these trade-offs, there is no single ideal source to draw recruiters from, and all recruiters need training to compensate for inevitable shortcomings.

Training Recruiters

Many recruiters who come from areas outside HR do not have any specialized training in HR. Hence, the training of recruiters is essential. Unfortunately, very few recruiters ever receive any training. Based on current organizational practices, recruiters should receive training in the following areas:[8] interviewing skills, job analysis, interpersonal aspects of recruiting, laws and regulations, forms and reports, company and job characteristics, and recruitment targets. Beyond these traditional areas, it is critical that recruiters receive training in some "nontraditional" areas: technology skills, marketing skills, working with other departments, and ethics.

First, in terms of technology skills, though access to large recruiting Web sites like *Monster.com* is to be expected, it must be recognized that many recruiters are mining these sites. Thus, recruiters must be instructed on accessing "niche" sites that specialize in a particular candidate cohort or personal Web pages, or even infiltrating corporate Web sites. In surfing the Internet, there are strategies to be learned, including "flipping" (finding résumés with links to a particular company), "peeling" (finding links to staff directories in URLs), and "x-raying" (identifying key employees by accessing those places on a company's Web site not directly accessible via links on the main Web page).

Second, recruiters must be trained in marketing and sales techniques.[9] Some of these techniques are very simple, such as surfing résumé sites to get a leg up on the competition. Recruiters also need to be trained on how to be more creative in identifying candidates. For example, in tight labor markets, some recruiters are creative enough to stake out airports, temples and churches, and health clubs. One recruiter even flies from airport to airport just to "raid" the airport clubs for potential recruits. More generally, recruiters need instruction on how to sell their jobs to candidates. For example, recruiters can be trained on how to do market research, how to find job candidates in the market, and how to identify what candidates want. In developing their marketing skills, recruiters can be shown how to link up with other departments, such as marketing and public relations. For example, recruiters may be able to collaborate with marketing efforts to achieve a brand image that not only sells products to customers but sells the organization to prospective hires as well.

Finally, in their efforts to recruit more creatively, recruiters need training on ethical issues in recruitment. Is it ethical for a recruiter to recruit at a competitor's place of business? In parking lots? At weddings or funerals? Some recruiters will even lie to applicants in an effort to lure them. Some might even argue that the Internet strategies of "peeling," "flipping," and "x-raying" cross the ethical line. To ensure that recruiters behave ethically, standards should be developed and recruiters should be trained on these standards.[10]

STRATEGY DEVELOPMENT

Once the recruitment planning phase is complete, the next phase is the development of a strategy. In essence, strategy development helps assess those issues that are fundamental to the organization: open versus targeted recruitment, recruitment sources, and recruiting metrics. Each of these issues will be addressed in turn.

Open Versus Targeted Recruitment

Once a requisition has been received, one of the most difficult aspects of recruitment is knowing where to look for applicants. In theory, the pool of potential job applicants is the eligible labor force (employed, unemployed, discouraged workers, new labor force entrants, and labor force reentrants). In practice, the organization must narrow down this vast pool into segments or strata of workers believed to be the most desirable applicants for the organization. To do so, organizations can use open or targeted recruitment methods.

Open Recruitment

With an open recruitment approach, organizations cast a wide net to identify potential applicants for specific job openings. Very little effort is made in segmenting the market into applicants with the most desirable KSAOs. This approach is very passive in that anyone can apply for an opening. All who apply for a position are considered regardless of their qualifications. The advantage to an open recruitment method is that applicants often see it as being "fair" in that everyone has the opportunity to apply. Open recruitment helps ensure that a diverse set of applicants—including disabled, minority teens, former retirees, veterans, and other overlooked employees groups—are given a fair shot at being considered. Another advantage of open recruitment is that it is useful—perhaps even essential—when large numbers of applicants must be hired. The disadvantage to this approach is that very large numbers of applications must be considered, and it is possible that qualified applicants may be overlooked in the process. Unfortunately, with the growth of Web-based recruiting, many employers have found that open recruiting yields too many applicants, making it very time consuming to review all the résumés and other application materials.[11]

Targeted Recruitment

A targeted recruitment approach is one whereby the organization identifies segments in the labor market where qualified candidates are likely to be. Often, this is done to find applicants with specific characteristics pertinent to person/job or person/organization match.

What are some of the objects of targeted recruitment? Below is a list of targeted recruitment groups (of course, these categories are not mutually exclusive):

- *Key KSAO shortages*—here, the objective is to identify applicants with specific new areas of knowledge or "hot" skills
- *Workforce diversity gaps*—often, one must go beyond open recruitment to reach diverse groups and make special efforts
- *Passive job seekers or noncandidates*—sometimes excellent candidates can be found in "trailing spouses" or other dual-career couples
- *Former military personnel*—especially those newly discharged with key competencies such as leadership
- *Employment discouraged*—long-term unemployed, homemakers, welfare recipients, teenagers, people with disabilities
- *Reward seekers*—those who are attracted to the organization's employee value proposition, which might offer benefits such as flexible work schedules and fully paid health care
- *Former employees*—those with good track records while they were employees
- *Reluctant applicants*—some individuals may have an interest in an organization but are conflicted; research shows that flexible work arrangements may help attract such conflicted individuals[12]

In addition to tailoring messages to reach employees with specific KSAO profiles, some organizations also target specific underrepresented groups, especially women and racioethnic minorities. Such efforts are among the most effective, and the least controversial, elements of affirmative action plans. One of the most common methods for increasing the diversity of applicant pools is to place advertisements in publications targeted at women and minorities. Surveys of job seekers show that women and minorities are especially interested in working for employers that endorse diversity through policy statements and in recruiting materials. Advertisements depicting groups of diverse employees are seen as more attractive to women and racioethnic minorities, which is probably why most organizations depict workforce diversity prominently in their recruiting materials. Effective depiction of diversity should take job functions into account as well; diversity advertisements that fail to show women and minorities in positions of organizational leadership send a negative message about the diversity climate at an organization.[13]

Making the Choice

The choice between open and targeted recruitment is important as it dictates recruiting methods and sources. This is not to suggest that they necessarily achieve different goals. Targeted recruitment can achieve the same ends of inclusion as open recruitment, though by a different mechanism. Whereas open recruitment achieves inclusiveness by encouraging everyone to apply, targeted recruitment may actually seek out particular groups. In theory, open and targeted recruitment can be used in combination. For example, an organization may encourage all applications by posting jobs on its Web site and advertising broadly, while still making special efforts to reach certain populations. Of course, by seeking out one group, one may in a way exclude another from the same consideration. So, before targeted recruitment is undertaken, the organization needs to carefully consider the groups to target, as well as the job skills necessary to perform the job(s) in question. Similarly, before open recruitment is selected, the organization needs to decide whether it is prepared to handle and fairly consider the large number of applications that may flow in.

Recruiting experts suggest that it is not necessary to use just one strategy.[14] Organizations might choose a very open strategy for jobs that are not core to their performance, such as clerical and administrative functions, but then use a much more targeted approach for employees who need highly specific KSAOs. Accenture consulting, for example, suggests that retailers should identify the most critical segments of the workforce and analyze the performance of the most successful employees, then target recruiting to attract employees sharing relevant characteristics with star performers in these high-leverage positions. For less critical positions, a less resource-intensive process might be advisable. Exhibit 5.4 reviews the advantages of open and targeted recruitment, along with suggestions for when each approach is most appropriate.

Recruitment Sources

Fortunately for employers, when conducting a search for applicants, they do not have to identify each possible job applicant. Instead, there are institutions in our economy where job seekers congregate. Moreover, these institutions often act as intermediaries between the applicant and the employer to ensure that a match takes place. These institutions are called recruitment sources or methods in staffing. Some are very conventional and have been around for a long time. Others are more innovative and have less of a track record.

Applicant Initiated

It is a common practice for employers to accept applications from job applicants who physically walk into the organization to apply for a job or who send in résumés. The usual point of contact for unsolicited walk-ins or résumé senders is the receptionist in smaller organizations and the employment office in larger organizations. When applications are accepted, a contact person who is responsible for processing such applicants needs to be assigned. Space needs to be created for walk-ins to complete application blanks and preemployment tests. Hours need to be established when applicants can apply for jobs. Procedures must be in place to ensure that data from walk-ins and résumé senders are entered into the applicant flow process. If walk-ins or résumé senders are treated as unexpected intruders, they may communicate a very negative image about the organization in the community.

Increasingly, unsolicited applications are received electronically. The primary transmission portal for electronic applications is via a company's Web site. When receiving electronic applications, organizations need to make sure that the applications don't get "lost in the system." They need to be regularly forwarded to recruiters or selection decision makers, and those who apply need to be contacted about the disposition of their application. Organizations that receive large numbers of applications submitted electronically will narrow the pool of applicants by scanning résumés for keywords or by requiring all applicants to respond to standardized preemployment questionnaires. Although surveys reveal that most employers believe their Web sites do a better job of attracting applicants than do job boards,[15]

EXHIBIT 5.4   Making the Choice Between Open and Targeted Recruiting

	Technique	Advantages	Best When
Open	Advertising positions with a message appealing to a wide variety of job seekers in a variety of media outlets that will reach the largest possible audience	Ensures that a diverse set of applicants are contacted and considered Lower resource and personnel cost per applicant located	Large numbers of applicants are required; pre-entry qualifications are not as important
Targeted	Focusing advertising and recruiting efforts by tailoring message content to attract segments of the labor market with specific KSAOs or demographic characteristics	Narrows the pool of potential applicants, allowing the organization to concentrate efforts on the most qualified Facilitates a more personal approach to each applicant	The organization needs specific skill sets that are in short supply; hiring for high-leverage positions

many of these Web sites do not live up to their potential. Many have been likened to little more than post office boxes where applicants can send their résumés. Many applicants receive no more than an automated reply.[16] A study of the best practices of the Web sites of 140 high-profile organizations indicates seven features of high-impact Web sites:

1. A site layout that is easily navigated and provides information about the organization's culture
2. A "job cart" function that allows prospective applicants to search and apply for multiple positions within the organization
3. Résumé builders where applicants can easily submit their education, background, and experience
4. Detailed information on career opportunities
5. Clear graphics
6. Personal search engines that allow applicants to create profiles in the organization's database and update the data later
7. Self-assessment inventories to help steer college graduates toward appealing career paths

Organizational Web sites can serve as a "make or break" recruiting opportunity for many organizations.[17] In addition to the principles for Web site design listed above, it is wise to emphasize the organization's employment brand by providing information about the organization's history, culture, and benefits of employment. The look and customization of an organization's Web site often determine whether job seekers decide to submit an application. To assess job seeker preferences, consultants from Brass Ring watch applicants go through the process of visiting company Web sites, with the applicants describing their thought processes aloud. The consultants' research indicates that recruits are often frustrated by complex application systems, especially those that require them to enter the same data multiple times. To keep potential applicants from feeling disconnected from the process of online recruiting, it is advisable to keep in touch with them at every stage of the process. To speed up the process, some organizations inform applicants immediately if there is a mismatch between the information they have provided through the application system and the job requirements, so that they can know immediately that they are not under consideration. Quickly eliminating unacceptable candidates also allows recruiters to respond more quickly to applicants who do have sufficient KSAOs. A review of online job solicitation found that the best Web site advertising offered special features to potential applicants, including opportunities to check where they are in the hiring process, examples of a typical "day in the life" at a company, and useful feedback to applicants regarding their potential fit with the company and job early in the process.

Many organizations have taken these suggestions to heart and are working to improve the functionality of their online recruiting efforts. For example, Red Lobster's recruiting site was revised as part of a comprehensive half-year effort to better leverage the organization's brand-based recruiting strategy. To facilitate exploring work options, candidates are directed through several job options on the basis of their level of experience and are provided detailed descriptions and requirements for each position before they apply. Comparing multiple jobs parallels the format many job seekers might be familiar with from e-commerce sites; essentially, applicants can "shop" for jobs. By encouraging potential applicants to carefully consider a variety of work options, there should be better eventual person-job match. Research also shows that candidates prefer organizational Web sites that allow them to customize the information that they receive. Candidates who consider many jobs might also self-select out of jobs that are not really of interest to them, which might help reduce the applicant pool to a set of more interested, qualified candidates and also reduce turnover down the line.

Employee Referrals

Employees currently working for an employer are a valuable source for finding job applicants. Most estimates suggest that referrals are one of the most commonly used recruiting methods. The vast majority of organizations accept referrals, though only about half have formal programs. SRA International has recruited nearly half of its employees through referrals. The employees can refer people they know to their employer for consideration. In some organizations, a cash bonus is given to employees who refer job candidates who prove to be successful on the job for a given period of time. To ensure that there are adequate returns on bonuses for employee referrals, it is essential that there be a good performance appraisal system in place to measure the performance of the referred new hire. There also needs to be a good applicant tracking system to ensure that new hire performance is maintained over time before a bonus is offered. Other organizations use more creative incentives. Lands' End, based in Dodgeville, Wisconsin, offers a drawing for each employee referral. The winner receives a free trip to a Green Bay Packers football game. Most bonuses range from a few hundred dollars to $1,000.

Referral programs have many potential advantages, including low cost/hire, high-quality hires, decreased hiring time, and an opportunity to strengthen the bond with current employees. Employee referral programs sometimes fail to work because current employees lack the motivation or ability to make referrals. Employees sometimes don't realize the importance of recruitment to the organization. As a result, the organization may need to encourage employee participation by providing special rewards and public recognition along with bonuses for successful referrals. Employees may not be able to match people with jobs, because they do not know about open vacancies or the requirements needed to fill them. Hence, communications regarding job vacancies and the requirements needed to fill those vacancies need to be constantly provided to employees.

Employee Networks

Though networks are not a formal referral program, many organizations use them to identify potential hires. These networks can be one's own network of personal contacts, or they can be formal programs that keep an active database of professional contacts.

Another way of finding applicants is through social networking, where friends or acquaintances are used to connect those looking for applicants to those looking for jobs. Many recruiters have turned to social networking Web sites such as *Jobster*, *LinkedIn*, and *Facebook* as sources for finding qualified job candidates.[18] The number of individuals using these sites has increased dramatically in recent years, especially among younger workers, making it difficult to obtain reliable data on just how many individuals are using these sites at any specific time. There are a number of advantages to using social networking sites. Because many of the connections between users are based on professional background or shared work experiences, networking sites often provide access to groups of potential employees with specific skill sets. Some social networking Web sites geared toward professionals encourage users to indicate the industry and area in which they work. Recruiters can set up their own profile pages with these Web sites, encouraging potential applicants to apply by making personal contacts. By accessing the social network of those already employed in the organization, it is possible to locate passive candidates who are already employed and not necessarily looking for new jobs at the time. In fields where the unemployment rate is very low, such as engineering, health care, and information technology (IT), these passive candidates may be the primary source of potential applicants. As with traditional referrals, a key advantage of using electronic networks is that employers can use their current employees as aids in the recruiting process. However, some recruiters find that these networking sites are not very efficient, because of the large number of passive candidates who are not interested in alternative employment offers. Organizations can face troubling legal and ethical quandaries when using social networking sites because candidates' personal information, such as marital status, health status, or demographics is often publicly available on personal pages. The long-range prospects of these networking sites will no doubt continue to change over time.

Advertisements

A convenient way to attract job applicants is to write an ad that can be placed in newspapers and trade journals and can appear as a banner ad on the Internet. Advertisements can also be recorded and played on radio or television. Cable television channels sometimes have "job shows." Advertisements can be very costly and need to be monitored closely for yield. Using marketing data on audience demographics, employers can diversify their applicant pool by placing ads in media outlets that reach a variety of applicant populations. Research suggests that applicants react more positively to ads that reflect their own demographic group, which should be taken into account when developing a media campaign.[19] By carefully monitoring the results of each ad, the organization can then make a more informed decision as to which ads should be run the next time a position is vacant. To track ads, each ad should be coded to assess the yield. Then, as résumés come into the organization in response to the ad, they can be recorded, and the yield for that ad can be calculated.

Coding an ad is a very straightforward process. For example, in advertising for a vice president of HR, ads may be placed in a variety of HR periodicals, such as *HR Magazine,* and business publications, such as the *Wall Street Journal.* To track responses sent, applicants for the vacant position are asked to respond to Employment Department A for *HR Magazine* or Employment Department B for the *Wall Street Journal*, depending on where they saw the ad. As résumés arrive, those addressed to Department A are coded as responses from *HR Magazine,* and those addressed to Department B are coded as responses from the *Wall Street Journal.*

Employment Web Sites

Millions of job seekers submit their résumés on the Web every year, and there are tens of thousands of job sites online. More than half of the résumés Microsoft receives are over the Internet. A growing problem for applicants is identity theft, where fake jobs are posted online in order to obtain vital information on a person or to extract a fake fee.

Employment Web sites have evolved from their original function as job boards and database repositories of jobs and résumés to become fully featured recruiting and screening centers.[20] For employers who pay a fee, many employment Web sites will provide services like targeted advertising, video advertising, preemployment screening examinations, and applicant tracking. For job seekers, there are resources to facilitate exploring different career paths, information about the communities where jobs are offered, and access to message boards where current and former employees can sound off on the culture and practices of different organizations. Millions of job seekers submit their résumés to employment Web sites every year, and there were at least 40,000 job sites online in 2007. Although it is difficult to obtain precise data on the use of employment Web sites, some recent estimates suggest that they are second only to referrals as a source of new hires. On the other hand, research does suggest that solicitations for employment from electronic bulletin boards are seen as especially low in credibility and informativeness relative to organization Web sites or face-to-face meetings at campus placement offices. Therefore, these methods should not be used without having some supporting practices that involve more interpersonal contact.[21]

One difficulty in the use of the Internet in recruiting is that many sites specifically designed for recruitment become defunct. Conversely, new employment Web sites come online on a nearly daily basis. Thus, one cannot assume that the sites a company has used in the past will be the best options in the future, or that they will even exist. Any attempt to summarize the current state of the Internet job posting board scene needs to be taken with a grain of salt, since the landscape for Internet recruiting is shifting very rapidly.

Posting Jobs on General Internet Employment Web Sites. Most readers of this book will be familiar with the biggest Internet employment Web sites, so it's easy to forget that as recently as 1994 Internet employment Web sites for recruiting were seen as a risky proposition that might not have any future. Since that time, a few early movers and larger entrants have grabbed the lion's share of the market. Three of the biggest employment Web sites are *Monster.com*, *CareerBuilder.com*, and *HotJobs.com*, which collectively are estimated to be responsible for a large portion of external Internet hires. *Monster.com*, which employers can access at *www.hiring.monster.com*, estimated in 2007 that it had over 73 million résumés in its database, and over a million job postings. *CareerBuilder.com*, which employers can access at *www.careerbuilder.com*, similarly estimates that at any time there are over 21 million unique visitors per month, and one million jobs at any time.

General employment Web sites are not limited to simple advertising, as noted earlier. Services are rapidly evolving for these employment Web sites, many now offer the ability to create and approve job requisitions online, manage recruiting tasks, track the progress of open positions and candidates, and report on recruiting metrics like time to hire, cost per hire, or equal employment opportunity (EEO). Several of the larger employment Web sites have developed extensive cross-listing relationships with local newspapers, effectively merging the advantages of local media in terms of credibility and name recognition with the powerful technological advances and large user base of employment Web sites.[22]

Posting Jobs on Niche Employment Web Sites. Although there are advantages to open recruitment, as described earlier, it is also possible to conduct a more targeted web-based recruitment effort through niche employment Web sites.[23] These niche sites focus on specific occupations (there are employment Web sites for jobs ranging from nurses to geologists to metal workers), by industry (sports, chemicals, transportation, human services), or by location (cities, states, or regions often have their own sites). Increasingly, employment Web sites are targeting blue-collar jobs as well. To see examples of niche job sites for a specific occupation, all recruiters need to do is an Internet search of "employment Web sites" coupled with the occupation of interest. Although any one niche job board is unlikely to have a huge number of posters, collectively these more specific niche employment Web sites have been estimated to account for 2/3 of internet hiring. Experienced recruiters claim that the audience for niche employment Web sites is often more highly qualified and interested in specific jobs than are applicants from more general job sites.

Niche job sites have also been developed that cater to specific demographic groups, including boards dedicated to women, African Americans, and Hispanics. Organizations seeking to improve the diversity of their work sites or that are under an affirmative action plan should consider posting in a variety of such specialized employment Web sites as part of their search strategy. Survey data suggest that applicants believe that companies that advertise on these targeted Web sites are more positively disposed toward workforce diversity, further serving to enhance the usefulness of diversity-oriented advertising.[24]

Searching Web-Based Databases.   As opposed to actively posting jobs online, another (but not mutually exclusive) means of recruiting on the Web is to search for applicants without ever having posted a position. Under this process, applicants submit their résumés online, which are then forwarded to employers when they meet the employer's criteria. Such systems allow searching the databases according to various search criteria, such as job skills, years of work experience, education, major, grade-point average, and so forth. It costs applicants anywhere from nothing to $200 or more to post their résumé or other information on the databases. For organizations, there is always a cost. The exact nature of the cost depends on both the database(s) to which the organization subscribes and the services requested. More databases allow organizations to search according to Boolean logic. For example, a recruiter interested in locating résumés of prospective HR managers for a Miami-based manufacturing facility might type "human resources + Miami + manufacturing." One potential pitfall is that online job candidates are not a random sample of the population—the most common user is a young white male. Thus, passive searching may not achieve a sufficiently diverse set of candidates.[25]

Mining Databases.   Though various ploys such as "flipping" and "peeling" are controversial, as noted earlier, many recruiters use them to mine organizational and other databases to obtain intelligence on passive candidates. The power of this strategy is that it allows organizations to identify passive candidates, who may be the best qualified but otherwise might not surface. The disadvantage is that many of these passive candidates may not be interested, and there are ethical issues to consider as well (how would you feel about competitors "x-raying" your Web site for information you never intended for them to have?).

Advantages and Disadvantages of Employment Web Sites.   Web-based recruiting offers many advantages to employers. There is no other method of reaching as many people as quickly as with a job posting. This advantage is particularly important when filling large numbers of positions, when the labor market is national or international, or when the unique nature of the necessary qualifications requires casting a wide net. Furthermore, using employment Web sites provides faster access to candidates. Most have résumés in their system within 24 hours of receipt and their searchable databases facilitate access to candidates with desired qualifications. It is commonly argued that Internet recruiting presents cost advantages, and if one is comparing the cost of an ad in the *Los Angeles Times* with the price for access to an online database, this is no doubt true. Finally, there is administrative convenience (many individuals in the same organization can access the database; it eliminates much "paper pushing").

Some of the past limitations of Web-based recruiting—specifically, that the vast majority of applicants are in the technology area and that most Web users are white males—seem to be improving. On the other hand, recruiting on the Web is not a magical solution for matching applicants to employers. Despite some claims to the contrary, decision makers need to be involved in the process. In fact, some large organizations have created new positions for individuals to manage the Internet sites and databases. It is important to remember that no matter what lofty promises a system makes for screening out undesirable applicants, the system is only as good as the search criteria, which generally make fairly rough cuts (e.g., based on years of experience, educational background, broad areas of expertise). Like all sources, employment Web sites must be evaluated against other alternatives to ensure that they are delivering on their considerable promise, and employers must remember that, for the time being, it is unlikely that the Web can be a sole source for recruiting applicants. The costs of employment Web sites must be weighed against the benefits, including the number of qualified applicants, the relative quality of these applicants, and other criteria such as offer acceptance rates, turnover, and so forth.

Colleges and Placement Offices

Colleges are a source of people with specialized skills for professional positions. Most colleges have a placement office or officer who is in charge of ensuring that a match is made between the employer's interests and the graduating student's interests. Research has shown that campus recruiting efforts are seen as more informative and credible than company Web sites or electronic bulletin boards.[26]

In most cases, the placement office is the point of contact with colleges. It should be noted, however, that not all students use the services of the placement office. Students sometimes avoid placement offices because they believe they will be competing against the very best students and will be unlikely to receive a job offer. Additional points of contact for students at colleges include individual professors, department heads, professional fraternities, honor societies, recognition societies, and national professional societies. Sometimes small colleges are overlooked as a recruitment source by organizations because the small number of students does not make it seem worth the effort to visit. In order to present a larger number of students to choose from, some small colleges have banded together in consortia. For example, the Oregon Liberal Arts Placement Consortia provides a centralized recruitment source for eight public and private small colleges and universities. It is essential that appropriate colleges and universities be selected for a visit.

The first decision an employer needs to make is which colleges and universities are to be targeted for recruiting efforts. This choice often is a difficult one. Some organizations focus their efforts on schools with the best return on investment, and invest in those programs more heavily. Other organizations, especially large organizations with relatively high turnover, find they need to cast a much broader net. In the end, the decision of breadth versus depth comes down to the number of individuals who need to be hired, the recruiting budget, and a strategic decision about whether to invest deeply in a few programs or more broadly in more programs. Some factors to consider when deciding which colleges and universities to target include the following:[27]

1. Past experiences with students at the school, including the quality of recent hires (measured in terms of performance and turnover), offer acceptance rates, and skills, experience, and training in the areas where job openings exist, should be factored in.

2. Rankings of school quality. *U.S. News and World Report, The Gorman Report,* and *Peterson's Guide* are comprehensive rankings of colleges and universities and various degree programs. *Business Week,* the *Wall Street Journal,* and the *Financial Times* provide rankings of business schools. Applicants recruited from highly ranked programs almost always come at a premium, so organizations need to make sure they are getting a good return on their investment.

3. Costs of recruiting at a particular school must be assessed. Colleges and universities that are nearby often mean substantially fewer resources expended on travel (both for recruiters traveling to the school and for bringing applicants in for interviews).

There are several ways an organization can establish a high-quality relationship on campus. A critical task is to establish a good relationship with the placement director. Although most placement directors are eager to make the organization's recruitment process productive and pleasant, there are also many aspects where they exert additional influence over the success of the organization's recruitment of high-quality graduates (e.g., informal discussions with students about good employers, alerting recruiters to impressive candidates). Another way to establish a high-quality relationship with a school is to maintain a presence. This presence can take various forms, and increasingly organizations are becoming more creative and aggressive in establishing relationships with universities and their students. Some investment banks, consulting firms, and other companies shell out $500,000 and more per school to fund career seminars, gifts for students, and fancy dinners. Ernst & Young built a study room at Columbia University, and GE sponsored an e-commerce lab at the University of Connecticut.[28] Other companies are using a nonconventional approach. UPS hired massage therapists to give students massages at job fairs. Ford allowed students to test-drive Fords and Jaguars. Dow held crayfish boils.

Of course, relationship building is not just about doling out money, and smaller organizations are not likely to have the resources. Beyond building a good relationship with the placement director and providing financial support, recruiters should build relationships with other key people (associate dean, other placement office staff, key faculty, members of student organizations). It is also important to keep in touch with these people beyond the day or week the recruiter visits campus. Finally, care must be taken to obtain permission for all activities. One dot-com company was banned from a prestigious MBA program for offering students signing bonuses of BMWs, among other nonconventional ploys, without alerting career services of its plans.[29]

Employment Agencies

A source of nonexempt employees and lower-level exempt employees is employment agencies. These agencies contact, screen, and present applicants to employers for a fee. The fee is contingent on successful placement of a candidate with an employer and is a percentage of the candidate's starting salary (around 25%). During difficult economic periods, employers cut back on the use of these agencies and/or attempt to negotiate lower fees in order to contain costs.

Care must be exercised in selecting an employment agency. It is a good idea to check the references of employment agencies with other organizations that have used their services. Allegations abound regarding the shoddy practices of some of these agencies. They may, for example, flood the organization with résumés. Unfortunately, this flood may include both qualified and unqualified applicants. A good agency will screen out unqualified applicants and not attempt to dazzle the organization with a large volume of résumés. Poor agencies may misrepresent the organization to the candidate and the candidate to the organization. Misrepresentation may take place when the agency is only concerned about a quick placement (and fee) and pays no regard to the costs of poor future relationships with clients. A good agency will be in business for the long run and not misrepresent information and invite turnover. Poor agencies may pressure managers to make decisions when they are uncertain or do not want to do so. Also, they may "go around" the HR staff in the organization to negotiate "special deals" with individual managers. Special deals may result in paying higher fees than agreed on with HR and overlooking qualified minorities and women. A good agency will not pressure managers, make special deals, or avoid the HR staff. Finally, it is important to have a signed contract in place where mutual rights and responsibilities are laid out.

Executive Search Firms

For higher-level professional positions or jobs with salaries of $100,000 and higher, executive search firms, or "headhunters," may be used. Like employment agencies, these firms contact, screen, and present résumés to employers. The difference between employment agencies and search firms lies in two primary areas. First, search firms typically deal with higher-level positions than those of employment agencies. Second, search firms are more likely to operate on the basis of a retainer rather than a contingency. Search firms that operate on a retainer are paid regardless of whether a successful placement is made. The advantage of operating this way, from the hiring organization's standpoint, is that it aligns the interests of the search firm with those of the organization. Thus, search firms operating on retainer do not feel compelled to put forward candidates just so their contingency fee can be paid. Moreover, a search firm on retainer may be less likely to give up if the job is not filled in a few weeks. Of late, business has been slow for executive search firms, partly due to the moderate economic growth and the bustling online recruiting business. That means that companies are able to negotiate smaller fees (retainers or contingencies).[30]

Whether contracting with a search firm on a contingency or retainer basis, organizations cannot take a completely hands-off approach to the recruitment process; they need to keep tabs on the progress of the search and, if necessary, "light a fire" under search firms. To expedite the search process, some organizations are going online. *Monster.com*'s Web site has an area that caters to executives. A disadvantage of most online databases is that they do not include passive candidates—executives who may be highly qualified for the position but who are not actively looking. Some companies, such as Direct Search of the United States, sell internal corporate telephone directories to organizations and search firms looking for executives. This practice is, of course, controversial, but it appears to be legal as a copyright on a directory generally covers only artwork and unique design features. For more information about executive recruiters, see *www.kennedypub.com*. This publication lists over 8,000 recruiters along with their specialty.

Increasingly, executive search firms are getting into the appraisal business, where a company pays the search firm to provide an assessment of the company's top executives. On one level this makes sense, since executive search firms are in the assessment business. The problem is that since the executive assessment pays much less than the retainer or contingency fees for hiring an executive, the search firms have an incentive to pronounce top executives substandard (so as to justify bringing in an outsider). This is exactly what happened with a top executive search firm whose executive recruiters negatively evaluated an executive, only to recommend hiring an outsider, for which the recruiters were compensated handsomely. Given these inherent conflicts of interest, organizations should avoid using the same company to hire new executives and appraise its existing executive team.[31]

Professional Associations and Meetings

Many technical and professional organizations have annual meetings around the country at least once a year. Many of these groups run a placement service for their members. There may be a fee to recruit at these meetings. This source represents a way to attract applicants with specialized skills or professional credentials. Also, some meetings represent a way to attract women and minorities. For example, the National Council of Black Engineers and Scientists holds an annual meeting.[32] In addition to having placement activities at annual conventions, professional associations may also have a placement function throughout the year. For example, it is a common practice in professional association newsletters to advertise both positions available and interested applicants. Others may also have a computerized job and applicant bank.

Social Service Agencies

All states have an employment or job service. These services are funded by employer-paid payroll taxes and are provided by the states to help secure employment for those seeking it, particularly those currently unemployed. Typically, these services refer low- to middle-level employees to employers. For jobs to be filled properly, the hiring organization must maintain a close relationship with the employment service. Job qualifications need to be communicated clearly to ensure that proper screening takes place by the agency. Positions that have been filled must be reported promptly to the agency so that résumés are not sent for closed positions. The federal Job Corps program is another option. Job Corps is designed to help individuals between 16 and 24 years of age obtain employment. The program targets individuals with lower levels of education and prepares them for entry-level jobs through a combination of work ethic training and general job skills. For employers, Job Corps can provide specialized training, prescreening of applicants, and tax benefits. Some agencies in local communities may also provide outplacement assistance for the unemployed who cannot afford outplacement services. The applicants who use these services may also be listed with a state employment service as well. Community agencies may also offer counseling and training.

The U.S. Department of Labor has provided the funding for states to develop one-stop career centers that will provide workers with various programs, benefits, and opportunities related to finding jobs. The centers' emphasis is on providing customer-friendly services that reach large segments of the population and are fully integrated with state employment services. For example, when Honda decided to build its Odyssey plant in Alabama, part of the deal was that the state would establish a close partnership with Honda to recruit and train employees.[33] Nissan has established similar relationships with the states of Mississippi and Tennessee. The state of Illinois provides customized applicant screening and referral to employers so efficiently that some employers, like Jewel Companies, a grocery store chain, use the service as an extension of their HR department.[34]

Outplacement Services

Some organizations retain an outplacement firm to provide assistance to employees who are losing their jobs. Outplacement firms usually offer job seekers assistance in the form of counseling and training to help facilitate a good person/job match. Most large outplacement firms have job banks, which are computerized listings of applicants and their qualifications. Registration by employers to use these job banks is usually free.

Larger organizations experiencing a downsizing may have their own internal outplacement function and perform the activities traditionally found in external outplacement agencies. They may also hold in-house job fairs. The reason for this in-house function is to save on the costs of using an external outplacement firm and to build the morale of those employees who remain with the organization and are likely to be affected by their friends' loss of jobs.

Job Fairs

Professional associations, schools, employers, the military, and other interested organizations hold career or job fairs to attract job applicants. Typically, the sponsors of a job fair will meet in a central location with a large facility in order to provide information, collect résumés, and screen applicants. Often, there is a fee for employers to participate. Job fairs may provide both short- and long-term gains. In the short run, the organization may identify qualified applicants. In the long run, it may be able to enhance its visibility in the community, which, in turn, may improve its image and ability to attract applicants for jobs.

For a job fair to yield a large number of applicants, it must be advertised well in advance. Moreover, advertisements may need to be placed in specialized publications likely to attract minorities and women. In order for an organization to attract quality candidates from all of those in attendance, the organization must be able to differentiate itself from all the other organizations competing for applicants at the job fair. To do so, giveaway items such as mugs and key chains with company logos can be distributed to remind the applicants of employment opportunities at a particular organization. An even better promotion may be to provide attendees at the fair with assistance in developing their résumés and cover letters.

One strength of job fairs is also a weakness—although a job fair enables the organization to reach many people, the typical job fair has around 1,600 applicants vying for the attention of about 65 employers. Given the ratio of 25 applicants for every employer, the typical contact with an applicant is probably shallow. In response, some employers instead (or also) devote their resources to information sessions geared toward a smaller group of specially qualified candidates. During these sessions, the organization presents information about itself, including its culture, working environment, and career opportunities. Small gifts and brochures are also typically given out. One recent research study showed that applicants who were favorably impressed by an organization's information session were significantly more likely to pursue employment with the organization. Other studies show that job fairs that allow for interpersonal interactions between job seekers and company representatives are seen as especially informative by job seekers. Thus, both applicants and employers find information sessions a valuable alternative, or complement, to job fairs.[35]

Increasingly, job fairs are being held online. Most online job fairs have preestablished time parameters. One online recruiting site held a job fair that included 240 participating companies. In these virtual job fairs, recruiters link up with candidates through chat rooms.

Co-ops and Internships

Students currently attending school are sometimes available for part-time work. Two part-time working arrangements are co-ops and internships. Under a co-op arrangement, the student works with one employer on an alternating quarter basis. In one quarter the student works full time, and in the next quarter the student attends school full time. Under an internship arrangement, the student has a continuous period of employment with an employer for a specified period of time. These approaches allow an organization to obtain services from a part-time employee for a short period of time, but they also allow the organization the opportunity to assess the person for a full-time position after graduation. One manager experienced in working with interns commented, "Working with them is one of the best talent-search opportunities available to managers."[36] In turn, interns have better employment opportunities as a result of their experiences.

Internships and co-op assignments can take a variety of different forms. One type of assignment is to have the student perform a part of the business that occurs on a periodic basis. For example, some amusement parks that operate only in the summer in northern climates may have a large number of employees who need to be hired and trained in the spring. A student with a background in HR could perform these hiring and training duties. Increasingly, colleges and universities are giving students college credit for, and even in some cases instituting a requirement for, working as a part of their professional degree.[37] A student in social work, for example, might be required to work in a social work setting. Occasionally, experience shows that some internships and co-op assignments do not provide these meaningful experiences that build on the qualifications of the student. Research shows that school-to-work programs often do not provide high utility to organizations in terms of benefit-cost ratios. Thus, organizations need to evaluate co-ops and internships not only in terms of the quality for the student but in terms of the cost-benefit economic perspective as well.[38]

Meaningful experiences benefit both the organization and the student. The organization gains from the influence of new ideas the student has been exposed to in his or her curriculum, and the student gains from having the experience of having to apply concepts while facing the realities of organizational constraints. For both parties to gain, it is important that a learning contract be developed and signed by the student, the student's advisor, and the corporate sponsor. The learning contract becomes, in essence, a job description to guide the student's activities. Also, it establishes the criteria by which the student's performance is assessed for purposes of grading by the academic advisor and for purposes of successful completion of the project for the organization. In the absence of a learning contract, internships can result in unrealistic expectations by the corporate sponsor, which, in turn, can result in disappointment when these unspoken expectations are not met.

To secure the services of students, organizations can contact the placement offices of high schools, colleges, universities, and vocational technology schools. Also, teachers, professors, and student chapters of professional associations can be contacted to obtain student assistance. Placement officials can provide the hiring organization with the policies that need to be followed for placements, while teachers and professors can give guidance on the types of skills students could bring to the organization and the organizational experiences the students would benefit from the most.

Alternative Sources

Several innovative sources might also be experimented with, particularly for purposes of widening the search.

Interest Groups. There are many associations that help facilitate the interests of their members. Two such groups are the American Association for Retired Persons (AARP) and the National Association for the Advancement of Colored People (NAACP). For example, when Home Depot was anticipating 35,000 new jobs, it partnered with AARP to help fill some of these positions.[39]

Realtors. Some realtors now offer employment services for trailing partners. When one person in a relationship must relocate to further a career, the Realtor may also help the trailing partner find a new job.

Alternative Media Outlets. Although most recruiters are familiar with the advantages of Internet, radio, television, and print advertising, there are other media outlets that have been explored less frequently that might offer a recruiter a competitive advantage for attracting candidates. For example, BNSF Railway finds that advertising for jobs in movie theaters is an effective way to reach a diverse group of candidates who might not otherwise consider working in the rail industry. The BNSF Railway recruiting method is notable for its use of movie theater advertisements to stimulate initial interest in employment opportunities, coupled with a Web site follow-up to provide more information about open positions. In another unusual example of innovative media recruiting, the U.S. Army has used a very popular online video game called "America's Army" to draw in thousands of recruits.[40]

Talent Pipeline. Some organizations develop a talent pipeline that includes individuals who may not take a job immediately but who the organization would like to attract into the organization in the future. Managing an organization's talent pipeline means establishing effective relationships even before positions come open. Some organizations try to develop an early relationship with incoming college freshmen in hopes that they will consider the organization as a potential employer when they graduate. Organizations that engage in large-scale collaborative research and development efforts with universities also cultivate relationships with faculty, with the hope of eventually luring them into private sector work at some point further down the line. Many organizations establish folders or databases of high-potential individuals who are either still receiving an education or work for other companies who have demonstrated potential, and then send materials to these employees regularly about potential career prospects within the company. For example, United Health Group maintains interest among high-potential employees by conducting exploratory interviews, sending routine e-mails about openings, and conducting seminars.[41]

Former Employees. Former employees can be an ideal source of future applicants, either by recruiting them to come back to the organization or by asking them if they can provide referrals. Former employees will be especially knowledgeable about the organization and jobs within the organization. As return employees, they will know the organization and its culture and will also be well known to those inside the organization. This will cut down on orientation costs and also means that they can get into the flow of work more quickly. As referral sources, they can convey their personal observations to other job seekers in advance, which means that those who decide to apply will be better informed. Using former employees as a recruiting source naturally means that the organization will need to ensure that it remains on good terms with departing employees and keeps channels of communication open after employees leave. Many organizations that undergo cyclical layoffs or downsizing in lean times might also seek to rehire those who were laid off previously when the organization returns to an expansionary strategy.[42]

Recruiting Metrics

Each recruiting source has strengths and weaknesses. Determining the best method for any organization entails assessing the costs and benefits of each method and then selecting the optimal combination of sources to meet the organization's strategic needs. Exhibit 5.5 provides an overview of the metrics that might be expected for the categories of recruiting activities along with issues to be considered relevant to each source. Our conclusions for the number and types of applicants drawn by each method are informed by a number of studies comparing recruiting sources.[43] Although broad generalizations can be made regarding quantity, quality, cost and impact on HR outcomes for different recruiting methods, each company's unique labor market situation will need to be considered since the meta-analytic evidence does show considerable variety in the effects of recruiting variables on applicant attraction.

Sufficient Quantity

The more broadly transmitted the organization's search methods, the more likely it is that a large number of individuals will be attracted to apply. Other methods of recruiting naturally tend to be more focused and will draw a comparatively small number of applicants. It should be noted that with the ability of some broad recruiting methods, like advertising and Internet postings, to reach thousands of individuals, it might be to an organization's advantage not to attract too many applicants, because of the costs associated with processing all of the applications.

Sufficient Quality

Recruiting methods that directly link employers to an employee base with exceptional skills will enable an employer to save some money on screening and selection processes, but the narrower the search, the more likely it is that the organization will be engaged in a long-term process of looking.

Cost

The costs of any method of recruiting are the direct expenses involved in contacting job seekers and processing their applications. Some sources, such as radio advertisements, sophisticated Web site portals that customize information and provide employees with feedback, and search firms, are quite expensive to develop. These methods may be worth the cost if the organization needs to attract a large number of individuals, if KSAOs for a job are in short supply, or if the job is crucial to the organization's success. On the other hand, organizations that need fewer employees or that require KSAOs that are easily found discover that lower-cost methods like applicant-initiated recruiting or referrals are sufficient to meet their needs. Some fee-based services, like employment agencies, are able to process applications inexpensively because the pool of applicants is prescreened for relevant KSAOs.

Impact on HR Outcomes

A considerable amount of research has been conducted on the effectiveness of various recruitment sources and can be used as a starting point as to which sources are likely to be effective. Research has defined effectiveness as the impact of recruitment sources on increased employee satisfaction, job performance, diversity, and retention. Evidence suggests that, overall, referrals and job trials are likely to attract employees who have a better understanding of the organization and its culture, and therefore they tend to result in employees who are more satisfied, more productive, and less likely to leave. Conversely, sources like newspaper advertising and employment agencies can produce employees who are less satisfied and productive. Any general conclusions regarding the effectiveness of recruitment sources should be tempered by the fact that the location of an organization, the compensation and benefits packages provided, the level of workers, and the typical applicant experience and education levels may moderate the efficacy of these practices.

EXHIBIT 5.5 Potential Recruiting Metrics for Different Sources

Recruiting Sources	Quantity	Quality	Costs	Impact on HR
Applicant initiated	Contingent on how widely the company's brand is known	Highly variable KSAO levels if no skill requirements are posted	Application processing and clerical staff time	Higher training costs, lower performance, higher turnover
Employee referrals	Generates a small number of applicants	Better fit because current employees will inform applicants about the culture	Signing bonuses are sometimes provided to increase quantity	Higher performance, higher satisfaction, lower turnover, lower diversity

(continued)

EXHIBIT 5.5   Continued

Recruiting Sources	Quantity	Quality	Costs	Impact on HR
Employee networks	Potentially a large number of individuals, depending on employee use of networks	Depends on whether networks are made up of others with similar skills and knowledge	Time spent searching through networks and soliciting applications	Potentially similar results to referrals, although results are unknown
Advertisements	Large quantity for general media ads, fewer applicants for specialized media outlets	Highly variable KSAO levels; can specify required skills in advertisement to limit applicant pool	Development of advertisement, media source costs	Lower job performance, higher turnover, can increase diversity
Employment Web sites	Often opens to very large pool, although niche sites have a more narrow pool	Can provide specific keywords to limit applications to those with specific KSAOs	Subscription fees or user fees from database services	Good tracking data, potentially lower satisfaction and higher turnover
Colleges and placement offices	About 50 individuals can be personally contacted at each university per day	High levels of job-relevant human capital, usually screened based on cognitive ability, little work experience	Time costs of establishing relationships, traveling to college locations	Initial training and development for inexperienced workers, can increase average KSAO levels
Employment agencies	Many applicants for lower-level jobs, fewer applicants available for managerial or executive positions	Applicants will be prescreened; organizations are often able to try out candidates as temps prior to hiring	Fees charged by employment agencies	Reduced costs of screening candidates, improved person/job match

(continued)

EXHIBIT 5.5 **Continued**

Recruiting Sources	Quantity	Quality	Costs	Impact on HR
Executive search firms	Only a small number of individuals will be contacted	Search firms will carefully screen applicants, usually experienced candidates	Fees for executive searches can be over 1/2 of the applicant's annual salary	Reduced staff time required because the search firm finds applicants; very high costs for firms
Professional associations and meetings	Comparatively few candidates will be identified for each job opening	Those attending professional meetings will be highly engaged and qualified	Cost of attending meetings and direct interviewing with staff can be very high	Superior performance, although those seeking jobs at meetings may be "job hoppers"
Social service agencies	There are usually a limited number of individuals available, although this varies by skill level	Applicants may have had difficulty finding jobs through other routes because of lack of skills	Often there are direct financial incentives for hiring from these agencies	Potentially greater training costs, higher levels of diversity
Outplacement services	A limited number of individuals available	Applicants are typically experienced workers, although there may be questions about why they were laid off	Registration for employers is typically free	Lower training costs because of experience; effects on job performance unknown
Job fairs	About 40 applicants can be personally contacted per recruiter per day	Often draws in individuals with some knowledge of the company or industry	Advertising and hosting costs are considerable, although this is an efficient way to screen many candidates	Higher levels of diversity if targeted to diverse audiences, effects on performance, satisfaction unknown
Co-ops and internships	Only a small number of interns can be used in most organizations	High levels of formal educational preparation, but few interns will have work experience	Cost of paid interns can be very high, unpaid interns are a huge cost savings although they often require staff time	Those who are hired will be prescreened, and should have higher performance and lower turnover

SEARCHING

Once the recruitment planning and strategy development phases are completed, it is time to actively conduct the search. Searching for candidates first requires the development of a message and then the selection of a medium to communicate that message. Each of these phases is considered in turn.

Communication Message

Types of Messages

The communication message to applicants could focus on conveying realistic, employment brand, or targeted information.

Realistic Recruitment Message.   A realistic recruitment message portrays the organization and job as they really are, rather than describing what the organization thinks job applicants want to hear. Organizations continue to describe themselves in overly positive terms, overstating desired values to applicants such as risk taking, while understating undesirable values such as rules orientation. Some would argue this is not the best message to send applicants on either moral or practical grounds. While hyping the benefits of joining up may work for the army, where recruits are obligated to remain for three to five years, employees generally have no such obligation.

A very well-researched recruitment message is known as a realistic job preview, or RJP.[44] According to this practice, job applicants are given a "vaccination" by being told verbally, in writing, or on videotape what the actual job is like.[45] An example of the attributes that might be contained in an RJP is shown in Exhibit 5.6. It shows numerous attributes for the job of elementary school teacher. Note that the attributes are quite specific and that they are both positive and negative. Information like this "tells it like it is" to job applicants.

EXHIBIT 5.6   Example of Job Attributes in an RJP for Elementary School Teachers

Positive Job Attributes
Dental insurance is provided
Innovative teaching strategies are encouraged
University nearby for taking classes
Large support staff for teachers

Negative Job Attributes
Salary growth has averaged only 2% in past three years
Class sizes are large
The length of the school day is long
Interactions with community have not been favorable

After receiving the vaccination, job applicants can decide whether they want to work for the organization. The hope with the RJP is that job applicants will self-select into and out of the organization. By selecting into the organization, the applicant may be more committed to working there than he or she might otherwise have been. When an applicant self-selects out, the organization does not face the costs associated with recruiting, selecting, training, and compensating an employee, only to then have him or her leave because the job did not meet his or her expectations.

A great deal of research has been conducted on the effectiveness of RJPs, which appear to lead to somewhat higher job satisfaction and lower turnover. This appears to be true because providing applicants with realistic expectations about future job candidates helps them better cope with job demands once they are hired. RJPs also appear to foster the belief in employees that their employer is concerned about them and honest with them, which leads to higher levels of organizational commitment.

RJPs may lead applicants to withdraw from the recruitment process, although a recent review suggests that they have little effect on attrition from the recruitment process. This may appear to be great news to employers interested in using RJPs: providing applicants with realistic information provides employers with more satisfied and committed employees while still maintaining applicant interest in the position. Where the situation may become problematic is when one considers the type of applicant "scared away" by the realistic message. It appears plausible that the applicants most likely to be repelled by the realistic message are high-quality applicants, because they have more options. In fact, research suggests that the negative effects of RJPs on applicant attraction are particularly strong for high-quality applicants (those whose general qualifications are especially strong) and those with direct experience or familiarity with the job.

Although RJPs appear to have both weakly positive consequences (slightly higher job satisfaction and lower turnover among new hires) and negative consequences (slightly reduced ability to hire high-quality applicants), these outcomes have been found to be affected by a number of factors. A recent review of 40 studies on the effectiveness of RJPs suggested that RJPs had weak effects, but to some extent these effects were affected by a number of factors. The following recommendations can be gleaned from these findings:

- RJPs presented very early in the recruitment process are less effective in reducing posthire turnover than those presented just before or just after hiring.
- Posthire RJPs lead to higher posthire levels of job performance than do RJPs presented before hiring.
- Verbal RJPs tend to reduce turnover more than written or videotaped RJPs.
- RJPs are less likely to lead to turnover when the organization "restricts" turnover for a period of time after the RJP (with contracts, above-market salaries, etc.).

In general, these findings suggest that RJPs should be given verbally (rather than in writing or by showing a videotape) and that it is probably best to reserve their use for later in the recruiting process (RJPs should not be part of the initial exposure of the organization to applicants).[46]

Employment Brand.   Organizations wishing to portray an appealing message to potential applicants may develop an "employment brand" to attract applicants. An employment brand is a "good company tag" that places the image of "being a great place to work" or "employer of choice" in the minds of job candidates. An organization's employment brand is closely related to its product market image. And like general product awareness, the more "customers" (in this case, potential applicants) are aware of an organization's employment brand, the more interested they are in pursuing a job.[47] Organizations that are well known by potential applicants may not need to engage in as much advertising for their jobs. Big-name organizations that market well-known products, such as Microsoft, Apple, Sony, and Disney, often have many more applicants than they need for most openings. Organizations with lower profiles may have to actively advertise their employment brand to bring in more applicants. One of the best ways for smaller organizations to emphasize their unique brand is to emphasize the organization's most attractive attributes. Experts in corporate branding also encourage employers to compare their own organizational employment offerings to the competition to see how they are unique, and then highlight these unique advantages in organizational recruiting messages. Under a branding strategy, the U.S. Marine Corps emphasized the Marines as an elite group of warriors rather than focusing on the financial advantages of enlistment, which had been done in the past.

One way to enhance an employment brand is to be named to *Fortune's 100 Best Companies to Work For* list. Being named to this list communicates to applicants that the organization treats its employees fairly, has employees who like their jobs, and offers good benefits. Obviously, this can be an enormous recruiting asset. Southwest Airlines, a longtime member of the list, enjoys 80 applicants for every opening.

Beyond reputation, another employment brand may be value- or culture-based. For example, GE has long promoted its high performance expectations in order to attract achievement-oriented applicants seeking commensurate rewards. Organization Web sites are often used as a method to convey information regarding an organization's culture and emphasize the employment brand. Most organizational Web sites provide information regarding their history, culture, diversity, benefits, and specific job information under a "careers" heading. It is informative to look through a series of these organizational Web sites to see how organizations cater to applicants. For example, Merck's corporate Web site shows an organization that is conveying a message of professional development and social responsibility, whereas Goldman Sachs emphasizes performance and success and Coca-Cola emphasizes global opportunities and fun.

There are several possible benefits to branding. Of course, establishing an attractive employment brand may help attract desired applicants to the organization. Moreover, having an established brand may help retain employees who were attracted to the brand to begin with. Research suggests that identifiable employment brands may breed organizational commitment on the part of newly hired employees.[48]

Research shows that having an employment brand can attract applicants to an organization, even beyond job and organizational attributes. Evidence also suggests that employers are most able to get their brand image out when they engage in early recruitment activities such as advertising or generating publicity about the company.[49]

Targeted Messages.   One way to improve upon matching people with jobs is to target the recruitment message to a particular audience. Different audiences may be looking for different rewards from an employer. This would appear to be especially true of special applicant populations, such as teenagers, older workers, welfare recipients, people with disabilities, homeless individuals, veterans, and displaced homemakers, who may have special needs. Older workers, for example, may be looking for employers that can meet their financial needs (e.g., supplement Social Security), security needs (e.g., retraining), and social needs (e.g., place to interact with people). College students appear to be attracted to organizations that provide rewards and promotions on the basis of individual rather than group performance. Also, most college students prefer to receive pay in the form of a salary rather than in the form of incentives.[50]

Choice of Messages

The different types of messages—realistic, branded, and targeted—are not likely to be equally effective under the same conditions. Which message to convey depends on the labor market, vacancy characteristics, and applicant characteristics.

A summary of the three types of messages is provided in Exhibit 5.7. If the labor market is tight and applicants are difficult to come by, then realism may not be an effective message, because to the extent that applicants self-select out of the applicant pool, fewer are left for an employer to choose from during an already-tight labor market. Hence, if the employment objective is simply to fill job slots in the short run and worry about turnover later, a realistic message will have counterproductive effects. Obviously, then, when applicants are in abundance and turnover is an immediate problem, a realistic message is appropriate.

During a tight labor market, branded and targeted messages are likely to be more effective in attracting job applicants. Attraction is strengthened as there are inducements in applying for a job. In addition, individual needs are more likely to be perceived as met by a prospective employer. Hence, the applicant is more motivated to apply to organizations with an attractive or targeted message than those without. During loose economic times when applicants are plentiful, the branded

---

EXHIBIT 5.7 **Comparing Choice of Messages**

	Information Conveyed	Applicant Reactions	Potential Drawback	Best For
Realistic	Both positive and negative aspects of a job and organization are described	Some applicants self-select out; those who remain will have a better understanding of the job and will be less likely to leave	The best potential applicants may be more likely to leave	Loose labor markets or when turnover is costly
Branded	An appealing description is developed based on marketing principles, emphasizing unique features of the organization	Positive view of the organization, increased intention to apply for jobs, and better prehire information about benefits of the job	Overly positive message may result in employee dissatisfaction after hire	Tight labor markets or for higher-value jobs
Targeted	Advertising themes are designed to attract a specific set of employees	Better fit between application message and specific applicant groups	May dissuade applicants who aren't interested in the work attributes featured in the message from applying	Specific KSAOs, or seeking a specific type of applicant

or targeted approaches may be more costly than necessary to attract an adequate supply of labor. Also, they may set up false expectations concerning what life will be like on the job, and thus lead to turnover.

Job applicants have better knowledge about the actual characteristics of some jobs than others. For example, service sector jobs, such as that of cashier, are highly visible to people. For these jobs, it may be redundant to give a realistic message. Other jobs, such as an outside sales position, are far less visible to people. They may seem very glamorous (e.g., sales commissions) to prospective applicants who fail to see the less glamorous aspects of the job (e.g., a lot of travel and paperwork).

Some jobs seem to be better suited to special applicant groups, and hence, a targeted approach may work well. For example, older employees may have social needs that can be well met by a job that requires a lot of public contact. Organizations, then, can take advantage of the special characteristics of jobs to attract applicants.

The value of the job to the organization also has a bearing on the selection of an appropriate recruitment message. Inducements for jobs of higher value or worth to the organization are easier to justify in a budgetary sense than inducements for jobs of lower worth. The job may be of such importance to the organization that it is willing to pay a premium through inducements to attract well-qualified candidates.

Some applicants are less likely than others to be influenced in their attitudes and behaviors by the recruitment message. In a recent study, for example, it was shown that a realistic message is less effective for those with considerable previous job experience.[51] A targeted message does not work very well if the source is seen as not being credible.[52] Inducements may not be particularly effective with applicants who do not have a family or have considerable wealth.

Communication Medium

Not only is the message itself an important part of the recruitment process, so, too, is the selection of a medium to communicate the message. The most common recruitment mediums are recruitment brochures, videos and videoconferencing, advertisements, direct contact, and online services.

Effective communication media are high in richness and credibility. Rich media channels allow for timely personal feedback and a variety of different methods of conveying messages (e.g., visual images, text, figures and charts), and they are customized to each respondent's specific needs. Credible media channels transmit information that is honest, accurate, and thorough. Research has shown that respondents will have more positive images of organizations that transmit information that is rich and credible.[53] If the information is seen as coming from the employees personally, rather than from the organization's recruiting offices, the message will likely be seen as more honest and unbiased. Experts on advertising also advise recruiters to remember that they need to constantly promote their brand to potential employees, because sheer repetition and consistency of a promotional message increase the effectiveness of the message.[54]

Recruitment Brochures
A recruitment brochure is usually sent or given directly to job applicants. Information in the brochure may be very detailed, and hence, the brochure may be lengthy. A brochure not only covers information about the job but also communicates information about the organization and its location. It may include pictures in addition to written narrative in order to illustrate various aspects of the job, such as the city

in which the organization is located and actual coworkers. These various means of demonstrating the features of the organization will enhance the richness of this recruiting technique.

The advantage of a brochure is that the organization controls who receives a copy. Also, it can be more lengthy than an advertisement. A disadvantage is that it can be quite costly to develop this medium. Also, because it is obviously a sales pitch made by the organization, it might be seen as less credible.

A successful brochure possesses (1) a unique theme or point of view relative to other organizations in the same industry and (2) a visual distinctiveness in terms of design and photographs. A good format for the brochure is to begin with a general description of the organization, including its history and culture (values, goals, "brand"), then include a description of the hiring process, then a characterization of pay/benefits and performance reviews, and conclude with contact information.

Videos and Videoconferencing

A video can be used along with the brochure but should not simply replicate the brochure. The brochure should be used to communicate basic facts and information. The video should be used to communicate the culture and climate of the organization. Professional Marketing Services, Inc., in Milwaukee, helps organizations develop a "profile" of themselves. As part of the profile they can highlight characteristics of the city that the organization resides in, such as the climate, housing market, school systems, churches, performing arts, spectator sports, nightlife, and festivals. This profile can be communicated to job seekers via videocassette, diskette, CD-ROM, CD-I, and the Internet.[55] Video diskettes can also be made interactive so that the job seeker can submit an application electronically, request additional information, or even arrange an interview.

A new form of communicating with job applicants is known as videoconferencing.[56] Rather than meeting in person with applicants, organizational representatives meet with applicants in separate locations, face to face on a television monitor. The actual image of the person in action appears on the screen, although the transmission appears to be in slow motion. The technology needed for videoconferencing is expensive, but the costs have decreased in recent years. Moreover, this technology makes it possible for the organization to screen applicants at multiple or remote locations without actually having to travel to those locations. Many college placement offices now have the equipment for videoconferencing. The equipment is also available at some FedEx Kinko's copy centers for applicants who do not have access to a college placement office.

Advertisements

Given the expense of advertising in business publications, ads are much shorter and to the point than are recruitment brochures. Unfortunately, because of the short duration of most advertisements, they typically cannot provide rich information. As a general rule, the greater the circulation of the publication, the greater the cost of advertising in it.

Ads appear in a variety of places other than business publications. Ads can be found in local, regional, and national newspapers; on television and radio; and in bargain shoppers, door hangers, direct mail, and welcome wagons. Advertisements can thus be used to reach a broad market segment. There are many different types of ads:[57]

1. *Classified advertisements.* These ads appear in alphabetical order in the "Help Wanted" section of the newspaper. Typically, they allow for very limited type and style selection and are usually only one newspaper column in width. These ads are used most often for the purpose of quick résumé solicitation for low-level jobs at a low cost. Most large- and medium-sized newspapers now place their classified ads online, potentially reaching many more prospective job candidates. Although there has been a major shift toward the use of electronic recruiting, surveys suggest that print ads remain a significant presence in the recruiting of hourly workers.

2. *Classified display ads.* A classified display ad allows more discretion in the type that is used and its location in the paper. A classified display ad does not have to appear in alphabetical order and can appear in any section of the newspaper. The cost of these ads is moderate; they are often used as a way to announce openings for professional and managerial jobs. An example of a classified display ad is shown in Exhibit 5.8.

3. *Display ads.* These ads allow for freedom of design and placement in a publication. Thus, they are very expensive and begin to resemble recruitment brochures. These ads are typically used when an employer is searching for a large number of applicants to fill multiple openings.

4. *Online ads.* More and more employers are choosing to place ads on the Internet. These ads can take several forms. One form is a clickable banner ad that appears on Web sites visited by likely prospects. Another form of advertising of sorts was reviewed earlier—posting positions using online Web sites such as *Monster.com.*

5. *Radio and television ads.* Organizations that advertise on the radio or on television purchase a 30- or 60-second time slot to advertise openings in specific job categories. Choice of stations and broadcast times will target specific audiences. For example, a classical music radio station will likely draw in different applicants than would a contemporary pop music radio station; an all-sports network will draw in different applicants than would a cooking program. Radio and television stations often have detailed demographic information available to potential advertisers. Some recruiting experts propose that advertising through a variety of community radio stations or cable access television programs is an ideal way to improve workforce diversity.[58] The advantage of radio and television advertisements is their reach. Help wanted ads are generally read by individuals who are already searching for jobs, whereas radio and television ads are more likely to be heard by those who are

---

EXHIBIT 5.8   Classified Display Ad for Human Resource Generalist

HUMAN RESOURCE GENERALIST

ABC Health, a leader in the health care industry, currently has a position available for an experienced **Human Resource Generalist.**

This position will serve on the human resources team, which serves as a business partner with our operational departments. Our team prides itself on developing and maintaining progressive and impactful human resources policies and programs.

Qualified candidates for this position will possess a bachelor's degree in business with an emphasis on human resource management, or a degree in a related field, such as industrial psychology. In addition, a minimum of three years of experience as a human resource generalist is required. This experience should include exposure to at least four of the following functional areas: compensation, employment, benefits, training, employee relations, and performance management.

In return for your contributions, we offer a competitive salary as well as comprehensive, flexible employee benefits. If you meet the qualifications and our opportunity is attractive to you, please forward your résumé and salary expectations to:

Human Resource Department
ABC Health
P.O. Box 123
Pensacola, FL 12345
An Equal Opportunity/Affirmative Action Employer

---

not currently looking for jobs. Being able to expand the potential job pool to include those who are not actively looking for work can be a real advantage in a tight labor market.[59]

Organizational Web Sites

The Web is somewhat unique in that it may function as both a recruitment source and a recruitment medium. When a Web page only serves to communicate information about the job or organization to potential applicants, it serves as a recruitment medium. However, when a Web page attracts actual applicants, particularly when applicants are allowed to apply online, it also functions as a recruitment source.

It may not be an overstatement to conclude that organizational Web sites have become the single most important medium through which companies communicate with potential applicants. Nearly every large organization has a careers page on its Web site, and many small organizations have company and point of contact information for job seekers. Web sites not only are a powerful means of communicating information about jobs, but they can also reach applicants who otherwise would not bother (or know how or where) to apply. Thus, care must be taken to ensure that the organizational Web site is appealing to potential job candidates.

The three core attributes driving the appeal of an organizational Web site are engagement, functionality, and content. First, the Web site must be vivid and attractive to applicants. Some experts have noted that in recruiting Web sites, engagement often takes a back seat. Second, while engagement is important, at the same time, the Web site must be functional, meaning that it is quick to load, easily navigated, and interactive. A Web site that is overly complex may be vivid, but it will only generate frustration if it is hard to decipher or slow to load. Third, an organizational Web site must convey the information prospective applicants would like to see, including current position openings, job requirements, and steps for applying. Finally, it's important to remember that your communication with an applicant shouldn't end with his or her online application. Apple's Web site, for example, allows applicants to track the status of their application for 90 days after they apply. Procter and Gamble does the same thing (online is the only way applicants can apply), using a process that is eased by the fact that software automatically scores its online applications. Perhaps these technological advances aren't feasible for every Web site, but applicants need to be informed in one way or another about the status of their application.[60]

One way to ensure that the Web site meets these requirements is to test it with "naïve" users—people who are not from the organization's IT department or recruiting staff. It is critical that the number of clicks is minimized, that the online application process is clear, and that animation and color are used effectively to engage the prospective applicant. However, it's important not to overdo it. When *Coach.com*, a leather retailer, removed flash graphics from its Web site, page visits increased by 45%.[61]

Of course, there is more to designing an organizational Web site than just the three attributes discussed above. Exhibit 5.9 provides a thorough list of factors to keep in mind when designing a Web site for organizational recruitment.

Direct Contact

In contrast to the methods of brochures, videos, Web sites, and advertising, some organizations use direct contact with respondents to enhance recruiting outcomes. The two most common media for direct contact are telephone messages and e-mail. These techniques are ideally much more personal than the other methods of recruiting because the applicants are specifically approached by the organization. Personal contacts are likely to be seen as more credible by respondents. In addition, messages delivered through direct contact often allow respondents to ask personally relevant questions, which obviously should enhance the richness of the information.

However, in the age of spamming, it is important to remember that most individuals will regard mass e-mailings or automated telephone messages with even less enthusiasm than junk mail. To make the most out of e-mail recruitment, it is

---

EXHIBIT 5.9   **Factors to Keep in Mind in Designing Organizational Web Sites**

1. *Keep it simple*—surveys reveal that potential job candidates are overwhelmed by complex, difficult-to-navigate Web sites; never sacrifice clarity for "jazziness"—remember, a good applicant is there for content of the Web site, not for the bells and whistles.
2. *Make access easy; Web page and links should be easy to download*—studies reveal that individuals will not wait more than eight seconds for a page to download, so that four-color page that looks great will backfire if it takes the user, working from a modem, time to download the page (also make sure that the link to the recruiting site on the home page is prominently displayed).
3. *Provide online application form*—increasingly, potential candidates expect to be able to submit an application online; online forms are not only desired by candidates, organizations can load them directly into searchable databases.
4. *Provide information about company culture*—allow applicants to self-select out if their values clearly do not match those of your organization; you wouldn't want them anyway.
5. *Include selected links to relevant Web sites*—the words "selected" and "relevant" are key here; things to include might be a cost-of-living calculator and a career advice area.
6. *Make sure necessary information is conveyed to avoid confusion*—clearly specify job title, location, etc., so applicants know the job for which they are applying and, if there are several jobs, they don't apply for the wrong job.
7. *Keep information current*—make sure position information is updated regularly (e.g., weekly).
8. *Evaluate and track the results*—periodically evaluate the performance of the Web site based on various criteria (number of hits, number of applications, application/hits ratio, quality of hires, cost of maintenance, user satisfaction, time to hire, etc.).

---

important to make the messages highly personal, reflecting an understanding of the candidate's unique qualifications. Providing a working response e-mail address or telephone number that allows respondents to ask a person questions about the job opening will also help increase the yield for the direct contact method. However, personalization and customized responding to questions obviously will increase the cost per individual contacted, so there are trade-offs in terms of cost that must be considered.

APPLICANT REACTIONS

An important source of information in designing and implementing an effective recruitment system is applicant reactions to the system. Both attitudinal and behavioral reactions to components of the recruitment system are important. Components of this system that have been studied include the recruiter and the recruitment process.

Reactions to Recruiters

Considerable research has been conducted and carefully reviewed on the reactions of job applicants to the behavior and characteristics of recruiters.[62] The data that have been collected have been somewhat limited by the fact that they focus primarily on reactions to college rather than noncollege recruiters. Despite this limitation, several key themes emerge in the literature.

First, though the recruiter does indeed influence job applicant reactions, he or she does not have as much influence on them as do actual characteristics of the job. Applicants' interest in a job is strongly predicted by the work environment, the organization's image, and location. This indicates that the recruiter cannot be viewed as a substitute for a well-defined and communicated recruitment message showing the actual characteristics of the job. It is not enough just to have good recruiters to attract applicants to the organization.

Second, the influence of the recruiter is more likely to be felt in the attitudes rather than the behaviors of the job applicant. That is, an applicant who has been exposed to a talented recruiter is more likely to walk away with a favorable impression of the recruiter than to accept a job on the basis of the interaction with a recruiter. This attitudinal effect is important, however, as it may lead to good publicity for the organization. In turn, good publicity may lead to a larger applicant pool to draw from in the future.

Third, demographic characteristics of the recruiter do not have much impact on applicant reactions. Respondents are largely indifferent regarding interviewer gender and function.

Fourth, two behaviors of the recruiter seem to have the largest influence on applicant reactions. The first is the level of warmth that the recruiter shows toward the job applicant. Warmth can be expressed by being enthusiastic, personable, empathetic, and helpful in dealings with the candidate. The second behavior is being knowledgeable about the job. This can be conveyed by being well versed with the job requirements matrix and the job rewards matrix. Finally, recruiters who show interest in the applicant are viewed more positively (one recruiter actually watched the World Series while "interviewing" an applicant).

Reactions to the Recruitment Process

Only some administrative components of the recruitment process have been shown to have an impact on applicant reactions.[63] Overall, research suggests that above all else, applicants want a system that is fair. First, job applicants are more likely to have favorable reactions to the recruitment process when the screening devices that are used to narrow the applicant pool are seen as job related. That is, the process that is used should be closely related to the content of the job as spelled out in the job requirements matrix. Applicants also see recruiting processes as more fair if they have an opportunity to perform or demonstrate their ability to do the job.

Second, delay times in the recruitment process do indeed have a negative effect on applicants' reactions. In particular, when long delays occur between the applicant's expression of interest and the organization's response, negative reactions are formed by the applicant. The negative impression formed is about the organization rather than about the applicant himself or herself. For example, with a long delay between an on-site visit and a job offer, an applicant is more likely to believe that something is wrong with the organization rather than with his or her personal qualifications. This is especially true of the better-qualified candidate, who is also likely to act on these feelings by accepting another job offer.

Third, simply throwing money at the recruitment process is unlikely to result in any return. There is no evidence that increased expenditures on the recruitment process result in more favorable attitudes or behaviors by job applicants. For expenditures to pay dividends, they need to be specifically targeted to effective recruitment practices, rather than indiscriminately directed to all practices.

Fourth, the influence of the recruiter on the applicant is more likely to occur in the initial rather than the latter stages of the recruitment process. In the latter stages, actual characteristics of the job carry more weight in the applicant's decision. At the initial screening interview, the recruiter may be the applicant's only contact with the organization. Later in the process, the applicant is more likely to have additional information about the job and company. Hence, the credibility of the recruiter is most critical on initial contact with applicants.

Finally, though little research is available, the increasing use of the Internet in recruitment, and that it is often the applicant's first exposure to an organization, suggests that applicants' reactions to an organization's Web site will increasingly drive their reactions to the organization's recruitment process. A survey revealed that 79% of college students and recent graduates indicated that the quality of a prospective employer's Web site was somewhat important (35%) or very important (44%) in their decision of whether to apply for a job.

Indeed, studies reveal that applicants are able to locate more relevant jobs on the Internet than in traditional sources such as print media. Moreover, applicants generally like the Internet, provided some provisos are kept in mind. As with general recruiting, perhaps the most important factor is the degree and speed of follow-up. Just as with other forms of recruiting, delays greatly harm the image of the recruiting organization, so organizations need to make sure that online applications are followed up. Also, research shows that job seekers are more satisfied with company Web sites when specific job information is provided and security provisions are taken to preserve the confidentiality of the information submitted. One key assurance is that the company will not share résumés with vendors that will spam applicants with various solicitations.[64]

TRANSITION TO SELECTION

Once a job seeker has been identified and attracted to the organization, the organization needs to prepare the person for the selection process. In preparation, applicants need to be made aware of the next steps in the hiring process and what will be required of them. If this transition step is overlooked by the recruiting organization, it may lose qualified applicants who mistakenly think that delays between steps in the hiring process indicate that the organization is no longer interested in them or are fearful that they "didn't have what it takes" to successfully compete during the next steps.

The city of Columbus, Ohio, has done an excellent job of preparing job seekers from external recruitment sources to become applicants for the position of firefighter. To become a firefighter, applicants must pass a series of physical ability exams, which require them to go through an obstacle course, carry heavy equipment up stairs, and complete a number of other timed physical exercises. Many applicants have never encountered these types of tests before and are fearful that they don't have the physical ability to successfully complete the tests.

To prepare job seekers and applicants for these tests, videotapes have been developed showing instructions on how to take the tests and a firefighter actually taking the tests. These tests are shown to those who have applied for the position, and they are also shown on public access television for those job seekers who are thinking about applying for the job. The city of Columbus also provides upper-body strength training, as this is a stumbling point for some job applicants in the selection process.

This example from the city of Columbus indicates that in order to successfully prepare people for the transition to selection, organizations should consider reviewing the selection method instructions with the applicants, showing them actual samples of the selection method, and providing them with practice or training if necessary. These steps should be followed not just for physical ability tests but for all selection methods in the hiring process likely to be unfamiliar or uncomfortable to applicants.

LEGAL ISSUES

External recruitment practices are subject to considerable legal scrutiny and influence. Through external recruitment, job applicants first establish contact with the organization and then become more knowledgeable about job requirements and rewards. During this process, there is ample room for the organization to exclude certain applicant groups (e.g., minorities, women, and people with disabilities), as well as deceive in its dealings with applicants. Various laws and regulations seek to place limits on these exclusionary and deceptive practices.

Legal issues regarding several of the practices are discussed in this section. These include definition of job applicants, affirmative action programs, electronic recruitment, job advertisements, and fraud and misrepresentation.

Definition of a Job Applicant

Both the Equal Employment Opportunity Commission (EEOC) and the Office of Federal Contract Compliance Programs (OFCCP) require the organization to keep applicant records so that adverse impact statistics can be computed. Exactly what is a job applicant? It is necessary to provide guidance on the answer to this question separately for traditional hard-copy and electronic applicants.

Hard Copy Applicants

The original (1979) definition of an applicant by the EEOC is in the Uniform Guidelines on Employee Selection Procedures (UGESP). It reads as follows: "The precise definition of the term 'applicant' depends on the user's recruitment and selection procedures. The concept of an applicant is that of a person who has indicated an interest in being considered for hiring, promotion, or other employment opportunities. This interest may be expressed by completing an application form, or might be expressed orally, depending on the employer's practice."

This definition was created prior to the existence of electronic job application. It remains in force for hard copy applications. Because it is so open ended, it could create a substantial record-keeping burden for the organization since any contact with the organization by a person might count as an application for enforcement purposes. Hence, it is advisable for the organization to formulate and strictly adhere to written application policies and procedures that are communicated to organizational representatives and to all persons acting as if they are job applicants. Several suggestions for doing this follow.

First, require a written application from all who seek to be considered, and communicate this policy to all potential applicants. Inform people who apply by other means that they must submit a written application in order to be considered. If this policy is not defined, virtually anyone who contacts the organization or expresses interest by any means could be considered an applicant. Second, require that the applicant indicate the precise position applied for, and establish written minimum qualifications for each position. In this way, the organization can legitimately refuse to consider as applicants those who do not meet these requirements. Third, establish a definite period for which the position will remain open, communicate this clearly to applicants, and do not consider those who apply after the deadline. Also, do not keep applications on hold or on file for future consideration. Fourth, return unsolicited applications through the mail. Finally, keep track of applicants who drop out of the process due to lack of interest or acceptance of another job. Such suggestions will help the organization limit the number of "true" applicants and reduce record keeping while also fostering legal compliance.[65]

Internet Applicants

The OFCCP regulations provide a definition of an Internet applicant for federal contractors, as well as establish record-keeping requirements. The EEOC has not yet provided a definition of an Internet applicant, though it is in the process of developing one.

According to the OFCCP, an individual must meet all four of the following criteria in order to be considered an Internet applicant:

- The individual submits an expression of an interest in employment through the Internet or related electronic technologies
- The employer considers the individual for employment in a particular position
- The individual's expression of interest indicates that the individual possesses the basic qualifications for the position
- The individual at no point in the employer's selection process prior to receiving an offer of employment from the employer removes himself or herself from further consideration or otherwise indicates that he or she is no longer interested in the position

Numerous amendments to these criteria have been suggested.[66] First, some propose that the employer should be able to establish a set procedure for how expressions of interest must be submitted by the applicant, and if that procedure is not followed by the applicant, the employer may disregard that application. For example, the employer could require the applicant to identify the specific position being applied for, require a statement of minimum salary requirements and geographic location preferences, and have an application deadline. Second, it has been proposed that if the employer advertises a position vacancy, the advertisement must include all the basic qualifications. Basic qualifications must be objective (such as an educational degree or experience requirement), relevant to the performance of the particular job, and enable the employer to accomplish its business goals. Employment test results are often not considered basic qualifications. Third, lack of interest by the applicant could be expressed by stating no further interest in the position, declining an interview or job offer, or not responding to follow-up contact by the employer. Lack of interest by the applicant might be inferred by the employer based on the applicant's stated salary requirements, type of position sought, or geographic location preference/willingness to relocate.

The OFCCP regulations also require the employer to make every reasonable effort to gather race/gender/ethnicity data from both traditional and Internet applicants. The preferred method for doing so is voluntary self-disclosure, such as through tear-off sheets on an application form, postcards, short forms to request the information, or as part of an initial telephone screen.

Finally, the OFCCP regulations make detailed record-keeping and adverse impact calculations requirements. In terms of record-keeping, the employer must retain the following:

- All expressions of interest submitted through the Internet
- Internal résumé databases—including date of entry, the position for which each search was made, the date of the search, and the search criteria used
- External résumé databases—position for which each search was made, the date of the search, search criteria used, and the records for each person who met the basic qualifications for the position

In terms of adverse impact calculations, the employer must keep records relating to adverse impact calculations for internet applicants and for all test takers.

Affirmative Action Programs

The Affirmative Action Programs regulations from the OFCCP require the organization to establish placement (hiring and promotion) goals for job groups in which there are disparities between the percentages of women and minorities actually employed and those available for employment. These placement goals are staffing objectives that should be incorporated into the organization's overall staffing planning. The regulations also require that the organization identify problem areas impeding EEO and undertake action-oriented programs to correct these problem areas and achieve the placement goals. While recruitment is mentioned as one of those potential problem areas, the regulations say little else specifically about recruitment activities. Based on former (now expired) regulations, however, the OFCCP offered considerable guidance to the organization for its recruitment actions. Suggested actions include the following:

- Update job descriptions and ensure their accuracy.
- Widely circulate approved job descriptions to hiring managers and recruitment sources.
- Carefully select and train all personnel included in staffing.
- Reach out to organizations prepared to refer women and minority applicants, such as the Urban League, state employment (job) services, National Organization for Women, sectarian women's groups, and so forth.
- Conduct formal briefings, preferably on organization premises, for representatives from recruiting sources.
- Encourage women and minority employees to refer job applicants.
- Include women and minorities on the HR department staff.
- Actively participate in job fairs.
- Recruit actively at secondary schools and community colleges with predominantly minority and women enrollment.
- Use special employment programs, such as internships, work/study, and summer jobs.
- Include minorities and women in recruitment brochures.
- Expand help wanted advertising to include women and minority news media.

Taken in total, the OFCCP suggestions indicate that organizations with AAPs should undertake targeted recruitment programs using recruitment staff trained in affirmative action recruiting.

Electronic Recruitment

Usage of electronic recruitment technologies has the potential to create artificial barriers to employment opportunities.[67] First, online recruitment and application procedures assume that potential applicants have access to computers and the skills necessary to make online applications. Research suggests these may be poor assumptions, especially for some racial minorities and the economically disadvantaged. Whether such implicit denial of access to job application opportunities is illegal is an open question due to the newness of the issue. To guard against legal challenge and to ensure accessibility, there are several things the organization might do. One action is to supplement online recruitment with recruitment via other widely used sources, such as newspaper advertisements or other sources that organizational experience indicates are frequently used by women and minorities. Alternately, online recruitment and application could be restricted to certain jobs that have strong computer-related KSAO requirements, such as word processing, programming, spreadsheets, and Internet searches. Many managerial, professional, and technical jobs are likely to have such requirements; applicants in all likelihood will have easy access to computers and online recruitment, as well as the skills necessary to successfully navigate and complete the application.

A second potential legal issue is the use of recruitment software that conducts résumé searches within an applicant database using keyword search criteria. Organizational representatives, such as staffing specialists or hiring managers, often specify the search criteria to use, and they could select non-job-related criteria that cause adverse impact against women, minorities, or people with disabilities. Examples of such criteria include preferences for graduation from elite colleges or universities, age, and physical requirements. To guard against such a possibility, the organization should be certain that a job analysis has been done to ensure that every job vacancy lists current KSAO requirements, restrict the type of search criteria that may be used by organizational representatives, and train those representatives in the appropriate specification and usage of search criteria.

A third issue is that the visually impaired may have difficulty navigating online help wanted ads and other recruitment information, because not all Web sites are compatible with screen reader software that translates computerized text and images into speech or Braille. The solution (required of federal contractors and many states) is to make the organization's Web site compatible with screen readers. This is usually quite simple to accomplish with existing technology.

A final issue is that of video résumés being submitted by job applicants. Video résumés can reveal protected class characteristics (e.g., race, sex, color, disability) about applicants that can easily enter into the screening decision by recruiters and managers, resulting in illegal discrimination. To guard against this possibility, the organization needs to take certain steps. First, create specific KSAO requirements against which applicants can be screened. Second, redesign the initial screening process so that the applicant's résumé or application only is reviewed; allow use of the video résumé only later in the hiring process. Third, provide training to recruiters and managers on how to evaluate applicants' video résumé information against the job's KSAOs and on the need for great care in not allowing protected class information to enter into their evaluations of applicants.

Job Advertisements

Some of the earliest (and most blatant) examples of discrimination come from job advertisements. Newspaper employment ads were once listed under separate "Help Wanted—Male" and "Help Wanted—Female" sections, and the content of the ads contained statements like "Applicant must be young and energetic." Such types of ads obviously discouraged certain potential applicants from applying because of their gender or age.

The EEOC has issued policy statements regarding age- and sex-referent language in advertising.[68] It bans the use of explicit age- or sex-based preferences. It also addresses more subtle situations in which ads contain implicit age- or sex-based preferences, such as "junior executive," "recent college graduate," "meter maid," and "patrolman." These are referred to in the policy statements as trigger words, and their use may deter certain individuals from becoming applicants. The statements make clear that trigger words, in and of themselves in an advertisement, are not illegal. However, the total context of the ad in which trigger words appear must not be discriminatory, or the trigger words will be a violation of the law.

The EEOC provides the following as an example of an advertisement with a trigger word: "Wanted: Individuals of all ages. Day and evening hours available. Full- and part-time positions. All inquiries welcomed. Excellent source of secondary income for retirees."

Use of the trigger word "retiree" in this ad is considered permissible because the context of the ad makes it clear that applicants of all ages are welcome to apply.

Fraud and Misrepresentation

Puffery, promises, half-truths, and even outright lies are all encountered in recruitment under the guise of selling the applicant on the job and the organization. Too much of this type of selling can be legally dangerous. When it occurs, under workplace tort law, applicants may file suit claiming fraud or misrepresentation.[69] Claims may cite false statements of existing facts (e.g., the nature and profitability of the employer's business) or false promises of future events (e.g., promises about terms and conditions of employment, pay, promotion opportunities, and geographic location). It does not matter if the false statements were made intentionally (fraud) or negligently (misrepresentation). Both types of statements are a reasonable basis for a claim by an applicant or newly hired employee.

To be successful in such a suit, the plaintiff must demonstrate that

1. A misrepresentation occurred
2. The employer knew, or should have known, about the misrepresentation
3. The plaintiff relied on the information to make a decision or take action, and
4. The plaintiff was injured because of reliance placed on the statements made by the employer.[70]

Though these four requirements may appear to be a stiff set of hurdles for the plaintiff, they are by no means insurmountable, as many successful plaintiffs can attest. Avoidance of fraud and misrepresentation claims in recruitment requires straightforward action by the organization and its recruiters. First, provide applicants with the job description and specific, truthful information about the job rewards. Second, be truthful about the nature of the business and its profitability. Third, avoid specific promises about future events, regarding terms and conditions of employment or business plans and profitability. Finally, make sure that all recruiters follow these suggestions when they recruit job applicants.

SUMMARY

The objective of the external recruitment process is to identify and attract qualified applicants. To meet this objective the organization must conduct recruitment planning. At this stage, attention must be given to both organizational issues (e.g., centralized versus decentralized recruitment function) and administrative issues (e.g., size of the budget). Particular care needs to be taken in the selection and training of recruiters.

The next stage in external recruitment is the development of a strategy. The strategy should consider open versus targeted recruitment, recruitment sources, and the choice of sources. Multiple sources should be used to identify specific applicant populations. There are trade-offs involved in using any source to identify applicants, which should be carefully reviewed prior to using it.

The next stage is to develop a message to give to the job applicants and to select a medium to convey that message. The message may be realistic, branded, or targeted. There is no one best message; it depends on the characteristics of the labor market, the job, and the applicants. The message can be communicated through brochures, videos, advertisements, voice messages, videoconferencing, online services, radio, or e-mail, each of which has different strengths and weaknesses.

Applicants are definitely influenced by characteristics of recruiters and the recruitment process. Through proper attention to these characteristics, the organization can help provide applicants with a favorable recruitment experience. That experience can be continued by carefully preparing applicants for the selection process.

Recruitment practices and decisions come under intense legal scrutiny because of their potential for discrimination at the beginning of the staffing process. The legal definition of a job applicant creates record-keeping requirements for the organization that, in turn, have major implications for the design of the entire recruitment process. Affirmative Action Program regulations likewise affect the entire recruitment process, prodding the organization to set targeted placement goals for women and minorities, and to be aggressive in recruitment outreach actions. Electronic recruitment has the potential to create legal quagmires, including lack of access to online application and recruitment by some disadvantaged applicants, résumé searches of databases using keyword search criteria that may be exclusionary of women, minorities, and the disabled; Web sites that are not screen-reader friendly for the visually impaired; and video résumés that reveal protected class characteristics to recruiters and hiring managers. Job advertisements may not contain applicant preferences regarding protected characteristics such as age and gender. Finally, recruitment communication with applicants must be careful to avoid false statements or promises, lest problems of fraud and misrepresentation arise.

DISCUSSION QUESTIONS

1. List and briefly describe each of the administrative issues that needs to be addressed in the planning stage of external recruiting.
2. List 10 sources of applicants that organizations turn to when recruiting. For each source, identify needs specific to the source, as well as pros and cons of using the source for recruitment.
3. In designing the communication message to be used in external recruiting, what kinds of information should be included?
4. What are the advantages of conveying a realistic recruitment message as opposed to portraying the job in a way that the organization thinks that job applicants want to hear?
5. What nontraditional inducements are some organizations offering so that they are seen as family-friendly organizations? What result does the organization hope to realize as a result of providing these inducements?

ETHICAL ISSUES

1. Many organizations adopt a targeted recruitment strategy. For example, some organizations have targeted workers 50 and older in their recruitment efforts, which includes advertising specifically in media outlets frequented by older individuals. Other organizations target recruitment messages at women,

2. minorities, or those with desired skills. Do you think targeted recruitment systems are fair? Why or why not?

2. Most organizations have in place job boards on their Web page where applicants can apply for jobs online. What ethical obligations, if any, do you think organizations have to individuals who apply for jobs online?

APPLICATIONS

Improving a College Recruitment Program

The White Feather Corporation (WFC) is a rapidly growing consumer products organization that specializes in the production and sales of specialty household items such as lawn furniture cleaners, spa (hot tub) accessories, mosquito and tick repellents, and stain-resistant garage floor paints. The organization currently employs 400 exempt and 3,000 nonexempt employees, almost all of whom are full time. In addition to its corporate office in Clucksville, Arkansas, the organization has five plants and two distribution centers at various rural locations throughout the state.

Two years ago WFC created a corporate HR department to provide centralized direction and control for its key HR functions—planning, compensation, training, and staffing. In turn, the staffing function is headed by the senior manager of staffing, who receives direct reports from three managers: the manager of nonexempt employment, the manager of exempt employment, and the manager of EEO/AA. The manager of exempt employment is Marianne Collins, who has been with WFC for 10 years and has grown with the organization through a series of sales and sales management positions. She was chosen for her current position as a result of the WFC's commitment to promotion from within, as well as her broad familiarity with the organization's products and customers. When Marianne was appointed her key area of accountability was defined as college recruitment, with 50% of her time to be devoted to it.

In her first year, Marianne developed and implemented WFC's first-ever formal college recruitment program. Working with the HR planning person, WFC decided there was a need for 40 college graduate new hires by the end of the year. They were to be placed in the production, distribution, and marketing functions; specific job titles and descriptions were to be developed during the year. Armed with this forecast, Marianne began the process of recruitment planning and strategy development. The result was the following recruitment process.

Recruitment was to be conducted at 12 public and private schools throughout the state. Marianne contacted the placement office(s) at each school and set up a one-day recruitment visit for each school. All visits were scheduled during the first week in May. The placement office at each school set up 30-minute interviews (16 at each school) and made sure that applicants completed and had on file a standard application form. To visit the schools and conduct the interviews, Marianne selected three young, up-and-coming managers (one each from production, distribution, and marketing) to be the recruiters. Each manager was assigned to four of the schools. Since none of the managers had any experience as a recruiter, Marianne conducted a recruitment briefing for them. During that briefing she reviewed the overall recruitment (hiring) goal, provided a brief rundown on each of the schools, and then explained the specific tasks the recruiters were to perform. Those tasks were to pick up the application materials of the interviewees at the placement office prior to the interviews, review the materials, conduct the interviews in a timely manner (the managers were told they could ask any questions they wanted to that pertained to qualifications for the job), and at the end of the day complete an evaluation form on each applicant. The form asked for a 1–7 rating of overall qualifications for the job, written comments about strengths and weaknesses, and a recommendation of whether to invite the person for a second interview in Clucksville. These forms were to be returned to Marianne, who would review them and decide which people to invite for a second interview.

After the campus interviews were conducted by the managers, problems began to surface. Placement officials at some of the schools contacted Marianne and lodged several complaints. Among those complaints were that (1) one of the managers failed to pick up the application materials of the interviewees; (2) none of the managers were able to provide much information about the nature of the jobs they were recruiting for, especially jobs outside their own functional area; (3) the interviewers got off schedule early on, so applicants were kept waiting and others had shortened interviews as the managers tried to make up time; (4) none of the managers had any written information describing the organization and its locations; (5) one of the managers asked female applicants very personal questions about marriage plans, use of drugs and alcohol, and willingness to travel with male coworkers; (6) one of the managers talked incessantly during the interviews, leaving the interviewees little opportunity to present themselves and their qualifications; and (7) all of the managers told the interviewees that they did not know when they would be contacted about decisions on invitations for second interviews. In addition to these complaints, Marianne had difficulty getting the managers to complete and turn in their evaluation forms (they claimed they were too busy, especially after being away from the job for a week). Based on the reports she did receive, Marianne extended invitations to 55 of the applicants for second interviews. Of these, 30 accepted the invitation. Ultimately, 25 of these were given job offers, and 15 of them accepted the offers.

To put it mildly, the first-ever college recruitment program was a disaster for WFC and Marianne. In addition to her embarrassment, Marianne was asked to meet with her boss and the president of WFC to explain what went wrong and to receive "guidance" from them as to their expectations for the next year's recruitment program. Marianne subsequently learned that she would receive no merit pay increase for the year and that the three managers all received above-average merit increases.

To turn things around for the second year of college recruitment, Marianne realized that she needed to engage in a thorough process of recruitment planning and strategy development. As she began this undertaking, her analysis of past events led her to the conclusion that one of her key mistakes was to naively assume that the three managers would actually know how to be good recruiters and were motivated to do the job effectively. Marianne first decided to use 12 managers as recruiters, assigning one to each of the 12 campuses. She also decided that she cannot send them off to the campuses with just a recruitment "briefing." She determined that an intensive, one-day training program must be developed and given to the managers prior to the beginning of the recruitment "season."

You are a professional acquaintance of Marianne's, and you work in HR at another organization in Clucksville. Knowing that you have had some experience in both college recruiting and training, Marianne calls you for some advice. She asks you if you would be willing to meet and discuss the following questions:

1. What topics should be covered in the training program?
2. What materials and training aids will be needed for the program?
3. What skills should the trainees actually practice during the training?
4. Who should conduct the training?
5. What other changes might have to be made to ensure that the training has a strong impact on the managers and that during the recruitment process they are motivated to use what they learned in training?

Internet Recruiting

Selma Williams is a recruiter for Mervin/McCall-Hall (MMH), a large publisher of textbooks for education (K–12 and college). Fresh out of college, Selma has received her first big assignment at MMH, and it is a tough one—to develop an Internet recruitment strategy for the entire organization. Previously, MMH had relied on the traditional recruitment methods—college recruiting, word-of-mouth, newspaper advertisements, and search firms. As more and more of MMH's textbook business is connected to the Web, however, it became clear to Selma's boss, Jon Beerfly, that MMH needs to consider upgrading its recruitment process. Accordingly, after Selma had acclimated herself to MMH and had worked on a few smaller recruitment projects (including doing a fair amount of recruiting at college campuses in the past three months), Jon described her new assignment to her, concluding, "Selma, I really don't know much about this. I'm going to leave it to you to come up with a set of recommendations about what we oughtta be doing. We just had a new intern come into the office for a stint in HR, and I'm going to assign this person to you to help on this assignment." Assume that you are the intern.

At your first meeting, you and Selma discuss many different issues and agree that regardless of whatever else is done, MMH must have a recruitment area on the MMH corporate Web site. After further discussion, Selma has given you several assignments toward this objective:

1. Look at three to five corporate Web sites that have a recruitment area and note their major features, strengths, and weaknesses (see Exhibit 5.7).
2. Interview three to five students who have used the recruitment area on a corporate Web site and ask them what they most liked and disliked about the recruitment areas.
3. Prepare a brief report that (a) summarizes your findings from assignments #1 and #2 and (b) recommends the design features that you and Selma will develop for inclusion in the MMH Web site.

TANGLEWOOD STORES CASE

You have just learned about many of the major methods organizations use to encourage individuals to apply for vacancies. The recruiting case will provide an opportunity to see how staffing managers can use organizational data to resolve an internal dispute regarding which recruiting methods work best. In addition, the assignment will demonstrate how contextual factors can bring out different strengths of the various recruiting methods.

The Situation

Tanglewood is engaged in a process of centralization. Previously, most staffing decisions were made by each individual store, but the corporate offices would like to see more consistency. They also believe that there is a great deal the stores can learn by comparing their experiences across locations. You are provided data from Tanglewood's recruiting outcomes from four different geographic regions. These data are supplemented with narrative reports from the organization's managerial focus groups pertaining to the fit between applicants and the unique requirements of Tanglewood's culture.

Your Tasks

You will assess the information about recruitment sources and the recruitment process provided by four divisions of Tanglewood Stores. You will then make recommendations regarding which methods of recruiting are likely to be most successful, and also provide suggestions on whether the organization should use open or targeted recruiting. Once you have concluded what the best course of action will be, you will create a recruitment guide for the organization like the one presented in Exhibit 5.3. Finally, you will develop recruiting messages by considering the message and the medium by which information will be provided. The background information for this case, and your specific assignment, can be found at *www.mhhe.com/heneman6e*.

ENDNOTES

1. J. S. Arthur, "Chamber Aid," *Human Resource Executive,* Feb. 2001, pp. 124–128; E. B. Coleman, "Fight or Fix? The Competition for Teachers," *The School Administrator,* Jan. 2001, pp. 28–32; C. Joinson, "Reeling in the Talent," *HR Magazine,* July 1999, pp. 46–52; A. S. Wellner, "Focus on Recruitment and Hiring," *HR Magazine,* Jan. 2001, pp. 87–96.

2. M. N. Martinez, "Recruiting Here and There," *HR Magazine,* Sept. 2002, pp. 95–100.

3. "Cutting Corners to the Best Candidates," *Weddle's,* Oct. 5, 2004 (*www.weddles.com*).

4. I. J. Shaver, "Innovative Techniques Lure Quality Workers to NASA," *Personnel Journal,* Aug. 1990, pp. 100–106.

5. R. D. Gatewood, M. A. Gowen, and G. Lautenschlager, "Corporate Image, Recruitment Image, and Initial Job Choice Decisions," *Academy of Management Journal,* 1993, 36(2), pp. 414–427.

6. Coopers and Lybrand, *Employment Policies, Turnover, and Cost-per-Hire* (New York: Coopers and Lybrand Compensation Resources, 1992).

7. J. A. Breaugh, *Recruitment: Science and Practice* (Boston: PWS-Kent, 1992); R. E. Thaler-Carter, "In-House Recruiters Fill a Specialized Niche," *HR Magazine,* Apr. 1998, pp. 72–78.

8. S. L. Rynes and J. W. Boudreau, "College Recruiting Practices in Large Organizations: Practice, Evaluation, and Research Implications," *Personnel Psychology,* 1986, 39(3), pp. 286–310.

9. J. Sullivan, "Becoming a Great Recruiter," in N. C. Burkholder, P. J. Edwards, and L. Sartain (eds.), *On Staffing* (Hoboken, NJ: Wiley, 2004), pp. 6–67.

10. C. Patton, "Recruiter Attack," *Human Resource Executive,* Nov. 2000, pp. 106–109; E. Zimmerman, "Fight Dirty Hiring Tactics," *Workforce,* May 2001, pp. 30–34.

11. D. H. Freedman, "The Monster Dilema," *Inc.*, May 2007, pp. 77–78; J. Barthold, "Waiting in the Wings," *HR Magazine,* Apr. 2004, pp. 89–95; A. M. Chaker, "Luring Moms Back to Work," *New York Times,* Dec. 30, 2003, pp. D1–D2; B. McConnell, "Hiring Teens? Go Where They Are Hanging Out," *HR-News,* June 2002, p. 16; J. Mullich, "They Don't Retire Them They Hire Them," *Workforce Management,* Dec. 2003, pp. 49–57; R. Rodriguez, "Tapping the Hispanic Labor Pool," *HR Magazine,* Apr. 2004, pp. 73–79; C. Wilson, "Rehiring Annuitants," *IPMA-HR News,* Aug. 2003, pp. 1–6.

12. B. L. Rau and M. M. Hyland, "Role Conflict and Flexible Work Arrangements: The Effects on Applicant Attraction," *Personnel Psychology,* 2002, 55, pp. 111–136.

13. P. F. McKay and D. R. Avery, "What Has Race Got to Do With It? Unraveling the Role of Racioethnicity in Job Seekers' Reactions to Site Visits." *Personnel Psychology,* 2006, 59, pp. 395–429; D. R. Avery, "Reactions to Diversity in Recruitment Advertising: Are the Differences Black and White?" *Journal of Applied Psychology,* 2003, 88, pp. 672–679; D. R. Avery and P. F. McKay, "Target Practice: An Organizational Impression Management Approach to Attracting Minority and Female Job Applicants," *Personnel Psychology,* 2006, 59, pp. 157–187.

14. F. Hansen, "Recruiting the Closer: Dealing With a Deal Maker," *Workforce Management Online,* Oct. 2007 (*www.workforce.com/archive/feature/25/18/58/index.php*).

15. R. T. Cober, D. J. Brown, P. E. Levy, and J. H. Shalhoop, *HR Professionals' Attitudes Toward and Use of the Internet for Employee Recruitment,* Executive Report, University of Akron and Society for Human Resource Management Foundation, 2003.

16. K. Maher, "Online Job Hunting Is Tough. Just Ask Vinnie," *Wall Street Journal,* June 24, 2003, pp. B1, B10.

17. M. Franse-Blunt, "Make a Good First Impression," *HR Magazine,* Apr. 2004, pp. 81–86; D. S. Onley, "Improving Your Online Application Process," *HR Magazine,* Oct. 2005 (*www.shrm.org/hrmagazine/articles/1005/1005hrtech.asp*); J. Post, "Online, In-house," *Workforce Management,* May 2005, pp. 49–51; G. Ruiz, "Studies Examine the Online Job Hunting Experience," *Workforce Management Online,* July 2006 (*www.workforce.com/archive/feature/24/45/31/index.php*).

18. F. Hansen, "Using Social Networking to Fill the Talent Acquisition Pipeline," *Workforce Management Online,* Dec. 2006 (*www.workforce.com/archive/feature/24/60/64/index.php*); E. Frauenheim, "Company Profile: Recruiters Get LinkedIn in Search of Job Candidates," *Workforce Management Online,* Nov. 2006 (*www.workforce.com/archive/feature/24/58/49/index.php*); A. Leung, "Different Ties for Different Needs: Recruitment Practices of Entrepreneurial Firms at Different Developmental Phases," *Human Resource Management,* 2003, 42, pp. 303–320.

19. D. R. Avery, "Reactions to Diversity in Recruitment Advertising: Are the Differences Black and White?" *Journal of Applied Psychology,* 2003, 88, pp. 672–679; D. R. Avery and P. F. McKay, "Target Practice: An Impression Management Approach to Attracting Minority and Female Job Applicants," *Personnel Psychology,* 2006, 59, pp. 157–187.

20. Freedman, "The Monster Dilemma," pp. 77–78; R. Zeidner, "Companies Tell Their Stories in Recruitment Videos," *HR Magazine,* Dec. 2007, p. 28; J. Borzo, "Taking on the Recruiting Monster," *Fortune Small Business,* May 2007, p. 89.

21. D. M. Cable and K.Y.T. Yu, "Managing Job Seekers' Organizational Image Beliefs: The Role of Media Richness and Media Credibility," *Journal of Applied Psychology,* 2006, 91, pp. 828–840.

22. G. Ruiz, "Newspapers, Job Boards Step Up Partnerships," *Workforce Management,* Dec. 11, 2006, pp. 17–18.

23. P. Babcock, "Narrowing the Pool: Employers Ponder Worth of Niche Job Sites, and Many Take the Plunge" *SHRM Online HR Technology Focus Area,* May 2007 (*www.shrm.org/outsourcing/library/*).

24. Avery and McKay, "Target Practice: An Organizational Impression Management Approach to Attracting Minority and Female Job Applicants," pp. 157–187.

25. E. Krell, "Recruiting Outlook: Creative HR for 2003," *Workforce,* Dec. 2002, pp. 40–45.

26. D. M. Cable and K. Y. T. Yu, "Managing Job Seekers' Organizational Image Beliefs: The Role of Media Richness and Media Credibility."

27. J. Flato, "Key Success Factors for Managing Your Campus Recruiting Program: The Good Times and Bad," in Burkholder, Edwards, and Sartain (eds.), *On Staffing,* pp. 219–229; J. Floren, "Constructing a Campus Recruiting Network," *EMT,* Spring 2004, pp. 29–31; C. Joinson, "Red Hot College Recruiting," *Employment Management Today,* Oct. 4, 2002 (*www.shrm.org/emt*); J. Mullich, "College Recruitment Goes for Niches," *Workforce Management,* Feb. 2004 (*www.workforce.com*).

28. A. Sanders, "We Luv Booz," *Forbes,* Jan. 24, 2000, p. 64; M. Schneider, "GE Capital's E-Biz Farm Team," *Business Week,* Nov. 27, 2000, pp. 110–111.

29. R. Buckman, "What Price a BMW? At Stanford, It May Only Cost a Resume," *Wall Street Journal,* Aug. 19, 2000, p. A1; S. Grabczynski, "Nab New Grads by Building Relationships With Colleges," *Workforce,* May 2000, pp. 98–103.

30. D. L. McLain, "Headhunters Edge Toward Consulting," *Wall Street Journal,* May 5, 2002, p. B4–18; S. J. Wells, "Slow Times for Executive Recruiting," *HR Magazine,* Apr. 2003, pp. 61–68.

31. L. Gomes, "Executive Recruiters Face Built-In Conflict Evaluating Insiders," *Wall Street Journal,* Oct. 14, 2002, p. B1.

32. Deutsch, Shea, and Evans, *Human Resources Manual* (New York: author, 1992–1993).

33. R. J. Grossman, "Made From Scratch," *HR Magazine,* Apr. 2002, pp. 44–52.

34. L. Q. Doherty and E. N. Sims, "Quick, Easy Recruitment Help—From a State?" *Workforce,* May 1998, pp. 35–42.

35. D. Aberman, "Smaller, Specialized Recruiting Events Pay Off in Big Ways," *EMA Today,* Winter 1996, pp. 8–10; T. A. Judge and D. M. Cable, "Role of Organizational Information Sessions in Applicant Job Search Decisions," Working paper, Department of Management and Organizations, University of Iowa; D. M. Cable and K. Y. T. Yu, "Managing Job Seekers' Organizational Image Beliefs: The Role of Media Richness and Media Credibility."

36. S. Armour, "Employers Court High School Teens," *Arizona Republic,* Dec. 28, 1999, p. E5; C. Hymowitz, "Make a Careful Search to Fill Internships: They May Land a Star," *Wall Street Journal,* May 23, 2000, p. B1; "In a Tight Job Market, College Interns Wooed," *IPMA News,* Nov. 2000, p. 22.

37. P. J. Franks, "Well-Integrated Learning Programs," in N. C. Burkholder, P. J. Edwards, and L. Sartain (eds.), *On Staffing,* pp. 230–238.

38. L. J. Bassi and J. Ludwig, "School-to-Work Programs in the United States: A Multi-Firm Case Study of Training, Benefits, and Costs," *Industrial and Labor Relations Review,* 2000, 53, pp. 219–239.

39. C. Johansson, "Retailer Shops for Older Employees," *Wisconsin State Journal,* June 7, 2004, p. C8.

40. Post, "Online, in-house," pp. 49–51.

41. S. Overman, "Keep Hot Prospects on Tap," *Staffing Management,* Jan. 2007, pp. 19–21.

42. P. Weaver, "Tap Ex-Employees Recruitment Potential," *HR Magazine,* July 2006, pp. 89–91.

43. D. S. Chapman, K. L. Uggerslev, S. A. Carroll, K. A. Piasentin, and D. A. Jones, "Applicant Attraction to Organizations and Job Choice: A Meta-Analytic Review of the Correlates of Recruiting Outcomes," *Journal of Applied Psychology,* 2005, 90, pp. 928–944; M. A. Zottoli and J. P. Wanous, "Recruitment Source Research: Current Status and Future Directions," *Human Resource Management Review,* 2000, 10, pp. 353–382.

44. S. L. Premack and J. P. Wanous, "A Meta-Analysis of Realistic Job Preview Experiments," *Journal of Applied Psychology,* 1985, 70, pp. 706–719.

45. J. P. Wanous, *Recruitment, Selection, Orientation, and Socialization of Newcomers,* second ed. (Reading, MA: Addison-Wesley, 1992).

46. R. D. Bretz, Jr., and T. A. Judge, "Realistic Job Previews: A Test of the Adverse Self-Selection Hypothesis," *Journal of Applied Psychology,* 1998, 83, pp. 330–337; D. M. Cable, L. Aiman-Smith, P. W. Molvey, and J. R. Edwards, "The Sources and Accuracy of Job Applicants' Beliefs About Organizational Culture," *Academy of Management Journal,* in press; "The Fit Factor of Online Recruiting," *Weddle's,* July 2001, pp. 3–4; Y. Ganzach, A. Pazy, Y. Ohayun, and E. Brainin, "Social Exchange and Organizational Commitment: Decision-Making Training for Job Choice as an Alternative to the Realistic Job Preview," *Personnel Psychology,* 2002, 55, pp. 613–637; P. W. Hom, R. W. Griffeth, L. E. Palich, and J. S. Bracker, "An Exploratory Investigation Into Theoretical Mechanisms Underlying Realistic Job Previews," *Personnel Psychology,* 1998, 51, pp. 421–451; B. M. Meglino, E. C. Ravlin, and A. S. DeNisi, "A Meta-Analytic Examination of Realistic Job Preview Effectiveness: A Test of Three Counter-Intuitive Propositions," *Human Resource Management Review,* 2000, 10, pp. 407–434; J. M. Phillips, "Effects of Realistic Job Previews on Multiple Organizational Outcomes: A Meta-Analysis," *Academy of Management Journal,* 1998, 41, pp. 673–690.

47. C. J. Collins, "The Interactive Effects of Recruitment Practices and Product Awareness on Job Seekers' Employer Knowledge and Application Behaviors," *Journal of Applied Psychology,* 2007, 92, pp. 180-190; C. J. Collins and C. K. Stevens, "The Relationship Between Early Recruitment-Related Activities and the Application Decisions of New Labor-Market Entrants: A Brand Equity Approach to Recruitment," *Journal of Applied Psychology*, 2002, 87, pp. 1121–1133; P. J. Kiger, "Talent Acquisition Special Report: Burnishing the Brand" *Workforce Management,* Oct. 22, 2007, pp. 39–45.

48. Corporate Leadership Council, *The Employment Brand: Building Competitive Advantage in the Labor Market* (Washington, DC: author, 1999); E. Silverman, "Making Your Mark," *Human Resource Executive,* Oct. 16, 2004, pp. 32–36; M. Spitzmüller, R. Hunington, W. Wyatt, and A. Crozier, "Building a Company to Attract Talent," *Workspan,* July 2002, pp. 27–30.

49. C. J. Collins and C. K. Stevens, "The Relationship Between Early Recruitment-Related Activities and the Application Decisions of New Labor-Market Entrants: A Brand Equity Approach to Recruitment," *Journal of Applied Psychology,* 2002, 87, pp. 1121–1133; F. Lievens and S. Highhouse, "The Relation of Instrumental and Symbolic Attributes to a Company's Attractiveness as an Employer," *Personnel Psychology,* 2003, 56, pp. 75–102.

50. R. H. Bretz and T. A. Judge, "The Role of Human Resource Systems in Job Applicant Decision Processes," *Journal of Management,* 1994, 20, pp. 531–551; D. Cable and T. Judge, "Pay Preferences and Job Search Decisions: A Person-Organization Fit Perspective," *Personnel Psychology,* 1994, 47, pp. 648–657; T. J. Thorsteinson, M. A. Billings, and M. C. Joyce, "Matching Recruitment Messages to Applicant Preferences," Poster presented at 16th annual conference of Society for Industrial and Organizational Psychology, San Diego, 2001.

51. R. J. Vandenberg and V. Scarpello, "The Matching Model: An Examination of the Processes Underlying Realistic Job Previews," *Journal of Applied Psychology,* 1990, 75(1), pp. 60–67.

52. D. R. Ilgen, C. D. Fisher, and M. S. Taylor, "Consequences of Individual Feedback on Behavior in Organizations," *Journal of Applied Psychology,* 1979, 64, pp. 349–371.

55. College Placement Council, College Relations and Recruitment Sourcebook; College Placement Council, "Technology," *Spotlight on Career Planning, Placement, and Recruitment,* 1995, 18(1), p. 2.

56. College Placement Council, "Technology"; D. Kelly, "High Tech Hits Recruiting," *Human Resource Executive,* Apr. 1994, pp. 43–45; K. O. Magnusen and K. G. Kroeck, "Videoconferencing Maximizes Recruiting," *HR Magazine,* Aug. 1995, pp. 70–72.

57. Wernimont, "Recruitment Policies and Practices"; G. Ruiz, "Print Ads See Resurgence as Hiring Source," *Workforce Management,* Mar. 26, 2007, pp. 16–17.

60. R. T. Cober, D. J. Brown, and P. E. Levy, "Form, Content, and Function: An Evaluative Methodology for Corporate Employment Web Sites," *Human Resource Management,* 2004, 43, pp. 201–218; R. T. Cober, D. J. Brown, P. E. Levy, A. B. Cobler, and K. M. Keeping, "Organizational Web Sites: Web Site Content and Style as Determinants of Organizational Attraction," *International Journal of Selection and Assessment,* 2003, 11, pp. 158–169.

61. "A 'Shopper Friendly' Web Site," *Weddle's,* Oct. 2002, p. 1; "KISS Your Web Site Visitors," *Weddle's,* Apr. 2002, p. 1.

62. S. L. Rynes, "Recruitment, Job Choice, and Post-Hire Decisions," in M. D. Dunnette and L. M. Hough (eds.), *Handbook of Industrial and Organizational Psychology,* Vol. 2 (Palo Alto, CA: Consulting Psychologists Press, 1991), pp. 399–444; J. L. Scott, "Total Quality College Relations and Recruitment Programs: Students Benchmark Best Practices," *EMA Journal,* Winter 1995, pp. 2–5; J. P. Wanous, *Organizational Entry,* second ed. (Reading, MA: Addison-Wesley, 1992).

63. D. S. Chapman, K. L. Uggerslev, S. A. Carroll, K. A. Piasemtin, and D. A. Jones, "Applicant Attraction to Organizations and Job Choice: A Meta-Analytic Review of the Correlates of Recruiting Outcomes," *Journal of Applied Psychology,* 2005, 90, pp. 928–944; W. R. Boswell, M. V. Roehling, M. A. Le Pine, and L. M. Moynihan, "Individual Job-Choice Decisions and the Impact of Job Attributes and Recruitment Practices: A Longitudinal Field Study," *Human Resource Management,* 2003, 42, pp. 23–37; A. M. Ryan, J. M. Sacco, L. A. McFarland, and S. D. Kriska, "Applicant Self-Selection: Correlates of Withdrawal From a Multiple Hurdle Process," *Journal of Applied Psychology,* 2000, 85, pp. 163–179; S. L. Rynes, "Recruitment, Job Choice, and Post-Hire Decisions"; S. L. Rynes, "Who's Selecting Whom? Effects of Selection Practices in Applicant Attitudes and Behaviors," in N. Schmitt, W. Borman, and Associates (eds.), *Personnel Selection in Organizations* (San Francisco: Jossey-Bass, 1993), pp. 240–276; S. L. Rynes, R. D. Bretz, and B. Gerhart, "The Importance of Recruitment and Job Choice: A

Different Way of Looking," *Personnel Psychology,* 1991, 44, pp. 487–521; M. S. Taylor and T. J. Bergmann, "Organizational Recruitment Activities and Applicant Reactions to Different Stages of the Recruiting Process," *Personnel Psychology,* 1988, 40, pp. 261–285.

64. B. Dineen, S. R. Ash, and R. A. Noe, "A Web of Applicant Attraction: Person-Organization Fit in the Context of Web-Based Recruitment," *Journal of Applied Psychology,* 2002, 87, pp. 723–734; D. C. Feldman and B. S. Klaas, "Internet Job Hunting: A Field Study of Applicant Experiences With On-Line Recruiting," *Human Resource Management,* 2002, 41, pp. 175–192; K. Maher, "The Jungle," *Wall Street Journal,* July 18, 2002, p. B10; D. L. Van Rooy, A. Alonso, and Z. Fairchild, "In With the New, Out With the Old: Has the Technological Revolution Eliminated the Traditional Job Search Process?" *International Journal of Selection and Assessment,* 2003, 11, pp. 170–174.

65. R. H. Glover and R. A. Schwinger, "Defining an Applicant: Maintaining Records in the Electronic Age," *Legal Report,* Society for Human Resource Management, Summer 1996, pp. 6–8; G. P. Panaro, *Employment Law Manual,* second ed. (Boston: Warren Gorham Lamont, 1993), pp. I-51 to I-57.

66. V. J. Hoffman and G. M. Davis, "OFCCP's Internet Applicant Definition Requires Overhaul of Recruitment and Hiring Policies," *Legal Report,* Society for Human Resource Management, Jan./Feb. 2006; D. Reynolds, "OFCCP Guidance on Defining a Job Applicant in the Internet Age: The Final Word?" *The Industrial/Organizational Psychologist,* 2006, 43(3), pp. 107–113.

67. J. Arnold, "Online Job Sites: Convenient but Not Accessible to All," *Society for Human Resource Management,* July 31, 2007 (*shrm.org/hrtx/library_published/nonIC/CMS_022275.asp*); K. Gurchiek, "Video Resumes Spark Curiosity, Questions," *HR Magazine,* May 2007, pp. 28–30; J. McGregor, "Because of That Video Resume," *Business Week,* June 11, 2007, p. 12; Bureau of National Affairs, "Resume Scanning, Tracking Software Raises New Discrimination Issues," *Daily Labor Report,* Mar. 17, 1998, pp. C1–C2; J. Click, "Blend Established Practices With New Technologies," *HR Magazine,* Nov. 1997, pp. 59–64; R. L. Hogler, C. Henle, and C. Bemus, "Internet Recruiting and Employment Discrimination: A Legal Perspective," *Human Resource Management Review,* 1998, 8, pp. 149–164; J. M. Stanton, "Validity and Related Issues in Web-Based Hiring," *The Industrial-Organizational Psychologist,* 1999, 36, pp. 69–77.

68. Bureau of National Affairs, *Fair Employment Practices* (Washington, DC: author, periodically updated), pp. 405:4027–4033; 405:6847–6848.

69. R. M. Green and R. J. Reibstein, *Employer's Guide to Workplace Torts* (Washington, DC: Bureau of National Affairs, 1992), pp. 40–61, 200, 254–255.

70. A. G. Feliu, *Primer on Individual Employee Rights* (Washington, DC: Bureau of National Affairs, 1992), p. 270.

CHAPTER SIX

Internal Recruitment

Recruitment Planning
   Organizational Issues
   Administrative Issues
   Timing

Strategy Development
   Closed, Open, and Targeted Recruitment
   Recruitment Sources
   Recruitment Metrics

Searching
   Communication Message
   Communication Medium

Applicant Reactions

Transition to Selection

Legal Issues
   Affirmative Action Programs Regulations
   Bona Fide Seniority Systems
   The Glass Ceiling

Summary

Discussion Questions

Ethical Issues

Applications

The objective of the internal recruitment process is to identify and attract applicants from among individuals already holding jobs with the organization. The nearly ubiquitous presence of internal labor markets underscores the importance of effective internal recruiting. Many organizations have recognized that careful management of their existing employee base may be a cost-effective way to fill upper-level managerial and professional vacancies. One survey of 725 human resource (HR) professionals found that as a result of rising recruiting, selection, training, and development costs, companies are increasingly looking internally to staff positions.[1] A majority of those surveyed reported that managing their internal talent pool was either a high (45.6%) or very high (27.7%) strategic priority in their organization. Typically, the development of internal talent was seen as one of the top talent management tasks (63% of respondents), even more so than acquisition of talent (49.4% of respondents). Unfortunately, despite the imperative placed on improving talent management, this survey also showed that only 25.7% of companies have a formal talent management strategy, and only 13.8% of small businesses have a formal talent management system. The first step in this process is recruitment planning, which addresses both organizational and administrative issues. Organizational issues include mobility paths and mobility path policies. Administrative issues include requisitions, number and types of contacts, budgets, and the recruitment guide.

The second step in the internal recruitment process is strategy development. Attention is directed to where, when, and how to look for qualified internal applicants. Knowing where to look requires an understanding of open, closed, and targeted internal recruitment systems. Knowing how to look requires an understanding of job postings, intranets and intraplacement, a talent management system, nominations, in-house temporary pools, replacement and succession plans, and career development centers. Knowing when to look requires an understanding of lead time and time sequence concerns.

The third step in the process is searching for internal candidates. This step consists of the communication message and medium for notification of the job vacancy. The message can be realistic, branded, or targeted. The medium for delivery can be a job posting, other written documents, and potential supervisors and peers.

The fourth step in the process is developing a system to make the transition to selection for job applicants. Making a transition requires a well-developed job posting system and providing applicants with an understanding of the selection process and how to best prepare for it.

The fifth step in the process is the consideration of legal issues. Specific issues to be addressed include Affirmative Action Programs regulations, bona fide seniority systems, and the glass ceiling. All three of these issues deal with mechanisms for enhancing the identification and attraction of minorities and women for higher-level jobs within the organization.

RECRUITMENT PLANNING

Prior to identifying and attracting internal applicants to vacant jobs, attention must be directed to organizational and administrative issues that facilitate the effective matching of internal applicants with vacant jobs.

Organizational Issues

Just as the external labor market can be divided into segments or strata of workers believed to be desirable job applicants, so, too, can the internal labor market of an organization. This division is often done inside organizations on an informal basis. For example, managers might talk about the talented pool of managerial trainees this year and refer to some of them as "high-potential employees." As another example, people in the organization talk about their "techies," an internal collection of employees with the technical skills needed to run the business.

At a more formal level, organizations must create a structured set of jobs for their employees and paths of mobility for them to follow as they advance in their careers. To do this, organizations create internal labor markets. Each internal labor market has two components: mobility paths and mobility policies. Mobility paths depict the paths of mobility between jobs. Mobility policies cover the operational requirements needed to move people between jobs.

Mobility Paths

A mobility path consists of possible employee movements within the internal labor market structure. Mobility paths are determined by many factors, including workforce, organization, labor union, and labor market characteristics. Mobility paths are of two types: hierarchical and alternative. Both types of mobility paths determine who is eligible for a new job in the organization.

Hierarchical Mobility Paths.   Examples of hierarachial mobility paths are shown in Exhibit 6.1. As shown, the emphasis is primarily on upward mobility in the organization. Due to the upward nature of hierarchial mobility paths, they are often labeled promotion ladders. This label implies that each job is a step toward the top of the organization. Upward promotions in an organization are often seen by employees as prizes because of the promotions' desirable characteristics. Employees receive these prizes as they compete against one another for available vacancies. For example, a promotion might lead to a higher rate of pay, and a transfer may result in a move to a better work location. Research has shown that these competitions may be contested, as opportunities for upward advancement are limited in most organizations.[2]

An exception to the primarily upward mobility in the promotion ladders in Exhibit 6.1 shows the lateral moves that sometimes occur for the staff member who has both generalist and specialist experiences as well as corporate and division

EXHIBIT 6.1 **Hierarchical Mobility Paths**

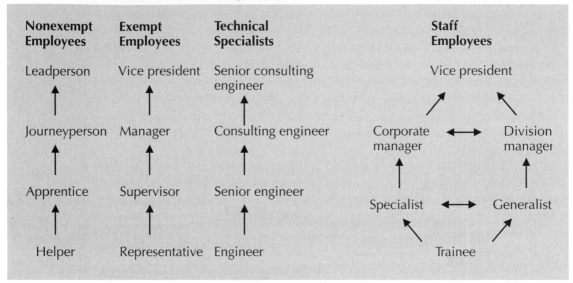

experience. This staff member is considered more well-rounded and better able to work within the total organization. Experience as a specialist helps the person be familiar with technical issues that arise. Experience as a generalist gives the employee a breadth of knowledge about many matters in the staff function. Corporate experience provides a policy and planning perspective, whereas division experience provides greater insight on day-to-day operational matters.

Hierarchical mobility paths make it very easy, from an administrative vantage point, to identify where to look for applicants in the organization. For promotion, one looks at the next level down in the organizational hierarchy, and over, for transfer. Although such a system is straightforward to administer, it is not very flexible and may inhibit the matching of the best person for the job. For example, the best person for the job may be at two job levels down and in another division from the vacant job. It is very difficult to locate such a person under a hierarchical mobility path.

Alternative Mobility Paths. Examples of alternative mobility paths are shown in Exhibit 6.2. The emphasis here is no longer simply on upward mobility. Instead, movement in the organization may be in any direction, including up, down, and from side to side. Employee movement is emphasized to ensure continuous learning by employees such that each can make the greatest contribution to the organization. This is in direct contrast to the hierarchical promotion ladder, where the goal is for each person to achieve a position with ever-higher status. Many organizations have shifted to alternative mobility paths for two reasons: (1) There is the need to

---

EXHIBIT 6.2   Alternative Mobility Paths

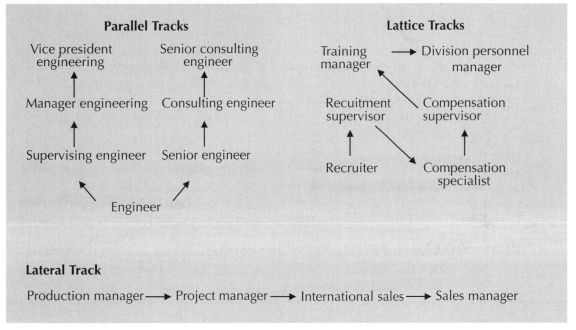

be flexible given global and technological changes, and (2) slower organizational growth has made it necessary to find alternative ways to utilize employees' talents. Parallel tracks allow for employees to specialize in technical work or management work and advance within either. Historically, technical specialists had to shift away from technical to managerial work if they wanted to receive higher-status job titles and pay. In other words, being a technical specialist was a dead-end job. Under a parallel track system, both job titles and salaries of technical specialists are elevated to be commensurate with their managerial counterparts.

With a lateral track system, there may be no upward mobility at all. The individual's greatest contribution to the organization may be to stay at a certain level of the organization for an extended period of time while serving in a variety of capacities, as shown in Exhibit 6.2.

A lattice mobility path has upward, lateral, and even downward movement. For example, a recruiter may be promoted to a recruitment supervisor position, but to continue to contribute to the organization, the person may need to take a lateral step to become knowledgeable about all the technical details in compensation. After mastering these details, the person may then become a supervisor again, this time in the compensation area rather than in recruitment. From a previous company, the person may have experience in training and be ready to take the next move to training manager without training experience internal to the organization. Finally, the person may take a lateral move to manage all the human resources (HR) functions (recruitment, compensation, training) in a division as a division personnel manager.

Increasingly, some organizations have abandoned career structures altogether. In these team-based kinds of jobs, employees do not occupy traditional jobs but are "bonded" together with other employees, depending on the project. In this structure, employees are essentially entrepreneurial consultants, and the organization facilitates their activities. One example of such a cellular organization is TCG, based in Sydney, Australia. TCG partners with other organizations to provide computer assistance. TCG employees work on particular projects, depending on their expertise, and are rewarded based on the success of the project. These rewards may involve assignment to larger projects in the future, which is a form of promotion.[3]

The downside to alternative mobility paths, such as those discussed, is that they are very difficult to administer. Neat categories of where to look do not exist to the same degree as with hierarchical mobility paths. On the positive side, however, talented inside candidates who may not have been identified within a hierarchical system are identified because the system is flexible enough to do so.

When upward mobility is limited in an organization, as with many organizations using alternative mobility paths, special steps need to be taken to ensure that work remains meaningful to employees. If steps are not taken, the organization with limited promotional opportunities risks turnover of good employees. Examples of steps to make work more meaningful include the following:

1. *Alternative reward systems.* Rather than basing pay increases on promotions, pay increases can be based on knowledge and skill acquisition and contribution to the organization as a team member and individual. An example of a career system focused on skill development is the Skill-Based Career Development system, established by the Sony Technology Center in Pittsburgh. When employees start their careers at the technology center, their first three years are devoted to learning core skills such as technical and team skills. During this time, their pay is based on acquisition of these core skills. After three years, employees can choose from several options: (1) continue to develop technical skills on an individual basis, (2) continue to develop team skills, or (3) bid for an opportunity in another Sony business unit. With the first two options, pay continues to be based on skill acquisition but is more individually tailored than during the first three years. This program has been so successful that Sony is using it in other divisions within the company.[4]

2. *Team building.* Greater challenge and autonomy in the workplace can be created by having employees work in teams where they are responsible for all aspects of work involved in providing a service or product, including self-management.

3. *Counseling.* Workshops, self-directed workbooks, and individual advising can be used by organizations to ensure that employees have a well-reasoned plan for movement in the organization.

4. *Alternative employment.* Arrangements can be made for employee leaves of absence, sabbaticals, and consulting assignments to ensure that workers remain challenged and acquire new knowledge and skills.

Mobility Policies

Mobility paths show the relationship among jobs, but they do not show the rules by which people move between jobs. These rules are specified in written policies, which must be developed and should specify eligibility criteria.

Development. A well-defined mobility path policy statement is needed for both hierarchical and alternative mobility paths and has the following characteristics:

1. The intent of the policy is clearly communicated.
2. The policy is consistent with the philosophy and values of top management.
3. The scope of the policy, such as coverage by geographic region, employee groups, and so forth, is clearly articulated.
4. Employees' responsibilities and opportunities for development are clearly defined.
5. Supervisors' responsibilities for employee development are clearly stated.
6. Procedures are clearly described, such as how employees will be notified of openings, time deadlines and data to be supplied by the employee, how requirements and qualifications will be communicated, how the selection process will work, and how job offers will be made.
7. Rules regarding compensation and advancement are included.
8. Rules regarding benefits and benefit changes as they relate to advancement are included.

A well-articulated and well-executed mobility path policy is likely to be seen by employees as being fair. A poorly developed or nonexistent policy is likely to lead to employee claims of favoritism and discrimination.

Eligibility Criteria. An important component of an effective mobility policy is a listing of the criteria by which the organization will decide who is eligible to be considered for an open vacancy in a mobility path. In essence, these criteria restrict eligibility for recruitment to certain individuals. Usually these criteria are based on the amount of seniority, level of experience, KSAOs (knowledge, skill, ability, and other characteristics), or job duties required for the job. For example, to be considered for an international assignment, the applicant may be required to have been with the organization a certain length of time, have experience in a functional area in which there is a vacancy, be proficient in a foreign language, and be interested in performing new duties. These criteria need to be made very clear in the policy, otherwise unqualified people will apply and be disappointed when they are not considered. Also, the organization may be flooded with the paperwork and processing of applicants who are not eligible.

Administrative Issues

Mobility paths and mobility policies must be established as part of the planning process, and so, too, must administrative matters. Those administrative matters include requisitions, coordination, the budget, and the recruitment guide.

Requisitions

A requisition or authorization to fill a position by higher-level management is essential to the internal recruitment process. Without a formal requisition, it is far too easy for managers to make promises or "cut deals" with employees, contrary to organizational objectives. For example, managers may promote their employees into new job titles that have not been authorized by top management. In doing so, they may create perceptions of unfairness among those with similar backgrounds who were not promoted. This action thus runs contrary to the organizational goal of fair HR systems. Thus, formal requisitions should always be used in internal recruitment, just as they are in external recruitment.

Coordination

Internal and external recruitment efforts need to be coordinated and synchronized via the organization's staffing philosophy (see Chapter 3). If this coordination is not done, disastrous results can occur. For example, if independent searches are conducted internally and externally, then two people may be hired for one open vacancy. If only an external recruitment search is conducted, the morale of existing employees may be reduced when they feel that they have been passed over for a promotion. If only an internal recruitment search is conducted, the person hired may not be as qualified as someone from the external market. Because of these possibilities, internal *and* external professionals must work together with the line manager to coordinate efforts before the search for candidates begins.

To coordinate activities, two steps should be taken. First, internal staffing specialist positions should be designated to ensure that internal candidates are considered in the recruitment process. External staffing specialists are called recruiters; internal staffing specialists are often known as placement or classification professionals, to acknowledge the fact that they are responsible for placing or classifying existing employees rather than bringing in or recruiting employees from outside the organization.

Second, policies need to be created that specify the number and types of candidates sought internally and the number and types of candidates sought externally. For example, at Honeywell's Systems and Research Center in Bloomington, Minnesota, a management team meets regularly as part of the planning and development process to make these determinations.[5]

Budget

An organization's internal recruitment budgeting process should also closely mirror the budgeting process that occurs with external recruitment. The cost per hire may, however, differ between internal and external recruitment. The fact that internal recruitment targets candidates already working for the organization does not mean that the cost per hire is necessarily less than the cost per hire for external recruitment. Sometimes internal recruitment can be more costly than external recruitment because some of the methods involved in internal recruitment can be quite expensive. For example, when internal candidates are considered for the job but not hired, they need to be counseled on what to do to further develop their careers to become competitive for the position the next time it is vacant. When an external candidate is rejected, a simple and less costly rejection letter usually suffices.

Recruitment Guide

As with external recruitment, internal recruitment activities involve the development of a recruitment guide, a formal document that details the process to be followed to attract applicants to a vacant job. Included in the plan are details such as the time, money, and staff activities required to fill the job, as well as the steps to be taken to fill the vacancy created by the internal candidate leaving to take the new job. An example of an internal recruitment guide is shown in Exhibit 6.3.

EXHIBIT 6.3 **Internal Recruitment Guide**

Position Reassignments Into New Claims Processing Center

Goal: Transfer all qualified medical claims processors and examiners from one company subsidiary to the newly developed claims processing center. Terminate those who are not well qualified for the new positions and whose existing positions are being eliminated.

Assumptions: That all employees have been notified that their existing positions in company subsidiary ABC are being eliminated and they will be eligible to apply for positions in the new claims processing center.

Hiring responsibility: Manager of Claims Processing and Manager of Claims Examining.

Other resources: Entire human resource department staff.

Time frames:
Positions posted internally on April 2, 2007
Employees may apply until April 16, 2007
Interviews will be scheduled/coordinated during week of April 19, 2007
Interviews will occur during the week of April 26, 2007
Selections made and communicated by last week in May
Total number of available positions: 60

(continued)

EXHIBIT 6.3 **Continued**

Positions available and corresponding qualification summaries:

6 claims supervisors—4-year degree with 3 years of claims experience, including 1 year of supervisory experience.

14 claims data entry operators—6 months of data entry experience. Knowledge of medical terminology helpful.

8 hospital claims examiners—12 months of claims data entry/processing experience. Knowledge of medical terminology necessary.

8 physician claims examiners—12 months of claims data entry/processing experience. Knowledge of medical terminology necessary.

8 dental claims examiners—12 months of claims data entry/processing experience and 6 months of dental claims examining experience. Knowledge of dental terminology necessary.

8 mental health claims examiners—12 months of claims data entry/processing experience and 6 months of mental health claims experience. Knowledge of medical and mental health terminology necessary.

8 substance abuse claims examiners—12 months of claims data entry/processing experience and 6 months of substance abuse experience. Knowledge of medical terminology necessary.

Transfer request guidelines: Internal candidates must submit internal transfer requests and an accompanying cover page listing all positions for which they are applying, in order of preference. Internal candidates may apply for no more than five positions.

Transfer requests must be complete and be signed by the employee and the employee's supervisor.

Candidate qualification review process: Transfer requests from internal candidates will be reviewed on a daily basis. Those not qualified for any positions for which they applied will be notified by phone that day, due to the large volume of requests.

All transfer requests and accompanying cover pages will be filed by the position to which they refer. If internal candidates applied for more than one position, their transfer packet will be copied so that one copy is in each position folder.

Once all candidate qualifications have been received and reviewed, each candidate's transfer packet will be copied and transmitted to the managers for review and interview selection. Due to the large number of candidates, managers will be required to interview only those candidates with the best qualifications for the available positions. Managers will notify human resources with the candidates with whom they would like interviews scheduled. Whenever possible, the manager will interview the candidate during one meeting for all of the positions applied and qualified for.

Selection guidelines: Whenever possible, the best-qualified candidates will be selected for the available positions.

The corporation has committed to attempting to place all employees whose positions are being eliminated. Managers reserve the right to not select employees currently on disciplinary probationary periods. Employees should be slotted in a position with a salary grade comparable to their current salary grade. Employees' salaries shall not be reduced due to the involuntary nature of the job reassignment.

Notification of nonselection: Candidates not selected for a particular position will be notified by electronic message.

Selection notifications: Candidates selected for a position will be notified in person by the human resource staff and will be given a confirmation letter specifying starting date, position, reporting relationship, and salary.

Timing

A final strategic consideration an organization must make is when to look for internal candidates. As with external recruitment, consideration involves calculation of lead time and time sequence concerns.

Lead Time Concerns

A major difference between internal and external recruitment is that internal recruitment not only fills vacancies but also creates them. Each time a vacancy is filled with an internal candidate, a new vacancy is created in the spot vacated by the internal candidate.

As a result of this difference, it is incumbent on the organization to do HR planning along with internal recruitment. This planning involves elements of succession planning (see Chapter 3). Such planning is essential for effective internal recruitment.

Time Sequence Concerns

As previously noted, it is essential that internal and external recruitment activities be properly coordinated. This proper coordination is especially true with the timing and sequencing of events that must be laid out carefully for both recruitment and placement personnel. Many organizations start with internal recruitment followed by external recruitment to fill a vacancy. Issues that need to be addressed include how long the internal search will take place, whether external recruitment can be done concurrently with internal recruitment, and who will be selected if both an internal and external candidate are identified with relatively equal KSAOs.

STRATEGY DEVELOPMENT

After organizational and administrative issues have been covered in the planning phase of internal recruitment, an organization must develop a strategy to locate viable internal job applicants. It must consider where to look, how to look, and when to look.

Closed, Open, and Targeted Recruitment

The strategy for where to look must be conducted within the constraints of the general eligibility criteria for mobility. Within these constraints it requires a knowledge of closed, open, and targeted systems.

Closed Internal Recruitment System

Under a closed internal recruitment system, employees are not made aware of job vacancies. The only people made aware of promotion or transfer opportunities are those who oversee placement in the HR department, line managers with vacancies, and contacted employees. The way a vacancy is typically filled under a closed system is shown in Exhibit 6.4.

EXHIBIT 6.4 **Closed Internal Recruitment System**

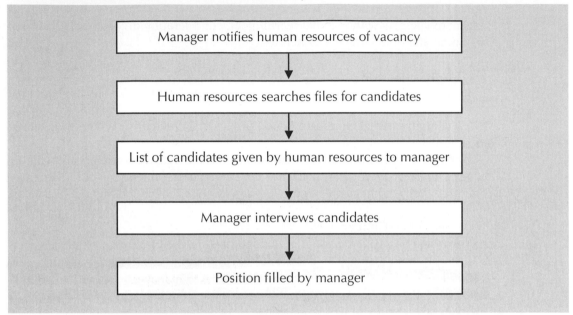

A closed system is very efficient. There are only a few steps to follow, and the time and cost involved are minimal. However, a closed system is only as good as the files showing candidates' KSAOs. If inaccurate or out-of-date files are kept, qualified candidates may be overlooked.

Open Internal Recruitment System

Under an open internal recruitment system, employees are made aware of job vacancies. Usually this is accomplished by a job posting and bidding system. The typical steps followed in filling a vacancy under an open internal recruitment system are shown in Exhibit 6.5.

An open system gives employees a chance to measure their qualifications against those required for advancement. It helps minimize the possibility of supervisors selecting only favorite employees for promotion or transfer. Hidden talent is often uncovered.

An open system may, however, create unwanted competition among employees for limited advancement opportunities. It is a very lengthy and time-consuming process to screen all candidates and provide them with feedback. Employee morale may be decreased among those who are not advanced.

EXHIBIT 6.5   Open Internal Recruitment System

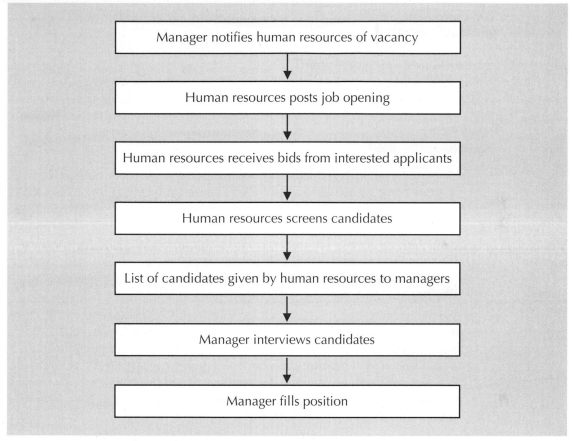

Targeted System of Internal Recruitment

Under a targeted system, both open and closed steps are followed at the same time. Jobs are posted, and the HR department conducts a search outside the job posting system. Both systems are used to cast as wide a net as possible. The large applicant pool is then narrowed down by KSAOs, seniority eligibility, demographics, and availability of applicants.

A targeted system is used by the Englehard Corporation. At Englehard, an HR council meets each month to discuss open positions and possible internal candidates. The council includes the CEO and directors of Englehard's business units to ensure that viable candidates are identified and that the moves make sense for the organization. At the same time, jobs are posted internally so interested (and perhaps overlooked) employees can apply.[6]

A targeted system has three advantages: a thorough search is conducted, people have equal opportunity to apply for postings, and hidden talent is uncovered. The major disadvantage with a targeted system is that it entails a very time-consuming and costly process.

Criteria for Choice of System

In an ideal world with unlimited resources, one would choose a targeted system of internal recruitment. However, resource constraints often make this choice impossible, so organizations must choose between open and closed systems. There are several criteria that need to be thoroughly considered before selecting an internal recruitment system:

1. A closed system is the least expensive in terms of search costs. However, it may lead to high legal costs if minorities and women do not have equal access to jobs. An open system is more costly; a targeted system costs the most.

2. Many managers want a person to start work immediately when they have a vacancy; a closed system offers the quickest response.

3. An open system is more likely than a closed system to identify more candidates, and hidden talent is less likely to be overlooked.

4. Some openings may require a very narrow and specialized KSAO set. A closed system may be able to identify these people quickly. An open system may be very cumbersome when only a select few meet the minimum qualifications needed to perform the job.

5. An open system may motivate migration of labor from jobs that are critical and difficult to fill. If so, then employees may create vacancies in critical areas, which in turn may create new recruitment problems.

6. A labor agreement or contract is a legally binding agreement. Whatever system is specified within must be followed.

7. An open system, where rules and regulations are known, enhances perception of fairness.

Although the choice between open and closed systems is important, with the advent of staffing software (see Chapter 13), bridges between these systems may be built so as to take advantage of the best features of each.

Recruitment Sources

Once it has been specified where and how in the organization individuals are likely to be found, there are several major methods that can be used to decide how to look for them: job postings, intranet and intraplacement, a talent management system, nominations, replacement and succession plans, career development centers, and in-house temporary pools.

Job Postings

A job posting is very similar to the advertisement used in external recruitment. It spells out the duties and requirements of the job and shows how applicants can apply. Its content should be based on the job requirements matrix. A job posting begins when a job vacancy occurs. A position announcement is then posted. This posting may be through a bulletin board, newsletter, e-mail, or intranet (see subsequent section). At this step, organizations must decide whether to first limit the posting or advertise it throughout the organization. If the first posting is limited to a department, location, or work area and the job is not filled, then it should be posted more broadly. Applicants respond to job postings using a bid sheet like the one shown in Exhibit 6.6.

At Home Depot, computer kiosks located in break rooms are used to list job openings. Employees can view these job postings during breaks or before or after shifts. If there is a job that appeals to an employee, he or she can take a computerized test for an opening at the kiosk. If the employee makes the cut, his or her application is forwarded. If the employee fails, the supervisor is notified and the employee may be offered training so he or she can compete successfully for the position in the future.[7]

Even advanced job posting systems may have some problems in administration. Examples of such difficulties include situations where employees believe that someone has been selected before the job was posted (a "bagged" job), cumbersome systems where managers and HR personnel are overwhelmed with résumés of unqualified candidates, and criticisms that the HR department is not doing an effective job of screening candidates for positions.

Some of these problems again point to the critical importance of the job requirements matrix. A good job posting system will clearly define the requisite KSAOs needed to perform the job. By having a job requirements matrix, employees, HR staff, and managers can do a more effective and efficient job of screening.

Another important issue with posting systems is feedback. Not only do employees need to know whether they have received the job, but those who do not receive the job need to be made aware of *why* they did not. Providing this feedback serves two purposes. First, it makes job posting part of the career development system of the organization. Second, it invites future bidding on postings by candidates. If employees are not given feedback, they may be less likely to bid for another job because they feel that their attempts to do so are futile.

An empirical study shows the characteristics of job posting systems that lead to high satisfaction by users.[8] Key characteristics include the adequacy of job descriptions, the adequacy of job notification procedures, the treatment received during the interview, the helpfulness of counseling, and the fairness of the job posting system. These characteristics should be treated as requirements of a good job posting policy.

EXHIBIT 6.6 Example of Bidding Form

INTERNAL APPLICATION FORM COVER SHEET

To apply for a posted position, interested employees should:

1. Look at the job posting notebook(s) or postings posted on the bulletin boards and choose the job or jobs that you are qualified for and interested in applying for. (Check the Qualifications section of the posting.) Make note of the deadline for applying for this position, which is indicated on the posting.

2. Complete one Internal Application Form to apply for a position or positions. This form acts as a résumé/application form. Obtain your direct supervisor's signature before turning the form into human resources.

3. Indicate below the priority of the jobs for which you would like to be given consideration.

   (Priority: 1 = first choice, 2 = second choice, 3 = third choice)

Priority   Job Title

_____   _____

_____   _____

_____   _____

_____   _____

_____   _____

4. Attach this cover sheet to the UHC Internal Application Form and turn both in to Karen in human resources by the application deadline appearing on the job posting.

5. Sign and date below:

_____   _____

Employee Signature   Date

SOURCE: Reprinted with permssion from United HealthCare Corporation and Physicians Health Plan of Ohio, Inc., Columbus, Ohio.

As indicated, job posting can be done traditionally by physically posting job openings in a convenient location. Such an approach, however, can be very slow, inefficient, and create a large amount of paperwork. A faster and more efficient way to post jobs is to put them on personal computers, which also gives employees 24-hours-a-day access to job postings.

Intranet and Intraplacement

An intranet is similar to the Internet, except that it is confined to the organization. This makes it ideal for internal recruitment because jobs can be quickly posted for all employees to see. Some companies have expanded their intranet to include an online career center, where employees not only view job postings but also gain access to information about KSAOs needed for positions that might interest them; it may even include modules that will assist employees in acquiring these KSAOs.

A company's internal e-mail and intranet capabilities provide an ideal tool to remind employees about prospects inside the organization, and they also serve as a counter to other organizations' efforts to acquire high-potential employees. Whirlpool set up an intranet system so that managers who have an opening can enter the criteria into the system, and employees can find a list of jobs that might match their skills and interests. Other companies such as BMW, Kellogg, Hyatt, and Hewlett-Packard have followed suit. Some vendors, such as Recruitsoft, SAP, Oracle, and *hire.com*, have developed software specifically for this application.

Some tips for ensuring that companies make the best use of their intranet include impressing on managers the importance of competing for internal talent (so they will be motivated to use the system), encouraging employees to use the system and emphasizing that it is for them, and making sure the interested employees get personal attention (even if they are not selected).[9]

Talent Management System

A talent management system is a comprehensive method for monitoring and tracking the utilization of employee skills and abilities throughout the organization.[10] The process of talent management is closely aligned with replacement and succession planning—talent management systems track the KSAOs of the workforce, and then replacement and succession planning translates information from the talent management system into concrete action plans for specific job roles. Although talent management involves performance management and training processes in addition to managing the internal recruiting process, tracking employees' knowledge, skills, and abilities and their use in the organization is the key component to talent management systems.

Although a number of different models for implementing talent management systems exist, there are a few key processes common to most. The first stage of the process is identifying the KSAOs required for all jobs in the organization. This information can be obtained from job descriptions and job specifications. The complete set of KSAOs required across the organization will then be compiled into a master list. Then the current workforce will need to be assessed for its competence in this set of KSAOs, usually as an adjunct to routine performance evaluations. When positions come open, managers make a query to the talent management system to determine which employees are ready to come into open positions. There should also be a process in place to make regular comprehensive examinations of the changing nature of KSAO requirements throughout the organization. Information from these analyses can then be used as a springboard for developing comprehensive plans for training and development experiences.

There has been such a strong integration of database software for talent management systems that when staffing managers refer to talent management systems, they are often talking about the specific human resources information system (HRIS) that is used to facilitate tracking KSAOs in the workforce. While these database applications offer great promise for coordinating information, many managers find operating talent management systems challenging. Most of the problems in implementing talent management systems in practice do not come from a lack of technology, but rather, an excess of technology that cannot be understood by line managers. There are a few principles that should be borne in mind when developing or evaluating a user-friendly talent management system:

- Keep the format for entering data as simple as possible.
- Have an easy method for updating basic information with each performance evaluation cycle.
- Make it easy to perform database queries.
- Provide varied formats for obtaining reports.
- Ensure that information is confidential.
- It should be possible to perform statistical analyses using relational databases.
- The data should be integrated with other HR files.

Nominations

Nominations for internal candidates to apply for open positions can be solicited from potential supervisors and peers. These individuals may be an excellent source of names of internal candidates, as they have a great deal of familiarity with what is required to be successful in the position. They can help establish the criteria for eligibility and then, through their contacts in the organization, search for eligible candidates. Self-nominations are also very useful in that they ensure that qualified candidates are not inadvertently overlooked using other applicant searching methods. Self-nomination is an especially important consideration in the internal recruitment of minorities and women.

Using employees to refer potential hires to the organization is a common method of looking for candidates in external recruitment. Though it has not been used much in internal recruitment, more companies are using employees' referrals to staff positions internally. One system that helps companies do this is CareerRewards. CareerRewards uses Web-based software that rewards employees who refer other employees within the company for open positions. Employees log onto their company's CareerRewards site and make referrals. If a referral is hired, the employee is rewarded (rewards differ from company to company). There are other providers of internal referral systems.[11] Regardless of what system is used, as with external recruitment, employee referral programs used internally may need to rely on formal programs with recognition for participation to get employees actively participating in making referrals. Moreover, they need to be educated on eligibility requirements to ensure that qualified personnel are referred.

In-House Temporary Pools

In-house temporary pools are not only important to the temporary staffing of organizations as the temporary need for personnel arises periodically, but they are also an excellent source of permanent internal employment. Unlike employees hired through external staffing agencies, those who are employed through in-house temporary pools are legally treated as employees. Therefore, the full legal liability for these employees falls exclusively on the employer. However, there are a number of advantages that have been identified for the use of in-house temporary employees.[12] Internal temporary employees require less orientation to the organization than would external hires. Staffing agencies typically charge an employer an hourly fee for each temporary employee. But with an internal system, because the employer does not have to pay an external agency for each hour the temporary employees work, the cost savings can be applied to higher levels of compensation and benefits. It is also easier for an organization to ensure the quality and person/organization fit for employees from an in-house pool relative to a pool of external hires. Temporary employment can also serve as an "audition" for full-time employment, allowing the temporary employees to try out a number of positions until the employee and the organization agree that there is a good person/job match. For example, Carroll County, Maryland, set up an in-house temporary pool to deal with absences, vacations, and vacancies. Rather than relying on costly temporary agencies, Carroll County has five entry-level employees who fill in wherever needed. The city of Little Rock, Arkansas, has a similar program.[13] In health care, it is common to have "float" staff who are assigned to different units regularly, depending on the organization's needs. Substitute teachers are staffed in a similar manner. Such employees must be adaptable to different situations, and the organization must ensure that there is sufficient work for the employees. Also, extra training may be needed for these employees since they are expected to have a broad range of skills in their repertoire.

Replacement and Succession Plans

A critical source of internal recruitment is provided by the results of replacement and succession planning. Most succession plans include replacement charts (see Chapter 3), which indicate positions and who is scheduled to fill those slots when they become vacant. Replacement charts usually also indicate the time until the individual is ready for the assignment. Succession plans are organized by position and list the skills needed for the prospective position (i.e., "for the employee to be ready for promotion into this position from her current position, these are the skills she needs to process or develop"). Dow Chemical's succession plan, for example, includes a list of "now ready" candidates; where there are jobs with similar competencies, it clusters roles and lists candidates for these roles as well. Dow has formal succession plans for 50–60 jobs that it has identified as critical corporate roles and also has plans for another 200–300 jobs that are identified as needing continuity.

It is critical that succession planning be future oriented, lest the organization plan be based on historical competencies that fail to meet new challenges. Software exists to assist companies with succession planning. Saba Succession is a succession planning package that interfaces with a company's HR information system to provide replacement charts and competency libraries that allow an organization to identify developmental activities and assignments for individuals in the replacement charts. Many Fortune 500 companies use Saba Succession.

CEO succession has always been an important issue for organizations, but never more so than today. The need for employee development has heightened as an increasing proportion of the workforce is approaching retirement. There is a very strong concern among career development specialists that the mass retirement of baby boomers will lead to a loss of organizational memory and knowledge built up with experience. Having strong succession planning techniques that will enable the more recently hired workforce to acquire knowledge from its experienced coworkers before moving into managerial positions is one way to minimize the impact of mass retirements. For example, at Bristol-Myers Squibb, a talent management program has been developed that provides employees with feedback on how to learn from great managers and leaders, and widely announces internal promotions with descriptions of the demonstrated leadership skills that led to the promotion being granted.[14] Many large, successful corporations lack clear succession plans. The problem may be even more severe in Asia, where many large conglomerates and family-owned businesses are run by aging chief executives without a clear succession plan in place.[15]

The key to avoiding potential fiascoes is to have a succession plan for CEOs. However, a poll of 518 companies indicated that only 42% had such a formal succession plan in place. According to a study by the National Association of Corporate Directors, a succession plan should begin with a thorough job analysis and a listing of the characteristics and behaviors of a successful CEO. The company should not leave it to the CEO to identify a successor. CEOs are typically not trained or experienced in staffing, and they may have selfish motives in appointing a successor. Or, they may avoid appointing a successor altogether, thus keeping themselves in the job. Therefore, the board must be deeply involved in the selection process. Boards also need to realize that the succession process should begin well before the CEO departs; in fact, it should be a continuous process.

Career Development Centers

To facilitate internal transfers, many organizations have an internal office of career development that helps employees explore the career options available within the organization.[16] Career development centers provide employees with opportunities to take interest inventories, assess their personal career goals, and interview with representatives across the organization. The goal of career development centers is twofold. First, employees learn about themselves and have a chance to think about what they really want to achieve in their careers. Second, employers have a chance to explain the career options within the organization and develop methods to structure internal career paths that match the interests of their employees. Surveys conducted in numerous organizations consistently demonstrate that employees are more satisfied when their employers provide them with ample communication and opportunities for internal advancement—an interactive career development center can provide both.[17]

The interest inventories provided in career development centers often take the form of multiple choice questionnaires that ask employees to indicate which work activities they prefer. For example, respondents might be asked to identify whether they prefer tasks that involve analytical processes like analyzing financial data or more social tasks like motivating a group of workers. After completing these surveys, employees compare their work preferences to the profile of activities in a variety of jobs. Career development counselors can also help talk employees through their thoughts and concerns about job options. Ideally, these career development inventories, coupled with careful analysis of KSAOs, will be paired with job analysis information to improve the person/job match. If employees lack the required KSAOs, career development counselors can suggest developmental work experiences or training opportunities.

Any assessment of career development centers needs to take the organization's bottom line into account.[18] Having full-time career development staff is a significant cost for any organization, and it is unlikely that small or medium-sized organizations will find it cost effective to develop a comprehensive career development center. For smaller organizations, it is more advisable to develop smaller-scale informal initiatives based on personal interactions. Smaller organizations can make use of some career development tools by bringing in external career coaches or consultants to deal with individuals who are especially interested in career development within the organization. To reduce costs, it is possible to have employees take their career development profiles and receive initial feedback through Web-based surveys. These electronic survey options save money by reducing staff needs, and employees will not need to go to the career development offices to receive initial counseling.

Although career development centers are complicated to develop and expensive to maintain, they do offer organizations an opportunity to help employees learn about a large spectrum of career offerings. By providing employees with a clear sense of how they can direct their own careers, it is hoped that job satisfaction will increase, which in turn will hopefully lead to increased retention. Because of the cost of career development services, it is especially important to keep track of the return on investment for these services.

Recruiting Metrics

As with external recruiting sources, each internal recruiting source has strengths and weaknesses. Exhibit 6.7 provides an overview of the metrics that might be expected for the categories of recruiting activities along with issues to be considered relevant to each source. There is far less research on the costs and benefits of internal recruiting techniques, so our comments here are necessarily somewhat speculative; it is likely that each organization will need to consider its unique needs even more thoroughly than it would when selecting external recruiting methods.

Sufficient Quantity

Because the organization's pool of employees will necessarily be smaller than the general labor market, most internal recruiting methods will have far lower quantity yields. Techniques that permit job postings and intranets will likely produce far more candidates for promotion and advancement than will succession plans.

Sufficient Quality

The degree to which the organization utilizes its own internal information on candidate qualifications and job performance to narrow the pool will determine how qualified the applicants will be. Most organizations that have internal recruiting systems will have a huge advantage in assessing applicant characteristics over organizations that use external recruiting systems, so the ability of each source to draw in qualified internal candidates should capitalize on the additional capacity to carefully observe candidates. Regular performance appraisals of all employees, coupled with talent management systems to track KSAOs, are a vital part of an effective internal recruiting system.

Cost

Internal recruitment methods have a completely different set of costs than external recruitment methods. In some ways, internal recruitment can be far less expensive than external recruitment, because usually the organization's own internal communication systems can be utilized. It costs very little to send an e-mail to all qualified staff informing them of job opportunities or to post job advertisements on either a physical or electronic bulletin board. However, systems that are more sophisticated, such as a corporate intranet or comprehensive talent management systems, will take more personnel resources to set up and maintain. Career development centers are very costly propositions, and only organizations with considerable internal placement needs will find them cost effective.

Impact on HR Outcomes

There has been very little research on the effectiveness of various internal recruitment sources. Thus, it is imperative that organizational leaders consider how their internal recruiting systems are impacting turnover rates, job performance, and

---

EXHIBIT 6.7 **Potential Recruiting Metrics for Different Sources**

Recruiting Method	Quantity	Quality	Costs	Impact on HR
Job posting	Often will be the company's entire workforce	Because all employees will be able to apply, quality is variable	Staff time to develop the recruiting message	May reduce turnover, reduced time to full performance
Intranet and intraplacement	Similar to job posting, although will weed out those who don't like the job characteristics	Better than job postings because applicants have more customized advance knowledge	Sophisticated interface systems will cost more in development time	May reduce turnover, reduced time to full performance
Talent management system	Identifies knowledge, skills, and abilities across all employees	High; preselection of applicants based on identified skill sets	Maintenance of databases can be very time and resource intensive	Higher performance, reduced downtime, reduced training costs
Nominations	Limited to those who receive positive appraisals by supervisors or coworkers	If supervisors make accurate assessments, will be very good person job match	Many companies keep routine records of employee performance	Can actively identify those who will be good performers and target identified training needs
In-house temporary pools	Based on organization's need for temporary staff coverage	Higher quality if in-house temps receive better benefits than what external staffing firms provide	Start-up costs can be significant; reduces payments to external agencies	More accountability relative to external agencies; increased internal flexibility
Replacement and succession plans	A small number of select workers seen as having high potential	Able to assess skill sets very carefully and consider configurations	HRIS start-up costs, data entry, and checking	Reduces gaps in leadership, protects against shocks due to turnover, reduced turnover
Career development centers	The set of employees who are interested in career development	Assesses employee KSAOs and preferences	Start-up costs, cost of staff, system maintenance	Significant reduction in turnover, increased match between KSAOs and work requirements

diversity. Despite the lack of research, because it is easier to directly measure the applicant pool contacted through internal methods, it should be easier to monitor these outcomes directly. Some preliminary conclusions can be drawn regarding the advantages of internal placement based on anecdotal observations. There is some evidence that internal career opportunities can reduce turnover intentions. Internal recruitment methods may reduce the time it takes for employees to reach full performance once placed, because they will already be familiar with the organization and may know more about the job in question than would an external hire. Any costs of internal recruitment should be compared against the costs of external recruiting, and the replacement of the employee who takes an internal position should also be taken into account.

SEARCHING

Once the planning and strategy development phases are conducted, it is time to conduct the search. As with external recruitment, the search for internal recruits is activated with a requisition. Once the requisition has been approved, the message and medium must be developed to communicate the vacancy to applicants.

Communication Message

As with external recruitment, the message to be communicated can be realistic, targeted, or branded. A realistic message portrays the job as it really is, including positive and negative aspects. A targeted message is one that points out how the job matches the needs of the applicant. A branded message emphasizes the value, culture, and identity of the unit so as to attract applicants who fit the brand label.

Realistic messages can be communicated using a technique like a realistic job preview (RJP). This technique needs to be applied carefully for internal recruitment because, as a result of their already being a member of the organization, applicants may have an accurate picture of the job. Hence, an RJP may not be needed. It should not, however, be automatically assumed that all internal candidates have accurate information about the job and organization. Hence, RJPs are appropriate for internal applicants when they move to an unknown job, a newly created job, or a new geographic area, including an international assignment.

Targeted messages along with inducements are likely to attract experienced internal employees. Targeted messages about the desirability of a position and the actual rewards should come directly from the job rewards matrix. Clearly, the information in the job rewards matrix needs to be communicated by the hiring manager who hopes to catch an experienced employee, rather than offers of elaborate promises that the manager may not be able to keep.

Communication Medium

The actual method or medium used to communicate job openings internally may be a job posting, other written documents, potential supervisors and peers, and informal systems. In a job posting, the duties and requirements of the job should be clearly defined, as should the eligibility requirements. To ensure consistency and fair treatment, job postings are usually coordinated by the HR department.

Other written documents used to communicate a vacancy may include a description of the organization and location as well as a description of the job. A brochure, videocassette, or diskette can be created to actually show and describe what the organization and the location of the organization is really like. This message may be of critical importance to the applicant, who may, for example, be asked to relocate to a new geographic area or to accept an international assignment.

Potential supervisors and peers can be used to describe to the internal applicant how the position he or she is considering fits into the larger organizational picture. Supervisors will have knowledge about how the position fits with the strategic direction of the organization. Hence, they can communicate information regarding the expansion or contraction of the business unit within which the organization resides. Moreover, supervisors can convey the mobility paths and requirements for future movement by the applicants within the business unit, should they be hired. Peers can be used to supplement these supervisory observations to give candidates a realistic look at what actually happens by way of career development.

Informal systems exist in organizations where organizational members communicate with one another about job vacancies to be filled internally in the absence of verifiable information. The problem with "word of mouth," the "grapevine," or "hall talk" is that it can be a highly selective, inaccurate, and haphazard method of communicating information. It is selective because, by accident or design, not all employees hear about vacant jobs. Talented personnel, including minorities and women, may thus be overlooked. It is inaccurate because it relies on second- or thirdhand information; important details, such as actual job requirements and rewards, are omitted or distorted as they are passed from person to person. Informal methods are also haphazard in that there is no regular communication channel specifying set times for communicating job information. As a result of these problems, informal systems are not to be encouraged.

APPLICANT REACTIONS

A glaring omission in the research literature is a lack of attention paid to studying the reactions of applicants to the internal recruitment process. This lapse stands in stark contrast to the quantity of research conducted on reactions to the external recruitment process. One notable exception in the internal recruitment process is the study of perceived fairness. Given limited opportunities for promotion and transfer, issues of fairness often arise over mobility decisions within an organization. Issues of fairness can be broken down into the categories of distributive and procedural justice. Distributive justice refers to how fair the employee perceives the actual decision to be (e.g., promote or not promote). This particular aspect of fairness is very salient today because there are a large number of baby boomers competing for the few positions at the tops of organizational hierarchies. At the same time, many organizations are eliminating middle management positions. Procedural justice refers to how fair the employee perceives the process (e.g., policies and procedures) that leads to the promotion or transfer decision to be. Reviews of the evidence suggest that procedures may be nearly as great a source of dissatisfaction to employees as decisions.[19] In some organizations, dissatisfaction arises as a result of the fact that there is no formal policy regarding promotion and transfer opportunities. In other organizations, there may be a formal policy, but it may not be closely followed. In yet other organizations, it may be who you know rather than what you know that serves as the criterion that determines advancement. Finally, in some organizations there is outright discrimination against women and minorities. All of these examples are violations of procedural justice and are likely to be perceived as unfair.

TRANSITION TO SELECTION

As with external recruitment, once a job seeker has been identified and attracted to a new job, the organization needs to prepare the person for the selection process. It should not be assumed that just because job seekers come from inside the organization they will automatically know and understand the selection procedures. With the rapid advances being made in selection methods, the applicant may be unaware of new methods being used that are different from those used previously to hire the applicant to a previous job. Even if the same selection methods are being used, the applicant may need to be "refreshed" on the process, as a considerable period of time may have elapsed between the current and previous selection decisions.

An example of an organization that has done an excellent job of preparing internal job seekers to become applicants is the Public Works Agency for the county of Sacramento, California.[20] The county uses a panel of interviewers together, rather than a series of individual interviews, to make selection decisions. For many lower-level employees in the maintenance department, this approach was a first-time experience. Consequently, they were apprehensive about this process because they had no previous experience with the internal selection process. In response to this situation, the HR group initially conducted training classes to describe the process to applicants. However, this was a very time-consuming process for the staff, so they replaced the classroom training with videos. One major component of the video was the preparation required prior to the panel interview. Instructions here included appropriate dress and materials to review. Another major component of the video depicted what happens to the applicant during the panel interview. This component included instructions on types of questions to be asked, the process to be followed, and do's and don'ts in answering the panel interview questions. A final component of the video was testimonials from previous exam takers who have become managers. They explain from an organizational perspective what the organization is looking for, as well as study tips and strategies.

LEGAL ISSUES

The mobility of people within the organization, particularly upward, has long been a matter of equal employment opportunity/affirmative action (EEO/AA) concern. The workings of the internal labor market rely heavily on internal recruitment activities. As with external recruitment, internal recruitment activities can operate in exclusionary ways, resulting in unequal promotion opportunities, rates, and results for certain groups of employees, particularly women and minorities. The Affirmative Action Programs regulations specifically address internal recruitment as part of the federal contractor's AAP. Seniority systems are likewise subject to legal scrutiny, particularly regarding the determination of what constitutes a bona fide system under the law. More recently, promotion systems have been studied as they relate to the "glass ceiling" effect and the kinds of barriers that have been found to stifle the rise of minorities and women upward in organizations.

Affirmative Action Programs Regulations

Regulations on Affirmative Action Programs from the Office of Federal Contract Compliance Programs (OFCCP) require promotion placement goals where there are discrepancies between percentages of minorities and women employed and available internally in job groups. Accompanying these goals must be an identification of problem areas and action-oriented programs to correct the problem areas. As in the case of external recruitment, the regulations are virtually silent on indications of specific steps the organization might take to correct promotion system problems. Previous (now expired) regulations provide many useful ideas.

Suggestions include the following:

- Post or otherwise announce promotion opportunities.
- Make an inventory of current minority and female employees to determine academic, skill, and experience levels of individual employees.
- Initiate necessary remedial job training and work-study programs.
- Develop and implement formal employee evaluation programs.
- Make certain that "worker specifications" have been validated on job performance–related criteria (neither minority nor female employees should be required to possess higher qualifications than those of the lowest qualified incumbent).

- When apparently qualified minority or female employees are passed over for upgrading, require supervisory personnel to submit written justification.
- Establish formal career counseling programs to include attitude development, education aid, job rotation, buddy systems, and similar programs.
- Review seniority practices and seniority clauses in union contracts to ensure such practices or clauses are nondiscriminatory and do not have a discriminatory effect.

As can be seen, the previous regulations contained a broad range of suggestions for reviewing and improving promotion systems. In terms of recruitment itself, the previous regulations appeared to favor developing KSAO-based information about employees as well as an open promotion system characterized by job posting and cautious use of seniority as a basis for governing upward mobility.

Bona Fide Seniority Systems

Title VII (see Chapter 2) explicitly permits the use of bona fide seniority systems as long as they are not the result of an intention to discriminate. This position presents the organization with a serious dilemma. Past discrimination in external staffing may have resulted in a predominantly white male workforce. A change to a nondiscriminatory external staffing system may increase the presence of women and minorities within an organization, but they will still have less seniority there than the white males. If eligibility for promotion is based on seniority and/or if seniority is an actual factor considered in promotion decisions, then those with less seniority will have a lower incidence of promotion. Thus, the seniority system will have an adverse impact on women and minorities, even though there is no current intention to discriminate. Is such a seniority system bona fide?

Two points are relevant here. First, the law never defines the term "seniority system." Generally, however, any established system that uses length of employment as a basis for making decisions (such as promotion decisions) is interpreted as a seniority system. Promotions based on ad-hoc judgments about which candidates are "more experienced," however, would not likely be considered a bona fide seniority system.[21] Seniority systems can and do occur outside the context of a collective bargaining agreement.

Second, current interpretation is that, in the absence of a discriminatory intent, virtually any seniority system is likely to be bona fide, even if it causes adverse impact.[22] This interpretation creates an incentive for the organization not to change its current seniority-based practices or systems. Other pressures, such as the Affirmative Action Program regulations or a voluntary AAP, create an incentive to change in order to eliminate the occurrence of adverse impact in promotion. The organization thus must carefully consider exactly what its posture will be toward seniority practices and systems within the context of its overall AAP.

Under the Americans With Disabilities Act (ADA) there is potential conflict between needing to provide reasonable accommodation to an employee (such as job reassignment) and provisions of the organization's seniority system (such as bidding for jobs on the basis of seniority). According to the Supreme Court, it will ordinarily be unreasonable (undue hardship) for a reassignment request to prevail over the seniority system unless the employee can show some special circumstances that warrant an exception.

The Glass Ceiling

The "glass ceiling" is a term used to characterize strong but invisible barriers for women and minorities to promotion in the organization, particularly to the highest levels. Evidence demonstrating the existence of a glass ceiling is substantial. Some evidence on the existence of the glass ceiling is as follows. The overall labor force is 74% white and 54% male. At the very top in large corporations, senior-level managers are overwhelmingly white males. As one goes down the hierarchy and across industries, a more mixed pattern of data emerges. Equal Employment Opportunity Commission (EEOC) data show that on a nationwide basis, the percentage of women who are officials and managers has increased to a present-day 36.4%. In some industries, particularly health care, department stores, legal services, and banking, the percentage of women managers is substantially higher, ranging from 47 to 77%. In other industries, such as manufacturing, trucking, and architectural/engineering services, the percentage of women managers is much lower (13 to 18%).[23] Unfortunately, similar kinds of data for minorities are not available, though few doubt a general underrepresentation of minorities as well in managerial roles. Thus, the closer to the top of the hierarchy, the thicker the glass in the ceiling. At lower levels, the glass becomes much thinner. There are substantial variations in this pattern, though, across industries.

Where glass ceilings exist, there are two important questions to ask: What are the reasons for a lack of upward mobility and representation for minorities and women at higher levels of the organization? What changes need to be made, especially staffing-related ones, to help shatter the glass ceiling?

Barriers to Mobility

An obvious conclusion from such data is that there are barriers to mobility, many of them originating within the organization. The Federal Glass Ceiling Commission conducted a four-year study of glass ceilings and barriers to mobility. It identified many barriers: lack of outreach recruitment practices, mentoring training in revenue-generating areas, and access to critical developmental assignments; initial selection for jobs in staff areas outside the upward pipeline to top jobs; biased performance ratings; little access to informal networks; and harassment by colleagues.[24] Added to this list should be another important barrier, namely, childrearing and domestic responsibilities that create difficult work/life balance choices.

An instructive illustration of these barriers, particularly the internal ones, comes from a 21-company study of men and women in sales careers.[25] The study found that 41% of women and 45% of men were eager to move into management, but the women were much less optimistic of their chances of getting promoted. Whereas the sales forces studied were 26% female, only 14% of sales managers were female. The study portrayed "a survivalist culture where career paths are more like obscure jungle trails and where most women say they experience sexual harassment." The study also found "recruiters' use of potentially discriminatory screening tests, managers' negative stereotypes about women, women's lack of access to career-boosting mentors and networks, and difficulty entertaining customers in traditional ways such as fishing and golf outings." Saleswomen were also highly dependent on their mostly male managers for job and territory assignments, which were often based on stereotypes about willingness to travel, relocate, and work long hours.

Overcoming Barriers

It is generally recognized that multiple actions, many of them beyond just staffing-system changes, will be needed to overcome barriers to mobility. Exhibit 6.8 shows a listing of such actions, many of which are consistent with recommendations of the Glass Ceiling Commission.[26]

In terms of specific staffing practices that are desirable for eliminating the glass ceiling, we offer the following suggestions. Barriers to upward mobility can be addressed and removed, at least in part, through internal recruitment activities. Internal recruitment planning needs to involve the design and operation of internal labor markets that facilitate the identification and flows of people to jobs throughout the organization. This may very well conflict with seniority-based practices or seniority systems, both of which are likely to be well entrenched. Organizations simply have to make hard and clear choices about the role(s) that seniority will play in promotion systems.

In terms of recruitment strategy, where to look for employees looms as a major factor in potential change. The organization must increase its scanning capabilities and horizons to identify candidates to promote throughout the organization. In particular, this requires looking across functions for candidates, rather than merely promoting within an area (from sales to sales manager to district manager, for example). Candidates should thus be recruited through both hierarchial and alternative career paths.

Recruitment sources have to be more open and accessible to far-ranging sets of candidates. Informal, word-of-mouth, and "good old boy" sources do not suffice. Job posting and other recruitment strategies that encourage openness of vacancy notification and candidate application will become necessary.

Recruitment changes must be accompanied by many other changes.[27] Top male managers need to fully understand that women executives differ from them

EXHIBIT 6.8   Ways to Improve Advancement for Women and Minorities

Examine the Organizational Culture
- Review HR policies and practices to determine if they are fair and inclusive.
- Examine the organization's informal culture: look at subtle behaviors, traditions and norms that may work against women.
- Discover men's and women's perceptions about the organization's culture, their career expectations, and what drives their intentions to stay or leave.
- Identify the organization's best practices that support women's advancement.

Drive Change Through Management Commitment
- Support top-management commitment to talent management, including women in senior positions.
- Ensure that diversity (including women in senior positions) is a key business measurement for success that is communicated to all employees by top management.
- Require line management accountability for advancement of women by incorporating it in performance goals.
- Train line managers to raise awareness and understand barriers to women's advancement.

Foster Inclusion
- Establish and lead a change-management diversity program for managers and employees.
- Affirm diversity inclusion in all employment brand communications.
- Develop a list of women for succession planning.
- Develop and implement retention programs for women.

Educate and Support Women in Career Development
- Emphasize the importance of women acquiring line management experience.
- Encourage mentoring via informal and formal programs.
- Acknowledge successful senior-level women as role models.
- Support the development and utilization of women's networks inside and outside the organization.
- Create and implement leadership development programs for women, including international assignments, if applicable.

Measure for Change
- Monitor the impact of recruiting strategies designed to attract women to senior levels of the organization.
- Track women's advancement in the organization (hiring, job rotation, transfers, international assignments, promotions).
- Determine who gets access to leadership and management training and development opportunities.
- Evaluate differences between salary of men and women at parallel levels within the organization.
- Measure women's turnover against men's.
- Explore reasons why women leave the organization.

SOURCE: Adapted from N. Lockwood, *The Glass Ceiling* (Alexandria, VA: Society for Human Resource Management, 2004), pp. 8–9. Used with permission.

in what they perceive to be the major barriers to advancement. Research suggests that women executives are more likely to see an exclusionary climate (male stereotyping and preconceptions of women, exclusion from informal networks, and inhospitable corporate culture) as a critical barrier, whereas top male managers are more likely to point to experience deficiencies (lack of significant general management and line experience, not being in the pipeline long enough) as the culprit. Hence, top management must take steps to not only create better experience-generating opportunities for women, but also develop and foster a more inclusive climate for women, such as through mentoring and providing access to informal networks. To encourage such changes and improve advancement results for women and minorities, managers must be held formally accountable for their occurrence.

An example of a far-reaching diversity initiative to expand the internal diversity pipeline is the "Championing Change for Women: An Integrated Strategy" program in Safeway, a retail grocery giant. A focal point is the Retail Leadership Development (RLD) Program, a formal full-time career development program for entry-level grocery store employees to prepare them for moving up into the management ranks (90% of store managers and above come through the program). The program has a particular focus on women and people of color. They apply for the program by taking a retail knowledge and skill exam. Those who complete the program are immediately assigned to a store as an assistant manager—the stepping stone to further advancement. To support the advancement program, all managers attend a managing diversity workshop, receive additional on-the-job education, and have access to a toolkit to help them incorporate diversity discussions into their staff meetings. Managers are evaluated in part on their success in meeting diversity goals, and bonus money is riding on that success. Every manager is also expected to serve as a mentor, helping mentees acquire the KSAOs necessary for continued advancement. Other elements of the program include strong support and participation from the CFO, women's leadership network groups (for black, Asian, Hispanic, and LGBT employees), modification of a requirement to relocate in order to gain experience, and work/life balance initiatives for employees with and without children. Since the program was initiated, the number of women who qualified for and completed the RLD program rose 37%, and the number of women store managers increased by 42% (31% for white women and 92% for women of color).[28]

In summary, solutions to the glass ceiling problem require myriad points of attack. First, women and minorities must have visibility and support at top levels—from the board of directors, the CEO, and senior management. That support must include actions to eliminate prejudice and stereotypes. Second, women and minorities must be provided the job opportunities and assignments that will allow them to develop the depth and breadth of KSAOs needed for ascension to, and success in, top management positions. These developmental experiences include assignments in multiple functions, management of diverse businesses, line management experience with direct profit-loss and bottom-line accountability, diverse geographic assignments, and international experience. Naturally, the relative importance of these experiences will vary according to type and size of the organization. Third, the organization must provide continual support for women and minorities to help ensure positive person/job matches. Included here are mentoring, training, and flexible work hours systems. Fourth, the organization must gear up its internal recruitment to aggressively and openly track and recruit women and minority candidates for advancement. Finally, the organization must develop and use valid methods of assessing the qualifications of women and minority candidates (see Chapters 8 and 9).[29]

SUMMARY

The steps involved in the internal recruitment process closely parallel those in the external recruitment process. These steps include planning, strategy development, and communication. With internal recruitment, the search is conducted inside rather than outside the organization. Where both internal and external searches are conducted, they need to be coordinated with each other.

The planning stage requires that the applicant population be identified. Doing so requires an understanding of mobility paths in the organization and mobility path policies. To get access to the internal applicant population, attention must be devoted in advance of the search to requisitions, number and types of contacts, the budget, development of a recruitment guide, and timing.

In terms of strategy development, a closed, open, or targeted system can be used to decide where to look. How to look requires a knowledge of recruitment sources, such as job postings, intranet and intraplacement, nominations, a talent management system, in-house temporary pools, replacement and succession plans, and career development centers. Just as with external recruitment, there are multiple criteria to be considered in choosing internal sources.

When searching for candidates, the message to be communicated can be realistic, targeted, or branded. Which approach is best to use depends on the applicants, job, and organization. The message is usually communicated with a job posting. It should, however, be supplemented with other media, including other written documents and potential peers' and supervisors' input. Informal communication methods with information that cannot be verified or with incomplete information are to be discouraged.

The organization needs to provide the applicant with assistance for the transition to selection. This assistance requires that the applicant be made fully aware of the selection process and how to best prepare for it. Taking this step, along with providing well-developed job postings and clearly articulated mobility paths and policies in the organization, should help applicants see the internal recruitment system as fair.

Internal recruitment activities have long been the object of close legal scrutiny. Past and current regulations make several suggestions regarding desirable promotion system features. The relevant laws permit bona fide seniority systems, as long as they are not intentionally used to discriminate. Seniority systems may have the effect of impeding promotions for women and minorities because these groups have not had the opportunity to accumulate an equivalent amount of seniority to that of white males. The glass ceiling refers to invisible barriers to upward advancement, especially to the top levels, for minorities and women. Studies of promotion systems indicate that internal recruitment practices contribute to this barrier. As a portion of an overall strategy to shatter the glass ceiling, changes are now being experimented with for opening up internal recruitment. These include actions to eliminate stereotypes and prejudices, training and developmental experiences, mentoring, aggressive recruitment, and use of valid selection techniques.

DISCUSSION QUESTIONS

1. Traditional career paths emphasize strict upward mobility within an organization. How does mobility differ in organizations with innovative career paths? List three innovative career paths discussed in this chapter, describing how mobility occurs in each.

2. A sound policy regarding promotion is important. List the characteristics necessary for an effective promotion policy.

3. Compare and contrast a closed internal recruitment system with an open internal recruitment system.

4. What information should be included in the targeted internal communication message?

5. Exhibit 6.8 contains many suggestions for improving the advancement of women and minorities. Choose the three suggestions you think are most important and explain why.

ETHICAL ISSUES

1. Let's say a company called MDN, Inc. is considering two employees for the job of senior manager. An internal candidate, Julie, has been with MDN for 12 years and has received very good performance evaluations. The other candidate, Raoul, works for a competitor and has valuable experience in the product market into which MDN wishes to expand. Do you think MDN has an obligation to promote Julie? Why or why not?

2. Do organizations have an ethical obligation to have a succession plan in place? If no, why not? If so, what is the *ethical* obligation, and to whom is it owed?

APPLICATIONS

Recruitment in a Changing Internal Labor Market

Mitchell Shipping Lines is a distributor of goods on the Great Lakes in the United States. Not only does it distribute goods but it also manufactures shipping containers used to store the goods while in transit. The name of the subsidiary that manufactures those containers is Mitchell-Cole Manufacturing, and the president and CEO is Zoe Brausch.

Brausch is in the middle of converting the manufacturing system from an assembly line to autonomous work teams. Each team will be responsible for producing a separate type of container, and each team will have different tools, machinery, and manufacturing routines for its particular type of container. Members of each team will have the job title "assembler," and each team will be headed by a permanent "leader." Brausch would like all leaders to come from the ranks of current employees, in terms of both the initial set of leaders and the leaders in the future as vacancies arise. In addition, she wants employee movement across teams to be discouraged in order to build team identity and cohesion. The current internal labor market, however, presents a formidable potential obstacle to her internal staffing goals.

Based on a long history in the container manufacturing facility, employees are treated like union employees even though the facility is nonunion. Such treatment was desired many years ago as a strategy to remain nonunion. It was management's belief that if employees were treated like union employees, there should be no need for employees to vote for a union. A cornerstone of the strategy is use of what everyone in the facility calls the "blue book." The blue book looks like a typical labor contract, and it spells out all terms and conditions of employment. Many of those terms apply to internal staffing and are very typical of traditional mobility systems found in unionized work settings. Specifically, internal transfers and promotions are governed by a facility-wide job posting system. A vacancy is posted throughout the facility and remains open for 30 days; an exception to this is identified entry-level jobs that are filled only externally. Any employee with two or more years of seniority is eligible to bid for any posted vacancy; employees with less seniority may also bid, but they are considered for positions only if no two-year-plus employees apply or are chosen. Internal applicants are assessed by the hiring manager and a representative from the HR department. They review applicants' seniority, relevant experience, past performance appraisals, and other special KSAOs. The blue book requires that the most senior employee who meets the desired qualifications receive the transfer or promotion. Thus, seniority is weighted heavily in the decision.

Brausch is worried about this current internal labor market, especially for recruiting and choosing team leaders. These leaders will likely be required to have many KSAOs that are more important than seniority, and KSAOs likely to not even be positively related to seniority. For example, team leaders will need to have advanced computer, communication, and interpersonal skills. Brausch thinks these skills will be critical for team leaders to have, and that they will more likely be found among junior rather than senior employees. Brausch is in a quandary. She asks for your responses to the following questions:

1. Should seniority be eliminated as an eligibility standard for bidding on jobs—meaning no longer giving the two-year-plus employees priority?
2. Should the job posting system simply be eliminated? If so, what should it be replaced with?
3. Should a strict promotion-from-within policy be maintained? Why or why not?
4. How could career mobility paths be developed that would allow across-team movement without threatening team identity and cohesion?
5. If a new internal labor market system is to be put in place, how should it be communicated to employees?

Succession Planning for a CEO

Lone Star Bank, based in Amarillo, is the fourth largest bank in Texas. The president and CEO of Lone Star, Harry "Tex" Ritter, has been with the company for 30 years, the last 12 in his current position as president and CEO. The last three years have been difficult for Lone Star, as earnings have been below average for the industry, and shareholders have grown increasingly impatient. Last month's quarterly earnings report was the proverbial last straw for the board. Particularly troublesome was Ritter's failure to invest enough of Lone Star's assets in higher-yielding investments. Though banks are carefully regulated in terms of their investment strategies, Ritter's investment strategy was conservative even for a bank.

In a meeting last week, the board decided to allow Ritter to serve out the last year of his contract and then replace him. An attractive severance package was hastily put together; when it was presented to Ritter, he agreed to its terms and conditions. Although the board feels it has made a positive step, it is unsure how to identify a successor. When they met with Ritter, he indicated that he thought the bank's senior vice president of operations, Bob Bowers, would be an able successor. Some members of the board think they should follow Ritter's suggestion because he knows the inner workings of the bank better than anyone on the board. Others are not sure what to do.

1. How should Lone Star go about finding a successor to Ritter? Should Bowers be recruited to be the next CEO?
2. How should other internal candidates be identified and recruited?
3. Does Lone Star need a succession plan for the CEO position? If so, how would you advise the board in setting up such a plan?
4. Should Lone Star have a succession plan in place for other individuals at the bank? If so, why and for whom?

ENDNOTES

1. BMP Forum and Success Factors, *Performance and Talent Management Trend Survey 2007* (San Mateo, CA: author, 2007).

2. W. T. Markham, S. L. Harlan, and E. J. Hackett, "Promotion Opportunity in Organizations: Causes and Consequences," in K. M. Rowland and G. R. Ferris (eds.), *Research in Personnel and Human Resources Management,* 1987, 5, pp. 223–287.

3. B. R. Allred, C. C. Snow, and R. E. Miles, "Characteristics of Managerial Careers in the 21st Century," *Academy of Management Executive,* 1998, 10, pp. 17–27.

4. A. Healey, "Implementing a Skill-Based Career Development Program," *ACA News,* May 1998, pp. 15–20.

5. National Foreman's Institute, "The Need for Hiring: A Second Look," *Employee Relations and Human Resources Bulletin* (Waterford, CT: author), Feb. 21, 1993, Report No. 1778, Section 1, p. 7.

6. J. Cook, "Crossover Success," *Human Resource Executive,* Sept. 2000, pp. 117–122.

7. E. R. Silverman, "Break Requests," *Wall Street Journal,* Aug. 1, 2000, p. B1.

8. L. W. Kleinman and K. J. Clark, "Users' Satisfaction With Job Posting," *Personnel Administrator,* 1984, 29(9), pp. 104–110.

9. M. Frase-Blunt, "Intranet Fuels Internal Mobility," *EMT,* Spring 2004, pp. 16–21; L. G. Klaff, "New Internal Hiring Systems Reduce Cost and Boost Morale," *Workforce Management,* July 2004, pp. 17–20; C. Waxer, "Inside Jobs," *Human Resource Executive,* Sept. 2004, pp. 36–41; S. Overman, "Keep Hot Prospects on Tap," Jan. 2007, *Staffing Management,* pp. 19–21.

10. U.S. Office of Personnel Management, *Human Capital Assessment and Accountability Framework* (Washington, DC: author, 2005); A. Gakovic and K. Yardley, "Global Talent Management at HSBC," *Organization Development Journal,* 2007, 25, pp. 201–206; E. Frauenheim, "Talent Management Keeping Score With HR Analytics Software," *Workforce Management,* May 21, 2007, pp. 25–33; K. Oakes, "The Emergence of Talent Management," *T + D,* Apr. 2006, pp. 21–24.

11. B. Calandra, "Reeling Them In," *Human Resource Executive,* May 16, 2000, pp. 58–62; "You've Got Friends," *HR Magazine,* Aug. 2001, pp. 49–55.

12. N. Glube, J. Huxtable, and A. Stanard, "Creating New Temporary Hire Options Through In-House Agencies," Society for Human Resource Management White Paper, 2002 (*www.shrm.org/hrresources/whitepapers_published/CMS_000353.asp#P-4_0*).

13. P. Lindsay, "Personnel Services: An Innovative Alternative to Temporary Staffing Problems," *IPMA-HR News,* Dec. 2003, p. 19; "Temporary or Contingent Workers," *IPMA-HR News,* June 2004, p. 7.

14. E. Goldberg, "Why You Must Build Management Capability," *Workforce Management Online,* Nov. 2007 (*www.workforce.com/archive/feature/25/22/23/index.php?ht=*); M. Toosi, "Labor Force Projections to 2014: Retiring Boomers," *Monthly Labor Review,* 2005, 128(11), pp. 25–44; P. J. Kiger, "With Baby Boomers Graying, Employers Are Urged to Act Now to Avoid Skills Shortages," *Workforce Management,* 2005, 84(13), pp. 52–54.

15. S. McBride, "In Corporate Asia, a Looming Crisis Over Succession," *Wall Street Journal,* Aug. 7, 2003, pp. A1, A6.

16. F. Anseel and F. Lievens, "An Examination of Strategies for Encouraging Feedback Interest After Career Assessment," *Journal of Career Development,* 2007, 33, pp. 250–268; T. F. Harrington and T. A. Harrigan, "Practice and Research in Career Counseling and Development—2005," *Career Development Quarterly,* 2006, 55, pp. 98–167.

17. T. Minton-Eversole, "Continuous Learning—in Many Forms—Remains Top Recruiting, Retention Tool," *SHRM Online Recruiting & Staffing Focus Area,* Feb. 2006 (*www.shrm.org*); Society for Human Resource Management, *2007 Job Satisfaction* (Alexandria, VA: author, 2007).

18. I. Speizer, "The State of Training and Development: More Spending, More Scrutiny," *Workforce Management,* May 22, 2006, pp. 25–26.

19. F. K. Foulkes, *Personnel Policies in Large Nonunion Companies* (Englewood Cliffs, NJ: Prentice-Hall, 1980); M. London and S. A. Stumpf, *Managing Careers* (Reading, MA: Addison Wesley, 1982); Markham, Harlan, and Hackett, "Promotion Opportunity in Organizations: Causes and Consequences"; S. A. Stumpf and M. London, "Management Promotions: Individual and Organizational Factors Influencing the Decision Process," *Academy of Management Review,* 1981, 6(4), pp. 539–549.

20. "Panic or Pass—Preparing for Your Oral Board Review," *IPMA News,* July 1995, p. 2.

21. D. J. Walsh, *Employment Law for Human Resource Practice*, second ed. (Mason, OH: Thompson Higher Education, 2007), p. 207.

22. Bureau of National Affairs, *Fair Employment Practices*, pp. 421:161–166.

23. Equal Employment Opportunity Commission, *Glass Ceilings: The Status of Women as Officials and Managers in the Private Sector* (Washington, DC: author, 2004).

24. Federal Glass Ceiling Commission, "Good for Business: Making Full Use of the Nation's Human Capital—Fact-Finding Report of the Federal Glass Ceiling Commission," *Daily Labor Report,* Bureau of National Affairs, Mar. 17, 1995, Special Supplement, p. S6.

25. S. Shellenberger, "Sales Offers Women Fairer Pay, but Bias Lingers," *Wall Street Journal*, Jan. 24, 1995, p. B1.

26. Federal Glass Ceiling Commission, "Good for Business: Making Full Use of the Nation's Human Capital," p. S19.

27. P. Digh, "The Next Challenge: Holding People Accountable," *HR Magazine,* Oct. 1998, pp. 63–69; B. R. Ragins, B. Townsend, and M. Mattis, "Gender Gap in the Executive Suite: CEOs and Female Executives Report on Breaking the Glass Ceiling," *Academy of Management Executive,* 1998, 12, pp. 28–42.

28. A. Pomeroy, "Cultivating Female Leaders," *HR Magazine,* Feb. 2007, pp. 44–50.

29. K. L. Lyness and D. E. Thompson, "Climbing the Corporate Ladder: Do Male and Female Executives Follow the Same Route?" *Journal of Applied Psychology,* 2000, 85, pp. 86–101; S. J. Wells, "A Female Executive Is Hard to Find," *HR Magazine,* June 2001, pp. 40–49; S. J. Wells, "Smoothing the Way," *HR Magazine,* June 2001, pp. 52–58.

The Staffing Organizations Model

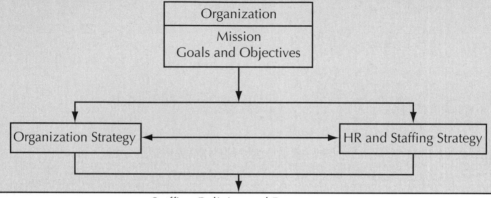

PART FOUR

Staffing Activities: Selection

CHAPTER SEVEN

Measurement

Importance and Use of Measures

Key Concepts
Measurement
Scores
Correlation Between Scores

Quality of Measures
Reliability of Measures
Validity of Measures
Validation of Measures in Staffing
Validity Generalization
Staffing Metrics and Benchmarks

Collection of Assessment Data
Testing Procedures
Acquisition of Tests and Test Manuals
Professional Standards

Legal Issues
Disparate Impact Statistics
Standardization and Validation

Summary

Discussion Questions

Ethical Issues

Applications

Tanglewood Stores Case I

Tanglewood Stores Case II

In staffing, measurement is a process used to gather and express information about persons and jobs in numerical form. A common example in which management employs measurement is to administer a test to job applicants and evaluate their responses to determine a test score for each of them. The first part of this chapter presents a view of the process of measurement in staffing decisions.

After showing the vital importance and uses of measurement in staffing activities, three key concepts are then discussed. The first concept is that of measurement itself, along with the issues raised by it—standardization of measurement, levels of measurement, and the difference between objective and subjective measures. The second concept is that of scoring and how to express scores in ways that help in their interpretation. The final concept is that of correlations between scores, particularly as expressed by the correlation coefficient and its significance. Calculating correlations between scores is a very useful way to learn even more about the meaning of scores.

What is the quality of the measures used in staffing? How sound an indicator of the attributes measured are they? Answers to these questions lie in the reliability and validity of the measures and the scores they yield. There are multiple ways of doing reliability and validity analysis; these are discussed in conjunction with numerous examples drawn from staffing situations. As these examples show, the quality of staffing decisions (e.g., who to hire or reject) depends heavily on the quality of measures and scores used as inputs to these decisions. Some organizations rely only on common staffing metrics and benchmarks—what leading organizations are doing—to measure effectiveness. Though benchmarks have their value, reliability and validity are the real keys in assessing the quality of selection measures.

An important practical concern involved in the process of measurement is the collection of assessment data. There are various decisions about testing procedures (who is qualified to test applicants, what information should be disclosed to applicants, how to assess applicants with standardized procedures) that need to be made. The collection of assessment data also includes the acquisition of tests and test manuals. This process will vary depending on whether paper-and-pencil or computerized selection measures are utilized. Finally, in the collection of assessment data, organizations need to attend to professional standards that govern their proper use.

Measurement concepts and procedures are directly involved in legal issues, particularly equal employment opportunity and affirmative action (EEO/AA) ones. This requires collection and analysis of applicant flow and stock statistics. Requirements for doing these analyses, as expressed in the Uniform Guidelines on Employee Selection Procedures (UGESP) and Affirmative Action Programs regulations, are reviewed. Also reviewed are implications of the results of disparate impact analysis for standardization and validation of measures, particularly as required by the UGESP.

IMPORTANCE AND USE OF MEASURES

Measurement is one of the key ingredients for, and tools of, staffing organizations. Staffing organizations is highly dependent on the availability and use of measures. Indeed, it is virtually impossible to have any type of systematic staffing process that does not use measures and an accompanying measurement process.

Measures are methods or techniques for describing and assessing attributes of objects that are of concern to us. Examples include tests of applicants' KSAOs (knowledge, skill, ability, and other characteristics), evaluations of employees' job performance, and applicants' ratings of their preferences for various types of job rewards. These assessments of attributes are gathered through the measurement process. That process consists of (1) choosing an attribute of concern, (2) developing an operational definition of the attribute, (3) constructing a measure of the attribute (if no suitable measure is available) as it is operationally defined, and (4) using the measure to actually gauge the attribute.

Results of the measurement process are expressed as numbers or scores—for example, applicants' scores on an ability test, employees' performance evaluation rating scores, or applicants' ratings of rewards in terms of their importance. These scores become the indicators of the attribute. Through the measurement process, the initial attribute and its operational definition have been transformed into a numerical expression of the attribute.

KEY CONCEPTS

This section covers a series of key concepts in three major areas: measurement, scores, and correlation between scores.

Measurement

In the preceding discussion, the essence of measurement and its importance and use in staffing were described. It is now important to define the term "measurement" more formally and explore implications of that definition.

Definition

Measurement may be defined as the process of assigning numbers to objects to represent quantities of an attribute of the objects.[1] Exhibit 7.1 contains a depiction of the general process of the use of measures in staffing, along with an example for the job of maintenance mechanic. Following from the definition of measurement provided above, the first step in measurement is to choose and define an attribute (sometimes also called a construct) to be measured. In the example, this is knowledge of mechanical principles. Then, a measure must be developed for the attribute, and at that point the attribute can physically be measured. In the example,

EXHIBIT 7.1   Use of Measures in Staffing

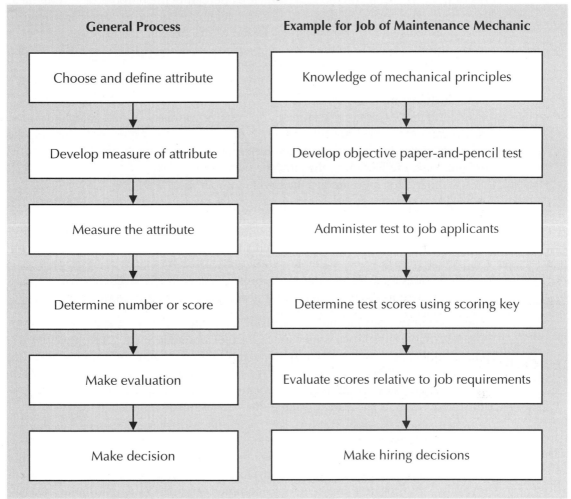

General Process	Example for Job of Maintenance Mechanic
Choose and define attribute	Knowledge of mechanical principles
Develop measure of attribute	Develop objective paper-and-pencil test
Measure the attribute	Administer test to job applicants
Determine number or score	Determine test scores using scoring key
Make evaluation	Evaluate scores relative to job requirements
Make decision	Make hiring decisions

a paper-and-pencil test may be developed to measure mechanical knowledge, and this test is then administered to applicants. Once the attribute is physically measured, numbers or scores are determined (in the example, the mechanical test is scored). At that point, scores are available on the applicants, so an evaluation can be made of the scores (which scores meet the job requirements) and a selection decision can be made (e.g., hire a maintenance mechanic).

Of course, in practice, this textbook process is often not followed explicitly. When this happens, selection errors are more likely. For example, if the methods used to determine scores on an attribute are not explicitly determined and evaluated, the scores themselves may be incorrectly determined. Similarly, if the evaluation of the scores is not systematic, each selection decision maker may put his or her own "spin" on the scores, thereby defeating the purpose of careful measurement. The best way to avoid these problems is for all of those involved in selection decisions to go through each step of the measurement process depicted in Exhibit 7.1, apply it to the job(s) in question, and reach agreement at each step of the way.

Standardization

The hallmark of sound measurement practice is standardization.[2] Standardization is a means of controlling the influence of outside or extraneous factors on the scores generated by the measure and ensuring that, as much as possible, the scores obtained are a reflection of the attribute measured.

A standardized measure has three basic properties:

1. The content is identical for all objects measured (e.g., all job applicants take the same test).
2. The administration of the measure is identical for all objects (e.g., all job applicants have the same time limit on a test).
3. The rules for assigning numbers are clearly specified and agreed on in advance (e.g., a scoring key for the test is developed before it is administered).

These seemingly simple and straightforward characteristics of standardization of measures have substantial implications for the conduct of many staffing activities. These implications will become apparent throughout the remainder of this text. For example, assessment devices, such as the employment interview and letters of reference, often fail to meet the requirements for standardization, and organizations must undertake steps to make them more standardized.

Levels of Measurement

There are varying degrees of precision in measuring attributes and in representing differences among objects in terms of attributes. Accordingly, there are different levels or scales of measurement.[3] It is common to classify any particular measure as falling into one of four levels of measurement: nominal, ordinal, interval, or ratio.

Nominal. With nominal scales, a given attribute is categorized, and numbers are assigned to the categories. With or without numbers, however, there is no order or level implied among the categories. The categories are merely different, and none is higher or lower than the other. For example, each job title could represent a different category, with a different number assigned to it: managers = 1, clericals = 2, sales = 3, and so forth. Clearly, the numbers do not imply any ordering among the categories.

Ordinal.   With ordinal scales, objects are rank ordered according to how much of the attribute they possess. Thus, objects may be ranked from "best" to "worst" or from "highest" to "lowest." For example, five job candidates, each of whom has been evaluated in terms of overall qualification for the job, might be rank ordered from 1 to 5, or highest to lowest, according to their job qualifications.

Rank orderings only represent relative differences among objects, and they do not indicate the absolute levels of the attribute. Thus, the rank ordering of the five job candidates does not indicate exactly how qualified each of them is for the job, nor are the differences in their ranks necessarily equal to the differences in their qualifications. The difference in qualifications between applicants ranked 1 and 2 may not be the same as the difference between those ranked 4 and 5.

Interval.   Like ordinal scales, interval scales allow us to rank order objects. However, the differences between adjacent points on the measurement scale are now equal in terms of the attribute. If an interval scale is used to rank order the five job candidates, the differences in qualifications between those ranked 1 and 2 are equal to the differences between those ranked 4 and 5.

It should be pointed out that there are many instances in which the level of measurement falls somewhere between an ordinal and interval scale. That is, objects can be clearly rank ordered, but the differences between the ranks are not necessarily equal throughout the measurement scale. In the example of the five job candidates, the difference in qualifications between those ranked 1 and 2 might be slight compared with the distance between those ranked 4 and 5.

Unfortunately, this in-between level of measurement is characteristic of many of the measures used in staffing. Though it is not a major problem, it does signal the need for caution in interpreting the meaning of differences in scores among people.

Ratio.   Ratio scales are like interval scales in that there are equal differences between scale points for the attribute being measured. In addition, however, ratio scales have a logical or absolute true zero point. Because of this, how much of the attribute each object possesses can be stated in absolute terms.

Normally, ratio scales are involved in counting or weighing things. There are many such examples of ratio scales in staffing. Assessing how much weight a candidate can carry over some distance for physically demanding jobs such as fire fighting or general construction is an example of this. Perhaps the most common example is counting how much previous job experience (general or specific) job candidates have had.

Objective and Subjective Measures

Frequently, staffing measures are described as being either "objective" or "subjective." Often, the term "subjective" is used in disparaging ways ("I can't believe how subjective that interview was; there's no way they can rate me fairly on the basis of it"). Exactly what is the difference between so-called objective and subjective measures?

The difference, in large part, pertains to the rules used to assign numbers to the attribute being assessed. With objective measures, the rules are predetermined and usually communicated and applied through some sort of scoring key or system. Most paper-and-pencil tests are considered objective. The scoring systems in subjective measures are more elusive and often involve a rater or judge who assigns the numbers. Many employment interviewers fall in this category, especially those with an idiosyncratic way of evaluating people's responses, one that is not known or shared by other interviewers.

In principle, any attribute can be measured objectively, or subjectively, and sometimes both are used. Research shows that when an attribute is measured by both objective and subjective means, there is often relatively low agreement between scores from the two types of measures. A case in point pertains to the attribute of "job performance." It may be measured objectively through quantity of output, and it may be measured subjectively through performance appraisal ratings. A review of the research shows that there is very low correlation between scores from the objective and subjective performance measures.[4] Undoubtedly, the raters' lack of sound scoring systems for rating job performance was a major contributor to the lack of obtained agreement.

It thus appears that whatever type of measure is being used to assess attributes in staffing, serious attention should be paid to the scoring system or key that is used. This requires nothing more, in a sense, than having a firm knowledge of exactly what the organization is trying to measure in the first place. This is true for both paper-and-pencil (objective) measures and judgmental (subjective) measures, such as the employment interview. It is simply another way of emphasizing the importance of standardization in measurement.

Scores

Measures yield numbers or scores to represent the amount of the attribute being assessed. Scores are thus the numerical indicator of the attribute. Once scores have been derived, they can be manipulated in various ways to give them even greater meaning and to help better describe characteristics of the objects being scored.[5]

Central Tendency and Variability

Assume that a group of job applicants was administered a test of the knowledge of mechanical principles. The test is scored using a scoring key, and each applicant receives a score on the test, known as a raw score. Their scores are shown in Exhibit 7.2.

Some features of this set of scores may be summarized through the calculation of summary statistics. These pertain to central tendency and variability in the scores and are also shown in Exhibit 7.2.

EXHIBIT 7.2   Central Tendency and Variability: Summary Statistics

Data		Summary Statistics
Applicant	**Test Score (x)**	
A	10	A. Central tendency
B	12	Mean ($\bar{x}$) = 338/20 = 16.9
C	14	Median = middle score = 17
D	14	Mode = most frequent score = 15
E	15	
F	15	B. Variability
G	15	Range = 10 to 24
H	15	Standard deviation (SD) =
I	15	
J	17	$\sqrt{\dfrac{\Sigma\,(x-\bar{x})^2}{n-1}} = 3.52$
K	17	
L	17	
M	18	
N	18	
O	19	
P	19	
Q	19	
R	22	
S	23	
T	24	
Total (Σ) = 338		
N = 20		

The indicators of central tendency are the mean, median, and mode. Since it was assumed that the data were interval level data, it is permissible to compute all three indicators of central tendency. Had the data been ordinal, the mean should not be computed. For nominal data, only the mode would be appropriate.

The variability indicators are the range and the standard deviation. The range shows lowest to highest actual score for the job applicants. The standard deviation shows, in essence, the average amount of deviation of individual scores from the average score. It summarizes the amount of "spread" in the scores. The larger the standard deviation, the greater the variability, or spread, in the data.

Percentiles

A percentile score for an individual is the percentage of people scoring below the individual in a distribution of scores. Refer again to Exhibit 7.2, and consider applicant C. That applicant's percentile score is the 10th percentile (2/20 × 100). Applicant S is in the 90th percentile (18/20 × 100).

Standard Scores

When interpreting scores, it is natural to compare individuals' raw scores to the mean, that is, to ask whether scores are above, at, or below the mean. But a true understanding of how well an individual did relative to the mean takes into account the amount of variability in scores around the mean (the standard deviation). That is, the calculation must be "corrected" or controlled for the amount of variability in a score distribution to accurately present how well a person scored relative to the mean.

Calculation of the standard score for an individual is the way to accomplish this correction. The formula for calculation of the standard score, or Z, is as follows:

$$Z = \frac{X - \overline{X}}{SD}$$

Applicant S in Exhibit 7.2 had a raw score of 23 on the test; the mean was 16.9 and the standard deviation was 3.52. Substituting into the above formula, applicant S has a Z score of 1.7. Thus, applicant S scored about 1.7 standard deviations above the mean.

Standard scores are also useful for determining how a person performed, in a relative sense, on two or more tests. For example, assume the following data for a particular applicant:

	Test 1	Test 2
Raw score	50	48
Mean	48	46
SD	2.5	.80

On which test did the applicant do better? To answer that, simply calculate the applicant's standard scores on the two tests. The Z score on test 1 is .80, and the Z score on test 2 is 2.5. Thus, while the applicant got a higher raw score on test 1 than on test 2, the applicant got a higher Z score on test 2 than on test 1. Viewed in this way, it is apparent that the applicant did better on the second of the two tests.

Correlation Between Scores

Frequently in staffing there are scores on two or more measures for a group of individuals. One common occurrence is to have scores on two (or often, more than two) KSAO measures. For example, there could be a score on the test of knowledge of mechanical principles and also an overall rating of the applicant's probable job success based on the employment interview. In such instances, it is logical to ask whether there is some relation between the two sets of scores. Is there a tendency for an increase in knowledge test scores to be accompanied by an increase in interview ratings?

As another example, an organization may have scores on a particular KSAO measure (e.g., the knowledge test) and a measure of job performance (e.g., performance appraisal ratings) for a group of individuals. Is there a correlation between these two sets of scores? If there is, then this would provide some evidence about the probable validity of the knowledge test as a predictor of job performance. This evidence would help the organization decide whether to incorporate the use of the test into the selection process for job applicants.

Investigation of the relationship between two sets of scores proceeds through the plotting of scatter diagrams and through calculation of the correlation coefficient.

Scatter Diagrams

Assume two sets of scores for a group of people, scores on a test and scores on a measure of job performance. A scatter diagram is simply the plot of the joint distribution of the two sets of scores. Inspection of the plot provides a visual representation of the type of relationship that exists between the two sets of scores. Exhibit 7.3 provides three different scatter diagrams for the two sets of scores. Each X represents a test score and job performance score combination for an individual.

Example A in Exhibit 7.3 suggests very little relationship between the two sets of scores. Example B shows a modest relationship between the scores, and example C shows a somewhat strong relationship between the two sets of scores.

Correlation Coefficient

The relationship between two sets of scores may also be investigated through calculation of the correlation coefficient. The symbol for the correlation coefficient is r. Numerically, r values can range from r = −1.0 to r = 1.0. The larger the absolute value of r, the stronger the relationship. When an r value is shown without the plus or minus sign, the value is assumed to be positive.

Naturally, the value of r bears a close resemblance to the scatter diagram. As a demonstration of this, Exhibit 7.3 also shows the approximate r value for each of the three scatter diagrams. In example A, a low r is indicated (r = .10). The r in example B is moderate (r = .25), and the r in example C is high (r = .60).

Actual calculation of the correlation coefficient is straightforward. An example of this calculation and the formula for r are shown in Exhibit 7.4. In the exhibit, there are two sets of scores for 20 people. The first set of scores is the set of test scores for the 20 individuals in Exhibit 7.2. The second set of scores is an overall job performance rating (on a 1–5 rating scale) for these people. As can be seen from the calculation, there is a correlation of r = .58 between the two sets of scores.

The calculation of the correlation coefficient is straightforward. The resultant value of r succinctly summarizes both the strength of the relationship between two sets of scores and the direction of the relationship. Despite the simplicity of its calculation, there are several notes of caution to sound regarding the correlation.

First, the correlation does not connote a proportion or percentage. An r = .50 between variables X and Y does not mean that X is 50% of Y or that Y can be

EXHIBIT 7.3   Scatter Diagrams and Corresponding Correlations

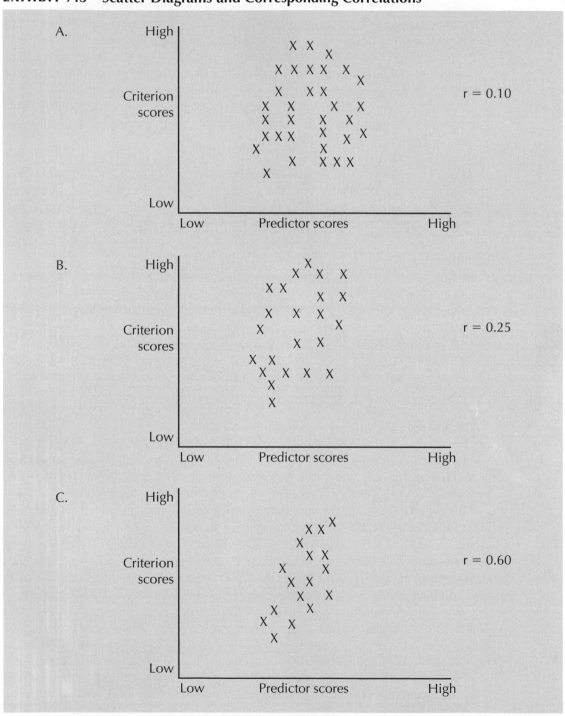

EXHIBIT 7.4 Calculation of Product-Moment Correlation Coefficient

Person	Test Score (X)	Performance Rating (Y)	(X²)	(Y²)	(XY)
A	10	2	100	4	20
B	12	1	144	1	12
C	14	2	196	4	28
D	14	1	196	1	14
E	15	3	225	9	45
F	15	4	225	16	60
G	15	3	225	9	45
H	15	4	225	16	60
I	15	4	225	16	60
J	17	3	289	9	51
K	17	4	289	16	68
L	17	3	289	9	51
M	18	2	324	4	36
N	18	4	324	16	72
O	19	3	361	9	57
P	19	3	361	9	57
Q	19	5	361	25	95
R	22	3	484	9	66
S	23	4	529	16	92
T	24	5	576	25	120
	$\Sigma X = 338$	$\Sigma Y = 63$	$\Sigma X^2 = 5948$	$\Sigma Y^2 = 223$	$\Sigma XY = 1109$

$$r = \frac{N\Sigma XY - (\Sigma X)(\Sigma Y)}{\sqrt{[N\Sigma X^2 - (\Sigma X)^2][N\Sigma Y^2 - (\Sigma Y)^2]}} = \frac{20(1109) - (338)(63)}{\sqrt{[20(5948) - (338)^2][20(223) - (63)^2]}} = .58$$

predicted from X with 50% accuracy. The appropriate interpretation is to square the value of r, for r^2, and then say that the two variables share that percentage of common variation in their scores. Thus, the proper interpretation of r = .50 is that the two variables share 25% ($.5^2 \times 100$) common variation in their scores.

Second, the value of r is affected by how much variation there actually is in each set of scores. Other things being equal, the less variation there is in one or both sets of scores, the smaller the calculated value of r will be. At the extreme, if there is no variation in one of the sets of scores, the correlation will be r = .00. That is, for there to be a correlation, there must be variation in both sets of scores. The lack of variation in scores is called the problem of restriction of range.

Third, the formula used to calculate the correlation in Exhibit 7.4 is based on the assumption that there is a linear relationship between the two sets of scores. This may not always be a good assumption; something other than a straight line may best capture the true nature of the relationship between scores. To the extent that two sets of scores are not related in a linear fashion, use of the formula for calculation of the correlation will yield a value of r that understates the actual strength of the relationship.

Finally, the correlation between two variables does not imply causation between them. A correlation simply says how two variables covary or corelate; it says nothing about one variable necessarily causing the other one.

Significance of the Correlation Coefficient

The statistical significance of a correlation refers to the likelihood that a correlation exists in a population, based on knowledge of the actual value of r in a sample from that population. Concluding that a correlation is indeed statistically significant means that there is most likely a correlation in the population. That means if the organization were to use a selection measure based on a statistically significant correlation, the correlation is likely to be significant when used again to select another sample (e.g., future job applicants).

More formally, r is calculated in an initial group, called a sample. From this piece of information, the question arises whether to infer that there is also a correlation in the *population*. To answer this, compute the t value of our correlation using the following formula,

$$t = \frac{r}{\sqrt{(1-r^2)/n-2}}$$

where r is the value of the correlation, and n is the size of the sample.

A t distribution table in any elementary statistics book shows the significance level of r.[6] The significance level is expressed as p < some value, for example, p < .05. This p level tells the probability of concluding that there is a correlation in the population when, in fact, there is not a relationship. Thus, a correlation with p < .05 means there are fewer than 5 chances in 100 of concluding that there is a relationship in the population when, in fact, there is not. This is a relatively small probability and usually leads to the conclusion that a correlation is indeed statistically significant.

It is important to avoid concluding that there is a relationship in the population when in fact there is not. Therefore, one usually chooses a fairly conservative or stringent level of significance that the correlation must attain before one can conclude that it is "significant." Typically, a standard of p < .05 or less (another common standard is p < .01) is chosen. The actual significance level (based on the t value for the correlation) is then compared to the desired significance level, and a decision is reached as to whether the correlation is statistically significant. Here are some examples:

Desired Level	Actual Level	Conclusion About Correlation
p < .05	p < .23	Not significant
p < .05	p < .02	Significant
p < .01	p < .07	Not significant
p < .01	p < .009	Significant

Although statistical significance is important in judging the usefulness of a selection measure, caution should be exercised in placing too much weight on this. With very large sample sizes even very small correlations will be significant, and with very small samples even strong correlations will fail to be significant. The absolute size of the correlation matters as well.

QUALITY OF MEASURES

Measures are developed and used to gauge attributes of objects. Results of measures are expressed in the form of scores, and various manipulations may be done to them. Such manipulations lead to better understanding and interpretation of the scores, and thus the attribute represented by the scores.

In staffing, for practical reasons, the scores of individuals are treated as if they were, in fact, the attribute itself, rather than merely indicators of the attribute. For example, scores on a mental ability test are interpreted as being synonymous with how intelligent individuals are. Or, individuals' job performance ratings from their supervisors are viewed as indicators of their true performance.

Treated in this way, scores become a major input to decision making about individuals. For example, scores on the mental ability test are used and weighted heavily to decide which job applicants will receive a job offer. Or, performance ratings may serve as a key factor in deciding which individuals will be eligible for an internal staffing move, such as a promotion. In these and numerous other ways, management acts on the basis of scores to guide the conduct of staffing activities in the organization. This is illustrated through such phrases as "let the numbers do the talking," "we manage by the numbers," and "never measured, never managed."

The quality of the decisions and the actions taken are unlikely to be any better than the quality of the measures on which they are based. Thus, there is a lot at stake in the quality of the measures used in staffing. Such concerns with the quality of measures are best viewed in terms of reliability and validity of measures.[7]

Reliability of Measures

Reliability of measurement refers to the consistency of measurement of an attribute.[8] A measure is reliable to the extent that it provides a consistent set of scores to represent an attribute. Rarely is perfect reliability achieved, because of the occurrence of measurement error. Reliability is thus a matter of degree.

Reliability of measurement is of concern both within a single time period in which the attribute is being measured and between time periods. Moreover, reliability is of concern for both objective and subjective measures. These two concerns help create a general framework for better understanding reliability.

The key concepts for the framework are shown in Exhibit 7.5. In the exhibit, a single attribute, "A" (e.g., knowledge of mechanical principles), is being measured. Scores are available for 15 individuals, and scores range from 1 to 5. A is being measured in time period 1 (T_1) and time period 2 (T_2). In each time period, A may be measured objectively, with two test items, or subjectively, with two raters. The same two items or raters are used in each time period. (In reality, more

EXHIBIT 7.5   Framework for Reliability of Measures

	Scores on Attribute A							
	Objective (Test Items)				Subjective (Raters)			
	Time 1		Time 2		Time 1		Time 2	
Person	X_1	Y_1	X_2	Y_2	X_1	Y_1	X_2	Y_2
A	5	5	4	5	5	5	4	5
B	5	4	4	3	5	4	4	3
C	5	5	5	4	5	5	5	4
D	5	4	5	5	5	4	5	5
E	4	5	3	4	4	5	3	4
F	4	4	4	3	4	4	4	3
G	4	4	3	4	4	4	3	4
H	4	3	4	3	4	3	4	3
I	3	4	3	4	3	4	3	4
J	3	3	5	3	3	3	5	3
K	3	3	2	3	3	3	2	3
L	3	2	4	2	3	2	4	2
M	2	3	4	3	2	3	4	3
N	2	2	1	2	2	2	1	2
O	1	2	3	2	1	2	3	2

NOTE: X_1 and X_2 are the same test item or rater; Y_1 and Y_2 are the same test item or rater. The subscript "1" refers to T_1, and the subscript "2" refers to T_2.

than two items or raters would probably be used to measure A, but for simplicity, only two are used here.) Each test item or rater in each time period is a submeasure of A. There are thus four submeasures of A—designated $X_1, X_2, Y_1,$ and Y_2—and four sets of scores. In terms of reliability of measurement, the concern is with the consistency or similarity in the sets of scores. This requires various comparisons of the scores.

Comparisons Within T_1 or T_2

Consider the four sets of scores as coming from the objective measure, which used test items. Comparing sets of scores from these items in either T_1 or T_2 is called internal consistency reliability. The relevant comparisons are X_1 and Y_1, and X_2 and Y_2. It is hoped that the comparisons will show high similarity, because both items are intended to measure A within the same time period.

Now treat the four sets of scores as coming from the subjective measure, which relied on raters. Comparisons of these scores involve what is called interrater reliability. The relevant comparisons are the same as with the objective measure scores, namely, X_1 and Y_1, and X_2 and Y_2. Again, it is hoped that there will be high agreement between the raters because they are focusing on a single attribute at a single moment in time.

Comparisons Between T_1 and T_2

Comparisons of scores between time periods involve assessment of measurement stability. When scores from an objective measure are used, this is referred to as test–retest reliability. The relevant comparisons are X_1 and X_2, and Y_1 and Y_2. To the extent that A is not expected to change between T_1 and T_2, there should be high test–retest reliability.

When subjective scores are compared between T_1 and T_2, the concern is with intrarater reliability. Here, the same rater evaluates individuals in terms of A in two different time periods. To the extent that A is not expected to change, there should be high intrarater reliability.

In summary, reliability is concerned with consistency of measurement. There are multiple ways of treating reliability, depending on whether scores from a measure are being compared for consistency within or between time periods and depending on whether the scores are from objective or subjective measures. These points are summarized in Exhibit 7.6. Ways of actually computing agreement between scores will be covered shortly, after the concept of measurement error is explored.

Measurement Error

Rarely will any of the comparisons among scores discussed previously yield perfect similarity or reliability. Indeed, none of the comparisons in Exhibit 7.6 visually shows complete agreement among the scores. The lack of agreement among the scores may be due to the occurrence of measurement error. This type of error

EXHIBIT 7.6   **Summary of Types of Reliability**

	Compare scores within T_1 or T_2	Compare scores between T_1 and T_2
Objective measure (test items)	Internal consistency	Test–retest
Subjective measure (raters)	Interrater	Intrarater

represents "noise" in the measure and measurement process. Its occurrence means that the measure did not yield perfectly consistent scores, or so-called true scores, for the attribute.

The scores actually obtained from the measure thus have two components to them, a true score and measurement error. That is,

$$\text{actual score} = \text{true score} + \text{error}$$

The error component of any actual score, or set of scores, represents unreliability of measurement. Unfortunately, unreliability is a fact of life for the types of measures used in staffing. To help understand why this is the case, the various types or sources of error that can occur in a staffing context must be explored. These errors may be grouped under the categories of deficiency and contamination error.[9]

Deficiency Error.   Deficiency error occurs when there is failure to measure some portion or aspect of the attribute assessed. For example, if knowledge of mechanical principles involves gear ratios, among other things, and our test does not have any items (or an insufficient number of items) covering this aspect, then the test is deficient. As another example, if an attribute of job performance is "planning and setting work priorities," and the raters fail to rate people on that dimension during their performance appraisal, then the performance measure is deficient.

Deficiency error can occur in several related ways. First, there can be an inadequate definition of the attribute in the first place. Thus, the test of knowledge of mechanical principles may fail to get at familiarity with gear ratios because it was never included in the initial definition of mechanical principles. Or, the performance measure may fail to require raters to rate their employees on "planning and setting work priorities" because this attribute was never considered an important dimension of their work.

A second way that deficiency error occurs is in the construction of measures used to assess the attribute. Here, the attribute may be well defined and understood, but there is a failure to construct a measure that adequately gets at the totality of the attribute. This is akin to poor measurement by oversight, which happens when measures are constructed in a hurried, ad hoc fashion.

Deficiency error also occurs when the organization opts to use whatever measures are available because of ease, cost considerations, sales pitches and promotional claims, and so forth. The measures so chosen may turn out to be deficient.

Contamination Error. Contamination error represents the occurrence of unwanted or undesirable influence on the measure and on individuals for whom the measure is being used. These influences muddy the scores and make them difficult to interpret.

Sources of contamination abound, as do examples of them. Several of these sources and examples are shown in Exhibit 7.7, along with some suggestions for how they might be controlled. These examples show that contamination error is multifaceted, making it difficult to minimize and control.

Calculation of Reliability Estimates

There are numerous procedures available for calculating actual estimates of the degree of reliability of measurement.[10] The first two of these (coefficient alpha, interrater agreement) assess reliability within a single time period. The other

EXHIBIT 7.7   Sources of Contamination Error and Suggestions for Control

Source of Contamination	Example	Suggestion for Control
Content domain	Irrelevant material on test	Define domain of test material to be covered
Standardization	Different time limits for same test	Have same time limits for everyone
Chance response tendencies	Guessing by test taker	Impossible to control in advance
Rater	Rater gives inflated ratings to people	Train rater in rating accuracy
Rating situation	Interviewees are asked different questions	Ask all interviewees same questions

two procedures (test–retest, intrarater agreement) assess reliability between time periods.

Coefficient Alpha.   Coefficient alpha may be calculated in instances in which there are two or more items (or raters) for a particular attribute. Its formula is

$$\alpha = \frac{n\,(\bar{r})}{1 + \bar{r}\,(n-1)}$$

where $\bar{r}$ is the average intercorrelation among the items (raters) and n is the number of items (raters). For example, if there are five items (n = 5), and the average correlation among those five items is $\bar{r}$ = .80, then coefficient alpha is .95.

It can be seen from the formula and the example that coefficient alpha depends on just two things—the number of items and the amount of correlation between them. This suggests two basic strategies for increasing the internal consistency reliability of a measure—increase the number of items and increase the amount of agreement between the items (raters). It is generally recommended that coefficient alpha be at least .80 for a measure to have an acceptable degree of reliability.

Interrater Agreement.   When raters serve as the measure, it is often convenient to talk about interrater agreement, or the amount of agreement among them. For example, if members of a group or panel interview independently rate a set of job applicants on a 1–5 scale, it is logical to ask how much they agreed with one another.

A simple way to determine this is to calculate the percentage of agreement among the raters. An example of this is shown in Exhibit 7.8.

There is no commonly accepted minimum level of interrater agreement that must be met in order to consider the raters sufficiently reliable. Normally, a fairly high level should be set—75% or higher. The more important the end use of the ratings, the greater the agreement required should be. Critical uses, such as hiring decisions, demand very high levels of reliability, well in excess of 75% agreement.

Test–Retest Reliability.   To assess test–retest reliability, the test scores from two different time periods are correlated through calculation of the correlation coefficient. The r may be calculated on total test scores, or a separate r may be calculated for scores on each item. The resultant r provides an indication of the stability of measurement; the higher the r, the more stable the measure.

Interpretation of the r value is made difficult by the fact that the scores are gathered at two different points in time. Between those two time points, the attribute being measured has an opportunity to change. Interpretation of test–retest reliability thus requires some sense of how much the attribute may be expected to change, and what the appropriate time interval between tests is. Usually, for very short time

---

EXHIBIT 7.8   Calculation of Percentage Agreement Among Raters

Person (ratee)	Rater 1	Rater 2	Rater 3
A	5	5	2
B	3	3	5
C	5	4	4
D	1	1	5
E	2	2	4

$$\% \text{ Agreement} \quad \frac{\# \text{ agreements}}{\# \text{ agreements} + \# \text{ disagreements}} \times 100$$

% Agreement
 Rater 1 and Rater 2 = 4/5 = 80%
 Rater 1 and Rater 3 = 0/5 = 0%
 Rater 2 and Rater 3 = 1/5 = 20%

---

intervals (hours or days), most attributes are quite stable, and a large test–retest r (r = .90 or higher) should be expected. Over longer time intervals, it is usual to expect much lower r's, depending on the attribute being measured. For example, over six months or a year, individuals' knowledge of mechanical principles might change. If so, there will be lower test–retest reliabilities (e.g., r = .50).

Intrarater Agreement.   To calculate intrarater agreement, scores assigned the same people by a rater in two different time periods are compared. The calculation could involve computing the correlation between the two sets of scores, or it could involve using the same formula as for interrater agreement (see Exhibit 7.8).

Interpretation of intrarater agreement is made difficult by the time factor. For short time intervals between measures, a fairly high relationship is expected (e.g., r = .80, or percentage agreement = 90%). For longer time intervals, the level of reliability may reasonably be expected to be lower.

Implications of Reliability

The degree of reliability of a measure has two implications. The first of these pertains to interpreting individuals' scores on the measure and the standard error of measurement. The second implication pertains to the effect that reliability has on the measure's validity.

Standard Error of Measurement.   Measures yield scores, which, in turn, are used as critical inputs for decision making in staffing activities. For example, in Exhibit 7.1 a test of knowledge of mechanical principles was developed and administered to job applicants. The applicants' scores were then used as a basis for making hiring decisions.

The discussion of reliability suggests that measures and scores will usually have some amount of error in them. Hence, scores on the test of knowledge of mechanical principles most likely reflect both true knowledge and error. Since only a single score is obtained from each applicant, the critical issue is how accurate that particular score is as an indication of the applicant's true level of knowledge of mechanical principles alone.

The standard error of measurement (SEM) addresses this issue. It provides a way to state, within limits, a person's likely score on a measure. The formula for the SEM is

$$SEM = SD_x \sqrt{1 - r_{xx}}$$

where SD_x is the standard deviation of scores on the measure and r_{xx} is an estimate of the measure's reliability. For example, if $SD_x = 10$, and $r_{xx} = .75$ (based on coefficient alpha), then SEM = 5.

With the SEM known, the range within which any individual's true score is likely to fall can be estimated. That range is known as a confidence interval or limit. There is a 95% chance that a person's true score lies within ±2 SEM of his or her actual score. Thus, if an applicant received a score of 22 on the test of knowledge of mechanical principles, the applicant's true score is most likely to be within the range of 22 ± 2(5), or 12–32.

Recognition and use of the SEM allows for care in interpreting people's scores, as well as differences between individuals in terms of their scores. For example, using the preceding data, if the test score for applicant 1 is 22 and the score for applicant 2 is 19, what should be made of the difference between the two applicants? Is applicant 1 truly more knowledgeable of mechanical principles than applicant 2? The answer is probably not. This is because of the SEM and the large amount of overlap between the two applicants' intervals (12–32 for applicant 1, and 9–29 for applicant 2).

In short, there is not a one-to-one correspondence between actual scores and true scores. Most measures used in staffing are sufficiently unreliable, meaning that small differences in scores are probably due to error of measurement and should be ignored.

Relationship to Validity.   The validity of a measure is defined as the degree to which it measures the attribute it is supposed to be measuring. For example, the validity of the test of knowledge of mechanical principles is the degree to which it measures that knowledge. There are specific ways to investigate validity; these are discussed in the next section. Here, it simply needs to be recognized that the reliability with which an attribute is measured has direct implications for the validity of the measure.

The relationship between the reliability and validity of a measure is

$$r_{xy} \leq \sqrt{r_{xx}}$$

where r_{xy} is the validity of a measure and r_{xx} is the reliability of the measure. For example, it had been assumed previously that the reliability of the test of knowledge of mechanical principles was r = .75. The validity of that test thus cannot exceed $\sqrt{.75} = 86$.

Thus, the reliability of a measure places an upper limit on the possible validity of a measure. It should be emphasized that this is only an upper limit. A highly reliable measure is not necessarily valid. Reliability does not guarantee validity; it only makes validity possible.

Validity of Measures

The validity of a measure is defined as the degree to which it measures the attribute it is intended to measure.[11] Refer back to Exhibit 7.1, which involved the development of a test of knowledge of mechanical principles that was then to be used for purposes of selecting job applicants. The validity of that test is the degree to which it truly measures the attribute or construct "knowledge of mechanical principles."

Judgments about the validity of a measure occur through the process of gathering data and evidence about the measure to assess how it was developed and whether accurate inferences can be made from scores on the measure. This process can be illustrated in terms of concepts pertaining to accuracy of measurement and accuracy of prediction. These concepts may then be used to demonstrate how validation of measures occurs in staffing.

Accuracy of Measurement

How accurate is the test of knowledge of mechanical principles? This question asks for evidence about the accuracy with which the test portrays individuals' true levels of that knowledge. This is akin to asking about the degree of overlap between the attribute being measured and the actual measure of the attribute.

Refer to Exhibit 7.9. It shows the concept of accuracy of measurement in Venn diagram form. The circle on the left represents the construct "knowledge of mechanical principles," and the circle on the right represents the actual test of knowledge of mechanical principles. The overlap between the two circles represents the degree of accuracy of measurement for the test. The greater the overlap, the greater the accuracy of measurement.

Notice that perfect overlap is not shown in Exhibit 7.9. This signifies the occurrence of measurement error with the use of the test. These errors, as indicated in the exhibit, are the errors of deficiency and contamination previously discussed.

So how does accuracy of measurement differ from reliability of measurement since both are concerned with deficiency and contamination? There is disagreement among

EXHIBIT 7.9 Accuracy of Measurement

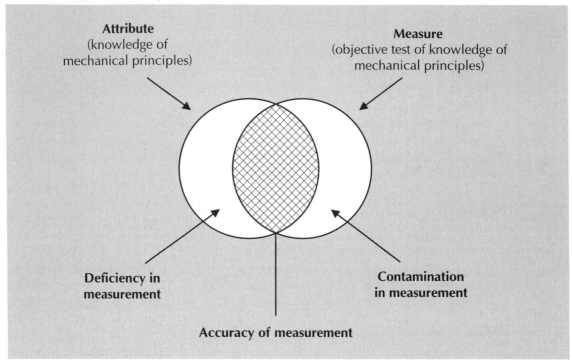

people on this question. Generally, the difference may be thought of as follows. Reliability refers to consistency among the scores on the test, as determined by comparing scores as previously described. Accuracy of measurement goes beyond this to assess the extent to which the scores truly reflect the attribute being measured—the overlap shown in Exhibit 7.9. Accuracy requires reliability, but it also requires more by way of evidence. For example, accuracy requires knowing something about how the test was developed. Accuracy also requires some evidence concerning how test scores are influenced by other factors—for example, how do test scores change as a result of employees attending a training program devoted to providing instruction in mechanical principles? Accuracy thus demands greater evidence than reliability.

Accuracy of Prediction

Measures are often developed because they provide information about people that can be used to make predictions about those people. In Exhibit 7.1, the knowledge test was to be used to help make hiring decisions, which are actually predictions about which people will be successful at a job. Knowing something about the accuracy with which a test predicts future job success requires examining the relationship between scores on the test and scores on some measure of job success for a group of people.

Accuracy of prediction is illustrated in the top half of Exhibit 7.10. Where there is an actual job success outcome (criterion) to predict, the test (predictor) will be used to predict the criterion. Each person is classified as high or low on the predictor and high or low on the criterion, based on predictor and criterion scores. Individuals falling into cells A and C represent correct predictions, and individuals falling into cells B and D represent errors in prediction. Accuracy of prediction is the percentage of total correct predictions. Accuracy can thus range from 0% to 100%.

The bottom half of Exhibit 7.10 shows an example of the determination of accuracy of prediction using a selection example. The predictor is the test of knowledge

---

EXHIBIT 7.10   Accuracy of Prediction

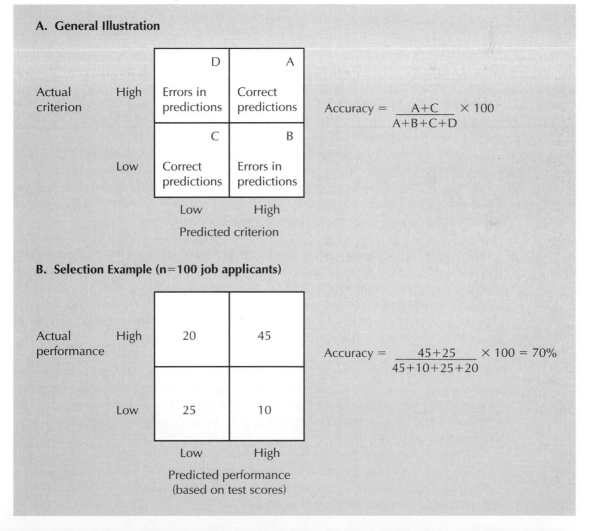

A. General Illustration

		D	A
Actual criterion	High	Errors in predictions	Correct predictions
		C	B
	Low	Correct predictions	Errors in predictions
		Low	High
		Predicted criterion	

$$\text{Accuracy} = \frac{A+C}{A+B+C+D} \times 100$$

B. Selection Example (n=100 job applicants)

Actual performance	High	20	45
	Low	25	10
		Low	High
		Predicted performance (based on test scores)	

$$\text{Accuracy} = \frac{45+25}{45+10+25+20} \times 100 = 70\%$$

of mechanical principles, and the criterion is an overall measure of job performance. Scores on the predictor and criterion measures are gathered for 100 job applicants and are dichotomized into high or low scores on each. Each individual is placed into one of the four cells. The accuracy of prediction for the test is 70%.

Validation of Measures in Staffing

In staffing, there is concern with the validity of predictors in terms of both accuracy of measurement and accuracy of prediction. It is important to have and use predictors that are accurate representations of the KSAOs to be measured, and those predictors need to be accurate in their predictions of job success. The validity of predictors is explored through the conduct of validation studies.

There are two types of validation studies typically conducted. The first of these is criterion-related validation, and the second is content validation. A third type of validation study, known as construct validation, involves components of reliability, criterion-related validation, and content validation. Each component is discussed separately in this book, and thus no further reference is made to construct validation.

Criterion-Related Validation

Exhibit 7.11 shows the components of criterion-related validation and their usual sequencing.[12] The process begins with job analysis. Results of job analysis are fed into criterion and predictor measures. Scores on the predictor and criterion are obtained for a sample of individuals; the relationship between the scores is then examined to make a judgment about the predictor's validity.

Job Analysis.　Job analysis is undertaken to identify and define important tasks (and broader task dimensions) of the job. The KSAOs and motivation thought to be necessary for performance of these tasks are then inferred. Results of the process of identifying tasks and underlying KSAOs are expressed in the form of the job requirements matrix. The matrix is a task × KSAO matrix; it shows the tasks required, combined with the relevant KSAOs for each task.

Criterion Measures.　Measures of performance on tasks and task dimensions are needed. These may already be available as part of an ongoing performance appraisal system, or they may have to be developed. However these measures are gathered, the critical requirement is that they be as free from measurement error as possible.

Criterion measures need not be restricted to performance measures. Others may be used, such as measures of attendance, retention, safety, and customer service. As with performance-based criterion measures, these alternative criterion measures should also be as error free as possible.

EXHIBIT 7.11   **Criterion-Related Validation**

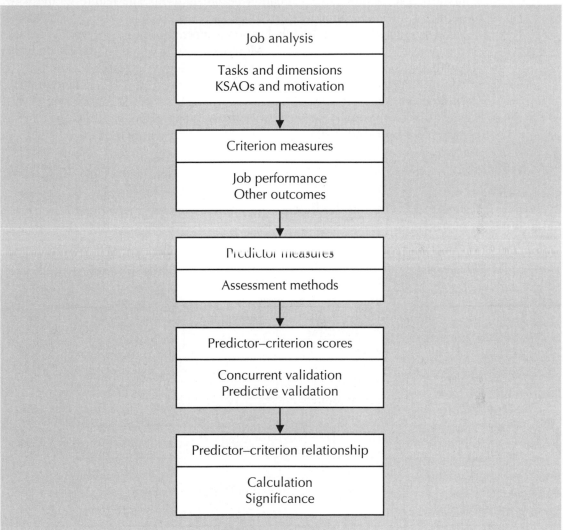

Predictor Measure.   The predictor measure is the measure whose criterion-related validity is being investigated. Ideally, it taps into one or more of the KSAOs identified in job analysis. Also, it should be the type of measure most suitable to assess the KSAOs. Knowledge of mechanical principles, for example, is probably best assessed with some form of written, objective test.

Predictor–Criterion Scores.   Predictor and criterion scores must be gathered from a sample of current employees or job applicants. If current employees are used, this involves use of a concurrent validation design. Alternately, if job applicants are used, a predictive validation design is used. The nature of these two designs is shown in Exhibit 7.12.

Concurrent validation definitely has some appeal. Administratively, it is convenient and can often be done quickly. Moreover, results of the validation study will be available soon after the predictor and criterion scores have been gathered.

Unfortunately, some serious problems can arise with use of a concurrent validation design. One problem is that if the predictor is a test, current employees may not be motivated in the same way that job applicants would be in terms of desire to perform well. Yet, it is future applicants for whom the test is intended to be used.

EXHIBIT 7.12 **Concurrent and Predictive Validation Designs**

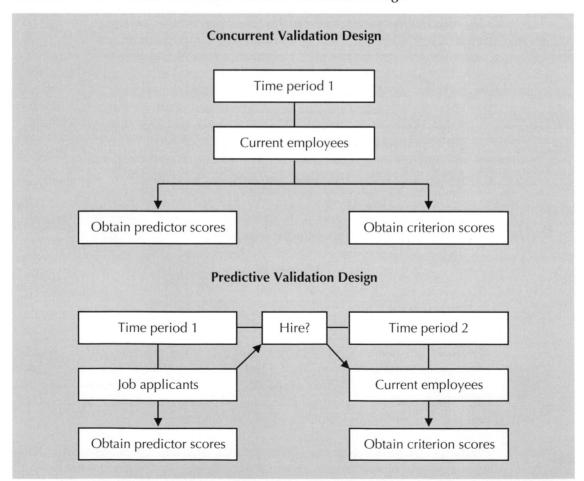

In a related vein, current employees may not be similar to, or representative of, future job applicants. Current employees may differ in terms of demographics such as age, race, sex, disability status, education level, and previous job experience. Hence, it is by no means certain that the results of the study will generalize to future job applicants. Also, some unsatisfactory employees will have been terminated, and some high performers may have been promoted. This leads to restriction of range on the criterion scores, which in turn will lower the correlation between the predictor and criterion scores.

Finally, current employees' predictor scores may be influenced by the amount of experience and/or success they have had on their current job. For example, scores on the test of knowledge of mechanical principles may reflect not only that knowledge but also how long people have been on the job and how well they have performed it. This is undesirable because one wants predictor scores to be predictive of the criterion rather than a result of it.

Predictive validation overcomes the potential limitations of concurrent validation since the predictor scores are obtained from job applicants. Applicants will be motivated to do well on the predictor, and they are more likely to be representative of future job applicants. And applicants' scores on the predictor cannot be influenced by success and/or experience on the job, because the scores are gathered prior to their being on the job.

Predictive validation is not without potential limitations, however. It is neither administratively easy nor quick. Moreover, results will not be available immediately, as some time must lapse before criterion scores can be obtained. Despite these limitations, predictive validation is considered the more sound of the two designs.

Predictor–Criterion Relationship. Once predictor and criterion scores have been obtained, the correlation r, or some variation of it, must be calculated. The value of the r is then referred to as the validity of the scores on the predictor. For example, if an r = .35 was found, the predictor would be referred to as having a validity of .35. Then, the practical and statistical significance of the r should be determined. Only if the r meets desired levels of practical and statistical significance should the predictor be considered "valid" and thus potentially usable in the selection system.

Illustrative Study. A state university civil service system covering 20 different institutions sought to identify predictors of job performance for clerical employees. The clerical job existed within different schools (e.g., engineering, humanities) and nonacademic departments (e.g., payroll, data processing). The goal of the study was to have a valid clerical test in two parallel forms that could be administered to job applicants in one hour.

The starting point was to conduct a job analysis, the results of which would be used as the basis for constructing the clerical tests (predictors) and the job performance ratings (criteria). Based on observation of the job and previous job descriptions, a task-based questionnaire was constructed by subject matter experts (SMEs) and administered to clerical incumbents and their supervisors throughout the system. Task statements were rated in terms of importance, frequency, and essentialness (if it was essential for a newly hired employee to know how to do this task). Based on statistical analysis of the ratings' means and standard deviations, 25 of the 188 task statements were retained as critical task statements. These critical task statements were the key input to the identification of key KSAOs and the dimension of job performance.

Analysis of the 25 critical task statements indicated there were five KSAO components of the job: knowledge of computer hardware and software, ability to follow instructions and prioritize tasks, knowledge and skill in responding to telephone and reception scenarios, knowledge of English language, and ability to file items in alphabetical order. A test was constructed to measure these KSAOs as follows:

- Computer hardware and software—17 questions
- Prioritizing tasks—18 questions
- Route and transfer calls—14 questions
- Record messages—20 questions
- Give information on the phone—20 questions
- Correct sentences with errors—22 questions
- Identify errors in sentences—71 questions
- Filing—44 questions
- Typing—number of questions not reported

To develop the job performance (criterion) measure, a behavioral performance rating scale (1–7 rating) was constructed for each of the nine areas, ensuring a high content correspondence between the tests and the performance criteria they sought to predict. Scores on these nine scales were summed to yield an overall performance score.

The nine tests were administered to 108 current clerical employees to obtain predictor scores. A separate score on each of the nine tests was computed, along with a total test score for all tests. In addition, total scores on two short (50-question) forms of the total test were created (Form A and Form B).

Performance ratings of these 108 employees were obtained from their supervisors, who were unaware of their employees' test scores. The performance ratings were summed to form an overall performance rating. Scores on each of the nine tests, on the total test, and on Forms A and B of the test were correlated with the overall performance ratings.

Results of the concurrent validation study are shown in Exhibit 7.13. It can be seen that seven of the nine specific tests had statistically significant correlations with overall performance (filing and typing did not). Total test scores were significantly correlated with overall performance, as were scores on the two short forms

EXHIBIT 7.13 **Clerical Test Concurrent Validation Results**

Test	Correlation With Overall Performance
Computer software and hardware	.37**
Prioritize tasks	.29*
Route and transfer calls	.19*
Record messages	.31**
Give information on phone	.35**
Correct sentences with errors	.32**
Identify errors in sentences	.44**
Filing	.22
Typing	.10
Total test	.45**
Form A	.55**
Form B	.49**

NOTE: *p < .05, **p < .01

SOURCE: Adapted from J. E. Pynes, E. J. Harrick, and D. Schaefer, "A Concurrent Validation Study Applied to a Secretarial Position in a State University Civil Service System," *Journal of Business and Psychology,* 1997, 12, pp. 3–18.

of the total test. The sizes of the statistically significant correlations suggest favorable practical significance of the correlations as well.

Content Validation

Content validation differs from criterion-related validity in one important respect: there is no criterion measure used in content validation. Thus, predictor scores cannot be correlated with criterion scores as a way of gathering evidence about a predictor's validity. Rather, a judgment is made about the probable correlation, had there been a criterion measure. For this reason, content validation is frequently referred to as judgmental validation.[13]

Content validation is most appropriate, and most likely to be found, in two circumstances: when there are too few people to form a sample for purposes of criterion-related validation, and when criterion measures are not available, or they are available but are of highly questionable quality. At an absolute minimum, an n = 30 is necessary for criterion-related validation.

Exhibit 7.14 shows the two basic steps in content validation—conducting a job analysis and choosing or developing a predictor. These steps are commented on next. Comparing the steps in content validation with those in criterion-related validation (see Exhibit 7.11) shows that the steps in content validation are a part of criterion-related validation. Because of this, the two types of validation should be thought of as complementary, with content validation being a subset of criterion-related validation.

EXHIBIT 7.14 Content Validation

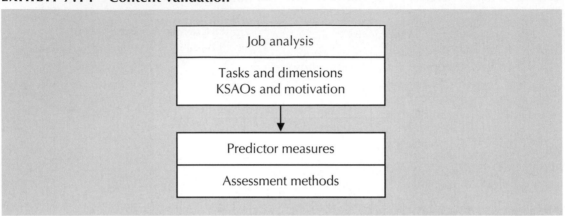

Job Analysis. As with criterion-related validation, content validation begins with job analysis, which, in both cases, is undertaken to identify and define tasks and task dimensions and to infer the necessary KSAOs and motivation for those tasks. Results are expressed in the job requirements matrix.

Predictor Measures. Sometimes the predictor will be one that has already been developed and is in use. An example here is a commercially available test, interviewing process, or biographical information questionnaire. Other times, there will not be such a measure available. This occurs frequently in the case of job knowledge, which is usually very specific to the particular job involved in the validation.

Lacking a readily available or modifiable predictor means that the organization will have to construct its own predictors. At this point, the organization has built predictor construction into the predictor validation process. Now, content validation and the predictor development processes occur simultaneously. The organization becomes engaged in test construction, a topic beyond the scope of this book.[14]

A final note about content validation emphasizes the importance of continually paying attention to the need for reliability of measurement and standardization of the measurement process. Though these are always matters of concern in any type of validation effort, they are of paramount importance in content validation. The reason for this is that without an empirical correlation between the predictor and the criterion, only the likely r can be judged. It is important, in forming that judgment, to pay considerable attention to reliability and standardization.

Illustrative Study. The Maryland Department of Transportation sought to develop a series of assessment methods for identifying supervisory potential among candidates for promotion to a first-level supervising position anywhere within the department. The content validation process and outputs are shown in Exhibit 7.15.

EXHIBIT 7.15   Content Validation Study

Job Analysis: First-Level Supervisor—Maryland Department of Transportation

Seven performance dimensions and task statements:
>   Organizing work; assigning work; monitoring work; managing consequences; counseling, efficiency reviews, and discipline; setting an example; employee development

Fourteen KSAOs and definitions:
>   Organizing; analysis and decision making; planning; communication (oral and written); delegation; work habits; carefulness; interpersonal skill; job knowledge; organizational knowledge; toughness; integrity; development of others; listening

Predictor Measures: Five Assessment Methods

Multiple-choice in-basket exercise
>   (assume role of new supervisor and work through in-basket on desk)

Structured panel interview
>   (predetermined questions about past experiences relevant to the KSAOs)

Presentation exercise
>   (make presentation to a simulated work group about change in their work hours)

Writing sample
>   (prepare a written reprimand for a fictitious employee)

Training and experience evaluation exercise
>   (give examples of training and work achievements relevant to certain KSAOs)

SOURCE: Adapted from M. A. Cooper, G. Kaufman, and W. Hughes, "Measuring Supervisory Potential," *IPMA News,* December 1996, pp. 8–18. Reprinted with permission of *IPMA News,* published by the International Personnel Management Association (IPMA), 703-549-7100, *www.ipma-hr.org.*

As shown in the exhibit, job analysis was first conducted to identify and define a set of performance dimensions and then infer the KSAOs necessary for successful performance in those dimensions. Several SMEs met to develop a tentative set of task dimensions and underlying KSAOs. The underlying KSAOs were in essence general competencies required of all first-level supervisors, regardless of work unit within the department. Their results were sent to a panel of experienced human resource (HR) managers within the department for revision and finalization. Three assessment method specialists then set about developing a set of assessments that would (1) be efficiently administered at locations throughout the state, (2) be reliably scored by people at those locations, and (3) emphasize the interpersonal skills important for this job. As shown in Exhibit 7.15, five assessment methods were developed: multiple-choice in-basket exercise, structured panel interview, presentation exercise, writing sample, and training and experience evaluation exercise.

Candidates' performance on the exercises was to be evaluated by specially chosen assessors at the location where the exercises were administered. To ensure that candidates' performance was skillfully observed and reliably evaluated by the assessors, an intensive training program was developed. The program provided both a written user's manual and specific skill training.

Validity Generalization

In the preceding discussions of validity and validation, an implicit premise is being made that validity is situation specific, and therefore validation of predictors must occur in each specific situation. All of the examples involve specific types of measures, jobs, individuals, and so forth. Nothing is said about generalizing validity across those jobs and individuals. For example, if a predictor is valid for a particular job in organization A, would it be valid for the same type of job in organization B? Or is validity specific to the particular job and organization?

The situation-specific premise is based on the following scenario, which, in turn, has its origins in findings from decades of previous research. Assume a large number of criterion-related validation studies have been conducted. Each study involves various predictor measures of a common KSAO attribute (e.g., general mental ability) and various criterion measures of a common outcome attribute (e.g., job performance). The predictor will be designated "X," and the criterion will be designated "Y." The studies are conducted in many different situations (types of jobs, types of organizations), and they involve many different samples (sample sizes, types of employees). In each study, r_{xy} is calculated. The results from all the studies reveal a wide range of r_{xy} values, though the average is $\bar{r}_{xy} = .25$. These results suggest that while on average there seems to be some validity to X, the validity varies substantially from situation to situation. Based on these findings, the best conclusion is that validity most likely is situation specific and thus cannot be generalized across the situations.

The concept of validity generalization questions this premise.[15] It says that much of the variation in the r_{xy} values is due to the occurrence of a number of methodological and statistical differences across the studies. If these differences were controlled for statistically, the variation in values would shrink and converge toward an estimate of the true validity of X. If that true r is significant (practically and statistically), one can indeed generalize validity of X across situations. Validity thus is not viewed as situation specific. The logic of this validity generalization premise is shown in Exhibit 7.16.

The distinction between situation-specific validity and validity generalization is important for two related reasons. First, from a scientific viewpoint, it is important to identify and make statements about X and Y relationships in general, without always having to say that everything depends on the sample, criterion measure, and so on. In this regard, validity generalization clearly allows greater latitude than does situation specificity. Second, from a practical standpoint, it would be conve-

EXHIBIT 7.16 **The Logic of Validity Generalization**

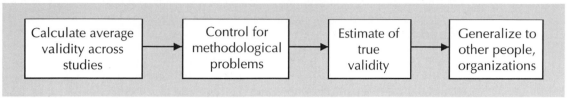

Calculate average validity across studies → Control for methodological problems → Estimate of true validity → Generalize to other people, organizations

nient and less costly not to have to conduct a separate validation study for predictor X in every situation in which its use was a possibility. Validity generalization allows that to happen, whereas situation specificity does not.

Evidence is beginning to surface that is supportive of the validity generalization premise. Some experts argue that validity generalization reduces or even eliminates the need for an organization to conduct its own validation study. If validity generalization shows that a selection measure has a statistically significant and practically meaningful correlation with job performance, the reasoning goes, why go to the considerable time and expense to reinvent the wheel (to conduct a validation study when evidence clearly supports use of the measure in the first place)? There are two caveats to keep in mind in accepting this logic. First, organizations or specific jobs (for which the selection measure in question is intended) can sometimes be unusual. To the extent that the organization or job was not reflected in the validity generalization effort, the results may be inapplicable to the specific organization or job. Second, validity generalization efforts, while undoubtedly offering more evidence than a single study, are not perfect. For example, validity generalization results can be susceptible to "publication bias," where test vendors may only report statistically significant correlations. Although procedures exist for correcting this bias, they assume evidence and expertise usually not readily available to an organization.[16] Thus, as promising as validity generalization is, we think organizations, especially if they think the job in question differs from comparable organizations, may still wish to conduct validation studies of their own.

A particular form of validity generalization that has proved useful is called meta-analysis. In meta-analysis the focus is on determining the average correlation between X and Y (i.e., $\bar{r}_{xy}$) noted above, such as between a particular selection technique (X) and job performance (Y) after controlling for methodological problems in the validation studies. For example, the average validity of general cognitive ability tests for predicting job performance is $\bar{r}_{xy} = .50$ (see Chapter 9). This represents our best statement of the average degree of validity found for mental ability tests to date, as well as an expectation of the validity we would likely find for general mental ability tests in future validation studies. We can also compare this $\bar{r}_{xy}$ to the $\bar{r}_{xy}$ of another selection technique, such as the unstructured interview, as a way of indicating the relative validity of the two techniques. Meta-analysis results and comparisons for numerous selection techniques are presented in Chapters 8 and 9.

Staffing Metrics and Benchmarks

For some time now, HR as a business area has sought to prove its value through the use of metrics, or quantifiable measures that demonstrate the effectiveness (or ineffectiveness) of a particular practice or procedure. Staffing is no exception. Fortunately, many of the measurement processes described in this chapter represent excellent metrics. Unfortunately, most HR managers, including many in staffing, may have limited (or no) knowledge of job analysis, validation, and measurement. The reader of this book can "show his or her stuff" by educating other organizational members about these metrics in an accessible and nonthreatening way. The result may be a more rigorous staffing process, producing higher levels of validity, and kudos for you.

Many who work in staffing are more familiar with another type of metric, namely, those produced by benchmarking. Benchmarking is a process where organizations evaluate their practices (in this case, staffing practices) against those used by industry leaders. Some commonly used benchmarks include cost per hire, forecasted hiring, and vacancies filled. Traditionally, most benchmarking efforts have focused on quantity of employees hired and cost. That situation is beginning to change. Companies such as Reuters and Dell are tracking "quality of hire," or the performance levels of those who are hired. Eventually, if enough organizations track such information, they can form a consortium so they can benchmark off one another's metrics for both quantity and quality.[17]

More generally, the SHRM regularly offers conferences and mini-conferences on staffing that provide benchmarks of current organizational practices. At a recent SHRM conference, Robyn Corr, VP of global staffing for Starbucks, discussed the company's approach to staffing, including how the company hires over 300 employees every day.

Such benchmarks can be a useful means of measuring important aspects of staffing methods or the entire staffing process. However, they are no substitute for the other measurement principles described in this chapter, including reliability and validity. Reliability, validity, utility, and measurement principles are more enduring, and more fundamental, metrics of staffing effectiveness.

COLLECTION OF ASSESSMENT DATA

In staffing decisions, the process of measurement is put into practice by collecting assessment data on external or internal applicants. To this point in this chapter, we have discussed how selection measures can be evaluated. To be sure, thorough evaluation of selection measures is important. Selection decision makers must be knowledgeable about how to use the assessment data that have been collected; otherwise the potential value of the data will lie dormant. On the other hand, to put these somewhat theoretical concepts to use in practice, selection decision makers must know how to collect the assessment data. Otherwise, the decision maker may find himself or herself in the unenviable "Big Hat, No Cattle" situation—knowing how to analyze and evaluate assessment data but not knowing where to find the data in the first place. Thus, knowing how to evaluate selection measures goes hand in hand with knowing where to find good assessment data in the first place.

In collecting assessment data, if a predictor is purchased, support services are needed. Consulting firms and test publishers can provide support for scoring of tests. Also necessary is legal support to ensure compliance with laws and regulations. Validity studies are important to ensure the effectiveness of the measures. Training on how to administer the predictor is also needed.

Beyond these general principles, which apply no matter what assessment data are collected, there is other information that the selection decision maker must know about the tangible process of collecting assessment data. Collection of data with respect to testing procedures, tests and test manuals, and professional standards are discussed.

Testing Procedures

In the past, most data concerning selecting testing procedures were in reference to paper-and-pencil tests. With the growth of computerization and the Internet, however, more and more selection measures are available on the personal computer (PC) and on the Web. Accordingly, in the sections that follow, we separate our discussion of the collection of testing procedures data into paper-and-pencil measures and PC- or Web-based procedures.

Paper and Pencil

Predictors cannot always be purchased by any firm that wants to use them; many test publishers require the purchaser to have certain expertise to properly use the test. For example, they may want the user to hold a PhD in a field of study related to the test and its use. For smaller organizations, this means hiring the consulting services of a specialist to use a particular test.

Care must be taken to ensure that correct answers for predictors are not shared with job applicants in advance of administration of the predictor. Any person who has access to the predictor answers should be fully trained and should sign a predictor security agreement. Also, a regular inventory procedure needs to be established to ensure that predictor materials are not inappropriately dispersed. Should a breach of security take place, use of the predictor should be abandoned and a new one should be used.

The predictor itself should be kept secure, but so should the results of the predictor in order to ensure the privacy of the individual. The results of the predictor should be used only for the intended purposes and by persons qualified to interpret them. Though feedback can be given to the candidate concerning the results, the individual should not be given a copy of the predictor or the scoring key.

Finally, it is imperative that all applicants be assessed with standardized procedures. This means that not only should the same or a psychometrically equivalent predictor be used, but individuals should take the test under the same circumstances. The purpose of the predictor should be explained to applicants, and they should be put at ease, held to the same time requirements to complete the predictor, and take the predictor in the same location.

PC- and Web-Based

Many selection measures can now be administered on the PC. Some of these tools are used by organizations to make initial cuts among applicants, as is the case with résumé- and application-screening software. In these systems, applicants complete the requested information, and then the software system, with input from the organization as to selection criteria and cutoffs, screens out unqualified applicants. Acclaim, for example, is an interactive program that tries to simulate the give-and-take of an initial screening interview. The software might pose a hypothetical situation (e.g., a rude customer) and ask the applicant for a response. Job applicants for hourly positions at Kmart, Albertson's, and the Sports Authority take an electronic assessment marketed by Unicru at in-store kiosks.

Other PC- and Web-based selection measures are formal tests. Many of the test publishers mentioned below offer selection decision makers the choice of paper-and-pencil or PC-based tests. For example, the *Wonderlic Personnel Test* has a version of the test that is administered and scored using a PC. It includes testing and scoring software and a user's manual. Typically, the cost of purchasing such tests is not much more than the paper-and-pencil version of the test.

Still other programs are a hybrid of these two systems, where applicants first complete initial information and if they are deemed to be at least minimally qualified, they then take a formal test. ePredix, for example, has applicants take a 15-minute initial screening test. Those who pass this hurdle are then asked to complete more detailed assessments. Although collecting assessment data in such a manner has the benefit of immediacy of results, organizations that choose to outsource preemployment screening on the Web need to ensure that the data are legally compliant, valid, and secure. Additionally, applicants may be concerned over privacy issues or may lack familiarity with the Web or be uncomfortable with tests administered via the Web. Finally, there is a concern about faking, such as the case when an individual other than the applicant takes the test. If organizations are concerned about individuals other than the applicant taking the test, verification procedures can be implemented, including mandating that the applicant take the test at a site that allows verification of identification.

In general, research suggests that Web-based tests work as well as paper-and-pencil tests, as long as they are validated in the same manner as other selection measures. Some organizations, however, in their rush to use such tests, fail to validate them. The results can be disastrous. The Transportation Security Administration (TSA), created after the September 11 attacks, has been criticized for its "inane" online test. Many questions on the test were obvious to a grade-school student. For example, one question was: Why is it important to screen bags for improvised explosive devices (IEDs)?

a. The IED batteries could *leak and damage* other passenger bags.
b. The wires in the IED could *cause a short* to the aircraft wires.
c. IEDs can cause *loss of lives*, property and aircraft.
d. The *ticking timer* could worry other passengers.

Obviously, the correct answer is "c." This test came about because the TSA farmed out the test to a vendor without asking for validation evidence. TSA's justification was, "We administered the test the way we were told to [by the vendor]." Thus, PC- and Web-based testing can work well and has many advantages, but organizations need to ensure that the tests are rigorously developed and validated.[18]

Acquisition of Tests and Test Manuals

The process of acquiring tests and test manuals requires some start-up costs in terms of the time and effort required to contact test publishers. Once one is on a mailing list, however, brochures from the publishers keep the selection decision maker updated on the latest developments and ordering information. In making decisions about which tests to acquire, a decision must be made not only about the particular type of test, but also the manner in which it will be administered and scored—paper and pencil versus PC-based.

Paper and Pencil

Most paper-and-pencil tests are acquired by contacting the publisher of the tests. Some publishers of paper-and-pencil tests used in selection decisions are Wonderlic (*www.wonderlic.com*), Consulting Psychologists Press (*www.cpp-db.com*), Institute for Personality and Ability Testing (*www.ipat.com*), Psychological Assessment Resources (*www.parinc.com*), NCS Assessments (*www.ncs.com*), Hogan Assessment Systems (*www.hoganassessments.com*), and Psychological Services, Inc. (*www.psionline.com*). All of these organizations have brochures that describe the products available for purchase. Most publishers will provide sample copies of the tests and a user's manual that selection decision makers may consult before purchasing the test. Costs of paper-and-pencil tests vary widely depending on the test and the number of copies ordered. One test that can be scored by the selection decision maker, for example, costs $100 for testing 25 applicants and $200 for testing 100 applicants. Another test that comes with a scoring system and interpretive report costs from $25 each for testing 5 applicants to $17 each for testing 100 applicants. Presumably, greater discounts are available for testing larger numbers of applicants.

Any test worth using will have a professional user's manual that accompanies it. This manual should describe the development and validation of the test, including validity evidence in selection contexts. A test manual should also include administration instructions, scoring instructions or information (many test marketers will score tests for organizations [for an additional fee]), interpretation information, and normative data. All of this information is crucial to make sure that the test is appropriate and that it is used in an appropriate (valid, legal) manner. Avoid using a test that has no professional manual, as it is unlikely to have been validated. Using a test without a proven track record is akin to hiring an applicant sight unseen. The *Wonderlic Personnel Test User's Manual* is an excellent example of a professional user's manual. It contains information about various forms of the *Wonderlic Personnel Test* (see Chapter 9), how to administer the test and interpret and use the scores, validity and fairness of the test, and various norms by age, race, gender, and so on.

PC- or Web-Based

When selection measures are administered on the PC or Web, acquisition is simple since copies of the measures are contained in the software. Thus, once an organization decides to administer selection measures in this manner, the consulting firm or test publisher arranges for access to the tests. Generally, organizations are given special user names that applicants use to complete the measures (along with their own identifying information). In some cases, the user's manuals for PC- or Web-based tests are provided on the computer. In other cases, only hard copies of the manuals are available. Irrespective of how the tests were acquired or administered, organizations must make sure they validate the tests. Selection decision makers should not accept vague claims regarding the accuracy of selection measures. The SHRM has launched the SHRM Assessment Center, whereby SHRM members can review and receive discounts on more than 200 Web-based tests.[19]

Professional Standards

Revised in 2003 by the Society for Industrial and Organizational Psychology (SIOP) and approved by the American Psychological Association (APA), the *Principles for the Validation and Use of Personnel Selection Procedures* is a guidebook that provides testing standards for use in selection decisions. The *Principles* covers test choice, development, evaluation, and use of personnel selection procedures in employment settings. The specific topics covered in the *Principles* include the various ways selection measures should be validated, how to conduct validation studies, what sources can be used to determine validity, generalizing validation evidence from one source to another, test fairness and bias, how to understand worker requirements, data collection for validity studies, ways in which validity information can be analyzed, the appropriate uses of selection measures, and an administration guide.

The *Principles* was developed by many of the world's leading experts on selection, and therefore any selection decision maker would be well advised to consult this important document, which is written in practical, nontechnical language.

The *Principles*, which is free, can be ordered from SIOP by visiting its Web site (*www.siop.org*).

A related set of standards has been promulgated by the APA. Formulated by the Joint Committee on Testing Practices, *The Rights and Responsibilities of Test Takers: Guidelines and Expectations* enumerates 10 rights and 10 responsibilities of test takers. One of the rights is for the applicant to be treated with courtesy, respect, and impartiality. Another right is to receive prior explanation for the purpose(s) of the testing. One responsibility is to follow the test instructions as given. In addition to enumerating test-taker rights and responsibilities, the document also provides guidelines for organizations administering the tests. For example, the standards stipulate that organizations should inform test takers about the purpose of the test. This document is available online at *www.apa.org/science/ttrr.html*. Organizations testing applicants should consult these guidelines to ensure, wherever possible, these rights are provided.

LEGAL ISSUES

Staffing laws and regulations, particularly EEO/AA laws and regulations, place great reliance on the use of measurement concepts and processes. Here, measurement is an integral part of (1) judging an organization's compliance through the conduct of disparate impact analysis, and (2) requiring standardization and validation of measures.

Disparate Impact Statistics

In Chapter 2, disparate (adverse) impact was introduced as a way of determining whether staffing practices were having potentially illegal impacts on individuals because of race, sex, and so forth. Such a determination requires the compilation and analysis of statistical evidence, primarily applicant flow and applicant stock statistics.

Applicant Flow Statistics
Applicant flow statistical analysis requires the calculation of selection rates (proportions or percentages of applicants hired) for groups, and the subsequent comparison of those rates to determine if they are significantly different from one another. This may be illustrated by taking the example from Exhibit 2.5:

	Applicants	**Hires**	**Selection Rate**
Men	50	25	.50 or 50%
Women	45	5	.11 or 11%

It can be seen in this example that there is a sizable difference in selection rates between men and women (.50 as opposed to .11). Does this difference indicate adverse impact?

The UGESP speak directly to this question. Several points need to be made regarding the determination of disparate impact analysis.

First, the UGESP require the organization to keep records that will permit calculation of such selection rates, also referred to as applicant flow statistics. These statistics are a primary vehicle by which compliance with the law (Civil Rights Act) is judged.

Second, the UGESP require calculation of selection rates (1) for each job category, (2) for both external and internal selection decisions, (3) for each step in the selection process, and (4) by race and sex of applicants. To meet this requirement, the organization must keep detailed records of its staffing activities and decisions. Such record keeping should be built directly into the organization's staffing system routines.

Third, comparisons of selection rates among groups in a job category for purposes of compliance determination should be based on the 80% rule in the UGESP, which states that "a selection rate for any race, sex or ethnic group which is less than four-fifths (4/5) (or eighty percent) of the rate for the group with the highest rate will generally be regarded by federal enforcement agencies as evidence of adverse impact, while a greater than four-fifths rate will generally not be regarded by federal enforcement agencies as evidence of adverse impact."

If this rule is applied to the previous example, the group with the highest selection rate is men (.50). The rate for women should be within 80% of this rate, or .40 (.50 × .80 = .40). Since the actual rate for women is .11, this suggests the occurrence of adverse impact.

Fourth, the 80% rule is truly only a guideline. Note the use of the word "generally" in the rule with regard to differences in selection rates. Also, the 80% rule goes on to provide for other exceptions, based on sample size considerations and issues surrounding statistical and practical significance of difference in selection rates. These exceptions represent recognition of the fact that adverse impact statistics may be unstable sample estimates of the amount of true adverse impact occurring. More precise methods of assessing adverse impact are needed. Despite these exceptions, organizations are encouraged to use the 80% rule with stringency for purposes of self-analysis. Deviations from the rule should be treated as red flags that trigger an investigation into possible reasons for their occurrence.

Applicant Stock Statistics

Applicant stock statistics require the calculation of the percentages of women and minorities (1) employed and (2) available for employment in the population. These percentages are compared to identify disparities. This is referred to as utilization analysis.

To illustrate, the example from Exhibit 2.3 is shown here:

	Employed	**Availability**
Nonminority	90%	70%
Minority	10%	30%

It can be seen that 10% of employees are minorities, whereas their availability is 30%. A comparison of these two percentages suggests an underutilization of minorities.

Utilization analysis of this sort is an integral part of not only compliance assessment but also affirmative action plans (AAPs). Indeed, utilization analysis is the starting point for the development of AAPs. This may be illustrated by reference to the Affirmative Action Programs regulations.

The regulations require the organization to conduct a formal utilization analysis of its workforce. That analysis must be (1) conducted by job group and (2) done separately for women and minorities. Though calculation of the numbers and percentages of persons employed is relatively straightforward, determination of their availability is not. The regulations require that the availabilities take into account at least the following factors: (1) the percentage of women or minorities with requisite skills in the recruitment area and (2) the percentage of women or minorities among those promotable, transferable, and trainable within the organization. Accurate measurement and/or estimation of availabilities that take into account these factors is difficult.

Despite these measurement problems, the regulations require comparison of the percentage of women and minorities employed with their availability. When the percentage of minorities or women in a job group is less than would reasonably be expected given their availability, underutilization exists and placement (hiring and promotion) goals must be set. Thus, the organization must exercise considerable discretion in the determination of adverse impact through the use of applicant stock statistics. It would be wise to seek technical and/or legal assistance for conducting utilization analysis (see also "Affirmative Action Plans" in Chapter 3).

Standardization and Validation

When it has been determined that an organization is in noncompliance with the law, such as through adverse impact statistics, it must take certain steps to move toward compliance. While the specific steps will obviously depend on the situation, measurement activities invariably will be actively involved in them. These activities will revolve around standardization and validation of measures.

Standardization
A lack of consistency in treatment of applicants is one of the major factors contributing to the occurrence of discrimination in staffing. This is partly due to a lack of

standardization in measurement, in terms of both what is measured and how it is evaluated or scored.

An example of inconsistency in what is measured is that the types of background information required of minority applicants may differ from that required of nonminority applicants. Minority applicants may be asked about credit ratings and criminal conviction records, while nonminority applicants are not. Or, the type of interview questions asked of male applicants may be different from those asked of female applicants.

Even if information is consistently gathered from all applicants, it may not be evaluated the same for all applicants. A male applicant who has a history of holding several different jobs may be viewed as a "career builder," while a female with the same history may be evaluated as an unstable "job-hopper." In essence, different scoring keys are being used for men and women applicants.

Reducing, and hopefully eliminating, such inconsistency requires a straightforward application of the three properties of standardized measures discussed previously. Through standardization of measurement comes consistent treatment of applicants, and with it, the possibility of lessened adverse impact.

Validation

Even with standardized measurement, adverse impact may occur. Under these circumstances, the question is whether adverse impact is still justified. The UGESP address this issue directly. When there is adverse impact, the organization must either eliminate it or justify it through presentation of validity evidence regarding the measure(s) causing the adverse impact.

The types of validity evidence required under the UGESP are precisely those presented in this chapter. There are also detailed technical standards governing the conduct of these validation studies in the UGESP. The purpose of these requirements is to ensure that if an organization's staffing system is causing adverse impact, it is for job-related reasons. Evidence of job relatedness thus becomes the employer's rebuttal to the plaintiff's charges of discrimination. In the absence of such validation evidence, the employer must take steps to eliminate the adverse impact. These steps will involve various recruitment, selection, and employment activities that will be discussed throughout the remainder of the book. A detailed review of the UGESP is provided in Chapter 9.

SUMMARY

Measurement, defined as the process of using rules to assign numbers to objects to represent quantities of an attribute of the objects, is an integral part of the foundation of staffing activities. Standardization of the measurement process is sought. This applies to each of the four levels of measurement: nominal, ordinal, interval, and ratio. Standardization is also sought for both objective and subjective measures.

Measures yield scores that represent the amount of the attribute being measured. Scores are manipulated in various ways to aid in their interpretation. Typical manipulations involve central tendency and variability, percentiles, and standard scores. Scores are also correlated to learn about the strength and direction of the relationship between two attributes. The significance of the resultant correlation coefficient is then assessed.

The quality of measures involves issues of reliability and validity. Reliability refers to consistency of measurement, both at a moment in time and between time periods. Various procedures are used to estimate reliability, including coefficient alpha, interrater and intrarater agreement, and test–retest. Reliability places an upper limit on the validity of a measure.

Validity refers to accuracy of measurement and accuracy of prediction, as reflected by the scores obtained from a measure. Criterion-related and content validation studies are conducted to help learn about the validity of a measure. In criterion-related validation, scores on a predictor (KSAO) measure are correlated with scores on a criterion (HR outcome) measure. In content validation, there is no criterion measure, so judgments are made about the content of a predictor relative to the HR outcome it is seeking to predict. Traditionally, results of validation studies were treated as situation specific, meaning that the organization ideally should conduct a new and separate validation study for any predictor in any situation in which the predictor is to be used. Recently, however, results from validity generalization studies have suggested that the validity of predictors may generalize across situations, meaning that the requirement of conducting costly and time-consuming validation studies in each specific situation could be relaxed. Staffing metrics such as cost per hire and benchmarks, representing how leading organizations staff positions, can be useful measures. But they are no substitutes for reliability and validity.

Various practical aspects of the collection of assessment data were described. Decisions about testing procedures and the acquisition of tests and test manuals require the attention of organizational decision makers. The collection of assessment data and the acquisition of tests and test manuals vary depending on whether paper-and-pencil or computerized selection measures are utilized. Finally, organizations need to attend to professional standards that govern the proper use of the collection of assessment data.

Measurement is also said to be an integral part of an organization's EEO/AA compliance activities, as the UGESP make clear. When adverse impact is found, changes in measurement practices may be legally necessary. As specified in the UGESP, these changes will involve movement toward standardization of measurement and the conduct of validation studies.

DISCUSSION QUESTIONS

1. Imagine and describe a staffing system for a job in which there are no measures used.
2. Describe how you might go about determining scores for applicants' responses to (a) interview questions, (b) letters of recommendation, and (c) questions about previous work experience.
3. Give examples of when you would want the following for a written job knowledge test: (a) a low coefficient alpha (e.g., $\alpha = .35$), and (b) a low test–retest reliability.
4. Assume you gave a general ability test, measuring both verbal and computational skills, to a group of applicants for a specific job. Also assume that because of severe hiring pressures, you hired all of the applicants, regardless of their test scores. How would you investigate the criterion-related validity of the test?
5. Using the same example as in question four, how would you go about investigating the content validity of the test?
6. What information does a selection decision maker need to collect in making staffing decisions? What are the ways in which this information can be collected?

ETHICAL ISSUES

1. Do individuals making staffing decisions have an ethical responsibility to know measurement issues? Why or why not?
2. Is it unethical for an employer to use a selection measure that has high empirical validity but lacks content validity? Explain.

APPLICATIONS

Evaluation of Two New Assessment Methods for Selecting Telephone Customer Service Representatives

The Phonemin Company is a distributor of men's and women's casual clothing. It sells exclusively through its merchandise catalog, which is published four times per year to coincide with seasonal changes in customers' apparel tastes. Customers may order merchandise from the catalog via mail or over the phone. Currently, 70% of orders are phone orders, and the organization expects this to increase to 85% within the next few years.

The success of the organization is obviously very dependent on the success of the telephone ordering system and the customer service representatives (CSRs) who staff the system. There are currently 185 CSRs; that number should increase to about 225 CSRs to handle the anticipated growth in phone order sales. Though the CSRs are trained to use standardized methods and procedures for handling phone orders, there are still seemingly large differences among them in their job performance. The CSRs' performance is routinely measured in terms of error rate, speed of order taking, and customer complaints. The top 25% and lowest 25% of performers on each of these measures differ by a factor of at least three (e.g., the error rate of the lowest group is three times as high as that of the top group). Strategically, the organization knows that it could enhance CSR performance (and ultimately sales) substantially if it could improve its staffing "batting average" by more accurately identifying and hiring new CSRs who are likely to be top performers.

The current staffing system for CSRs is straightforward. Applicants are recruited through a combination of employee referrals and newspaper ads. Because turnover among CSRs is so high (50% annually), recruitment is a continuous process at the organization. Applicants complete a standard application blank, which asks for information about education and previous work experience. The information is reviewed by the staffing specialist in the HR department. Only obvious misfits are rejected at this point; the others (95%) are asked to have an interview with the specialist. The interview lasts 20–30 minutes, and at the conclusion the applicant is either rejected or offered a job. Due to the tightness of the labor market and the constant presence of vacancies to be filled, 90% of the interviewees receive job offers. Most of those offers are accepted (95%), and the new hires then attend a one-week training program before being placed on the job.

The organization has decided to investigate fully the possibilities of increasing CSR effectiveness through sounder staffing practices. In particular, it is not pleased with its current methods of assessing job applicants; it feels that neither the interview nor the application blank provides the accurate and in-depth assessments of the KSAOs truly needed to be an effective CSR. Consequently, it has engaged the services of a consulting firm that offers various methods of KSAO assessment, along with validation and installation services. In cooperation with the HR staffing specialist, the consulting firm conducted the following study for the organization.

A special job analysis led to the identification of several specific KSAOs likely to be necessary for successful performance as a CSR. Three of these (clerical speed, clerical accuracy, interpersonal skills) were singled out for further consideration because of their seemingly high impact on job performance. Two new methods of assessment, provided by the consulting firm, were chosen for experimentation. The first was a paper-and-pencil clerical test assessing clerical speed and accuracy. It was a 50-item test with a 30-minute time limit. The second was a brief work sample that could be administered as part of the interview process. In the work sample the applicant must respond to four different phone calls: from a customer irate about an out-of-stock item, from a customer wanting more product information about an item than was provided in the catalog, from a customer who wants to change an order placed yesterday, and from a customer with a routine order to place. The applicant is rated by the interviewer (using a 1–5 rating scale) in terms of tactfulness (T) and in terms of concern for customers (C). The interviewer is provided with a rating manual containing examples of exceptional (5), average (3), and unacceptable (1) responses by the applicant.

A random sample of 50 current CSRs were chosen to participate in the study. At Time 1 they were administered the clerical test and the work sample; performance data were also gathered from company records for error rate (number of errors per 100 orders), speed (number of orders filled per hour), and customer complaints (number of complaints per week). At Time 2, one week later, the clerical test and the work sample were readministered to the CSRs. A member of the consulting firm sat in on all the interviews and served as a second rater of applicants' performance on the work sample at Time 1 and Time 2. It was expected that the clerical test and work sample would have positive correlations with speed and negative correlations with error rate and customer complaints.

Results for Clerical Test

	Time 1	Time 2
Mean score	31.61	31.22
Standard deviation	4.70	5.11
Coefficient alpha	.85	.86
Test–retest r		.92**
r with error rate	−.31**	−.37**
r with speed	.41**	.39**
r with complaints	−.11	−.08
r with work sample (T)	.21	.17
r with work sample (C)	.07	.15

Results for Work Sample (T)

	Time 1	Time 2
Mean score	3.15	3.11
Standard deviation	.93	1.01
% agreement (raters)	88%	79%
r with work sample (C)	.81**	.77**
r with error rate	−.13	−.12
r with speed	.11	.15
r with complaints	−.37**	−.35**

Results for Work Sample (C)

	Time 1	Time 2
Mean score	2.91	3.07
Standard deviation	.99	1.10
% agreement (raters)	80%	82%
r with work sample (C)	.81**	.77**
r with error rate	−.04**	−.11**
r with speed	.15	.14**
r with complaints	−.40	−.31

(Note: ** means that r was significant at $p < .05$)

Based on the description of the study and results above,

1. How do you interpret the reliability results for the clerical test and work sample? Are they favorable enough for Phonemin to consider using them "for keeps" in selecting new job applicants?
2. How do you interpret the validity results for the clerical test and work sample? Are they favorable enough for Phonemin to consider using them "for keeps" in selecting new job applicants?
3. What limitations in the above study should be kept in mind when interpreting the results and deciding whether to use the clerical test and work sample?

Conducting Empirical Validation and Adverse Impact Analysis

Yellow Blaze Candle Shops provide a full line of various types of candles and accessories such as candle holders. There are 150 shops located in shopping malls and strip malls throughout the country. There are over 600 salespeople staffing these stores, each of which has a full-time manager. Staffing the manager's position, by policy, must occur by promotion from within the sales ranks. The organization is interested in trying to improve its identification of salespeople most likely to be successful store managers. It has developed a special technique for assessing and rating the suitability of salespeople for the manager's job.

To experiment with this technique, the regional HR department representative met with the store managers in the region to review and rate the promotion suitability of each manager's salespeople. They reviewed sales results, customer service orientation, and knowledge of store operations for each salesperson, and then assigned a 1–3 promotion suitability rating (1 = not suitable, 2 = maybe suitable, 3 = definitely suitable) on each of these three factors. A total promotion suitability (PS) score, ranging from 3 to 9, was then computed for each salesperson.

The PS scores were gathered, but not formally used in promotion decisions, for all salespeople. Over the past year 30 salespeople have been promoted to store manager. Now it is time for the organization to preliminarily investigate the validity of the PS scores and to see if their use might lead to the occurrence of adverse impact against women or minorities. Each store manager's annual overall performance appraisal rating, ranging from 1 (low performance) to 5 (high performance), was used as the criterion measure in the validation study. The following data were available for analysis:

Employee ID	PS Score	Performance	Sex M/F	Minority Status (M = Minority NM = Nonminority)
11	9	5	M	NM
12	9	5	F	NM
13	9	1	F	NM
14	9	5	M	M
15	8	4	F	M
16	8	5	F	M
17	8	4	M	NM
18	8	5	M	NM
19	8	3	F	NM
20	8	4	M	NM
21	7	5	F	M
22	7	3	M	M
23	7	4	M	NM
24	7	3	F	NM
25	7	3	F	NM
26	7	4	M	NM
27	7	5	M	M
28	6	4	F	NM
29	6	4	M	NM
30	6	2	F	M
31	6	3	F	NM
32	6	3	M	NM
33	6	5	M	NM
34	6	5	F	NM
35	5	3	M	NM
36	5	3	F	M
37	5	2	M	M
38	4	2	F	NM
39	4	1	M	NM
40	3	4	F	NM

Based on the above data, calculate:

1. Average PS scores for the whole sample, males, females, nonminority, and minority.
2. The correlation between PS scores and performance ratings, and its statistical significance (an r = .37 or higher is needed for significance at p < .05).

3. Adverse impact (selection rate) statistics for males and females, and non-minorities and minorities. Use a PS score of 7 or higher as a hypothetical passing score (the score that might be used to determine who will or will not be promoted).

Using the data, results, and description of the study, answer the following questions:

1. Is the PS assessment a valid predictor of performance as a store manager? Would you recommend the PS be used in the future to select salespeople for promotion to store manager?
2. With a cut score of 7 on the PS, would its use lead to adverse impact against women? Against minorities? If there is adverse impact, does the validity evidence justify use of the PS anyway?
3. What are limitations of this study?
4. Would you recommend that Yellow Blaze now actually use the PS for making promotion decisions? Why or why not?

TANGLEWOOD STORES CASE I

Identifying the methods that select the best employees for the job is indisputably one of the central features of the organizational staffing process. The measurement chapter described statistical methods for assessing the relationship between organizational hiring practices and important outcomes. The case will help you see exactly how these data can be analyzed in an employment setting, and show how the process differs depending on the job being analyzed.

The Situation

As you read in the recruiting case, Tanglewood has a history of very divergent staffing practices among stores, and it is looking to centralize its operations. For most stores, the only information collected from applicants is an application blank with education level and prior work experience. After a brief unstructured interview with representatives from the operations and HR departments, store managers make a hiring decision. Many managers have complained that the result of this system is that many individuals are hired who have little understanding of Tanglewood's position in the retail industry and whose personalities are completely wrong for the company's culture. To improve its staffing system, Tanglewood has selected certain stores to serve as prototypes for an experimental selection system that includes a much more thorough assessment of applicant qualifications.

Your Tasks

The case considers concurrent validation evidence from the existing hiring system for store associates as well as predictive validation evidence from the proposed hiring system. You will determine whether the proposed selection system represents a real improvement in the organization's ability to select associates who will perform well. Your willingness to generalize the results to other stores will also be assessed. An important ancillary activity in this case is ensuring that you communicate your statistical analyses in a way that is easy for a nonexpert to comprehend. Finally, you will determine if there are any other outcomes you would like to assess with the new staffing materials, such as the potential for adverse impact and the reactions of store managers to the new system. The background information for this case, and your specific assignment, can be found at *www.mhhe.com/heneman6e*.

TANGLEWOOD STORES CASE II

Adverse Impact

One of the most significant equal employment opportunity concerns for any organization is when a large class of employees gathers together to propose that they have been discriminated against. In this case, you will assess a complaint of adverse impact proposed by the nonwhite employees of Tanglewood in Northern California.

The Situation

This case revolves around analyzing data about the promotion pipeline at Tanglewood Stores and trying to decide if there is a glass ceiling in operation. As you saw in the introduction and planning case, Tanglewood's top management is deeply concerned about diversity, and they want to ensure that the promotion system does not discriminate. They have provided you with background data that will help you assess the situation.

Your Tasks

Using the information in this chapter, you will assess the proportional representation of women and minorities by analyzing concentration statistics and promotion rates. As in the measurement and validation case, an important activity in this case is ensuring that you communicate your statistical analyses in a way that is easy for management to comprehend. After making these assessments, you will provide specific recommendations to the organization regarding elements of planning, culture change, and recruiting. The background information for this case, and your specific assignment, can be found at *www.mhhe.com/heneman6e*.

ENDNOTES

1. E. F. Stone, *Research Methods in Organizational Behavior* (Santa Monica, CA: Goodyear, 1978), pp. 35–36.
2. F. G. Brown, *Principles of Educational and Psychological Testing* (Hinsdale, IL: Dryden, 1970), pp. 38–45.
3. Stone, *Research Methods in Organizational Behavior,* pp. 36–40.
4. W. H. Bommer, J. L. Johnson, G. A. Rich, P. M. Podsakoff, and S. B. McKenzie, "On the Interchangeability of Objective and Subjective Measures of Employee Performance: A Meta-Analysis," *Personnel Psychology,* 1995, 48, pp. 587–606; R. L. Heneman, "The Relationship Between Supervisory Ratings and Results-Oriented Measures of Performance: A Meta-Analysis," *Personnel Psychology,* 1986, 39, pp. 811–826.
5. This section draws on Brown, *Principles of Educational and Psychological Testing,* pp. 158–197; L. J. Cronbach, *Essentials of Psychological Testing,* fourth ed. (New York: Harper and Row, 1984), pp. 81–120; N. W. Schmitt and R. J. Klimoski, *Research Methods in Human Resources Management* (Cincinnati: South-Western, 1991), pp. 41–87.
6. J. T. McClave and P. G. Benson, *Statistics for Business and Economics,* third ed. (San Francisco: Dellan, 1985).
7. For an excellent review, see Schmitt and Klimoski, *Research Methods in Human Resources Management,* pp. 88–114.
8. This section draws on E. G. Carmines and R. A. Zeller, *Reliability and Validity Assessment* (Beverly Hills, CA: Sage, 1979).
9. D. P. Schwab, "Construct Validity in Organization Behavior," in B. Staw and L. L. Cummings (eds.), *Research in Organizational Behavior* (Greenwich, CT: JAI Press, 1980), pp. 3–43.
10. Carmines and Zeller, *Reliability and Validity Assessment*; J. M. Cortina, "What Is Coefficient Alpha? An Examination of Theory and Application," *Journal of Applied Psychology,* 1993, 78, pp. 98–104; Schmitt and Klimoski, *Research Methods in Human Resources Management,* pp. 89–100.
11. This section draws on R. D. Arvey, "Constructs and Construct Validation," *Human Performance,* 1992, 5, pp. 59–69; W. F. Cascio, *Applied Psychology in Personnel Management,* fourth ed. (Englewood Cliffs, NJ: Prentice-Hall, 1991), pp. 149–170; H. G. Heneman III, D. P. Schwab, J. A. Fossum, and L. Dyer, *Personnel/Human Resource Management,* fourth ed. (Homewood, IL: Irwin, 1989), pp. 300–329; N. Schmitt and F. J. Landy, "The Concept of Validity," in N. Schmitt, W. C. Borman, and Associates, *Personnel Selection in Organizations* (San Francisco: Jossey-Bass, 1993), pp. 275–309; Schwab, "Construct Validity in Organization Behavior"; S. Messick, "Validity of Psychological Assessment," *American Psychologist,* Sept. 1995, pp. 741–749.
12. Heneman, Schwab, Fossum, and Dyer, *Personnel/Human Resource Management,* pp. 300–310.
13. I. L. Goldstein, S. Zedeck, and B. Schneider, "An Exploration of the Job Analysis-Content Validity Process," in N. Schmitt, W. C. Borman, and Associates, *Personnel Selection in Organizations,* pp. 3–34; Heneman, Schwab, Fossum, and Dyer, *Personnel/Human Resource Management,* pp. 311–315; D. A. Joiner, *Content Valid Testing for Supervisory and Management Jobs: A Practical/Common Sense Approach* (Alexandria, VA: International Personnel Management Association, 1987); P. R. Sackett and R. D. Arvey, "Selection in Small N Settings," in Schmitt, Borman, and Associates, *Personnel Selection in Organizations,* pp. 418–447.
14. R. S. Barrett, "Content Validation Form," *Public Personnel Management,* 1992, 21, pp. 41–52; E. E. Ghiselli, J. P. Campbell, and S. Zedeck, *Measurement Theory for the Behavioral Sciences* (San Francisco: W. H. Freeman, 1981).

15. R. M. Guion, "Personnel Assessment, Selection and Placement," in M. D. Dunnette and L. M. Hough (eds.), *Handbook of Industrial and Organizational Psychology,* Vol. 2 (Palo Alto, CA: Consulting Psychologists Press, 1991), pp. 360–365; F. L. Schmidt and J. E. Hunter, "Development of a General Solution to the Problem of Validity Generalization," *Journal of Applied Psychology,* 1977, 62, pp. 529–540; Schmitt, Borman, and Associates, *Personnel Selection in Organizations,* pp. 295–296.

16. M. A. McDaniel, H. R. Rothstein, and D. L. Whetzel, "Publication Bias: A Case Study of Four Test Vendors," *Personnel Psychology,* 2006, 59, pp. 927–953.

17. C. Winkler, "Quality Check: Better Metrics Improve HR's Ability to Measure—and Manage—the Quality of Hires," *HR Magazine,* May 2007, pp. 93–98; *SHRM Human Capital Benchmarking Study* (Alexandria, VA: Society for Human Resource Management, 2005).

18. B. Calandra, "Boosting Better Hires," *Human Resource Executive,* Aug. 2003, pp. 17–19; K. Kersting, "How Do You Test on the Web? Responsibly," *APA Monitor,* Mar. 2004, pp. 26–27; K. Maher, "Web-Based Tools Help Find the Right Person for the Job," *Wall Street Journal,* Nov. 26, 2002, p. B8; M. Martinez, "Screening for Quality on the Web," *EMT,* Winter 2004, pp. 12–17; J. A. Naglieri, F. Drasgow, M. Schmit, L. Handler, A. Prifitera, A. Margolis, and R. Velasquez, "Psychological Testing on the Internet," *American Psychologist,* Apr. 2004, 59, pp. 150–162; R. E. Ployhart, J. A. Weekley, B. C. Holtz, and C. Kemp, "Web-Based and Paper-and-Pencil Testing of Applicants in a Proctored Setting: Are Personality, Biodata, and Situational Judgment Tests Comparable?" *Personnel Psychology,* 2003, 56, pp. 733–752; S. Power, "Federal Official Faults TSA Screener Testing as 'Inane,'" *Wall Street Journal,* Oct. 9, 2003, pp. B1–B2.

19. S. B. Morrise and R. E. Lobsenz, "Significance Tests and Confidence Intervals for the Adverse Impact Ratio," *Personnel Psychology,* 2000, 53, pp. 89–111.

CHAPTER EIGHT

External Selection I

Preliminary Issues
   The Logic of Prediction
   The Nature of Predictors
   Development of the Selection Plan
   Selection Sequence

Initial Assessment Methods
   Résumés and Cover Letters
   Application Blanks
   Biographical Information
   Reference and Background Checks
   Genetic Screening
   Initial Interview
   Choice of Initial Assessment Methods

Legal Issues
   Disclaimers
   Reference and Background Checks
   Preemployment Inquiries
   Bona Fide Occupational Qualifications

Summary

Discussion Questions

Ethical Issues

Applications

External selection refers to the assessment and evaluation of external job applicants. A variety of different assessment methods are used. Preliminary issues that guide the use of these assessment methods will be discussed. These issues include the logic of prediction, the nature of predictors, development of the selection plan, and the selection sequence.

Initial assessment methods are used to select candidates from among the initial job applicants. The initial assessment methods that will be reviewed are résumés and cover letters, application blanks, biographical information, letters of recommendation, reference and background checks, genetic screening, and initial interviews. The factors that should guide the choice of initial assessment methods will be reviewed. These factors are frequency of use, cost, reliability, validity, utility, applicant reactions, and adverse impact.

The use of assessment methods also requires a firm understanding of legal issues. One method of preventing legal difficulties—the use of disclaimers as a means of protecting employer rights—is described. Due to myriad legal issues surrounding their use, reference and background checks and preemployment inquiries require special attention to numerous details in using these methods of initial assessment. The most important of these details will be reviewed. Finally, bona fide occupational qualifications (BFOQs) have particular relevance to initial assessment because such qualifications are usually assessed during the initial stages of selection. The legal issues involved in establishing such qualifications will be reviewed.

PRELIMINARY ISSUES

Many times, selection is equated with one event, namely, the interview. Nothing could be further from the truth if the best possible person/job match is to be made. For the best possible match to be achieved, a series of well-thought-out activities needs to take place. Hence, selection is a process rather than an event. It is guided by a logic that determines the steps that need to be taken. The logic applies to all predictors that might be used, even though they differ in terms of several characteristics. Actual implementation of the logic of prediction requires that predictors be chosen through development of a selection plan. Implementation also requires creation of a selection sequence, which is an orderly flow of people through the stages of applicant, candidate, finalist, and offer receiver.

The Logic of Prediction

In Chapter 1, the selection component of staffing was defined as the process of assessing and evaluating people for purposes of determining the likely fit between the person and the job. This process is based on the logic of prediction, which holds that indicators of a person's degree of success in past situations should be predictive of how successful he or she will likely be in new situations. Application of this logic to selection is illustrated in Exhibit 8.1.

A person's knowledge, skills, abilities, and other characteristics (KSAOs) and motivation are the product of experiences of past job, current job, and nonjob situations. During selection, samples of these KSAOs and motivation are identified, assessed, and evaluated by the organization. The results constitute the person's overall qualifications for the new situation or job. These qualifications are then used to predict how successful the person is likely to be in that new situation or job regarding the human resource (HR) outcomes. The logic of prediction works in practice if the organization accurately identifies and measures qualifications relative to job requirements, and if those qualifications remain stable over time so that they are carried over to the new job and used on it.

An example of how this logic can be followed in practice comes from a national communications organization with sales volume in the billions of dollars.[1] It was very interested in improving on the prediction of job success (sales volume) for its salespeople, whose sales figures had stagnated. To do so, it constructed what it labeled a "sales competency blueprint," or selection plan, to guide development of a new selection process. The blueprint depicted the KSAOs that needed to be sampled from previous jobs in order to predict sales success in a telemarketing sales job. The blueprint was established on the basis of a thorough job analysis in which subject matter experts (SMEs) identified the KSAOs thought necessary to be a successful telemarketer (e.g., knowledge of the product, how it was developed, and how it compared to the competitors' products). Then a structured interview was developed to sample the extent to which applicants for sales jobs in telemarketing had acquired the necessary KSAOs. In turn, the interview was used in selection to predict the likely success of applicants for the job.

The logic of prediction shown in Exhibit 8.1 demonstrates how critical it is to carefully scrutinize the applicant's past situation when making selection decisions. For example, in selecting someone for a police officer position, the success

EXHIBIT 8.1   The Logic of Prediction

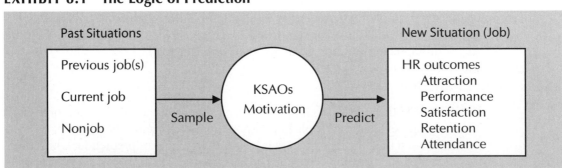

of the applicant in a previous security guard position might be considered a relevant predictor of the likelihood that the applicant will succeed in the new police officer position. Alternatively, the fact that the person was previously successful as a homemaker might be viewed as totally irrelevant to the job of police officer. Surprisingly, considering the homemaker role to be irrelevant might well be an incorrect assessment. Research shows that there is a close correspondence between the homemaker and the police officer position. Specifically, thorough job analysis showed that both jobs rely heavily on troubleshooting and emergency handling skills. Hence, in the absence of a sound job analysis, many qualified applicants may inadvertently be overlooked even though they have some of the characteristics needed to perform the job. Nonjob experience in the home, in the community, and in other institutions may be as valuable as or more valuable than previous employment experiences.

Job titles such as homemaker are not nearly specific enough for making selection decisions. Similarly, the fact that someone has a certain number of years of experience usually does not provide sufficient detail to make selection decisions. What counts, and what is revealed through job analysis, is the specific types of experiences required and the level of successfulness at each. Similarly, the fact that someone was paid or not paid for employment is not relevant. What counts is the quality of the experience as it relates to success on the new job. In short, the logic of prediction indicates that a point-to-point comparison needs to be made between requirements of the job to be filled and the qualifications that applicants have acquired from a variety of past situations.

Not only is the logic of prediction important to selection, but it is important to recruitment as well. One study showed that applicant reactions to selection procedures were determined in part by the job relatedness of the selection procedure. If applicants see the selection process as job related, which should occur if the logic of prediction is used, then they are more likely to view the selection process as being fair.[2] It would be expected that applicants who view the selection procedure as fair are more likely to accept a job offer and/or encourage others to apply for a job in the organization.

Finally, the logic of prediction means separating recruitment from selection. For example, many organizations use employee referrals to identify prospective hires (recruitment), to select among those who have applied (selection), or both. Though there is nothing wrong with using referrals, how they are evaluated as a recruitment device will differ from how they are evaluated as a selection measure (often in the form of references).

The Nature of Predictors

As will be seen shortly, there is a wide variety of different types of predictors used in external selection, ranging from interviews to genetic screening. These types can be differentiated from one another in terms of content and form.

Content

The substance or content of what is being assessed with a predictor varies considerably and may range from a sign to a sample to a criterion.[3] A sign is a predisposition of the person that is thought to relate to performance on the job. Personality as a predictor is a good example here. If personality is used as a predictor, the prediction is that someone with a certain personality (e.g., "abrasive") will demonstrate certain behaviors (e.g., "rude to customers") leading to certain results on the job (e.g., "failure to make a sale"). As can be seen, a sign is very distant from actual on-the-job results. A sample is closer than a sign to actual on-the-job results. Observing a set of interactions between a sales applicant and a customer to see if sales are made provides an example of a sample. The criterion is very close to the actual job performance, such as sales during a probationary period for a new employee.

Form

The form or design of the predictor may vary along several different lines.

Speed Versus Power. A person's score on some predictors is based on the number of responses completed within a certain time frame. One event in a physical abilities test may, for example, be the number of bench presses completed in a given period of time. This is known as a speed test. A power test, on the other hand, presents individuals with items of increasing difficulty. For example, a power test of numerical ability may begin with addition and subtraction, move on to multiplication and division, and conclude with complex problem-solving questions. A speed test is used when speed of work is an important part of the job, and a power test is used when the correctness of the response is essential to the job. Of course, some tests (see the *Wonderlic Personnel Test* in Chapter 9) can be both speed and power tests, in which case few individuals would finish.

Paper and Pencil Versus Performance. Many predictors are of the paper-and-pencil variety; applicants are required to fill out a form, write an answer, or complete multiple choice items. Other predictors are performance tests, where the applicant is asked to manipulate an object or equipment. Testing running backs for the NFL on their time in the 40-yard dash is a performance test. Paper-and-pencil tests are frequently used when psychological abilities are required to perform the job; performance tests are used when physical and social skills are required to perform the job.

Objective Versus Essay. An objective paper-and-pencil predictor is one in which multiple choice questions or true/false questions are used. These tests should be used to measure specific knowledge in specific areas. Another form of a predictor is an essay, where a written answer is required of the respondent. Essays are best used to assess written communication, problem-solving, and analytical skills.[4]

Oral Versus Written Versus Computer.   Responses to predictor questions can be spoken, written, or entered into the computer. For example, when conducting interviews, some organizations listen to oral responses, read written responses, or read computer printouts of typed-in responses to assess applicants. As with all predictors, the appropriate form depends on the nature of the job. If the job requires a high level of verbal skill, then oral responses should be solicited. If the job requires a large amount of writing, then written responses should be required. If the job requires constant interaction with the computer, then applicants should enter their responses into the computer.[5]

Development of the Selection Plan

To translate the results of a job analysis into the actual predictors to be used for selection, a selection plan must be developed. A selection plan describes which predictor(s) will be used to assess the KSAOs required to perform the job. The recommended format for a selection plan, and an example of such a plan for the job of secretary, is shown in Exhibit 8.2. In order to establish a selection plan, three steps are followed. First, the KSAOs are written in the left-hand column. This list comes directly from the job requirements matrix. Second, for each KSAO, a "yes" or "no" is written to show whether this KSAO needs to be assessed in the selection process. Sometimes the answer is no because it is a KSAO the applicant will acquire once on the job (e.g., knowledge of company policies and procedures). Third, possible methods of assessment are listed for the required KSAOs, and the specific method to be used for each of these KSAOs is then indicated.

Although selection plans are costly and time consuming to develop, organizations are increasingly finding that the benefits of developing a selection plan outweigh the costs. As a result, it is and should be a required step in the selection process. For example, a selection plan or "niche testing" was used to select tellers and customer service representatives by Barnett Bank in Jacksonville, Florida. It found that an essential KSAO for both positions is the ability to make judgments when interacting with the public. For this KSAO, a niche test was developed in which applicants watch actual dealings with the public on video and then decide on the appropriate course of action. Their responses are graded and used to predict their likelihood of success in either position.

Selection Sequence

Usually, a series of decisions is made about job applicants before they are selected. These decisions are depicted in Exhibit 8.3. The first decision that is reached is whether initial applicants who have applied for the job become candidates or are rejected. A candidate is someone who has not yet received an offer, but who possesses the minimum qualifications to be considered for further assessment.

EXHIBIT 8.2 Selection Plan Format and Example for Secretarial Position

Major KSAO Category	Necessary for Selection? (Y/N)	Method of Assessment								
		WP	CT	DB	LTR	TEF	ML	EM	TM	Interview
1. Ability to follow oral directions/ listening skills	Y			X					X	
2. Ability to read and understand manuals/guidelines	Y	X	X	X	X	X	X	X		
3. Ability to perform basic arithmetic operations	Y			X		X				
4. Ability to organize	Y			X			X			
5. Judgments/priority setting/decision-making ability	Y			X		X				
6. Oral communication skills	Y									X
7. Written communication skills	Y		X		X			X	X	
8. Interpersonal skills	Y									X
9. Typing skills	Y	X	X		X					
10. Knowledge of word processing, graphics, database, and spreadsheet software	Y	X	X	X	X	X				
11. Knowledge of company policies and procedures	N									
12. Knowledge of basic personal computer operations	Y	X	X	X	X	X		X		
13. Knowledge of how to use basic office machines	N									
14. Flexibility in dealing with changing job demands	Y						X	X	X	
15. Knowledge of computer software	Y	X	X	X	X	X		X		
16. Ability to attend to detail and accuracy	Y	X	X	X	X	X	X	X	X	

WP = Word processing test, CT = Correction test, DB = Database exam, LTR = Letter, TEF = Travel expense form, ML = Mail log, EM = Electronic mail messages, and TM = Telephone messages.

Source: Adapted from N. Schmitt, S. Gilliland, R. S. Landis, and D. Devine, "Computer-Based Testing Applied to Selection of Secretarial Positions," *Personnel Psychology*, 1993, 46, pp. 149–165.

EXHIBIT 8.3   Assessment Methods by Applicant Flow Stage

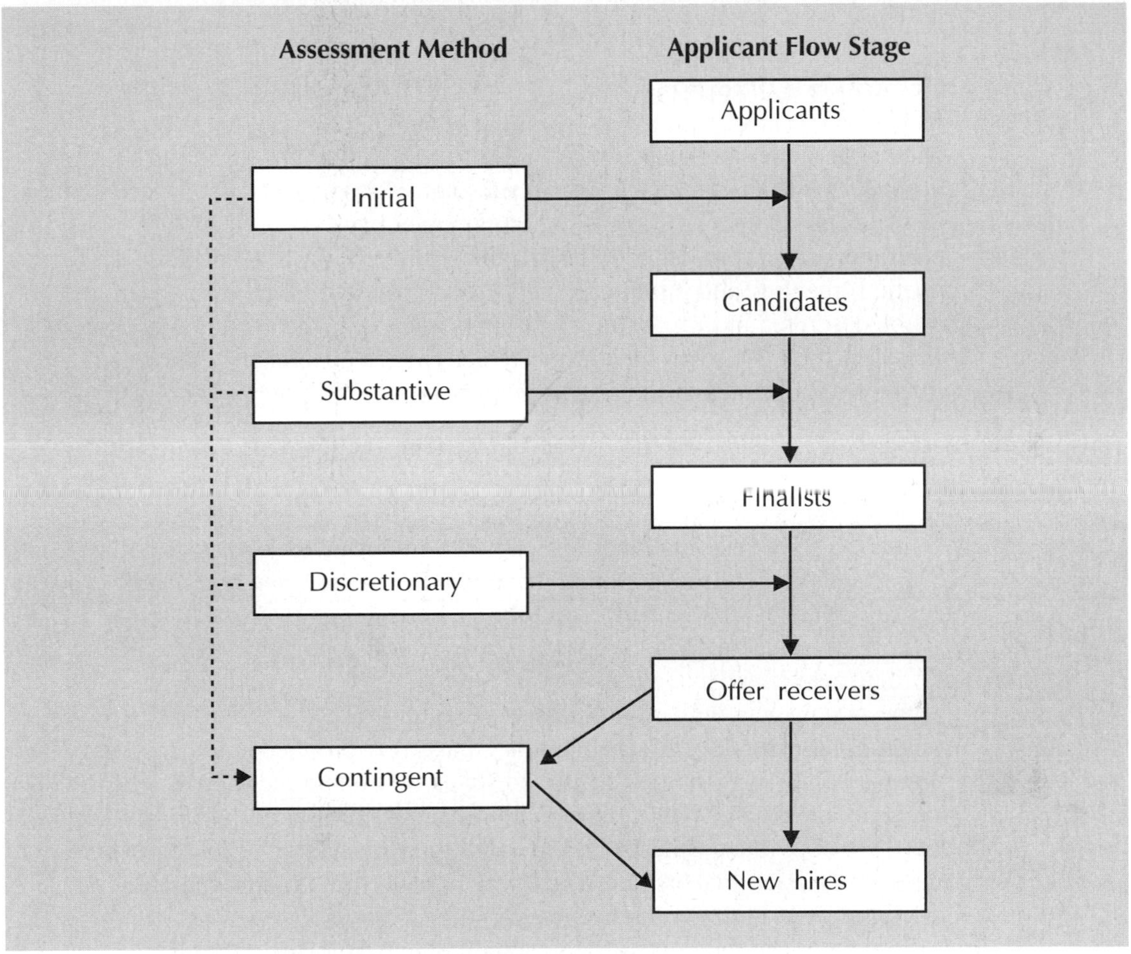

Assessment Method	Applicant Flow Stage
	Applicants
Initial	Candidates
Substantive	Finalists
Discretionary	Offer receivers
Contingent	New hires

Initial assessment methods are used to choose candidates (these will be discussed later in this chapter). The second decision made is which candidates become finalists. A finalist is someone who meets all the minimum qualifications and whom the organization considers fully qualified for the job. Substantive assessment methods are used to select finalists. These methods will be discussed in the next chapter. The third decision made is which finalist receives the actual job offer. Offer receivers are those finalists to whom the organization extends an offer of employment. Discretionary methods are used to select finalists and will be described in the next chapter. Contingent methods are sometimes used, meaning the job offer is subject to certain qualifications, such as passing a medical exam or drug test, before the offer receiver can become a new hire. Use of contingent methods, in particular drug testing and medical exams, will be reviewed in the next chapter. Finally, some offer receivers become new hires when they decide to join the organization.

INITIAL ASSESSMENT METHODS

Initial assessment methods, also referred to as preemployment inquiries, are used to minimize the costs associated with substantive assessment methods by reducing the number of people assessed. Predictors typically used to screen candidates from applicants include application blanks, biographical information, reference reports, genetic screening, and initial interviews. Each of these initial assessment methods will be described in turn. Using meta-analysis results, the average validity (i.e., $\bar{r}$) of each method is also provided if possible. Then, a general evaluation will be presented to help guide decisions about which initial assessment methods to use.

Résumés and Cover Letters

The first introduction of the applicant to the organization is often a cover letter and résumé. This introduction is controlled by the applicant as to the amount, type, and accuracy of information provided. As a result, résumés and cover letters always need to be verified with other predictors, such as background checks, to ensure that there are accurate and complete data across all job applicants with which to make informed selection decisions.

One major issue with résumés as a selection tool is the volume that organizations must process. Some organizations make few provisions for how to file and organize résumés as they filter in, and for how to store them once a hiring decision is made. Most organizations are well advised to produce and maintain an electronic copy of résumés received, both to ease sharing of information among selection decision makers and to track applicants should any questions (legal or otherwise) arise once the applicant is hired.

Employers can also outsource résumé collection to résumé-tracking services. These services scan résumés, but most do more than that—including scoring applicant résumés and placing a percentage next to an applicant's name reflecting the number of criteria each résumé meets. Though such methods have powerful time- and cost-saving advantages, there are disadvantages, such as rejection of résumés that the software has trouble reading (e.g., those on colored paper or with special formatting like bullets) and applicants who try to beat the system by loading their résumé with every conceivable skill that appears in the advertisement. Despite these drawbacks, the efficiencies of such services make them particularly attractive for organizations facing large volumes of résumés.

The vast majority of large employers, and even many medium-size employers, encourage submission of résumés via e-mail or through online forms on the organization's Web site. For example, on the Toys "R" Us Web site, applicants can search an online database for openings and then apply either by completing an online form or, for managerial positions, by attaching their résumé to an e-mail message.

Even if applicants submit an electronic résumé to an employer (by uploading it to the organization's Web site or attaching it to an e-mail message), they need to make sure it is electronically scan-ready. This means applicants should avoid unusual fonts and formatting. With today's résumés, form definitely should follow function. Moreover, as opposed to the traditional emphasis on action verbs ("managed," "guided," etc.), applicants should use nouns to describe noteworthy aspects of their background ("nonprofit," "3.75 GPA," "environmental science experience") because nouns are more likely to be identified as keywords in scanning software. If the applicant believes his or her résumé is likely to be scanned, then the résumé needs to be built around such keywords that will be the focus of the scan.

Video Résumés. Video résumés are getting considerable attention in the business press. Some sites, like *WorkBlast.com,* help applicants put together video résumés where applicants talk about their qualifications directly to the camera or in a simulated interview. Lucy Cherkasets sent a video résumé to organizations in the New York area that had openings that particularly interested her. "I used it to apply for the jobs I wanted the most," she said. She is now working as an HR manager for LaForce & Stevens, a public relations firm in Manhattan.

While the topic of video résumés is fashionable, few employers have any experience with them, and there is no research on their effectiveness. Although a survey indicated that many hiring managers would view a video résumé, a majority (58%) of those admitted they would do so out of "sheer curiosity." As one career advisor noted, "Most employers don't have much direct familiarity with them yet. Folks are still trying to figure out where the video résumé falls in the calculus in applicant selection." Some employers refuse to view video résumés for fear of introducing subjective biasing factors (appearance, race, disability) into their decisions. Other job applicants have submitted video résumés only to be the subject of ridicule by their potential employers. Aleksey Vayner, a finance major at Yale, sent a video résumé to bank giant UBS, only to have it posted on blogs and be mocked by others.[6]

Thus, while video résumés are receiving a lot of attention in the press, the pitfalls involved for employers and applicants, for the time being at least, might cause them to be considered more of a fad than the "wave of the future."

Résumé Issues. Although résumés have the advantage of allowing the applicant control over information that is presented to employers, in preparing or evaluating a résumé, there are two issues that applicants and employers should keep in mind: how to deal with fabrications/distortions and how to get a résumé noticed. We consider each of these issues and how to address them below.

Résumé Fabrications and Distortions. Because résumés are prepared by applicants and follow no set-in-stone form, and because there are incentives for applicants to present themselves in a favorable light, distortions are a significant problem. For example, David J. Edmondson, CEO of RadioShack, was fired after a newspaper investigation revealed that he padded his résumé with two degrees he never earned, from a university he never attended. Edmondson is not alone. In the past few years, the same thing happened to the CEO of Bausch and Lomb, the former head football coach of Notre Dame, the dean of admissions for MIT, the CEO of R. H. Donnelly, and the opponent of Senator Hillary Clinton in the most recent New York Senate race. These are just the visible cases—and the ones who got caught. ResumeDoctor, an online company that assists applicants in preparing résumés, checked the accuracy of applicants' résumés posted on its Web site, and found that nearly half (42.7%) had "significant inaccuracies." A background checking agency found that 56% of résumés contained a falsehood of some kind.[7]

Like the truth, résumés come in various degrees of accuracy, ranging from small, unintentional mistakes to outright fabrications. Some degree of what we might call "fudging" is commonplace. For example, Ellie Strauss's two more recent full-time jobs lasted less than six months. Ellie represented these as freelance jobs, under the heading "Senior Project Manager" to make them look like contract positions. Some might call this deception. Others might call it "creative marketing" or "tailoring." Whatever you call it, padding happens a lot. People even fudge their education for wedding announcements. Recently, the *New York Times* had to print a correction because a bride indicated she graduated from the University of Pennsylvania and received a doctorate in neuroscience from the University of Southern California, neither of which was true. If people will lie on a wedding announcement, imagine what they will do on a résumé!

According to a recent survey, the three biggest areas of distortion or misinformation are the following:[8]

1. Inflated titles
2. Inaccurate dates to cover up job hopping or employment gaps
3. Half-finished degrees, inflated education, or "purchased" degrees

The best way to combat résumé fraud or fudging is to conduct careful background checks. Also, applying a "smell" test to any suspicious information is a wise policy. For example, in light of the false information submitted by coaches, colleges are giving résumés much closer scrutiny. On the University of Louisville's athletic department application forms, a new warning has been inserted: "If a discrepancy is found after the background check, the employee is subject to dismissal." In short, the best protection against résumé fraud is for the hiring organization to do its homework.[9]

Getting a Résumé Noticed. The conscientious job seeker may wonder how to best prepare a résumé. Although there are as many theories on the ingredients of a perfect résumé as there are résumé readers, a few general guidelines may be helpful.

First, realize that typos and other minor mistakes can kill an applicant's chances. A survey revealed that 84% of hiring managers exclude applicants from further consideration with just two typographical errors on their résumé; 47% of these managers exclude applicants with just a single error. Second, make sure to customize your résumé to the position if at all possible (try to address how your background, skills, and accomplishments fit the specific job requirements). Third, although résumés are getting somewhat longer, recognize that brevity is highly valued among hiring managers—many hiring managers refuse to read résumés that are longer than two pages, and some won't read a résumé longer than a page. Third, as we noted above, be factual and truthful. Where judgment is required, err on the side of accuracy. As one expert put it, "People are lying when they don't have to." Most hiring managers understand that no résumé is perfect. And even if being truthful hurts you in the short run, better to pay the price now rather than later when you might have an entire career at stake. Finally, though taking care to be truthful, a résumé is no time to underplay one's accomplishments—it is often wise not to simply list one's job duties but to identify one's accomplishments as well. Consider your impact on your division or group: What would not have happened had you not been there? What are you proudest of? Can you identify your own strengths from your performance review? Are there skills demonstrated during college that might be described? For example, the global head of recruiting for Accenture says he looks for evidence of teamwork skills in hiring: "I'd have to put the ability to work in a team environment toward the very top of what we look for," he says. Since most college students do some of their work in teams, why not list that as a skill acquired?[10]

Evaluation.   Almost no research exists on the validity and reliability of résumés and cover letters. Nor is there information on their costs or adverse impact. A review did indicate relatively low validity for applicant self-reports of grades, class standing, and test scores, but this does not address other information—such as self-reported work experience—often provided in applications and résumés. This situation is unfortunate given the pervasive use of résumés and cover letters in certain types of jobs, especially entry-level management, professional, and technical positions. Thus, organizations using résumés and cover letters in selection should carefully evaluate their effectiveness and make sure to independently verify information they are using in hiring decisions.[11]

Application Blanks

Most application blanks request in written form the applicant's background in regard to educational experiences, training, and job experiences. This information is often on the résumé as well and may seem unnecessarily duplicated. This is not the case. An application can be used to verify the data presented on the résumé and can also be used to obtain data omitted on the résumé, such as employment dates. The major advantage of application blanks over résumés is that the organization, rather than the applicant, dictates what information is presented. As a result, information critical to success on the job is less likely to be omitted by the applicant or overlooked by the reviewer of the résumé. The major issue with application blanks is to make sure that information requested is critical to job success, following the logic of prediction discussed earlier.

A sample application blank is provided in Exhibit 8.4. As with most application blanks, the major sections of the application are personal information, employment desired, educational background, special interests and abilities, work experience, and suggested references. The only information sought from the application blank should be KSAOs that can be demonstrated as relevant to the job. This not only avoids wasting the organization's and the applicant's time but also protects the employer from charges of unfair discrimination (see "Legal Issues" at the end of this chapter). It is important to take note of the statement at the bottom of the application blank, known as a disclaimer statement. It provides certain legal protections to the organization, which are discussed in "Legal Issues." Asking applicants to sign a disclaimer may also decrease the incentive to distort or falsify information.

Educational Requirements

Special care needs to be taken in wording items on an application blank when soliciting information about educational experiences and performance.[12] Following are discussed several particularly important areas pertaining to educational requirement information on application blanks.

Level of Education. Level of education or degree is one element of educational performance used to predict job performance. Often, level of education is measured by the attainment of a degree. The degree should be assessed in conjunction with other educational requirements. A high-level degree from a nonaccredited school may be an indication of a lesser accomplishment than a lower-level degree from an accredited school. Research indicates that level of education is weakly related to job performance ($\bar{r} = 13$).[13]

Grade Point Average. Classroom grades are measured using a grade point average (GPA). Care should be exercised in the interpretation of GPA information. For example, a GPA in one's major in college may be different (usually higher) from one's GPA for all classes. Grades also vary widely by field (e.g., grades in engineering tend to be lower than in other fields). Further, a GPA of 3.5 may be good at one school but not at another. Research suggests that the validity of GPA in predicting job performance may be as high as the mid .30s. College grades are no more valid than high school grades, and grades are most valid in predicting early job performance. Although there is variability from employer to employer, evidence indicates that GPA does not play a large role in most recruiters' evaluations. GPAs do tend to have adverse impact against minorities, and, as with all selection measures with adverse impact, the validity evidence must be balanced against adverse impact implications.[14]

EXHIBIT 8.4   Application for Employment

PERSONAL INFORMATION

DATE _____

NAME _____
LAST   FIRST   MIDDLE

SOCIAL SECURITY
NUMBER _____

PRESENT ADDRESS _____
STREET   CITY   STATE   ZIP

PERMANENT ADDRESS _____
STREET   CITY   STATE   ZIP

PHONE NO. _____   ARE YOU 18 YEARS OR OLDER?   Yes ☐   No ☐

ARE YOU PREVENTED FROM LAWFULLY BECOMING EMPLOYED
IN THIS COUNTRY BECAUSE OF VISA OR IMMIGRATION STATUS?   Yes ☐   No ☐

EMPLOYMENT DESIRED

POSITION _____   DATE YOU
CAN START _____   SALARY
DESIRED _____

ARE YOU EMPLOYED NOW? _____   IF SO MAY WE INQUIRE
OF YOUR PRESENT EMPLOYER? _____

APPLIED TO THIS COMPANY BEFORE? _____   WHERE? _____   WHEN? _____

REFERRED BY _____

EDUCATION

	NAME AND LOCATION	NO. OF YEARS ATTENDED	DID YOU GRADUATE?	SUBJECTS STUDIED
GRAMMAR SCHOOL				
HIGH SCHOOL (GED)				
COLLEGE				
OTHER				

(continued)

EXHIBIT 8.4 **Continued**

GENERAL

SUBJECTS OF SPECIAL STUDY

SPECIAL SKILLS

ACTIVITIES: (CIVIC, ATHLETIC, ETC.)

U.S. MILITARY OR
NAVAL SERVICE   RANK

PRESENT MEMBERSHIP IN
NATIONAL GUARD OR RESERVES

FORMER EMPLOYERS (LIST BELOW LAST 3 EMPLOYERS, STARTING WITH THE LAST ONE FIRST)

DATE	NAME & ADDRESS	SALARY	POSITION	REASON FOR LEAVING
FROM				
TO				
FROM				
TO				
FROM				
TO				

REFERENCES (GIVE THE NAMES OF 3 PERSONS NOT RELATED TO YOU)

	NAME	ADDRESS	BUSINESS	YEARS ACQUAINTED
1				
2				
3				

"I certify that all the information submitted by me on this application is true and complete, and I understand that if any false information, omissions, or misrepresentations are discovered, my application may be rejected and, if I am employed, my employment may be terminated at any time. In consideration of my employment, I agree to conform to the company's rules and regulations, and I agree that my employment and compensation can be terminated, with or without cause, and with or without notice, at any time, at either my or the company's option. I also understand and agree that the terms and conditions of my employment may be changed, with or without cause, and with or without notice, at any time by the company. I understand that no company representative, other than its president, and only when in writing and signed by the president, has any authority to enter into any agreement for employment for any specific period of time, or to make any agreement contrary to the foregoing."

DATE   SIGNATURE

Quality of School.   In recent times, much has been said and written about the quality of various educational programs. For example, *U.S. News and World Report* annually publishes the results of a survey showing ratings of school quality. A more comprehensive source on school quality is *The Gourman Report.*[15] *The Gourman Report* assigns numerical scores (ranging from 1.00 = unacceptable to 5.00 = perfect) to virtually every degree-granting university in the United States on the basis of 18 criteria (e.g., faculty qualifications, admission standards, curriculum, quality of instruction). *The Gourman Report* includes ratings for undergraduate and graduate programs in many fields.

The huge wage premiums for MBA degrees in particular, but also educational degrees in general, are commanded by graduates from prestigious universities. Sixty percent of corporate recruiters cite the reputation of the school as the top reason for recruiting at a particular university. As one article concluded, "It's not necessarily what you learn in an MBA program, but where you learn it."

Although the overwhelming majority of people who earn MBAs say it was worth it (89% in a recent survey), they generate mixed sentiments from employers. Some employers believe that universities are glorified placement services—merely a collection node for smart people. In response, more employers are weighing applicants' entrance exam scores (e.g., SAT, ACT) to measure mental ability more directly. One job posting on *HotJobs.com* for an entry-level investment banking position required a minimum SAT score of 1350.

Major Field of Study.   The more specialized the knowledge requirements of a particular position, the more important an applicant's major field of study is likely to be as a predictor. An English major may do very well as an editor but may be unsuccessful as a physician. It should also be noted that choice of a major does not guarantee that a certain number or type of classes have been taken. The number and type of classes needed for a major or minor varies from school to school and needs to be carefully scrutinized to ensure comparability across majors. The relationship between field of study and job performance is very difficult to assess; therefore, no conclusive validity evidence is available.

Extracurricular Activities.   The usefulness of extracurricular activities as a predictor depends on the job. Being a field hockey player may have little relevance to being a successful manager. However, being elected captain of a hockey team may indeed be a sign of leadership qualities needed to be a successful manager. Information about extracurricular activities taken from an application blank must be relevant to the job in question. Evidence suggests that participation in extracurricular activities is a demonstration of interpersonal skills, indicating that it may be more valid for jobs with a heavy social component.[17]

Training and Experience Requirements

Many past experiences predictive of future performance do not take place in a classroom. Instead, these experiences come from life experiences in other institutions, which, fortunately, can also be captured on an application blank. A great deal of weight is often put on training and experience requirements on the theory that actions speak louder than words. Experienced surgeons tend to make better surgeons, for example. A study found that the mortality rate of procedures was about twice as high for inexperienced surgeons as for experienced surgeons. As with other jobs, though, the benefits of experience tend to be at the low levels of experience. Beyond a certain level, added experience doesn't help much. The drawback of putting too much emphasis on previous work experience, however, is that the amount of experience and training an applicant has may be overstated. Also, applicants with high potential may be overlooked because they have not had the opportunity to gain the training or experience needed.

Various methods can be used to measure training and experience. Since training and experience information is not directly equivalent across applicants, all methods require the judgment of selection decision makers. These decision makers render judgments about how to classify and weight different levels of experience. An approach termed the "behavioral consistency method" has shown the highest degree of validity because it focuses on determining the quality of an applicant's previous training and experience. One of the means by which the behavioral consistency method determines quality is by asking applicants to complete a supplemental application wherein they describe their most significant accomplishments relative to a list of key job behaviors. Due to their involved nature, however, behavioral consistency ratings are time consuming and expensive to administer, and they require the applicant to possess some degree of analytical ability and writing skills. Thus, the choice of weighting methods rests on a trade-off between accuracy and ease and cost of administration.[18]

Licensing, Certification, and Job Knowledge

Many professions and occupations require or encourage people to demonstrate mastery of a certain body of knowledge. Such mastery is commonly measured by two distinct methods: licensure and certification. A license is required of people by law to perform an activity, whereas a certification is voluntary in the sense that law does not mandate it (though an individual employer may require it). The purpose of a license is to protect the public interest, whereas the purpose of a certification is to identify those people who have met a minimum standard of proficiency. Licensing exams and certification exams are usually developed by SMEs in conjunction with testing specialists. Licensure and certification are to be distinguished from job knowledge tests. While licensure and certification demonstrate mastery of a general body of knowledge applicable to many organizations, job knowledge tests assess a specific body of knowledge within a particular organization. Job knowledge tests are usually used in the public sector as an initial screening device. In the private sector, they are used primarily for promotion purposes. Although mentioned here, job knowledge tests will be covered in detail in Chapter 9.

The actual use of licensing and certification requirements depends on whether they are used as an initial or a contingent assessment method. As an initial method, licensing and certification requirements are used to eliminate applicants who fail to possess these credentials. For example, a car repair shop electing to hire only certified mechanics might initially screen out individuals who fail to have the proper certification. When licensing and certification requirements are used as a contingent method, the selection process proceeds on the assumption that the applicant has the requisite credential (or will have it by the time of hire). This is then verified after an initial offer decision has been made. For example, rather than verifying that each applicant for a nursing position possesses a valid state license, a hospital may assess applicants based on the assumption that they have a valid license and then verify this assumption after a contingent job offer has been made. Thus, the difference between using licensing and certification requirements as initial or contingent assessment methods depends on when the information is considered in the selection process.

Increasingly, organizations are using voluntary professional certification as a method of verifying competence in various occupations. There are more than 1,000 professional certifications. Most of these voluntary certifications are issued on the basis of experience and education. The vast majority of certifications also require examinations.

There are several practical problems or limitations in using licensing and certification requirements in selection. First, one cannot assume that simply because an applicant has a license or certification he or she is qualified for the position. That assumption places full confidence in the licensing and certification standards of the professional organization. Licensing and certification requirements vary greatly in their rigor, and one should not accept on faith that the fulfillment of those requirements ensures professional competency. Moreover, even if the requirements did perfectly measure professional competence, because licenses and certifications are issued to those passing some minimum threshold, they do not discriminate between the minimally qualified and the exceptionally well qualified. If you had to choose between Dr. Smith, who barely passed his board exam on the fourth try, and Dr. Jones, who earned the top score in her class, wouldn't you usually prefer Dr. Jones? Yet, all the patient (and selection decision maker) knows is that both Dr. Smith and Dr. Jones are licensed. The upshot: The wise selection decision maker may require licensure or certification but will also assess competency and job knowledge in other ways.

A second difficulty with licensing and certification requirements is that, like job titles, there has been significant proliferation. This is particularly true with certifications. For example, among financial advisors there are certified financial planners (CFPs), certified financial analysts (CFAs), certified investment management analysts (CIMAs), chartered financial consultants (ChFCs), chartered retirement planning counselors (CRPCs), and so forth. Indeed, there are more than 100 such titles used by financial professionals. No central regulator monitors these titles, and some can be earned by simply spending a few hours taking an online course. Massachusetts took steps to regulate one of these certifications—certified senior advisors (CSAs)—because it determined that the certification requirements were somewhat lax and that many of the CSAs were steering their clients toward high-commission investments. This example illustrates our point: If selection decision makers wish to require certification, they need to research the types and meanings of certifications that may exist for a job.

Finally, there are practice effects with repeated tries at a licensing or certification exam, and the effects may be quite strong. One study of medical professionals found that for one certification exam, second-time examinees improved their scores by 0.79 standard deviations. For another exam, the average gain was 0.48 standard deviations. Translating first gain (0.79SD) into a standard normal distribution, this would mean that someone who scored at the 34th percentile the first time out would be expected to score at the 66th percentile on the second try. For the second exam (0.48SD), the improvement would be from the 34th percentile to the 53rd percentile. Unlike some standardized tests, where scores may be reported for each time the test is taken, there generally is no way for a selection decision maker to know how many times an applicant has taken a licensing or certification exam (nor, as noted above, can one determine a test taker's exact score).

We are not arguing that selection decision makers should ignore licensing and certification requirements. They are important—even necessary—for many jobs. However, selection decision makers need to be informed consumers for those areas where they require licensure and certification, and supplement licensure and certification with other information to ascertain knowledge and competency.[19]

Weighted Application Blanks

Not all of the information contained on an application blank is of equal value to the organization in making selection decisions. Depending on the organization and job, some information predicts success on the job better than other information. Procedures have been developed that help weight application blank information by the degree to which the information differentiates between high- and low-performing individuals.[20] This scoring methodology is referred to as a weighted application blank and is useful not only in making selection decisions but also in developing application blanks. The statistical procedures involved help the organization discern which items should be retained for use in the application blank and which should be excluded, on the basis of how well they predict performance.

Evaluation of Application Blanks

Evidence suggests that scored evaluations of the unweighted application blank are not particularly valid predictors of job performance (average validity ranges from r̄ = .10 to r̄ = .20).[21] This is not surprising given the rudimentary information that is collected in application blanks. Another factor that may undermine the validity of application blanks is distortion. Evidence suggests that about one-third of the investigations into the background of applicants suggested that misrepresentation occurred on the application blank. Subsequent studies have suggested that the most common questions that are misrepresented include previous salary, education, tenure on previous job, and reasons for leaving previous job. Some individuals even go beyond misrepresentation to outright invention. One study revealed that 15% of supposedly previous employers of applicants indicated that the individual never worked for them.[22] Thus, application information that is given heavy weight in selection decisions should be verified.

The validity evidence for weighted application blanks is much more positive.[23] In a sense, this would almost have to be true since items in the weighted application blank are scored and weighted based on their ability to predict job performance. Thus, as long as *some* of the items are predictive, the scoring and weighting schemes embedded in the weighted application blank will ensure that the overall score is predictive. Because the process used to develop the weighted application blank is time consuming and expensive, more cost-benefit studies need to be conducted on the weighted application blank. Is the validity worth the cost? Unfortunately, there is little recent research on the weighted application blank, so answers to this question are difficult to attain.

The relatively poor validity of unweighted application blanks also should not be taken as an indication that they are useless in selection decisions. Unweighted application blanks are a very inexpensive means of collecting basic information on job applicants. Most organizations use unweighted application blanks only for initial screening decisions (to rule out applicants who are obviously unqualified for the job). Thus, it is not necessarily appropriate to condemn unweighted application blanks based on a criterion for which they are rarely used (i.e., used by themselves to make substantive selection decisions about applicants). As long as application blanks are used in this context (and not relied on to a significant degree in making substantive hiring decisions), they can be a useful method of making initial decisions about applicants.

Biographical Information

Biographical information, often called biodata, is personal history information on an applicant's background and interests. Results from a biodata survey provide a general description of a person's life history. The principal assumption behind the use of biodata is the axiom "The best predictor of future behavior is past behavior." These past behaviors may reflect ability or motivation. Biodata inventories are thought to measure applicant motivation that can be inferred from past choices. However, research also suggests that many ability items are included in biodata inventories.[24]

Like application blanks, biographical information blanks ask applicants to report on their background. Responses to both of these questionnaires can provide useful information in making initial selection decisions about applicants. Unlike application blanks, however, biographical information can also be fruitfully used for substantive selection decisions. In fact, if scores on a biodata inventory are predictive of subsequent job performance (which, as we will see, is often the case), it may be somewhat limiting to use biodata scores only for initial assessment decisions. Thus, although biographical information is as much a substantive assessment method as it is an initial assessment method, because it shares many similarities with application blanks, we have included it in this section. Nevertheless, it should also be considered in deliberations about which substantive assessment methods are to be used.

Biographical information also has similarities and differences with background tests (see the section on reference reports). Biodata and background checks are similar in that both look into an applicant's past. However, the two types of selection methods differ in their general purpose and measurement. First, whereas a background check is often used to turn up any "buried bones" in an applicant's background, biodata is used to predict future performance. Second, whereas reference checks are conducted through records checks, and conversations with references, biodata information is collected by survey. Thus, biodata inventories and background checks are distinct methods of selection that must be considered separately.

The type of biographical information collected varies a great deal from inventory to inventory and often depends on the job. For example, a biographical survey for executives might focus on career aspirations, accomplishments, and disappointments. A survey for blue-collar workers might focus on training and work experience. A biodata inventory for federal government workers might focus on school and educational experiences, work history, skills, and interpersonal relations. As can be seen from these examples, most biodata surveys consider individual accomplishments, group accomplishments, disappointing experiences, and stressful situations.[25] The domains in which these attributes are studied often vary from job to job but can range from childhood experiences to educational or early work experiences to current hobbies or family relations.

Measures

Typically, biographical information is collected in a questionnaire that applicants complete. Exhibit 8.5 provides example biodata items. As can be seen, the items are quite diverse. It has been suggested that each biodata item can be classified according to 10 criteria:

- *History* (does the item describe an event that has occurred in the past, or a future or hypothetical event?)
- *Externality* (does the item address an observable event or an internal event such as values or judgments?)

EXHIBIT 8.5   Examples of Biodata Items

1. In college, my grade point average was:
   a. I did not go to college or completed less than two years
   b. Less than 2.50
   c. 2.50 to 3.00
   d. 3.00 to 3.50
   e. 3.50 to 4.00

2. In the past five years, the number of different jobs I have held is:
   a. More than five
   b. Three–five
   c. Two
   d. One
   e. None

3. The kind of supervision I like best is:
   a. Very close supervision
   b. Fairly close supervision
   c. Moderate supervision
   d. Minimal supervision
   e. No supervision

4. When you are angry, which of the following behaviors most often describes your reaction:
   a. Reflect on the situation for a bit
   b. Talk to a friend or spouse
   c. Exercise or take a walk
   d. Physically release the anger on something
   e. Just try to forget about it

5. Over the past three years, how much have you enjoyed each of the following (use the scale at right below):
   a. ____ Reading   1 = Very much
   b. ____ Watching TV   2 = Some
   c. ____ Home improvements 3 = Very little
   d. ____ Music   4 = Not at all
   e. ____ Outdoor recreation

6. In most ways is your life close to ideal?
   a. Yes
   b. No
   c. Undecided or neutral

- *Objectivity* (does the item focus on reporting factual information or subjective interpretations?)
- *Firsthandedness* (does the item seek information that is directly available to the applicant rather than an evaluation of the applicant's behavior by others?)
- *Discreteness* (does the item pertain to a single, unique behavior or a simple count of events as opposed to summary responses?)
- *Verifiability* (can the accuracy of the response to the item be confirmed?)
- *Controllability* (does the item address an event that was under the control of the applicant?)
- *Equal accessibility* (are the events or experiences expressed in the item equally accessible to all applicants?)
- *Job relevance* (does the item solicit information closely tied to the job?)
- *Invasiveness* (is the item sensitive to the applicant's right to privacy?)[26]

Most selection tests simply score items in a predetermined manner and add the scores to arrive at a total score. These total scores then form the basis of selection decisions made about the applicants. With most biodata inventories, the process of making decisions on the basis of responses to items is considerably more complex. Essentially, the development of a biodata inventory is a bit of a fishing expedition where current employees are given many items to complete and the inventory used for future hiring decisions is based on those items—and the specific responses within items or questions—that seem to discriminate between high performers and low performers.

Google developed its biodata inventory by first asking its employees 300 questions and then correlating employee responses to their job performance. Once it isolated items that predicted the job performance of current employees, Google then began asking applicants a smaller set of questions that range from the age when an applicant first got excited about computers to whether the applicant has ever turned a profit at his or her own side-business.[27]

Evaluation of Biodata

Research conducted on the reliability and validity of biodata is quite positive.[28] Responses tend to be reliable (test–retest coefficients range from .77 to .90). More important, past research suggests that biodata inventories are valid predictors of job performance. A number of meta-analyses have been conducted, and the average validity has ranged from $\bar{r} = .32$ to $\bar{r} = .37$.[29]

Because biodata inventories are developed and scored on the basis of a particular job and sample, it has commonly been argued that the validity of a particular inventory in one organization is unlikely to generalize to another organization. However, one study demonstrated that biodata inventories can be constructed in a way that will lead to generalizability across organizations if the items are chosen based on their generalizability.[30]

One of the more important issues in evaluating the usefulness of biodata is the issue of falsification, or "faking good."[31] Because responses to most biodata items are difficult, if not impossible, to verify (e.g., "Did you collect coins or stamps as a child?"), it is conceivable that applicants distort their responses to tell prospective employers what they want to hear. In fact, research clearly shows that such faking does occur. Research also suggests, though, that faking can be reduced in a couple of ways: by using items that are more objective and verifiable, and by warning applicants against faking.[32]

Reference and Background Checks

Background information about job applicants can come not only from the applicant but also from people familiar with the applicant in previous situations (e.g., employers, creditors, neighbors). Organizations often solicit this information on their own or use the services of agencies that specialize in investigating applicants. Background information solicited from others consists of letters of recommendation, reference checks, and background testing.

Letters of Recommendation

A very common reference check in some settings (e.g., academic institutions) is to ask applicants to have letters of recommendation written for them. There are two major problems with this approach. First, these letters may do little to help the organization discern the more-qualified applicants from the less-qualified applicants. The reason for this is that only very poor applicants are unable to arrange for positive letters about their accomplishments. Second, most letters are not structured or standardized. What this means is that the organization receives data from letter writers that are not consistent across organizations. For example, a letter about one applicant may concern the applicant's educational qualifications, whereas a letter about another applicant may focus on work experience. Comparing the qualifications of applicants A and B under these circumstances is like comparing apples and oranges.

The problem with letters of recommendation is demonstrated dramatically in one study that showed there was a stronger correlation between two letters written by one person for two different applicants than between two different people writing letters for the same person.[33] This finding indicates that letters of recommendation have more to do with the letter writer than with the person being written about. In fact, one study revealed that letter writers who had a dispositional tendency to be positive wrote consistently more favorable letters than letter writers with a tendency to be critical or negative.[34]

Such problems indicate that organizations should downplay the weight given to letters unless a great deal of credibility and accountability can be attached to the letter writer's comments. Also, a structured form should be provided so that each writer provides the same information about each applicant.

Another way to improve on letters of recommendation is to use a standardized scoring key. An example of one is shown in Exhibit 8.6. Using this method, categories of KSAOs are established and become the scoring key (shown at the bottom of the exhibit). Then the adjectives in the actual letter are underlined and classified

---

EXHIBIT 8.6   Scoring Letters of Recommendation

Dear Personnel Director:

Mr. John Anderson asked that I write this letter in support of his application as assistant manager and I am pleased to do so. I have known John for six years as he was my assistant in the accounting department.

John always had his work completed <u>accurately</u> and <u>promptly</u>. In his years here, he <u>never missed a deadline</u>. He is very <u>detail</u> oriented, <u>alert</u> in finding errors, and <u>methodical</u> in his problem-solving approach. Interpersonally, John is a very <u>friendly</u> and <u>helpful</u> person.

I have great confidence in John's ability. If you desire more information, please let me know.

MA _0_   CC _2_   DR _6_   U _0_   V _0_

Dear Personnel Director:

Mr. John Anderson asked that I write this letter in support of his application as assistant manager and I am pleased to do so. I have known John for six years as he was my assistant in the accounting department.

John was one of the most <u>popular</u> employees in our agency as he is a <u>friendly, outgoing, sociable</u> individual. He has a great sense of <u>humor</u>, is <u>poised</u>, and is very <u>helpful</u>. In completing his work, he is <u>independent, energetic</u>, and <u>industrious</u>.

I have great confidence in John's ability. If you desire more information, please let me know.

MA _0_   CC _2_   DR _0_   U _5_   V _3_

Key   MA = mental ability
CC = consideration-cooperation
DR = dependability-reliability
U = urbanity
V = vigor

SOURCE: M. G. Aumodt, D. A. Bryan, and A. J. Whitcomb, "Predicting Performance with Letters of Recommendation," *Public Personnel Management,* 1993, 22, pp. 81–90. Reprinted with permission of *Public Personnel Management,* published by the International Personnel Management Association.

into the appropriate category. The number of adjectives used in each category constitutes the applicant's score.

Reference Checks

With reference checking, a spot check is made on the applicant's background. Usually the person contacted is the immediate supervisor of the applicant or is in the HR department of current or previous organizations with which the applicant has had contact. Surveys reveal that 96% of organizations conduct reference checks. A roughly equal number conduct the checks in-house (by human resources) versus a third-party vendor. The most common information sought is verification of employment eligibility, criminal background, verification of former employers, verification of dates of previous employment, and verification of former job titles.[35] Exhibit 8.7 provides a sample reference request. Although this reference request was developed for checking references by mail, the questions contained in the request could easily be adapted for use in checking references via the telephone.

Both of the problems that occur with letters of recommendation take place with reference checks as well. An even more significant concern, however, is the reluctance of organizations to give out the requested information because they fear a lawsuit on grounds of invasion of privacy or defamation of character. Recall the survey results reported above indicating that 96% of employers always check references. The same survey indicated that 93% of employers refuse to provide reference information for fear of being sued. As one executive stated, "There's a dire need for better reference information but fear of litigation keeps employers from providing much more than name, rank, and serial number."[36] As a result of employers' reluctance to provide reference information, reference checkers claim to receive inadequate information roughly half of the time. To a large degree, this concern over providing even rudimentary reference information is excessive—less than 3% of employers have had legal problems with reference checks (see "Legal Issues" at the end of this chapter). It is important to remember that if every organization refused to provide useful reference information, a potentially important source of applicant information would lose any of its potential value.

It's still the case that most reference checking is done over the telephone. There is evidence, though, that this situation is changing. Increasingly, employers are mining networking Web sites such as Facebook, MySpace, and LinkedIn not only to find out more about an applicant but also to locate references to contact. T-Mobile, for example, regularly mines "public" information on applicants' profile pages. These networking Web sites have "changed everything" about how T-Mobile conducts reference checks, according to one hiring manager.[37] No matter the source or method used to gather the information, it's critical that the questions be job related and that the same information is asked about all applicants. When properly structured and job-relevant, references can have moderate levels of validity.[38]

EXHIBIT 8.7 **Sample Reference Request**

TO BE COMPLETED BY APPLICANT

NAME (PRINT): SOCIAL SEC. NUMBER:

I have made application for employment at this company. I request and authorize you to release all information requested below concerning my employment record, reason for leaving your employ, or my education. I hereby release my personal references, my former employers and schools, and all individuals connected therewith, from all liability for any damage whatsoever for furnishing this information.

SIGNATURE _____ DATE _____

SCHOOL REFERENCE
DATES ATTENDED
FROM: TO: GRADUATED? YES ☐ NO ☐
DEGREE AWARDED:

EMPLOYMENT REFERENCE
POSITION HELD: EMPLOYMENT DATES:

IMMEDIATE SUPERVISOR'S NAME

REASON FOR LEAVING DISCHARGED ☐ RESIGNED ☐ LAID OFF ☐

FORMER EMPLOYER OR SCHOOL—Please complete the following. Thank you.

IS THE ABOVE INFORMATION CORRECT? YES ☐ NO ☐

If not, give correct information: _____

_____

PLEASE CHECK	EXCEL.	GOOD	FAIR	POOR	COMMENTS:
ATTITUDE	____	____	____	____	
QUALITY OF WORK	____	____	____	____	
COOPERATION	____	____	____	____	
ATTENDANCE	____	____	____	____	

WOULD YOU RECOMMEND FOR EMPLOYMENT? YES ☐ NO ☐

ADDITIONAL COMMENTS

_____

_____

SIGNATURE OF EMPLOYER OR SCHOOL REPRESENTATIVE TITLE

Background Checks

How would you feel if you found out that the organization you had hoped to join was having your traffic record and moral character investigated? How would you feel if an organization did *not* investigate the backgrounds of guards to be selected for the gun storage depot of the U.S. military base near your home? Some organizations do a very thorough job of checking applicants' backgrounds even when security is not a particular issue. The U.S. Department of Education, for example, engages in very thorough background testing, which includes fingerprinting, credit checking, and examining medical records.[39]

Although background checking may seem to be a very invasive procedure, such checks have become a thriving business after the September 11, 2001, terrorist attacks and, more recently, in light of ethics problems and incidents of workplace violence that have affected organizations. Surveys indicate that the number of background checks has nearly tripled since 2000. In many industries, the percentage of applicants identified to have some problem (criminal record, discrepancy in past employment or education) is surprisingly high. According to one source, more than half (51.7%) of the applicants in the nonprofit industry had significant discrepancies between their self-reported and actual employment history, and nearly half (48.9%) of the applicants in the construction industry had a major motor vehicle violation (involving license suspension).[40]

For a more concrete example, consider the case of Wal-Mart. In two separate incidents in South Carolina, Wal-Mart employees were accused of sexually assaulting young girls. Both of the accused employees had past criminal convictions for sexually related offenses. In response, Wal-Mart instituted criminal background checks on all of its employees.

Some organizations do background checks on their own, while others employ agencies to do so. Background checks cost anywhere from $25 to $1,000 per hire, depending on the type of position and the information sought. One practical problem in background checks is that different information is contained in different databases. Criminal records are kept at the county or federal level, depending on the nature of the crime. Credit histories and educational data must also be searched separately. Various firms provide comprehensive background checking services, with fees depending on what databases are checked. For example, Bed, Bath, & Beyond uses Sterling to conduct its background checks; FedEx uses Infomart. Some of the other large background checking services include USIS, ChoicePoint, ADP, and First Advantage. Whether the organization conducts its own background checks or works through a vendor, extreme care needs to be taken in the use of such measures because of the limited validity reports available to date, as well as legal constraints on preemployment inquiries (see "Legal Issues" at the end of this chapter).

Background checks do have limitations. First, the records can be wrong or misinterpreted. For example, sometimes peoples' identities are mixed up. Unless someone has an unusual name, there are probably many others with the same name in the population. Also, sometimes the records contain misleading information. Johnnie Ulrigg was denied a job in Missoula, Montana, because his background check turned up a list of probation violations. It turns out that several counties in the state list failure to pay a traffic ticket as a probation violation. It took Ulrigg two years to clear his record. Second, because background checks have become more commonplace, they can place a seemingly permanent bar on the reemployment of reformed criminals. Peter Demain was sentenced to six years for possessing 21 pounds of marijuana. While in prison, he was so adept in the prison kitchen that he quickly rose to head baker. Once out of prison, though, Demain was unable to find a job at bagel shops, coffeehouses, grocery stores, and bakeries. Is it fair for reformed criminals, no matter how long ago or the nature of the offense, to be banned from employment?[41] Such questions are difficult to answer.

Finally, many labor unions resist background checking. In 2007, major league baseball owners clashed with the umpires union about background checks. Conversely, when in the same year, the Transportation Security Administration (TSA) instituted mandatory background checks for all airport workers (including pilots, mechanics, flight attendants, and even gift shop clerks), the pilot's union welcomed the change.[42]

More and more organizations are conducting *posthire* background checks. In some cases, these occur when an applicant is being considered for a promotion. Increasingly, though, organizations are finding it necessary to expand background checks to current employees even if they haven't changed jobs. For example, Fresh Direct, which delivers groceries to apartment-dwelling New Yorkers, found out that one of its drivers was charged with (and later pleaded guilty to) stalking and harassing numerous female customers. Fresh Direct had used an outside agency to conduct its background check on this employee, but the check did not reveal the truth that this employee had previous misdemeanor and felony convictions. As a result, Fresh Direct regularly verifies the backgrounds of its current employees. Many other organizations also verify their employees' backgrounds or pay vendors, such as Verified Person, that promise to continuously monitor employees and provide automatic updates revealing any convictions.[43]

One way to ameliorate some of these problems is to limit background checks to that information that is job related (it may be difficult to establish that a spotty credit history is important to jobs that mostly involve manual labor) and to use multiple sources to verify the accuracy of the background data.

Evaluation of Recommendations, References, and Background Checks

The empirical data that do exist on the validity of reference checks suggest that their validity is low to moderate. A meta-analysis of a number of studies revealed that the validity coefficients of reference data ranged from $\bar{r} = .16$ to $\bar{r} = .26$. Another study suggested that when reference reports are structured (the same questions were asked about every applicant), their validity was $\bar{r} = .25$. To some degree, the validity depends on who is providing the information. If it is the personnel officer, coworker, or relative, the information is not very valid. On the other hand, reference reports from supervisors and acquaintances are somewhat more valid. The validity of personnel officers may be less valid because they are less knowledgeable about the applicant (their past employee); the reports of coworkers and relatives probably are less valid because these individuals are positively biased toward the applicant.

Although references do not have high validity, we need to take a cost-benefit approach. In general the quality of the information may be low, but in the few cases where reference information changes a decision, the payoff can be significant. An executive with the U.S. Postal Service once told one of the authors that many of the acts of violence by Postal Service employees would have been avoided if a thorough background check had been conducted. Thus, since references are a relatively cheap method of collecting information on applicants, screening out the occasional unstable applicants or in a few cases learning something new and important about an applicant may make reference checks a good investment. As with unweighted application blanks, though, using reference checks requires employers to turn elsewhere to obtain suitable information for making final decisions about applicants.

Genetic Screening

Due to advances in medical technology, it is now possible for employers to screen people on the basis of their genetic code. The testing is done to screen out people who are susceptible to certain diseases (e.g., sickle cell anemia) due to exposure to toxic substances at work.[44] Screening out susceptible people is one way to ensure that workers do not become ill. Another way is to eliminate the toxic substances. Although the use of genetic screening is not widespread, companies such as Du Pont and Dow Chemical experimented with it to protect their employees.[45] Organizations also experimented with genetic screening because of the huge costs associated with work-related diseases and illnesses. However, a recent court decision has ruled that genetic screening is prohibited under the Americans With Disabilities Act (ADA).[46] Further, a California court of appeals ruled that genetic testing is permissible only when consent has been granted by the applicant or when test results directly bear on an applicant's ability to perform the job.[47] Federal legislation under consideration would limit employers' ability to conduct genetic testing, so employers should exercise considerable caution in using genetic screening.

Initial Interview

The initial interview occurs very early in the initial assessment process and is often the applicant's first personal contact with the organization and its staffing system. At this point, applicants are relatively undifferentiated to the organization in terms of KSAOs. The initial interview will begin the process of necessary differentiation, a sort of "rough cut."

The purpose of the initial interview is, and should be, to screen out the most obvious cases of person/job mismatches. To do this, the interview should focus on an assessment of KSAOs that are absolute requirements for the applicant. Examples of such minimum levels of qualifications for the job include certification and licensure requirements and necessary (not just preferred) training and experience requirements.

These assessments may be made on the basis of information gathered from written means (e.g., application blank or résumé), as well as the interview per se. Care should be taken to ensure that the interviewer focuses only on this information as a basis for decision making. Evaluations of personal characteristics of the applicant (e.g., race, sex), as well as judgments about an applicant's personality (e.g., she seems so outgoing and "just right" for this job), are to be avoided. Indeed, to ensure that this focus happens, some organizations (e.g., civil service agencies) have basically eliminated the initial interview altogether and make the initial assessment only on the basis of written information provided by the applicant.

One of the limitations with the initial interview is that it is perhaps the most expensive method of initial assessment. One way to reduce costs is to use companies, such as Gallup, that conduct an initial screening interview via the telephone (applicants dial a toll-free number and answer a series of questions); the company then reports results back to the employer. Some consulting firms use interactive voice technology so that interviews are computerized. When Nike opened a store in Las Vegas, it used the technology to screen 6,000 applicants for 250 positions.[48] Given that the validity evidence for such types of interviews is not particularly impressive, such cost-saving methods appear worthwhile.

Video and Computer Interviews

One means of reducing the costs of initial interviews is to use video interviews. Video interviews can take at least two forms. One form of the video interview is to link the applicant and the recruiter via remote video access. This sort of videoconferencing allows the applicant and the recruiter to see each other on a monitor and, in some cases, even exchange documents. Viewnet of Madison, Wisconsin, has sold its video interview technology to more than 70 colleges to use as an alternative selection device. A variant of this type of video interview is to hire a consulting firm to conduct the video interviews for the organization. Under this approach, the organization identifies the candidates (perhaps after screening their applications or résumés) and submits their names to the consulting firm. The firm then videotapes the interviews and submits the tapes to the organization. In general, one of the advantages of video-based interviews is that they can dramatically lower the cost of initial interviews. This is particularly true for employers that may wish to interview only a few applicants at a given location. Another advantage of these interviews is that they can be arranged on short notice (no travel and no schedule rearrangements). Of course, a disadvantage of these interviews is that they do not permit face-to-face contact. The effect of this limitation on validity and applicant reactions is unknown.

Another form of video interviews takes the process a step further. Computer-based interviews utilize software that asks applicants questions (e.g., "Have you ever been terminated for stealing?") or presents realistic scenarios (e.g., an irate customer on the screen) while recording applicants' responses. These responses are then forwarded to selection decision makers for use in initial screening. The software can also be configured to inform applicants about job duties and requirements. It can even track how long it takes an applicant to answer each question. Retailers are beginning to use computerized interviews on-site, where applicants walk into a store, enter a kiosk, and submit information about their work habits and experiences. As with video interviews, computer-based interviews can offer dramatic savings (although start-up costs to customize such programs can be high). As before, though, the accuracy of these high-tech interviews as compared to the old standby, the person-to-person variety, is unclear. The same holds true for how applicants will react to these relatively impersonal methods.

Evaluation of Initial Interview

Whether high-tech or traditional, the interview has benefits and limitations. Nearly all of the research evaluating the interview in selection has considered it a substantive method (see the "Structured Interview" section in Chapter 9). Thus, there is little evidence about the usefulness of the initial interview. However, organizations using the initial interview in selection are likely to find it more useful by following a few guidelines:

1. Ask questions that assess the most basic KSAOs identified by job analysis. This requires separating what is required from what is preferred.
2. Stick to basic, qualifying questions suitable for making rough cuts (e.g., "Have you completed the minimum certification requirements to qualify for this job?") rather than subtle, subjective questions more suitable for substantive decisions (e.g., "How would this job fit within your overall career goals?"). Remember, the purpose of the initial interview is closer to cutting with a saw than operating with a scalpel. Ask only the most fundamental questions now, and leave the fine-tuning for later.
3. Keep interviews brief. Most interviewers make up their minds quickly and, given the limited usefulness and the type of information collected, a long interview (e.g., 45–60 minutes) is unlikely to add much over a shorter one (15–30 minutes).
4. As with all interviews, the same questions should be asked of all applicants, and EEO compliance must be monitored.

Choice of Initial Assessment Methods

As described, there is a wide range of initial assessment methods available to organizations to help reduce the applicant pool to bona fide candidates. A range of formats is available as well. Fortunately, with so many choices available to organizations, research results are available to help guide choices of methods to use. This research has been reviewed many times and is summarized in Exhibit 8.8. In Exhibit 8.8, each initial assessment method is rated according to several criteria. Each of these criteria will be discussed in turn.

Use

Use refers to how frequently surveyed organizations use each predictor. Use is probably an overused criterion in deciding which selection measures to adopt. Benchmarking—basing HR decisions on what other companies are doing—is a predominant method of decision making in all areas of HR, including staffing. However, is this a good basis on which to make decisions about selection methods? Although it is always comforting to do what other organizations are doing, relying on information from other organizations assumes that they know what they are doing. Just because many organizations use a selection measure does not necessarily make it a good idea for a particular organization. Circumstances differ from organization to organization. Perhaps more important, many organizational decision makers (and HR consultants) either lack knowledge about the latest findings in HR research or have decided that such findings are not applicable to their organization. It is also difficult to determine whether a successful organization that uses a particular selection method is successful because it uses this method or is successful for some other reason. Thus, from a research standpoint, there may be real strategic advantage in relying on "effectiveness" criteria (e.g., validity, utility, adverse impact) rather than worrying about the practices of other organizations.

Another reason to have a healthy degree of skepticism about the use criterion is that there is a severe lack of timely and broad surveys of selection practices (i.e., coverage of many industries and regions in the United States). The Bureau of National Affairs (BNA) has conducted broad surveys of selection practices, but the most recent was in 1988. Other surveys of selection practices are available, but they generally cover only a single selection practice (e.g., drug testing) or lack adequate scope or breadth. In providing conclusions about use of various selection methods in organizations, we are forced to make judgment calls concerning which survey to rely on. In the case of some selection measures (e.g., application blanks), there is little reason to believe the BNA figures have changed much. With other predictors, the use figures have shown a fair degree of volatility and change from year to year. Thus, in classifying the use of assessment methods, we rely on the most recent surveys that achieve some degree of breadth. For purposes of classifying the predictors, high use refers to use by more than two-thirds of organizations, moderate is use by one-third to two-thirds of organizations, and low use refers to use by less than one-third of organizations.

EXHIBIT 8.8   Evaluation of Initial Assessment Methods

Predictors	Use	Cost	Reliability	Validity	Utility	Reactions	Adverse Impact
Level of education	High	Low	Moderate	Low	Low	?	Moderate
Grade point average	Moderate	Low	Moderate	Moderate	?	?	?
Quality of school	?	Low	Moderate	Low	?	?	Moderate
Major field of study	?	Low	Moderate	Moderate	?	?	?
Extracurricular activity	?	Low	Moderate	Moderate	?	?	?
Training and experience	High	Low	High	Moderate	Moderate	?	Moderate
Licensing and certification	Moderate	Low	?	?	?	?	?
Weighted application blanks	Low	Moderate	Moderate	Moderate	Moderate	?	?
Biographical data	Low	High	High	High	High	Negative	Moderate
Letters of recommendation	Moderate	Low	?	Low	?	?	?
Reference checks	High	Moderate	Low	Low	Moderate	Mixed	Low
Background checks	Low	High	?	?	?	Mixed	Moderate
Résumés and cover letters	Moderate	Low	Moderate	?	?	Moderate	?
Initial interview	High	Moderate	Low	Low	?	Positive	Moderate
Genetic screening	Low	High	Moderate	?	?	?	High

Now that we've issued these caveats about the use criterion, Exhibit 8.8 reveals clear differences in the use of various methods of initial assessment. The most frequently used methods of initial assessment are education level, training and experience, reference checks, and initial interview. These methods are considered, to some degree, in selection decisions for most types of positions. Licensing and certification requirements, letters of recommendation, and résumés and cover letters have moderate levels of use. All three of these methods are widely used in filling some types of positions but infrequently used in filling many others. The least widely used initial assessment methods are weighted application blanks, biographical information, background checks, and genetic screening. It is relatively unusual for organizations to use these methods for initial screening decisions. There are no reliable figures on the use of quality of school, major field of study, and extracurricular activity in initial selection decisions; thus, their use could not be estimated.

Cost

Cost refers to expenses incurred in using the predictor. Although most of the initial assessment methods may seem relatively cost free since the applicant provides the information on his or her own time, this is not entirely accurate. For most initial assessment methods, the major cost associated with each selection measure is administration. Consider an application blank. It is true that applicants complete application blanks on their own time, but someone must be present to hand out applications, answer inquiries in person and over the phone about possible openings, and collect, sort, and forward applications to the appropriate person. Then the selection decision maker must read each application, perhaps make notes and weed out the clearly unacceptable applicants, and then make decisions about candidates. Thus, even for the least expensive methods of initial assessment, costs associated with their use are far from trivial.

On the other hand, utility research has suggested that costs do not play a large part in evaluating the financial benefit of using particular selection methods. This becomes readily apparent when one considers the costs of hiring a poor performer. For example, a secretary who performs one standard deviation below average (16th percentile, if performance is normally distributed) may cost the organization $8,000 in lost productivity per year. This person is likely to remain on the job for more than one year, multiplying the costs. Considered in this light, spending an extra few hundred dollars to accurately identify good secretaries is an excellent investment. Thus, although costs need to be considered in evaluating assessment methods, more consideration should be given to the fact that valid selection measures pay off handsomely and will return many times their cost.

As can be seen in Exhibit 8.8, the least costly initial assessment methods include information that can be obtained from application blanks (level of education, grade point average, quality of school, major field of study, extracurricular activity, training and experience, licensing and certification) and other applicant-provided information (letters of recommendation, résumés, and cover letters). Initial assessment methods of moderate cost include weighted application blanks, reference checks, and initial interviews. Biographical information, background checks, and genetic screening are relatively expensive assessment methods.

Reliability

Reliability refers to consistency of measurement. As was noted in Chapter 7, reliability is a bound for validity, so it would be very difficult for a predictor with low reliability to have high validity. By the same token, it is unlikely that a valid predictor would have low reliability. Unfortunately, the reliability information on many initial assessment methods is lacking in the literature. Some researchers have investigated distortion of applicant-reported information (application blanks and résumés). One study found that nearly half of the items on application blanks were distorted by 20% of the applicants. Other studies have suggested that one-third of application blanks contain some inaccuracies.[49] Thus, it is probably reasonable to infer that applicant-supplied information in application blanks and résumés is of moderate reliability. The reliability of reference checks appears to be relatively low. In terms of training and experience evaluations, while distortion can occur if the applicant supplies training and experience information, interrater agreement in evaluating this information is quite high.[50] Biographical information also generally has high reliability. The initial interview, like most unstructured interviews, probably has a relatively low level of reliability.

Validity

Validity refers to the strength of the relationship between the predictor and job performance. Low validity refers to validity in the range of about .00 to .15. Moderate validity corresponds to validity in the range of about .16 to .30, and high validity is .31 and above. As might be expected, most initial assessment methods have moderate to low validity because they are used only for making "rough cuts" among applicants rather than for final decisions. Perhaps the two most valid initial assessment methods are biodata and training and experience requirements; their validity can range from moderate to high.

Utility

Utility refers to the monetary return associated with using the predictor, relative to its cost. According to researchers and decision makers, when comparing the utility of selection methods, validity appears to be the most important consideration.[51] In short, it would be very unusual for a valid selection method to have low utility. Thus, as can be seen in Exhibit 8.8, high, moderate, and low validities tend to directly correspond to high, moderate, and low utility values, respectively. Question marks predominate this column in the exhibit because relatively few studies have directly investigated the utility of these methods. However, based on the argument that validity should be directly related to utility, it is likely that high validity methods will also realize large financial benefits to organizations that choose to use them. Research does indicate that training and experience requirements have moderate (or even high) levels of utility, and reference checks have moderate levels of utility.

Applicant Reactions

Reactions refers to the favorability of applicants' reactions to the predictor. Applicant reactions are an important evaluative criterion because research has indicated that applicants who feel positively about selection methods and the selection process report higher levels of satisfaction with the organization, are more likely to accept a position with the organization, and are more likely to recommend the organization to others.[52]

Research suggests that selection measures that are perceived as job related, present applicants with an opportunity to perform, are administered consistently, and provide applicants with feedback about their performance are likely to generate favorable applicant reactions.[53] Although research on applicants' reactions to specific selection procedures is lacking, evidence has been accumulating and suggests that applicants react more positively to some initial assessment methods, such as interviews, résumés, and references, than to others, such as biodata.[54]

Adverse Impact

Adverse impact refers to the possibility that a disproportionate number of protected-class members may be rejected using this predictor. Several initial assessment methods have moderate degrees of adverse impact against women and/or minorities, including level of education, quality of school, training and experience, biographical information, and the initial interview. Genetic screening may have a high degree of adverse impact, while reference and background checks appear to have little adverse impact.

LEGAL ISSUES

Initial assessment methods are subject to numerous laws, regulations, and other legal considerations. Four major matters of concern pertain to using disclaimers, conducting reference checks, making preemployment inquiries, and making bona fide occupational qualifications claims.

Disclaimers

During the initial stages of contact with job applicants, it is important for the organization to protect itself legally by clearly identifying rights it wants to maintain for itself. This involves the use of disclaimers. Disclaimers are statements (usually written) that provide or confer explicit rights to the employer as part of the employment contract and that are shown to job applicants. The organization needs to decide (or reevaluate) which rights it wants to retain and how these will be communicated to job applicants.

Three areas of rights are usually suggested for possible inclusion in a disclaimer policy. These are (1) employment-at-will (right to terminate the employment relationship at any time, for any reason); (2) verification consent (right to verify information provided by the applicant); and (3) false statement warning (right to not hire, terminate, or discipline prospective employee for providing false information to the employer). Examples of disclaimer statements in these three areas are shown at the bottom of the application blank in Exhibit 8.4. Care should be exercised in the development of disclaimers and their communication to job applicants and employees. The language must be clear, understandable, and unambiguous. Disclaimers must be communicated directly, such as on the application blank and in the employee handbook, and there should be an acknowledgment of receipt in writing. Also, the disclaimers must be conspicuous to the applicant or employee, such as with a visible location and highlighted print.[55]

Reference and Background Checks

Separate legal concerns arise for reference checks (conducted by a member of the organization) and background checks (conducted by a third party, such as a consumer reporting agency, on behalf of the organization).

Reference Checks

Reference checking creates a legal quagmire for organizations. Current or former employers of the job applicant may be reluctant to provide a reference (especially one with negative information about the applicant) because they fear the applicant may file a defamation suit against them. Hence, the organization may view requesting references to be somewhat fruitless. On the other hand, failure to conduct a reference check opens up the organization to the possibility of a negligent hiring suit, in which it is claimed that the organization hired a person it should have known would cause harm to other employees or customers. To deal with such problems and obtain thorough, accurate information, the following suggestions are offered.

First, gather as much information as possible directly from the applicant, along with a verification consent. In this way, use of reference providers and information demands on them are minimized.

Second, be sure to obtain written authorization from the applicant to check references. The applicant should sign a blanket consent form for this purpose. Also, the organization could prepare a request-for-reference form that the applicant would give to the person(s) being asked to provide a reference. That form would authorize the person(s) to provide requested information, release the person from any liability for providing the information, and be signed by the applicant (see Exhibit 8.7).

Third, specify the type of information being requested and obtain the information in writing. That information should be specific, factual, and job related in content; do not seek health or disability information.

Fourth, limit access to reference information to those making selection decisions.

Finally, check relevant state laws about permissible and impermissible reference check practices. Also, determine if your organization is covered by state reference immunity laws—these provide some degree of immunity from civil liability to organizations that in good faith provide information about the job performance and professional conduct of former or current employees. Organizations in these states (currently 39) may be more willing to request and provide reference information.[56]

Background Checks

General Checks.   The first legal requirement for the organization is to comply with the federal Fair Credit Reporting Act ([FCRA]; see Chapter 2). The FCRA governs the gathering and use of background information on applicants and employees (*www.ftc.gov*). Its requirements apply to both "consumer reports" and "investigative consumer reports." Consumer reports are prepared from accessible databases by a consumer reporting agency and bear on the person's creditworthiness and standing, character, general reputation, personal information, and mode of living. Investigative consumer reports are a subset of consumer reports; they obtain information about the applicant's or employee's general reputation, character, personal characteristics, or mode of living via personal interviews with friends, neighbors, or business associates.

Before obtaining a consumer report, the organization must (1) give the applicant clear notice in writing that a report may be obtained and used in hiring or promotion procedures, and (2) obtain the applicant's written authorization to obtain the report. These notification requirements do not apply to an organization conducting a third-party investigation of suspected employee misconduct. The consumer reporting agency may not furnish a consumer report to the organization unless the organization certifies to the agency that it has given the required notice and received authorization. Before taking any "adverse action," such as denial of employment, based in whole or part on the report received, the organization must wait a reasonable amount of time and then provide the applicant with a copy of the report and a written description of his or her consumer rights put forth by the Federal Trade Commission. After taking an adverse action, the organization must (1) notify (by written, oral, or electronic means) the applicant of the adverse action, (2) provide the name, address, and phone number of the consumer reporting agency to the applicant, and (3) provide notice of the applicant's right to obtain a free copy of the report from the agency and to dispute the accuracy and completeness of the reports. The organization is not required to inform the applicant which information in the report led to the adverse action, but it must inform the applicant that the agency had no part in the decision.

Another legal requirement for the organization is to comply with the state and local laws that govern background checks. This should include the state/locale in which the individual being investigated resides, the reporting agency conducts business, and the requesting organization is incorporated and conducts business.[57]

Criminal Checks.   Criminal background checks seek to uncover information about an applicant's interactions with the law. The FCRA governs these checks, as do myriad state and local laws. It is important to distinguish between the gathering and the use of arrest information, and it is also important to distinguish between the gathering and the use of conviction information. Although arrest information may be gathered, it cannot be used in staffing decisions. Conviction information may also be gathered, and generally it might be permissible to use it in staffing decisions. An exception to the use of conviction information is that the Equal Employment Opportunity Commission (EEOC) is of the opinion that such information may have a disparate impact on minorities and thus should not be used without a business necessity justification. In claiming this justification, the employer must consider the following.

- The nature and gravity of the offense(s)
- The time that has passed since the conviction and/or completion of a sentence
- The nature of the job assignment

These factors suggest that the organization should decide on a job-by-job basis whether to seek a criminal background check, carefully communicate to the background screening firm exactly what information it wishes to receive, and decide in advance exactly how it will use that information in a way that will serve the best interest of the organization within the complex legal environment governing criminal background checks.

Preemployment Inquiries

The term "preemployment inquiry" (PI), as used here, pertains to both content and method of assessment. Regarding content, PI refers to applicants' personal and background data. These data cover such areas as demographics (race, color, religion, sex, national origin, age), physical characteristics (disability, height, weight), family and associates, residence, economic status, and education. The information could be gathered by any method; most frequently, it will be gathered with an initial assessment method, particularly the application blank, biodata questionnaire, or preliminary interview. At times, PIs may also occur as part of an unstructured interview.

PIs have been singled out for particular legal (equal employment opportunity and affirmative action [EEO/AA]) attention at both the federal and state levels. The reason for this is that PIs have great potential for use in a discriminatory manner early on in the selection process. Moreover, research continually finds that organizations make inappropriate and illegal PIs. One study, for example, found that out of 48 categories of application blank items, there was an average of 5.4 inadvisable items used by employers on their application blanks for customer service jobs.[58] It is thus critical to understand the laws and regulations surrounding the use of PIs.

Federal Laws and Regulations

The laws and their interpretation indicate that it is illegal to use PI information that has a disparate impact based on a protected characteristic (race, color, etc.), unless such disparate impact can be shown to be job related and consistent with business necessity. The emphasis here is on the potentially illegal use of the information rather than on its collection per se.

The EEOC makes the following general points about PIs:[59]

1. It is reasonable to assume that all requests for information on an application form or in a preemployment interview are for some purpose and that selection or hiring decisions are being made on the basis of the answers given. In an investigation of charges of discrimination, the burden of proof is on the employer to show that answers to all questions on application forms or in oral interviews are not used in making hiring and placement decisions in a discriminatory manner prohibited by law.
2. To seek information other than that which is essential to effectively evaluate a person's qualifications for employment is to make oneself vulnerable to charges of discrimination and consequent legal proceedings.
3. It is, therefore, in an employer's own self-interest to carefully review all procedures used in screening applicants for employment, eliminating or altering any not justified by business necessity.

These principles are reflected in two sets of regulations and guidelines: the *EEOC Guide to Preemployment Inquiries* and *ADA Regulations*.

EEOC Guide to Preemployment Inquiries.　This guide provides the principles just given above. It then provides specific guidance (do's and don't's) on PIs regarding race, color, religion, sex, national origin, age, height and weight, marital status, number of children, provisions for child care, English language skill, educational requirements, friends or relatives working for the employer, arrest records, conviction records, discharge from military service, citizenship, economic status, and availability for work on weekends or holidays.[60]

ADA Regulations.　There appears to be a fine line between permissible and impermissible information that may be gathered, and between appropriate and inappropriate methods for gathering it, under the Americans With Disabilities Act (ADA). To help employers, the EEOC has developed specific enforcement guidance on these matters.[61]

The general thrust of the guidance is that the organization may not ask disability-related questions and may not conduct medical examinations until after it makes a conditional job offer to a person. Once that offer is made, however, the organization may ask disability-related questions and conduct medical examinations so long as this is done for all entering employees in the job category. When such questions or exams screen out a person with a disability, the reason for rejection must be job related and consistent with business necessity. A person may be rejected for safety reasons if the person provides a direct threat of substantial harm to himself or herself or others. We will have more to say about the legality of medical examinations in the next chapter.

More specific guidance is provided for the preoffer stage as follows. Disability-related questions cannot be asked, meaning questions (1) about whether a person has a disability, (2) that are likely to elicit information about a disability, or (3) that are closely related to a disability. Along with these general prohibitions, it is impermissible to ask applicants whether they will need reasonable accommodation to perform the functions of the job or can perform major life activities (e.g., lifting, walking), to ask about lawful use of drugs, to ask about workers' compensation history, or to ask third parties (e.g., former employers, references) questions that cannot be asked of the applicant.

Alternatively, preoffer it is permissible to ask the following:

- If the applicant can perform the job, with or without reasonable accommodation
- The applicant to describe or demonstrate how he or she would perform the job (including any needed reasonable accommodation)
- If the applicant will need reasonable accommodation for the hiring process (unless there is an obvious disability or the applicant discloses a disability)
- The applicant to provide documentation of a disability if requesting reasonable accommodation for the hiring process
- If the applicant can meet the organization's attendance requirement
- The applicant for certifications and licenses
- About the applicant's current illegal use of drugs (but not past addiction)
- About the applicant's drinking habits (but not alcoholism)

State Laws and Regulations

There is a vast cache of state laws and regulations pertaining to PIs.[62] These requirements vary substantially among the states. They are often more stringent and inclusive than federal laws and regulations. The organization thus must become familiar with and adhere to the laws for each state in which it is located.

An example of Ohio state law regarding PIs is shown in Exhibit 8.9. Notice how the format of the example points out both lawful and unlawful ways of gathering PI information.

EXHIBIT 8.9 **Ohio Preemployment Inquiry Guide**

INQUIRIES BEFORE HIRING	LAWFUL	UNLAWFUL*
1. NAME	Name.	Inquiry into any title which indicates race, color, religion, sex, national origin, handicap, age, or ancestry.
2. ADDRESS	Inquiry into place and length at current address.	Inquiry into any foreign addresses which would indicate national origin.
3. AGE	Any inquiry limited to establishing that applicant meets any minimum age requirement that may be established by law.	A. Requiring birth certificate or baptismal record before hiring. B. Any inquiry which may reveal the date of high school graduation. C. Any other inquiry which may reveal whether applicant is at least 40 and less than 70 years of age.
4. BIRTHPLACE, NATIONAL ORIGIN, OR ANCESTRY		A. Any inquiry into place of birth. B. Any inquiry into place of birth of parents, grandparents, or spouse. C. Any other inquiry into national origin or ancestry.
5. RACE OR COLOR		Any inquiry which would indicate race or color.
6. SEX		A. Any inquiry which would indicate sex. B. Any inquiry made of members of one sex, but not the other.

(continued)

EXHIBIT 8.9   Continued

INQUIRIES BEFORE HIRING	LAWFUL	UNLAWFUL*
7. HEIGHT AND WEIGHT	Inquiries as to ability to perform actual job requirements.	Being a certain height or weight will not be considered to be a job requirement unless the employer can show that no employee with the ineligible height or weight could do the work.
8. RELIGION— CREED		A. Any inquiry which would indicate or identify religious denomination or custom. B. Applicant may not be told any religious identity or preference of the employer. C. Request pastor's recommendation or reference.
9. HANDICAP	Inquiries necessary to determine applicant's ability to substantially perform specific job without significant hazard.	A. Any inquiry into past or current medical conditions not related to position applied for. B. Any inquiry into worker's compensation or similar claims.
10. CITIZENSHIP	A. Whether a U.S. citizen. B. If not, whether applicant intends to become one. C. If U.S. residence is legal. D. If spouse is citizen. E. Require proof of citizenship after being hired. F. Any other requirement mandated by the Immigration Reform and Control Act of 1986, as amended.	A. If native-born or naturalized. B. Proof of citizenship before hiring. C. Whether parents or spouse are native-born or naturalized.
11. PHOTOGRAPHS	May be required after hiring for identification.	Require photograph before hiring.

(continued)

EXHIBIT 8.9 Continued

INQUIRIES BEFORE HIRING	LAWFUL	UNLAWFUL*
12. ARREST AND CONVICTIONS	Inquiries into *conviction* of specific crimes related to qualifications for the job applied for.	Any inquiry which would reveal arrests without convictions.
13. EDUCATION	A. Inquiry into nature and extent of academic, professional, or vocational training. B. Inquiry into language skills such as reading and writing of foreign languages, if job-related.	A. Any inquiry which would reveal the nationality or religious affiliation of a school. B. Inquiry as to what mother tongue is or how foreign language ability was acquired.
14. RELATIVES	Inquiry into name, relationship, and address of person to be notified in case of emergency.	Any inquiry about a relative which would be unlawful if made about the applicant.
15. ORGANIZATIONS	Inquiry into membership in professional organizations and offices held, excluding any organization, the name or character of which indicates the race, color, religion, sex, national origin, handicap, age, or ancestry of its members.	Inquiry into every club and organization where membership is held.
16. MILITARY SERVICE	A. Inquiry into service in U.S. Armed Forces when such service is a qualification for the job. B. Require military discharge certificate after being hired.	A. Inquiry into military service in armed service of any country but U.S. B. Request military service records. C. Inquiry into type of discharge.
17. WORK SCHEDULE	Inquiry into willingness or ability to work required work schedule.	Any inquiry into willingness or ability to work any particular religious holidays.

(continued)

EXHIBIT 8.9   Continued

INQUIRIES BEFORE HIRING	LAWFUL	UNLAWFUL*
18. MISCELLANEOUS	Any question required to reveal qualifications for the job applied for.	Any non-job-related inquiry which may elicit or attempt to elicit any information concerning race, color, religion, sex, national origin, handicap, age, or ancestry of an applicant for employment or membership.
19. REFERENCES	General personal and work references which do not reveal the race, color, religion, sex, national origin, handicap, age, or ancestry of the applicant.	Request references specifically from clergy or any other persons who might reflect race, color, religion, sex, national origin, handicap, age, or ancestry of applicant.

I. Employers acting under bona fide Affirmative Action Programs or acting under orders of Equal Employment law enforcement agencies of federal, state, or local governments may make some of the prohibited inquiries listed above to the extent that these inquiries are required by such programs or orders.

II. Employers having federal defense contracts are exempt to the extent that otherwise prohibited inquiries are required by federal law for security purposes.

III. Any inquiry is prohibited although not specifically listed above, which elicits information as to, or which is not job-related and may be used to discriminate on the basis of race, color, religion, sex, national origin, handicap, age, or ancestry in violation of law.

*Unless bona fide occupational qualification is certified in advance by the Ohio Civil Rights Commission.

SOURCE: Ohio Civil Rights Commission, 1989.

Bona Fide Occupational Qualifications

Title VII of the Civil Rights Act explicitly permits discrimination on the basis of sex, religion, or national origin (but not race or color) if it can be shown to be a BFOQ "reasonably necessary to the normal operation" of the business. The Age

Discrimination in Employment Act (ADEA) contains a similar provision regarding age. These provisions thus permit outright rejection of applicants because of their sex, religion, national origin, or age, as long as the rejection can be justified under the "reasonably necessary" standard. Exactly how have BFOQ claims by employers fared? When are BFOQ claims upheld as legitimate? Several points are relevant to understanding the BFOQ issue.

The burden of proof is on the employer to justify any BFOQ claim, and it is clear that the BFOQ exception is to be construed narrowly. Thus, it does not apply to the following:[63]

- Refusing to hire women because of a presumed difference in comparative HR outcomes (e.g., women are lower performers, have higher turnover rates)
- Refusing to hire women because of personal characteristic stereotypes (e.g., women are less aggressive than men)
- Refusing to hire women because of the preferences of others (customers or fellow workers)

To amplify on the above points, an analysis of BFOQ claims involving sex reveals four types of justifications usually presented by the employer. These involve inability to perform the work, personal contact with others that requires the same sex, customers' preference for dealing with one sex, and pregnancy or fertility protection concerns.[64]

Inability to Perform
The general employer claim here is that one gender (usually women) is unable to perform the job due to job requirements such as lifting heavy weights, being of a minimum height, or working long hours. The employer must be able to show that the inability holds for most, if not all, members of the gender. Moreover, if it is possible to test the required abilities for each person, then that must be done rather than having a blanket exclusion from the job based on gender.

Same-Sex Personal Contact
Due to a job requirement of close personal contact with other people, the employer may claim that employees must be the same sex as those people with whom they have contact. This claim has often been made, but not always successfully defended, for the job of prison guard. Much will depend on an analysis of just how inhospitable and dangerous the work environment is (e.g., minimum security versus maximum security prisons). Same-sex personal conflict claims have been made successfully for situations involving personal hygiene, health care, and rape victims. In short, the permissibility of these claims depends on a very specific analysis of the job requirements matrix (including the job context portion).

Customer Preference
Organizations may argue that customers prefer members of one sex, and this preference must be honored in order to serve and maintain the continued patronage

of the customer. This claim might occur, for example, for the job of salesperson in women's sportswear. Another example, involving religion, is a refusal to hire people who wear turbans or hijabs, due to a fear that customers will not want to interact with them. Usually, customer preference claims cannot be successfully defended by the employer.

Pregnancy or Fertility

Exclusion of pregnant applicants could be a valid BFOQ claim, particularly in jobs where the risk of sudden incapacitation due to pregnancy poses threats to public safety (e.g., airline attendant). A threat to fertility of either sex generally cannot be used as a basis for sustaining a BFOQ claim. For example, an employer's fetal protection policy that excluded women from jobs involving exposure to lead in the manufacture of batteries was held to not be a permissible BFOQ.[65]

The discussion and examples here should make clear that BFOQ claims involve complex situations and considerations. The organization should remember that the burden of proof is on it to defend BFOQ claims. BFOQ provisions in the law are and continue to be construed very narrowly. The employer thus must have an overwhelming preponderance of argument and evidence on its side in order to make and successfully defend a BFOQ claim.

SUMMARY

This chapter reviews the processes involved in external selection and focuses specifically on methods of initial assessment. Before candidates are assessed, it is important to base assessment methods on the logic of prediction and to use selection plans. The logic of prediction focuses on the requisite correspondence between elements in applicants' past situations and KSAOs critical to success on the job applied for. The selection plan involves the process of detailing the required KSAOs and indicating which selection methods will be used to assess each KSAO. The selection sequence is the means by which the selection process is used to narrow down the initial applicant pool to candidates, then finalists, and, eventually, job offer receivers.

Initial assessment methods are used during the early stages of the selection sequence to reduce the applicant pool to candidates for further assessment. The methods of initial assessment were reviewed in some detail. The methods include résumés and cover letters, application blanks, biographical data, letters of recommendation, reference and background checks, genetic screening, and initial interviews. Initial assessment methods differ widely in their usefulness. The means by which these methods can be evaluated for potential use include frequency of use, cost, reliability, validity, utility, applicant reactions, and adverse impact.

Legal issues need to be considered in making initial assessments about applicants. The use of disclaimers as a protective mechanism is critical. Also, three areas of initial assessment that require special attention are reference and background checking, preemployment inquiries, and BFOQs.

DISCUSSION QUESTIONS

1. A selection plan describes which predictor(s) will be used to assess the KSAOs required to perform the job. What are the three steps to follow in establishing a selection plan?
2. In what ways are the following three initial assessment methods similar and in what ways are they different: application blanks, biographical information, and reference and background checks?
3. Describe the criteria by which initial assessment methods are evaluated. Are some of these criteria more important than others?
4. Some methods of initial assessment appear to be more useful than others. If you were starting your own business, which initial assessment methods would you use and why?
5. How can organizations avoid legal difficulties in the use of preemployment inquiries in initial selection decisions?

ETHICAL ISSUES

1. Is it wrong to "pad" one's résumé with information that, while not an outright lie, is an enhancement? For example, would it be wrong to term one's job "maintenance coordinator" when in fact one simply emptied garbage cans?
2. Do you think employers have a right to check into applicants' backgrounds? Even if there is no suspicion of misbehavior? Even if the job poses no security or sensitivity risks? Even if the background check includes driving offenses and credit histories?

APPLICATIONS

Reference Reports and Initial Assessment in a Start-Up Company

Stanley Jausneister owns a small high-tech start-up company, called BioServer-Systems (BSS). Stanley's company specializes in selling Web server space to clients. The server space that Stanley markets runs from a network of personal computers. This networked configuration allows BSS to more efficiently manage its server space and provides greater flexibility to its customers, who often want weekly or even daily updates of their Web sites. The other innovation Stanley brought to BSS is special security encryption software protocols that make the BSS server space nearly impossible for hackers to access. This flexibility is particularly attractive to organizations that need to manage large, security-protected databases with multiple points of access. Stanley has even been contacted by the government, which is interested in using BSS's systems for some of its classified intelligence.

Due to its niche, BSS has experienced rapid growth. In the past year, BSS hired 12 programmers and 2 marketers, as well as a general manager, an HR manager, and other support personnel. Before starting BSS, Stanley was a manager with a large pharmaceutical firm. Because of his industry connections, most of BSS's business has been with drug and chemical companies.

Yesterday, Stanley received a phone call from Lee Rogers, head of biotechnology for Mercelle-Poulet, one of BSS's largest customers. Lee is an old friend, and he was one of BSS's first customers. Yesterday when Lee called, he expressed concern about BSS's security. One area of Mercelle-Poulet's biotech division is responsible for research and development on vaccines for various bioterrorist weapons such as anthrax and the plague. Because the research and development on these vaccines require the company to develop cultures of the biotech weapons themselves, Lee has used BSS to house information for this area. A great deal of sensitive information is housed on BSS's servers, including in some cases the formulas used in developing the cultures.

Despite the sensitivity of the information on BSS's servers, given BSS's advanced software, Stanley was very surprised to hear Lee's concern about security. "It's not your software that worries me," Lee commented, "It's the people running it." Lee explained that last week a Mercelle-Poulet researcher was arrested for attempting to sell certain cultures to an overseas client. It turns out that this individual had been dismissed from a previous pharmaceutical company for unethical behavior, but this information did not surface during the individual's background check. This incident not only caused Lee to reexamine Mercelle-Poulet's background checks, but it also made him think of BSS, as certain BSS employees have access to Mercelle-Poulet's information.

Instantly after hearing Lee's concern, Stanley realized he had a problem. Like many small employers, BSS did not do thorough background checks on its employees. It assumed that the information provided on the application was accurate and generally only called the applicant's previous employer (often with ineffective results). Stanley realized he needed to do more, not only to keep Lee's business but to protect his company and customers.

1. What sort of background testing should BSS conduct on its applicants?
2. Is there any information BSS should avoid obtaining for legal or EEO reasons?

3. How can BSS know that its background testing programs are effective?
4. In the past, BSS has used the following initial assessment methods: application blank, interviews with Stanley and other BSS managers, and a follow-up with the applicant's former employer. Beyond changes to its background testing program, would you suggest any other alterations to BSS's initial assessment process?

Developing a Lawful Application Blank

The Consolidated Trucking Corporation, Inc. (CTCI) is a rapidly growing short-haul (local) firm within the greater Columbus, Ohio, area. It has grown primarily through the acquisitions of numerous small, family-owned trucking companies. Currently it has a fleet of 150 trucks and over 250 full-time drivers. Most of the drivers were hired initially by the firms that CTCI acquired, and they accepted generous offers to become members of the CTCI team. CTCI's expansion plans are very ambitious, but they will be fulfilled primarily from internal growth rather than additional acquisitions. Consequently, CTCI is now faced with the need to develop an external staffing system that will be geared up to hire 75 new truckers within the next two years.

Terry Tailgater is a former truck driver for CTCI who was promoted to truck maintenance supervisor, a position he has held for the past five years. Once CTCI's internal expansion plans were finalized, the firm's HR director (and sole member of the HR department), Harold Hornblower, decided he needed a new person to handle staffing and employment law duties. Terry Tailgater was promoted by Harold to the job of staffing manager. One of Terry's major assignments was to develop a new staffing system for truck drivers.

One of the first projects Terry undertook was to develop a new, standardized application blank for the job of truck driver. To do this, Terry looked at the many different application blanks the current drivers had completed for their former companies. (These records were given to CTCI at the time of acquisition.) The application blanks showed that a large amount of information was requested and that the specific information sought varied among the application forms. Terry scanned the various forms and made a list of all the questions the forms contained. He then decided to evaluate each question in terms of its probable lawfulness under federal and state (Ohio) law. Terry wanted to identify and use only lawful questions on the new form he is developing.

Shown below is the list of questions Terry developed, along with columns labeled "probably lawful" and "probably unlawful." Assume that you are Terry and are deciding on the lawfulness of each question. Place a check mark in the appropriate column for each question and prepare a justification for its mark as "probably lawful" or "probably unlawful."

Questions Terry Is Considering Including on Application Blank

Question About	Probably Lawful	Probably Unlawful
Birthplace	——	——
Previous arrests	——	——
Previous felony convictions	——	——
Distance between work and residence	——	——
Domestic responsibilities	——	——
Height	——	——
Weight	——	——
Previous work experience	——	——
Educational attainment	——	——
High school favorite subjects	——	——
Grade point average	——	——
Received workers' compensation in past	——	——
Currently receiving workers' compensation	——	——
Child care arrangements	——	——
Length of time on previous job	——	——
Reason for leaving previous job	——	——
Age	——	——
Sex	——	——
Home ownership	——	——
Any current medical problems	——	——
History of mental illness	——	——
OK to seek references from previous employer?	——	——
Have you provided complete/truthful information?	——	——
Native language	——	——
Willing to work on Easter and Christmas	——	——
Get recommendation from pastor/priest	——	——

ENDNOTES

1. G. J. Myszkowski and S. Sloan, "Hiring by Blueprint," *HR Magazine,* May 1991, pp. 55–58.

2. J. W. Smither, R. R. Reilly, R. E. Millsap, K. Pearlman, and R. Stoffey, "Applicant Reactions to Selection Procedures," *Personnel Psychology,* 1993, 46, pp. 49–76.

3. P. F. Wernimont and J. P. Campbell, "Signs, Samples, and Criteria," *Journal of Applied Psychology,* 1968, 52, pp. 372–376.

4. State of Wisconsin, Chapter 134, *Evaluating Job Content for Selection,* Undated.

5. State of Wisconsin, *Evaluating Job Content for Selection.*

6. A. Ellin, "Lights! Camera! It's Time to Make a Résumé," *New York Times,* Apr. 21, 2007, pp. B1, B6; K. Gurchiek, "Video Résumé Use Rises, but So Do Big Questions," *SHRM Online,* Apr. 12, 2007, pp. 1–2; M. J. de la Merced, "Student's Video Résumé Gets Attention (Some of It Unwanted)," *New York Times,* Oct. 21, 2006, pp. B1, B6.

7. R. Strauss, "When the Résumé Is Not to Be Believed," *New York Times,* Sept. 12, 2006, p. 2; K. J. Winstein and D. Golden, "MIT Admissions Dean Lies on Résumé in 1979, Quits," *New York Times,* Apr. 27, 2007, pp. B1, B2; M. Villano, "Served as King of England, Said the Résumé," *New York Times,* Mar. 19, 2006, p. BU9.

8. "Resume Fraud," *Gainesville Sun,* Mar. 5, 2006, pp. 5G, 6G.

9. "Editor's Note," *New York Times,* Mar. 21, 2004, p. ST13; "Getting Jail Time for This Resume Lie?" *Netscape Careers & Jobs,* Mar. 18, 2004 (*channels.netscape.com/ns/careers*); "Lying on Your Resume," *Netscape Careers & Jobs,* Mar. 18, 2004 (*channels.netscape.com/ns/careers*); K. Maher, "The Jungle," *Wall Street Journal,* May 6, 2003, p. B5; E. Stanton, "If a Résumé Lies, Truth Can Loom Large," *Wall Street Journal,* Dec. 29, 2002, p. B48; T. Weir, "Colleges Give Coaches' Résumés Closer Look," *USA Today,* May 28, 2002, p. C1.

10. "Survey Finds a Single Resume Typo Can Ruin Job Prospects," *IPMA-HR Bulletin,* Sept. 15, 2006, p. 1; C. Soltis, "Eagle-Eyed Employers Scour Résumés for Little White Lies," *Wall Street Journal,* Mar. 21, 2006, p. B7; D. Mattioli, "Standing Out in a Sea of CVs," *Wall Street Journal,* Jan. 16, 2007, p. B8; D. Mattioli, "Hard Sell on 'Soft' Skills Can Primp a Resume," *Wall Street Journal,* May 15, 2007, p. B6.

11. N. R. Kuncel, M. Credé, and L. L. Thomas, "The Validity of Self-Reported Grade Point Averages, Class Ranks, and Test Scores: A Meta-Analysis and Review of the Literature," *Review of Educational Research*, 2005, 75, pp. 63–82.

12. A. Howard, "College Experiences and Managerial Performance," *Journal of Applied Psychology,* 1986, 71, pp. 530–552; R. Merritt-Halston and K. Wexley, "Educational Requirements: Legality and Validity," *Personnel Psychology,* 1983, 36, pp. 743–753.

13. R. T. Schneider, *The Rating of Experience and Training: A Review of the Literature and Recommendations on the Use of Alternative E & T Procedures* (Alexandria, VA: International Personnel Management Association, 1994); J. Sullivan, "Experience—It Ain't What It Used to Be," *Public Personnel Management,* 2000, 29, pp. 511–516.

14. A. E. McKinney, K. D. Carlson, R. L. Meachum, N. C. D'Angelo, and M. L. Connerly, "Recruiters' Use of GPA in Initial Screening Decisions: Higher GPAs Don't Always Make the Cut," *Personnel Psychology,* 2003, 56, pp. 823–845; P. L. Roth, C. A. BeVier, F. S. Switzer, and J. S. Schippmann, "Meta-Analyzing the Relationship Between Grades and Job Performance," *Journal of Applied Psychology,* 1996, 81, pp. 548–556; P. L. Roth and P. Bobko, "College Grade Point Average as a Personnel Selection Devise: Ethnic Group Differences and Potential Adverse Impact," *Journal of Applied Psychology,* 2000, 85, pp. 399–406.

15. J. Gourman, *The Gourman Report* (Los Angeles: National Education Standards, 1994).

16. K. Dunham, "More Employers Ask Job Seekers for SAT Scores," *Wall Street Journal,* Oct. 28, 2003, pp. B1, B10; M. Jackson, "Can a Test Gauge the Value of an MBA?" *Wall Street Journal,* Sept. 8, 2002, p. B12; S. Jaschik, "The B-School Hierarchy," *New York Times,* Apr. 25, 2004, pp. 36–40; J. Merritt, "What's an MBA Really Worth?" *Business Week,* Sept. 22, 2003, pp. 90–102; J. Pfeffer and C. T. Fong, "The End of Business Schools? Less Success Than Meets the Eye," *Academy of Management Learning and Education,* 2002, 1(1), pp. 78–95.

17. R. S. Robin, W. H. Bommer, and T. T. Baldwin, "Using Extracurricular Activity as an Indicator of Interpersonal Skill: Prudent Evaluation or Recruiting Malpractice?" *Human Resource Management,* 2002, 41(4), pp. 441–454.

18. R. A. Ash, "A Comparative Study of Behavioral Consistency and Holistic Judgment Methods of Job Applicant Training and Work Experience Evaluation," *Public Personnel Management,* 1984, 13, pp. 157–172; M. A. McDaniel, F. L. Schmidt, and J. E. Hunter, "A Meta-Analysis of the Validity of Methods for Rating Training and Experience in Personnel Selection," *Personnel Psychology,* 1988, 41, pp. 283–314; R. Tomsho, "Busy Surgeons Are Good for Patients," *Wall Street Journal,* Nov. 28, 2003, p. B3.

19. M. R. Raymond, S. Neustel, and D. Anderson, "Retest Effects on Identical and Parallel Forms in Certification and Licensure Testing," *Personnel Psychology,* 2007, 60, pp. 367–396; J. D. Opdyke, "'Wait, Let Me Call My ChFC,'" *Wall Street Journal,* Jan. 28, 2006, pp. B1, B3; J. McKillip and J. Owens, "Voluntary Professional Certifications: Requirements and Validation Activities," *The Industrial-Organizational Psychologist,* July 2000, pp. 50–57.

20. G. W. England, *Development and Use of Weighted Application Blanks* (Dubuque, IA: W. M. C. Brown, 1961).

21. J. E. Hunter and R. F. Hunter, "Validity and Utility of Alternative Predictors of Job Performance," *Psychological Bulletin,* 1984, 96, pp. 72–98.

22. I. L. Goldstein, "The Application Blank: How Honest Are the Responses?" *Journal of Applied Psychology,* 1974, 59, pp. 491–494.

23. G. W. England, *Development and Use of Weighted Application Blanks,* revised ed. (Minneapolis: University of Minnesota Industrial Relations Center, 1971).

24. B. K. Brown and M. A. Campion, "Biodata Phenomenology: Recruiters' Perceptions and Use of Biographical Information in Resume Screening," *Journal of Applied Psychology,* 1994, 79, pp. 897–908.

25. C. J. Russell, J. Mattson, S. E. Devlin, and D. Atwater, "Predictive Validity of Biodata Items Generated From Retrospective Life Experience Essays," *Journal of Applied Psychology,* 1990, 75, pp. 569–580.

26. F. A. Mael, "A Conceptual Rationale for the Domain and Attributes of Biodata Items," *Personnel Psychology,* 1991, 44, pp. 763–792.

27. S. Hansell, "Google Answer to Filling Jobs Is an Algorithm," *New York Times,* Jan. 3, 2007, pp. A1, C9.

28. M. A. Oviedo-García, "Internal Validation of a Biodata Extraversion Scale for Salespeople," *Social Behavior and Personality,* 2007, 35, pp. 675–692; C. M. Harold, L. A. McFarland, and J. A. Weekley, "The Validity of Verifiable and Non-verifiable Biodata Items: An Examination Across Applicants and Incumbents," *International Journal of Selection and Assessment,* 2006, 14, pp. 336–346.

29. J. E. Hunter and R. F. Hunter, "Validity and Utility of Alternative Predictors of Job Performance"; R. R. Reilly and G. T. Chao, "Validity and Fairness of Some Alternative Selection Procedures," *Personnel Psychology,* 1982, 35, pp. 1–62.

30. K. D. Carlson, S. Sculten, F. L. Schmidt, H. Rothstein, and F. Erwin, "Generalizable Biographical Data Validity Can Be Achieved Without Multi-Organizational Development and Keying,"

Personnel Psychology, 1999, 52, pp. 731–755; H. R. Rothstein, F. L. Schmidt, F. W. Erwin, W. A. Owens, and C. P. Sparks, "Biographical Data in Employment Selection: Can Validities Be Made Generalizable?," *Journal of Applied Psychology,* 1990, 75, pp. 175–184.

31. N. Schmitt, F. L. Oswald, B. H. Kim, M. A. Gillespie, L. J. Ramsay, and T. Yoo, "Impact of Elaboration on Socially Desirable Responding and the Validity of Biodata Measures," *Journal of Applied Psychology,* 2003, 88, pp. 979–988.

32. T. E. Becker and A. L. Colquitt, "Potential Versus Actual Faking of a Biodata Form: An Analysis Along Several Dimensions of Item Type," *Personnel Psychology,* 1992, 45, pp. 389–406.

33. J. C. Baxter, B. Brock, P. C. Hill, and R. M. Rozelle, "Letters of Recommendation: A Question of Value," *Journal of Applied Psychology,* 1981, 66, pp. 296–301.

34. T. A. Judge and C. A. Higgins, "Affective Disposition and the Letter of Reference," *Organizational Behavior and Human Decision Processes,* 1998, 75, pp. 207–221.

35. M. E. Burke, "2004 Reference Check and Background Testing," Society for Human Resource Management, 2005; P. J. Taylor, K. Pajo, G. W. Cheung, and P. Stringfield, "Dimensionality and Validity of a Structured Telephone Reference Check Procedure," *Personnel Psychology,* 2004, 57, pp. 745–772.

36. J. Click, "SJRM Survey Highlights Dilemmas of Reference Checks," *HR News,* July 1995, p. 13.

37. A. Athavaley, "Job References You Can't Control," *Wall Street Journal,* Sept. 27, 2007, pp. D1, D2.

38. P. J. Taylor, K. Pajo, G. W. Cheung, and P. Stringfield, "Dimensionality and Validity of a Structured Telephone Reference Check Procedure," *Personnel Psychology,* 2004, 57, pp. 745–772.

39. J. D. Glater, "Critics Question Breadth of Background Checks for Hiring at Education Department," *New York Times,* Feb. 11, 2007, p. 18.

40. "Employers Increase Use of Background Checks," *USA Today,* Apr. 26, 2007, p. 1B; T. Minton-Eversole, "More Background Screening Yields More 'Red Tape,'" *SHRM News,* July 2007, pp. 1–5.

41. K. Maher, "The Jungle," *Wall Street Journal,* Jan. 20, 2004, p. B8; A. Zimmerman, "Wal-Mart to Probe Job Applicants," *Wall Street Journal,* Aug. 12, 2004, pp. A3, B6; A. Zimmerman and K. Stringer, "As Background Checks Proliferate, Ex-Cons Face Jobs Lock," *Wall Street Journal,* Aug. 26, 2004, pp. B1, B3.

42. L. Schwarz, "Baseball and Umpires Clash Over Background Checks," *New York Times,* Aug. 7, 2007, p. C15; T. Frank, "Aviation Workers Soon to Get More Criminal Checks," *USA Today,* Nov. 28, 2007, p. 1A.

43. J. McGregor, "Background Checks That Never End," *Business Week,* Mar. 20, 2006, p. 40.

44. Office of Technology Assessment, *Genetic Monitoring and Screening in the Workplace* (Washington, DC: U.S. Congress, 1990).

45. S. Dentzer, B. Cohn, G. Raine, G. Carroll, and V. Quade, "Can You Pass This Job Test?" *Newsweek,* May 5, 1986, pp. 46–53.

46. V. Kiernan, "US Bans Gene Prejudice at Work," *New Scientist,* 1995, 146, p. 4.

47. M. Minehan, "The Growing Debate Over Genetic Testing," *HR Magazine,* Apr. 1998, p. 208.

48. L. Thornburg, "Computer-Assisted Interviewing Shortens Hiring Cycle," *HR Magazine,* Feb. 1998, pp. 73–79.

49. Goldstein, "The Application Blank: How Honest Are the Responses?"; W. Keichel, "Lies on the Resume," *Fortune,* Aug. 23, 1982, pp. 221–222, 224; J. N. Mosel and L. W. Cozan, "The Accuracy of Application Blank Work Histories," *Journal of Applied Psychology,* 1952, 36, pp. 365–369.

50. R. A. Ash and E. L. Levine, "Job Applicant Training and Work Experience Evaluation: An Empirical Comparison of Four Methods," *Journal of Applied Psychology,* 1985, 70, pp. 572–576.

51. G. P. Latham and G. Whyte, "The Futility of Utility Analysis," *Personnel Psychology,* 1994, 47, pp. 31–46.

52. Smither, Reilly, Millsap, Pearlman, and Stoffey, "Applicant Reactions to Selection Procedures."

53. S. W. Gilliland, "Fairness From the Applicant's Perspective: Reactions to Employee Selection Procedures," *International Journal of Selection and Assessment,* 1995, 3, pp. 11–19.

54. D. A. Kravitz, V. Stinson, and T. L. Chavez, "Evaluations of Tests Used for Making Selection and Promotion Decisions," *International Journal of Selection and Assessment,* 1996, 4, pp. 24–34; D. D. Steiner and S. W. Gilliland, "Fairness Reactions to Personnel Selection Techniques in France and the United States," *Journal of Applied Psychology,* 1996, 81, pp. 134–141.

55. G. P. Panaro, *Employment Law Manual,* second ed. (Boston: Warren Gorham Lamont, 1993), pp. 1–29 to 1–42; M. G. Danaher, "Handbook Disclaimer Dissected," *HR Magazine,* Feb. 2007, p. 116; D. J. Walsh, *Employment Law for Human Resource Practice* (Mason, OH: Thompson Higher Education, 2007).

56. J. E. Bahls, "Available Upon Request," *HR Magazine Focus,* Jan. 1999, p. 206; W. M. Mercer, Inc., "Hazards of Giving Employee Health References," *The Mercer Report,* July 22, 1998, p. 8; Panaro, *Employment Law Manual,* pp. 2–101 to 2–106; M. E. Burke and L. A. Weatherly, *Getting to Know the Candidate: Providing Reference Checks* (Alexandria, VA: Society for Human Resource Management, 2005).

57. T. B. Stivarius, J. Skonberg, R. Fliegel, R. Blumberg, R. Jones, and K. Mones, "Background Checks: Four Steps to Basic Compliance in a Multistate Environment," *Legal Report,* Society for Human Resource Management, Mar.–Apr. 2003.

58. J. C. Wallace and S. J. Vadanovich, "Personal Application Blanks: Persistence and Knowledge of Legally Inadvisable Application Blank Items," *Public Personnel Management,* 2004, 33, pp. 331–349.

59. Bureau of National Affairs, "EEOC Guide to Pre-Employment Inquiries," *Fair Employment Practices* (Washington, DC: author, periodically updated), pp. 443:65–80. G. M. Davis, "Criminal Background Checks for Employment Purposes," *Legal Report,* Society for Human Resource Management, July-Aug. 2006; D. Cadrain, "Full Disclosure," *HR Magazine,* Sept. 2007, pp. 60-64.

60. Bureau of National Affairs, "EEOC Guide to Pre-Employment Inquiries," pp. 443:65–80.

61. Equal Employment Opportunity Commission, *ADA Enforcement Guidance: Pre-Employment Disability Related Questions and Medical Examinations* (Washington, DC: author, 1995).

62. Bureau of National Affairs, *Fair Employment Practices* (Washington, DC: author, periodically updated), 454: whole section.

63. Bureau of National Affairs, *Fair Employment Practices,* pp. 421:352–356.

64. N. J. Sedmak and M. D. Levin-Epstein, *Primer on Equal Employment Opportunity* (Washington, DC: Bureau of National Affairs, 1991), pp. 36–40.

65. Bureau of National Affairs, *Fair Employment Practices,* pp. 405:6941–6943.

CHAPTER NINE

External Selection II

Substantive Assessment Methods
  Personality Tests
  Ability Tests
  Job Knowledge Tests
  Performance Tests and Work Samples
  Situational Judgment Tests
  Integrity Tests
  Interest, Values, and Preference Inventories
  Structured Interview
  Choice of Substantive Assessment Methods

Discretionary Assessment Methods

Contingent Assessment Methods
  Drug Testing
  Medical Exams

Legal Issues
  Uniform Guidelines on Employee Selection Procedures
  Selection Under the Americans With Disabilities Act (ADA)
  Drug Testing

Summary

Discussion Questions

Ethical Issues

Applications

Tanglewood Stores Case

The previous chapter reviewed preliminary issues surrounding external staffing decisions made in organizations, including the use of initial assessment methods. This chapter continues the discussion of external selection by discussing in some detail substantive assessment methods. The use of discretionary and contingent assessment methods, collection of assessment data, and legal issues will also be considered.

Whereas initial assessment methods are used to reduce the applicant pool to candidates, substantive assessment methods are used to reduce the candidate pool to finalists for the job. Thus, the use of substantive methods is often more involved than using initial methods. Numerous substantive assessment methods will be discussed in depth, including various tests (personality, ability, job knowledge, performance/work samples, situational judgment, integrity); interest, values, and preference inventories; structured interviews; and assessment for team environments. The average validity (i.e., $\bar{r}$) of each method and the criteria used to choose among methods will be reviewed.

Discretionary assessment methods are used in some circumstances to separate those who receive job offers from the list of finalists. The applicant characteristics that are assessed when using discretionary methods are sometimes very subjective. Several of the characteristics most commonly assessed by discretionary methods will be reviewed.

Contingent assessment methods are used to make sure that tentative offer recipients meet certain qualifications for the job. Although any assessment method can be used as a contingent method (e.g., licensing/certification requirements, background checks), perhaps the two most common contingent methods are drug tests and medical exams. These procedures will be reviewed.

All forms of assessment decisions require the collection of assessment data. The procedures used to make sure this process is properly conducted will be reviewed. In particular, several issues will be discussed, including support services, training requirements in using various predictors, maintaining security and confidentiality, and the importance of standardized procedures.

Finally, many important legal issues surround the use of substantive, discretionary, and contingent methods of selection. The most important of these issues will be reviewed. Particular attention will be given to the Uniform Guidelines on Employee Selection Procedures (UGESP) and staffing requirements under the Americans With Disabilities Act (ADA).

SUBSTANTIVE ASSESSMENT METHODS

Organizations use initial assessment methods to make "rough cuts" among applicants—weeding out the obviously unqualified. Conversely, substantive assessment methods are used to make more precise decisions about applicants—among those who meet minimum qualifications for the job, which are the most likely to be high performers if hired? Because substantive methods are used to make fine distinctions among applicants, the nature of their use is somewhat more involved than initial assessment methods. As with initial assessment methods, however, substantive assessment methods are developed using the logic of prediction outlined in Exhibit 8.1 and the selection plan shown in Exhibit 8.2. Predictors typically used to select finalists from the candidate pool include personality tests; ability tests; job knowledge tests; performance tests and work samples; situational judgment tests; integrity tests; interest, values, and preference inventories; structured interviews; team assessments; and clinical assessments. Each of these predictors is described next in some detail.

Personality Tests

Until recently, personality tests were not perceived as a valid selection method. Historically, most studies estimated the validity of personality tests to be between .10 and .15, which would rank them among the poorest predictors of job performance—only marginally better than a coin toss.[1] Starting with the publication of an influential review in the 1960s, personality tests were not viewed favorably, nor were they widely used.[2]

Recent advances, however, have suggested much more positive conclusions about the role of personality tests in predicting job performance. Mainly, this is due to the widespread acceptance of a major taxonomy of personality, often called the Big Five. The Big Five are used to describe behavioral (as opposed to emotional or cognitive) traits that may capture up to 75% of an individual's personality. The Big Five factors are *emotional stability* (disposition to be calm, optimistic, and well adjusted), *extraversion* (tendency to be sociable, assertive, active, upbeat, and talkative), *openness to experience* (tendency to be imaginative, attentive to inner feelings, intellectually curious and independent), *agreeableness* (tendency to be altruistic, trusting, sympathetic, and cooperative), and *conscientiousness* (tendency to be purposeful, determined, dependable, and attentive to detail). The Big Five are a reduced set of many more specific traits. The Big Five are very stable over time, and there is even research to suggest a strong genetic basis of the Big Five traits (roughly 50% of the variance in the Big Five traits appears to be inherited).[3] Because job performance is a broad concept that comprises many specific behaviors, it will be best predicted by broad dispositions such as the Big Five. In fact, some research evidence supports this proposition.[4]

Measures of Personality

Although personality can be measured in many ways, for personnel selection, the most practical measures are self-report surveys. There are several survey measures of the Big Five traits that are used in selection. The *Personal Characteristics Inventory* (PCI) is a self-report measure of the Big Five that asks applicants to report their agreement or disagreement (using a "strongly disagree" to "strongly agree" scale) with 150 sentences.[5] The measure takes about 30 minutes to complete and has a fifth- to sixth-grade reading level. Exhibit 9.1 provides sample items from the PCI. Another commonly used measure of the Big Five is the *NEO Personality Inventory* (NEO), of which there are several versions that have been translated into numerous languages.[6] A third alternative is the *Hogan Personality Inventory* (HPI), which is also based on the Big Five typology. Responses to the HPI can be scored to yield measures of employee reliability and service orientation.[7] All three of these measures have shown validity in predicting job performance in various occupations.

Traditionally, personality tests are administered to applicants on-site, with a paper-and-pencil survey. Some companies, such as Gallup, market a phone personality test that they administer and score, and then report the results to the hiring organization. Increasingly, personality tests are administered online, which is cheaper for the organization and more convenient for the applicant.

EXHIBIT 9.1   Sample Items for Personal Characteristics Inventory

Conscientiousness
I can always be counted on to get the job done.
I am a very persistent worker.
I almost always plan things in advance of work.

Extraversion
Meeting new people is enjoyable to me.
I like to stir up excitement if things get boring.
I am a "take-charge" type of person.

Agreeableness
I like to help others who are down on their luck.
I usually see the good side of people.
I forgive others easily.

Emotional Stability
I can become annoyed at people quite easily (reverse-scored).
At times I don't care about much of anything (reverse-scored).
My feelings tend to be easily hurt (reverse-scored).

Openness to Experience
I like to work with difficult concepts and ideas.
I enjoy trying new and different things.
I tend to enjoy art, music, or literature.

SOURCE: M. K. Mount and M. R. Barrick, *Manual for Personal Characteristics Inventory* (December 1995). Reprinted with permission of the Wonderlic Personnel Test, Inc.

However, because most online testing is unmonitored, there are three potential problems: (a) test security might be compromised (e.g., test items posted on a blog); (b) applicants may find it easier to cheat or be more motivated to cheat online; and (c) applicants may not tolerate long online personality tests. There are no "silver bullet" remedies to these problems. Because each of these problems is less of an issue with paper-and-pencil tests, organizations may be well advised to use paper-and-pencil tests where feasible.

Where traditional paper-and-pencil personality testing is infeasible, several steps can be taken to ameliorate the problems with online testing. First, experts recommend keeping online personality tests as brief as possible. If the test takes more than 20 minutes, applicants may grow impatient. Second, it is important to assign applicants identification codes, to collect basic background data, and to break the test into sections. These steps increase accountability (lessening the odds of faking) and ensure that if the applicant loses the Internet connection while taking the test, the portions completed will not be lost. Finally, the probability of faking can be reduced by following some of the steps outlined shortly. These steps are especially important for online testing. Finally, many experts recommend the use of "item banking" (variation in specific items used to measure each trait) to enhance test security; to further reduce faking, inform test takers that their online scores will be verified with a paper-and-pencil test, should they advance further in the selection process.[8]

Evaluation of Personality Tests

Many comprehensive reviews of the validity of personality tests have been published. Nearly all of the recent reviews focus on the validity of the Big Five.[9] Although there are some inconsistencies across reviews, the results can be summarized in Exhibit 9.2. As the exhibit shows, each of the Big Five traits has advantages and disadvantages. However, the traits differ in the degree to which they are a "mixed blessing." Specifically, whereas the disadvantages of agreeableness and openness appear to offset their advantages, there are fewer downsides for conscientiousness, emotional stability, and, to some degree, extraversion than there are advantages. These three traits also happen to have the strongest correlates with overall job performance. Conscientiousness and emotional stability, in particular, appear to be useful across a wide range of jobs. Thus, in general, the personality traits of conscientiousness, emotional stability, and extraversion—in that order—appear to be the most useful for selection contexts. Of course, in certain situations—such as where adaptability or creativity may be highly valued, or where cooperative relations are crucial—openness and agreeableness may be important to assess as well.

Today there is widespread acceptance regarding the validity and utility of personality tests in personnel selection. This does not mean that the area is free of its critics, however: A few researchers continue to argue that personality traits are not useful selection tools.[10] Here we evaluate three of the most important criticisms against the use of personality tests in selection decisions: the validities are trivial,

EXHIBIT 9.2   Implications of Big Five Personality Traits at Work

Big Five Trait	Advantages	Disadvantages
Conscientiousness	• Better overall job performers • Higher levels of job satisfaction • More likely to emerge as leaders • Fewer "deviant" work behaviors • Higher retention (lower turnover)	• Lower adaptability
Emotional stability	• Better overall job performers • Higher levels of job satisfaction • More effective leaders • Higher retention (lower turnover)	• Less able to identify threats
Extraversion	• Perform better in sales • More likely to emerge as leaders • Higher levels of job satisfaction	• Higher absenteeism • More accidents
Agreeableness	• More valued as team members • More "helping" behaviors • Fewer "deviant" work behaviors	• Lower career success • Less able to cope with conflict • Give more lenient ratings
Openness	• Higher creativity • More effective leaders • More adaptable	• Less committed to employer • More "deviant" work behaviors • More accidents

faking undermines the usefulness of personality tests, and applicants react negatively to personality tests.

Trivial Validities. One set of critics has argued that validities of personality traits are so small as to border on the trivial, rendering them of limited usefulness as selection devices. These researchers note, "Why are we now suddenly looking at personality as a valid predictor of job performance when the validities still haven't changed and are still close to zero?"[11] While this is an extreme position, it does contain a grain of truth: The validities are far from perfect. For example, our best estimate of the validity of conscientiousness in predicting overall job performance is $\bar{r} = .23$. By no means would this be labeled a strong validity (though, in fairness, we are not aware of any personality researchers who have done so). Does this mean that the validity of personality measures, though, are trivial? We do not believe so, for four reasons.

First, because applicants can complete an entire Big Five inventory in less than 30 minutes in most selection situations, the entire Big Five framework is used, or at least more than a single trait is assessed. So, it is important to look at the multiple correlations between the set of Big Five traits and criteria such as job performance. For example, the multiple correlation between the Big Five and criteria such as overall job performance and leadership is roughly R = .50. This is hardly trivial.[12]

Second, as with any selection measure, one can find situations in which a personality trait does not predict job performance. Even though personality tests generalize across jobs, this doesn't mean they will work in every case. And sometimes when they work and when they don't is counterintuitive. For example, evidence suggests that conscientiousness and positive self-concept work well in predicting player success in the NFL but not so well in predicting the performance of police officers.[13] Organizations need to perform their own validation studies to ensure that the tests are working as hoped. In general, personality is more predictive of performance in jobs that have substantial autonomy, meaning that individuals have discretion in deciding how—and how well—to do their work.[14]

Third, the Big Five do not exhaust the set of potentially relevant personality traits. Research suggests, for example, that a trait termed proactive personality (degree to which people take action) predicts performance and career success, even controlling for the Big Five traits.[15] Another trait, termed core self-evaluations (a reflection of individuals' self-confidence and self-worth), has also been linked to job performance. The Core Self-Evaluations Scale is shown in Exhibit 9.3. Research indicates that core self-evaluations are predictive of job performance, and the Core Self-Evaluations Scale appears to have validity equivalent to that of conscientiousness. A further advantage of this measure is that it is nonproprietary (free).[16]

Finally, personality is not intended to be a stand-alone selection tool. In nearly all cases it is part of a selection battery consisting of other substantive selection measures. No reasonable person would recommend that applicants be hired solely on the basis of scores on a personality test. But by the same token, personality measures do appear to add to the validity of other selection measures.[17]

Faking. Another frequent criticism of personality measures is that they are "fakeable"—applicants will distort their responses to increase their odds of being hired. This concern is apparent when one considers personality items (see Exhibits 9.1 and 9.3) and the nature of the traits. Few individuals would want to describe themselves as disagreeable, neurotic, closed to new experiences, and unconscientious. Furthermore, since answers to these questions are nearly impossible to verify (e.g., imagine trying to verify whether an applicant prefers reading a book to watching television), the possibility of "faking good" is quite real. This then leads to the perverse outcome that the applicants most likely to be hired are those who enhanced their responses (faked) the most.

There is a voluminous literature on faking. The results of this literature can be summarized as follows. First, there is little doubt that some faking or enhance-

EXHIBIT 9.3   The Core Self-Evaluations Scale

Instructions: Below are several statements about you with which you may agree or disagree. Using the response scale below, indicate your agreement or disagreement with each item by placing the appropriate number on the line preceding that item.

1	2	3	4	5
Strongly Disagree	Disagree	Neutral	Agree	Strongly Agree

1. _____I am confident I get the success I deserve in life.
2. _____Sometimes I feel depressed. (r)
3. _____When I try, I generally succeed.
4. _____Sometimes when I fail, I feel worthless. (r)
5. _____I complete tasks successfully.
6. _____Sometimes I do not feel in control of my work. (r)
7. _____Overall, I am satisfied with myself.
8. _____I am filled with doubts about my competence. (r)
9. _____I determine what will happen in my life.
10. _____I do not feel in control of my success in my career. (r)
11. _____I am capable of coping with most of my problems.
12. _____There are times when things look pretty bleak and hopeless to me. (r)

Note: r = reverse-scored (for these items, 5 is scored 1, 4 is scored 2, 2 is scored 4, and 1 is scored 5).

SOURCE: T. A. Judge, A. Erez, J. E. Bono, and C. J. Thoresen, "The Core Self-Evaluations Scale: Development of a Measure," *Personnel Psychology,* 2003, 56, pp. 303–331.

ment does occur. Studies suggest that applicants consistently score higher on socially desirable personality traits (like conscientiousness, emotional stability, and agreeableness) than do current employees (in most situations, there is no reason to believe that applicants should score more favorably on personality tests than employees—if anything, the reverse would be expected). Also, when individuals are informed that their scores matter (might be used in selection decisions), their scores on personality tests increase.[18]

But what is the outcome of this enhancement? Does the fact that some applicants fake their responses destroy the validity of personality measures in selection? Interestingly, the answer to this question appears to be quite clearly no. In short, though applicants do try to look good by enhancing their responses to personality tests, it seems clear that such enhancement does not significantly detract from the validity of the tests. Why might this be the case? Evidence suggests that socially desirable responding, or presenting oneself in a favorable light, doesn't end once someone takes a job. So, the same tendencies that cause someone to present themselves in a somewhat favorable light on a personality test also help them do better on the job.[19]

Because faking does not appear to undermine personality validities, some of the proposed solutions to faking may be unnecessary or may cause more problems than they solve. For example, some have proposed correcting applicant scores for faking. However, the literature is quite clear that such corrections do not improve the validity of personality measures.[20] Another proposed solution—using forced choice personality measures, where an applicant must choose between evaluating themselves as, say, conscientious and evaluating themselves as emotionally stable—also appears to be fraught with considerable problems.[21] The third possible method of reducing faking—warning applicants that their scores will be verified—appears to reduce faking (by as much as 30%) without undermining validities. Thus, it is not clear that faking is as pervasive or as problematic as critics allege. However, if faking is to be addressed, warning applicants against faking appears to be the least problematic method.[22]

Negative Applicant Reactions.   Finally, it is important to evaluate personality tests not only in terms of their validity but also from the applicant's perspective. From an applicant's standpoint, the subjective and personal nature of the questions asked in these tests may cause questions about their validity and concerns about invasiveness. In fact, the available evidence concerning applicants' perceptions of personality tests suggests that they are viewed relatively negatively compared to other selection measures.[23] To some degree, applicants who react the most negatively are those who believe they have scored the worst.[24] But in general, applicants do not perceive personality measures to be as face-valid as other selection measures. Thus, while personality tests—when used properly—do have validity, this validity does not seem to translate into favorable applicant perceptions. More research is needed into the ways that these tests could be made more acceptable to applicants.

Ability Tests

Ability tests are measures that assess an individual's capacity to function in a certain way. There are two major types of ability tests: aptitude and achievement. Aptitude tests look at a person's innate capacity to function, whereas achievement tests assess a person's learned capacity to function. In practice, these types of abilities are often difficult to separate. Thus, it is not clear that this is a productive, practical distinction for ability tests used in selection.

Surveys reveal that between 15% and 20% of organizations use some sort of ability test in selection decisions.[25] Organizations that use ability tests do so because they assume the tests assess a key determinant of employee performance. Without a certain level of ability, innate or learned, performance is unlikely to be acceptable, regardless of motivation. Someone may try extremely hard to do well in a very difficult class (e.g., calculus), but will not succeed unless he or she has the ability to do so (e.g., mathematical aptitude).

There are four major classes of ability tests: cognitive, psychomotor, physical, and sensory/perceptual.[26] As these ability tests are quite distinct, each will be considered separately below. Because most of the research attention—and public controversy—has focused on cognitive ability tests, they are discussed below in considerable detail.

Cognitive Ability Tests

Cognitive ability tests refer to measures that assess abilities involved in thinking, including perception, memory, reasoning, verbal and mathematical abilities, and the expression of ideas. Is cognitive ability a general construct or does it have a number of specific aspects? Research shows that measures of specific cognitive abilities, such as verbal, quantitative, reasoning, and so on, appear to reflect general intelligence (sometimes referred to as IQ or "g").[27] One of the facts that best illustrate this finding is the relatively high correlations among scores on measures of specific facets of intelligence. Someone who scores well on a measure of one specific ability is more likely to score well on measures of other specific abilities. In other words, general intelligence causes individuals to have similar scores on measures of specific abilities.

Measures of Cognitive Ability. There are many cognitive ability tests that measure both specific cognitive abilities and general mental ability. Many test publishers offer an array of tests. For example, the Psychological Corporation sells the *Employee Aptitude Survey*, a test of 10 specific cognitive abilities (e.g., verbal comprehension, numerical ability, numerical and verbal reasoning, word fluency). Each of these specific tests is sold separately and takes no more than five minutes to administer to applicants. Each of the 10 specific tests is sold in packages of 25 for about $44 per package. The Psychological Corporation also sells the *Wonderlic Personnel Test*, perhaps the most widely used test of general mental ability for selection decisions. The Wonderlic is a 12-minute, 50-item test. Items range in type from spatial relations to numerical problems to analogies. Exhibit 9.4 provides examples of items from one of the forms of the Wonderlic. In addition to being a speed (timed) test, the Wonderlic is also a power test—the items get harder as the test progresses (very few individuals complete all 50 items). The Wonderlic has been administered to more than 2.5 million applicants, and normative data are available from a database of more than 450,000 individuals. Cost of the Wonderlic ranges from approximately $1.50 to $3.50 per applicant, depending on whether the organization scores the test itself. Costs of other cognitive ability tests are similar. Although cognitive ability tests are not entirely costless, they are among the least expensive of any substantive assessment method.

There are many other tests and test publishers in addition to those reviewed above. Before deciding which test to use, organizations should seek out a reputable testing firm. An association of test publishers has been formed with bylaws to help

---

EXHIBIT 9.4 **Sample Cognitive Ability Test Items**

Look at the row of numbers below. What number should come next?

8   4   2   1   1/2   1/4   ?

Assume the first 2 statements are true. Is the final one: (1) true, (2) false, (3) not certain?
The boy plays baseball. All baseball players wear hats. The boy wears a hat.

One of the numbered figures in the following drawing is most different from the others. What is the number in that drawing?

A train travels 20 feet in 1/5 second. At this same speed, how many feet will it travel in three seconds?

How many of the six pairs of items listed below are exact duplicates?

3421	1243
21212	21212
558956	558956
10120210	10120210
612986896	612986896
356471201	356571201

The hours of daylight and darkness in SEPTEMBER are nearest equal to the hours of daylight and darkness in

(1) June   (2) March   (3) May   (4) November

Source: Reprinted with permission from C. F. Wonderlic Personnel Test, Inc., *1992 Catalog: Employment Tests, Forms, and Procedures* (Libertyville, IL: author—Charles F. Wonderlic, 1992).

ensure this process.[28] It is also advisable to seek out the advice of researchers or testing specialists. Many of these individuals are members of the American Psychological Association or the American Psychological Society. Guidelines are for deciding which test to use.[29]

Evaluation of Cognitive Ability Tests

The findings regarding general intelligence have had profound implications for personnel selection. A number of meta-analyses have been conducted on the validity of cognitive ability tests. Although the validities found in these studies have fluctuated to some extent, the most comprehensive reviews have estimated the "true" validity of measures of general cognitive ability to be roughly $\bar{r} = .50$.[30] The conclusions from these meta-analyses are dramatic:

1. Cognitive ability tests are among the most valid, if not *the* most valid, methods of selection.
2. Cognitive ability tests appear to generalize across all organizations, all job types, and all types of applicants; thus, they are likely to be valid in virtually any selection context.
3. Cognitive ability tests appear to generalize across cultures, with validities in Europe at least as high as those in the United States.
4. Organizations using cognitive ability tests in selection enjoy large economic gains compared to organizations that do not use them.

These conclusions are not simply esoteric speculations from the ivory tower. They are based on hundreds of studies of hundreds of organizations employing hundreds of thousands of workers. Thus, whether an organization is selecting engineers, customer service representatives, or meat cutters, general mental ability is likely the single most valid method of selecting among applicants. A large-scale quantitative review of the literature suggested relatively high average validities for many occupational groups:[31]

- Manager, $\bar{r} = .53$
- Clerk, $\bar{r} = .54$
- Salesperson, $\bar{r} = .61$
- Protective professional, $\bar{r} = .42$
- Service worker, $\bar{r} = .48$
- Trades and crafts, $\bar{r} = .46$
- Elementary industrial worker, $\bar{r} = .37$
- Vehicle operator, $\bar{r} = .28$
- Sales clerk, $\bar{r} = .27$

These results show that cognitive ability tests have some degree of validity for all types of jobs. The validity is particularly high for complex jobs (e.g., manager, engineer), but even for simple jobs the validity is positive. The same review also revealed that cognitive ability tests have very high degrees of validity in predicting training success—$\bar{r} = .37$ for vehicle operators to $\bar{r} = .87$ for protective professionals. This is due to the substantial learning component of training and the obvious fact that smart people learn more.[32]

Whereas cognitive ability tests are more valid for jobs of medium complexity (e.g., police officers, salespersons) and high complexity (e.g., computer programmers, pilots), they are even valid for jobs of relatively low complexity (e.g., bus driver, factory worker). Why are cognitive ability tests predictive even for relatively simple jobs where intelligence would not appear to be an important attribute? The fact is that some degree of intelligence is important for *any* type of job. The validity of cognitive ability tests even seems to generalize to performance on and of athletic teams (see Exhibit 9.5). Additionally, one study found that college basketball teams high in cognitive ability

---

EXHIBIT 9.5 Cognitive Ability Testing in the NFL

As ardent football fans know, each year the NFL holds a draft to select college players for its teams. As part of that draft, potential draftees go through a "combine" where their skills are tested: They bench press, they run, they jump through hoops (literally), and they complete an intelligence test (the *Wonderlic Personnel Test*). Although the test has its critics, it continues to be used by NFL teams.

Although players for all positions take the Wonderlic, NFL teams pay particular attention to quarterbacks' scores because of the importance of decision making and memory for that position (an NFL playbook is quite extensive).

Here's a select sample of how some NFL quarterbacks scored on the Wonderlic (scores for some NFL quarterbacks, like Jeff Garcia, were unavailable):

30 and higher (very intelligent)
Alex Smith: 40, Eli Manning: 39, Charlie Frye: 38, Matt Leinart: 35, Tom Brady: 33, J. P. Losman: 31, Josh McCown: 30, Philip Rivers: 30, Tony Romo: 30, Matt Schaub: 30

25–29 (intelligent)
Marc Bulger: 29, Rex Grossman: 29, Matt Hasselbeck: 29, Brady Quinn: 29, Drew Brees: 28, Peyton Manning: 28, Jason Campbell: 27, Jay Cutler: 26, Carson Palmer: 26, Damon Huard: 25, Byron Leftwich: 25, Chad Pennington: 25, Ben Roethlisberger: 25

20–24 (above average)
JaMarcus Russell: 24, Luke McCown: 24; Brett Favre: 22, Michael Vick: 20

Less than 20 (average to below average)
Tarvaris Jackson: 19, Donovan McNabb: 16, Vince Young: 16, Steve McNair: 15; David Garrard: 14

It's clear that NFL quarterbacks are smart—they score well above average relative to the U.S. population (the population average is 19). Do differences among the quarterbacks predict success? Judging from the recent seasons, it's not clear, though the "smart" quarterbacks did acquit themselves well during the 2007–2008 playoffs: The average Wonderlic score for the four starting quarterbacks in the AFC and NFC championship games was a lofty 31, and the quarterback with the second-highest score (Eli Manning) led his team to a Super Bowl victory.

Of course, like all selection methods, cognitive ability tests have their limits. George Young, general manager of the New York Giants, was the individual responsible for convincing the NFL to use the Wonderlic. He recalled a game where a defensive lineman with a low test score went up against an offensive lineman with a high score. According to Young, "The defensive lineman told the offensive lineman, 'Don't worry. After I hit you a few times, you'll be just as dumb as I am.'"

SOURCES: M. Mirabile, "NFL Quarterback Wonderlic Scores" (*www.macmirabile.com/Wonderlic.htm*); J. Saraceno, "Who Knows if This Longhorn Is Short on IQ," *USA Today*, Mar. 1, 2006, p. 2C; B. Plaschke and E. Almond, "Has the NFL Become a Thinking Man's Game?" *Los Angeles Times*, Apr. 21, 1995.

performed better than teams low in cognitive ability.[33] Thus, cognitive ability may be unimportant to performance in some jobs, but if this is true, we have yet to find them.

Why do cognitive ability tests work so well in predicting job performance? Research has shown that most of the effect of cognitive ability tests is due to the fact that intelligent employees have greater job knowledge.[34] Another important issue in understanding the validity of cognitive ability tests is the nature of specific versus general abilities. As was noted earlier, measures of specific abilities are available and continue to be used in selection. These specific measures will likely have some validity in predicting job performance, but this is simply because these tests measure general mental ability. Research has suggested rather conclusively that specific abilities do not explain additional variance in job performance over and above that explained by measures of general cognitive ability.[35] Thus, in most cases, organizations would be better served by using a measure of general cognitive ability than measures of specific abilities.

Potential Limitations

If cognitive ability tests are so valid and cheap, one might be wondering why more organizations aren't using them. One of the main reasons is concern over the adverse impact and fairness of these tests. In terms of adverse impact, regardless of the type of measure used, cognitive ability tests have severe adverse impact against minorities. Specifically, blacks on average score 1 standard deviation below whites, and Hispanics on average score .72 standard deviations below whites. This means that only 10% of blacks score above the average score for whites.[36] Historically, this led to close scrutiny—and sometimes rejection—of cognitive ability tests by the courts. The issue of fairness of cognitive ability tests has been hotly debated and heavily researched. One way to think of fairness is in terms of accuracy of prediction of a test. If a test predicts job performance with equal accuracy for two groups, such as whites and blacks, then most people would say the test is "fair." The problem is that even though the test is equally accurate for both groups, the average test score may be different between the two groups. When this happens, use of the test will cause some degree of adverse impact. This causes a dilemma: Should the organization use the test because it is an accurate and unbiased predictor, or should it not be used because it would cause adverse impact?

Research shows that cognitive ability tests are equally accurate predictors of job performance for various racial and ethnic groups.[37] But research also shows that blacks and Hispanics score lower on such tests than whites. Thus, the dilemma noted above is a real one for the organization. It must decide whether to (1) use the cognitive ability test and experience the positive benefits of using an accurate predictor; (2) not use the cognitive ability test, to avoid adverse impact, and substitute a different measure that has less adverse impact; or (3) use the cognitive ability test in conjunction with other predictors that do not have adverse impact, thus lessening adverse impact overall. Unfortunately, current research does not offer clear guidance on which approach is best. Research suggests that while using other selection measures in conjunction with cognitive ability tests reduces the adverse impact of cognitive ability tests, it by no means eliminates adverse impact.[38]

Although the apparent trade-off between diversity and validity is not likely to disappear anytime soon, there are two positive developments in the cognitive ability testing area. First, one study suggests that tests constructed in an open-ended manner—where the test taker writes in a response—reduces black-white differences in test scores by 39% while producing equivalent levels of validity, compared to the traditional multiple-choice tests. Evidence suggests that open-ended tests reduce group differences because they generate more positive reactions from minority test takers (minority test takers are more likely to see open-ended tests as fair and are more motivated to do well on them). Though this line of research is still in its early stages, and scoring open-ended tests does pose certain logistical and cost issues, it does suggest one possible solution to the validity-diversity trade-off associated with cognitive ability tests.[39] Second, some evidence suggests that the gap in test scores between whites and blacks is narrowing, perhaps by as much as 10%. Though controversy exists over this issue, if it was true, it would mean that future employers may still face a validity-diversity trade-off, but the trade-off may be less severe.[40]

Another aspect of using cognitive ability tests in selection is concern over applicant reactions. Research on how applicants react to cognitive ability tests is scant and somewhat mixed. One study suggested that 88% of applicants for managerial positions perceived the Wonderlic as job related.[41] Another study, however, demonstrated that applicants thought companies had little need for information obtained from a cognitive ability test.[42] Perhaps one explanation for these conflicting findings is the nature of the test. One study characterized eight cognitive ability tests as either concrete (vocabulary, mathematical word problems) or abstract (letter sets, quantitative comparisons) and found that concrete cognitive ability test items were viewed as job related while abstract test items were not.[43] Thus, while applicants may have mixed reactions to cognitive ability tests, concrete items are less likely to be objectionable. In general, applicants perceive cognitive ability tests to be more valid than personality tests but less valid than interviews or work samples.[44]

Conclusion

In sum, cognitive ability tests are one of the most valid selection measures across jobs; they also predict learning and training success, and predict retention.[45] But they also have some troubling "side effects," notably that applicants aren't wild about the tests and the tests have substantial adverse impact against minorities.

A recent survey of 703 members of the main professional association in which cognitive ability tests are used generated some interesting findings. Among the experts, there were several areas of consensus:[46]

1. Cognitive ability is measured reasonably well by standardized tests.
2. General cognitive ability will become increasingly important in selection as jobs become more complex.

3. The predictive validity of cognitive ability tests depends on how performance is defined and measured.

4. The complex nature of job performance means that cognitive ability tests need to be supplemented with other selection measures.

5. There is more to intelligence than what is measured by a standard cognitive ability test.

Given such prominent advantages and disadvantages, cognitive ability tests are here to stay. But so is the controversy over their use.

Other Types of Ability Tests

In the following section we consider tests that measure other types of abilities. Following the earlier classification of abilities into cognitive, psychomotor, physical, and sensory/perceptual, and having just reviewed cognitive ability tests, we now consider the other types of ability tests.

Psychomotor Ability Tests. Psychomotor ability tests measure the correlation of thought with bodily movement. Involved here are processes such as reaction time, arm-hand steadiness, control precision, and manual and digit dexterity. An example of testing for psychomotor abilities is the test used by the city of Columbus, Ohio, to select firefighters. The test mimics coupling a hose to a fire hydrant, and it requires a certain level of processing with psychomotor abilities to achieve a passing score. Some tests of mechanical ability are psychomotor tests. For example, the *MacQuarrie Test for Mechanical Ability* is a 30-minute test that measures manual dexterity. Seven subtests require tracing, tapping, dotting, copying, and so on.

Physical Abilities Tests. Physical abilities tests measure muscular strength, cardiovascular endurance, and movement quality.[47] An example of a test that requires all three is the test given to firefighters in the city of Milwaukee. The test measures upper-body strength (bench press, a lat pulldown, and grip strength pressure), abdominal strength (sit-ups), aerobic endurance (five-minute step tests), and physical mobility (roof ladder placement).[48]

Physical abilities tests are becoming increasingly common to screen out individuals susceptible to repetitive stress injuries, such as carpal tunnel syndrome. One company, Devilbiss Air Power, found that complaints of repetitive stress injuries dropped from 23 to 3 after it began screening applicants for repetitive strain.[49] Physical abilities tests may also be necessary for equal employment opportunity (EEO) reasons.[50] Although female applicants typically score 1.5 standard deviations lower than male applicants on a physical abilities test, the distributions of scores for male and female applicants overlap considerably. Therefore, all applicants must be given a chance to pass requirements and not be judged as a class. Another reason to use physical abilities tests for appropriate jobs is to avoid injuries on the job. Well-designed tests will screen out applicants who have applied for positions that are poorly suited to their physical abilities. Thus, fewer injuries should result. In fact, one study using a concurrent validation approach on a sample of railroad workers found that 57% of all injury costs were due to the 26% of current employees who failed the physical abilities test.[51]

When carefully conducted for appropriate jobs, physical abilities tests can be highly valid. One comprehensive study reported average validities of $\bar{r} = .39$ for warehouse workers to $\bar{r} = .87$ for enlisted army men.[52] Applicant reactions to these sorts of tests are unknown.

Sensory/Perceptual Abilities Tests.   Sensory/perceptual abilities tests assess the ability to detect and recognize environmental stimuli. An example of a sensory/perceptual ability test is a flight simulator used as part of the assessment process for airline pilots. Some tests of mechanical and clerical ability can be considered measures of sensory/perceptual ability, although they take on characteristics of cognitive ability tests. For example, the most commonly used mechanical ability test is the *Bennett Mechanical Comprehension Test,* which contains 68 items that measure an applicant's knowledge of the relationship between physical forces and mechanical objects (e.g., how a pulley operates, how gears function). In terms of clerical tests, the most widely known is the *Minnesota Clerical Test.* This timed test consists of 200 items in which the applicant is asked to compare names or numbers to identify matching elements. For example, an applicant might be asked (needing to work under time constraints) to check the pair of number series in the following list that is the same:

109485_____	104985
456836_____	456836
356823_____	536823
890940_____	890904
205837_____	205834

These tests of mechanical and clerical ability and others like them have reliability and validity data available that suggest they are valid predictors of performance within their specific area.[53] The degree to which these tests add validity over general intelligence, however, is not known.

Emotional Intelligence.   Some have argued that traditional measures of cognitive ability do a poor job of measuring the kind of intelligence that is important to work. It would be more useful, these critics allege, to measure a type of social or emotional intelligence. Though these researchers have labeled their concepts somewhat differently and have used different frameworks, here we focus on the type of intelligence that has generated the most attention: emotional intelligence (EI).

One of the most prominent EI researchers defines EI as "the ability to monitor one's own and others' feelings, to discriminate among them, and to use this information to guide one's thinking and action."[54] Thus, individuals who have high EI are self-aware (good at recognizing their own emotions), other aware (good at recognizing others' emotions), and good at making use of or managing this awareness. It's not hard to understand that this concept is important. Wouldn't nearly every employee be more effective if he or she could readily sense what he or she was feeling (and why), sense what others were feeling, and manage his or her own—and others'—emotions?

Some evidence suggests that EI is related to job performance.[55] One study found that EI predicted the performance of employees in a cigarette factory in China. Another study found that being able to recognize emotions in others' facial expressions and to emotionally "eavesdrop" (pick up subtle signals about people's emotions) predicted coworkers' ratings of how valuable these people were to their organization. Finally, a review of 59 studies indicated that, overall, EI correlated moderately ($\bar{r}=.23$) with job performance.[56]

On the other hand, there are many criticisms of EI.[57] First, many have criticized EI measures. Some EI measures are very similar to items contained in a personality test, and, indeed, one review found that such EI items are strongly related to personality, especially to emotional stability. Other EI items—for example, those that involve describing the emotional qualities of certain sounds and images—bear less similarity to personality measures, but these measures have been criticized for having poor reliability and for their content validity (one measure asks test takers to identify the emotions of colors).[58] Second, for many researchers, it's not clear what EI is. Is it really a form of intelligence? Most of us wouldn't think that being self-aware or sensitive to others' emotions is a matter of intellect. Beyond this definitional ambiguity, different EI researchers have studied a dizzying array of concepts—including emotion recognition, self-awareness, empathy, self-control, and self-discipline. One reviewer noted, "The concept of EI has now become so broad and the components so variegated that . . . it is no longer even an intelligible concept."[59]

Finally, some critics argue that because EI is so closely related to intelligence and personality, once you control for these factors, EI has nothing unique to offer. There are now scores of studies on EI, but very few have controlled for either personality or cognitive ability. To be sure, there are a few studies that show that EI predicts performance, controlling for either personality or cognitive ability,[60] but we are unaware of studies that have controlled for both.

Still, among consulting firms and in the popular press, EI is wildly popular. For example, one company's promotional materials for an EI measure claimed, "EI accounts for more than 85 percent of star performance in top leaders."[61] To say the least, it's hard to validate this statement with the research literature. Weighing the arguments for and against EI, it's still too early to tell whether the concept is useful. It *is* clear, though, that more and more organizations are using EI measures in selection decisions.

Job Knowledge Tests

Job knowledge tests attempt to directly assess an applicant's comprehension of job requirements. Job knowledge tests can be one of two kinds. One type asks questions that directly assess knowledge of the duties involved in a particular job. For example, an item from a job knowledge test for an oncology nurse might be, "Describe the five oncological emergencies in cancer patients." The other type of job knowledge test focuses on the level of experience with, and corresponding knowledge about, critical job tasks and tools/processes necessary to perform the job. For example, the state of Wisconsin uses an *Objective Inventory Questionnaire* (OIQ) to evaluate applicants on the basis of their experience with tasks, duties, tools, technologies, and equipment that are relevant to a particular job.[62] OIQs ask applicants to evaluate their knowledge about and experience using skills, tasks, tools, and so forth by means of a checklist of specific job statements. Applicants can rate their level of knowledge on a scale ranging from "have never performed the task" to "have trained others and evaluated their performance on the task." An advantage of OIQs is that they are fast and easy to process and can provide broad content coverage. A disadvantage of an OIQ is that applicants can easily falsify information. Thus, if job knowledge is an important prerequisite for a position, it is necessary to verify this information independently.

There has been less research on the validity of job knowledge tests than on most other selection measures. One study, however, provided relatively strong support for the validity of job knowledge tests. A meta-analytic review of 502 studies indicated that the "true" validity of job knowledge tests in predicting job performance is .45. These validities were found to be higher for complex jobs and when job and test content were similar.[63]

Performance Tests and Work Samples

Performance tests are mechanisms to assess actual performance rather than underlying capacity or disposition. As such, they are more akin to samples rather than signs of work performance. For example, Chrysler asks applicants for its assembly-line jobs to try assembling auto parts, whereas applicants for executive-level positions undergo a "day in the life" simulation in which they play the role of plant manager, a process that has been followed by Hyundai and Mitsubishi.[64] Exhibit 9.6 provides examples of performance tests and work samples for a variety of jobs. As can be seen in the exhibit, the potential uses of these selection measures is quite broad in terms of job content and skill level.

Types of Tests

Performance Test Versus Work Sample. A performance test measures what the person actually does on the job. The best examples of performance tests are

---

EXHIBIT 9.6   Examples of Performance Tests and Work Samples

Professor
  Teaching a class while on a campus interview
  Reading samples of an applicant's research
Mechanic
  Repairing a particular problem on a car
  Reading a blueprint
Clerical
  Typing test
  Proofreading
Cashier
  Operating a cash register
  Counting money and totaling a balance sheet
Manager
  Performing a group problem-solving exercise
  Reacting to memos and letters
Airline Pilot
  Pilot simulator
  Rudder control test
Taxi Cab Driver
  Driving test
  Street knowledge test
TV Repair Person
  Repairing a broken television
  Finger and tweezer dexterity test
Police Officer
  Check police reports for errors
  Shooting accuracy test
Computer Programmer
  Programming and debugging test
  Hardware replacement test

internships, job tryouts, and probationary periods. Although probationary periods have their uses when one cannot be completely confident in an applicant's ability to perform a job, they are no substitute for a valid prehire selection process. Discharging and finding a replacement for a probationary employee is expensive and has numerous legal issues.[65] A work sample is designed to capture parts of the job, for example, a drill press test for machine operators and a programming test for computer programmers.[66] A performance test is more costly to develop than a work sample, but it is usually a better predictor of job performance.

Motor Versus Verbal Work Samples. A motor work sample test involves the physical manipulation of things. Examples include a driving test and a clothes-making test. A verbal work sample test involves a problem situation requiring language skills and interaction with people. Examples include role-playing tests that simulate contact with customers, and an English test for foreign teaching assistants.

High- Versus Low-Fidelity Tests. A high-fidelity test uses very realistic equipment and scenarios to simulate the actual tasks of the job. Therefore, it elicits actual responses encountered in performing the task.[67] A good example of a high-fidelity test is one being developed to select truck drivers in the petroleum industry. The test is on the computer and mimics all the steps taken to load and unload fuel from a tanker to a fuel reservoir at a service station.[68] It is not a test of perfect high fidelity, because fuel is not actually unloaded. It is, however, a much safer test because the dangerous process of fuel transfer is simulated rather than performed. Most of Station Casino's applicants (more than 800 per week) are customers, so the casino starts off with a very short high-fidelity test (five minutes behind a bank-type counter); applicants then pass through successive simulations, such as assembling a jigsaw puzzle in a group, to assess teamwork skills.[69]

A low-fidelity test is one that simulates the task in a written or verbal description and elicits a written or verbal response rather than an actual response. An example of a low-fidelity test is describing a work situation to job applicants and asking them what they would do in that particular situation. This was done in writing in a study by seven companies in the telecommunications industry for the position of manager.[70] Low-fidelity work samples bear many similarities to some types of structured interviews, and in some cases they may be indistinguishable (see "Structured Interview" section).

Work sample tests are becoming more innovative. Increasingly, work sample tests are being used for customer service positions. For example, Aon Consulting has developed a Web-based simulation called REPeValuator in which applicants assume the role of a customer service specialist. In the simulation, the applicant takes simulated phone calls, participates in Internet "chat," and responds to e-mails. The test takes 30 minutes to complete and costs $20 per applicant. The test provides scores on rapport, problem solving, communication, empathy, and listening skills.[71] Another interesting work sample resembles a job tryout, except that the applicant is not hired or compensated. For example, one small business actually took a promising applicant on a sales call. In this case, although the applicant looked perfect on paper, the sales call revealed troubling aspects to the applicant's behavior, and she wasn't hired.[72] Finally, some technology companies are hosting "coding competitions" at colleges, where in return for a hefty prize (first-place awards can be as high as $50,000) and a job offer, students can try to develop software or solve a programming problem. The company gets a chance to spread its brand name and a crack at hiring the best applicants who have just proved themselves.[73]

Computer Interaction Performance Tests Versus Paper-and-Pencil Tests. As with ability testing, the computer has made it possible to measure aspects of work that are not possible to measure with a paper-and-pencil test. The computer can capture the complex and dynamic nature of work. This is especially true in work where perceptual and motor performance is required.

An example of how the computer can be used to capture the dynamic nature of service work comes from Suntrust Bank. Suntrust has applicants perform some of the same tasks its tellers perform, such as looking up account information and entering customer data. The candidates' reactions to the scenarios, both mental (e.g., comprehension, coding, calculation) and motor (e.g., typing speed and accuracy), are assessed.[74]

The computer can also be used to capture the complex and dynamic nature of management work. On videotape, Accu Vision shows the candidate actual job situations likely to be encountered. In turn, the candidate selects a behavioral option in response to each situation. The response is entered in the computer and scored according to what it demonstrates of the skills needed to successfully perform as a manager.[75]

Evaluation

Research indicates that performance or work sample tests have a high degree of validity in predicting job performance. One meta-analysis of a large number of studies suggested that the average validity was $\bar{r} = .54$ in predicting job performance.[76] Because performance tests measure the entire job and work samples measure a part of the job, they also have a high degree of content validity. Thus, when one considers the high degree of empirical and content validity, work samples are perhaps the most valid method of selection for many types of jobs.

Performance tests and work samples have other advantages as well. Research indicates that these measures are widely accepted by applicants as being job related. One study found that no applicants complained about performance tests when 10% to 20% complained about other selection procedures.[77] Another study of American workers in a Japanese automotive plant concluded that work sample tests are best able to accommodate cross-cultural values and therefore are well suited for selecting applicants in international joint ventures. Another possible advantage of performance tests and work samples is that they have low degrees of adverse impact, though some recent evidence suggests that they may have more adverse impact than is commonly thought.[78]

Work samples do have several limitations. The costs of the realism embedded in work samples are high. The closer a predictor comes to simulating actual job performance, the more expensive it becomes to use it. Actually having people perform the job, as with an internship, may require paying a wage. Using videotapes and computers adds cost as well. As a result, performance tests and work samples are among the most expensive means of selecting workers. The costs of performance tests and work samples are amplified when one considers the lack of generalizability of such measures. Probably more than any other selection method, performance tests and work samples are tied to the specific job at hand. This means that a different test, based on a thorough analysis of the job, will need to be developed for each job. While their validity may well be worth the cost, in some circumstances the costs of work samples may be prohibitive. One means of mitigating the administrative expense associated with performance tests or work samples is to use a two-stage selection process whereby the full set of applicants is reduced using relatively inexpensive tests. Once the initial cut is made, performance tests or work samples can be administered to the smaller group of applicants who demonstrated minimum competency levels on the first-round tests.[79]

The importance of safety must also be considered as more realism is used in the selection procedure. If actual work is performed, care must be taken so that the candidate's and employer's safety are ensured. When working with dangerous objects or procedures, the candidate must have the knowledge to follow proper procedures. For example, in selecting nurse's aides for a long-term health care facility, it would not be wise to have candidates actually move residents in and out of their beds. Both the untrained candidate and the resident may suffer physical harm if proper procedures are not followed.

Finally, most performance tests and work samples assume that the applicant already possesses the knowledge, skill, ability, and other characteristics (KSAOs) necessary to do the job. If substantial training is involved, applicants will not be able to perform the work sample effectively, even though they could be high performers with adequate training. Thus, if substantial on-the-job training is involved and some or many of the applicants would require this training, work samples simply will not be feasible.

Situational Judgment Tests

A hybrid selection procedure that takes on some of the characteristics of a job knowledge test as well as some of the aspects of a work sample is the situational judgment test. These tests place applicants in hypothetical, job-related situations. Applicants are then asked to choose a course of action from several alternatives. For example, applicants for a 911 operator position may listen to a series of phone calls and be asked to choose the best response from a series of multiple-choice alternatives. Or, applicants to be a member of a project team may be confronted with a scenario in which the team is in conflict and the applicant is asked to choose a method to resolve the conflict. Exhibit 9.7 provides two examples of situational judgment test items.

As one can see, there are similarities between situational judgment tests and job knowledge tests and work samples, so much so that the main differentiation in type of situational judgment tests reflects whether the tests assess knowledge (more similar to job knowledge tests) or behavioral tendency (more similar to work samples). Still, there are distinctions between situational judgment tests and

EXHIBIT 9.7   Examples of Situational Judgment Test Items

Retail Industry Manager

You are the assistant manager of a large department store. One weekend day while you are in charge of the store a customer seeks to return a pair of tennis shoes. The employee in charge of the customer service department refused to accept the return. The customer asked to speak to the manager, and so the employee paged you. Upon meeting the customer—who is clearly agitated—you learn that the customer does not have a receipt, and, moreover, you see that the shoes are clearly well worn. When you ask the customer why she is returning the shoes, she tells you that she has bought many pairs of shoes from your store, and in the past they have "held up much better over time than these." You recognize the shoes as a brand that your store has stocked, so you have no reason to believe the customer is lying when she says that she bought them from your store. Still, the shoes have clearly been worn for a long time. Should you:

a. Issue a refund to the customer
b. Check with your boss—the store manager—when he is at the store on Monday
c. Deny a refund to the customer, explaining that the shoes are simply too worn to be returned
d. Inform the customer of the current sale prices on comparable tennis shoes

Park Ranger

You are a park ranger with the National Park Service, stationed in Yellowstone National Park. One of your current duties is to scout some of the park's more obscure trails to look for signs of lost hikers, to detect any malfeasance, and to inspect the conditions of the trails. It is mid-September, and you're inspecting one of the more remote trails in the Mount Washburn area to determine whether it should be closed for the season. When you set out on your hike, the forecast called for only a slight chance of snow, but midway through your hike, an early fall blizzard has struck. For a time you persisted on, but later you took refuge under a large lodgepole pine tree. Although the storm is now abating, it is near dark. Which of the following would be your best course of action?

a. Stay put until help comes
b. Reverse course and hike back to the ranger station
c. Once the clouds clear, locate the North Star, and hike north to the nearest ranger station
d. Use your matches to build a fire, and hike back in the morning

job knowledge tests and work samples. A job knowledge test more explicitly taps the content of the job (areas that applicants are expected to know immediately upon hire), whereas situational judgment tests are more likely to deal with future hypothetical job situations. Furthermore, job knowledge tests are less "holistic" than situational judgment tests in that the latter are more likely to include video clips and other more realistic material. Situational judgment tests differ from work samples in that the former present applicants with multiple-choice responses to the scenarios, whereas in the latter, applicants actually engage in behavior that is observed by others.

The principal argument in favor of situational judgment tests is to capture the validity of work samples and cognitive ability tests in a way that is cheaper than work samples and that has less adverse impact than cognitive ability tests. How well are these aims achieved? A recent meta-analysis of the validity of situational judgment tests indicated that such tests were reasonably valid correlates of job performance $\bar{r} = .26$).[80] Research also suggests that situational judgment tests have less (but not zero) adverse impact against minorities.[81] Furthermore, video-based situational judgment tests appear to generate positive applicant reactions.[82]

One possible limitation with using situational judgment tests is that while they are easier to administer than work sample tests, and have less adverse impact and more positive applicant reactions than cognitive ability tests, they are not as valid as work sample tests or job knowledge tests. Moreover, because situational judgment tests are generally significantly correlated with cognitive ability ($\bar{r} = .32$) and personality (especially conscientiousness, $\bar{r} = .27$),[83] there is reason to worry about whether situational judgment tests have incremental validity beyond cognitive ability and personality. Some studies have shown that they do.[84] However, other studies have shown little or no incremental validity.[85] In aforementioned meta-analysis, the average incremental validity contributed by situational judgment tests over cognitive ability and personality tests was only $\Delta R = .02$. As the authors note, this is not the last word on the incremental validity of situational judgment tests. However, given the recent attention focused on situational judgment tests, one might well wonder, "Where's the beef?"

If situational judgment tests are used, two operational issues that must be considered are format and scoring. The two main formats of situational judgment tests are written and video. With video tests, applicants first view a video clip that typically involves a role-play episode (e.g., an employee whom the applicant is assumed to supervise asks for advice about a personal matter) and then are asked to choose from a list of responses. Some evidence suggests that video-based situational judgment tests have less adverse impact than written ones and may have higher levels of incremental validity.[86]

Because each possible response must be evaluated for its superiority over the alternatives, scoring situational judgment tests is no small feat. Care needs to be taken in ensuring that the presumed scoring scheme (what's been called the "theoretical scoring scheme") holds up over time. One way to do this, similar to biodata, is to examine the responses chosen by high- vs. low-performing current employees (a so-called empirical scoring scheme).[87]

Integrity Tests

When asked to identify the qualities desired in ideal job applicants, employers routinely put honesty and integrity at the top of their list. In a recent survey, college recruiters were asked to rate the importance of various skills/qualities in job candidates on a 1 = *not important* to 5 = *extremely important* scale. The following skills/qualities were the six most highly rated:[88]

1.	Honesty/integrity	4.7
2.	Communication skills (oral and written)	4.7
3.	Interpersonal skills (relates well to others)	4.5
4.	Motivation/initiative	4.5
5.	Strong work ethic	4.5
6.	Teamwork skills	4.5

Clearly, integrity is an important quality in applicants; integrity tests are designed to tap this important attribute.

Integrity tests are paper-and-pencil or computerized tests that attempt to assess an applicant's honesty and moral character. They are alternatives to other methods—such as polygraph (so-called lie detector) tests or interviewer evaluations that attempt to ascertain an applicant's honesty and morality. For most employers, polygraph tests are prohibited by law. Even if they were legal, polygraphs are so invasive that negative applicant reactions would weigh against their use in most situations. Interviewer evaluations of applicant integrity are, of course, not illegal, but they are unreliable as a method of detecting dishonesty, as dishonesty is very hard to detect. Even experts such as FBI agents, judges, and psychologists scarcely perform above chance in detecting lying. A recent review of 108 studies revealed that people detect lies at a rate that is only 4.2% better than chance.[89] For these reasons, integrity tests are seen as a superior alternative to polygraph tests and interviews, and indeed the use of integrity tests in selection decisions has grown dramatically in the past decade. The tests are especially likely to be used where theft, safety, or malfeasance is an important concern. For example, retail organizations lose an estimated $19 billion per year to employee theft, and it might surprise you to learn that theft due to employees accounts for roughly half (46.8%) of all inventory shrinkage—much greater than that attributed to shoplifting (31.6%).[90] So-called acts of organizational deviance are not just a problem in retailing—nearly every industry has experienced acts of employee theft, sabotage, violence, and other wrongdoing.[91] The promise of integrity testing is that it will weed out those most prone to these counterproductive work behaviors.

Measures
There are two major types of integrity tests: clear purpose (sometimes called overt) and general purpose (sometimes called veiled purpose or personality-oriented). Exhibit 9.8 provides examples of items from both types of measures. Clear purpose tests directly assess employee attitudes toward theft. Such tests often consist of two sections: (1) questions of antitheft attitudes (see items 1–5 in Exhibit 9.8)

EXHIBIT 9.8   Sample Integrity Test Questions

Clear Purpose or Overt Test Questions

1. Do you think most people would cheat if they thought they could get away with it?
2. Do you believe a person has a right to steal from an employer if he or she is unfairly treated?
3. What percentage of people take more than $5 per week (in cash or supplies) from their employer?
4. Do you think most people think much about stealing?
5. Are most people too honest to steal?
6. Do you ever gamble?
7. Did you ever write a check knowing there was not enough money in the bank?
8. Did you make a false insurance claim for personal gain?
9. Have you ever been in serious indebtedness?
10. Have you ever stolen anything?

Veiled Purpose or Personality-Based Test Questions

11. Would you rather go to a party than read a newspaper?
12. How often do you blush?
13. Do you almost always make your bed?
14. Do you like to create excitement?
15. Do you like to take chances?
16. Do you work hard and steady at everything you do?
17. Do you ever talk to authority figures?
18. Are you more sensible than adventurous?
19. Do you think taking chances makes life more interesting?
20. Would you rather "go with the flow" than "rock the boat"?

and (2) questions about the frequency and degree of involvement in theft or other counterproductive activities (see items 6–10 in Exhibit 9.8).[92] General or veiled purpose integrity tests assess employee personality with the idea that personality influences dishonest behavior (see items 11–20 in Exhibit 9.8). The most commonly used clear purpose or overt integrity tests are the *Personnel Selection Inventory* (PSI), the *Reid Report,* and the *Stanton Survey.* The most commonly used general or veiled purpose tests are the *Personnel Reaction Blank,* the *PDI Employment Survey,* and the *Reliability Scale of the Hogan Employment Inventory.*[93]

Some have suggested that integrity represents a sixth personality factor, something unique from the Big Five traits.[94] However, most researchers believe that scores on integrity tests reflect a broad or "compound" personality trait that is a combination of several Big Five personality traits. Specifically, integrity test scores appear to reflect conscientiousness, agreeableness, and emotional stability.[95] Regardless of what aspects of personality integrity tests measure, it appears that integrity tests predict workplace deviance or counterproductive behaviors better than any of the individual Big Five traits.

Validity of Integrity Tests

A major meta-analysis of more than 500,000 people and more than 650 individual studies suggests that integrity tests have surprising levels of validity.[96] The principal findings from this study are the following:

1. Both clear and general purpose integrity tests are valid predictors of counterproductive behaviors (actual and admitted theft, dismissals for theft, illegal activities, absenteeism, tardiness, workplace violence). The average validity for clear purpose measures ($\bar{r} = .55$) was higher than for general purpose ($\bar{r} = .32$).
2. Both clear and general purpose tests were valid predictors of job performance ($\bar{r} = .33$ and $\bar{r} = .35$, respectively).
3. Limiting the analysis to estimates using a predictive validation design and actual detection of theft lowers the validity to $\bar{r} = .13$.
4. Integrity tests have no adverse impact against women or minorities and are relatively uncorrelated with intelligence. Thus, integrity tests demonstrate incremental validity over cognitive ability tests and reduce the adverse impact of cognitive ability tests.

Results from this comprehensive study suggest that organizations would benefit from using integrity tests for a wide array of jobs. Since most of the individual studies included in the meta-analysis were conducted by test publishers (who have an interest in finding good results), however, organizations using integrity tests should consider conducting their own validation studies.

Criticisms and Concerns

Faking. One of the most significant concerns with the use of integrity tests is the obvious possibility that applicants might fake their responses. Consider answering the questions in Exhibit 9.8. Now consider answering these questions in the context of applying for a job that you desire. It seems more than plausible that applicants might distort their responses in such a context (particularly given that most of the answers would be impossible to verify). This possibility becomes a real concern when one considers the prospect that the individuals most likely to "fake good" (people behaving dishonestly) are exactly the type of applicants organizations would want to weed out.

Embedded within the issue of faking are three questions: (1) Can integrity tests be faked? (2) Do applicants fake or enhance their responses to integrity tests? and (3) Does faking harm the validity of the tests, such that a "perverse inversion" occurs where those who get high scores are those who have the least integrity (fake the most)?

First, it is clear that applicants can fake their scores when instructed or otherwise sufficiently motivated to do so, just as they can with personality tests. Studies that compare individuals who are asked to respond honestly with those who are told to "fake good" reveal that, unsurprisingly, integrity test scores in the "fake condition" situation are higher.

Secondly, a problem with interpreting whether applicants *can* fake is that it doesn't tell us whether they indeed *do* fake. After all, job applicants certainly aren't told to "fake good" when completing employment tests, and many applicants may not purposely enhance their responses out of moral reasons (they feel it would be wrong to enhance) or practical reasons (they believe enhancements would be detected). Unfortunately, there is much less evidence on this second question. As one review noted, "A generally unanswered question is whether job applicants actually do fake on integrity tests."[97]

Finally, in terms of whether faking matters, if faking was pervasive, integrity test scores would either have no validity in predicting performance from applicant scores, or have *negative* validity (honest applicants reporting worse scores than dishonest applicants). The fact that validity was positive for applicant samples suggests that if faking does occur, it does not severely impair the predictive validity of integrity tests. It has been suggested that dishonest applicants do not fake more than honest applicants because they believe that everyone is dishonest and therefore they are reporting only what everyone else already does. No matter what the reason, it does seem clear that if faking is a problem, it is not sufficient enough to undermine the validity of the tests.

Misclassification and Stigmatization. Some object to integrity tests on the basis of applicants being misclassified as dishonest.[98] In a sense, this is an odd objection in that all selection procedures involve misclassification of individuals because all selection methods are imperfect (have validities less than 1.0). We think the larger issue is the possible stigmatization of applicants who are thought to be dishonest based on their test scores. These problems can be avoided with proper procedures for maintaining the security and confidentiality of test scores (which, of course, should be done in any case).

Negative Applicant Reactions. A meta-analysis compared applicant reactions to 10 selection procedures, including interviews, work samples, cognitive ability tests, and integrity tests. The results revealed that applicants react negatively to integrity tests—indeed, their favorability ratings were lower than all methods except graphology (handwriting analysis).[99] It is likely that applicants react quite differently to various kinds of integrity test questions, and that applicants' negative reactions might be mollified with explanations and administrative instructions. Unfortunately, there is little published research on these issues.

Interest, Values, and Preference Inventories

Interest, values, and preference inventories attempt to assess the activities individuals prefer to do both on and off the job. This is in comparison with predictors that measure whether the person can do the job. However, just because a person can do a job does not guarantee success on the job. If the person does not want to do the job, that individual will fail regardless of ability. Although interests seem important, they have not been used very much in human resource (HR) selection.

Standardized tests of interests, values, and preferences are available. Many of these measure vocational interests (e.g., the type of career that would motivate and satisfy someone) rather than organizational interests (e.g., the type of job or organization that would motivate and satisfy someone). The two most widely used interest inventories are the *Strong Vocational Interest Blank* (SVIB) and the *Myers-Briggs Type Inventory* (MBTI). Rather than classify individuals along continuous dimensions (e.g., someone is more or less conscientious than another), both the SVIB and the MBTI classify individuals into distinct categories based on their responses to the survey. With the MBTI, individuals are classified into 16 types that have been found to be related to the Big Five personality characteristics discussed earlier.[100] Example interest inventory items are provided in Exhibit 9.9. The SVIB classifies individuals into six categories (realistic, investigative, artistic, social, enterprising, and clerical) that match jobs that are characterized in a corresponding manner. Both of these inventories are used extensively in career counseling in high school, college, and trade schools.

Past research has suggested that interest inventories are not valid predictors of job performance. The average validity of interest inventories in predicting job performance appears to be roughly $\bar{r} = .10$.[101] This does not mean that interest inventories are invalid for all purposes. Research clearly suggests that when individuals' interests match those of their occupation, they are happier with their jobs and are more likely to remain in their chosen occupation.[102] Thus, although interest inventories fail to predict job performance, they do predict occupational choices and job satisfaction levels. Undoubtedly, one of the reasons why vocational interests are poorly related to job performance is because the interests are tied to the occupation rather than the organization or the job.

Research suggests that while interest inventories play an important role in vocational choice, their role in organizational selection decisions is limited. However, a more promising way of considering the role of interests and values in the staffing process is to focus on person/organization fit.[103] As was discussed in Chapter 1, person/organization fit argues that it is not the applicants' characteristics alone that influence performance but rather the interaction between the applicants' characteristics and those of the organization. For example, an individual with a strong interest in social relations at work may perform well in an organization that emphasizes cooperation and teamwork, but the same individual might do poorly in an organization whose culture is characterized by independence or rugged individualism. Thus, interest and value inventories may be more valid when they consider the match between applicant values and organizational values (person/organization fit).[104]

EXHIBIT 9.9   Sample Items From Interest Inventory

1. Are you usually:
   (a) A person who loves parties
   (b) A person who prefers to curl up with a good book?

2. Would you prefer to:
   (a) Run for president
   (b) Fix a car?

3. Is it a higher compliment to be called:
   (a) A compassionate person
   (b) A responsible person?

4. Would you rather be considered:
   (a) Someone with much intuition
   (b) Someone guided by logic and reason?

5. Do you more often:
   (a) Do things on the "spur of the moment"
   (b) Plan out all activities carefully in advance?

6. Do you usually get along better with:
   (a) Artistic people
   (b) Realistic people?

7. With which statement do you most agree?
   (a) Learn what you are, and be such.
   (b) Ah, but a man's reach should exceed his grasp, or what's a heaven for?

8. At parties and social gatherings, do you more often:
   (a) Introduce others
   (b) Get introduced?

Structured Interview

The structured interview is a very standardized, job-related method of assessment. It requires careful and thorough construction, as described in the sections that follow. It is instructive to compare the structured job interview with an unstructured or psychological interview. This comparison will serve to highlight the differences between the two.

A typical unstructured interview has the following characteristics:

- It is often unplanned, informal, and quick, and the interviewer often spends little time preparing for it.
- Rather than being based on the requirements of the job, questions are based on interviewer "hunches" or "pet questions" in order to psychologically diagnose applicant suitability.

- It consists of casual, open-ended, or subjective questioning (e.g., "Tell me a little bit about yourself.").
- It has obtuse questions (e.g., "What type of animal would you most like to be, and why?").
- It has highly speculative questions (e.g., "Where do you see yourself 10 years from now?").
- The interviewer makes a quick, and final, evaluation of the candidate (often in the first couple of minutes).

Despite its continued prevalence—it remains the most widely used substantive selection procedure—research shows that organizations clearly pay a price for the use of the unstructured interview, namely, lower reliability and validity.[105] Interviewers using the unstructured interview are unable to agree among themselves in their evaluation of job candidates and cannot predict the job success of candidates with any degree of consistent accuracy.

Over the years, research has unraveled the reasons why the unstructured interview does not work well and what factors need to be changed to improve reliability and validity. Sources of error or bias in the unstructured interview include the following:[106]

- Reliability of the unstructured interview is relatively low. Interviewers base their evaluations on different factors, have different hiring standards, and differ in the degree to which their actual selection criteria match their intended criteria.
- Applicant physical attractiveness has consistently been shown to predict interviewer evaluations.
- Negative information receives more weight than positive information in the interview. Research suggests it takes more than twice as much positive information as negative information to change an interviewer's initial impression of an applicant. As a result, the unstructured interview has been labeled a "search for negative evidence."
- Interviewers tend to make snap decisions—people's first impressions form after only 1/10 of one second, and the majority of interviewers make their decisions after the first few minutes of the interview.
- Interviewers place weight on superficial background characteristics such as names and the presence of accents. One study found that when responding to actual employment ads in Boston and Chicago, fictitious applicants with the first names of Allison and Brad were twice as likely to receive interview invitations than individuals with the first names of Kenya and Hakim, even though the résumés were otherwise identical.
- Similarity effects, where applicants who are similar to the interviewer with respect to race, gender, or other characteristics receive higher ratings, also exist.

- Poor recall by interviewers often plagues unstructured interviews. One study demonstrated this by giving managers an exam based on factual information after watching a 20-minute videotaped interview. Some managers got all 20 questions correct, but the average manager got only half right.

Thus, the unstructured interview is not very valid, and research has identified the reasons why this is so. The structured interview is an attempt to eliminate the biases inherent in unstructured formats by standardizing the process.

Characteristics of Structured Interviews

There are numerous hallmarks of structured interviews. Some of the more prominent characteristics are (1) questions are based on job analysis; (2) the same questions are asked of each candidate; (3) the response to each question is numerically evaluated; (4) detailed anchored rating scales are used to score each response; and (5) detailed notes are taken, particularly focusing on interviewees' behaviors.[107]

There are two principal types of structured interviews: situational and experience based. Situational interviews assess an applicant's ability to project what his or her behavior would be in future hypothetical situations.[108] The assumption behind the use of the situational interview is that the goals or intentions individuals set for themselves are good predictors of what they will do in the future.

Experience-based or job-related interviews assess past behaviors that are linked to the prospective job. The assumption behind the use of experience-based interviews is the same as that for the use of biodata—past behavior is a good predictor of future behavior. It is assumed that applicants who are likely to succeed have demonstrated success with past job experiences similar to the experiences they would encounter in the prospective job. An example of an experience-based interview is the *Patterned Behavior Description Interview,* which collects four types of experiential information during the interview: (1) *credentials* (objective verifiable information about past experiences and accomplishments); (2) *experience descriptions* (descriptions of applicant's normal job duties, capabilities, and responsibilities); (3) *opinions* (applicant's thoughts about his or her strengths, weaknesses, and self-perceptions); (4) *behavior descriptions* (detailed accounts of actual events from the applicant's job and life experiences).[109]

Situational and experience-based interviews have many similarities. Generally, both are based on the critical incidents approach to job analysis, where job behaviors especially important to (as opposed to typically descriptive of) job performance are considered. Also, both approaches attempt to assess applicant *behaviors* rather than feelings, motives, values, or other psychological states. Finally, both methods have substantial reliability and validity evidence in their favor.

On the other hand, situational and experience-based interviews have important differences. The most obvious difference is that situational interviews are future oriented ("what *would* you do if?"), whereas experience-based interviews are past oriented ("what *did* you do when?"). Also, situational interviews are more standardized in that they ask the same questions of all applicants, while many experience-based interviews place an emphasis on discretionary probing based on responses to particular questions. Presently, there is little basis to guide decisions about which of these two types of structured interviews should be adopted. However, one factor to consider is that experience-based interviews may only be relevant for individuals who have had significant job experience. It does not make much sense to ask applicants what they did in a particular situation if they have never been in that situation. Another relevant factor is complexity of the job. Situational interviews fare worse than experience-based interviews when the job is complex. This may be because it is hard to simulate the nature of complex jobs.

Evaluation

Traditionally, the employment interview was thought to have a low degree of validity. Recently, however, evidence for the validity of structured (and even unstructured) interviews has been much more positive. Meta-analyses have suggested the following conclusions:[110]

1. The average validity of interviews is $\bar{r} = .37$.
2. Structured interviews are more valid ($\bar{r} = .31$) than unstructured interviews ($\bar{r} = .23$).
3. The literature on whether situational or experienced-based interviews are more valid is not consistent. The largest meta-analysis found that situational interviews were more valid ($\bar{r} = .35$) than experience-based interviews ($\bar{r} = .28$). However, a more recent meta-analysis found the opposite.
4. Panel interviews may be *less* valid ($\bar{r} = .22$) than individual interviews ($\bar{r} = .31$).

Given the advantages of structured interviews, their lack of use is perplexing—whereas 99% of organizations indicate they use the interview in selection, only slightly more than half (55%) claim to use a structured interview. As one review concluded, "Structured interviews are infrequently used in practice." Like all of us, selection decision makers show considerable inertia and continue to use the unstructured interview because they always have, and because they favor expediency over quality. Thus, a cycle of past practice generating continued use needs to be broken by changing the climate. The best way to do this is to educate decision makers about the benefits of structured interviews.[111]

Applicants tend to react very favorably to the interview, whether it is structured or not. Research suggests that most applicants believe the interview is an essential component of the selection process, and most view the interview as the most suitable measure of relevant abilities. As a result, the interview has been rated by applicants as more job related than any other selection procedure.[112]

The interview appears to have moderate adverse impact against minorities—more than personality tests but considerably less than cognitive ability tests.[113]

The process of structuring an interview requires that organizations follow a systematic and standardized process. For purposes of illustration, we describe development of a situational interview.

Constructing a Structured Interview

The structured interview, by design and conduct, standardizes and controls for sources of influence on the interview process and the interviewer. The goal is to improve interview reliability and validity beyond that of the unstructured interview. Research shows that this goal can be achieved; doing so requires following each of these steps: consult the job requirements matrix, develop the selection plan, develop the structured interview plan, select and train interviewers, and evaluate effectiveness. Each of these steps is elaborated on next.

The Job Requirements Matrix and Selection Plan

The starting point for the structured interview is the job requirements matrix. It identifies the tasks and KSAOs that define the job requirements around which the structured interview is constructed and conducted.

Because the selection plan flows from the KSAOs identified in the job requirements matrix, it helps identify which KSAOs are necessary to assess during selection, and whether the structured interview is the preferred method of assessing them.

Is the KSAO Necessary? Some KSAOs must be brought to the job by the candidate, and others can be acquired on the job (through training and/or job experience). The bring-it/acquire-it decision must be made for each KSAO. This decision should be guided by the importance indicator(s) for the KSAOs in the job requirements matrix.

Is the Structured Interview the Preferred Method? It must be decided if the structured interview is the preferred method of assessing each KSAO necessary for selection. Several factors should be considered when making this decision. The structured interview is probably best suited for assessing only the more interpersonal or face-to-face skills and abilities, such as communication and interpersonal skills.

An example of a selection plan for the job of sales associate in a retail clothing store is shown in Exhibit 9.10. While there were five task dimensions for the job in the job requirements matrix (customer service, use of machines, use of customer service outlets, sales and departmental procedures, cleaning and maintenance), the selection plan is shown only for the dimension of customer service.

Note in the exhibit that the customer service dimension has several required KSAOs. However, only some of these will be assessed during selection, and only

EXHIBIT 9.10   Partial Selection Plan for Job of Retail Store Sales Associate

Task Dimension: Customer Service

KSAO	Necessary for Selection?	Method of Assessment
1. Ability to make customer feel welcome	Yes	Interview
2. Knowledge of merchandise to be sold	Yes	Written test
3. Knowledge of location of merchandise in store	No	None
4. Skill in being cordial with customers	Yes	Interview
5. Ability to create and convey ideas to customers ...	Yes	Interview

some of those will be assessed by the structured interview. The method of assessment is thus carefully targeted to the KSAO to be assessed.

The Structured Interview Plan

Development of the structured interview plan proceeds along three sequential steps: construction of interview questions, construction of benchmark responses for the questions, and weighting of the importance of the questions. The output of this process for the sales associate job is shown in Exhibit 9.11 and is referred to in the discussion that follows.

Constructing Questions.   One or more questions must be constructed for each KSAO targeted for assessment by the structured interview. Care must be taken to ensure that questions reflect a sampling of the candidate's behavior, as revealed by past situations (behavioral description) or what the candidate reports would be his or her behavior in future situations (situational). The questions ask in essence, "What have you done in this situation?" and "What would you do if you were in this situation?"

The key to constructing both types of questions is to create a scenario relevant to the KSAO in question and to ask the candidate to respond to it by way of answering a question. If one plans on considering applicants with limited prior experience, future-oriented or situational questions should be favored over behavioral description questions, since not all applicants will have been in the situation previously.

Exhibit 9.11 shows three questions for the KSAOs to be assessed by the interview, as determined by the initial selection plan for the job of sales associate in a retail store. As can be seen, all three questions present very specific situations that a sales associate is likely to encounter. The content of all three questions is clearly job relevant, a logical outgrowth of the process that began with the development of the job requirements matrix.

EXHIBIT 9.11 Structured Interview Questions, Benchmark Responses, Rating Scale, and Question Weights

Job: Sales Associate
Task Dimension: Customer Service

	Rating Scale				Rating	×	Weight	=	Score
	1	2	3	4	5				

Question No. One (KSAO 1)
A customer walks into the store. No other salespeople are around to help the person, and you are busy arranging merchandise. What would you do if you were in this situation?

Rating scale: 1 — Keep on arranging merchandise; 3 — Keep working, but greet the customer; 5 — Stop working, greet customer, and offer to provide assistance.
Rating 5 × Weight 1 = Score 5

Question No. Two (KSAO 4)
A customer is in the fitting room and asks you to bring her some shirts to try on. You do so, but by accident bring the wrong size. The customer becomes irate and starts shouting at you. What would you do if you were in this situation?

Rating scale: 1 — Tell customer to "keep her cool"; 3 — Go get correct size; 5 — Apologize, go get correct size.
Rating 3 × Weight 1 = Score 3

Question No. Three (KSAO 5)
A customer is shopping for the "right" shirt for her 17-year-old granddaughter. She asks you to show her shirts that you think would be "right" for her. You do this, but the customer doesn't like any of them. What would you do if you were in this situation?

Rating scale: 1 — Tell customer to go look elsewhere; 3 — Explain why you think your choices are good ones; 5 — Explain your choices, suggest gift certificate as alternative.
Rating 5 × Weight 2 = Score 10

Total: 18

Benchmark Responses and Rating Scales. The interviewer must somehow evaluate or judge the quality of the candidate's response to the interview questions. Prior development of benchmark responses and corresponding rating scales is the method for providing firm guidance to the interviewer in doing this task. Benchmark responses represent qualitative examples of the types of candidate responses that the interviewer may encounter. They are located on a rating scale (usually 1–5 or 1–7 rating scale points) to represent the level or "goodness" of the response.

Exhibit 9.11 contains benchmark responses, positioned on a 1–5 rating scale, for each of the three interview questions. Note that all the responses are quite specific, and they clearly suggest that some answers are better than others. These responses represent judgments on the part of the organization as to the desirability of behaviors its employees could engage in.

Weighting Responses. Each candidate will receive a total score for the structured interview. It thus must be decided whether each question is of equal importance in contributing to the total score. If so, the candidate's total interview score is simply the sum of the scores on the individual rating scales. If some questions are more important than others in assessing candidates, then those questions receive greater weight. The more important the question, the greater its weight relative to the other questions.

Exhibit 9.11 shows the weighting decided on for the three interview questions. As can be seen, the first two questions receive a weight of 1, and the third question receives a weight of 2. The candidate's assigned ratings are multiplied by their weights and then summed to determine a total score for this particular task dimension. In the exhibit, the candidate receives a score of 18 (5 + 3 + 10 = 18) for customer service. The candidate's total interview score would be the sum of the scores on all the dimensions.

Selection and Training of Interviewers

Some interviewers are more accurate in their judgments than others. In fact, several studies have found significant differences in interviewer validity.[114] Thus, rather than asking, "How valid is the interview?" it might be more appropriate to ask, "Who is a valid interviewer?" Answering this question requires selecting interviewers based on characteristics that will enable them to make accurate decisions about applicants. Little research is available regarding the factors that should guide selection of interviewers. Perhaps not surprisingly, cognitive ability has been linked to accuracy in evaluating others. It would also be possible to design an interview simulation where prospective interviewers are asked to analyze jobs to determine applicant KSAOs, preview applications, conduct hypothetical interviews, and evaluate applicants.

Training interviewers is another means of increasing the validity of structured interviews. Interviewers will probably need training in the structured interview process, as the process is probably quite different from what they have encountered and/or used; training becomes a way of introducing them to the process. Logical program content areas to be covered as part of the training are the following:

- Problems with the unstructured interview
- Advantages of the structured interview
- Development of the structured interview
- Use of note taking and elimination of rating errors
- Actual practice in conducting the structured interview

Research on whether interviewer training works is inconsistent. One review concluded that the evidence regarding the ability of training programs to reduce rating errors showed that these programs "have achieved at best mixed results."[115] However, a more recent study revealed that an interviewer training program was effective, in no small part because it increased the degree to which a structured format was followed.[116] Given that interviewers tend not to use structured formats, this is a key advantage.

Evaluating Effectiveness

As with any assessment device, there is a constant need to learn more about the reliability, validity, and utility of the structured interview. This is particularly so because of the complexity of the interview process. Thus, evaluation of the structured interview's effectiveness should be built directly into the process itself.

Selection for Team Environments

Decades ago, when companies like W. L. Gore and General Foods used work teams, it was news. Nowadays, of course, teams are pervasive. One of the main reasons organizations have turned to teams is that they feel teams are more flexible and responsive to changing events. They may also believe that teams operate more efficiently than individuals working alone. Or, they may wish to make teamwork a part of their culture as a way to democratize themselves and increase employee motivation.[117]

There are as many types of teams as there are configurations of individuals. However, teams can be clustered into four categories:[118] (1) *problem-solving teams*, or teams where members share ideas or offer suggestions on how work processes can be improved (though they rarely have the authority to unilaterally implement any of their suggested actions); (2) *self-managed work teams*, where groups of typically 10–15 employees perform highly related or interdependent jobs and take on many of the responsibilities of their former supervisors; (3) *cross-functional teams*, or teams made up of employees from roughly the same hierarchical level but from different work areas or functions; and (4) *virtual teams*, or teams that use computers to tie together physically dispersed members in order to achieve a common goal or work on a single project.

No matter the reason for the existence of teams, or the type of team involved, teamwork means revisiting the way work is done in an organization, which necessarily affects how positions are staffed.

The first step in understanding the proper steps for selection in team-based environments is to understand the requirements of the job. A recent analysis of the KSAOs for teamwork is presented in Exhibit 9.12. Identified in the exhibit are 2 major categories of KSAs for teamwork, 5 subcategories, and 14 specific KSAs (the "other" category was not considered in the study). Thus, in order to be effective in a teamwork assignment, an employee needs to demonstrate *interpersonal KSAs* (consisting of conflict resolution, collaborative problem solving, and communication KSAs) and *self-management KSAs* (consisting of goal setting and performance management KSAs and planning and task coordination KSAs). The implication of this framework for selection is that existing selection processes and methods may need to be revamped to incorporate these KSAs.

One means of incorporating team-based KSAs into the existing selection process has been developed.[119] Exhibit 9.13 provides some sample items from the 35-item test. This test has been validated against three criteria (teamwork performance, technical performance, and overall performance) in two studies.[120] The teamwork test showed substantial validity in predicting teamwork and overall performance in one of the studies, but no validity in predicting any of the criteria in the other study. (It is not clear why the teamwork test worked well in one study and not in the other.) It should be noted that tests are not the only method of measuring teamwork KSAs. Other methods of assessment that some leading companies have used in selecting team members include structured interviews, assessment centers, personality tests, and biographical inventories.[121] For example, the PCI personality test described earlier has a special scale that is designed to predict team performance. Furthermore, a study of 51 manufacturing teams revealed that teams composed of members who, on average, scored high on agreeableness, conscientiousness, and emotional stability outperformed other teams.[122] Thus, personality testing may be a useful means of staffing team positions.

Another important decision in team member selection is who should make the hiring decisions. In many cases, team assessments are made by members of the self-directed work team in deciding who becomes a member of the group. An example of an organization following this procedure is South Bend, Indiana–based I/N Tek, a billion-dollar steel-finishing mill established in a joint venture between the United States' Inland Steel and Japan's Nippon Steel. Employees in self-directed work teams, along with managers and HR professionals, interview candidates as a final step in the selection process. This approach is felt to lead to greater satisfaction with the results of the hiring process because employees have a say in which person is selected to be part of the team.[123]

Thus, staffing processes and methods in team environments require modifications from the traditional approaches to selection. Before organizations go to the trouble and expense of modifying these procedures, however, it would be wise to examine whether the team initiatives are likely to be successful. Many teams fail because they are implemented as an isolated practice.[124] Thus, before overhauling

---

EXHIBIT 9.12   Knowledge, Skill, and Ability (KSA) Requirements for Teamwork

I. INTERPERSONAL KSAs
  A. Conflict-Resolution KSAs
    1. The KSA to recognize and encourage desirable, but discourage undesirable, team conflict.
    2. The KSA to recognize the type and source of conflict confronting the team and to implement an appropriate conflict-resolution strategy.
    3. The KSA to employ an integrative (win-win) negotiation strategy rather than the traditional distributive (win-lose) strategy.

  B. Collaborative Problem-Solving KSAs
    4. The KSA to identify situations requiring participative group problem solving and to utilize the proper degree and type of participation.
    5. The KSA to recognize the obstacles to collaborative group problem solving and implement appropriate corrective actions.

  C. Communication KSAs
    6. The KSA to understand communication networks and to utilize decentralized networks to enhance communication where possible.
    7. The KSA to communicate openly and supportively, that is, to send messages which are: (1) behavior- or event-oriented, (2) congruent, (3) validating, (4) conjunctive, and (5) owned.
    8. The KSA to listen nonevaluatively and to appropriately use active listening techniques.
    9. The KSA to maximize consonance between nonverbal and verbal messages and to recognize and interpret the nonverbal messages of others.
    10. The KSA to engage in ritual greetings and small talk and a recognition of their importance.

II. SELF-MANAGEMENT KSAs
  D. Goal-Setting and Performance-Management KSAs
    11. The KSA to help establish specific, challenging, and accepted team goals.
    12. The KSA to monitor, evaluate, and provide feedback on both overall team performance and individual team member performance.

  E. Planning and Task-Coordination KSAs
    13. The KSA to coordinate and synchronize activities, information, and task interdependencies between team members.
    14. The KSA to help establish task and role expectations of individual team members and to ensure proper balancing of workload in the team.

Source: M. J. Stevens and M. A. Campion, "The Knowledge, Skill, and Ability Requirements for Teamwork: Implications for Human Resource Management," *Journal of Management*, 1994, 20, pp. 503–530. With permission from Elsevier Science.

EXHIBIT 9.13 Example Items Assessing Teamwork KSAs

1. Suppose that you find yourself in an argument with several coworkers about who should do a very disagreeable but routine task. Which of the following would likely be the most effective way to resolve this situation?
   A. Have your supervisor decide, because this would avoid any personal bias.
   B. Arrange for a rotating schedule so everyone shares the chore.
   C. Let the workers who show up earliest choose on a first-come, first-served basis.
   D. Randomly assign a person to do the task and don't change it.

2. Your team wants to improve the quality and flow of the conversations among its members. Your team should:
   A. Use comments that build on and connect to what others have said.
   B. Set up a specific order for everyone to speak and then follow it.
   C. Let team members with more to say determine the direction and topic of conversation.
   D. Do all of the above.

3. Suppose you are presented with the following types of goals. You are asked to pick one for your team to work on. Which would you choose?
   A. An easy goal to ensure the team reaches it, thus creating a feeling of success.
   B. A goal of average difficulty so the team will be somewhat challenged, but successful without too much effort.
   C. A difficult and challenging goal that will stretch the team to perform at a high level, but attainable so that effort will not be seen as futile.
   D. A very difficult, or even impossible goal so that even if the team falls short, it will at least have a very high target to aim for.

Source: M. J. Stevens and M. A. Campion, "The Knowledge, Skill, and Ability Requirements for Teamwork: Implications for Human Resource Management," *Journal of Management*, 1994, 20, pp. 503–530. With permission from Elsevier Science.

selection practices in an effort to build teams, care must be taken to ensure the proper context for these environments in the first place.

Choice of Substantive Assessment Methods

As with the choice of initial assessment methods, there has been a large amount of research conducted on substantive assessment methods that can help guide organizations in the appropriate methods to use. Reviews of this research, using the same criteria that were used to evaluate initial assessment methods, are shown in Exhibit 9.14. Specifically, the criteria are use, cost, reliability, validity, utility, applicant reactions, and adverse impact.

EXHIBIT 9.14 Evaluation of Substantive Assessment Methods

Predictors	Use	Cost	Reliability	Validity	Utility	Reactions	Adverse Impact
Personality tests	Low	Low	High	Moderate	?	Negative	Low
Ability tests	Low	Low	High	High	High	Negative	High
Job knowledge tests	Moderate	Moderate	High	High	?	Neutral	?
Performance tests and work samples	Moderate	High	High	High	High	Positive	Low
Situational judgment tests	Low	High	Moderate	Moderate	?	Positive	Moderate
Integrity tests	Low	Low	High	High	High	Negative	Low
Interest, value, and preference inventories	Low	Low	High	Low	?	?	Low
Structured interviews	Moderate	High	Moderate	High	?	Positive	Mixed
Team assessments	Low	Moderate	?	?	?	Positive	?

Use

As can be seen in Exhibit 9.14, there are no widely used (at least two-thirds of all organizations) substantive assessment methods. Job knowledge tests, structured interviews, and performance tests and work samples have moderate degrees of use. The other substantive methods are only occasionally or infrequently used by organizations.

Cost

The costs of substantive assessment methods vary widely. Some methods can be purchased from vendors quite inexpensively (personality tests; ability tests; interest, value, and preference inventories; integrity tests)—often for less than $2 per applicant. (Of course, the costs of administering and scoring the tests must be factored in.) Some methods, such as job knowledge tests or team assessments, can vary in price depending on whether the organization develops the measure itself or purchases it from a vendor. Other methods, such as structured interviews, performance tests and work samples, and situational judgment tests, generally require extensive time and resources to develop; thus, these measures are the most expensive substantive assessment methods.

Reliability

The reliability of all the substantive assessment methods is moderate or high. Generally, this is true because many of these methods have undergone extensive development efforts by vendors. However, whether an organization purchases an assessment tool from a vendor or develops it independently, the reliability of the method must be investigated. Just because a vendor claims a method is reliable does not necessarily mean it will be so within a particular organization.

Validity

Like cost, the validity of substantive assessment methods varies a great deal. Some methods, such as interest, value, and preference inventories, have demonstrated little validity in past research. As was noted when reviewing these measures, however, steps can be taken to increase their validity. Some methods, such as personality tests and structured interviews, have at least moderate levels of validity. Some structured interviews have high levels of validity, but the degree to which they add validity beyond cognitive ability tests remains in question. Finally, ability tests, performance tests and work samples, job knowledge tests, and integrity tests have high levels of validity. As with many structured interviews, while the validity of job knowledge tests is high, the degree to which job knowledge is important in predicting job performance beyond cognitive ability is suspect. Integrity tests are moderate to high predictors of job performance; their validity in predicting other important job behaviors (counterproductive work behaviors) appears to be quite high.

Utility

As with initial assessment methods, the utility of most substantive assessment methods is unknown. A great deal of research has shown that the utility of ability tests (in particular, cognitive ability tests) is quite high. Performance tests and work samples and integrity tests also appear to have high levels of utility.

Applicant Reactions

Research is just beginning to emerge concerning applicant reactions to substantive assessment methods. From the limited research that has been conducted, however, applicants' reactions to substantive assessment methods appear to depend on the particular method. Relatively abstract methods that require an applicant to answer questions not directly tied to the job (i.e., questions on personality tests, most ability tests, and integrity tests) seem to generate negative reactions from applicants. Thus, research tends to suggest that personality, ability, and integrity tests are viewed unfavorably by applicants. Methods that are manifestly related to the job for which applicants are applying appear to generate positive reactions. Thus, research suggests that applicants view performance tests and work samples and structured interviews favorably. Job knowledge tests, perhaps because they are neither wholly abstract nor totally experiential, appear to generate neutral reactions.

Adverse Impact

A considerable amount of research has been conducted on adverse impact of some substantive assessment methods. In particular, research suggests that personality tests, performance tests and work samples, and integrity tests have little adverse impact against women or minorities. In the past, interest, value, and preference inventories had substantial adverse impact against women, but this problem has been corrected. Conversely, ability tests have a high degree of adverse impact. In particular, cognitive ability tests have substantial adverse impact against minorities, while physical ability tests have significant adverse impact against women. The adverse impact of structured interviews was denoted as mixed. While evidence suggests that many structured interviews have little adverse impact against women or minorities, other evidence suggests some adverse impact. Furthermore, since even structured interviews have an element of subjectivity to them, the potential always exists for interviewer bias to enter into the process. There are too few data to draw conclusions about the adverse impact of clinical assessments and job knowledge tests.

   A comparison of Exhibits 8.8 and 9.14 is instructive. In general, both the validity and the cost of substantive assessment procedures are higher than those of initial assessment procedures. As with the initial assessment procedures, the economic and social impact of substantive assessment procedures is not well understood. Many initial assessment methods are widely used, whereas most substantive assessment methods have moderate or low degrees of use. Thus, many organizations rely on initial assessment methods to make substantive assessment decisions.

This is unfortunate, because, with the exception of biographical data, the validity of substantive assessment methods is higher. This is especially true of the initial interview relative to the structured interview. At a minimum, organizations need to supplement the initial interview with structured interviews. Better yet, organizations should strongly consider using ability, performance, personality, and work sample tests along with either interview.

DISCRETIONARY ASSESSMENT METHODS

Discretionary assessment methods are used to separate those who receive job offers from the list of finalists. Sometimes discretionary methods are not used, because all finalists may receive job offers. When used, discretionary assessment methods are typically highly subjective and rely heavily on the intuition of the decision maker. Thus, factors other than KSAOs may be assessed. Organizations intent on maintaining strong cultures may wish to consider assessing the person/organization match at this stage of the selection process.

Another interesting method of discretionary assessment that focuses on person/organization match is the selection of people on the basis of likely organizational citizenship behavior.[125] With this approach, finalists not only must fulfill all of the requirements of the job but also are expected to fulfill some roles outside the requirements of the job, called organizational citizenship behaviors. These behaviors include things like doing extra work, helping others at work, covering for a sick coworker, and being courteous.

Discretionary assessments should involve use of the organization's staffing philosophy regarding equal employment opportunity and affirmative action (EEO/AA) commitments. Here, the commitment may be to enhance the representation of minorities and women in the organization's workforce, either voluntarily or as part of an organization's affirmative action plans and programs (AAPs). At this point in the selection process, the demographic characteristics of the finalists may be given weight in the decision about to whom the job offer will be extended. Regardless of how the organization chooses to make its discretionary assessments, they should never be used without being preceded by initial and substantive methods.

CONTINGENT ASSESSMENT METHODS

As was shown in Exhibit 8.3, contingent methods are not always used, depending on the nature of the job and legal mandates. Virtually any selection method can be used as a contingent method. For example, a health clinic may verify that an applicant for a nursing position possesses a valid license after a tentative offer has been made. Similarly, a defense contractor may perform a security clearance check on applicants once initial, substantive, and discretionary methods have been exhausted. While these methods may be used as initial or contingent methods, depending on the preferences of the organization, two selection methods, drug testing and medical exams, should be used exclusively as contingent assessment methods for legal compliance. When drug testing and medical exams are used, considerable care must be taken in their administration and evaluation.

Drug Testing

More than 70% of substance abusers hold jobs, and substance abuse has been identified as a major cause of workplace violence, accidents, absenteeism, and increased health care costs. A workplace study revealed that the average drug user was 3.6 times more likely to be involved in an accident, received 3 times the average level of sick benefits, was 5 times more likely to file a workers' compensation claim, and missed 10 times as many work days as nonusers.[126] One comprehensive study found that over an 11-year period, approximately 50 train accidents were attributed to workers under the influence of drugs or alcohol. These accidents resulted in 37 people killed, 80 injured, and the destruction of property valued at $34 million. A National Transportation Safety Board study found that 31% of all fatal truck accidents were due to alcohol or drugs.[127]

As a result of the manifold problems caused by drug use, many employers have drug testing programs to screen out drug users. Drug testing grew dramatically throughout the 1980s and 1990s, though there is reason to believe that its growth has peaked. A study by the American Management Association found that drug testing in the workplace peaked in 1996, when 81% of employers screened workers and applicants, and then declined steadily to 62% in 2004 (it was up slightly, to 66%, by 2006).[128]

One of the reasons drug testing has declined is shown in Exhibit 9.15.[129] As the exhibit shows, drug tests do not "catch" many people. Far and away, the highest positive test rate is marijuana, and it is only 2.54%—meaning that only 2.54% of applicants tested positive for marijuana. Overall, only 3.8% tested positive (the positive results in the exhibit add up to more than 3.8% because some applicants tested positive for more than one drug). The 3.8% positive rate means that if an organization tested 100 applicants, only about 4 would fail the test (i.e., test positive). The positive rate has dropped over time—indeed, the largest provider of employer drug testing says that positive tests are at a 17-year low. The decline is probably due to a combination of factors, including lower drug use in the population and the deterrent effect of the drug tests themselves (if an individual has used drugs recently and is aware that the organization tests for drugs, he or she won't apply). It may also reflect applicants "gaming" the tests (diluting, adulterating, substituting samples); though, as we note shortly, if properly conducted, drug tests are difficult to fake.

Types of Tests
There are a variety of tests to ascertain substance abuse. The major categories of tests are the following:[130]

EXHIBIT 9.15   Percent of Applicants Testing Positive by Drug Category

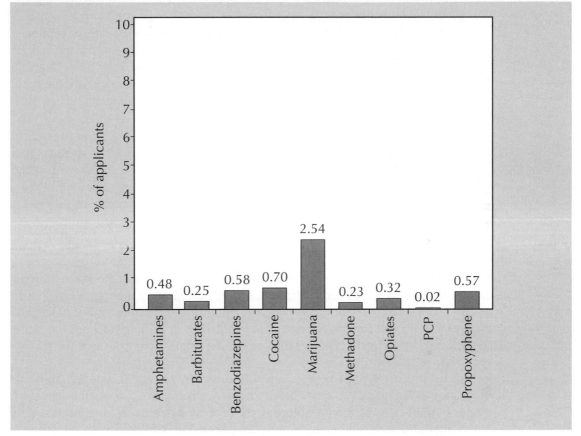

SOURCE: *Amphetamines Use Declined Significantly Among U.S. Workers in 2005, According to Quest Diagnostics' Drug Testing Index,* Quest Diagnostics Incorporated, 2006.

1. *Body fluids.* Both urine and blood tests can be used. Urine tests are by far the most frequently used method of detecting substance abuse. There are different types of measures for each test. For example, urine samples can be measured using the enzyme-multiplied immunoassay technique or the gas chromatography/spectrometry technique. The latest innovation in drug testing allows companies to test applicants and receive results on the spot. It uses a strip that is dipped into a urine sample, similar to a home pregnancy test.

2. *Hair analysis.* Samples of hair are analyzed using the same techniques as are used to measure urine samples. Chemicals remain in the hair as it grows, so it can provide a longer record of drug use (however, hair analysis is more expensive than urinalysis).

3. *Pupillary reaction test.* The reaction of the pupil to light is assessed. The pupils will react differently when the applicant is under the influence of drugs than when the applicant is drug free.

4. *Performance tests.* Hand-eye coordination is assessed to see if there is impairment compared with the standard drug-free reactions. One of the limitations of performance tests in a selection context is that there may be no feasible means of establishing a baseline against which performance is compared. Thus, performance tests are usually more suitable for testing employees than applicants.

5. *Integrity test.* Many integrity tests contain a section that asks applicants about drug use. The section on substance abuse often includes 20 or so items that inquire about past and present drug use (e.g., "I only drink at work when things get real stressful") as well as attitudes toward drug use (e.g., "How often do you think the average employee smokes marijuana on the job?"). Of course, such tests are susceptible to denial or deliberate falsification.

Administration

For the results of drug tests to be accurate, precautions must be taken in their administration. When collecting samples to be tested, care must be exercised to ensure that the sample is authentic and not contaminated. To do so, the U.S. Department of Health and Human Services has established specific guidelines that must be followed by federal agencies (and are good guidelines to follow in the private sector as well).[131]

The testing itself must be carefully administered as well. Large labs process thousands of samples per day. Hence, human error can occur in the detection process. Also, false-positive results can be generated due to cross-reactions. This means that a common compound (e.g., poppy seeds) may interact with the antibodies and mistakenly identify a person as a substance abuser. Prescription medications may also affect drug test results. One new complicating factor in evaluating drug test results is the use of adulterants that mask the detection of certain drugs in the system. Although most adulterants can be tested, not all are easily detected, and many firms are unaware they can ask drug companies to test for adulterants.

In order for the testing to be carefully administered, two steps need to be taken. First, care must be taken in the selection of a reputable drug testing firm. Various certification programs, such as the College of American Pathologists and the National Institute for Drug Abuse (NIDA), exist to ensure that accurate procedures are followed. More than 50 drug testing laboratories have been certified by NIDA. Second, positive drug tests should always be verified by a second test to ensure reliability.

What would a well-conducted drug testing program look like?[132] Samples are first submitted to screening tests, which are relatively inexpensive ($25–$45 per applicant), but yield many false positives (test indicates drug use when none occurred) due to the cross-reactions described above. Confirmatory tests are then used, which are extremely accurate but more expensive. Error rates for confirmatory tests with reputable labs are very low. It should be noted that to avoid false positives, most organizations have nonzero cutoff levels for most drugs. Thus, if a mistake does occur, it is much more likely to be a false negative (testing negative when in fact drug use did occur) than a false positive. Thus, some applicants who occasionally use drugs may pass a test, but it is very rare for an individual who has never used the drug to fail the test—assuming the two-step process described above is followed. Exhibit 9.16 outlines the steps involved in a well-designed drug testing program. In this example:

- Applicants are advised in advance of testing.
- All applicants are screened by urine testing.
- Prescreening is done in-house; positives are referred to an independent lab.
- A strict chain of custody is followed.
- Verified positive applicants are disqualified.
- Disqualified applicants cannot reapply for two years.

EXHIBIT 9.16   Example of an Organizational Drug Testing Program

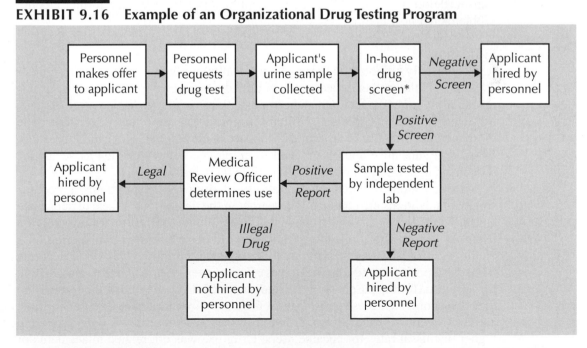

* Most organizations screen for five drugs: amphetamines, cocaine, cannabinoids (e.g., marijuana, hashish), opiates (morphine, heroin), and phencyclidine (PCP).

The Other Drugs: Smoking and Alcohol

Some employers are beginning to ban smokers from hiring consideration. A recent study estimated that about 6% of employers will not hire smokers (urinalysis also picks up nicotine). Such policies are usually aimed at cutting insurance costs (smoking costs employers $27 billion annually), absence rates (smokers' absence rates are 50% higher than those of nonsmokers), and potential liability due to the dangers of secondary smoke. However, about half the states have passed laws prohibiting discrimination against off-the-job smoking. Thus, while some employers may wish to screen out smokers to lower health care costs, the myriad legal and ethical issues make it a risky selection practice.

As for alcohol, few employers test applicants for alcohol use for two reasons. First, because alcohol use is legal, and far more socially accepted than use of other mood-altering drugs, most employers have no desire to test applicants for alcohol; doing so would exclude large numbers of applicants. A second reason alcohol testing is infrequently used is because alcohol remains in the system for only a day. Recently, however, a test called EtG has been developed. The advantage of this test is that rather than scanning for the presence of alcohol, EtG scans for a by-product of the metabolization of alcohol, ethyl glucuronide, which remains in the system for about 80 hours. To date, the only companies using the EtG test are those that prohibit or restrict alcohol use in certain jobs (e.g., some health care positions, transportation jobs), and for those with applicants who have had former alcohol problems but now claim to be sober.[133]

Evaluation

It is commonly believed that drug testing results in a large number of false positives. But if the proper procedures (as already outlined) are followed, drug test results are extremely accurate and error rates are very low. Accuracy of the test, however, is not the same as its validity in predicting important job criteria. The most accurate drug test in the world will be a poor investment if it cannot be established that substance abuse is related to employee behaviors such as accidents, absenteeism, tardiness, impaired job performance, and so on.

Although more research on the validity of drug testing programs is needed, some organizations are conducting research on the deleterious effects of substance abuse. The U.S. Postal Service conducted an evaluation of its drug testing program using applicants who applied for positions in 21 sites over a six-month period.[134] A quality control process revealed that the drug testing program was 100% accurate (zero false positives and false negatives). Ten percent of applicants tested positive for drug use (for the purposes of the study, applicants were hired without regard to their test scores). Of those positive tests, 65% were for marijuana, 24% for cocaine, and 11% were for other drugs. It found higher absenteeism for drug users and higher dismissal rates for cocaine users. Drug use was not related to accidents or injuries. A cost-benefit analysis suggested that full implementation of the program would save the Postal Service several million dollars per year in lower absenteeism and turnover rates.

The validity of performance and psychological drug tests is not well established. As with integrity tests, a major concern is faking, but an advantage of psychological drug tests is that they are likely to be perceived as less intrusive by applicants. Of those organizations that drug test, few rely on physical or psychological tests.

In considering the validity of drug tests, one should not assume that the logical criterion against which the tests are validated is job performance. Typically, the criterion of job performance is central to evaluating the validity of most selection measures, yet drug tests have not been validated against job performance. Thus, it is far from clear that drug tests do a good job of discerning good from poor performers. Drug tests do appear to predict other work behaviors, however, including absenteeism, accidents, and other counterproductive behavior. For the purposes for which they are suited, then, validity of drug tests can be concluded to be high.

Finally, as with other assessment methods, two other criteria against which drug testing should be evaluated are adverse impact and applicant reactions. The adverse impact of drug testing is not universally accepted, but the Postal Service study indicated that drug testing programs did have a moderate to high degree of adverse impact against black and Hispanic applicants. Research on applicant reactions to drug tests shows that if applicants perceive a need for drug testing, they are more likely to find such a program acceptable.[135] Thus, organizations that do a good job explaining the reasons for the tests to applicants are more likely to find that applicants react favorably to the program.

Recommendations for Effective Drug Testing Programs

Though drug testing may have peaked, it is likely to continue as one of the most commonly used selection methods, especially among large employers. In an effort to make organizations' drug testing programs as accurate and effective as possible, six recommendations are outlined as follows:

1. Emphasize drug testing in safety-sensitive jobs as well as positions where the link between substance abuse and negative outcomes (e.g., as was the case with the Postal Service study described earlier) has been documented.
2. Use only reputable testing laboratories, and ensure that strict chain of custody is maintained.
3. Ask applicants for their consent and inform them of test results; provide rejected applicants with the opportunity to appeal.
4. Use retesting to validate positive samples from the initial screening test.
5. Ensure that proper procedures are followed to maintain the applicant's right to privacy.
6. Review the program and validate the results against relevant criteria (accidents, absenteeism, turnover, job performance); conduct a cost-benefit analysis of

the program, as a very small number of detections may cause the program to have low utility.

Medical Exams

Medical exams are often used to identify potential health risks in job candidates. Care must be taken to ensure that medical exams are used only when a compelling reason to use them exists. This is to ensure that individuals with disabilities unrelated to job performance are not screened out. As a result of these sorts of potential abuses, the use of medical exams is strictly regulated by the ADA (discussed later in this chapter).

Although many organizations use medical exams, they are not particularly valid, because the procedures performed vary from doctor to doctor.[136] Also, medical exams are not always job related.[137] Finally, the emphasis is usually on short-term rather than long-term health. A promising new development has recently taken place in medical exams. This development is known as job-related medical standards.[138] Under this procedure, physical health standards have been developed that are highly job related. Physicians' manuals have been developed that provide information on the specific diseases and health conditions that prohibit adequate functioning on specific jobs or clusters of tasks. This procedure should not only improve content validity (because it is job related) but also improve reliability because it standardizes diagnosis across physicians. Along with the manuals, useful data-gathering instruments have been developed to properly assess applicants' actual medical conditions. Again, this helps standardize assessments by physicians, which should improve reliability.

LEGAL ISSUES

This section discusses three major legal issues. The first of these is the UGESP, a document that addresses the need to determine if a selection procedure is causing adverse impact, and if so, the validation requirements for the procedure. The second issue is selection in conformance with the ADA as pertains to reasonable accommodation to job applicants and the use of medical tests. The final issue is that of drug testing for job applicants.

Uniform Guidelines on Employee Selection Procedures

The UGESP is a comprehensive set of federal regulations specifying requirements for the selection systems of organizations covered under the Civil Rights Acts and under E.O. 11246 (see *www.eeoc.gov/policy/regs* for the full text of the UGESP). There are four major sections to the UGESP, namely, general principles, technical standards, documentation of impact and validity evidence, and definitions of terms. Each of these sections is summarized next. An excellent review of the

UGESP in terms of court cases and examples of acceptable and unacceptable practices is available and should be consulted. The organization should also consult research that reviews how the UGESP have been interpreted, criticized, and used since their passage.[139]

General Principles

1. *Summary.* The organization must keep records that allow it to determine if its selection procedures are causing adverse impact in employment decisions. If no adverse impact is found, the remaining provisions of the UGESP generally do not apply. If adverse impact is found, the organization must either validate the selection procedure(s) causing the adverse impact or take steps to eliminate the adverse impact (such as stopping use of the procedure or using an alternate selection procedure that has less adverse impact).

2. *Scope.* The scope of the UGESP is very broad in that the guidelines apply to selection procedures used as the basis for any employment decisions. Employment decisions include hiring, promotion, demotion, and retention. A selection procedure is defined as "any measure, combination of measures, or procedure used as a basis for any employment decision." The procedures include "the full range of assessment techniques from traditional paper-and-pencil tests, performance tests, training programs, or probationary periods and physical, educational, and work experience requirements through informal or casual interviews and unscored application forms."

3. *Discrimination defined.* In general, any selection procedure that has an adverse impact is discriminatory unless it has been shown to be valid. There is a separate section for procedures that have not been validated.

4. *Suitable alternative selection procedures.* When a selection procedure has adverse impact, consideration should be given to the use of any suitable alternative selection procedures that may have lesser adverse impact.

5. *Information on adverse impact.* The organization must keep impact records by race, sex, and ethnic group for each of the job categories shown on the EEO-1 form (see Chapter 13).

6. *Evaluation of selection rates.* For each job or job category, the organization should evaluate the results, also known as the "bottom line," of the total selection process. The purpose of the evaluation is to determine if there are differences in selection rates that indicate adverse impact. If adverse impact is not found, the organization usually does not have to take additional compliance steps, such as validation of each step in the selection process. If overall adverse impact is found, the individual components of the selection process should be evaluated for adverse impact.

7. *Adverse impact and the four-fifths rule.* To determine if adverse impact is occurring, the organization should compute and compare selection rates for

race, sex, and ethnic groups. A selection rate that is less than four-fifths (or 80%) of the rate for the group with the highest rate is generally regarded as evidence of adverse impact. There are exceptions to this general rule, based on sample size (small sample) considerations and on the extent to which the organization's recruitment practices have discouraged applicants disproportionately on grounds of race, sex, or ethnic group.

8. *General standards for validity studies.* There are three types of acceptable validity studies: criterion related, content, and construct. There are numerous provisions pertaining to standards governing these validity studies, as well as the appropriate use of selection procedures.

9. *Procedures that have not been validated.* This section discusses the use of alternative selection procedures to eliminate adverse impact. It also discusses instances in which validation studies cannot or need not be performed.

10. *Affirmative action.* Use of validated selection procedures does not relieve the employer of any affirmative action obligation it may have. The employer is encouraged to adopt and implement voluntary affirmative action plans.

Technical Standards

This section contains a lengthy specification of the minimum technical standards that should be met when conducting a validation study. There are separate standards given for each of the three types of validity (criterion-related, content, construct) studies.

Documentation of Impact and Validity Evidence

For each job or job category, the employer is required to keep detailed records on adverse impact and, where adverse impact is found, evidence of validity. Detailed record-keeping requirements are provided.

There are two important exceptions to these general requirements. First, a small employer (fewer than 100 employees) does not have to keep separate records for each job category, but only for its total selection process across all jobs. Second, records for race or national origin do not have to be kept for groups constituting less than 2% of the labor force in the relevant labor area.

Definitions

This section provides definitions of terms (25 total) used throughout the UGESP.

Summary

In totality, the UGESP make substantial demands of an organization and its staffing systems. Those demands exist to ensure organizational awareness of the possibility of adverse impact in employment decisions. When adverse impact is found, the UGESP provide mechanisms (requirements) for coping with it. The UGESP thus should occupy a place of prominence in any covered organization's EEO/AA policies and practices.

Selection Under the Americans With Disabilities Act (ADA)

The ADA, as interpreted by the Equal Employment Opportunity Commission (EEOC), creates substantial requirements and suggestions for compliance pertaining to external selection.[140] The general nature of these is identified and commented upon next.

General Principles

There are two major, overarching principles pertaining to selection. The first principle is that it is unlawful to screen out individuals with disabilities, unless the selection procedure is job related and consistent with business necessity. The second principle is that a selection procedure must accurately reflect the KSAOs being measured, and not impaired sensory, manual, or speaking skills, unless those impaired skills are the ones being measured by the procedure.

The first principle is obviously very similar to principles governing selection generally under federal laws and regulations. The second principle is important because it cautions the organization to be sure that its selection procedures do not inadvertently and unnecessarily screen out applicants with disabilities.

Access to Job Application Process

The organization's job application process must be accessible to individuals with disabilities. Reasonable accommodation must be provided to enable all persons to apply, and applicants should be provided assistance (if needed) in completing the application process. Applicants should also be told about the nature and content of the selection process. This allows them to request reasonable accommodation to testing, if needed, in advance.

Reasonable Accommodation to Testing

In general, the organization may use any kind of test in assessing job applicants. These tests must be administered consistently to all job applicants for any particular job.

A very important provision of testing pertains to the requirement to provide reasonable accommodation, if requested, by an applicant to take the test. The purpose of this requirement is to ensure that the test accurately reflects the KSAO being measured, rather than an impairment of the applicant. Reasonable accommodation, however, is not required for a person with an impaired skill if the purpose of that test is to measure that skill. For example, the organization does not have to provide reasonable accommodation on a manual dexterity test to a person with arthritis in the fingers and hands if the purpose of the test is to measure manual dexterity.

There are numerous types of reasonable accommodation that can be made, and there is organizational experience and research in providing reasonable accommodation.[141] Examples of what might be done to provide reasonable accommodation include substituting an oral test for a written one (or vice versa); providing extra time to complete a test; scheduling rest breaks during a test; administering tests in large print, in Braille, or by reader; and using assistive technologies to adapt computers, such as a special mouse or screen magnifier.

Inquiries About Disabilities

Virtually all assessment tools and questions are affected by the ADA. A summary of permissible and impermissible practices is shown in Exhibit 9.17. Note that permissibility depends on the assessment tool, whether the tool is being used for an external applicant or employee, and whether the tool is being used pre–or conditional post–job offer. Also note the many stipulations governing usage. Another useful source of information is "Job Applicants and the Americans With Disabilities Act" (*www.eeoc.gov*).

Medical Examinations: Job Applicants

There are substantial regulations surrounding medical exams, both before and after a job offer. Prior to the offer, the organization may not make medical inquiries or require medical exams of an applicant. The job offer, however, may be conditional, pending the results of a medical exam.

Postoffer, the organization may conduct a medical exam. The exam must be given to all applicants for a particular job, not just individuals with a known or suspected disability. Whereas the content of the exam is not restricted to being only job related, the reasons for rejecting an applicant on the basis of the exam must be job related. A person may also be rejected if exam results indicate a direct threat to the health and safety of the applicant, or others such as employees or customers. This rejection must be based on reasonable medical judgment, not a simple judgment that the applicant might or could cause harm. There must be an individual assessment of each applicant in order to determine if the applicant's impairment creates a significant risk of harm and cannot be accommodated through reasonable accommodation. Results of medical exams are to be kept confidential, held separate from the employee's personnel file, and released only under very specific circumstances.

It is difficult to determine whether something is a medical examination and thus subject to the above requirements surrounding its use. The EEOC defines a medical examination as "a procedure or test that seeks information about an individual's physical or mental impairments or health."[142] The following factors are suggestive of a selection procedure that would be considered a medical examination:

- It is administered by a health care professional and/or someone trained by such a professional.
- It is designed to reveal an impairment of physical or mental health.
- It is invasive (e.g., requires drawing blood, urine, or breath).
- It measures the applicant's physiological responses to performing a task.

EXHIBIT 9.17   Inquiries About Disabilities

What Inquiries Can Be Made About Disabilities?

Type	External Applicant (Pre-Offer Stage)	External Applicants (Post-Conditional Offer Stage)	Employees
AA data (self-ID and requests)	Yes	Yes	Yes
Physical exam	No	Yes (C, D)	Yes (B, E)
Psychological exam	No	Yes (C, D)	Yes (B, E)
Health questionnaire	No	Yes (C, D)	Yes (B, E)
Work comp history	No	Yes (C, D)	Yes (B, E)
Physical agility test	Yes (A, C)	Yes (A, C)	Yes (A, C)
Drug test	Yes	Yes	Yes
Alcohol test	No	Yes (B, D)	Yes (B, E)
Specific questions (oral and written):			
About existence of a disability, its nature	Yes	Yes (A,C)	Yes (B, E)
About ability to perform job-related functions (essential and nonessential)	Yes	Yes	Yes
About smoking (but not allergic to it)	Yes	Yes	Yes
About history of illegal drug use	No	Yes (B, D)	Yes (B, E)
Specific requests:			
Describe how you would perform job-related functions (essential and nonessential) with or without reasonable accommodation	Yes (D, F)	Yes (C, D)	Yes (B, E)
Provide evidence of not currently using drugs	Yes	Yes	Yes

A. If given to all similarly situated applicants/employees
B. If job related and consistent with business necessity
C. If only job-related criteria consistent with business necessity are used afterwards to screen out/ exclude the applicant, at which point reasonable accommodation must be considered.
D. If all entering employees in the same job category are subjected to it and subjected to same qualification standard
E. But only for the following purposes:
  a. To determine fitness for duty (still qualified or still able to perform essential functions)
  b. To determine reasonable accommodation
  c. To meet requirements imposed by federal, state, or local law (DOT, OSHA, EPA, etc.)
  d. To determine direct threat
F. Can be requested of a particular individual if the disability is known and may interfere with or prevent performance of a job-related function.

SOURCE: S. K. Willman, "Tips for Minimizing Abuses Under the Americans With Disabilities Act," *Society for Human Resource Management Legal Report,* Jan.-Feb. 2003, p. 8. Used with permission.

- It is normally given in a medical setting, and/or medical equipment is used.
- It tests for alcohol consumption.

Though closely allied with medical examinations, several types of tests fall outside the bounds of medical examinations; these may be used pre–offer. These include physical agility tests, physical fitness tests, vision tests, drug tests for current illegal use of controlled substances, and tests that measure honesty, tastes, and habits.

A gray area involves the use of psychological tests, such as personality tests. They are considered medical if they lead to identifying a medically recognized mental disorder or impairment, such as those in the American Psychiatric Association's *Diagnostic and Statistical Manual of Mental Disorders*. Future regulations and court rulings may help clarify which types of psychological tests are medical exams.

Medical Examinations: Current Employees

This enforcement guidance applies to employees generally, not just employees with disabilities.[143] An employee who applies for a new (different) job with the same employer should be treated as an applicant for a new job and thus subject to the provisions described above for job applicants. An individual is not an applicant where she or he is entitled to another position with the same employer (e.g., because of seniority or satisfactory performance in her or his current position) or when returning to a regular job after being on temporary assignment in another job. Instead, these individuals are considered employees.

For employees, the employer may make disability-related inquiries and require medical examinations only if they are job related and consistent with business necessity. Any information obtained, or voluntarily provided by the employee, is a confidential medical record. The record may only be shared in limited circumstances with managers, supervisors, first aid and safety personnel, and government officials investigating ADA compliance. Generally, a disability-related inquiry or medical examination is job related and consistent with business necessity when the employer has a reasonable belief, based on objective evidence, that (1) an employee's ability to perform essential job functions will be impaired by a medical condition or (2) an employee will pose a direct threat due to a medical condition.

A medical examination for employees is defined the same way as for job applicants. Examples of disability-related inquiries include the following:

- Asking an employee whether she or he was disabled (or ever had a disability) or how she or he became disabled or asking about the nature or severity of an employee's disability
- Asking employees to provide medical documentation regarding their disability
- Asking an employee's coworkers, family members, doctor, or another person about an employee's disability

- Asking about an employee's genetic information
- Asking about an employee's prior workers' compensation history
- Asking if an employee is taking any medication or drugs or has done so in the past
- Asking an employee broad information that is likely to elicit information about a disability

Drug Testing

Drug testing is permitted to detect the use of illegal drugs. The law, however, is neutral as to its encouragement.

UGESP

The UGESP do not apply to the ADA or its regulations. This means that the guidance and requirements for employers' selection systems under the Civil Rights Act may or may not be the same as those that end up being required for compliance with the ADA.

Drug Testing

Drug testing is surrounded by an amalgam of laws and regulations at the federal and state levels. Special law for the Department of Transportation requires alcohol and drug testing for transportation workers in safety-sensitive jobs.[144] The organization should seek legal and medical advice to determine if it should do drug testing, and if so, what the nature of the drug testing program should be. Beyond that, the organization should require and administer drug tests on a contingency (postoffer) basis only, to avoid the possibility of obtaining and using medical information illegally. For example, positive drug test results may occur because of the presence of a legal drug, and using these results preoffer to reject a person would be a violation of the ADA.

SUMMARY

This chapter continues discussion of proper methods and processes to be used in external selection. Specifically, substantive, discretionary, and contingent assessment methods are discussed, as well as collection of assessment data and pertinent legal issues.

Most of the chapter discusses various substantive methods, which are used to separate finalists from candidates. As with use of initial assessment methods, use of substantive assessment methods should always be based on the logic of prediction and the use of selection plans. The substantive methods that are reviewed include personality tests; ability tests; job knowledge tests; performance tests and work samples; situational judgment tests; integrity tests; interest, values, and preference inventories; structured interview; and assessment for team environments. As with initial assessment methods, the criteria used to evaluate the effectiveness of substantive assessment methods are frequency of use, cost, reliability, validity, utility, applicant reactions, and adverse impact. In general, substantive assessment methods show a marked improvement in reliability and validity over initial assessment methods. This is probably due to the stronger relationship between the sampling of the applicant's previous situations and the requirements for success on the job.

Discretionary selection methods are somewhat less formal and more subjective than other selection methods. When discretionary methods are used, two judgments are most important: Will the applicant be a good organization "citizen," and do the values and goals of this applicant match those of the organization?

Though discretionary methods are subjective, contingent assessment methods typically involve decisions about whether applicants meet certain objective requirements for the job. The two most common contingent methods are drug testing and medical exams. Particularly in the case of drug testing, the use of contingent methods is relatively complex from an administrative and legal standpoint.

Regardless of predictor type, attention must be given to the proper collection and use of predictor information. In particular, support services need to be established, administrators with the appropriate credentials need to be hired, data need to be kept private and confidential, and administration procedures must be standardized.

Along with administrative issues, legal issues need to be considered as well. Particular attention must be paid to regulations that govern permissible activities by organizations. Regulations include those in the UGESP and the ADA.

DISCUSSION QUESTIONS

1. Describe the similarities and differences between personality tests and integrity tests. When is each warranted in the selection process?
2. How would you advise an organization considering adopting a cognitive ability test for selection?
3. Describe the structured interview. What are the characteristics of structured interviews that improve on the shortcomings of unstructured interviews?
4. What are the selection implications for an organization that has recently adopted a total quality management program?
5. What are the most common discretionary and contingent assessment methods? What are the similarities and differences between the use of these two methods?
6. How should organizations apply the general principles of the UGESP to practical selection decisions?

ETHICAL ISSUES

1. Do you think it's ethical for employers to select applicants on the basis of questions such as "Dislike loud music" and "Enjoy wild flights of fantasy" even if the scales that such items measure have been shown to predict job performance? Explain.

2. Cognitive ability tests are one of the best predictors of job performance, yet they have substantial adverse impact against minorities. Do you think it's fair to use such tests? Why or why not?

APPLICATIONS

Assessment Methods for the Job of Human Resources Director

Nairduwel, Inoalot, and Imslo (NII) is a law firm specializing in business law. Among other areas, it deals in equal employment opportunity law, business litigation, and workplace torts. The firm has more than 50 partners and approximately 120 employees. It does business in three states and has law offices in two major metropolitan areas. The firm has no federal contracts.

NII has plans to expand into two additional states with two major metropolitan areas. One of the primary challenges accompanying this ambitious expansion plan is how to staff, train, and compensate individuals who will fill the positions in the new offices. Accordingly, the firm wishes to hire an HR director to oversee the recruitment, selection, training, performance appraisal, and compensation activities accompanying the business expansion, as well as supervise the HR activities in the existing NII offices. The newly created job description for the HR director is listed in the accompanying exhibit.

The firm wishes to design and then use a selection system for assessing applicants that will achieve two objectives: (1) create a valid and useful system that will do a good job of matching applicant KSAOs to job requirements, and (2) be in compliance with all relevant federal and state employment laws.

The firm is considering numerous selection techniques for possible use. For each method listed below, decide whether you would or would not use it in the selection process and state why.

1. Job knowledge test specifically designed for HR professionals that focuses on an applicant's general knowledge of HR management

2. Medical examination and drug test at the beginning of the selection process in order to determine if applicants are able to cope with the high level of stress and frequent travel requirements of the job and are drug free

3. Paper-and-pencil integrity test

4. A structured behavioral interview that will be specially designed for use in filling only this job

5. General cognitive ability test

6. Personal Characteristics Inventory

7. A set of interview questions that the firm typically uses for filling any position:

    (a) Tell me about a problem you solved on a previous job.

    (b) Do you have any physical impairments that would make it difficult for you to travel on business?

    (c) Have you ever been tested for AIDS?

    (d) Are you currently unemployed, and if so, why?

    (e) This position requires fresh ideas and energy. Do you think you have those qualities?

    (f) What is your definition of success?

    (g) What kind of sports do you like?

    (h) How well do you work under pressure? Give me some examples.

Exhibit

Job Description for Human Resources Director

JOB SUMMARY

Performs responsible administrative work managing personnel activities. Work involves responsibility for the planning and administration of HRM programs, including recruitment, selection, evaluation, appointment, promotion, compensation, and recommended change of status of employees, and a system of communication for disseminating information to workers. Works under general supervision, exercising initiative and independent judgment in the performance of assigned tasks.

TASKS

1. Participates in overall planning and policy making to provide effective and uniform personnel services.

2. Communicates policy through organization levels by bulletin, meetings, and personal contact.

3. Supervises recruitment and screening of job applicants to fill vacancies. Supervises interviewing of applicants, evaluation of qualifications, and classification of applications.

4. Supervises administration of tests to applicants.

5. Confers with supervisors on personnel matters, including placement problems, retention or release of probationary employees, transfers, demotions, and dismissals of permanent employees.
6. Initiates personnel training activities and coordinates these activities with work of officials and supervisors.
7. Establishes effective service rating system and trains unit supervisors in making employee evaluations.
8. Supervises maintenance of employee personnel files.
9. Supervises a group of employees directly and through subordinates.
10. Performs related work as assigned.

JOB SPECIFICATIONS

1. *Experience and Training*

   Should have considerable experience in area of HRM administration. Six years minimum.

2. *Education*

   Graduation from a four-year college or university, with major work in human resources, business administration, or industrial psychology. Master's degree in one of these areas is preferable.

3. *Knowledge, Skills, and Abilities*

   Considerable knowledge of principles and practices of HRM, including staffing, compensation, training, and performance evaluation.

4. *Responsibility*

   Supervises the human resource activities of six office managers, one clerk, and one assistant.

Choosing Among Finalists for the Job of Human Resources Director

Assume that Nairduwel, Inoalot, and Imslo (NII), after weighing its options, decided to use the following selection methods to assess applicants for the HR director job: résumé, cognitive ability test, job knowledge test, structured interview, and questions (f) and (g) from the list of generic interview questions.

NII advertised for the position extensively, and out of a pool of 23 initial applicants, it was able to come up with a list of three finalists. Shown in the accompanying exhibit are the results from the assessment of the three finalists using these selection methods. In addition, information from an earlier résumé screen is included for possible consideration. For each finalist, you are to decide whether you would be willing to hire the person and why.

Exhibit

Results of Assessment of Finalists for Human Resource Director Position

	Finalist 1— Lola Vega	Finalist 2— Sam Fein	Finalist 3— Shawanda Jackson
Résumé	GPA 3.9/Cornell University B.S. Human Resource Mgmt. 5 years' experience in HRM • 4 years in recruiting	GPA 2.8/SUNY Binghamton B.B.A. Finance 20 years' experience in HRM • Numerous HR assignments • Certified HR professional	GPA 3.2/Auburn University B.B.A. Business and English 8 years' experience in HRM • 3 years HR generalist • 4 years compensation analyst
	No supervisory experience	15 years' supervisory experience	5 years' supervisory experience
Cognitive ability test	90% correct	78% correct	84% correct
Knowledge test	94% correct	98% correct	91% correct
Structured Int. (out of 100 pts)	85	68	75
Question (f)	Ability to influence others	To do things you want to do	Promotions and earnings
Question (g)	Golf, shuffleboard	Spectator sports	Basketball, tennis

TANGLEWOOD STORES CASE

In our second chapter on external selection, you read how structured interviews are developed. However, following these steps is more complex than you might think. By using the procedures described in the chapter, you will better understand the challenges posed by developing a good structured interview. You will also be able to see the advantages of using a structured protocol.

The Situation

Tanglewood is looking to revise its method for selecting department managers. Currently, external candidates are assessed by an application blank and unstructured interview. Neither of these methods is satisfactory to the organization, and it would like to use your knowledge of structured interviews to help design a more reliable, valid selection procedure.

Your Tasks

First, you should carefully examine the job description for the position in Appendix A and then create a selection plan as shown in Exhibit 9.10. Then, you will write situational and experience-based interview questions designed to assess candidates' knowledge, skills, and abilities for the department manager position, like those in Exhibit 9.11. After writing up these initial questions and behavioral rating scales, you will try them out on a friend to see how he or she reacts to the questions as either an applicant or an interviewer. Based on the comments of your "test subject," you will revise the content of the questions and make recommendations on the process to be followed in conducting the interview. The background information for this case, and your specific assignment, can be found at *www.mhhe. com/heneman6e.*

ENDNOTES

1. L. M. Hough, "The 'Big Five' Personality Variables—Construct Confusion: Description Versus Prediction," *Human Performance,* 1992, 5, 139–155.

2. R. M. Guion and R. F. Gottier, "Validity of Personality Measures in Personnel Selection," *Personnel Psychology,* 1965, 18, pp. 135–164.

3. P. T. Costa, Jr., and R. R. McCrae, "Four Ways Five Factors Are Basic," *Personality and Individual Differences,* 1992, 13, pp. 653–665.

4. D. S. Ones and C. Viswesvaran, "Bandwidth-Fidelity Dilemma in Personality Measurement for Personnel Selection," *Journal of Organizational Behavior,* 1996, 17, pp. 609–626.

5. M. K. Mount and M. R. Barrick, *Manual for the Personal Characteristics Inventory* (Iowa City, IA: author, 1995).

6. P. T. Costa, Jr., and R. R. McCrae, *Revised NEO Personality Inventory (NEO-PI-R) and NEO Five-Factor (NEO-FFI) Inventory Professional Manual* (Odessa, FL: Psychological Assessment Resources, 1992).

7. J. Hogan and R. Hogan, "How to Measure Employee Reliability," *Journal of Applied Psychology,* 1989, 74, pp. 273–279.

8. N. T. Tippins, J. Beaty, F. Drasgow, W. M. Gibson, K. Pearlman, D. O. Segall, and W. Shepherd, "Unproctored Internet Testing in Employment Settings," *Personnel Psychology,* 2006, 59, pp. 189–225; S. Overman, "Online Screening Saves Time and Money," *Staffing Management,* July–Sept. 2005, pp. 18–22.

9. Exhibit 9.2 and the review here are based on C. M. Berry, D. S. Ones, and P. R. Sackett, "Interpersonal Deviance, Organizational Deviance, and Their Common Correlates: A Review and Meta-Analysis," *Journal of Applied Psychology,* 2007, 92, pp. 410–424; C. Viswesvaran, J. Deller, and D. S. Ones, "Personality Measures in Personnel Selection: Some New Contributions," *International Journal of Selection and Assessment,* 2007, 15, pp. 354–358; N. M. Dudley, K. A. Orvis, J. E. Lebiecki, and J. M. Cortina, "A Meta-Analytic Investigation of Conscientiousness in the Prediction of Job Performance: Examining the Intercorrelations and the Incremental Validity

of Narrow Traits," *Journal of Applied Psychology,* 2006, 91, pp. 40–57; D. S. Ones, C. Viswesvaran, and S. Dilchert, "Personality at Work: Raising Awareness and Correcting Misconceptions," *Human Performance,* 2005, 18, pp. 389–404; M. G. Rothstein and R. D. Goffin, "The Use of Personality Measures in Personnel Selection: What Does Current Research Support?" *Human Resource Management Review,* 2006, 16, pp. 155–180.

10. For a review of these criticisms and responses to them, see F. P. Morgeson, M. A. Campion, R. L. Dipboye, J. R. Hollenbeck, K. Murphy, and N. Schmitt, "Reconsidering the Use of Personality Tests in Personnel Selection Contexts," *Personnel Psychology,* 2007, 60, pp. 683–729; D. S. Ones, S. Dilchert, C. Viswesvaran, and T. A. Judge, "In Support of Personality Assessment in Organizational Settings," *Personnel Psychology,* 2007, 60, pp. 995–1027; R. P. Tett and N. D. Christiansen, "Personality Tests at the Crossroads: A Response to Morgeson, Campion, Dipboye, Hollenbeck, Murphy, and Schmitt (2007)," *Personnel Psychology,* 2007, 60, pp. 967–993.

11. Morgeson et al., "Reconsidering the Use of Personality Tests in Personnel Selection Contexts," p. 694.

12. D. S. Ones, S. Dilchert, C. Viswesvaran, and T. A. Judge, "In Support of Personality Assessment in Organizational Settings"; M. R. Barrick, M. K. Mount, and T. A. Judge, "Personality and Performance at the Beginning of the New Millennium: What Do We Know and Where Do We Go Next?" *International Journal of Selection & Assessment,* 2001, 9, pp. 9–30.

13. G. V. Barrett, R. F. Miguel, J. M. Hurd, S. B. Lueke, and J. A. Tan, "Practical Issues in the Use of Personality Tests in Police Selection," *Public Personnel Management,* 2003, 32, pp. 497–517; V. M. Mallozzi, "This Expert in Scouting Athletes Doesn't Need to See Them Play," *New York Times,* Apr. 25, 2004, pp. SP3, SP7.

14. M. R. Barrick and M. K. Mount, "Autonomy as a Moderator of the Relationships Between the Big Five Personality Dimensions and Job Performance," *Journal of Applied Psychology,* 1993, 78, pp. 111–118.

15. D. Chan, "Interactive Effects of Situational Judgment Effectiveness and Proactive Personality on Work Perceptions and Work Outcomes," *Journal of Applied Psychology,* 2006, 91, pp. 475–481; J. A. Thompson, "Proactive Personality and Job Performance: A Social Capital Perspective," *Journal of Applied Psychology,* 2005, 90, pp. 1011–1017; S. E. Seibert, M. L. Kraimer, and J. M. Crant, "What Do Proactive People Do? A Longitudinal Model Linking Proactive Personality and Career Success," *Personnel Psychology,* 2001, 54, pp. 845–874.

16. T. A. Judge and J. E. Bono, "Relationship of Core Self-Evaluations Traits—Self-Esteem, Generalized Self-Efficacy, Locus of Control, and Emotional Stability—With Job Satisfaction and Job Performance: A Meta-Analysis," *Journal of Applied Psychology,* 2001, 86, pp. 80–92; T. A. Judge, A. Erez, J. E. Bono, and C. J. Thoresen, "The Core Self-Evaluations Scale: Development of a Measure," *Personnel Psychology,* 2003, 56, pp. 303–331.

17. S. A. Birkeland, T. M. Manson, J. L. Kisamore, M. T. Brannick, and M. A. Smith, "A Meta-Analytic Investigation of Job Applicant Faking on Personality Measures," *International Journal of Selection and Assessment,* 2006, 14, pp. 317–335; S. Stark, O. S. Chernyshenko, and F. Drasgow, "Examining Assumptions About Item Responding in Personality Assessment: Should Ideal Point Methods Be Considered for Scale Development and Scoring?" *Journal of Applied Psychology,* 2006, 91, pp. 25–39.

18. Rothstein and Goffin, "The Use of Personality Measures in Personnel Selection: What Does Current Research Support?"

19. J. E. Ellingson, D. B. Smith, and P. R. Sackett, "Investigating the Influence of Social Desirability on Personality Factor Structure," *Journal of Applied Psychology,* 2001, 86, pp. 122–133; D. B.

Smith and J. E. Ellingson, "Substance Versus Style: A New Look at Social Desirability in Motivating Contexts," *Journal of Applied Psychology,* 2002, 87, pp. 211–219.

20. N. Schmitt and F. L. Oswald, "The Impact of Corrections for Faking on the Validity of Noncognitive Measures in Selection Settings," *Journal of Applied Psychology,* 2006, 91, pp. 613–621.

21. E. D. Heggestad, M. Morrison, C. L. Reeve, and R. A. McCloy, "Forced-Choice Assessments of Personality for Selection: Evaluating Issues of Normative Assessment and Faking Resistance," *Journal of Applied Psychology,* 2006, 91, pp. 9–24; S. Dilchert, D. S. Ones, C. Viswesvaran, and J. Deller, "Response Distortion in Personality Measurement: Born to Deceive, yet Capable of Providing Valid Self-Assessments?" *Psychology Science*, 2006, 48, pp. 209–225.

22. S. A. Dwight and J. J. Donovan, "Do Warnings Not to Fake Reduce Faking?" *Human Performance,* 2003, 16, pp. 1–23; J. Hogan, P. Barrett, and R. Hogan, "Personality Measurement, Faking, and Employment Selection," *Journal of Applied Psychology,* 2007, 92, pp. 1270–1285; J. E. Ellingson, P. R. Sackett, and B. S. Connelly, "Personality Assessment Across Selection and Development Contexts: Insights into Response Distortion," *Journal of Applied Psychology,* 2007, 92, pp. 386–395.

23. "Workers Question Validity of Personality Tests," *Staffing Management,* Jan.–Mar. 2007, p. 11.

24. J. P. Hausknecht, D. V. Day, and S. C. Thomas, "Applicant Reactions to Selection Procedures: An Updated Model and Meta-Analysis," *Personnel Psychology,* 2004, 57, pp. 639–683.

25. P. M. Rowe, M. C. Williams, and A. L. Day, "Selection Procedures in North America," *International Journal of Selection and Assessment,* 1994, 2, pp. 74–79.

26. E. A. Fleishman and M. E. Reilly, *Handbook of Human Abilities* (Palo Alto, CA: Consulting Psychologists Press, 1992).

27. M. J. Ree and J. A. Earles, "The Stability of Convergent Estimates of g," *Intelligence,* 1991, 15, pp. 271–278.

28. F. Wonderlic, Jr., "Test Publishers Form Association," *Human Resource Measurements* (Supplement to the Jan. 1993 *Personnel Journal*), p. 3.

29. B. Azar, "Could 'Policing' Test Use Improve Assessments?" *APA Monitor,* June 1994, p. 16.

30. L. S. Gottfredson, "Societal Consequences of the g Factor in Employment," *Journal of Vocational Behavior,* 1986, 29, pp. 379–410; J. F. Salgado, N. Anderson, S. Moscoso, C. Bertua, F. de Fruyt, and J. P. Rolland, "A Meta-Analytic Study of General Mental Ability Validity for Different Occupations in the European Community," *Journal of Applied Psychology,* 2003, 88, pp. 1068–1081.

31. J. E. Hunter, "Cognitive Ability, Cognitive Aptitudes, Job Knowledge, and Job Performance," *Journal of Vocational Behavior,* 1986, 29, pp. 340–362.

32. M. J. Ree and J. A. Earles, "Predicting Training Success: Not Much More Than g," *Personnel Psychology,* 1991, 44, pp. 321–332.

33. P. M. Wright, G. McMahan, and D. Smart, "Team Cognitive Ability as a Predictor of Performance: An Examination of the Role of SAT Scores in Determining NCAA Basketball Team Performance," Working paper, Department of Management, Texas A&M University.

34. Hunter, "Cognitive Ability, Cognitive Aptitudes, Job Knowledge, and Job Performance"; F. L. Schmidt and J. E. Hunter, "Development of a Causal Model of Processes Determining Job Performance," *Current Directions in Psychological Science,* 1992, 1, pp. 89–92.

35. J. J. McHenry, L. M. Hough, J. L. Toquam, M. A. Hanson, and S. Ashworth, "Project A Validity Results: The Relationship Between Predictor and Criterion Domains," *Personnel Psychology,* 1990, 43, pp. 335–354.

36. P. L. Roth, C. A. BeVier, P. Bobko, F. S. Switzer, and P. Tyler, "Ethnic Group Differences in Cognitive Ability in Employment and Educational Settings: A Meta-Analysis," *Personnel Psychology,* 2001, 54, pp. 297–330; P. R. Sackett and S. L. Wilk, "Within-Group Norming and Other Forms of Score Adjustment in Preemployment Testing," *American Psychologist,* 1994, 49, pp. 929–954.

37. R. D. Arvey and P. R. Sackett, "Fairness in Selection: Current Developments and Perspectives," in N. Schmitt, W. C. Borman, and Associates (eds.), *Personnel Selection in Organizations* (San Francisco: Jossey-Bass, 1993), pp. 171–202; R. P. DeShon, M. R. Smith, D. Chan, and N. Schmitt, "Can Racial Differences in Cognitive Test Performance Be Reduced by Presenting Problems in a Social Context?" *Journal of Applied Psychology,* 1998, 83, pp. 438–451; F. L. Schmidt, "The Problem of Group Differences in Ability Test Scores in Employment Selection," *Journal of Vocational Behavior,* 1988, 33, pp. 272–292.

38. P. Bobko, P. L. Roth, and D. Potosky, "Derivation and Implications of a Meta-Analytic Matrix Incorporating Cognitive Ability, Alternative Predictors, and Job Performance," *Personnel Psychology,* 1999, 52, pp. 561–589; D. S. Ones, C. Viswesvaran, and F. L. Schmidt, "Comprehensive Meta-Analysis of Integrity Test Validities: Findings and Implications for Personnel Selection and Theories of Job Performance," *Journal of Applied Psychology* (monograph), 1993, 78, pp. 531–537; A. M. Ryan, R. E. Ployhart, and L. A. Friedel, "Using Personality to Reduce Adverse Impact: A Cautionary Note," *Journal of Applied Psychology,* 1998, 83, pp. 298–307.

39. B. D. Edwards and W. Arthur, Jr., "An Examination of Factors Contributing to a Reduction in Subgroup Differences on a Constructed-Response Paper-and-Pencil Test of Scholastic Achievement," *Journal of Applied Psychology,* 2007, 92, pp. 794–801.

40. W. T. Dickens and J. R. Flynn, "Black Americans Reduce the IQ Gap," *Psychological Science,* 2006, 17, pp. 913–920; J. P. Rushton and A. R. Jensen, "The Totality of Available Evidence Shows the Race IQ Gap Still Remains," *Psychological Science,* 2006, 17, pp. 921–922. See also E. Hunt and J. Carlson, "Considerations Relating to the Study of Group Differences in Intelligence," *Perspectives on Psychological Science,* 2007, 2, pp. 194–213.

41. T. A. Judge, D. Blancero, D. M. Cable, and D. E. Johnson, "Effects of Selection Systems on Job Search Decisions." Paper presented at the Tenth Annual Conference of the Society for Industrial and Organizational Psychology, Orlando, FL, 1995.

42. Rynes and Connerley, "Applicant Reactions to Alternative Selection Procedures."

43. Smither et al., "Applicant Reactions to Selection Procedures."

44. J. P. Hausknecht, D. V. Day, and S. C. Thomas, "Applicant Reactions to Selection Procedures: An Updated Model and Meta-Analysis," *Personal Psychology,* 2004, 57, pp. 639–683.

45. S. M. Gully, S. C. Payne, and K. L. K. Koles, "The Impact of Error Training and Individual Differences on Training Outcomes: An Attribute-Treatment Interaction Perspective," *Journal of Applied Psychology,* 2002, 87, pp. 143–155; J. P. Hausknecht, C. O. Trevor, and J. L. Farr, "Retaking Ability Tests in a Selection Setting: Implications for Practice Effects, Training Performance, and Turnover," *Journal of Applied Psychology,* 2002, 87, pp. 243–254; J. F. Salgado, N. Anderson, and S. Moscoso, "International Validity Generalization of GMA and Cognitive Abilities: A European Community Meta-Analysis," *Personnel Psychology,* 2003, 56, pp. 573–605.

46. K. R. Murphy, B. E. Cronin, and A. P. Tam, "Controversy and Consensus Regarding Use of Cognitive Ability Testing in Organizations," *Journal of Applied Psychology,* 2003, 88, pp. 660–671.

47. J. Hogan, "Physical Abilities," in M. D. Dunnette and L. M. Hough (eds.), *Handbook of Industrial and Organizational Psychology,* Vol. 2 (Palo Alto, CA: Consulting Psychologists Press, 1991), pp. 753–831.

48. N. Henderson, M. W. Berry, and T. Malic, "Field Measures of Strength and Fitness Predict Firefighter Performance on Physically Demanding Tasks," *Personnel Psychology,* 2007, 60, pp. 431–473.

49. R. Britt, "Hands and Wrists Are Thrust Into the Hiring Process," *New York Times,* Sept. 21, 1997, p. 11.

50. M. A. Campion, "Personnel Selection for Physically Demanding Jobs: Review and Recommendations," *Personnel Psychology,* 1987, 36, pp. 527–550.

51. T. A. Baker, "The Utility of a Physical Test in Reducing Injury Costs," Paper presented at the Ninth Annual Meeting of the Society for Industrial and Organizational Psychology, Nashville, TN, 1995.

52. B. R. Blakley, M. A. Quinones, M. S. Crawford, and I. A. Jago, "The Validity of Isometric Strength Tests," *Personnel Psychology,* 1994, 47, pp. 247–274.

53. E. E. Ghiselli, "The Validity of Aptitude Tests in Personnel Selection," *Personnel Psychology,* 1973, 61, pp. 461–467.

54. P. Salovey and D. Grewal, "The Science of Emotional Intelligence," *Current Directions in Psychological Science,* 2005, 14, p. 281.

55. K. S. Law, C. Wong, and L. J. Song, "The Construct and Criterion Validity of Emotional Intelligence and Its Potential Utility for Management Studies," *Journal of Applied Psychology,* 2004, 89, pp. 483–496; H. A. Elfenbein and N. Ambady, "Predicting Workplace Outcomes From the Ability to Eavesdrop on Feelings," *Journal of Applied Psychology,* 2002, 87, pp. 963–971.

56. D. L. Van Rooy and C. Viswesvaran, "Emotional Intelligence: A Meta-Analytic Investigation of Predictive Validity and Nomological Net," *Journal of Vocational Behavior,* 2004, 65, pp. 71–95.

57. M. Zeidner, G. Matthews, and R. D. Roberts, "Emotional Intelligence in the Workplace: A Critical Review," *Applied Psychology: An International Review,* 2004, 53, pp. 371–399.

58. J. M. Conte, "A Review and Critique of Emotional Intelligence Measures," *Journal of Organizational Behavior,* 2005, 26(1), pp. 433–440; M. Davies, L. Stankov, and R. D. Roberts, "Emotional Intelligence: In Search of an Elusive Construct," *Journal of Personality and Social Psychology,* 1998, 75(4), pp. 989–1015.

59. E. A. Locke, "Why Emotional Intelligence Is an Invalid Concept," *Journal of Organizational Behavior,* 2005, 26, p. 426.

60. S. Côté and C. T. H. Miners, "Emotional Intelligence, Cognitive Intelligence, and Job Performance," *Administrative Science Quarterly,* 2006, 51, pp. 1–28; D. Rosete and J. Ciarrochi, "Emotional Intelligence and Its Relationship to Workplace Performance Outcomes of Leadership Effectiveness," *Leadership & Organization Development Journal,* 2005, 26, pp. 388–399.

61. F. J. Landy, "Some Historical and Scientific Issues Related to Research on Emotional Intelligence," *Journal of Organizational Behavior,* 2005, 26, p. 421.

62. Wisconsin Department of Employment Relations, *Developing Wisconsin State Civil Service Examinations and Assessment Procedures* (Madison, WI: author, 1994).

63. D. M. Dye, M. Reck, and M. A. McDaniel, "The Validity of Job Knowledge Measures," *International Journal of Selection and Assessment,* 1993, 1, pp. 153–157.

64. E. White, "Walking a Mile in Another's Shoes," *Wall Street Journal,* Jan. 16, 2006, p. B3.

65. R. Miller, "The Legal Minefield of Employment Probation," *Benefits and Compensation Solutions,* 1998, 21, pp. 40–43.

66. J. J. Asher and J. A. Sciarrino, "Realistic Work Sample Tests: A Review," *Personnel Psychology,* 1974, 27, pp. 519–533.

67. S. J. Motowidlo, M. D. Dunnette, and G. Carter, "An Alternative Selection Procedure: A Low-Fidelity Simulation," *Journal of Applied Psychology,* 1990, 75, pp. 640–647.

68. W. Arthur, Jr., G. V. Barrett, and D. Doverspike, "Validation of an Information Processing-Based Test Battery Among Petroleum-Product Transport Drivers," *Journal of Applied Psychology,* 1990, 75, pp. 621–628.

69. J. Cook, "Sure Bet," *Human Resource Executive,* Jan. 1997, pp. 32–34.

70. Motowidlo et al., "An Alternative Selection Procedure: A Low-Fidelity Simulation."

71. "Making a Difference in Customer Service," *IPMA News,* May 2002, pp. 8–9.

72. P. Thomas, "Not Sure of a New Hire? Put Her to a Road Test," *Wall Street Journal,* Jan. 2003, p. B7.

73. S. Greengard, "Cracking the Hiring Code," *Workforce Management,* June 2004 (*www.workforce.com/archive/article/23/74/45.php*).

74. C. Winkler, "Job Tryouts Go Virtual," *HR Magazine,* Sept. 2006, pp. 131–134.

75. Electronic Selection Systems Corporation, *Accu Vision: Assessment Technology for Today, Tomorrow, and Beyond* (Maitland, FL: author, 1992).

76. J. E. Hunter and R. F. Hunter, "Validity and Utility of Alternative Predictors of Job Performance," *Psychological Bulletin,* 1984, 96, pp. 72–98.

77. W. Cascio and W. Phillips, "Performance Testing: A Rose Among Thorns?" *Personnel Psychology,* 1979, 32, pp. 751–766.

78. P. Bobko, P. L. Roth, and M. A. Buster, "Work Sample Tests and Expected Reduction in Adverse Impact: A Cautionary Note," *International Journal of Selection and Assessment,* 2005, 13, pp. 1–24.

79. K. A. Hanisch and C. L. Hulin, "Two-Stage Sequential Selection Procedures Using Ability and Training Performance: Incremental Validity of Behavioral Consistency Measures," *Personnel Psychology,* 1994, 47, pp. 767–785.

80. M. A. McDaniel, N. S. Hartman, D. L. Whetzel, and W. L. Grubb, "Situational Judgment Tests, Response Instructions, and Validity: A Meta-Analysis," *Personnel Psychology,* 2007, 60, pp. 63–91.

81. D. L. Whetzel, M. A. McDaniel, and N. T. Nguyen, "Subgroup Differences in Situational Judgment Test Performance: A Meta-Analysis," *Human Performance,* in press.

82. F. Lievens and P. R. Sackett, "Video-Based Versus Written Situational Judgment Tests: A Comparison in Terms of Predictive Validity," *Journal of Applied Psychology,* 2006, 91, pp. 1181–1188.

83. McDaniel et al., "Situational Judgment Tests, Response Instructions, and Validity: A Meta-Analysis."

84. D. Chan and N. Schmitt, "Situational Judgment and Job Performance," *Human Performance,* 2002, 15, pp. 233–254; J. A. Weekley and C. Jones, "Further Studies of Situational Tests," *Personnel Psychology,* 1999, 52, pp. 679–700; J. Clevenger, G. M. Pereira, D. Wiechmann, N. Schmitt, and V. S. Harvey, "Incremental Validity of Situational Judgment Tests," *Journal of Applied Psychology,* 2001, 86, pp. 410–417.

85. M. S. O'Connell, N. S. Hartman, M. A. McDaniel, W. L. Grubb, and A. Lawrence, "Incremental Validity of Situational Judgment Tests for Task and Contextual Job Performance," *International Journal of Selection and Assessment,* 2007, 15, pp. 19–29.

86. F. Lievens and P. R. Sackett, "Video-Based Versus Written Situational Judgment Tests: A Comparison in Terms of Predictive Validity."

87. M. E. Bergman, F. Drasgow, M. A. Donovan, J. B. Henning, and S. E. Juraska, "Scoring Situational Judgment Tests: Once You Get the Data, Your Troubles Begin," *International Journal of Selection and Assessment,* 2006, 14, pp. 223–235.

88. "Employers Cite Communication Skills, Honesty/Integrity as Key for Job Candidates," *IPMA-HR Bulletin,* Mar. 23, 2007, p. 1.

89. M. G. Aamodt and H. Custer, "Who Can Best Catch a Liar?: A Meta-Analysis of Individual Differences in Detecting Deception," *The Forensic Examiner,* Spring 2006, pp. 6–11.

90. R. C. Hollinger, "2006 National Retail Security Survey Final Report," Survey Research Project, University of Florida (downloaded January 8, 2008, from *http://web.crim.ufl.edu/research/srp/srp.html*).

91. C. M. Berry, D. S. Ones, and P. R. Sackett, "Interpersonal Deviance, Organizational Deviance, and Their Common Correlates: A Review and Meta-Analysis," *Journal of Applied Psychology,* 2007, 92, pp. 410–424.

92. P. R. Sackett and J. E. Wanek, "New Developments in the Use of Measures of Honesty, Integrity, Conscientiousness, Dependability, Trustworthiness, and Reliability for Personnel Selection," *Personnel Psychology,* 1996, 49, pp. 787–829.

93. C. M. Berry, P. R. Sackett, and S. Wiemann, "A Review of Recent Developments in Integrity Test Research," *Personnel Psychology,* 2007, 60, pp. 271–301.

94. B. Marcus, K. Lee, and M. C. Ashton, "Personality Dimensions Explaining Relations Between Integrity Tests and Counterproductive Behavior: Big Five, or One in Addition?" *Personnel Psychology,* 2007, 60, pp. 1–34.

95. D. S. Ones, C. Viswesvaran, and S. Dilchert, "Personality at Work: Raising Awareness and Correcting Misconceptions," *Human Performance,* 2005, 18, pp. 389–404.

96. Ones, Viswesvaran, and Schmidt, "Comprehensive Meta-Analysis of Integrity Test Validities: Findings and Implications for Personnel Selection and Theories of Job Performance."

97. Berry et al., "A Review of Recent Developments in Integrity Test Research."

98. R. J. Karren and L. Zacharias, "Integrity Tests: Critical Issues," *Human Resource Management Review,* 2007, 17, pp. 221–234.

99. J. P. Hausknecht, D. V. Day, and S. C. Thomas, "Applicant Reactions to Selection Procedures: An Updated Model and Meta-Analysis," *Personnel Psychology,* 2004, 57, pp. 639–683.

100. R. R. McCrae and P. T. Costa, Jr., "Reinterpreting the Myers-Briggs Type Indicator From the Perspective of the Five-Factor Model of Personality," *Journal of Personality,* 1989, 57, pp. 17–40.

101. Hough, "The 'Big Five' Personality Variables—Construct Confusion: Description Versus Prediction."

102. M. Assouline and E. I. Moir, "Meta-Analysis of the Relationship Between Congruence and Well-Being Measures," *Journal of Vocational Behavior,* 1987, 31, pp. 319–332.

103. See B. Schneider, H. W. Goldstein, and D. B. Smith, "The ASA Framework: An Update," *Personnel Psychology,* 1995, 48, pp. 747–773.

104. D. M. Cable, "The Role of Person-Organization Fit in Organizational Entry," Unpublished doctoral dissertation, Cornell University, Ithaca, New York, 1995.

105. R. W. Eder and M. Harris (eds.), *The Employment Interview Handbook* (Thousand Oaks, CA: Sage, 1999).

106. M. Hosoda, E. F. Stone-Romero, and G. Coats, "The Effects of Physical Attractiveness on Job-Related Outcomes: A Meta-Analysis of Experimental Studies," *Personnel Psychology,* 2003, 56, pp. 431–462; J. R. Burnett and S. J. Motowidlo, "Relation Between Different Sources of Information in the Structured Selection Interview," *Personnel Psychology,* 1998, 51, pp. 963–980; A. J. Prewett-Livingston, H. S. Feild, J. G. Veres, and P. M. Lewis, "Effects of Race on Interview Ratings in a Situational Panel Interview," *Journal of Applied Psychology,* 1996, 81, pp. 178–186; "Survey Finds Employers Form Opinions of Job Interviewees Within 10 Minutes," *IPMA-HR Bulletin,* Apr. 21, 2007, p. 1; M. Bertrand and S. Mullainathan, "Are Emily and Greg More Employable Than Lakisha and Jamal? A Field Experiment on Labor Market Discrimination," *American Economic Review,* 2004, 94, pp. 991–1013; S. L. Purkiss, P. L. Perrewé, T. L. Gillespie, B. T. Mayes, and G. R. Ferris, "Implicit Sources of Bias in Employment Interview Judgments and Decisions," *Organizational Behavior and Human Decision Processes,* 2006, 101, pp. 152–167.

107. M. A. Campion, D. K. Palmer, and J. E. Campion, "A Review of Structure in the Selection Interview," *Personnel Psychology,* 1997, 50, pp. 655–702.

108. G. P. Latham, L. M. Saari, E. D. Pursell, and M. A. Campion, "The Situational Interview," *Journal of Applied Psychology,* 1980, 65, pp. 422–427; S. D. Maurer, "The Potential of the Situational Interview: Existing Research and Unresolved Issues," *Human Resource Management Review,* 1997, 7, pp. 185–201.

109. A. I. Huffcutt, J. N. Conurey, P. L. Roth, and U. Klehe, "The Impact of Job Complexity and Study Design on Situational and Behavior Description Interview Validity," *International Journal of Selection and Assessment,* 2004, 12, pp. 262–273.

110. M. A. McDaniel, D. L. Whetzel, F. L. Schmidt, and S. D. Maurer, "The Validity of Employment Interviews: A Comprehensive Review and Meta-Analysis," *Journal of Applied Psychology,* 1994, 79, pp. 599–616; A. I. Huffcutt, J. M. Conway, P. L. Roth, and U. Klehe, "The Impact of Job Complexity and Study Design on Situational and Behavior Description Interview Validity," *International Journal of Selection and Assessment,* 2004, 12, pp. 262–273.

111. K. I. van der Zee, A. B. Bakker, and P. Bakker, "Why Are Structured Interviews So Rarely Used in Personnel Selection?" *Journal of Applied Psychology,* 2002, 87, pp. 176–184; F. Lievens and A. De Paepe, "An Empirical Investigation of Interviewer-Related Factors That Discourage the Use of High Structure Interviews," *Journal of Organizational Behavior,* 2004, 25, pp. 29–46; N. Smith, "Using Structured Interviews to Increase Your Organization's Hiring Investments," *HR Weekly,* Oct. 2006, pp. 1–3.

112. J. P. Hausknecht, D. V. Day, and S. C. Thomas, "Applicant Reactions to Selection Procedures: An Updated Model and Meta-Analysis."

113. A. I. Huffcutt and P. L. Roth, "Racial Group Differences in Interview Evaluations," *Journal of Applied Psychology,* 1998, 83, pp. 179–189.

114. E. D. Pulakos, N. Schmitt, D. Whitney, and N. Smith, "Individual Differences in Interviewer Ratings: The Impact of Standardization, Consensus Discussion, and Sampling Error on the Validity of a Structured Interview," *Personnel Psychology,* 1996, 49, pp. 85–102; C. H. Van Iddekinge, C. E. Sager, J. L. Burnfield, and T. S. Heffner, "The Variability of Criterion-Related Validity Estimates Among Interviewers and Interview Panels," *International Journal of Selection and Assessment,* 2006, 14, pp. 193–205.

115. M. Harris, "Reconsidering the Employment Interview: A Review of Recent Literature and Suggestions for Future Research," *Personnel Psychology,* 1989, 42, pp. 691–726.

116. D. S. Chapman and D. I. Zweig, "Developing a Nomological Network for Interview Structure: Antecedents and Consequences of the Structured Selection Interview," *Personnel Psychology,* 2005, 58, pp. 673–702.

117. S. P. Robbins and T. A. Judge, *Organizational Behavior,* thirteenth ed. (Upper Saddle River, NJ: Prentice-Hall, 2008).

118. Robbins and Judge, *Organizational Behavior.*

119. M. J. Stevens and M. A. Campion, "The Knowledge, Skill, and Ability Requirements for Teamwork: Implications for Human Resource Management," *Journal of Management,* 1994, 20, pp. 503–530.

120. M. J. Stevens, "Staffing Work Teams: Testing for Individual-Level Knowledge, Skill, and Ability Requirements for Teamwork," Unpublished doctoral dissertation, Purdue University, West Lafayette, Indiana, 1993.

121. R. S. Wellens, W. C. Byham, and G. R. Dixon, *Inside Teams* (San Francisco: Jossey-Bass, 1995).

122. M. R. Barrick, G. L. Stewart, M. J. Neubert, and M. K. Mount, "Relating Member Ability and Personality to Work-Team Processes and Team Effectiveness," *Journal of Applied Psychology,* 1998, 83, pp. 377–391.

123. S. M. Colarelli and A. L. Boos, "Sociometric and Ability-Based Assignment to Work Groups: Some Implications for Personnel Selection," *Journal of Organizational Behavior Management,* 1992, 13, pp. 187–196; M. Levinson, "When Workers Do the Hiring," *Newsweek,* June 21, 1993, p. 48.

124. B. Dumaine, "The Trouble With Teams," *Fortune,* Sept. 5, 1994, pp. 86–92.

125. W. C. Borman and S. J. Motowidlo, "Expanding the Criterion Domain to Include Elements of Contextual Performance," in N. Schmitt, W. Borman, and Associates (eds.), *Personnel Selection in Organizations* (San Francisco: Jossey-Bass, 1993), pp. 71–98.

126. "Why Worry About Drugs and Alcohol in the Workplace?" Facts for Employers, American Council for Drug Education, 2007 (*www.acde.org/employer/DAwork.htm*).

127. Smithers Institute, "Drug Testing: Cost and Effect," *Cornell/Smithers Report,* Vol. 1 (Ithaca, NY: Cornell University, 1992), pp. 1–5.

128. "U.S. Corporations Reduce Levels of Medical, Drug and Psychological Testing of Employees," American Management Association, 2007 (*www.amanet.org/press/archives/reduce.htm*).

129. *Amphetamines Use Declined Significantly Among U.S. Workers in 2005, According to Quest Diagnostics' Drug Testing Index,* Quest Diagnostics Incorporated, 2006.

130. L. Paik, "Organizational Interpretations of Drug Test Results," *Law & Society Review,* Dec. 2006, pp. 1–28.

131. *Mandatory Guidelines and Proposed Revisions to Mandatory Guidelines for Federal Workplace Drug Testing Programs,* Department of Health and Human Services, Substance Abuse and Mental Health Services Administration, 2004.

132. S. Overman, "Debating Drug Test ROI," *Staffing Management,* Oct.–Dec. 2005, pp. 19–22.

133. K. Helliker, "A Test for Alcohol—and Its Flaws," *Wall Street Journal,* Aug. 12, 2006, pp. A1, A6.

134. J. Normand, S. D. Salyards, and J. J. Mahoney, "An Evaluation of Preemployment Drug Testing," *Journal of Applied Psychology,* 1990, 75, pp. 629–639.

135. J. M. Grant and T. S. Bateman, "An Experimental Test of the Impact of Drug-Testing Programs on Potential Job Applicants' Attitudes and Intentions," *Journal of Applied Psychology,* 1990, 75, pp. 127–131; K. R. Murphy, G. C. Thornton III, and D. H. Reynolds, "College Students' Attitudes Toward Employee Drug Testing Programs," *Personnel Psychology,* 1990, 43, pp. 615–631.

136. E. A. Fleishman, "Some New Frontiers in Personnel Selection Research," *Personnel Psychology,* 1988, 41, pp. 679–701.

137. M. A. Campion, "Personnel Selection for Physically Demanding Jobs: Review and Recommendations," *Personnel Psychology,* 1983, 36, pp. 527–550.

138. Fleishman, "Some New Research Frontiers in Personnel Selection."

139. W. F. Cascio and H. Aquinis, "The Federal Uniform Guidelines on Employee Selection Procedures: An Update on Selected Issues," *Review of Public Personnel Administration,* 2001, 21, pp. 200–218; C. Daniel, "Separating Law and Professional Practice From Politics: The Uniform Guidelines Then and Now," *Review of Public Personnel Administration,* 2001, 21, pp. 175–184; A. I. E. Ewoh and J. S. Guseh, "The Status of the Uniform Guidelines on Employee Selection Procedures: Legal Developments and Future Prospects," *Review of Public Personnel Administration,* 2001, 21, pp. 185–199; G. P. Panaro, *Employment Law Manual,* second ed. (Boston: Warren Gorham Lamont, 1993), pp. 3-28 to 3-82.

140. Equal Employment Opportunity Commission, *Technical Assistance Manual of the Employment Provisions (Title 1) of the Americans With Disabilities Act* (Washington, DC: author, 1992), pp. 51–88; J. G. Frierson, *Employer's Guide to the Americans With Disabilities Act* (Washington, DC: Bureau of National Affairs, 1992); D. L. Stone and K. L. Williams, "The Impact of the ADA on the Selection Process: Applicant and Organizational Issues," *Human Resource Management Review,* 1997, 7, pp. 203–231.

141. L. Daley, M. Dolland, J. Kraft, M. A. Nester, and R. Schneider, *Employment Testing of Persons With Disabling Conditions* (Alexandria, VA: International Personnel Management Association, 1988); L. D. Eyde, M. A. Nester, S. M. Heaton, and A. V. Nelson, *Guide for Administering Written Employment Examinations to Persons With Disabilities* (Washington, DC: U.S. Office of Personnel Management, 1994).

142. Equal Employment Opportunity Commission, *ADA Enforcement Guidance: Preemployment Disability Related Questions and Medical Examinations* (Washington, DC: author, 1995).

143. Equal Employment Opportunity Commission, *Enforcement Guidance on Disability-Related Inquiries and Medical Examinations of Employees Under the Americans With Disabilities Act* (Washington, DC: author, 2001).

144. J. E. Balls, "Dealing With Drugs: Keep It Legal," *HR Magazine,* Mar. 1998, pp. 104–116; A. G. Feliu, *Primer on Employee Rights* (Washington, DC: Bureau of National Affairs, 1998), pp. 137–166.

CHAPTER TEN

Internal Selection

Preliminary Issues
The Logic of Prediction
Types of Predictors
Selection Plan

Initial Assessment Methods
Skills Inventory
Peer Assessments
Self-Assessments
Managerial Sponsorship
Informal Discussions and Recommendations
Choice of Initial Assessment Methods

Substantive Assessment Methods
Seniority and Experience
Job Knowledge Tests
Performance Appraisal
Promotability Ratings
Assessment Centers
Interview Simulations
Promotion Panels and Review Boards
Choice of Substantive Assessment Methods

Discretionary Assessment Methods

Legal Issues
Uniform Guidelines on Employee Selection Procedures
The Glass Ceiling

Summary

Discussion Questions

Ethical Issues

Applications

nternal selection refers to the assessment and evaluation of employees from within the organization as they move from job to job via transfer and promotion systems. Many different assessment methods are used to make internal selection decisions. Preliminary issues we will discuss to guide the use of these assessment methods include the logic of prediction, the nature of predictors, and the development of a selection plan.

Initial assessment methods are used to select internal candidates from among the internal applicants. Initial assessment methods that will be reviewed include skills inventories, peer and self-assessments, managerial sponsorship, and informal discussions and recommendations. The criteria that should be used to choose among these methods will be discussed.

Substantive assessment methods are used to select internal finalists from among the internal candidates. Various methods will be reviewed, including seniority and experience, job knowledge tests, performance appraisal, promotability ratings, assessment centers, interview simulations, and promotion panels and review boards. The criteria used to choose among the substantive assessment methods will also be discussed.

Discretionary assessment methods are used to select offer recipients from among the finalists. The factors on which these decisions are based, such as equal employment opportunity and affirmative action (EEO/AA) concerns, whether the finalist had previously been a finalist, and second opinions about the finalist by others in the organization, will be considered.

All of these assessment methods require the collection of a large amount of data. Accordingly, attention must be given to support services, the required expertise needed to administer and interpret predictors, security, privacy and confidentiality, and the standardization of procedures.

The use of internal selection methods requires a clear understanding of legal issues. In particular, the Uniform Guidelines on Employee Selection Procedures (UGESP) and the glass ceiling are reviewed.

PRELIMINARY ISSUES

The Logic of Prediction

The logic of prediction described in Chapter 8 is equally relevant to the case of internal selection. Specifically, indicators of internal applicants' degree of success in past situations should be predictive of their likely success in new situations. Past situations importantly include previous jobs, as well as the current one, held by the applicant with the organization. The new situation is the internal vacancy the applicant is seeking via the organization's transfer or promotion system.

There may also be similarities between internal and external selection in terms of the effectiveness of selection methods. As you may recall from Chapters 8 and 9, three of the most valid external selection measures are biographical data, cognitive ability tests, and work samples. These methods also have validity in internal selection decisions. Personality measures have been found to be a valid predictor in selecting top corporate leaders. Research indicates that cognitive ability is strongly predictive of long-term job performance and advancement. Finally, work samples are valid predictors of advancement.[1] In this chapter we focus on processes and methods of selection that are unique to promotion and transfer decisions. However, in considering these methods and processes, it should be kept in mind that many of the techniques of external selection may be relevant as well.

Although the logic of prediction and the likely effectiveness of selection methods are similar for external and internal selection, in practice there are several potential advantages of internal over external selection. In particular, the data collected on internal applicants in their previous jobs often provide greater depth, relevance, and verifiability than the data collected on external applicants. This is because organizations usually have much more detailed and in-depth information about internal candidates' previous job experiences.

Along with depth and relevance, another positive aspect of the nature of predictors for internal selection is variability. Rather than simply relying on the opinion of one person as to the suitability of an internal candidate for the job, multiple assessments may be solicited. Opinions about the suitability of the candidate can also be solicited from other supervisors and peers. By pooling opinions, it is possible to get a more complete and accurate picture of a candidate's qualifications.

While internal selection has important advantages over external selection, there are two factors that can derail the logic of prediction. First, impression management and organizational politics can play important roles in who gets promoted in organizations. Although impression management also plays a role in external hiring (especially in employment interviews), internal "apple polishers" have a much greater opportunity to work their magic, with more targets for their influence and over a longer period of time, than external candidates. Thus, decision makers selecting internal candidates need to make sure they are not being "played" by internal candidates. A second factor that can undermine the logic of prediction for internal selection is title inflation. A recent study revealed that the job responsibilities of nearly half (46%) of recently promoted executives remained roughly the same after their new titles. Although there may be no great harm in such title inflation, the newly promoted, with no corresponding change in pay or responsibilities, should see these "promotions" for what they are. Being given a title of "process change manager" may mean little more than words.[2]

Types of Predictors

The distinctions made between types of predictors used in external selection are also applicable to types of internal predictors. One important difference to note between internal and external predictors pertains to content. There is usually greater depth and relevance to the data available on internal candidates. That is, the organization can go to its own files or managers to get reports on the applicants' previous experiences.

Selection Plan

Often it seems that internal selection is done on the basis of "who you know" rather than relevant knowledge, skill, ability, and other characteristics (KSAOs). Managers tend to rely heavily on the subjective opinions of previous managers who supervised the internal candidate. When asked why they rely on these subjective assessments, the answer is often, "Because the candidate has worked here for a long time, and I trust his supervisor's feel for the candidate."

Decision errors often occur when relying on subjective feelings for internal selection decisions. For example, in selecting managers to oversee engineering and scientific personnel in organizations, it is sometimes felt that those internal job candidates with the best technical skills will be the best managers. This is not always the case. Some technical wizards are poor managers and vice versa. Sound internal selection procedures need to be followed to guard against this error. A sound job analysis will show that both technical and managerial skills need to be assessed with well-crafted predictors.

Feel, hunch, gut instinct, intuition, and the like do not substitute for well-developed predictors. Relying solely on others' "feelings" about the job applicant may result in lowering hiring standards for some employees, discrimination against protected-class employees, and decisions with low validity. Therefore, it is imperative that a selection plan be used for internal as well as external selection. As described in Chapter 8, a selection plan lists the predictors to be used for assessment of each KSAO.

INITIAL ASSESSMENT METHODS

The internal recruitment process may generate a large number of applications for vacant positions. This is especially true when an open rather than a closed recruitment system is used—where jobs are posted for employees to apply. Given the time and cost of rigorous selection procedures, organizations use initial assessment methods to screen out applicants who do not meet the minimum qualifications needed to become a candidate. Initial assessment methods for internal recruitment typically include the following predictors: skills inventories, peer evaluations, self-assessments, managerial sponsorship, and informal discussions and recommendations. Each of these predictors will be discussed in turn, followed by a general evaluation of all predictors.

Skills Inventory

An immediate screening device in applicant assessment is to rely on existing data on employee skills. These data can be found in personnel files, which are usually on the computer in larger organizations and in file drawers in smaller organizations. The level of sophistication of the data kept by organizations varies considerably, depending on the method used. A traditional skills inventory is a listing of the KSAOs held by each employee in the organization. Usually, the system records a small number of skills listed in generic categories, such as education, experience, and supervisory training received. One of the problems with traditional skills inventories is that they often quickly become outdated. For a skills inventory to be useful (rather than simply another bureaucratic form to complete), managers must systematically enter the latest skills acquired by employees into the database as soon as they are developed. Another limitation with the traditional skills inventory is that the KSAOs are rather general or generic. Increasingly, the broad skills in a traditional skills inventory are being replaced or augmented with a customized skills assessment, where specific skill sets are recorded for specific jobs. Because specific skills can change even more quickly than general ones, it is even more imperative that customized inventories be regularly updated.

Peer Assessments

Assessments by peers or coworkers can be used to evaluate the promotability of an internal applicant. A variety of methods can be used, including peer ratings, peer nominations, and peer rankings.[3] Examples of all three are shown in Exhibit 10.1.

As can be seen in Exhibit 10.1, whereas peers are used to make promotion decisions in all three methods of peer assessments, the format of each is different. With peer ratings, readiness to be promoted is assessed for each peer using a rating scale. The person with the highest ratings is deemed most promotable. On the other hand, peer nominations rely on voting for the most promotable candidates. Peers receiving the greatest number of votes are the most promotable. Finally, peer rankings rely on a rank ordering of peers. Those peers with the highest rankings are the most promotable.

Peer assessments have been used extensively in the military over the years and to a lesser degree in industry. A virtue of peer assessments is that they rely on raters who presumably are very knowledgeable of the applicants' KSAOs due to their day-to-day contact with them. A possible downside to peer assessments, however, is that they may encourage friendship bias. Also, they may undermine morale in a work group by fostering a competitive environment.

Another possible problem with peer assessment is that the criteria by which assessments are made are not always made clear. For peer assessments to work, care should be taken in advance to carefully spell out the KSAOs needed for successful performance in the position the peer is being considered for. To do so, a job requirements matrix should be used.

A probable virtue of peer assessments is that peers are more likely to feel that the decisions reached are fair, because they had an input into the decision. The decision is thus not seen as a "behind the back" maneuver by management. Therefore, peer assessments are used more often with open rather than closed systems of internal recruitment.

EXHIBIT 10.1 **Peer Assessment Methods**

Peer Rating

Please consider each of the following employees and rate them using the following scale for the position of manager described in the job requirements matrix:

	Not Promotable		Promotable in One Year		Promotable Now
	1	2	3	4	5
Jean	1	2	3	4	5
John	1	2	3	4	5
Andy	1	2	3	4	5
Herb	1	2	3	4	5

Peer Nominations

Please consider each of the following employees and mark an X for the one employee who is most promotable to the position of manager as described in the job requirements matrix:

    Joe   _____
    Nishant   _____
    Carlos   _____
    Suraphon _____
    Renee   _____

Peer Ranking

Please rank order the following employees from the most promotable (1) to the least promotable (5) for the position of manager as described in the job requirements matrix:

    Ila   _____
    Karen   _____
    Phillip   _____
    Yi-Chan   _____
    Kimlang   _____

Self-Assessments

Job incumbents can be asked to evaluate their own skills as a basis for determining promotability. This procedure is sometimes used with open recruitment systems. An example of this approach is shown in Exhibit 10.2. Caution must be exercised in using this process for selection, as it may raise the expectations of those rating themselves that they will be selected. As one VP of human resources (HR) noted,

EXHIBIT 10.2   Self-Assessment Form Used for Application in Job Posting System

SUPPLEMENTAL QUESTIONNAIRE

This supplemental questionnaire will be the principal basis for determining whether or not you are highly qualified for this position. You may add information not identified in your SF-171 orexpand on that which is identified. You should consider appropriate work experience, outside activities, awards, training, and education for each of the items listed below.

1. Knowledge of the Bureau of Indian Affairs' mission, organization, structure, policies, and functions, as they relate to real estate.
2. Knowledge of technical administrative requirements to provide technical guidance in administrative areas, such as personnel regulations, travel regulations, time and attendance requirements, budget documents, Privacy Act, and Freedom of Information Act, etc.
3. Ability to work with program directors and administrative staff and ability to apply problem solving techniques and management concepts; ability to analyze facts and problems and develop alternatives.
4. Ability to operate various computer programs and methodology in the analysis and design of automated methods for meeting the information and reporting requirements for the division.
5. Knowledge of the bureau budget process and statistical profile of all field operations that impact in the Real Estate Services program.

On a separate sheet of paper, address the above items in narrative form. Identify the vacancy announcement number across the top. Sign and date your Supplemental Questionnaire.

SOURCE: Department of the Interior, Bureau of Indian Affairs. Form BIA-4450 (4/22/92).

"Some people think a lot more highly of their skills and talent" than is warranted. Employees' supervisors should encourage upward mobility (not "hoard" talent), but they also need to ensure that employees are realistic in their self-assessments.[4]

Managerial Sponsorship

Increasingly, organizations are relying on higher-ups in the organization to identify and develop the KSAOs of those at lower levels in the organization. Historically, the higher-up has been the person's immediate supervisor. Today, however, the higher-up may be a person at a higher level of the organization who does not have direct responsibility for the person being rated. Higher-ups are sometimes labeled coaches, sponsors, or mentors, and their roles are defined in Exhibit 10.3. In some organizations, there are formal mentorship programs where employees are assigned

---

EXHIBIT 10.3 **Employee Advocates**

Coach

- Provides day-to-day feedback
- Diagnoses and resolves performance problems
- Creates opportunities for employees using existing training programs and career development programs

Sponsor

- Actively promotes person for advancement opportunities
- Guides person's career rather than simply informing them of opportunities
- Creates opportunities for people in decision-making capacities to see the skills of the employee (e.g., lead a task force)

Mentor

- Becomes personally responsible for the success of the person
- Available to person on and off the job
- Lets person in on "insider" information
- Solicits and values person's input

SOURCE: Reprinted with permission from Dr. Janina Latack, PhD, Nelson O'Connor & Associates/ Outplacement International, Phoenix/Tucson.

coaches, sponsors, and mentors. In other organizations, these matches may naturally occur, often progressing from coach to sponsor to mentor as the relationship matures. Regardless of the formality of the relationship, these individuals are often given considerable influence in promotion decisions. Their weight is due to their high organizational level and in-depth knowledge of the employee's KSAOs. Not only is the judgment of these advocates important but so, too, are their behaviors. Mentors, for example, are likely to put employees in situations where they receive high visibility. That visibility may increase the applicants' chances of promotion.

Informal Discussions and Recommendations

Not all promotion decisions are made on the basis of formal HR policy and procedures. For many promotions, much or all of the decision process occurs outside normal channels, through informal discussions and recommendations. For example, Celeste Russell, VP of HR for Good Times Entertainment, a New York home video and direct marketing company, invites employees out for coffee. "It's like a sales call," she says. Although such informal discussions are a common means of internal selection decisions, especially in small companies, they may have limited validity because they are quite subjective. Although Russell prides herself on knowing the names of employees' pets and other personal information, it seems likely the personal and subjective nature of these conversations compromises her ability to make internal selection decisions relative to "cold and hard" data such as skills, accomplishments, abilities, and so forth. Such is the case with many, if not most, informal approaches to selection.[5]

Choice of Initial Assessment Methods

As was discussed, there are several formal and informal methods of initial assessment available to screen internal applicants to produce a list of candidates. Research has been conducted on the effectiveness of each method, which will now be presented to help determine which initial assessment methods should be used. The reviews of this research are summarized in Exhibit 10.4.

In Exhibit 10.4, the same criteria are applied to evaluating the effectiveness of these predictors as were used to evaluate the effectiveness of predictors for external selection. Cost refers to expenses incurred in using the predictor. Reliability refers to the consistency of measurement. Validity refers to the strength of the relationship between the predictor and job performance. Low validity refers to validity in the range of about .00 to .15, moderate validity corresponds to validity in the range of about .16 to .30, and high validity is .31 and above. Utility refers to the monetary return, minus costs, associated with using the predictor. Adverse impact refers to the possibility that a disproportionate number of women and minorities are rejected using this predictor. Finally, reaction refers to the likely impact on applicants.

Two points should be made about the effectiveness of initial internal selection methods. First, skills inventories and informal methods are used extensively. This suggests that many organizations continue to rely on closed rather than open internal recruitment systems. Certainly this is a positive procedure when administrative ease is of importance. However, it must be noted that these approaches may result in overlooking talented applicants. Also, there may be a discriminatory impact on women and minorities.

The second point to be made is that peer assessment methods are very promising in terms of reliability and validity. They are not frequently used, but need to be given more consideration by organizations as a screening device. Perhaps this will take place as organizations continue to decentralize decision making and empower employees to make business decisions historically made only by the supervisor.

SUBSTANTIVE ASSESSMENT METHODS

The internal applicant pool is narrowed down to candidates using the initial assessment methods. A decision as to which internal candidates will become finalists is usually made using the following substantive assessment methods: seniority and

EXHIBIT 10.4 Evaluation of Initial Assessment Methods

Predictors	Use	Cost	Reliability	Validity	Utility	Reactions	Adverse Impact
Self-nominations	Low	Low	Moderate	Moderate	?	Mixed	?
Skills inventories	High	High	Moderate	Moderate	?	?	?
Peer assessments	Low	Low	High	High	?	Negative	?
Managerial sponsorship	Low	Moderate	?	?	?	Positive	?
Informal methods	High	Low	?	?	?	Mixed	?

experience, job knowledge tests, performance appraisal, promotability ratings, assessment centers, interview simulations, and review boards. After each of these methods is discussed, an evaluation is made.

Seniority and Experience

At first blush the concepts of seniority and experience may seem the same. In reality, they may be quite different. Seniority typically refers to length of service or tenure with the organization, department, or job. For example, company seniority is measured as length of continuous employment in an organization and is operationalized as the difference between the present date of employment and the date of hire. Thus, seniority is a purely quantitative measure that has nothing to do with the type or quality of job experiences.

Conversely, experience generally has a broader meaning. While seniority may be one aspect of experience, experience also reflects *type* of experience. Two employees working at the same company for 20 years may have the same level of seniority but very different levels of experience if one employee has performed a number of different jobs, worked in different areas of the organization, enrolled in various training programs, and so on. Thus, experience includes not only length of service in the organization or in various positions in the organization but also the kinds of activities employees have undertaken in those positions. Thus, although seniority and experience are often considered synonymous, they are quite different, and—as we will see in the following discussion—these differences have real implications for internal selection decisions.

Use and Evaluation

Seniority and experience are among the most prevalent methods of internal selection. In most unionized companies, heavy reliance is placed on seniority over other KSAOs for advancement.[6] Between two-thirds and four-fifths of union contracts stipulate that seniority be considered in promotion decisions, and about one-half mandate that it be the determining factor. In policy, nonunion organizations claim to place less weight on seniority than other factors in making advancement decisions. In practice, however, at least one study showed that regardless of the wording in policy statements, heavy emphasis is still placed on seniority in nonunion settings.[7] Research has shown that seniority is more likely to be used for promotions in small, unionized, and capital-intensive companies.[8] Although few data are available, there is reason to believe that experience is also frequently considered in internal selection decisions.

There are various reasons why seniority and experience are so widely used as methods of internal selection decisions. First, organizations believe that direct experience in a job content area reflects an accumulated stock of KSAOs necessary to perform the job. In short, experience may be content valid because it reflects on-the-job experience. Second, seniority and experience information is easily and cheaply obtained. Furthermore, unions believe that reliance on objective measures such as seniority and experience protects the employee from capricious treatment and favoritism. Finally, promoting experienced or senior individuals is socially acceptable because it is seen as rewarding loyalty. In fact, it has been found that most decision makers feel that negative repercussions would result if a more junior employee is promoted over a more senior employee.

In evaluating seniority and experience as methods of internal selection, it is important to return to our earlier distinction between the two concepts. Several studies have found that seniority is unrelated to job performance.[9] In fact, one study of unionized plants found that 97% of the promotions went to the most senior employee, yet in nearly half the cases this person was not the highest performer. Thus, seniority does not seem to be a particularly valid method of internal selection. In fact, the "Big Three" automakers cite abandoning seniority for promotions as a reason for their improved performance in the mid-1990s.[10]

As compared to seniority, evidence for the validity of experience is more positive. A large-scale review of the literature has shown that experience is moderately related to job performance.[11] Research suggests that experience is predictive of job performance in the short run but is followed by a plateau during which experience loses its ability to predict job performance. It appears that most of the effect of experience on performance is due to the fact that experienced employees have greater job knowledge. However, while experience may result in increased performance due to greater job knowledge, it does not remedy performance difficulties due to low ability; initial performance deficits of low-ability employees are not remedied by increased experience over time.[12] Thus, while experience is more likely to be related to job performance than seniority, neither ranks among the most valid predictors for internal selection decisions.

Based on the research evidence, several conclusions about the use of seniority and experience in internal selection decisions seem appropriate:

1. Experience is a more valid method of internal selection than seniority (although unionized employers may have little choice but to use seniority).
2. Experience is better suited to predict short-term rather than long-term potential.
3. Experience is more likely to be content valid if the past or present jobs are similar to the future job.
4. Employees seem to expect that promotions will go to the most senior or experienced employee, so using seniority or experience for promotions may yield positive reactions from employees.
5. Experience is unlikely to remedy initial performance difficulties of low-ability employees.

Job Knowledge Tests

Job knowledge measures one's mastery of the concepts needed to perform certain work. Job knowledge is a complex concept that includes elements of both ability (capacity to learn) and seniority (opportunity to learn). It is usually measured with a paper-and-pencil test. To develop a paper-and-pencil test to assess job knowledge, the content domain from which test questions will be constructed must be clearly identified. For example, a job knowledge test used to select sales managers from among salespeople must identify the specific knowledge necessary for being a successful sales manager.

An innovative video-based job knowledge test to be used as part of the promotion system was developed by Federal Express.[13] Federal Express developed the interactive video test to assess employees' ability to deal with customers. The test is based on job analysis data derived from the critical tasks necessary to deliver high levels of customer service. The test, termed QUEST (Quality Using Electronic Systems Training), presents employees with a menu of modules on CD-ROM (e.g., delivering packages, defensive driving). A 90% competency level on the test is established as the expectation for minimum performance—and subsequent promotability. This suggests that such assessments could fruitfully be used in internal selection decisions when promoting employees into customer-sensitive positions. The greater the employee's portfolio of customer skills, the better able he or she should be to help Federal Express meet its customer service goals.

Although job knowledge is not a well-researched method of either internal or external employee selection, it holds great promise as a predictor of job performance. This is because it reflects an assessment of previous experiences of an applicant and an important KSAO, namely, cognitive ability.[14]

Performance Appraisal

One possible predictor of future job performance is past job performance. This assumes, of course, that elements of the future job are similar to the past job. Data on employees' previous performance are routinely collected as part of the performance appraisal process and thus available for use in internal selection.

One advantage of performance appraisals over other internal assessment methods is that they are readily available in many organizations. Another desirable feature of performance appraisals is that they probably capture both ability and motivation. Hence, they offer a very complete look at the person's qualifications for the job. Care must still be taken in using performance appraisals because there is not always a direct correspondence between the requirements of the current job and the requirements of the position applied for. Performance appraisals should only be used as predictors when job analysis indicates a close relationship between the current job and the position applied for.

For example, performance in a highly technical position (e.g., scientist, engineer) may require certain skills (e.g., quantitative skills) that are required in both junior- and senior-level positions. Thus, using the results of the performance appraisal of the junior position is appropriate in predicting the performance in the senior position. It is not, however, appropriate to use the results of the performance appraisal for the junior-level technical job to predict performance in a job, requiring a different set of skills (e.g., planning, organizing, staffing), such as that of manager.

Although there are some advantages to using performance appraisal results for internal selection, they are far from perfect predictors. They are subject to many influences that have nothing to do with the likelihood of success in a future job.[15]

The well-known "Peter Principle"—that individuals rise to their lowest level of incompetence—illustrates another limitation with using performance appraisal as a method of internal staffing decisions.[16] The argument behind the Peter Principle is that if organizations promote individuals on the basis of their past performance, the only time that people stop being promoted is when they are poor performers at the job into which they were last promoted. Thus, over time, organizations will have internally staffed positions with individuals who are incompetent. In fact, the authors have data from a Fortune 100 company showing that less than one-fifth of the variance in an employee's current performance rating can be explained by the performance ratings previous three years. Thus, although past performance may have some validity in predicting future performance, the relationship may not be overly strong.

This is not to suggest that organizations should abandon using performance ratings as a factor in internal staffing decisions. Rather, the validity of using performance appraisal as an internal selection method may depend on a number of considerations. Exhibit 10.5 provides several questions that should be used in deciding how much weight to place on performance appraisal as a means of making internal selection decisions. Affirmative answers to these questions suggest that past performance may be validly used in making internal selection decisions.

An advance over simple use of performance ratings is to review past performance records more thoroughly, including an evaluation of various dimensions of performance that are particularly relevant to job performance (where the dimensions are based on job analysis results). For example, a study of police promotions used a pool of six supervisors to score officers on four job-relevant police officer performance dimensions—supervisory-related education and experience, disciplined behavior, commendatory behavior, and reliability—with the goal of predicting future performance. Results of the study indicated that using ratings of past performance records was an effective method of promoting officers.[17] Such a

---

EXHIBIT 10.5   Questions to Ask in Using Performance Appraisal as a Method of Internal Staffing Decisions

- Is the performance appraisal process reliable and unbiased?
- Is present job content representative of future job content?
- Have the KSAOs required for performance in the future job(s) been acquired and demonstrated in the previous job(s)?
- Is the organizational or job environment stable such that what led to past job success will lead to future job success?

method might be adapted to other positions and provide a useful means of incorporating past performance data into a more valid prediction of future potential.

Promotability Ratings

In many organizations, an assessment of promotability (assessment of potential for a higher-level job) is made at the same time that performance appraisals are conducted. Replacement and succession planning frequently use both types of assessments (see Chapter 3).

Promotability ratings are useful not only from a selection perspective but also from a recruitment perspective. By discussing what is needed to be promotable, employee development may be encouraged as well as coupled with organizational sponsorship of the opportunities needed to develop. In turn, the development of new skills in employees increases the internal recruitment pool for promotions.

Caution must be exercised in using promotability ratings as well. If employees receive separate evaluations for purposes of performance appraisal, promotability, and pay, the possibility exists of mixed messages going out to employees that may be difficult for them to interpret. For example, it is difficult to understand why one receives an excellent performance rating and a solid pay raise, but at the same time is rated as not promotable. Care must be taken to show employees the relevant judgments that are being made in each assessment. In the example presented, it must be clearly indicated that promotion is based not only on past performance but also on skill acquisition and opportunities for advancement.

Assessment Centers

An elaborate method of employee selection, primarily used internally, is an assessment center. An assessment center is a collection of predictors used to forecast success, primarily in higher-level jobs. It is used for higher-level jobs because of the high costs involved in conducting the center. The assessment center can be used to select employees for lower-level jobs as well, though this is rarely done.

The theory behind assessment centers is relatively straightforward. Concern is with the prediction of an individual's behavior and effectiveness in critical roles, usually managerial. Since these roles require complex behavior, multiple KSAOs will predict those behaviors. Hence, there is a need to carefully identify and assess those KSAOs. This will require multiple methods of assessing the KSAOs, as well as multiple assessors. The result should be higher validity than could be obtained from a single assessment method or assessor.

As with any sound selection procedure, the assessment center predictors are based on job analysis to identify KSAOs and aid in the construction of content valid methods of assessment for those KSAOs. As a result, a selection plan must be developed when using assessment centers. An example of such a selection plan is shown in Exhibit 10.6.

EXHIBIT 10.6   Selection Plan for an Assessment Center

KSAO	Writing Exercise	Speech Exercise	Analysis Problem	In-Basket Tent.	In-Basket Final	Leadership Group Discussion Management Problems	Leadership Group Discussion City Council
Oral communications					X	X	X
Oral presentation		X				X	
Written communications	X		X	X	X		
Stress tolerance				X	X	X	X
Leadership					X	X	
Sensitivity			X	X	X	X	X
Tenacity				X	X	X	
Risk taking			X	X	X	X	X
Initiative			X	X	X	X	X
Planning & organization			X	X	X	X	X
Management control			X	X	X		
Delegation				X	X		
Problem analysis			X	X	X	X	X
Decision making			X	X	X	X	X
Decisiveness			X	X	X	X	X
Responsiveness			X	X	X	X	X

Source: Department of Employment Relations, State of Wisconsin.

Characteristics of Assessment Centers

Whereas specific characteristics vary from situation to situation, assessment centers generally have some common characteristics. Job candidates usually participate in an assessment center for a period of days rather than hours. Most assessment centers last two to three days, but some may be as long as five days. As we describe shortly, a big part of assessment centers is simulations, where employees participate in exercises, and trained assessors evaluate their performance. Assessors are usually line managers, but sometimes psychologists are used as well. The average ratio of assessors to assessees ranges from 1:1 to 4:1.

The participants in the center are usually managers who are being assessed for higher-level managerial jobs. Normally, they are chosen to participate by other organization members, such as their supervisor. Often selection is based on an employee's current level of job performance.

At the conclusion of the assessment center, the participants are evaluated by the assessors. Typically, this involves the assessor examining all of the information gathered about each participant. The information is then translated into a series of ratings on several dimensions of managerial jobs. Typical dimensions assessed include communications (written and oral), leadership and human relations, and planning, problem solving, and decision making. In evaluating these dimensions, assessors are trained to look for critical behaviors that represent highly effective or ineffective responses to the exercise situations in which participants are placed. There may also be an overall assessment rating that represents the bottom-line evaluation for each participant. Assessment center dimensions are relatively highly correlated with one another, though evidence suggests that the dimensions do add to the prediction of performance beyond the overall score.[18] Exhibit 10.7 provides a sample rating form.

A variety of different exercises are used at a center. Experts argue that the simulation is the key to an assessment center, though exactly how future performance is simulated varies from assessment center to assessment center.[19]

Although many assessment centers contain written tests and interviews—and thus may include some of the external selection techniques we discussed in Chapters 8 and 9—the simulation exercises are the heart of assessment centers. The most frequently used exercises are the in-basket exercise, group discussion, and case analysis. Each of these exercises will be briefly described.

In-Basket Exercise.   The most commonly used assessment center exercise is the in-basket (according to one study, used in 82% of assessment centers). The in-basket (sometimes called "inbox") usually contains memoranda, reports, phone calls, and letters that require a response. When this in-basket material is presented to a candidate, he or she is asked to respond to the items by prioritizing them, drafting responses, scheduling meetings, and so forth. It is a timed exercise, and usually the candidate has two to three hours to respond. Even when used alone, the in-basket exercise seems to forecast ascendancy, one of the key criteria of assessment centers.[20]

EXHIBIT 10.7   Sample Assessment Center Rating Form

Participant Name: _____

Personal Qualities:
    1. Energy   _____
    2. Risk taking   _____
    3. Tolerance for ambiguity   _____
    4. Objectivity   _____
    5. Reliability   _____

Communication Skills:
    6. Oral   _____
    7. Written   _____
    8. Persuasion   _____

Human Relations:
    9. Teamwork   _____
   10. Flexibility   _____
   11. Awareness of social environment   _____

Leadership Skills:
   12. Impact   _____
   13. Autonomy   _____

Decision-Making Skills:
   14. Decisiveness   _____
   15. Organizing   _____
   16. Planning   _____

Problem-Solving Skills:
   17. Fact finding   _____
   18. Interpreting information   _____

Overall Assessment Rating:
Indication of potential to perform
effectively at the next level is:
    Excellent   _____
    Good   _____
    Moderate   _____
    Low   _____

Group Discussion.   In a group discussion, a small group of candidates is given a problem to solve. The problem is one they would likely encounter in the higher-level position for which they are applying. As they work on the problem, assessors sit around the perimeter of the group and evaluate how each candidate behaves in an unstructured setting. They look for skills such as leadership and communication. Roughly 60% of assessment centers include a group discussion. Some group discussion exercises assign candidates specific roles to play; others are "leaderless" in that no one is assigned a particular role. An example of the former is where participants are part of a project team and each participant assumes a role (IT, HR, marketing, etc.). An example of the latter is a "lost in the wilderness" exercise, where a group of individuals is presented a scenario in which they are lost and have a few resources on which they can survive and find their way home. Both assigned role and leaderless group discussions assess the skills of leadership, judgment, persuasive oral communication, teamwork, and interpersonal sensitivity.

Case Analysis.   Cases of actual business situations can also be presented to the candidates. Each candidate is asked to provide a written analysis of the case, describing the nature of the problem, likely causes, and recommended solutions. Not only are the written results evaluated but the candidate's oral report is scored as well. The candidates may be asked to give an oral presentation to a panel of managers and to respond to their questions, comments, and concerns. Case analyses are used in roughly half of all assessment centers.

Validity and Effective Practices

In a study of 50 different assessment centers, their average validity was very favorable ($\overline{r} = .37$). This study showed that the validity of the assessment center was higher when multiple predictors were used, when assessors were psychologists rather than managers, and when peer evaluations as well as assessor evaluations were used. The latter results call into question the common practice of using only managers as assessors. The finding suggests that multiple assessors be used, including psychologists and peers as well as managers. Such usage provides a different perspective on participants' performance, one that may be overlooked by managers.[20] Assessment centers have incremental validity in predicting performance and promotability beyond personality traits and cognitive ability tests, though the incremental validity may be relatively small because assessment center scores are substantially correlated with cognitive ability.[21]

Another advantage of assessment centers is that they appear to have little or no adverse impact against women and minorities. Indeed, one recent study of nearly 2,000 managers found that female candidates generally performed better than mal candidates.

Research has uncovered some problems with assessment centers.[23] One of the most commonly cited problems is the "crown prince or princess" syndrome. Here, it is alleged, decision makers may know how people did on the assessment center and therefore promote those who did well versus those who did not do well. Thus, assessment centers could be a self-fulfilling prophecy—they are valid only because decision makers think they are. However, research indicates that assessment centers are valid even when the results of the assessment center are "blind" to decision makers. Thus, due to the validity of assessment centers, they should be seriously considered in making promotion decisions—if they can be afforded.

One of the biggest limitations with assessment centers is their cost. The nature of the individualized assessment and the requirement of multiple assessors make them cost prohibitive for many organizations. One way some organizations are mitigating the costs of assessment centers is through other, related assessments. Some organizations videotape assessees' performance so that assessors can evaluate their performance when convenient. This saves coordination and travel costs. A practice that results in even greater cost savings is to use situational judgment tests, where assessees are given various exercises in written, video, or computerized form. An analysis of 102 studies suggested that the validity of situational judgment tests ($\bar{r} = .34$) is about as high as the validity of assessment centers.[24]

Another way to reduce the costs of the assessment center is to use off-the-shelf assessments provided by vendors. For example, Assessment Center Exercises (AC-ESX) is a vendor that sells more than 150 assessment center exercises, including instructions on how to train assessors, administer the exercises, and score responses. The exercises include the three most common exercises noted above, as well as scheduling exercises, interview simulations, and fact-finding exercises. While using such off-the-shelf products may save money, it is critical that assessors have proper training. Without the right training, the resulting assessment or score derived from the assessment may be so scattershot as to be useless.

There is little research that has examined participant reactions to assessment centers. However, it is commonly noted that although assessment centers are stressful to participants, they generate positive reactions for assessors and assessees. This probably is partly due to the fact that they are seen as valid by participants. Furthermore, they may result in increased self-confidence for participants, even for those who are not promoted as a result of the assessment center. The positive effects of assessment centers on employee attitudes and self-confidence may be relatively fleeting, however, as one study of British managers found. Thus, it is possible that the positive impact of assessment centers on assessees wanes over time. The International Task Force on Assessment Center Guidelines has published a set of guidelines for the development and use of assessment centers. They are a useful tool for those wishing to ensure that an assessment center is conducted in a valid, fair, and effective manner. Another group of experts has discussed common pitfalls in using assessment centers and has provided recommendations to avoid these problems.[25]

Assessment for Global Assignments

When assessment centers were developed, little thought was given to the prospect of using assessment data to forecast job success in a foreign environment. As globalization continues, however, organizations increasingly are promoting individuals into positions overseas. A survey indicated that 80% of midsize and large companies send professionals abroad, and many plan on increasing this percentage. Because overseas assignments present additional demands on an employee beyond the typical skills and motivations required to perform a job in the host country, staffing overseas positions presents special challenges for employers. Indeed, one study revealed that cultural factors were much more important to success in an overseas assignment than were technical skills factors. Although many competencies are important to expatriate success, such as family stability/support and language skills, the most important competency is cultural adaptability and flexibility.

One means of predicting success in overseas assignments is a personality test. For example, employees who respond positively to items such as "It is easy for me to strike up conversations with people I do not know" or "I find it easy to put myself in other people's position" may better navigate the challenges of overseas assignments. Personnel Decisions International has developed a personality test designed to assess whether employees will be successful in overseas assignments. The company reports a positive relationship between scores on the test and success in overseas assignments. Another tool is simulations or interviews designed to simulate conditions overseas or typical challenges that arise.[26] As one can see, bringing these methods together may make the assessment process for global assignments closely resemble an assessment center.

Interview Simulations

An interview simulation simulates the oral communication required on the job. It is sometimes used in an assessment center, but less frequently than in-baskets, leaderless group discussions, and case analysis. It is also used as a predictor separate from the assessment center. There are several different forms of interview simulations.[27]

Role-Play

With a role-play, the job candidate is placed in a simulated situation where he or she must interact with a person at work, such as the boss, a subordinate, or a customer. The interviewer or someone else plays one role, and the job candidate plays the role of the person in the position applied for. So, for example, in selecting someone to be promoted to a supervisory level, the job candidate may be asked to role-play dealing with a difficult employee.

Fact Finding

In a fact-finding interview, the job candidate is presented with a case or problem with incomplete information. It is the job of the candidate to solicit from the interviewer or a resource person the additional facts needed to resolve the case. If one was hiring someone to be an EEO manager, one might present him or her with a case where adverse impact is suggested, and then evaluate the candidate according to what data he or she solicits to confirm or disconfirm adverse impact.

Oral Presentations

In many jobs, presentations need to be made to customers, clients, or even boards of directors. To select someone to perform this role, an oral presentation can be required. This approach would be useful, for example, to see what sort of "sales pitch" a consultant might make or to see how an executive would present his or her proposed strategic plan to a board of directors.

Given the importance of interpersonal skills in many jobs, it is unfortunate that not many organizations use interview simulations. This is especially true with internal selection, where the organization knows if the person has the right credentials (e.g., company experiences, education, and training) but may not know if the person has the right interpersonal "chemistry" to fit in with the work group. Interview simulations allow for a systematic assessment of this chemistry rather than relying on the instinct of the interviewer. To be effective, these interviews need to be structured and evaluated according to observable behaviors identified in the job analysis as necessary for successful performance.

Promotion Panels and Review Boards

In the public sector, it is a common practice to use a panel or board of people to review the qualifications of candidates. Frequently, a combination of both internal and external candidates are being assessed. Typically, the panel or board consists of job experts, HR professionals, and representatives from constituencies in the community that the board represents. Having a board such as this to hire public servants, such as school superintendents or fire and police officials, offers two advantages. First, as with assessment centers, there are multiple assessors with which to ensure a complete and accurate assessment of the candidate's qualifications. Second, by participating in the selection process, constituents are likely to be more committed to the decision reached. This "buy-in" is particularly important for community representatives with whom the job candidate will interact. It is hoped that by having a say in the process, they will be less likely to voice objections once the candidate is hired.

Choice of Substantive Assessment Methods

Along with research on initial assessment methods, there has also been research conducted on substantive assessment methods. The reviews of this research are summarized in Exhibit 10.8. The same criteria are applied to evaluating the effectiveness of these predictors as were used to evaluate the effectiveness of initial assessment methods.

An examination of Exhibit 10.8 indicates that there is no single best method of narrowing down the candidate list to finalists. What is suggested, however, is that some predictors are more likely to be effective than others. In particular, job knowledge, promotability ratings, and assessment centers have a strong record in terms of reliability and validity in choosing candidates. A very promising development for internal selection is use of job knowledge tests. The validity of these tests appears to be substantial, but, unfortunately, few organizations use them for internal selection purposes.

The effectiveness of several internal selection predictors (case analysis, interview simulations, panels and review boards) is not known at this stage. Interview simulations appear to be a promising technique for jobs requiring public contact skills. All of them need additional research. Other areas in need of additional research are the utility, reactions, and adverse impact associated with all of the substantive assessment methods.

DISCRETIONARY ASSESSMENT METHODS

Discretionary methods are used to narrow down the list of finalists to those who will receive job offers. Sometimes all finalists will receive offers, but at other times, there may not be enough positions to fill for each finalist to receive an offer. As with external selection, discretionary assessments are sometimes made on the basis of organizational citizenship behavior and staffing philosophy regarding EEO/AA.

Two areas of discretionary assessment differ from external selection and need to be considered in deciding job offers. First, previous finalists who do not receive job offers do not simply disappear. They may remain with the organization in hopes of securing an offer the next time the position is open. At the margin, this may be a factor in decision making because being bypassed a second time may create a disgruntled employee. As a result, a previous finalist may be given an offer over a first-time finalist, all other things being equal.

Second, multiple assessors are generally used with internal selection. That is, not only can the hiring manager's opinion be used to select who will receive a job offer but so can the opinions of others (e.g., previous manager, top management) who are knowledgeable about the candidate's profile and the requirements of the current position. As a result, in deciding which candidates will receive job offers, evaluations by people other than the hiring manager may be accorded substantial weight in the decision-making process.

EXHIBIT 10.8 **Evaluation of Substantive Assessment Methods**

Predictors	Use	Cost	Reliability	Validity	Utility	Reactions	Adverse Impact
Seniority	High	Low	High	Low	?	?	High
Experience	High	Low	High	Moderate	High	Positive	Mixed
Job knowledge tests	Low	Moderate	High	High	?	?	?
Performance appraisal	Moderate	Moderate	?	Moderate	?	?	?
Promotability ratings	Low	Low	High	High	?	?	?
Assessment center	Low	High	High	High	High	?	?
In-basket exercise	Low	Moderate	Moderate	Moderate	High	Mixed	Mixed
Leaderless group discussion	Low	Low	Moderate	Moderate	?	?	?
Case analysis	Low	Low	?	Moderate	?	?	?
Global assignments	High	Moderate	?	?	?	?	?
Interview simulations	Low	Low	?	?	?	?	?
Panels and review boards	Low	?	?	?	?	?	?

LEGAL ISSUES

From a legal perspective, methods and processes of internal selection are to be viewed in the same way as those of external selection. The laws and regulations make no major distinctions between them. Consequently, most of the legal influences on internal selection have already been treated in Chapters 8 and 9. There are, however, some brief comments to be made about internal selection legal influences. Those influences are the UGESP and the glass ceiling.

Uniform Guidelines on Employee Selection Procedures

It should be remembered that the UGESP define a "selection procedure" in such a way that virtually any selection method, be it used in an external or internal context, is covered by the requirements of the UGESP. It should also be remembered that the UGESP apply to any "employment decision," which explicitly includes promotion decisions.

When there is adverse impact in promotions, the organization is given the option of justifying it through the conduct of validation studies. These are primarily criterion-related or content validity studies. Ideally, criterion-related studies with predictive validation designs will be used, as has been partially done in the case of assessment centers. Unfortunately, this places substantial administrative and research demands on the organization that are difficult to fulfill most of the time. Consequently, content validation appears to be a better bet for validation purposes.

Many of the methods of assessment used in internal selection attempt to gauge KSAOs and behaviors directly associated with a current job that are felt to be related to success in higher-level jobs. Examples include seniority, performance appraisals, and promotability ratings. These are based on current, as well as past, job content. Validation of these methods, if legally necessary, likely occurs along content validation lines. The organization thus should pay particular and close attention to the validation and documentation requirements for content validation in the UGESP.

The Glass Ceiling

In Chapter 6, the nature of the glass ceiling was discussed, as well as staffing steps to remove it from organizational promotion systems. Most of that discussion centered on internal recruitment and supporting activities that could be undertaken. Surprisingly, selection methods used for promotion assessment are rarely mentioned in literature on the glass ceiling.

This is a major oversight. Whereas the internal recruitment practices recommended may enhance the identification and attraction of minority and women candidates for promotion, effectively matching them to their new jobs requires application of internal selection processes and methods. The Equal Employment

Opportunity Commission's (EEOC's) policy on nondiscriminatory promotions is (1) the KSAOs to be assessed must be job related and consistent with business necessity; (2) there must be uniform and consistently applied standards across all promotion candidates.[28] How might the organization operate its internal selection system to seek compliance with EEOC policy?

The first possibility is for greater use of selection plans. As discussed in Chapter 8, these plans lay out the KSAOs required for a job, which KSAOs are necessary to bring to the job (as opposed to being acquired on the job), and of those necessary, the most appropriate method of assessment for each. Such a plan forces an organization to conduct job analysis, construct career ladders or KSAO lattices, and consider alternatives to many of the traditional methods of assessment used in promotion systems.

A second suggestion is for the organization to back away from use of these traditional methods of assessment as much as possible, in ways consistent with the selection plan. This means a move away from casual, subjective methods such as supervisory recommendation, typical promotability ratings, quick reviews of personnel files, and informal recommendations. In their place should come more formal, standardized, and job-related assessment methods. Examples here include assessment centers, promotion review boards or panels, and interview simulations.

A final suggestion is for the organization to pay close attention to the types of KSAOs necessary for advancement, and undertake programs to impart these KSAOs to aspiring employees. These developmental actions might include key job and committee assignments, participation in conferences and other networking opportunities, mentoring and coaching programs, and skill acquisition in formal training programs. Internal selection methods would then be used to assess proficiency on these newly acquired KSAOs, in accordance with the selection plan.

SUMMARY

The selection of internal candidates follows a process very similar to the selection of external candidates. The logic of prediction is applied, and a selection plan is developed and implemented.

One important area where internal and external selection methods differ is in the nature of the predictor. Predictors used for internal selection tend to have greater depth and more relevance and are better suited for verification. As a result, there are often different types of predictors used for internal selection decisions than for external selection decisions.

Initial assessment methods are used to narrow down the applicant pool to a qualified set of candidates. Approaches used are skills inventories, peer assessments, self-assessments, managerial sponsorship, informal discussions and recommendations, and career concepts. Of these approaches, no single approach is particularly strong in predicting future performance. Hence, consideration should be given to using multiple predictors to verify the accuracy of any one method. These results also point to the need to use substantive as well as initial assessment methods in making internal selection decisions.

Substantive assessment methods are used to select finalists from the list of candidates. Predictors used to make these decisions include seniority and experience, job knowledge tests, performance appraisals, promotability ratings, the assessment center, interview simulations, and panels and review boards. Of this set of predictors, ones that work well are job knowledge tests, promotability ratings, and assessment centers. Organizations need to give greater consideration to the latter three predictors to supplement traditional seniority and experience.

Although very costly, the assessment center seems to be very effective. It is so effective because it is grounded in behavioral science theory and the logic of prediction. In particular, samples of behavior are analyzed, multiple assessors and predictors are used, and predictors are developed on the basis of job analysis.

Internal job applicants have the potential for far greater access to selection data than do external job applicants due to their physical proximity to the data. As a result, procedures must be implemented to ensure that manual and computer files with sensitive data are kept private and confidential.

Two areas of legal concern for internal selection decisions are the UGESP and the glass ceiling. In terms of the UGESP, particular care must be taken to ensure that internal selection methods are valid if adverse impact is occurring. To minimize glass ceiling effects, organizations should make greater use of selection plans and more objective internal assessment methods, as well as help impart the KSAOs necessary for advancement.

DISCUSSION QUESTIONS

1. Explain how internal selection decisions differ from external selection decisions.
2. What are the differences among peer ratings, peer nominations, and peer rankings?
3. Explain the theory behind assessment centers.
4. Describe the three different types of interview simulations.
5. Evaluate the effectiveness of seniority, assessment centers, and job knowledge as substantive internal selection procedures.
6. What steps should be taken by an organization that is committed to shattering the glass ceiling?

ETHICAL ISSUES

1. Given that seniority is not a particularly valid predictor of job performance, do you think it's unethical for a company to use it as a basis for promotion? Why or why not?

2. Vincent and Peter are sales associates and are up for promotion to sales manager. In the last five years, on a 1 = poor to 5 = excellent scale, Vincent's average performance rating was 4.7 and Peter's was 4.2. In an assessment center that was meant to simulate the job of sales manager, on a 1 = very poor to 10 = outstanding scale, Vincent's average score was 8.2 and Peter's was 9.2. Other things being equal, who should be promoted? Why?

APPLICATIONS

Changing a Promotion System

Bioglass Inc. specializes in sales of a wide array of glass products. One area of the company, the commercial sales division (CSD), specializes in selling high-tech mirrors and microscope and photographic lenses. Sales associates in CSD are responsible for selling the glass products to corporate clients. In CSD there are four levels of sales associates, ranging in pay from $28,000 to $76,000 per year. There are also four levels of managerial positions in CSD; those positions range in pay from $76,000 to $110,000 per year (that's what the division president makes).

Tom Caldwell has been a very effective sales associate. He has consistently demonstrated good sales techniques in his 17 years with Bioglass and has a large and loyal client base. Over the years, Tom has risen from the lowest level of sales associate to the highest. He has proved himself successful at each stage. An entry-(first-) level management position in CSD opened up last year, and Tom was the natural candidate. Although several other candidates were given consideration, Tom was the clear choice for the position.

However, once in the position, Tom had a great deal of difficulty being a manager. He was not accustomed to delegating and rarely provided feedback or guidance to the people he supervised. Although he set goals for himself, he never set performance goals for his workers. Morale in Tom's group was low, and group performance suffered. The company felt that demoting Tom back to sales would be disastrous for him and present the wrong image to other employees; firing such a loyal employee was considered unacceptable. Therefore, Bioglass decided to keep Tom where he was, but never promote him again. It was also considering enrolling Tom in some expensive managerial development programs to enhance his management skills.

Meanwhile, Tom's replacement, although successful at the lower three levels of sales associate positions, was having a great deal of difficulty with the large corporate contracts that the highest-level sales associates must service. Two of

Tom's biggest clients had recently left Bioglass for a competitor. CSD was confused about how such a disastrous situation had developed when they seemed to make all the right decisions.

Based on this application and your reading of this chapter, answer the following questions:

1. What is the likely cause of CSD's problems?
2. How might CSD, and Bioglass more generally, make better promotion decisions in the future? Be specific.
3. In general, what role should performance appraisals play in internal selection decisions? Are there some cases in which they are more relevant than others? Explain.

Promotion From Within at Citrus Glen

Mandarine "Mandy" Pamplemousse is vice president of human resources for Citrus Glen, a juice producer based in south Florida that supplies orange and grapefruit juice to grocery stores, convenience stores, restaurants, and food processors throughout the United States. Citrus Glen has been growing rapidly over the last few years, leading Mandy to worry about how to hire and promote enough qualified individuals to staff the ever-expanding array of positions within the company.

One of the ways Mandy has been able to staff positions internally is by contracting with Staffing Systems International (SSI), a management consulting firm based in Charlotte, North Carolina. When positions open up at Citrus Glen that are appropriate to staff internally, Mandy sends a group of candidates for the position up to SSI to participate in its assessment center. The candidates return from SSI three days later, and a few days after that, SSI sends Mandy the results of the assessment with a recommendation. Though Mandy has never formally evaluated the accuracy of the promotions, it is her feeling that the process is pretty accurate. Of course, for $5,500 per candidate, Mandy thought, it should be accurate.

A few days ago, Mandy was hosting Thanksgiving, and her brother-in-law, Vin Pomme, joined them. Vin is a doctoral student in industrial psychology at Ohio International University. After Thanksgiving dinner, while Mandy, Vin, and their family were relaxing on her lanai and enjoying the warm Florida sunshine, Mandy was talking to Vin about her difficulties in promoting from within and the cost of SSI's assessment process. Vin quickly realized that SSI was using an assessment center. He was also aware of research suggesting that once one takes an applicant's personality and cognitive ability into account, assessment center scores may contribute little additional validity. Given the high cost of assessment centers, he reasoned, one must wonder whether this "incremental" validity (the validity that assessment centers contribute beyond the validity provided by personality and cognitive ability tests) would prove cost effective. After Vin conveyed these impressions to Mandy, she felt that after the holidays she would reexamine Citrus Glen's internal selection processes.

Questions

1. Drawing from concepts presented in Chapter 7 (Measurement), how could Mandy more formally evaluate SSI's assessment process, as well as the alternative presented to her by Vin?

2. Construct a scenario in which you think Mandy should continue her business relationship with SSI. On the other hand, if Mandy decides on an alternative assessment process, what would that process be? How would she evaluate whether that process was effective?

3. Citrus Glen has considered expanding its operations into the Caribbean and Latin America. One of Mandy's concerns is how to staff such positions. If Citrus Glen does expand its operations to different cultures, how should Mandy go about staffing such positions? Be specific.

ENDNOTES

1. A. Howard and D. W. Bray, "Predictions of Managerial Success Over Long Periods of Time: Lessons From the Management Progress Study," in K. E. Clark and M. B. Clark (eds.), *Measures of Leadership* (West Orange, NJ: Leadership Library of America, 1990), pp. 113–130; C. J. Russell, "Selecting Top Corporate Leaders: An Example of Biographical Information," *Journal of Management,* 1990, 16, pp. 73–86; J. S. Schippman and E. P. Prien, "An Assessment of the Contributions of General Mental Ability and Personality Characteristics to Management Success," *Journal of Business and Psychology,* 1989, 3, pp. 423–437.

2. "Nearly Half of Newly-Promoted Executives Say Their Responsibilities Are Same," *IPMA-HR Bulletin,* Dec. 22, 2006, p. 1.

3. J. J. Kane and E. E. Lawler, "Methods of Peer Assessment," *Psychological Bulletin,* 1978, 85, pp. 555–586.

4. L. Grensing-Pophal, "Internal Selections," *HR Magazine,* Dec. 2006, p. 75.

5. C. Patton, "Standout Performers: HR Professionals Are Testing Unconventional Strategies for Finding Employees With Leadership Potential," *Human Resource Executive,* Aug. 1, 2005, pp. 46–49.

6. Bureau of National Affairs, *Basic Patterns in Union Contracts* (Washington, DC: author, 1995).

7. F. K. Folkes, *Personnel Policies in Large Non-Union Companies* (Englewood Cliffs, NJ: Prentice-Hall, 1985).

8. C. Ichniowski, J. T. Delaney, and D. Lewin, "The New Resource Management in US Workplaces: Is It Really New and Is It Only Nonunion?" *Industrial Relations,* 1989, 44, pp. 97–119.

9. K. G. Abraham and J. L. Medoff, "Length of Service and Promotions in Union and Nonunion Work Groups," *Industrial and Labor Relations Review,* 1985, 38, pp. 408–420; M. E. Gordon and W. J. Fitzgibbons, "An Empirical Test of the Validity of Seniority as a Factor in Staffing Decisions," *Journal of Applied Psychology,* 1982, 67, pp. 311–319.

10. A. Lienert, "From Rust to Riches," *Management Review,* 1994, 83, pp. 10–14.

11. M. A. Quinones, J. K. Ford, and M. S. Teachout, "The Relationship Between Work Experience and Job Performance: A Conceptual and Meta-Analytic Review," *Personnel Psychology,* 1995, 48, pp. 887–910; P. E. Tesluk and R. R. Jacobs, "Toward an Integrated Model of Work Experience," *Personnel Psychology,* 1998, 51, pp. 321–355.

12. F. L. Schmidt, J. E. Hunter, and A. N. Outerbridge, "Joint Relation of Experience and Ability with Job Performance: Test of Three Hypotheses," *Journal of Applied Psychology,* 1988, 73, pp. 46–57.

13. W. Wilson, "Video Training and Testing Supports Customer Service Goals," *Personnel Journal,* 1994, 73, pp. 47–51.

14. F. L. Schmidt and J. E. Hunter, "Development of a Causal Model of Processes Determining Job Performance," *Current Directions in Psychological Science,* 1992, 1, pp. 89–92.

15. K. R. Murphy and J. M. Cleveland, *Performance Appraisal: An Organizational Perspective* (Boston: Allyn and Bacon, 1991).

16. L. J. Peter and R. Hull, *The Peter Principle* (New York: William Morrow, 1969).

17. G. C. Thornton III and D. M. Morris, "The Application of Assessment Center Technology to the Evaluation of Personnel Records," *Public Personnel Management,* 2001, 30, pp. 55–66.

18. W. Arthur, Jr., E. A. Day, T. L. McNelly, and P. S. Edens, "A Meta-Analysis of the Criterion-Related Validity of Assessment Center Dimensions," *Personnel Psychology,* 2003, 56, pp. 125–154.

19. D. A. Joiner, "Assessment Center: What's New?" *Public Personnel Management,* 2003, 31, pp. 179–185.

20. B. B. Gaugler, D. B. Rosenthal, G. C. Thornton III, and C. Bentson, "Meta-Analysis of Assessment Center Validity," *Journal of Applied Psychology,* 1987, 72, pp. 493–511.

21. K. Dayan, R. Kasten, and S. Fox, "Entry Level Police Candidate Assessment Center: An Efficient Tool or a Hammer to Kill a Fly?" *Personnel Psychology,* 2002, 55, pp. 827–849; R. D. Goffin, M. G. Rothstein, and N. G. Johnson, "Personality Testing and the Assessment Center: Incremental Validity for Managerial Selection," *Journal of Applied Psychology,* 1996, 81, pp. 746–756; H. W. Goldstein, K. P. Yusko, E. P. Brauerman, D. B. Smith, and B. Chung, "The Role of Cognitive Ability in Subgroup Differences and Incremental Validity of Assessment Center Exercises," *Personnel Psychology,* 1998, 51, pp. 357–374; F. L. Schmidt and J. E. Hunter, "The Validity and Utility of Selection Methods in Personnel Psychology: Practical and Theoretical Implications of 85 Years of Research Findings," *Psychological Bulletin,* 1998, 124, pp. 262–274.

22. N. Anderson, F. Levens, K. van Dam, and M. Born, "A Construct-Driven Investigation of Gender Differences Leadership-Role Assessment Center," *Journal of Applied Psychology,* 2006, 91, pp. 555–566.

23. Gaugler et al., "Meta-Analysis of Assessment Center Validity"; A. Howard, "An Assessment of Assessment Centers," *Academy of Management Journal,* 1974, 17, pp. 115–134; R. Klimoski and M. Brickner, "Why Do Assessment Centers Work? The Puzzle of Assessment Center Validity," *Personnel Psychology,* 1987, 40, pp. 243–260; P. R. Sackett, "A Critical Look at Some Common Beliefs About Assessment Centers," *Public Personnel Management,* 1988, 11, pp. 140–146.

24. M. A. McDaniel and N. T. Nguyen, "Situational Judgment Tests: A Review of Practice and Constructs Assessed," *International Journal of Selection and Assessment*, 2001, 9, pp. 103–113.

25. C. Fletcher, "Candidates' Reactions to Assessment Centres and Their Outcomes: A Longitudinal Study," *Journal of Occupational Psychology,* 1991, 64, pp. 117–127; "Guidelines and Ethical Considerations for Assessment Center Operations," *Public Personnel Management,* 2000, 29, pp. 315–331; C. Caldwell, G. C. Thornton III, and M. L. Gruys, "Ten Classic Assessment Center Errors," *Public Personnel Management,* 2003, 32, pp. 73–88.

26. J. E. Abueva, "Return of the Native Executive," *New York Times,* May 17, 2000, pp. B1, B8; P. Caligiuri and W. F. Cascio, "Sending Women on Global Assignments," *WorldatWork,* Second Quarter 2001, pp. 34–41; J. A. Hauser, "Filling the Candidate Pool: Developing Qualities in Potential International Assignees," *WorldatWork,* Second Quarter 2000, pp. 26–33; M. Mukuda,

"Global Leaders Wanted. . . Apply Within," *Workspan,* Apr. 2001, pp. 36–41; C. Patton, "Match Game," *Human Resource Executive,* June 2000, pp. 36–41.

27. G. C. Thornton, *Assessment Centers in Human Resource Management* (Reading, MA: Addison-Wesley, 1992).

28. EEOC Compliance Manual-Section 15 (*eeoc.gov/policy/docs/ract-color.html*); J. A. Segal, "Land Executives, Not Lawsuits," *HR Magazine,* Oct. 2006, pp. 123–130.

The Staffing Organizations Model

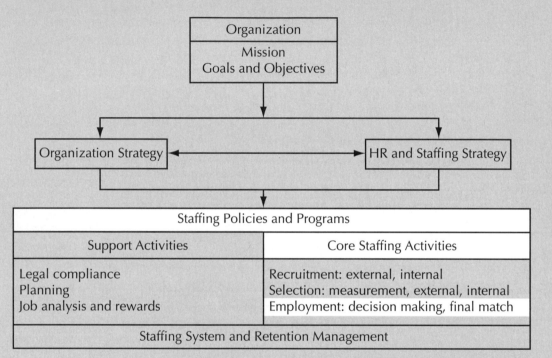

PART FIVE

Staffing Activities: Employment

CHAPTER ELEVEN

Decision Making

Choice of Assessment Method
Validity Coefficient
Face Validity
Correlation With Other Predictors
Adverse Impact
Utility

Determining Assessment Scores
Single Predictor
Multiple Predictors

Hiring Standards and Cut Scores
Description of the Process
Consequences of Cut Scores
Methods to Determine Cut Scores
Professional Guidelines

Methods of Final Choice
Random Selection
Ranking
Grouping

Decision Makers
Human Resource Professionals
Managers
Employees

Legal Issues
Uniform Guidelines on Employee Selection Procedures
Diversity and Hiring Decisions

Summary

Discussion Questions

Ethical Issues

Applications

Tanglewood Stores Case

I ndividuals flow through the staffing process, passing through several stages: applicant, candidate, finalist, offer receiver, and new hire. To implement and manage this flow, key decisions that must be made in several areas will be discussed. First, the factors that determine the choice of assessment methods to be used will be reviewed. Discussion will focus on the important considerations of validity, the correlation of one assessment method with other methods, likely adverse impact, and the utility of the method.

Once assessment data have been collected from applicants, decisions must be made about how to determine assessment scores. The process of translating predictor scores into assessment scores will be discussed for using single predictors and multiple predictors. In the case of multiple predictors, methods to combine predictor scores will be considered. Methods that will be reviewed are a compensatory model, multiple hurdles, and a combined approach. Each has distinct strengths and weaknesses.

Hiring standards and cut scores must be established to determine passing levels for the assessment scores. The process used to determine cut scores will be described, as well as the consequences of cut scores and methods to determine cut scores. Methods that will be covered are minimum competency, top-down, and banding. Professional guidelines for determining cut scores will also be reviewed.

Methods of final choice must be considered to determine who from among the finalists will receive a job offer. Methods of final choice that will be reviewed include random selection, ranking, and grouping. Each method may be advantageous, depending on one's objectives.

For all of the preceding decisions, consideration must be given to who should be involved in the decision process. The role of various potential decision makers will be discussed, including human resource (HR) professionals, line managers, and employees. In general, decisions about the staffing procedures to be followed are determined by HR professionals. Actual hiring decisions are usually made by managers. Increasingly, employees are being involved in both decisions.

Finally, legal issues should also guide the decision making. Particular consideration will be given to the Uniform Guidelines on Employee Selection Procedures (UGESP) and to the role of diversity considerations in hiring decisions.

CHOICE OF ASSESSMENT METHOD

In our discussions of external and internal selection methods, we listed multiple criteria to consider when deciding which method(s) to use (e.g., validity, utility). Some of these criteria require more amplification, specifically validity, correlation with other predictors (newly discussed here), adverse impact, and utility.

Validity Coefficient

Validity refers to the relationship between predictor and criterion scores. Often this relationship is assessed using a correlation (see Chapter 7). The correlation between predictor and criterion scores is known as a validity coefficient. The usefulness of a predictor is determined on the basis of the practical significance and statistical significance of its validity coefficient. As was noted in Chapter 7, reliability is a necessary condition for validity. Selection measures with questionable reliability will have questionable validity.

Practical Significance

Practical significance refers to the extent to which the predictor adds value to the prediction of job success. It is assessed by examining the sign and the magnitude of the validity coefficient.

Sign.   The sign of the validity coefficient refers to the direction of the relationship between the predictor and the criterion. A useful predictor is one where the sign of the relationship is positive or negative and is consistent with the logic or theory behind the predictor.

Magnitude.   The magnitude of the validity coefficient refers to its size. It can range from 0 to 1.00, with a coefficient of 0 being the least desirable and a coefficient of 1.00 being the most desirable. The closer the validity coefficient is to 1.00, the more useful the predictor. Predictors with validity coefficients of 1.00 are not to be expected given the inherent difficulties in predicting human behavior. Instead, as shown in Chapters 8 and 9, validity coefficients for current assessment methods range from 0 to about .60. Any validity coefficient above 0 is better than random selection and may be somewhat useful. Validities above .15 are of moderate usefulness, and validities above .30 are of high usefulness.

Statistical Significance

Statistical significance, as assessed by probability or p values (see Chapter 7), is another factor that should be used to interpret the validity coefficient. If a validity coefficient has a reasonable p value, chances are good that, it would yield a similar validity coefficient if the same predictor was used with different sets of job applicants. That is, a reasonable p value indicates that the method of prediction, rather than chance, produced the observed validity coefficient. Convention has it that a reasonable level of significance is $p < .05$. This means there are fewer than 5 chances in 100 of concluding there is a relationship in the population of job applicants when, in fact, there is not.

It should be pointed out that caution must be exercised in using statistical significance as a way to gauge the usefulness of a predictor. Research has clearly shown that nonsignificant validity coefficients may simply be due to the small samples of employees used to calculate the validity coefficient. Rejecting the use of a predictor solely on the basis of a small sample may lead to the rejection of a predictor that would have been quite acceptable had a larger sample of employees been used to test for validity.[1] These concerns over significance testing have led some researchers to recommend the use of "confidence intervals," for example, showing that one can be 90% confident that the true validity is no less than .30 and no greater than .40.[2]

Face Validity

Face validity concerns whether the selection measure appears valid to the applicant. Face validity is potentially important to selection decision making in general, and choice of selection methods in particular, if it affects applicant behavior (willingness to continue in the selection process, performance, and turnover once hired). Judgments of face validity are closely associated with applicant reactions.

Correlation With Other Predictors

If a predictor is to be considered useful, it must add value to the prediction of job success. To add value, it must add to the prediction of success above and beyond the forecasting powers of current predictors. In general, a predictor is more useful if it has a smaller correlation with other predictors and a higher correlation with the criterion.

In order to assess whether the predictor adds anything new to forecasting, a matrix showing all the correlations between the predictors and the criteria should always be generated. If the correlations between the new predictor and the existing predictors are higher than the correlations between the new predictor and the criterion, then the new predictor is not adding much that is new. There are also relatively straightforward techniques, such as multiple regression, that take the correlation among predictors into account.[3]

Predictors are likely to be highly correlated with one another when their domain of content is similar. For example, both biodata and application blanks may focus on previous training received. Thus, using both biodata and application blanks as predictors may be redundant, and neither one may augment the other much in predicting job success.

Adverse Impact

A predictor discriminates between people in terms of the likelihood of their success on the job. A predictor may also discriminate by screening out a disproportionate number of minorities and women. To the extent that this happens, the predictor has adverse impact, and it may result in legal problems. As a result, when the validity of alternative predictors is the same and one predictor has less adverse impact than the other predictor, then the predictor with less adverse impact should be used.

A very difficult judgment call arises when one predictor has high validity and high adverse impact while another predictor has low validity and low adverse impact. From the perspective of accurately predicting job performance, the former predictor should be used. From an equal employment opportunity and affirmative action (EEO/AA) standpoint, the latter predictor is preferable. Balancing the trade-offs is difficult and requires use of the organization's staffing philosophy regarding EEO/AA. Later in this chapter we consider some possible solutions to this important problem.

Utility

Utility refers to the expected gains to be derived from using a predictor. Expected gains are of two types: hiring success and economic.

Hiring Success Gain

Hiring success refers to the proportion of new hires who turn out to be successful on the job. Hiring success *gain* refers to the increase in the proportion of successful new hires that is expected to occur as a result of adding a new predictor to the selection system. If the current staffing system yields a success rate of 75% for new hires, how much of a gain in this success rate will occur by adding a new predictor to the system? The greater the expected gain, the greater the utility of the new predictor. This gain is influenced not only by the validity of the new predictor (as already discussed) but also by the selection ratio and base rate.

Selection Ratio.   The selection ratio is simply the number of people hired divided by the number of applicants (sr = number hired / number of applicants). The lower the selection ratio, the more useful the predictor. When the selection ratio is low, the organization is more likely to be selecting successful employees.

If the selection ratio is low, then the denominator is large or the numerator is small. Both conditions are desirable. A large denominator means that the organization is reviewing a large number of applicants for the job. The chances of identifying a successful candidate are much better in this situation than when an organization hires the first available person or reviews only a few applicants. A small numerator indicates that the organization is being very stringent with its hiring standards. The organization is hiring people likely to be successful rather than hiring anyone who meets the most basic requirements for the job; it is using high standards to ensure that the very best people are selected.

Base Rate.   The base rate is defined as the proportion of current employees who are successful on some criterion or HR outcome (br = number of successful employees / number of employees). A high base rate is desired for obvious reasons. A high base rate may come about from the organization's staffing system alone or in combination with other HR programs, such as training and compensation.

When considering possible use of a new predictor, one issue is whether the proportion of successful employees (i.e., the base rate) will increase as a result of using the new predictor in the staffing system. This is the matter of hiring success gain. Dealing with it requires simultaneous consideration of the organization's current base rate and selection ratio, as well as the validity of the new predictor.

The Taylor-Russell tables provide the necessary assistance for addressing this issue. An excerpt from the Taylor-Russell tables is shown in Exhibit 11.1.

The Taylor-Russell table shows in each of its cells the percentage of new hires who will turn out to be successful. This is determined by a combination of the validity coefficient for the new predictor, the selection ratio, and the base rate. The top matrix (A) shows the percentage of successful new hires when the base rate is low (.30), the validity coefficient is low (.20) or high (.60), and the selection ratio is low (.10) or high (.70). The bottom matrix (B) shows the percentage of successful new hires when the base rate is high (.80), the validity coefficient is low (.20) or high (.60), and the selection ratio is low (.10) or high (.70). Two illustrations show how these tables may be used.

The first illustration has to do with the decision whether to use a new test to select computer programmers. Assume that the current test used to select programmers has a validity coefficient of .20. Also assume that a consulting firm has approached the organization with a new test that has a validity coefficient of .60. Should the organization purchase and use the new test?

EXHIBIT 11.1   Excerpts From the Taylor-Russell Tables

A.

	Base Rate = .30 Selection Ratio	
Validity	**.10**	**.70**
.20	43%	33
.60	77	40

B.

	Base Rate = .80 Selection Ratio	
Validity	**.10**	**.70**
.20	89%	83
.60	99	90

SOURCE: H. C. Taylor and J. T. Russell, "The Relationship of Validity Coefficients to the Practical Effectiveness of Tests in Selection," *Journal of Applied Psychology,* 1939, 23, pp. 565–578.

At first blush, the answer might seem to be affirmative, because the new test has a substantially higher level of validity. This initial reaction, however, must be gauged in the context of the selection ratio and the current base rate. If the current base rate is .80 and the current selection ratio is .70, then, as can be seen in the lower matrix (B) of Exhibit 11.1, the new selection procedure will only result in a hiring success gain from 83% to 90%. The organization may already have a very high base rate due to other facets of HR management it does quite well (e.g., training, rewards). Hence, even though it has validity of .20, the base rate of its current predictor is already .80.

On the other hand, if the existing base rate of the organization is .30 and the existing selection ratio is .10, then it should strongly consider use of the new test. As shown in the top matrix (A) in Exhibit 11.1, the hiring success gain will go from 43% to 77% with the addition of the new test.

A second illustration using the Taylor-Russell tables has to do with recruitment in conjunction with selection. Assume that the validity of the organization's current predictor, a cognitive ability test, is .60. Also assume that a new college recruitment program has been very aggressive. As a result, there is a large swell in the number of applicants, and the selection ratio has decreased from .70 to .10. The decision the organization faces is whether to continue this college recruitment program.

An initial reaction may be that the program should be continued because of the large increase in applicants generated. As shown in the top matrix of Exhibit 11.1, this answer would be correct if the current base rate is .30. By decreasing the selection ratio from .70 to .10, the hiring success gain increases from 40% to 77%. On the other hand, if the current base rate is .80, the correct decision may be to not continue the program. The hiring success increases from 90% to 99%, which may not justify the very large expense associated with aggressive college recruitment campaigns.

The point of these illustrations is that when confronted with the decision of whether to use a new predictor, the decision depends on the validity coefficient, base rate, and selection ratio. They should not be considered independent of one another. HR professionals should carefully record and monitor base rates and selection ratios. Then, when asked by management whether they should be using a new predictor, the HR professionals can respond appropriately. Fortunately, the Taylor-Russell tables are for any combination of validity coefficient, base rate, and selection ratio values. The values shown in Exhibit 11.1 are excerpts for illustration only. When other values need to be considered, the original tables should be consulted to provide the appropriate answers.

Economic Gain

Economic gain refers to the bottom line or monetary impact of a predictor on the organization. A predictor is more useful the greater the economic gain it produces. Considerable work has been done over the years on assessing the economic gain associated with predictors. The basic utility formula used to estimate economic gain is shown in Exhibit 11.2.

At a general level, the economic gain formula shown in Exhibit 11.2 works as follows. Economic gains derived from using a valid predictor versus random selection (the left-hand side of the equation) depend on two factors (the right-hand side of the equation). The first factor (the entry before the subtraction sign) is the revenue generated by hiring productive employees using the new predictor. The second factor (the entry after the subtraction sign) is the costs associated with using the new predictor. Positive economic gains are achieved when revenues are maximized and costs are minimized. Revenues are maximized by using the most valid selection procedures. Costs are minimized by using the predictors with the least costs. To estimate actual economic gain, values are entered into the equation for each of the variables shown. Values are usually generated by experts in HR research relying on the judgments of experienced line managers.

Several variations on the economic gain (utility) formula shown in Exhibit 11.2 have been developed. For the most part, these variations require consideration of additional factors such as assumptions about tax rates and applicant flows. In all of these models, the most difficult factor to estimate is the dollar value of job performance, which represents the difference between productive and nonproductive employees in dollar value terms. A variety of methods have been proposed, ranging from manager estimates of employee value to percentages of compensation (usually 40% of base pay).[4] Despite this difficulty, economic gain formulas represent a significant way of estimating the economic gains that may be anticipated with the use of a new (and valid) predictor.

EXHIBIT 11.2 Economic Gain Formula

$$\Delta U\ (T \times N_n \times r_{xy} \times SD_y \times \overline{Z}_s) - (N_a \times C_y)$$
Where:

ΔU = expected dollar value increase to the organization using the predictor versus random selection

T = average tenure of employees in position

N_n = number of people hired

r_{xy} = correlation between predictor and job performance

SD_y = dollar value of job performance

$\overline{Z}_s$ = average standard predictor score of selected group

N_a = number of applicants

C_y = cost per applicant

Adapted from C. Handler and S. Hunt, "Estimating the Financial Value of Staffing Assessment Tools," *Workforce Management*, Mar. 2003 (*www.workforce.com*).

Limitations With Utility Analysis

Although utility analysis can be a powerful method to communicate the bottom-line implications of using valid selection measures, it is not without its limitations. Perhaps the most fundamental concern among researchers and practitioners is that utility estimates lack realism because of the following:

1. Virtually every organization uses multiple selection measures, yet existing utility models assume that the decision is whether to use a single selection measure rather than selecting applicants by chance alone.[5]
2. There are many important variables missing from the model, such as EEO/AA concerns and applicant reactions.[6]
3. The utility formula is based on many assumptions that are probably overly simplistic, including that validity does not vary over time,[7] that nonperformance criteria such as attendance, trainability, applicant reactions, and fit are irrelevant,[8] and that applicants are selected in a top-down manner and all job offers are accepted.[9]

Perhaps as a result of these limitations, several factors indicate that utility analysis may have a limited effect on managers' decisions about selection measures. For example, a survey of managers who stopped using utility analysis found that 40% did so because they felt that utility analysis was too complicated, whereas 32% discontinued use because they believed that the results were not credible.[10] Other studies have found that managers' acceptance of utility analysis is low; one study found that reporting simple validity coefficients was more likely to persuade HR decision makers to adopt a particular selection method than was reporting utility analysis results.[11]

These criticisms should not be taken as arguments that organizations should ignore utility analysis when evaluating selection decisions. However, decision makers are much less likely to become disillusioned with utility analysis if they are informed consumers and realize some of the limitations inherent in such analyses. Researchers have the responsibility of better embedding utility analysis in the strategic context in which staffing decisions are made, while HR decision makers have the responsibility to use the most rigorous methods possible to evaluate their decisions.[12] By being realistic about what utility analysis can and cannot accomplish, the potential to fruitfully inform staffing decisions will increase.

DETERMINING ASSESSMENT SCORES

Single Predictor

Using a single predictor in selection decisions makes the process of determining scores easy. In fact, scores on the single predictor *are* the final assessment scores. Thus, concerns over how to combine assessment scores are not relevant when a single predictor is used in selection decisions. Although using a single predictor has the advantage of simplicity, there are some obvious drawbacks. First, few employers would feel comfortable hiring applicants on the basis of a single attribute. In fact, almost all employers use multiple methods in selection decisions. A second and related reason for using multiple predictors is that utility increases as the number of valid predictors used in selection decisions increases. In most cases, using two valid selection methods will result in more effective selection decisions than using a sole predictor. For these reasons, although basing selection decisions on a single predictor is a simple way to make decisions, it is rarely the best one.

Multiple Predictors

Given the less-than-perfect validities of predictors, most organizations use multiple predictors in making selection decisions. With multiple predictors, decisions must be made about combining the resultant scores. These decisions can be addressed through consideration of compensatory, multiple hurdles, and combined approaches.

Compensatory Model

With a compensatory model, scores on one predictor are simply added to scores on another predictor to yield a total score. What this means is that high scores on one predictor can compensate for low scores on another. For example, if an employer is using an interview and grade point average (GPA) to select a person, an applicant with a low GPA who does well in the interview may still get the job.

The advantage of a compensatory model is that it recognizes that people have multiple talents and that many different constellations of talents may produce success on the job. The disadvantage to a compensatory model is that, at least for some jobs, the level of proficiency for specific talents cannot be compensated for by other proficiencies. For example, a firefighter requires a certain level of strength that cannot be compensated for by intelligence.

In terms of making actual decisions using the compensatory model, there are four procedures that may be followed: clinical prediction, unit weighting, rational weighting, and multiple regression. The four methods differ from one another in terms of the manner in which predictor scores (raw or standardized) are weighted before being added together for a total or composite score.

The following example will be used to illustrate these procedures. In all four, raw scores are used to determine a total score. Standard scores (see Chapter 7) may need to be used rather than raw scores if each predictor variable uses a different method of measurement or is measured under different conditions. Differences in weighting methods are shown in Part A of Exhibit 11.3. In Part B of Exhibit 11.3, there is a selection system consisting of interviews, application blanks, and recommendations. For simplicity, assume that scores on each predictor range from 1 to 5. Scores on these three predictors are shown for three applicants.

EXHIBIT 11.3   Four Compensatory Model Procedures for Three Predictors

A. Models

Clinical Prediction

$P_1 \rightarrow P_2 \rightarrow P_3 \rightarrow$ Total Score

Unit Weighting

$P_1 + P_2 + P_3 =$ Total Score

Rational Weighting

$w_1 P_1 + w_2 P_2 + w_3 P_3 =$ Total Score

Multiple Regression

$a + b_1 P_1 + b_2 P_2 + b_3 P_3 =$ Total Score

Where :   P = predictor score
        w = rational weight
        a = intercept
        b = statistical weight

B. Raw Scores for Applicants on Three Predictors

	Predictors		
Applicant	Interview	Application Blank	Recommendation
A	3	5	2
B	4	3	4
C	5	4	3

Clinical Prediction.   Returning to Exhibit 11.3, note that with a clinical prediction, managers use their expert judgment to arrive at a total score for each applicant. That final score may or may not be a simple addition of the three predictor scores shown in Exhibit 11.3. Hence, applicant A may be given a higher total score than applicant B even though simple addition shows that applicant B had one point more $(4 + 3 + 4 = 11)$ than applicant A $(3 + 5 + 2 = 10)$.

Frequently, clinical prediction is done by initial screening interviewers or hiring managers. These decision makers may or may not have "scores" per se, but they have multiple pieces of information on each applicant, and they make a decision on the applicant by "taking everything into account." In initial screening decisions, this summary decision is whether the applicant gets over the initial hurdle and passes on to the next level of assessment. For example, when making an initial screening decision on an applicant, a manager at a fast food restaurant might subjectively combine his or her impressions of various bits of information about the applicant on the application form. A hiring manager for a professional position might focus on a finalist's résumé and answers to the manager's interview questions to decide whether to extend an offer to the finalist.

The advantage to the clinical prediction approach is that it draws on the expertise of managers to weight and combine predictor scores. In turn, managers may be more likely to accept the selection decisions than if a mechanical scoring rule (e.g., add up the points) was used. The problem with this approach is that the reasons for the weightings are known only to the manager. Also, clinical predictions have generally been shown to be less accurate than mechanical decisions; although there are times when using intuition and a nuanced approach is necessary or the only option, in general, one is well advised to heed former GE CEO Jack Welch's advice for making hiring decisions: "Fight like hell against . . . using your gut. Don't!".[13]

Unit Weighting. With unit weighting, each predictor is weighted the same at a value of 1.00. What this means is shown in Exhibit 11.3 (Part A): the predictor scores are simply added together to get a total score. So, in Exhibit 11.3 (Part B), the total scores for applicants A, B, and C are 10, 11, and 12, respectively. The advantage to unit weighting is that it is a simple and straightforward process to follow and makes the importance of each predictor explicit to decision makers. The problem with this approach is that it assumes that each predictor contributes equally to the prediction of job success, which often will not be the case.

Rational Weighting. With rational weighting, each predictor receives a differential rather than equal weighting. Managers and other subject matter experts (SMEs) establish the weights for each predictor according to the degree to which each is believed to predict job success. These weights (w) are then multiplied by each raw score (P) to yield a total score, as shown in Exhibit 11.3 (Part A).

For example, the predictors in Exhibit 11.3 (Part B) may be weighted .5, .3, and .2 for the interview, application blank, and recommendation. Each applicant's raw score in Exhibit 11.3 (Part B) is multiplied by the appropriate weight to yield a total score. For example, the total score for applicant A is $(.5)3 + (.3)5 + (.2)2 = 3.4$.

The advantage to this approach is that it considers the relative importance of each predictor and makes this assessment explicit. The downside, however, is that it is an elaborate procedure that requires managers and SMEs to agree on the differential weights to be applied.

Multiple Regression. Multiple regression is similar to rational weighting in that the predictors receive different weights. With multiple regression, however, the weights are established on the basis of statistical procedures rather than on the basis of judgments by managers or other SMEs. The statistical weights are developed on the basis of (1) the correlation of each predictor with the criterion, and (2) the correlations among the predictors. As a result, regression weights provide optimal weights in the sense that the weights are those that will yield the highest total validity.

The calculations result in a multiple regression formula like the one shown in Exhibit 11.3 (Part A). A total score for each applicant is obtained by multiplying the statistical weight (b) for each predictor by the predictor (P) score and summing these along with the intercept value (a). As an example, assume the statistical weights are .9, .6, and .2 for the interview, application blank, and recommendation, respectively, and that the intercept is .09. Using these values, the total score for applicant A is .09 + (.9)3 + (.6)5 + (.2)2 = 6.19.

Multiple regression offers the possibility of a much higher degree of precision in the prediction of criterion scores than do the other methods of weighting. Unfortunately, this level of precision is realized only under a certain set of circumstances. In particular, for multiple regression to be more precise than unit weighting, there must be a small number of predictors, low correlations between predictor variables, and a large sample.[14] Many selection settings do not meet these criteria, so in these cases consideration should be given to unit or rational weighting, or to alternative regression-based weighting schemes that have been developed—general dominance weights or relative importance weights.[15] In situations where these conditions are met, however, multiple regression weights can produce higher validity and utility than the other weighting schemes.

Choice Among Weighting Schemes. The choice from among different weighting schemes is important because how various predictor combinations are weighted is critical in determining the usefulness of the selection process. Despite the limitations of regression weighting schemes noted above, one analysis of actual selection measures revealed that when scores on cognitive ability and integrity tests are combined by weighting them equally, the total validity increases to .65, an increase of 27.6% over the validity of the cognitive ability test alone.[16] When scores are weighted according to multiple regression, however, the increase in validity becomes 28.2%. In fact, the study revealed that when supplementing cognitive ability tests with additional selection procedures, using multiple regression to establish weights always yields higher validity than unit weighting. While these results do not prove that multiple regression weighting is a superior method in all circumstances, they do help illustrate that the choice of the best weighting scheme is consequential and likely depends on answers to the most important questions about clinical, unit, rational, and multiple regression schemes (in that order):

- Do selection decision makers have considerable experience and insight into selection decisions, and is managerial acceptance of the selection process important?
- Is there reason to believe that each predictor contributes relatively equally to job success?

- Are there adequate resources to use relatively involved weighting schemes such as rational weights or multiple regression?
- Are the conditions under which multiple regression is superior (relatively small number of predictors, low correlations among predictors, large sample) satisfied?

Answers to these questions—and the importance of the questions themselves—will go a long way toward deciding which weighting scheme to use. We should also note that while statistical weighting is more valid than clinical weighting, the combination of both methods may yield the highest validity. One study indicated that regression-weighted predictors were more valid than clinical judgments, but clinical judgments contributed uniquely to performance controlling for regression-weighted predictors. This suggests that both statistical and clinical weighting might be used. Thus, the weighting schemes are not necessarily mutually exclusive.[17]

Multiple Hurdles Model

With a multiple hurdles approach, an applicant must earn a passing score on each predictor before advancing in the selection process. Such an approach is taken when each requirement measured by a predictor is critical to job success. Passing scores are set using the methods to determine cut scores (discussed in the next section). With multiple hurdles, unlike the compensatory model, a high score on one predictor cannot compensate for a low score on another predictor.

Multiple hurdles are used to prevent false-positive errors. They are costly and time consuming to set up. As a result, they are used to select people for jobs where the occupational hazards are great (e.g., astronaut) or the consequences of poor performance have a great impact on the public at large (e.g., police officers and firefighters).

Combined Model

For jobs where some but not all requirements are critical to job success, a combined method may be used involving both the compensatory and multiple hurdles models. The process starts with the multiple hurdles and ends with the compensatory method.

An example of the combined approach for the position of recruitment manager is shown in Exhibit 11.4. The selection process for recruitment manager starts with two hurdles that must be passed, in succession, by applicants. These are the application blank and the job knowledge test. Failure to clear either hurdle results in rejection. Applicants who pass receive an interview and have their references checked. Information from the interview and the references is combined in a compensatory manner. Those who pass are offered jobs, and those who do not pass are rejected.

EXHIBIT 11.4   Combined Model for Recruitment Manager

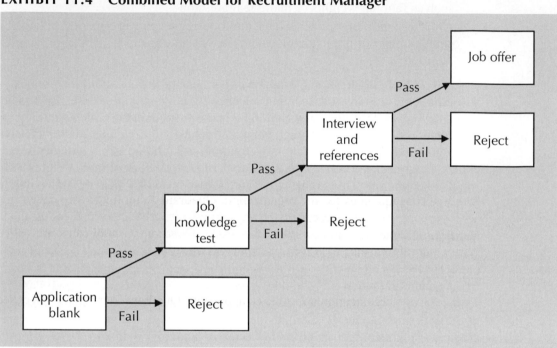

HIRING STANDARDS AND CUT SCORES

Hiring standards or cut scores address the issue of what constitutes a passing score. The score may be a single score from a single predictor or a total score from multiple predictors. To address this, a description of the process and the consequences of cut scores are presented. Then, methods that may be used to establish the actual cut score are described.

Description of the Process

Once one or more predictors have been chosen for use, a decision must be made as to who advances in the selection process. This decision requires that one or more cut scores be established. A cut score is the score that separates those who advance in the process (e.g., applicants who become candidates) from those who are rejected. For example, assume a test is used on which scores may range from 0 to 100 points. A cut score of 70 would mean that those applicants with a 70 or higher would advance, while all others would be rejected for employment purposes.

Consequences of Cut Scores

Setting a cut score is a very important process, as it has consequences for the organization and the applicant. The consequences of cut scores can be shown using Exhibit 11.5, which contains a summary of a scatter diagram of predictor and criterion scores. The horizontal line shows the criterion score at which the organization has determined whether an employee is successful or unsuccessful—for example, a 3 on a 5-point performance appraisal scale where 1 is the low performance and 5 is the high performance. The vertical line is the cut score for the predictor—for example, a 3 on a 5-point interview rating scale where 1 reveals no chance of success and 5 a high chance of success.

The consequences of setting the cut score at a particular level are shown in each of the quadrants. Quadrants A and C represent correct decisions, which have positive consequences for the organization. Quadrant A applicants are called true positives because they were assessed as having a high chance of success using the predictor and would have succeeded if hired. Quadrant C applicants are called true negatives because they were assessed as having little chance for success and, indeed, would not be successful if hired.

Quadrants D and B represent incorrect decisions, which have negative consequences to the organization and affected applicants. Quadrant D applicants are called

---

EXHIBIT 11.5   Consequences of Cut Scores

Criterion	Predictor Cut Score	
	D False negatives	A True positives
Successful		
	C True negatives	B False positives
Unsuccessful		
	No hire	Hire

Predictor

false negatives because they were assessed as not being likely to succeed, but had they been hired, they would have been successful. Not only was an incorrect decision reached, but a person who would have done well was not hired. Quadrant B applicants are called false positives. They were assessed as being likely to succeed, but would have ended up being unsuccessful performers. Eventually, these people would need to receive remedial training, be transferred to a new job, or even be terminated.

How high or low a cut score is set has a large impact on the consequences shown in Exhibit 11.5, and trade-offs are always involved. Compared with the moderate cut score in Exhibit 11.5, a high cut score results in fewer false positives but a larger number of false negatives. Is this a good, bad, or inconsequential set of outcomes for the organization? The answer depends on the job open for selection and the costs involved. If the job is an astronaut position for NASA, then it is essential that there be no false positives. The cost of a false positive may be the loss of human life.

Now consider the consequences of a low cut score, relative to the one shown in Exhibit 11.5. There are fewer false negatives and more true positives, but more false positives are hired. In organizations that gain competitive advantage in their industry by hiring the very best, this set of consequences may be unacceptable. Alternatively, for EEO/AA purposes it may be desirable to have a low cut score so that the number of false negative minorities and women is minimized.

In short, when setting a cut score, attention must be given to the consequences. As indicated, these consequences can be very serious. As a result, different methods of setting cut scores have been developed to guide decision makers. These will now be reviewed.[18]

Methods to Determine Cut Scores

There are three methods that may be used to determine cut scores: minimum competency, top-down, and banding. Each of these is described below, along with professional guidelines for setting cut scores.

Minimum Competency

Using the minimum competency method, the cut score is set on the basis of the minimum qualifications deemed necessary to perform the job. SMEs are usually used to establish a minimum competency score. This approach is often needed in situations where the first step in the hiring process is the demonstration of minimum skill requirements. Exhibit 11.6 provides an illustration of the use of cut scores in selection. The exhibit lists the scores of 25 applicants on a particular test. Using the minimum competency method, the cut score is set at the level at which applicants who score below the line are deemed unqualified for the job. In this case, a score of 75 was determined to be the minimum competency level necessary. Thus, all applicants who scored below 75 are deemed unqualified and rejected, and all applicants who scored 75 or above are deemed at least minimally qualified. Finalists and ultimately offer receivers can then be chosen from among these qualified applicants on the basis of other criteria.

EXHIBIT 11.6   Use of Cut Scores in Selection Decisions

Rank	Test Scores	Minimum Competency		Top-Down			Banding*
1.	100	100		100	1st	choice	100
2.	98	98		98	2nd	choice	98
3.	97	97		97	3rd	choice	97
4.	96	96		96	4th	choice	96
T5.	93	93		95	5th	choice	93
T5.	93	93		95	5th	choice	93
7.	91	91		91	''		91
T8.	90	90		90	''		90
T8.	90	90		90	''		90
10.	88	88	Qualified	88	''		88
11.	87	87		87	''		87
T12.	85	85		85	''		85
T12.	85	85		85	''		85
14.	83	83		83	''		83
15.	81	81		81	''		81
16.	79	79		79	''		79
T17.	77	77		77	''		77
T17.	77	77		77	''		77
19.	76	76		76	''		76
20.	75	75	Min. competency	75	''		75
21.	74	74		74	21st	choice	74
22.	71	71		71	22nd	choice	71
23.	70	70	Unqualified	70	23rd	choice	70
24.	69	69		69	24th	choice	69
25.	65	65		65	25th	choice	65

*All scores within brackets treated as equal; choice of applicants within brackets (if necessary) can be made on the basis of other factors, such as EEO/AA considerations.

A variation of the minimum competency approach is hiring the first acceptable candidate. It is often used when candidates come to the attention of the hiring person sequentially, one at a time, rather than having a total pool of candidates from which to choose the finalists. It is also used when the organization is desperate for "warm bodies" and willing to hire anyone who meets some threshold. Although at times a rush to hire is understandable, the consequences can be most unfortunate. For example, due to the difficulty in finding telemarketers, a home mortgage call center had a policy of hiring the first acceptable candidate. The hiring manager at this call center overheard a newly hired employee tell a customer, "If I had a rate as high as yours, I'd slit my wrists, then climb to the top of the highest building and jump off." It turned out this employee had recently chipped his front tooth from his favorite experiment—seeing how close he could get to a fast-moving train.[19] So, while hiring the first acceptable candidate may seem necessary, it is far from an ideal hiring strategy and the costs may not be revealed until it is too late—as in the above example of the newly hired telemarketer.

Another variant on the minimum competency approach is to impose a sort of *maximum* competency on "overqualified" applicants. The assumption here is that the job will not be sufficiently rewarding, and the overqualified employee will quickly quit. Care needs to be taken per se selecting out seemingly overqualified applicants. We are not aware of any scientific evidence that employees can be too smart or too conscientious or too positive for a job. It is possible that some seemingly overqualified applicants are not serious about a job. But this hypothesis needs to be tested directly, rather than assuming that a well-qualified applicant is not serious. Sometimes people are interested in a job for reasons that the hiring manager does not know (without asking). There are also legal dangers, as many apparently overqualified applicants are over 40. As one manager said, "I think it's a huge mistake not to take a second look at overqualified candidates. Certainly there are valid reasons to reject some candidates, but it shouldn't be a blanket response."[20]

Top-Down

Another method of determining at what level the cut score should be set is to simply examine the distribution of predictor scores for applicants and set the cut score at the level that best meets the demands of the organization. Demands of the organization may include the number of vacancies to be filled and EEO/AA requirements. This top-down method of setting cut scores is illustrated in Exhibit 11.6. As the exhibit shows, under top-down hiring, cut scores are established by the number of applicants that need to be hired. Once that number has been determined, applicants are selected from the top based on the order of their scores until the number desired is reached. The advantage of this approach is that it is a system that is easy to administer. It also minimizes judgment required because the cut score is determined on the basis of the demand for labor. The big drawback to this approach is that validity has often not been established prior to the use of the predictor. Also, there may be overreliance on the use of a single predictor and cut score, while other potentially useful predictors are ignored.

A well-known example of a top-down method is the Angoff method.[21] In this approach, SMEs are used to set the minimum cut scores needed to proceed in the selection process. These experts go through the content of the predictor (e.g., test items) and determine which items the minimally qualified person should be able to pass. Usually 7 to 10 SMEs (e.g., job incumbents, managers) are used, and they must agree on the items to be passed. The cut score is the sum of the number of items that must be answered correctly.

There are several problems with this particular approach and subsequent modifications to it. First, it is a time-consuming procedure. Second, the results are dependent on the SMEs. It is a very difficult matter to get members of the organization to agree on who are "the" SMEs. Which SMEs are selected may have a bearing on the actual cut scores developed. Finally, it is unclear how much agreement there must be among SMEs when they evaluate test items. There may also be judgmental errors and biases in how cut scores are set. If the Angoff method is used, it is important that SMEs are provided with a common definition of minimally competent test takers, and that SMEs are encouraged to discuss their estimates. Each of these steps has been found to increase the reliability of the SME.[22]

Banding and Other Alternatives to Top-Down Selection

The traditionally selected cut score method is the top-down approach. For both external hiring and internal promotions, the top-down method will yield the highest validity and utility. This method has been criticized, however, for ignoring the possibility that small differences between scores are due to measurement error. Another criticism of the top-down method is its potential for adverse impact, particularly when cognitive ability tests are used. As we noted in Chapter 9, there is perhaps no greater paradox in selection than the fact that the single most valid selection measure (cognitive ability tests) is also the measure with the most adverse impact. The magnitude of the adverse impact is such that, on a standard cognitive ability test, if half the white applicants are hired, only 16% of the black applicants would be expected to be hired.[23]

One suggestion for reducing the adverse impact of top-down hiring is to use different norms for minority and majority groups; thus, hiring decisions are based on normatively defined (rather than absolute) scores. For example, a black employee who achieved a score of 75 on a test where the mean of all black applicants was 50 could be considered to have the same normative score as a white applicant who scored a 90 on a test where the mean for white applicants was 60. However, this "race norming" of test scores, which was a common practice in the civil service and among some private employers, is expressly forbidden by the Civil Rights Act of 1991. As a result, another approach, termed "banding," has been promulgated.

Banding refers to the procedure whereby applicants who score within a certain score range or band are considered to have scored equivalently. A simple banding procedure is provided in Exhibit 11.6. In this example, using a 100-point test, all applicants who score within the band of 10-point increments are considered to have scored equally. For example, all applicants who score 91 and above could be assigned a score of 9, those who score 81–90 are given a score of 8, and so on. (In essence, this is what is done when letter grades are assigned based on exam scores.) Hiring within bands could then be done at random or, more typically, could be based on race or sex in conjunction with other factors (e.g., seniority or experience). Banding might reduce the adverse impact of selection tests because such a procedure tends to reduce differences between higher- and lower-scoring groups (as is the case with whites and minorities on cognitive ability tests). In practice, band widths are usually calculated on the basis of the standard error of measurement.

Research suggests that banding procedures result in substantial decreases in the adverse impact of cognitive ability tests, while, under certain conditions, the losses in terms of utility are relatively small. Various methods of banding have been proposed, but the differences between these methods are relatively unimportant.[24]

Perhaps the major limitation with banding is that it sacrifices validity, especially when the selection measure is reliable. Because the standard error of the difference between test scores is partly a function of the reliability of the test, when test reliability is low, band widths are wider than when the reliability of the test is high. For example, if the reliability of a test is .80, at a reasonable level of confidence, nearly half the scores on a test can be considered equivalent.[25] Obviously, taking scores on a 100-point test and lumping applicants into only two groups wastes a great deal of important information on applicants (it is unlikely that an applicant who scores a 51 on a valid test will perform the same on the job as an applicant who scores 99). Therefore, if the reliability of a test is even moderately high, the validity and utility decrements that result from banding become quite severe. There is also evidence that typical banding procedures overestimate the width of bands, which of course exacerbates the problem.[26]

The scientific merit of test banding is hotly debated.[27] It is unlikely that we could resolve here the myriad ethical and technical issues underlying its use. Organizations considering the use of banding in personnel selection decisions must weigh the pros and cons carefully, including the legal issues (a review of lawsuits concerning banding found that banding was generally upheld by the courts).[28] In the end, however, there may be a values choice to be made: To optimize validity (to some detriment to diversity) or to optimize diversity (with some sacrifice in validity). As one review noted, though "there is extensive evidence supporting the validity" of cognitive tests, "adverse impact is unlikely to be eliminated as long as one assesses" cognitive abilities in the selection process.[29]

In an effort to resolve this somewhat pessimistic trade-off, some researchers have recently developed nonlinear models that attempt to find optimal solutions that maximize validity and diversity. One effort produced a statistical algorithm that attempts to achieve an optimal trade-off between validity and adverse impact by differentially weighting the selection measures. Although such algorithms may reduce the price to be paid in the values (between optimizing validity and diversity), the "silver bullet" solution remains elusive.[30]

Professional Guidelines

Much more research is needed on systematic procedures that are effective in setting optimal cut scores. In the meantime, a sound set of professional guidelines for setting cut scores is shown in Exhibit 11.7.

METHODS OF FINAL CHOICE

The discussion thus far has been on decision rules that can be used to narrow down the list of people to successively smaller groups that advance in the selec-

---

EXHIBIT 11.7   Professional Guidelines for Setting Cutoff Scores

1. It is unrealistic to expect that there is a single "best" method of setting cutoff scores for all situations.
2. The process of setting a cutoff score (or a critical score) should begin with a job analysis that identifies relative levels of proficiency on critical knowledge, skills, abilities, or other characteristics.
3. The validity and job relatedness of the assessment procedure are crucial considerations.
4. How a test is used (criterion-referenced or norm-referenced) affects the selection and meaning of a cutoff score.
5. When possible, data on the actual relation of test scores to outcome measures of job performance should be considered carefully.
6. Cutoff scores or critical scores should be set high enough to ensure that minimum standards of job performance are met.
7. Cutoff scores should be consistent with normal expectations of acceptable proficiency within the workforce.

SOURCE: W. F. Cascio, R. A. Alexander, and G. V. Barrett, "Setting Cutoff Scores: Legal, Psychometric, and Professional Issues and Guidelines," *Personnel Psychology,* 1988, 41, pp. 21–22. Used with permission.

tion process from applicant to candidate to finalist. How can the organization now choose from among the finalists to decide which of them will receive job offers? Discretionary assessments about the finalists must be converted into final choice decisions. The methods of final choice are the mechanisms by which discretionary assessments are translated into job offer decisions.

Methods of final choice include random selection, ranking, and grouping. Examples of each of these methods are shown in Exhibit 11.8 and are discussed here.

Random Selection

With random selection, each finalist has an equal chance of being selected. The only rationale for the selection of a person is the "luck of the draw." For example, the six names from Exhibit 11.8 could be put in a hat and the finalist drawn out. The one drawn out would be the person selected and tendered a job offer. This approach has the advantage of being quick. Also, with random selection, one cannot be accused of favoritism, because everyone has an equal chance of being selected. The disadvantage to this approach is that discretionary assessments are simply ignored.

EXHIBIT 11.8 Methods of Final Choice

Random	Ranking	Grouping
Casey	1. Keisha	Keisha
Keisha	2. Meg	Meg] Top choices
Buster	3. Buster	
Lyn Aung ⟩ Pick one	4. Lyn Aung	Buster
Meg	5. Casey	Lyn Aung] Acceptable
Luis	6. Luis	
		Casey
		Luis] Last resorts

Ranking

With ranking, finalists are ordered from the most desirable to the least desirable based on results of discretionary assessments. As shown in Exhibit 11.8, the person ranked 1 (Keisha) is the most desirable, and the person ranked 6 (Luis) is the least desirable. It is important to note that desirability should be viewed in the context of the entire selection process. When this is done, persons with lower levels of desirability (e.g., ranks of 3, 4, 5) should not be viewed necessarily as failures. Job offers are extended to people on the basis of their rank ordering, with the person ranked 1 receiving the first offer. Should that person turn down the job offer or suddenly withdraw from the selection process, then the finalist ranked 2 receives the offer, and so on.

The advantage to ranking is that it provides an indication of the relative worth of each finalist for the job. It also provides a set of backups should one or more of the finalists withdraw from the process.

It should be remembered that backup finalists may decide to withdraw from the process to take a position elsewhere. Although ranking does give the organization a cushion if the top choices withdraw from the process, it does not mean that the process of job offers can proceed at a leisurely pace. Immediate action needs to be taken with the top choices in case they decide to withdraw and there is a need to go to backups. This is especially true in tight labor markets where there is a strong demand for the services of people on the ranking list.

Grouping

With the grouping method, finalists are banded together into rank-ordered categories. For example, in Exhibit 11.8, the finalists are grouped according to whether they are top choices, acceptable, or last resorts. The advantage of this method is that it permits ties among finalists, thus avoiding the need to assign a different rank to each person. The disadvantage is that choices still have to be made from among the top choices. These might be made on the basis of factors such as probability of each person accepting the offer.

DECISION MAKERS

A final consideration in decision making for selection is who should participate in the decisions. That is, who should determine the process to be followed (e.g., establishing cut scores) and who should determine the outcome (e.g., who gets the job offer). The answer is that both HR professionals and line managers must play a role. Although the two roles are different, both are critical to the organization. Employees may play certain roles as well.

Human Resource Professionals

As a general rule, HR professionals should have a high level of involvement in the processes used to design and manage the selection system. They should be consulted in matters such as which predictors to use and how to best use them. In particular, they need to orchestrate the development of policies and procedures in the staffing areas covered. These professionals have or know where to find the technical expertise needed to develop sound selection decisions. Also, they have the knowledge to ensure that relevant laws and regulations are being followed. Finally, they can also represent the interests and concerns of employees to management.

Although the primary role to be played by HR professionals is in terms of the process, they should also have some involvement in determining who receives job offers. One obvious area where this is true is with staffing the HR function. A less obvious place where HR professionals can play an important secondary role is in terms of providing input into selection decisions made by managers.

HR professionals may be able to provide some insight on applicants that is not always perceived by line managers. For example, they may be able to offer some insight on the applicants' people skills (e.g., communications, teamwork). HR professionals are sensitive to these issues because of their training and experience. They may have data to share on these matters as a result of their screening interviews, knowledge of how to interpret paper-and-pencil instruments (e.g., personality test), and interactions with internal candidates (e.g., serving on task forces with the candidates).

The other area where HR professionals may make a contribution to outcomes is in terms of initial assessment methods. Many times, HR professionals are and should be empowered to make initial selection decisions, such as who gets invited into the organization for administration of the next round of selection. Doing so saves managers time in which to carry out their other responsibilities. Also, HR professionals can ensure that minorities and women applicants are actively solicited and not excluded from the applicant pool for the wrong reasons.

Managers

As a general rule, a manager's primary involvement in staffing is in determining who is selected for employment. Managers are the SMEs of the business, and they are thus held accountable for the success of the people hired. They are far less involved in determining the processes followed to staff the organization, because they often do not have the time or expertise to do so. The average manager can also be expected to have no knowledge of staffing research whatsoever, though that doesn't mean he or she is uninterested in learning.[31]

Although they may not play a direct role in establishing process, managers can and should be periodically consulted by HR professionals on process issues. They should be consulted because they are the consumers of HR services. As such, they should be provided with input into the staffing process to ensure that it is meeting their needs in making the best possible person/job matches.

There is an additional benefit to allowing management a role in process issues. As a result of their involvement, managers may develop a better understanding of why certain practices are prescribed by HR professionals. When they are not invited to be part of the process to establish staffing policy and procedures, line managers may view HR professionals as obstacles to hiring the right person for the job.

It should also be noted that the degree of managers' involvement usually depends on the type of assessment decisions made. Decisions made using initial assessment methods are usually delegated to the HR professional, as just discussed. Decisions made using substantive assessment methods usually involve some degree of input from the manager. Decisions made using discretionary methods are usually the direct responsibility of the manager. As a general rule, the extent of managerial involvement in determining outcomes should only be as great as management's knowledge of the job. If managers are involved in hiring decisions for jobs with which they are not familiar, then legal, measurement, and morale problems are likely to be created.

Employees

Traditionally, employees are not considered part of the decision-making process in staffing. Slowly this tradition is changing. For example, in team assessment approaches (see Chapter 8), employees may have a voice in both process and outcomes. That is, they may have ideas about how selection procedures are established and make decisions about or provide input into who gets hired. Employee involvement in the team approach is encouraged because it may give a sense of ownership of the work process and help employees to better identify with organizational goals. Also, it may result in the selection of members who are more compatible with the goals of the work team. In order for employee involvement to be effective, employees need to be provided with staffing training just as managers are (see Chapter 9).

LEGAL ISSUES

The legal issue of major importance in decision making is that of cut scores or hiring standards. These scores or standards regulate the flow of individuals from applicant to candidate to finalist. Throughout this flow, adverse impact may occur. When it does, the UGESP come into play. In addition, the organization could form a multipronged strategy for increasing workforce diversity.

Uniform Guidelines on Employee Selection Procedures

If there is no adverse impact in decision making, the UGESP are essentially silent on the issue of cut scores. The discretion exercised by the organization as it makes its selection decisions is thus unconstrained legally. If there is adverse impact occurring, however, then the UGESP become directly applicable to decision making.

Recall that under conditions of adverse impact, the UGESP require the organization to either eliminate its occurrence or justify it through the conduct of validity studies. As part of the general standards for such validity studies, the UGESP say the following about cut scores:

> Where cutoff scores are used, they should normally be set as to be reasonable and consistent with normal expectations of acceptable proficiency within the workforce. Where applicants are ranked on the basis of properly validated selection procedures and those applicants scoring below a higher cutoff score than appropriate in light of such expectations have little or no chance of being selected for employment, the higher cutoff score may be appropriate, but the degree of adverse impact should be considered.

This provision suggests that the organization should be cautious in general about setting cut scores that are above those necessary to achieve acceptable proficiency among those hired. In other words, even with a valid predictor, the organization should be cautious that its hiring standards are not so high that they create needless adverse impact. This is particularly true with ranking systems. Use of random, or to a lesser extent grouping, methods would help overcome this particular objection to ranking systems.

Whatever cut score procedure is used, the UGESP also require that the organization be able to document its establishment and operation. Specifically, the UGESP say that "if the selection procedure is used with a cutoff score, the user should describe the way in which normal expectations of proficiency within the workforce were determined and the way in which the cutoff score was determined."

The preceding validation and cut score approach is one option for dealing with problems of adverse impact. The UGESP also suggest two other options, both of which seek to eliminate adverse impact rather than justify it as in the validation and cut score approach. The next option is "alternative procedures." Here, the organization must consider using an alternative selection procedure that causes less adverse impact (e.g., work sample instead of a written test) but has roughly the same validity as the procedure it replaces.

The final selection option is that of affirmative action. The UGESP do not relieve the organization of any affirmative action obligations it may have. Also, the UGESP strive to "encourage the adoption and implementation of voluntary affirmative action programs" for organizations that do not have any affirmative action obligations.

Diversity and Hiring Decisions

There has been considerable controversy and litigation over the issue of whether it is permissible for a legally protected characteristic such as race or gender to enter into a staffing decision at all, and if so, under exactly what circumstances. At the crux of the matter is whether staffing decisions should be based solely on a person's qualifications, or qualifications and the protected characteristic. It is argued that allowing the protected characteristic to receive some weight in the decision would serve to create a more diverse workforce, which many public and private organizations claim is something they have a compelling interest in and responsibility to do (refer back to Chapter 3 and the discussion of affirmative action).

It can be concluded that unless the organization is under a formal affirmative action plan, protected characteristics (e.g., race, sex, religion) should not be considered in selection decision making. This conclusion is consistent with Equal Employment Opportunity Commission (EEOC) policy that the organization should use job-related hiring standards and that the same selection techniques and weights must be used for all people.[33]

How should the organization proceed, especially if it wants to not only comply with the law but also increase the diversity of its workforce? Several things might be done. First, carefully establish KSAOs (knowledge, skill, ability, and other characteristics) for jobs so that they are truly job related, and as part of that process attempt to establish some job-related KSAOs that may correlate with protected characteristics, such as diversity in experience and customer contacts. For example, a KSAO for the job of marketing manager might be "substantial contacts within diverse racial and ethnic communities." Both white and nonwhite applicants could potentially meet this requirement, increasing the chances of recruiting and selecting a person of color for the job. Second, use recruitment (both external and internal) as a tool for attracting a more qualified and diverse applicant pool. Third, use valid methods of KSAO assessment, derived from a formal selection plan. Fourth, avoid clinical or excessively subjective prediction in making the assessment and deriving a total assessment or score for candidates. Instead, establish and use the same set of predictors and weights for them to arrive at the final assessment. Fifth, provide training in selection decision making for hiring managers and staffing managers. Content of the training should focus on overcoming usage of stereotypes, learning how to gather and weight predictor information consistently for all candidates, and looking for red flags about acceptance or rejection based on vague judgments about the candidate being a "good fit." Sixth, use a diverse group of hiring and staffing managers to gather and evaluate KSAO information, including a diverse team to conduct interviews. Finally, monitor selection decision making and challenge those decision makers who reject candidates who would enhance diversity, to demonstrate that the reasons for rejection are job related.[34]

When the organization is under an affirmative action plan, either voluntary or court imposed, the above recommendations are still appropriate. Attempts to go even further and provide a specific "plus" to protected characteristics should not be undertaken without a careful examination and opinion of whether this would be legally permissible.

SUMMARY

The selection component of a staffing system requires that decisions be made in several areas. The critical concerns are deciding which predictors (assessment methods) to use, determining assessment scores and setting cut scores, making final decisions about applicants, considering who within the organization should help make selection decisions, and complying with legal guidance.

In deciding which assessment methods to use, consideration should be given to the validity coefficient, face validity correlation with other predictors, adverse impact, utility, and applicant reactions. Ideally, a predictor would have a validity coefficient with large magnitude and significance, high face validity, low correlations with other predictors, little adverse impact, and high utility. In practice, this ideal situation is hard to achieve, so decisions about trade-offs are necessary.

How assessment scores are determined depends on whether a single predictor or multiple predictors are used. In the case of a single predictor, assessment scores are simply the scores on the predictor. With multiple predictors, a compensatory, multiple hurdles, or combined model must be used. A compensatory model allows a person to compensate for a low score on one predictor with a high score on another predictor. A multiple hurdles model requires that a person achieve a passing score on each successive predictor. A combined model uses elements of both the compensatory and multiple hurdles models.

In deciding who earns a passing score on a predictor or a combination of predictors, cut scores must be set. When doing so, the consequences of setting different levels of cut scores should be considered, especially those of assessing some applicants as false positives or false negatives. Approaches to determining cut scores include minimum competency, top-down, and banding methods. Professional guidelines are reviewed on how best to set cut scores.

.

Methods of final choice involve determining who will receive job offers, from among those who have passed the initial hurdles. Several methods of making these decisions are reviewed, including random selection, ranking, and grouping. Each has advantages and disadvantages.

Multiple individuals may be involved in selection decision making. HR professionals play a role primarily in determining the selection process to be used and in making selection decisions based on initial assessment results. Managers play a role primarily in deciding whom to select during the final choice stage. Employees are becoming part of the decision-making process, especially in team assessment approaches. A basic legal issue is conformance with the UGESP, which provide guidance on how to set cut scores in ways that help minimize adverse impact and allow the organization to fulfill its EEO/AA obligations. In the absence of an affirmative action play, protected class characteristics must not enter into selection decision making. That prohibition notwithstanding, there are numerous steps organizations might take to increase workforce diversity.

DISCUSSION QUESTIONS

1. Your boss is considering using a new predictor. The base rate is high, the selection ratio is low, and the validity coefficient is high for the current predictor. What would you advise your boss and why?
2. What are the positive consequences associated with a high predictor cut score? What are the negative consequences?
3. Under what circumstances should a compensatory model be used? When should a multiple hurdles model be used?
4. What are the advantages of ranking as a method of final choice over random selection?
5. What roles should HR professionals play in staffing decisions? Why?
6. What guidelines do the UGESP offer to organizations when it comes to setting cut scores?

ETHICAL ISSUES

1. Do you think companies should use banding in selection decisions? Defend your position.
2. Is clinical prediction the fairest way to combine assessment information about job applicants, or are the other methods (unit weighting, rational weighting, multiple regression) fairer? Why?

APPLICATIONS

Utility Concerns in Choosing an Assessment Method

Randy May is a 32-year-old airplane mechanic for a small airline based in Nantucket Island, Massachusetts. Recently, Randy won $2 million in the New England lottery. Because Randy is relatively young, he decided to invest his winnings in a business to create a future stream of earnings. After weighing many investment decisions, Randy opted to open up a chain of ice cream shops in the Cape Cod area. (As it turns out, Cape Cod and the nearby islands are short of ice cream shops.) Based on his own budgeting, Randy figured he had enough cash to open shops on each of the two islands (Nantucket and Martha's Vineyard) and two shops in small towns on the Cape (Falmouth and Buzzards Bay). Randy contracted with a local builder and the construction/renovation of the four shops is well under way.

The task that is occupying Randy's attention now is how to staff the shops. Two weeks ago, he placed advertisements in three area newspapers. So far, he has received 100 applications. Randy has done some informal HR planning and figures he needs to hire 50 employees to staff the four shops. Being a novice at this, Randy is unsure how to select the 50 people he needs to hire. Randy consulted his friend Mary, who owns the lunch counter at the airport. Mary advised Randy that she used the interview to get "the most knowledgeable people possible" and recommended it to Randy because her people had "generally worked out well." While Randy greatly respected Mary's advice, on reflection several questions came to mind. Does Mary's use of the interview mean that it meets Randy's requirements? How could Randy determine whether his chosen method of selecting employees was effective or ineffective?

Confused, Randy also sought the advice of Professor Ray Higgins, from whom Randy took an HR management course while getting his business degree. After learning of the situation and offering his consulting services, Professor Higgins suggested that Randy choose one of two selection methods (after paying Professor Higgins's consulting fees, he cannot afford to use both methods). The two methods Professor Higgins recommended are the interview (as Mary recommended) and also a work sample test that entails scooping ice cream and serving it to the customer. Randy estimates that it would cost $100 to interview an applicant and $150 per applicant to administer the work sample. Professor Higgins told Randy that the validity of the interview is $r = .30$ while the validity of the work sample is $r = .50$. Professor Higgins also informed Randy that if the selection ratio is .50, the average score on the selection measure of those applicants selected is $z = .80$ (.80 standard deviations above the mean). Randy plans to offer employees a wage of $6.00 per hour. (Over the course of a year, this would amount to a $12,000 salary.)

Based on the information presented above, Randy would really appreciate it if you could help him answer the following questions:

1. How much money would Randy save using each selection method?
2. If Randy can use only one method, which should he use?

3. If the number of applicants increases to 200 (more applications are coming in every day), how would your answers to questions 1 and 2 change?

4. What limitations are inherent in the estimates you have made?

Choosing Entrants Into a Management Training Program

Come As You Are, a convenience store chain headquartered in Fayetteville, Arkansas, has developed an assessment program to promote nonexempt employees into its management training program. The minimum entrance requirements into the program are five years of company experience, a college degree from an accredited university, and a minimum acceptable job performance rating (3 or higher on a 1–5 scale). Any interested applicant into the management program can enroll in the half-day assessment program, where the following assessments are made:

1. Cognitive ability test
2. Integrity test
3. Signed permission for background test
4. Brief (30-minute) interview by various members of the management team
5. Drug test

At the Hot Springs store, 11 applicants have applied for openings in the management training program. The selection information on the candidates is provided in the following exhibit. (The scoring key is provided at the bottom of the exhibit.) It is estimated that there are three slots in the program available for qualified candidates from the Hot Springs location. Given this information and what you know about external and internal selection, as well as staffing decision making, answer the following questions:

1. How would you go about the process of making decisions about whom to select for the openings? In other words, without providing your decisions for the individual candidates, describe how you would weigh the various selection information to reach a decision.

2. Using the decision-making process from the previous question, which applicant would you select into the training program? Explain your decision.

3. Although the data provided in the exhibit reveal that all selection measures were given to all 11 candidates, would you advise Come As You Are to continue to administer all the predictors at one time during the half-day assessment program? Or, should the predictors be given in a sequence so that a multiple hurdles or combined approach could be used? Explain your recommendation.

EXHIBIT

Predictor Scores for Eleven Applicants to Management Training Program

Name	Company Experience	College Degree	Performance Rating	Cognitive Ability Test	Integrity Test	Background Test	Interview Rating	Drug Test
Radhu	4	Yes	4	9	6	OK	6	P
Merv	12	Yes	3	3	6	OK	8	P
Marianne	9	Yes	4	8	5	Arrest '95	4	P
Helmut	5	Yes	4	5	8	OK	4	P
Siobhan	14	Yes	5	7	8	OK	8	P
Galina	7	No	3	3	4	OK	6	P
Raul	6	Yes	4	7	8	OK	2	P
Frank	9	Yes	5	2	5	OK	7	P
Osvaldo	10	Yes	4	10	7	OK	3	P
Byron	18	Yes	3	3	6	OK	6	P
Aletha	11	Yes	4	7	6	OK	5	P
Scale	Years	Yes–No	1–5	1–10	1–10	OK–Other	1–10	P–F

TANGLEWOOD STORES CASE

The cases you have considered up to this point have involved making aggregated decisions about a large number of applicants. After gathering relevant information, there is still the important task of determining how to combine this information to arrive at a set of candidates. This case combines several concepts from the chapters on selection and decision making.

The Situation

Tanglewood is faced with a situation in which 11 qualified applicants have advanced to the candidate stage for the job of store manager. These individuals have submitted résumés, completed several standardized tests similar to those described in the case on measurement, and engaged in initial interviews. There is considerable debate among the regional management staff that is responsible for selecting store managers about which of these candidates are best qualified to make it to the finalist stage, and they have asked you to help them reach a more informed decision.

Your Tasks

You will select the top candidates for the finalist pool by using various combinations of the predictors. The methods for combining predictors will include clinical prediction, unit weighting, rational weighting, and a multiple hurdles model. In your answers you will provide detailed descriptions of how you made decisions and also assess how comfortable you are with the results. You will also describe what you think are appropriate minimal "cut scores" for each of the predictors. The background information for this case, and your specific assignment, can be found at *www.mhhe.com/heneman6e*.

ENDNOTES

1. F. L. Schmidt and J. E. Hunter, "Moderator Research and the Law of Small Numbers," *Personnel Psychology,* 1978, 31, pp. 215–232.
2. J. Cohen, "The Earth Is Round (p <.05)," *American Psychologist,* 1994, 49, pp. 997–1003; F. L. Schmidt, "Quantitative Methods and Cumulative Knowledge in Psychology: Implications for the Training of Researchers," Paper presented at the meeting of the American Psychological Association, Los Angeles, CA, 1994.
3. L. G. Grimm and P. R. Yarnold, *Reading and Understanding Multivariate Statistics* (Washington, DC: American Psychological Association, 1995).
4. C. Handler and S. Hunt, "Estimating the Financial Value of Staffing-Assessment Tools," *Workforce Management,* Mar. 2003 (*www.workforce.com*); J. Sullivan, "The True Value of Hiring and Retaining Top Performers," *Workforce Management,* Aug. 2002 (*www.workforce.com*).
5. M. C. Sturman and T. A. Judge, "Utility Analysis for Multiple Selection Devices and Multiple Outcomes," Working paper, Cornell University, 1994.

6. J. Hersch, "Equal Employment Opportunity Law and Firm Profitability," *Journal of Human Resources,* 1991, 26, pp. 139–153.

7. G. V. Barrett, R. A. Alexander, and D. Doverspike, "The Implications for Personnel Selection of Apparent Declines in Predictive Validities Over Time: A Critique of Hulin, Henry, and Noon," *Personnel Psychology,* 1992, 45, pp. 601–617; C. L. Hulin, R. A. Henry, and S. L. Noon, "Adding a Dimension: Time as a Factor in Predictive Relationships," *Psychological Bulletin,* 1990, 107, pp. 328–340; C. T. Keil and J. M. Cortina, "Degradation of Validity Over Time: A Test and Extension of Ackerman's Model," *Psychological Bulletin,* 2001, 127, pp. 673–697.

8. J. W. Boudreau, M. C. Sturman, and T. A. Judge, "Utility Analysis: What Are the Black Boxes, and Do They Affect Decisions?," in N. Anderson and P. Herriot (eds.), *Assessment and Selection in Organizations* (Chichester, England: Wiley, 1994), pp. 77–96.

9. K. M. Murphy, "When Your Top Choice Turns You Down," *Psychological Bulletin,* 1986, 99, pp. 133–138; F. L. Schmidt, M. J. Mack, and J. E. Hunter, "Selection Utility in the Occupation of US Park Ranger for Three Modes of Test Use," *Journal of Applied Psychology,* 1984, 69, pp. 490–497.

10. T. H. Macan and S. Highhouse, "Communicating the Utility of Human Resource Activities: A Survey of I/O and HR Professionals," *Journal of Business and Psychology,* 1994, 8, pp. 425–436.

11. K. C. Carson, J. S. Becker, and J. A. Henderson, "Is Utility Really Futile? A Failure to Replicate and an Extension," *Journal of Applied Psychology,* 1998, 83, pp. 84–96; J. T. Hazer and S. Highhouse, "Factors Influencing Managers' Reactions to Utility Analysis: Effects of SDy Method, Information Frame, and Focal Intervention," *Journal of Applied Psychology,* 1997, 82, pp. 104–112; G. P. Latham and G. Whyte, "The Futility of Utility Analysis," *Personnel Psychology,* 1994, 47, pp. 31–46; G. Whyte and G. Latham, "The Futility of Utility Analysis Revisited: When Even an Expert Fails," *Personnel Psychology,* 1997, 50, pp. 601–610.

12. C. J. Russell, A. Colella, and P. Bobko, "Expanding the Context of Utility: The Strategic Impact of Personnel Selection," *Personnel Psychology,* 1993, 46, pp. 781–801.

13. J. Sawyer, "Measurement and Predictions, Clinical and Statistical," *Psychological Bulletin,* 1966, 66, pp. 178–200; D. Westen and J. Weinberger, "When Clinical Description Becomes Statistical Prediction," *American Psychologist,* 2004, 59, pp. 595–613; J. Welch and S. Welch, "Hiring Wrong-and Right," *Business Week,* Jan. 29, 2007, p. 102.

14. F. L. Schmidt, "The Relative Efficiency of Regression and Sample Unit Predictor Weights in Applied Differential Psychology," *Educational and Psychological Measurement,* 1971, 31, pp. 699–714.

15. J. M. LeBreton, M. B. Hargis, B. Griepentrog, F. L. Oswald, and R. E. Ployhart, "A Multidimensional Approach for Evaluating Variables in Organizational Research and Practice," *Personnel Psychology,* 2007, 60, pp. 475–498.

16. D. S. Ones, F. L. Schmidt, and K. Yoon, "Validity of an Equally-Weighted Composite of General Mental Ability and a Second Predictor" and "Predictive Validity of General Mental Ability Combined With a Second Predictor Based on Standardized Multiple Regression," Working paper, University of Iowa, Iowa City, 1996.

17. Y. Ganzach, A. N. Kluger, and N. Klayman, "Making Decisions From an Interview: Expert Measurement and Mechanical Combination," *Personnel Psychology,* 2000, 53, pp. 1–20.

18. W. F. Cascio, R. A. Alexander, and G. V. Barrett, "Setting Cutoff Scores: Legal, Psychometric, and Professional Issues and Guidelines," *Personnel Psychology,* 1988, 41, pp. 1–24.

19. J. Bennett, "Scientific Hiring Strategies Are Raising Productivity While Reducing Turnover," *Wall Street Journal,* Feb. 10, 2004, p. B7.

20. S. J. Wells, "Too Good to Hire?" *HR Magazine,* Oct. 2004, pp. 48–54.

21. W. H. Angoff, "Scales, Norms, and Equivalent Scores," in R. L. Thorndike (ed.), *Educational Measurement* (Washington, DC: American Council on Education, 1971), pp. 508–600; R. E. Biddle, "How to Set Cutoff Scores for Knowledge Tests Used in Promotion, Training, Certification, and Licensing," *Public Personnel Management,* 1993, 22, pp. 63–79.

22. J. P. Hudson, Jr., and J. E. Campion, "Hindsight Bias in an Application of the Angoff Method for Setting Cutoff Scores," *Journal of Applied Psychology,* 1994, 79, pp. 860–865; G. M. Hurtz and M. A. Auerbach, "A Meta-Analysis of the Effects of Modifications to the Angoff Method on Cutoff and Judgment Consensus," *Educational and Psychological Measurement,* 2003, 63, pp. 584–601.

23. P. R. Sackett and S. L. Wilk, "Within-Group Norming and Other Forms of Score Adjustment in Preemployment Testing," *American Psychologist,* 1994, 49, pp. 929–954.

24. K. R. Murphy, K. Osten, and B. Myors, "Modeling the Effects of Banding in Personnel Selection," *Personnel Psychology,* 1995, 48, pp. 61–84.

25. K. R. Murphy," Potential Effects of Banding as a Function of Test Reliability," *Personnel Psychology,* 1994, 47, pp. 477–495.

26. P. Bobko, P. L. Roth, and A. Nicewander, "Banding Selection Scores in Human Resource Management Decisions: Current Inaccuracies and the Effect of Conditional Standard Errors," *Organizational Research Methods,* 2005, 8, pp. 259–273.

27. W. F. Cascio, I. L. Goldstein, and J. Outtz, "Social and Technical Issues in Staffing Decisions," in H. Aguinis (ed.), *Test-Score Banding in Human Resource Selection: Technical, Legal, and Societal Issues* (Westport, CT, 2004), pp. 7–28; K. R. Murphy, "Conflicting Values and Interests in Banding Research and Practice," in H. Aguinis (ed.), *Test-Score Banding in Human Resource Selection: Technical, Legal, and Societal Issues,* pp. 175–192; F. Schmidt and J. E. Hunter, "SED Banding as a Test of Scientific Values in I/O Psychology," in H. Aguinis (ed.), *Test-Score Banding in Human Resource Selection: Technical, Legal, and Societal Issues,* pp. 151–173.

28. C. A. Henle, "Case Review of the Legal Status of Banding," *Human Performance,* 2004, 17, pp. 415–432.

29. P. R. Sackett, N. Schmitt, J. E. Ellingson, and M. B. Kabin, "High-Stakes Testing in Employment, Credentialing, and Higher Education," *American Psychologist,* 2001, 56, pp. 302–318.

30. W. De Corte, F. Lievens, and P. R. Sackett, "Combining Predictors to Achieve Optimal Trade-Offs Between Selection Quality and Adverse Impact," *Journal of Applied Psychology,* 2007, 92, pp. 1380–1393; H. Aguinis and M. A. Smith, "Understanding the Impact of Test Validity and Bias on Selection Errors and Adverse Impact in Human Resource Selection," *Personnel Psychology,* 2007, 60, pp. 165–190.

31. M. D. Nowicki and J. G. Rosse, "Managers' Views of How to Hire: Building Bridges Between Science and Practice," *Journal of Business and Psychology,* 2002, 17, pp. 157–170.

CHAPTER TWELVE

Final Match

I n the previous chapter, the focus was on organizational aspects of decision making regarding the likely match or fit between an individual and an organization. The emphasis was on reducing the initial applicant pool to a smaller set of candidates and identifying one or more job finalists from that candidate set to whom to offer employment.

A final match occurs when the offer receiver and the organization have determined that the probable overlap between the person's knowledge, skill, ability, and other characteristics (KSAOs)/motivation and the job's requirements/rewards is sufficient to warrant entering into the employment relationship. Once this decision has been made, the organization and the individual seek to become legally bound to each other through mutual agreement on the terms and conditions of employment. They thus enter into an employment contract, and each expects the other to abide by the terms of the contract.

The formation of, and agreement on, the employment contract occurs in both external and internal staffing. Any time the matching process is set in motion, either through external or internal staffing, the goal is establishment of a new employment relationship.

Knowledge of employment contract concepts and principles is central to understanding the final match. This chapter begins with an overview of such material, emphasizing the essential requirements for establishing a legally binding employment contract, as well as some of the nuances in doing so. A strategic approach to job offers is then presented, followed by a discussion of the major components of a job offer and points to address in it. As is apparent, staffing organizations effectively demands great skill and care by the employer as it enters into employment contracts. The employer and offer receiver are accorded great freedom in the establishment of terms and conditions of employment; both parties have much to decide and agree on pertaining to job offer content.

Through the job offer process, these terms and conditions are proposed, discussed, negotiated, modified, and, ultimately, agreed on. The process, therefore, is frequently complex, requiring planning by those responsible for it. Elements and considerations in this process are discussed next.

Once agreement on the terms and conditions of employment has been reached, the final match process is completed, and the formal employment relationship is established. In a sense, staffing activities end at this point. In another sense, however, it is important to phase these activities into initial post-employment activities that help the new employee adapt and adjust to the new job. Employee orientation and socialization activities are discussed as ways to facilitate this.

The chapter concludes with a discussion of specific legal issues that pertain not only to the establishment of the employment contract but also to potential long-term consequences of that contract that must be considered at the time it is established.

EMPLOYMENT CONTRACTS

The establishment and enforcement of employment contracts is a very complex and constantly changing undertaking. Covered next are some very basic, yet subtle, issues associated with this undertaking. It is crucial to understand the elements that compose a legally enforceable contract and to be able to identify the parties to the contract (employees or independent contractors, third-party representatives), the form of the contract (written, oral), disclaimers, fulfillment of other conditions, reneging on an offer or acceptance, and other sources (e.g., employee handbooks) that may also constitute a portion of the total employment contract.

Requirements for an Enforceable Contract

There are three basic elements required for a contract to be legally binding and enforceable: offer, acceptance, and consideration.[1] If any one of these is missing, there is no binding contract.

Offer

The offer is usually made by the employer. It is composed of the terms and conditions of employment desired and proposed by the employer. The terms must be clear and specific enough to be acted on by the offer receiver. Vague statements and offers are unacceptable (e.g., "Come to work for me right now; we'll work out the details later"). The content of newspaper ads for the job and general written employer material, such as a brochure describing the organization, probably are also too vague to be considered offers. Both the employer and the offer receiver should have a definite understanding of the specific terms being proposed.

Acceptance

To constitute a contract, the offer must be accepted on the terms as offered. Thus, if the employer offers a salary of $50,000 per year, the offer receiver must either accept or reject that term. Acceptance of an offer on a contingency basis does not constitute an acceptance. If the offer receiver responds to the salary offer of $50,000 by saying, "Pay me $52,500, and I'll come to work for you," this is not an acceptance. Rather, it is a counteroffer, and the employer must now either formally accept or reject it.

The offer receiver must also accept the offer in the manner specified in the offer. If the offer requires acceptance in writing, for example, the offer receiver must accept it in writing. Or, if the offer requires acceptance by a certain date, it must be accepted by that date.

Consideration

Consideration entails the exchange of something of value between the parties to the contract. Usually, it involves an exchange of promises. The employer offers or promises to provide compensation to the offer receiver in exchange for labor, and the offer receiver promises to provide labor to the employer in exchange for compensation. The exchange of promises must be firm and of value, which is usually quite straightforward. Occasionally, consideration can become an issue. For example, if the employer makes an offer to a person that requires a response by a certain date, and then does not hear from the person, there is no contract, even though the employer thought that they "had a deal."

Parties to the Contract

Two issues arise regarding the parties to the contract: whether the employer is entering into a contract with an "employee" or with an "independent contractor," and whether an outsider or "third party" can execute or otherwise play a role in the employment contract.[2]

Employee or Independent Contractor

Individuals are acquired by the organization as either employees or independent contractors. Both of these terms have definite legal meanings that should be reviewed (see Chapter 2) prior to entering into a contractual relationship. The organization should be clear in its offer whether the relationship being sought is that of employer–employee or employer–independent contractor. Care should be taken to avoid misclassifying the offer receiver as an independent contractor when in fact the receiver will be treated practically as an employee (e.g., subject to specific direction and control by the employer). Such a misclassification can result in substantial tax and other legal liability problems for the organization.

Third Parties

Often, someone other than the employer or offer receiver speaks on their behalf in the establishment or modification of employment contracts. These people serve as agents for the employer and offer receiver. For the employer, this may mean the use of outsiders such as employment agencies, executive recruiters, or search consultants; it also usually means the use of one or more employees, such as the human resource (HR) department representative, the hiring manager, higher-level managers, and other managers within the organization. For the offer receiver, it may mean the use of a special agent, such as a professional agent for an athlete or an executive. These possibilities raise three important questions for the employer.

First, who, if anyone, speaks for the offer receiver? This is usually a matter of checking with the offer receiver as to whether any given person is indeed authorized by the offer receiver to be a spokesperson, and what, if any, limits have been placed on that person regarding terms that may be discussed and agreed on with the employer.

Second, who is the spokesperson for the employer? In the case of its own employees, the employer must recognize that from a legal standpoint, any of them could be construed as speaking for the employer. Virtually anyone could thus suggest and agree to contract terms, knowingly or unknowingly. This means that the employer should formulate and enforce explicit policies as to who is authorized to speak on its behalf.

Third, exactly what is that person authorized to say? Here, the legal concept of apparent authority is relevant. If the offer receiver believes that a person has the authority to speak for the employer, and there is nothing to indicate otherwise, that person has the apparent authority to speak for the employer. In turn, the employer may be bound by what that person says and agrees to, even if the employer did not grant express authority to do so to this person. It is thus important for the organization to clarify to both the offer receiver and the designated spokespersons what the spokesperson is authorized to discuss and agree to without approval from other organizational members.

Form of the Contract

Employment contracts may be written, oral, or even a combination of the two.[7] All may be legally binding and enforceable. Within this broad parameter, however, are numerous caveats and considerations.

Written Contracts

As a general rule, the law favors written contracts over oral ones. This alone should lead an organization to use only written contracts whenever possible.

A written contract may take many forms, and all may be legally enforceable. Examples of a written document that may be construed as a contract include a letter of offer and acceptance (the usual example), a statement on a job application blank (such as an applicant voucher to the truthfulness of information provided), internal job posting notices, and statements in employee handbooks or other personnel manuals. The more specific the information and statements in such documents, the more likely they are to be considered employment contracts.

Unintended problems may arise with these documents. They may become interpreted as enforceable contracts even though that was not their intent (perhaps the intent was merely informational). Or, statements on a given term or condition of employment may contradict one another in various documents.

An excellent illustration of these kinds of problems involves the issue of employment-at-will. Assume an employer wishes to be, as a matter of explicit policy, a strict at-will employer. That desire may be unintentionally undercut by written documents that imply something other than an employment-at-will relationship. For example, correspondence with an applicant may talk of "continued employment after you complete your probationary period." This statement might be legally interpreted as creating something other than a strict at-will employment relationship. To further muddy the waters, the employee handbook may contain an explicit at-will statement, thus contradicting the policy implied in the correspondence with the applicant.

Care must thus be taken to ensure that all written documents accurately convey only the intended meanings regarding terms and conditions of employment. To this end, the following suggestions should be heeded:[4]

- Before putting anything in writing, ask, Does the company mean to be held to this?
- Choose words carefully; where appropriate, avoid using words that imply binding commitment.
- Make sure all related documents are consistent with one another.
- Always have a second person review what another has written.
- Form the habit of looking at the entire hiring procedure and consider any writings within that context.

Oral Contracts

While oral contracts may be every bit as binding as written contracts, there are two notable exceptions that support placing greater importance on written contracts.

The first exception is the one-year rule, which comes about in what is known as the statute of frauds.[5] Under this rule, a contract that cannot be performed or fulfilled within a one-year interval is not enforceable unless it is in writing. Thus, oral agreements for any length greater than one year are not enforceable. Because of this rule, the organization should not make oral contracts that are intended to last more than one year.

The second exception involves the concept of parole evidence, which pertains to oral promises that are made about the employment relationship.[6] Legally, parole evidence (e.g., the offer receiver's claim that "I was promised that I wouldn't have to work on weekends") may not be used to enforce a contract if it is inconsistent with the terms of a written agreement. Thus, if the offer receiver's letter of appointment explicitly stated that weekend work was required, the oral promise of not having to work weekends would not be enforceable.

Note, however, in the absence of written statements to the contrary, oral statements may indeed be enforceable. In the preceding example, if the letter of appointment was silent on the issue of weekend work, then the oral promise of no weekend work might well be enforceable.

More generally, oral statements are more likely to be enforceable as employment contract terms in the following situations:[7]

- When there is no written statement regarding the term (e.g., weekend work) in question
- When the term is quite certain ("You will not have to work on weekends," as opposed to, "Occasionally, we work weekends around here")
- When the person making the oral statement is in a position of authority to do so (e.g., the hiring manager as opposed to a coworker)

- The more formal the circumstances in which the statement was made (the manager's office as opposed to around the bar or dinner table as part of a recruiting trip)
- The more specific the promise ("You will work every other Saturday from 8:00 to 5:00," as opposed to, "You may have to work from 8:00 to the middle of the afternoon on the weekends, but we'll try to hold that to a minimum")

As this discussion makes clear, from a legal perspective, oral statements are a potential minefield in establishing employment contracts. They obviously cannot be avoided (employer and applicant have to speak to each other), and they may serve other legitimate and desired outcomes, such as providing realistic recruitment information to job applicants. Nonetheless, the organization should use oral statements with extreme caution and alert all members to its policies regarding their use. As further protection, the organization should include in its written offer that, by accepting the offer, the employee agrees the organization has made no other promises than those contained in the written offer.

Disclaimers

A disclaimer is a statement (oral or written) that explicitly limits an employee right and reserves that right for the employer.[8] Disclaimers are often used in letters of appointment, job application blanks, and employee handbooks.

A common, and increasingly important, employee "right" that is being limited through the use of a disclaimer is that of job security. Here, through its policy of employment-at-will, the employer explicitly makes no promise of any job security and reserves the right to terminate the employment relationship at its own will. The following is an example of such a disclaimer that survived legal challenge:

> In consideration of my employment, I agree to conform to the rules and regulations of Sears, Roebuck and Company, and recognize that employment and compensation can be terminated, with or without cause, and with or without notice, at any time, at the option of either the company or myself. I understand that no store manager or representative of Sears, Roebuck and Company, other than the president or vice-president of the company, has any authority to enter into any agreement for employment for any specified period of time, or to make any agreement contrary to the foregoing.[9]

An employment-at-will disclaimer should appear in the job offer letter. It should also appear on the application blank, along with two other disclaimers (see Chapter 8). First, there should be a statement of consent by the applicant for the organization to check provided references, along with a waiver of the right to make claims against them for anything they said. Second, there should be a so-called false statement warning, indicating that any false statement, misleading statement, or material omission may be grounds for dismissal.

Disclaimers are generally enforceable. They can thus serve as an important component of employment contracts. Their use should be guided by the following set of recommendations:[10]

1. They should be clearly stated and conspicuously placed in appropriate documents.
2. The employee should acknowledge receipt and review of the document and the disclaimer.
3. The disclaimer should state that it may be modified only in writing and by whom.
4. The terms and conditions of employment, including the disclaimer, as well as limits on their enforceability, should be reviewed with offer receivers and employees.

It would be wise to obtain legal counsel for drafting language for all disclaimers.

Contingencies

Often, the employer may wish to make a job offer that is contingent on certain other conditions being fulfilled by the offer receiver.[11] Examples of such contingencies include (1) passage of a particular test, such as a licensure exam (e.g., CPA or bar exam); (2) passage of a medical exam, including alcohol/drug/screening tests; (3) satisfactory background and reference checks; and (4) proof of employability under the Immigration Reform and Control Act (IRCA).

Though contingencies to a contract are generally enforceable, contingencies to an employment contract (especially those involving any of the preceding examples) are exceedingly complex and may be made only within defined limits. For this reason, contingencies should not be used in employment contracts without prior legal counsel.

Other Employment Contract Sources

As alluded to previously, employment contract terms may be established through multiple sources, not just the letters of job offer and acceptance. Such establishment may be the result of both intentional and unintentional acts by the employer. Moreover, these terms may come about not only when the employment relationship is first established but also during the course of the employment relationship.[12]

The employer thus must constantly be alert to the fact that terms and conditions of employment may come into being and be modified through a variety of employment contract sources. Sources worth reiterating here are employee handbooks (and other written documents) and oral statements made by employer representatives. Job advertisements and job descriptions are generally not considered employment contracts.

In the case of employee handbooks, the employer must consider whether statements in them are legally enforceable or merely informational. While there is legal opinion on both sides of this question, handbooks are being considered increasingly as a legally enforceable part of the employment contract. To avoid this occurrence, the employer may wish to place an explicit disclaimer in the handbook that states the intent to provide only information to employees and that the employer will not be bound by any of the statements contained in the handbook.

In the case of oral statements, their danger and the need for caution in their use have already been addressed. It should be remembered that oral statements may present legal problems and challenges when made not only at the time of the initial employment contract but also throughout the course of the employment relationship. Of particular concern here are oral promises made to employees regarding future events, such as job security ("Don't worry, you will always have a place with us") or job assignments ("After training, you will be assigned as the assistant manager at our new store"). With oral statements, there is thus a constant need to be careful regarding the messages being delivered to employees, as well as who delivers those messages.

Unfulfilled Promises

Since the staffing process in general, and the job offer process in particular, involves the making of promises to offer receivers about terms and conditions of employment, it is important for the organization to (1) not make promises it is unwilling to keep, and (2) be sure that promises made are actually kept. Unfulfilled promises may spur the disappointed person to pursue a legal action against the organization. Three types of claims might be pursued.[13]

The first claim is that of breach of contract, and it may be pursued for both written and oral promises. The employee will have to show that both parties intended to be legally bound by the promise and that it was specific enough to establish an actual oral agreement. The second claim is that of promissory estoppel. Here, even if there is no enforceable oral contract, employees may claim that they relied on promises made by the organization, to their subsequent detriment, since the actual or presumed job offer was withdrawn (such withdrawal is known as reneging). Examples of detrimental effects include resigning from one's current employer, passing up other job opportunities, relocating geographically, and incurring expenses associated with the job offer. When the offer receiver experiences such detrimental reliance, the person may sue the employer for compensatory damages; actual hiring of the person is rarely sought. The final claim is that of fraud, where the employee claims the organization made promises it had no intention of keeping. Employees may legally pursue fraud claims and seek both compensatory and punitive damages.

JOB OFFERS

A job offer is an attempt by the organization to induce the offer receiver into the establishment of an employment relationship. Assuming that the offer is accepted and that consideration is met, the organization and offer receiver will have established their relationship in the form of a legally binding employment contract. That contract is the culmination of the staffing process. The contract also signifies that the person/job match process has concluded and that the person/job match is now about to become a reality. That reality, in turn, becomes the start of, and foundation for, subsequent employee effectiveness on the various HR outcomes. For these reasons, the content and extension of the job offer become critical final parts of the overall staffing process.

This section discusses first a strategic approach to job offers. It shows the numerous factors that should be considered in the determination of the content of job offers. Then the actual content of job offers is discussed, along with some of the complexities associated with that.

Strategic Approach to Job Offers

The organization has considerable discretion in the content of the offers that it "puts together" to present to finalists. Rather than hastily crafting job offers, often in the heat of the hiring moment and desire to fill the vacancy now, it is better to think a bit more strategically as to job offer content. Such an approach has a better possibility of serving the interests of both the organization and the finalists and not locking them into a contract either will come to regret. Another benefit of the strategic approach is that it will help the organization decide whether there will be a standard offer for all finalists or whether "enhanced" offers will be possible for some finalists, and the circumstances that will give rise to such offers.

Shown in Exhibit 12.1 is the strategic approach to job offers, or the employee value proposition (EVP). Recall from Chapter 4 that the EVP is the total package of extrinsic and intrinsic rewards that the offered job will provide to the finalist if the job offer is accepted. Technically, the job offer is not the same as the EVP, because it is difficult to reduce to writing in the job offer letter the nature of the intrinsic rewards that will be provided, and because a job offer contains information in addition to job rewards (e.g., starting date, date the offer lapses, disclaimers). Nonetheless, the major thrust and purpose of the job offer is to convey to the finalist the nature of the rewards "deal" being promised if the offer is accepted. First and foremost, the job offer must be a compelling one—an EVP the finalist will find enticing and difficult to turn down. The offer thus must present a package of rewards with the right combination of magnitude, mix, and distinctiveness to be compelling to the offer receiver.

Exhibit 12.1 indicates that labor market conditions, organization needs, applicant needs, and legal issues are forces to consider in the creation of job offers generally. As to labor markets, the simple availability of potential offer receivers needs to be considered, for often there may be shortages that will require the organization to "sweeten the deal" if it is to have a chance of filling vacancies. Coupled with that is consideration of the overall "tightness" or "looseness" of the labor market. Tight

EXHIBIT 12.1   **Strategic Approach to Job Offers**

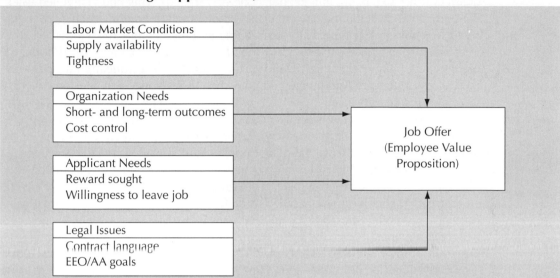

labor markets will serve to exacerbate limited supply availability, for applicants in the limited supply pool will likely have many job offer alternatives. On the other hand, with plentiful supply and a loose labor market, the organization will be in a position to provide standard offers, and ones that are lower in cost.

The organization has multiple needs it must seek to identify and fulfill in the formation of the employment relationship. Some of these are short-term outcomes—such as filling vacancies quickly or at any cost. To what extent does the organization want to respond to such pressures? The answer will clearly shape the content of job offers. Long-term outcomes such as the likely performance level of the new employee, the extent to which the employee fits in with the organization and work unit, the promotion success of the employee, and employee job satisfaction and retention all need to be considered. To what extent does the organization wish to craft job offers that are likely to enhance these longer-term outcomes? Finally, cost control must come into play. All job offers, if accepted, will cost the organization, so how much is it willing to spend? And is the organization willing to spend more for finalists that it thinks will more likely deliver the short-term and/or long-term outcomes it seeks?

In terms of applicant needs, the organization must seek to identify the rewards likely sought by applicants. Here, it is useful to consider the full range of rewards possible and to gather information about reward preferences of applicants (see Chapter 4). Strategically, it will be helpful to identify some rewards with a distinctiveness that may be particularly alluring. For example, in the case of over-the-road (long distance) truck drivers, common driver complaints (and causes of turnover) were long stretches on the road without a return home, and cramped and inhospitable quarters ("It's like being in a kennel," one driver said). This knowledge led trucking companies to begin making changes in the nature of the EVP, such as changing routes to provide less time away from home and equipping cabs with televisions, microwaves, and closets to provide a friendlier work environment. In addition, the magnitude of some extrinsic rewards was increased. The mileage rate paid was increased (drivers are paid by the mile), and health insurance and pension coverage were provided or enhanced.[14] Such job offer improvements required strategic information gathering and analysis, plus extended lead times to implement them.

Coupled with the assessment of applicant needs should be an assessment of the finalists' willingness to leave their current jobs. If the finalist is relatively willing, or even eager to leave, the job offer may not need to be as compelling in magnitude, mix, or distinctiveness. On the other hand, if the finalist is satisfied with the current job and current geographic location, the need to craft a compelling offer rises dramatically. Basically, such offers must provide an EVP that stirs in the finalist a dissatisfaction with the current job and boosts the willingness to change locations, both by pointing out positive features of the new location and by minimizing the costs of making the move.

Finally, legal issues come into play. The contract language will need to be reviewed for clarity and completeness of rewards promised and other terms of the offer, and for consistency with organizational employment policies, especially those with a legal basis. In addition, a review of the organization's equal employment opportunity and affirmative action (EEO/AA) policies, and progress toward hiring and promotion goals, should be made as the offer is being constructed. Being behind on these goals might well signal a need for more aggressive job offers.

Job Offer Content

The organization has considerable latitude in the terms and conditions of employment that it may offer to people. That latitude, of course, should be exercised within the organization's particular applicant attraction strategy, as well as the rewards generally available and shown in the job rewards matrix.

With some degree of latitude in terms and conditions offered for almost any job, it is apparent that job offers should be carefully constructed. There are definite rewards that can, and for the most part should, be addressed in any job offer. Moreover, the precise terms or content of the offer to any given finalist requires careful forethought. What follows is a discussion of the types of rewards to address, as well as some of their subtleties and complexities.

Starting Date

Normally, the organization desires to control when the employment relationship begins. To do so, it must provide a definite starting date in its offer. If it does not, acceptance and consideration of the offer occur at the time the new hire actually begins work. Normally, the starting date is one that allows the offer receiver at least two weeks to provide notification of resignation to a current employer.

Duration of Contract

As noted in Chapter 2, employment contracts may be of a fixed term (i.e., have a definite ending date) or indeterminate term (i.e., have no definite ending date). The decision about duration is intimately related to the employment-at-will issue.

A fixed-term contract provides certainty to both the new hire and the organization regarding the length of the employment relationship. Both parties decide to and must abide by an agreed-on term of employment. The organization can then (according to common law) terminate the contract prior to its expiration date for "just cause" only. Determination and demonstration of just cause can be a complicated legal problem for the organization.

Most organizations are unwilling to provide such employment guarantees. They much prefer an employment-at-will relationship, in which either party may terminate the employment relationship at any time without having to demonstrate just cause.[15] Should the organization decide to have indeterminate-term employment contracts, it should carefully state in its written offer that the duration is indeterminate and that it may be terminated by either party at any time, for any reason. Because of the overriding importance of this issue, all wording should be approved at the highest organizational level.

A compromise between a fixed-term and an indefinite-term provision is to have a contract provision that states it is for an indefinite term, that the employer may terminate the agreement at any time for good cause, and that either the employer or the employee may terminate the contract on 30 days' (or some other time period) written notice. Such a provision provides protection to the employee against arbitrary, immediate termination, and to the employer against a sudden and unanticipated loss of an employee.[16]

Compensation

Compensation is the most important reward that the organization has to offer in its attraction strategy. It is a multifaceted reward that may be presented to the offer receiver in many forms. Sometimes that may consist of a standard pay rate and benefits package, which must be simply accepted or rejected. Other times the offer may be more tailor made, often negotiated in advance.

It should be remembered that job seekers carry with them a set of pay preferences and expectations that shape how they respond to the compensation components of the job offer. For example, a study of engineering and hotel administration soon-to-graduate job seekers found that they would respond more favorably to a pay package that had (1) a high, fixed rate of pay that was not contingent on the success of the organization; (2) pay pegged to a particular job rather than the number of skills they possessed; (3) pay raises based on individual rather than group performance; and (4) a flexible, as opposed to standard, benefits package.[17]

The compensation portion of the job offer should thus be carefully thought out and planned in advance. This pertains to starting pay, variable pay, and benefits.

Starting Pay: Flat Rate. In flat-rate job offers, all persons are offered an identical rate of pay, and variance from this is not permitted. Starting pay is thus offered on a "take it or leave it" basis.

Use of flat rates is appropriate in many circumstances, such as the following examples:

- Jobs for which there is a plentiful supply of job applicants
- Where applicants are of quite similar KSAO quality
- Where there is a desire to avoid creating potential inequities in starting pay among new employees

It should also be noted that under some circumstances, use of flat rates may be mandatory. Examples here include pay rates under many collective bargaining agreements and for many jobs covered by civil service laws and regulations.

Starting Pay: Differential Rates. Organizations often opt out of flat rates, despite their simplicity, and choose differential starting pay rates. In general, this occurs under three sets of circumstances.

First, there are situations where the organization thinks there are clear qualitative (KSAO) differences among finalists. Some finalists are thus felt to be worth more than others, and starting pay differentials are used in recognizing this. A good example here involves new college graduates. Research clearly shows that differences in major and previous work experience lead to starting pay differentials among new graduates.[18] Another example involves differences in starting pay for MBA graduates that reflect the quality of the MBA program from which they graduated. On the assumption that graduates from the elite programs (top 25 nationally ranked schools) represent better "raw business talent" than the mass of graduates from the other schools, the elite program graduates are receiving starting pay offers about twice the amount of other program graduates ($120,000 versus $60,000). A final example is paying a premium for applicants with bilingual language skills. The city of Los Angeles provides a bilingual pay premium to ensure that city services are accessible to non-English speakers. New hires (and current employees) who are required to speak, write, or interpret a language other than English receive a 5.5% bilingual premium.[19]

The second situation occurs when the organization is concerned about attraction outcomes, almost regardless of applicant KSAO differences. Here, the organization is under intense pressure to acquire new employees and fill vacancies promptly. To accomplish these outcomes, flexibility in starting pay rate offers is used to be responsive to finalists' demands, to sweeten offers, and to otherwise impress applicants with an entrepreneurial spirit of wheeling and dealing. Hence, the organization actively seeks to strike a bargain with the offer receiver, and differential starting pay rates are a natural part of the attraction package.

The third situation involves geographic pay differentials. For organizations with multiple facilities in different geographic areas, the starting pay rate for any particular job may need to vary because of average pay differentials across geographic areas. For example, for the job of human resources manager, which has an average national rate of $88,500, pay varies from $57,300 in Montana to $103,500 in Delaware.[20] Clearly, starting pay must take into account geographic pay variation.

Use of differential starting pay rates requires attention to several potential problems.[21] One problem is that offer receivers, though similarly qualified, may have different pay "mix" preferences. Some offer receivers may place higher (or lower) value on salary than on stock options or benefits, leading them to demand higher (or lower) salaries. The organization must decide how much it is willing to provide offer receivers salary trade-offs for other forms of compensation. A second problem, often heightened by the first one, is that issues of fairness and internal equity among employees may arise when there is too much discretion in the range of starting salaries that exist. Naturally, similarly qualified employees receiving wide differences in starting pay is a guaranteed recipe for perceived pay inequities, and paying new hires starting salaries that exceed those of current "leapfrogged" employees also fuels the perceived inequity flames. Finally, research shows that starting pay expectations are often lower among women than men applicants. For example, a survey of 1,600 undergraduate and graduate students found that the average starting pay expectation for men was $55,950, compared to $49,190 for women. If these expectations shape salary negotiations and acceptances, the average starting pay for women will be lower than that for men, and "catch up" for women may be difficult since raises are usually a percentage of one's salary. These represent potential salary discrimination issues confronting the organization.

For such reasons, whenever differential rates of starting pay are used, there is the need for the organization to carefully consider what is permissible and within bounds. At times, the organization may choose to provide minimal guidance to managers making the offers. Often, however, there is a need for some constraints on managers. These constraints may specify when differential starting pay offers may be made and where within a pay range starting pay rates must fall. Exhibit 12.2 contains examples of such starting pay policies.

Variable Pay: Short Term.   Short-term variable pay may be available on jobs, and if so, the organization should address this in the job offer.

Prior to the job offer itself, the organization should give serious thought to whether there should be variable pay in the first place. This is a major issue that transcends staffing per se, but it does have important implications for the likely effectiveness of staffing activities.

Consider an organization with sales jobs, a classic example of a situation in which incentive or commission pay systems might be used. The mere presence/

EXHIBIT 12.2   Example of Starting Pay Policies

The Wright Company

The following policies regarding starting pay must be adhered to:

1. No person is to be offered a salary that is below the minimum, or above the midpoint, of the salary range for the job.
2. Generally, persons with reasonable qualifications should be offered a salary within the first quartile (bottom 25%) of the salary range for the job.
3. Salary offers above the first quartile, but not exceeding the midpoint, may be made for exceptionally well-qualified persons, or when market conditions dictate.
4. Salary offers should be fair in relation to other offers made and to the salaries paid to current employees.
5. Salary offers below the first quartile may be made without approval; offers at or above the first quartile must be approved in advance by the manager of compensation.
6. Counteroffers may not be accepted without approval of the manager of compensation.

absence of such a pay plan will likely affect the motivation/job rewards part of the matching process. Different "breeds of cats" may be attracted to jobs providing incentive plans as opposed to those that do not.

More generally, research shows that the use of short-term incentive pay is quite common, with almost 90% of private sector, 76% of partnerships, and 44% of public sector organizations offering incentive pay plans of various sorts. Of these organizations, 95% provide cash payments via individual incentive pay and bonuses, based on financial, customer service, production, goal attainment, efficiency, and cost reduction measures. Two of the major reasons these organizations provide for such short-term incentive offerings are to compete for qualified employees and to retain employees.[22] Usage of these types of incentive systems is increasing.[23]

If there are to be short-term variable pay plans, the organization should communicate this in the offer letter. Beyond that, the organization should give careful consideration to how much detail about such plans, including payout formulas and amounts, it wants to include in the job offer. The more specific the information, the less flexibility the organization will have in the operation or modification of the plan.

Variable Pay: Long Term. Long-term variable pay plans provide employees ownership opportunity and the opportunity to increase their income as the value of the organization increases. Applicable only in the private sector, the most commonly used long-term variable pay plan is stock options—either an incentive stock option or a nonqualified stock option.[24] A stock option is a right to purchase a share of stock for a predetermined price at a later date; there is both a time span during which the right may be exercised (e.g., 10 years) and a waiting period before the employee is eligible (vested) to make purchases (e.g., 1 year). Incentive stock option plans provide special tax treatment for the employee, primarily regarding capital gains when the employee sells the purchased stock (hopefully at a net gain), but these plans place many statutory restrictions on employers. Nonqualified stock options do not have to meet statutory requirements like those of incentive stock option plans, thus providing the organization greater flexibility in granting options. But nonqualified options do not qualify for special tax treatment for the employee, whereas the organization can receive a tax deduction for the corporation expense of the stock options.

Though stock options provide potential incentive value to offer receivers, some may prefer cash in the form of base pay or short-term variable pay incentives. In addition, stock options only have actual value to the recipient if the value of the stock appreciates beyond the purchase price and if the employee remains eligible to participate in the plan—such as through remaining with the organization for a specified time period.

The use of stock options has been waning. In its place are numerous other long-term variable pay plans—performance options, stock appreciation rights, stock grants, restricted stock, delayed issuance awards, employee stock ownership, and employee stock purchase. Each of these types of plans has both strong and weak points, and careful analysis of the objectives sought (e.g., employee retention) should occur prior to its use and presentation to job offer receivers.[25] As with short-term variable pay plans, the job offer letter should mention the right or requirement to participate in these plans, but not go into too much detail about them.

Inclusion of stock options or other types of long-term variable pay in the job offer requires considerable care and expertise. Experts should draft the actual language in the offer, and the organization should take special steps to ensure that the offer receiver actually understands what is being offered.

Benefits. Normally there is a fixed benefits package for a job, and it is offered as such to all offer receivers. Examples include health insurance and retirement and work/life plans. When a fixed or standard benefits package is offered, the offer letter should not spell out all of the specific benefit provisions. Rather, it should state that the employee will be eligible to participate in the benefit plans maintained by the organization, as provided in written descriptions of these plans. In this way, the job offer letter does not inadvertently make statements or promises that contradict or go beyond the organization's actual benefits plan.

Sometimes the offer may provide not only standard benefits but also additional custom-made benefits or other perquisites, known as "perks." These deal sweeteners may be offered to all potential new hires in a job category, or they may be tailor-made to the preferences of the individual offer receiver. In other instances, they may be offered in direct response to requests or demands from the offer receiver. The number and value of perks offered (or demanded) varies with the degree of difficulty in successfully attracting new hires. Perks are most likely provided to top executives, managers, and professionals. The set of perks used by organizations is almost endless. Commonly used perks are shown in Exhibit 12.3. More exotic perks used for enticing executive stars to relocate include providing a family clothing allowance, moving pet horses, covering a housekeeper's medical insurance, paying children's tuition at private schools, and reimbursing for financial counseling services and tax preparation.

Whether to offer perks, which ones, and to whom are perplexing issues. Although they may have definite applicant enticement appeal, they increase hiring costs, raise numerous tax issues, and may cause feelings of inequity and jealousy among other employees.

Hours

Statements regarding hours of work should be carefully thought out and worded. For the organization, such statements will affect staffing flexibility and cost. In terms of flexibility, a statement such as "Hours of work will be as needed and scheduled" provides maximum flexibility. Designation of work as part time, as opposed to full time, may affect cost because the organization may provide restricted, if any, benefits to part-time employees.

Factors other than just number of hours may also need to be addressed in the job offer. If there are to be any special, tailor-made hours of work arrangements, these need to be clearly spelled out. Examples include "Weekend work will not be required of you," and "Your hours of work will be from 7:30 to 11:30 A.M. and 1:30 to 5:30 P.M." Overtime hours requirements and overtime pay, if applicable, could also be addressed.

Hiring Bonuses. Hiring, signing, or "up-front" bonuses are one-time payments offered and subsequently paid on acceptance of the offer. Typically, the bonus is in the form of an outright cash grant; the bonus may also be in the form of a cash advance against future expected earnings. Top executives are likely to receive not only a cash bonus but restricted stock and/or stock options as well.

EXHIBIT 12.3   Examples of Perquisites

- First-class air travel
- Paid meals
- Country club membership
- Automobile
- Cell phone
- Tuition reimbursement
- Pay-off of student loans
- Specially equipped computer
- Fax machine at home
- Adoption assistance
- Corporate plane
- Housing supplement
- Interest-free loans
- Selling home

For recent college graduates, hiring bonuses range from $1,000 to $10,000, with an average of $3,568. Roughly half (46.4%) of college recruiters say they use hiring bonuses to recruit college graduates.[26]

Generally, as labor markets tighten and employee shortages increase, hiring bonuses become more prevalent and of larger size. For example, in information technology (IT), hiring bonuses are the norm, with 65% of IT employers offering them. However, hiring bonuses can happen at all job levels, including nondegree jobs such as fast food workers, butchers, bartenders, hairstylists, and pizza cooks.[27] The converse is also true, with looser labor markets and employee surpluses leading to smaller or disappearing hiring bonuses.

In addition to simply helping attract highly desired individuals (monetary flattery), hiring bonuses can provide an offset for something the offer receiver may give up by changing jobs, such as a pending pay raise or a promotion. Also, hiring bonuses might be a useful way to lure people to rural areas or to offset relocation costs or a higher cost of living. Finally, use of a hiring bonus might help in avoiding a permanent elevation in base pay, thus holding down labor costs.

Offers of hiring bonuses should be used judiciously, or they will lose their particular distinctiveness as part of the EVP, as well as lead to other problems. For example, while it is desirable to maintain a policy of flexibility as to the use and amount of hiring bonuses, it is necessary to carefully monitor them so that they do not get out of control. Also, it is important to avoid getting into overly spirited hiring bonus bidding wars with competitors—the other rewards of the job need to be emphasized in addition to the bonus. Another danger is that hiring bonuses might give rise to feelings of jealousy and inequity, necessitating retention bonuses if existing employees get wind of the bonuses being given to new hires. To avoid this possibility, hiring bonuses should be considered confidential.[28] Another potential problem is that bonus recipients may be tempted to "take the money and run," and their performance motivation may be lessened because their bonus money is not contingent on their job performance. Debra Ortega, vice president (VP) of HR at Huntington Hospital in Pasadena, California, stopped using hiring bonuses for exactly that reason. "Although sign-on bonuses are common in our industry because of the labor shortages, we find that the practice can almost encourage job hopping from bonus to bonus," she said.

To address these problems, the organization may place restrictions on the bonus payment, paying half up front and the other half after some designated time period, such as 6 or 12 months; another option is to make payment of a portion or all of the bonus contingent on meeting certain performance goals within a designated time period. Such payment arrangements should help other employees see the hiring bonus as not a total "freebie" and should encourage only serious and committed offer receivers to actually accept the offer. Although such "clawbacks" are awkward, and some employers have had difficulties enforcing such agreements, they are generally necessary in some form because the very labor markets in which bonuses are most likely to be used (tight labor markets) are the same markets in which job hopping is very easy to do.[29]

Relocation Assistance. Acceptance of the offer may require a geographic move and entail relocation costs for the offer receiver. The organization may want to provide assistance to conduct the move, as well as totally or partially defray moving costs. Thus, a relocation package may include assistance with house hunting, guaranteed purchase of the applicant's home, a mortgage subsidy, actual moving cost reimbursement, and a cost-of-living adjustment if the move is to a higher-cost area. To simplify things, a lump-sum relocation allowance may be provided, thus reducing record keeping and other paperwork.[30]

Recently, relocation has become even more difficult in dual-career circumstances.[31] With both people working, it may be necessary to move both the offer receiver and the accompanying partner. Such a move may entail employing both people or providing job search assistance to the accompanying partner. The problem is likely to grow in magnitude.

Hot Skill Premiums. A hot skill premium is a temporary pay premium added to the regular base pay to account for a temporary market escalation in pay for certain skills in extreme shortage. An example of a field where hot skill premiums might be used is the IT arena. The job offer should clearly indicate the amount of base pay that constitutes the premium, the length of time the premium will be in effect, and the mechanism by which the premium will be halted or phased out. Before offering such premiums, it is wise to recognize that there will likely be pressure to maintain rather than discontinue the premium and that careful communication with the offer receiver about the temporary nature of the premium will be necessary.[32]

Severance Packages. Terms and conditions that the organization states the employee is entitled to upon departure from the organization constitute a severance package. Content of the package typically includes one or two weeks of pay for every year of service, earned vacation and holiday pay, extended health insurance coverage and premium payment, and outplacement assistance in finding a new job.[33] What is the organization willing to provide?

In pondering this question, a few points should be borne in mind. Severance packages for top executives are usually expected and provided, and their provisions can be quite complex. For lower-level managers and nonmanagers, there appear to be heightened awareness and expectations of severance packages. In other words, these packages are being considered part of the EVP by job applicants. This expectation is probably due to a realization of how marketable their KSAOs are, as well as increased concerns about job security and layoff protection. Unmet severance expectations may translate into demands by candidates for a severance package to be included in their job offer, or a refusal to even consider a job offer that does not provide some form of severance benefit.[34]

Other thorny issues surround these packages. When does an employee become eligible for the package? Will severance be granted for voluntary or involuntary termination, or both? If involuntary, are there exceptions, such as for unacceptable job performance or misconduct? Questions such as those above illustrate the need to very carefully craft the terms that will govern the package and define its contents.

Restrictions on Employees

In some situations, the organization may want to place certain restrictions on employees to protect its own interests. These restrictions should be known, and agreed to, by the new employee at the time of hire. Thus, they should be incorporated into the job offer and resultant employment contract. Because of the potential complexities in these restrictions and the fact that they are subject to state contract laws, legal counsel should be sought to guide the organization in drafting appropriate contract language. Several types of restrictions are possible.[35]

One form of restriction involves so-called confidentiality clauses that prohibit current or departing employees from the unauthorized use or disclosure of confidential information during or after employment. Confidential information is any information not made public and that gives the organization an advantage over its competitors. Examples of such information include trade secrets, customer lists, secret formulas, manufacturing processes, marketing and pricing plans, and business forecasts. It will be necessary to spell out, in some degree, exactly what information the organization considers confidential, as well as the time period after employment for which confidentiality must be maintained.

Another restriction, known as a noncompete agreement, seeks to keep departed employees from competing against the organization. For example, former Microsoft VP Kai-Fu Lee signed a noncompete agreement when he first joined Microsoft. When Lee left Microsoft to run a Google research facility in China, Microsoft sued Google and Lee for violating his noncompete agreement. Google and Microsoft eventually settled out of court, but the case showed that not all noncompete agreements are enforceable. For example, some states (Alabama, California, Georgia, Montana, Nebraska, North Dakota, Oklahoma, and Texas) bar noncompetes. If an employee signs a noncompete agreement in a state that allows them, but relocates to a state that bars them, the employer may be out of luck—which is exactly what happened to Convergys Corp. when an employee signed a noncompete agreement with Convergys in Ohio and then moved to work for a competitor in Georgia, which bars such agreements.[36]

More generally, noncompete agreements cannot keep departed employees from practicing their trade or profession completely or indefinitely, for this would in essence restrict the person from earning a living in a chosen field. Accordingly, the noncompete agreement must be carefully crafted in order to be enforceable. The agreement should probably not be a blanket statement that applies to all employees; rather, the agreement should apply to those employees who truly could turn into competitors, such as high-level managers, scientists, and technical staff. Also, the agreement must be limited in time and geography. The time should be of short duration (less than two years), and the area should be limited to the geographic area of the organization's competitive market. For example, the VP of sales for an insurance agency with locations in two counties of a state might have a non-compete agreement that prohibits working with any other agencies within the two counties, and the solicitation of the agency's policyholders, for one year.

A final type of restriction is the "golden handcuff," or payback agreement. The intent of this restriction is to retain new hires for some period of time and to financially discourage them from leaving the organization, particularly soon after they have joined. A typical golden handcuff will require the employee to repay (in full or pro rata) the organization for any up-front payments made at the time of hire if the employee departs within the first year of employment. These payments might include hiring bonuses, relocation expenses, tuition reimbursements, or any other financial hiring lures. Executive pay packages might contain even more restrictions designed to tie the executive to the organization for an extended period of time. Annual bonuses might be deferred for two or three years and be contingent on the executive not leaving during that time, or an executive may forfeit accrued pension benefits if he or she departs before a particular date.

Other Terms and Conditions

Job offers are by no means restricted to the terms and conditions discussed so far. Virtually any terms and conditions may be covered and presented in a job offer, provided they are legally permissible. Hence, the organization should carefully and creatively think of other terms it may wish to offer. None of these other possible terms should be offered, however, unless the organization is truly willing to commit itself to them as part of a legally binding contract.

The organization should also give careful thought to the possible use of contingencies, which, as mentioned previously, are terms and conditions that the applicant must fulfill before the contract becomes binding (e.g., passage of a medical exam). As was noted, inclusion of these contingencies should not be done without prior knowledge and understanding of their potential legal ramifications (e.g., in the case of a medical exam, potential factors to consider under the Americans With Disabilities Act [ADA]).

Acceptance Terms

The job offer should specify terms of acceptance required of the offer receiver. For reasons previously noted regarding oral contracts, acceptances should normally be required in writing only. The receiver should be required to accept or reject the offer in total, without revision. Any other form of acceptance is not an acceptance, merely a counteroffer. Finally, the offer should specify the date, if any, by which it will lapse. A lapse date is recommended so that certainty and closure are brought to the offer process.

Sample Job Offer Letter

A sample job offer letter is shown in Exhibit 12.4 that summarizes and illustrates the previous discussion and recommendations regarding job offers. This letter should be read and analyzed for purposes of becoming familiar with job offer letters, as well as gaining an appreciation for the many points that need to be addressed in such a letter. Remember that, normally, whatever is put in the job offer letter, once accepted by the receiver, becomes a binding employment contract. Examples of more complex job offer letters, more relevant to executives, might also be consulted.

JOB OFFER PROCESS

Besides having a knowledge of the types of issues to address in a job offer, it is equally important to have an understanding of the total job offer process. The content of any specific job offer must be formulated within a broad context of considerations. Once these have been taken into account, the specific offer must be developed and presented to the finalist. Following this, there will be matters to address in terms of either acceptance or rejection of the offer. Finally, there will be an occasional need to deal with the unfortunate issue of reneging, either by the organization or by the offer receiver.

Formulation of the Job Offer

When the organization puts together a specific job offer, several factors should be explicitly considered. These factors are knowledge of the terms and conditions offered by competitors, applicant truthfulness about KSAOs and reward information provided, the receiver's likely reaction to the offer, and policies on negotiation of job offer content with the offer receiver.

Knowledge of Competitors

The organization competes for labor within labor markets. The job offer must be sensitive to the labor demand and supply forces operating, for these forces set the overall parameters for job offers to be extended.

On the demand side, this requires becoming knowledgeable about the terms and conditions of job contracts offered and provided by competitors. Here, the organization must confront two issues: exactly who are the competitors, and exactly what terms and conditions are they offering for the type of job for which the hiring organization is staffing?

Assume the hiring organization is a national discount retailer, and it is hiring recent (or soon-to-be) college graduates for the job of management trainee. It may identify as competitors other retailers at the national level (e.g., Sears), as well as national discount retailers (e.g., Target, Wal-Mart, and Kmart). There may be fairly

---

EXHIBIT 12.4   Example of Job Offer Letter

The Wright Company

Mr. Vern Markowski
152 Legion Lane
Clearwater, Minnesota

Dear Mr. Markowski:

We are pleased to offer you the position of Human Resource Specialist, beginning March 1, 2005. Your office will be located here in our main facility at Silver Creek, Minnesota.

This offer is for full-time employment, meaning you will be expected to work a minimum of 40 hours per week. Weekend work is also expected, especially during peak production periods.

You will receive a signing bonus of $2,500, half payable on March 1, 2005, and the other half on August 1, 2005, if you are still an employee of the company. Your starting pay will be $3,100 per month. Should you complete one year of employment, you will then participate in our managerial performance review and merit pay process. You will be eligible to participate in our benefit plans as provided in our written descriptions of those plans.

Should you choose to relocate to the Silver Creek area, we will reimburse you for one house/apartment hunting trip for up to $1,000. We will also pay reasonable and normal moving expenses up to $7,500, with receipts required.

It should be emphasized that we are an employment-at-will employer. This means that we, or you, may terminate our employment relationship at any time, for any reason. Only the president of the Wright Company is authorized to provide any modification to this arrangement.

This offer is contingent on (a) your receiving certification as a professional in human resources (PHR) from the Human Resource Certification Institute prior to March 1, 2005, and (b) your passing a company-paid and -approved medical exam prior to March 1, 2005.

We must have your response to this offer by February 1, 2005, at which time the offer will lapse. If you wish to accept our offer as specified in this letter, please sign and date at the bottom of the letter and return it to me (a copy is enclosed for you). Should you wish to discuss these or any other terms prior to February 1, 2005, please feel free to contact me.

Sincerely yours,

Mary Kaiser
Senior Vice President, Human Resources

I accept the employment offer, and its terms, contained in this letter. I have received no promises other than those contained in this letter.

_____   _____
Signed   Date

direct competitors in other industries as well (e.g., banking, insurance) that typically place new college graduates in training programs.

Once such competitors are identified, the organization needs to determine, if possible, what terms and conditions they are offering. This may be done through formal mechanisms such as performing salary surveys, reading competitors' ads and Web sites, or consulting with trade associations. Information may be gathered informally as well, such as through telephone contacts with competitors, and conversations with actual job applicants, who have firsthand knowledge of competitors' terms.

The organization may quickly acquire salary information through use of free online salary sites (e.g., *salary.com, wageweb.com, salaryexpert.com*) or ones that charge fees (e.g., *towers.com, haygroup.com*). Listings of the sites and discussions of their advantages and disadvantages are available.[37] Generally, the user should be cautious in his or her use of these data, being careful to assess salary survey characteristics such as sample nature and size, currency of data, definitions of terms and job descriptions, and data presentation. It should also be remembered that job seekers can and will access these data, making the job seeker a very knowledgeable "shopper" and negotiator.

Through all of the above mechanisms, the organization becomes "marketwise" regarding its competitors. Invariably, however, the organization will discover that for any given term or condition there will be a range of values offered. For example, starting pay might range from $30,000 to $40,500 per year, and the length of the training program may vary from three months to two years. The organization will thus need to determine where within these ranges it wishes to position itself in general, as well as for each particular offer receiver.

On the labor supply side, the organization will need to consider its needs concerning both labor quantity and quality (KSAOs and motivation). In general, offers need to be attractive enough that they yield the head count required. Moreover, offers need to take into account the KSAOs each specific receiver possesses and what these specific KSAOs are worth in terms and conditions offered the person. This calculation is illustrated in Exhibit 12.2, which shows an example of an organization's policies regarding differential starting pay offers among offer receivers. Such differential treatment, and all the issues and questions it raises, applies to virtually any other term or condition as well.

Applicant Truthfulness

Throughout the recruitment and selection process, information about KSAOs and other factors (e.g., current salary) is being provided by the applicant. Initially, this information is gathered as part of the assessment process, whose purpose is to determine which applicants are most likely to provide a good fit with job requirements and rewards. For applicants who pass the hurdles and are to receive job offers, the information that has been gathered may very well be used to decide the specific terms and conditions to include in a job offer. Just how truthful or believable is this information? The content and cost of job offers depends on how the organization answers this question.

There is little solid evidence on the degree of applicant truthfulness. However, there are some anecdotal indications that lack of truthfulness by applicants may be a problem, especially for current salary, salary history, job title, and job duties and accomplishments.

Consider the case of starting pay. Quite naturally, the organization may wish to base its starting pay offer on knowledge of what the offer receiver's pay is currently. Will the person be truthful or deceitful in reporting current salary? Indications are that deceit may be common. People may embellish or enhance not only their reported salaries but also their KSAOs to provide an artificially high base or starting point for the organization as it prepares its job offer. A production analyst earning $55,000 did this and obtained a new job at $150,000, with a company car and a country club membership also included in the package.[38]

To combat such deceit by applicants, organizations are becoming increasingly prone to pursue verification of all applicant information, including salary, and may go to extremes to do so. At the executive level, for example, some organizations now require people to provide copies of their W-2 income forms that are used for reporting to the Internal Revenue Service. The organization should not act on finalist-provided information in the preparation of job offers unless it is willing to assume, or has verified, that the information is accurate.

Likely Reactions of Offer Receivers

Naturally, the terms and conditions to be presented in an offer should be based on some assessment of the receiver's likely reaction to it. Will the receiver jump at it, laugh at it, or respond somewhere in between?

One way to gauge likely reactions to the offer is to gather information about various preferences from the offer receiver during the recruitment/selection process. Such preliminary discussions and communications will help the organization construct an offer that is likely to be acceptable. At the extreme, the process may lead to almost simultaneous presentation and acceptance of the offer. Another way to assess likely reactions to offers from offer receivers is to conduct research on reward importance to employees and applicants (see Chapter 4).

Policies on Negotiations and Initial Offers

Prior to making job offers, the organization should decide whether it will negotiate on them. In essence, the organization must decide whether its first offer to a person will also be its final offer.

To help make this decision, it is useful to consider what components of the salary and benefits part of the offer are considered open to negotiation by organizations. An example of such data, based on a survey of HR professionals in n = 418 organizations of all sizes, is shown in Exhibit 12.5. It can be seen that salary is

EXHIBIT 12.5   **Negotiable Components of Salary and/or Benefits According to HR Professionals**

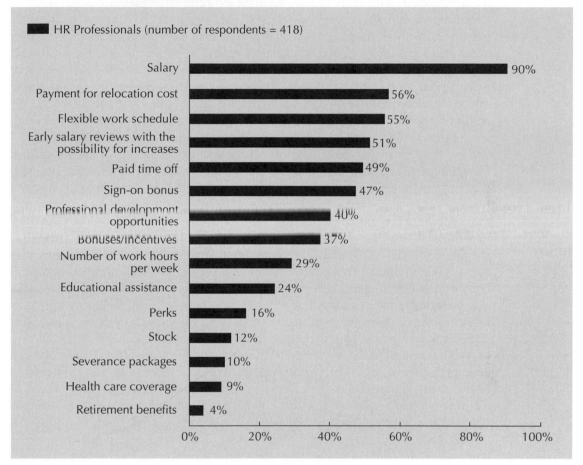

■ HR Professionals (number of respondents = 418)

Component	Percentage
Salary	90%
Payment for relocation cost	56%
Flexible work schedule	55%
Early salary reviews with the possibility for increases	51%
Paid time off	49%
Sign-on bonus	47%
Professional development opportunities	40%
Bonuses/incentives	37%
Number of work hours per week	29%
Educational assistance	24%
Perks	16%
Stock	12%
Severance packages	10%
Health care coverage	9%
Retirement benefits	4%

Source: E. Esen, *Job Negotiation Survey Findings: A Study by SHRM and CareerJournal.com* (Alexandria, VA: Society for Human Resource Management, 2004), p. 9. Used with permission.

almost uniformly considered negotiable. A majority also considers negotiable payment for relocation costs, flexible work schedules, and early salary reviews with the possibilities for increases. The openness to negotiation of other components then trails off from there.

Several considerations should also be kept in mind when formulating strategies and policies for making job offers. First, remember that job offers occur for both external and internal staffing. For external staffing, the job offer is intended to convert the offer receiver into a new hire. For internal staffing, the job offer is being made to induce the employee to accept a new job assignment or to attempt to retain the employee by making a counteroffer to an offer the employee has received from another organization. These separate types of job offers (new hires, new assignment, retention) will likely require separate job offer strategies and policies.

Second, consider fully the costs of not having a job offer be accepted by the offer receiver. Are there other equally qualified individuals available as backup offer receivers? How long can the organization afford to let a position remain vacant? How will current employees feel about job offers being rejected—will they, too, feel rejected, or will they feel that something they are unaware of is amiss in the organization? Will those next in line to receive an offer feel like second-class citizens or choices of desperation and last resort? Answers to such questions will often suggest it may be desirable to negotiate (up to a point) with the offer receiver.

Third, recognize that many people to whom you will be making offers may in turn be seeking and receiving counteroffers from their current employer. Anecdotal evidence suggests that counteroffers are being used much more frequently in attempts to retain increasingly less loyal employees. ("People are jumping jobs so frequently these days that U.S. business is beginning to look like a French bedroom farce. The new morality says that you have to be more loyal to your career than to your company, and the new math adds, if you are typical, you'll have about ten employers during your working life. So even if you're not hopping around now, you may soon be."[39]) Shortages of qualified replacements and the high cost of hiring replacements also contribute to the counteroffer wave. Hence, the organization should recognize that any offer it makes may lead to a bidding war of sorts with other organizations.

Fourth, a currently employed offer receiver normally incurs costs for leaving and will expect a "make whole" offer from the organization. Often these costs can amount to 20–30% of the offer receiver's current base pay. In addition to relocation or higher commuting costs, the offer receiver may forfeit employer contribution to a retirement plan, vacation time and holidays, various perks, and so forth. In addition, there may be waiting periods before the offer receiver would be eligible for various benefits, leading to opportunity costs of lost coverage and possibly paying the costs (e.g., health insurance premiums) out of pocket until coverage begins.

Finally, job seekers are often quite sophisticated in formulating and presenting their demands to the organization. They will know what it truly costs them to leave their current job and frame their demands accordingly. They will be aware of the particular KSAOs that they uniquely have to offer, make these acutely known to the organization, and demand a high price for them. The terms demanded (or more politely, "proposed") may focus not only on salary but on myriad other possibilities, including vacation time, a flexible work schedule to help balance work and family pressures, guaranteed expenditures on training and development, higher employer matching to a 401(k) retirement plan, and so on. In short, unless it is illegal, it is negotiable, and the organization must be prepared to handle demands from job seekers on virtually every term and condition of employment.

Presumably, each term or condition contained in an offer is a mini-offer itself. For each term or condition, therefore, the organization must decide the following:

- Whether it will negotiate on this term or condition
- If it negotiates, what are its lower and (especially) upper bounds

Once these questions have been answered, the organization may determine its posture regarding the presentation of the initial offer to the receiver. There are three basic strategies to choose from: lowball, competitive, and best shot.

Lowball.   The lowball strategy involves offering the lower bounds of terms and conditions to the receiver. Advantages to this strategy include getting acceptances from desperate or unknowledgeable receivers, minimizing initial employment costs, and leaving plenty of room to negotiate upward. Dangers to the lowball strategy include failing to get any acceptances, driving people away from and out of the finalist pool, developing an unsavory reputation among future potential applicants, and creating inequities and hard feelings that the reluctant accepter may carry into the organization, which may then influence postemployment attraction outcomes, such as retention.

Competitive.   With a competitive strategy, the organization prepares an offer that it feels is "on the market," neither too high nor too low. The competitive strategy should yield a sufficient number of job offer acceptances overall, though not all of the highest-quality (KSAO) applicants. This strategy leaves room for subsequent negotiation, should that be necessary. Competitive offers are unlikely to offend or excite the receiver, and they probably will not have negative consequences for postemployment outcomes.

Best Shot.   With the best-shot strategy, the organization "goes for broke" and gives a high offer, one right at the upper bounds of feasible terms and conditions. Accompanying this offer is usually a statement to the receiver that this is indeed the organization's "best shot," thus leaving little or no room for negotiation. These offers should enhance both preemployment attraction outcomes (e.g., filling vacancies quickly) and postemployment outcomes (e.g., job satisfaction). Best-shot offers obviously increase employment costs. They also leave little or no room for negotiation or for "sweetening" the offer. Finally, they may create feelings of inequity or jealousy among current employees.

None of these initial offer strategies is inherently superior. But the organization does need to make some choices as to which to generally use. It could also choose to tailor a strategy to fit the finalist pursued, as well as other circumstances. For example, the best-shot strategy may be chosen (1) for high-quality finalists, (2) when there are strong competitive hiring pressures from competitors, (3) when the organization feels great pressure to fill vacancies quickly, and (4) as part of an aggressive EEO/AA recruitment program.

Presentation of the Job Offer

Presentation of the offer may proceed along many different paths. The precise path chosen depends on the content of the offer, as well as factors considered in formulating the offer. To illustrate, two extreme approaches to presenting the job offer—the mechanical and the sales approaches—are detailed.

Mechanical Approach

The mechanical approach is a dry, sterile one that relies on simple one-way communication from the organization to the offer receiver. Little more than a standard, or "form," written offer is sent to the person. The organization then awaits a response. Little or no input about the content of the offer is received from the person, and after the offer has been made, there is no further communication with the person. If the person rejects the offer, another form letter acknowledging receipt of the rejection is sent. Meanwhile, the offer process is repeated anew, without modification, for a different receiver.

Sales Approach

The sales approach treats the job offer as a product that must be developed and sold to the customer (i.e., receiver). There is active interaction between the organization and the receiver as the terms and conditions are developed and incorporated into an offer package. There is informal agreement that unfolds between the receiver and the organization, and reduction of that agreement into an actual job offer is a mere formality. After the formal offer has been presented, the organization continues to have active communication with the receiver. In this way, the organization can be alert to possible glitches that occur in the offer process, and continue to sell the job to the receiver.

As the mechanical and sales approaches to job offer presentation make clear, the organization has considerable discretion in choosing how it delivers the offer. When it develops its job offer presentation process, it should be ever mindful of the strategic job offer process (Exhibit 12.1), and its emphasis on labor market conditions, organization and applicant need, and legal issues, all as factors affecting applicant attraction outcomes.

Job Offer Acceptance and Rejection

Ultimately, of course, job offers are accepted and rejected. How this happens and how it is handled are often as important as the outcomes themselves.

Provided next are some general suggestions and recommendations about acceptances and rejections. These are intended to serve as advice about additional practices and issues involved in the job offer process.

Acceptance

When the offer receiver accepts a job offer, the organization should do two important things. First, it should check the receiver's actual acceptance to ensure that it has been accepted as required in the offer. Thus, the acceptance should not come in the form of a counteroffer or with any other contingencies attached to it. Also, the acceptance should occur in the manner required (normally in writing), and it should arrive on or before the date specified.

Second, the organization must maintain contact with the new hire. Initially, this means acknowledging receipt of the acceptance. Additional communication may also be appropriate to further "cement the deal" and build commitment to the new job and organization. Examples of such continued communication include soon-to-be coworkers calling and offering congratulations to the new hire, sending work materials and reports to the new hire to help phase the person into the new job, and inviting the new hire to meetings and other activities prior to that person's starting date.

Rejection

The organization may reject the finalist, and the finalist may reject the organization.

By the Organization. Depending on the decision-making process used, the acceptance of an offer by one person means that the organization will now have to reject others. This should be done promptly and courteously. Moreover, the organization should keep records of those it rejects. This is necessary for legal purposes (e.g., applicant flow statistics) and for purposes of building and maintaining a pool of potential applicants that the organization may wish to contact about future vacancies.

The content of the rejection message (usually a letter) is up to the discretion of the organization. Most organizations opt for short and vague content that basically mentions a lack of fit between the applicant's KSAOs and the job's requirements. Providing more specific reasons for rejection should only be done with caution. The reasons provided should be candid and truthful, and they should match with the reasons recorded and maintained on other documents by the organization.

By the Offer Receiver. When the receiver rejects the job offer, the organization must first decide whether it wants to accept the rejection or extend a new offer to the person. If the organization's position on negotiations has already been determined, as ideally it should, then the organization simply needs to carry out its plan to either extend a new offer or move on to the next candidate.

When the rejection is accepted, it should be done so in a prompt and courteous manner. Moreover, records should also be kept of these rejections, for the same reasons they are kept when rejection by the organization occurs.

Reneging

Occasionally, and unfortunately, reneging occurs. Organizations rescind offers extended, and receivers rescind offers accepted. Solid evidence on reneging, and exactly why it occurs, is lacking. Sometimes reneging is unavoidable. The organization may experience a sudden downturn in business conditions, which causes planned-on jobs to evaporate. Or, the offer receiver may experience sudden changes in circumstances requiring reneging, such as a change in health status.

To illustrate how reneging is a tricky business and how tensions created by reneging can escalate, consider the case of Dianna Abdala. In 2005, Abdala graduated from Suffolk University's law school and passed the bar exam. She interviewed with a law firm started by William Korman, a former state prosecutor, and was offered a job. Abdala accepted the offer, but when she later reneged, sparks flew. Exhibit 12.6 provides the e-mail communications between Abdala and Korman. Korman later forwarded the e-mail exchange to several colleagues, and it quickly spread exponentially.[40]

While some reneging by the organization may be necessary, we believe that the organization can and should take steps to lessen its occurrence. If these steps are insufficient, we believe there are other actions the organization should take to handle reneging. Examples of these actions are shown in Exhibit 12.7. They represent attempts to be fair to the offer receiver while still representing the interests of the organization.

For the offer receiver, high standards of fairness are also required. The receiver should not be frivolous, just going through the application process "for the experience." Nor should the receiver accept an offer as a way of extracting a counteroffer out of his or her current employer. Indeed, organizations should be aware of the fact that some of the people to whom they make job offers will receive such counteroffers, and this should be taken into account during the time the offer is initially formulated and presented. Finally, the receiver should do a careful assessment of probable fit for the person/job match prior to accepting an offer.

NEW EMPLOYEE ORIENTATION AND SOCIALIZATION

Establishment of the employment relationship through final match activities does not end a concern with the person/job match. Rather, that relationship must now be nurtured and maintained over time to ensure that the intended match becomes and remains effective. The new hires become newcomers, and their initial entry into the job and organization should be guided by orientation and socialization activities. Orientation and socialization may be concurrent, overlapping activities that occur for the newcomer. Orientation is typically more immediate, while socialization is more long term.

EXHIBIT 12.6   The Messy Process of Reneging

```
-----Original Message-----
From: Dianna Abdala
Sent: Friday, February 03, 2006 9:23 p.m.
To: William A. Korman
Subject: Thank you

Dear Attorney Korman,

At this time, I am writing to inform you that I will not be accepting
your offer. After careful consideration, I have come to the conclusion
that the pay you are offering would neither fulfill me nor support the
lifestyle I am living in light of the work I would be doing for you. I
have decided instead to work for myself, and reap 100% of the benefits
that I sew.

Thank you for the interviews.

Dianna L. Abdala, Esq.
--------End Message-------
```

```
-----Original Message-----
From: William A. Korman
To: Dianna Abdala
Sent: Monday, February 06, 2006 12:15 p.m.
Subject: RE: Thank you

Dianna --

Given that you had two interviews, were offered and accepted the job
(indeed, you had a definite start date), I am surprised that you chose
an e-mail and a 9:30 p.m. voicemail message to convey this information
to me. It smacks of immaturity and is quite unprofessional. Indeed, I
did rely upon your acceptance by ordering stationary and business cards
with your name, reformatting a computer and setting up both internal
and external e-mails for you here at the office. While I do not quarrel
with your reasoning, I am extremely disappointed in the way this played
out. I sincerely wish you the best of luck in your future endeavors.

Will Korman
--------End Message-------
```

```
-----Original Message-----
From: Dianna Abdala
Sent: Monday, February 06, 2006 4:01 p.m.
To: William A. Korman
Subject: Re: Thank you

A real lawyer would have put the contract into writing and not
exercised any such reliance until he did so.

Again, thank you.
--------End Message-------
```

(continued)

EXHIBIT 12.6   Continued

```
-----Original Message-----
From: William A. Korman
To: Dianna Abdala
Sent: Monday, February 06, 2006 4:18 p.m.
Subject: RE: Thank you

Thank you for the refresher course on contracts. This is not a bar exam
question. You need to realize that this is a very small legal
community, especially the criminal defense bar. Do you really want to
start pissing off more experienced lawyers at this early stage of your
career?
--------End Message-------

-----Original Message-----
From: Dianna Abdala
To: William A. Korman
Sent: Monday, February 06, 2006 4:28 p.m.
Subject: Re: Thank you

bla bla bla
--------End Message-------
```

EXHIBIT 12.7   Organization Actions to Deal with Reneging

A. To Lessen the Occurrence of Reneging

Extend offers only for positions known to exist and be vacant.
Require top management approval of all reneging.
Conduct thorough assessments of finalists prior to job offer.
Honor outstanding offers but make no new ones.
Discourage offer receiver from accepting offer.
Defer starting date and provide partial pay in interim.
Keep offer open but renegotiate or reduce salary and other economic items.
Stagger new hire starting dates to smooth out additions to payroll.

B. To Handle Reneging

Communicate honestly and quickly with offer receiver.
Provide consolation or apology package (e.g., hiring bonus, three months salary).
Pay for any disruption costs (e.g., relocation).
Hire as consultant (independent contractor), convert to employee later.
Guarantee priority over other applicants when future vacancies occur.

It should be remembered that the newcomer is likely entering a situation of uncertainties and unknowns. Research indicates that how the organization reduces these will have an important impact on how well the newcomer will adapt to the job and remain with the organization. Several factors have been identified as influencing the likely effectiveness of orientation and socialization:[41]

- Providing realistic recruitment information about job requirements and rewards (orientation begins before the job does)
- Clarifying for the newcomer job requirements and knowledge and skills to be acquired
- Socializing for the newcomer to learn sources of influence in the organization and to develop friendships
- Integrating the newcomer into the work unit and team
- Providing more information about job rewards to newcomers
- Conducting active mentoring for the newcomer

Elaboration on these points, as well as many examples, are provided below.

Orientation

Orientation requires considerable advanced planning in terms of topics to cover, development of materials for the newcomer, and scheduling of the myriad activities that contribute to an effective orientation program. Often, the HR department is responsible for the design and conduct of the orientation, and it will seek close coordination of actual orientation activities and schedules with the newcomer's supervisor.

Exhibit 12.8 contains a far-ranging set of suggested topics of information for an orientation program, delivery of which is accomplished via written materials, online services, training programs, meetings with various people, and visual inspection. Note that these activities are spaced out rather than concentrated in just the first day of work for the newcomer. An effective orientation program will foster an understanding of the organization's culture and values, help the new employee understand his or her role and how he or she fits into the total organization, and help the new employee achieve objectives and shorten the learning curve.

Socialization

Socialization of the newcomer is a natural extension of orientation activities. Like orientation, the goal of socialization is to achieve effective person/job and person/organization matches. Whereas orientation focuses on the initial and immediate aspects of newcomer adaptation, socialization emphasizes helping the newcomer fit into the job and organization over time. The emphasis is on the long haul, seeking to gain newcomers' adaptation in ways that will make them want to be successful, long-term contributors to the organization.[42] Research has shown that when

EXHIBIT 12.8   New Employee Orientation Guidelines

Before the Employee Arrives

- Notify everyone in your unit that a new person is starting and what the person's job will be; ask the other staff members to welcome the new employee and encourage their support
- Prepare interesting tasks for the employee's first day
- Provide new employee with a copy of the job description, job performance standards, organization chart, and your department's organization chart
- Enroll the employee in any necessary training programs
- Make sure the employee's work location is available, clean, and organized
- Make sure a copy of the appropriate personnel policy manual or contract is available for the employee
- Have a benefits information package available
- If possible, identify a staff member to act as a buddy for the first week
- Put together a list of key people the employee should meet and interview to get a broader understanding of their roles
- Arrange for a building pass, parking pass, and IDs if necessary
- Draft a training plan for the new employee's first few months

First Day on the Job

- Give a warm welcome and discuss the plan for the first day
- Tour the employee's assigned work space
- Explain where rest rooms, vending machines, and break areas are located
- Provide required keys
- Arrange to have lunch with the new employee
- Tour the building and immediate area and introduce the new employee to other staff members
- Introduce the new employee to the person you've identified as a mentor (if appropriate)
- Review job description
- Review the department's (or office's) organizational chart
- Review your office's policies and procedures involving working hours, telephone, e-mail and Internet use, office organization, office resources, and ethics

During the First Week

- Review employee work area to ensure needed equipment is in place
- Set up a brief meeting with the employee and the assigned buddy to review the first week's activities (if appropriate)
- Schedule meeting with human resources office to complete required paperwork, review personnel policies and procedures, learn about benefits, obtain credentials, and explain other policies and procedures

<hr>

EXHIBIT 12.8   Continued

Within the First Month of Employment

- Meet with employee to review:
  - ❏ Job description
  - ❏ Performance standards
  - ❏ Work rules
  - ❏ Organization structure
  - ❏ Health and safety
  - ❏ Benefits overview

Within Six Months of Starting

- Revisit performance standards and work rules
- Schedule performance appraisal meeting

SOURCE: Based on "Guide to Managing Human Resources: New Employee Orientation," Human Resources, University of California, Berkeley (*http://hrweb.berkeley.edu/guide/orient.htm*).

socialization programs are effective, they facilitate new employee adjustment by increasing employees' role clarity (clarify job duties and performance expectations), by enhancing their self-efficacy (their belief that they can do the job), and by fostering their social acceptance (making employees believe that they are valued members of the team).[43]

To increase new employee role clarity, self-efficacy, and social acceptance, there are two key issues to address in developing and conducting an effective socialization process. First, what are the major elements or contents of socialization that should occur? Second, how can the organization best deliver those elements to the newcomer?

Content

While the content of the socialization process should obviously be somewhat job- and organization-specific, there are several components that are likely candidates for inclusion. From the newcomer's perspective these are the following:[44]

1. *People*—meeting and learning about coworkers, key contacts, informal groups and gatherings, and networks; becoming accepted and respected by these people as "one of the gang"
2. *Performance proficiency*—becoming very familiar with job requirements; mastering tasks; having impacts on performance results; and acquiring necessary KSAOs for proficiency in all aspects of the job
3. *Organization goals and values*—learning of the organization's goals; accepting these goals and incorporating them into my "line of sight" for performance

proficiency; learning about values and norms of desirable behavior (e.g., working late and on weekends; making suggestions for improvements)

4. *Politics*—learning about how things "really work"; becoming familiar with key players and their quirks; taking acceptable shortcuts; schmoozing and networking

5. *Language*—learning special terms, buzzwords, and acronyms; knowing what not to say; learning the jargon of people in my trade or profession

6. *History*—learning about the origins and growth of the organization; becoming familiar with customs, rituals, and special events; understanding the origins of my work unit and the backgrounds of people in it

Many of the above topics overlap with the possible content of an orientation program, suggesting that orientation and socialization programs be developed in tandem so that they are synchronized and seamless as the newcomer passes from orientation into socialization.

Delivery

Delivery of socialization to the newcomer should be the responsibility of several people. First, it should be the responsibility of the newcomer's supervisor to personally socialize the newcomer, particularly in terms of performance proficiency and organization goals and values. The supervisor is intimately familiar with and the "enforcer" of these key elements of socialization. It is important that the newcomer and supervisor communicate directly, honestly, and formally about these elements.

Peers in the newcomer's work unit or team are promising candidates for assisting in socialization. They can be most helpful in terms of politics, language, and history, drawing on and sharing their own accumulated experiences with the newcomer. They can also make their approachability and availability known to the newcomer when he or she wants to ask questions or raise issues in an informal manner.

To provide a more formal information and support system to the newcomer, but one outside of a chain of command, a mentor or sponsor may be assigned to (or chosen by) the newcomer. The mentor functions as an identifiable point of contact for the newcomer, as well as someone who actively interacts with the newcomer to provide the inside knowledge, savvy, and personal contacts that will help the newcomer settle into the current job and prepare for future job assignments. Mentors can also play a vital role in helping shatter the glass ceiling of the organization.

Given the advances in computer technology and the increasing geographic dispersion of an organization's employees, organizations might be tempted to conduct their orientation programs online. Though some of this may be necessary, depending on the job, research suggests that socialization programs are less effective when conducted online—both in the eyes of the employees and in the eyes of their supervisors. As would be expected, when compared with in-person programs, online socialization programs do a particularly poor job of socializing employees to the personal aspects of the job and organization, such as organizational goals and values, politics, and how to work well with others.[45]

Finally, the HR department can be very useful to the socialization process. Its representatives can help establish formal, organization-wide socialization activities such as mentoring programs, special events, and informational presentations. Also, representatives may undertake development of training programs on socialization topics for supervisors and mentors. Representatives might also work closely, but informally, with supervisors and coach them in how to become successful socializers of their own newcomers.

Examples of Programs

The Sonesta Hotels chain developed a formal program to help newcomers adapt to their jobs during their first 100 days. At the end of 30 days the hotel site HR director meets with the newcomer to see if his or her expectations are being met and if he or she has the resources needed to do the job. At 60 days the newcomers participate in a program called the Booster, which focuses on developing customer service and communication skills. Then at the end of 90 days the newcomer meets with the supervisor to do performance planning for the rest of the year. In addition, managers are encouraged to take the newcomer and the rest of the department out to lunch during the first month.[46]

The president and chief executive officer of Southcoast Hospitals Group in Fall River, Massachusetts, decided to develop an "owner's manual" about himself that was to be given to the new VP of performance improvement that he was recruiting for. The one-page manual gave tips to the new VP on how to work for the president. It was developed on the basis of self-assessment and feedback from colleagues and direct reports. These people began using the completed manual immediately in their interactions with the president. The manual was given to the finalist for the VP job two days before the job offer was actually extended. The finalist took the job and commented on how helpful the manual was in saving him time figuring out what the president thinks of things.[47]

The National City Corporation in Cleveland, a bank and financial services organization, experienced high turnover among newcomers within the first 90 days on the job. These early-exiting employees were referred to as "quick quits" in the HR department. To combat this problem, a program was designed for entry-level, nonexempt newcomers, called Early Success. Newcomers attend a series of custom-made training programs to provide them the necessary knowledge and skills. Examples of the programs are Plus (overview of the organization's objectives, employee benefits, and brand); People, Policies, and Practices (augment the employee handbook and reinforce the organization as an employer of choice); and Top-Notch Customer Care (focus on customer service delivery and how to be a team player). Another component of the program is a buddy system that matches a newcomer with a peer; buddies then attend workshops to learn coaching skills. Finally, the hiring managers of the newcomers also attend workshops on such topics as how to select a buddy for the newcomer, how to communicate and create a supportive work environment, and how to help the newcomer assume more job responsibilities and achieve career goals. The program has reduced turnover 50% and improved attendance 25%, saving over $1.6 million per year.[48]

LEGAL ISSUES

The employment contract establishes the actual employment relationship and the terms and conditions that will govern it. In the process of establishing it, there are certain obligations and responsibilities that the organization must reckon with. These pertain to (1) employing only those people who meet the employment requirements under the IRCA, (2) avoiding the negligent hiring of individuals, and (3) maintaining the organization's posture toward employment-at-will. Each of these is discussed in turn.

Authorization to Work

Under the IRCA (see Chapter 2), the organization is prohibited from hiring or continuing to employ an alien who is not authorized to work in the United States. Moreover, the organization must verify such authorization for any person hired (after November 6, 1986, only), and it must not discriminate against individuals on the basis of national origin or citizenship status. There are specific federal regulations detailing the requirements and methods of compliance.

Compliance with these regulations means the following for the organization. First, the organization must verify the employability status of each new employee (not just aliens). This is accomplished through the completion of the I-9 verification form, which in turn requires documents that verify the new employee's identity and eligibility. Both identity and eligibility must be verified. Some documents (e.g., U.S. passport) verify both identity and eligibility; other documents verify only identity (e.g., state-issued driver's license or ID card) or employment eligibility (e.g., original Social Security card or birth certificate).

Second, verification must occur within three days of being hired. Note, however, that verification need not occur at the time of the extension of the job offer. Offers extended without verification should contain a contingency clause making the offer contingent on satisfactory employment verification.

Third, the organization must maintain I-9 records in its own files for three years after the date of hire and one year after the employee's termination date. Records may be kept in paper or electronic form.

Finally, to avoid possible national origin or citizenship discrimination, it is best not to ask for proof of employment eligibility prior to making the offer. The reason for this is that many of the identity and eligibility documents contain personal information that pertains to national origin and citizenship status, and such personal information might be used in a discriminatory manner. As a further matter of caution, the organization should not refuse to make a job offer to a person based on that person's foreign accent or appearance.

Negligent Hiring

Negligent hiring is a workplace torts issue (see Chapter 2) involving claims by an injured plaintiff (e.g., customer or employee) that the plaintiff was harmed by an unfit employee who was negligently hired by the organization. The employer is claimed to have violated its common-law duty—to protect its employees and customers from injury—by hiring an employee it knew (or should have known) posed a threat of risk to them.[49] To have a successful suit, there are several things that the plaintiff must prove:

1. The person was, in fact, an employee of the organization.
2. The employee was, in fact, incompetent, as opposed to being a competent employee who acted in a negligent manner.
3. The employer knew, or should have known, of the employee's incompetence.
4. The employer had a legal duty to select competent employees.
5. The injury or harm was a foreseeable consequence of hiring the unfit employee.
6. The hiring of the unfit employee was the proximate cause of the injury or harm.

Examples of negligent hiring cases abound, particularly extreme ones involving violence, bodily injury, physical damage, and death. As a specific example, negligent hiring of nursing aides in nursing homes appears to be an acute problem, with nursing home patients suffering crimes ranging from theft to physical abuse to death. Some states have even passed legislation requiring background investigations of applicants for nursing home jobs. Illinois mandates background checks for nursing assistants, and the law specifies 74 employment-disqualifying crimes, from theft to first-degree murder. Under this law, of the 56,008 checks made, 2,670 applicants were found to have a disqualifying background for the job, though 42% of the applicants were allowed to take the job anyway.[50]

What should the organization do to minimize negligent hiring occurrences? There are several straightforward recommendations that can be made.[51] First, staffing any job should be preceded by a thorough analysis that identifies all the KSAOs required by the job. Failure to identify or otherwise consider KSAOs prior to the final match is not likely to be much of a defense in a negligent hiring lawsuit.

Second, particular attention should be paid to the *O* part of KSAOs, such as licensure requirements, criminal records, references, unexplained gaps in employment history, and alcohol and illegal drug usage. Of course, these should be derived separately for each job rather than applied identically to all jobs.

Third, methods for assessing these KSAOs that are valid and legal must be used. This is difficult to do in practice because of lack of knowledge about the validity of some predictors, or their relatively low levels of validity. Also, difficulties arise because of legal constraints on the acquisition and use of preemployment inquiries, as explained in Chapter 8.

Fourth, require all applicants to sign disclaimer statements allowing the employer to check references and otherwise conduct background investigations. In addition, have the applicant sign a statement indicating that all provided information is true and that the applicant has not withheld requested information.

Fifth, apply utility analysis to determine whether it is worthwhile to engage in the preceding recommendations to try to avoid the (usually slight) chance of a negligent hiring lawsuit. Such an analysis will undoubtedly indicate great variability among jobs in terms of how many resources the organization wishes to invest in negligent hiring prevention.

Finally, when in doubt about a finalist and whether to extend a job offer, do not extend it until those doubts have been resolved. Acquire more information from the finalist, verify more thoroughly existing information, and seek the opinions of others on whether to proceed with the job offer.

Employment-at-Will

As discussed in this chapter and in Chapter 2, employment-at-will involves the right of either the employer or the employee to unilaterally terminate the employment relationship at any time, for any legal reason. In general, the employment relationship is at-will, and usually the employer wishes it to remain that way. Hence, during the final match (and even before) the employer must take certain steps to ensure that its job offers in fact clearly establish the at-will relationship. These steps are merely a compilation of points already made regarding employment contracts and employment-at-will.

The first thing to be done is to ensure that job offers are for an indeterminate time period, meaning that they have no fixed term or specific ending date. Second, include in the job offer a specific disclaimer stating that the employment relationship will be strictly at-will. Third, review all written documents (e.g., employee handbook, application blank) to ensure that they do not contain any language that implies anything but a strictly at-will relationship. Finally, take steps to ensure that organizational members do not make any oral statements or promises that would serve to create something other than a strictly at-will relationship.[52]

SUMMARY

During the final match, the offer receiver and the organization move toward each other through the job offer/acceptance process. They seek to enter into the employment relationship and become legally bound to each other through an employment contract.

Knowledge of employment contract principles is central to understanding the final match. The most important principle pertains to the requirements for a legally enforceable employment contract (offer, acceptance, and consideration). Other important principles focus on the identity of parties to the contract, the form of the contract (written or oral), disclaimers by the employer, contingencies, reneging by the organization or offer receiver, other sources that may also specify terms and conditions of employment (e.g., employee handbooks), and unfulfilled promises.

Job offers are designed to induce the offer receiver to join the organization. Offers should be viewed and used strategically by the organization. In that strategy, labor market conditions, organization and applicant needs, and legal issues all converge to shape the job offer and EVP.

Job offers may contain virtually any legal terms and conditions of employment. Generally, the offer addresses terms pertaining to starting date, duration of contract, compensation, hours, special hiring inducements (if any), other terms (such as contingencies), and acceptance of the offer.

The process of making job offers can be complicated, involving a need to think through multiple issues prior to making formal offers. Offers should take into account the content of competitors' offers, potential problems with applicant truthfulness, likely reactions of the offer receiver, and the organization's policies on negotiating offers. Presentation of the offer can range from a mechanical process all the way to a major sales job. Ultimately, offers are accepted and rejected, and all offer receivers should receive prompt and courteous attention during these events. Steps should be taken to minimize reneging by either the organization or the offer receiver.

Acceptance of the offer marks the beginning of the employment relationship. To help ensure that the initial person/job match starts out and continues to be effective, the organization should undertake both orientation and socialization activities for newcomers.

From a legal perspective, the organization must be sure that the offer receiver is employable according to provisions of the IRCA. Both identity and eligibility for employment must be verified. The potential negligent hiring of individuals who, once on the job, cause harm to others (employees or customers) is also of legal concern. Those so injured may bring suit against the organization. There are certain steps the organization can take in an attempt to minimize the occurrence of negligent hiring lawsuits. There are limits on these steps, however, such as the legal constraints on the gathering of background information about applicants. Finally, the organization should have its posture, policies, and practices regarding employment-at-will firmly developed and aligned. There are numerous steps that can be taken to help achieve this.

DISCUSSION QUESTIONS

1. If you were the HR staffing manager for an organization, what guidelines might you recommend regarding oral and written communication with job applicants by members of the organization?

2. If the same job offer content is to be given to all offer receivers for a job, is there any need to use the strategic approach to job offers? Explain.

3. What are the advantages and disadvantages to the sales approach in the presentation of the job offer?

4. What are examples of orientation experiences you have had as a new hire that have been particularly effective (or ineffective) in helping to make the person/job match happen?

5. What are the steps an employer should take to develop and implement its policy regarding employment-at-will?

ETHICAL ISSUES

1. A large financial services organization is thinking of adopting a new staffing strategy for entry into its management training program. The program will provide the trainees all the knowledge and skills they need for their initial job assignment after training. The organization has therefore decided to do college recruiting at the end of the recruiting season. It will hire those who have not been fortunate enough to receive any job offers, pay them a salary 10% below market, and provide no other inducements such as a hiring bonus or relocation assistance. The organization figures this strategy and EVP will yield a high percentage of offers accepted, low cost per hire, and considerable labor cost savings due to below market salaries. Evaluate this strategy from an ethical perspective.

2. An organization has a staffing strategy in which it overhires by 10% the number of employees it will actually need in any job category in order to ensure it meets its hiring needs. It reasons that some of the new hires will renege on the accepted offer and that the organization can renege on some of its offers if need be, to end up with the right number of new hires. Evaluate this strategy from an ethical perspective.

APPLICATIONS

Making a Job Offer

Clean Car Care (3Cs) is located within a western city of 175,000 people. The company owns and operates four full-service car washes in the city. The owner of 3Cs, Arlan Autospritz, has strategically cornered the car wash market, with his only competition being two coin-operated car washes on the outskirts of the city. The unemployment rate in the city and surrounding area is 3.8%, and it is expected to go somewhat lower.

Arlan has staffed 3Cs by hiring locally and paying wage premiums (above market wages) to induce people to accept job offers and to remain with 3Cs. Hiring occurs at the entry level only, for the job of washer. If they remain with 3Cs, washers have the opportunity to progress upward through the ranks, going from washer to shift lead person to assistant manager to manager of one of the four car wash facilities. Until recently, this staffing system worked well for Arlan. He was able to hire high-quality people, and a combination of continued wage premiums and promotion opportunities meant he had relatively little turnover (under 30% annually). Every manager at 3Cs, past or present, had come up through the ranks. But that is now changing with the sustained low unemployment and new hires, who just naturally seem more turnover prone. The internal promotion pipeline is thus drying up, since few new hires are staying with 3Cs long enough to begin climbing the ladder.

Arlan has a vacancy for the job of manager at the north-side facility. Unfortunately, he does not think that any of his assistant managers are qualified for the job, and he reluctantly concluded that he has to fill the job externally.

A vigorous three-county recruitment campaign netted Arlan a total of five applicants. Initial assessments resulted in four of those being candidates, and two candidates became finalists. Jane Roberts is the number one finalist, and the one to whom Arlan has decided to extend the offer. Jane is excited about the job and told Arlan she will accept an offer if the terms are right. Arlan is quite certain Jane will get a counteroffer from her company. Jane has excellent supervisory experience in fast-food stores and a light manufacturing plant. She is willing to relocate, a move of about 45 miles. She will not be able to start for 45 days, due to preparing for the move and the need to give adequate notice to her present employer. As a single parent, Jane wants to avoid work on either Saturday or Sunday each week. The number two finalist is Betts Cook. Though she lacks the supervisory experience that Jane has, Arlan views her as superior to Jane in customer service skills. Jane has told Arlan she needs to know quickly if she is going to get the offer, since she is in line for a promotion at her current company and she wants to begin at 3Cs before being offered and accepting the promotion.

Arlan is mulling over what kind of an offer to make to Jane. His three managers make between $28,000 and $35,000, with annual raises based on a merit review conducted by Arlan. The managers receive one week's vacation the first year, two weeks of vacation for the next four years, and three weeks of vacation after that. They also receive health insurance (with a 20% employee co-pay on the premium). The managers work five days each week, with work on both Saturday and Sunday frequently occurring during peak times. Jane currently makes $31,500, receives health insurance with no employee co-pay, and has one week's vacation (she is due to receive two weeks shortly, after completing her second year with the company).

She works Monday through Friday, with occasional work on the weekends. Betts earns $34,500, receives health insurance fully paid by her employer, and has one week of vacation (she is eligible for two weeks in another year). Weekend work, if not constant, is acceptable to her.

Arlan is seeking input from you on how to proceed. Specifically, he wants you to:

1. Recommend whether Jane should receive a best-shot, competitive, or lowball offer, and why.
2. Recommend other inducements beyond salary, health insurance, vacation, and hours schedule that might be addressed in the job offer, and why.
3. Draft a proposed job offer letter to Jane, incorporating your recommendations in points (1) and (2) above, as well as other desired features that should be part of a job offer letter.

Evaluating a Hiring and Variable Pay Plan

Effective Management Solutions (EMS) is a small, rapidly growing management consulting company. EMS has divided its practice into four areas: management systems, business process improvement, human resources, and quality improvement. Strategically, EMS has embarked on an aggressive revenue growth plan, seeking a 25% revenue increase in each of the next five years for each of the four practice areas. A key component of its plan involves staffing growth, since most of EMS's current entry-level consultants (associates) are at peak client loads and cannot take on additional clients; the associates are also at peak hours load, working an average of 2,500 billable hours per year.

Staffing strategy and planning have resulted in the following information and projections. Each practice area currently has 25 associates, the entry-level position and title. Each year, on average, each practice area has five associates promoted to senior associate within the area (there are no promotions or transfers across areas, due to differing KSAO requirements), and five associates leave EMS, mostly to go to other consulting firms. Replacement staffing thus averages 10 new associates in each practice area, for a total of 40 per year. To meet the revenue growth goals, each practice area will need to hire 15 new associates each year, or a total of 60. A total of 100 associate new hires will thus be needed each year (40 for replacement and 60 for growth).

Currently, EMS provides each job offer receiver a generous benefits package plus what it deems to be a "competitive" salary that is nonnegotiable. About 50% of such offers are accepted. Most of those who reject the offer are the highest-quality applicants; they take jobs in larger, more established consulting firms that provide somewhat below-market salaries but high upside monetary potential through various short-term variable-pay programs, plus rapid promotions.

Faced with these realities and projections, EMS recognizes that its current job offer practices need to be revamped. Accordingly, it has asked Manuel Rodriguez, who functions as a one-person HR "department" for EMS, to develop a job offer proposal for the EMS partners to consider at their next meeting. The partners tell Rodriguez they want a plan that will increase the job offer acceptance rate, slow down the outflow of associates to other firms, and not create dissatisfaction problems among the currently employed associates.

In response, Rodriguez developed the proposed hiring and variable pay (HVP) program. It has as its cornerstone varying monetary risk/reward packages through a combination of base and short-term variable (bonus) pay plans. The specifics of the HVP program are as follows:

- The offer receiver must choose one of three plans to be under, prior to receiving a formal job offer. The plans are the high-risk, standard, and low-risk.
- The high-risk plan provides a starting salary from 10% to 30% below the market average and participation in the annual bonus plan with a bonus range from 0 to 60% of current salary.
- The standard plan provides a starting salary of ±10% of the market average and participation in the annual bonus plan with a bonus range from 0 to 20% of current salary.
- The low-risk plan provides a starting salary that is 5% above the market average and no participation in the annual bonus plan.
- The average market rate will be determined by salary survey data obtained by HR.
- The individual bonus amount will be determined by individual performance on three indicators: number of billable hours, number of new clients generated, and client-satisfaction survey results.
- The hiring manager will negotiate starting salary for those in the high-risk and standard plans, based on likely person/job and person/organization fit and on need to fill the position.
- The hiring manager may also offer a "hot skills" premium of up to 10% of initial starting salary under all three plans—the premium will lapse after two years.
- Switching between the three plans is permitted only once every two years.
- Current associates may remain in their current plan or opt into one of the new plans at their current salary.

Evaluate the HVP program as proposed, answering the following questions:

1. If you were an applicant, would the HVP program be attractive to you? Why or why not? If you were going to be an offer receiver, which of the three plans would you choose and why?
2. Will the HVP program likely increase the job offer acceptance rate? Why or why not?
3. Will the HVP program likely reduce turnover? Why or why not?
4. How will current associates react to the HVP program, and why?

5. What issues and problems will the HVP plan create for HR? For the hiring manager?
6. What changes would you make in the HVP program, and why?

ENDNOTES

1. M. W. Bennett, D. J. Polden, and H. J. Rubin, *Employment Relationships: Law and Practice* (New York: Aspen, 2004), pp. 3-3 to 3-4; A. G. Feliu, *Primer on Individual Employee Rights,* second ed. (Washington, DC: Bureau of National Affairs, 1996), pp. 7–29; G. P. Panaro, *Employment Law Manual* (Boston, MA: Warren, Gorham and Lamont, 1993), pp. 4-2 to 4-4.

2. Panaro, *Employment Law Manual,* pp. 4-61 to 4-63.

3. Bennett, Polden, and Rubin, *Employment Relationships: Law and Practice,* pp. 3-22 to 3-23; Panaro, *Employment Law Manual,* pp. 4-5 to 4-60.

4. Panaro, *Employment Law Manual,* pp. 4-18 to 4-19.

5. Feliu, *Primer on Individual Employee Rights,* pp. 23–25; Panaro, *Employment Law Manual,* pp. 4-30 to 4-31.

6. Feliu, *Primer on Individual Employee Rights,* pp. 26–28.

7. Feliu, *Primer on Individual Employee Rights,* pp. 48–51.

8. Bennett, Polden, and Rubin, *Employment Relationships: Law and Practice,* pp. 3-30 to 3-32; Feliu, *Primer on Individual Employee Rights,* pp. 22–25.

9. Feliu, *Primer on Individual Employee Rights,* p. 24.

10. Feliu, *Primer on Individual Employee Rights,* p. 26.

11. Panaro, *Employment Law Manual,* pp. 4-66 to 4-136.

12. Bennett, Polden, and Rubin, *Employment Relationships: Law and Practice,* pp. 3-24 to 3-34; Feliu, *Primer on Individual Employee Rights,* pp. 39–50.

13. J. A. Segal, "An Offer They Couldn't Refuse," *HR Magazine,* Apr. 2001, pp. 131–144.

14. A. W. Matthews, "Wanted: 400,000 Long Distance Truck Drivers," *Wall Street Journal,* Sept. 11, 1997, p. B1; R. Romell, "Truckers in the Driver's Seat," *Milwaukee Journal Sentinel,* Nov. 30, 1997, p. 1D.

15. Bennett, Polden, and Rubin, *Employment Relationships: Law and Practice,* pp. 2-11 to 2-49.

16. D. S. Fortney and B. Nuterangelo, "Written Employment Contracts: When?, How?, Why?" *Legal Report,* Society for Human Resource Management, Spring 1998, pp. 5–8.

17. D. M. Cable and T. A. Judge, "Pay Preferences and Job Search Decisions: A Person–Organization Fit Perspective," *Personnel Psychology,* 1994, 47, pp. 317–348.

18. P. D. Gardner, *Recruiting Trends 2000–2001* (East Lansing, MI: Michigan State University Student Services, 2000).

19. S. Nasar, "A Top MBA Is a Hot Ticket as Pay Climbs," *New York Times,* Aug. 2, 1998, p. B1; E. Price, "Paying for Bilingual Skills: Job Requirement or Added Value?" *International Personnel Management Association News,* Feb. 1997, p. 10.

20. *http://online.onetcenter.org/.*

21. Y. J. Dreazen, "When #$%+! Recruits Earn More," *Wall Street Journal,* July 25, 2000, p. B1; K. J. Dunham, "Back to Reality," *Wall Street Journal,* Apr. 12, 2001, p. R5; M. Gasser, N. Flint, and R. Tan, "Reward Expectations: The Influence of Race, Gender, and Type of Job," *Journal of Business and Psychology,* 2000, 15, pp. 321–329; E. R. Silverman, "Great Expectations," *Wall Street Journal,* July 25, 2000.

22. Society for Human Resource Management, *Strategic Compensation Survey* (Alexandria, VA: author, 2000), pp. 35–47.

23. E. E. Lawler III, "Pay Practices in Fortune 1000 Companies," *WorldatWork Journal,* 2003, Fourth Quarter, pp. 45–53.

24. M. A. Jacobs, "The Legal Option," *Wall Street Journal,* Apr. 12, 2001, p. R9; Society for Human Resource Management, *Strategic Compensation Survey,* pp. 48–57.

25. B. Jones, M. Staubus, and D. N. Janich, "If Not Stock Options, Then What?" *Workspan,* Fall 2003, pp. 26–32; R. Simon, "With Options on the Outs, Alternatives Get a Look," *Wall Street Journal,* Apr. 28, 2004, p. D2.

26. "Employers Say Increased Competition Not Likely to Translate Into Signing Bonuses for New College Graduates," *IPMA-HR Bulletin,* Dec. 1, 2006, p. 1.

27. F. Hansen, "Smarter About Hiring Bonuses," *Workforce Management,* Mar. 27, 2006, pp. 39–42.

28. Hansen, "Smarter About Hiring Bonuses"; J. R. Bratkovich and J. Ragusa, "The Perils of the Signing Bonus," *Employment Management Today,* Spring 1998, pp. 22–25.

29. L. Morsch, "Return of the Signing Bonus?" Sept. 24, 2007, *www.careerbuilder.com.*

30. L. G. Klaff, "Tough Sell," *Workforce Management,* Nov. 2003, pp. 47–50; J. S. Lublin, "The Going Rate," *Wall Street Journal,* Jan. 11, 2000, p. B14.

31. J. S. Lublin, "As More Men Become 'Trailing Spouses,' Firms Help Them Cope," *Wall Street Journal,* Apr. 13, 1993, p. A1.

32. L. Rivenbark, "Short Term Pay Hikes Can Last Indefinitely," *HR News,* July 2000, p. 16.

33. J. S. Lublin, "You Should Negotiate a Severance Package—Even Before the Job Starts," *Wall Street Journal,* May 1, 2001, p. B1.

34. C. Patton, "Parting Ways," *Human Resource Executive,* May 20, 2002, pp. 50–51.

35. T. D. Egler, "A Manager's Guide to Employment Contracts," *HR Magazine,* May 1996, pp. 28–33; J. J. Meyers, D. V. Radack, and P. M. Yenerall, "Making the Most of Employment Contracts," *HR Magazine,* Aug. 1998, pp. 106–109; D. R. Sandler, "Noncompete Agreements," *Employment Management Today,* Fall 1997, pp. 14–19; S. G. Willis, "Protect Your Firm Against Former Employees' Actions," *HR Magazine,* Aug. 1997, pp. 117–122.

36. A. Smith, "Noncompetes Can Be Tough to Enforce When Former Employees Move," *HR News,* Apr. 10, 2006 (*www.shrm.org/hrnews*).

37. S. J. Marks, "Can the Internet Help You Hit the Salary Mark?" *Workforce,* Jan. 2001, pp. 86–93; A. S. Wellner, "Salaries in Site," *HR Magazine,* May 2001, pp. 89–96.

38. J. A. Lopez, "The Big Lie," *Wall Street Journal,* Apr. 21, 1993, pp. R6–R8.

39. B. Kelley, "Is Your Counter Productive?" *Human Resource Executive,* Apr. 1995, pp. 57–61; M. Loeb, "The Smart Way to Change Jobs," *Fortune,* Sept. 4, 1995, p. 139; G. McWilliams, "To Have and to Hold," *Business Week*, June 19, 1995, p. 43.

40. "Dianna Abdala," Wikipedia (*http://en.wikipedia.org/wiki/Dianna_Abdala*); J. Sandberg, "Infamous Email Writers Aren't Always Killing Their Careers After All," *Wall Street Journal,* Feb. 21, 2006, p. B1.

41. J. Kammeyer-Mueller and C. Wanberg, "Unwrapping the Organizational Entry Process: Disentangling Multiple Antecedents and Their Pathways to Adjustment," *Journal of Applied Psychology,* 2003, 88, pp. 779–794; M. J. Lankau and T. A. Scanduva, "An Investigation of Personal Learning in Mentoring Relationships: Content, Antecedents, and Consequences," *Academy of Management Journal,* 2002, 45, pp. 779–790; E. W. Morrison, "Newcomer Relationships: The Role of Social Network Ties During Socialization," *Academy of Management Journal,* 2002, 45, pp. 1149–1160; C. Wanberg, J. Kammeyer-Mueller, and M. Marchese, "Predictors and Outcomes of Mentoring in a Formal Mentoring Program," 2004, unpublished manuscript, Industrial Relations Center, University of Minnesota.

42. C. L. Adkins, "Previous Work Experience and Organizational Socialization: A Longitudinal Examination," *Academy of Management Journal,* 1995, 38, pp. 839–862.

43. T. N. Bauer, T. Bodner, B. Erdogan, D. M. Truxillo, and J. S. Tucker, "Newcomer Adjustment During Organizational Socialization: A Meta-Analytic Review of Antecedents, Outcomes, and Methods," *Journal of Applied Psychology,* 2007, 92, pp. 707–721.

44. G. T. Chao, A. M. O'Leary-Kelly, S. Wolf, H. J. Klein, and P. D. Gardner, "Organizational Socialization: Its Content and Consequences," *Journal of Applied Psychology,* 1994, 79, pp. 730–743.

45. M. J. Wesson and C. I. Gogus, "Shaking Hands With a Computer: An Examination of Two Methods of Organizational Newcomer Orientation," *Journal of Applied Psychology,* 2005, 90, pp. 1018–1026.

46. J. Mullich, "They're Hired: Now the Real Recruiting Begins," *Workforce Management Online,* Feb. 9, 2004 (*www.workforce.com*).

47. J. S. Lublin, "Job Candidates Get Manual From Boss: How to Handle Me," *Wall Street Journal,* Jan. 7, 2003, p. B1.

48. M. Hammers, "Optimas Award Financial Impact: National City Corporation," *Workforce Management Online,* Feb. 9, 2004 (*www.workforce.com*).

49. Feliu, *Primer on Individual Employee Rights,* pp. 283–285; R. M. Green and R. J. Reibstein, *Employers Guide to Workplace Torts* (Washington, DC: Bureau of National Affairs, 1992), pp. 1–18, 198–200, 245–250; A. M. Ryan and M. Lasek, "Negligent Hiring and Defamation: Areas of Liability Related to Preemployment Inquiries," *Personnel Psychology,* 1991, 44, pp. 293–319; W. J. Woska, "Negligent Employment Practices," *Labor Law Journal,* 1991, 42, pp. 603–610.

50. M. Moss, "Many Elders Receive Care at Criminals' Hands," *Wall Street Journal,* Mar. 18, 1998, p. B1.

51. Bureau of National Affairs, "Recruiting Exposure to Negligent Hiring Suits Requires Preventive Action, Practitioner Says," *Daily Labor Report,* June 18, 1998, p. C1; F. Hansen, "Taking 'Reasonable Action' to Avoid Negligent Hiring Claims," *Workforce Management,* Dec. 11, 2006, pp. 31–33.

52. Bennet, Polden, and Rubin, *Employment Relationships: Law and Practice,* pp. 2-1 to 2-65.

The Staffing Organizations Model

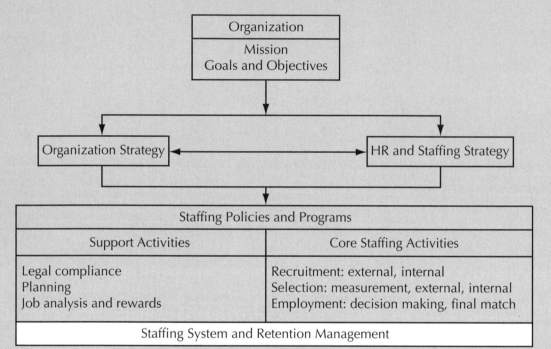

PART SIX

Staffing System and Retention Management

CHAPTER THIRTEEN

Staffing System Management

Administration of Staffing Systems
Organizational Arrangements
Jobs in Staffing
Policies and Procedures
Technology
Outsourcing

Evaluation of Staffing Systems
Staffing Process
Staffing Process Results
Calculating Staffing Metrics
Customer Satisfaction

Legal Issues
Record Keeping and Privacy
Audits
Training for Managers and Employees
Dispute Resolution

Summary

Discussion Questions

Ethical Issues

Applications

S taffing systems involve complex processes and decisions that require organizational direction, coordination, and evaluation. Most organizations must create mechanisms for managing their staffing system and its components. Such management of staffing systems requires consideration of both administration and evaluation, as well as legal issues.

Regarding administration, this chapter shows how the staffing (employment) function is one of the key areas within the human resources (HR) department. It provides illustrations of typical organizational arrangements for the staffing function. Various jobs held by people in the staffing function are also described. The role and nature of staffing policies and procedures in administering the staffing function are explained, as is the use of staffing technology and software to enhance efficient operation of staffing systems. Finally, outsourcing specific staffing activities to other organizations is described as a way of streamlining the staffing function.

Presented next is a discussion of ways to evaluate the effectiveness of the staffing function. Evaluation of how standardized the staffing process is and developing a flowchart of the process to guide identification of practices that deviate from it or cause bottlenecks are ways to gauge effectiveness. Various results of the staffing process are examined to gauge the effectiveness of staffing systems. Compilation and analysis of staffing system costs are also suggested as an evaluation technique. Last, assessment of customer (hiring managers, applicants) satisfaction is presented as a new, innovative approach to the evaluation of staffing systems.

Legal issues, as always, surround the management of staffing systems. Partly, this involves matters of compiling various records and reports and of conducting legal audits of staffing activities. Also discussed are training for managers and employees, and mechanisms for dispute resolution.

ADMINISTRATION OF STAFFING SYSTEMS

Organizational Arrangements

Organizational arrangements refers to how the organization structures itself to conduct HR and staffing activities, often within the HR department. The arrangements vary considerably, and both organization size and type (integrated or multiple business) make a difference in the likely type of organizational arrangement used.

Consider the following data from the U.S. Small Business Administration on organization size (*www.sba.gov*). The vast majority of organizations (5.5 million) have fewer than 100 employees, and those organizations employ about 36% of total employees. At the other extreme, only 17,000 organizations have 500+ employees, and they employ about 50% of total employees. In between are about 85,000 organizations that have 100–499 employees.

In organizations with fewer than 100 employees, regardless of purpose, research suggests that staffing is most likely to be conducted by the owner, president, or work unit manager. Only a small percentage (13%) of organizations will have an HR department in which responsibility for staffing might be housed. And staffing activities are quite varied among these small organizations in terms of establishing job requirements, recruitment sources, recruitment communication techniques, selection methods, decision making, and job offers. The presence of an HR department leads these organizations to adopt staffing practices different from those without an HR department.[1]

As organization size increases, so does the likelihood of there being an HR department and a unit within it responsible for staffing. But the exact configuration of the HR department and staffing activities will depend on whether the organization is composed of business units pursuing a common business product or service (an integrated business organization) or a diverse set of products or services (a multiple business organization).[2] Because of its diversity, the multiple business organization will likely not try to have a major, centralized corporate HR department. Rather, it will have a small corporate HR department, with a separate, decentralized HR department within each business unit. In this arrangement, staffing activities will be quite decentralized, with some guidance and expertise from the corporate HR department.

In an integrated business organization, there will likely be a highly centralized HR department at the corporate level, with a much smaller HR presence at the plant or site level. As pertains to staffing, such centralization creates economies of scale and consistency in staffing policies and processes, as well as hiring standards and new hire quality.

Sun Trust Bank in Atlanta provides an excellent example of an organization that moved from a decentralized to a centralized HR function and created a new corporate employment department to manage staffing throughout its 1,200 branches.[3] Previously, Sun Trust operated with 28 regional charters, and each region had its own HR department and staffing function. This created a muddle of inconsistency in technologies, services, and expertise, as well as quality of its job candidates. Through centralization, the bank sought to achieve greater consistency, along with a common vision and strategic focus, while still allowing some flexibility in operation among the regions. HR managers from the regional HR departments who had served as generalists were moved into specialist roles, some of them in the new employment department, with the assistance of considerable training in new policies and procedures. Job descriptions, qualifications, and recruitment strategies were standardized, and competency models were created to identify ideal candidates' personality traits, interests, and skills. Also, standardized guidelines, checklists, and candidate evaluation tools were developed. But some latitude was allowed for individual banks and staffing managers, such as decisions on how and when to recruit within their own territory. It appears as though the centralization worked well. The new head of the HR function said, "We tried to balance the push-pull between the corporate vision and the real-world banking realities. We did not want one side or the other to hold all the cards. . . . The bank managers unanimously say they are now getting better candidates and our new, more precise recruiting system has enabled us to reduce advertising and sourcing expenditures, while increasing the amount of assessments on each candidate. So in effect we end up spending less but getting more." It is also reported that full-time teller turnover decreased, the average time to fill a position dropped, and the average cost to fill a nonexempt position was reduced.

A more detailed example of a centralized organizational arrangement for an integrated-business, multiplant manufacturing organization is shown in Exhibit 13.1. At the corporate level, the HR department is headed by the vice president (VP) of human resources. Reporting to the VP are directors of employment and equal employment opportunity/affirmative action (EEO/AA), compensation and benefits, training and development, labor relations, and HR information systems. These directors, along with the vice president, formulate and coordinate HR strategy and policy, as well as manage their own functional units.

The director of employment and EEO/AA has three direct reports: the managers of exempt, nonexempt, and EEO/AA employment areas. Each manager, in turn, is responsible for the supervision of specialists and assistants. The manager of exempt employment, for example, handles external and internal staffing for managerial and professional jobs. There are two specialists in this unit, college recruiter and internal placement specialist, plus an administrative assistant. The manager of nonexempt employment is responsible for external and internal staffing for hourly paid employees. Reporting to this manager are four specialists (recruiter, interviewer, testing specialist, and consultant) plus two administrative assistants. The EEO/AA manager has a consultant and an administrative assistant as direct reports. The consultants are individuals who serve in liaison roles with the line managers of units throughout the organization when hiring is occurring. Functioning as internal customer service representatives to these managers, the consultants help the managers understand corporate employment policies and procedures, determine specific staffing needs, handle special staffing problems and requests, and answer questions.

At the plant level, there is a single HR manager and an administrative assistant who perform all HR activities, including staffing. This HR manager is a true generalist and works closely with the plant manager on all issues involving people concerns. Regarding staffing, the dotted line shows that the HR manager has an indirect reporting relationship to the director of employment and EEO/AA (as well as the other corporate-level HR directors, not shown). Very importantly, these directors will work with the HR manager to develop policies and programs (including staffing) that are consistent with corporate strategy and are also tailor-made to the particular needs and workforce of the plant.

EXHIBIT 13.1   **Example of HR Department and Employment (Staffing) Function**

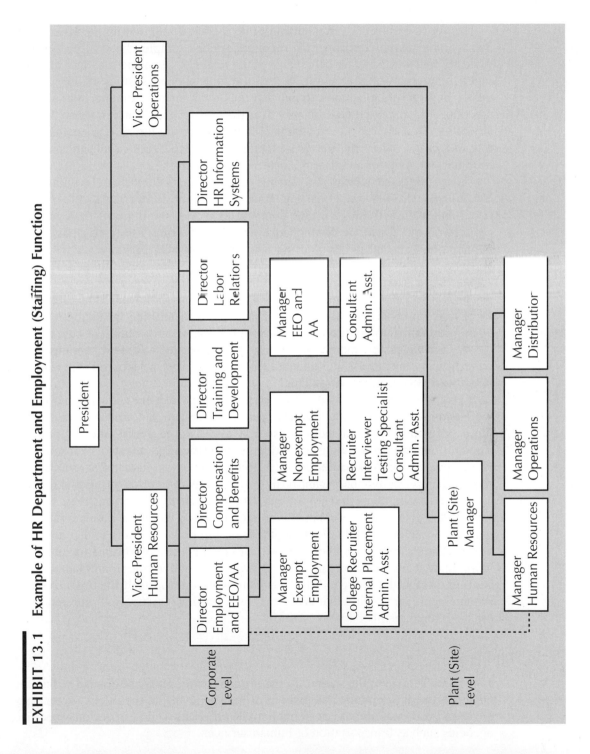

The above example shows staffing to be a critical area within the HR department, and research confirms this importance. For example, the staffing function typically receives a greater percentage of the total HR department budget than any other function, averaging about 20% of the total budget. A study of HR departments in large organizations found that the focus on recruitment and selection activities had increased significantly over the past several years, more so than for any other HR activity.[4] Salaries for people in the staffing function are comparable to those in the other HR functions. Increasingly, employees in all HR areas are becoming eligible for short-term incentives and bonuses.[5]

Those employed within the staffing function must work closely with members of all the other functional HR areas. For example, staffing members must coordinate their activities with the compensation and benefits staff in developing policies on the economic components of job offers, such as starting pay, hiring bonuses, and special perks. Staffing activities must also be closely coordinated with the training and development function. This will be needed to identify training needs for external, entry-level new hires, as well as for planning transfer and promotion-enhancing training experiences for current employees. The director of labor relations will work with the staffing area to determine labor contract language pertaining to staffing issues (e.g., promotions and transfers) and to help resolve grievances over staffing procedures and decisions. Record keeping, staffing software, and EEO/AA statistics requirements will be worked out with the director of HR information systems.

It should also be noted that although staffing activities are concentrated within the HR department, members of any specific organizational unit for which staffing is occurring will (and should) also play a role in the overall staffing process. The unit manager will submit the hiring authorization request, work closely with HR in developing the knowledge, skill, ability, and other characteristics (KSAOs) required/preferred for the vacant position, and actively participate in making discretionary assessments and job offers. Other members of the unit may provide input to the unit manager on KSAOs sought, formally meet and interact with candidates for recruiting and attracting purposes, and provide inputs to the unit manager on their preferences about who should receive the job offer. In team-based work units, team members may play an even more active role in all phases of the staffing process. Each organization needs to work out for itself the organizational arrangements for staffing that best fit its own staffing strategy and preferences of organizational members.

Jobs in Staffing

Jobs in staffing are quite varied. In the private sector, most are housed within the HR department (corporate and plant or office site level). In the public sector, they are found within the central personnel or HR office, as well as in various specified agencies such as transportation or human services.

The types and scope of tasks and responsibilities in staffing jobs are also varied. Some jobs are specialist ones, involving a functional specialty such as interviewing, recruiting, or college relations. These are often entry-level jobs as well. Other jobs may have a more generalist flavor to them, particularly in smaller organizations or smaller units (plant or office) of a larger organization. In such units, one person may handle all staffing-related activities. At higher organizational levels, both specialist and generalist jobs are found. Examples of specialist positions include test development and validation, executive assessment, and affirmative action. Generalists usually have broader managerial responsibilities that cut across specialties; the job of staffing manager is one example.

Exhibit 13.2 provides job descriptions for two staffing jobs—junior recruiter/HR generalist, and corporate manager of staffing (western region)—at Science Applications International Corporation (SAIC), taken from the SAIC Web site (*www.saic.com*). The first job is an entry-level staffing job, and the second is a generalist, corporate-level staffing job. SAIC is a Fortune 500, employee-owned research and engineering organization with offices in over 150 cities worldwide.

Entry into staffing jobs normally occurs at the specialist rank in the areas of recruiting and interviewing, in both private and public organizations. Staffing of these jobs may come from the new hire ranks of the organization. It may also come from an internal transfer from a management training program, from a line management job, or from another HR function. In short, there is no fixed point or method of entry into staffing jobs.

Mobility within staffing jobs may involve both traditional and nontraditional career tracks. In a traditional track, the normal progression is from entry-level specialist up through the ranks to staffing manager, with assignments at both the corporate and operating unit level. A nontraditional track might involve entry into a staffing specialist job, lateral transfer after a year to another functional HR area, rotation from there into an entry-level supervisory position, advancement within the supervisory ranks, and then promotion to the job of staffing manager. In short, there is often no established upward mobility track. One should expect the unexpected.

If a person advances beyond or outside the staffing function, this will usually serve the person well for advancement to the highest HR levels (director or vice president). At these levels, job occupants have typically held varied assignments, including working outside HR in managerial or professional capacities. The work outside HR has been in a diverse set of areas, including customer service, operations, finance, sales/marketing, and HR consulting.[6]

It should be noted that jobs in staffing (and other areas of HR) are becoming increasingly more customer focused and facilitative in nature. As staffing activities become more decentralized and subject to line management control, holders of staffing jobs will exist to provide requested services and act as consultants to the service requesters. This will be a challenge because many of those newly responsible for staffing (line managers and team leaders) will be untrained and inexperienced in staffing matters.

EXHIBIT 13.2 Staffing Jobs at Science Applications International Corporation

A. Junior Recruiter/HR Generalist

Job Description:
Performs technical and administrative recruiting for the Pacific Programs Division. Recruits for several different locations throughout the Pacific to include Hawaii, Alaska, Guam, California, Korea, and Japan. Responsibilities include job requisition tracking, job posting and ad placement, pre-screening candidates, coordinating with hiring manager on scheduling and conducting interviews and conducting reference checks. Secondary responsibility includes performing HR Generalist job duties which may include benefits, compensation and employee relations.

Education:
Bachelor's degree preferred.

Required Skills:
One to three years of recruiting experience. Ability to establish effective working relationships with peers, applicants and hiring managers. Must project a positive professional image through written and verbal communication and must be able to work independently with minimal supervision. Must be proficient in MS Office (Word, Excel, Power Point). Some travel may be required.

Desired Skills:
Recruiting for technical positions to include systems engineers, software engineers and systems administrators. Experience working with Resumix or other automated recruitment and staffing tools.

Job Category: Human Resources   **Ref. No:**
Location: Honolulu, Hawaii, US
Contact:

Part Time or Temporary: Full-time (1st shift)

Must be able to obtain clearance level: Secret
SAIC is an Equal Opportunity/Affirmative Action Employer

B. Corporate Manager of Staffing—Western Region (San Diego Based)

Job Description:
The incumbent provides strategic staffing support to HR managers, recruiters and generalists within SAIC Western Region. Analyzes, develops, implements and evaluates the effectiveness of employment process addressing the business needs of Sectors and Groups within the Western Region, while meeting legal and corporate compliance requirements. Coordinates College Relations and College Recruitment activities, including advertising strategies, within the Region. Develops and coordinates Regional print and Internet advertising strategies, diversity

(continued)

EXHIBIT 13.2   Continued

and professional recruiting processes, employee referral programs, student internships and the collection of employment metrics. Develops and implements tools and processes to improve ROI [Return on Investment] by optimizing recruiting strategies. Will be required to travel to meet business needs supporting any incumbent captures, acquisitions, outsourcing, and other engagements with critical hiring needs. The incumbent will have a dual reporting relationship to the Corporate Staffing Director and Director of HR, Western Region. Directly supervises regional service center recruiting and administrative staff. In addition, responsible for ensuring all recruiters receive timely training and refresher courses for Applicant Tracking Information System (e.g., Resumix) operations. Will develop and lead a team of superusers, providing user support and development, upgrade, implementation requirements, and some vendor relations.

Education:
BA/BS in a relevant field plus a minimum of 10 years of experience, with a minimum of 3 years in a supervisory capacity required. Masters degree in HR or a related area is desirable.

Required Skills:
Must have supervisory experience leading a successful high volume recruiting team in a tight labor market. Experience with electronic applicant tracking systems required, Resumix preferred. Must be well organized with excellent interpersonal skills. Must be a team player with outstanding persuasive, negotiation, and motivational skills. Must possess the ability to manage a team and achieve results through influence, without the benefit of direct management authority. Must possess the proven ability to facilitate the exchange of information through leadership of meetings, and in the development and delivery of effective training and information sessions. Must be knowledgeable of EEO, labor laws and immigration compliance practices.

Desired Skills:
Prefer experience with managing IT industry high volume recruiting programs.

Job Category: Human Resources   **Ref. No:**
Location: San Diego, California, US
Contact:

Part Time or Temporary: Full-time (1st shift)
SAIC is an Equal Opportunity/Affirmative Action Employer

SOURCE: Science Applications International Corporation. Used with permission.

Increasing numbers of staffing jobs are found in staffing firms. One such firm is Staffmark, a large, diversified staffing firm with offices nationwide (*www.Staffmark.com*). Services offered by Staffmark include supplemental staffing (short and long term), supplemental to direct staffing, direct hire, executive search, on-site managed programs, national multisite workforce management, and training programs. Exhibit 13.3 provides a job description for the entry-level job of staffing specialist

EXHIBIT 13.3 Staffing Job at Staffmark

Job Title: Staffing Specialist

Job Summary:
This position is responsible for taking complete and accurate job orders and identifying and placing temporary associates on temporary assignments or direct placement with client companies according to specified job orders and requirements and identifying business development opportunities through penetration of existing accounts.

Essential Duties and Responsibilities:
1. Carries out such functions as identifying qualified applicants, conducting screening interviews, administering tests, checking references, and evaluating applicant qualifications.
2. Hires qualified temporary associates and establishes appropriate pay rates for temporary associates based on skills, abilities, and experience.
3. Makes job offer to associate explaining full job description, term of assignment, pay rate, benefits.
4. Obtains complete and accurate information from clients placing job orders and matches best temporary associate to the client job order. May quote and explain base rates to client.
5. Determines appropriate client placement of qualified associates (may be through skill marketing) and conducts basic associate orientation.
6. Monitors associate activity at client, e.g. track attendance, performance, etc.
7. Maintains current, accurate data in the computer of client activity and associate inventory.
8. Conducts regular service calls (retail accounts <$500,000) to assigned clients to ensure quality service, identify any problems, and obtain feedback.
9. Completes quality control procedures including check-in calls and follow-up calls on completed job orders.
10. Completes accurate payroll processing for temporary associates.
11. Follows and communicates all safety rules and regulations as established by Staffmark to associates.
12. Ensures worker's compensation claims are properly filed.
13. Under the supervision of management, will counsel associates and handle conflict resolution.
14. At the direction of Branch Manager, will record drug testing results and follow drug testing policy.
15. Performs telephone marketing and recruiting in order to identify suitable temporary associates for current and prospective clients.
16. Represents the company in a professional manner at various professional, academic, and/or civic activities as requested.

(continued)

EXHIBIT 13.3   Continued

Other Duties and Responsibilities:

1. Occasionally, may be given responsibility for handling worker's compensation or unemployment compensation hearings.
2. Needs to be available for on-call duty after hours and on weekends.
3. May require shift work.

Note: Additional responsibilities not listed here may be assigned at times.

Supervisory Responsibilities:

Supervises temporary associates including monitoring extension or completion of assignments, addressing problems or concerns of temporary associates, coaching, counseling, and taking corrective action with temporary associates. Terminates temporary associates when appropriate. Does not have responsibility for supervising internal Staffmark employees.

Required Competencies:

Utilizes independent judgment and exhibits sound reasoning. Has a working knowledge of Staffmark's unemployment compensation and worker's compensation filing process.

Required Qualifications:

To perform this job successfully, an individual must be able to perform each essential duty satisfactorily. The requirements listed below are representative of the knowledge, skill, and/or ability required. Reasonable accommodations may be made to enable individuals with disabilities to perform the essential functions.

Education and/or Experience:

High school diploma or general education degree (GED); or one to three months' related experience and/or training; or equivalent combination of education and experience.

Language Skills:

Ability to read and interpret documents such as safety rules, operating and maintenance instructions, and procedure manuals. Ability to write routine reports and correspondence. Ability to speak effectively before groups of customers or employees of organization.

Mathematical Skills:

Ability to add, subtract, multiply, and divide in all units of measure, using whole numbers, common fractions, and decimals. Ability to compute rate, ratio, and percent and to draw and interpret bar graphs.

Reasoning Ability:

Ability to apply common sense understanding to carry out detailed but uninvolved written or oral instructions. Ability to deal with problems involving a few concrete variables in standardized situations.

(continued)

EXHIBIT 13.3 Continued

Computer Skills:
Microsoft Word, Microsoft Outlook, Caldwell, Excel, Powerpoint, and Internet.

Certificates, Licenses, Registrations:
Must have current, valid driver's license. Position requires travel to and from client companies and civic events.

Physical Demands:
The physical demands described here are representative of those that must be met by an employee to successfully perform the essential functions of this job. Reasonable accommodations may be made to enable individuals with disabilities to perform the essential functions.

While performing the duties of this job, the employee is regularly required to sit; use hands to finger, handle, or feel; and talk or hear. The employee is frequently required to walk and reach with hands and arms. The employee is occasionally required to stand; climb or balance and stoop, kneel, crouch, or crawl. The employee must frequently lift and/or move up to 10 pounds and occasionally lift and/or move up to 25 pounds. Specific vision abilities required by this job include close vision, distance vision, color vision, peripheral vision, depth perception and ability to adjust focus.

Work Environment:
The work environment characteristics described here are representative of those an employee encounters while performing the essential functions of this job. Reasonable accommodations may be made to enable individuals with disabilities to perform the essential functions. While performing the duties of this job, the employee is occasionally exposed to wet and/or humid conditions; moving mechanical parts; outside weather conditions; extreme cold and extreme heat. The noise level in the work environment is usually moderate. On occasion, duties may require the wearing of proper safety equipment in areas where such equipment is required.

Needs to be available for on-call duty after hours and on weekends. May require shift work.

SOURCE: Staffmark. Used with permission.

for Staffmark. More advanced jobs include senior staffing specialist, direct hire recruiter, on-site staffing supervisor, and staffing manager. Individuals in on-site staffing roles work directly with the client's HR department to conduct all phases of staffing. Use of such specialists occurs when the client lacks staffing expertise or is seeking to hire large numbers of new employees quickly.[7]

Another new type of staffing job is that of chief talent officer or vice president for talent acquisition. Organizations that are critically dependent on talent, such as those in technology and entertainment, and that need to conduct specialized talent searches outside the mainstream of the normal staffing processes are creating such positions. One organization, America Online, went even further and created a special talent acquisition department of 35 people who conduct both external and internal searches. It is suggested that such individuals have a background in recruiting, understand accountability in organizations, possess some marketing experience to help sell the organization and build relationships, and can draw on an ability to think "outside the box" and devise a strategic vision for recruits and their roles within the organization.[8]

Policies and Procedures

It is highly desirable to have written policies and procedures to guide the administration of staffing systems. Understanding the importance of policies and procedures first requires definition of these terms.

A policy is a selected course or guiding principle. It is an objective to be sought through appropriate actions. For example, the organization might have a promotion-from-within policy as follows: It is the intent of XXX organization to fill from within all vacancies above the entry level, except in instances of critical, immediate need for a qualified person unavailable internally. This policy makes it clear that promotion from within is the desired objective; the only exception is the absence of an immediately available qualified current employee.

A procedure is a prescribed routine or way of acting in similar situations. It provides the rules that are to govern a particular course of action. To carry out the promotion-from-within policy, for example, the organization may have specific procedures to be followed for listing and communicating the vacancy, identifying eligible applicants, and assessing the qualifications of the applicants.

Policies and procedures can improve the strategic focus of the staffing area. When there are clearly articulated systems of policies and procedures, it is possible to consider the meaning and function of the entire system at a strategic level. On the other hand, poorly thought out or inconsistent policies and procedures mean that HR managers will spend an inordinate amount of time playing catch-up or "putting out fires," as inconsistent behavior across organizational units inevitably leads to employee complaints. Without clear staffing policies, managers scramble to develop solutions to recruiting or selection needs at the last minute. Dealing with these routine breakdowns in procedures will mean that there is insufficient time to consult organizational goals or consider alternatives. The final result is inefficiency and wasted time.

The existence of policies and procedures can also do a great deal to enhance the perceived justice of staffing activities. Research conducted in a wide variety of organizations has consistently shown that organizational decision-making is perceived as most fair by employees when decisions are based on facts rather than social influence or personal biases, when decision-making criteria are clearly communicated, and when the process is consistently followed across all affected individuals.[9] The use of well-articulated policies and procedures can increase perceived justice considerably if they meet all of the requirements for perceived justice. There are bottom-line implications of perceived justice. Employee perceptions of organizational justice have been linked to increased intention to pursue a job in the recruiting context, increased intention to accept a job in the selection context, increased satisfaction and commitment for job assignments, and decreased intention to sue a former employer in the layoff context.[10]

The scope of staffing actions and practices is large, ranging across a broad spectrum of recruitment, selection, and employment issues, both external and internal. Consequently, the organization's staffing policies and procedures also need to be broad in scope. To illustrate this, Exhibit 13.4 provides an overview of the content of CompuServe's staffing policies. The total statement of these policies, and accompanying procedures, consumes more than 20 pages in CompuServe's policies and procedures manual.

Technology

Staffing activities generate and use considerable information, often in paper form. Job descriptions, application materials, résumés, correspondence, applicant profiles, applicant flow and tracking, and reports are examples of the types of information that are necessary ingredients for the operation of a staffing system. Naturally, problems regarding what types of information to generate, along with how to file, access, and use it, will arise when managing a staffing system. Addressing and solving these problems have important implications for paperwork burdens, administrative processing costs, and speed in filling job vacancies. Thus, management of a staffing system involves management of an information system.

For many organizations, the information system will continue to be a primarily paper-based manual system. This will most likely occur in smaller organizations, single-site organizations, and organizations where there is a limited amount of staffing activity (few vacancies to fill) in a given time period. These systems should be carefully scrutinized to determine if they require excessive and duplicative paper documents, as well as unnecessary files and logs.

As organizations increase in size, complexity (e.g., multiple sites), and level of staffing activity, the paperwork, paper flows, and manual handling become expensive and burdensome. Moreover, the number of individuals needed to operate the staffing system and take care of its paper becomes excessive. These problems cause the organization to seek staffing system efficiencies through adoption of staffing technology.

The primary improvements come about through a combination of conversion to electronic information and automation of staffing tasks and processes. A central feature is the creation of electronic databases of applicant and employee information. Computer systems will also be needed to provide data entry, access, and manipulation. Also, relevant software will need to be developed or purchased commercially through vendors. These information system requirements naturally mean that HR information system specialists will need to work closely with members of the staffing function.

EXHIBIT 13.4 **Staffing Topics in CompuServe's HR Policy Manual**

Affirmative Action	Personnel Records and Files
Affirmative Action Plan	Procedures
Americans With Disabilities Act	Internal Moves
Associate Status	Job Descriptions
Exempt/Nonexempt	Promotion
Full-time/Part-time	Recruiting and Selecting
Independent Contractor	Transfer
Internship	Promotion
Temporary Agencies	Reasonable Accommodation
Balanced Workforce	Recruiting and Selecting
Charges of Discrimination	Associate Referrals
Confidential Information	Classified Advertising
Diversity	Employment Agencies
Employment Agencies	Former Associates
Employment-at-Will	Interviews
Equal Employment and Affirmative Action	Relatives
Essential Functions of the Job	Screening
External Recruiting	Targeted Selection
Flextime	Testing
Immigration	Reference Checks
Internal Moves	Release of Information: Personnel Files
Internal Recruiting	Relocation
Interviews	Right to Privacy
Job Descriptions	Secondary Job
Job Posting	Selection of Candidates
Letter of Recommendation	Temporary Agencies
Offers of Employment	Testing
Outreach Programs: EEO/AA	Valuing Diversity
Performance Reviews	Visa Status

Source: Compliments of CompuServe, Columbus, OH. Used with permission.

Most organizations with a sufficient number of employees to warrant a dedicated HR department have integrated the function with human resources information systems (HRISs). Many vendors have developed specialized HRIS interfaces that can track the critical processes and outcomes involved in staffing, as shown in Exhibit 13.5. The features listed in Exhibit 13.5 are meant to be illustrative rather than exhaustive; new functionality is continually being added to HRISs. Providing hard data on staffing system outcomes can increase the credibility of staffing services in organizations. The increased availability of data on staffing processes following from the use of HRISs means that organizations will also be able to

EXHIBIT 13.5 **Human Resources Information Systems for Staffing Tasks**

Staffing Tasks	HRIS Functionality
Legal compliance	EEO data analysis and reports
	Policy and procedure writing guides
	Statistical analysis for demonstrating job relatedness
Planning	Tracking historical demand for employees
	Forecasting workforce supply
	Replacement and succession planning
Job analysis	Database of job titles and responsibilities
	Database of competencies across jobs
	Compare job descriptions to O*Net
External recruitment and selection	Job posting reports
	Time-to-fill hiring requisitions
	Applicant logs, status, and tracking reports
	Recruitment source effectiveness
	Electronic résumé routing
	Keyword scanning of applications
	New hire reports (numbers, qualifications, assignments)
	Validation of selection systems
Internal recruitment and selection	Employee succession planning
	Intranet for job postings
	Skills databases
	Tracking progress through assessment centers
	Job performance reports
	Individual development plans
Final match	Tracking job acceptance rates
	Contract development
	Tracking employee socialization progress
Staffing system management	System cost reports
	Return on investments
	Record-keeping functions
Retention	Collection and analysis of job satisfaction data
	Track differences in turnover rates across locations and time
	Document performance management and/or progressive discipline

accurately track the efficacy of policies and procedures. Staffing policies that do not show returns on investments can be eliminated, whereas those that show positive results can be expanded. Organizations that have outsourced staffing functions should also be aware of the information provided by HRISs and should ensure that they are receiving accurate and comprehensive reports from their vendors' HRIS database. Organizations considering outsourcing options should request historical data showing the efficacy of staffing systems in other organizations before committing resources toward any particular vendor. If an outsourcing service provider cannot provide these data, this may be a sign that the service provider does not communicate well or may not be very rigorous about evaluating the quality of its services.

Web-based staffing management systems are also available from application service providers (ASPs). With such systems, the vendor provides both the hardware (e.g., servers, scanners) and the software, as well as day-to-day management of the system. Recruiters and hiring managers access the system through a Web browser. One example of such a system is the Enterprise system from Brass Ring, Inc. (*www.brassring.com*). The system posts job openings to job boards and other Web sites. It accepts all forms of résumés (paper, fax, e-mail, Web-based), scans and codes them, and stores them in a relational database on a secure server. In addition to résumé information, a talent record may include information pertaining to work samples, background checks, test scores, training, certification, performance reviews, and references. The hiring manager or recruiter can then access the database to submit job requisitions, perform literal and conceptual searches based on specified KSAOs, schedule interviews, conduct correspondence with applicants, forward résumés to others, track the search status of current applicants, track current employee KSAOs, and conduct various recruitment reports, such as average cost per hire for each recruitment source used and EEO compliance.

Effectiveness

Surveys of organizations' experiences with new staffing technologies and case studies of their adoption, implementation, and operation provide a comprehensive overview of how well the new technologies are working.[11] What emerges from the data is a very "mixed bag" of evidence, with numerous positive and negative experiences being reported.

Staffing technologies may have a multitude of positive and negative effects. Many of these effects extend beyond process improvement (e.g., speed of staffing) and cost reduction. While these two potential advantages are very important, they need to be considered within the context of other potential advantages, and especially the myriad potential disadvantages. Based on the evidence, it is very clear that the organization should proceed with caution and due diligence in deciding whether to move toward use of new staffing technologies, evaluating products and vendors, establishing service agreements with vendors, and conducting careful planning prior to implementation. It is also clear that even once the staffing technologies are implemented, monitoring and system improvement will need to be periodically undertaken.

Outsourcing

Outsourcing refers to contracting out work to a vendor or third-party administrator. In the chapter on planning we discussed outsourcing work for noncore organizational processes. Here we consider the case when certain staffing functions are outsourced. There are many examples of the outsourcing of specific staffing activities. These include seeking temporary employees, executive search, drug testing, skill testing, background checks, conducting job fairs, employee relocation, assessment centers, and affirmative action planning. Other examples continue to emerge. For example, on-demand recruiting services provide short-term assistance in conducting executive searches, but payment for these services is based on a fixed fee or time rate, rather than on a percentage of the new hire's salary.[12] A number of factors that influence the decision of whether to outsource are reviewed in Exhibit 13.6. Outsourcing decisions require consideration of organizational strategy, size, and the skills required. As you can see, the decision about whether to outsource is not an all-or-nothing proposition; there are some staffing functions that make more sense for outsourcing than others, so most organizations use outsourcing for some tasks but not for others.

One of the benefits of outsourcing is that it frees the internal HR department from performing day-to-day administrative activities that could be more efficiently managed by an external organization. A survey of HR representatives showed that the major advantages of outsourcing include access to superior information from specialists, access to technology and services that are difficult to implement internally, and general cost reduction.[13] By eliminating the day-to-day work of maintaining staffing systems, it is possible to dedicate more energy to analyzing and improving the effectiveness of the staffing system as a whole. Because specialized staffing firms work with the same processes all the time, they can develop specialized, highly efficient systems that can deliver results more quickly and more cheaply than an organization's in-house staffing services. An external staffing firm will have more resources to keep up with developments in its area. For example, a firm that specializes in EEO compliance will always have the latest information regarding the latest court decisions and changing precedents.

These advantages of outsourcing should always be weighed against the potential downfalls of outsourcing too many staffing functions or outsourcing functions too rapidly. Companies that outsource should hold external providers accountable by keeping track of staffing metrics, especially since specialized staffing firms should have access to better systems for managing and reporting staffing data. There should also always be someone inside the organization who has final, bottom-line accountability for any outsourced services. In many organizations, there is

EXHIBIT 13.6   Comparing Outsourced vs. In-House Staffing

	Outsourced	**In-House**
Strategy	Staffing functions not linked to core organizational competencies	Staffing functions linked to core organizational competencies
Size	Small organizations, organizations without a centralized HR function, or organizations with continual hiring needs	Large organizations where economies of scale will pay off or for executive selection tasks where knowledge of the organization is crucial
Skills required	General human capital, such as that easily obtained through education	Firm-specific human capital, such as knowledge of organizational policies or specific personality traits
Examples	• Recruiting packaging employees in a small warehouse • Screening registered nurses for a long-term-care facility • Developing a Web site for automatically screening entry-level candidates • Providing temporary employees for a highly cyclical manufacturing organization	• Recruiting creative talent for an advertising firm • Selecting members of the organization's executive team • Providing employee orientation • Recruiting and selecting employees for a large retail organization • Recruiting and selecting individuals for an interdependent work team

resistance to outsourcing, and employees may feel that the company is treating them impersonally if questions or concerns about employment are directed to an external vendor. Thus, if employees have complaints or concerns about staffing services, there should be someone inside the organization who can respond to them.

It is worth noting that staffing is not one of the first activities most organizations outsource. The same surveys noted earlier demonstrate that the most commonly outsourced HR services are payroll and pension plans. It is also more common for organizations to outsource their recruiting function than selection. This makes sense when one considers the comparative advantages of internal and outsourced services: Most organizations do not have much access to the external labor market, so a specialized staffing firm can provide superior recruiting. But the choice of who will or will not work in an organization is often made based on a complex assessment of fit with the job and work group that would be more accurately made by internal HR representatives.

An emerging type of vendor is the professional employer organization (PEO), formerly referred to as an employee leasing firm. It is similar to a staffing firm, but differs from it by providing a wider range of HR services and having a long-term commitment to the client. Under a typical arrangement, the client organization enters into a contractual relationship with a PEO to conduct some or all HR activities and functions. The client and the PEO are considered coemployers of record. A PEO is particularly appealing to small employers because it can provide special HR expertise and technical assistance, conduct the administrative activities and transactions of an HR department, provide more affordable employee benefits, meet legal obligations (payroll, withholding, workers' compensation, unemployment insurance), and manage legal compliance. PEOs are licensed in many states.[14]

There is also experimentation with total outsourcing of the staffing function. An example is Kellogg (cereal and convenience foods), which selected a single vendor to which the entire staffing process was outsourced. Kellogg worked with the vendor at the outset to develop a staffing strategy and fit it into the vendor's staffing technology, implement the total staffing solution, and then modify the system as experience with it revealed problems requiring adjustment. Assessment and hiring of finalists, however, remained in the hands of the hiring manager. Within three years, over 95% of jobs available at Kellogg were being filled by the vendor.[15]

Consider the example of Charmant, which is a moderate-sized organization (130 employees) that was seeking to update its outmoded HRISs.[16] Like most organizations of this size, Charmant has a relatively small HR department, consisting of only two individuals. Its old systems were poorly integrated, required a great deal of redundant work to access information from multiple systems (e.g., recruiting, performance management, benefits, and payroll were completely separate applications), and had a user interface that was difficult to understand. Through a relationship with a specialized software provider, it was able to obtain a seamless integration of all its HR systems, which simultaneously reduced the amount of staff time required for routine HR processes while increasing access to data for decision making. The new system made it possible to update records for payroll and benefits simultaneously when new employees were hired or employees left, which makes managing head count and related HR functions more straightforward. Using an external vendor also facilitated the posting of internal jobs with recruiting providers like Monster and made conducting background checks easier. In sum, tasks that this medium-sized organization's HR representatives could not complete as readily, especially information systems integration, were performed by an external vendor, thereby allowing in-house HR individuals to concentrate more of their time on core business operations. This example demonstrates how outsourcing for specific HR services can be used to facilitate in-house staffing effectiveness for companies that do not have resources to devote to a large HR department.

At the outset, it is important to remember that the agreement (often called a service-level agreement, or SLA) with the vendor is almost always negotiable, and that flaws in the negotiating stage are responsible for many problems that may subsequently occur in the relationship. Using some form of legal or consulting assistance might be desirable, especially for the organization that has little or no staffing outsourcing experience.

There are many issues to discuss and negotiate. Awareness of these factors and advance preparation with regard to the organization's preferences and requirements are critical to a successful negotiation with a potential vendor. The factors include the actual staffing services sought and provided, client control rights (e.g., monitoring of the vendor's personnel; software to be used), fees and other costs, guaranteed improvements in service levels and cost savings, benchmarking metrics and performance reviews, and willingness to hire the organization's own employees to provide expertise and coordination. On top of these factors, the choice of vendor should take into account the vendor's past track record and familiarity with the organization's industry.[17]

EVALUATION OF STAFFING SYSTEMS

Evaluation of staffing systems refers to the effectiveness of the total system. The evaluation should focus on the operation of the staffing process, the results and costs of the process, and the satisfaction of customers of the staffing system.

Staffing Process

The staffing process establishes and governs the flow of employees into, within, and out of the organization. Evaluation of the process itself requires a mapping out of the intended process, identifying any deviations from the intended process, and planning corrective actions to reduce or eliminate the deviations. The intent of such an evaluation is to ensure standardization of the staffing process, remove bottlenecks in operation, and improve speed of operation.

Standardization refers to the consistency of operation of the organization's staffing system. Use of standardized staffing systems is desirable for several reasons. First, standardization ensures that the same KSAO information is gathered from all job applicants, which, in turn, is a key requirement for reliably and validly measuring these KSAOs. Second, standardization ensures that all applicants receive the same information about job requirements and rewards. Thus, all applicants can make equally informed evaluations of the organization. Third, standardization will enhance applicants' perceptions of the procedural fairness of the staffing system and of the decisions made about them by the organization. Having applicants feel they were treated fairly and got a "fair shake" can reap substantial benefits for the organization. Applicants will speak favorably of their experience and the organization to others, they may seek employment with the organization in the future (even if rejected), they may be more likely to say yes to job offers, and they may become organizational newcomers with a very upbeat frame of mind as they begin their new jobs. Finally, standardized staffing systems are less likely to generate legal challenges by job applicants; if they are challenged, they are more likely to successfully withstand the challenge.

Mapping out the staffing process involves construction of a staffing flowchart. An example of a staffing flowchart is shown in Exhibit 13.7. It depicts the staffing system of a medium-sized (580 employees) high-tech printing and lithography company. It shows the actual flow of staffing activities, and both organization and applicant decision points, from the time a vacancy occurs until the time it is filled with a new hire.

A detailed inspection of the chart reveals the following information about the organization's staffing system:

1. It is a generic system used for both entry-level and higher-level jobs.
2. For higher-level jobs, vacancies are first posted internally (thus showing a recruitment philosophy emphasizing a commitment to promotion from within). Entry-level jobs are filled externally.
3. External recruitment sources (colleges, newspaper ads, employment agencies) are used only if the current applicant file yields no qualified applicants.
4. Initial assessments are made using biographical information (application blanks, résumés), and results of these assessments determine who will be interviewed.
5. Substantive assessments are made through the interview(s) conducted by the HR manager and the hiring supervisor, and results of these assessments determine who receives the job offer.
6. The applicant may counteroffer, and acceptance by the applicant of the final offer is conditional on passing drug/alcohol and physical tests.
7. The new hire undergoes a six-month probationary employment period before becoming a so-called permanent employee.

A more fine-grained analysis is then conducted to indicate the specific steps and actions that should be taken throughout the staffing process. For example, it can be seen in Exhibit 13.7 that non-entry-level manufacturing jobs are posted internally, so the more fine-grained analysis would involve a description of the job posting process—content of the posting, timing of the posting, mechanisms for circulating and displaying the posting, and person responsible for handling the posting. As another example, the staffing process involves contacting qualified applicants for an interview, inviting them for an interview, and interviewing them. The more fine-grained analysis would involve identification of the amount of time between the initial contact and completion of interviews, who conducts the interview, and the nature/content of the interview (such as a structured, situational interview). After the fine-grained analysis is complete, there would be a detailed specification of the staffing process in flow terms, along with specific events, actions, and timing that should occur over the course of the process.

EXHIBIT 13.7 **Staffing Flowchart for Medium-Sized Printing Company**

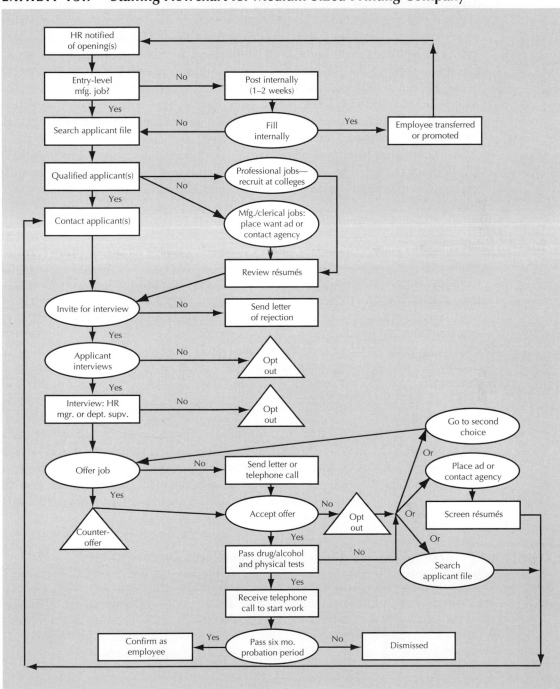

Once the staffing process has been mapped out, the next step is to check for deviations from it that have actually occurred. This will require an analysis of some past staffing "transactions" with job applicants, following what was done and what actions were taken as the applicants entered and flowed through the staffing system. All identified deviations should be recorded. It might be found, for example, that the content of the job postings did not conform to specific requirements for listing tasks and necessary KSAOs, or that interviews were not being conducted within the required one-week period from date of first contact with a qualified applicant, or that interviewers were conducting unstructured interviews rather than the required structured, situational interview.

The next step is to analyze all discovered deviations and determine the reason(s) for their occurrence. The final step is to determine and make changes in the staffing system in order to reduce deviations, enhance standardization, and remove bottlenecks.

Staffing Process Results

In the past it was commonly argued that most of the processes involved in staffing were too subjective or difficult to quantify. As a result, staffing managers had problems interfacing with representatives from finance and accounting, who demanded hard cost-effectiveness data. Fortunately, a dramatic increase in the availability and functionality of database software in recent years means that staffing system effectiveness can be assessed much more readily. HRISs can catalog and quickly display recruiting, hiring, retention, and job performance data. HR scholars have developed standardized metrics based on these sources of information that can help staffing managers communicate the business case for staffing services across the organization.[18]

Exhibit 13.8 provides a flowchart for using metrics to evaluate and update staffing processes. The first stage of the process is assessing the organization's needs and strategic goals at both the job and organization level. This stage was covered in organizational planning. Once organizational priorities are established, a set of policies and procedures is developed designed to achieve these ends. The next

---

EXHIBIT 13.8 **Staffing Process Results Evaluation Flowchart**

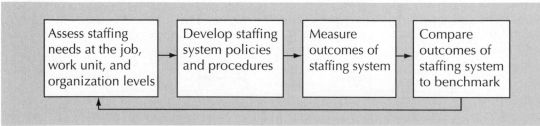

stage is to measure the outcomes of the staffing system. Consulting staffing system metrics will then serve as the basis for assessing future organizational needs, priorities and goals, and will also be used to revise staffing system policies and procedures. After measurements have been obtained, they should be compared to benchmark figures. These benchmarks can be obtained from split sample techniques, longitudinal techniques, or external benchmarking, which we will cover shortly. This strategic planning and evaluation process is an essential component of staffing system management. If there are no attempts to monitor and check the outcomes of staffing systems, it is likely that systems that may have been effective in the past will remain in place long after they have failed to obtain desired results. Of course, there is no guarantee that HR programs will prove to be effective when put to the test; experienced managers who have used staffing system metrics often find that new staffing systems may not represent a significant improvement.

One method for evaluating the efficacy of staffing programs is to use the scientific technique of split samples.[19] As an example, a split sample analysis might begin with the premise that a new recruiting program will affect operational outcomes by attracting more qualified employees, improving the organization's ability to respond to staffing requisitions quickly, and reducing long-range turnover. The specific metrics for this proposed program include measures of employee qualifications, time-to-hire for position openings taken from the organization's HRIS, and unit turnover rates. In a split sample analysis, the target employee population is split in half, and the new HR program is initiated with only one of these halves. In this case, perhaps one region of a national chain would serve as the experimental group for the new recruiting program, and their outcomes will be compared with the rest of the organization, which would not use the new recruiting program. After the program has had an opportunity to work, representatives from HR can compare the metrics from the experimental sample to areas of the company where the new recruiting system was not employed. The split sample technique is not just useful for evaluating new programs. To assess the effectiveness of an existing program, it is always possible to selectively discontinue the program in one location or business unit while maintaining it in another section. If the temporary elimination of a costly program does not appreciably alter business outcomes, it may be wise to eliminate the program permanently.

If it is not possible to use the split sample technique because the workforce does not have geographically or operationally distinct units, it is still possible to use metrics to assess the efficacy of proposed system changes. Staffing managers can compare long-run data on a single business unit's effectiveness before and after a change has been initiated. This is called a longitudinal design, or simply put, a measure of change. To make valid inferences, benchmark data should be taken over a long period of time, so that changes in staffing metrics can be reliably attributed to the program implementation rather than just routine variability in organizational performance.

A final strategy for assessing the effectiveness of HR programs is to compare organizational results to external benchmarks. The Society for Human Resource Management (SHRM) has developed a number of guidelines for developing and interpreting staffing metrics. Its Web site provides a number of benchmarking studies every year, including surveys that outline the use and perceived efficacies ranging across a number of practices, such as retention initiatives, e-recruiting, and diversity management. More detailed metrics can also be obtained from SHRM surveys of human capital benchmarks. Learning what organizations are doing may not always be especially informative for determining the effectiveness of these policies and procedures for the organization. Many practices that work in one context may not be as useful in another context, and the research on HR bundling suggests that policies need to be implemented into a comprehensive system rather than just implementing individual practices in isolation. So, although it is helpful to have some benchmark information, any new policies should be investigated for how well they are working in one's own organization.

Over the course of the staffing process it is possible to develop quantitative indicators that show how effectively and efficiently the staffing system is operating. For example, how many applicants does a given vacancy attract, on average? Or, what percentage of job offers are accepted? What is the average number of days it takes to fill a vacancy? What percentage of new hires remain with the organization for one year posthire? Answers to such questions can be determined by tracking and analyzing applicant flows through the staffing pipeline.

In Exhibit 13.9 we offer some suggestions for the types of financial and process data that might be most useful for assessing the effectiveness of staffing systems overall. These suggestions are based on established research on best practices in the field. Following from several other writers, we divided the outcomes into four key categories: cost, timeliness, outcomes, and reactions. For each category, we present some representative metrics that might be useful, although there are many other measurable outcomes that might be relevant depending on an organization's goals.

Exhibit 13.10 shows the required layout for this tracking and analysis, as well as some staffing process results that may be easily calculated. In the upper part of the exhibit (A), the steps in the staffing process start with announcement of a vacancy and run through a sequential flow of selection, job offer, offer acceptance, start as new hire, and retention. Also shown is a timeline, in average number of days, for completion of each step. For illustration purposes, it is assumed that there are 25 vacancies that have been filled and that these vacancies attracted 1,000 applicants who then proceeded through the staffing process. Ultimately, all 25 vacancies were filled, and these new hires were then tracked to see how many of them remained with the organization for six months and one year posthire.

At the bottom of Exhibit 13.10 (B) are staffing process results indicators, also referred to as metrics, along with their calculations using data from the example. The first indicator is applicants per vacancy, which averaged 40. This is an indication of

---

EXHIBIT 13.9   Common Staffing Metrics

	Cost	**Timeliness**	**Outcomes**	**Reactions**
Staffing system	Staffing budget Staffing-to-employee ratios Staffing expenses for full-time equivalents (FTEs)	Time to respond to requests	Evaluation of employee readiness for strategic goals	Communication Satisfaction with services provided
Recruiting	Advertising expenses Cost per applicant	Recruits per week	Number of recruits	Applicant quality
Selection	Test costs per candidate Interview expenses Cost per candidate	Time to hire Days to fill	Competence Workforce diversity	Candidate quality Satisfaction with tests
Final match	Training costs per hire Cost per hire	Days to start Time to perform	Number of positions filled Job performance	New employee satisfaction
Retention	Exit interview expenses Replacement costs	Timely response to external offers	Voluntary separation rate Involuntary separation rate	Employee job satisfaction

the effectiveness of recruitment activities to attract people to the organization. The second indicator is the yield ratio; it indicates the percentage of people who moved on to one or more of the next steps in the staffing process. For example, the percentage of applicants who became candidates is 20%; the percentage of job offers accepted is 83.3%. The third indicator, time lapse (or cycle time), shows the average amount of time lapsed between each step in the staffing process. It can be seen that the average days to fill a vacancy is 44. The final indicator is retention rate; for the new hires it can be seen that the six-month retention rate is 80%, and the one-year rate fell to 52%.

These types of metrics are very useful barometers for gauging the pulse of the staffing flow. They have an objective, "bottom-line" nature that can be readily communicated to managers and others in the organization. These types of data are also very useful for comparative purposes. For example, the relative effectiveness and efficiency of staffing systems in two different units of the organization could be assessed by comparing their respective yield ratios and so forth. Another comparison could be the same staffing system compared to itself over time. Such time-based comparisons are useful for tracking trends in effectiveness and efficiency. These comparisons are also used to help judge how well changes in staffing practices have actually worked to improve staffing process performance.

EXHIBIT 13.10 **Evaluation of Staffing Process and Results: Example**

A. Staffing Process Example
No. of vacancies filled = 25

Process step	Vacancy announced (1)	Applicants (2)	Candidates (3)	Finalists (4)	Offer receiver (5)	Offer acceptance (6)	Start as new hire (7)	On the job Six months (8)	One Year (9)
No. of people	0	1,000	200	125	30	25	25	20	13
Process time Avg. no. of days	0	14	21	28	35	42	44		

B. Staffing Process Results

Applicants/Vacancy = 1,000/25 = 40

Yield ratio: candidates/applicant = 20%; new hires/applicant = 2.5%; offers accepted/received = 83.3%

Time lapse: avg. days to offer = 35; avg. days to start = 44 (cycle time)

Retention rate: $\dfrac{\text{on job six months}}{\text{new hires}}$ = 80% for six months; $\dfrac{\text{on job one year}}{\text{new hires}}$ = 52% for first year

For example, Mirage Resorts in Las Vegas was going to conduct a mass, one-time staffing process to hire 9,600 employees when it opened its luxury resort, the Bellagio. Mirage Resorts' previous mass hire had taken nine months; it sought to design a new staffing process that would shorten the staffing time and cost. A new, computerized staffing process was developed that accomplished the staffing objective within five-and-one-half months, at a cost savings of $600,000. The system operated as follows: From a newspaper help-wanted ad, interested applicants called a toll-free number to schedule an appointment to apply in person. Up to 1,200 applicants daily completed an application on a computer screen, then went to an HR checkout desk to make sure they had completed the application appropriately and to have their appearance and behavior noted. Applicants were placed in a database, which was searched by individual hiring departments. Viable candidates were interviewed by one of 180 specially trained interviewers; interview results were fed back into the database. Background checks were then conducted, and those chosen as finalists by hiring managers in the hiring departments took a drug test. Job offers were then extended by departments, though this took up to a few months after the interview. Only 3% of the initial applicants who were favorably evaluated by Mirage withdrew somewhere along the staffing process.[20]

Increasingly, organizations are emphasizing time to fill vacancies as a key indicator of staffing effectiveness based on the reasonable assumption that the shorter the vacancy time, the less the employee contribution foregone. Vacancies in sales jobs, for example, often mean lost sales and revenue generation, so shortening the time to fill means lessening the revenue foregone. Reducing time to fill vacancies has led organizations to develop "speed hiring" and continuous hiring programs, which in turn causes them to redesign their staffing systems to eliminate any excessive delays or bottlenecks in the process.[21]

Finally, surveys of organizational practice in calculating staffing metrics should be consulted to learn about the many nuances involved.[22]

Calculating Staffing Metrics

We have already outlined methods for assessing the costs and benefits of staffing policies and procedures. Below we present more specific methods for calculating these metrics.[23] Number of positions filled is a straightforward count of the number of individuals who accepted positions during the fiscal year. These data are collected for both internal and external candidates. Time-to-fill openings is estimated by assessing the number of days it takes for a job requisition to result in a job acceptance by a candidate. Hiring cost estimates are the sum of advertising, agency fees, employee referrals, travel costs for applicants and staff, relocation costs, and pay and benefits for recruiters. Hiring cost estimates are often indexed by dividing by the number of positions filled. As we noted in the chapter on recruiting, it is possible to subdivide these cost estimates in a number of ways to get a better idea of which portions of the staffing process are comparatively more expensive.

Turnover rates are also often used as staffing metrics. The annual turnover rate is estimated by dividing the number of separations per month by the average number of individuals employed each month and then taking the sum of these average month rates. Turnover rates are often differentiated based on whether they represent voluntary or involuntary turnover, which we cover in the next chapter. Other cost data, and how to calculate them, are also available.[24]

Another staffing cost metric is the staffing cost or efficiency ratio.[25] It takes into account that recruiting applicants for higher compensation level jobs might cost more due to such costs as executive search fees, recruitment advertising, relocation, and so forth. The formula for the staffing cost ratio is total staffing cost ratio = total staffing costs/total compensation recruited. Though the cost per hire may be greater for one job category than for another job category, their staffing cost ratios may be the same. This is illustrated in Exhibit 13.11. It can be seen that if just cost per hire is considered, it appears that recruitment for the repair job is more effective than for the sales manager job. But by also calculating the staffing cost ratio, it can be seen that recruitment is at the same level of efficiency for both job categories—that is, recruitment for each source is incurring the same relative expense to "bring in" the same amount of compensation via new hires.

Customer Satisfaction

Staffing systems, by their very nature, influence users of them. Such users can be thought of as customers of the system. Two of the key customers are managers and job applicants. Managers look to the staffing system to provide them the right numbers and types of new hires to meet their own staffing needs. Job applicants expect the staffing system to recruit, select, and make employment decisions about them in ways that are fair and legal. For both sets of customers, therefore, it is important to know how satisfied they are with the staffing systems that serve them. Detection of positive satisfaction can reinforce the usage of current staffing practices. Discovering areas of dissatisfaction, alternately, may serve as a trigger for needed changes in the staffing system and help pinpoint the nature of those changes.

EXHIBIT 13.11 Comparison of Cost per Hire and Staffing Cost Ratio

Job Category	New Hires	Staffing Cost	Cost per Hire	Compensation per Hire	Staffing Cost Ratio
Repair	500	$500,000	$1,000	$20,000	5%
Sales Manager	100	$300,000	$3,000	$60,000	5%

Customer satisfaction with staffing systems is of fairly recent origin as an organizational concern. Rarely in the past were managers and job applicants even thought of as customers, and rarer yet were systematic attempts made to measure their customer satisfaction as a way of evaluating the effectiveness of staffing systems. Recently, that has begun to change. Described next are examples of measures of customer satisfaction for managers and for job applicants.

Managers

The state of Wisconsin Department of Employment Relations houses the Division of Merit Recruitment and Selection (DMRS), which is the central agency responsible for staffing the state government. Annually, it helps the 40 state agencies to fill about 4,000 vacancies through hiring and promoting. Managers within these agencies, thus, are customers of the DMRS and its staffing systems.

To help identify and guide needed staffing system improvements, the DMRS decided to develop a survey measure of managers' satisfaction with staffing services. Through the use of focus groups, managers' input on the content of the survey was solicited. The final survey had 53 items on it, grouped into five areas: communication, timeliness, candidate quality, test quality, and service focus. Examples of the survey items are shown in Exhibit 13.12.

The survey was administered via internal mail to 645 line and HR managers throughout the agencies. Statistical analyses provided favorable psychometric evidence supporting usage of the survey. Survey results served as a key input to implementation of several initiatives to improve staffing service delivery. These initiatives led to increases in the speed of filling vacancies, elimination of paperwork, higher reported quality of job applicants, and positive applicant reactions to the staffing process.[26]

Job Applicants

As with managers, it is best to develop a tailor-made survey for job applicants, one that reflects the specific characteristics of the staffing system being used and the types of contacts and experiences job applicants will have with it. Consultation of a staffing flowchart (Exhibit 13.7) would be helpful in this regard. If possible, the survey should be given to three different applicant groups: candidates who were rejected, candidates who accepted a job offer, and candidates who declined a job offer. Examples of questions that might be included on the survey are in Exhibit 13.13. Separate analysis of responses from each group should be done. Online assistance in survey design, survey administration, and analysis of results is available from SurveyMonkey (*www.surveymonkey.com*) and Zoomerang (*www.zoomerang.com*). Many Web-based recruiting systems provide applicants with surveys or open-ended text boxes where they can share their reactions to the recruiting process. Because these systems provide immediate feedback to the organization, it may be possible to make real-time improvements to a recruiting drive.

EXHIBIT 13.12 **Examples of Survey Items for Assessing Manager's Satisfaction With Staffing Services**

Communication: How well are you kept informed on the staffing process?

How satisfied are you with:

1. The clarity of instructions and explanation you receive on the staffing process
2. Your overall understanding of the steps involved in filling a vacancy
3. The amount of training you receive in order to effectively participate in the total staffing process

Timeliness: How do you feel about the speed of recruitment, examination, and selection services?

How satisfied are you with the time required to:

1. Obtain central administrative approval to begin the hiring process
2. Score oral and essay exams, achievement history questionnaires, or other procedures involving scoring by a panel of raters
3. Hire someone who has been interviewed and selected

Candidate Quality: How do you feel about the quality (required knowledges and skills) of the job candidates?

How satisfied are you with:

1. The number of people you can interview and select from
2. The quality of candidates on new register
3. Your involvement in the recruitment process

Test Quality: How do you feel about the quality of civil service exams (tests, work samples, oral board interviews, etc.)?

How satisfied are you with:

1. Your involvement in exam construction
2. The extent to which the exams assess required KSAOs
3. The extent to which the exams test for new technologies used on the job

Service Focus: To what extent do you believe your personnel/staffing representatives are committed to providing high-quality service?

How satisfied are you with:

1. The accessibility of a staffing person
2. The expertise and competence of the staffing representative
3. Responses to your particular work unit's needs

SOURCE: H. G. Heneman III, D. L. Huett, R. J. Lavigna, and D. Ogsten, "Assessing Managers' Satisfaction With Staffing Services," *Personnel Psychology*, 1995, 48, pp. 170–173. (c) *Personnel Psychology*, 1995. Used with permission.

EXHIBIT 13.13   Sample Job Applicant's Satisfaction Survey Questionnaire

1. What prompted you to apply to Organization X?

    ___ company Web site   ___ advertisement   ___ employee referral
    ___ job fair   ___ campus recruitment   ___ other (indicate)

2. Was the information you got from this source valuable?

    ___ very   ___ somewhat   ___ no

3. Please indicate your level of agreement with each of the following on the 1– 5 scale, where 1 = strongly disagree and 5 = strongly agree

	strongly disagree				strongly agree
The applicant process was easy to use.	1	2	3	4	5
I received a prompt response to my application.	1	2	3	4	5
My first interview was promptly scheduled.	1	2	3	4	5
My first interview covered all my qualifications.	1	2	3	4	5
The test I took was relevant to the job.	1	2	3	4	5
The test process was fair.	1	2	3	4	5
I received prompt feedback about my test scores.	1	2	3	4	5
I always knew where I stood in the selection process.	1	2	3	4	5
My interview with the hiring manager was thorough.	1	2	3	4	5
The hiring manager represented Organization X well.	1	2	3	4	5
I was treated honestly and openly.	1	2	3	4	5
Overall, I am satisfied with the selection process.	1	2	3	4	5
I would recommend Organization X to others as a place to work.	1	2	3	4	5

4. Please describe what you liked most about your experience seeking a job with Organization X.

5. Please describe what you liked least about your experience seeking a job with Organization X.

LEGAL ISSUES

Record Keeping and Privacy

In staffing systems, substantial information is generated, used, recorded, and disclosed. There are numerous legal constraints and requirements surrounding staffing information. These pertain to record keeping and privacy concerns.

Record Keeping

A wide range of information is created by the organization during staffing and other HR activities. Examples include personal data (name, address, date of birth, dependents, etc.), KSAO information (application blank, references, test scores, etc.), medical information, performance appraisal and promotability assessments, and changes in employment status (promotion, transfers, etc.). Why should records of such information be created?

Basically, records should be created and maintained for two major legal purposes in staffing. First, they are necessary for legal compliance. Federal, state, and local laws specify what information should be kept, and for how long. Second, having records allows the organization to provide documentation to justify staffing decisions or to defend these decisions against legal challenge. For example, performance appraisal and promotability assessments might be used to explain to employees why they were or were not promoted. Or, these same records might be used as evidence in a legal proceeding to show that promotion decisions were job related and unbiased.

It is strongly recommended that two sets of records be created. These records can be kept in paper or electronic form. The first set should be the individual employee's personnel file. It should comprise only documents that relate directly to the job and the employee's performance of it. To determine which documents to place in the personnel file, ask if it is a document on which the organization could legally base an employment decision. If the answer is "no," "probably no," or "unsure," the document should not be placed in the employee's personnel file. The second set of records should contain documents that cannot be used in staffing decisions. Examples include documents pertaining to medical information (both physical and mental), equal employment opportunity (e.g., information about protected characteristics such as age, sex, religion, race, color, national origin, and disability), and information about authorization to work (e.g., I-9 forms).[27]

Any document that is to be placed in an employee's personnel file should be reviewed before it becomes part of that record. Examine the document for incomplete, inaccurate, or misleading information, as well as potentially damaging notations or comments about the employee. All such information should be completed, corrected, explained, or, if necessary, eliminated. Remember that any document in the personnel file is a potential court exhibit that may work either for or against the employer's defense of a legal challenge.[28]

Federal EEO/AA laws contain general record-keeping requirements. Though the requirements vary somewhat from law to law, major subject areas for which records are to be kept (if created) are shown in Exhibit 13.14. Requirements by the Office of Federal Contract Compliance Programs (OFCCP) are broader than those shown, and records must be maintained for at least two years.

The various laws also have requirements about length of retention of records. As a general rule, most records must be kept for a minimum of one year from the date a document is made or a staffing action is taken, whichever is later. Exceptions to the one-year requirements all provide for even longer retention periods. If a charge of discrimination is filed, the records must be retained until the matter is finally resolved.

Privacy Concerns

The organization must observe legal requirements governing employees' and others' access to information in personnel files, as well as guard against unwarranted disclosure of the information to third-party requesters (e.g., other employers) of it. Information access and disclosure matters raise privacy concerns under both constitutional and statutory law.[29]

Several (not all) states have laws guaranteeing employees reasonable access to their personnel files. The laws generally allow the employee to review and copy pertinent documents; some documents such as letters of reference or promotion plans for the person may be excluded from access. The employee may also have a right to seek to correct erroneous information in the file. Where there is no state law permitting access, employees are usually allowed access to their personnel file only if the organization has a policy permitting it. Disclosure of information in

---

EXHIBIT 13.14   Federal Record-Keeping Requirements

Records that should be kept include the following:

- Applications for employment (hire, promote, transfer)
- Reasons for refusal to hire, promote, transfer
- Tests and test scores, plus other KSAO information
- Job orders submitted to labor unions and employment agencies
- Medical exam results
- Advertisements or other notices to the public or employees about job openings and promotion opportunities
- Requests for reasonable accommodation
- Impact of staffing decisions on protected groups (adverse impact statistics)
- Records related to filing of a discrimination charge

All records should be kept for a minimum of one year.

personnel files to third parties is often regulated as well, requiring such procedures as employees' written consent for disclosure.

At the federal level, numerous laws and regulations restrict access to and disclosure of employee personnel information. An example here is the Americans With Disabilities Act (ADA) and its provisions regarding the confidentiality of medical information. There is, however, no general federal privacy law covering private employees. Public employees' privacy rights are protected by the Privacy Act of 1974.

Reports

Under the Civil Rights Act and Affirmative Action Programs regulations, private employers with more than 100 employees (50 for federal contractors) are required to file an annual report with the Equal Employment Opportunity Commission (EEOC). The basis of the report is the revised EEO-1 form, especially the section requesting employment data, shown in Exhibit 13.15.[30] Data are to be reported for combinations of job categories and race/ethnicity classifications. The data may be gathered from organization records, visual inspection, or a self-report. Detailed instructions and questions and answers are available online (*www.eeoc.gov*). They cover issues such as definitions of job categories and race/ethnicity classification, and data collection. While the report is to be included in the federal contractor's affirmative action plan (AAP), the OFCCP has not yet provided guidance on how to incorporate the data from the revised EEO-1 form into availability determination, establishment of placement goals, identification of problem areas, or development of action-oriented programs (see Chapter 3). The EEOC has moved to a Web-based system for reporting and will now accept paper forms only if Internet access is not available to an employer. This method provides several advantages for employers. Electronic filing can be more efficient because employers do not need to re-enter data from previous years that have not changed. The Web-based system also allows employers to retrieve the full information from these previous reports, which facilitates the examination of trends.

Audits

It is highly desirable to periodically conduct audits or reviews of the organization's degree of compliance with laws and regulations pertaining to staffing. The audit forces the organization to study and specify what in fact its staffing practices are and to compare these current practices against legally desirable and required practices. Results can be used to identify potential legal trouble spots and to map out changes in staffing practices that will serve to minimize potential liability and reduce the risk of lawsuits being filed against the organization. Note that development of AAPs and reports includes a large audit and review component. They

EXHIBIT 13.15 Employer Information Report EEO-1 Form

Number of Employees
(Report employees in only one category)

Job Categories		Hispanic or Latino		Race/Ethnicity — Not-Hispanic or Latino												Total Col A-N
				Male						Female						
		Male	Female	White	Black or African American	Native Hawaiian or other Pacific Islander	Asian	American Indian or Alaska Native	Two or more races	White	Black or African American	Native Hawaiian or other Pacific Islander	Asian	American Indian or Alaska Native	Two or more races	
		A	B	C	D	E	F	G	H	I	J	K	L	M	N	O
Executive/Senior Level Officials and Managers	1.1															
First/Mid-Level Officials and Managers	1.2															
Professionals	2															
Technicians	3															
Sales Workers	4															
Administrative Support Workers	5															
Craft Workers	6															
Operatives	7															
Laborers and Helpers	8															
Service Workers	9															
TOTAL	10															
PREVIOUS YEAR TOTAL	11															

do not, however, cover the entire legal spectrum of staffing practices, nor do they require sufficient depth of analysis of staffing practices in some areas. For these reasons, AAPs and reports are not sufficient as legal audits, though they are immensely important and useful inputs to a legal audit.

The audit could be conducted by the organization's own legal counsel. Alternately, the HR department might first conduct a self-audit, then review its findings with legal counsel. Conducting an audit after involvement in employment litigation is also recommended.[31]

Training for Managers and Employees

Training for managers and employees in employment law and compliance requirements is not only a sound practice, but increasingly a defense point for the organization in employment litigation. The following statement illustrates this: "Recent judicial and agency activity make clear that training is no longer a discretionary HR activity—it is essential. The question is not whether your company is going to provide it, but how long will it have to suffer the costly consequences of neglect. A carefully crafted, effectively executed, methodically measured, and frequently fine-tuned employment practices training program for managers and employees is a powerful component of a strategic HRD (human resource development) plan that aligns vital corporate values with daily practices. The costs of neglect are serious. The benefits are compelling and fundamental to long-term success. . . . Adequate, effective, and regularly scheduled employment law and practices training is now the rule, not the exception."[32] While this need for training arose from within the realm of sexual harassment prevention, it has gradually encompassed all forms of discrimination, including that which might occur in staffing the organization.

Though the requirements for employment law training are still developing, it appears as though there are several desirable components to be incorporated into it: (1) the training should be for all members of the organization; (2) basic harassment and discrimination training should be given immediately to new employees, managers should receive additional training, and refresher training should occur periodically and when special circumstances arise, such as a significant change in policy or practice; (3) the trainers should have special expertise in employment law and practice; (4) the training content should be substantive and cover EEO practices in several staffing areas—such as recruitment, hiring, succession planning, promotion—as pertains to the numerous EEO laws and regulations; training in other areas of HR, such as compensation and benefits, should also be provided; and (5) the training materials should also be substantive, incorporate the organization's specific harassment and discrimination policies, and allow for both information presentation and active practice by the participants.[33] Trainees should learn which EEO actions they can implement on their own and which actions should be referred to the HR department. Finally, the training should be matched with diversity initiatives to avoid an overly legalistic perspective.[34]

Dispute Resolution

Employment laws and regulations naturally lead to claims of their violation by job applicants and employees. If the claim is filed with an external agency, such as the EEOC, the dispute resolution procedures described in Chapter 2 (Laws and Regulations) are applied. In the case of the EEOC, by providing mediation as an alternative dispute resolution (ADR) procedure (*www.eeoc.gov*), it seeks to settle disputes quickly and without formal investigation and litigation. The EEOC provides, without fee, a trained mediator to help the employer and the job applicant (or employee) reconcile their differences and reach a satisfactory resolution. The process is confidential, any records or notes are destroyed at its conclusion, and nothing that is revealed may be used subsequently in investigation or litigation should the dispute not be resolved. About 70% of the disputes are resolved through mediation. However, employers are reluctant to participate in mediation—only about 30% accept an offer of mediation, compared to about 83% of applicants or employees.[35]

For claims of discrimination (or other grievances) made internally, the organization will likely offer some form of ADR to resolve the dispute.[36] Exhibit 13.16 shows the numerous approaches to ADR that might be used. Research shows that most organizations do in fact use one or more of these procedures, with negotiation and fact finding being the most prevalent by far. Peer review and mediation are used substantially less, and arbitration is the least used.[37]

Despite the attraction of ADR as a replacement for more formal enforcement mechanisms, such as filing complaints with enforcement agencies and litigation, a major stumbling block to its adoption occurs if individuals are required to use the

EXHIBIT 13.16 Alternative Dispute Resolution Approaches

Approach	Description
Negotiation	Employer and employee discuss complaint with goal of resolving complaint.
Fact finding	A neutral person, from inside or outside the organization, investigates a complaint and develops findings that may be the basis for resolving the complaint.
Peer review	A panel of employees and managers work together to resolve the complaint.
Mediation	A neutral person (mediator) from within or outside the organization helps the parties negotiate a mutually acceptable agreement. Mediator is trained in mediation methods. Settlement is not imposed.
Arbitration	A neutral person (arbitrator) from within or outside the organization conducts formal hearing and issues a decision that is binding on the parties.

ADR system and forgo the right to use other mechanisms. Such a possibility exists when new hires are required as part of an employment contract to sign a provision waiving their protected rights under civil rights laws to file or participate in a proceeding against the organization and to instead use only a specified ADR system to resolve complaints. The EEOC has issued guidance indicating that such waiver provisions are null and void, and that their existence cannot stop the EEOC from enforcing the law.[38] So the EEOC may pursue a discrimination claim even when there is an ADR waiver signed by the employee.

The Special Case of Arbitration

With arbitration as the ADR procedure, the employer and the job applicant (or employee) agree in advance to submit their dispute to a neutral third-party arbitrator, who will issue a final and binding decision. Such arbitration agreements usually include statutory discrimination claims, meaning that the employee agrees to not pursue charges of discrimination against the employer by any means (e.g., lawsuit) except arbitration. The courts have ruled that such arbitration agreements generally are legally permissible and enforceable. However, such agreements do not serve as a bar to pursuit by the EEOC of a discrimination claim seeking victim-specific relief.

If the organization decides to require mandatory arbitration agreements from job applicants and employees, it should be aware that there are many specific, suggested standards that the arbitration agreement and process must meet in order to be enforceable.[39] For example, the agreement must be "knowing and voluntary," meaning that it is clearly written, obvious as to purpose, and presented to the employee as a separate document for a signature. Examples of other suggested standards include the following:

- The arbitrator must be a neutral party.
- The process should provide for more than minimal discovery (presentation of evidence).
- The same remedies as permitted by the law should be allowed.
- The employee should have the right to hire an attorney and the employer should reimburse the employee a portion of attorney's fees.
- The employee should not have to bear excessive responsibility for the cost of the arbitrator.
- The types of claims (e.g., sex discrimination, retaliation) subject to arbitration should be indicated.
- There should be a written award issued by the arbitrator.

The above points are complex and only illustrative of all of the issues. Because of this, legal counsel should be sought prior to use of arbitration agreements. In addition, it should be noted that arbitration agreements, the arbitration process, and reasons for it must be carefully explained to employees in order to help ensure employee understanding and acceptance.

SUMMARY

The multiple and complex set of activities collectively known as a staffing system must be integrated and coordinated throughout the organization. Such management of the staffing system requires both careful administration and evaluation, as well as compliance with legal mandates.

To manage the staffing system, the usual organizational arrangement in all but very small organizations is to create an identifiable staffing or employment function and place it within the HR department. That function then manages the staffing system at the corporate and/or plant and office level. Numerous types of jobs, both specialist and generalist, are found within the staffing function. Entry into these jobs, and movement among them, is very fluid and does not follow any set career mobility path.

The myriad staffing activities require staffing policies to establish general staffing principles and procedures to guide the conduct of those activities. Lack of clear policies and procedures can lead to misguided and inconsistent staffing practices, as well as potentially illegal ones. Staffing technology can help achieve these consistencies and aid in improving staffing system efficiency. Electronic systems are increasingly being used to conduct a wide range of staffing tasks; they have a mixed bag of advantages and disadvantages. Outsourcing of staffing activities is also being experimented with as a way of improving staffing system operation and results.

Evaluation of the effectiveness of the staffing system should proceed along several fronts. First is assessment of the staffing system from a process perspective. Here, it is desirable to examine the degree of standardization (consistency) of the process, as well as a staffing flowchart in order to identify deviations in staffing practice and bottlenecks. The results of the process according to indicators such as yield ratios and time lapse (cycle time), along with the costs of staffing system operation, should also be estimated. Finally, the organization should consider assessing the satisfaction of staffing system users, such as managers and job applicants.

Various laws require maintenance of numerous records and protection of privacy. It is desirable to periodically conduct an actual legal audit of all the organization's staffing activities. This will help identify potential legal trouble spots that require attention. Employment law training for managers and employees is increasingly necessary. Methods for addressing employment disputes, known as ADRs, should be explored.

DISCUSSION QUESTIONS

1. What are the advantages of having a centralized staffing function, as opposed to letting each manager be totally responsible for all staffing activities in his or her unit?
2. What are examples of staffing tasks and activities that cannot or should not be simply delegated to a staffing information system for their conduct?
3. What would be the advantages and disadvantages of outsourcing the entire staffing system to a vendor?
4. In developing a report on the effectiveness of the staffing process being conducted for entry-level jobs, what factors would you address and why?
5. How would you try to get individual managers to be more aware of the legal requirements of staffing systems and to take steps to ensure that they themselves engage in legal staffing actions?

ETHICAL ISSUES

1. It has been suggested that the use of staffing technology and software is wrong because it dehumanizes the staffing experience, making it nothing but a mechanical process that treats applicants like digital widgets. Evaluate this assertion.
2. Since there are no standard ways of creating staffing process results and cost metrics, is there a need for some sort of oversight of how these data are calculated, reported, and used within the organization? Explain.

APPLICATIONS

Learning About Jobs in Staffing

The purpose of this application is to have you learn in detail about a particular job in staffing currently being performed by an individual. The individual could be a staffing job holder in the HR department of a company or public agency (state or local government), a nonprofit agency, a staffing firm, an employment agency, a consulting firm, or the state employment (job) service. The individual may perform staffing tasks full time, such as a recruiter, interviewer, counselor, employment representative, or employment manager. Or, the individual may perform staffing duties as part of the job, such as the HR manager in a small company or an HR generalist in a specific plant or site.

Contact the job holder and arrange for an interview with that person. Explain that the purpose of the interview is for you to learn about the person's job in terms of job requirements (tasks and KSAOs) and job rewards (both extrinsic and intrinsic). To prepare for the interview, review the examples of job descriptions for staffing jobs in Exhibit 13.2 and 13.3, obtain any information you can about the organization, and then develop a set of questions that you will ask the job holder. Either before or at the interview, be sure to obtain a copy of the job holder's job description if one is available. Based on the written and interview information, prepare a report of your investigation. The report should cover the following:

1. The organization's products and services, size, and staffing (employment) function
2. The job holder's job title, and why you chose that person's job to study
3. A summary of the tasks performed by the job holder and the KSAOs necessary for the job
4. A summary of the extrinsic and intrinsic rewards received by the job holder
5. Unique characteristics of the job that you did not expect to be a part of the job

Evaluating Staffing Process Results

The Keepon Trucking Company (KTC) is a manufacturer of custom-built trucks. It does not manufacture any particular truck lines, styles, or models. Rather, it builds trucks to customers' specifications; these trucks are used for specialty purposes such as snow removal, log hauling, and military cargo hauling. One year ago KTC received a new, large order that would take three years to complete and required the external hiring of 100 new assemblers. To staff this particular job, the HR department manager of nonexempt employment hurriedly developed and implemented a special staffing process for filling these new vacancies. Applicants were recruited from three different sources: newspaper ads, employee referrals, and a local employment agency. All applicants generated by these methods were subjected to a common selection and decision-making process. All offer receivers were given the same terms and conditions in their job offer letters and were told there was no room for any negotiation. All vacancies were eventually filled.

After the first year of the contract, the manager of nonexempt employment, Dexter Williams, decided to pull together some data in an attempt to determine how well the staffing process for the assembler jobs had worked. Since he had not originally planned on doing any evaluation, Dexter was able to retrieve only the following data to help him with his evaluation:

Exhibit
Staffing Data for Filling the Job of Assembler

Method	Applicants	Offer receivers	Start as new hires	Remaining at six months
Newspaper ads				
No. apps.	300	70	50	35
Avg. no. days	30	30	10	
Employee referral				
No. apps.	60	30	30	27
Avg. no. days	20	10	10	
Employment agency				
No. apps.	400	20	20	8
Avg. no. days	40	20	10	

1. Determine the yield ratios (offer receivers/applicants, new hires/applicants), time lapse or cycle times (days to offer, days to start), and retention rates associated with each recruitment source.
2. What is the relative effectiveness of the three sources in terms of yield ratios, cycle times, and retention rates?
3. What are possible reasons for the fact that the three sources differ in their relative effectiveness?
4. What would you recommend that Dexter do differently in the future to improve his evaluation of the staffing process?

ENDNOTES

1. H. G. Heneman III and R. A. Berkley, "Applicant Attraction Practices and Outcomes Among Small Businesses," *Journal of Small Business Management,* Jan. 1999, pp. 53–74.
2. E. E. Lawler III and A. A. Mohrman, *Creating a Strategic Human Resources Organization* (Stanford, CA: Stanford University Press, 2003), pp. 15–20.
3. M. Hammers, "Sun Trust Bank Combines 28 Recruiting and Screening Systems Into One," Dec. 3, 2003 (*www.workforce.com*).
4. Lawler and Mohrman, *Creating a Strategic Human Resources Organization,* p. 33.
5. J. Vocino, "HR Compensation Continues to Rise," *HR Magazine,* Nov. 2004, pp. 72–88.
6. Mercer Human Resource Consulting, *Transforming HR for Business Results* (New York: author, 2004), p. 9.
7. A. Rosenthal, "Hiring Edge," *Human Resource Executive,* Apr. 2000, pp. 96–98.
8. J. S. Arthur, "Title Wave," *Human Resource Executive,* Oct. 2000, pp. 115–118; K. J. Dunham, "Tapping Talent," *Wall Street Journal,* Apr. 10, 2001, p. B14.

9. J. A. Colquitt, "On the Dimensionality of Organizational Justice: A Construct Validation of a Measure," *Journal of Applied Psychology,* 2001, 86, pp. 386–400; J. A. Colquitt, D. E. Conlon, M. J. Wesson, C. O. Porter, and N. K. Yee, "Justice at the Millennium: A Meta-Analytic Review of 25 Years of Organizational Justice Research," *Journal of Applied Psychology,* 2001, 86, pp. 425–445.

10. R. E. Ployhart and A. M. Ryan, "Toward an Explanation of Applicant Reactions: An Examination of Organizational Justice and Attribution Frameworks," *Organizational Behavior and Human Decision Processes,* 1997, 72, pp. 308–335; D. M. Truxillo, T. N. Bauer, M. A. Campion, and M. E. Paronto, "Selection Fairness Information and Applicant Reactions: A Longitudinal Field Study," *Journal of Applied Psychology,* 2002, 87, pp. 1020–1031; T. N. Bauer, D. M. Truxillo, R. J. Sanchez, J. Craig, P. Ferrara, and M. A. Campion, "Applicant Reactions to Selection: Development of the Selection Procedural Justice Scale (SPJS)," *Personnel Psychology,* 2001, 54, pp. 387–419; S. W. Gilliland, "Effects of Procedural and Distributive Justice on Reactions to a Selection System," *Journal of Applied Psychology,* 1994, 79, pp. 691–701; C. W. Wanberg, L. W. Bunce, and M. B. Gavin, "Perceived Fairness of Layoffs Among Individuals Who Have Been Laid Off: A Longitudinal Study," *Personnel Psychology,* 1999, 52, pp. 59–84; J. Brockner, S. L. Grover, and M. D. Blonder, "Predictors of Survivors' Job Investment Following Layoffs: A Field Study," *Journal of Applied Psychology,* 1988, 73, pp. 436–442.

11. *BrassRing,* "Measuring the Value of a Talent Management System," Jan. 7, 2005 (*www.brassring. com*); P. Buckley, K. Minette, D. Joy, and J. Michaels, "The Use of an Automated Employment Recruiting and Screening System for Temporary Professional Employees: A Case Study," *Human Resource Management,* 2004, 43, pp. 233–241; D. Chapman and J. Webster, "The Use of Technologies in the Recruiting, Screening, and Selection Processes for Job Candidates," *International Journal of Selection and Assessment,* 2003, 11, pp. 113–120; S. Greengard, "Seven Myths About Recruiting Technology," *Workforce,* Aug. 10, 2004 (*www.workforce.com*); J. W. Jones and K. D. Dages, "Technology Trends in Staffing and Assessment, A Practical Note," *International Journal of Selection and Assessment,* 2003, 11, pp. 247–252; B. Roberts, "A Sure Bet," *HR Magazine,* Aug. 2004, pp. 115–119.

12. M. Frase-Blunt, "A Recruiting Spigot," *HR Magazine*, Apr. 2003, pp. 71–79.

13. WorldatWork, *The State of Human Resources Outsourcing: 2004–2005* (Scottsdale, AZ: author, 2005); J. Koch, "Why HR Is Turning to Outsourcing," *Personnel Journal,* Sept. 1993, 72, pp. 92–101; E. Zimmerman, "B of A and Big-Time Outsourcing," *Workforce*, Apr. 2001, pp. 51–54; B. E. Rosenthal, "How to Outsource Everything in HR," *SHRM HR Outsourcing Library,* Aug., 2006 (*www.shrm.org*).

14. B. S. Klaas, J. McClendon, T. Gainey, and H. Yang, *HR Outsourcing in Small and Medium Enterprises: A Field Study of the Use and Impact of Professional Employer Organizations* (Alexandria, VA: Society for Human Resource Management Foundation, 2004).

15. B. Siegel, "Outsourced Recruiting," in N. C. Burkholder, P. J. Edwards, and L. Sartain (eds.), *On Staffing* (Hoboken, NJ: Wiley, 2004), pp. 116–132.

16. J. Harney, "Integrating Payroll With Benefits Administration Transforms HR for Charmant," *Outsourcing Journal,* Dec. 2007 (*www.outsourcing-journal.com/dec2007-hr.html*).

17. P. Babcock, "Slicing Off Pieces of HR," *HR Magazine,* July 2004, pp. 71–76; J. C. Berkshire, "Seeking Full Partnership," *HR Magazine,* July 2004, pp. 89–96; D. Dell, *HR Outsourcing* (New York: The Conference Board, 2004); E. Esen, *Human Resource Outsourcing* (Alexandria, VA: Society for Human Resource Management, 2004); S. Greengard, "Pulling the Plug," *Workforce Management,* July 2004, pp. 43–46; R. J. Grossman, "Sticker Shock," *HR Magazine,* July 2004, pp. 79–86; T. Starner, "Measuring Success," *Human Resource Executive,* Oct. 16, 2004, pp. 49–50.

18. S. Caudron, "Introducing the Human Capital Metrics Consortium," *Workforce Management,* Apr. 2004, p. 51; E. Zimmerman, "What Are Employees Worth?" *Workforce,* Feb. 2001, pp. 32–36; J. Fitz-enz, *The ROI of Human Capital: Measuring the Economic Value of Employee Performance* (New York: AMACOM, 2000); J. E. Edwards, J. C. Scott, and N. S. Raju, *The Human Resources Program-Evaluation Handbook* (Thousand Oaks, CA: Sage Publications, 2003); M. A. Huselid, B. E. Becker, and R. W. Beatty, *The Workforce Scorecard: Managing Human Capital to Execute Strategy* (Boston: Harvard Business School Press, 2005); Society for Human Resource Management, *SHRM Human Capital Benchmarking Study* (Alexandria, VA: author, 2007).

19. J. Sullivan, "HR's Burden of Proof," *Workforce Management,* Jan. 2007, p. 26; I. L. Goldstein and Associates, *Training and Development in Organizations* (San Francisco: Jossey-Bass, 1991).

20. E. P. Gunn, "How Mirage Resorts Sifted 75,000 Applicants to Hire 9,600 in 24 Weeks," *Fortune,* Oct. 12, 1998, p. 195.

21. L. Micco, "Lockheed Wins the Best Catches," *Employment Management Association Today,* Spring 1997, pp. 18–20; E. R. Silverman, "The Fast Track," *Human Resource Executive*, Oct. 1998, pp. 30–34.

22. L. Klutz, *Time to Fill/Time to Start: 2002 Staffing Metrics Survey* (Alexandria, VA: Society for Human Resource Management, 2003).

23. Fitz-enz, *The ROI of Human Capital: Measuring the Economic Value of Employee Performance;* Society for Human Resource Management, *SHRM Human Capital Benchmarking Study.*

24. Society for Human Resource Management, *2002 SHRM/EMA Staffing Metrics Study* (Alexandria, VA: author, 2003); Staffing.Org, *2003 Recruiting Metrics and Performance Benchmark Report* (Willow Grove, PA: author, 2003).

25. K. Burns, "Metrics Are Everything: Why, What and How to Choose," in Burkholder, Edwards, and Sartain (eds.), *On Staffing,* pp. 364–371.

26. H. G. Heneman III, D. L. Huett, R. J. Lavigna, and D. Ogsten, "Assessing Managers' Satisfaction With Staffing Service," *Personnel Psychology,* 1995, 48, pp. 163–172.

27. H. P. Coxson, "The Double-Edged Sword of Personnel Files and Employee Records," *Legal Report* (Alexandria, VA: Society for Human Resource Management, 1992); Warren Gorham Lamont, *How Long Do We Have to Keep These Records?* (Boston: author, 1993).

28. Coxson, "The Double-Edged Sword of Personnel Files and Employee Records."

29. International Personnel Management Association, "Employee Privacy and Recordkeeping—I and II," *IPMA News,* Aug. and Sept. 1998, pp. 16–18, 17–18.

30. V. J. Hoffman, "Equal Opportunity Reporting: New Requirements, New Best Practices," *Legal Report,* Society for Human Resource Management, July-Aug. 2006 (*www.shrm.org/hrresources/lrpt_published/CMS_018229.asp#P-10_0*); R. Zeidner, "EEO-1 Changes," *HR Magazine,* May 2006, pp. 61–64.

31. J. W. Janove, "It's Not Over, Even When It's Over," *HR Magazine,* Feb. 2004, pp. 123–131.

32. W. K. Turner and C. S. Thrutchley, "Employment Law and Practices Training: No Longer the Exception—It's the Rule," *Legal Report,* Society for Human Resource Management, July-Aug. 2002, p. 1.

33. S. K. Williams, "The New Law of Training," *HR Magazine,* May 2004, pp. 115–118.

34. J. A. Segal, "Unlimited Check-Writing Authority for Supervisors?" *HR Magazine,* Feb. 2007, pp. 119–124; J. C. Ramirez, "A Different Bias," *Human Resource Executive,* May 16, 2006, pp. 37–40.

35. M. Barrier, "The Mediation Disconnect," *HR Magazine,* May 2003, pp. 54–58; "EEOC's Efforts to Expand Mediation Gain Momentum" (no author), *HR Magazine,* May 2003, pp. 32–34.

36. M. W. Bennett, D. J. Polden, and H. J. Rubin, *Employment Relationships: Law and Practice* (New York: Aspen, periodically updated), pp. 13-1 to 13-33.

37. U.S. Government Printing Office, *Employment Discrimination: Most Private Sector Employers Use Alternative Dispute Resolution* (Washington, DC: author, 1995).

38. Equal Employment Opportunity Commission, *EEOC Enforcement Guidance on Non-Waivable Employee Rights Under EEOC Enforcement Statutes* (Washington, DC: author, 1997).

39. M. E. Bruno, "The Future of ADR in the Workplace," *Compensation and Benefits Review,* Nov.-Dec. 2001, pp. 46–59; C. Hirschman, "Order in the Hear," *HR Magazine,* July 2001, pp. 58–64; L. P. Postol, "To Arbitrate Employment Disputes or Not, That Is the Question," *Legal Report,* Society for Human Resource Management, Sept.-Oct. 2001, pp. 5–8.

CHAPTER FOURTEEN

Retention Management

Turnover and Its Causes
Nature of the Problem
Types of Turnover
Causes of Turnover

Analysis of Turnover
Measurement
Reasons for Leaving
Costs and Benefits

Retention Initiatives: Voluntary Turnover
Current Practices and Deciding to Act
Desirability of Leaving
Ease of Leaving
Alternatives

Retention Initiatives: Discharge
Performance Management
Progressive Discipline

Retention Initiatives: Downsizing
Weighing Advantages and Disadvantages
Staffing Levels and Quality
Alternatives to Downsizing
Employees Who Remain

Legal Issues
Separation Laws and Regulations
Performance Appraisal

Summary

Discussion Questions

Ethical Issues

Applications

Tanglewood Stores Case

R etention of employees is the final component of an overall staffing system. While some loss of employees is both inevitable and desirable, retention management seeks to ensure that the organization is able to keep enough employees with important knowledge, skill, ability, and other characteristics (KSAOs) to generate future success.

In this chapter, turnover and its causes are first discussed. Three types of turnover are identified—voluntary, discharge, and downsizing. Each type of turnover has different causes or drivers, and these are identified and discussed. Particular attention is paid to voluntary turnover and its three primary causes, namely, ease of leaving, cost of leaving, and alternatives.

Retention management must be based on a thorough analysis of the organization's turnover. The analyses discussed are measuring turnover, determining employees' reasons for leaving, and assessing the costs and benefits of turnover.

Attention then turns to retention initiatives, with the first discussion focused on ways of enhancing retention by reducing voluntary turnover. Examples of current organization practices and a decision process to follow for deciding whether to move forward with such practices are presented. This is followed by numerous examples of how to increase retention by attacking its underlying causes.

The next retention initiative discussed is that of reducing the occurrence of employee discharges. This is shown to involve use of both performance management and progressive discipline initiatives.

The final retention initiative is the matter of downsizing. Here, the first concern is with keeping a sufficiently high number and quality of employees that the organization does not go overboard, shedding so many employees that the ability to rebound is threatened. Also, there are many alternatives to downsizing that might be used. How to treat employees who survive a downsizing is also discussed.

The final topic is that of legal issues. The first issue is a complex one, reminding those responsible for staffing of the myriad laws and regulations pertaining to employee separation from the organization. The second issue is that of performance appraisal, a matter of critical importance for organizations seeking to retain their best performers.

TURNOVER AND ITS CAUSES

Nature of the Problem

The focus of this book so far has been on acquiring and deploying people in ways that contribute to organizational effectiveness. Attention now shifts to retaining employees as another part of staffing that can contribute to organizational effectiveness. Although turnover is often seen exclusively as a detriment to organizational performance, there are several positive, functional outcomes. An extremely important part of employee retention strategy and tactics thus must involve careful assessment of both retention costs and benefits and the design of retention initiatives that provide positive benefits at reasonable cost to the organization. Moreover, retention strategies and tactics must focus not only on how many employees are retained but exactly who is retained. Both within and between jobs and organization levels, some employees are "worth" more than others in terms of their contributions to job and organizational effectiveness. Another important matter for the retention agenda is thus making special efforts to retain what we call "high-value" employees.

Retention must be tackled realistically, however, since some amount of employee turnover is simply inevitable.[1] People constantly move out of organizations voluntarily, and organizations shed employees as well. For example, for employees between the ages of 18 and 34, the Department of Labor estimates that (1) the median number of years they have been with their current employer (called tenure) is 3–5 years, and (2) they have held an average of 9.2 jobs. While job-hopping decreases and median tenure increases with age, some amount of turnover persists throughout workers' careers. In some industries, high voluntary turnover is a continual fact of life and cost of doing business. Turnover among sit-down restaurant managers, for example, hovers around 50% annually year after year. It is not clear that even costly retention initiatives, such as substantial pay level increases or converting managers to franchisees, can reduce this turnover. A final example is that in 2000 the Department of Labor estimates there were over 5,500 mass layoffs (those involving 50 or more employees), creating over one million unemployed workers. This was a relatively low number of mass layoffs due to generally favorable economic conditions that year.

When people voluntarily leave the organization, they do so for a variety of reasons, only some of which are potentially avoidable (controllable) by the organization. Sound retention management thus must be based on a gathering and analysis of employees' reasons for leaving. Specific retention initiatives then must be tailor-made to address these reasons and hopefully neutralize them and take them "out of play," but in a cost-effective way. Against this backdrop we now turn to a more detailed discussion of types of turnover and their causes.

Types of Turnover

There are many different types of employee turnover. Exhibit 14.1 provides a basic classification of these types.[2] It can be seen that turnover is either voluntary, being initiated by the employee, or involuntary, being initiated by the organization.

Voluntary

Voluntary turnover, in turn, is broken down into avoidable and unavoidable turnover. Avoidable turnover is that which potentially could have been prevented by certain organization actions, such as a pay raise or a new job assignment. Unavoidable turnover represents employee quits that the organization probably could not

EXHIBIT 14.1 Types of Employee Turnover

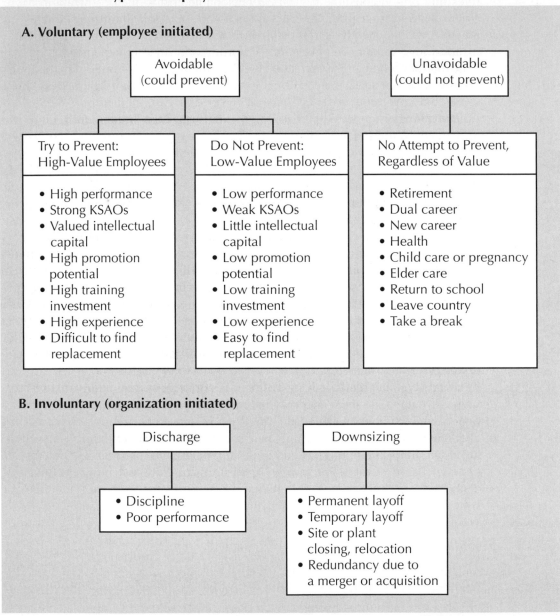

A. Voluntary (employee initiated)

Avoidable (could prevent)		Unavoidable (could not prevent)

Try to Prevent: High-Value Employees	Do Not Prevent: Low-Value Employees	No Attempt to Prevent, Regardless of Value
• High performance • Strong KSAOs • Valued intellectual capital • High promotion potential • High training investment • High experience • Difficult to find replacement	• Low performance • Weak KSAOs • Little intellectual capital • Low promotion potential • Low training investment • Low experience • Easy to find replacement	• Retirement • Dual career • New career • Health • Child care or pregnancy • Elder care • Return to school • Leave country • Take a break

B. Involuntary (organization initiated)

Discharge	Downsizing
• Discipline • Poor performance	• Permanent layoff • Temporary layoff • Site or plant closing, relocation • Redundancy due to a merger or acquisition

have prevented, such as people who quit and withdraw from the labor force through retirement or returning to school. Other examples of unavoidable turnover are people who quit due to dual career problems, pursuit of a new and different career, health problems that require taking a different type of job, child care and elder care responsibilities, or leaving the country. The line of demarcation between avoidable and unavoidable is fuzzy and depends on decisions by the organization as to exactly what types of voluntary turnover it thinks it could potentially prevent.

A further line of demarcation involves just avoidable turnover, in which the organization explicitly chooses to either try to prevent or not try to prevent employees from quitting. As shown in Exhibit 14.1, the organization will try to prevent high-value employees from quitting—those employees with high job performance, strong KSAOs, key intellectual capital, high promotion potential, high training and development invested in them, high experience, and who are difficult to find replacements for. Retention attempts for low-value employees are less likely to be made—this is a specific decision the organization must make.

Involuntary

Involuntary turnover is split into discharge and downsizing types. Discharge turnover is aimed at the individual employee, due to discipline and/or job performance problems. Downsizing turnover typically targets groups of employees and is also known as reduction in force (RIF). It occurs as part of an organizational restructuring or cost-reduction program to improve organizational effectiveness and increase shareholder value (stock price). RIFs may occur as permanent or temporary layoffs for the entire organization, or as part of a plant or site closing or relocation. RIFs may also occur as the result of a merger or acquisition, in which some employees in the combined workforces are viewed as redundant in the positions they hold. It is important to recognize that even though the organization is considering terminating employees through discharge and downsizing, it can take many steps to lessen or eliminate discharges or downsizing, thereby having positive employee-retention impacts.

It is apparent that there are many different types of turnover, and these types have different underlying causes. Because of this, the organization must think very selectively in terms of the different types of retention strategies and tactics it wishes to deploy. It is first necessary to explore the underlying causes of turnover, since knowledge of those causes is necessary for developing and implementing those retention strategies and tactics.

Causes of Turnover

Separate models of turnover causes are presented next for each of the three turnover types that the organization may seek to influence with its retention strategies and tactics. These are voluntary, discharge, and downsizing turnover.

Voluntary Turnover

Through considerable research, various models of voluntary turnover have been developed and tested.[3] The model shown in Exhibit 14.2 is a distillation of that research.

The employee's intention to quit depends on three general factors: the perceived desirability of leaving, the perceived ease of leaving, and alternatives available to the employee. The perceived desirability of leaving is often an outgrowth of a poor person/job or person/organization match. One form of the mismatch may be a difference between the rewards provided by the job and the rewards desired by the employee, leading to job dissatisfaction. In addition to mismatches, certain shocks may occur to the employee that trigger a more impulsive intention to quit, such as finding out that the organization is being acquired and one's job might be eliminated. Interpersonal conflicts with coworkers or supervisors are another type of shock that could lead to turnover. Finally, employees may find it desirable to leave for personal, nonjob reasons that are unavoidable.

The perceived ease of leaving represents a sense of lack of barriers to leaving and the likelihood of being able find a new job. Labor market conditions, specifically the tightness or looseness of the labor market, are very important types of information for the employee in helping to frame an intention to quit. Tight labor

EXHIBIT 14.2 Causes (Drivers) of Voluntary Turnover

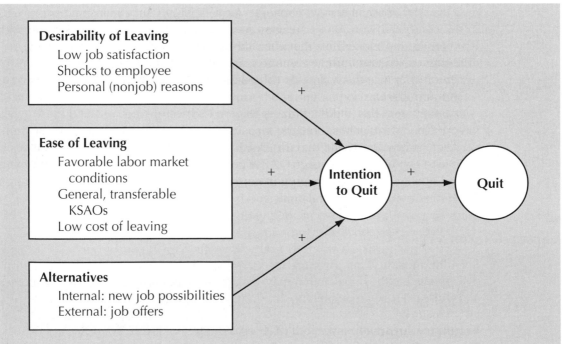

NOTE: The relative importance of the drivers and how they interact to determine the decision to quit varies across situations.

markets fuel the intention-to-quit flames, and loose labor markets douse the flames. The flames may also be doused by the employee knowing that many of his or her KSAOs are specific and only useful to the current employer. Ease of leaving may also be heightened by a low cost of leaving, such as not having to give up valuable benefits, because none were provided by the organization. In short, the ease of leaving will be higher when labor market conditions provide plentiful job opportunities with other organizations, when the employee possesses KSAOs that are transferable to other organizations, and when leaving is not a very costly proposition for the employee. Employees who are highly "embedded" in their jobs, organizations, and communities are less likely to leave. Some of the factors that increase embeddedness can be influenced by the organization, such as interpersonal relationships with supervisors and coworkers or levels of training in company-specific human capital. Other factors are beyond the organization's control, such as ties to the local community.[4]

Finally, the intention to quit will depend on other job alternatives available to the employee within and outside the organization. Specifically, availability of promotion, transfer, and relocation alternatives may lessen or eliminate any intentions to quit by the employee, even though the employee is very dissatisfied with the current job. Also, actual or potential receipt of a job offer from another employer represents a clear external alternative for the employee.

The final stage of the turnover process is the formation of intention to turnover, which is accompanied by a search for alternatives. Job searching has been empirically identified as a close correlate of turnover. However, employers should not assume that it is too late to make efforts to keep an employee who is seeking another job. Directly addressing what changes would be necessary to keep an employee is a good strategy in this case. Many employees who are looking for alternative jobs would be willing to stay with their current employers if their jobs were modified sufficiently.

The model in Exhibit 14.2 illustrates both avoidable and unavoidable turnover. Retention initiatives must be directed toward the avoidable types of turnover. Using the model, that will be turnover due to job dissatisfaction, employee possession of general and transferable KSAOs, a low cost of leaving, the availability of other job opportunities within the organization, and the employee's receipt of a job offer.

Discharge Turnover

Discharge turnover is due to extremely poor person/job matches, particularly the mismatch between job requirements and KSAOs. One form of the mismatch involves the employee failing to follow rules and procedures. These requirements range from the relatively minor (e.g., dress code violations, horseplay) to the very serious (e.g., bringing a firearm to work). Often it is the cumulative effect of multiple incidents that results in the discharge.

The other form of discharge turnover involves unacceptable job performance. Here, the KSAO–job requirements mismatch is severe. In fact, the employee's performance is so deficient that the organization has decided that it is intolerable and the only solution is termination.

Downsizing Turnover

Downsizing turnover is a reflection of a staffing level mismatch in which the organization actually is, or is projected to be, overstaffed. In other words, the head count available exceeds the head count required. Overstaffing may be due to (1) a lack of forecasting and planning, (2) inaccuracies in forecasting and planning, or (3) unanticipated changes in labor demand and/or labor supply. For example, optimistic forecasts of demand for products and services that do not materialize may lead to overstaffing, as may sudden unanticipated downturns in demand that create sudden excess head count. Or, increasing looseness in the labor market may reduce the ease of movement, causing fewer employees to leave the organization—an unanticipated decrease in the voluntary turnover rate and thus an increase in workforce head count available. Quite naturally, these types of demand/supply imbalances create strong downsizing pressure on the organization to which it must respond.

ANALYSIS OF TURNOVER

Analysis of turnover requires that the three types be measured and benchmarked, that specific reasons for employees' leaving be identified, and that costs and benefits of each type of turnover be assessed.

Measurement

Formula

Since turnover involves the discrete action of leaving or staying with the organization, it is expressed as the proportion or percentage of employees who leave the organization in some time period. Thus:

$$\text{turnover rate} = \frac{\text{number of employees leaving}}{\text{average number of employees}} \times 100$$

Use of this formula to calculate turnover rates will require data on, and decisions about, (1) what is the time period of interest (e.g., month, year), (2) what is an employee that "counts" (e.g., full time only? part time? seasonal?), and (3) how to calculate the average number of employees over the time period, such as straight or weighted average.

Breakouts and Benchmarks

Analysis and interpretation of turnover data are aided by making breakouts of the data according to various factors, including (1) type of turnover: voluntary—avoidable and unavoidable; involuntary—discharge; involuntary—downsizing, (2) type of employee (e.g., exempt–nonexempt, demographics, KSAOs, performance level), (3) job category, and (4) geographic location. Such breakouts help in identifying how much variation in turnover there is around the overall average and pockets of the most and least severe turnover. Such data are the foundation for development of strategic retention initiatives. Because human resources information systems (HRISs) are designed to process and track employee departures, data are often readily available regarding when, where, and even why employee turnover is occurring.

It is also useful to benchmark turnover data in order to have comparative statistics that will aid in interpretation of the organization's turnover data. One benchmark is an internal one, looking at the trends in the organization's own turnover data over time. Such trend analysis is very useful for identifying where turnover problems are worsening or improving and for evaluating the effectiveness of retention initiatives. Internal benchmarking requires a commitment to a sustained data collection process.

The other form of benchmarking is external, in which the organization compares its own data to the current rates and turnover trends of other organizations. One major external benchmarking source is the data from the Job Openings and Labor Turnover Survey (JOLTS), collected and published by the U.S. Department of Labor (*www.bls.gov/jlt*). The JOLTS is conducted monthly among 16,000 business establishments. It provides data on total employment, job openings, hires, quits, layoffs and discharges, and other separations. Exhibit 14.3 provides representative data from the JOLTS for the period between 2001 and 2006. It should be noted that on the Web site the data are broken down by region and industry but not by occupation.

Reasons for Leaving

It is important to ascertain, record, and track the various reasons why employees leave an organization. These data are essential for measuring and analyzing turnover. At a minimum, the exit of each employee should be classified as a voluntary, discharge, or downsizing exit, thus permitting the calculation of turnover rates for these three major types of turnover. In order to learn more about the specific reasons underlying exit decisions, however, more in-depth probing of employee motivations is necessary. Three tools for conducting such probing are exit interviews, postexit surveys, and employee satisfaction surveys.[5] All three tools can be used to help gauge whether the decision to leave was voluntary, and if so, the specific reasons—thus allowing a determination of avoidable and unavoidable turnover.

EXHIBIT 14.3   Data From Job Openings and Labor Turnover Survey

Annual	Hires	Quits	Layoff and Discharge	Other Separations
2001	41.4%	23.4%	15.1%	2.9%
2002	38.1%	20.6%	14.6%	2.9%
2003	37.9%	19.1%	15.2%	2.8%
2004	41.6%	21.3%	15.3%	2.8%
2005	43.0%	23.1%	15.0%	2.8%
2006	43.6%	23.7%	13.9%	3.1%

NOTE: Percentages of total nonfarm employment.

Exit Interviews

Exit interviews are formally planned and conducted interviews with departing employees. In addition to helping to learn about the employee's reasons for leaving, exit interviews are used to explain such things as rehiring rights, benefits, and confidentiality agreements. One major implication of potentially inaccurate measurement is that organizations should not dramatically alter retention strategies based on any one interview. Rather, the overall pattern of results that emerges over many interviews should be used.

It is important to ensure that exit interviews are conducted carefully. Research suggests that there are differences between the reasons for turnover that employees provide in exit interviews and the reasons employees provide in anonymous surveys.[6] Departing employees are reluctant to complain about their former employers because they will want to avoid burning bridges and don't want to jeopardize future references. In response, employees may claim that they are leaving for higher pay, when in fact they are leaving because of poor working conditions or interpersonal conflicts with supervisors and coworkers.

The following are suggestions for conducting an appropriate interview that will hopefully elicit truthful information from the interviewee: (1) the interviewer should be a neutral person (normally someone from the human resources [HR] department or an external consultant) who has been trained in how to conduct exit interviews; (2) the training should cover how to put the employee at ease and explain the purposes of the interview, how to follow the structured interview format and avoid excessive probing and follow-up questions, the need for taking notes, and how to end the interview on a positive note; (3) there should be a structured interview format that contains questions about unavoidable and avoidable reasons for leaving, and for the avoidable category, the questions should focus on desirability of leaving, ease of leaving, and job alternatives (Exhibit 14.4 contains an example of structured exit interview questions, with questions focused on desirability of leaving, ease of leaving, and alternatives); (4) the interviewer

EXHIBIT 14.4   Examples of Exit Interview Questions

1. Current job title _____ Department/work unit _____
2. Length of time in current job _____ Length of time with organization _____
3. Are you leaving for any of the following reasons?
   retirement _____ dual career _____ new career _____ health _____
   child care or pregnancy _____ elder care _____ return to school _____
   leave the country _____ take a break _____
4. Do you have another job lined up? _____ New employer _____
5. What aspects of your new job will be better than current job? _____
6. Before deciding to leave did you check the possibility of
   job transfer _____ promotion _____ relocation _____
7. Was it easy to find another job? _____ Why? _____
8. Did many of your current skills fit with your new job? _____
9. What aspects of your job have been most satisfying? _____
   least satisfying? _____
10. What could the company have done to improve your job satisfaction? _____
11. How satisfactory has your job performance been since your last review? _____
12. What are things the company or your manager could have done to help you improve
    your performance? _____
13. If you could have had a different manager, would you have been more likely to stay
    with the company? _____
14. Are you willing to recommend the company to others as a place to work? _____
15. Would you be willing to hire back with the company? _____
16. Is there anything else you would like to tell us about your decision to leave the com-
    pany? _____

should prepare for each exit interview by reviewing the interview format and the interviewee's personnel file; (5) the interview should be conducted in a private place, before the employee's last day; and (6) the interviewee should be told that the interview is confidential and that only aggregate results will be used to help the organization better understand why employees leave and to possibly develop new retention initiatives. The organization must decide whether to conduct exit interviews with all departing employees or only those who are leaving voluntarily. The advantage of including all departing employees is that it expands the sample from which information is drawn, and even employees leaving involuntarily can provide useful information. Conducting the interview before an employee's last day can sometimes bring up issues that, if addressed, could prevent the interviewee from leaving. For example, if an exit interview reveals that an employee is only leaving for higher pay, the company has an opportunity to make a counteroffer.

Postexit Surveys

To minimize departing employees' concerns about confidentiality in exit interviews and possible employer retaliation, postexit surveys might be used. It is recommended that (1) the survey cover the same areas as the exit interview; (2) the survey be sent shortly after the employee's last day; (3) a cover letter explain the purpose of the survey, use of only aggregate results, and confidentiality of individual responses; and (4) a stamped, pre-addressed envelope be included for return of the survey. It is unknown what types of response rates are typical for postexit surveys.

Employee Satisfaction Surveys

Since employee job dissatisfaction (desirability of leaving) is known to be a potent predictor of voluntary turnover, conduct of job satisfaction surveys is an important way to discover the types of job rewards that are most dissatisfying to employees and might therefore become reasons for leaving. Conducting job satisfaction surveys has the advantage of learning from all employees (at least those who respond to the survey), rather than just those who are leaving. Satisfaction survey results also give the organization information it can use to hopefully preempt turnover by making changes that will increase job satisfaction. Designing, conducting, analyzing, and interpreting results from these surveys require substantial organizational resources and should only be undertaken with the guidance of a person explicitly trained in job satisfaction survey techniques. Oftentimes there will be a consultant retained for this purpose.

Costs and Benefits

Costs and benefits may be estimated for each of the three turnover types. These costs are both financial and nonfinancial in nature. Most involve actual costs or benefits, though some are potential, depending on how events transpire. Some of the costs and benefits may be estimated financially, a useful and necessary exercise. Such financial analysis must be supplemented with a careful consideration of the other costs and benefits to arrive at a reasonable estimate of the total costs and benefits of turnover. It may well turn out that the nonfinancial costs and benefits outweigh the financial ones in importance and impact for the development of retention strategies and tactics.

Voluntary Turnover

Exhibit 14.5 shows the major types of costs and benefits that can occur when an employee leaves the organization.[7] An assessment of these costs and benefits could be used in the case of an individual employee who is threatening to leave for avoidable reasons; the assessment will help frame decisions about whether a retention attempt should be made, and if so, how far the organization is willing to go in that attempt. Or, at the aggregate level the costs and benefits assessment could be developed for

---

EXHIBIT 14.5   Voluntary Turnover: Costs and Benefits

I. Separation Costs
  A. Financial Costs
  - HR staff time (e.g., exit interview, payroll, benefits)
  - Manager's time (e.g., retention attempts, exit interview)
  - Accrued paid time off (e.g., vacation, sick pay)
  - Temporary coverage (e.g., temporary employee; overtime for current employees)

  B. Other Costs
  - Production and customer service delays or quality decreases
  - Lost or unacquired clients
  - Leaves—goes to competitor or forms competitive business
  - Contagion—other employees decide to leave
  - Teamwork disruptions
  - Loss of workforce diversity

II. Replacement Costs
  - Staffing costs for new hire (e.g., cost-per-hire calculations)
  - Hiring inducements (e.g., bonus, relocation, perks)
  - Hiring manager and work-unit employee time
  - Orientation program time and materials
  - HR staff induction costs (e.g., payroll, benefits enrollment)

III. Training Costs
  - Formal training (trainee and instruction time, materials, equipment)
  - On-the-job training (supervisor and employee time)
  - Mentoring (mentor's time)
  - Socialization (time of other employees, travel)
  - Productivity loss (loss of production until full proficient employee)

IV. Benefits
  - Replacement employee better performer and organization citizen than last employee
  - New KSAO and motivation infusion to organization
  - Opportunity to restructure work unit
  - Savings from not replacing employee
  - Vacancy creates transfer or promotion opportunity for others
  - Replacement less expensive in salary and seniority-based benefits

the work or business unit, division, or total organization. Results may then be used to communicate with top management about the nature and severity of employee turnover and to help fashion the development of retention strategies and tactics.

Inspection of Exhibit 14.5 shows that on the cost side there are separation, replacement, and training costs, both financial and nonfinancial. The financial costs mainly involve the cost of people's time, cost of materials and equipment, cash outlays, and productivity losses. The other costs are less discernable and harder to estimate but may entail large negative impacts on organizational effectiveness, such as loss of clients. On the benefits side, a number of positive things may occur, including finding a higher-quality, less-expensive replacement for the departing employee(s).

Accurate cost and benefit calculations require diligence and care in development, particularly those involving people's time. To estimate time costs, it is necessary to know the average amount of time spent by each person in the specific activity, plus each person's compensation (pay rate plus benefits). Consider the case of an exit interview, a separation cost. Assume that (1) the staffing manager spends one hour conducting the interview and writing up a brief summary to add to the voluntary turnover data file, (2) the staffing manager's salary is $46,000 ($23/hour) and the employee's salary is $50,000 ($25/hour), and (3) benefits are 30% of pay ($6.90/hour for the staffing manager and $7.50/hour for the employee). The time cost of the exit interview is $62.40. At the aggregate level, if the staffing manager conducts 100 exit interviews annually, and the average pay rate of those interviewed is $20/hour, the annual time cost of exit interviews is $5,590 (staffing manager pay = $2,300 and benefits = $690; employee's pay = $2,000 and benefits = $600).

Materials and equipment costs are likely to be most prevalent in replacement and training costs. For example, they will be a part of staffing costs in such things as recruitment brochures and testing materials, orientation program materials, and induction materials such as benefits enrollment forms. Formal training may involve the use of both materials and equipment that must be costed. Cash outlays include paying for (1) the departing employee's accrued but unused paid time off, (2) possible temporary coverage for the departed employee, and (3) hiring inducements for the replacement employee.

On the benefits side, the primary immediate benefit is the labor cost savings from not having the departing employee on the payroll. This will save the organization labor costs until a permanent replacement is hired (if ever). The organization will also save on labor costs if a temporary replacement at a lower pay rate can fill the position until a permanent replacement is acquired. And the hired permanent replacement may be hired at a lower wage or salary than the departing employee, resulting in additional pay and benefit savings. The other benefits shown in Exhibit 14.5 are less tangible but potentially very important in a longer-run sense of improved work-unit and organizational effectiveness.

Exhibit 14.6 shows the cost estimates for a single incident of voluntary turnover for a hypothetical industrial supplies organization that employs 40 salespeople who receive $20/hour on average and bring in approximately $8,000,000 in total annual sales. The three categories of the turnover and replacement process (separation, replacement, and training) are described in terms of their time costs, materials and equipment costs, and other costs.

EXHIBIT 14.6   Example of Financial Cost Estimates for One Voluntary Turnover

	Time Hours	Cost ($)	Materials and Equipment ($)	Other Costs ($)
A. Separation Costs				
Staffing manager	1	25		
HR staff	1	15		
Employee's manager	3	120		
Accrued paid time off	160	2,400		
Processing			30	
B. Replacement Costs				
Temporary replacement				
Compensation difference	160	(800)		
Staffing manager	1	25		
Employee's manager	1	40		
Staffing firm fee (markup)				800
Permanent replacement				
Compensation difference	960	(4,800)		
Cost-per-hire				4,500
Hiring bonus				3,000
Laptop computer				2,000
Employee's manager	3	120		
Orientation	8	160		
C. Training Costs				
Training program				
Trainee	80	1,200		
Instructor	100	1,600		
Mentor	52	1,040		
Productivity/sales loss			1,000	
Permanent replacement				50,000
Temporary replacement				2,000
D. Total Costs		1,145	1,030	62,300

Separation costs include the time of employees who process turnover ($25 + $15) and the former employee's manager ($120). There is also accrued time off paid to the departing individual ($160). Replacement costs include both a temporary fill-in and a permanent replacement. It takes an average of four weeks to find a permanent replacement. During these four weeks (160 hours), a temporary replacement is hired from a staffing firm for $15/hour plus a 33.3% markup. While this temporary employee is paid less than the average salesperson, temporary salespeople typically make $2,000 less in sales over the four-week period. A permanent new hire receives an average of $15/hour less for the first six months of employment until he or she gets up to speed ($5/hour less × 960 hours = $4,800 in savings). However, each new hire costs $4,500, and newcomers receive a hiring bonus of $3,000 and a laptop computer worth $2,000. Each new salesperson's manager typically has an additional three hours devoted to orienting the newcomer, along with an eight-hour organizational orientation session.

Training costs include the materials and equipment required for the program ($1,000), two weeks (80 hours) of paid time in the class, and the pay for an instructor who devotes 100 hours to the program. Additionally, an experienced salesperson acts as a mentor during the transition period, averaging one hour per week over the course of a year. It takes the new permanent replacement 24 weeks (24 weeks × 40 hours = 960 hours) to reach the average sales proficiency of $200,000; this means that $50,000 in sales is lost during this period. Overall, the estimated total costs for this organization for a single salesperson turnover incident come to $62,300. The data for this organization also suggest that time costs and material costs are a fairly trivial contribution to the total expense of turnover. Lost productivity makes up 81% of the cost of turnover (i.e., 52,000/64,475 = 81%). This figure will, of course, vary considerably depending on the job under consideration.

It should be recognized that turnover cost estimates require considerable judgment and "guesstimates." Nonetheless, the example above illustrates that many turnover costs are hidden in (1) the time demands placed on the many employees who must handle the separation, replacement, and training activities, and (2) the sales or productivity losses experienced. Such costs might be offset, at least in part, through the acquisition of less-expensive temporary and permanent replacement employees, at least for a while. It should also be noted that when turnover costs for a single employee loss are aggregated to an annual level for multiple losses, the costs can be substantial. In the above example, if the sales unit experienced just a 20% annual voluntary turnover rate, it would lose eight employees at a total cost of $519,000, or 6.5% of annual sales.

Discharge

In the case of an employee discharge, some of the costs and benefits are the same as for voluntary turnover. Referring to Exhibit 14.7, it can be seen that separation, replacement, and training costs are still incurred. There may be an additional

---

EXHIBIT 14.7   Discharge: Costs and Benefits

I. Separation Costs

A. Financial Costs

- Same as for voluntary turnover plus
- Contract buyout (salary, benefit, perks)

B. Other Costs

- Manager and HR staff time handling problem employee
- Grievance, alternative dispute resolution
- Possibility of lawsuit, loss of lawsuit, settlement or remedy
- Damage to harmonious labor–management relations

II. Replacement Costs

- Same as for voluntary turnover

III. Training Costs

- Same as for voluntary turnover

IV. Benefits

- Departure of low-value employee
- High-value employee replacement possibility
- Reduced disruption for manager and work unit
- Improved performance management and disciplinary skills

separation cost for a contract buyout of guarantees (salary, benefits, perks) made in a fixed-term contract. Such buyouts are very common for high-level executives and public sector leaders such as school superintendents. These guarantees are negotiated and used to make the hiring package more attractive and to reduce the financial risk of failure for the new hire. Such guarantees can drive up the costs of discharge substantially and reinforce the need for careful selection decisions followed by support to help the new hire turn out to be a successful performer who will remain with the organization for at least the full term of the contract.

It is the other costs that are potentially very large. A discharge is usually preceded by the manager and others spending considerable time, often unpleasant and acrimonious, with the employee in seeking to change the person's behavior through progressive discipline or performance management activities. The discharge may be followed by a lawsuit, such as a claim that the discharge was tainted by discrimination based on the race or sex of the dischargee. The time costs for handling the matter, and the potential cash outlays required in a settlement or court-imposed remedy, can be substantial.[8] In short, compared to voluntary turnover, discharge is a more costly, and unpleasant, type of turnover to experience. Moreover, in unionized settings, discharge problems may pose a serious threat to labor–management relations.

Against these often large costs are many potential benefits. First and foremost is that the organization will be rid of a truly low-value employee whose presence has caused considerable disruption, ineffective performance, and possibly declines in organizational effectiveness. A following benefit is the opportunity to replace the discharge with a high-quality new hire who will hopefully turn out to be a high-value employee. A side benefit of a discharge experience is that many members of the organization will gain improved disciplinary and performance management skills, and the HR department's awareness of the need for better discipline and performance management systems may be heightened and lead to these necessary changes.

Downsizing

Downsizing costs are concentrated in separation costs for a permanent RIF since there will presumably be no replacement hiring and training. These costs are shown in Exhibit 14.8, along with potential benefits.[9] The major economic cost areas are time costs, cash outlays for various severance and buyout packages, and increased unemployment compensation insurance premiums. The time costs involve both HR staff and managers' time in planning, implementing, and handling the RIF.

Severance costs may take numerous forms. First, employees can be paid for accrued time off. Second, early retirement packages may be offered to employees as an inducement to leave early. Third, employees ineligible for early retirement may be offered a voluntary severance package as an inducement to leave without being laid off. A typical severance package includes one week's pay for each year of service, continued health insurance coverage and premium payment, and outplacement assistance. More generous terms may be provided to key executives, such as two weeks' pay for each year of service and a lump-sum exit bonus. A danger with both early retirement and voluntary severance packages is that their provisions may turn out to be so attractive that more employees take them and leave than had been planned for in the RIF.

If the early retirement and voluntary severance packages do not serve as an adequate inducement to sufficient numbers of employees, the organization may also institute an involuntary RIF with a severance package, oftentimes not as generous as the voluntary package offered. It is customary to inform employees of the content of both the voluntary and involuntary packages at the time the RIF is announced so they may decide which to take. Some employees may decide to take their chances by not accepting the voluntary package and gambling that they won't be laid off (and if they are, being willing to live with the involuntary severance package).

EXHIBIT 14.8 Downsizing: Costs and Benefits

I. Separation Costs

A. Financial Costs

- HR staff time in planning and implementing layoff
- Managers' time in handling layoff
- Accrued paid time off (e.g., vacation, sick pay)
- Early retirement package
- Voluntary severance package (e.g., one week pay/year of service, continued health insurance, outplacement assistance)
- Involuntary severance package
- Contract buyouts for fulfillment of guarantees
- Higher unemployment insurance premiums
- Change in control (CIC) guarantees for key executives during a merger or acquisition

B. Other Costs

- Shareholder value (stock price) may not improve
- Loss of critical employees and KSAOs
- Inability to respond quickly to surges in product and service demand; restaffing delays and costs
- Contagion—other employees leave
- Threat to harmonious labor–management relations
- Possibility of lawsuit, loss of lawsuit, costly settlement or remedy
- Decreased morale, increased feelings of job insecurity
- Difficulty in attracting new employees

II. Benefits

- Lower payroll and benefit costs
- Increased production and staffing flexibility
- Ability to relocate facilities
- Improved promotion and transfer opportunities for stayers
- Focus on core businesses, eliminate peripheral ones
- Spread risk by outsourcing activities to other organizations
- Flatten organization hierarchy—especially among managers
- Increase productivity

Some employees may receive special severance consideration. For those on a fixed-term contract, a contract buyout will be necessary. Others, usually key executives, may have change in control (CIC) clauses in their contract that must be fulfilled if there is a merger or acquisition; CICs are also known as "golden parachutes." In addition to the terms in typical severance packages, a CIC may provide for immediate vesting of stock options, a retirement payout sweetener or buyout, bonus payments, continuation of all types of insurance for an extended time period, and maintenance of various perks.

Severance costs can be considerable. The Wall Street securities firm Merrill Lynch and Company reduced its workforce 14% over a two-year period as part of a restructuring effort. About 15,000 employees were cut, at a severance cost of $1.2 billion ($80,000 per employee).[10]

Other costs of downsizing shown in Exhibit 14.8 may also be considerable. Shareholder value (stock price) may not improve, suggesting the stock market views the probable effectiveness of the restructuring as low. There will be a critical talent loss and an inability to respond quickly to the need for workforce additions to cover new demand surges. And a reputation for job instability among job seekers will create added difficulties in attracting new employees. Terminated employees may pursue legal avenues, claiming, for example, that decisions about whom to lay off were tainted by age discrimination. Employees who survive the job cuts may have damaged morale and may fear even more cuts, which may harm performance and cause them to look for another job with a more secure organization. Finally, as with discharges, downsizing may place great strains on labor–management harmony.

Against this backdrop of heavy costs are many potential benefits. There will in fact be lower payroll and benefits costs. The organization may gain production and staffing flexibility, an ability to outsource parts of the business that are not mission critical, and opportunities to redesign and relocate facilities. The restructuring may also entail a flattening of the organization hierarchy through elimination of management layers, leading to increased speed in decision making and productivity boosts. Finally, new promotion and transfer opportunities may open up as the restructuring leads to the hoped-for rebound in organizational effectiveness.

Summary

Despite their many potential benefits, voluntary turnover, discharges, and downsizing are typically costly propositions. Time costs, materials costs, performance and revenue losses, severance costs, legal costs, and so forth can create substantial cost challenges and risks for the organization. Potentially even more important are the human costs of frayed relationships, critical talent losses, performance declines, disruptive discipline, the contagion effect of other employees leaving along with the departing employee, and the risk of not being able to locate, attract, and hire high-quality replacements.

The organization must carefully weigh these costs and benefits generally for each type of turnover, as well as specifically for separate employee groups, job categories, and organizational units. Clear cost-benefit differences in turnover will likely emerge from these more fine-grained analyses. Such analyses will help the organization better understand its turnover, determine where and among whom turnover is most worrisome, and learn how to fashion tailor-made retention strategies and tactics.

RETENTION INITIATIVES: VOLUNTARY TURNOVER

For most organizations, of the three types of turnover, voluntary turnover is the most prevalent and the one they choose to focus on in the continual "war for talent." Described below are examples of retention initiatives undertaken by organizations. These are vast in number, but little is known about how organizations actually decide to act on a turnover problem and go forth with one or more retention initiatives. To fill this void, a retention decision process is described that will help the organization more systematically and effectively pursue the right retention initiatives. Based on the causes of turnover model (Exhibit 14.2), ways to influence the three primary turnover drivers—desirability of leaving, ease of leaving, and alternatives—are suggested for retention initiatives.

Current Practices and Deciding to Act

Turnover analysis does not end with the collection and analysis of data. These activities are merely a precursor to the critical decision of whether to act to solve a perceived turnover problem, and if so, how to intervene to attack the problem and ultimately assess how effective the intervention was. Presented first are some examples of organization retention initiatives that illustrate the breadth and depth of attempts to address retention concerns. Then a systematic decision process for retention initiatives is provided as a framework to help with deciding whether to act. Such decision guidance is necessary given the complexity of the retention issue and the lack of demonstrated best practices for improving retention.

What Do Organizations Do?

Several descriptive surveys provide glimpses and hints of what actions organizations decide to take to address retention. These examples come mostly from relatively large organizations, so what happens in small organizations is more of an unknown. Nonetheless, the data provide interesting illustrations of organization tenacity and ingenuity, along with a willingness to commit resources, in their approaches to retention.

SHRM Survey. The Society for Human Resource Management (SHRM) surveyed HR professionals in 432 organizations nationwide.[11] A multitude of reasons for turnover were given. The top 10 reasons, and percentage of HR professionals citing each, were as follows: career opportunity elsewhere (51%), better compensation elsewhere (50%), dissatisfaction with potential for career development at the organization (31%), burnout from current job (23%), poor management (16%), conflict with supervisors (16%), difficulty balancing work/life issues (14%), not feeling appreciated (14%), ready for a new experience (13%), and better benefits package elsewhere (13%). It is interesting to compare HR managers' responses with those provided by employees in this same survey. The responses of line managers and other employees were typically very similar to those provided by HR managers, although the line managers and employees thought turnover was also often driven by being ready for new experiences and boredom with an old job, neither of which was highlighted as a major driver of turnover by HR managers. It is not entirely clear why there was this inconsistency between the opinions of HR managers and the opinions of other employees, but it should be noted that most research supports the perspective of employees, showing that employees who are dissatisfied with their work assignments are considerably more likely to quit.

What do these organizations do about retention problems and threats? Exhibit 14.9 shows the perceived most and least effective retention practices.

Although there are few intrinsic rewards mentioned in the SHRM survey, this does not mean that such rewards do not reduce turnover in the aggregate. In fact, research generally suggests that there is a strong relationship between job enrichment efforts from organizations and employee satisfaction. Employee perceptions that their jobs provide them with high levels of intrinsic satisfiers are consistently related to job satisfaction across multiple studies.[12] In addition, research suggests that individuals who hold jobs that are intrinsically satisfying are less likely to leave.[13]

WorldatWork Survey. WorldatWork conducts regular surveys of HR managers regarding the implementation and success of retention initiatives. A survey conducted with a sample of 649 respondents in 2007 focused on benefits and work/life programs.[14] Paid vacation and medical benefits were both very widely used, and both were seen as extremely effective tools for improving retention. Deferred

---

EXHIBIT 14.9   Most and Least Effective Retention Initiatives

Most Effective Retention Initiatives
- Competitive merit increases/salary adjustments
- Career development opportunities
- Promoting qualified employees
- Competitive merit increases
- Increasing health care benefits
- Offering schedules conducive to work/life balance
- Bonuses

Least Effective Retention Initiatives
- Telecommuting
- Childcare
- Early eligibility for benefits
- Stock options
- Miscellaneous competitive benefits

compensation plans, such as defined benefit pensions, were also rated as highly effective in reducing turnover. Not many organizations offered flex-time and tele-commuting, but those that did believe that these flexible work options increased retention. Although a large number of organizations provided flexible spending accounts for childcare, this was not seen by HR managers as an especially effective retention tool.

The Best 100 Companies. Each year *Fortune* magazine publishes the report "The Best 100 Companies to Work For."[15] Organizations apply to be on the list, and their score is based on randomly chosen employees' responses to the Great Place to Work Trust Index survey and an evaluation of a Culture Audit. Winners are ranked in order according to their final score, and brief descriptions are provided about the number of U.S. employees (including percentage of women and percent-age of minorities), job growth, annual number of job applicants and voluntary turnover rate, average number of employee training hours, entry-level salary for production and for professional employees, revenues, and what makes the organi-zation stand out.

Unfortunately, the study does not provide specific information on patterns of usage and effectiveness of retention initiatives among the 100 organizations. How-ever, comments about "what makes the organization stand out" provide intriguing tidbits as to special practices that might contribute to enhanced retention. Google, which was the top-rated organization for 2007, provides employees with an impres-sive array of perquisites, including gourmet cafeterias, laundry and dry-cleaning facilities, concierge services, car washing and oil changes, massage therapists, and weekly parties on-site with live music. To avoid turnover, Google is also taking steps to provide specialized sabbaticals and bonuses for longer tenure focused on high-performing employees. *Fortune* also highlighted Capital One's Future of Work project as a retention tool. This program aims to increase satisfaction and decrease stress by providing employees with a laptop computer with wireless Internet capability, a BlackBerry handheld computer, and an iPod, all of which promote flexible scheduling. All of these forms of technology allow employees to work away from the office, and open-space floor plans for regional offices mean that employees can work in different desks, booths, couches, or wherever is con-venient for that day. Capital One provides employees with opportunities to use this technology to access internal quarterly company reports and to take distance learning courses from top business schools. The reader should consult the 100 Best Companies results each year to gain glimpses such as these into what organizations are doing to make themselves attractive to job applicants and employees, which may aid in retention enhancement.

Retention Bundles. The retention initiatives up to this point have been described in terms of individual practices, such as either providing rewards linked to tenure or matching offers from other organizations. This should not be taken to suggest that retention initiatives should be offered in isolation. To be effective, retention practices need to be integrated into a comprehensive system, or as a "bundle" of practices. As an example, research has shown that the best performers are least likely to quit when an organization both rewards performance with higher compensation *and* widely communicates its compensation practices. Focusing on only compensation or communication did not have these effects—the procedures are much more effective as a bundle.[16] One study grouped steel minimills into those that used a bundle of commitment-oriented staffing practices (including programs to foster social relationships, employee participation, and general training) as opposed to minimills that used control-oriented practices (including programs that focused on reducing employment costs through minimal investment in employee programs). Turnover was two times higher in control-oriented organizations relative to commitment-oriented organizations.[17] A study examining a more diverse set of firms focused on an alternative effective set of bundles, including extensive recruiting, careful use of validated selection strategies, attitude assessments, incentive compensation, organizational communication, and use of formal job analysis procedures. Each standard deviation increase in the use of this bundle of high-performance work practices resulted in a 7% decrease in the turnover rate relative to the average turnover rates.[18]

In practical terms, managers need to examine all the characteristics in the work environment that might lead to turnover and address them in a comprehensive manner. Organizations that provide strong investments in their staffing methods may find their investments are lost if they do not support this strategy with an equally strong commitment to providing newcomers with sufficient orientation material to become adjusted to their new jobs. Organizations that provide numerous benefits in a poorly integrated fashion may similarly find that the intended effects are lost if managers and employees believe that the programs fail to address their needs.

Specific Retention Initiatives.   To further illustrate policies that organizations might adopt to control turnover, Exhibit 14.10 summarizes practices from a number of organizations that have been able to significantly improve retention outcomes.[19] One noteworthy feature of these programs is the use of both extrinsic and intrinsic rewards.

Decision Process

Exhibit 14.11 provides a suggested decision process that can help navigate the complex trade-offs inherent in developing retention intitiatives.

The first question—do we think turnover is a problem?—requires consideration and analysis of several types of data. It is necessary to judge whether the turnover rate(s) are increasing and/or high relative to internal and external benchmarks such as industry or direct competitor data. If turnover is relatively high or getting higher, this is cause for concern. Additional information is now necessary, such as whether managers are complaining about retention problems, whether mostly high-value

EXHIBIT 14.10 Retention Initiative Examples

Organization	Initiative	Results
Cedant	Flexible working schedule and work/life balance program designed around employee survey feedback	Annual turnover decreased from approximately 30% to less than 10%
Fleet Bank	Career growth opportunities and ensuring that employees are able to establish long-term relationships with their managers	Turnover fell by 40% among salaried employees and by 25% among hourly employees
New York Presbyterian Hospital	Flexible working schedule and tuition assistance to help employees attend skill-building courses	Annual turnover rate fell from 15.25% to 10.25%
Outback Steakhouse	Provide adequate information on job characteristics prior to hiring, extensive opportunities for employee voice	Turnover rates at approximately half of industry norms
SAP Americas	Increase communication regarding the organization's strategic direction and goals, provide rewards for retention, improve supervisor–employee relationship	Voluntary annual turnover rates fell from 14.9% to 6.1%
UPS	Provide well-above-market wages, ample vacation time, free health insurance, and pension	Typical annual turnover rate of 1.8%
Wegman's	Provide a comprehensive menu of health care benefits far above industry norms	Turnover rates at approximately 60% of industry norms

employees are leaving, and whether there are demographic disparities among the leavers. If these indicators also show trouble signs, then it is likely that turnover is a problem. The final analysis should involve the type of costs/benefits described earlier. Even though turnover may be high, in the final analysis it is only a problem if its costs are judged to exceed the benefits.

The second question—how might we attack the problem?—requires consideration of desirability of leaving, ease of leaving, and alternative turnover causes. Also, within each of these areas, which specific factors is it possible to change? Referring to Exhibit 14.11, for desirability of leaving it shows that increasing job satisfaction, improving organizational justice, and improving the social environment are

EXHIBIT 14.11 **Decision Process for Retention Initiatives**

Do We Think Turnover Is a Problem?	How Might We Attack the Problem?	What Do We Need to Decide?	Should We Proceed?	How Should We Evaluate the Initiatives?

• Turnover high or increasing relative to internal and external benchmarks
• Managers complain about retention problems
• High-value employees are leaving
• Demographic disparities among leavers
• Overall costs exceed benefits of turnover
	• Lower desirability of leaving?
	  Increase job satisfaction—yes
	  Decrease shocks—no
	  Personal reasons—no
	  Improve organizational justice—yes
	  Improve social environment at work—yes
	• Lower ease of leaving?
	  Change market conditions—no
	  Provide organization-specific KSAOs—yes
	  Make leaving more costly—yes
	• Change alternatives?
	  Promotion and transfers—yes
	  Respond to job offers—yes
		• Turnover goals
		• Targeted to units and groups
		• High-value employees
		• General and targeted retention initiatives
		• Lead, match, or lag the market
		• Supplement or supplant
		• HR and managers' roles
			• Feasibility
			• Probability of success
			• Timing
			• Costs
				• Lower proportion of turnover if avoidable
				• Turnover low or decreasing compared to benchmarks
				• Fewer complaints about retention problems
				• Fewer high-value employees leaving
				• Reduced demographic disparities
				• Lower costs relative to benefits

possible, but it is likely not possible to change personal shocks or personal reasons for leaving. Likewise, for ease of leaving it is possible to provide organization-specific KSAOs and to increase the cost of leaving for the employee.

Question three—what do we need to decide?—crosses the boundary from consideration to possible implementation. First to be decided are specific numerical turnover (retention) goals in the form of desired turnover rates. Retention programs without retention goals are bound to fail. Then it must be decided whether the goals and retention programs will be across the board, targeted to specific organization units and employee groups, or applied to both. Examples of targeted groups include certain job categories in which turnover is particularly troublesome, women and minorities, and first-year employees (newcomers)—a group that traditionally experiences high turnover. Next to be considered is if and how high-value employees will be treated. Many organizations develop special retention initiatives for high-value employees, on top of other retention programs, and it will have to be decided whether to follow this path of special treatment for such employees.[20] Having identified organizational units, targeted groups, and high-value employees (and established turnover goals for them), the retention program specifics must be designed. These may be general (across-the-board) initiatives applicable to all employees, or they may be targeted ones. For each such initiative, it must then be decided how to position the organization's initiatives relative to the marketplace. Will it seek to lead, match, or lag the market? For example, will base pay on average be set to be higher than the market average (lead), to be the same as the market average (match), or be lower than the market average (lag)? Likewise, will new variable pay plans try to outdo competitors (e.g., more favorable stock option plan) or simply match them? Adding to the complexity of the decision process is the delicate issue of whether new retention initiatives will supplement (add on to) or supplant (replace) existing rewards and programs. If the latter, the organization should be prepared for the possibility of employee backlash against what employees may perceive as "take-backs" of rewards they currently have and must give up. Finally, the respective rules of HR and individual managers will have to be worked out, and this may vary among the retention initiatives. If the initiative involves responding to job offers, for example, line managers may demand a heavy or even exclusive hand in making them. Alternatively, some initiatives may be HR driven; examples here include hours of work and variable pay plans.

Should we proceed? is question four in the decision process. It will depend on judgments about feasibility, such as ease of implementation. Judgments about probability of success will also enter in, and having specific turnover (retention) goals will be of immense help in making the decision. Finally, matters of timing should enter in. Even if judged to be feasible and a likely success, a retention program may not be launched immediately. Other HR problem areas and initiatives may have emerged and taken on higher priority. Or, turnover problems may have lost urgency because looser labor markets may have intervened to reduce turnover at the very time the retention initiatives were being planned. The cost of these initiatives will also be a major consideration.

The final question—how should we evaluate the initiatives?—should be considered *before* any plan is implemented. Answers will provide focus to the design of the intervention and agreed-upon criteria on which to later judge intervention effectiveness. Ideally, the same criteria that led to the conclusion that turnover was a problem (question one) will be used to determine if the solution that has been chosen actually works (question five).

Desirability of Leaving

Employees' desire to leave depends on their job satisfaction, shocks they experience, and personal (nonjob) reasons. Of these, only job satisfaction can usually be meaningfully influenced by the organization. So the first strategy for improving retention is to improve job satisfaction. The myriad examples of retention initiatives used by organizations described above represent mostly attempts to improve job satisfaction through delivery of various rewards to employees.

It is critical to understand that merely "throwing" more or new rewards at employees is not a sound retention initiative. Which rewards are chosen, and how they are delivered to employees, will determine how effective they are in improving job satisfaction. Accordingly, guidelines for reward choice and delivery are also described. Exhibit 14.12 summarizes the guidelines for increasing job satisfaction and retention.

Guidelines for Increasing Job Satisfaction and Retention

Recalling our discussion in Chapter 4, there are a variety of extrinsic and intrinsic rewards that can be brought to bear on the question of job satisfaction. Rather than reiterating these specific rewards here, we instead discuss the manner in which organizations can provide both categories of rewards consistent with the best practices identified by research and experience.

One important point must be borne in mind for both intrinsic and extrinsic rewards. The person/job match model emphasizes that job satisfaction results from a match between the rewards desired by employees and the rewards provided by the job. Employee reward preferences may be assessed at all stages of the staffing process by (1) asking applicants what attracted them to the organization, (2) asking current employees about the most important sources of job satisfaction, and (3) assessing reasons for turnover during exit interviews. It is also important to provide rewards large enough to be meaningful to the recipient. For example, an employee earning $50,000 who receives a gross 4% raise of $2,000 will realize a raise of 2.8% if inflation and taxes combined are at 30%. Such a net raise may not be very meaningful.

Extrinsic Rewards. To have attraction and retention power, extrinsic rewards must be unique and unlikely to be offered by competitors. The organization must benchmark against its competitors to determine what others are offering. Base pay levels are an important component in this process. Organizations may attempt to "lead the market" by providing wages above the market level. This leader strategy allows the organization to attract a higher-quality workforce, provides a workforce that is very satisfied with its pay, and minimizes the attractiveness of alternatives because employees cannot find comparable salaries elsewhere. This market leader strategy can be pursued for any reward and can be tailored to particular employee and industry demands. For example, if an organization is a seasonal employer in the recreation and tourism industry, it may concede pay leadership and lead with benefits such as free use of equipment (e.g., boats, bikes), clothing at cost, and free passes for use of facilities. A survey of 1,223 employed adults also revealed that employee benefits were a key driver of employee retention. In particular, 40% of respondents indicated that 401(k) matching decreased their odds of turnover; health care coverage and competitive salary also topped the list.[21]

Rewards can be even more powerfully attached to employee retention if they explicitly take seniority into account. For example, employees who have been with the organization longer may receive more vacation hours, career advancement opportunities, and increased job security. A more subtle way of rewarding employee retention is to make the reward contingent on the person's base pay level. Base pay levels typically increase over time through a combination of promotions and merit pay increases. Defined benefit retirement plans, for example, typically calculate retirement pay as some percentage (say, 50%) of the average person's three highest years of pay multiplied by years of service. Specific retention bonuses are also used to encourage longer-term relationships.

Rewards can also be linked to employee job performance. Organizations with a strong performance management culture thrive on high performance expectations, coupled with large rewards (e.g., base pay raises, bonuses, commissions, stock options) for high performers. Because lesser performers receive lower wages in these organizations, they are more likely to leave, whereas superior performers are more likely to stay.[22] Organizations may even more specifically target key performers by providing special retention bonuses, new job assignments, and additional perks if it appears that top performers are likely to leave.[23]

Intrinsic Rewards.   The intrinsic rewards described in Exhibit 4.19 should not be overlooked. There is consistent evidence that employee dissatisfaction with the intrinsic quality of their jobs is strongly related to turnover.[24]

Improving the work environment involves assigning employees to jobs that better meet their intrinsic-reward preferences. For example, employees with high needs for skill variety could be assigned to more complex jobs or projects within a work unit, or employees with high autonomy needs could be assigned to supervisors with a very "hands-off" style of leadership. Job redesign can also improve the work environment. To increase skill variety, managers may broaden the scope of tasks and responsibility for longer-term employees, allowing for personal growth on the job. Job rotation programs also help reduce perceived monotony on the job. Some organizations combine intrinsic and extrinsic rewards through the development of formal knowledge- and skill-based plans. In these plans, specific knowledge or skills are designated as critical, and employees receive a predetermined increase in base pay for demonstrated proficiency or acquisition of the knowledge or skill. For example, many school districts provide teachers with increases in their base compensation level for receiving master's degrees. Enhancing job autonomy might be facilitated by establishing formal performance goals for the job while giving employees minimal direction or oversight for the methods required to achieve these goals. A survey of 593 retail managers in three distinct organizations found that employees who were involved in management development programs that provided opportunities to learn and develop new skills were less likely to leave. Similar methods for improving task identity, task significance, and feedback should also be considered.

One of the closest correlates of employee commitment is the perception that the organization engages in fair treatment of its employees and provides them with support. Two forms of justice are necessary.[25] Distributive justice refers to perceptions that the individual reward levels are consistent with employee contributions to the organization. Procedural justice refers to perceptions that the process for allocating rewards and punishments is administered consistently, follows well-defined guidelines, and is free from bias. A sense that these justice principles have been violated can create dissatisfaction and may result in turnover or a lawsuit.

A crucial component to increasing employees' perception of justice is clear communication. Communication must begin early in the staffing process by providing employees with honest information about their job conditions. Evidence suggests that employees who receive adequate information regarding job conditions perceive their employers as more honest and may be less likely to leave.[26] If reward systems are going to increase satisfaction, employees must know why the system was developed, the mechanics of the system, and the payouts to be expected. Such knowledge and understanding require continuous communication. Research shows that a very common form of employee dissatisfaction with reward systems is a failure to understand them, or actual misinformation about them.[27] Any retention initiative designed to increase job satisfaction must have a solid communication component. On a broader level, communication regarding the organization's strategic direction can reduce turnover. Surveys at SAP Software indicated that employees who felt that the organization had a clear vision for the future and believed that top management supported them were more likely to report that they were engaged in their work.[28]

Justice perceptions are also strongly influenced by reward system design. Distributive justice requires that there be a rational and preferably measurable basis for reward decisions. Seniority-based rewards score high here because many employees believe seniority is a legitimate way to distinguish employees, and because it can be objectively measured. Objective measures of job performance, such as sales figures, are also likely to be accepted as legitimate. Rewards based on managerial performance reviews may be more problematic if employees question the legitimacy of the performance measurement system, or if they believe that these rewards create divisive comparisons among employees. When managerial reviews are part of the rewards process, the procedures involved in the review should be clearly communicated to employees. The importance of system fairness has been demonstrated in many contexts. Although much of the research on justice has been conducted in the United States and Canada, studies from China, Korea, Japan, and Pakistan have also shown that perceived justice increases job satisfaction and decreases turnover intentions.[29]

It is said that employees don't quit their jobs, they quit their bosses. Thus, interpersonal compatibility or chemistry between the employee and the supervisor can be a critical part of the employee's decision to stay or leave. The same could be said for coworkers. Employees who believe that they fit with the social environment in which they work are more likely to see their jobs as a source of significant social rewards. The resultant sense of camaraderie with the supervisor and coworkers may make them reluctant to leave the organization.

The supervisor is also a source of justice perceptions because of his or her role as a direct source of reward or punishment. The supervisor functions as an intermediary between the employee and the organization's compensation and promotion systems. This is because the supervisor decides the process for assessing employees, as well as the amount of rewards to be provided on the basis of these assessments. The supervisor will also serve as a key communication conduit regarding reward systems. If supervisors communicate the purpose and mechanics of the system, employees will be able to understand the process of reward distribution and also understand what they need to do if they wish to receive rewards in the future. Employees who believe that their supervisors use motivational language regularly have lower intentions to leave.[30]

Supervisors and coworkers in the social setting can also engage in abusive or harassing behaviors that are threatening or discomforting to the employees. Research suggests that employees who believe that their supervisors are abusive are more likely to leave.[31] Examples of abusive supervisor behavior that are frequently cited in surveys include "tells me my thoughts and feelings are stupid," "puts me down in front of others," and "tells me I'm incompetent." More extreme behaviors, such as sexual harassment, will have even stronger negative impacts on an employee's desire to remain on the job. Turnover due to interpersonal conflicts at work tends to come especially quickly; many employees who have such conflicts will bypass the process of searching for and considering alternative jobs and will instead quit immediately. Employees who are isolated from others in their racial, ethnic, or gender group are more likely to leave, whereas pro-diversity workplace climates tend to reduce turnover intentions.

For many employees, trying to balance work tasks with their personal lives contributes to stress, dissatisfaction, and a desire to leave.[32] Therefore, many organizations hoping to reduce turnover develop programs to help employees integrate their work and nonwork lives. These work/life balance programs allow employees to take time off from work if needed, create flexible scheduling options, and facilitate opportunities to work from remote locations. Many organizations have made family-friendly benefits and flexible work arrangements centerpieces of their retention strategy, and surveys suggest that making efforts to help employees balance their work and family lives can pay off in terms of lower turnover. For example, a survey of 393 professional-level employees demonstrated that individuals who made use of telework options experienced lower levels of work exhaustion and had lower intentions to leave. Data from 3,504 individuals who responded to the National Study of the Changing Workforce found that employees who had access to family-friendly work benefits experienced less stress and had lower turnover intentions relative to employees who did not have access to these benefits. Despite evidence supporting their use, it should be remembered that these work/life programs do not come without costs. Restructuring the workforce can disrupt productivity and may require investments in new technology to facilitate off-site work. Research has also shown that some employees who choose not to take advantage of telework options resent their coworkers who are not in the office regularly, and this resentment can lead to increased intention to leave.

Ease of Leaving

The decision process (Exhibit 14.11) indicates two points of attack on ease of leaving—providing organization-specific training and increasing the cost of leaving. The third possible factor, changing labor market conditions, cannot be influenced and represents a variable that will continuously influence the organization's voluntary turnover.

Organization-Specific Training

Training and development activities provide KSAOs to employees that they did not possess at the time they entered the organization as new hires. Training and development seek to increase labor quality in ways that will enhance employees' effectiveness. As shown previously, training represents a substantial investment (cost) that evaporates when an employee leaves the organization.

The organization may invest in training to provide KSAOs that vary along a continuum of general to organization specific. The more general the KSAOs, the more transferable they are to other organizations, thus increasing the likelihood they improve the employee's marketability and raise the probability of leaving. Organization-specific KSAOs are not transferable, and possession of them does not improve employee marketability. Hence, it is possible to lower the employee's ease of leaving by providing, as much as possible, only organization-specific training content that has value only as long as the employee remains with the organization.

This strategy needs to be coupled with a selection strategy in which any general KSAOs required for the job are assessed and selected on so that they will not have to be invested in once the employee is on the job. For example, applicants for an entry-level sales job might be assessed and selected for general sales competencies

EXHIBIT 14.12   Guidelines for Increasing Job Satisfaction and Retention

A. Extrinsic Rewards

- Reward must be meaningful and unique.
- Reward must match individual preferences.
- Link rewards to retention behaviors.
- Link reward to performance.

B. Intrinsic Rewards

- Assign employees to jobs that meet their needs for work characteristics.
- Provide clear communications with employees.
- Design fair reward allocation systems.
- Ensure supervisors provide a positive environment.
- Provide programs to enhance work/life balance.

such as written and verbal communication and interpersonal skills. Those hired may then receive more specialized training in such areas as product knowledge, specific software, and knowledge of territories. To the extent such organization-specific KSAOs become an increasingly large proportion of the employee's total KSAO package over time, they help restrict the employee's mobility.

This strategy entails some risk. It assumes the general KSAOs are available and affordable among applicants. It also assumes these applicants will not be turned off by the job if they learn about the organization-specific training and development they will receive.

Increased Cost of Leaving

Driving up the cost of leaving is a way to make it less easy to leave. Providing above-market pay and benefits is one way to do this since employees will find it difficult to find better-paying jobs elsewhere. Any form of deferred compensation, such as deferred bonuses, will also raise the cost of leaving since the compensation will be lost if the employee leaves prior to being eligible to receive it.

Retention bonuses might also be used. Normally, these are keyed to high-value employees whose loss would wreak organizational havoc. Such may be the case during mergers and acquisitions, when retention of key managers is essential to a smooth transition. For example, when TransWorld Airlines (TWA) sold itself to American Airlines, TWA had a plan to pay retention bonuses of 15% to 30% of annual salaries to 100 key managers. The bonuses were paid in three phases over a one-year period. In addition, a separate $500,000 discretionary fund was used to pay other people retention bonuses.[33]

Another long-term way to make leaving costly is to locate the organization's facilities in an area where it is the dominant employer and other amenities (housing, schools, health care) are accessible and affordable. This may entail location in the outer rings of suburban areas or relatively small and rural communities. Once employees move to and settle into these locations, the cost of leaving is high because of the lack of alternative jobs within the area and a need to make a costly geographic shift in order to obtain a new job.

Alternatives

In confronting outside alternatives available to employees, the organization must fashion ways to make even better internal alternatives available and desirable. Two key ways to do this involve internal staffing and responding to outside job offers.

Internal Staffing

The nature and operation of internal staffing systems have already been explored. It is important to reiterate that open systems serve as a safety valve, retentionwise, in that employees are encouraged to look internally for new job opportunities and managers benefit by seeking internal candidates rather than going outside the organization. The organization should also think of ways outside the realm of its traditional internal staffing systems to provide attractive internal alternatives to its employees.

For example, Mercer Management Consulting has developed a rotational externship program for some of its consultants. These consultants are allowed to take on a full-time operational role for a client for 6 to 24 months, rather than handle multiple clients, allowing the consultant the satisfaction of seeing a project through to completion and to gain valuable operating experience. It is hoped that these consultants will return to Mercer at the end of the project, based on the bird-in-the-hand theory—if you love it, let it go; if it loves you, it will come back. Another example is a temporary internal transfer system used by Interbrand Group, Inc., a unit of Omnicom Group, Inc. Certain high-performance employees are offered short-term transfers to any of its 26 offices worldwide. The lateral moves last from three months to one year. The transfers allow employees to get a change of life without having to quit their jobs.[34] Illustrating this point, a study of 205 individuals employed in diverse work settings found that those who were unhappy with their work environments did not translate this dissatisfaction into an intention to leave if they believed that there were opportunities for mobility within their organization. In a sense, one could say that these dissatisfied individuals saw internal transfers as a way to quit a disliked job, but without the costs to the employer that typically come with turnover.[35]

Response to Job Offers

When employees receive an actual outside job offer or are on the verge of receiving one, they clearly have a solid job alternative in hand. How should the organization respond, if at all, in order to make itself the preferred alternative?

The organization should confront this dilemma with some carefully thought through policies in advance. This will help prevent some knee-jerk, potentially regrettable actions being taken on the spot when an employee brings forth a job offer and wants to use it for leverage.

First, the organization should decide whether it will be willing to respond to job offers. Some organizations choose not to, thereby avoiding bidding wars and counteroffer games; even if the organization successfully retained the employee, the employee may now lack commitment to the organization, and other employees may resent the special retention deal that was cut. Other organizations choose to respond to job offers, not wanting to automatically close out an opportunity to at least respond to, and hopefully retain, the employee. Other times, job offers are welcomed because they help the organization sort out who its stars are and what kinds of offer packages it may have to give other recruits in order to lure them into the organization's fold. There is even an example of an organization that pays $1,000 "notification bonuses" to employees who disclose receiving an outside offer so that it can learn its content and have the option of being able to respond to it.[36] The price for such an openness to outside offers is that it may encourage employees to actively solicit them in order to try to squeeze a counteroffer out of the organization, thus improving the "deal."

The second major policy issue is for which employees will the organization respond to outside offers. Will it be all employees or only select ones, and if it is the latter, which select ones? Here, the focus should likely be on high-value employees.

A third set of policy issues pertains to who will put together the counteroffer and what approval process must be followed. While individual managers will likely want wide latitude over these issues, the HR function will need to be an important player for cost-control purposes, as well as for ensuring procedural and distributive justice overall.

RETENTION INITIATIVES: DISCHARGE

Performance Management

Performance management is used by many organizations to help ensure that the initial person/job match made during staffing yields an effectively performing employee, to facilitate employee performance improvement and competency growth, and to detect and hopefully remedy performance problems. Performance management systems focus most of their attention on planning, enabling, appraising, and rewarding employee performance.[37] Having a performance management system in place, however, also allows the organization to systematically detect and treat performance problems that employees exhibit before those problems become so harmful and intractable that discharge is the only recourse. The discharge prevention possibilities of a performance management system make it another important retention initiative to use within an overall retention program. Also, a sound performance management system can be very useful in helping an organization successfully defend itself against legal challenges to discharges that do occur.

Exhibit 14.13 portrays the performance management process. Organization strategy drives work-unit plans, which in turn become operational and doable for employees through a four-stage process. Stage one—performance planning—involves setting performance goals for each employee and identifying specific competencies the employee will be evaluated on. After performance planning, stage two—performance execution—begins. Here the focus is on the employee actually performing the job. Assistance to the employee could or should be made in the form of resources to aid in job performance, coupled with coaching and feedback from the employee's manager, peers, and others. To be effective, performance feedback should be provided frequently and should always be accompanied by specific suggestions for how to improve. At the end of the performance period, such as quarter or year, stage three begins and a formal performance review is con-

EXHIBIT 14.13   Performance Management Process

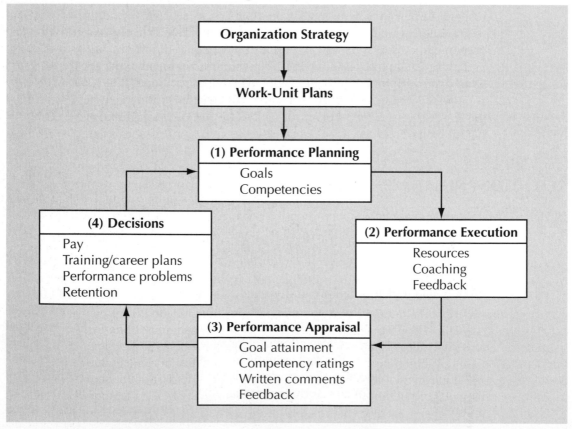

ducted, usually by the manager. In this stage, an assessment is made of the employee's success in reaching established goals, ratings of the employee's competencies are made, written comments are developed to explain ratings and provide suggestions for performance improvement, and feedback of the assessment is provided to the employee. Collectively, these actions are known as performance appraisal. In stage four, the information developed during the performance review is used to help make decisions that will affect the employee. Most likely, these decisions pertain to pay raises and to training and career plans. They may also pertain to formal identification of performance problems, where the employee has shown, or is headed toward, unacceptable performance. In reality, this process is ongoing, with each decision leading to a new cycle of performance planning.

It should be noted that the design, implementation, and operation of a performance management system is a complex undertaking, and the specific ways that the four stages described above are actually carried out vary among organizations.[38] For purposes here, however, the performance management system depicted in Exhibit 14.13 shows how such a system can be a critical retention tool for the organization when it is confronted with employees who are having severe performance problems that place them on the cusp of termination.

Specifically, it may be decided that an employee has severe performance problems (stage four), and this can then set in motion a focused performance-improvement process throughout the next performance management cycle. The process of performance counseling and discipline can be conceptualized in six stages, as shown in Exhibit 14.14. It is important for managers to consider different types of performance problems when developing a counseling and disciplinary plan, because each dimension requires different responses. The model in Exhibit 14.14 breaks job performance into three categories.[39] Task performance includes the completion of job tasks that are specifically included in the job description. Citizenship reflects the psychological and social environment of work created by employees, which might be only indirectly reflected in written job descriptions but is important for maintaining a smoothly functioning work group. Counterproductivity represents actions that directly violate organizational rules or that undermine performance. The first imperative for managers is to continually monitor employee performance and identify problems. Next, managers should determine why it is that employee performance has become unacceptable. This process should involve the employees' input as well. If problems are occurring because of lack of knowledge or skills, it may be possible to use corrective action based on training or counseling; problems involving lack of motivation or negative attitudes require the use of rewards and punishments, and problems involving personality or lack of ability may require reassignment to a different job. Regardless of which corrective actions are taken, employees need to be clearly informed about the consequences for continued failure to perform adequately, and the entire counseling and disciplinary process needs to be documented. Hopefully, there will be improvements in performance, but if not, the organization will need to consider the possibility of terminating employment.

EXHIBIT 14.14 Performance Counseling and Disciplinary Processes

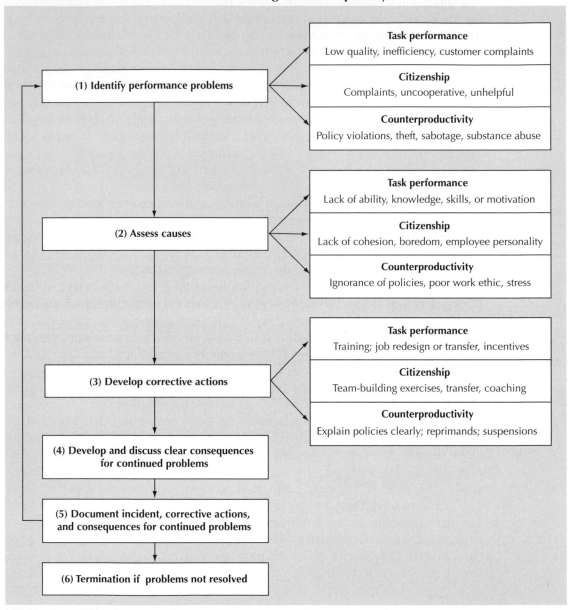

Manager Training and Rewards

There are many components required for a successful performance management system. None are probably more critical than training and rewards for the managers who will be users of the performance management system with employees in their work units.[40]

Performance management requires a complex set of knowledges and skills that managers must possess, particularly for the performance execution and performance appraisal stages. Training for managers is essential to provide them these requisites to being effective performance managers. Examples of training content include purposes of performance management, policies and procedures of the performance management system, appraisal forms and how to complete them, keeping records of employee performance incidents, rating accuracy, coaching techniques, finding and providing resources, methods of providing feedback, goal setting, and legal compliance requirements. It is especially important to stress exactly why and how performance management is to be used as a retention initiative that seeks to prevent discharge through intensive performance improvement attempts.

Managers must also be provided incentives for using these new knowledges and skills to effectively conduct performance management. At a minimum it is necessary to formally make performance management a part of the manager's job during the performance planning stage so that he or she will have performance management as an area of responsibility requiring attention and that the manager's own performance appraisal results will depend on how well he or she practices performance management.

Another important part of training should be concerned with employee termination. Here, managers must come to understand that a decision to discharge an employee for performance problems falls outside the normal performance management process (Exhibit 14.13) and is not a decision that can or should be made alone by the individual manager. Terminations require separate procedural and decision-making processes.[41] These could also be covered as part of a regular performance management training program, or a separate program devoted to termination could be conducted.

Progressive Discipline

Employee discipline pertains to problems of behavioral conduct that violate rules, procedures, laws, and professional and moral standards.[42] Discipline may also come into play for performance problem employees. Progressive discipline has a series of penalties for misconduct that increase in severity if the misconduct is repeated, starting with an informal warning and going all the way up to termination. In progressive discipline, employees are given notice of their misconduct and are provided the opportunity (and often the assistance) to change their behavior; termination is a last resort.

Progressive discipline systems are rooted in major principles of fairness and justice that can be summarized in the following five requirements for a progressive discipline system: (1) give employees notice of the rules of conduct and misconduct, (2) give employees notice of the consequences of violation of the rules, (3) provide equal treatment for all employees, (4) allow for full investigation of the alleged misconduct and defense by the employee, and (5) provide employees the right to appeal a decision.[43]

Actions to Take

To address those fairness requirements, several things should be done. First, establish what constitutes misconduct and the penalties for misconduct. The penalties start with an oral warning and progress through a written warning, suspension, and termination. Second, provide training to employees and managers so that they are aware of the types of misconduct, penalties, investigation and documentation requirements, and appeal rights. Third, work with managers to ensure that there is consistency of treatment (no favoritism) of employees, meaning that similar misconduct results in similar penalties for all employees. Finally, establish an appeals procedure in which employees may challenge disciplinary actions if one is not already in place.

Documentation by the manager is critical in all but the least severe instances of misconduct (e.g., first-time minor offense with an oral warning).[44] Thus, the manager must investigate allegations of misconduct, gather evidence, and write down and keep records of what was learned. Allegations of tardiness, for example, might involve inspection of time cards and interviews with other employees. The time cards and interview notes should then be kept as part of the documentation record. Employees should have the right to see all documentation and provide written documentation in self-defense.

Performance problems could be incorporated into, or dovetailed with, the progressive discipline system.[45] Here, it would be wise if possible to first adhere to the normal performance management cycle so that correction of performance deficiencies is done in a consultative way between the employee and the manager, and the manager assumes major responsibility for providing resources to the employee, as well as for attentive coaching and feedback. If performance improvement is not forthcoming, then shifting to the progressive discipline system will be necessary. For very serious performance problems, it may be necessary for the manager to address them with an expedited performance management cycle, coupled with a clear communication to the employee that failure to correct performance problems could lead immediately to the beginning of formal disciplinary actions.

Employee termination is the final step in progressive discipline, and ideally it would never be necessary. Rarely, if ever, will this be the case. The organization thus must be prepared for the necessity of conducting terminations. Termination processes, guidelines, training for managers, and so forth must be developed and implemented. Considerable guidance is available to help the organization in this regard.[46]

RETENTION INITIATIVES: DOWNSIZING

Downsizing involves reduction in the organization's staffing levels through layoffs (RIFs). Many factors contribute to layoff occurrences: decline in profits, restructuring of the organization, substitution of the core workforce with a flexible workforce, obsolete job or work unit, mergers and acquisitions, loss of contracts and clients, technological advances, productivity improvements, shortened product life cycles, and financial markets that favor downsizing as a positive organizational action.[47] While downsizing obviously involves the elimination of jobs and employees, it also encompasses several retention matters. These involve balancing the advantages and disadvantages of downsizing, staffing levels and quality, alternatives to layoffs, and dealing with employees who remain after downsizing.

Weighing Advantages and Disadvantages

There are multiple advantages (benefits) and disadvantages (costs) of downsizing; refer back to Exhibit 14.8 for a review. A thoughtful consideration of these makes it clear that if downsizing is to be undertaken, it should be done with great caution. It is simply not usually an effective "quick fix" to financial performance problems confronting the organization.

Moreover, research suggests that the presumed and hoped-for benefits of downsizing may not be as great as they might seem.[48] For example, one study looked at how employment level changes affected profitability and stock returns of 537 organizations over a 14-year period. Downsizing did not significantly improve profitability, though it did produce somewhat better stock returns. But organizations that combined downsizing with asset restructuring fared better. Another study looked at the incidence of downsizing across the regional sales offices of a large financial services organization and found that layoffs ranged from 0 to 29% of the workforce, with an average of 7%. It was also found that the amount of downsizing had a significant negative impact on sales offices' profitability, productivity, and customer satisfaction. Additional research has found that downsizing has negative impacts on employee morale and health, workgroup creativity and communication, and workforce quality.[49]

In short, downsizing is not a panacea for poor financial health. It has many negative impacts on employees and should be combined with a well-planned total restructuring if it is to be effective. Such conclusions suggest the organization should carefully ponder if in fact it wants to downsize; if so, by how much and which employees it should seek to retain.

Staffing Levels and Quality

Reductions in staffing levels should be mindful of retention in at least two ways. First, enthusiasm for a financial quick fix needs to be tempered by a realization that, once lost, many downsized employees may be unlikely to return later if economic circumstances improve. The organization will then have to engage in costly restaffing, as opposed to potentially less costly and quicker retention initiatives. At a minimum, therefore, the organization should consider alternatives to downsizing simultaneously with downsizing planning. Such an exercise may well lead to lesser downsizing and greater retention.

Staffing level reductions should also be thought of in selective or targeted terms, rather than across the board. Such a conclusion is a logical outgrowth of HR planning, through which it is invariably discovered that the forecasted labor demand and supply figures lead to differing HR head-count requirements across organizational units and job categories. Indeed, it is possible that some units or job categories may be confronting layoffs while others will actually be hiring. Such an occurrence is increasingly common in organizations.[50]

If cuts are to be made, who should be retained? Staffing quality and employee acceptance concerns combine to produce some alternatives to choose from. The first alternative would be to retain the most senior employees and cut the least senior employees in each work unit. Such an approach explicitly rewards the most senior employees, thus likely enhancing long-run retention efforts by signaling job security commitments to long-term employees. Such seniority-based retention also likely meets with strong employee acceptance. On the downside, the most senior employees may not be the best performers, and looking ahead, the most senior employees may not have the necessary qualifications for job requirement changes that will be occurring as part of the restructuring process. In addition, seniority-based layoffs raise important but thorny procedural internal labor market issues, such as how to exactly count seniority and what (if any) "bumping" rights employees targeted for layoff might have. Bumping is a process by which an employee may avoid layoff by taking over the job of another employee, usually one with less seniority, who will be laid off instead. In unionized settings, such issues are typically spelled out at length in the labor contract.[51]

A second alternative would be to make performance-based retention decisions. Employees' current and possibly past performance appraisals' would be consulted in each work unit. The lowest-performing employees would be designated for layoff. This approach seeks to retain the highest-quality employees, those who through their performance are contributing most to organizational effectiveness. It may meet with less employee acceptance than the first alternative among some employees because of perceived injustice in the performance appraisal process. It also assumes that the current crop of best performers will continue to be so in the future, even though job requirements might be changing. And legal challenges may arise, as discussed later.

A third alternative focuses on retaining what are called "high-value employees" and concentrating layoffs on "low-value employees" (Exhibit 14.1). Here, multiple criteria of value are used, rather than a single criterion such as seniority or performance, though both of these value indicators would likely be included in the value assessments of employees. Recognition of multiple indicators of value is more encompassing in terms of employees' likely future contributions to organizational effectiveness, and because of this it may also meet with high employee acceptance. Use of this approach, however, requires a complex and potentially burdensome process. Indeed, the process is directly akin to an internal selection system in which the value indicators must be identified, assessed, scored, and weighted to come up with a composite value score for each employee that would then be used as the basis for the retention decision. Cut scores are also probably required.

Alternatives to Downsizing

A no-layoffs or guaranteed employment policy as an organization strategy is the most dramatic alternative to downsizing. Several major organizations pursue this strategy, including S.C. Johnson, Pella, Nucor, Northwestern Mutual, Enterprise Rent-A-Car, Erie Insurance, and Lincoln Electric.[52] At Lincoln Electric, every employee who has three or more years of continuous service is guaranteed a minimum of 75% of a normal workweek. This guarantee is for a job, not a specific position, so cross-training with flexible internal mobility is practical. To create a staffing buffer, during peak times overtime is paid rather than staffing up with new employees; during downturns, overtime hours, but not employees, are cut. Incentive pay systems are used, along with letting go of people who don't meet performance expectations. Senior executives have a higher percentage of their pay in profit sharing than the rest of the workforce, which functions as an economic buffer during downturns.

No-layoff strategies require considerable organization and HR planning, along with a commitment to a set of programs necessary for successfully implementing the strategy. The strategies also require a gamble and bet that, if lost, could severely damage employee loyalty and trust.

Other organizations are unwilling to make a no-layoff guarantee but pursue layoff minimization through many different programs. Exhibit 14.15 provides an example, based on a survey of 226 organizations. It can be seen that multiple steps were taken prior to layoff, headed by attrition (not replacing employees who leave), employment freezes, and nonrenewal of contract workers. A series of direct and indirect pay changes (e.g., salary reduction, early retirement) also played some role in their layoff minimization. Other actions are also possible, such as temporary layoff with some proportion of pay and benefits continued, substitution of stock options for bonuses, conversion of regular employees to independent contractors, temporary assignments at a reduced time (and pay) commitment, and off-site Internet employees who temporarily convert to work-at-home on a reduced time (and pay) basis.[53]

Employees Who Remain

Employees who remain either in their prelayoff or in a redeployed job after a downsizing must not be ignored. Doing otherwise creates a new retention problem—survivors who are stressed and critical of the downsizing process. One study of survivors found that less than 50% of them rated management's honesty as positive in regard to layoffs, felt support for remaining staff was adequate, and thought their organizations recognized the value of remaining employees. Moreover, almost half

EXHIBIT 14.15   Layoff Minimization Examples

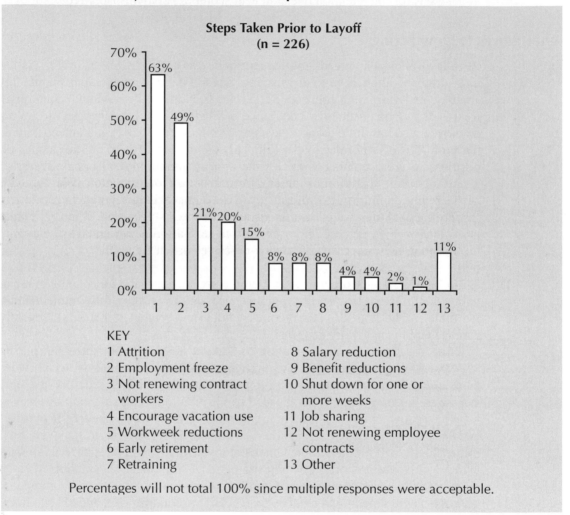

Steps Taken Prior to Layoff
(n = 226)

KEY

1 Attrition	8 Salary reduction
2 Employment freeze	9 Benefit reductions
3 Not renewing contract workers	10 Shut down for one or more weeks
4 Encourage vacation use	11 Job sharing
5 Workweek reductions	12 Not renewing employee contracts
6 Early retirement	13 Other
7 Retraining	

Percentages will not total 100% since multiple responses were acceptable.

Source: Society for Human Resource Management, *Layoffs and Job Security Survey* (Alexandria, VA: author, 2001), p. 9. Used with permission.

of the survivors learned about the downsizing through rumors or word of mouth.[54] In terms of stress, it is heightened by loss of coworkers and friends, higher work-loads, new locations and work hours, new and/or more responsibilities, and fear of job loss just around the corner.

These many examples of "survivor sickness" suggest a need to anticipate and attack it directly within downsizing planning. One survey reported that organizations sought to meet survivors' needs through enhanced communication programs, morale-boosting events, promotion of the employee assistance program, and stress-related training. Surprisingly, 30% of organizations surveyed reported they took no steps to deal with survivors.[55] Unless steps are taken to help survivors plan for and adjust to the new realities they will confront, heightened job dissatisfaction seems inevitable. In turn, voluntary turnover may spike upward, increasing even more the cost of downsizing.

LEGAL ISSUES

Retention initiatives are closely intertwined with the occurrence of employee separations since the result of an unsuccessful retention initiative is the voluntary or involuntary separation of the employee from the organization. The organization's retention initiatives thus must be guided in part by the laws and regulations governing separations. A brief overview of these is provided. Then a detailed look at the role of performance appraisal in separation is presented since a thrust of this chapter has been performance-based retention.

Separation Laws and Regulations

A desire to provide protection and safeguards to employees leaving the organization, especially for discharge and downsizing, has led to myriad laws and regulations governing the separation process.[56] These include the following:

- Public policy restrictions on employment-at-will
- Employment discrimination laws and regulations
- Affirmative action requirements
- Employment contract principles
- Labor contract provisions
- Civil service laws and regulations
- Negligent supervision and retention
- Advanced warning about plant closings

A basic tenet underlying restrictions on employee separation is the need for fair and consistent treatment of employees. Included here are concerns for ensuring procedural fairness and for basing separations on legitimate bases, such as merit, seniority, or performance. The organization should be thoroughly familiar with these numerous laws and regulations, and their underlying principles, as it designs and administers its retention initiatives. There is evidence that even after taking tenure and job performance into account, African Americans and Hispanics are more likely to be laid off than whites or Asians, adding to these concerns.[57] Although statistics show that older workers are less likely to be laid off, organizations should be wary of potential disparate impact against older workers if older facilities are being downsized.[58]

Performance Appraisal

Organizations often favor retention and separation systems and decisions being driven by employee performance. Laws and regulations generally uphold or even encourage such a role for performance. However, the law as interpreted also insists that the performance appraisals, and the performance appraisal system generally, be fair and equitable in application to employees undergoing separation. Interpretations come about from a combination of court decisions and governmental regulations that have evolved around the issue of performance appraisal in practice.

Based on these decisions and regulations, numerous specific suggestions have been put forth to guide the organization in the design and use of its performance appraisal (or management) system:[59]

- Appraisal criteria should be job related, specific, and communicated in advance to the employee.
- The manager (rater) should receive training in the overall performance appraisal process and in how to avoid common rating errors.
- The manager should be familiar with the employee's job description and actual performance.
- There should be agreement among different raters in their evaluation of the employee's performance.
- Evaluations should be in writing.
- The employee should be able to review the evaluation and comment on it before it becomes final.
- The employee should receive timely feedback about the evaluation and an explanation for any outcome decision (e.g., retention or separation).
- There should be an upward review of the employee's appraisal.
- There should be an appeal system for employees dissatisfied with their evaluation.

Conforming to the above recommendations will help (not guarantee) provide a fair evaluation process and the defensible evaluation decisions pertaining to retention and separation. If the organization wants to manage a performance-driven retention system, it would be wise to ensure the adequacy of its performance appraisal system relative to the above recommendations.

SUMMARY

Retention management seeks to control the numbers and types of employees who leave and who remain with the organization. Employee loss occurs via voluntary turnover or involuntary turnover in the form of discharge or downsizing. Voluntary turnover is caused by a combination of perceived desirability of leaving, ease of leaving, and alternatives to one's current job. Some of these reasons are avoidable, and others are not. Avoidable turnover can also be said to occur among high- and low-value employees. Discharge occurs for performance- and discipline-related problems. Downsizing or RIF comes about because the organization is, or is projected to be, overstaffed in head-count terms.

It is important for the organization to conduct thorough analyses of its turnover. Using a simple formula, turnover rates can be calculated, both overall and broken down by types of turnover, types of employees, job categories, and geographic location. It is also useful to benchmark the organization's turnover rates internally and externally. Another form of analysis is determining reasons that people leave. This can be done via exit interviews, postexit surveys, and employee satisfaction surveys. Analysis of costs and benefits of each of the three types of turnover should also be done. The three major cost categories are separation, replacement, and training. Within each category numerous costs, both financial and nonfinancial, may be estimated. Likewise, each type of turnover has both financial and nonfinancial benefits associated with it that must be weighed against the many costs. A thorough understanding of costs and benefits will help the organization determine where and among whom turnover is the most worrisome, and how to fashion retention strategies and tactics.

To reduce voluntary turnover, organizations engage in numerous retention initiatives centered around direct and variable pay programs, benefits, hours of work schedules, and training and development. Little is known about attempts to increase intrinsic rewards. A decision process may be followed to help decide which, if any, retention initiatives to undertake. The process follows five basic questions: Do we think turnover is a problem? How might we attack the problem? What do we need to decide? Should we proceed? How should we evaluate the programs? To influence the desirability of leaving, the organization must raise job satisfaction by providing both extrinsic and intrinsic rewards. Ease of leaving can possibly be reduced by providing organization-specific training and by increasing the costs of leaving. Finally, retention might be improved by providing more internal job alternatives to employees and by responding forcefully to other job offers they receive.

Discharges might be reduced via formal performance management and progressive discipline systems. The performance management system involves four stages—performance planning, performance execution, performance appraisal, and decisions about the employee. This helps prevent, and correct, performance problems. A progressive discipline system addresses problems of behavioral conduct that violate rules, procedures, laws, and professional and moral standards. It has a series of penalties for misconduct that progress up to termination, which the system seeks to prevent if at all possible.

While downsizing seems to have some obvious benefits, research indicates that there are many costs as well, so the organization should carefully consider whether it really wants to downsize, and if so, by how much in terms of employee numbers and quality. Staffing levels should be achieved in a targeted way rather than across the board. From a staffing quality perspective, cuts could be based on seniority, job performance, or a more holistic assessment of who are the high-value employees the organization desires to retain. There are also many alternatives to downsizing that could be pursued. Attention must be paid to employees who survive a downsizing, or they might create a new retention problem for the organization by starting to leave.

Legally, employee separation from the organization, especially on an involuntary basis, is subject to myriad laws and regulations that the organization must be aware of and incorporate into its retention strategy and tactics. If the organization wishes to base retention decisions on employees' job performance, it should recognize that laws and regulations require performance management systems to be fair and equitable to employees during separation. Based on regulations and court decisions, there are numerous recommendations to be followed for a performance management system to have a chance at withstanding legal challenges and scrutiny.

DISCUSSION QUESTIONS

1. For the three primary causes of voluntary turnover (desirability of leaving, ease of leaving, alternatives), might their relative importance depend on the type of employee or type of job? Explain.
2. Which of the costs and benefits of voluntary turnover are most likely to vary according to type of job? Give examples.
3. If a person says to you, "It's easy to reduce turnover, just pay people more money," what is your response?
4. Why should an organization seek to retain employees with performance or discipline problems? Why not just fire them?
5. Discuss some potential problems with downsizing as an organization's first response to a need to cut labor costs.

ETHICAL ISSUES

1. Consider a circumstance where your organization is doing exit interviews and has promised confidentiality to all who respond. You are responsible for conducting the exit interviews. Your supervisor has asked you to give her the name of each respondent so she can assess the information in conjunction with the person's supervisor. What obligation do corporate HR employees have to keep information confidential in such circumstances?

2. There are numerous negative organizational consequences to firing employees, including the discomfort of the supervisor who needs to deliver the termination information, conflict or sabotage from the departing employee, and the potential for a lawsuit. In response, many supervisors provide problem employees unpleasant work tasks, reduce working hours, or otherwise negatively modify their jobs in hopes that the problem employees will simply quit. What are the ethical issues raised by this strategy?

APPLICATIONS

Managerial Turnover: A Problem?

HealthCareLaunderCare (HCLC) is a company that specializes in picking up, cleaning, and delivering all the laundry for health care providers, especially hospitals, nursing homes, and assisted-care facilities. Basically, these health care providers have outsourced their laundry operations to HCLC. In this very competitive business, a typical contract between HCLC and a health care provider is only two years, and HCLC experiences a contract nonrenewal rate of 10%. Most nonrenewals occur because of dissatisfaction with service costs and especially quality (e.g., surgical garb that is not completely sterilized).

HCLC has 20 laundry facilities throughout the country, mostly in large metropolitan areas. Each laundry facility is headed by a site manager, and there are unit supervisors for the intake, washing, drying, inspection and repair, and delivery areas. An average of 100 nonexempt employees are employed at each site.

Operation of a facility is technologically sophisticated and very health and safety sensitive. In the intake area, for example, employees wear protective clothing, gloves, and eyewear because of all the blood, tissue, and germs on laundry that comes in. The washing area is composed of huge washers in 35-foot stainless steel tunnels with screws that move the laundry through various wash cycles. Workers in this area are exposed to high temperatures and must be proficient in operation of the computer control systems. Laundry is lifted out of the tunnels by robots and moved to the drying room area, where it is dried, ironed, and folded by machines tended by employees. In the inspection and repair area, quality inspection and assurance occurs. Laundry is inspected for germs and pinholes (in the case of surgical garb—pinholes could allow blood and fluids to come into contact with the surgeon), and other employees complete repairs on torn clothing and sheets. In the delivery area, the laundry is hermetically sealed in packages and placed in delivery vans for transport.

HCLC's vice president of operations, Tyrone Williams, manages the sites, and site and unit managers, with an iron fist. Mr. Williams monitors each site with a weekly report of a set of cost, quality, and safety indicators for each of the five areas. When he spots what he thinks are problems or undesirable trends, he has a conference telephone call with both the site manager and the area supervisor. In the decidedly one-way conversation, marching orders are delivered and are expected to be fulfilled. If a turnaround in the "numbers" doesn't show up in the next weekly report, Mr. Williams gives the manager and the supervisor one more week to improve. If sufficient improvement is not forthcoming, various punitive actions are taken, including base pay cuts, demotions, reassignments, and terminations. Mr. Williams feels such quick and harsh justice is necessary to keep HCLC competitive and to continually drive home to all employees the importance of working "by the numbers." Fed up with this management system, many managers have opted to say "bye-bye numbers!" by leaving HCLC.

Recently, the issue of retention of site and unit managers came up on the radar screen of HCLC's president, Roman Dublinski. Mr. Dublinski glanced at a payroll report showing that 30 of the 120 site and unit managers had left HCLC in the past year, though no reasons for leaving were given. In addition, Mr. Dublinski had received a few copies of angry resignation letters written to Mr. Williams. Having never confronted or thought about possible employee retention problems or how to deal with them, Mr. Dublinski calls you (the corporate manager of staffing) to prepare a brief written analysis that will then be used as the basis for a meeting between the two of you and the vice president of HR, Debra Angle (Ms. Angle recommended this). Address the following questions in your report:

1. Is the loss of 30 managers out of 120 in one year cause for concern?
2. What additional data should we try to gather to learn more about our managerial turnover?
3. What are the costs of this turnover? Might there be any benefits?
4. Are there any lurking legal problems?
5. If retention is a serious problem for HCLC, what are the main ways we might attack it?

Retention: Deciding to Act

Wally's Wonder Wash (WWW) is a full-service, high-tech, and high-touch car wash company owned solely by Wally Wheelspoke. Located in a midwestern city of 200,000 people (with another 100,000 in suburbs and more rural towns throughout the county), WWW currently has four facilities within the city. Wally has plans to add four more facilities within the city in the next two years, plus plans a little farther out to begin placing facilities in suburban locations and the rural towns. Major competitors include two other full-service car washes (different owners), plus three touchless automatic facilities (same owner) in the city.

Wally's critical strategy is to provide the very best to customers who want and relish extremely clean and "spiffy" vehicles and to have customers feel a positive experience each time they come to WWW. To do this, WWW seeks to provide high-quality car washes and car detailing and to generate considerable repeat business through competitive prices combined with attention to customers. To make itself accessible to customers, WWW is open seven days a week, 8:00 A.M. to 8:00 P.M. Peak periods, volumewise, are after 1:00 on weekdays and 10:00 to 5:00 on weekends. In addition, Wally uses his workforce to drive his strategy. Though untrained in HR, Wally knows that he must recruit and retain a stable, high-quality workforce if his current businesses, let alone his ambitious expansion plans, are to succeed.

WWW has a strong preference for full-time employees, who work either 7:30 to 4:00 or 11:00 to 8:00. Part-timers are used occasionally to help fill in during peak demand times and during the summer when full-timers are on vacation. There are two major jobs at WWW—attendant (washer) and custom service specialist (detailer). Practicing promotion from within, WWW promotes all specialists from the attendant ranks. There are currently 70 attendants and 20 customer service specialists at WWW. In addition, each facility has a manager. Wally has filled the manager's job by promotion-from-within (from either attendant or custom service specialist ranks) but is unsure if he will be able to continue doing this as he expands.

The job of attendant is a demanding one. Attendants vacuum vehicles from front to rear (and trunk if requested by the customer), wash and dry windows and mirrors, dry vehicles with hand towels, apply special cleaning compounds to tires, wipe down the vehicle's interior, and wash or vacuum floor mats. In addition, attendants wash and fold towels, lift heavy barrels of cleaning compounds and waxes, and perform light maintenance and repair work on the machinery. Finally, and very important, attendants consistently provide customer service by asking customers if they have special requests and by making small talk with them. A unique feature of customer service at WWW is that the attendant must ask the customer to personally inspect the vehicle before leaving to ensure that the vehicle is satisfactorily cleaned (attendants also correct any mistakes pointed out by the customer). The attendants work as a team, with each attendant being expected to be able to perform all of the above tasks.

Attendants start at a base pay of $8.00/hour, with automatic $.50 raises at six months and one year. They receive a brief training from the manager before starting work. Custom service specialists start at $9.00/hour, with $.50 raises after six months and one year. Neither attendants nor custom service specialists receive performance reviews. Managers at each facility all receive a salary of $27,000, plus an annual "merit" raise based on a very casual performance review conducted by Wally (whenever he gets around to it). All attendants share equally in a customer tip pool; custom service specialists receive individual tips. The benefits package is composed of (1) major medical health insurance with a 20% employee co-pay on the premium, (2) paid holidays for Christmas, Easter, July 4, and Martin Luther King, Jr.'s birthday, and (3) a generous paid sick pay plan of two days per month (in recognition of high illness due to extreme working conditions).

In terms of turnover, Wally has spotty and general data only. WWW experienced an overall turnover rate the past year of 65% for attendants and 20% for custom service specialists; no managers left. Though lacking data further back, Wally thinks the turnover rate for attendants has been increasing. WWW's managers constantly complain to Wally about the high level of turnover among attendants and the problems it creates, especially in fulfilling the strong customer-service orientation for WWW. Though the managers have not conducted exit interviews, the major complaints they hear from attendants are (1) pay is not competitive relative to the other full-service car washes or many other entry-level jobs in the area, (2) training is hit-or-miss at best, (3) promotion opportunities are limited, (4) managers provide no feedback or coaching, and (5) customer complaints and mistreatment of attendants by customers are on the rise.

Wally is frustrated by attendant turnover and its threat to his customer service and expansion strategies. Assume he calls on you for assistance in figuring what to do about the problem. Use the decision process shown in Exhibit 14.10 to help develop a retention initiative for WWW. Address each of the questions in the process, specifically:

1. Do we think turnover is a problem?
2. How might we attack the problem?
3. What do we need to decide?
4. Should we proceed?
5. How should we evaluate the initiatives?

TANGLEWOOD STORES CASE

The final stage of the staffing process is ensuring that you are able to retain those individuals you have carefully recruited and selected. This chapter described some of the most well-documented correlates of employee turnover, including perceptions of organizational reward systems, the work environment, communication and justice, and the social environment.

The Situation

Although some retail organizations are comfortable with fairly high turnover, Tanglewood is very concerned about losing the talent and cultural knowledge of its managerial employees. The leaders of the organization are especially worried that competing retail firms have recognized the quality of Tanglewood's employee development plans and are enticing away the best store managers with large salary offers. Corporate staffing representatives have collected information regarding turnover rates and job satisfaction scores for all of its stores. In addition to the raw turnover rates, they have also provided you with data on those employees who have left, including their job performance levels and exit interviews.

Your Tasks

First and foremost, Tanglewood wants you to see if turnover is a serious concern by looking at the relationship between performance and turnover. Once you have determined how much of a concern turnover is, you will investigate why employees are leaving. You will assess what the available information tells you about the reasons for turnover, and also assess what new information Tanglewood might gather in the future to improve its understanding of why turnover occurs. Using Exhibit 14.12 as a guide, you will develop recommendations for how Tanglewood can improve retention with a combination of intrinsic and extrinsic rewards. The background information for this case, and your specific assignment, can be found at *www.mhhe.com/heneman6e*.

ENDNOTES

1. U.S. Department of Labor, "Employee Tenure Study," *News*, Aug. 29, 2000; U.S. Department of Labor, "Mass Layoffs in October 2001," *News*, Nov. 30, 2001; U.S. Department of Labor, "Number of Jobs Held, Labor Market Activity, and Earnings Growth Over Two Decades: Results From a Longitudinal Survey Summary," *News*, Apr. 25, 2000; B. Wysocki, Jr., "When the Job Is From Hell, Recruiting Is Tough," *Wall Street Journal,* July 10, 2001, p. B1.

2. P. W. Hom and R. W. Griffeth, *Employee Turnover* (Cincinnati, OH: South-Western, 1995), pp. 1–12; Saratoga Institute, *Human Capital Benchmarking Report* (Santa Clara, CA: author, 2001).

3. R. W. Griffeth, P. W. Hom, and S. Gaertner, "A Meta-Analysis of Antecedents and Correlates of Employee Turnover," *Journal of Management,* 2000, 26, pp. 463–488; Hom and Griffeth, *Employee Turnover,* pp. 51–107; J. D. Kammeyer-Mueller, C. R. Wanberg, T. M. Glomb, and D. A. Ahlburg, "Turnover Processes in a Temporal Context: It's About Time," *Journal of Applied Psychology,* 2005, 90, pp. 644–658; T. W. Lee and T. R. Mitchell, "An Alternative Approach: The Unfolding Model of Employee Turnover," *Academy of Management Review,* 1994, 19, pp. 51–89; J. G. March and H. A. Simon, *Organizations* (New York: Wiley, 1958); T. R. Mitchell, B. C. Holtom, and T. W. Lee, "How to Keep Your Best Employees: Developing an Effective Retention Policy," *Academy of Management Executive,* 2001, 15(4), pp. 96–107; C. O. Trevor, "Interactions Among Actual Ease of Movement Determinants and Job Satisfaction in the Prediction of Voluntary Turnover," *Academy of Management Journal,* 2001, 44, pp. 621–638.

4. C. D. Crossley, R. J. Bennett, S. M. Jex, and L. Burnfield, "Development of a Global Measure of Job Embeddedness and Integration Into a Traditional Model of Voluntary Turnover," *Journal of Applied Psychology,* 2007, 92, pp. 1031–1042; W. S. Harman, T. W. Lee, T. R. Mitchell, W. Felps, and B. P. Owens, "The Psychology of Voluntary Employee Turnover," *Current Directions in Psychological Science,* 2007, 16, pp. 51–54; F. Niederman, M. Sumner, and C. P. Maertz, Jr., "Testing and Extending the Unfolding Model of Voluntary Turnover to IT Professionals," *Human Resource Management,* 2007, 46, pp. 331–347; C. P. Maertz and M. A. Campion, "Profiles in Quitting: Integrating Content and Process Turnover Theory," *Academy of Management Journal,* 2004, 47, pp. 566–582.

5. N. Drake and I. Robb, *Exit Interviews*, White Paper (Alexandria, VA: Society for Human Resources, 2001); R. W. Griffeth and P. W. Hom, *Retaining Valued Employees* (Cincinnati, OH: South-Western, 2001), pp. 203–222.

6. M. A. Campion, "Meaning and Measurement of Turnover: Comparison and Recommendations for Research," *Journal of Applied Psychology,* 1991, 76, pp. 199–212; H. R. Nalbantian and A. Szostak, "How Fleet Bank Fought Employee Flight," *Harvard Business Review,* Apr. 2004, pp. 116–125; S. Wescott, "Goodbye and Good Luck," *Inc.,* Apr. 2006, pp. 40–41.

7. W. F. Cascio, *Costing Human Resources,* fourth ed. (Cincinnati, OH: South-Western, 2000), pp. 23–57; Griffeth and Hom, *Retaining Valued Employees,* pp. 10–22; Hom and Griffeth, *Employee Turnover,* pp. 13–35.

8. Cascio, *Costing Human Resources,* pp. 83–105; P. C. Gibson and K. S. Piscitelli, *Basic Employment Law Manual for Managers and Supervisors* (Chicago: Commerce Clearing House, 1997); E. E. Schuttauf, *Performance Management Manual for Managers and Supervisors* (Chicago: Commerce Clearing House, 1997).

9. J. N. Barron and D. M. Kreps, *Strategic Human Resources* (New York: Wiley, 1999), pp. 421–445; Cascio, *Costing Human Resources,* pp. 23–57; J. A. Schmidt (ed.), *Making Mergers Work* (New York: Towers, Perrin, Foster and Crosby, 2001), pp. 257–268.

10. S. Craig and J. Singer, "Merrill Confirms 9,000 Job Cuts, Earnings Charge of 2.2 Billion," *Wall Street Journal,* Jan. 10, 2002, p. C1.

11. E. Esen, *U.S. Job Recovery and Retention: Poll Findings* (Alexandria, VA: SHRM Research, 2005).

12. T. A. Judge, J. E. Bono, and E. A. Locke, "Personality and Job Satisfaction: The Mediating Role of Job Characteristics," *Journal of Applied Psychology,* 2000, 85, pp. 237–249; B. T. Loher, R. A. Noe, N. L. Moeller, and M. P. Fitzgerald, "A Meta-Analysis of the Relation of Job Characteristics to Job Satisfaction," *Journal of Applied Psychology,* 1985, 70, pp. 280–289.

13. M. A. Campion and M. M. Mitchell, "Management Turnover: Experiential Differences Between Former and Current Managers," *Personnel Psychology,* 1986, 39, pp. 57–69; Kammeyer-Mueller, Wanberg, Glomb, and Ahlburg, "Turnover Processes in a Temporal Context: It's About Time"; P. E. Spector and S. M. Jex, "Relations of Job Characteristics From Multiple Data Sources With Employee Affect, Absence, Turnover Intentions, and Health," *Journal of Applied Psychology,* 1991, 76, pp. 46–53.

14. WorldatWork, *Attraction and Retention: The Impact and Prevalence of Work-Life & Benefit Programs* (Scottsdale, AZ: author, 2007).

15. A Lashinsky, "Search and Enjoy," *Fortune*, Jan. 22, 2007, pp. 70–84; A. Fisher, "Playing for Keeps," *Fortune,* Jan. 22, 2007, pp. 85–93.

16. J. D. Shaw and N. Gupta, "Pay System Characteristics and Quit Patterns of Good, Average, and Poor Performers," *Personnel Psychology,* 2007, 60, pp. 903–928.

17. J. B. Arthur, "Effects of Human Resource Systems on Manufacturing Performance and Turnover," *Academy of Management Journal,* 1994, 37, pp. 670–687.

18. M. A. Huselid, "The Impact of Human Resource Management Practices on Turnover, Productivity, and Corporate Financial Performance," *Academy of Management Journal,* 1995, 38, pp. 635–672.

19. D. Cadrain, "An Acute Condition: Too Few Nurses," *HR Magazine,* Dec. 2002, pp. 69–71; E. R. Demby, "The Insider: Benefits," *Workforce Management,* Feb. 2004, pp. 57–59; Nalbantian and Szostak, "How Fleet Bank Fought Employee Flight"; S. Overman, "Outback Steakhouse Grills Applicants, Caters to Employees to Keep Turnover Low," SHRM News Online, Oct. 2004 (*www.shrm.org/ema/news_published/CMS_008306.asp*); T. Rutigliano, "Tuning Up Your Talent Engine," *Gallup Management Journal,* Fall 2001, pp. 12–14; G. Strauss, "UPS' Pay, Perks Make It a Destination Job for Many," *Wall Street Journal,* Oct. 14, 2003, pp. B1–B2; E. Zimmerman, "The Joy of Flex," *The Workforce Management 2004 Optimas Awards,* pp. 4–5.

20. H. Axel, "Strategies for Retaining Critical Talent," *The Conference Board,* 1998, 6(2), pp. 4–18; P. Cappelli, "A Market-Driven Approach to Retaining Talent," *Harvard Business Review,* Jan.–Feb. 2000, pp. 103–111; T. Wilson, "Brand Imaging," *ACA News,* May 2000, pp. 44–48.

21. Harris Interactive, *Working in America: The Key to Employee Satisfaction* (Rochester, NY: author, 2007).
22. C. O. Trevor, B. Gerhart, and J. W. Boudreau, "Voluntary Turnover and Job Performance: Curvi-linearity and the Moderating Influences of Salary Growth and Promotions," *Journal of Applied Psychology,* 1997, 82, pp. 44–61; S. J. Peterson and F. Luthans, "The Impact of Financial and Nonfinancial Incentives on Business-Unit Outcomes Over Time," *Journal of Applied Psychology,* 2006, 91, pp. 156–165; Shaw and Gupta, "Pay System Characteristics and Quit Patterns of Good, Average, and Poor Performers"; J. D. Shaw, N. Gupta, and J. E. Delery, "Pay Dispersion and Work Force Performance: Moderating Effects of Incentives and Interdependence," *Strategic Management Journal,* 2002, 23, pp. 491–512; J. D. Shaw, N. Gupta, and J. E. Delery, "Alternative Conceptualizations of the Relationship Between Voluntary Turnover and Organizational Performance," *Academy of Management Journal,* 2005, 48, pp. 50–68.
23. Cappelli, "A Market-Driven Approach to Retaining Talent"; L. Gomez-Mejia and D. Balkin, *Compensation, Organizational Strategy, and Firm Performance* (Cincinnati, OH: South-Western, 1992), pp. 290–307; B. Klaas and J. McClendon, "To Lead, Lag, or Match: Estimating the Financial Impact of Pay Level Policies," *Personnel Psychology,* 1996, 49, pp. 121–140.
24. S. L. Peterson, "Managerial Turnover in U.S. Retail Organizations," *Journal of Management Development,* 2007, 26, pp. 770–789; Griffeth and Hom, *Retaining Valued Employees,* pp. 31–45; Kammeyer-Mueller, Wanberg, Glomb, and Ahlburg, "Turnover Processes in a Temporal Context: It's About Time"; Harman, Lee, Mitchell, Felps, and Owens, "The Psychology of Voluntary Employee Turnover"; Niederman, Sumner, and Maertz, Jr., "Testing and Extending the Unfolding Model of Voluntary Turnover to IT Professionals"; Maertz and Campion, "Profiles in Quitting: Integrating Content and Process Turnover Theory."
25. R. Folger and R. Cropanzano, *Organizational Justice and Human Resource Management* (Thousand Oaks, CA: Sage, 1998); R. A. Postuma, C. P. Maertz, Jr., and J. B. Dworkin, "Procedural Justice's Relationship With Turnover: Explaining Past Inconsistent Findings," *Journal of Organizational Behavior,* 2007, 28, pp. 381–398.
26. Hom and Griffeth, *Employee Turnover,* pp. 93–103; G. Paré and M. Tremblay, "The Influence of High-Involvement Human Resources Practices, Procedural Justice, Organizational Commitment, and Citizenship Behaviors on Information Technology Professionals' Turnover Intentions," *Group & Organization Management,* 2007, 32, pp. 326–357; N. P. Podsakoff, J. A. LePine, and M. A. LePine, "Differential Challenge Stressor-Hindrance Stressor Relationships With Job Attitudes, Turnover Intentions, Turnover, and Withdrawal Behavior: A Meta-Analysis," *Journal of Applied Psychology,* 2007, 92, pp. 438–454.
27. S. Fournier, "Keeping Line Managers in the Know," *ACA News,* 2000, 43(3), pp. 1–3; K. D. Scott, D. Morajda, and J. W. Bishop, "Increase Company Competitiveness," *WorldatWork Journal,* 2002, 11(1), pp. 35–42.
28. Rutigliano, "Tuning Up Your Talent Engine."
29. J. Choi and C. C. Chen, "The Relationships of Distributive Justice and Compensation System Fairness to Employee Attitudes in International Joint Ventures," *Journal of Organizational Behavior,* 2007, 28, pp. 687–703; A. A. Chughtai and S. Zafar, "Antecedents and Consequences of Organizational Commitment Among Pakistani University Teachers," *Applied H.R.M. Research,* 2006, 11, pp. 39–64; T. Kim and K. Leung, "Forming and Reacting to Overall Fairness: A Cross-Cultural Comparison," *Organizational Behavior and Human Decision Processes,* 2007, 104, pp. 83–95.
30. J. Mayfield and M. Mayfield, "The Effects of Leader Communication on a Worker's Intent to Stay: An Investigation Using Structural Equation Modeling," *Human Performance,* 2007, 20, pp. 85–102.

31. B. J. Tepper, "Consequences of Abusive Supervision," *Academy of Management Journal,* 2000, 43, pp. 178–190; J. S. Leonard and D. I. Levine, "The Effect of Diversity on Turnover: A Large Case Study," *Industrial and Labor Relations Review,* 2006, 59, pp. 547–572; P. F. McKay, D. R. Avery, S. Toniandel, M. A. Morris, M. Hernandez, and M. R. Hebl, "Racial Differences in Employee Retention: Are Diversity Climate Perceptions the Key?" *Personnel Psychology,* 2007, 60, pp. 35–62.

32. C. A. Thompson and D. J. Prottas, "Relationships Among Organizational Family Support, Job Autonomy, Perceived Control, and Employee Well-Being," *Journal of Occupational Health Psychology,* 2006, 11, pp. 100–118; N. P. Podsakoff, J. A. LePine, and M. A. LePine, "Differential Challenge Stressor-Hindrance Stressor Relationships With Job Attitudes, Turnover Intentions, Turnover, and Withdrawal Behavior: A Meta-Analysis," *Journal of Applied Psychology,* 2007, 92, pp. 438–454; S. Aryee, V. Luk, and R. Stone, "Family-Responsive Variables and Retention-Relevant Outcomes Among Employed Parents," *Human Relations,* 1998, 51, pp. 73–87; J. Hughes and N. Bozionelos, "Work-Life Balance as Source of Job Dissatisfaction and Withdrawal Attitudes: An Exploratory Study on the Views of Male Workers," *Personnel Review,* 2007, 36, pp. 145–154; T. D. Golden, "Avoiding Depletion in Virtual Work: Telework and the Intervening Impact of Work Exhaustion on Commitment and Turnover Intentions," *Journal of Vocational Behavior,* 2006, 69, pp. 176–187; T. Golden, "Co-workers Who Telework and the Impact on Those in the Office: Understanding the Implications of Virtual Work for Co-worker Satisfaction and Turnover Intentions," *Human Relations,* 2007, 60, pp. 1641–1667.

33. D. J. Hanford, "Stay. Please," *Wall Street Journal,* Apr. 12, 2001, p. R8.

34. E. R. Silverman, "Mercer Tries to Keep Its Employees Through Its 'Externship' Program," *Wall Street Journal,* Nov. 7, 2000, p. B18.

35. A. R. Wheeler, V. C. Gallagher, R. L. Brover, and C. J. Sablynski, "When Person-Organization (Mis)Fit and (Dis)Satisfaction Lead to Turnover: The Moderating Role of Perceived Job Mobility," *Journal of Managerial Psychology,* 2007, 22, pp. 203–219.

36. J. S. Lublin, "In Hot Demand, Retention Czars Face Tough Job," *Wall Street Journal,* Sept. 12, 2000, p. B1.

37. M. Armstrong, *Performance Management,* second ed. (London: Kogan-Page, 2000); D. Grote, *The Complete Guide to Performance Appraisal* (New York: AMACOM, 1996); G. P. Latham and K. N. Wexley, *Increasing Productivity Through Performance Appraisal,* second ed. (Reading, MA: Addison-Wesley, 1994); Schuttauf, *Performance Management Manual for Managers and Supervisors.*

38. Grote, *The Complete Guide to Performance Appraisal,* Society for Human Resource Management, *Performance Management Survey* (Alexandria, VA: author, 2000).

39. M. Rotundo and P. R. Sackett, "The Relative Importance of Task, Citizenship, and Counterproductive Performance to Global Ratings of Job Performance: A Policy Capturing Approach," *Journal of Applied Psychology,* 2002, 87, pp. 66–80; J. W. Johnson, "The Relative Importance of Task and Contextual Performance Dimensions to Supervisor Judgments of Overall Performance," *Journal of Applied Psychology,* 2001, 86, pp. 984–996; P. R. Sackett, C. M. Berry, S. A. Wiemann, and R. M. Laczo, "Citizenship and Counterproductive Behavior: Clarifying Relations Between the Two Domains," *Human Performance,* 2006, 19, pp. 441–464; F. Lievens, J. M. Conway, and W. De Corte, "The Relative Importance of Task, Citizenship, and Counterproductive Performance to Job Performance Ratings: Do Rater Source and Team-Based Culture Matter?" *Journal of Occupational and Organizational Psychology* (in press).

40. G. A. Stoskopf, "Taking Performance Management to the Next Level," *Workspan,* Feb. 2002, pp. 26–33.

41. F. T. Coleman, *Ending the Employment Relationship Without Ending Up in Court* (Alexandria, VA: Society for Human Resource Management, 2001); J. G. Frierson, *Preventing Employment Lawsuits* (Washington, DC: Bureau of National Affairs, 1997); Gibson and Piscitelli, *Basic Employment Law Manual for Managers and Supervisors.*

42. Gibson and Piscitelli, *Basic Employment Law Manual for Managers and Supervisors,* pp. 51–53.

43. Frierson, *Preventing Employment Lawsuits*, pp. 140–141.

44. Schuttauf, *Performance Management Manual for Managers and Supervisors,* pp. 43–45.

45. Frierson, *Preventing Employment Lawsuits,* pp. 358–365; Gibson and Piscitelli, *Basic Employment Law Manual for Managers and Supervisors,* pp. 48–53.

46. Coleman, *Ending the Employment Relationship Without Ending Up in Court,* pp. 51–84.

47. Barron and Kreps, *Strategic Human Resources,* pp. 421–443; Society for Human Resource Management, *Layoffs and Job Security Survey* (Alexandria, VA: author, 2001).

48. W. F. Cascio, L. E. Young, and J. R. Morris, "Financial Consequences of Employment-Change Decisions in Major U.S. Corporations," *Academy of Management Journal,* 1997, 40, pp. 1175–1189; J. C. McElroy, P. C. Morrow, and S. N. Rude, "Turnover and Organizational Performance: A Comparative Analysis of the Effects of Voluntary, Involuntary, and Reduction-in-Force Turnover," *Journal of Applied Psychology,* 2001, 86, pp. 1294–1299.

49. Barron and Kreps, *Strategic Human Resources,* pp. 424–430.

50. P. Barta, "In This Expansion, As Business Booms, So Do the Layoffs," *Wall Street Journal,* Mar. 13, 2000, p. A1; L. Uchitelle, "Pink Slip? Now It's All in a Day's Work," *New York Times,* Aug. 5, 2001, p. BU1.

51. Bureau of National Affairs, *Basic Patterns in Union Contracts* (Washington, DC: author, 1995), pp. 67–88; J. A. Fossum, *Labor Relations,* eighth ed. (Burr Ridge, IL: McGraw-Hill/Irwin, 2002), pp. 126–127.

52. M. Conlin, "Where Layoffs Are a Last Resort," *Business Week,* Oct. 8, 2001, p. 42; Q. Hardy, "Cease Firing," *Fortune,* Nov. 26, 2001; "How No Layoffs Can Work," Nov. 6, 2001 (*www.businessweek.com/careers*).

53. F. Crandall and M. J. Wallace, Jr., "Down(sized) but Not Out," *Workspan,* Nov. 2001, pp. 31–35.

54. A. Freedman, "Serving the Survivors," *Human Resource Executive,* Dec. 2001, p. 47.

55. Freedman, "Serving the Survivors."

56. Coleman, *Ending the Employment Relationship Without Ending Up in Court;* Frierson, *Preventing Employment Lawsuits;* S. C. Kahn, B. B. Brown, and M. Lanzarone, *Legal Guide to Human Resources* (Boston: Warren, Gorham and Lamont, 2001), pp. 9-3 to 9-82; D. P. Twomey, *Labor and Employment Law,* eleventh ed. (Cincinnati, OH: South-Western, 2001); E. Lipsig, M. E. Dollarhide, and B. K. Seifert, *Reductions in Force in Employment Law* (Washington, DC: BNA Books, 2007).

57. M. M. Elvira and C. D. Zatrick, "Who's Displaced First? The Role of Race in Layoff Decisions," *Industrial Relations,* 2002, 41, pp. 329–361.

58. D. Rodriguez and M. Zavodny, "Changes in Age and Education Profiles of Displaced Workers," *Industrial and Labor Relations Review,* 2003, 56, pp. 498–510.

59. Kahn, Brown, and Lanzarone, *Legal Guide to Human Resources,* pp. 6-2 to 6-58; D. C. Martin, K. M. Bartol, and P. E. Kehoe, "The Legal Ramifications of Performance Appraisal," *Public Personnel Management,* 2000, 29, pp. 379–406; J. M. Werner and M. C. Bolino, "Explaining U.S. Courts of Appeals Decisions Involving Performance Appraisals: Accuracy, Fairness, and Validation," *Personnel Psychology,* 1997, 50, pp. 1–24; J. Marquez, "Is G.E.'s Ranking System Broken?" *Workforce Management,* June 25, 2007, pp. 1–3; M. Orey, "Fear of Firing," *Business Week*, Apr. 23, 2007, pp. 52–62.

NAME INDEX

SUBJECT INDEX

50
Great Ghost
Stories

EDITED BY
JOHN CANNING

BELL PUBLISHING COMPANY · NEW YORK

Contents

CONTENTS

CONTENTS

Editor's Note

In the process of sifting the material for a book such as this, one becomes aware inevitably of the amount of evidence there is in support of ghosts. (I use the word "ghosts" not only in its normally accepted meaning of the ethereal presentation of a dead person to the living, but in the wider sense of psychic manifestations generally —precognition, telepathy, astral wanderings, clairvoyance, clairaudience, the psychical propulsion of physical objects, etc.)

Scientific circles, for so long sceptical, have shown a greater tendency than ever before to believe that there may be at least a field here for investigation. The Society for Psychical Research in London made a start in 1882; the researches of J. B. Rhine at Duke University have been notable, whilst in Europe the work of Whately Carington and S. G. Soal has attracted attention; and the University of Utrecht has set up a laboratory for the study of parapsychological phenomena.

Distinguished men brought up in the disciplines of science, such as Sir Arthur Conan Doyle and Sir Oliver Lodge, have been among the whole-hearted believers in psychic phenomena and life beyond the grave. And in any event the orientation of science has changed to provide an atmosphere much more favourable to the existence of paranormal occurrences. The old Newtonian conception of a universe of three-dimensional space separated absolutely from time has given place in physics to a universe of space-time in which space and time are indissolubly linked.

Dunne in his absorbing study of precognition through dreams,* argues impressively for a four-dimensional "serial" universe in which the dreamer, freed from the waking habit of viewing time from moment to moment in a one-directional stream, slips into a four-dimensional space-time consciousness which allows him to travel freely about time both forwards and backwards. Such a consciousness extended occasionally into the waking state could account for such happenings as are recounted in some of the stories in this book—"The Ghosts of Versailles", " 'Steer Nor'West' ", "The Return of Richard Tarwell", and a number of others. (It is interesting to speculate about the changes in men's lives and attitudes if such a faculty were in the course of evolution to become as established in their mental structure as, say, rational thought.)

However, when all is said and done, this is a book intended neither to prove nor disprove anything but simply to entertain. And I hope the reader will feel that this is what it does.

JOHN CANNING

*An Experiment with Time, J. W. Dunne.

Ghosts of Ancient Egypt

The obsession which the ancient Egyptians had with the other world seems to have created powerful supernatural forces which have lasted for thousands of years. Some of the most sinister and potent ghostly activity reported in modern times stems from Ancient Egypt, whose ageless hauntings have spanned fifty centuries and more.

The Cult of the Dead, which originated in India, reached its apotheosis in Egypt. At first the Egyptians believed that only members of the royal family and certain chosen companions were privileged to enjoy eternal life. Later the hereafter became democratized and at first nobles and high officials, and finally all "good men" were permitted through the eternal gates.

It is strange that, for all their preoccupation with eternity, the Egyptians never evolved a sophisticated religion. They were not however alone in considering life on earth merely as a brief preparation for the great hereafter. Their chief god became Osiris, who ruled in the region of the dead and who was believed to have fathered all the Pharaohs. The Egyptians were so obsessed with this Cult of the Dead that they turned the teeming and fruitful valley of the Nile into a place devoted to the dead.

They believed that a soul could not enter the blessed region of Osiris unless his body remained intact in the place where he had lived on earth, and therefore very great importance was placed upon the preservation of the body and the inviolability of the tomb. To despoil a tomb and remove a mummy from its coffin was to the

Egyptians an act of terrible desecration. The awful and solemn ceremonies which took place at the entombment included the most terrible curses on the tomb-breakers, and these curses were inscribed upon the walls of the death chambers.

In view of the intensity of their feeling on this subject, it is not surprising that we hear stories of spirits disturbed in their eternal rest by the despoliation of their earthly tombs, perhaps many thousands of years after their burial, and returning to earth to seek vengeance.

The dread inscriptions on the tombs were supposed to have an especial potency owing to the deep belief the ancient Egyptians had in the magic of the written word. They believed that the very act of writing down the curses would ensure their effectiveness.

Such imprecations were made at the rich and splendid funeral of Tutenkhamen in the middle of the fourteenth century B.C. This unimportant sovereign was only eighteen at his death. He was the son-in-law and successor of Akhnaton, one of the most remarkable of the Pharaohs.

Both the splendour of Tutenkhamen's unspoiled tomb and his father-in-law's religious convictions, which shook Egypt to its foundations, had strange echoes in the twentieth century, with stories which suggested that those ancient Nile curses had a remarkable and far-reaching power.

Akhnaton forsook the ancient gods of Egypt—including the sacred Osiris—and worshipped the sun-god Aton. He abandoned Thebes, the magnificent city of the god Ammon, and transferred the country's religious centre to Al Amarna in the plain of Hermopolis, where he built splendid temples to Aton.

But the ancient religion was not readily abandoned by the ordinary superstitious Egyptians, and the old priesthood, though temporarily dispossessed and forced to remain silent, worked relentlessly in the background against the heretic Pharaoh.

Akhnaton is regarded by many as an enlightened prophet who foresaw the truth of monotheism, an inspired intellectual in an age of priest-ridden superstition. His Queen was the beautiful and famous Nefertiti. Akhnaton had no son, but six daughters who constantly appeared with him in the religious ceremonies at Amarna. Entirely wrapped up in his religious activities, Akhnaton neglected his country and lost his empire in Syria, which fell to the Hittite hordes, while Akhnaton wrote poems to Aton.

He had made many enemies in Egypt, where a dangerous situation was brewing. In an attempt to combat this, he married his

eldest daughter to the young Tutenkhamen, one of his favourites, and whom he appointed co-regent with himself when the boy was merely twelve years of age.

Akhnaton was faced with family as well as national dissension. It seems certain that his Queen Nefertiti fell into disfavour, for it has been discovered that her name was removed from some of the family monuments at Amarna. The inference is that the family trouble was religious. This was reinforced by another more sensational story which was told later.

One of Akhnaton's daughters turned violently against her father over the religious question. Akhnaton is said to have treated her with shocking brutality and had her raped and killed. His priests then cut off her right hand and buried it secretly in the Valley of the Kings. As she had reverted to the old religion, this would effectively exclude her from entering the blessed region of Osiris as her body was not intact at her burial.

Akhnaton did not live for long, dying in 1358 B.C. in the seventeenth year of his reign, and at about the age of thirty. His son-in-law, Tutenkhamen, succeeded him and reigned for about six years and was consigned to his magnificent and famous tomb.

The hand of his sister-in-law remained buried in the secret place in the Valley of the Kings under a curse that it was never to be re-united to the body of the princess, who was thus excluded from paradise. For more than three thousand years apparently the princess awaited at the gates of Osiris, her inexhaustible vigil being finally rewarded in a remarkable, if incredible, manner.

The story was told by Count Louis Hamon, a well-known occultist of the day, that in the 1890s he was in Luxor where he became friendly with one of the local sheikhs. The sheikh caught malaria and Hamon was able to cure him. The sheikh expressed his gratitude by presenting to him a mummified hand which, he said, had belonged to a princess of Ancient Egypt, the daughter of Akhnaton, who had been killed and mutilated for opposing her father's heretical religious faith.

This curious gift did not in any way repulse Count Hamon, who had a great interest in the religion of ancient Egypt, the priests of which he believed possessed knowledge and power undreamed of by modern man. He thanked the grateful sheikh and added the mummified hand of the princess to his treasures and curiosities which he had collected during his world travels in search of the unknown and the unfathomable.

In the 1920s Hamon and his wife were living in England, and in

1922 he noticed that the hand which had been shrivelled and mummified for the last thirty-two centuries began to soften and to his amazement and incredulity blood appeared in the veins under the skin.

Hamon and his wife were not unnaturally disturbed at this miraculous development. The count was well acquainted with the workings of the occult, and he decided to bring the matter to a head by burning the hand on the night of Halloween. This is the night when witches and spirits are abroad, and the night, too, when according to some ancient tradition, the souls of the lost are released from their eternal bondage to return to the earth. Hamon knew the story of the daughter of Nefertiti and that according to her deeply-held religion she was one of the lost.

Hamon cast the hand on the fire and read over it prayers from the Egyptian Book of the Dead. Upon that very moment, he says, the doors burst open with a sudden uprising of wind and in the door-way stood the figure of the princess from Ancient Egypt.

Nefertiti's daughter made a splendid appearance in her ancient royal apparel, with the serpent of the House of the Pharaohs glittering on her head-dress. As she went over to the fire Hamon noticed that her right arm ended at the wrist, just as she had been mutilated those many centuries ago. The phantom bent over the fire, and then in a moment was gone. Instantly Hamon went to the fire and found that the mummified hand had also gone.

This was on the last day of October, 1922, and a few days later Hamon read that Lord Carnarvon's expedition had discovered the tomb of King Tutenkhamen in the Valley of the Kings.

Why did the princess's hand come to life at this particular moment during her eternal vigil outside the gates of Osiris? Count Hamon did not pretend to know the answer to this riddle, but he believed that the ancient Egyptians possessed strange and remarkable powers, and had the key to many mysteries unknown to modern man. He obviously connected this weird and fantastic story with the discovery by modern Egyptologists of the tomb of the princess's brother-in-law, Tutenkhamen.

Now this famous tomb had an unusual history. As everyone knows, the Egyptians had for centuries buried their kings in the pyramids, which were just huge shells of masonry built around the royal burial chamber. But they had been a singularly ineffective form of protection, for every pyramid had been plundered of its treasures by generations of tomb robbers, who thrived in Ancient Egypt undeterred by the awful curses laid by the priests upon those

who disturb the holy sleep of the royal departed. The Pharaohs eventually abandoned pyramid burial and made their tombs in the cliffs of the Nile. Even so, the tomb plunderers sought them out, and at the time of the fall of the Egyptian Empire (1150 B.C.) not one royal tomb remained unplundered.

It was quite by accident that the burial place of Tutenkhamen remained undisturbed throughout the centuries. Shortly after his burial had taken place, tomb robbers broke into the splendid sepulchre, and were discovered in the act. The grim fate of the robbers can be left to the imagination. The loot was all replaced, with the exception of some of the gold vessels which apparently proved too much of a temptation for certain officials and mysteriously disappeared during the replacement of the treasures. After that the tomb remained undisturbed, and probably well guarded. Two hundred years later the excavations for the tomb of Rameses VI resulted in the tomb of Tutenkhamen being completely buried underneath tons of limestone rubble.

The actual discovery of the tomb on 4 November, 1922—four days after the princess retrieved the precious hand which would at long last gain her access to the realms of Osiris—was made by Howard Carter, a well-known Egyptologist whose expedition in the Nile Valley was financed by Lord Carnarvon. The richness and beauties of Tutenkhamen's tomb had long been told in legend. It was said that it had been filled with the most priceless treasures. A story had been told for centuries that Akhnaton had chosen Tutenkhamen to succeed him because he possessed some kind of supernatural powers, and that these powers had protected his sacred tomb throughout the ages. The opening of the tomb therefore was surrounded by foreboding from the start.

When he read of the imminent opening of Tutenkhamen's tomb Count Hamon wrote urgently to Lord Carnarvon recounting his fantastic experience with the hand of the dead Pharaoh's sister-in-law, and begged him not to defy the curse and enter the forbidden tomb, which he would do at the risk of his life.

"The ancient Egyptians possessed knowledge and powers of which we today have no comprehension," wrote Hamon. "Take care not to offend their spirits."

Carnarvon was at first so impressed by this warning that he decided not to open the tomb and tempt the ancient curse, but Carter would not listen. He had no intention of giving up years of labour on account of an ancient curse which was calculated to frighten the superstitious and the ignorant. Carter was so deter-

mined that Carnarvon gave in. After all, he had given his warning.

On 22 February, 1923, they entered the tomb, Carnarvon being first, followed by Carter (the order was apparently important), the event being accompanied by a blaze of world-wide publicity. This was the first and only time that such a tomb had been found intact, and even the archaeologists who knew more or less what to expect were astonished at the unparalleled magnificence of the tomb furnishings of the young Pharaoh.

It was a sombre moment when these artistic wonders and treasures of the ancient world were revealed once more to human eyes after their three-thousand-year entombment in the Nile cliffs. Tutenkhamen lay in a splendid sarcophagus of blue and gold. The outer coffin richly wrought in gold was uniquely beautiful. The mummy case, made in his likeness, was inlaid with gold and lapis lazuli.

For many long and devoted months Carter worked among these ancient and mysterious splendours, salvaging the magnificent treasure, most of which was put in the National Museum at Cairo. When he opened the mummy-case, he found that the consecration balm had through the centuries hardened into a pitchlike substance which had made the body adhere to the bottom of the golden coffin. The examination of the body showed that Tutenkhamen had been about eighteen years old, and no sign could be discovered that he had not met a natural death.

Carter immersed himself in these fascinating excavations which occupied him until 1924, completely undisturbed by the curse which was presumed to have descended upon him.

It is not to be supposed that such spirits as have an eternal vigil at these ancient places of burial are less perturbed when the plunder takes place in the interests of archaeology. Taking a mummy from its coffin was considered an act of the most appalling desecration, the perpetrator of which was threatened with swift and fearful retribution, whatever his motive might be.

During the excavation of Tutenkhamen's tomb Lord Carnarvon was bitten by a mosquito, and after several months of illness he died in Cairo on 5 April, 1923. A few years later his brother committed suicide and his stepmother died after another mysterious insect bite.

Naturally much was made of the ancient curse. But Carter, an inveterate tomb-opener, and who had done the real work of excavating Tutenkhamen's tomb, suffered no ill-effects and continued his work until 1939 when he died at the age of sixty-six.

But those who believe in the tomb curse say that it applies to the

first man to enter the burial chamber, and Lord Carnarvon, whose expedition it was, claimed that honour himself and was swiftly struck down.

Nevertheless the fact remains that many tombs of the Pharaohs upon which the solemn curse was laid have been opened and plundered with apparent impunity throughout the ages. Carnarvon seems to have believed in the curse, and it has been observed that people who believe in curses are more likely to be struck down by them.

More effective was the curse laid upon those who handled the mummy-case of another princess of Ancient Egypt who had been a high-priestess in the Temple of Amon-Ra. She was supposed to have lived in Thebes in about 1600 B.C. The outside of the case bore her image worked in gold and enamel. It was in an unusually good state of preservation and was bought by the late Douglas Murray many years ago while on a visit to Egypt.

Murray knew nothing about the curse at the time, and though he confessed to a slight aversion of this object of ancient curiosity, he could not resist the temptation to acquire it, which he did and had it packed up and sent to London.

Much has been written about this particular mummy-case, and it has been said that nearly everyone who had anything to do with it suffered accident or misfortune. Certainly Douglas Murray came by a terrible accident when, a few days after he had bought it, he went on a shooting expedition up the Nile and the gun he was carrying exploded unaccountably in his hand. Murray lay in great agony while the boat was hastily turned round to return to Cairo for him to have urgent medical attention, but head-winds of unusual force persistently held them up and it was ten days before they reached Cairo, by which time gangrene had set in. Murray suffered weeks of agony in hospital and his arm had to be amputated above his elbow.

Disaster also befell his companions, both of whom died during the voyage back to England and were buried at sea. Two Egyptian servants who had handled the mummy-case also died within a year. When the ship arrived at Tilbury it was found that valuable Egyptian curiosities Murray had bought in Cairo had been stolen.

But the mummy-case was there awaiting him. Whatever he had lost, he had not lost that, and he said that when he had looked at the carved face of the priestess which was upon it, her eyes seemed to come to life and look at him with a malevolence that turned his blood cold. He promptly gave the fatal mummy-case away to a

lady, upon whom disaster immediately befell. Her mother broke her leg and died after months of prolonged suffering. The lady lost her fiancé, who for no apparent reason declined to marry her. Her pets died and she became ill herself with an undiagnosable complaint which wasted her away so much that she feared death and instructed her lawyer to make her will.

The lawyer, hearing the story, agreed to make the will, but at the same time insisted on packing up the mummy-case and returning it to Douglas Murray. The lady thereupon recovered, but Murray, whose health was broken, wanted to have nothing more to do with the accursed relic, and presented it to the British Museum, which was presumably too impersonal and scientific an institution to be affected by such superstitions as ancient Egyptian curses.

But, it seems, everyone who had anything to do with this mummy-case encountered disaster in some shape or form. A photographer who took pictures of it, which when developed showed living, malevolent eyes in the carved face of the priestess, died mysteriously a few weeks later. Likewise an Egyptologist who looked after the exhibit while awaiting the Museum's decision to accept it, was shortly afterwards found dead in bed. The Museum finally accepted it and spent much time subsequently denying stories of strange and unaccountable things taking place in the Egyptian Section. Eventually they had it removed to the cellars.

Many other strange stories were told about this famous mummy-case. It was even said that the British Museum presented the unwanted thing to the New York Museum and sent it over on the ill-starred *Titanic*. But perhaps it is stretching things a little to blame the ancient Egyptians for that particular disaster.

Chased by a Prehistoric Horseman

Ghosts of pre-history are scarce. Most of them, one presumes, are so old that they have become worn out. The Devil is the exception who proves the rule.

I have never met a man who has seen a Druidic ghost under the standing stones of Stonehenge on a lonely night of moon and stars, but I know a strange, incredibly ancient grove of gnarled and witch-like oaks in an old park meadow at the back of a little manor-house on the edge of the Essex marshes. The church is tiny, forlorn and derelict. When I knew it first some of the window-panes were of horn. The nearby heronry is in a little wood surrounded by double moats. And in the park at the back of Hall and church where the lines of ancient oaks are planted as to pattern, there was, the legend says, once a Druid altar where blood ran.

I have had the shooting on that remote, marshland estate for many years. I have crossed that old, small park under the moon, in snow-mist, in bright sunlight and in the glimmer of dawn. It has an atmosphere like that of no other place I know. It literally smells of pre-history. But I have never seen a ghost of a Druid or of any man of Ancient Britain.

I know a pictish broch on a high moor above Donside in Aberdeenshire built like a great stone beehive. There dwelt the Little Men, the Picts, long before Scottish history was written. I would not care to sleep in that broch alone.

We may count the Pixies of Cornwall and Devon and the fairies of elsewhere not so much as prehistoric people since they belong to

all time, but when one speaks of prehistoric ghosts one thinks of spectres of the Ancient Briton, the little Pict creeping through the heather, the dark Girvii of the Eastern fens and the rest of the tribesmen of pre-Roman days and the lower, more brutal types, of mankind who were their predecessors.

I know a lonely island called Vallay, across a wide, seaweed-strewn strand of sand and shining pools off the coast of North Uist in the Outer Hebrides. On that island stands a great empty house, alone with the winds and the booming surges. In the heart of the island is a hollow where you will see the ruined walls and downcast stones of beehive-shaped dwellings.

There I have shot curlew and golden plover, wild duck and the grey geese, and seen the raven hunt the tide-line and the golden eagle pass over, lordly in the high sun. Vallay is a rare place for wild birds and wild beauty. There are sheep upon it and cattle, wild-eyed as hawks. Once a rich man, something of a hermit, but a very good naturalist and a keen sportsman, lived in that great house which now stands empty. One day he was drowned and his body was cast up on the rocks. Since then no one has lived in the Great House.

A year or two back, when I was shooting on Vallay, I said to the gamekeeper and the ghillie with him:

"The tide's right. The geese will be in soon. There are thousands of duck out at sea waiting to come in to the lochan. We'll stay for the flight and go home by the moon."

They refused point-blank. Two strong Hebridean men who would round up a bull, climb a mountain, walk the bogs and moors all day, launch a boat in an Atlantic blow and think nothing of climbing up to an eagle's eyrie. But the thought of an hour of dusk, let alone full night, on Vallay terrified them. Not once, but several times, politely but firmly, they hustled me off the island and across the sands to North Uist long before the sun had set.

"Is it the ghost of the drowned laird?" I asked them. It was not. They confessed in the end that "the auld people, the wee men" came out of those ruined stone beehives under the moon. Not for a handful of five-pound notes would they stay a night on Vallay. The ghosts of pre-history walked there.

Here and there, particularly in downland country and in ancient woodlands, you will come across places which have more than a hint, more than a whisper, of Diana and her nymphs, of the ancient gods of Rome.

My lamented friend, the late Patrick Chalmers, that graceful poet of gun and rod who knew and loved the corners of forgotten England,

wrote, in one of his enchanting verses, of the wind in the pine tops:

> Its song was of wayside altars (the pine-tops sighed like the surf),
> Of little shrines uplifted, of stone and scented turf,
> Of youths divine and immortal, of maids as white as the snow
> That glimmered among the thickets, a mort of years ago.
> All in the cool of dawn, all in the twilight grey,
> The gods they came from Italy along the Roman way.

But, alas, on ancient hills and in Druidic groves, on hill-top camps and moorland brochs, on Badbury Rings and Arbor Low, on Avebury Downs and by classic streams:

> The altar smoke it has drifted and faded afar on the hill;
> No wood-nymph haunts the hollows; the reedy pipes are still;
> No more the youth, Apollo, shall walk in the sunshine clear;
> No more the maid, Diana, shall follow the fallow-deer.

Nymphs and fairies, Picts and pixies survive as charming beliefs seen by few, immortalized by poets.

No one sings a song to the Ancient Briton, yet he was a triumph of survival. He lived in a land hideous with wolves. His only weapons were flint-tipped arrows, a flint axe or a bronze-shod spear. He was a master of the art of survival. Wolves, those grey forest skulkers, "the witches' horses", who galloped under the moon, were not his sole enemies. We cannot say, within a thousand years, when the Stone Age merged into the Bronze Age, but it is probable that the man of the Bronze Age had to fight not only the grey wolves of the forest who swept down upon his flocks, more terrible than the Assyrians in purple and gold, but against the brown bear, shambling from its cave. It is possible even that cave lions and sabre-toothed tigers made his life a private hell.

We do know that the Bronze Age man could tame and ride a horse, bare-backed and possibly without bit or bridle. Even more incredible, he tamed the giant aurochs, *bos primigenius*, that vast shaggy animal who dwarfed the American bison of today. That much we know from Lydekker.

During the Bronze Age, which according to Montelius lasted from 2000 B.C. to 800 B.C., three-quarters of England was dark with forests or drowned by swampy moors and misty fens, haunts of wolves and boars, brown bears and yellow fevers. The Ancient Briton not only had a job to live, but few places wherein he could live with comparative safety.

That is why so many of his barrows, tumuli, camps, weapons, cooking-pots, ornaments and pathetic household goods are found

on the high chalk downs. Chalk meant few trees. Where there were few trees there were few wolves.

So the Ancient Briton built his huts, fortified his camp, tended his herds of sheep, swine and goats, trained his wild horses, knapped his flints and lived his life mainly on the bare chalk, the thymy downs. There the winds blew free. Larks sang. Harebells danced in the summer breeze, like fields of asphodel. Conies burrowed in the chalk and were there for the catching. The night dews filled the dew ponds with sweet water. His children gambolled on the short turf in the bright sun. His stockade of pointed stakes was a barrier by day against foes, even as his glinting fire, leaping in red and yellow tongues, was the terror of wolves by night.

Far below, in the valley or on the outflung green and sullen waves of the wealden plains, there lurked every sort of terror that could menace a man and his family. Up here on the downs, where a man might see for miles, ambush and sudden attack were not easy. Astride his fleet horse, bow in hand, dagger in belt, hound at heel, the Bronze Age man was, in his far-off, fustian way, a knightly fellow.

Now, although the chalk downs of Wiltshire and Gloucestershire, of Dorset and Hampshire and all those wide and windy miles of still-lovely England are studded with the burial mounds, the ancient camps and the shadows in the grass that mean their vanished homes, although Stonehenge still stands against the stars in ghastly grandeur and cromlech and dolemn tell the bloody tale of far-off sacrifices, ghosts and hauntings are few and far between.

Here and there the Romans left their spirits behind. I know of a centurion who still walks the Roman Strood between Mersea Island and the mainland, with ringing steps on moonlight nights, and I could take you to a mud-flat on the Thames where a Viking in winged helm wades ashore under the moon, in endless quest for his vanished longship. But although I have stood in Stonehenge by night, and walked the glimmering woodland aisles of that ancient wood of the Druids which they call Staverton Forest in East Suffolk, I have never met man or woman who had any true tale to tell of a ghost of Ancient Britain, of a haunting of pre-Saxon days, until there came a letter in the post in August, 1956. The writer was Mr R. C. C. Clay, who lives at the Manor House, Fovant, near Salisbury. Mr Clay is not only an extremely busy professional man with a practice which covers a wide extent of that country of chalk downs nd glimmering plains, but he is a Fellow of the Society of Antiquaries.

In his letter, Mr Clay said: "In response to your letter in the *Salisbury Journal* of 24 August, I am sending you an account of a personal encounter with a prehistoric horseman, just over the Dorset border. Three episodes with 'ghosts' in my own house, which were not witnessed by others, would not come within the scope of your inquiry and I have not included them."

Mr Clay then went on to give the following account of the appearance of a prehistoric horseman, probably of the Bronze Age. It is, I believe, unique in the annals of ghost-hunters. Here it is.

"In 1924, I was in charge of the excavations carried out by the Society of Antiquaries on the Late Bronze Urnfield at Pokesdown, near Bournemouth. Every afternoon I drove down to the site and returned at dusk.

"One evening I was motoring home along the straight road which cuts the open downland between Cranborne and Sixpenny Handley. I had reached the spot between the small clump of beeches on the east and the pine-wood on the west, where the road dips before rising to cross the Roman road from Badbury Rings to Old Sarum. I saw away to my right a horseman travelling on the downland towards Sixpenny Handley, that is to say, he was going in the same direction as I was going. Suddenly he turned his horse's head, and galloped as if to reach the road ahead of me, and to cut me off.

"I was so interested that I changed gear to slow down so that we should meet, and that I should be able to see who the man was. However, before I had drawn level with him, he turned his horse again to the north, and galloped along parallel to me and about fifty yards from the road.

"I could see that he was no ordinary horseman, for he had bare legs, and wore a long, loose cloak. His horse had a long mane and tail, but I could see neither bridle nor stirrup. His face was turned towards me, but I could not see his features. He seemed to be threatening me with some implement, which he waved in his right hand above his head.

"I now realized that he was a prehistoric man, and I did my best to identify the weapon so that I could date him. After travelling along-side my car for about one hundred yards, the rider and horse suddenly vanished. I noted the spot, and found next day, when I drove along the road in daylight, that it coincided with a low, round barrow which I had never noticed before.

"Many times afterwards at all hours of the day, when I was weary, and when I was alert, I tried to see my horseman again. I

tried to find some bush or other object which my tired brain could have transformed into a horseman. I had no success.

"I made inquiries in the district, and after a few months, Mr Young, the well-known iron craftsman of Ebbesbourne Wake, told me that he had asked many of his friends in Sixpenny Handley if anyone had ever seen a ghost on the downs between the village and Cranborne, and that one old shepherd had replied:

" 'Do you mean the man on the horse that comes out of the opening in the pinewood?'

"A year or two later a friend of mine, a well-known archaeologist, wrote to me as follows:

" 'Your horseman has turned up again. Two girls, cycling from Handley to a dance at Cranborne one night lately, have complained to the police that a man on a horse had followed them over the downs and had frightened them.' "

This record is of the first importance. Not only is it vouched for by a highly qualified eye-witness, but it has the additional value of being corroborated by other witnesses. In short, it is probably the best and, possibly, the first example of a Stone Age or Bronze Age haunting in the country.

Two significant points emerge from the evidence. The first is that Mr Clay saw man and horse both suddenly vanish near "a low, round barrow". The second is that the old shepherd apparently knew the ghost well and had often seen it come "out of the opening in the pinewood . We may deduce from this, first, that the horseman had probably been mortally wounded whilst in the woodland —the eternal haunt and hiding-place of the enemies of his race and time—and secondly, that he lies buried, with his horse, "in the low, round barrow". Thus his spectral ride from the pinewood to the barrow probably signifies his last living journey on earth.

There is no doubt that men of the Bronze Age, probably chieftains, were often buried not only with their horses, but with a pig to give them pork, deer to give them venison and goats to give them milk in the life hereafter. Frequently they were incinerated before burial. When, for example, the Money Hill Barrow on Therfield Heath on the Cambridgeshire–Hertfordshire borders was excavated by Mr Beldam, the local squire, in 1861, he found a cist cut in the chalk, 2 feet long by 18 inches in depth and width, containing the cremated bones of a child aged about two years, placed in an elaborately decorated cinerary urn. The barrow, which was 15 feet high and 100 feet in diameter, was apparently a family "vault" of the Bronze Age, in which numerous people, presumably of a noble or chieftainly

family, had been buried. When the diggers got down through successive layers of clay, charcoal, ashes and decayed turf, they found not only clear evidence of other human burials, but the bones of pig, horse, roe deer and goat. Similar evidences of domestic animals and deer, including horses, being buried in Bronze and Iron Age barrows are by no means uncommon. The chances are, therefore, that if Mr Clay's low, round barrow were excavated today we should discover the remains not only of the spectral horseman, but also of his horse.

Now comes a very different sort of haunting, but equally well authenticated, from more or less the same wide, bright country of chalk downs and fertile plains.

Nor far from the village of Langley Burrell, a few miles from Chippenham in Wiltshire, there stands on a hill a remarkable monument. It is a tall, stone column, toppped by the stone figure of a little old lady, with a basket of eggs and lace beside her. It is the visible memorial of Maud Heath, a village higgler, who died more than a century ago.

She walked each week to Chippenham market, sold her eggs and home-made lace, and walked home again, in winter dark and autumn rainstorms, to her cottage in the village street. More than once she waded waist-deep through swollen brooks. So towards the end of her days this indomitable old woman made a vow that, should she ever leave any money, it should be spent on making a good footpath from her village to Chippenham, so that other poor persons like herself might walk to market in winter in comfort.

Maud did, in fact, leave a small fortune. The footpath and the monument are the results.

Now comes the up-to-date story of this little old lady who died when the last century was very young. Mrs V. Carrington of Biddestone, near Chippenham, widow of the late Brigadier Carrington, D.S.O., O.B.E., has very kindly sent me a cutting of an article which she contributed to a local journal some little time ago. It concerns Maud Heath. Mrs Carrington wrote:

"Not so very long ago I returned from an excellent day's fox-hunting, and as the fox had been a good one, we had all enjoyed a splendid run—almost to the Wiltshire Downs.

"I was not one of the more fortunate ones who could telephone for my horse-box to bring me home, and I turned my weary horse towards Chippenham in which neighbourhood we then lived.

"Alas, my horse was very tired, to say nothing of its rider. Night coming on and it was getting darker and darker.

"Down the hill we almost stumbled, past Maud Heath on her monument and on along by her path.

"Soon the good and faithful friend who had carried me well got so tired he could only go at a walk, and I began to think we'd never get home.

"Suddenly, to my astonishment, he snorted and began prancing across the road.

"I thought this strange, knowing how very tired he had been only a few minutes before.

"Could it be a car coming up behind?—for there seemed a strange light shining on the very quaintest of old women walking a few yards ahead of us on the footpath. But no, there was no car in sight, neither could I hear one.

"On looking at the strange old lady, I wondered at her old-fashioned dress.

"Was it some eccentric old village woman walking with her basket to shop?

"The dress that I could see by the quite mauvish-yellow light on her was of a strange coarse material not made nowadays. Her headgear was unusual; her shawl . . . those odd little steps she took!

"But, above all, the basket at her side. I could see large, white eggs and thick, heavily-made lace hung out from the basket.

"After a good deal of cross words and rough handling I at last got my horse to trot.

"I tried to overtake the strange lady, but to my utter astonishment the figure in front kept exactly the same distance away.

"On coming into the high road, the old lady became one long, shining shadow, and disappeared over the hedge opposite.

"My horse, although in a 'muck sweat', as the grooms say, became again the weary animal he had been before, and the groom told me afterwards that the horse kept breaking out in a sweat all night.

"Had it been myself alone I might have thought I was mistaken, but my horse that night, I know, was convinced there was someone not human just in front of us.

"Had I seen the ghost of Maud Heath, or was this just one of those optical illusions sometimes experienced in certain conditions by tired persons?"

Hauntings Royal

Henry VIII's matrimonial reputation is not of the best. His dealings with his six wives, two of whom he did to death, have certainly put him, according to popular opinion, among the arch-villains of history.

When he died at the no great age of fifty-six, he was an enormous mass of flesh, so fat and diseased that he could hardly move. The royal corpse was taken from Westminster to Windsor, and the ponderous coffin was placed upon a trestle in Syon House. During the night so great was the weight of the contents that the coffin burst open and the dogs scrambled forward to lick the dead king's blood. Syon House had once been an Abbey. It had been appropriated by Henry during the Dissolution of the Monasteries, and many people thought that his body being thus dishonoured, as Ahab's had been, was of some dread significance.

Nevertheless Henry's spirit has apparently rested in peace. This has surprised some who thought that the ghost of such a man would surely return to haunt the scenes of his wrong-doings.

It is in fact the two wives he executed—Anne Boleyn and Catherine Howard—who have remained behind to haunt the world with their disturbed spirits, while the lord and master who put them to death sleeps peacefully in his royal tomb.

We should not be surprised at this apparent injustice. It is the wronged, rather than the wrong-doers, whose spirits are uneasy, and it is not for us to question this inequitable arrangement on the

part of the eternal forces. Also, it should be remembered that neither of these young Queens of England could with all honesty maintain their innocence of the immorality with which they were charged. Resentful they undoubtedly were at the treatment Henry meted out to them, but their conduct during their lifetime was hardly befitting that of Queens of England. Whether this merited death is another matter and one we are not concerned with here.

Anne and Catherine were cousins. Neither had had the kind of sheltered upbringing which is usual for future Queens of England, though of course neither girl dreamed in her youth that she would become the King's Consort.

Anne's father was Sir Thomas Boleyn. Her mother was the daughter of Thomas Howard, the second Duke of Norfolk (who was also Catherine Howard's grandfather). At a tender age Anne went to the French Court and was exposed to the influence of an elegant and unmoral society. Her sister Mary became Henry's mistress, and when Henry cast his eyes desirously upon Anne, she thought she would go one better than Mary and become the King's wife. She had not been to Paris for nothing, and she succeeded in becoming Queen after playing a remarkable game of hard-to-get with this redoubtable seducer, which lasted six years. Of course she would never have become the Queen of England if Henry himself had not been desirous of taking another wife, Catherine of Aragon having failed to produce a male heir.

It certainly appeared at first that Anne had had a more glorious success than her sister. But though Mary lost her reputation, she at least kept her head on her shoulders. Poor Anne in the end lost both head and reputation. She was accused of the worst of crimes—incest and witchcraft as well as adultery.

Her true crime was the same as Catherine of Aragon's—the inability to produce the all-important male heir. Henry turned from her in disgust, not suspecting that the despised daughter she gave birth to would turn out to be England's finest Queen—a better monarch than he, and a child he certainly would have been proud that he fathered.

There has always been controversy over Anne's guilt, but of her instability of character there is general agreement. Becoming Queen went to her head. She became arrogant, overbearing, and caused endless trouble at Court by her jealousies and improprieties.

Anne Boleyn has not only become England's most famous ghost, but her name has been loaded with infamy these past four hundred years. She lived at a time when the dangers of withcraft and sorcery

were looming large in men's minds. It was all started by Henry, who in his anxiety to rid himself of her said she had bewitched him and that he had been a victim of her devilish sorcery. The fact that she is said to have possessed a third nipple, and a sixth finger on her left hand, lent colour to the belief that she was a witch. They said that as a child she had a curious dislike of church-bells, an aversion common to witches apparently, which is not surprising considering that they are supposed to have entered into a pact with the Devil.

In order to marry Anne, Henry broke with Rome and thus brought Protestantism to England. Anne was never forgiven for her incidental part in bringing about the Reformation. Her character has been traduced by centuries of Roman Catholic writers. Unspeakable crimes were attributed to her. When Bishop Fisher was beheaded in 1536 for refusing to acknowledge Henry as head of the Church, they said she had his severed head brought to her on a dish so that she could stick a silver bodkin through the tongue. She was also accused of trying to poison Queen Catherine and the Princess Mary. The diplomatic gossips of the time freely branded "the concubine" as they called her, as a witch who was devoted to the foullest diabolism. These fantastic stories were put about by Papists who held her responsible for England breaking away from the true Church.

Whatever might be said against Anne Boleyn, she did not deserve these calumnies. She went to her death with a scornful courage which aroused great admiration. She wore a gay robe of damask over an underskirt of red and upon her wonderful black hair she had a pearl-embroidered hood. It was a clement May morning in 1536 as she stood there on the scaffold, her dark eyes shining, laughing in the very face of death, making a joke about her little neck and the skill of the executioner. Her bravery on the scaffold caused the Governor of the Tower, Sir William Kingston, to write: "I have seen many men and also women executed, and they all have been in great sorrow; and to my knowledge this lady has much joy and pleasure in death."

Of course this courage in the face of death was open to various interpretations by the superstitious minds of the age. There were some who thought that it merely proved that she was a witch, anxious to go to that other world to her true consort, the Prince of Darkness. A fanciful theory indeed.

But whatever be the truth of Anne Boleyn, her restless spirit has haunted the world ever since, and has been seen in various places, particularly at the several homes where she had lived. At Blickling

Hall in Norfolk her much-travelled ghost is said to make a spectacular appearance every year upon the anniversary of her death,
driving up the avenue to the hall in a coach. She sits holding her head
in her lap, and the coach is drawn by headless horses. The whole
grisly equipage pulls up in front of Blickling Hall and then vanishes
into the air. Phantom coaches and headless horses have by tradition
been associated with withcraft and devil worship.

She has also been seen driving furiously along the roads of
Norfolk, headless in her spectral coach, followed by a strange blue
light. Her ghost has also been reported in Kent, this time being
driven up the avenue of Hever Castle at a furious pace in a funeral
coach drawn by six black headless horses. Hever, a thirteenth-
century castle near Edenbridge, was once her home. Here Henry
wooed both Anne and her sister Mary. The great oak under which
he courted Anne still stands, and they say that her ghost is seen
there every Christmas-time.

The Rochford district of Essex is said to be haunted by the ghost
of a headless witch, clad in a rich silken gown, and no one would
go near the grounds of Rochford Hall for twelve nights after
Christmas on account of a terrifying apparition in white which
haunted the place. Witches were burnt as a rule, not beheaded, and
they did not usually wear silken apparel. Anne Boleyn had lived at
Rochford Hall when she was a girl, and this story may just have
been put about by the superstitious countryfolk to add colour to the
accusation that she was a witch.

But Anne's most persistent haunting is in the Tower where she
met her death with such scornful courage. She was buried in the
Church of St Peter ad Vincular, which is within the Tower itself. Many
years later, it is said, her coffin was opened and she was identified
by the remains of the famous—or infamous—sixth finger.

She is said to haunt this little church in particular when a death is
imminent. A ghostly ritual is then held in the aisle.

This was witnessed by a nineteenth-century officer of the guard
who noticed a light shining inside the church and asked the sentry
outside the church what it was. The soldier said he did not know.
Nor did he wish to investigate. Queer things took place inside that
church, he said. The officer decided to investigate himself. He ordered
the sentry to fetch a ladder. The officer mounted the ladder and
peered into the window of the church.

The church was filled with an eerie glowing light, and the officer
saw a procession of people dressed in Elizabethan costume moving
along the aisle. At the head of the procession was a splendidly

dressed and bejewelled woman whose face, the officer said, was like that of the portrait of Anne Boleyn. This phantom procession passed along the aisle, then suddenly vanished, together with the ghostly light by which it had been illuminated, leaving the little church in utter darkness.

It was noted that Anne was seen this time unmutilated, and as she had been at the height of her success and power. But her ghostly appearances as a rule are more horrific, and many soldiers on guard at the Tower have been terrified when they encountered her. In 1817 a sentry had a fatal heart attack after meeting her on a stairway, and in 1864 a soldier was court-martialled for being found asleep on duty. He claimed to have been in a swoon after encountering Anne Boleyn.

The story was told to an incredulous, half-amused court-martial. The man said he was at his post near the Lieutenant's Lodgings when he was suddenly confronted by a white figure. He made the usual challenge, but, receiving no reply, he made a thrust with his fixed bayonet, whereupon there was a "fiery flash" which ran up his rifle and gave him such a burning shock that he dropped the weapon. After that he remembered no more. Further questioned about the appearance of the figure in white, he said: "It was the figure of a woman wearing a queer-looking bonnet, but there wasn't no head inside the bonnet."

This description was greeted with laughter in court, but the amusement ceased when the offending soldier called evidence to corroborate what he said. Several witnesses told the court that they had seen a headless woman in white near the Lieutenant's Lodgings that night.

An officer gave sensational evidence to the effect that he was in his room in the Bloody Tower when he heard the challenge: "Who goes there?" He looked out of the window and saw the sentry confronted by a figure in white. He saw the sentry thrusting at the ghostly intruder with his bayonet. The figure, he said, not only walked through the bayonet, but through the sentry as well. He then saw the soldier collapse unconscious. The soldier was found in this position and accused of sleeping while on duty.

The court-martial found him not guilty and he was acquitted. Whether the court believed the story is not recorded, but they must have come to the conclusion that something inexplicable had been going on at the Tower that night.

Anne Boleyn's ghost apparently made another appearance at the Tower in 1933 when, according to newspaper reports, she walked

straight into the bayonet of a guard and scared him so much that he dropped his rifle and fled from his post into the guardroom shouting for help.

Considering its grim history, there are relatively few ghosts at the Tower. One of them is said to be the unfortunate Margaret, Countess of Salisbury, another of Henry VIII's numerous victims. She was a niece of Edward IV, was the last of the Plantagenets, and had a better title to the throne of England than Henry himself, his father Henry VII having usurped it from its lawful inheritors.

The Countess of Salisbury's son, the famous Cardinal Pole, offended Henry by opposing his political religious policies. Henry determined to exterminate the whole family, and the Countess, who was sixty-eight, and certainly too near to the throne for Henry's comfort, was executed at the Tower in 1541.

It was perhaps the most macabre beheading on record. The venerable lady, who had done nothing to justify execution, was dragged, violently protesting, to the scaffold. Unlike most of Henry's victims she not only refused to make the usual hypocritical declaration of loyalty to the King, but she flatly refused to do anything which showed that she consented to her death. When she was told to lay her head on the block, she replied: "No, my head never committed treason. If you want it, you must take it as you can."

The executioner tried to grab her, but she darted round the block, tossing her head from side to side, while he struck at her with his axe, as did the guards with their weapons.

At last, brutally wounded, covered with blood, she was forcibly held down crying out: "Blessed are those who suffer persecution for righteousness's sake," and the headsman hacked off her head.

There are those who claim to have seen this whole dreadful scene in a kind of spectral tableau at the Tower, a remarkable effort indeed on the part of the spirit world which would seem at times to have a decidedly theatrical bent.

Henry's vengeance fell upon the Boleyn family too, after he had executed Anne, but her father, Sir Thomas Boleyn, continued to live at Hever Castle after his daughter's death. He could not have had a very easy conscience about his craven behaviour, for he had publicly declared his belief in his daughter's guilt at the trial of her reputed lovers, as indeed did Anne's uncle, the Duke of Norfolk. Maybe they had to do this to save their own heads.

Anne's father has had no peace after his death apparently, for according to tradition he is doomed to ride the countryside pursued by hordes of screaming devils. After Henry had executed Anne's

brother, Lord Rochford, it is said that his blood-bespattered, headless corpse was to be seen dragged across the countryside by four headless horses.

A few days after he had disposed of the unfortunate—but apparently not unhappy—Anne Boleyn, Henry married Jane Seymour, who died of puerperal fever in the following year (1537) after giving birth to the child who became Edward VI. It was said that her life was deliberately sacrificed by the performance of a Caesarean operation in order to ensure the safety of the precious boy heir.

It was said that Jane herself had an uneasy conscience concerning the circumstances in which she supplanted Anne, and that after her death her worried and anxious spirit remained earthbound seeking to make contact with the ghost of Anne. She is said to haunt the Silver Stick Gallery in Hampton Court Palace every year on the birthday of the baby prince whose birth had meant her death. Dressed in white, she carries a lighted candle in her hand, ascends the staircase leading to the Gallery, along which she is said to glide wreathed in a silvery light, to vanish from sight at the end of the gallery. All this, despite the fact that she had a most lavish funeral and 1,200 masses were paid for to ensure that her soul had the peace it was considered it deserved.

Unlike the formidable Anne Boleyn, Jane Seymour is an elusive ghost, and can be seen, it appears, only by those with extra-sensory perception.

In 1540 Henry was married briefly to Anne of Cleves, and in the following year he made Catherine Howard his Queen. She was Anne Boleyn's cousin, daughter of a younger son of the 2nd Duke of Norfolk, and was a lush attractive girl upon whom Henry doted. She was his "rose without a thorn", and he did not dream of the scandalous youth she had spent under the disorderly household of the ancient Duchess of Norfolk, where, unknown to her grace, Catherine indulged in fun and games with various young men of the household. Before Henry married her, she had been enjoyed by a variety of men from spinet-teachers to page-boys. Her reputation for immorality was the talk of the Court, and when she became Queen it could not be concealed from the King. Henry wept, but sent her to the block, together with her lovers, past and present. She had after all taken a lover after becoming his Queen and was thus guilty of treason.

Catherine, young and in love with her cousin Thomas Culpepper, did not want to die, and the story is told how when she was arrested at Hampton Court she broke away from the guards and ran along

a gallery to the chapel where Henry—"the professional widower"—with a typical touch of Tudor hypocrisy, was on his knees praying for her soul. She tried to get to him to make a last plea for her life, but the guards seized her and dragged her screaming from the chapel where Henry pretended not to notice the disturbance.

Shrieking and lamenting, Catherine was hurried from the royal presence, into a barge and then down the Thames to the Tower, and, on 13 February, 1542, to the block.

Many say that there was a Protestant conspiracy against Catherine Howard, who came from a powerful Catholic family, the Norfolks. Undoubtedly the Protestants feared any Romanist influence on the King, and exploited Catherine's youthful indiscretions for their own political ends. Unhappily for the foolish, amorous Catherine—a lovely young girl married to a fat, diseased man twice her age—she provided her enemies with plenty of evidence with which to destroy her.

She went to her death bravely enough, but her young protesting spirit soon returned to haunt Hampton Court Palace, where she was seen time and time again running frantically along that same gallery, pursued by spectral soldiers, her screams and shrieks chilling the spines of those who heard them.

This Haunted Gallery was closed up as a consequence of this formidable invasion by the other-worldly spirit of the hapless Catherine, and for many years it was used as a lumber-room for worn-out furniture and moth-eaten tapestries. For centuries the rats and mice of that neglected part of Hampton Court seemed to live happily with the unquiet spirit of Catherine, while the other inhabitants of the old Palace retreated from the sound of her distressing screams.

In the twentieth century, however, the Office of Works, who don't believe in ghosts, had the Haunted Gallery cleared out and renovated, and it was opened to the public in April, 1918. Apparently this assault on her old stomping-ground had the effect of laying Catherine's noisy ghost, for she does not seem to have been seen or heard since in the Haunted Gallery.

She has also been seen in more tranquil fashion flitting about the famous Hampton Court gardens on sunny afternoons, re-living the memories of more pleasant times before she was sent on her sad way to the Tower.

Henry VIII, the arch-villain of all these beheadings—for apart from her lovers past and present, some members of Catherine's family lost their heads in the general mêlée of her execution—sleeps peacefully in his grave. At least we have no reports to the contrary.

So does his son, born to Jane Seymour, the sickly, interesting, precociously clever Edward VI, who died of consumption in his sixteenth year. But there is an interesting ghost story connected with Edward VI's foster-mother.

It will be recalled that Edward's mother died as a consequence of his birth, being deliberately sacrificed, they said, in order to ensure the survival of the much more important heir to the throne. Henry appointed Mistress Sibell Penn as the child's foster-mother. Mrs Penn was an excellent woman in every respect, devoted to her charge, and respected by the King with whom she remained in high favour. When Edward himself came to the throne at the tender age of nine she became an important personage at Court, and when the young King died she mourned him as though he had been her own son. Afterwards she lived in a grace-and-favour residence at Hampton Court, dying in 1562 of smallpox and being buried in an imposing tomb in the old church of Hampton-on-Thames.

There the worthy soul rested in peace for a full two and a half centuries until in 1829 when the old church was demolished and the present church erected in its place. During the demolition, Mrs Penn's tomb was disturbed—some say rifled—and the stately monument which had been erected over it moved to another part of the church.

This disturbance of her tomb disturbed also, it seems, the soul of this excellent and respected matron who had been well rewarded on earth for her many virtues, and who had no reason to have her eternal peace disturbed. But disturbed it was.

Very soon after her grave had been so unceremoniously opened, Mrs Penn's ghost returned to her old rooms at Hampton Court. At first nothing but angry mutterings were heard and the sound of a spinning-wheel. These sounds were so persistent and mysterious that eventually the authorities made an investigation in the apartments were they seemed to be coming from. They discovered a secret door leading to a room which had been closed and forgotten for centuries, in which was found an ancient spinning-wheel together with a variety of sixteenth-century curiosities.

Investigation of the Hampton Court records showed that this room had been occupied by Mrs Penn who had often used a spinning-wheel. Indeed the old oak flooring in the forgotten room had been worn away by the treadle where it had touched the boards.

Mrs Penn's ghost has been seen several times since, and people sleeping in the Palace have been awoken by icy hands placed upon their faces, and over them bends Mrs Penn, a luminous figure clad in grey—a frightening experience.

The Phantoms of Littlecote

Littlecote is one of Wiltshire's most historic stately homes. It has had many owners, among them people distinguished by wealth or birth—or by sheer iniquity. The wicked and the famous have left their ghostly mark in those old rooms, corridors and staircases. Replete with legend, with whispers of satanic deeds and secret murders, Littlecote sits in its woodland splendour, oblivious to the passing years, haunted, they say, to the end of time by the wickedness of those who have lived there.

For two centuries or more Littlecote, which is near Hungerford, was owned by the Darrell family, and it was they who finally beghosted not only the house but also the neighbourhood—even as far as the Hungerford to Salisbury road.

Wild Will Darrell, an Elizabethan rake, is the villain of Littlecote. The Darrell family had acquired Littlecote early in the sixteenth century. Through Wild Will's crimes they lost it, and local legend has it that had it not been for him the Darrells would be living at Littlecote to this day. Latterly Littlecote was owned by the Wills family, Sir Ernest Wills dying there in 1958.

The Wills family were troubled by the ghost. When Major George Wills was staying there his dog began to bark in the middle of the night, awaking not only the Major, but the whole household. In vain the Major tried to pacify the dog. The animal stood in front of the closed bedroom door, its hair standing on end, quivering in terror.

The Major opened the door and saw the Littlecote phantom pass

by—a woman in a shift, wringing her hands, appearing to be looking for someone.

The woman's spectral search had its quite horrible origin one night four hundred years previously. It began with a thunderous knocking upon the door of the cottage of a Mrs Barnes in the little Berkshire village of Great Shefford.

Now Mrs Barnes was known as the village gamp—a midwife of few scruples and even fewer qualifications. She was not unused to being aroused in the middle of the night to perform her doubtful services for the unwise as well as the under-privileged.

She opened her door to be confronted by two arrogant young men, warmly as well as expensively cloaked, while behind them a pair of furiously-driven horses steamed in the cold night air as they pawed the ground, straining at carriage traces.

Mrs Barnes did not like the look of her visitors. Moreover their request aroused Mrs Barnes's suspicions. She was required immediately to attend professionally upon a lady who lived not far from Great Shefford. But she must be taken there blindfolded and even permit herself to be conducted to the bedside blindfolded. When she asked who the lady might be, she was informed that it was Lady Knyvett.

Now it is not likely that Mrs Barnes believed this. She knew of Lady Knyvett, the wife of Sir Harry Knyvett, Bart., of Charlton. It was highly improbable that such a lady would call upon her services.

What finally made Mrs Barnes agree to the proposition was her natural cupidity. When gold was thrust into her hands, she agreed to attend upon the lady, whoever she might be, in the manner demanded of her.

A bandage was placed over her eyes and she was led to the carriage which was promptly driven off at a furious pace. She was unable to tell in which direction she was being taken. When the carriage finally stopped, she found herself being conducted into what was obviously a great mansion. She was led through rooms, through galleries and corridors, and up a staircase. Carefully the curious Mrs Barnes, now convinced that she was not at Lady Knyvett's, counted thirty-one steps.

Of all the great houses in the district, only Littlecote contained a staircase of thirty-one steps. Mrs Barnes did not know this at the time. Nor did she know the masked young lady lying in the four-poster in the bedroom where her bandage was finally removed.

Mrs Barnes only knew that the lady was unmarried, for no legitimate birth in a great house would take place in this manner.

She became aware that a man was awaiting in an ante-room, in the hearth of which a fierce fire was burning. Every now and then the impatient father—for who else could he be?—piled more fuel upon the roaring fire.

Quickly and unhygienically Mrs Barnes delivered the masked woman of her child. No sooner had this been done than the man strode in from the ante-room and seized the infant roughly from the midwife's hands.

He took it straight into the ante-room, placed the little body on the fire and crushed it into the burning coals with his foot. In a few moments the briefly-lived life was extinct, and in a little while more the small body was consumed by the flames.

Mrs Barnes was not a woman of great conscience or reputation, which was why she had been chosen, but she was not inhuman. She was outraged at this act of barbarity.

She screamed and to her screams were added those of the distracted and terrified mother. Their screams rang through stricken Littlecote, the inhabitants of which listened in fear, knowing that the master of the house was up to some fresh devilry.

Mrs Barnes did not know Wild Will Darrell. She described him as being tall and slender with a dark and angry face. This was a fair description and helped to confirm the tale she later told. Mrs Barnes did not even know that she was at Littlecote, though she must have had her suspicions, for the tales of what went on in that house were the talk of the countryside. She was certain only that she was not at Lady Knyvett's.

Having performed her duty, Mrs Barnes was then seized at Wild Will's command to be blindfolded once more. She was now terrified as well as angry. For all she knew, she might well be put to death herself as the witness of this outrage. Nevertheless she vowed that this child slayer should not go unpunished if it should ever be within her power to help bring him to justice.

There was little indeed that she could do. If she had an idea that she was at Littlecote she had no means of proving it. She did not know the face of the murderer, or of the men who had come for her, nor the identity of the now-stricken and appalled mother whose new-born had been so brutally destroyed practically before her eyes.

As they seized her, Mrs Barnes turned once more to the distracted mother, her hands clutching desperately at the chintz curtains of the four-poster on which the woman lay. The curtains had an unusual

pattern, and with sudden inspiration Mrs Barnes snipped a piece out of them, surreptitiously and unobserved.

She was then blindfolded again and led back to the carriage, the piece of chintz clutched in her hand. Once again she counted the thirty-one steps of the staircase.

Then she was driven back to her cottage in Great Shefford where she was informed in a forcible manner of the dire consequences which would fall upon her if she spoke one word to a living soul of what had happened that night.

Thus intimidated, Mrs Barnes kept silent, no doubt considering herself fortunate in escaping with her life.

But she could not forget. The infamy of that night haunted her for the rest of her days. But it was not until she was on her deathbed, at last out of the reach of Wild Will, that she told the story to a magistrate named Bridges, who recorded it on paper.

Now Bridges was Wild Will Darrell's cousin, and in view of this family connexion it is not likely that he would have officially recorded Mrs Barnes's story had he not thought that there might be some truth in it. Her remembrance of a staircase of thirty-one steps, and the piece of the chintz curtain—found to fit exactly a hole in the curtains of a certain four-poster at Littlecote—bore out the sinister stories which had long been rumoured about Wild Will Darrell.

The Knyvetts now came into the story. Sir Harry Knyvett and Darrell were bad friends. Sir Harry had long complained about Darrell's wild behaviour at Littlecote.

There must have been great bitterness between the two families, which explains why Darrell slandered Lady Knyvett by trying to persuade the midwife that she was the masked lady who had been so inconveniently with child.

Sir Harry Knyvett wrote a letter to Sir John Thynne of Longleat, whose family took the title of the Marquess of Bath in 1789, and later became the Dukes of Bedford. This letter was found at Longleat in the 1870s and was written in 1578 about the time of the Barnes's deathbed confession. Its subject was the suspected crimes and wicked behaviour of Will Darrell which had scandalized the counties of Wiltshire and Berkshire.

In Sir John Thynne's household at Longleat was a man named Bonham, whose sister had become Darrell's mistress. The girl's treatment at Littlecote and the murder of at least one illegitimate child she had borne was widely known.

Was it not time, wrote Sir Harry Knyvett, that Mr Bonham

should be urged to do something about his sister's "usage at Will Darrell's, the birth of her children, how many there were, and what became of them, for that the report of the murder of one of them was increasing foully and would touch Will Darrell to the quick".

This letter seemed to substantiate the deathbed story of the Great Shefford gamp. Wild Will Darrell was brought to trial. But the evidence against him was pretty slender. The tragically used Miss Bonham was unwilling to give evidence against him, or had died, her restless spirit, they said, already haunting Littlecote in search of her murdered child.

Darrell escaped justice, mainly, it was thought, through bribery and corruption. Returning to Littlecote, he continued his wild and reckless life.

But he did not live for long, and was thrown from his horse while riding in Littlecote Park and killed instantly. It was said that his horse had seen the ghost of his victim and reared up in terror, throwing Darrell to his death.

Littlecote then passed out of the hands of the Darrell family, but Wild Will's phantom has never left the place of his crimes, orgies and misdeeds. He is said to haunt the ante-chamber where he burnt his unwanted child, and the infant's bloodstains have been reported to appear in some mysterious fashion every now and then upon the floor before the fireplace, shedding blood that was apparently never shed in life.

Wild Will has also been seen haunting the place where his horse threw him to his death at the sight of the infant its rider had murdered.

And in the long gallery of Littlecote walks the ghost of the inconsolable Miss Bonham in search of her child. The screams of mother and midwife on that terrible night have echoed through the rooms and galleries of Littlecote for centuries, and are heard to this day, if we are to believe numbers of persons over the intervening years who said that they have heard them.

Littlecote has exercised a strange supernatural fear over people who never see its ghosts. Its domestic staff have always been affected by the hauntings and have refused to go into certain rooms.

It is always difficult to keep staff in haunted houses, and there was once an order at Littlecote that on every sunny day each of its three hundred and sixty-five windows should be opened, and closed by nightfall. Only one maid could be persuaded to perform this duty as none of them would dare to go into the haunted rooms when it was getting dark. This particular maid confessed that these rooms filled her with an unaccountable fear.

In 1914 Princess Marie Louise had a strange experience at Littlecote which she told in her book, *My Memories of Six Reigns* (Evans Brothers).

Her lady-in-waiting, Mrs Evelyn Adams, was the cousin of Sir Ernest Wills, then the owner of Littlecote. The Princess had never been to the house, nor had she ever seen a drawing or a picture of it. Sir Ernest invited her to lunch.

The Princess motored over with Mrs Adams, and as they approached it she experienced that not-unknown sensation that she had been there before. Littlecote and its surroundings were quite new to her, or should have been, yet they were strikingly, disturbingly familiar. In some strange way she felt that she knew the place.

Luncheon was served in the great hall, in honour of the royal guest, who confessed both then and afterwards that every detail of the place was known to her.

Naturally talk reverted to the story of Wild Will Darrell and the tale told by the gamp of Great Shefford on her deathbed, and after lunch Sir Ernest offered to show the Princess over the house, an offer which the Princess eagerly accepted in view of her strange feeling of having been there before.

Finally they came to the long gallery where the ghost of the wretched Miss Bonham walks in search of her child. Lady Wills pointed to a door at the far end of the gallery and said that that was where Mrs Barnes came up.

"Oh no, you are quite mistaken," contradicted the Princess. "This is where she was brought up." She pointed to another door.

She now closed her eyes and walked along the gallery, warning Mrs Adams that there were two steps ahead of them, and that she must take care not to fall. Eyes still closed, the Princess opened a door and stepped into a small room.

"Here is the fireplace where Wild Will Darrell burnt the child," she exclaimed. Then she crossed the room, still with her eyes closed, and took hold of the chintz bed-curtains, pointing to the hole made in it by Mrs Barnes nearly four hundred years previously.

Then she opened her eyes. She was quite unable to explain how she could have known these things. She could only assume that she must have been Mrs Barnes in a previous existence—perhaps because of her being able to go there with her eyes closed, as Mrs Barnes had been taken there blindfolded.

Princess Marie Louise is now dead herself and may or may not know the answer to questions which arise out of her story.

It will be remembered that Mrs Barnes never saw the interior of

Littlecote, being blindfolded, and there is no reason to suppose that she ever saw the interior of it during her lifetime, so she could not have known what it looked like.

Yet it was all familiar to the Princess. Her assumption that she must have been the gamp in a previous existence was probably a false one.

It is more likely—if we are to believe in previous existences—that she had once been Miss Bonham, for Miss Bonham would know the things the Princess claimed to know about Littlecote, and the gamp would not. Miss Bonham would certainly know the interior of Littlecote, which Mrs Barnes had never seen.

If this was so, then perhaps some recompense was made to the tragic Miss Bonham by becoming a Princess in another life. But if this was the case, would her troubled spirit continue to haunt Littlecote? We shall never know the answer to such questions.

Phantom Lovers

Throughout the ages lovers have been victims of disapproving parents, and recalcitrant lovers have often been dealt with in a cruel and heartless manner. Acts of violence, even murder, have been committed against those who have put love before obedience to parental authority. These tragic victims of love, whose happiness was so brief in life, may seek and find each other in the spirit world, their unhappy souls haunting the place where they once had met and loved, and were warm flesh and blood, delighting in each other's embraces.

Just such a tragic love story was that of the Lady Dorothy, daughter of Sir John Southworth of Samlesbury Hall, Lancashire, and Robert, the handsome son of a noble family who owned a large estate nearby. One would have thought the match to be ideal, and that the most choosy of parents would have welcomed such a union, especially as the young pair were so much in love. But this was not the case with Sir John, one-time Sheriff of the County Palatine of Lancaster, who held high military commands in the service of Queen Elizabeth I. The trouble was that he was a strict Catholic and Robert's parents were Protestants.

In those days there was great bitterness between members of the old Roman faith and the reformed anti-Papist church which had supplanted it. The conflict was as much political as it was religious and was one which was to drag on for centuries. The fact that the diplomatic and clever Queen Elizabeth employed both Protestants and Catholics in her service did little to damp down the feeling in

the country, and Sir John Southworth felt more strongly than most. He belonged to the old school and regarded the Protestants as heretics whose souls were destined for the eternal fires.

Imagine his consternation therefore when this young man from a staunch Protestant family called at Samlesbury asking for Dorothy's hand. When Sir John learned that his daughter had been freely associating with the young heretic and had fallen in love with him, he made no bones about the way he felt to the young suitor. Suppressed anger turned his ruddy complexion into purple, and his neat beard bristled and twitched above his starched white ruff. How dare a Protestant even enter his house—let alone approach him as a prospective son-in-law!

"You seem to be under a misapprehension, young sir. No daughter of mine would dream of forming an attachment for someone not of the true faith. You must know that the Southworths are devout Romanists. If my daughter Dorothy is known to you, she has never divulged her association to me, and as her father I would have forbidden such a friendship. As to marriage, that is absolutely out of the question. Marry a Protestant! I would rather see her dead."

Robert was taken aback by Sir John's outburst. He had not expected anything like this, though Dorothy had warned him that her father would object to a proposal from anyone who was not a Catholic. But he had been optimistic. After all, it wasn't as if he was a penniless nobody. Sir John was treating him as though he was the stable boy. But he was determined for Dorothy's sake to keep his own temper in check.

"But surely, sir, you do not refuse your sanction to your daughter's marriage solely because I am a Protestant? I love Dorothy, and she has given me to understand that she returns my love. We wish to become——"

"That is enough, sir! How dare you force your way into my house and confront me with such falsehoods! My daughter would never flout her father's wishes. And I say that she will marry a Papist, or she will not marry at all."

"Does not your daughter's happiness mean anything to you, sir? Since the English prayer-book has been revised, the Church embraces the Catholics as well as the Protestant-minded. Could you not be all-embracing, for your daughter's sake?" Robert was quite pale. He felt as though he was pleading for his very life.

"I am the best judge of where my daughter's happiness lies and it is not in the arms of a heretical Protestant. The revision of the English prayer-book has not been recognized by the Holy Father, so enough

of your false reasoning, young man. I forbid you ever to see my daughter again. She will soon forget you. I shall make sure of that. And now you will oblige me by leaving my house, never to enter it again."

"I will leave now, sir, as you wish. But I beg you to reconsider. Think of Dorothy. We truly love each other, and we will not be parted for long."

Sir John's colour deepened once more. "Get out of my house, you insolent young dog," he exclaimed, "or I will have you thrown out. My daughter will never marry you, and you will not see her again."

The heartbroken Dorothy was confined to her room for several days after this by her irate parent, but somehow her loved one managed to smuggle a letter to her in which he suggested a secret meeting in the woods surrounding the Hall, which in the sixteenth century was situated in the midst of a great forest of oaks. (Today Samlesbury Hall stands beside the main road between Preston and Blackburn.) An obliging maid-servant, who was walking out with one of the neighbouring knight's footmen, delivered her young mistress's reply into the hands of her sweetheart, who passed it on to Robert, and thus a meeting between the parted lovers was arranged.

They met under a particular tree in the woods, far enough from the Hall so that it would be most unlikely for anyone to pass that way, and where they could find a little privacy surrounded by the broad sheltering trunks and enveloping branches of the friendly oak trees.

Sir John's opposition to their attachment made them even more determined to marry, and after two or three meetings they planned to elope. Sir John was going to be away for a few days on business of state, and the lovers made their plans accordingly.

But they reckoned without Dorothy's brother, as rigid a Romanist as his father, and totally opposed to his sister's marriage into a family which espoused the hated Protestant faith.

One evening the two lovers met in their usual secret place and planned the details of their elopement, unaware of the fact that the trees which sheltered them also concealed an eavesdropper—Dorothy's brother. Overhearing their plans to run away together, and well knowing of his father's objection to such a union, which he certainly shared himself, he decided that he must prevent the elopement at all costs. He knew that his father would commend him for doing so, for protecting the family honour in his absence. The brother laid his own plans accordingly.

Meanwhile Dorothy, blissfully unaware that her secret had been

discovered, went about her own preparations with a light heart. By the time her father returned to Samlesbury she would be far away with the man she loved. She dressed in white, as befitted a bride, and ventured out of her room and along the broad corridors, choosing the right moment when both members of the family and the servants were otherwise occupied. Her wide-skirted dress with the fulness held out from a tight bodice by the fashionable farthingale, made her appear as though she was floating across the long gallery and down the wide staircase, so quickly did her dainty feet carry her, her heart beating fast with excitement, fearing every moment that she would be discovered and her happy plan frustrated.

But she met no one and let herself out quietly by a little used side door which she had chosen so that the nearby bushes would give as much concealment to her as possible. So she hurried across the park into the woods where her lover was awaiting her in the company of two trusted friends who were there to help them and to speed them on their way to happiness.

Alas, neither of the three young men was armed. But Dorothy's brother, watching from a vantage point, was. His sword was at the ready. He was an excellent and experienced swordsman, and the fact that he had three men to contend with did not deter him in the least. On the contrary, his triumphant fight for the Southworth honour would be the more glorious.

When Dorothy arrived and was greeting her lover, the waiting swordsman sprang out to the attack, and was upon them before they realized what was happening. The three unarmed men were defenceless before the flashing steel of the determined brother. Robert's two friends went down mortally wounded from well-aimed sword-thrusts. Robert's first thought was to protect his loved one, and he fell at her feet with her brother's sword plunged into his heart.

Dorothy knew nothing of what happened after that, for she swooned and when she recovered her senses she was back in her room at Samlesbury, crying out the name of her lover who would never again embrace her.

That night the bodies of the three men were secretly buried within the precincts of the domestic chapel attached to Samlesbury Hall.

Lady Dorothy never really recovered from the shock of witnessing her lover's death at the hands of her own brother. She was ill for a long time, a prisoner in her room. Her father's reaction to the tragedy and the part his over-zealous son played in it, is not on record; but he was a man of importance at the court of Queen Elizabeth, and could not afford a domestic scandal of this kind. The

Queen did not desire to widen the already wide breach between the Protestants and the adherents of the old religion.

Whatever Sir John might have thought of the violent and murderous manner in which his impetuous son dealt with the situation in his absence, it was not possible to do anything about it. He did not wish such a scandal in the delicate political balance which existed in England just then.

As for the unfortunate, broken-hearted Dorothy, there was only one thing to do, and her parents had no hesitation in doing it. She was bundled into a convent. It was the conventional solution for such circumstances in those days, though what Dorothy's parents must have thought at having to do it in these particular circumstances can well be imagined, for it must not be assumed that they were insensitive or without any feelings towards their wronged daughter.

They decided to send her abroad, where, it is said, she was kept under strict surveillance, for she was showing signs that her mind was breaking under her desperate grief. "The name of her murdered lover," said Harland in his *Lancashire Legends*, "was ever on her lips". Her great grief finally drove her right out of her mind, and she died, her lover's name being the last word she spoke.

According to legend, Lady Dorothy's ghost was seen in her old home and the surrounding woods immediately after her death, when her spirit returned to seek her lost love. On quiet, clear evenings—the same as that happy evening when she had tip-toed starry-eyed for that last meeting with her lover—many people have seen a white lady gliding down the corridors and the galleries of Samlesbury Hall, descending the staircase, floating across the entrance hall and through the door out into the grounds, where she is met by a handsome young knight who receives her on his bended knees, and then accompanies her on her ghostly walk.

She has been seen in the woods accompanied by this ghostly knight dressed in Elizabethan garb. Some have said that at the end of their walk together the two phantom lovers embrace and lie down in each other's arms under the great oak tree where they had met and embraced in their lifetime; and it is said that at this time the air is filled with mournful sighs of despair and sorrowful whisperings among the branches above, where they eventually disappear together, still clasped in each other's arms.

This very romantic and fanciful story received a certain confirmation about two hundred years later when Samlesbury Hall fell upon bad times and was neglected, eventually becoming a farmhouse. Later it was restored to its original condition, it being a unique

example of the ancient type of Lancashire manor-house of the late fourteenth century. Workmen re-inforcing a wall near the old chapel came across a skeleton, and later two more skeletons were found. Local opinion considered the finding of the three skeletons to be ample confirmation of the basic facts of the tragedy of Dorothy Southworth and her unfortunate lover.

Another romantic haunting came about as the result of the un-fortunate love affair between the Lady Arabella Stuart and Sir William Seymour, whose romance ended in imprisonment in the Tower and death from madness for the doomed Arabella, whose only crime was that she was born too near the throne.

Descended from Henry VII's eldest daughter, Margaret Stuart, the Countess of Lennox, Arabella was next in succession to James VI of Scotland (James I of England), and she became the subject of intrigues by those who would not accept James as Elizabeth's successor. When Arabella was only ten, Elizabeth paraded her at her court as the heir to the throne, mainly to provoke James, whom she regarded in the same odious light as she did Mary Queen of Scots, his mother.

Lady Arabella had many requests for her hand, but all her suits, commoners and royal princes alike, were repulsed by both Elizabeth and James whose policy was to keep her unmarried, because the child of such a union would be a claimant to the throne which would complicate the succession.

Arabella pretended that marriage did not interest her, for she was clever enough to realize that any other policy would land her in trouble, so she devoted herself to literature, poetry, and even theology, a subject more fashionable in those days than now, for theology was changing the face of England in a way which we find it difficult to imagine.

When, upon Elizabeth's death, James was safely in possession of the throne, he acted more liberally towards Arabella, allowing her apartments in the palace and settling an allowance upon her. James's Queen, Anne of Denmark, liked Arabella and enjoyed her lively and intelligent companionship, for Arabella was always ready to participate in the masques and pageants which the Queen liked so much, and she became very popular at Court where she met again an old childhood acquaintance, the handsome Sir William Seymour, son of Lord Beauchamp, and their renewed attachment quickly turned into something more serious. They were in love.

At first they managed to keep their affair secret, but an alarmed

James at length came to hear of it, and also the highly disturbing news that they were planning to get married. Such a marriage he saw as a threat to his own safety on the throne, for Sir William Seymour was also descended from Henry VII, and any offspring of such a marriage would be dangerous indeed.

James summoned each of the offending lovers before his Council, and they were told in no uncertain manner that such a marriage between them could not be countenanced unless the King gave his express permission. In order to disarm suspicion Arabella and Seymour agreed to part.

They well knew that James would never under any circumstances permit them to marry, and so they married secretly. Eventually this came to the ears of James, who, incensed at their duplicity, ordered their arrest. Seymour was sent to St Thomas's Tower and Arabella to Lambeth Palace under the guard of Sir Thomas Parry. This was in the summer of 1610.

There was a great deal of sympathy for the young couple, and it was made quite easy for them to meet secretly. All their friends were ready to help them, and Seymour did not have much difficulty in leaving the Tower to go to Lambeth. All he had to do was to bribe his jailer, who was then quite willing to turn a blind eye to the absence of his charge.

The two lovers often met in the gardens of Lambeth and sometimes in the Palace. These meetings were as happy as they could be under the circumstances, and during their walks together beside the banks of the Thames they talked of the day when they would be able to live a normal, happy life together. It seemed that the only solution was to escape to the Continent.

Meanwhile their friends at Court—even the Queen herself—were trying to intercede for them and to persuade James to adopt a more lenient attitude. But James, afraid for his throne, was adamant. It was inevitable that news of their stolen meetings should eventually come to his ears, and he ordered a stricter guard to be put on Seymour, and that Arabella should be moved to Durham under the surveillance of the Bishop, who was ordered to keep a firm watch upon her.

But Arabella, being of strong character, refused to be sent to the north of England where she would not be able to see her husband. When ordered to go, she flatly refused to get out of her bed. So her bed was carried out of Lambeth, with her in it, placed in a boat and rowed up the river.

Poor Arabella became extremely agitated at such forthright and

demoralizing treatment and by the time they reached Barnet she appeared to be really ill with a high temperature. A doctor was called, diagnosed a fever, and pronounced her too ill to travel. James therefore arranged for her to be taken care of in the home of the Earl of Essex at Highgate, stating that he would allow her to remain there for only a month, after which time it was reckoned she would be strong enough to continue her journey to Durham.

This respite brought about a swift recovery in Arabella's health, and she instantly got in touch with her husband through their many friends, of whom James probably had much to fear, for he had proved a disappointing King to many people. Apart from being extremely unprepossessing and scandalous in his private life, he had broken many promises and made many enemies.

Sir William Seymour realized that he and Arabella must make their escape plans quickly. With the help of their friends they arranged both to escape at the same time and to meet at Blackwall where they would board a ship for France. The day chosen was one when the Bishop was to go to Durham to prepare for Lady Arabella's reception, and thus Arabella's escape was made much easier.

She disguised herself as a man, wearing a large black hat and a cloak. She wore also a peruque, doublet and hose and a sword, and passing very well as a young blade of the times, she set off with one retainer as an escort to an inn at Crompton where horses were waiting. They rode to Blackwall and arrived at the agreed time, but there was no sign of Seymour. After inquiring for him at the inn, they boarded the French ship which was to take them across the water. Arabella waited for her husband, anxiously scanning the riverside as the precious time went by, watching the tide go down, and praying desperately that her beloved would get there in time.

The French captain was concerned about other things than the tide. He was worried about the serious nature of his commission, and despite Arabella's entreaties he moved his ship further down river to the mouth of the Thames.

Meanwhile Sir William's escape from St Thomas's Tower had been planned with the help of a carter who delivered cartloads of faggots and hay. The carter had been bribed to exchange places with the prisoner on an outward journey. However, the switchover took longer than anticipated and the coast had to be quite clear before the carter would part with his smock and enveloping hat and hide himself under the hay. Seymour, dressed in the carter's clothing, and wearing a peruque and a black beard, walked out of the Tower

with the empty cart without a hitch, though well behind the agreed time.

When he reached Blackwall, he was too late. The French barque with Arabella on board had sailed without him. He eventually managed to bribe the captain of a collier to take him to Ostend. It cost him forty pounds—a large sum in those days—and after many delays he finally landed on the Continent, and made his way to Calais where he reckoned his wife would be awaiting him.

But Arabella's luck had deserted her. Her inquiry for Seymour at the inn at Blackwall had come to the ears of Admiral Monson, to whom a courier had been dispatched telling him to be on the look-out for the Lady Arabella and Sir William, whose flight was already known to James and was causing him the greatest consternation, for he was certain that a new conspiracy against him was afoot. Couriers had in fact been sent in all directions in an effort to intercept the runaway couple.

The Admiral immediately ordered H.M.S. *Adventure* to pursue the French ship, which the swift naval frigate overhauled in mid-channel and ordered it to heave-to. After some resistance the French ship was boarded and the unhappy Arabella was seized and brought back to London and lodged in the Bell Tower, where she was closely guarded.

At first her imprisonment did not bother her too much. At least her husband had escaped and she knew that he would leave no stone unturned until he could get her release, for he had influential friends. Arabella did not relax her efforts to appeal to James for her liberty and the Queen did her utmost to this end.

But James was adamant. He had been scared, quite certain that Arabella and her husband had been party to a conspiracy to seize the throne. It has been said that the fugitives were to have been received in the Netherlands by the Spanish commander, at the instigation of the King of Spain and the Papists, whose plan had been to bring them back to London at the head of a Catholic host. James was determined that nothing like that should happen if he could help it. While it is true that in the case of Arabella his fears on this score were groundless, it is just as true that his fears of a conspiracy against his throne in order to place a Roman Catholic monarch upon it were very real. There were several such conspiracies actively afoot, both in England and on the Continent.

At first Arabella bore her imprisonment well, but as time went by and James showed no sign of relenting and the Queen was unable to influence him, for he was convinced that Arabella's only wish was

to take his place on the throne, all hope gradually left her, and she sank into the deepest melancholy. Of her husband she never heard again. He had to go into hiding on the Continent on account of the activities of James's agents, and he was unable to lift a finger to help her.

Arabella's end is wrapped in mystery. It is said that her splendid and sensitive mind eventually gave way and she became hopelessly insane. The only certainty is that she died on 27 September, 1615, after having been four years in the Tower, and she was buried in the tomb of Mary Queen of Scots in Henry VII's Chapel in Westminster Abbey.

Arabella Stuart's ghost has been seen several times since her death terminated her sad romance. Occasionally a lady in grey is seen at a certain window in the Bell Tower. She does not, however, often show herself, but doors are sometimes opened by unseen hands and the tapping of heels is heard along the corridors.

She is seen more often in Lambeth Palace where she roams the corridors and staircases in a rustling grey gown looking for her lost love. Sometimes the two lovers are seen in the Palace gardens as dusk gathers, walking hand in hand.

The White Lady of Berlin

At the end of the Unter den Linden in Berlin stands a huge, imposing quadrangular building known as the Old Palace. But the only palatial thing about it now is its appearance. After 1919 it was turned over to government offices, and later became a museum. But once it knew great splendours: Frederick, first King of Prussia, began to build it in 1699 with the aim of rivalling Versailles itself. Here lived the powerful race of Hohenzollerns, and here flourished their courts. They ruled by absolute authority—an authority that could proclaim to the nobles of the land: "I am king and lord, and will do what I wish! Holiness is God's, but all else must be mine!"

It is not surprising that in a place where passions ran strongly they should leave strong currents behind them. Frederick, its builder, was a wild, vicious and cruel man. In a tower of the Palace, known as the Tower of the Green Hat, he kept an Iron Maiden, that terrible instrument of torture and death shaped roughly like a woman and lined with steel spikes, which pierced and crushed its victims. These would often be innocent people against whom a court had not been able to find sufficient evidence. Beneath the Maiden a trap-door let down the torn remains of the Maiden's prey into the engulfing darkness of an oubliette.

But the phantom of the Old Palace, who is said to have come from the Tower of the Green Hat, was not one of these victims. The White Lady who has appeared to so many Berliners is said by some to be the model for the Iron Maiden, a beautiful woman whose likeness was used to make that horrid travesty of womanhood.

After her death, her mission was to visit the descendants of Frederick, her inventor, and warn them of their coming fate. According to some who saw her, she was dressed in the white robe and veil of the Virgin, because the statue had been so made, and the victim, as he was pressed into it, had been told to "Return thanks to our Holy Mother". So a profanation was punished.

There are other stories, however, of the White Lady's origin. Some say she was Anna Sidow, the lovely, low-born mistress of Elector Joachim II, a half-mad ruler of the sixteenth century, who squandered his people's gold on her. But the pious son who followed him had Anna imprisoned in Spandau, and she died miserably there. It may be that her spirit travelled from the royal dwelling on the outskirts of Berlin to the Palace built long after her time.

Also before the stones of the Old Palace rose was the wrong done that caused the third claimant to the White Lady's title to "walk". One of the early Hohenzollerns was Margrave Albert, known as the Beautiful, who fell in love with a young widow, the Countess d'Orlamunde, who had two children. Unthinkingly, he remarked to someone that he would gladly marry her, if he were not held back by the influence of *four eyes*. Hearing of this, the widow took it to refer to her children; and her way of disposing of these obstacles to her ennoblement was to kill them by running a gold pin into their heads. It was only after she had done this that she found out the Margrave's true meaning—he had been referring to his parents' opposition to the marriage. Nature had its way—Agnes d'Orlamunde went mad, and wanders without rest.

But whoever she may have been—artist's model, unhappy prisoner, or crazed mother—the White Lady has been seen by many, usually on occasions when tragedy threatened the Hohenzollern princes. The first recorded appearance was in 1619, in the reign of John Sigismund. A cheeky young page was sauntering down a corridor of the Old Palace when he turned a corner and came face to face with a silent white figure, gliding towards him with a fold of its veil drawn across its features. He knew instantly who—or what —it was; and knew that those who had seen her in the past had drawn aside, trembling, to let her pass. But the page did not see why he should be frightened by a mere white shadow. He stood in her way, checked her with a hand on her arm, and inquired briskly, "And where might you be going, madam?"

The White Lady lowered the hand with which she had been holding the veil over her face. She held in it a great key—the key that was said to unlock for her each one of the castle's six hundred

doors—and she brought it down heavily upon the page's head. He fell to the ground, dead; just as two horrified fellow-servants appeared round the corner. They had more sense than the dead boy. They stood back as the White Lady flitted past them and disappeared.

On the next day, Elector John Sigismund died.

There is no story of the White Lady's appearance in the reign of Frederick William, the Great Elector, a strong ruler and a simple man. Nor did she visit his son and grandson, with their extravagances and eccentricities; nor Frederick the Great, perhaps because he was well known to be a sceptic.

Yet it seems that after death Frederick's scepticism must have been considerably modified. His nephew, Frederick William II, had invaded Champagne, during the French revolutionary period, with such success that he was able to announce his army's victorious arrival under the walls of Paris. He himself was staying at a Verdun inn. Dissatisfied with the wine that had been brought to him, he went down to the cellar of the inn to choose a better vintage; and there, to his horror, slowly materialized before him, against an unlikely background of bottles and barrels, the figure of his uncle, the Great Frederick.

"Unless you call off the Prussian army from Paris, nephew," said the spirit, "you may expect to see someone who will not be welcome to you."

The terrified Frederick William stammered that he did not know what was meant.

"I mean," replied Frederick, "the White Lady of the Old Palace, and I am sure you know what *her* visit implies." And he faded away into a cloudy shape less substantial than the cobwebs festooned from the cellar beams.

Frederick William took the warning seriously. He called off his troops, returned to Berlin, and lived another five years.

From this story, and that of the White Lady's next appearance, it would almost seem that she held some watching brief over France. For in the early autumn of 1806 she was seen several times. It was just before the Battle of Jena, when the Prussians were threatening to drive Napoleon's army "with whip-lashes" back to the Seine. At a party, Prince Louis of Prussia gaily asked a young girl to play on the pianoforte as many tunes as he would kill Frenchmen the next day. She played until dawn. The Prince, as he rode away, called: "Forward, gentlemen, to crush Napoleon!" The next night he lay dead at Saalfeld. Elector Frederick William III took the White Lady's hint, and fled from Berlin; and Napoleon himself moved into

the Old Palace and stayed two months. The White Lady was quiet; perhaps French occupation pleased her.

When the White Lady was seen again in June, 1914, Kaiser William II may well have expected his own death to follow. But the victim this time was the Archduke Francis Ferdinand, heir to the throne of Austria. William lamented his friend, but kept on with his violently militarist policy, and in August, 1918, its results broke upon the world—war between Germany and England. The White Lady's prophesy of disaster had been more accurate than ever this time. Four years later the defeated William left his empty title and the Old Palace behind him for ever. It is not recorded whether the White Lady ever appeared again during his lifetime. Perhaps she had no need to, for the long exile at Doorn was as fantastically tragic an end to the rule of the Hohenzollerns as even she could have wished.

There is a story that on 29 April, 1945, as Berlin's death agony approached its end and the fires of Allied bombing blazed brightly, the White Lady walked once more in the no longer princely corridors of the Old Palace. Their glory was departed, like the glory of the Hohenzollerns, and the man who was to die ignominiously in the ruins of the Reich Chancellery was a low-born person of the name of Schickelgruber. It is hardly likely that she would have troubled to warn *him*. Perhaps this time she appeared in triumph, for the enemies of France and England and the true Germany were slain upon the high places.

School for Ghosts

It is no surprise that China, for many centuries so remote and isolated, should have developed a ghost lore different from the Western world. Chinese ghosts are not usually the frightening apparitions so familiar to us. European ghosts frequently appear in the guise of the dead, with faces of the dead, clad sometimes in grave-clothes, sometimes without their heads, and to the accompaniment of terrifying noises.

But Chinese ghosts as a rule—for there are exceptions—are not like this. They are often indistinguishable from the living. They are frequently beautiful maidens who return from the other world, not to frighten man, but to play with him, tease him, make love to him, or even help him in the endless and burdensome examinations which the men of Old China had to pass before they could reach any status in their country.

Chinese ghosts are not the insubstantial wraiths of Western tradition. They are ghosts of flesh and blood, and they are often ghosts of animals, particularly of foxes, for the Chinese believe that all creatures have spirits.

A collection of these ghost stories was made by Pu Sung-ling, who lived in the seventeenth century, and who recorded the incidents from the people who reported them. The following two stories, which I have broadly adapted from his collection, are typical of these quaint and romantic tales of the supernatural.

When Yang Shien heard about the haunted house, once the home

of a high official, but now empty and deserted, he decided that he would approach the owner to allow him to live there as a caretaker, for it was just the sort of home Yang had dreamed that one day he would own. Yang secured an interview with the owner of the house and put his proposition before him.

At first the high official would not hear of it. "Young man," he said, "no one has been able to live there for years. The spirits which occupy it are such that they bring trouble to anyone who stays in the house."

"I am prepared to risk that. It is a great pity that such a lovely house should be left to spirits who care nothing if it falls into ruins. I will look after it for you."

The older man shrugged his shoulders. "I have nothing to lose, young man. I have warned you, and seeing that you still insist, you can have the key. But at the first sign of trouble you must leave. Otherwise I would not want to be responsible for you."

Yang was jubilant and immediately moved his belongings into his new home. He had to make several journeys back and forth, carrying everything himself, for he could not afford to hire a cart, and it was past sunset when he returned with his last load.

Yang's books were his pride and joy, and he had carefully placed them upon a table which he had decided would be admirable for his studies, but when he returned with his last load they were no longer there. He hunted high and low, but they were not to be found in the house and there was no sign of anyone having broken in. When however he returned to the room where he had left the missing books, they were back on the table. Puzzled, but happier now at the return of his most precious possessions, he went to the kitchen to cook some rice for his supper, and when he returned to his room where he thought he would read a while before retiring, he found his books had again vanished. He then heard the patter of light foot-steps and saw two beautiful young girls carrying his books in their arms. They were laughing together as they quietly replaced the books on the table.

They turned round and gazed straight at him, looking so human in the half-light of dusk that he could hardly believe they were ghosts at all; but knowing that they were, he turned his head away and would not return their saucy looks. Whereupon they laughed at him and came closer.

Yang's heart bumped against his ribs with fear, as he remembered the warning of the owner of the house. One of the girls prodded his body with her finger. The other one stroked his face, and they

started walking around him trying to make him look at them, touching him and laughing as they did so.

Yang had now revised his disbelief in spirits, and if he had not seen them with his own eyes walk right through the door just now, he would not have believed they were ghosts. However, they seemed as harmless as little children and he decided to treat them as such.

"Get out of my sight, you silly ghosts," he exclaimed. "How dare you come here to disturb me?" He made his voice sound as cross and belligerent as he possibly could. All the same, he did not expect them to take fright and scuttle away as quickly as they did.

His confidence returned, Yang lit a lamp and began to read, but all the time he was aware of other presences in the room and conscious of flitting shadows in the dark corners. He tried to concentrate on his book, but could not quite ignore those now quiet but eerie spirits which were around him. He soon gave up trying to read and got ready for bed.

He was very tired after his busy day, but no sooner had he closed his eyes than he was disturbed by a tickling sensation on his nose. Many times he brushed away whatever was tickling him, but it always returned. Eventually he sneezed and in the darkness he heard sounds of suppressed laughter. He got up, lit a candle and went back to bed again, closing his eyes and listening.

Presently he heard a faint sound and he opened his eyes. One of the girls was coming towards him with a feather in her delicate little hand. Immediately he jumped out of bed and shouted at her, and she ran away. Eventually he managed to get off to sleep, only to be awakened by a tickling sensation, this time on his ear. And so it went on all night. He couldn't get any sleep for the wretched little ghosts, until cock-crow, and then all was peaceful, and he relapsed into a deep sleep, not waking until long past noon.

The rest of the day was quiet and normal and Yang did some cleaning, arranging everything to his liking. Then he settled down to study, realizing that he would probably be plagued again by his ghostly visitors after sunset. He was reading when he became aware of a presence, and looking up from his book he beheld his beautiful visitors of the previous night watching him. He ignored them and continued reading. Then suddenly one of them came up to him and closed his book.

He jumped up in anger. "Am I to have no peace in this house?" he shouted. "I have important work to do, so go away."

They ran off, but no sooner had he returned to his book when they

returned. Yang held on to his book, determined to continue his reading, but one of them came up behind him and put her cool hands over his eyes. Again he jumped up in anger, but they only laughed at him. So he tried a different approach.

"I have work to do and must study to pass my examinations," he told them in a friendly manner. "So why don't you be good girls and leave me in peace? Go and do something useful."

This approach surprised them and they stopped laughing and looked at him in a contemplative way. One of them whispered in the other's ear and they both smiled sweetly at him and then left the room. Presently he heard sounds of activity in the kitchen and he went back to his work, thankful that he was getting a little peace at last.

About half an hour later the two pretty ghosts came back and started to lay out a meal on the low table. It all looked delicious, but even though Yang was hungry he was a little dubious about eating a meal cooked by ghosts. They might poison him! He thanked them and told them how clever he thought they were. "But I am not hungry", he said, going back to his book.

"If you do not trust us, how can you expect us to be good?' asked the one who seemed to be the elder of the two.

Yang looked up in surprise, for she had spoken in a sweet, tinkling voice. "Of course I trust you," he felt obliged to reply.

"Then if you trust us, you will eat the food we have laboured to prepare for you."

Yang thought that if he refused to eat, he would continue to be plagued by them and would be unable to stay there. He took up a bowl of rice and chop-sticks and tasted some of the food, and, feeling no ill effects, he pronounced it excellent and perfectly cooked, and the two little ghosts were delighted.

After he had finished his meal, they sat together and talked, but they would say little about themselves. He learned that the name of the older one was Ching-Yen and the younger one was Shai-Lu; but of their families they would tell him nothing, saying that as they were only spirits his interest in them could not be marriage—therefore why was he so curious?

"As I never thought to meet such charming spirits when I came here, it is natural that I am curious about you, especially as we are to live together in this house."

To this Ching-Yen replied: "Fortunately for you, the other spirits which occupied this house have been recalled to the world below by the Black Judge, while we await whatever fate is in store for us.

But if you wish to stay here, we will continue to serve you."

And so Yang was able to settle down and work, and the girls—for he could no longer think of them as ghosts—came every evening after sunset and cleaned and cooked for him, taking an interest in his work, disturbing him no longer, and he was very happy.

One day he had to go out and did not return until well after sunset. He found the younger girl, Shai-Lu, seated at his desk laboriously copying from the book which he had been transcribing. She showed him what she had been doing and he praised it. "But there is much room for improvement," he told her with a smile, "and if you like, I will teach you."

Shai-Lu was delighted at the suggestion and Yang, seating her on his knee, held her hand and showed her how to hold the brush correctly. Just then Ching-Yen came into the room and, on seeing them thus, her face flushed up to the roots of her shiny black hair as though she was jealous of the younger girl.

On seeing this, Yang set Shai-Lu on her feet again and offered his knee to Ching-Yen. "Let me see how well you can wield the brush, my dear," he said to her, and smilingly the girl wrote with Yang guiding her wrist.

Seeing that they were both very interested, Yang gave them a piece of paper each and told them to copy a verse, and while they laboured at their tasks he was able to continue with his own studies. When they had finished, they brought their work to him and he gave them marks. The younger girl's work got the higher marks and again Yang had to placate Ching-Yen with encouraging words, telling her that if she worked hard she would soon improve.

Thus Yang became the teacher to the two young ghosts, and when their writing improved he taught them how to read. They were apt pupils and once they had grasped anything they did not forget it.

One evening Ching-Yen brought her young brother, Song, a handsome youth of about sixteen years, but also, alas, like his attractive sister, a ghost, having departed this life at a tender age. Could Song also be Yang's pupil? Yang agreed, and Song proved to be a very intelligent boy. Before long he was reading the classics and writing poems.

Yang was delighted with the success of his school for ghosts. The lessons kept these naughty spirits occupied and out of mischief, and Yang was able to continue with his studies and also earn a little money writing poems of satire on current affairs, which became quite well known, but not always popular.

Eventually the day came when Yang had to leave to take his examinations, and say good-bye to his phantom pupils. He was gratified to find how badly they took his news. The girls wept and Song was full of forebodings, begging him not to go. "The Gods are not with you at this time," he said, "and if you go now some dreadful calamity will befall you."

But Yang would not listen and the next day left the house to keep his appointment with the examiner. When Yang arrived at the capital he learned that his works of satire had enraged a prefect of great influence in the district, and his examiner, far from being sympathetic, accused Yang of improper conduct. Yang was thrown into prison, and, penniless, without food, becoming weaker every day, he wished that he had taken heed of Song's warning.

One night he thought he was dreaming when he saw Ching-Yen, but when she gave him food he knew it was really her. She told him that his examiner had been bribed to accuse him of improper conduct and that her brother, Song, had gone to the court to plead for his release. She would return the next night to tell him how Song had fared.

When she had gone he ate the food which gave him new strength and hope. But Ching-Yen did not return the following night as she had promised. Neither did she come the next night or the next, and Yang became even weaker—all hope gone.

Then one night Shai-Lu came to him, but she was very sad and downcast. She told him that Song's request for Yang's release had fallen on deaf ears and he also had been taken into custody. Ill had also befallen Ching-Yen, who on her way back from visiting Yang had been accosted by the Black Judge and had been carried off to be his concubine, but, refusing to submit, she too had been imprisoned.

Yang, weak as he was, tried to console Shai-Lu, taking the blame upon himself. She gave him some money, so that he could buy food and then left him, saying that she must go back to watch over Song.

The next day Yang was brought before the Judge who asked him who was the young man called Song Tsai, who had pleaded for his release. Yang, not wanting to cause any more trouble for his spirit pupils, pretended that he did not know, whereupon the Judge told him that the young man had been brought before him to be beaten, but, throwing himself upon the ground, he had disappeared. Yang still kept silent, and the Judge, thinking that Song's disappearance was a sign to indicate Yang's innocence, told him he was free to go.

Yang could hardly believe his good fortune. He went back to his house as quickly as he could, arriving there just after dusk, but no one was there to greet him. When he went to bed that night he could hear the sound of weeping, but when he got up and lit his candle he could see no one.

Henceforth Yang often heard in the night the sound of quiet weeping, and it made him feel very sad and helpless. He was not visited by his little ghost maidens any more, and he missed them very much, and often thought of them when he sat alone at his studies in the evening. He thought of taking a wife, but how could he afford to do so when he had not yet passed his examinations? He began to work harder than ever, dreaming of the wife he would be able to have one day, and she always looked like either Ching-Yen or Shai-Lu.

One night the sound of weeping was louder than usual, but it came from outside the house. Yang got up and went to the door to investigate. A young girl was there. He asked her whence she came.

"I have travelled a long way and now I am so tired that I cannot walk another step. I was told that you would give me refuge."

Yang invited her inside and saw that she was very beautiful, with lovely eyes and teeth like pearls. "Who told you to come to me?" he asked, thinking how pale she looked and wondering if she was another ghost.

But the girl fell at his feet with exhaustion and he lifted her on to his bed. He watched over her all through the night and in the morning when she awoke he made gruel for her. He knew now that she was not a ghost, and yet she had talked in her sleep calling him by name and reciting verses which had been written by his spirit pupils and known only by him. He was mystified and could hardly wait to ask her again how she had come to him and from where.

"I only know that I was very ill, indeed near to death, when a girl came to me and told me of Yang and his teachings. She said that you needed me and that I must come to you. She seemed to enter into my body and give me the strength, and here I am."

Yang was amazed at what he heard and asked: "Did the girl who came to you tell you her name?"

"She told me her name was Shai-Lu. Do you know of her?"

"Yes, I know of her. Did she say anything else?"

The girl blushed and lowered her eyes. "She said that you would want to take me for your wife."

And Yang knew that nothing would make him happier. "But,"

he said to her regretfully, "your family would not want you to marry a poor man."

"I will not marry anyone but you," she told him.

And so a messenger was despatched to the girl's parents who soon came to fetch her away, but she would not go with them, and therefore they had to agree to the marriage, which took place the next day.

But one thing marred their happiness, and that was the sound of weeping which haunted the house every evening until they were blessed with their first child, and then the weeping ceased.

The child was a girl and she strongly resembled Ching-Yen.

*   *   *   *   *

Nui Chang was a personable young man of an age when he should have been thinking of marriage, but he seemed to have little interest in the opposite sex, apparently quite content to live alone reading and studying in the hope that he would pass his examinations and get his degree, thus attaining high office and honour in the state at an earlier age than most.

His neighbour who visited him occasionally was always telling him that he should take a wife, warning him that a student young and unmarried and living alone as he did might well be visited by ghosts or foxes. Nui told him that he was not afraid and laughed at his neighbour, who, thinking to teach him a lesson, arranged that a local singing girl should one night call on Nui and when he saw her she should pretend to be a ghost.

The girl came and knocked on his door asking to be let in, but Nui was wary and would not let her in no matter how much she entreated him. For, although he had laughed at his neighbour, he knew that foxes had the power to turn into beautiful girls, and he did not want to have anything to do with such creatures.

The next day the neighbour called to find out what had happened. Nui told him of his ghostly visitor and that he had been afraid to go to sleep that night. His neighbour was highly amused, and, laughing heartily, he spoke of the beauty of the singing girl who had called on him, and of the delights he might have enjoyed with her.

Several nights later Nui was visited by another girl, and thinking his neighbour was playing the same game upon him, he this time opened his door and invited her in. He was astounded at the beauty of this girl. Never in his wildest dreams had he expected to be confronted by so much loveliness. He asked her who she was and from whence she came.

"My name is Lien," she replied. "I am a singing girl from the district west of the town, and I have come to relieve your loneliness." Her eyes were bright and bewitching and her smile inviting.

Nui believed what she told him, thinking that his neighbour had not over-praised the girl's beauty in any way. She untied his robe and her touch was soft and warm and he was filled with desire. She extinguished the lantern and they retired to his bed. When she left him some hours later she promised that she would come to him again in a few days' time. She visited him three times during the next two weeks.

Nui always worked at his studies when Lien did not come, and one night he was immersed in his work when someone softly entered the house. Naturally he thought it was Lien, but the girl who stood before him was only about fifteen years of age, with loose flowing hair as befitted a virgin. He knew that she could not be a singing girl, and she looked so delicate and moved with such grace that he did not think she could be a fox. He asked her who she was.

"I come from an honourable family," said the girl in a voice of dulcet tones. "And my name is Ying. Having heard of your lonely diligence with your books, I have long admired and respected you and wished to know you. As it seemed impossible for us to meet, I have come to you without the knowledge of my parents. I am yours to command, for I already love you."

Nui was touched at such devotion and his blood quickened at the thought of embracing such a young and delicate maiden. He took her hand in his and remarked upon its coldness, and she reminded him that she had come through the chilly night air to be near him, and he could soon warm her with his love.

Overjoyed at his good fortune, Nui took her to his bed, and lay with her, drinking of her cool, sweet fragrance to his heart's content. Later, when she had to leave him, she gave him one of her dainty shoes and told him that he had only to hold it in his hands when he wanted her and she would know that he was thinking of her and would come to him. But only at night, she said, when her parents would not know that she was not in her own bed. "Does anyone else visit you?" she asked of him.

"Sometimes a singing girl comes to me, but not very often," Nui replied truthfully, for the wide-eyed innocence of her lovely eyes gazing into his own forbade him to tell her a lie. He need not have worried for she was quite unconcerned about his other visitor, but warned him that it would not do for the two ever to meet. "I must

c   65

be careful not to come when she is here and you must keep my visits secret. I would not want to be classed with a singing girl."

Nui promised that he would honour her wishes and the next evening Lien did not come and so he took out Ying's dainty shoe and thinking of her stroked it lovingly, his fingers caressing its delicate curves as though it was Ying herself whom he was caressing. He wished that she would again honour him with her presence, and almost as soon as the thought had formulated in his mind she was there beside him. He marvelled at her swift and silent arrival.

Ying gave a tinkling laugh. "I knew that you would wish to see me again, and I have been waiting in case your singing girl should come. As she did not, here I am."

And so Ying again embraced her and he was enraptured by her delicacy and her beauty. They took pleasure in each other as on the previous night, and she came to him night after night. He had only to stroke her shoe and there she was.

Then one night Lien, the singing girl, came to him once more and when she set eyes on him she exclaimed in dismay:"Whatever have you been doing with yourself since I last saw you?" she cried. "Are you not sleeping well? You look quite ill."

Nui replied that perhaps he had not been eating as well as usual and every night he was deep in his studies, working into the small hours.

"It is obvious that you are not taking care of yourself. Since my mother is sick and I will not be able to see you again for at least a week, I want you to promise me that you will not work so hard and that you will have your meals regularly."

But when Lien saw him again she was shocked at his appearance, saying that he was even worse than before. "You are so frail and ill-looking, I am sure you have the spirit sickness. I think you have been playing the love game with someone else and that is why you have become so weak. Tell me truthfully if you have and who she is, and I can help you."

But Nui denied that he was seeing anyone else, for had he not promised Ying that he would keep her visits secret? In any case, how could anyone so delicate and fragile as she was be the cause of his sickness?

Lien did not believe him and the next night she waited hidden by a tree outside his window. She was determined to find out if Nui had lied to her and she did not have long to wait before she saw Nui take out Ying's shoe from its secret hiding place, and as he stroked it with his thin hand a truly beautiful girl appeared as if by

magic and Lien knew that her worst fears had been realized. She made her presence known to them and immediately Ying took fright and left.

Lien told him: "She is a ghost. No wonder you have the spirit sickness. You are being slowly poisoned by contact with her, and you must give her up immediately. Fortunately the poison has not yet penetrated too deeply into your system and I can drive it out of your body with some special herbs. I will bring them to you tomorrow and will nurse you until you are well again. But you must promise me that you will not see your ghost maiden again."

Nui did not think that Ying would come to him again in any case, for she would be too frightened of being seen by Lien. He promised not to see her again, for he was too weak to do anything else. So Lien brought the herbs and nursed him back to health and in time he was quite better and eating well, his vigour returned as before. The day came when Lien said that she must return to her home and that she would not be seeing him for a few days. She warned him once more about the folly of associating with his ghost maiden.

But Nui did not believe that he had been suffering from the spirit sickness and still less did he believe that Ying was a ghost. He had to know if the shoe could still bring her to him. He took it from its hiding place once more and fondled it, thinking of the beauty of its owner, and Ying appeared as before.

As soon as Lien saw him again she knew that he had not kept his promise to her. "You must be besotted with love for this maid of the underworld, and you must want to die," she told him sorrowfully. "Before long you will again suffer from the spirit sickness and this time I will not be there to help you." And with that she left him.

Lien's words came true and some weeks later Nui was indeed very ill once more. He lay on his bed getting weaker and weaker, praying that Lien would come back to him and eventually she did, but only to tell him that his end was near. He begged her to save him and she told him that he had not heeded her warning and why should she nurse him back to health so that he could again go back to his ghost girl?

Nui told Lien about the shoe, saying that he would not summon Ying to him ever again, and Lien must take the shoe and burn it. Lien took the shoe and no sooner had she touched it than Ying appeared. Lien upbraided her, saying that she was the cause of Nui's illness and why did she not admit it?

"I do admit it," said Ying with tears in her lovely eyes, "and I have come only to beg you to save him. If you do, I promise that I will

return to the underworld never to see him again, for I do not wish to be the cause of his death."

Lien, somewhat mollified by Ying's obvious distress, for she was now on her knees pleading to Lien to do what she could to save Nui, who was in great pain and having difficulty in breathing. Lien agreed to try to save Nui and together they worked, making herbal medicines, massaging his heart and lungs, but he still seemed unable to breathe properly.

Lien then put her mouth to his and forced her own breath into his lungs until she was exhausted, but she had given him the breath of life and he was now breathing more easily, and eventually he dozed off into a natural sleep.

Ying, seeing that Lien had indeed managed to save his life, told her that she must now go and never would return. "I thank you for your goodness," she said to Lien. "I had no idea that beings like yourself could be so forgiving and so clever in healing the sick.

Lien looked at Ying in surprised dismay, for the ghost girl obviously knew *her* secret, but she did not feel strong enough after her efforts on Nui's behalf to deny anything. "We are just the same when it comes to loving, and caring for the sick," she said.

Ying told her that she need have no fear. Nui would never know from her. She would keep her promise and would be happy knowing that Nui was in good hands.

Lien nursed Nui day and night, and as Nui regained his strength so Lien gradually lost hers, until eventually it was Nui who was nursing Lien. But nothing he did for her could save her and she became weaker and weaker.

Lien knew that she was dying and with her last breath she told him the truth about herself. And so it was that her now wasted body lying on the bed changed into that of a fox.

Vengeful Ghosts

One cannot generalize about ghosts any more than one can about the living, for spirits have various reasons for returning to haunt this earth, and some seem to have a definite purpose. The following story is of one who sought vengeance against a tardy lover who lived to regret deserting his sweetheart when he thought his own life was in danger.

Caisho Burroughes was said to be one of the most handsome men in the England of his day, extremely valiant, though proud and bloodthirsty. Even so, the ghost of his sweetheart was to reduce him to a trembling wreck of his former self. His father was Sir John Burroughes, Garter King of Arms during the reign of Charles I, and Keeper of the Records at the Tower of London. He was sent by King Charles to Germany as English Envoy to the Emperor.

Caisho was the eldest of two sons and two daughters, and Sir John was persuaded to take Caisho along with him, journeying by way of Italy, where he left the young man in Florence in order that he should learn the Italian language. If Sir John had had the slightest idea what was going to be the devastating effect of his son's handsome looks upon a certain beautiful courtesan and the tragedy which would ensue, he might have had second thoughts about continuing his journey without him.

Caisho, with his good looks and proud family background, was soon received into the highest social circles, and made many influential friends. He was entertained royally and his studies took second place, especially when he met the beautiful mistress of the

Grand Duke of Tuscany, with whom he soon became deeply involved, and who fell so passionately in love with him that she cast caution to the winds and was constantly to be seen in his company.

Their affair became so public that it inevitably came to the ears of the Grand Duke, an extremely proud and jealous man. He was something of a diplomat and had no desire to offend King Charles by taking direct measures against this inconvenient young English blade. The most discreet way out of the awkward situation would be for Caisho to encounter a fatal accident in one of the less reputable Florentine haunts which he was in the habit of frequenting.

Mutual friends came to hear of the Duke's plan to have Caisho murdered, and warned him that his life was in danger if he continued to stay in Florence. Caisho did not at first believe that the Duke would go to such lengths to stop his affair with his mistress; but on the very night of the warning he was innocently involved in a brawl and an attempt was made to stab him. Fortunately for him he had two men friends with him, and when the would-be assassin found himself outnumbered, he made off as fast as his legs could carry him. The three friends laughed at the sight, but Caisho was now in no doubt of the seriousness of his position. He did not wish to die just yet, in the full flower of his youth. Life was far too sweet and no woman was worth dying for—especially another man's mistress. Even though she had given him to understand that she was willing to give up everything for his sake, he was not in the position to keep a mistress. She would be a luxury he could not afford.

He left for England immediately.

Meanwhile his lady love waited and pined for him in vain. He had left Florence in such haste that he had not even said goodbye to her, nor sent her a message telling of his impending departure. As for her, she knew nothing of the Duke's design, and she waited as usual for her lover, miserable and unhappy because he did not come, for all her hopes and thoughts had been centred around the handsome young Caisho. She no longer cared for the Grand Duke, nor for her envied position as his mistress, for she loved Caisho as she had never loved anyone before.

It was the Grand Duke himself who informed her of her lover's flight. He had been disappointed that his prey had escaped him and he had been robbed of taking his revenge. He took it out on his mistress instead, deriding her for her treachery and faithlessness, and reproaching her for choosing so unworthy a young man—a coward who ran away at the slightest sign of danger, and who did not even wait to say goodbye to her.

The poor girl was heartbroken and bitterly disappointed at the way her lover had deserted her. She knew that the Grand Duke would never permit her to leave and follow Caisho to England—and life with the Duke after this would be unbearable. She might as well be dead. So in despair she took her own life, hopeful perhaps that in death she would find her lover again.

Meanwhile Caisho had returned to London and was sharing a room with a friend, a Colonel Remes, a member of Parliament. One night they were in bed together when the ghost of his Florentine sweetheart appeared before them.

At first Caisho thought it was really her, and he asked her how she had known where to find him and what was she doing in England? Whereupon the beautiful ghost solemnly told him that she had killed herself because he had deserted her and left her to the vengeance of the Grand Duke, who after he had found out about their love affair had treated her shamefully, making her life miserable. She had preferred to die than to face life without Caisho.

"You, too, will die soon," she told her now frightened gallant. "You will be killed in a duel. But until that time comes, I shall haunt you and you will regret having left me without so much as a word. Every day that is left to you, you will regret it." She thereupon vanished with her words of doom and foreboding echoing in the wretched Caisho's ears.

If Caisho had been alone he might have dismissed the incident from his mind, putting it down to a bad dream after over-indulgence in the taverns. But Colonel Remes had seen the apparition as well, and was very much affected by what they had both seen. They tried to make jokes about their visitor from the other world, saying the next time she came they would invite her to join them in bed, but neither of them could shake off the fear of the unknown which the visitation had given them.

In the morning they were more inclined to dismiss it as a temporary hallucination probably evoked by a sorceress, who perhaps had been paid to use her withcraft on them by some of their devil-may-care friends, who were perhaps at this moment laughing themselves silly after hearing of their reaction to the bedside apparition. The following night Caisho made some inquiries among his friends, but it was obvious that they knew nothing about the incident, and he returned to his lodgings a little the worse for drink.

Colonel Remes was already asleep and Caisho fell into bed beside him, but he had hardly closed his eyes when he was vividly and frighteningly aware of a presence in the room. Blearily he opened his

eyes and once more saw the ghost of the woman from Florence.

Terrified, he shrieked at her, waking his friend, and they both saw her sad and beautiful face, and heard again her words of denunciation and her forecast of death for Caisho.

Caisho, still in his cups, jumped out of bed as though to attack her, but when he reached out he grasped nothing, and felt only a breath of icy air upon his face as she vanished before his sight, her words echoing in his ears: "You, too, will soon die. You will be killed in a duel. But until that time comes, I will haunt you . . . haunt you . . . haunt you."

"If this sort of thing is going to happen every night," said Colonel Remes, in the morning, "I shall be looking for new lodgings." He was as good as his word, for the ghostly visitations continued, and Caisho was becoming more and more terror-stricken, crying out as soon as he saw her. He dared not sleep alone at night and after Remes left he persuaded his younger brother John to sleep with him, and he too saw and heard the vengeful ghost of Caisho's dead sweetheart.

Caisho was indeed regretting his callous desertion of her. Death in some dark alley in Florence would have been preferable to this continued assault from the spirit world which was gradually driving him out of his mind. He would cry out in anguish every time he saw her, his whole body shaking with fear. "Oh, God! Here she comes! Here she comes!"

The story of the haunting was now the talk of London. It even aroused the interest of King Charles. John Aubrey (1626–97) wrote in his book *Miscellanies upon Various Subjects*: "The story was so common that King Charles I sent for Caisho Burroughes's father, whom he examined as to the truth of the matter; who did (together with Colonel Remes) aver the matter of fact to be true, so that the King thought it worth his while to send to Florence to inquire at what time this unhappy lady killed herself; it was found to be the same minute that she first appeared to Caisho in bed with Colonel Remes. This relation I had from my worthy friend Mr Monson, who had it from Sir John's own mouth, brother of Caisho; he had also the same account from his own father, who was intimately acquainted with old Sir John Burroughes, and both his sons, and says, as often as Caisho related this, he wept bitterly."

Caisho went to pieces and spent the nights with the women of the town and drinking in the taverns, rather than go back to his lodgings to face his nightly visitor from the other world. One night he became involved in an argument with a stranger who challenged him to a

duel, and on returning to his room in the early hours, hoping to get some rest, for he was in no fit shape to wield a sword just then, the ghost appeared again, this time telling him that his end was at hand and that he would die that very day.

Perhaps he did not wish to live, having been thoroughly demoralized by this terrible campaign of revenge, or perhaps his health did not permit him to fight with his usual sureness and precision; but whatever it was he appeared to be quite unable to protect himself from his opponent, whose sword soon found its mark deep in Caisho's heart.

As he died on the grass, the early morning mist seemed to gather around Caisho's body, and some who witnessed the sight said the mist was more of a wraith, a phantom form bending over him as he died, and it was believed that his ghost-sweetheart had come to claim in death what she had lost in life.

Ghosts would be legion if everyone who had suffered and died in consequence of a treacherous act inflicted by another came back from the nether world to haunt the guilty person. That a number do come back is generally accepted, for many wrong-doers have experienced terrifying ordeals which seem to prove that the dead can and do return to exact vengeance. Engine-driver Brierly was not at heart a dishonourable man, yet through him his best friend, Jim Robson, had killed his wife and child and then himself, returning from the spirit world to take a terrible revenge.

If anyone had ever told Brierly that he would become obsessed by another man's wife he would not have believed him, for his own wife was a good woman and he loved her and their little daughter very much indeed. Jim was his best friend and drove the Night Express regularly, and had got him a job in the same yard as himself as a driver on one of the local trains. John Brierly was a happy man and when Jim got married he was his best man. The Brierlys were the first friends to visit the happy couple when they went to live in a cottage on the main line.

It was Jim who first threw them together. The Robsons had been visiting the Brierlys and Jim asked John to see his wife home for him. Both men were going back on duty and John's train, being a local, made its first stop at the station near the Robsons' cottage, which was close enough to the station for John to see her safely to the door.

After that it became a habit for John to call on Jim's wife for a chat every time his local stopped at the station. At first there was

nothing between them, and she did not encourage him, but Jim was away a lot, only seeing his wife two or three times a week, and she was lonely. Brierly saw her at every opportunity, and their friendship soon ripened into something more serious.

John Brierly continued to visit her even when she was expecting Jim's child, and inevitably there was gossip, which eventually came to the ears of the husband.

Jim was not a church-going man, but he was strict about morals and marital fidelity, and he could not believe that his wife was carrying on with his best friend.

But when Jim tackled Brierly, he could not deny that he had visited the cottage at every opportunity. Jim told him never to go there again. He was white to the lips, his grey eyes cold and hostile as he looked at the man he had thought was his friend.

"You must ask for a transfer, Brierly, or as God is my judge I shall have my revenge on you." He turned angrily on his heels and walked away.

The next morning John Brierly asked for the transfer, and was put on a train running to the Midlands and back on the same day. But he still had to pass the cottage every night and every morning. The cottage was situated on a bend in the line which necessitated slowing down the train to quarter speed as they approached, and John would blow the whistle and lean out of the cab for a glimpse of Jim's wife. She was always there standing in the doorway of the cottage waving to him as he passed by, and every night she put a light in the cottage window for him to see.

But it was torture for him having only a glimpse of her, and Brierly was not content with this state of affairs for long. He started to write to her, pouring out his heart in wild words of love, forgetting the danger, thinking only of the woman he was obsessed with, heedless of the fact that his letters might be found and read by her husband.

A premonition of disaster came one dark Saturday night when for the first time there was no light in the cottage window. Brierly pulled the whistle as he had always done, so that she might hear him coming, but there was still no welcoming gleam. The cottage was in pitch darkness.

He continued his journey with a feeling of dread and foreboding, and when he reached the terminus the first thing that caught his eyes was a news bill in big black letters which said: ENGINE DRIVER KILLS WIFE, CHILD AND SELF. He knew without reading the newspaper that it was Jim.

Of course he should have gone right away when Jim first found out about his affair with her. It was his own fault. He was to blame for his weakness in not being able to leave her alone. If only he had been strong enough this terrible tragedy would never have happened. She would still be alive, and so would the child and Jim.

As fate would have it Brierly was promoted to take his friend's place as driver of the Night Express and he was asked to take over immediately, on the very night after the tragedy. He did not funk taking over Jim's engine and having Jim's fireman on the footplate with him; but he felt dead inside, with no heart and feeling left.

He did the usual things before starting out on his first trip, automatically, feeling more like a machine than a man, for life now seemed to have lost its meaning. He alone was to blame for what had happened, and there was nothing he could do about it now. It was too late.

Under his hand the great locomotive moved forward as it pounded out of the station, the wheels quickly gathering momentum. Soon he was reducing speed as they approached the bend in the line, where the cottage stood, a dark blur, where no welcoming light would ever shine for him again from the window. Tears welled up in his eyes and he quickly wiped them away with the back of his hand, glancing at the fireman to see if he had noticed. But the fireman was standing cap in hand, also wiping away a tear as they passed. The two men self-consciously grasped each other's hands, and without a word went back to their respective jobs which ensured the safe arrival of the express at its destination.

Every night the express swept by the cottage, and after some weeks of uneventful monotony a frightening thing happened.

They were approaching the bend near the cottage one dark night, and as usual Brierly pulled back the lever to reduce speed. He still made a habit of leaning out of the cab as they went round the bend at quarter speed, staring at the cottage and thinking of Jim's wife, as though hoping to see her once more.

His thoughts were this time interrupted by the voice of the fireman shouting at him: "For God's sake, look at the lever!"

Brierly jerked back into the cab, for he had already felt the steam valves opening, and he could see to his horror that the regulator lever was being pulled open as if by an unseen hand. He leapt at the lever to close it, as the engine rapidly gained a speed much too high for the curve. Trying to close the lever was like pulling against an

75

irresistible force. He slammed on the brakes, and the engine rounded the curve swaying from side to side and bucking dangerously, while the long train followed, rocking on its bogeys, brakes hissing and grinding.

Both men thought the engine was going off the rails. Brierly had to pull with all his might to shut off the steam against the force of the unseen hand, but they got round the bend without disaster with both men white to the lips. Never was a train crew more thankful to pull safely into the terminus at the other end of the run.

Brierly had more reason to be afraid than the fireman, because he knew that there was no natural cause for such a thing to have happened. He was certain that the unseen hand which had fought to open the regulator lever against him was Jim's, and he was equally certain that it would happen again. Would he always be able to hold it?

From that time he often had to fight against the unseen force which tried to gain control of the lever. He hung on like grim death every time they approached the bend near the cottage, and never took his hand off it on that particular stretch of the line. But he realized that each succeeding time it happened the force was stronger, and he knew that one day he would not be able to hold it.

He decided to quit and go up North. He should have done this long ago. It was the only way of avoiding disaster—a disaster which would involve not only him but a trainload of trusting passengers.

Soon he was going on his last journey driving the Night Express for the last time, and for the last time he would drive past the cottage with its memories and its horrors. His wife and little daughter were travelling with him and were seated in the first coach nearest to the engine, and they had it to themselves.

Brierly had kissed them both before climbing up into the monster of steel and settling himself behind the controls. The final whistle sounded and he put his hand on the lever, gripping it hard, for the feel of it made him shudder despite the intense heat which came from the roaring furnace being tended by the fireman. There was a great hiss of steam and then another before the mighty engine started to move and then, gaining momentum, pounded away into the night.

The train was travelling at sixty miles an hour when it approached the bend, and according to the fireman there was nothing either of them could do to close the regulator. They both hung on to it with all their might, but it opened full and they could not move it to

shut the steam off. They were pushing helplessly against an irresistible force.

The engine and the first carriage jumped the track. The fireman was thrown clear, but John Brierly, his wife and child were killed. Though the train was derailed there were no other casualties.

Jim Robson had had his revenge.

Pearlin Jean

The great house of Allanbank, which for over a hundred years had been the seat of the Stuarts, a family of Scottish baronets, stood grim and imposing in the bright moonlight of a June night. A few lighted windows showed that the family had not yet retired; it was the hour of card-playing for the ladies, and of the enjoyment of a fine old port by the gentlemen. The children slept in the nurseries, and below stairs the servants chatted, their work over for the day.

Allanbank was blessed with extensive gardens, and beyond them lay a large orchard. On this beautiful night the moon "tipped with silver all the fruit-tree tops" and made shining ornaments of the ripening apples. It was a night for lovers' meetings, and young Thomas Blackadder, standing beneath a particularly large apple-tree, was hoping for just such an encounter. On the bark of the tree a ray of moonlight picked out the initials "J.M." and "T.B." surrounded by the outline of a heart. Thomas had carved them, and Thomas was waiting for his sweetheart, Jenny Mackie. Every night at this time, when Jenny's duties as a still-room maid at Allanbank permitted, they would meet here and stroll beneath the trees, talking of their coming wedding-day and of the small cottage which Thomas's master had promised them. Jenny was well known as being the prettiest girl in the district, and what with this and the cottage Thomas considered himself a lucky man.

Jenny was late tonight, however. Thomas had no watch and could not have told the time if he had possessed one. But he was a countryman, and by the place of the moon in the sky and the

gradual silencing of even the latest-singing blackbird, he knew that he was being kept waiting. A sharp little breeze was rising, and Thomas's coat was thin; he shivered slightly.

Suddenly, through the trees, a white glimmer caught his eye—the glimmer of a dress. At last Jenny had come! "Here I am, my lass," he cried, and ran forward with open arms, eager to embrace her. She halted and stood waiting for him to reach her, a few yards away; then, just as he approached her, she vanished.

Thomas stood as if spellbound. One minute she had been there, the next she was gone. What was she playing at, and where was she? He began to run about among the trees, calling "Jenny! Jenny! Come oot, I ken ye're there!" But no Jenny replied, and Thomas began to be angry, and to think of the sharp things he would say to her when she chose to reappear. Just then he saw her again—a faint white figure at the far end of the orchard, almost half an acre off. How could she have run there in the time? He started towards her, calling her name, and all the time she stood motionless; but once again, when he was within ten or twelve yards of her, she melted into the darkness. There was nothing to be seen of her in a light that was almost as bright as day—neither shawled head nor white skirts—and the orchard was silent as death.

Thomas could not have told at what moment he was struck by a chill of horror that made him quite forget his anger with Jenny. But after a moment of contemplating the empty air where the white girl had stood, he turned on his heel and ran, never stopping until he reached the farmstead where he worked, a mile away through the village.

A few minutes after his abrupt flight, a white dress again gleamed out among the tree-trunks, and a hurried step rustled through the grass.

"Thomas! Where are ye? I'm sorry I'm late!"

But neither searching nor calling produced any sign of Thomas, and soon Jenny went home, puzzled and cross. Tomorrow, she decided, she would demand a full explanation.

But to her surprise she found Thomas reproachful instead of apologetic when they met on the following evening.

"Why did ye lead me on, lass, and then rin awa'? It was no' like ye to dae sic a thing," he complained.

"I never did! I never set eyes on ye, Thomas, and well you know it!"

They were anxious to believe the best of each other, and Jenny listened patiently to Thomas's account of his Vanishing Lady.

When he had finished telling her of the final disappearance, and of his flight, her face changed.

"Guid help us, Thomas! Ye saw Pearlin Jean!"

And so for the first time Thomas heard the story of the ghost of Allanbank. Jenny had never told him of it before, knowing him to be of a nervous, sensitive disposition, such as avoids graveyards at night-time. But she consoled herself with the thought that he would in any case have heard the tale sooner or later, for it was known to all the domestics at Allanbank and to most of the villagers.

Nearly a hundred years before, in the 1670s, young Mr Robert Stuart set out from his home, Allanbank, to finish his education as a gentleman, by making a tour of foreign cities. He was a gay, handsome young man, with bright dark eyes and a face of almost feminine beauty, well set off by the long curled wig of the time and the foppish clothes which had adorned men since the Restoration. There was not much life in Scotland for a rich and frivolous young man, and Mr Stuart was glad enough to escape to the Continent.

He had explored Italy to his own satisfaction, spending a very little time in its famous churches and a great deal in its fashionable salons, and had made his way to that Mecca of young men, Paris.

The brilliant Court of Versailles reckoned little of the wars with Spain and Holland that raged intermittently throughout those years. Luxurious living, witty conversation, and amorous intrigue were the main occupations of Louis XIV's courtiers, and the latter diversion, in particular, appealed to Mr Stuart. A strict Scottish upbringing had not been able to quench a strong natural enthusiasm for feminine beauty, and he was delighted to find the ladies of France a good deal more accommodating and accessible than those of his native country.

It was not, however, a court lady who made the sun of Paris shine most brightly for Mr Stuart. The windows of his lodgings in a tall, ancient house, once the home of a noble Parisian family, overlooked a long garden belonging to a neighbouring convent. Every morning and afternoon the nuns and novices walked there in sedate groups. As they walked, some read their breviaries, some meditated. But among those who had not yet taken their vows there were eyes that wandered—eyes as yet undimmed by the shadows of the cloister. One particular pair of eyes was often raised to Mr Stuart's windows, and the vision which frequently appeared there of a young man as handsome as any archangel—to eyes as unsophisticated as these. They were blue eyes, very large, and the

hair that peeped beneath the severe hood was corn-yellow and curled softly into something suspiciously like modish ringlets. Altogether, Mlle Jeanne de la Salle was a most un-nun-like young lady. Deeply emotional and romantic, she had at the age of fourteen developed a wild attachment for one Soeur Thérèse, a teacher at the convent school which Jeanne attended. Nothing would do but that Jeanne must follow her into the cloister, and live a life of rapt piety, clad in radiant white and with her charming face surrounded by a highly becoming wimple.

But convent life, so far, had proved to be ever so slightly dull. Jeanne found her devotional rapture distinctly weak at the unheard-of hours at which a relentless bell summoned her to prayer. Perhaps she had made a mistake in thinking she had a vocation. When her eyes met the dark eyes of Mr Stuart, and held them, she was sure she had made a mistake.

Very soon a wordless rendezvous was kept every day between the young man at the window and the girl in the garden. Before two weeks had passed, a convent servant had been bribed to bring Mr Stuart a note telling him at what hour Mademoiselle would walk in the garden alone, and which garden gate would be left unlatched. On Monday of the third week, the little bell called Jeanne to prayer in vain. Her narrow bed was empty. But the more ample bed of Mr Stuart, hung with rosy curtains and watched by carven Cupids, was by no means empty.

Jeanne threw herself into the business of being Robert Stuart's mistress with the same concentrated devotion that she had at first given to her novitiate. To him, her simple sweetness and extravagant adoration brought more pleasure than had the easy favours of the Court beauties. He was as much in love as it was possible for him to be. He transferred his servants, his luggage, his lady and himself to a hotel discreetly far away from the convent, and for some two months the lovers led an idyllic life.

Ironically enough, it was the very simplicity and intensity which had attracted Robert Stuart to Jeanne which now began to repel him. He began to exchange glances with other young ladies, in public places. He invented important errands which kept him out in the evenings, while Jeanne sat in their lodgings, tapping her foot impatiently, adding a few stitches to her embroidery, then dropping her needle to sigh. Then he would come home to find her weeping and reproachful, and a quarrel would break out.

It was cowardly of Mr Stuart not to tell Jeanne that he was leaving her—that their affair was ended. He thought seriously of it

one evening, when she had been more vehement than usual in her reproaches, protestations of love, and pleas for marriage.

"I left the convent for you—I broke my vows! And now, having led me into mortal sin, you won't keep your promise and marry me."

"I have told you a hundred times," said Mr Stuart patiently, "that I cannot marry you without my father's consent. He would be mortally offended, and I should lose my inheritance."

"Then take me back to Scotland with you! He will not refuse when he knows that I am a demoiselle of good family."

"I have told you I cannot. How would it seem if we travelled to Scotland together, unmarried? You must let me go back myself, while you remain here."

Jeanne wept and pleaded, but in vain. In the early hours of next morning, when it was still hardly light, a carriage drew up at the door of the hotel, and the muffled figure of Mr Stuart stepped into it. Just as the postilion was about to whip up the horses, another figure appeared in the hotel doorway. Jeanne, her face tear-streaked and her hair dishevelled, and still wearing the dress in which she had thrown herself down on the bed the night before, ran to the coach door and frantically shook the handle.

"Let me in! Take me with you! You are going to Scotland, I know it. Robert, don't leave me—don't leave me!"

But he held fast to the handle, and made wild signals to the bewildered postilion.

"You shan't go!" she shrieked. "I tell you this, Robert Stuart— if you marry any woman but me I shall come between you to the end of your days!" And she leapt on to the fore-wheel of the carriage, one foot on the hub, clinging to the top of the wheel with both hands.

"Drive on! Drive on!" cried Stuart. The postilion, half-dazed with sleep and surprise, obeyed him. As the wheels turned Jeanne fell— not to the side of the carriage, but directly in front of it. To the end of his life Robert Stuart heard her scream, as the wheel went over her forehead.

It was a dusky autumn evening, two or three weeks later, when another carriage bore him along a quiet, hilly road towards Allanbank. He was more quietly dressed than in his Paris days, but not a whit less jaunty. As a pretty shepherd lass herded her flock together to let the coach pass, he swept off his feathered hat to her and gave her a smile which irradiated her life for many a week. And why, after all, should he not smile? He was going home, after a highly

instructive—and amusing—tour, marred only by one unfortunate incident of the sort which could happen to any man of the world, and which is best forgotten. His parents would be awaiting him with a warm welcome, there would be charming girls produced for his inspection. The spacious estates of Allanbank awaited him. As the coach turned a corner, the familiar arched gateway came in sight, and he leaned forward eagerly to see it.

Up the road rumbled the coach; then, thirty yards or so from the gateway, one of the horses gave a frightened neigh, and reared. A second later the other echoed it.

"Get on, ye daft cattle! What ails ye?" shouted the driver, lashing out with his whip. But both horses were as though riveted to the ground, their eyes rolling with fear.

"What is it? Are the horses mad?" Mr Stuart put his head out of the window. There was nothing to account for the animals' behaviour—no highwayman in the road, no flapping scarecrow. Suddenly his eye took in an unfamiliar object; something white and red on top of the gateway, that he had never seen there before. He stared, and stared again, and his face grew as pale as the rich lace skirts that moved softly in the breeze, as Jeanne stretched out her arms to him in welcome, and bent her terrible head, from which the blood streamed on to her white shoulders and her white bodice.

It is not recorded how Mr Stuart made his way home that night, but the celebrations for his return were not held; nor was he ever again the same confident young man who had driven up to the gateway of Allanbank.

Nor was Allanbank the same. It had been a placid house, where nothing more eventful than domestic births and deaths had ever taken place. Now it became a place to be feared at night. Unaccountable things happened. Doors opened and shut with a great noise, at midnight—a hideous scream was sometimes heard, enough to chill the blood—and the rustling of silks and pattering of high heels were heard in rooms and passages. For some time nothing was seen; then one night a maid, on her way to bed, met face to face an apparition which frightened her into shrieking hysterics. For hours she could say nothing but "The pearlin dress! The pearlin dress!" At last she managed to explain that the figure had been clad in a dress made of pearlin, or thread-lace.

The worst of the hauntings occurred when the master of Allanbank was at home. During his absences in Edinburgh or London the noises abated and the form of "Pearlin Jean", as she was now known, was seldom seen. But as soon as he returned the footsteps

and rustlings began again, doors slammed, furniture moved—nobody could be sure of a good night's rest. The whole household suffered, and servants were hard to replace. But Robert Stuart suffered worst of all; he lived in constant fear of a glimpse of his dead love's lacy skirts, or of the whole dreadful figure appearing to him, as it sometimes did.

It was with a certain relief that he took to himself a wife. She was a young lady of excellent background, highly suited to become Lady Stuart—for in 1687 Robert Stuart had been created a baronet. Her temperament, fortunately, was calm, even phlegmatic. She had been told of the ghostly disturbances at Allanbank—indeed, it would have been hard to keep the information from her—but regarded them as something in the nature of a household nuisance, like jackdaws in the chimney. "Pearlin Jean" seemed furious at Lady Stuart's arrival, and redoubled her efforts to annoy; but the young lady of Allanbank refused to be put out even by a full-scale appearance of the ghost.

Sir Robert was pleased with his wife. He had her portrait, in satin and pearls, painted by a London artist, and hung with his own in the Long Gallery. On the day it went on the wall, all hell broke loose at Allanbank—objects were hurled about, tables and chairs moved of themselves, china ornaments fell and smashed—and the insistent angry footsteps paced rapidly from room to room, through halls and corridors, running down stairs and up stairs, only pausing to stamp on or kick whatever lay in their way.

Sir Robert became desperate. Finally he decided to resort to exorcism. Seven ministers of the Church of Scotland agreed to come to Allanbank and attempt, with solemn ceremonies, to send the spirit of Jeanne back to its Paris grave or to a better world. But all in vain: "they did no mickle guid," as Jenny the maid told Thomas Blackadder long after. The hauntings continued as though the reverend gentlemen had never been.

In desperation, Sir Robert sought about for another solution. The last words Jeanne had ever spoken came back to him: "If you marry any woman but me I shall come between you to the end of your days." Could she, perhaps, be pacified by appearing to "come between" himself and his wife—if only in paint? It was a strange, macabre idea, but worth trying. He nervously explained it to his wife, who with her usual calm good temper agreed that he must be prepared to try anything that would stop the nuisance. Accordingly, Sir Robert consulted a portrait-painter who was only too glad of a commission. No portrait of Jeanne was in Sir Robert's possession—

not surprisingly—but he gave the painter a full description of her as she had been, and in rough masculine fashion sketched out the style of her dress. (He had seen it often enough, Heaven knew!) Working on this, the artist produced a full-length painting, not the most accurate likeness of Jeanne, but sufficiently like, Sir Robert hoped, to please her. This he had hung in the Long Gallery between the portraits of himself and his wife.

The effect was immediate. The ghost became comparatively quiet. She made no appearances, and for the first time the Stuarts were able to go to bed with a reasonable expectation of sleeping through the night. This happy state of things continued so long that Sir Robert's confidence began to return. Now that Jeanne was pacified, he thought, might not the portrait be removed? After all, awkward questions were often asked about it, and now that his young family was growing up it was a little embarrassing for them to have the picture of a strange woman hung prominently between those of their mother and father. The picture was accordingly removed, and banished to an attic.

In the hour in which it was taken down, the hauntings returned. For some reason long forgotten, the picture was not restored to its place, and Allanbank continued to be a pestered house. If Jeanne did not actually succeed in coming between her false lover and his lady, she made their life extremely uncomfortable, and may even have hastened his death. Even after he was gone, Jeanne continued her perambulations. They extended to the grounds and gardens, as witness the teasing of young Thomas Blackadder—though, to do her justice, she did not appear to him in her full horror.

Long after Thomas and his Jenny were man and wife—somewhere about the year 1790—two ladies paid a visit to Allanbank, which had now passed out of the Stuart family. No word of the ghost had been mentioned to them, but the night they spent there was made hideous by the constant pacing of someone unseen up and down their bedroom. In the nineteenth century the ghost was both seen and heard, but by now her power was failing and she was regarded almost affectionately. Time creeps like ivy over the memory of all wrongs—even the cruel one that had been done to poor "Pearlin Jean".

Child Ghosts

All ghosts frighten most people, but the ghosts of children, whose young lives have been tragically cut short, excite pity as well. There is always tragedy in the death of a child.

In olden times there were many of these young ghosts, but it is an interesting fact that the number of ghostly children has considerably decreased through the centuries, and the reasons for this are not hard to find.

Peoples of the ancient world did not care for their children in the way we do in modern times. It was not unusual to sacrifice a child to ensure protection from the gods and to ward off evil spirits. Children were used as foundation sacrifices and walled-up live in buildings, even in churches, and small skeletons have often been found in ancient walls as horrifying evidence of this pagan practice of long ago. The ghosts of these unfortunate children were relied upon to haunt the buildings in which they were immured and ward off the evil spirits. In some cases the haunting has gone on for centuries.

Relatives of the unwanted could be equally cruel to children in their charge, and everyone knows the legend of the Babes in the Wood, who were Norfolk children and whose rascally uncle paid two cut-throats to take them into Wayland Wood and murder them. However, their innocence and sweetness so touched the heart of one of the paid killers that he persuaded the other that instead of killing the children they should leave them to their fate. The children never found their way out of the wood, and ever after it

was haunted by the two little ghosts wailing and bemoaning their fate.

Another well-known story is that of the little Princes in the Tower—twelve-year-old Edward V and his ten-year-old brother, Richard Duke of York—who were believed to have been murdered at the command of their uncle, Richard III. According to the narrative of Sir Thomas More, the Constable of the Tower, Sir Richard Brackenbury, had refused to have anything to do with Richard's plan to kill the Princes. The unsavoury task was said to have been undertaken by Sir James Tyrrell, one of whose ancestors was said to have murdered William Rufus. Tyrrell hired two ruffians, Miles Forest and John Dighton, who smothered the boys with their pillows as they slept. The Bloody Tower was haunted for centuries by these two pathetic boy ghosts. In 1674, during certain structural alterations at the Tower, a wooden chest was discovered inside which were found two small skeletons. It was presumed at the time that these were the remains of the two Princes, and Charles II had them buried in Henry VII's chapel, after which the Princes' ghosts were never seen again in the Bloody Tower.

The cessation of the haunting might have been considered reason enough to believe that the skeletons found in 1674 actually were those of young Edward V and his brother. But the authorities needed further proof apparently and the urn containing the skeletons was opened and examined in 1933. A celebrated anatomist concluded that the remains were those of two brothers of the age of the young Princes, and that the skull of the elder boy bore traces of death by suffocation. In December, 1964, the remains of eight-year-old Anne Mowbray, the child bride of the younger Prince, Richard, Duke of York, were found in a casket on a Stepney building site. It is not known how this unfortunate little girl met her death. Some think that she, too, may have been murdered, thus completing the circle of death which encompassed the innocent lives of these tragic royal children.

It is worth noting incidentally that the examination of the remains of the Princes in the Tower in 1933 was completed in five days. Three months after the discovery of the body of Anne Mowbray in 1964, the experts were still at work on the remains, despite protests by Lord Mowbray, Anne's descendant. But the authorities pleaded historical and scientific necessity.

In medieval times children were often given in marriage at a tender age for political and other reasons. Girls were considered to be grown up at fifteen and it is evident that they ripened more

quickly in those days. Well-to-do families often sent their daughters away to be educated at a convent where they would learn to read and write, spin, embroider and sing.

Boys were also boarded at monasteries, or they might be sent away as pages to a nobleman's household, or taught at home by the chaplain. One boy who was sent to be a page at Hayne, in Devon, ended up haunting the Manor where he had worked and from where he had vanished together with a quantity of his master's silver.

When the master first started to see the ghost of his missing page boy he took no notice, thinking that he was dreaming, or that his imagination was playing tricks, as he had been considerably upset by the loss of his valuables. But the page-boy ghost was not to be ignored and appeared more and more persistently, always at the foot of his bed and beckoning to his old master as though asking him to follow him when he left the room.

Impatient at his continual loss of sleep, the man eventually got out of bed and followed the ghostly page-boy, who went ahead along the passage, down the stairs, across the hall and through the great front door, constantly turning back and beckoning, obviously anxious to lead his former master to some place. The man opened the front door and went out into the night to find the apparition awaiting him in the garden. The boy ghost beckoned again and continued on its way, always a little ahead of the man, whom he led into a nearby wood. Eventually the ghost stopped at the foot of a large hollow tree, and there he vanished.

Convinced now that the ghost of the page-boy was trying to tell him something, the man had the tree chopped down, and inside the hollow trunk were the remains of the page boy, who obviously had been murdered. Underneath the body was some of the missing silver, the recovery of which, with the help of the ghostly page boy, eventually led to the culprit—the butler, who had been taking the silver and hiding it in the hollow tree piece by piece until he could dispose of it. The page-boy had found out and the butler murdered him to silence him and put his body in the tree along with what was left of the stolen silver. The page-boy had returned from the dead to clear his name.

Some little ghosts are able to convey to the living what has happened to them, or what appears to worry them. Others are not able to do so, as in the case of the unhappy little girl who haunts St Helen's Church in Worcester. She is often to be seen wearing dark clothes, grovelling about on the floor of the aisle as though

searching for something. She has been seen by several visitors to the church, most of whom do not realize that she is not of this world. Her white, unhappy little face as she searches the floor with tears in her eyes has brought many sympathetic words from visitors who want to know what the little girl has lost and whether they can help her to find it. Some have even offered her money, thinking that she looked ill and under-nourished, but any approach always sends her running off in the direction of the chancery where she disappears. But she returns again another day to begin her search all over again. No one knows who she is or what she is looking for.

Another sad little ghost is that of William Hoby, the boy who blotted his copybook. He was a son of Sir Thomas Hoby, whom Queen Elizabeth I appointed Ambassador to France, and Elizabeth, one of the five brilliant daughters of Sir Anthony Cooke of Essex, and who was tutor to the young and ailing King Edward VI.

The Hoby family lived at Bisham Abbey, near Marlow, Bucks, once owned by Henry VIII, who gave it to Anne of Cleves, from whom Sir Thomas Hoby acquired it.

Poor little William showed none of the brilliance of his parents, and he was so nervous when he was doing his lessons under the eagle eye of his clever mother that he always made ink blots on his copybook. Lady Hoby was a brilliant French scholar who could write verse in Latin and Greek, and the fact that her small son not only did not take after her intellectually, but could not even keep his work free from blots and inkstains, annoyed her beyond reason. One day she completely lost her temper with him, and beat him so hard and so long that the boy died.

Bisham Abbey is now haunted not only by the mournful William, but also by his mother, majestic and penitent in coif, weeds and a wimple. Lady Hoby glides through the corridors of the Abbey and along the banks of the river, for ever wringing her hands, as though trying to wash away the blood of her small son. Other reports say that she is washing her hands in blood.

In the nineteenth century a number of badly-blotted copy-books were found hidden behind the wainscoting in one of the rooms at the Abbey. One of the books had ink blots on almost every line, and it is thought that this is the one that belonged to William.

In 1946 Bisham Abbey was taken over by the Central Council for Physical Recreation, and it is used by athletes who go there for training. More alterations were being made to the Abbey in 1964-65 in order to build a gymnasium and hostel for students, when it was

hoped that more papers would be discovered to throw additional light on this colourful legend.

Child ghosts are sometimes accompanied by the ghosts of older people, in many cases the mother. Watton Abbey in Yorkshire sheltered both monks and nuns in medieval times. Their vows of chastity were reinforced by a wall separating the two communities. The ghost of a headless nun, believed to be that of the beautiful Elfreda, who committed the unforgivable sin of getting over the forbidden wall, falling in love with a monk and having a child by him, still haunts the ruins of Watton Abbey. In the seventeenth century the Lady of Watton and her child were murdered by Roundheads, and their ghosts also haunt the ruins of the Abbey. It is not unusual for ghosts of different times to haunt the same place, and it would be interesting to know what, if anything, they think when they encounter each other.

Perhaps the best known of Yorkshire's many hauntings can be seen through a window in Holy Trinity Church, Micklegate, York. The window in question has four divisions of stained glass, and a strip of plain glass about two inches wide separates each division. Through this window, sometimes in broad daylight, a hooded robed figure, apparently female, has been seen passing from north to south, and then returning across the window again, this time with a child. The woman wears a long, trailing and transparent robe, and her approach is heralded by a bright light. When she is alone, she glides rapidly by the windows, but when she has the child with her she takes a little longer. They stop for a brief moment at the last pane but one and then vanish.

Many stories have been told to explain these ghosts, and one account recalls the plunder of the convent attached to the church by a party of soldiers during the reign of Henry VIII. Thomas Cromwell was the king's instrument in the dissolution of the monasteries and convents, which were a source of wealth to Henry, whose ego-mania had brought him inevitable money troubles. When Cromwell's men burst into the convent at Micklegate, they were faced bravely by the Abbess, who told them they would only enter her convent over her dead body, and that if they did kill her, she would haunt them for the rest of their lives and that her ghost would haunt the defiled convent until a new holy building took its place. Undeterred by her words, Cromwell's men slew her in brutal fashion. A terror-stricken child hiding in a corner witnessed the barbarous death of the Abbess, and was dealt with in similar manner.

Many believe the Abbess haunted the convent until it was demolished, and that she is the hooded figure who still haunts Holy Trinity Church accompanied by the ghost of the child who was killed so barbarously with her.

The ghosts of a woman and her babe in arms have long haunted the churchyard and mill-stream of Ebbw Vale in South Wales. People who have seen her say that she is clad in misty white and cradles her precious bundle in her arms, walking lightly but steadily along the path by the mill stream, looking neither to right nor to left. The stream bends near a bridge and here the phantoms disappear briefly, to reappear on the other side, the woman still clasping the ghostly child in her arms. Finally the ghostly pair come to the churchyard on the other side of the village, pass through the closed gates and walk a short distance up the path leading to the church, where they disappear.

A 'sad and truly Victorian legend is linked with this ghostly mother and her babe and their unsuccessful attempts to get to the altar of the church at Ebbw Vale.

They say she was a pretty Welsh country girl who had an affair with the son of a wealthy farmer. The young man's name was William, and at first he was quite serious and honourable in his intentions. The girl was much in love with William, but William's father had other plans for his son and wanted him to marry the daughter of a sea captain.

The young man's desire for the pretty dark-eyed Welsh girl was aroused and his intentions became debased to those of mere seduction. But the girl was virtuous and refused to give herself to the hot-blooded young man except in marriage. So intent was he on getting his way with her that William conceived a plan of going through a form of illegal marriage with her. This the innocent girl fell for under a pledge of secrecy, and thus William got what he wanted.

At first he visited the girl regularly at her home, much to the indignation of her father, whose reproaches she endured with fortitude, for she believed that she was William's wife in law and before the sight of God, and that the day was not far distant when she would be accepted as such.

Soon, as was only to be expected, William tired of her, and began to visit her less. His manner towards her changed, and he was cold, even cruel to her. In vain she pleaded with him to let the world know about their marriage, but he told her that his father would

disinherit him if he found out. One day he told her that it was finished and that he did not want to see her again, and he left before she had been able to tell him that she was expecting his child.

When her child was born, her father threatened to turn her out of the house for the disgrace she had brought upon him. She was forced then to break her promise and tell him about the secret marriage.

Her father instantly went to William's father and told him the story. The farmer coldly assured the girl's father that there was no question of his son marrying the girl, who was beneath his station in life. Other plans had been made for William's marriage. William, summoned before the two men, admitted going through an illegal form of marriage in order to gain the girl's favours.

In vain the girl's father pleaded that William should be made to do the right thing by his ill-used daughter, but though the farmer undertook to deal with his erring son, there could be no question of him marrying beneath him. His marriage with the sea-captain's daughter was already arranged.

The girl's father solemnly laid a curse upon William, and his forthcoming marriage, and then returned home to tell his daughter how she had been so basely deceived, and to comfort her as best he could.

Just before William was to be married to the sea-captain's daughter the young abandoned mother went to see her false lover. Perhaps she thought even at that late hour that he might change his mind on seeing his own child, or perhaps she threatened to tell his future wife. What transpired was never known, but she was never seen again. The bodies of her and her child were found in the mill-stream near her home. It was never known whether the despairing girl committed suicide, or whether, as many believe, mother and child were murdered.

Poltergeists have been a source of trouble and terror throughout the ages, and when they attach themselves to places of business, such as inns, the trouble and embarrassment they cause are magnified a hundredfold.

An old inn called "The Jolly Collier" at Dudley, Worcestershire, was, according to legend, beset by such phenomena, causing visitors to be thrown out of their beds, objects hurled about the rooms, crockery broken, bells ringing unaccountably at all hours. It became so bad that no one would stay at the inn. The landlord's wife had died leaving him a young daughter.

It has been long believed that poltergeists are attracted towards

children. In many cases they only operate when children are in the house. It certainly seemed to be so in the haunting at "The Jolly Collier".

Business was so bad that the distraught landlord got into debt, and eventually, threatened by bailiffs and debtors' prison, he killed his daughter and then took his own life. The poltergeists then left the inn which has ever since been haunted by a flaxen-haired girl and a man in a brown suit.

The mortality rate in Europe was very high right up to the end of the nineteenth century. The parish registers tell a frightful story of whole families of children dying one after the other from poverty and the diseases it brought. The Industrial Revolution which brought about a great increase in child labour made things worse than they had been in the previous century. The Napoleonic wars also caused great poverty all over Europe, particularly among the poorer classes. Children were always the first victims of the pestilences which followed in the wake of Napoleon's armies. The factories brought no prosperity to the working people, only hard and grinding work in conditions of labour and hours of work which their grandparents, let alone their descendants, would not have tolerated. This had such an effect upon a whole generation that people born in the eighteenth century were much stronger than either their children or their grandchildren. The cholera epidemic of 1832 took a dreadful toll, affecting the rich as well as the poor. The children went down like flies. Perhaps one or other of these circumstances might account for the grisly discovery in the following story.

A mother and her two daughters went to stay in a certain house in the north of England during the middle of the nineteenth century. The house was rather full and their hostess asked if the older girl, May, would mind sharing a room with her small sister. During the night May was awakened by feeling that a child's head was resting upon her shoulder. Thinking it was her younger sister, she asked why the child had come into her bed? Was she afraid as they were in a strange house? On getting no reply and not being able to feel her sister in bed with her, May lit her candle and saw that her sister was sleeping peacefully in the bed next to her. Thinking she had been dreaming, she put out her candle and went back to sleep, only to be awakened again by the same feeling of a child's head resting on her shoulder. She put out her hand, but there was no child there. She decided that it was all in her imagination and eventually went to sleep. But the next night the same thing happened. She kept waking up convinced that a child's head rested on her shoulder.

She had very little sleep that night and in the morning she told her hostess, who then moved her to another room where she slept soundly and undisturbed.

Some time later the house was pulled down and under the floor of the room where May had slept with her little sister were found the skeletons of five children.

The Club of Dead Men

Cambridge is full of ghosts. What else could one expect of that enchanting city of chiming bells and soaring spires, of echoing courts and oaken stairways. Cambridge will hold my heart for the rest of my days, even as it captured it when young. It is the city of eternal youth, of grace and beauty, dusty with age, bright beneath its blue East Anglian sky. It has a spirit and an atmosphere a world away from this drab, standardized modern world of birdcage architecture, mediocrity and hyena pop-singers.

You might expect, therefore, that its attitude towards ghosts is rather different. It was put, blandly, by a College "bedder" when I woke up one morning in a small room in the oldest part of Corpus. As she put my cup of tea down by the bed I remarked cheerfully: "There's a ghost on the next staircase, isn't there—the old man who looks out of a window?"

"Lord! Bless you, sir," said she cheerfully. "There's a ghost next door all right, but there ought to be one in that there very bed you're a-sleeping in! One of the gentlemen shot hisself in that bed on'y a few years ago. Sech a nice gennleman too. He left £5 to me and the other bedder with his apologies for the mess he made a-shootin hisself."

I have sat up in the ancient house of the Ghostly Squire and dozed in the room where a White Nun walks. I have heard chains rattle in a cellar as midnight struck from all the bells of Cambridge.

I know the ghastly tale of The Man Who Changed Into a Cat and I know a room in Scrope Terrace where extremely odd things

happen. The most macabre of all the ghosts of Cambridge is The Club of Dead Men. I heard of it first on a bright May morning when I sat at the feet of the Sage of English Literature.

"Spend a night in Cow Lane if you want to write about ghosts," said "Q", with an amused twinkle. He pushed a Georgian decanter of Warre's '08 gently across the table. It reflected roses in a silver bowl. The year was 1920, so the wine was in its prime. "You'll see enough there to keep you busy writing about them for a year," he added, "if you come out alive!"

Through the windows, the sun lit that oaken-floored, panelled room of his in Jesus and made pools of light on the polished floor. The long refectory table bore, as always, its bright picture of roses in silver, and port wine winking in cut-glass.

The late Sir Arthur Quiller-Couch, that master of English literature, did not, I fancy, ever believe in ghosts, although in 1900 he wrote a book called *Old Fires and Profitable Ghosts*, when this scribe was at the thoughtful age of one year. Then came *Q's Mystery Stories* in 1937. Whether he believed in ghosts or not, he made them profitable. Perhaps not such money-spinners as *Troy Town*, *The Splendid Spur*, *The Golden Pomp*, *The Ship of Stars* and those others with shining titles. Nonetheless, ghosts to him were fun.

The man who held a Master of Arts degree at both Oxford and Cambridge and was a Doctor of Literature of the Universities of Bristol, Aberdeen and Edinburgh, as well as Professor of English Literature at Cambridge, and author of some fifty-three books and editor of the Oxford Book of Prose, never quite grew up.

That fact and his love of lordly language, his devotion to the beauty of simple English and his infinite wisdom, made him unforgettable. He had no peer. Such another will not soon arise.

I went off to look for Cow Lane. It is not, as you might suppose, a twisting alleyway of cobblestones, such as might have led once to a cattle-market or a buttercup meadow among the river willows, but a staircase. Neck-breakingly steep, it rises in headlong flight from the stone floor in the angle of the cloister next to the Hall of Jesus College at Cambridge. You could pass it by easily, without glance or thought. If you did glance it is unlikely that you would think of climbing that steep and sudden flight of stairs, which, half-way up, is crossed by a great beam so that you must duck your head or be brained.

Yet if you climb those stairs, as I did, rosy with port, ducking your head on the way, you will come to a massive oaken door on the right of the landing on the top floor. When I climbed it first,

more than forty years ago, a great padlock on a chain closed the door like a prison. I stood, frustrated.

Then came footsteps climbing the steep stairs from below. A "gyp", swinging a key in his hand, whistling gently between his teeth, ducked his head beneath that murderous beam and, in a few steps, was on the landing and fitting the key into the padlock. He swung the door open.

"Ah!" I said. "Just what I wanted! May I have a look in that room?"

"You may, sir," he chirruped cheerfully, for he was a bird-like little man, with a striped waistcoat which somehow made one think of a chaffinch. "Not at there's much to see, sir, 'cept jugs and basins, plates and bowls, cups and saucers—an' a few dozen domestic bedroom-ware—them what the young gennlemen likes to 'ang up of a dark night over the front door of the Senate House, the day before Degree Day, or 'oist to the pinnacles of King's Chapel. We keep our reserves of sich in 'ere."

A gloomy room with, if I remember rightly, a great stone fire-place, a lot of old oak and a window which was either walled up or heavily curtained. The bare oak floor was stacked with glimmering, ghostly piles of crockery, chinaware and those bulbous unmentionables in which the "gyp" seemed to take a personal pride.

"This 'ere is the Ghost Room," he remarked brightly. "It's where the Everlastin' Club meets, once a year. They 'ave met 'ere for two 'undred years or more. 'Orrible goings on! When them ghostly gennlemen gather in this room, they kick up such a 'ell of a row that you'd think they was smashin' up all this 'ere china and cuttin' each other's throats. That's why it ain't used any longer as gennlemen's chambers but jest a storeroom.

"I 'ave 'eard," he went on, drawing in his breath between his teeth and sucking an invisible lollipop with ghastly relish, "as 'ow the last gennleman as 'kept' in these 'ere rooms was so 'orrified by the 'orrible crew of ghosts as met 'ere one midnight, when he wasn't expectin' of 'em, that 'e bolted out of this 'ere door, went down them stairs three at a time, bashed his blessed 'ead on that there beam, stunned 'isself cold and rolled over and over to the bottom of the stairs where 'e lay for dead. Pore gennleman! Never was right in the 'ead arter that lark."

He whistled brightly, obviously delighted with his own story, dusted a few dozen plates with lightning flicks of a napkin, balanced a monstrous pile of them on both hands, from his navel to his chin, and asking me to lock the door behind him trotted gaily down the stairs like a circus artiste. I slammed the door, turned the key in the

padlock, descended those cliff-like stairs, taking care not to 'bash my 'ead', and joined the little man in the cloister.

"Sir Arthur says I ought to spend a night in those rooms," I remarked, conversationally. "But as I'm not a member of this College, I suppose I'd better get the Master's permission."

"Wot flowers would you like on your cawfin, Sir?" the little man inquired brightly. "Carnations, pinks, lilies or jest a bunch o' roses? I'd like to remember you, sir, when you passes over!"

He suddenly became serious. "I wouldn't sleep in that there room for all the tea in China, all the suvvereigns in the Bank o' England. No, sir! And don't you do it neither. Anyway, the Master wouldn't let yer."

That little chat took place more than forty years ago. Today, I believe, the rooms at the top of Cow Lane are occupied by an undergraduate, who, so far as I could find out on a visit to the College in 1955, slept well at night. He had not, in the year of 1955 at any rate, bashed out his brains in headlong midnight flight.

It was not always thus. As you will have gathered from the "gyp's" spirited description and Sir Arthur Quiller-Couch's quizzical suggestion, the rooms at the top of Cow Lane have a certain cachet.

Cachets, however, like cliches, wear thin with the passing of time. What is a fad in one decade is a bore in the next. Old gods are overthrown. New gods arise. Sometimes sheer atheism takes their place. It may be, therefore, that the ghosts of Cow Lane have given up the ghost. So let us unravel the tale before it is all forgotten.

It began in the days of George II, or of his successor, the third George; the days of brocade and powdered wigs, knee breeches, silk stockings and buckled shoes, clouded canes and curious clubs.

Cambridge University, like that other place somewhere on the upper reaches of the Thames, has always been a hot-bed of clubs. Literary Clubs, Debating Clubs—who remembers the Magpie and Stump nowadays?—Political Clubs, Dilettante Clubs, Wine Bibbing Clubs, Dining Clubs, Clubs for Fox-hunters and Beaglers, Clubs for Fossil Diggers and Bird Worriers, Card-playing Clubs, Highbrow Clubs for Pale Ineffectuals—any, and every, excuse is good enough to found a club.

So it was in the days of George II and his poor Queen Caroline, who, I am sure, often wished herself back in her father's Margravate of Brandenburg-Anspach. The Georgian undergraduates had their clubs for dining, wining, talking, gambling, reading, debating, dicing and dancing, in College rooms and inn-parlours, in raftered halls and the panelled rooms of pleasant private houses, new-risen

in their Georgian red brick. They were all harmless enough—except the Everlasting Club. It was evil, a callow sort of evil.

It aped that other Hell Fire Club of Medmenham Abbey, not far from that other place on the upper reaches of the Thames. But this pale, Cambridge shadow of the gilded, gaudy evil spawned by that other place, boasted no Barrymore, no Dashwood, no orgiastic revels in the underground caverns of West Wycombe Park, or bawdy profanation of abbey cloisters. It merely met in the rooms at the top of the landing, on the right-hand side, as you go up the stairs called Cow Lane—without bumping your head. There were seven members only. They were all young and foolish, between twenty-two and thirty years of age. One was a Fellow of Jesus named Charles Bellasis, a sprig of that noble family which produced the Lords Bellasis, more than one of whom died on the point of a sword in riot and wine. Another was a young Cambridgeshire squire. The third member was a Fellow-Commoner of Trinity. The next two were Fellows of other colleges. The sixth was a young Cambridge doctor.

The Founder and President of this Club was the Honourable Alan Dermot, the son of an Irish peer, who had a nobleman's degree at the University, which meant that he wore a tuft in his "square" or academic cap. Hence the word "tuft-hunter", to describe those who fawned and fattened on noble undergraduates in the days when they were distinguished by dress and privilege from the common run. Dermot, an idle fellow, was vain, cruel and wicked. He learnt nothing but vice, lived for naught but folly, and died with a rapier in his stomach, coughing out his blood, in Paris in 1743. You may regard him as the evil genius of the other six members.

It was the duty of the secretary of this foolish, futile, but nonetheless Everlasting Club to keep a Minute Book. That book, detailing the Club's activities from the years 1738 to 1766 was, according to the late Arthur Gray, until recent years Master of Jesus College, "a stout duodecimo volume, bound in red leather and fastened with red, silken strings". There were forty pages of goose-quill writing, in a plain, legible, educated hand. They ended abruptly with the date 2 November, 1766.

The first pages of this book set out the laws of the Club. Here they are:

"1. This Society consisted of seven Everlastings, who may be Corporeal or Incorporeal, as Destiny shall determine.

"2. The rules of the Society, as herein written, are immutable and Everlasting.

"3. None shall hereafter be chosen into the Society and none shall cease to be members.

"4. The Honourable Alan Dermot is the Everlasting President of the Society.

"5. The Senior Corporeal Everlasting, not being the President, shall be the Secretary of the Society, and in this Book of Minutes shall record its transactions, the date at which any Everlasting shall cease to be Corporeal, and all fines due to the Society. And when such Senior Everlasting shall cease to be Corporeal he shall, either in person or by some sure hand, deliver this Book of Minutes to him who shall be next Senior and at the time Corporeal, and he shall in like manner record the transactions therein and transmit it to the next Senior. The neglect of these provisions shall be visited by the President with fine or punishment according to his discretion.

"6. On the second day of November in every year, being the Feast of All Souls, at ten-o'clock post meridium, The Everlastings shall meet at supper in the place of residence of that Corporeal member of the Society to whom it shall fall in order of rotation to entertain them and they shall all subscribe in this Book of Minutes their names and present place of abode.

"7. It shall be the obligation of every Everlasting to be present at the yearly entertainment of the Society, and none shall allege for excuse that he has not been invited thereto. If any Everlasting shall fail to attend the yearly meeting, or in his turn shall fail to provide entertainment for the Society, he shall be mulcted at the discretion of the President.

"8. Nevertheless, if in any year, in the month of October and not less than seven days before the Feast of All Souls, the major part of the Society, that is to say, four at the least, shall meet and record in writing in these Minutes that it is their desire that no entertainment be given in that year, then, notwithstanding the two rules last rehearsed, there shall be no entertainment in that year, and no Everlasting shall be mulcted on the ground of his absence."

There are other rules, but they are either too impious or childish to be worth printing. They do show, however, the remarkable levity with which the Everlastings took on their fantastic obligations.

Morals were bad enough throughout England in the first half of the eighteenth century. The reflex in the University was equally bad. Nonetheless, the behaviour of the seven members of the Everlasting Club scandalized even that lax age. The College authorities came down heavily on them. Charles Bellasis was "sent down". Somehow he contrived to retain his Fellowship.

Other members were sent down by their various colleges as the years went on. Yet, each year, they met in the rooms of whoever might be Secretary at the time. There they drank and sang far into the night and scandalized the college and the stars alike with their riotous debaucheries.

The Minutes were kept religiously; perhaps one should say irreligiously, for not only is there a record of attendances, fines inflicted and the rest of the Club business, but each page carries obscene and irreverent remarks.

The first entry which begins to give a hint of the terrible end of the Club is that under the date of 2 November, 1743. That night the members dined in the house of the young Cambridge doctor. One member, Henry Davenport, a Fellow-Commoner of Trinity, was not there. He had been an officer in King George's army, and had been killed at the Battle of Dettingen, the last battle, incidentally, in which the British Army was led in person by the Monarch.

The members did not know, when they sat down to dine, that Davenport was dead. He was absent, so he had to be fined. And he was. The Minutes contained the simple entry: "Mulctatus propter absentiam per Presidentem, Hen. Davenport."

Did the ghost of the dead Davenport, now an Incorporeal Everlasting, sit down to dine that night, as he had sworn in life to do? It seems likely, for on the next page there is this entry: "Henry Davenport, by a Cannon-shot, became an Incorporeal Member; 3 November, 1743."

How, you may ask, could the members know of his death within a few hours of their dining that night, unless he, Davenport, appeared in spirit that night, at the dinner table, to tell them that he was either dead or about to die? He may, indeed, have been dead by the time the dinner was finished, since they went on well into the early hours of 3 November, when the second entry was written.

There was no telephone, no wireless, no railways, no aeroplanes, no means of communication save couriers, who took days on horseback and aboard sailing ships to bring such news so swiftly in so short a time.

So it seems likely enough that the six Everlastings, those still alive sat down to dine that night in the young Cambridge doctor's house with Dermot at the head of the table—and one empty chair. They dined and they drank wine. The "claretted and punched", topped up with black-strap and dosed themselves with brandy, sang their ribald songs and screamed their insults to God until the stars wheeled in their courses.

At some time, probably at the beginning of the dinner, the Secretary formally reported the absence of Henry Davenport, The President, equally formally, inflicted his fine. Then they drank their sherry and sat down to dinner.

One may imagine the decanter of claret or burgundy or Rhenish being pushed round the table in its Georgian silver coaster—until it came to the empty chair.

Then a ghostly hand, silvery, impermanent in the yellow candle-light, reached out, lifted the decanter, filled the empty glass—and raised it to the slowly-seen, grinning spectral lips of Henry Davenport. There he sat, gradually taking shape, in his tarnished regimentals, his powdered wig, sardonically smiling, the first Everlasting to become an Incorporeal Everlasting.

Consider the gasp which went round that suddenly chilled table. The blanched whiteness of six frightened faces. The stuttering attempts to recapture the old, profane defiance of God and Death.

Then, perhaps, Davenport spoke. Probably he called them, poked fun at them, reminded them that they had all sworn to turn up each year at the dinner, *dead or alive*.

And so, said he, here am I, Henry Davenport, one-time Fellow-Commoner of Trinity, for all time the first Incorporeal Everlasting come to honour my pledge—*as you must all do*—dead or alive, each year throughout eternity.

If that were not horrible enough to contemplate, what does one make of that other entry in the book, on the same date, 2 November in the same year, 1743, for there, boldly written, in his own unmistakable handwriting at the top of the list, is the signature of "Alan Dermot, President at the Court of His Royal Highness".

Now it is an historical fact that the Honourable Alan Dermot was at the Court of Prince Charles Edward Stuart, the Young Pretender, in Paris, in October, 1743. It is equally a fact that he was killed in a duel in Paris on 28 October—*five days before the Club met*. The news of his death cannot have reached the Club on the night on which it met and dined, 2 November, for, under the date 10 November appears this entry: "This day was reported that the President was become an Incorporeal by the hands of a French chevalier." It was followed by a sudden written gasp from the Secretary, for, in his goose-quill handwriting, he slapped down the unexpected prayer: "The Good God shield us from ill."

Yet how came the President's handwriting, unmistakably his own, to appear at the top of the list, when the entries of attendance were written down at that dinner of 2 November? In short, the

President must have been there, *although dead*, in his normal, earthly, human form and semblance of being. He must have eaten and drunk with them, cracked his wicked jokes, uttered his profanities, cursed his God and generally behaved as the man whom they all knew—leaving them to find out later that they had dined not with a living man but with *a ghost*. That is the sort of ghastly joke one would expect from Dermot.

The news that they had dined with a dead man, who seemed in every sense to be a live man, shattered the Club. The five remaining members were paralysed with fear. They left Cambridge. They buried themselves on their distant country estates—for most of them were landed men. The Cambridge doctor tried to banish from his mind the memory of the dead man sitting at the head of his table, leering and laughing as though alive. Better, far, the pale, half-seen, ethereal wisp in the empty chair that might, or might not have been, Henry Davenport. He, at any rate, had not signed *his* name in the book. Had he seemed to have been there, it might so well have been a mere trick of the wine. Yet no matter how the doctor might seek to forget these things by dedicating himself to his patients and his medical researches; no matter how the other four members might hunt the fox, shoot their pheasants with long, single-barrelled muzzle-loaders, play cards at night with their neighbours, devote themselves to their home farms or to the bottle, each man knew that unless he wished once more to face the hateful, leering presence of the President, at the Annual Dinner on 2 November, he and the others must not fail to turn up and record their objections to the dinner being held each year "in the month of October and not less than seven days before the Feast of All Souls".

So for five years, five wretched men met annually in October, lodged their formal objection to the holding of the dinner and the Secretary duly recorded it in the Minute Book. Then another member died and, like the little nigger boys, "then there were four".

For eighteen years after, the four haunted, wretched survivors continued to meet each October and record their protests. Among them was Charles Bellasis. He had become middle-aged and respectable. Jesus College had once more admitted its one-time renegade Fellow to its ancient bosom. He was a model of decorum. He lived in the rooms at the top of Cow Lane.

Finally, we come to the year 1766. Under the date of 27 January appears this entry in the Minute Book:

"Jan. 27th. On this day, Francis Witherington, Secretary, became an Incorporeal Member. The same day this Book was delivered to

me, James Harvey." Harvey died a month later. On 7 March is another entry, which tells us that William Catherston is the new Secretary. He lived little more than two months. For, on 18 May, Charles Bellasis sets down the fact that Catherston had died on that date and that he, Bellasis, was now the last Corporeal of the Club and therefore the Secretary.

Now you will remember that under Rule 8 it was laid down, hard and fast, that an objection to the holding of the annual Dinner could only be lodged by "the major part of the Society, that is to say four at least." So long as four of them were alive, they were safe. When Francis Witherington died on 27 January in that year of 1766, it left only Harvey, Catherston and Bellasis. Harvey and Catherston, by now middle-aged, were probably so terrified out of their wits at having to face the ghastly banquet in November that they died of heart failure or sheer terror—perhaps by their own hands.

Bellasis was a tougher type. He determined to live. Moreover, he determined to defy the rules of the Club. He was now a respected, honoured and more or less welcome Fellow of Jesus. The young generation knew nothing of his past. The older ones had either forgotten or forgiven him.

What happened behind the heavy oaken door at the top of those steep stairs in Cow Lane in that dark panelled room on the night of 2 November will never be known. One would have thought, to begin with, that Bellasis would either have left College that night altogether and stayed elsewhere with a friend in a house full of lively people or, at the least, would have slept that night in the rooms of another Don or Fellow of the College. He was not that sort. It may be that the spark of his old youthful spirit of devil-may-care still flickered bravely. At any rate he stayed in his rooms and "sported his oak".

At ten o'clock, precisely, pandemonium broke out. Shouts and yells, oaths and bawdy songs, blasphemies against God, the crashing of glass and the breaking of furniture horrified the night.

Dons shivered in the Senior Common Room. Undergraduates quaked in their beds. The Master fumed in his Lodge. The porters and other college servants trembled in their shoes. None dare climb the steep stairs of Cow Lane, to discover what unholy visitors were revelling in the rooms of Charles Bellasis, Fellow of the College. Dead on midnight, the uproar stopped. The College slept uneasily the rest of that night.

When dawn came the Master and braver Dons, with some sturdy

workmen, crept up the steep staircase. They listened outside the stout, low, oak door of Bellasis's rooms. Not a sound. Quiet as the grave. They knocked. No answer. They rattled loudly on the door. There came no reply.

"Break the door down," the Master ordered.

A sledge-hammer splintered the lock. Crowbars sent the bolts starting from their sockets. The door splintered and swung open.

There, at the top of the long oaken table, sat Charles Bellasis. Dead. His head was bent low; his folded arms shielded his eyes. He had died in fear of the dreadful sight, whatever it may have been, which he had seen.

About the table were six other chairs, drawn up as though at a dinner. Some were turned upside down. Some were smashed. Broken glass glittered in the thin light of dawn. Smashed china littered the floor. The terrible smell of death was in the cold air.

On the table lay the red, leather-bound Minute Book, in front of Bellasis. Goose-quill pen, a silver ink-pot and a sand-sprinkler were beside it. On the last page, dated 2 November, were written, for the first time since 1742, the full names of the seven members of the Everlasting Club. None had given his address. In the bold hand of the President, Alan Dermot, was written these words:

"Mulctatus per Presidentem propter neglectum obsonii, Car. Bellasis."

That was the end of the Everlasting Club. From that day until at least 1920, and possibly twenty years after that, the rooms remained tenantless. They were used, as I have said, for storage. The legend persisted that, annually on the night of 2 November, "sounds of unholy revelry" were heard from Bellasis's chamber. That, I believe, is a fiction. No one has been able to pin down any witness who can swear that he heard any sounds from the room on the night of any 2 November. Indeed, if one reads the Minute Book, it is quite clear that no provision was made for the holding of the Annual Dinner after the last Everlasting had become an Incorporeal. As for the Minute Book itself, Arthur Gray says:

"The Minute Book was secured by the Master of the College, and I believe that he alone was acquainted with the nature of its contents. The scandal reflected on the College by the circumstances revealed in it caused him to keep the knowledge rigidly to himself."

He addes: "And though, so far as I am aware, it is no longer extant, I have before me a transcript of it which, though it is in a recent handwriting, presents in a bald shape such a singular array of facts that I must ask you to accept them as veracious."

For myself, having known and loved Cambridge for more than half a century, I can affirm that this tale is a living legend. It endures to this day. Not one, but many members of Jesus College and of its staff have assured me that the rooms at the head of Cow Lane, the last meeting place on earth of the Everlasting Club, are not the rooms in which they would choose to sleep. Why else were they left untenanted for nearly two hundred years?

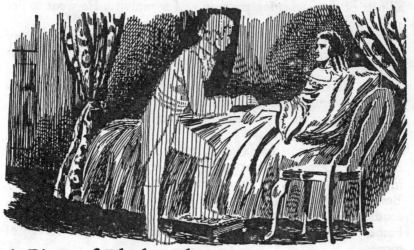

A Piece of Black Velvet

Why I tie about thy wrist
Julia, this silken twist
'Tis to show thee how in part
Thou my pretty captive art,

quoted Sir Tristram Beresford, looking admiringly across the breakfast-table at his young wife. Even at this time in the morning, and clad in a simple loose sacque, she was appealingly beautiful. But a little pale and distrait today, thought Sir Tristram; perhaps she had slept badly. As he spoke she gave a little start.

"I was not attending; what did you say?" she asked.

"I was only quoting Herrick, my dear—as being relevant to your new ornament." His eyes went to her wrist, about which was tightly bound a piece of black velvet ribbon, hiding the white skin for some two inches. Lady Beresford's pale face flushed, then paled again.

"I——" she began, then bit her lip, and seemed unable to go on. Sir Tristram waited patiently. She rose from the table, walked to the window, and stood looking out unseeingly. Then she turned to face her husband.

"Tristram," she said, "I have something to ask of you. Never inquire of me why I wear this ribbon. I shall wear it always—you will never see me without it—but I cannot tell you why—I *cannot*."

Sir Tristram was a kindly man, much in love with his wife, and prepared to make every allowance for women's fancies. When their two daughters had been born Nicola had had strange whims—it was

all part of the fascinating panorama of femininity. He went to her and patted her shoulder affectionately.

"What you do not wish to tell me I shall not ask, now or at any time, my love," he said. "Now pray do sit down and finish your breakfast."

Lady Beresford obeyed him, though without much appetite. After a few mouthfuls she laid down her knife.

"Has the post come yet?" she asked nervously.

"Not yet, my dear."

"Oh. I thought, as I was up so late, it would have been here by now." Sir Tristram was not unduly curious about his wife's interest in the post. They were on a visit, this October of 1693, to Lady Beresford's sister, Lady Macgill, at Gill Hall, in the County Down, southern Ireland. It was natural that she should want letters from home, where their two children had remained in the charge of nurses.

Lady Beresford sipped her chocolate abstractedly, then laid down her cup and rang the handbell which was beside her on the table. In a moment her maid appeared.

"Have the letters come yet, Bridget?" she asked.

"No, my lady, not yet."

"Bring them to me as soon as they arrive."

When the girl had left the room Sir Tristram looked humorously at his wife.

"Really, my love, I shall begin to think you are expecting a communication from some gallant, if you continue to show this anxiety," he said.

"Don't joke!" she flashed at him. "If you knew——"

"If I knew what?" he asked gently. "Won't you tell me, my dear? What is it you expect to hear in a letter today?"

His wife's head drooped, and her fingers strayed to the black-bound wrist.

"I expect," she said in a low voice, "I expect to hear of Lord Tyrone's death."

"Of Tyrone's death? Your old playfellow? But, my dear Nicola, why should you anticipate his death? Surely he is only the same age as yourself. You have always told me you were brought up by the same guardian as if you had been twins."

"We were born in the same year," she replied. "Nevertheless, I know that he is dead. And that he died on Tuesday."

Sir Tristram came round the table and sat by his wife's side, with his arm about her shoulders.

"My sweet Nicola, this is not like you. You have never been super-stitious—in fact I think our good chaplain believes you to be rather too worldly for your soul's welfare."

"Yes," she answered tonelessly, "I have never been a true church-woman. I was brought up to think freely of spiritual matters. But now you will see, I shall be different."

"You've been dreaming, my love. That is all. Get dressed now, and we'll go for a ride in the Park. The exercise will restore you."

At this moment the door opened, and Sir Tristram, seeing his servant, said: "Oh, Patrick, see that the horses are brought round in half an hour, will you?"

"Yes, sir. The letters have arrived, sir."

He laid them on the table, and Lady Beresford eagerly snatched at them. Among them was one sealed with black wax.

"It is the Tyrone crest!" she cried hysterically. "You'll see, he is dead. Open it, Tristram, for I cannot!"

Sir Tristram did as she asked. As he read the letter, his face changed. He laid down the letter and looked at her gravely.

"God knows how you knew, my dear; but it is true. Tyrone's steward writes that he died in Dublin on Tuesday, at four in the afternoon."

"I knew it! I knew it!" she cried, and burst into tempestuous weeping. As Sir Tristram tried to console her, his mind was busy. Strange things had been known in this fairy-haunted land of Ireland, and strange prophecies had been made in dreams. It was not for him to deride his wife's premonition. Young Tyrone and she had been brought up together, and had had for each other the deepest affection—as deep as though they had been truly sister and brother. The fact that their guardian had reared them in the principles of Deism, and not in the Christian faith, had only bound them closer together, making them allies in a world that condemned them. There must, Sir Tristram reflected, be a strong soul-tie between them, and it was quite possible that in a vivid dream the news of Tyrone's death had been conveyed to the woman who had been his "sister Nicola".

Lady Beresford had become calmer. Drying her tears, she assured her husband that she felt relieved now that she knew the worst. "And I have something else to tell you," she added with a rainbow smile, "something that will please you."

"What's that, my dear?"

"I am with child," she replied. "And it will be a boy."

Her husband was almost speechless with delight and amazement.

If her premonition of death had been true, why should not this happier premonition of birth? At last perhaps he would have the son he longed for. He rang the bell for the servant.

"The horses may go back to the stables," he said. "My lady will not ride today."

Soon afterwards they left Gill Hall for their own home in Derry. In the following July, true to her prophecy, Lady Beresford bore a son, Marcus. Six years later Sir Tristram died.

Only thirty-four years old, and still beautiful, Lady Beresford might have been expected to make an early second marriage. But it seemed to her friends that she wished to avoid even the possibility of it. Even when the period of mourning was over she refused invitations to social gatherings, dressed in black, and lived as quietly as possible in the company of her three children. Close friends found that she did not relish their society any longer; and her only intimates were now a Mr and Mrs Jackson, of Coleraine. Mr Jackson, a clergyman, was one of the town's leading citizens, and was related to the late Sir Tristram on his mother's side. His wife had a brother, Colonel Richard Gorges, a young man who had risen rapidly in his Army career. He was handsome, charming, slightly dissolute, and a good many years younger than the pretty widow; but it soon became obvious that he was paying court to her. One day Mrs Jackson and Lady Beresford were sitting together at tea when Lady Beresford, who had been very silent for some minutes, rose from her chair and seated herself on the sofa by her friend.

"Jane," she said, "I have some news for you. I think you will not find it hard to guess."

Mrs Jackson looked at her apprehensively.

"Nicola, it is not—Richard?"

"Yes. We are to be married."

"But, my dear, have you thought? He is so much younger—and so—though he is my own relative, I cannot think he will make you a good husband. Pray do consider this carefully!"

"I have considered it," said Lady Beresford. "I have given it earnest thought and prayer." (For some years now she had been a devout member of the Church.) "It is my conviction that Richard and I are destined to be husband and wife, and that our mutual love will compensate for the difference in our ages."

"Will you not at least wait another year—six months?" urged Mrs Jackson. Lady Beresford shook her head.

"The marriage is to be in six weeks. I have quite made up my mind."

Mrs Jackson sighed. She knew her brother only too well.

Her fears, and those of Lady Beresford's other friends, were justified. For a short time after their marriage in 1704 the ill-assorted couple seemed happy enough; it was apparent that the former Lady Beresford was infatuated with her young husband, and in order to get control of her money and possessions it suited him to please her for a time. But soon, in spite of the birth of two daughters, they began to drift apart. Colonel Gorges treated her cruelly and contemptuously, laughing at her tears and reproaches when some fresh evidence of his infidelity came to her ears. The children were brought into contact with his roistering companions, who came to stay at the house and behaved shamefully there. At last, goaded into action, Nicola Gorges insisted on a separation.

Their parting lasted for several years, during which Mrs Gorges reverted to her former quiet life. But her infatuation for the unworthy man she had married never quite died. He had now risen to the rank of General, and his way of life seemed to have steadied somewhat. When he came to her and fell on his knees, begging her to forgive his past faults and take him back, and promising most solemnly to be a reformed character and a model husband in the future, she at first wavered and then relented. In 1715 they once more lived together as man and wife; and a year later Nicola Gorges, though now middle-aged, became the mother of a second son. All was joy. General Gorges appeared pleased, and treated his wife with particular affection. The Jacksons said to each other that perhaps they had been wrong, after all, since this apparently ill-fated marriage had been blessed so late and so unexpectedly.

Mrs Gorges was happy beyond expression, and particularly so because her fiftieth birthday, that milestone in a woman's life, was past, and here was she restored to youth by the gift of a baby son to her arms. She kept her bed for three weeks, as was the custom of ladies in that age, but a month to the day after her son's birth she felt so well that she decided to hold a small celebration. A party was planned, to include her son Sir Marcus Beresford—now twenty-two—and her married daughter, Lady Riverston. Also invited was Dr King, the Archbishop of Dublin, who had become a great friend of Mrs Gorges since her conversion to the church; and of course the Jacksons could not be left out.

About noon on the day of the party Mr Jackson called to inquire after the hostess's health. He found her up and dressed, blooming and youthful in a white satin dress laced with pink, the only sombre note in her costume the black ribbon which still bound her wrist. Mrs

Gorges rang for Madeira and biscuits to be served, and a nurse was summoned to exhibit the baby for Mr Jackson's admiration.

"My dear madam," said the clergyman. "This is indeed a happy day."

"Indeed it is," replied the beaming mother. "And what is more, it is my birthday."

"Of course—I had forgotten. But Jane no doubt has remembered and will bring you a gift this afternoon."

"I want no gift but my son," she said, looking fondly down at the occupant of the cradle. "Tell me, do you think I look my age? Has he not waved the wand of youth over me?"

"Whatever age you are, madam," replied Mr Jackson gallantly, "I can assure you that you do not look it."

"Well then," she said, smiling, "I am fifty-one years old."

Mr Jackson's eyebrows rose. "Fifty-one? I had not thought—let me see, I had a discussion with your mother, many years ago, upon this very point. What was the issue, now? She declared that you had been born in 1665."

"That is so. Lord Tyrone and I were almost twins."

"But I assured her that it was not so" said Mr Jackson. "Indeed, I confirmed it by consulting the baptismal register, in which it was clearly stated that you were born in 1666. I remember it well, because it was about the time we had news of the great Fire raging in London."

Mrs Gorges paled, and her youthful radiance seemed to fade in a moment. "Then," she said tremblingly, "I am not fifty-one years old, but only fifty."

"That is the case, madam. Are you not glad to find yourself a year younger than you imagined?"

Nicola Gorges rose and walked slowly to the window. She stood looking out at the pleasant garden and the pearly clouds sweeping above the trees, as though she had never seen them before. After a few moments she turned, and said in a calm voice:

"You have signed my death-warrant, Mr Jackson. I have not much longer to live. No,"—cutting short his anxious exclamations—"there is nothing you can do to help me, except to send my son and daughter here to me as soon as you can. And send word to the Archbishop that I shall not be able to entertain him today."

Puzzled and alarmed, Mr Jackson obeyed her orders. The two young people were soon at their mother's side, distressed to see such a change in her since earlier in the morning. She kissed her

baby, bade the nurse take it away, and, telling her son and daughter to sit down, solemnly addressed them.

"I have something most important to tell you, my dears, before I die."

"Die, Mamma!" exclaimed young Sir Marcus. "Pray don't jest with us.'

"It is no jest, my son. Be patient, and listen to me. You know that as a child I was brought up with Lord Tyrone like sister and brother —indeed, I doubt if you two, fond though you are, are as attached as we were. Our guardian was a free-thinking man who held that the beliefs of the Church were all superstition, and that only a materialistic view of existence could be held by sensible people. Now, a great many of our friends were shocked by his views, and lost no opportunity of putting their own to us. Poor confused children that we were, we did not know what to believe; particularly as regarded a future life. One day, after talking for a long time, we made a pact, as young people will. Whichever of us died first would, if permitted, appear to the other and tell him or her what were the real great truths.

"Years passed. We grew up, and I married your father, Sir Tristram. John—that is, Lord Tyrone—and I saw little of each other, though we kept up our friendship by letters.

"Now comes the strange and dreadful part of my tale. One night, in October, 1693, your father and I were on a visit to your Aunt Arabella at Gill Hall. We had gone to bed as usual, and were sleeping soundly, when I suddenly awoke with the consciousness that somebody else was in the room with us. I sat up—and saw Lord Tyrone, sitting by the side of the bed. I did not know what to think, but I was very frightened, and screamed out. Your father did not stir, and even shaking his shoulder could not wake him. Then Lord Tyrone, bending on me a solemn look, said:

"'It is myself and no other, Nicola.'

"'But why are you here at this time of night, John?' I asked, trembling.

"'Have you forgotten our youthful promise to each other? I died on Tuesday, at four o'clock. I have been permitted to appear to you thus to let you know that the Church's religion is the true and only one by which we can be saved. And I am allowed to tell you something else. You are with child, and will bear a son, who will marry my daughter.'

"'But——' interrupted Sir Marcus.

"'Peace, son. You will see it will come true.' Then Lord Tyrone

told me that Sir Tristram would not long survive after the child's birth, and that in the course of time I should marry again, and die as a result of childbirth in my fiftieth year. 'Good Heavens,' I said, 'cannot I prevent this?' 'Of course you can,' he replied, 'you are a free agent and may resist any temptation to a second marriage, but your passions are strong.' 'Oh, tell me——' I began; but he held up his hand (which was perfectly solid, and could not be seen through) and said: 'More I cannot tell you, but one thing—that if you persist in your present opinions your fate in the next world will be miserable indeed.' 'Are you happy yourself, John?' I asked. He smiled. 'Had it been otherwise I would not have been permitted to appear to you.'

" 'But now,' I said, 'when morning comes, shall I be convinced that your appearance has been real, and not a mere phantasm of my imagination?' 'Will not the news of my death be sufficient to convince you?' he asked. 'No,' I replied. 'I might have had such a dream, and that dream might accidentally have come to pass. I want some stronger proof of your presence.' 'You shall have it,' he said. He waved his hand, and the crimson velvet bed-curtains were instantly drawn through a large iron hook by which the oval tester of the bed was suspended. 'Now you cannot be mistaken,' he said. 'No mortal arm could have done that.' 'True,' I replied, 'but in sleep we are often far stronger than in waking. Awake, I could not have done it—asleep, I might—and therefore I shall still doubt.' Then he said: 'You have a pocket-book here in which I shall write. You know my handwriting?' 'Yes,' I said. He then wrote his signature on one of the leaves. 'Still,' I objected, 'in the morning I may doubt. When I am awake I cannot imitate your handwriting, but asleep it's possible that I might.' 'You are hard to convince,' he said with a smile. 'I might—but I must not touch you, for that would mark you for life.' 'I don't mind a small blemish,' I replied. 'You are a brave woman, Nicola,' he said, 'hold out your hand.' I did so. He touched my wrist lightly with his hand, which was as cold as marble, and in a moment the sinews shrank up and the nerves withered. 'Now,' he cautioned me, 'let no mortal eye see that wrist, while you live.' I looked down at my injured wrist, then back to him—but he had vanished.

"While he was with me I was perfectly calm and collected, but the moment he was gone I felt chilled with horror and dismay. A cold sweat came over me, and again I tried to wake your father; but he would not stir. For a time I lay awake, weeping, and at last fell asleep.

"In the morning your father awoke and dressed himself without waking me—he apparently found nothing unusual about the bedcurtains. When I awoke they were still as Lord Tyrone had left them. I went into the gallery adjoining our bedroom, and found there a large cornice-broom, with the help of which I unhooked the curtains, fearing that their position might cause inquiry. Then I found a length of black velvet ribbon, and tied up my wrist with it before going down to breakfast.

"You, Marcus, came into the world exactly as Lord Tyrone told me you would, and your father died, as he had prophesied. Remembering his other warning, I tried to avoid society and not mingle again with the world, hoping to avoid the dreadful fate a second marriage would involve. But alas! At the house of my only real friends I met a man I found deeply attractive, and in a fatal moment—for my own peace—I married him. Then his conduct drove me to demand a separation, and again I hoped to escape the prophecy. I thought today that I *had* escaped it. But Mr Jackson has just told me that I am only fifty today, not fifty-one—all this time I have been mistaken about my age. I know, therefore, that I am about to die."

Sir Marcus and Lady Riverston wept, and protested that their mother must be mistaken. But she held to her story, and seemed now quite calm and resigned. One thing only she asked them.

"When I am dead, my dears, I want you, and you alone, to unbind this black ribbon from my wrist, and see what it covers."

Sadly, they promised, and left her alone to rest, as she requested; but at Lady Riverston's earnest plea she agreed to let a maidservant with with her in case she should need anything.

An hour after they had left her, the bell in her room rang violently. The brother and sister ran upstairs, to meet the frantic maid standing outside the door of Mrs Gorges's room and crying:"Oh, she is dead! My mistress is dead!"

Before Mrs Gorges's body was committed to the grave, Sir Marcus and Lady Riverston knelt alone beside it, and, as she had wished, unwound the black ribbon. There, in proof of her story, were the shrunken and withered sinews.

The last of Lord Tyrone's ghostly prophecies soon came true— his daughter married young Sir Marcus, and their daughter, Lady Betty Cobbe, allowed her grandmother's strange story to be known in 1806. It aroused widespread interest, and impressed Sir Walter

Scott sufficiently for him to base a poem on it, in which the verses occur:

> He laid his left palm on an oaken beam,
>   His right upon her hand—
> The lady shrunk, and fainting sunk,
>   For it scorched like a fiery brand.
>
> The sable score of fingers four
>   Remains on that board impressed;
> And for evermore that lady wore
>   A covering on her wrist.

The Ghost in Two Halves

At the physical heart of Scotland lies the county of Perth, and almost bisecting the county laterally is Glen Lyon, the largest of all the Scottish glens, whose cold clear stream, rising on the borders of Argyllshire, swells as it tumbles its way down eastwards, until it meets the River Tay as a considerable tributary just north of the northern tip of Loch Tay.

Even among the barbaric romanticism which characterizes so rawly the glens and their inhabitants, Glen Lyon's history has a special glow all its own. Originally the property of the Clan Macgregor, it was taken from them in the late sixteenth century, when, as a punishment for opposition to the throne, "letters of fire and sword" were issued against them, and those who escaped death were deprived of their patrimony, and dispersed. About a century later, some of the Highland chiefs took a deep dislike to the new regime of William and Mary. One of them, Alexander Macdonald of Glencoe, was so slow in taking the oath of allegiance to the monarchs that the government resolved to punish him and his men as technical traitors.

The Master of Stair, Sir John Dalrymple, the official responsible for ordering and organizing the Macdonalds' punishment, probably recalled the "letters of fire and sword" issued against the Macgregors, for he gave orders for the destruction of the clan. He bestowed the commission upon Captain Campbell of Glen Lyon, who went about his task with such devotion that he cheerfully resorted to treachery. Though the majority of the Macdonalds escaped with

their families to the hills, when Captain Campbell had finished forty Macdonalds were dead, and the Massacre of Glencoe remained a permanent blot on the already violent history of Scotland.

On his way to the homes and mountains of the Macdonalds, Captain Campbell had stayed the night at Meggernie Castle, which lies roughly half-way up Glen Lyon. The oldest parts of the castle date from the fifteenth century, and are characterized by walls of immense thickness. But additions were made later when Scots architects were under the influence of their counterparts among their French allies. For example, the square baronial tower, with its high-pointed roof and battlemented parapet, might well have graced a rather solid château.

Since Meggernie Castle was taken from the Macgregors it has passed through various hands, and in 1862 it was owned by a Mr Herbert Wood. Wood was an hospitable man, and enjoyed nothing so much as having a castle full of guests.

To one such party he invited a friend, E. J. Simons, who lived at Ullesthorpe, in Leicestershire. Simons was late in arriving, and by the time he reached Meggernie all the guest rooms had been allocated, with the exception of a large room in the tower.

"I hope you won't mind being tucked away up there," Wood said to his guest. "You won't be alone. In the adjoining room I've put a very good friend of mine, Beaumont Fetherstone."

"I don't mind at all," Simons assured Wood. "The tower is the oldest part of Meggernie, if I'm not mistaken. I shall find it most interesting."

"It is quite pleasant up there," Wood admitted. "There are fine views of the glen, and I'm sure you'll find Fetherstone a congenial sort of chap."

Shown to his room, Simons discovered that his host had, in fact, been too modest in describing the prospect it provided. From the north window he looked out on the hills at whose base the castle stood, and which sheltered it from the cold northerly blasts. From the south window was a view of the rich meadows and majestic park, with a swift silent stretch of the River Lyon beyond, at no farther distance than a long stone's throw. Across the river lay the heather-carpeted moors.

In the drawing-room before dinner, Simon found his fellow guest in the tower to be as agreeable, in his own way, as the room. Beaumont Fetherstone was a man of about his own age—in the early forties—good-looking, good-humoured, with a gay laugh and

lively eyes, giving an overall impression of levelheadedness. "A man after my own heart," Simons told himself.

It had been a long and tiring journey from the railhead at Perth to the castle, and not long after dinner Simons excused himself, saying that he would like a good night's rest to refresh for the stalk which had been arranged for the following day. Beaumont Fetherstone overheard him making his apologies and said that it was a good idea, and one that he himself would follow.

Together the two men made their way to their rooms in the tower, pausing outside Simons's to wish one another good night. In his room, Simons closed his door, and as he turned into the room his attention was caught by another door which he had not noticed earlier and which looked as though it should connect with Fetherstone's room next door.

Crossing to it, Simons discovered that it had been securely fastened and that even its keyhole had been blocked up. He knocked on it to attract his neighbour's attention, and when Fetherstone called out, asked, "Does this door lead into your room?"

"Well, yes and no!" Fetherstone replied. "It leads into a small cupboard which looks as if it might have been used as a powder closet. I tried it before you arrived, but it's securely screwed up on my side. Would you mind if I came and had a look at it from your side?"

"Certainly," Simons told him, and for the next twenty minutes or so the two men inspected door and cupboard, surmising this and that reason for its being securely walled up. Then once more they bade one another goodnight and prepared for bed.

How long Simons had actually been asleep he could never say, but in the early hours he was awakened by what felt like the light touch of a branding-iron on his cheek. The sensation was nevertheless so fierce that he believed that the flesh had been seared through to the bone.

It brought him to his senses with such force, however, that not fully realizing what he was doing, he leapt out of bed. And as he did so he saw distinctly the upper half of a woman's body drifting across the room towards the sealed-up door, through which it disappeared.

Simons rushed to the door, expecting to find it open. But it was as securely fastened as it had been when he and Fetherstone had carefully inspected it a few hours earlier.

He was, however, a man of cool courage, recognizing no misapprehension of phenomena for which at first sight there appeared

to be no rational explanation. At least that is the kind of man he seems to have been from his immediately subsequent behaviour.

For he did not call out, nor do anything to rouse his fellow guest next door, but having first lit his candle he went to the mirror above the dressing-table to examine his still smarting cheek, expecting to find some sign of the cause of the pain. To his complete surprise he found not the slightest mark.

At last it began to occur to him that what had happened seemed to have in it elements of the supernatural. This his cool-headedness could not accept, so taking up his candle he left the room and began to search the passages and staircases of the tower for some sign which would provide an acceptable explanation of the apparition.

When he had searched every corner of the tower and found nothing, he returned to his bed and passed the remaining hours till dawn sleepless and perplexed.

As soon as he heard Beaumont Fetherstone moving, he called out to him, "Fetherstone, I've had a terrible night!"

"What did you say?" Fetherstone called back through the sealed-up door.

Simons repeated that he had had a terrible night.

"That's what I thought you said, Fetherstone replied. "May I come round?"

"Of course," Simons told him.

A minute or two later Fetherstone came into the room, a splendid morning figure in a rich brocade dressing-gown which swept the floor. For the moment Simons forgot the reason for the visit.

"How very splendid!" he commented.

But clearly Fetherstone was less interested in his dressing-gown than in the experiences of the night. "Passed on by an ancient uncle," he said lightly and briefly, going on quickly, "Did your terrible night include a ghost?"

"I suppose you could call it that," Simons admitted. "But I've always thought of myself as a rational man, and ghosts are not submissive to reason."

"A woman would you say?" Fetherstone asked.

"Well, part . . ." Simons began.

Fetherstone held up his hand. "Don't say another word, old chap. I have an idea. We'll each tell our stories separately to Herbert Wood, and see what happens. Do you agree?

"Certainly," Simons replied. "It will be interesting, but I don't mind telling you that I am still disinclined to believe in ghosts."

"Then we're both in the same boat," Fetherstone said. "I didn't.

Reason tells me now not to. But . . . well, I'll go and dress. See you at breakfast."

Mrs Wood was already at the table when Simons went into the dining-room. Indicating a vacant place on her left, she said:"Herbert and Beaumont have gone to the library. They won't be long. I understand you had a disturbed night."

"I'm afraid so," Simons agreed, and was on the point of telling her when she put her hand on his arm."Later, Mr Simons, please!" Then in a whisper,"The servants are very superstitious."

Presently their host and Fetherstone came to the table. Wood was somewhat withdrawn, but Fetherstone seemed in the best of spirits.

At the conclusion of the meal, Wood reminded his men guests that the stalk would assemble at the main entrance of the castle in half an hour's time. Then looking towards Simon, he said:"Edward, Beaumont tells me you would like to speak to me in the library."

"If you can spare a moment,"Simons replied, now rather wishing that he had not agreed to Fetherstone's plan.

"Perhaps you will come too, my dear,"Wood suggested to his wife."You, of course, Beaumont."

In the library Wood said:"It was as I thought, my dear, our guests have had a disturbed night. Beaumont has told me his story. Edward will tell us his now. I thought it would interest you to hear it, my dear, in view of what the servants have been claiming recently."

Succinctly, but careful to leave out no detail, Simons related his experiences, and as he did so he noticed that Fetherstone was becoming more and more excited, though he did not interrupt; while Mrs Wood regarded the speaker with increasing bewilderment. When he had finished, Fetherstone exclaimed, "There, Herbert, the same in every detail!"

"In *almost* every detail,"Wood corrected him.

"In every essential detail,"Fetherstone persisted.

"What exactly happened to you?"Wood asked.

"Well, it was round about two o'clock," Fetherstone began. "I had been asleep for quite a time, when suddenly I woke up and realized that the room was faintly illuminated by a suffused pink light. At first I thought one of the out-houses had caught fire and the light was coming from the flames via the windows, until I remembered that I had not drawn back the curtains, which were still closed when I looked at them.

"It was as I turned from looking at the windows that my glance caught the figure of a woman standing at the foot of the bed. At first I thought it might be the housekeeper . . ."

"Mrs Menzies in a guest's room in the middle of the night!" Mrs Wood exclaimed. "My dear Beaumont, please never let her have the faintest whisper of your suspicions. She would be outraged!"

"I had no ill opinion of her motives, I assure you," Fetherstone exclaimed. "It struck me that she might be sleep-walking."

"I'm sorry, Beaumont," Mrs Wood smiled. "I'll not interrupt you again."

"As I was wondering what I might do for the best, for I have heard or read somewhere that it can be dangerous to waken a sleep-walker," Fetherstone went on, "she began to come round the side of the bed and as she came level with me started to incline towards me.

"A little alarmed by what I thought she intended to do, I sat up fully, the better to ward her off; and as I did so, she backed away and then turned and went hurriedly across the room towards the old powder closet. It was as she passed through the door into the closet that I realized I could not see her legs. In fact, she seemed to be walking on invisible legs."

Like Simons, however, though shaken, he lit his candle and when the lady did not emerge from the closet and not a sound came from that direction, he got out of bed and quietly made his way across the room. Though, under his night-shirt his flesh was covered with goose-pimples, he compelled himself to enter the little room.

"There was no one there!" he said. "The hip-bath and the clothes-horse were there, untouched, just as you saw them, Edward, and as you know there is no window; no opening, in fact, except the door into my room, the sealed-up door into Edward's room and the two long narrow loop-holes in the outside wall, which in any case are so narrow that not even the domestic cat could squeeze through them."

Mystified, and still not realizing that he had perhaps seen an apparition, he thought that while his attention was directed towards lighting the candle, the lady might have slipped out of the closet and concealed herself in the bedroom. So, before getting back into bed, he had made a thorough search of his room, even to the extent of looking under his bed. But all without result.

"She must have come to me after she had visited you," Simons remarked, "otherwise I should have heard you moving about. At least she spared you her burning kiss."

"I'm certain she intended it," Fetherstone said. "I seemed to have frightened her when I sat up in bed . . . Well, there you are, Herbert! Your castle is haunted by half a female ghost!"

"Exactly!" Wood replied. "The question is—which half?

Both the men looked at him sharply.

"Which half?" exclaimed Simons. "What do you mean? Fetherstone and I both saw the top half."

Wood glanced across to his wife with a faint smile. "You'd better tell them your story, my dear," he said.

"Why, have you seen her, too?" Fetherstone asked Mrs Wood.

"No, I have been spared that so far," Mrs Wood answered, "But one day last week one of the young housemaids ran screaming on the verge of hysterics into the still-room, where I was, crying out that she had seen a ghost."

"What time of day was it?" Fetherstone asked.

"Mid-morning," Mrs Wood replied. "It was a bright morning, too, full daylight, and I thought the simple girl had been frightened by a shadow, but when I had calmed her down she declared that what she had seen had been the *lower* part of a woman; that is to say, from the waist downwards, moving at speed along the north corridor leading from the tower. The lower part of the gown which covered the legs, she said, was covered with blood at the waist, or where the waist ought to have been.

"Somehow I managed to persuade her that she had been the victim of her imagination. I say persuaded her, but I don't think I did, really, for she gave in her notice before the day was out.

"Naturally, it was impossible to keep this sort of thing from the ears of the other servants, and I decided to warn my housekeeper what might be in store. She told me then that this was the first time the apparition had made its appearance for some years, but that, on the other hand, there were several among the older servants and people who live in the glen who claim that they have seen these ghostly legs not only wandering about the castle, but in the avenue of limes and in the graveyard. I must say it is a slight relief to know that there is an upper half also."

"Until this latest manifestation," Herbert Wood put in, "I had no idea at all that the castle was supposed to be haunted."

"The housemaid's experience," Mrs Wood went on, "has, as I am sure you will appreciate, unsettled the servants, and I'm afraid some may leave us. That was why I stopped you when you seemed on the point of telling me what had happened to you during the night, Edward."

"But you've lived here for five years now, Herbert," Fetherstone commented. "Had you really heard nothing until now?"

"Not a whisper?" Wood told him.

"I suppose you've made inquiries, Herbert," Simons said.

"No, I haven't," Wood answered. "I thought it best to leave well alone. You know what the folk up here are like. Start asking questions, and you'll let them know at once that something has happened. Tongues will begin to wag, and before long the servants will be frightened off. Situated as we are, we should never be able to replace them."

He looked at his watch.

"Well, it's time for us to be moving off. I can rely on you both I know, not to talk to any of the others about what has happened, and we must hope that the lady, whoever she is, will keep her top half and her bottom half well out of the way."

"Of course we'll say nothing," both men agreed.

"Fortunately," Mrs Wood said, the "Hawthornes are leaving today, so you will not have to spend another night in the tower."

Simons and Fetherstone protested that it was not necessary to move them, but Mrs Wood believed she detected a certain half-heartedness in their protests, and insisted.

"For my own peace of mind," she said, "I'll have your things brought down while you are out."

In the next few days Fetherstone's visit came to an end, but Simons stayed on for a week or two. Before he left the castle, he was to have yet another encounter with the legless ghost.

It was late at night and the other guests and their hosts had already gone to bed. Simons, however, wished to catch the next day's post, and went into the library to write his letters.

As he bent over the writing-table, presently he became aware that the atmosphere in the room had become so cold that he was beginning to shiver a little. Yet when he glanced towards the grate, a large log was blazing on a deep bed of glowing embers. And he became aware, too, that there was beginning to envelop him, some of the sensations of terror that had made him so uncomfortable during the night he had spent in the tower.

He glanced round the room, half-expecting to see the upper half of his former visitor. She was not there, but his attention was attracted and held to the heavy studded door to the library which was slowly and noiselessly opening.

As he stared at the door, unable to take his eyes from it, he saw pass down the corridor outside the upper half of a woman's body go gliding by. With a tremendous effort of will, he put down his pen, picked up the lamp by whose light he was writing, and frozen to the marrow he forced himself to set out for his bedroom, with the intention of taking refuge there.

To get to the room, however, he had to pass down a long flagged passage on the ground floor. The passage was lit by a single window, and as he passed it he saw peering in through the glass a woman's beautiful face, upon which was an expression of infinite sadness.

He recognized it at once as the face he and Beaumont Fetherstone had seen on the night they had spent in the tower. It brought him to a stop, but even the full beam of his lamp, which fell fully upon it, did not seem to disturb it, for it remained looking in through the window long enough for him to take a long look at its features. Then suddenly it was gone.

When he reported his experience to Herbert Wood next morning he begged him to let him make discreet inquiries to try to discover whether any local tradition existed which might provide an explanation for the haunting of the castle. Wood gave his permission on condition that Simons would be really careful not to say or do anything which might increase the superstitious misgivings with which, if the servants were a true guide, the inhabitants of Glen Lyon regarded Meggernie Castle.

It took Simons many days of skilful and cunning interrogation before he finally pieced together the story which clearly formed the basis of the haunting. It was, indeed, a gruesome tale.

In the days when Meggernie Castle formed part of the estates of the Clan Menzies, the then chief of the clan had a very beautiful wife. Though utterly innocent and completely modest, the lady attracted the attention of all the local gentlemen, who paid her gallant court.

Instead of taking this universal admiration as the compliment it was to himself as much as to his wife, the Menzies was constantly creating scenes which showed that his jealousy bordered on insanity. One of these scenes, in which he reached new heights of invective and accusation of infidelity, took place one day when the couple were in the room which Beaumont Fetherstone had occupied in the tower on his and Simons's first night at the castle.

On this occasion, the Menzies's jealousy roused him to a pitch of violence which surpassed all his previous attacks, and culminated in his striking his wife. She fell and caught her head, as she did so, against one of the bed posts.

Immediately his rage evaporated, and he ran to her and knelt beside her, imploring her to open her eyes and try to find it in her heart to forgive him. It was some minutes before he was sufficiently calm to realize that she was dead.

Jealousy was not the only flaw in his character, for now he began

to search for means by which he might be able to escape the consequences of what he had done. After some thought he formulated his plan.

In the powder closet, he knew, was a large chest-of-drawers; the same which still stood in the tiny room when Beaumont Fetherstone and Edward Simons inspected it that night. He dragged his wife's body across the room with the intention of concealing it in one of the drawers. But though his wife had been slightly built none of the drawers of the chest was large enough to take her.

The Menzies was now beside himself, and reacted with the stark ruthlessness which characterized so many of his contemporary countrymen. He fetched a saw, and sawed the body in two at the waist. One half he then put in one drawer; the other in the drawer above.

This gruesome task finished, he then nailed up the door leading from the closet to Simons's room, locked the door leading into Fetherstone's room, then left the bedroom, fastening its door securely behind him.

Going downstairs he ordered one of the grooms to bring round his wife's carriage, saying that she wished to visit a relative who lived farther up the glen. He told the groom that he would drive the carriage himself.

None of the servants saw the carriage go, and when the Menzies returned alone in it shortly before dinner time no one was surprised, either by the absence of Mistress Menzies, or by his further orders. These were to the effect that he and the mistress had decided to go on a visit abroad, that her maid was to pack a suitable selection of clothes, and that the carriage was to be ready shortly after dawn. Once more he announced that he would drive it himself, and added that as the visit would probably keep them away for several months, the servants were to be sent home on board-wages, and the castle shut up.

Early next morning the servants watched him drive away in the carriage. Seven months passed before they saw him again, and heard from him the sad news that the mistress had been drowned in a boating accident in Italy.

There was no reason why they should not believe him, and soon the glens-folk and neighbours were calling to offer the Menzies their condolences. The Menzies played the part of bereaved husband convincingly.

When life had settled down once more into the normal run, he decided that he must no longer delay in disposing permanently of

the evidence of his crime. So, one night, taking a dark lantern and a spade, after the servants were safely in bed, he went to the nearby kirkyard and prepared a shallow hole.

He then returned to the castle, and made his way to the tower. The room was still locked, as he had left it, and so was the closet, he noted with satisfaction. But some of his composure left him when he let himself into the closet and, on opening the lower drawer, smelt and saw the putrefaction of the limbs it contained.

It took some minutes for him to steel himself to lift the decaying flesh into a sheet. By the time he had deposited it in the grave in the kirkyard and covered it over, he had had more than he could stomach for one night, and decided that the second part of his task must be left for another occasion.

But he did not dare to put off the task too long, for the stench from the closet would undoubtedly betray its contents if it were not soon disposed of. So next night, fortifying himself well with whisky, he forced himself to prepare a second grave in the kirkyard.

Before going up to the tower, he went to the library where he poured himself another glass of whisky, which he swallowed at one gulp. He was so intent upon what he had to do that he was completely unaware of the dark shape which followed him silently, concealing itself in the shadows.

Despite the false courage which he had hoped the whisky would have given him, when he reached the powder closet and opened the drawer the state of what he found there was too much for him.

"I can't do it!" he muttered to himself. "But it can't stay here! What is to be done with it?"

As he spoke, he staggered back into the bedroom, and in doing so he stood on a loose floor-board. With a whimper of awesome joy, he pulled back the carpet and inspected the board. It was a half-section, newer than the rest of the floor, and whoever had been responsible for laying it, he had not nailed it down, for when the Menzies tried he found that he could prise it up with the point of his dirk.

Below was a deep cavity whose floor was the ceiling of the room beneath.

Hurrying to the closet, not daring to think of what he was doing, he dragged the stinking remains of his wife's torso from the drawer, thrust it between the joists, replaced the board, and drew back the carpet.

It was as he turned to take up the candle with which he had lighted his way that he saw the tall figure standing in the doorway.

Who the figure was, tradition does not say. It is clear, however, that the Menzies realized that he had been watched, and that his secret was no longer safe. He rushed at the figure, dirk in hand; but the figure was too quick for him. The servants, searching for him next morning found him dead in the already drying pool of blood which had seeped from the wound in his heart.

Thus the top half of the murdered Mistress Menzies lay beneath the floor-boards of the room in which she had been killed, while her lower half lay buried in the kirkyard. This, so tradition had it, was why the Meggernie ghost haunted the rooms of the tower, while the lower half wandered about the ground-floor corridors and the avenue of limes.

After the experience of Fetherstone and Simons, Mistress Menzies remained quiet for some time. But there are records of more recent manifestations, the most recent being to a local doctor who was called to the castle late one night in 1928, and accepted an invitation to stay the night.

He was put in a room in the tower below the one in which Fetherstone had slept. The doctor fell asleep, and after an hour or two suddenly awoke, and believed that he heard footsteps approaching his door. He expected that he was being summoned to his patient, but as he waited for the knock on his door which did not come he had the impression that someone had entered the room.

As he glanced about the dark room he saw, illuminated in a kind of aureole of pink light, a woman's head and shoulders gliding round the walls of the room, high up near the ceiling. As he watched it, suddenly it disappeared.

In more recent times there has been no sighting of the apparition, but successive occupants of the castle have heard occasional inexplicable rappings and knockings.

The Ghost of Nance

In the days when the fastest traffic on the Great North Road were the mail-coaches, one of the coachmen, Tom Driffield, was engaged to marry Nance, the daughter of a farmer at Sheriff Hutton in Yorkshire. The day was fixed for the third Sunday in May; the farmer had contracted with the local builder to build them a cottage in one of his fields standing back from the road, and Nance and her mother and sister were spending every spare minute sewing her trousseau.

Nance was some fifteen years younger than her husband-to-be, but she had no doubts on that score. He was handsome and strong, and no driver of the mails could match him in skill between Edinburgh and London. But it was neither his looks nor his strength nor his skill which had won the heart of Nance. It was the warm kindness that shone from his great brown eyes, the quiet kindness of his deep soft voice and the gentle kindness in the caresses of his broad hands.

The banns were to be called for the first time on the last Sunday in April.

"It's a pity you can't be at the church to hear them," Nance had said when Tom had told her that on that day he would be carrying the mails from York to London. "But I'll go and I'll think of you all the time, dear Tom."

She had arrived at the church for matins that Sunday morning with her father and mother, brothers and sisters, with few other thoughts besides those she had of Tom. But as the five-minute-bell

began to toll, there came striding down the aisle a young stranger. His jet black hair, shining with pommard, was drawn tightly down over his head into a queue in the nape of his slender neck, held in place by a splendid bow of crimson velvet. His coat sat with elegance upon his well-formed body; the calves encased in flashing white stockings were perfectly proportioned with swelling thighs and tapering ankles; his feet in their leather pumps glistening with silver buckles were the neatest to be seen on any man; the frills at his wrists, and the jabot at his throat, were of finest Brussels lace; while on the long slender index-finger of his right hand scintillated a diamond the size of a hedge-sparrow's egg, the only piece o jewellery about him.

The beadle, taking him to be gentry, conducted him to pews reserved for distinguished strangers, on the left side of the chancel steps which looked inwards and faced the squire's pews. He bowed to the beadle, who closed the door of the pew after him, then placing his black tricorne he was carrying on the seat, he knelt with his face in his hands for some seconds, before sitting back and allowing his gaze to wander over the congregation.

Presently his eyes came to rest on Nance, who had been regarding him frankly since the moment of his appearance. He held her gaze for a time, until a nudge from her younger sister brought her to her senses.

"You're staring, Nance," Prue scolded. "It's not polite."

"Who is he?" Nance whispered, lowering her eyes.

"Some London gentleman," Prue told her. "Been staying at the inn since Thursday."

(Prue was being courted by Dick Driver, son of the inn-keeper, and was always the first of the Tucker family to learn any news.)

The organ struck up, the choir emerged from the vestry, and soon matins were in full swing. Nance, staring hard at her prayer-book, did her best to concentrate on versicles, psalms and responses, but every so often she felt her gaze going across the aisle, and each time she looked up she saw that his eyes were on her. Only when she heard the Rector call Tom's name with hers as he read the banns did she remember to think of her future spouse, and she felt a spasm of shame. It was short-lived, however, for when she looked up, blushing, the young gentleman's eyes were still on her.

When the service was over, many of their neighbours in the village had waited by the porch to give her their good wishes for her happiness. She thanked them demurely, leaving her mother to

do the talking. And while they stood there, he came out of the church.

Seeing her he smiled, and in great trepidation she watched him coming towards her. His tricorne pressed lightly to his chest, he leaned forward in a bow.

"Ma'am," he said. "I believe I have the honour and great pleasure of addressing the fortunate young lady whose banns were called for the first time this morning?"

"Sir," she said, bobbing a curtsy. Then turning to Mrs Tucker, she went on, "My mother, sir."

He bowed again, and Mrs Tucker curtsied.

"Ma'am," he said, "may a stranger offer one of the prettiest girls he's ever set eyes on his most cordial wishes. Your future husband is the most fortunate of men."

"You are kind, sir," replied Mrs Tucker. "My daughter thanks you."

Once more he inclined towards her, smiled broadly at Nance, put on his tricorne and strode off down the path back to the inn.

"Fine manners these gentlemen have!" Mrs Tucker sniffed, "if many of them have little else besides."

"You saw his great diamond, mother?" Nance exclaimed.

"Glass, if the truth was known," said Mrs Tucker tersely.

But here she was wrong. It was a genuine stone, only lately come into the gentleman's possession.

Three days later Sheriff Hutton was thrown into an uproar.

Jill Thornton, who helped Mrs Tucker in the kitchen, had come scurrying down to her mother's cottage with the incredible news that during the night Nance Tucker had eloped with the fine stranger at the inn, who had decamped, incidentally, without settling his account. She had left behind a note telling her parents so, and a note for Tom Driffield, begging his forgiveness, but saying that she had lost her heart utterly.

On Sunday evening, Jill went on, Jane Croft, a maid at the inn, and a friend of hers, had come to the farm on the pretext of visiting her. At the first moment they were alone together, Jane had produced from her blouse a note which she begged Jill to give to Nance secretly as soon as possible.

"He's sent you this," Jane said, pressing into Jill's hand a silver crown piece.

Jill entered excitedly into the plot, and contrived an early opportunity to pass the note to Nance. After supper, when her work in the kitchen was finished, and she had gone up to her bedroom, as she was drawing the curtains she had seen a woman in a long hooded

black cloak glide quickly across the farmyard, making for the field behind the long barn.

When Tom Driffield learned that his Nance had forsaken him, he seemed to be broken. But there was in him a vein of stoicism and presently he told himself that nothing happens without good reason. So he continued to drive his coach from Edinburgh to London with the care and skill that he had always employed, maintaining his reputation as the fastest mail on the Great North Road, and in December he married a Thirsk girl, and made a home for her there.

Nothing was heard of Nance in Sheriff Hutton; no word came from her to her parents. It was as if she had vanished from the face of the earth.

Then one wet and miserable day in the following March, as Tom was driving his coach south and was a few miles from York, he saw a woman standing by the roadside with a baby in her arms. Though illness and exhaustion had much changed her appearance, he recognized her at once, and reined in his horses.

"Why, Nance," he exclaimed, jumping down. "You are ill. There's room in the coach. Get up and I'll take you to York to a doctor."

She was almost too weak to speak, but as he lifted her and her baby into the coach she whispered, "Dear Tom."

In York, when he had set down his passengers for the night, he took Nance and her child to the York Tavern, where the proprietress was a friend of his. While Nance was being put to bed, he fetched a physician, who, after examining her, took him seriously aside and told him that neither she nor the child could live long.

That evening he sat by her bedside, hoping to comfort her. He could not reproach her, and he asked her no questions. If she wished him to know how she had come to this plight she would be telling him, and this it seemed she wanted to do.

It was a pitiable story. The fine gentleman had proved to be a highwayman; but what was worse, after they had gone through a marriage ceremony at Northallerton and the child was already coming she had discovered that he was married already, and she had left him. Since then she had been working in service with a family in Oswaldkirk, over by Helmsley, but when the baby was born they had turned her out. Scarcely knowing what she was doing, she had wandered over the moors, and had reached the main road shortly before he had come along.

"If ever I set eyes on the scoundrel," he promised her, "I'll flog him within an inch of his life."

She took his hand and smiled at him wanly.

"Dear Tom," she said, "if you don't catch him, sooner or later the law will."

Throughout the night he dozed by her bed, and she was sleeping still when he had to leave her. Handing a sovereign to the landlady, he said: "Look after her well. Whatever more you spend, I will repay you when I return."

When he came again to York going north, and called at the Tavern, it was to be told that Nance and her baby had died three days after he had gone.

"Before she died she said to me," the landlady told him, " 'Dear Tom, he never uttered a word of reproach. Tell him that to repay his kindness, if ever he, or his son, or his grandson, are ever in any need of help, I will come back to help them.' "

Tom smiled.

"She'll keep her promise," the landlady said sharply, seeing him smile. "You see if her words don't come true."

During the next two years nothing happened, and then one day, as sometimes happened, Tom was given a special commisssion. He was to take a carriage to Durham and there pick up four very important passengers and drive them to York.

When he arrived at the Royal County Hotel in Durham, where his passengers were waiting for him, he found them very impatient to get to their destination as quickly as possible.

"How much will your charge be for the journey?" one of them asked.

"Four guineas, sir," Tom replied.

"Get us there by eight o'clock this evening and you shall have twenty!" the man declared.

It was a tall order, but it was a challenge. If the weather held, Tom might just do it, though no other driver on the Road could. So they set out, and Tom whipped up the horses, and all went well until at half-past six, when they were only seven miles from York, they ran into a thick fog.

Stopping the carriage, Tom got down and opening the door said to the passengers, "I'm sorry, gentlemen, unless the fog clears in the next quarter of an hour it will be impossible to reach York by eight o'clock."

"But you are going on, coachman?" the spokesman asked. "The fog may lift after a mile or so."

"We still shouldn't make it, sir. In normal circumstances I would wait here until the fog cleared. It's impossible to see more than a yard or two ahead, and it really is folly to go on ..."

"You must try, we beg you. It is a matter of life and death. You shall have thirty guineas."

"It's not a matter of money, sir; that wouldn't be much good to me if I were to be killed, would it? However, since you are so urgent, I will go on."

He closed the door, and climbed back on to the box. But through the mist he saw that someone else was already sitting there and had taken up the reins.

"Why, Nance," he said. "So you've kept your promise!"

She smiled at him, shook the reins and the horses broke at once into a gallop. For the next seven miles, through the swirling mist they kept up their mad pace.

From time to time Tom could hear the cries of alarm coming from inside the carriage as it swayed from side to side on the uneven road. But he grinned to himself, feeling no fear, having absolute faith in the driver who sat beside him.

There was even thicker fog enveloping York, but the horses abated their speed not one bit as they writhed and turned through the narrow cobbled streets of the ancient city, until they pulled up at last before the Black Swan Inn in Coney Lane.

Smiling at Tom again, Nance passed him the reins and vanished.

When he went to the carriage, he found his passengers still almost speechless with fright.

"You asked for it, gentlemen," he laughed. "But come, cheer up. It is five minutes to eight. I have kept my bargain, and it is all over now."

"We never thought," said the spokesman, "that when we urged you to go on you would drive through thick fog at such breakneck speed. I'll wager no other gentlemen in the North or South of England has ever had such an experience."

"No other gentlemen in the North or South of England," Tom replied, "have ever had such a coachman."

This was but the first of many appearances that Nance made to Tom before he retired, always coming when he stood in special need. When he handed over the private business he had acquired when he grew too old for the long journeys with the mail-coaches, he told his son the story of Nance.

"She has come to my aid many a time," he said. "She promised to come to your aid, too, and to the aid of your son. Whenever she comes, you must do exactly as she tells you. Even if she wishes to take the reins, you must let her."

There is no record that Nance ever appeared to Tom's son, but

there is one account of an appearance she made to his grandson.

Peter Jackson and his brother John one day took the coach, driven by Robert Driffield, from Pickering to York. As it was a fine night, the brothers took seats outside. Before they had set off from Pickering, Robert Driffield, who knew the Jackson brothers, had taken them privately on one side.

"I'm a bit anxious," he told them. "I've got a feeling about the man who's sitting beside me on the box. I don't know anything mind, but it won't surprise me if he's up to no good. So be ready for anything that happens."

Nothing happened, however, until as they were approaching Malton the horses suddenly swerved to avoid a woman standing in the middle of the roadway. Although it was bright moonlight, it was clear from their exclamations that none of the passengers had seen her but the Jackson brothers.

Driffield stopped the coach, and getting down made an inspection of the wheels and axles. While he was doing so, Peter Jackson went to him and said quietly, "Is anything wrong, Bob?"

"With the coach? No," Driffield replied. "But I've been warned."

"You mean the woman?"

"You saw her?"

"Yes. So did John. Where is she now?"

"I'll tell you about her presently," Driffield promised. "But now I'm going to drive back to the village on the excuse that something is wrong with the springs. Play up with me."

So he turned about, and when they came back to the village inn, he made another inspection, and then announced to the passengers that he regretted that they would have to pass the night at the inn as there was damage to the coach, and it would be dangerous to go on until it was put right.

All agreed that this was wise, except the man who had been riding on the box. He protested loudly that he must go on, as he had very important business in York early the next morning. He did not protest for long, however, for the Jackson brothers seized him, and the innkeeper, who had previously been taken into Driffield's confidence, showed them to one of the attics of the inn, where they locked their prisoner in.

When the passengers had gone to their rooms, Driffield, with the innkeeper's help once more, rounded up a party of stout villagers, and presently the coach, with the Jackson brothers the only outside passengers, set out again for York.

As they reached the spot where the horses had swerved they saw

the woman still there. This time, however, she was at the roadside, and made no attempt to stop them, but waved them on.

"But who is she?" Peter Jackson begged Driffield to tell them.

"Do you believe in ghosts?" he asked.

"No, of course not," John Jackson replied shortly.

"Well, you've just seen one," Driffield laughed, and told them the story of Nance.

As he came to the end of his account they were approaching Barton Corner.

"Watch out here!" Driffield warned them, and had scarcely spoken when three masked men rode out of the trees and barred the road.

As one of them pointed his pistol at the men outside his two companions opened the carriage doors.

"Is he in there?" the leader called, but his question went unanswered, for before they knew what was happening the labourers concealed inside the coach had leapt out and overpowered them. Putting his spurs to his horse, their leader was clearly intending to leave them to their fate, when Peter Jackson drew the pistol he had been holding under his cloak and took aim.

"He's out of range!" his brother exclaimed. "You're too slow."

Nevertheless, Peter fired, the fleeing horse stumbled, throwing his rider over his head, and leaving him lying motionless on the ground, galloped on.

"I hit him!" Peter Jackson cried triumphantly.

"No, you scared him," his brother corrected.

"Or Nance did," Driffield remarked. "Didn't you see her there, under the trees?"

The Haunting of Itchells Manor

Itchells Manor, in Hampshire, was a small but pleasant country mansion, standing in an estate of several hundred acres of parkland and farm-land.

Towards the very end of the seventeenth century, the lord of the manor of Itchells was a certain Squire Bathurst. The Bathursts had been squires of Itchells for several generations, but though they had been good husbandmen they had not laid up for themselves great treasure. This is not to say that they were not comfortably off, but they could not comport themselves so lavishly as many of the other county gentry could, and, in particular, their neighbours, the Bushnells.

All preceding Bathurst squires had chosen their wives carefully from among the Englishwomen of their acquaintance, so it came as something of a shock to the county when the father of our Squire Bathurst returned to Itchells from a tour of the continent, bringing with him an Italian wife who, besides possessing a small fortune, bore also the high-ranking title of Marchesa.

These were not the only attributes which set the new Mrs Bathurst apart from the usual run of Itchells chatelaines. She was dark, whereas the predominant colouring of the family was brunette or fair; she was exceptionally beautiful, rivalling in this respect the contemporary Countess of Southampton, who was one of the outstanding beauties of the times; and though she could be, and often was, the source or centre of laughter and merriment, there was in her composition an instability of temper and a broad streak of morose-

ness which she could not or would not control when thwarted in any degree.

Within a year of her arrival at Itchells she gave birth to a son, who was eventually to become our Squire Bathurst. In the two succeeding years, she presented her Squire with two daughters; and these three children represented her contribution to the family. Since nature seems to delight in contrariness, the boy was dark, selfish and uneven tempered like his mother; the girls had the fair colouring and sunny disposition of their father. It was not strange, therefore, when the mother made the son her favourite, though it was unfortunate, for she encouraged him to be more like herself than a Bathurst, and urged him to seek his friends among those of a more elevated station and wealth.

It was in this way that he first made the acquaintance of and then became on intimate terms with the Bushnell family, the birth of whose heir had almost coincided with his own. Robert Bushnell was not unlike Alexander Bathurst in many ways. At fifteen he was outgrowing his strength, which made him inordinately slim and pale, and kept him in a constant state of lassitude, so that he languished rather than lived. Though the physicians assured his parents that this was merely a passing phase, they did impress upon Sir George and Lady Bushnell the necessity for his being cosseted for the time-being.

Under the influence of this cosseting and from the effects of his general lack of stamina, the youth became spoiled and selfish. Soon he seemed to be enjoying his poor health, for he discovered that it was a formidable weapon for getting his own way. He used it first chiefly against his tutor, a poor timid wretch who was a distant cousin and who depended entirely on the largesse of his wealthy kinsman for his very existence.

Robert's campaign of tutor-baiting presently reached such a pitch that the young man felt that starvation would be the lesser of two evils and took his complaints to his employer. Sir George, the fourth baronet, was distressed, and talked seriously to his wife.

"The poor boy's bored, naturally," said Lady Bushnell, and suggested that Robert's two brothers should be brought home from Eton to keep him company. But Sir George would not hear of it.

Then Lady Bushnell had an inspiration. She ordered her carriage and called upon Mrs Bathurst, and at the end of a short conversation the two ladies had agreed that Alexander Bathurst should share Robert Bushnell's tutor in the hope that they would become friends.

By good fortune the two strange boys, so strange as to be almost

changelings to their respective families, took an immediate liking to one another, and were so absorbed in this new relationship that they had no time to devote to bullying their tutor; for it was a relationship of a kind neither of them had experienced before, but for which clearly both had been unconsciously yearning. In addition, Alexander Bathurst had a natural leaning towards learning, and fired Robert Bushnell with a new, if restrained, enthusiasm, so that the tutor found his task of instructing them no longer a chore, but a pleasure.

The initial arrangement was that Alexander should live with the Bushnells from Monday to Friday. Within a short time, however, the boys found that the deprivation of each other's company, even for two days out of seven, more than they could bear, so it was agreed that Alexander should remain permanently in what was quickly becoming his real home.

The two mothers were delighted. Only Sir George growled, "Don't be over-confident, Lady Bushnell. My view is that it is too good to last."

In holding this view, however, he was holding an erroneous one. The longer the relationship extended, the more inseparable did the boys become. To each other they were quite different from what they were towards others, though even in this respect they had changed. They never quarrelled, they did not behave selfishly, and they supported one another in every way.

It must be revealed, nevertheless, that Robert Bushnell was the dominant character, and of the two it was Alexander Bathurst who paved the way for harmony, by being prepared to give in and thus avoid any clash between them. But he was quite content with this role, for though his affection for Robert was genuine, he had good, if entirely private and secret, reasons for doing nothing which might lead to a breach between them.

His motive was a simple one. The Bushnells lived on a far more lavish scale than the Bathurst income would allow. There was no stinting of money, as there was intermittently at Itchells Manor when crops were bad, live-stock less productive or rents not forthcoming. Even the Marchesa's fortune was not sufficient to off-set these temporary set-backs, and when they occurred, not only the whole family, but the entire household were required to contribute to the general economies.

But what Mrs Bathurst called "these times of poverty" were not the main reason, though they were a tributary one, for her son's attitude towards his friends' family circumstances. It was the whole

atmosphere of comfort and well-being which enveloped the Bushnells. There was, for example, a large army of servants who were always on hand whenever one needed them. The furnishings were not shabby through generations of use and lack of funds to keep them in good shape, as were those at Itchells. The food was always exciting—the Bushnells' Swiss chef, brought back by Sir George on his return from a diplomatic mission to Berne, saw to that—and its service was impeccable. Finally, there was the ever-full purse of Robert himself, who at sixteen received an allowance of fifty pounds, which his mother privately doubled. Whatever his friend had a whim for, he could buy without humiliating application to his father.

The effect of all this on any perceptive boy must have been marked. On a boy brought up as the Marchesa had brought up her son, to believe his home surroundings to be unworthy of his aesthetic needs, they had an impact that was never to be eradicated. He learned the lesson that money not only spells power, but makes possible the kind of comfort he found he required not merely for his physical but for his mental well-being also. It was now that he determined that he would employ every means to avoid the cheese-paring which differentiated the Bathurst way of life from the way of life of the real aristocracy.

As the years went by the boys grew into young men, and when they were twenty, as the Bushnell dower-house was unoccupied, with Sir George's consent they moved into it and set up their own establishment, the bill for which was entirely footed by Robert. Though Alexander had to accept it—or part with his friend—he did so; but how much it irked him not to be able to pay his way, only he knew. It was no use Robert trying to persuade him that since they were more than friends, mundane considerations should never be allowed to enter their relationship; Alexander felt the indignity of living on Bushnell wealth more than he cared to admit to himself, and became all the more determined to put an end to this false position in which his comparative poverty confined him. Once he became squire of Itchells there would be changes.

Though his rank was not superior, the Bushnell wealth made Robert, at twenty-one, one of the most eligible bachelors in the county. To the chagrin of mothers of eligible daughters, he kept himself aloof from all female company. Balls and receptions were seldom honoured by his presence, he declined invitations to stay and he made it quite clear, if he did appear, that it was useless for mothers to hope that their daughters might find favour with him. Had they

asked him why, he would have told them, "So long as Alex and I have one another, we have no need of anyone else!" But mothers of daughters are particularly obstinate, and despite the warnings of their wiser husbands that they were tilting at a windmill, they continued to hope.

Their hopes, however, were destined to be short-lived. A year after they had moved into the dower-house, the two young men decided to embark on the Grand Tour. They went, they saw, they were conquered, particularly by Italy, and especially by Florence; and there they decided to stay until the spirit moved them.

Unfortunately, after they had been there for several months, Robert Bushnell was accidentally drowned in a boating accident. Devastated by the loss of his friend, for a time it seemed that Alexander Bathurst was in danger of going out of his mind. He was preserved from this fate, however, but was faced not only with loneliness, but with returning to Itchells and to the state of penury from which he had been protected for the last ten years. But there was nothing else he could do; it was a prospect which would have daunted many a more normal young man.

On his return to Itchells he found his sisters married, and the squire and Mrs Bathurst existing in a state of fragile armistice which inevitably infected the whole atmosphere of the manor. The chief cause of their estrangement was Mrs Bathurst's insistence on keeping up with the aristocratic Joneses and running into debt to do so. The death of Robert Bushnell exacerbated this unhappy situation, for the Marchesa foresaw that with her son's usefulness to the Bushnells terminated, her own relationship with the family might be changed, and she increased her social efforts to prevent this.

The reappearance of his son also affected the squire, who, robust countryman that he was, found exceptionally distasteful the widespread reputation Alexander had acquired as a result of his friendship with Robert Bushnell. While they had been boys, it could be ignored; while they were abroad and out of sight, it could be successfully put out of mind; but to have the dark, handsome young man in his foppish clothes sulking about the place, his white hands a constant reminder that he was not fitted to be a country squire who had the practical oversight of his estates, produced in him a profound irritation and incipient feelings of hatred, which he was too constitutionally ingenuous to be able to dissimulate. To comfort himself he increased his drinking.

Since this bibulousness can be traced directly to the man his heir had become, it can be said that Alexander Bathurst was responsible

for the deaths of his father and mother. For, a little less than a year and a half after Alexander's return to Itchells, one night the drunkard squire insisted on driving home from dinner with a nearby neighbour. He could hold his liquor as befits a gentleman, and though his companions knew that he had imbibed unwisely, they made no attempt to dissuade him from getting up on to the box himself, since he was only slightly uncertain in speech and gait. But as soon as he laid hold on the reins a devil seemed to possess him, and he whipped up the horses, which, surprised and frightened, leapt down the drive at tremendous pace. The groom beside the squire tried to seize the reins from his master's hands, and for his pains was flung from the box, broke his back and died. As the swaying carriage charged through the ornamental gateway guarding the exit to the drive a wheel struck a pillar, the squire was catapulted from the box and broke his neck in his fall, while Mrs Bathurst, inside the carriage, received head injuries which led to a haemorrhage of the brain, and after lying in a coma for several weeks she also died.

As soon as he had recovered from the shock, not of his parents' deaths, but from his unexpected elevation to the lordship of the manor of Itchells, Alexander Bathurst immediately set about implementing the plans which he had formulated secretly over the years against the time when he would be in control of whatever revenue the estates brought in. His main object was to increase his personal income until it would provide him with the standard of living which his friendship with Robert Bushnell had made possible for him. He realized that this he could never achieve by the working of the estates alone. He would have to invest, and for this he would need capital.

To raise the capital, he sold several hundred acres, raised the rents of his tenants, bought inferior grain and stock, and by this means acquired some thousands of pounds. With them he went to London and, to begin with, invested them in the East India Company. These investments secured him very reasonable returns, but even so he realized that it would take him a long time to acquire the fortune he needed.

By this time the South Sea Company had been started, but Squire Bathurst had had his doubts about the soundness of its transactions. However, when, in 1719, the company gained further concessions from the government, he allowed himself to be caught up in the speculation mania, which was now quickly approaching its peak, and he invested £8,000.

As everyone knows, the population of England went mad during

the first six months of 1720. Rich and poor alike scraped together every available penny to buy South Sea stock at any price, and by mid-summer £1100 was being offered for every £100 of the company's stock. Prime Minister Walpole did his best to warn the speculators of the risk they were running, but few took heed.

Though he could never afterwards explain why he disposed of his holdings when the stock was at its peak price, that was precisely what he did. Now worth some £90,000, he invested two-thirds of it in East India Company stock, and took himself to Florence with the sole intention of impressing the friends he and Robert Bushnell had made there, with his own financial status.

It took some time for news of the bursting of the South Sea Bubble to reach him, but when at last it did once again he suffered a profound shock. Wasting no time, accompanied by his young Italian valet, he returned to England. When he learned in London of the narrowness of his escape from absolute ruin, the first shock, instead of subsiding, increased, and had the effect of implanting in him an absolute distrust of all commercial ventures. Withdrawing all his investments from the East India Company, and converting it into gold coin, he withdrew to Itchells Manor.

Now that he had wealth enough and more, to surround himself with the luxuries he had learned to desire so ardently, his recent experiences seemed to have wrought such a change in his character as to turn him into a miser of classic mould. He dismissed his domestic staff with the exception of the Italian valet, and kept open only one room for himself, the kitchen and a room for the valet. He sold his horses and carriages, again keeping only one. To save the expense of a groom he looked after the horse himself, and he required the valet to cook and do such other duties about the house that would prevent it from becoming, in the complete absence of other servants, a veritable pig-sty. He never went out into society, and, in fact, very rarely emerged from the manor, certainly never leaving the estate.

As time went by, it became obvious to the valet that his master had become mad. There were constant quarrels over the cost of the simple foodstuffs which the valet insisted were essential to sustain life. When the valet asked for replacements of clothes, he narrowly escaped being horsewhipped.

It was inevitable, therefore, that sooner or later the valet would forsake his master, and presently this he planned to do. But he planned something else besides.

He had been aware of the arrival of heavy chests, iron-bound and

securely bolted, shortly after all the servants had been dismissed, and guessed that they contained valuables, for Squire Bathurst kept them in the room which served him as bedroom, study and dining-room. This room he was never allowed to enter except in the presence of his master. Its door was kept locked whenever the squire was not in it.

It did not take him long, either, to discover what the chests contained, for squire Bathurst formed the habit of counting the contents of one chest each night before he retired to bed. One evening, wishing to speak to the squire, the valet had knocked on the door, and receiving no answer had tried the door-handle, and found the door to be locked.

At first fearing that something might have happened to the squire, whom he believed to be in the room, since a light shone under the door, he bent down and put an eye to the keyhole. He could see nothing, because the key was in the lock, but on listening for any sound which might tell him that the squire was not unconscious, he heard the clinking of metal and Bathurst's murmured counting.

It was this discovery which set the valet thinking. No one came to the manor except the tenants with their rents. The master never left the estate and rarely the house. He himeslf went only to the village once a week to get supplies of food. If he gave it out that the squire had decided to go to London, and if he drove the carriage which would contain the money chests and a dummy made of the squire's clothes, only in case they were seen by a poacher as they passed through the countryside, he could be safely back in Italy long before anyone began to think that the squire was making a protracted stay in London. Of course, he would have to make certain that the squire's body was hidden in a place where it would never be found, and it was to this end that he spent much of his time during the next week on opening up the chimney-piece in one of the upstairs bedrooms.

His practical plans completed, on the chosen night shortly before eleven o'clock he went to the squire's room. In case the squire should be awake, he took with him a posset which he would beg his master to take, saying that he was worried about his health, which had indeed become generally undermined by lack of food. He expected that the door would be unlocked, because it invariably was when he took in the squire's so-called breakfast, and when, more often than not, the squire would still be asleep.

He opened the door with some difficulty, since he had to hold the

tankard containing the posset, and the candle-stick with which he had to light his way, in one hand. As he moved towards the bed, the squire made no move; but as he set down the posset and candle on the bedside table, and put up a hand to draw back the curtain, Alexander Bathurst awoke with a start, and with surprising agility sprang from the bed.

"Who is it? What do you want?" he shouted.

"It's Giuseppe, master. Quietly, quietly!" the valet soothed him.

"Oh God!" the squire exclaimed shakily. "I thought you were an intruder. What do you want?"

"You are looking ill, master, and I am anxious for your health," the valet told him. "I've brought you a posset which I beg you to drink."

"Who told you to make a posset?" Bathurst demanded. "Such things are luxuries I cannot afford!"

"A few pence, master, for the ale!" the valet remonstrated.

"You are not to make such things without my orders."

"No, master. But please, drink it. You will not have it waste?"

"Oh, very well," Bathurst grumbled.

"Get back into bed, master, and I will give it to you."

"No, no! You have unsettled me. Bring it to the table and I will sit there and drink it," the squire told him, as wrapping a coverlet from the bed about him, he went to the table and sat down.

The valet carried the tankard and the candle-stick to the table and seemed to be waiting.

"You needn't wait," Bathurst said, wanting the man to go so that he might check his chests.

But the last word had barely come from his tongue when he felt himself seized by the hair, his head jerked back and a momentarily sharp pain strike across his throat, as the valet drew the razor's edge across it.

In his nervous determination, for he had not intended to kill the madman thus—he had planned to smother him with a pillow, and had brought the razor only as a safeguard—the man had employed too great strength, so that the head was half-severed from the body. But his viciousness served the squire well, for he choked once, blood spurted from his mouth across the table, and he fell forward into the pool of it, dead.

With precise cold-blooded movements the valet went about his business. Binding a cover from the bed about the dead squire's neck and head, he hoisted the emaciated body of Alexander Bathurst over one shoulder, and with ease carried it upstairs to the hiding-

place he had prepared for it. He worked quickly and deftly, and within half an hour the hole he had made in the chimney-piece was bricked in.

This done, he hurried down to the coach-house and harnessed the horse to the carriage, which he drove round to the main entrance. Returning to the squire's room, which had formerly been the large drawing-room, he began to carry the chests out to the carriage. They were heavier than he had imagined they would be, and by the time he had taken four of them he was feeling the strain of his exertions. He was also aware that the weight of them was pressing down alarmingly on the springs of the dilapidated carriage, and reluctantly he decided that he must be content with them, though it pained him to have to leave two chests behind.

He returned to the squire's room, cleaned up the blood on the table to his satisfaction, made the bed and carried the candle and tankard to the kitchen, having locked the door of the room behind him. In the kitchen he put on his own great-coat and hat, took the dummy-figure he had already prepared from its hiding-place in a cupboard, and went out to the carriage.

As he went back to close and lock the entrance door, he was seized with a desire to make certain that he had left no trace of his work behind him in the bedroom. It was fortunate that he did so, for he discovered that he had forgotten to extinguish the candle by which he had worked, and that its wick was bent over, carrying the flame perilously near to some silk hangings. In another few minutes it must have fallen on to them and set them ablaze, and the manor with it. Hastily he extinguished it, and finding his way across the room by a bright beam of moonlight falling through a window he made for the door.

He was but a yard or two from the door when he was startled by loud bangs behind him, and he heard Squire Bathurst's voice calling out, "Let me out! Let me out!"

He slammed-to the door behind him, and with heart pounding and cold sweat breaking on his brow, he rushed, half-falling, down the staircase, locked the door and flung himself on to the carriage.

Across the park, on the brittle frosty air came the bells of the church clock striking the hour—midnight.

Urging the half-starved horse with whip and words, he drove the carriage down the drive. But neither horse nor carriage were equal to what was demanded of them, and less than a mile on the other side of the village the horse gave a sigh, stumbled and collapsed between the shafts, dead, like its master; and as the carriage stopped

suddenly thus, with slow, sharp-sounding rending noises, the floor-boards gave way under the weight of the chests.

Frightened out of his wits by the predicament he was now in, the valet wrenched open the lid of one of the chests, filled his pockets with gold coins, and drastically changing his plans set out on foot for Southampton.

The carriage and its contents were discovered not long after dawn by a farmer, who rode post-haste to the magistrate, Sir George Bushnell, who hurried to the spot. Examining the dummy found with the chests, he believed he knew at once what had happened, and rode straight to Itchells Manor. Having ordered an entrance to be gained to the house, and finding neither the squire nor his valet, as he had expected, he gave instructions for a "Hue and Cry" to be raised throughout the county, with special attention to be paid to the London and Southampton roads—the quarry, the valet.

Giuseppe Mancini was arrested in Southampton docks as he was trying to find a ship to carry him to France. Before his trial at Winchester assizes he made a full confession. The sentence of death he accepted with resignation.

"It is the just retribution of Squire Bathurst's spirit," he told the chaplain to whom he made his last confession.

Alexander Bathurst's assets now passed to his two sisters. Since both had married well and had households established in their husbands' family homes, an arrangement was reached whereby it was agreed that when the second son of Chloë Bathurst, Lady Foxendean, came of age, he should take over Itchells, live in the manor and manage the estate. This involved some complicated apportioning of the late squire's possessions, so that the sisters should receive a fair division after the arrangement had been taken into consideration, but all was done amicably and caused not the slightest dissension.

As Martin Foxendean was still a young boy, the house at Itchells was left unoccupied for several years. However, a couple were installed as caretakers, whose duty it was to keep all in order. A bailiff was put in to oversee the management of the estate, and after several years of hard work Itchells at last reverted to its original good shape.

The choice of Martin Foxendean as lord of Itchells Manor proved a wise one. From the time that he took occupation of the estate in 1735, for the next eighty years or so, he and his descendants gave it

the attention which former generations of Bathursts had lavished upon it. There was one great difference, however: the endowment of the estate with a portion of Squire Alexander's South Sea hoard obviated the intermittent financial difficulties which had bedevilled the Bathurst squires.

There can be but little doubt but that the Foxendeans would have continued as lords of Itchells Manor had not misfortune overtaken them in the early years of the nineteenth century. The then owner, Charles Foxendean, like his seventeenth-century forebear, fathered only one son among the bevy of daughters. This caused the family no anxiety, for the boy was strong and healthy and had every prospect of reaching maturity and marrying. At nineteen he was a robust and lively young man, restless, for ever seeking some diversion with which to satisfy his passion for physical activity. He was quickly absorbing the intricacies of estate management, but Itchells was too small to accommodate two strong-charactered Foxendeans, and hoping thereby to provide him with an interest for a year or two until maturity calmed his son down a little, Charles Foxendean proposed that he should embark upon the Grand Tour. To this the young man agreed, and in the spring of 1814 he crossed to the Continent.

The following year Richard Foxendean was in Austria when the news arrived of Napoleon Bonaparte's escape from Elba, and his arrival in France. Immediately young Foxendean set out for Belgium and there applied for, and was granted, a commission in the Duke of Wellington's army. On 18 June, 1815, he went into action at Waterloo, and shortly before six o'clock in the evening was killed defending the farm-house at La Haye Sainte.

Charles Foxendean never recovered from the shock of his son's death, and in the spring of 1818 he died. His widow, having no inclination to be burdened with the management of the estate, decided to dispose of it, and it was acquired by a family called Lefroy. For some reason or other which the records do not disclose, the Lefroys left the manor-house in the charge of caretakers for five years, and did not enter into occupation themselves until 1823.

They were the first "outsiders" to occupy Itchells for nearly three hundred years, and perhaps the fact that they were not of Bathurst stock has some bearing on their experiences throughout the greater part of the century. For until they acquired the place there is no record of the haunting of the house, which began within a month or two of their moving in.

Among their domestic staff was a young housemaid called

Margaret Smilie. Meg's parents lived in the village, and her father and brothers were employed on the estate, as previous Smilies had been for several generations. She was a happy-natured, level-headed girl of eighteen, physically sturdy and bright mentally. As Mrs Lefroy later said of her, "Meg Smilie had both feet firmly planted on the ground, and was the last person to succumb to imaginings."

Proud of their new possession, the Lefroys were naturally anxious to show it off to friends and relatives, so about Eastertide, 1823, they arranged a house-party for a dozen guests. This number meant that every bedroom in the house would be occupied.

Though the spring had come with bright sunshine and dry days that year, by evening the temperature dropped and there were several nights of sharp ground frost. The house, having been empty for so long, had not yet warmed itself, so to prevent her guests from suffering discomfort Mrs Lefroy had given orders for fires to be lit in all rooms from four o'clock.

It was the duty of the housemaids to bank up the fires for the night shortly before the guests retired, and they began their rounds for this purpose between half-past ten and quarter to eleven. So it was that Meg Smilie came into one of the bedrooms allotted to her shortly before eleven o'clock.

The fire had burned rather low, and she realized that if she made it up with dust in the condition it was in she would stand a good chance of putting it out altogether. So kneeling down before the hearth, she put on a log and began to blow some life into the embers with a pair of bellows. She was tired and would be glad to get to bed; nevertheless, as she blew on the fire, she hummed a tune to herself.

Presently her efforts were rewarded; the log burst into flame and was soon burning merrily. Carefully she arranged round it some smallish pieces of coal, and on these blew also, until they had caught.

It was as she was gingerly covering the whole conflagration with coal-dust that the banging began. At first she thought it must be Jess Richards making up the fire in the room below, but when the knocks continued in groups of three or four, now slow and measured, now quick and imperious, that she realized it could not be Jess, for no one in their right mind would treat a fire so. Besides, the sounds now seemed to be coming from too nearby for them to originate downstairs.

Puzzled, she surveyed the massive chimney-piece. (Only one other room in the house had a similar "piece", and that was the room above.) As she did so, another series of knockings began, and there

could be no doubt that they were coming from the left-hand side of the fire-place, just above her head.

Cool and level-headed though Meg was, she felt the blood in her veins beginning to run cold, the skin tightening across her skull, ice forming in her cheeks and her hands begin to tremble. For one or two terrible moments she imagined that she had been rooted to the spot, for she wished to get to her feet, yet her limbs would not obey the commands of her will.

The sounds of someone breathing heavily near to her were so loud and close that she thought for a brief second that she could feel the rush of air on the nape of her neck. Momentarily she was on the verge of panic, from which reason saved her as she realized that what she was hearing was the sound of her own breathing.

"Silly girl!" she told herself aloud, with a shamefaced laugh. "Pull yourself together, do!"

Taking a deep breath to quiet the pounding of her heart, she began to get up from her knees. As she did so, the heel of her shoe caught in the hem of her dress, and to save herself from stumbling headlong into the fire she put out a hand to the side of the chimney-piece, and steadied herself. But while her hand still pressed the brickwork, the knockings began again, and she felt distinctly the bricks under her hand tremble.

She drew back her hand as if she had been burned, and now all her fear returned, she stooped to pick up her pail and began to hurry from the room. Before she was half-way to the door, a man's voice called to her from the fire-place, "Let me out! Let me out!"

It was too much! With a cry, she dropped the pail and fire-irons and ran from the room, pulling the door shut after her with a bang, which only served to heighten her fear. Though normally she would have taken the back-stairs, the main staircase was nearer, and throwing obedience to her mistress's orders to the wind, she scurried down the carpeted stairs.

The noise of the falling pail and irons, and her shriek, had been heard throughout the house, and as she came to the last leg of the staircase she saw that all the guests were crowding from the drawing-room into the hall, and that some of the other servants had joined them from their quarters.

The sight of the anxious faces, and the sound of Mr Lefroy's voice calling up to her, asking what was amiss, restored her courage a little. But as she steadied herself by the bannister, suddenly she seemed to be pushed aside roughly, and as she began to stumble down

the remaining steps, she heard a avoice saying, "Oh, my God! Oh, my God!"

By the time that James Lefroy, one of the sons of the house, who had hurried forward to help her, caught her in his arms, she was in a dead faint. As he picked her up and began to carry her towards the drawing-room, the heavy front door blew open. An icy blast of night air swept in, and as the startled guests turned to see what had happened the door swung too with a loud bang, as quickly as it had opened.

A silence had fallen on the still company, and everyone there afterwards declared that they had heard a carriage moving off down the drive. Certainly Mr Lefroy heard it and he jumped towards the door to see who it could be. But when he tried to pull open the door he found that it had jammed, and that all his strength could not move it.

He rushed from the door to the drawing-room, and pulled back the curtains at one of the windows from which the whole length of the drive could be seen. Outside, under the bright moonlight, not a twig or bush or tree stirred, and the drive was completely empty.

Bewildered he returned to the hall, where Jevons, the butler, had gone to the door and was trying to open it.

"It will need tools," Mr Lefroy told him. "It's jammed fast."

"Yes, sir," Jevons agreed quietly. "May I have a private word with you, sir?"

As he went towards the servants' quarters, Mr Lefroy followed him, even more puzzled. When they reached the butler's pantry, Jevons closed the door behind him.

"What is it, Jevons?" Mr Lefroy asked, impressed by his butler's solemnity.

"I thought it best not to say so before the guests, sir," Jevons replied. "They are perturbed enough already. But the door is not jammed, sir. The key is turned in the lock."

"Are you sure, Jevons?"

"Perfectly, sir."

"But how can that be? Did any of the others go near the door after I went into the drawing-room?"

"No, sir."

"But I did not turn the lock, Jevons, I swear."

"No, sir. You couldn't, the key is still hanging on its hook to the right of the door, sir, where I keep it during the day."

"Are you quite sure you are not mistaken, Jevons?"

"I am quite certain, sir." He opened a drawer and took out a large key. "Here is the spare key, sir. I suggest that I take tools and feign unjamming the door, and under cover of my activities, sir, do you put this key in the lock and turn it. You will see that I am right."

And so he proved to be.

By this time Meg had been carried to a sofa in the drawing-room and restored to her senses. At first she could not speak for weeping, and though she was still trembling Lefroy asked her if she could walk to his study. She nodded, and Mrs Lefroy, supporting the girl, helped her from the room.

"I am sorry," Lefroy apologized to his guests. "The girl has obviously had a fright, and we must discover the cause of it. Will you forgive us if we desert you for a few moments?"

Above the murmur of assent, one of the men asked, "Whose carriage was it, Tom?"

"I didn't recognize it," Lefroy lied.

"Are you sure you saw a carriage, Tom?" someone else asked.

"I couldn't be sure. I thought so. Let's not frighten the ladies any more, gentlemen. Excuse me."

By the time he reached his study Mrs Lefroy had been able to coax Meg into talking. When the girl had finished her story, Mrs Lefroy said: "I'll have Mrs Smart make you a posset, and bring it to you in bed. Jessie sleeps with you, doesn't she, so you won't be alone. If anyone asks what frightened you, say you thought you saw a large rat."

When the butler had taken the girl away, Mrs Lefroy turned to her husband.

"Well, Tom, what do you make of it?" she asked.

"I don't know, my dear. Have you ever heard that the house is haunted?"

"Never. If it had been any of the other girls I would have said they were imagining things. But Meg has both feet firmly on the ground, and would be the last to succumb to imaginings."

"The rat was a good idea, Bess," Mr Lefroy said. "We will tell the others that that is what it was."

Though the guests pretended to be satisfied with this explanation, secretly they were not convinced, for it did not explain the sounds of the carriage moving down the drive, which all said they had heard. But so that their hosts should not be embarrassed, they did not refer to it when the Lefroys did not. But there was not one of them who was sorry when their visit came to an end.

The effect on Meg had been deeper than Mrs Lefroy had believed

it would be, and next morning the girl was all for giving in her notice. Fearing the effect this might have on the rest of her staff, Mrs Lefroy pleaded and coaxed, until at last Meg told her, "Very well, ma'am, I will stay so long as I never have to set foot in that room again."

"That I promise you," Mrs Lefroy replied. "Miss Nightingale leaves us today, and we will close up the room and not use it again."

As it turned out, the closing of the room had a not entirely satisfactory result, for knockings were heard in other parts of the house for several years, and on account of them many of the maid-servants left hurriedly. Then there seems to have followed a period of quiescence for Alexander Bathurst's ghost, for it is not until 1840 that there are further reports of it.

It would seem also that Meg's experience had not been remembered after nearly twenty years, for William Lefroy, now squire, had not been at home on the night of that occurrence, and if he was ever told, he had forgotten, for when a Captain Anstey arrived to stay he found the family in a state of upset.

"I hope you will be comfortable, John," his host greeted him. "But the truth is, we seem to have a ghost, and we cannot get servants to stay with us. So, please, overlook any shortcomings there may appear to be in our hospitality."

The mention of the ghost aroused the Captain's curiosity, and he insisted that William Lefroy should tell him all about it.

"I'd like to hear him," he said at last. "I hope you have put me in his room."

"Of course not," replied Lefroy.

"Then please do so."

"Nothing would make me, John. But what I will agree to, if you are game, is that we should both keep watch and try to find out what really happens, for to tell the truth none of us have heard it."

So the two men kept watch in the room. For three nights nothing happened, but on the fourth, about eleven o'clock, the bangings began.

"They come from the room downstairs," Anstey said when they had inspected the fire-place. "There must be some shaft which carries up the sound."

They listened for a time, and the knockings came again, slowly sometimes, urgently at others.

"Let's go downstairs and investigate," Anstey suggested. "And if we find nothing there, I'll wager that a bird has built its nest in the chimney-stack."

So saying he made for the door, followed by William Lefroy. As Anstey reached out his hand to the door-knob, both men were brought up suddenly by a voice demanding, "Let me out! Let me out!"

Though he had turned round, Anstey had kept his hand on the knob, and as he stood looking in bewilderment at his friend he felt himself being roughly pushed on one side, and the door was pulled open by some unseen hand, and then swung-to with a bang.

"God in heaven! he exclaimed. "No birds, William. You are haunted!"

"Listen!" Lefroy said sharply.

From the drive below them came the sounds of a carriage being driven away. They ran to the window and peered down—but the drive was empty.

The Brown Lady of Raynham

One of England's most celebrated ghosts is the wraith of a lady whose portrait used to hang in a room at Raynham Hall, Norfolk, the seat of the Marquesses of Townshend. According to the best authorities, she was Lady Dorothy Townshend, and her ghost which has haunted this particular stately home for nearly two hundred and fifty years once caused considerable affright to George IV, was shot at by the author Frederick Marryat, and later successfully photographed.

The lady, who has achieved such success on the spectral plane, had, according to her portrait, large and shining eyes, and was dressed in brown with yellow trimmings and a ruff around her throat. A harmless enough looking lady of the early eighteenth century, except when seen by candlelight, when a strange almost evil expression was seen upon her face. It was also said that when the candlelight was thrown upon the portrait from some angles the flesh appeared to shrink from the face and the eyes to disappear giving it almost the semblance of a skull.

This portrait was sold among the Townshend heirlooms at Christies in 1904 and was called "The Brown Lady—Dorothy Walpole, wife of the second and most famous Marquess of Townshend".

Dorothy Walpole was the daughter of Robert Walpole, Member of Parliament for Houghton in Norfolk. Her brother was the great Sir Robert Walpole, who was England's first Prime Minister, though the office was not recognized in those days.

When Dorothy was a young girl her father became the guardian to Viscount Charles Townshend, whose father died when the boy was thirteen. In the Walpole home two future statesmen were growing up and maturing, for young Charles Townshend achieved greatness in the political sphere as well.

There was also the beginning of a rather sad romance. Dorothy fell in love with Charles, but her father, so the legend went, forbade the match, for he did not want it to be thought that he was trying to gain a family advantage by marrying his daughter to his ward. Lord Townshend married a daughter of Baron Pelham of Laughton, but she died in 1711. A year or so later he married Dorothy Walpole, his first love.

But Dorothy in her disappointment had apparently gone off the rails. Unknown to Lord Townshend, already a rising young statesman, his mind fully occupied with such matters of high state as the negotiation of the Treaty of Utrecht, Dorothy had not apparently conducted herself as a young unmarried Georgian lady should. She had in fact acquired a somewhat tarnished reputation, having been, it was said, the mistress of a well-known profligate by the name of Lord Wharton, who had the doubtful distinction of being bitingly satirized by Pope. Wharton later fled the country, and his creditors, and lived in eccentric and disreputable exile, throwing in his lot with the Old Pretender.

Dorothy Walpole was twenty-six when she married Lord Townshend. The legend adds substance to the rumours of her reputation, for according to it there was an estrangement between her and her husband, who, having belatedly discovered about the Wharton episode, kept her locked in her apartments at Raynham Hall and treated her so badly that in 1726 she died of a broken heart. According to another story it was a broken neck, which she acquired by falling down the grand staircase at Raynham. A contemporary record, however, says she died of smallpox.

At that time her husband and her brother were ruling England between them, so she was a lady of some importance, and if her death had been, to say the least, inconvenient for someone, it is possible that the actual cause of it was concealed. The bewailing of her ghost ever since would suggest that this was so.

In 1730, after differences with his boyhood friend and brother-in-law, Walpole, Townshend retired to Raynham and devoted the rest of his life to agriculture.

We may never know whether Lady Dorothy Townshend died of smallpox, of a broken heart, or by falling—or being pushed—down

Raynham's grand staircase. Whatever unsettled her spirit for all time is something of a mystery. But, however she met her death, her ghost soon became the terror of the visitors and servants at the Hall. She has been seen by a number of persons for the better part of two and a half centuries, and is in fact an extremely well-established ghost—one of the few who have been tackled by both firearms and camera.

It is no use trying to shoot a ghost, of course. The celebrated author who tried to do so should have known better. But the photographer was more successful and achieved one of the rare ghost pictures which all the experts agreed had not been faked.

For her photograph the Brown Lady seems to have appeared in her bridal dress, though on the occasion of the foolish and rather ungallant attempt to shoot her she was dressed in brown as in her portrait.

The Townshends became marquesses in 1786, and their seat at Raynham Park, which is about four miles to the south-west of Fakenham, was one of the country's great houses, where royalty as well as the aristocracy were lavishly entertained. There George IV visited the Townshends when he was Regent, and the Brown Lady frightened him out of his wits.

His Royal Highness awoke Raynham in the middle of the night, saying that a lady dressed in brown"with dishevelled hair and a face of ashy paleness"had appeared at his bedside in the State bedroom. "I will not pass another hour in this accursed house,"he declared to the accompaniment of many vigorous Regency oaths."For tonight I have seen that which I hope to God I may never see again."

The Brown Lady, it was becoming clear, was no social asset. In those days of princely hospitality and great house parties it was a serious business for the family ghost to frighten away the First Gentleman of Europe.

They told a story of how some gentlemen of the household sat up for three nights in the corridors where the Brown Lady had been seen. They had gamekeepers stationed at the doors and played écarté to pass the time. On the third night they saw her.

She appeared to be coming through the wall at them. One of the gentlemen and the gamekeepers were petrified with terror, but the other gallant, bolder than the rest, stood resolutely in the path of the Brown Lady as she approached, but she passed right through him in a puff of icy smoke and disappeared through the wall beyond, leaving her bold challenger utterly devastated by his uncanny experience.

The Brown Lady made another appearance in 1835. It was appropriately enough at Christmas-time and there was a large house-party at Raynham Hall.

Among the guests of Lord and Lady Charles Townshend were Colonel and Mrs Loftus. Colonel Loftus was Lord Townshend's cousin and was also the brother of Lady Townshend. It was the practice of the aristocracy in those days to marry within narrow circles, and marriage between cousins was very common.

Loftus and another guest named Hawkins lingered late one night over a protracted game of chess and finally went upstairs. They saw the Brown Lady standing outside the door of Lady Townshend's room. The apparition turned and walked along the corridor, pursued by Loftus, but the old warrior had to give up, and the Brown Lady soon melted from his sight.

This night Loftus saw it only dimly, but the following night he came face to face with it on the grand staircase—a stately lady, he said, in rich brocade with a coif on her hair. "Although her features were clearly defined, where her eyes should have been were nothing but dark hollows.

During that spooky Christmas at Raynham the host himself reluctantly admitted to having seen the ghost. "I am forced to believe in it," he told one of the house guests, "for she ushered me to my room last night."

But the ghost caused great alarm among the servants, some of whom had seen it, and were horror-stricken at the sight of her face, which consisted of dark hollows and was truly macabre. The servants were all for leaving.

Normally there was no servant problem in those days, but a really frightening supernatural apparition could cause one. His lordship in desperation had all the locks changed at Raynham and even employed policemen disguised as manservants in case the ghost turned out to be a practical joker, though Townshend had little hope that this was the case. Certainly no practical joker was found and the Brown Lady continued to haunt.

Townshend then summoned the assistance of Captain Frederick Marryat, a local celebrity, who had recently settled in Norfolk at Langham Manor. Marryat, who had spent years at sea, had become famous for his sea stories and books for boys, such as *Mr Midshipman Easy* and *The Children of the New Forest*.

Captain Marryat, by no means the superstitious sailor, did not believe in ghosts. He thought some sort of trick was being played upon the Townshend family. He had a theory that it was connected

with the smugglers and poachers who abounded in that part of Norfolk in those days, and who were, he thought, using some old ruined buildings near the Hall for their hiding places. He was sure that there were ruffians lurking around who would have much to gain by frightening the Townshend family away from the Hall.

The story was later told in Marryat's biography, written by his daughter, Florence Marryat, herself a novelist with a keen interest in psychic phenomena.

Marryat was invited to stay at Raynham and he insisted upon sleeping in the room where hung the portrait of the Brown Lady— a splendid bedroom panelled in cedarwood.

How serious the celebrated author was about his theory that the apparitions were caused by some cunning trick of desperate smugglers anxious to frighten the Townshends away is open to question. The Townshend family had lived at Raynham for well over a century and the Brown Lady was part of the Townshend legend. She had even scared George IV out of the house in the middle of the night. It was not likely that anyone would believe that the Townshends, having endured the ghost for so long, would be scared away from their historic country seat by a few smugglers. It is not seriously to be supposed that Captain Marryat, that professional romancer, was foolish enough to entertain such improbable fancies.

Anyway, he got his coveted invitation to the Hall and ghost-hunting was good fun, so he enjoyed himself.

One night, after he had retired to his room and undressed except for his trousers and singlet, Lord Charles Townshend's two young nephews knocked on his door and asked him if he would go into their room and give an opinion about a new gun which one of them had just acquired.

During the evening there had been much talking and joking about the Brown Lady, and as he left his room Marryat picked up his loaded pistol, saying laughingly to the two young men: "In case we meet the Brown Lady."

After the Captain had inspected the gun, the two young men offered, in the same joking mood, to escort him safely back to his room— "in case you are kidnapped by the Brown Lady."

It was a long, dark corridor, and the lights had been extinguished, and as the three men walked along it they saw a woman approaching them carrying a lamp. They were in that part of the house reserved for the men guests, and the sight of the approaching woman caused them a little unease, especially Marryat in his vest and trousers. But

the Hall was full and it was possible that a lady had lost her way in the labyrinthine corridors and staircases of Raynham.

There was only one thing to do, consistent with modesty and gentlemanly behaviour, and that was to hide. The three of them stepped quickly into the open doorway of an empty room and stood there in the darkness waiting for the lady to pass by.

But the lady did not pass by. She stopped at the doorway, and when the three men saw the manner in which she was dressed they had no doubt at all as to who she was. Her resemblance to the portrait in Captain Marryat's bedroom was unmistakable—"the waxy countenance, the large shining eyes and the noiseless step". There was no reference this time to the hollows in the face. The spectral lady was plainly not in her macabre mood that night.

The Brown Lady held the lighted lamp before her face and then, said Marryat, looked straight into his eye and smiled at him. But it was a diabolical, a wicked smile, which so alarmed Marryat that he stepped into the corridor, pistol in hand, and discharged it point blank at her.

As the bullet passed through her insubstantial form, still evilly and mysteriously smiling, she disappeared, leaving nothing but a wisp of smoke, and a bullet-hole in the door behind her.

After that Captain Marryat entertained no doubts at all about the reality of the ghost at Raynham Hall. But the Brown Lady herself must have been affronted by such ungallant behaviour, for she did not return to her old haunts for many a long year after Marryat himself had joined her in the shades, which he did in 1848.

What should Captain Marryat have done? To shoot at a ghost is pointless. It has been said in his defence that he genuinely thought it was someone playing a prank, but if he had thought that his action was no more pardonable. One doesn't shoot people who play pranks, not even when they are played upon the aristocracy.

It is far more probable that Marryat was scared out of his wits and panicked, believing he was seeing the famous ghost and that his theories about the desperate smuggling characters had been wrong.

At all events, the Brown Lady of Raynham Hall, after her encounter with Captain Marryat in the 1830s, remained sulking on the eternal shores for the rest of the century and more before she troubled the haunted staircases and galleries of Raynham again.

It was in November, 1926, when she was next reported. The then Marquis Townshend, a boy at the time, encountered her on the famous staircase. With the Marquis was another boy, who also

saw the phantom. The Brown Lady's return caused something of a newspaper sensation. Both boys were carefully questioned. Neither had heard of the ghost story, or seen the picture, the family legend presumably having been all but forgotten. Their description of the Brown Lady was apparently the traditional one. It was not considered a boyish prank.

Ten years later the Brown Lady provided an even greater sensation by getting herself photographed.

Lady Townshend wanted a series of pictures taken of the interior of Raynham Hall and she commissioned Mr Indre Shira, a professional photographer, to take them. On the afternoon of 19 September, 1936, he and a Mr Provand were taking flash-light pictures of the grand staircase. Mr Provand was wielding the camera while Mr Shira was standing a little behind him, casting his professional eye upon the splendid staircase.

Provand took a picture and was putting in another plate and re-setting the camera and flash equipment, when Shira, looking up the first flight of the staircase, saw what he described as a vapoury form gradually assuming the appearance of a woman draped and veiled in some diaphanous material.

Down the staircase the figure glided with floating steps, and the excited Shira told his companion to aim his camera and get a shot quickly. Here was something which would make a sensational picture.

Provand had not seen the apparition, owing perhaps to the effect of the photo-flash, and wondered what had got Shira so excited. Nevertheless he aimed his camera at the required spot and took another picture. After the flash the spectre presumably disappeared.

Provand then asked Shira what all the fuss was about, and when Shira told him that he had seen a ghost descending the staircase, Provand pooh-poohed the idea. It must have been an optical illusion, he said, the effect of the flash, or perhaps even someone playing a mirror trick from the gallery above. Shira thereupon bet Provand five pounds that the ghost would appear on the plate.

Shira won his bet and the Brown Lady came out on the plate. This time she was not in her traditional brown brocade, but appeared, though only in outline, as a bride in white, enveloped in a clinging veil.

This photograph was reproduced in the magazine *Countrylife*, dated 16 December, 1936. It naturally aroused considerable controversy. A number of experts examined the plate, and all agreed that there was no fake about it. The figure—whatever it was—had

been photographed all right, or at least it appeared on the exposed plate. There was a suggestion that the ghost photograph had been caused by some freak of light or perhaps a flaw in the negative, which of course might be considered a possibility. But to accept this you would have to assume that Mr Shira made up the story, which is an assumption both unwarrantable and improbable, for he would have no reason to do such a thing.

The Brown Lady of Raynham, however, might well consider herself sufficiently well established and attested not to require photographic proof.

The fact that she would have appeared to have put on her wedding gown to pose before Mr Shira and his companion might be said to lend a little colour to one legend about her—that she had been a young and beautiful girl of the eighteenth century and forced to marry an old roué against her will and to endure a horrifying wedding night with him.

It cannot be said for certain that this photograph, if it is of a ghost, is that of the Brown Lady. While ghosts have been known to change their habits, they do not as a rule change their clothes.

The Return of Richard Tarwell

In the first half of the eighteenth century the well-known family of Harris of Heyne made their permanent headquarters at their ancient seat in Devon, not far from the borders of Cornwall. Though not ennobled, the Harrisses were a wealthy family and their broad acres stretched for several miles on every side of the mansion. They occupied a prominent place among the West Country gentry and were greatly respected by the discerning inhabitants of Devon and the neighbouring shires.

At this time, the head of the family, Mr George Harris, held an appointment at the Court of King George II, which obliged him to spend a part of the year in his town house in Sloane Square. When his attendance at Court was required, it was Mr Harris's custom to move the greater part of his establishment to London, leaving only a few servants behind in Devon in the charge of Richard Morris, who had been butler to the family for many years.

While in London to perform his duties in 1730, Mr Harris found among his post one day a letter from Richard Morris. Since he had instructed his butler that he need not bother to communicate except on a matter of urgency, Mr Harris broke the seals with some slight degree of trepidation and with a strong premonition that the butler's letter could only contain bad news. His premonition proved right. The news was of a kind which made him summon his carriage and hurry to the office of the Lord Great Chamberlain, whom he begged to act as his intercessor with His Majesty for permission to absent himself from Court for two or three weeks as he had totally

163

unexpected personal affairs to attend to at his home in Devon.

When the Lord Great Chamberlain heard the nature of this business, he agreed at once to seek an audience of the King, and having sent in his request, was informed that His Majesty would receive him at once. The King, too, was sympathetic to his petitioner's request, and early next morning Mr Harris set out for Devon, and arrived at his home five days later.

As soon as he had refreshed himself after his journey, he summoned the half-dozen servants, headed by Morris, to him in his study.

Now, Morris," he said, when the two footmen, the cook and two housemaids were drawn up before him. "Tell me what happened."

"One night some three weeks ago, sir," the butler began, "I was wakened in the night by noises which I was sure were coming from my pantry, which I do not need to tell you is below the room in which I sleep. At first I thought I must be mistaken, for immediately before I had retired for the night I had made my rounds of the house, as I always do, and checked that every window and door were secured. However, when the noises continued and it was certain that someone was in the room below, thinking it must be one of the servants who had no business to be there, I decided to go down to see what was afoot.

"When I came to the passage outside my pantry, it was clear to me that I had not been mistaken, for a light in the pantry was shining under the door. I also heard men's voices talking quietly, and was convinced that Eames and Barnwell, the two footmen, were going about some act, which I believed to be nefarious because of the time of night, the fact that no one is allowed in the pantry without first having asked my permission, and because of other sounds issuing from the room."

"What sounds?" Mr Harris interrupted him.

"Sounds which seemed to indicate to me, sir," the butler continued, "that one of the strong-boxes in which the silver plate is stowed was being broken into."

"Did you really suspect that the voices you heard were those of the footmen?" Harris again interrupted him.

"There were two men's voices, sir, and they were talking low so that I could not recognize them, but I fear that the thought came at once into my mind that it must be the footmen, because I could not imagine who else it could be. I am sorry now that I should have harboured such suspicions, since I realize that in thinking so I slandered their good names. I have apologized again and again, sir, but both of them have insisted on handing in their notices."

"Is that so?"Harris asked the two young men sternly. They looked embarrassed and nodded. "Then you are being very foolish. Morris has apologized, but you must admit that it was a justifiable mistake in the circumstances."

"With respect, sir, I do not think so,"Eames replied. "Mr Morris, by his suspicions, has virtually accused us of being thieves, or at least of being capable of dishonesty and of treachery to you and the family."

"What have you to say to that, Barnwell?"

"I agree, sir, with every word. We have been in your service now, myself for two years and Eames for nearly five,"Barnwell replied. "Mr Morris should know us well enough by this time to realize that our loyalty to the family, sir, is no less than his own, for all he has served you upwards of thirty years."

"I still think it was a justifiable mistake,"Harris told them. "Will you reconsider your decision if I add my apologies to his? I do so abominate having to engage new servants. Well?"

"I don't know, sir,"Eames said stubbornly.

"Well think about it, and we will talk of it again later. Continue, Morris."

The butler went on to explain that because he had (wrongly) supposed that the men in the pantry were the footmen, that it had not occurred to him to go for help. He was the only other male in the house, and the maidservants would have been too frightened to be of any assistance.

"But you must have known that whoever was in the pantry doing what you were sure they were doing—namely, breaking into the strong-boxes—would physically attack you or anyone else who interrupted them?"Harris commented.

The butler replied that that had occurred to him in the light of day, but that at the time he thought only of protecting his master's property.

"What you should have done was to arouse two of the maids and sent them post-haste to the village to fetch the constables, while you kept watch to see what the intruders did or where they went."

"Yes, sir, I realize that now,"the butler agreed, a tone of anguish in his voice.

"Mr Morris is wrong in saying that we were the only males in the house, sir," Barnwell said. "The boy was in the cubby-hole opposite Mr Morris's own room, so far as he knew then."

"The boy?"Harris asked.

"I engaged a young lad of fourteen, sir, a day or two after you

had gone, to help me in the pantry with the silver," the butler explained. "He came to the house one day with his father, whom I knew of slightly by reputation as a sound and honest man, to ask whether there was an opening for the lad. The other boy, Franklin, left to join the household of Mr Soames, the day you departed for London, so I offered this boy, Richard Tarwell, the position."

"Where is he now?" Harris asked. "Why isn't he here?"

"He's disappeared, sir," Morris replied.

"That night, sir," Barnwell added.

Seeing that he was in danger of confusing the butler with his interruptions, Harris determined to wait until the man had finished his relation before he asked more questions and told the man so.

Morris then described how he had approached the door of the pantry quietly, and then flung it open to take them, he hoped, by surprise. To his amazement, however, the two men he found there were not the two footmen, but men he had never seen before; and with them was the boy, Richard Tarwell.

Before he had had time to recover, one of the intruders had jumped on him brandishing an iron bar, and had struck him so hard about the head as to render him unconscious. When he had regained his senses, he found himself securely bound to a chair, and a gag tightly fixed in his mouth. Two of the strong-boxes had had their lids burst open, and he could see that their contents, or at least most of them, had gone.

"Did no one else hear any noise in the night?" Harris asked.

The footmen and the servants shook their heads.

"No, sir," said Mrs Coombes, the cook. "We heard nothing. I got up at seven and called Mary and Joan, as I always do, and went down to the kitchen to prepare breakfast for half-past seven. The two maids came down at about twenty minutes after the hour and busied themselves with some chore or other, and five minutes later the footmen came in. I think it was Eames who remarked, 'Isn't Mr Morris down yet?' and when I said no, he laughed and said, 'Escaped again!'."

"What do you think he meant by that?" Harris probed.

"Mr Morris is very strict about punctuality at meals, sir," the cook told him. "He always comes into the servants' hall, or the kitchen when the family is in London, five minutes before the appointed time, by when all the other servants must be assembled. Once or twice recently in the mornings, the footmen had cut it fine, sir, as they had this particular morning. Or I should say, would have cut it fine if Mr Morris had come in at his usual time.

"Still, I didn't think much about it as I was busy at the stove, until Eames said, 'What's happened to the old man? Has the miracle happened and he's overlain?'

"'He'll be here presently,' I said.'You'd best not draw up until he comes. He dislikes it if he does not sit down first.' So we waited and when ten minutes had gone by I did begin to wonder, so I asked Eames to go up and knock on Mr Morris's door and tell him politely what the time was."

Harris looked at Eames, who took up the tale.

"I went up to Mr Morris's room and knocked on the door, and when after two or three knockings I got no answer, I opened the door and looked in. He was not there, but I noticed that his bed had been slept in, When I came out of the room, I noticed that the boy's cubby-hole was empty, too, and recalling that the boy had not been in the kitchen waiting with us, as he usually was, I thought that perhaps Mr Morris and Tarwell had risen early and were working in the butler's pantry and had overlooked the time. So, I went downstairs to the pantry and found Mr Morris gagged and bound to the chair as he has told you, sir."

"The next thing we knew,"Mrs Coombes said,"was Eames's voice shouting something that sounded like *Help*! Barnwell rushed out of the kitchen first and the girls and I followed hard on his heels. When we got to the pantry, Eames had released Mr Morris and was just loosening the gag. Mr Morris's first words were, 'We've been robbed! Go for the constables!'

"'You go,' Eames said to Barnwell, and when Barnwell had run out, he helped Mr Morris to his feet. Mr Morris was very upset, and when he saw the strong-boxes were quite empty, I thought he was going to collapse."

"Did the constables come quickly?"Harris asked.

"Within the half-hour, sir. I told them what had happened, and what was missing, and that the boy, too, appeared to be gone. They began to make inquiries at once, but up to now they've uncovered no trace, sir."

"And what of the boy?"

"No trace of Tarwell either, sir. His father protests that his son is no thief. But I saw the boy in the pantry with the robbers, sir, with my own eyes."

"How had the thieves gained entry to the house?"Harris asked. Was a window broken?"

"No, sir. Through the side door, which was unlocked. The boy must have known they were coming and let them in,"Morris said.

"And what did they take?"

"The four great silver candle-sticks with the birds," Morris began to enumerate, "three entrée dishes of silver, two silver sauce-boats, the salt-bowls that were presented to Mr Joseph Harris by Her Majesty, Queen Anne . . ."

When he had come to the end of the list, Harris considered briefly. "I suppose it could have been worse," he said. "But it is bad enough. I regret the candle-sticks and the salt-bowls particularly."

"Perhaps they will be recovered," Mrs Coombes suggested.

Harris smiled for the first time. "Perhaps, Mrs Coombes," he replied. "We must hope for the best."

"I blame myself for taking the boy on without making more searching inquiries about his family and his character," the butler said. "But the father seemed honest enough."

"You mustn't blame yourself. God bless my soul, we are not the first family to be burgled, and I dare say we shall not be the last. Well, thank you. I will dine, Mrs Coombes, as soon as you are ready, and I warn you, I am famished. The rest of you may go. I would like Eames and Barnwell to remain."

When the other servants had gone, he looked at the two young men.

"Look here," he said. "I want you to change your minds about your notices. Morris is growing old, and he takes upon himself great responsibilities when I and the family are absent. You must do your best to excuse him."

"He at once thought we were the thieves," Eames reminded him. "It's that that sticks in my gullet, sir."

"Yes, I know. I add my apologies to his yet again. Would it make any difference if I also added a guinea to your year's wages?"

There was a brief silence, then Eames said with a smile, "Yes, sir".

"And you Barnwell?"

"Well yes, sir."

"Right. Then that's settled! I do so abominate having new servants about me, especially footmen. You may go now."

As they walked across to the door, he called after them, "Did the boy strike you that he might be a thief or a person likely to be in league with thieves?"

"No, sir," Eames turned and said. "He seemed a good, honest, simple boy, eager to please."

"He was happy enough, too, sir," Barnwell added. "He'd only been here a few weeks, but he was not backward in playing harmless jokes on Eames and me."

After two days of making his own inquiries, which revealed nothing, Mr Harris returned to London and completed his tour of duty at Court. Four months later, he and his family and household returned to Devon, there to learn that the authorities had lost all interest in the case and that they must resign themselves to the loss of their property.

Since they were tired after their long journey, Mr Harris suggested that he should pass the night on the bed that was always kept made up in his dressing-room, leaving to his wife the exclusive comfort of the four-poster. Mrs Harris, who was even more exhausted, had no objection, and shortly after dinner announced that she was going to retire.

"I'll go the rounds with Morris," Mr Harris told her, "and follow you up."

As the two men went round the house, Harris noted the meticulous care with which his butler examined every window-latch and shutter, and the lock on every outside door, even going to the extent of locking some of the inner doors as well. They spoke little, according to their usual custom while performing their nightly ritual, for it was at the end of the day and both were anxious to get to their beds. He supposed it must be one of the effects of the robbery that made him this evening take more notice of the butler's routine than he ever remembered doing before; for he found himself becoming more and more surprised by the butler's care.

"Have you always gone to these lengths, Morris?" he asked.

"Oh, most certainly, sir."

"Even to the extent of locking the inner doors?"

"Why, yes, sir!" The butler seemed surprised now. "Braunton, your father's butler, always made me do it, sir, for it was upon the late Mr Harris's instructions that the inner doors were locked—after another robbery, sir—and they have been every night for, I suppose, the last forty or fifty years."

"God bless my soul!" Harris exclaimed. "It shows how much I trust you, Morris, for tonight is the first time I have observed you locking the inner doors. Which ones do you lock?"

"Of the inner doors, sir? Those from the ball-room, those from the conservatory into the large drawing-room, those of the large drawing-room into the hall, the door to the servants' quarters, and the door to my pantry, sir."

"Indeed!" remarked Harris.

By this time they had returned to the hall, and saying good night to Morris, Mr Harris began to mount the stairs. As he went, he

heard Morris turning the key in the door closing off the corridor leading to the servants' quarters from the hall.

Mrs Harris was already in bed and had dismissed her maid when he went in to say good night to her.

"Do you know," he remarked as he perched himself on the edge o the great bed, "I've been going round locking up with Morris every night—at least while we're here—for the past thirty years, and I discovered for the first time this evening that besides checking every window and outer door downstairs he actually locks a number of the inner doors?"

"But I could have told you that, my dear," Mrs Harris yawned.

"Yes," he mused, preoccupied with his own thoughts, "even the door to his pantry! Good heavens, I must ask him about that in the morning!" he exclaimed.

"About what, my dear?" his dutiful wife asked.

"Where he keeps the key of the pantry at night after he has locked the door."

"Is it important, dear?"

"Very important!"

"Then I'll remind you in the morning. Kiss me and say good night, and get you to bed. You look as though you have need of some repose."

"Yes, you're right, my dear," he confessed, performed his connubial duties, drew the bed-curtain and went to the dressing-room. Within a quarter of an hour he was himself in bed and on the verge of sleep. Five minutes later, had Mrs Harris herself still been conscious, she would have heard the undeniable sounds of her spouse's unconcern for the problems of the world.

Rarely had Mr Harris slept so soundly; yet in the middle of the night he suddenly awoke. Relating the incident later, he declared that he was in an instant thoroughly wide-awake, though how or why he could never explain.

And by the light of a small lamp he had kept burning, he saw a young lad standing at the foot of his bed.

"Though I had never seen him before," he would say, "I knew at once that he was the boy, Richard Tarwell, who had disappeared on the night of the robbery four or five months previously."

Mr Harris's amazement was extreme, and the thought passed through his mind that the boy must have evaded capture with great cunning by hiding somewhere in the house, the last place anyone would ever think of looking for a fugitive from justice—the very site of his crime.

But he was puzzled, too, by the lad's coming to him now. If he had been an accomplice of the thieves, as Morris swore he had been, his master would surely be the last person he would come to.

Sitting up in bed he demanded, "What do you want with me at this time of night?"

The boy made no reply, but merely beckoned with his finger.

"Are you mute?" Mr Harris demanded now. "Tell me, why have you come to me at this hour?"

Again the boy did not speak, but beckoned once more and then turned and pointed to the door.

Thinking that perhaps the boy had suffered some fright that had deprived him of his speech, and understanding from the signs he made that he wished his master to follow him, Harris, with some feelings of exasperation, got out of bed, partly dressed himself, and taking his sword under his arm, followed the boy, still beckoning and pointing with his arm out of the room.

As he heard his own footsteps padding on the carpet covering the floor of the corridor, he became aware that the boy was moving without any sound whatsoever, despite the fact that he appeared to be wearing boots; and it was now that Harris suddenly began to wonder whether or not the boy was alive or an apparition.

"I felt no fear," he said afterwards, "for the boy, whether alive or spirit seemed to me a gentle creature. My strongest desire was to see where he would lead me and for what purpose."

With the boy leading several paces before him, the two went down the staircase, along a short passage to a side door, which to Harris's still mounting amazement was unlocked and open, though only a short while ago he had watched Morris lock it. So they passed into the park.

The boy led the way for about a hundred yards making for a very large oak, the trunk of which was surrounded and almost hidden by low shrubs and bushes, which had been allowed to grow wild there for time out of mind. At the tree the boy stopped, pointed to the ground with his forefinger, and still having spoken not a word seemed to pass round to the other side of the tree.

It was a bright starlit night, and Harris had been able to see his way without any difficulty since they had left the house. When, however, he followed the boy round the tree he had vanished.

"Richard Tarwell," Harris called out softly. "Where are you? Do you hear me?"

No answer came, nor when he called again. If the boy were alive it would be impossible for him to move through the tangle of

undergrowth without being heard; but though Harris listened intently, he heard no sound at all. He told himself then that it was an apparition he had seen.

Now he must discover what the boy's intention had been in bringing him here, but as there was nothing he could do at this hour, he returned to the house, locking the side door after him when he had gone in. Back in his bed, he did not sleep, but turned over in his mind the best course he should take.

As the first light of dawn began to penetrate the room by the window, whose curtains he had drawn back before getting into bed, he got up and dressed. Going quietly, he found his way to the room where the two footmen, Eames and Barnwell, slept.

When he had reassured them that they had nothing to fear, he said, "I want you to get up and come with me. Go very quietly, for I do not wish to rouse anyone else in the house".

When they joined him at the side door, he had already fetched two spades from the gardener's sheds.

"Take these," he said, "and follow me."

He led them to the oak to which only a short time before the ghost of Richard Tarwell had led him, and pointing to the spot to which the boy had pointed before he had vanished he said, "I want you to dig there".

Though they were puzzled, they asked no questions, but set to with the spades. Within a few minutes Barnwell exclaimed, "There is something buried here!"

"Ah!" Harris exclaimed quietly. "Go carefully, then. I fear you will be shocked as well as surprised by what you will find."

"There is clothing here!" Eames next remarked. Putting aside their spades, the two men knelt down and began to scoop the earth from the shallow hole, uncovering with each handful more and more of the clothing.

"Good God!" they both exclaimed together, as they recognized the coat which, though soiled and mildewed, could now be plainly seen; and Eames explained, "This is the boy's coat."

"And if I am not mistaken," Harris said, "his body will be in it."

Realizing what thoughts must be passing through their minds, as they worked Mr Harris told them briefly what had made him bring them here. "I fear," he said, "that we have been grossly deceived. For many years I have trusted Morris without question. Had anyone come to me and suggested however slightly that he was a dishonest man, I should have told them that they were no longer any friends of mine."

"But I found him tied up, upon my honour, sir!"Eames protested.

"I am not doubting you for a moment," Harris assured him. "What I believe happened was this. Morris had accomplices whom he let into the house. While they were robbing the strong-boxes, the boy came upon them. Naturally, they had to silence him to protect their own skins. Which of them did the terrible deed does not matter, since before the law they are all guilty. You will recall that when I questioned you Morris made no mention of the boy's bed being empty when he left his room, yet he must have noticed it. But he claimed to have been surprised when he found the boy in the pantry. You also corrected him when he said there was no other male in the house. Do you know where he keeps the key of his pantry after he has locked it for the night?"

"Always in the drawer of the commode by his bed," Eames replied.

"Then that fact will convict him more than any other," Harris commented, "because, for anyone to gain access to the pantry with the key, he must have got it from the drawer without disturbing Morris as he slept, a thing which it would be very difficult for an inexperienced boy to perform.

"Say nothing to any of the servants, and particularly to Morris, of what we have discovered. As soon as you have breakfasted, Eames, go at once to the village and bring the constables."

When the constables arrived and Morris was summoned to them and accused, he at first denied the accusation. But when they led him out to the oak, he broke down and confessed. It had happened as Harris had deduced. He had had two accomplices, whom he had let into the house by the side door; the boy had disturbed them and one of the men had attacked him and killed him; all three of them had buried the body under the oak. When they had done this, they talked for a time about what they should do now, and hit upon the plan of gagging Morris and binding him to the chair.

They were to have taken the silver to Plymouth and there disposed of it, sending the butler his share of the proceeds. But they had crossed him; he had heard no word from them.

Morris was found guilty at the next Exeter assizes, sentenced to death and hanged. His accomplices were never found, however, nor any trace discovered of the stolen property.

Every detail of this story is based on the transcript of Morris's trial, at which Harris gave evidence, avowing most solemnly his belief that Richard Tarwell had returned to avenge his own death.

Ghosts of Old France

La Clairon was one of the most famous actresses on the French stage during the reign of Louis XV. She acted in all the great roles of classical tragedy, created many parts in the plays of Voltaire, Marmontel and Saurin, and her talents were praised by Goldsmith and Garrick. She was for many years the toast of Paris theatre-lovers. Rich and elegant gallants from the Court of Versailles patronized her salons. She lived until the ripe age of eighty, and in 1798, a few years before her death, she wrote her memoirs in which she told a remarkable ghost story.

She was born Claire Leris in 1723 in the little town of Condé, near the Belgian frontier of France, the illegitimate daughter of a sergeant of King Louis's army. She made her first stage appearance at the Comédie Italienne when she was thirteen. For some years she lived the life of a demi-mondaine, as a consequence of which she had some difficulty in getting the title role in Racine's tragedy *Phèdre* at the Comédie Française in 1743.

La Clairon was singularly beautiful, and had, said Goldsmith, the most perfect female figure he had ever seen on any stage. She was, as can be imagined, much sought after by the voluptuaries of that luxurious and licentious age. But her ambition was set firmly upon a stage career. She was well aware of her talents in that direction.

It was in the year of her début at the Comédie Française at the age of twenty, when she was in the full bloom of her youthful beauty, that she was very ardently pursued by a young man whom she calls discreetly M. de S—— in her *Memoires d'Hippolyte Clairon*.

Now La Clairon had hosts of admirers. She could have become the mistress of many a rich aristocrat, and no doubt she had been. But her ambition lay in another profession, respectable as well as ancient; and, besides, she confesses, there was something about M. de S—— which quite turned her against him.

He was ashamed of his humble beginnings. His father was a prosperous merchant in Brittany, and M. de S—— had come to Paris to pose as a person of birth and quality, as apparently he was able to, for he had both the education and the manners to enable him to be accepted in the Parisian society of the day. He had realized all his assets and had come to Paris to climb the social ladder. He made a show of lavish living in order to be taken for someone who came from a higher class.

All this he confessed to the forthright Mademoiselle Clairon, without realizing that it was quite the wrong thing to say to her, for she had never troubled to conceal her own even more humble beginnings and wasn't ashamed of them. People took her for what she was, and the fact that she was a lovely and brilliantly talented girl who was taking Paris by storm meant that all society was at her feet. She did not have to indulge in the pretences of M. de S——.

It is likely that M. de S——'s method was the only means by which a man of humble birth could have been accepted in the snobbish society of eighteenth-century Paris. At all events, La Clairon could hardly be blamed for considering his ambition rather ignoble, even though her own mode of life was open to much criticism.

M. de S—— had other disadvantages which repelled the volatile, sought-after young actress. He wanted to have her completely to himself, and take her into the country away from her admirers, so that he could enjoy her by himself. It was not that he was a fascinating and entertaining person, or that his passion for her was romantically exciting. He was not an amusing or sophisticated companion. He was in fact often morose, and his obsession for her had made him more so.

La Clairon, who had no intention of entering into such a relationship with anyone at that particular time in her life, then began to discourage him. The affair had dragged on for a long time. She had known him for more than two years, and it was not that she had been ungenerous with her favours, but his passion for her grew and grew until it was the all-consuming thing of his life, and he was causing her both distress and embarrassment with his terrible jealousy and impossible demands.

Gradually, and with what tact as she could, she took steps to end the association. She refused his invitations, saw less of him, and devoted herself more ardently to her stage career, at which she was having her first great success at this time.

The rejected lover took it very badly indeed. His passion for her completely dominated his life. Without her, he was nothing. He became desperately ill. On top of this, he got into financial troubles. He had entrusted part of his money to his brother-in-law who failed to respond to his urgent requests for funds. M. de S—— would have starved on his sick-bed but for his former mistress, who with a warmness and generosity one would expect from such a girl immediately came to his aid and gave him money to help him out of his difficulties, though she was adamant in her refusal to resume the affair and would not even accept the letters he wrote to her.

She did not realize that her former lover was dying, and on the evening he sent a last pathetic message to her begging her to come round to see him for the last time, just for a few minutes so that he could look upon her once more, she was entertaining friends to a supper party at her house. She would have gone to him, but her friends stopped her, and, not liking to desert her guests, she did not insist.

M. de S——'s only companion as he lay dying was an elderly lady who had befriended him. He died at eleven o'clock, and just at that time La Clairon had been entertaining her guests with some of her delightful singing.

She had finished her song and bowed to the enthusiastic applause, and as the handclaps died away the clock on the mantel struck the hour of eleven. On the final stroke a loud and terrible cry echoed throughout the whole house. The cry seemed to come from the room itself and was one of such appalling, heart-broken anguish that it chilled the blood of all who heard it.

La Clairon herself fainted, having no doubt at all in her mind that her old lover had died and that the cry had in some way come from him and was intended for her to hear. Terrified and not wishing to be alone that night, she persuaded several of her friends to stay with her until morning.

Her friends were perhaps more puzzled at that dreadful cry than she, and when it was heard the following night at the same hour, and the night after, it became the talk of Paris. At first it was thought someone was playing a practical joke, because the cry could be heard not only in the house, but in the street where, night after night, it now was heard not only by her friends and her neighbours,

but also the police, who sought in vain for the person who uttered it. So great was the interest aroused by the strange cries that crowds gathered every night to hear them.

La Clairon had no doubt at all that she was being haunted, and she bitterly regretted that she had not responded to M. de S——'s dying appeal to pay him that last visit. One night she had been out to supper after the theatre, and as her escort was bidding her good-night at her doorway, she said that the terrible cry suddenly exploded between them. Her companion was as terrified as she, though he knew the story, as did all Paris, and he had to be assisted to his carriage in a state of collapse.

On another occasion she was driving to a friend's house near the Porte Sainte-Denis with one of her admirers, a young aristocrat who mocked at the supernatural and who was wittily sceptical about her ghost voice, challenging her to produce it for his benefit, before he would believe in it.

Half seriously, she accepted his challenge and the next instant the carriage was filled with the most appalling and pitiful screams. The coachman had difficulty in preventing the horses from bolting, and when they arrived at their destination Mlle Clairon said that she and her companion were found lying senseless in the carriage.

For some time after that the ghost voice left her in peace, and she heard it next, and for the last time, some months later at Versailles where she and the company of the Comédie Française had been commanded by Louis XV to give a performance on the occasion of the marriage of the Dauphin. They had to stay three nights at Versailles, and the town was overcrowded for the festivities. La Clairon had to share her room with one of the other actresses and her bed with her maid. She was joking about their cramped, uncomfortable quarters, and the weather being so foul. "I doubt if my ghost would ever find me here at the end of the world," she laughed.

Immediately, she says, the fearful cry once more burst upon their ears, and the whole house was in uproar, for everyone heard it, and none of them, she says, slept a wink that night.

When she returned to Paris, her ghost began the second phase of its vengeful campaign against her. Upon the first stroke of eleven one evening a week later when she was sitting in her house entertaining some friends, there was the sound of a musket being discharged outside her window. Everyone in the room not only heard the shot but saw the flash, and the men rushed gallantly to the protection of the idol of the Paris stage, thinking an attempt was

being made upon her life. But there was no bullet-hole in the window and outside was no sign of an assailant.

The police were immediately summoned by her alarmed companions, and though they made a rigorous investigation and questioned all the residents of the road, they could discover no explanation for the shot. Every night now at eleven o'clock the shot rang out and the flash was seen outside the window; and although the police were constantly on duty, they were unable to solve the mystery. They had no means of stopping the noise or of detecting its origin. Mlle Clairon declared in her memoirs that this continued every night for three months, and the proof of it is to be found in the records of the Paris Police of 1744.

She became so used to the phantom shot that eventually she looked upon it as something of a joke, and she recalls an incident which happened when she and a man friend were on the balcony of the haunted window at the appointed time making jokes about it. The shot rang out as the clock struck the hour, but the explosion this time was so great that they were both thrown back into the room and each felt a sharp blow on the side of the head which seemed to have been dealt them by a human hand. This brusque reprimand for their unseemly levity did not have the desired effect, for they both burst out laughing.

La Clairon was troubled by the phantom shot for the last time two nights later when passing in her carriage the very house where her former lover had died a couple of years previously. As she pointed out the house to her companion, the shot rang out once again, and the coachman, believing they were being ambushed by armed robbers, whipped the horses into a gallop.

The haunting continued for several months, but she heard no more shooting, only mysterious hand-clapping and the singing of a strange and curious song which was truly haunting, for it was an air which was both tantalizing and fascinating, and which she could never fully recall afterwards. This ghostly song ended the haunting which had begun two and a half years previously and to which its victim had now become thoroughly accustomed.

During this time La Clairon's success on the stage had brought her both wealth and fame, and she moved to a more luxurious house in a fashionable part of Paris. She decided to let her old home. A number of people came to look at the famous residence of La Clairon where the strange haunting had taken place, and it was not surprising that among the viewers were some who had no intention of renting the place.

With most of these her servants had no difficulty in dealing, but there was one lady of advancing years who was unusually persistent and seemed to be in a state of some agitation, demanding to see Mlle Clairon, saying she had been a friend of M. de S———. The young actress immediately saw her.

The lady told La Clairon that she had nursed and looked after her former lover during the last few weeks of his life and was with him when he died. She knew all about his affair with La Clairon and his hopeless love for her, and she had done her best to make him accept the inevitable and forget her, but in vain. On the contrary, he said he would never forget her in this life or in the next, and that he would return from the grave to haunt her.

But why? asked La Clairon, puzzled as well as distressed at what her visitor had told her.

The woman replied that if La Clairon had complied with the dying man's request to go and see him for the last time, he would have passed away in peace and he would have left her in peace too. When she refused his request, he declared with his dying breath that he would come back to haunt her and do so in a way which would alarm and frighten her. He would haunt her, he said, for the same length of time as he had been held enslaved under her spell.

As La Clairon recollected, his passion for her had lasted two and a half years, when it was terminated by his death, after which his spirit had terrorized her for another two and a half years before finally releasing her from its ghostly attentions.

Her experience had no effect upon her great success on the Paris stage during its golden years in the reign of Louis XV, when she herself reigned at the Comédie Française for twenty-two years. She retired in 1766 and opened a dramatic school in Paris which flourished for many years. La Clairon outlived the Revolution and died in the year 1803.

Eighteenth-century France was the setting for another interesting ghost story in which an English family was involved.

During the reign of Louis XV a young man inherited some property in and around Lille. He was placed under the guardianship of his uncle, who turned out to be a villain of the blackest hue, prepared to go to any lengths to rob his nephew of his inheritance, which included two imposing houses in Lille and an estate in the country.

The young heir was a weakling and was somewhat under the influence of his guardian, who tried to make him sign documents

to transfer the property, but the nephew was not such a fool as all that. The uncle then proceeded to sterner more ruthless measures. In the garret room of their house in the Place du Lion d'Or at Lille he installed one of those fearsome iron cages sometimes used in those days to confine human beings. This hideous contraption was eight feet high and four feet square and contained an iron collar attached to a chain. The whole apparatus was riveted to the wall. The wicked uncle then put his nephew in this cage and kept him in it, it is supposed, until he died.

Afterwards the murderer sold up all the property and disappeared. Such was the state of affairs in the *ancien régime* that he took little trouble to conceal his crime, which became the talk of Lille. The wretch did not even dismantle the iron cage in which he had killed his nephew. Nor in fact did the man who bought the house in the Place du Lion d'Or from him.

For many years the house was empty. No tenant would stay in it for more than a few days on account of the *revenant*. The house passed from father to son and vain attempts were made to let it. Its evil reputation lingered on through the century.

Then in the autumn of the year 1786 a wealthy and aristocratic English family came to Lille. They were Sir William and Lady Court and four of their children. They arrived in style in their coach with a retinue of six servants—coachman, groom, footman and three maids. Their object in coming to France was for the children to learn French, an accomplishment as desirable in Georgian times as it is today. In pursuit of this laudable object they were to remain there for the winter in the charge of Lady Court, while Sir William went elsewhere on business of his own.

The arrival of this cavalcade of English wealth and quality in the ancient town of Lille was a matter of some interest. They were looking for a house suitable for their needs and appropriate to their station, and the large and well-built residence in the Place du Lion d'Or seemed to meet both requirements. It was offered to Sir William at what seemed a ridiculously low rental. He took it and moved his family and servants into it without delay.

Having settled his family at Lille, Sir William furnished his wife with letters-of-credit which she could cash at the local bankers in order to meet her expenses, and then betook himself elsewhere. He may have returned to England on business, or he may have gone to enjoy the pleasures of Paris; but what he did is of no further importance to this story.

No sooner had the Courts settled themselves in the house than

they began to hear mysterious noises at night—particularly the sound of a slow, measured tread in the room above the large chamber which Lady Court shared with one of her daughters, Elizabeth. They may have been reduced to sleeping together in this way on account of the fact that they had so many servants to accommodate. Six domestics were not enough for their requirements, for they engaged in addition a cook, a butler, a footman and a house-boy, all of whom were French. The footsteps above therefore had not unduly disturbed Lady Court and her daughter, as they thought it was one of the man-servants walking about.

After they had been installed there for a short while, Lady Court and Elizabeth went to the bank to cash a letter-of-credit. The money was paid in six-franc pieces, the bulky coinage of the day, and the banker offered to send the money round to the house. When Lady Court told him that she lived in the Place du Lion d'Or he looked surprised, and said that the only house in that thoroughfare suitable for her ladyship's occupation was haunted and as a consequence had been impossible to let for many years.

Neither Lady Court nor her daughter believed in ghosts, and they greeted this piece of information with well-bred laughter, bordering on derision. They implored the banker to order his clerk to say nothing about the *revenant* to their servants, who being ignorant people were probably superstitious. On the way back Lady Court jokingly said to Elizabeth: "I suppose it must have been the ghost walking about over our heads that kept us awake."

They dismissed the matter as not really being worthy of their attention, though of course the footsteps which they heard again in the night above them brought it back to the mind of Lady Court, who was of a somewhat nervous disposition.

"Who sleeps in the room over us?" she demanded of Cresswell, her personal maid.

Cresswell looked at her in surprise. "No one, my lady. Above your room is a large garret which is quite empty."

Within a week the story of the ghost was the talk of the household and all the French servants were for leaving. It was then that Cresswell enlightened her ladyship about the story of the man in the iron cage, adding the thrilling information that the very cage itself was in the garret above her ladyship's head.

The children, of course, rushed upstairs to see this fascinating object of horror and Lady Court was not far behind them. The English sceptics gazed enraptured upon the rusty old iron cage which reminded them of a place in which beasts were kept. The very

thought that a human being had been imprisoned in it filled them with creepy horror.

But they did not believe that the house was haunted. Educated and intelligent people in the eighteenth century did not believe in ghosts. The Courts had a theory that the footsteps heard in the empty garret were made by someone who, for some reason, wished to keep the house untenanted—though why there should be such a human conspiracy against them they could not imagine. Nevertheless the Court family were convinced of it, and it was the thought that someone other than themselves and their gaggle of servants having access to the house, that made Lady Court decide to move elsewhere. But another house was difficult to find and she decided to stay where she was until she was successful.

Cresswell shared a room with a Mrs Marsh, who was Elizabeth's personal maid—for the favoured Court children each had a servant of their own—and a couple of nights after the discovery of the iron cage both the servants were woken in the middle of the night by the appearance of a tall, thin man in their room. He walked towards the door and disappeared through it. The terrified women hid under their bedclothes shivering with fright until morning.

When Cresswell recounted this story to Lady Court the next day, Elizabeth, who was there, burst out laughing, and this made Cresswell cry and say she could never sleep in that room again. Both mother and daughter comforted her and told her she could sleep in the little room next to theirs, and that they would soon be moving into a new house.

The door which opened into the room which had been occupied by Cresswell and the other maid was in a recess leading from a wide staircase which led to a passage where the main bedrooms were.

A night or two later Lady Court asked Elizabeth and her son Charles to go to her bedroom and bring down her large embroidery frame. It was dark, and as brother and sister started up the wide staircase they saw, by the light of the lamp fixed in the hall, a tall, thin man ascending the stairs in front of them. According to Elizabeth, the figure was wearing a powdering gown and wore his hair long at the back in the style of the mid-eighteenth century.

Neither of the young people believed it was a ghost. They thought it was Hannah, one of their maids, playing a trick on them. They called out: "It's no good, Hannah. You can't frighten us like that."

The ghost thereupon turned into the recess leading to the doorway of the room Cresswell had occupied, then melted into the door and disappeared.

Elizabeth and Charles continued on their way not disconcerted, still thinking it was one of Hannah's little jokes which had been brought off rather successfully in the uncertain light of the lamp at the foot of the stairs. When they returned with the embroidery frame they told their mother of the trick they imagined Hannah had played upon them, but Lady Court informed them that Hannah had gone to bed some time ago with a sick headache.

Elizabeth and Charles at once went to Hannah's room where they found another of the maids, Alice, with Hannah who was fast asleep, and had been so, Alice assured them, for more than an hour. Later they told Cresswell of the incident, and described the figure they had seen ascending the stairs. Cresswell went white and said that was exactly the same figure she had seen in her bedroom that night.

Brother Harry, who was Head Boy at Westminster School, now came to spend ten days with the family at Lille. After his first night in the house in the Place du Lion d'Or the youth appeared at breakfast in a state of high indignation, accusing his mother of sending "some Frenchy" to spy upon him and see that he put his candle out at the proper time. Harry had heard the footsteps in the passage, jumped out of bed and opened the door to see the figure in the loose gown. If he'd had any clothes on, he said, he would have gone after him and taught him a lesson. His mother assured him that she had sent no one to spy upon him.

A young English couple named Atkyns, who lived near Lille, visited them and upon hearing of the ghost, Mrs Atkyns recklessly offered to sleep in the room where Cresswell had been frightened. Lady Court agreed and Mrs Atkyns spent an extremely restless night, accompanied by her pet terrier, who was reduced to a state of terror, as was Mrs Atkyns, by the sinister movements and footsteps which were heard in the room during the night.

"Perhaps you dreamed it all," said her husband unsympathetically the next morning, and Lady Court was just as disbelieving, despite everything, and despite the fact also that she confessed that she would be terrified if there really was a ghost in the house. By now she had arranged to take over the house of a nobleman who was going to spend a few years in Italy, and during their last night in the house in the Place du Lion d'Or, Elizabeth saw the ghost in the bedroom she shared with her mother.

The ghost was standing with one arm resting upon the chest-of-drawers, and with its face turned towards Elizabeth as she sat bolt upright in her four-poster, eyes staring at it with terror. She saw

that it was the face of a young man, ghastly pale, and thin, with hollow cheeks and with an expression of infinite suffering and unhappiness—a ravaged and terrible face which made her think of that dreadful iron cage in the room above her head, in which he had been chained like an animal with the metal collar around his neck. The face of this wretched and unhappy ghost haunted Elizabeth for years.

But just then, though frightened out of her wits, she would have been even more frightened to have awoken her mother who, she was sure, would have had hysterics at the sight of the phantom standing by the chest-of-drawers—a melancholy but terrifying thing from that other world.

Elizabeth heard the clock strike four, and then, copying Cresswell, she suddenly slid down and lay under the bedclothes, shivering with terror. She lay like that for nearly an hour and when at last she ventured her head above the clothes and looked once more to the chest-of-drawers she saw nothing. Nor had she heard a sound. The bedroom door had not opened or closed. And then she heard the clock strike five.

She did not sleep that night, trying to persuade herself that what she had seen had been something human, and that she had omitted to lock their bedroom door, which was always done in that house.

In fact when Cresswell came in as usual to rouse them in the morning, she called out to the maid that she must have forgotten to lock the door, and so there was no need for her (Elizabeth) to get out of bed. But she had not forgotten. The door was locked and the key was in its usual place. It was impossible to get in from the outside.

When she heard about her daughter's experience during the night, Lady Court was most grateful that Elizabeth had not awoken her, for she believed the shock of witnessing such a sight would have killed her.

Elizabeth, still reluctant to believe in the supernatural, made a thorough search of the room with the help of Cresswell, to see if there was any concealed or secret way of getting into it, but they found nothing.

That day Lady Court with her children and domestics left the house for the more comfortable and certainly less sinister home of the nobleman who had gone to Italy.

Then followed the French Revolution and the Napoleonic Wars, but by this time the Court family were safely back in England, and these "disturbances", as they termed those momentous events, made

them forget their *revenant* at Lille, and it was not until some years later that the story was recalled, and was told in various forms, garbled and otherwise, during the ghost-conscious nineteenth century. A form of the story was told by the author S. Baring-Gould in a long-forgotten number of the *Cornhill Magazine*.

But in Lille, it was impossible to ignore the ghost. It will be recalled that in the case of a similar haunting at Hinton Ampner (q.v.) the owner pulled the place down when its spectral residents made the place uninhabitable for human beings. The French, however, are more practical people. They turned the haunted house in the Place du Lion d'Or at Lille into a hotel, and it remained so for many years during the nineteenth century. Of course the ghost still walked, although the sinister iron cage was removed. Doubtless a number of guests were thoroughly frightened by the spectral goings-on, but a haunted hotel is not necessarily bad for business. Many have thrived upon such a reputation.

The scene of the Court family's *revenant* now became the Hotel du Lion d'Or, and a small party of English people stayed there in the 1880s and described it as an old-fashioned, unpretentious hostelry. In those days the landlord was reticent about the ghost and kept the haunted room locked. The English guests noticed that it was approached by a recess, now full of the brooms and pails used by the housemaids.

In the night they were disturbed by the footsteps, slow and dragging. They had been assured that they were the only guests in that part of the hotel, and each of the men thought it was the other restlessly pacing his room unable to sleep. When they consulted each other in the middle of the night, they found that it was not so, and came to the conclusion that the footsteps were in the room above.

They went to sleep, lulled by that "stealthy dragging step" above them, not knowing until they later heard the story of the Court family, that their sleep had been troubled by the ghost of the man in the iron cage.

The Spirit of Sergeant Davies

When a war is over and won, the true reckoning begins. The Jacobite Rebellion of 1745 ended in total failure for the Stuart cause. Prince Charlie had fled back to France, leaving his faithful Highlanders to suffer unspeakable wrongs at the hands of the English victors, under their cruel leader "Butcher" Cumberland. Murder, rape, house-burning were the order of the day, and nothing was left undone that might break the spirit of the brave Clans. They might no longer wear their traditional tartans, nor carry swords—officially. But Highland blood is high, and the heaths and mountains hid as many broken and outlawed men as they did rabbits and foxes; each with some vestige of a knife or rusted gun, and each with hatred in his heart for the conquering Sassenach.

There is the tale of one Donald Ban and his wife, who were visited one night by a ghost, and sorely frightened. But the woman retained enough self-possession to beg the ghost to answer one question for her: "Will our Prince come again?" The phantom replied in the following lines:

> The wind has left me bare indeed,
> And blawn my bonnet off my heid,
> But something's hid in Hieland brae—
> The wind's no' blawn my sword away!

But this poetic spirit is not the ghost of our story.

By 1749, three years after the Rising was quelled, the English government was still uneasy about the Highlands. The feeling that "something's hid in Hieland brae" was only too strong upon them,

and an Army of Occupation still kept a sharp watch on the territory. It was as popular as Armies of Occupation usually are.

But an exception to the general label of "bluidy redcoat" was Sergeant Arthur Davies, of Guise's regiment, who in the summer of 1749 was posted from Aberdeen to Dubrach in Braemar, eight miles away from the nearest guard-station at Glenshee. Between the two places stretched a wild waste of bog and mountain, rock and river. Sergeant Davies was not perturbed by the difference between this savage land and his own gentle countryside, and soon settled down. He was quickly accepted, for he was one of those men born to be liked by their fellow-men—kindly, honest, fair in his dealings, and in his private life devoted to his young wife and fond of children. This last must have been a remarkable attribute in a country where a second Slaughter of the Innocents had just taken place. His wife later testified that "he and she lived together in as great amity and love as any couple could do, and he never was in use to stay away a night from her".

The sergeant, who was comfortably off in England, and of saving disposition, must have appeared very wealthy to hungry Highland eyes. He wore a silver watch, and two gold rings—one with a peculiar knob on it. His brogues had silver buckles, and, like Bobbie Shafto, he wore "silver buckles at his knee". On his striped lute-string waistcoat were two dozen silver buttons; his coat was a cheerful bright blue, his hat, with his initials cut into the felt was silver-laced, and his dark brown hair was gathered into a silk ribbon. He had saved fifteen guineas and a half—a huge sum for those days—and was in the habit of carrying it in a green silk purse and innocently displaying it to those interested. He carried a gun—an envied possession in those parts. Such was Sergeant Davies, "a pretty man", every detail of his appearance and attire noted by those who saw him leave his lodgings at Michael Farquharson's in Dubrach on 28 September, early in the morning. His wife, in her cap and bed-gown, came down to kiss him good-bye at the door. Did her arms hold more tightly and long around him than usual? Or did she watch him out of sight, with the uneasy feeling that this was the beginning of a very long journey? Probably not; she was an English-woman, not a Highland lass with "the sight". "Good-bye, Arthur—take good care of yourself," was more than likely to be all she said, before shutting the door and beginning her household tasks.

Sergeant Davies briskly collected four men, and set out towards Glenshee to meet the patrol which was coming from there. On the way he met a man called John Growar, and noticed that Growar

was wearing a tartan coat—a thing forbidden by law. Instead of arresting him, as most English officers would have done, Davies kindly advised him to take it off and not to wear it again, and then let him go on his way. Davies was by this time alone, having left his men temporarily because he thought he would like to cross the hill and try to get a stag—he fancied himself as a sportsman. He promised to rejoin the men later on their way to the rendezvous with the patrol.

But when they met with the patrol, Sergeant Davies had not rejoined them. They gave him an hour or two, then went back and searched the route. They called, they shouted, but no voice answered, only the frightened moorland birds. The sun of a late summer was hot on their heads, and by the end of the day they gave up, exhausted.

For three days it was expected that Sergeant Davies would return of his own accord; on the fourth day a band of soldiers from the combined forces of Dubrach and Glenshee went out on an intensive search for him. But no trace of him was found; the substantial Sergeant Davies had vanished as if the fairies had taken him. Some simple folk believed they had; others had darker ideas.

The weeks passed, and the months. It was June, 1750, and the rooms where Sergeant Davies had lodged were occupied by his replacement. Poor Mrs Davies had gone home to England; after waiting for months in Scotland for her lost husband to return, she had given up hope. Michael Farquharson's son, Donald, was at home when the servant came to tell him that there was a visitor asking for his father, one Alexander Macpherson. His father being away on business, Donald offered to see the man himself.

Alexander Macpherson was a middle-aged man who had so far stayed out of trouble with the English, and was living humbly but peacefully enough in a shepherd's hut among the hills. The story he had to tell was a strange one. He had, he said, been visited repeatedly at night by the ghost of Sergeant Davies, looking exactly as he had done in life but with an anxious, troubled expression. The ghost had begged Macpherson to go and look for his bones, which were buried in a peat moss, about half a mile from the road taken by the patrols. Macpherson, afraid, refused to do this. "Bury my bones! bury my bones!" repeated the ghost over and over, despairingly. "I will not—I am afraid," returned Macpherson. "Then you will find one who will. Go to Michael and Donald Farquharson at my old lodgings, and tell them to bury my bones—bury my bones!"

Donald Farquharson listened to this recital incredulously. He

was a level-headed person, and had heard many wild tales from his fellow-Highlanders. Frankly, he did not believe Macpherson, and said so.

"But at least come with me and see if the bones are there!" Macpherson pleaded. "If you could have seen and heard the ghost you would have believed!"

His insistence finally succeeded with Farquharson, who agreed to go with him. The next morning they set out, and within an hour or two arrived at the spot described by the ghost. They had brought spades, and now used them. Not far below the surface they turned up a shred of blue cloth. Deeper still they dug, until the peat yielded what the ghost had promised—the pathetic bones of Sergeant Davies, the brown hair still clinging to the skull, but the silk ribbon gone; the silk waistcoat almost intact, but without its silver buttons, and the buckles vanished from the bones of knee and foot. His murderers had torn the silver lacing from his hat and thrown the hat down beside him. There it lay, rotting, the initials "A.D." still clear.

Reverently, Farquharson and Macpherson dug a neat grave away from the peat moss, and it in they laid the poor bones, saying over them a service of prayer and committal; for they were both devout men. The rags and relics of clothing they collected and took back with them to Dubrach, as evidence of the murder that had been done.

A trial was held, and Alexander Macpherson was called upon to give evidence. His testimony differed substantially from the story he had told Donald Farquharson. According to what he now said, he had been visited late in May by a vision of a man clothed in blue, who said "I am Sergeant Davies!" At first he thought the figure was a real living man—a brother of Donald Farquharson's. He rose and followed the shape to the door, where it told him that its bones lay in a spot the direction of which it pointed out, and said that it wished them to be decently buried, and that Donald Farquharson would help to do this.

Next day Macpherson went out and found the bones, afterwards covering them up again. On his way back to his hut he met Growar, the man of the tartan coat whom Davies had encountered on his last day on earth. Growar said that if Macpherson did not keep quiet about the discovery, he himself would impeach Macpherson to Shaw of Daldownie, a magistrate. Macpherson, taking the wise course, went to Shaw himself and told his story; but Shaw told him to keep his mouth shut about the whole affair, and not give the district a bad name for harbouring rebels. Macpherson went home

with a disturbed mind. That night the ghost again appeared to him, reproaching him, and once again commanding him to get Donald Farquharson to bury the bones. He also—and this caused a sensation in the court—revealed the names of the two men who had murdered him, Duncan Clerk and Alexander Bain Macdonald.

At this point the magistrate interrupted to ask in what language the ghost had spoken to Macpherson.

"In the Gaelic," Macpherson replied. The magistrate wrote down his answer.

Then came an uncanny piece of evidence from Mistress Isobel MacHardie, for whom Macpherson worked as a shepherd. One night in June, 1750, she said, she had been sleeping in the sheiling (a hut for the use of shepherds) while Macpherson slept at the other end; a double watch was kept on the sheep. While she lay awake "she saw something naked come in at the door, which frighted her so much that she drew the clothes over her head. When it appeared it came in in a bowing posture, and next morning she asked Macpherson what it was that had troubled them in the night. He answered that she might be easy, for it would not trouble them any more".

Incredible as it may seem, no further inquiry was made into the doings of the men Clerk and Macdonald; the whole matter was suspended. Then, three years later, in September, 1753, they were suddenly arrested—on charges of rebellious behaviour, such as wearing the kilt! They were kept in Edinburgh's Tolbooth Prison until June, 1754, and then tried. At the trial it emerged that Clerk's wife wore Sergeant Davies's ring—the one with the characteristic knob—and that Clerk, after the murder, had suddenly become prosperous and had taken a farm. Witnesses came forward to swear that Clerk and Macdonald, armed, were on a hill in the neighbourhood of the murder on 28 September, 1749. And one Angus Cameron swore that he saw the murder committed, while he and another Cameron, now dead, had been hiding in a little hill-hollow all day, waiting for Donald Cameron, *who was afterwards hanged*, together with some of Donald's companions from Lochaber. The implication is that some underground Jacobite business was afoot. The watchers had seen Clerk and Macdonald strike and shoot a man in a blue coat and silver-laced hat, and then had run away.

Their evidence impressed the court greatly. But, 142 years later, it was contradicted by the story told by a very old lady, a descendant of one of the witnesses at the trial. She said that her ancestor had been out stag-shooting on 28 September, 1749, with gun and deerhound. He saw Clerk and Macdonald on the hill, and, thinking they

had got a stag, went towards them, his dog running in front of him. As he drew nearer, he saw *what it was they had*. He called to the dog, and began to run away, but they fired a shot after him and the dog was wounded. Then he ran home as fast as he could.

Between the story of 1754 and that of 1896 it seems more than likely that Clerk and Macdonald were guilty. Their lawyers were certainly convinced of their guilt. And yet, when the jury of Edinburgh tradesmen returned to give their verdict, it was that of— Not Guilty. The reason for their acquittal was that the ghost had spoken to Alexander Macpherson in Gaelic, *a language it did not know in life*.

And so the unfortunate Sergeant Davies, who had struggled back through the gates of death to beg for Christian burial and to denounce his murderers, had made his journey in vain; for his bones were never interred in a kirkyard, and Clerk and Macdonald went free. They lived in prosperity, for those times, on the proceeds of the sergeant's guineas, watch and rings, and the silver buckles and buttons for which they had killed him. Small wonder if his forlorn blue-coated spirit walks the Braemar hills to this day.

The Haunting at Hinton Ampner

The strange events which took place at the old manor house of Hinton Ampner between the years 1767 and 1771 constitute one of the best observed and most carefully checked ghost stories on record. After studying the reports of the various independent witnesses, there can be little doubt that something took place at Hinton Ampner Manor which cannot be accounted for by natural events—a haunting which has its echoes right down to the present century, even though the old beghosted manor, being long destroyed, is no more.

The fact that these events took place during the eighteenth century should not deter us, or make us think we can doubt the reliability of the accounts which have come down to us. On the contrary, the period of the story should make us take it more seriously than if it had taken place in almost any other century.

The eighteenth century was the Age of Reason. People were superficially religious, and certainly not superstitious. Materialism was the creed of most educated people. There was less belief in ghosts then than there is now.

The Georgian lady who set down the chronicle of this strange haunting at first steadfastly refused to accept that she was living in a haunted house. She plainly did not believe in ghosts, and when her servants came to her with weird stories of the eerie goings on in her house, she scornfully dismissed them as the superstitions and fears "to which the vulgar minds of the lower classes of people are so prone".

She was to learn very differently, and finally to be driven from the house by the terror of the unknown forces she at first despised and disbelieved in.

Hinton Ampner is a tiny Hampshire village which lies just off the main road between Winchester and Petersfield. The old manor-house was built in the 1620s during the reign of James I by Sir Thomas Stewkeley, Bart. It was a comfortable though not a large manor-house by the standards of the day, and the Stewkeleys lived there for about a century.

In 1719 Miss Mary Stewkeley, the eldest daughter of Sir Hugh Stewkeley, married Edward Stawell, the younger brother of Lord Stawell. As the latter had no children, Edward was the heir pre-sumptive to the title.

On her father's death, Mary inherited the property. Her younger sister, Honoria, came to live with them at Hinton, and after Mary's death in 1740 the attachment was such between Honoria and her widowed brother-in-law that she stayed on at Hinton, thus causing a great scandal.

Stories told by the servants at the manor spread throughout the district. They told not only of an immoral relationship between Stawell and his sister-in-law—incest no less, as the law did not permit them to marry—but also that a child had been born in consequence of their criminal affair. Worse, it was even whispered that the body of the child had been "done away with".

No one knows for sure whether there was any truth in this story, which spread like wildfire through the gossiping countryside, and which had a remarkable echo half a century later. It certainly seemed that the sad and disturbed spirits of the two lovers remained behind after their deaths to haunt the scene of some tragic and terrible happening.

In 1742 Edward Stawell's brother died and he inherited the title. He continued to live at Hinton Ampner with Honoria, who died in 1754. The following year Lord Stawell died of a stroke. He was fifty-six and the date was 2 April, 1755.

Shortly after his death his ghost was reported to be seen in the house "dressed in a drab coat".

Hinton Ampner Manor and the estate now passed into the hands of the Hon. Henry Bilson Legge, presumably as part of a marriage settlement, for he had married Lord Stawell's only daughter, Stawell's only son having died at Westminster School at the age of sixteen.

The Legges came to Hinton Ampner for only a few weeks every

year for the shooting season, and the place was looked after by three old family retainers, who lived there, and who had indeed lived there all their lives. They were Thomas Parfait and his wife Sarah, who had been coachman and housekeeper respectively to Lord Stawell, and had been with the family for forty years, and Elizabeth Banks, a housemaid, also an old family servant.

Legge died in 1764. His widow later married the Earl of Hillsborough, who apparently did not want Hinton Ampner as part of the price of marrying the lady. Nor did he desire to use the place, so she decided to let it furnished.

It is here where the heroine of this haunting comes into the story. She was Mary Jervis, a well-born young lady whose father was Swynfen Jervis, Solicitor to the Admiralty and treasurer of Greenwich Hospital, a man of some importance in London. Her brother, Captain John Jervis, R.N., who also had an encounter with the Hinton Ampner ghosts, was the brilliant naval officer who became the Earl St. Vincent—one of the most illustrious names of the British Navy. As Admiral Jervis, he led the Fleet to the great victory of the Battle of St. Vincent, at which Nelson served under him.

Mary Jervis married William Henry Ricketts, of Longwood, Hampshire, in 1757. He was a wealthy merchant whose affairs frequently took him to the West Indies. Mr and Mrs Ricketts had three children, and in January, 1765, they rented Hinton Ampner from Lady Hillsborough through the Hillsborough steward, a man named Sainsbury.

Mary Ricketts was then twenty-eight, an educated young lady who had been brought up in the sophisticated society of Georgian London—the London of Dr Johnson, Addison and Steele, Burke and Fielding. She had never been a country-girl, and she had the Londoner's contempt for countryfolk, their ways and their superstitious beliefs. In London she had mixed in an elegant, informed and reasoning society, which considered that it knew practically the sum total of knowledge about life and all that lay beyond—for was not Sir William Herschel already mapping the very shape of the Universe? Mary Ricketts was a product of this sophisticated and unhurried age. She scorned the very idea of ghosts, "knowing", as she put it, "how exploded such opinions were".

Not even after her devastating experience would she admit the supernatural. To her it was just "unexplained".

This is the great value of her testimony. Her one concern at all times was to tell the truth. Even before these events she had a widely recognized reputation for veracity.

The documentation of this story consists of letters from Mary Ricketts to her husband, to the Rector of Hinton Ampner and letters from her brother, John Jervis, to her husband in Jamaica, and also a "Narration" she wrote for posterity.

But as so often happens in such cases, posterity did not get it until a hundred years later. There were two copies of the "Narration" and they were jealously kept away from the public by the family until a garbled version appeared in 1870 in the biography of Richard Harris Barham, author of *The Ingoldsby Legends*. Mrs Ricketts's descendants then gave the complete "Narration" to *The Gentleman's Magazine* which published it in 1872.

It is the "Narration" which is the main source of this account.

When the Ricketts family took possession of Hinton Ampner Manor in January, 1765, Thomas Parfait, Lord Stawell's old coachman, was lying dead in his bed. It was not the best of omens. People these days, not even the eccentric aristocracy, are scarcely in the habit of letting furnished houses with dead bodies lying in the beds.

But the Ricketts were undeterred. The first thing they did was to get the old man buried and to pension off his widow Sarah, and also Elizabeth Banks, the ancient retainers who had lived in the manor all their lives and considered it their home, as was the custom of the times in such houses.

Shortly after their arrival at Hinton, Mary and her husband both heard noises in the night, particularly that of doors being slammed. This happened frequently and the master of the house got out of bed and searched, imagining robbers had broken in, or that irregularities were taking place in the servants' quarters. But he found no sign of intruders, and the servants were all in bed, and in their proper rooms.

When the noises continued Mary believed that some of the villagers had somehow acquired keys to the house and were coming in to make mischief, perhaps some sort of revenge for the importation of "foreign" servants. So they had all the locks in the house changed. But the strange noises continued nevertheless. They had to get used to them.

In the summer of 1765 the ghost of Lord Stawell again made its appearance in his old haunts of alleged incestuousness and infanticide.

He was seen first by Elizabeth Brelsford, the nurse to the Ricketts's eight-month-old son Henry. She was sitting by his cot in the nursery, the open door of which faced the yellow bedchamber used by the mistress of the house. It was a bright summer's evening and she plainly saw a man in "a drab coloured suit of clothes" go into the yellow room.

The nurse was not really surprised, imagining there was some strange visitor in the house, but when she and a fellow servant who assured her there was no stranger in the house, searched the yellow room immediately after the apparition had gone into it, they found no trace of the man in the drab-coloured suit.

A few months later George Turner, a groom, encountered the ghost while crossing the great hall to go to bed. He mistook his drab clothes for those worn by the butler while off duty, and thought indeed it was the butler. But when Turner got upstairs he found all the man servants, including the butler, were in their beds.

In the July of 1767 several of the servants were sitting in the kitchen when they heard a woman's footsteps come down the stairs towards the kitchen. It could not be one of the servants because they all heard the rustling of clothes which must have been made of the stiffest silk.

They looked to the door and all of them plainly saw a strange woman pass by. She was tall and she wore dark clothes. She went in the direction of the yard and the street. Almost immediately afterwards a man came through the door from the yard and could not have avoided seeing her, if she had been a live person. But he declared that he had seen no one.

The servants heard other eerie noises—dismal groans, and strange rustlings at night around their beds.

When they recounted these experiences to their mistress, Mary Ricketts treated the whole thing with ridicule. Ignorant, lower-class people were full of these stupid fears and superstitions.

In 1769 her husband went to Jamaica on one of his protracted business trips, and she remained alone at Hinton with her three young children and eight servants, all of whom were trusted and reliable, and none of whom came from the neighbourhood. Mary makes a great point of establishing the trustworthiness of her servants, as she long suspected that she was being made the victim of some kind of trickery, in which case her servants would be the first to be suspected.

Mary herself now began to hear the spectral noises in a way which thoroughly disturbed her. She heard people walking about in rooms which were subsequently found to be empty, and the rustling of those silken clothes was so pronounced and so loud that it often awakened her from sleep. As so many other people have found, locked and bolted doors could not keep out intruders of this nature.

During the winter of 1769-70 an old man came from the poor-house at West Meon, knocked upon the door of Hinton Ampner

Manor and desired to speak to the lady of the house upon a matter of importance touching upon the mysterious happenings at Hinton which had been the talk and the wonder of the countryside for miles around.

Mary, herself disturbed, though still suspecting she was the victim of some kind of conspiracy, condescended to see the old man, who then told her that he could not rest in his mind until he had acquainted her with something his late wife had once told him.

In her younger days, the old man said, his wife had known a carpenter who told her that Sir Hugh Stewkeley—the father of Honoria, whose ghost the servants in the kitchen had seen—had employed him to take up some floorboards in the dining room, and that Sir Hugh had concealed something underneath, after which the carpenter had been ordered to replace the floorboards. The carpenter imagined it was some kind of treasure which was hidden.

Mary's reaction to this piece of information was to write to the Mr Sainsbury, who was Lord Hillsborough's attorney, telling him what the old man had said, and suggesting that he might think it worth while to take up the floorboards and see whether there was any truth in the story. But neither Sainsbury nor the landlady herself seemed sufficiently interested in what they no doubt considered an idle tale.

Nor did Mary or her staff make any investigation, for she would certainly have recorded in her "Narrative" the finding of the thing that really was there under the floorboards all the time, and the cause—who knows?—of the terrifying haunting which then followed.

One night in the summer of 1770 Mary had just gone to bed in the yellow room and was wide awake, when she heard the heavy plodding footsteps of a man walking towards the end of her bed. She rushed from her room in terror into the nursery opposite, where the nursemaid, Hanna Streeter, was with the children.

Accompanied by Hannah and candles, she returned to the yellow room, but there was no one there. Nor was there any way by which an intruder could have got out of the yellow room unseen. This alarmed and perplexed her very much, as she had heard the footsteps so distinctly, being perfectly wide awake and her mind composed and collected at the time.

Nevertheless Mary refused to be frightened out of her yellow bedchamber, and even though she could easily have had one of her

domestics to sleep in the room with her, she determined to go to bed there alone. She heard nothing more that summer.

When the chills of winter came to Hinton Ampner, she moved into the chintz bedroom which was over the hall and was a warmer room. In this room she heard sounds of music, and one night three distinct and violent knocks, as though someone was hitting a door with a club.

During this winter she became aware of a strange and hollow murmuring which seemed to fill the whole house. This was not a wind, for it was heard on the calmest of nights. It was a sound, she said, such as she had never heard before, so eerie that she was unable to find words to describe it.

On the 2nd of April of that year—the sixteenth anniversary of Lord Stawell's fatal seizure—Mary was awakened at two o'clock in the morning by the sound of people walking about in the adjoining lobby. She got out of bed and listened at the door for twenty minutes or so, during which she heard distinctly the sound of walking and a noise like someone pushing up against the door. Only when she was certain that her senses were not being deceived did she ring the bell for her maid. Elizabeth Godin came in immediately.

Mary continues the story thus: "Thoroughly convinced there were persons in the lobby before I opened my door, I asked her if she saw no one there. On her replying in the negative, I went out to her, examined the window which was shut, looked under the couch, the only furniture of concealment there; the chimney board was fastened, and when removed all was clear behind it. She found the door into the lobby shut, as it was every night. After this examination, I stood in the middle of the room, pondering with astonishment, when suddenly the door that opens into the little recess leading to the yellow apartment sounded as if played to and fro by a person standing behind it. This was more than I could bear unmoved. I ran into the nursery and rang the bell there that goes into the men's apartment."

Mary was still sceptical that the phenomenon was being caused by a supernatural agency, for when her coachman, young Robert Camis, a big, stolid farmer's son, answered her ring, she informed him that she was sure someone had broken in. It should be noted that the landing door, to which Robert came in answer to her ring, was also locked and barred, so it was impossible for anyone to get into her apartments, except by way of the windows, which were all shut and locked.

She let Robert in, armed him with a light and a stout stick and

told him to go and investigate. But there was no one there. The yellow bedroom, from which the disturbance seemed to be coming, was bolted and locked as usual. Everything was in order. There was no intruder, and no place where one could have hidden. After dismissing Robert, she went to bed, but still heard the mysterious knocks. Other members of the household heard these noises.

Throughout the spring and summer of that year, the noises continued and increased, and were heard by several members of the household.

With midsummer, the noises became well-nigh intolerable. The great humming which Mary had noted before now seemed to be evolving into human sounds, articulate sounds, and both she and Elizabeth Godin were soon distinguishing human voices. There were three voices, one female and shrill and the other two male.

These three voices were conducting a conversation quite close to Mary and her maid, but neither of them could distinguish any of the words which were said—an incomprehensible, impassioned conversation, plucked from the past, and in some unfathomable way caught, imprisoned in that house in a kind of unending echo. These strange noises went on often all night, and continued until after daylight in the morning.

At night Mary's bed curtains rustled and it sounded as though some person was walking up against them, and yet no one was there. "I had taken every method to investigate the cause," she wrote. "And could not discover the least appearance of a trick. On the contrary, I became convinced it was beyond the power of any mortal agent to perform, but knowing how exploded such opinions are, I kept them in my own bosom, and hoped my resolution would enable me to support whatever might befall."

Her brother, Captain John Jervis, had just returned with his ship from the Mediterranean. Though eight years older than his sister, there had always been a very strong bond between them, but when he came to see her at Hinton she could not bring herself to tell him about the weird things which were taking place in the house, even though the noises continued while he was with her. But apparently he did not hear them on that occasion.

As light dawned on the day after he had returned to Portsmouth, even more violent sounds began at Hinton. "The most loud, deep, tremendous noise which seemed to rush and fall with infinite velocity and force upon the lobby door adjoining to my room." This was heard by both Mary and Elizabeth, who was too terrified to speak.

This extraordinary whirlpool of sound ended with a piercing scream which was repeated several times, growing fainter and fainter and seeming to sink into the floor.

The whole household was now in such a state of fear and alarm that Mary determined to tell her brother, who was expected back at Hinton within a week, what had happened.

This she did. With Captain Jervis was Captain Luttrell, a mutual friend, and when Mary told them the story they resolved to stay watch all night. They were armed, and with John Jervis was his personal servant John Bolton. Before they settled down to watch that night, the men searched every nook and cranny in the house.

The strange rustlings and noises took place that night, the same as before, and were heard and attested to by both Jervis and Luttrell as well as Bolton. Doors were slammed and banged unaccountably and John Jervis heard the most fearful groans as well as other weird and strange noises.

The gallant Captain sat up every night for a week to protect his sister from these unknown forces. During one of the nights she heard a pistol shot, followed by groans of agony, but no one had been shot at Hinton that night. One afternoon the Captain heard a tremendous noise as though some great weight had fallen through the ceiling into the room where he sat.

The man who was to rout the Spanish fleet off the Cape of St Vincent and thus establish British naval supremacy for a hundred years and more, retreated before the spectral hosts of Hinton Ampner, and urgently pressed his sister to leave the place.

This she did in the August of 1771. The story of course was the talk of the countryside.

With tenants unobtainable, Lady Hillsborough gave up the struggle with the supernatural forces and ordered Hinton Ampner Manor to be pulled down. During the demolition the housebreakers found a small skull under the floor of one of the rooms. It was said to be that of a monkey. But it was never professionally examined. Nor was any inquiry made into the circumstances and nature of the find.

It was said to have been found in a box, and near it were papers which had apparently been hidden under the floor during the Civil War.

The answer to the mystery of the skull of Hinton Ampner will never be known. One can only guess. The skull of a newly born baby could have been mistaken for that of a monkey by the ignorant workmen, and this might fully explain why the restless spirits of

the guilty parents haunted the place. Was that awful scream which so frightened Mary and Elizabeth the unwanted infant's first cry smothered in death?

At the end of the eighteenth century a new Hinton Ampner House was built about fifty yards from the old site. But in the new house strange noises were heard—and are still heard—usually about dawn. It seems that the restless spirits of Lord Stawell and the sad Honoria are still abroad at Hinton Ampner.

The Drunk who Lost his Way

Half-way between the west and east coasts of the western claw of
Cornwall, a few miles south of the line St Just–Penzance, lies the
little village of Sancreed. In 1783 undoubtedly the best-known
inhabitant of Sancreed, then known as San Crete, was John Thomas.

Thomas was a man of sixty-four, tough and vigorous, which
was surprising when one considers that for more than two-thirds
of his life he had been one of the most notorious drunkards in the
whole Duchy of Cornwall, a region renowned for its hard-drinking
men. It was the reputation which lifted his fame head and shoulders
above all the other villagers.

Thomas at this time had been a widower for approaching fifteen
years, and he had not yet accustomed himself to the loneliness which
the death of his wife had brought into his life. For despite his
drunkenness she had loved him deeply and he had worshipped the
ground she trod. There were some among the more sympathetic
who would excuse his failing by claiming that it was the loss of
Mary, at an age when she could have anticipated another quarter of a
century of life, that had increased his indulgence of ale and rough
cider when un-Customed brandy and armagnac were not to be
come by, and anything else he could lay hands on, maintaining that
it was only during the last decade and a half that he had taken no
measures to curb his weakness for strong drink. Their toleration
did them credit; unfortunately it led them into some error; for
there were those who had known John Thomas as a young man
who remembered the villagers running into their houses and

securing their doors as soon as it was known that the handsome, sturdy smallholder was roaring his way home.

The true facts were that from the first moment he had broached the keg of cognac which he had found washed up on the beach in Whitesand Bay after the wreck of a French merchantman on her way to Dublin, he had formed a passion for hard liquor. Before he was thirty his outbreaks of tipsiness had become part of the canon of local legend, and since then he had done nothing which might have helped the legend to fade.

Before Mary had died she had given him two sons and two daughters, all of whom, in 1783, were married with families of their own. His children having grown up with his excesses, had become accustomed to them, and, having watched their mother patiently drive the devil out, had had no fear of him when he was in his rampageous cups. Sons-in-law and daughters-in-law had come to share wives' and husbands' tolerance, and when he was left alone all of them had encouraged him to make his home with them, for all were aware of the profound, if somewhat strangely based, relationship that had existed between him and their mother, and knew that he would be lonely.

Their invitations had warmed him, but he had declined them.

"You know I can't keep off the drink," he told them, "and you know what I get like then. You've all young children, and it would not be right for them to see the degradation into which a man can fall when he's plagued with the thirst I have."

"What harm did it do us?" they asked.

"You were my flesh and blood, and hers," he said. "Besides, times are changing and, with them, people."

"You're changing, too, by all accounts," they pointed out. "Now, instead of getting drunk every night, you get drunk once a week."

"I told you people were changing," he grinned.

But they could not persuade him. The fact was that his talk of his drinking was an excuse. The real reason for his refusal was that he could not bear to leave the cottage where he and Mary had lived all their married lives, where every article had been found a place and put in it by her, where her spirit still seemed to hover with kindly protection, as in life she had always surrounded him with the guard of her understanding and love.

Once every other year, however, he visited his children and stayed a week, or two or three, as the fancy took him, at Easter and at Christmas. This Christmas it was the turn of his son Frank to have him for the festival.

"Come over on the Sunday before," Frank's wife had told him. "Maybe then you'll get here safely. If you wait for Christmas Eve those well-meaning friends of yours at Sancreed will want to drink with you, and like as not you'll spend the holiday in a stupor and we'll never see you. Besides, there'll be a wreck, I shouldn't wonder, and it would be useful to have an extra hand."

He saw the point of her argument about the drink, but it was her hint of the wreck that decided him.

"I'll come in the morning of Sunday," he answered her. "If I leave Sancreed at mid-morning, I'll be in St Just in time for dinner."

"And don't call at the inn on the way!" she warned him.

"I promise solemnly," he said.

They were right when they had said he had changed, and not only in the frequency of his bouts, but in the effects he exhibited after them. He no longer became pugnacious, wreaking his vengeance on anything or anyone that got in his way. And he seemed to have soaked up so much strong drink in the past that as much as he drank now, though he might sway and reel, he did not lose consciousness of what he was doing or must do. It was only when he reached the cottage, kicked off his boots and dropped into a chair, that he would sink into a sleep from which he might not wake from Saturday night to Monday morning.

From Monday morning to Saturday night he pottered about his garden patch or his little house, passing the time with odd jobs, gathering kindling and chopping logs and being in every sense a good neighbour. This was why it was that he only got drunk on Saturday nights, for, appreciative of the many good turns he did them, the inhabitants of Sancreed were always willing to pay all their indebtedness to him at the inn. Otherwise he could not have afforded to drink enough to get drunk.

They were surprised therefore when he had not appeared in the taproom on the eve of the Sunday before Christmas by the time the evening was nearly spent.

"Do you think the old man's ill?" someone asked.

"He wasn't just before dusk," he was told. "I came by his cottage and he'd lit his lamp and was sawing wood in the kitchen."

"Then why hasn't he come?"

"I seem to have heard someone say that he's spending Christmas with Frank at St Just, and has agreed to go over tomorrow. Maybe he intends to stay sober tonight so as to keep his promise tomorrow."

"Ah, that'll be it," it was agreed.

"Dang it, I owe him a drink," a man sitting on the settle before the

fire remarked. "He brought the missus two sacks of logs on Thursday. Well, I suppose it will wait until the New Year."

"If you don't forget," he was chaffed.

Meanwhile in his cottage the old man was waging a struggle with an appalling thirst. But Beth, Frank's wife, was his favourite. There was something in her manner that reminded him of Mary. He intended to keep his promise to her, no matter how much it cost him in suffering. So he tried to tell himself that it was not Saturday night and sat down in his chair and busied himself in putting the finishing touches to the head of a fox he was carving on a briar root, which he intended as a Christmas gift for one of his grandsons.

When he began to nod over his patient work, and he realized that he was ready for bed, he was surprised at the ease with which he had prevented himself from going down to the inn. Next morning he awoke earlier than usual and, wondering why, he presently recognized the craving which denoted his special thirst.

"I'll hang on now till I get to St Just," he told himself, and when he said the words he meant them in all sincerity.

He got out of bed, pulled on his breeches and boots, blew on the black embers on the hearth until they were red again, went to the pail he had drawn the previous afternoon from the well, took a hammer and chipped off lumps of ice into a black pot, which he hung over the flames.

When he had eaten, he pottered about the cottage until the gold time-piece, which he had taken from the body of a Spanish nobleman washed up on the shore of Mount's Bay, opposite Mousehole, more than thirty-five years ago, told him that it was time to set out. So he tied up his bundle of odds and ends he was taking with him for Frank's family, took his stick from the corner, and left the cottage.

It was unfortunate that the road that was to take him to St Just should bring him past the inn. It was more unfortunate still that at the moment of his passing a neighbour who owed him a drink should be entering the inn and caught sight of him.

"Well met!" the man called to him. "Come in and let me get out of your debt."

"That's kindly said," Thomas called back. "But I'm on my way to St Just. I'll see you when I come back."

"I'll have forgotten by then."

"Then I'll remind you," Thomas laughed.

"Come in and have just one," the neighbour urged. "It'll set you up. It'll be a cold walk if you're aiming to go over the dunes."

"No thanks," Thomas insisted. "I promised Beth . . ."

"Oh, come in! Just one drink! That won't harm you."

While they had been talking, the craving which had roused him had returned. It was true what the man said; it would be a cold walk; a drink would set him up. Well, he would have one! But only one!

"Only one then!" he cried to the neighbour. "Then I must be on my way."

But there were other neighbours in the inn, and yet others came in after them. Some called up drinks for him without asking him; some insisted on paying debts; some that he should drink with them for Christmas's sake, since he would not be there.

No one was more surprised than he when he found on next looking at his time-piece that it was three o'clock. He knew that he was drunk, for he read the swaying time only with difficulty. But he was not so drunk as to have forgotten that he must get to St Just.

"I must go," he shouted to the company. "Where are my bundle and stick? I said I'd be there for dinner. Beth will flay me for this. A happy feast to you, neighbours!"

They gave him his bundle and his stick, clapped him on the back and wished him well in return, and went with him to the door to put him on his way. It did not occur to any one of them that he could not now reach St Just before dark.

With the approach of night it had become colder. As he passed out into the fresh air, it rushed at him with a staggering blow. He steadied himself and strode out uncertainly, the frost striking him a fresh blow with every stride he took.

When he had come outside the village, his brain had become so befuddled that he sat down by the side of the track to rest, so that he might get some easement.

"Old fool!" he muttered. "Whatever happens you must get to St Just!"

He awoke to the brittle twinkling of stars, and scrambled to his feet with an oath. He searched the heavens for The Plough and when he found it muttered, "Half-way to midnight! But I must get to St Just!" and he strode off, steadier now, along the track.

But his head burned like a thunder-bolt must burn, and for minutes at a time he was only half-conscious of what he was doing for the pain of it.

When he had been walking about an hour, he suddenly realized that the landmarks about him were strange, and in a sobering moment

he knew that he had left the track. He stopped and looked about him, but could see nothing that he recognized.

Turning about, he began to retrace his steps, hoping that they would bring him back to the right track. What he did not know was that there was no path beneath his feet, that he was going off at a tangent and that when he looked up at the Pole star he was already more than a mile too far to the south.

In his anxiety at the thought that he would not now reach St Just by midnight, he began to panic a little. He plunged forward, not knowing where he was going, telling himself again and again that he must get to St Just come what may.

Then suddenly there was no ground at all beneath his feet. He was falling and falling until it never seemed as if he would stop, his cries deafening him with the fright. At last the ground struck him. It shook every bone in his body and he lay while the pain of it receded and his shaken brain cleared.

Gingerly he put out a hand and felt about him. There was solid earth beneath his hands, but what they touched were mostly stones. He knew then that he had fallen into one of the pits that the Romans had dug in their search for tin. It might be any one of half a dozen such pits, but not one of them was within a mile or more of the track over the dunes from Sancreed to St Just.

He put his weight on his hands to pull himself up, but as he tried to gather his legs under him, frightful pains burned their way through every limb, making red and green lights shudder before his eyes and his brain recoil. He sank down again with a groan.

The pain having eased a little, he tried again. This time the effects were more terrible than before, and he lost consciousness. When he came round he told himself that one or both of his legs were broken, and that he would not be able to move till help came.

The non-arrival of his father on Sunday, as he had promised, neither surprised nor worried Frank Thomas or his wife. He was not even perturbed when he had not arrived by bed-time on Monday.

"He'll not have been able to stay away from the inn on Saturday night," Frank remarked to Beth. "He'll be sleeping himself sober."

"I suppose you'll be right," Beth agreed. "But he did promise me solemnly, and this is the first time he has ever broken his promise to me."

"It is Christmas, you know," Frank reminded her. "They will have got him as drunk as a lord."

But when her father-in-law had not arrived by dinner-time on Tuesday, Beth did become anxious, and before the meal was over

she had persuaded her husband to take a lantern and go to Sancreed to see what was amiss.

"I feel it in my bones something has happened to him," she insisted.

At his father's cottage, Frank found all in darkness. From the general tidiness of the place, however, he surmised that his father had not been there that day, or had set out for St Just. But if the latter were the case, they must have met.

Puzzled, Frank went down to the inn. There he learned that his father had left at three o'clock on the Sunday afternoon. Certainly he had been drinking, but he knew what he was about; and if he was a bit unsteady in his gait, he knew the direction he must take.

"Then he must have gone off the track," Frank told them, "because there was no sign of him as I came over."

It was too late to do anything that night, but early next morning, as soon as it was light, the men and boys of Sancreed met at the inn, divided themselves into parties and set off in all directions. They returned at dusk, all to report failure. No sign of John Thomas had been found.

A similar search next day having similar results, they concluded that whatever had happened to the old man he must now be dead. All they could do was to wait until some wanderer stumbled on his skeleton.

The following Sunday, James Trethewy, one of John Thomas's neighbours, set out from Sancreed to visit his sister in St Buryon. Like the old man, he decided to cross the dunes.

Not far from the track which he was following there were two or three of the ancient workings, one of which he had to pass by quite close.

As he approached this pit, though was still some distance away, he saw a stranger sitting on the bank which had been thrown up round the edge of the pit on the track side, as a protection for travellers like himself. On his coming nearer, the man stood up and walked round to the other side of the pit, and disappeared behind a bush.

Thinking to warn him of the danger he was running, Trethewy left the track and hurried round the edge of the pit, but when he came to the place where he had last seen the man there was no one there, and though he went carefully round the edge of the pit, searching behind every bush, and looking in every direction, he could find no one, nor any indication that anyone had been there.

Bewildered, but wishing to be in St Buryon before darkness fell, Trethewy went on. He stayed the night with his sister, and in the

middle of Monday morning, set off back to Sancreed, following the way by which he had come.

It was a bright, sunny day, though the sun was low in the heavens, and the rays of it pale and feeble. Still, it was a practical day for practical people. On such a winter day there could be no possibility of seeing strange sights or hearing strange sounds, as could often be heard over the dunes when the skies were black and lowering, and heavy banks of clouds scudded over sea and land.

During his short stay with his sister, Trethewy had forgotten about the man who had been by the pit as he had come over the day before. But as he started to cross the dunes the scene brought the incident back to him, and as he went along whistling quietly to himself, stepping out with the exhilaration of the autumn borrowed day, he pondered upon who the stranger might be and where he had gone. Cornishmen, even today, do not take kindly to those they do not know or cannot identify as having legitimate business among them. In the times of which we are writing, when the smugglers and the wreckers were at the peak of their activities, they disliked even more anyone who might be an excise spy.

"It was obvious that he didn't want to speak to me, or to let me get a close look at him," Trethewy mused. "But what I can't make out is, how did he manage to disappear so completely? I've never heard of there being caves in or nearby the pits. This will keep Tom Blower happy for hour after hour."

Blower was the Sancreed parson's clerk, who, because he could read, write and cipher, believed himself to be, among his illiterate fellow-villagers, the fountain of all knowledge.

And so Trethewy went along, now creasing his forehead with answered questions, now smiling as he heard Blower from the chimney settle in the inn begin, "Well, my ignorant friends, it is like this, as you would know if any two of you had an A and a B between you . . ."

He was perhaps half a mile from the pit, when his eye caught something which made him stop in his tracks, and utter an oath.

"By St Michael! That's him again!"

There was no mistaking the man, who, despite the cold of the last days of December, wore no hat, a point about him which Trethewy had unconsciously taken note of the day before.

"What's he doing here? He must be an excise agent. I've heard that some of the Boskenna men have a hide-out hereabouts. If he is an excise man, they must be warned. I'll catch up with him and see what he has to say for himself."

So he began to walk more quickly, but the faster he went so the man walking before him seemed to go. He put his hands about his mouth and called out as loudly as his lungs would give, "Holla, there! Wait for me, and we can walk together."

But if the man heard he did not turn his head or stop, but hurried on.

Angry at the man's refusal, and more suspicious now than ever, and determined to come up with the man and have a look at him, Trethewy broke into a run. But though the man did not appear to be running himself, he came no nearer.

As the bank edging the pit came in sight, the man left the track and began to move round the top of the pit, exactly as he had done yesterday.

Trethewy swore aloud.

"He must have a hide-out there somewhere, and he's making for it," he said aloud between pants, for he was not so young as he had been. "I'll watch carefully where he goes."

So he slowed up to a walk, and moved from the track himself, keeping his eyes always on the man, who was now nearing the bush behind which he had seemed to disappear on that first occasion. But this time, when he reached the bush, he did not go behind it, but stood on the edge of the pit looking down, his back still turned to his pursuer.

Now at last Trethewy was coming up with him.

"Hi," he called. "Stand back from the edge. It's dangerous, man. If it breaks away, you'll be done for."

Still the man ignored him.

Trethewy had come within a dozen yards of him, and again he called out a warning.

Now the man turned, and Trethewy stopped dead in his tracks. He knew the man after all. But this was not as he was now, but as he had been thirty or more years ago.

"John Thomas!" he gasped. "You!"

While these words were being forced from his throat, the figure raised its right arm and pointed with its finger over the edge of the pit.

"What is it then, lad?" Trethewy asked, and found himself approaching against his will. He was near enough to touch the figure now. "What is it?" he asked again.

Gesturing with what seemed to be impatience, the figure looked him full in the face, its eyes shining, its brow creased with an expression of anger; and even as Trethewy peered back at it, slowly it

began to dissolve and disappear, until only the hand with the finger pointing downwards remained, disembodied. Then it, too, vanished.

If Trethewy lacked the learning of Tom Blower, he was not entirely devoid of commonsense. Throwing himself down at full length, he worked his way carefully towards the crumbling edge of the pit, but when he could see the bottom there was nothing but stones and clumps of coarse grass.

He was never able afterwards to explain why he called out, "Hallo, is there anyone down there?"

And then he received another shock, for faintly there came up to him a cry, "Help! It's me, John Thomas of Sancreed. Help!"

Trethewy pushed himself a little farther out, and now he could see, right up under the wall of the pit's side, the figure of a man lying, and what was more he recognized him as his neighbour, John Thomas, not as he was thirty years ago, but as he had last seen him in Sancreed inn nine days back.

"It's me, James Trethewy," he called down. "I'm going to fetch help. We'll be back in no time."

He scrambled to his feet and despite his paunch, he ran all the two miles to Sancreed. He had some difficulty in persuading his neighbours that he had spoken to John Thomas, but they could not deny that he had seen him at the bottom of the pit.

"We can't leave his corpse there," they said, "otherwise the old man will haunt us for the rest of our lives."

So they fetched ropes, and marched out to the pit. There they lowered two men with ropes, and when they heard the voices of the men excitedly calling up to them, "He's alive! James was right! He's alive!" no one could have been more surprised.

William Moore of Redruth gave the first account of this strange event in a letter to the *Arminian Magazine*, which was published within a month of its taking place, on 22 January, 1784. Mr Moore had taken the trouble to travel to Sancreed to interview Thomas and his friends before he wrote his description. He concluded his letter:

"As Thomas had been there in the pit more than eight days, he was very low when he was got out; but is now in a fair way to do well, his legs mending amazingly for so old a gentleman. In the bottom of the pit, near to where he fell, he found a small current of water; which he drank freely of. This, in all likelihood, was the means of keeping him alive."

There were few in Sancreed, however, who would credit this. "He has pickled himself over the years," they said. "That s what kept him alive."

Radiant Boys

Radiant Boys are a particular kind of ghost. They are the spirits of children murdered by their mothers, and their usual function is to warn those to whom they appear that a violent end threatens to overtake them.

Though far more numerous in German spirit-lore—where they are described as *Kindermorderinn*—English spirit-lore does contain a number of outstanding examples. It has been suggested that their presence in England has its origin in the Scandinavian and North-European settlers who came here in the ninth and tenth centuries, bringing their folk-lore with them.

This explanation can certainly be acceptable for one of the most famous of all English Radiant Boys, the one which, until the early years of the last century, haunted Corby Castle, which stands above the densely wooded banks of the River Eden, in Cumberland.

The Howard family have for many years been the owners of Corby. Nowadays the castle has the appearance of being the typical eighteenth-century country mansion that it chiefly is; but the site on which it stands has been the site of numerous ancient buildings, whose remains have been incorporated in successive ones. The first of these ancient buildings was a tower built by the Romans as part of their defensive system against marauding Picts and Scots. This tower was extended in Norman times into a castle, but when the Norman extensions fell into decay it remained and, with its massive walls, from eight to ten feet thick, and its spiral stone staircase, still forms part of the present so-called castle.

The room frequented by the Radiant Boy of Corby was in the older part of the castle adjoining the Roman tower. Its windows looked out on the inner courtyard. It was, therefore, neither remote nor solitary, but surrounded on all sides by rooms which were in constant use.

Reached by a passage cut through an eight-foot-thick wall, it measured twenty-one feet by eighteen. At the beginning of the nineteenth century it was used as a bedroom, but later as a study. When it took over the latter function, the current owner removed the bed and replaced some of the more ancient heavy dark furniture with modern pieces. Apart from this, however, the room remained as it had been for many years.

One wall of the room was hung with tapestry, the others with old family pictures and some pieces of embroidery thought to have been worked by nuns. Over a press, which had doors of Venetian glass, was a wooden carving of an ancient figure, with a battle-axe in his hand. This figure had been one of a number which the burgesses of Carlisle had placed on the walls of their city to give the impression to would-be invaders that the border-town was well guarded.

The owner had hoped that by taking away the bed and replacing some of the furniture he would remove "a certain air of gloom which I thought might have given rise to the unaccountable reports of apparitions and extraordinary noises which were constantly reaching us. But I regret that I did not succeed in banishing the nocturnal visitor."

The last authenticated appearance of the Radiant Boy was early in September, 1803. In this case, however, the Boy seems to have been behaving wilfully, for no calamity overtook the man who saw him. In fact, twenty years later, this man was still dining out on the strength of his experience.

A house-party had been invited to the castle, and among the guests were the Rector of Greystoke, near Penrith, and his wife. It was a large party and all the bedrooms of the castle had to be used. In her allocation of the rooms, Mrs Howard assigned that overlooking the courtyard to the parson and his wife. She did so without any deliberate intention, for her mind was completely void of any thoughts of the Boy.

On the morning after their arrival, the guests were at breakfast with their hosts in the dining-room when suddenly their attention was attracted by a commotion in the drive outside. A chaise-and-four was dashing up to the door at such speed that the driver seemed

to have difficulty in controlling the horses, for the carriage knocked down part of the fence protecting the flower-beds from the drive.

"Who on earth can it be arriving at this early hour?" Mr Howard remarked. "It would seem from the coachman's emulation of Jehu that he is the bearer of important tidings. Not ill, I hope," he concluded, smiling at his guests.

As he looked round the table, he noticed that the Rector of Greystoke had become very agitated. For a moment the parson could not speak, but as the chaise drew up on the gravel outside the windows he managed to stammer out: "I cannot expect you to forgive me, sir, but it is my chaise. I sent for it as soon as it was light. I fear we must leave at once. Come, my dear."

"But, Rector!" Mr Howard exclaimed. "Have you had bad news? Is there anything one might do to help you?"

"Nothing, sir," replied the Rector. "Except that you will not try to detain us."

"But something must be wrong, Mr A . . ." Mrs Howard said. "Have we offended you in any way? If so, we are extremely sorry and will do all we can to make amends."

"No, no," the Rector told her with increasing embarrassment, since all the guests were looking at him and his wife in silent bewilderment. "No, madam, you have been more than kind."

"Then why must you go?" asked Howard. "We were looking forward to your company for some days. Besides Colonel and Mrs S . . . are dining this evening especially to meet you. Pray, change your mind, there's a good fellow, and send the chaise away."

"I am truly sorry, sir," the Rector replied. "We realize that we are risking your friendship and kindness in responding to your hospitality in this way, but I implore you not to press us further, but to let us go."

"How can we do that unless you tell us what is wrong, for something so clearly is?" Howard persisted.

The Rector had already risen to his feet, and his wife, silent and weeping, followed his example.

"Forgive us," the Rector said, his voice catching a little, and left the table.

Mrs Howard, moved by Mrs A . . .'s obvious distress, followed and tried to comfort her. "If only you would tell us," she said.

Mrs A . . looked at her husband, but he shook his head. "Later, perhaps," he said, "but not now."

The Corby servants and the Rector's groom had already loaded the visitors' bags into the chaise, and holding out his hand to Mr

Howard, Mr A... attempted one last regret, but articulation failed him, and he turned abruptly, with a bow to Mrs Howard, and hurried to the carriage, where he helped his wife to mount. A moment later the chaise was hurtling down the drive.

Mr and Mrs Howard, perplexed and a little hurt, returned to their guests, whom they found discussing the strange occurrence among themselves.

As Howard sat down, one of the men asked, "Did he say anything to you out there?"

Howard shook his head. "Not a word," he said. "The Rector tried to assure us that nothing we had done was the cause of their sudden departure. But I am not so sure."

As he confided later to his diary, "They departed, leaving us in consternation to conjecture what could possibly have occasioned so sudden an alteration in their arrangements. I really felt quite uneasy lest anything should have given them offence; and we reviewed all the occurrences of the preceding evening in order to discover, if offence there was, whence it had arisen. But all our pains were vain; and after talking a great deal about it for some days, other circumstances banished the matter from our minds."

The "other circumstances" to which he referred was the entertainment of his guests, and when all had finally departed he discovered that he was still exercised in his mind by the Rector's hasty departure. For a day or two he tried to dismiss it from his thoughts, but eventually had to confess that he would know no peace of mind until he had learned the truth. So he decided that he must visit Greystoke and try to persuade the A...'s to be frank with him.

At Greystoke he was surprised and his bewilderment greatly increased by the warmth of the A...s reception.

"You will surmise why I have come," he said, as Mrs A... led the way to the drawing-room.

"Of course," the Rector told him. "Perhaps now we can set your mind at rest by proving that it was no default of your kind self which caused us to leave the castle so precipitously. I am sorry that we left as we did, but we had both been so much shaken by the experience—an experience which, I may say, both my reason and my profession ought to have rejected out of hand..."

As he heard these words, Howard understood at last what had happened.

"You saw the Radiant Boy!" he exclaimed, and was at a loss to imagine why this explanation had not occurred to him before,

except that he had not known which room the A...'s had been allotted.

"You mean you know that the castle is haunted by what you have so exactly described as a Radiant Boy, sir?" the Rector exclaimed.

"There is some sort of tradition at Corby that such an apparition does from time to time manifest itself,"Howard confessed,"but we— the family, that is—have always been somewhat sceptical about it, as it has never appeared to any Howard, but only to guests visiting the castle. He has not appeared for many years now, and I fear he did not cross my mind as a possible reason for your curtailing your visit so abruptly. I am sure, too, that Mrs Howard is equally innocent."

"My dear sir!" the Rector expostulated. "I do assure you that neither Mrs A ... nor I have ever entertained the thought that you deliberately set out to frighten us."

"Could you bear to tell me now what happened?"Howard asked.

"I am happy to say that we have long since recovered from the shock we had," replied the Rector. "But I hesitate to relate what occurred because as a man of intelligence and education, and more particularly as a priest, I feel I ought to reject the whole matter as a figment of the imagination."

"I feel much the same as you do,"Howard told him."On the other hand, I find it very difficult to dismiss as chimera the serious pro-testations of sensible men, and I do assure you that in the records of the Radiant Boy's manifestations, among the men and women who have declared they have seen him, are those whose level-headedness as well as their intellectual talents are beyond reproach or dispute. I will give you my solemn word that if you will tell me what you saw, I will breathe not a word of it to any living soul. My interest is purely in relating your account to previous ones."

The Rector, perceiving that it would be boorish of him not to comply with his visitor's request, agreed to accept Howard's assurances.

"Very well, sir,"he said."On those terms I will tell you. Soon after we went to bed, we fell asleep. It might be one or two in the morning when I awoke. I observed that the fire was totally extin-guished; but although that was the case, and we had no light, I saw a glimmer in the middle of the room, which suddenly increased to a bright flame.

"I looked out, apprehending that something had caught fire; when to my amazement I beheld a beautiful boy clothed in white, with bright locks resembling gold, standing by my bedside. He

remained in this position some minutes, fixing his eyes upon me with a mild and benevolent expression.

"He then glided gently towards the side of the chimney, where it is obvious there is no possible egress, and entirely disappeared. I found myself again in total darkness, and all remained quiet until the usual hour of rising.

"As soon as he had disappeared, I seemed to come suddenly to my senses. The vision was so real that at the time I could have reached out and touched him. It was the realization that it was no dream, that I had actually seen the Boy, as you call him, when I was in a state of complete awareness, which made my heart fail. I began to tremble and was so violent in my trembling that my wife awoke, and inquired what was wrong with me."

"I believed he had been struck with an ague," Mrs A . . . interpolated. "He was shaking uncontrollably. When he assured me that he was not ill, I became alarmed and pressed him to explain what had caused his trembling. For some minutes he refused."

"But I could not keep it to myself," the Rector went on. "I had to tell my wife, though I knew it would disturb her. Like me, she slept no more that night. I was in such a state that I could not risk a second experience by staying another night in the room, But we knew that all your other rooms must be occupied, so as soon as dawn broke I went down and dispatched one of your servants to summon my chaise.

"I had imagined that my groom could not possibly reach Corby until well after breakfast. His sudden and spectacular arrival while we were still at table frustrated our intention of slipping away quietly without disturbing you or your guests. I apologize sincerely for the embarrassment we caused you by leaving as we did, and for our refusal to give the reason. But as I have said, I was sure we should become laughing-stocks if I attempted an explanation. I fear I preferred to be thought impolite than to be the butt of jokes."

"I understand perfectly," Howard assured him. "Thank you for being so forthcoming now. You must pay us another visit at Corby and we will see that you do not occupy the Boy's room again."

Howard kept his word, and put the Rector's experience on record only in his personal journal. Whether the parson eventually decided that perhaps after all he had been too sensitive to the possible reactions of his neighbours, or his wife proved garrulous, not long after his revelations to Mr Howard he is found recounting his experiences in all kinds of company. As we have said, as late as 1824 he was still dining out on the story.

As for the Boy, throughout the next half-century he is recorded as having appeared to a variety of people, some of whom died in violent circumstances, but many of whom, like the Rector of Greystoke, found his manifestation a benevolent experience. Since the middle of the last century the Corby Boy seems to have deserted the castle altogether.

The origin of the Boy is explained neither in record nor in tradition. The same applies to the Radiant Boy who appeared to Lord Castlereagh many years before he cut his throat at North Cray Place, in 1822.

At the time, Castlereagh was still Captain Robert Stewart, second son of the Marquis of Londonderry, and was quartered in Ireland. He was fond of sport, and one day while out shooting he went so far into unfamiliar country that he lost his way. The weather, by the time he realized he was lost, had deteriorated, and this prompted him to seek shelter at a country house.

He sent in his card, with a request for shelter for the night, and Irish hospitality being what it is the master of the house received him warmly, though he pointed out that he already had many guests, and could not make Captain Stewart so comfortable as he would have wished. However, to such accommodation as he could give the Captain was heartily welcome.

"You are very kind, sir," Castlereagh assured him. "I shall be more than grateful for shelter, warmth and somewhere where I may stretch out."

"I am sure there must be a bed," his host replied, and rang for his butler, to whom he gave instructions to do his best for Captain Stewart.

As his host had said, the house was crammed, but the guests, some of whom were casual refugees from the weather like himself, made a good party. Over dinner, when his host asked him if he had to return to his regiment the next day, and learned that he had still three days of his leave left, he agreed with alacrity to accept the invitation to stay as long as he could, for he was promised some good shooting.

After an agreeable evening, the party at last went to bed, and the butler showed Stewart to his room. It was a large room, empty of furniture except for a couple of chairs and a press. In the wide grate, however, a magnificent peat fire was burning, and before it a mattress and a heterogeneous collection of cloaks and other covers had been made up. Rough though it was, to the weary Captain Stewart it was as inviting as the most comfortable of beds.

It seemed to him that the fire was blazing up the chimney in a rather alarming manner, so he removed some of the peat, and then stretched out on the mattress and was quickly asleep. He had slept about two hours, when he awoke suddenly and was startled by such a vivid light in the room that, like the Rector of Greystoke at Corby, he thought at first it must be the fire. But when he turned and looked at the grate he saw that the fire was quite dead.

As the light gradually grew brighter, he sat up, hoping to discover where it was coming from; and as he watched he saw that by degrees it was forming itself into a human form, which presently revealed itself as a very beautiful naked boy, surrounded by a cloud of light of the most dazzling radiance. The Boy gazed at him intently, and as the Captain gazed back, slowly the apparition began to fade until eventually it quite disappeared.

Stewart's first reaction was that his host and the other guests were amusing themselves at his expense, and were trying to frighten him. Naturally, he felt very indignant, and when he went down to breakfast next morning he showed by his demeanour that he was still displeased.

His host was puzzled by this change in his guest, who, the previous evening, had been the most genial member of the party; but when Stewart told him that he was leaving as soon as he had eaten, he realized that something was wrong.

"But, Captain Stewart!" he exclaimed. "You promised that you would join the party for two or three days!"

"I have changed my mind, sir,"Stewart replied, and so coldly that his host took him on one side and pressed him to tell him what had offended him.

All Stewart would say, however, was that he had been the victim of a practical joke, and that in his view this was quite unwarrantable treatment of one who was not only a guest, but also a stranger.

"By God, sir, you are right!"exclaimed his host. "Some of these young devils are quite thoughtless, and I apologize. If I make them present their apologies also, will you overlook the incident and continue to give us the pleasure of your company? I beg you to be so far generous. The shooting, I assure you, has never been excelled."

Stewart's fondness for sport persuaded him to be magnanimous. But when they returned to the breakfast room, and the host sternly demanded that those who had been responsible for the practical joke played on their distinguished fellow-guest during the night should apologize immediately, all the young men roundly protested their innocence.

Suddenly a thought struck the host, and clapping a hand to his forehead with a muttered imprecation he summoned the butler.

"Hamilton," he said to the servant, "where did Captain Stewart sleep last night?"

"Well, sir," the butler said, "you know the house was full. Some of the gentlemen were lying on the floor, three or four to a room. So I gave him the Boy's room. But," he went on hurriedly, "I lit a blazing fire, to keep him from coming out."

"But you know," his master told him angrily, "I have forbidden you to put anyone in the Boy's room. Why do you think I had all the furniture removed? If you do this again, Hamilton, we shall part company. Be good enough to come to my study, sir," he said to Stewart.

There he said, "Sir, I must offer you ten thousand apologies. You should not have been put in that room!"

"What's this about 'the Boy'?" Stewart asked.

"Forgive me, Captain, I would rather not go into particulars. Let us say that you saw the family ghost."

Stewart burst out laughing. "Come, sir, this really will not do, he said. "He was the prettiest ghost I am sure anyone ever saw."

"So others have deposed, sir," said his host. "When he took to haunting us, the family must have been on better days, for I am told that his golden suit . . ."

"Last night he was completely naked," Stewart interrupted him.

"Naked? That I have never heard before."

"Who is he?"

"He was the son of an ancestor, sir," his host explained. "Unhappily, his mother lost her reason, and in one of her most violent moods strangled the Boy, who was her youngest and favourite child, while he was asleep in the room where you passed the night. He was only nine or ten years old."

"And now he haunts the room. Does he trouble you?" Stewart asked, interested.

"He troubles us only if someone sees him," his host replied.

"Why only then?"

Once more his host seemed reluctant to answer him, and only when Stewart said that he would be offended if he would not satisfy his curiosity did the man acquiesce.

"Please remember that you have insisted. The tradition is that the Boy portends good and bad news. Whoever the Boy shows himself to experiences a period of the greatest prosperity. He will rise to the

summit of power, but at the very climax of his rise he will meet a violent death."

This reply seemed to sober Stewart. He was silent for some minutes, then he smiled, and said, "Well, sir, we've all to die sooner or later, and it does not seem to me to matter how death comes. If my period of prosperity makes life pleasant for me, then the end should be worth it. For you must know, sir, that I am only my father's second son, and my prospects are no better than any second son's. Indeed, at the moment it would appear that I shall spend the rest of my active career as a soldier. I am no great shakes at soldiering. A colonelcy is the most I can hope for."

Within a few years of the Boy's appearance, however, Captain Stewart's fortunes suddenly and spectacularly changed. His elder brother, the heir to the Marquisate of Londonderry, was drowned in a boating accident, and Stewart succeeded him, taking the courtesy title of Viscount Castlereagh.

The change in status brought a change in responsibilities, too, and soon the new Lord Castlereagh found himself occupying a prominent position in Irish affairs. The part he played in the political manoeuvres which resulted in 1800 in the Act of Union between England and Ireland was merely the opening of a brilliant career.

He now discovered that he possessed abilities of which he had been previously ignorant. These led him onward until he won a commanding position in successive English administrations. In 1805 he was appointed Secretary of War, and again in 1807; while from 1812 onwards, as Foreign Secretary, he conducted the country's foreign policy during one of the most important periods of its history.

Unfortunately, he developed into a man of cold, even actively antagonistic, manner, which caused him to be not merely unpopular, but cordially hated, even by the members of his own party. Yet he was not merely a strong man, such as the times demanded, but also successful in most of his schemes as a Minister for the welfare of the nation.

In 1821, on the death of his father, he became Marquess of Londonderry, though he remains best known as Castlereagh. There are two accounts as to the cause of his death. One states that towards the end of his life he suffered greatly from gout, and the continued anxieties of a long and trying public career began noticeably to tell upon him. His manner grew strange, and, on the suggestion of the Duke of Wellington, he sought medical advice, which did nothing to relieve his condition.

It was then seen that he appeared to be in imminent danger of losing his reason, and so serious did his condition become that he had to be confined to his country house, North Cray Place. As a precautionary measure, his razors were removed. This proved unavailing, however, and on 12 August, 1822, he cut his throat with a pen-knife.

The other version is less kind. It is purported by some social historians that he was a homosexual, and that he committed suicide as the result of blackmail. If this is true, the fact that the Radiant Boy appeared to him, alone of all its victims, naked adds a footnote which the psychiatrists will no doubt find interesting.

The third most famous manifestation of a Radiant Boy is recounted in connexion with Thomas, second Baron Lyttleton, known even during his life-time as The Bad Lord Lyttleton, on account of his dissipation, which he made no attempt to conceal. His affairs and his gambling were a scandal of the times, and the times—the latter half of the eighteenth century—were scandalous enough.

After an extremely colourful period on the continent—where his family had more or less banished him in an attempt to protect the good name of the Lyttletons—he returned to England and married a wealthy widow, named Apphia Peach, who possessed a fortune of £20,000. He refused to let her see her solicitor so that her money might be "tied up" in her favour, and under the laws of the times the £20,000 became legally his the moment he put the ring on Mrs Peach's finger. Within three months he had got through it all, and had so outraged his wife that she died shortly after.

The final curtain came down on this dissolute man in November, 1779. He had staying with him at his London home, Hill House, a Mrs Amphlett and her three young daughters, Elizabeth, who was nineteen, Christina, seventeen, and Margaret, fifteen.

Mrs Amphlett was more likely than not unhappy at the close proximity of her three pretty girls to the Wicked Lord. At all events, she cast such a wet blanket over the party that while she was lying down in her room, Lyttleton summoned his carriage, bundled in the three girls and hurried them down to his country house, Pit Place, not far from Epsom.

Just before midnight Lyttleton retired to bed. What happened next has been recounted by a friend, who was also staying in the house.

"He had been asleep only a short time," this account states, "when

he was awakened, by his own account, by a noise like the fluttering of a bird, outside the bed-curtains. He drew them back, and saw a figure dressed in white.

"Shocked, he demanded 'What do you want?' To which the apparition replied, 'Prepare to die. I am here to warn you that you have very little time left.' 'How long?' his lordship demanded in return. 'Weeks, months, perhaps a year?' 'You will die within three days,' the figure replied.

"His lordship was much alarmed, and called to a servant in a closet adjoining, who found him much agitated and in a profuse perspiration. The circumstance had a considerable effect all the next day upon his lordship's spirits. On the third day, which was a Saturday, his lordship was at breakfast with his guests, and was observed to have grown very thoughtful, but attempted to carry it off by the transparent ruse of accusing the others at table of unusual gravity. 'Why do you look so grave?' he asked. 'Are you thinking of the ghost? I am as well as ever I was in my life.'

"Later on he remarked, 'If I live over tonight, I shall have jockeyed the ghost, for this is the third day'.

"Early in the afternoon, his lordship experienced one of the suffocating fits which had troubled him during the preceding month. After a short interval he recovered, dined at five o'clock, and went to bed at eleven. When his servant was about to give him a dose of rhubarb and mint-water, his lordship, perceiving him stirring it with a tooth-pick, called him a slovenly dog, and bade him go and fetch a teaspoon.

"On the man's return, he found his master in a fit, and, the pillow being placed high, his chin bore hard upon his neck; when the servant, instead of relieving his lordship on the instant from his perilous situation, ran, in his fright, and called out for help; but on his return he found his lordship dead."

So, he did not "jockey the ghost", as he expressed it and as he might reasonably have hoped to do, for he was only thirty-five.

Another strange incident is told in connexion with his death. It would seem that Lord Lyttleton had proposed visiting an intimate friend, Miles Peter Andrews, who lived at Dartford, on the day of his death. His spirits were so low, however, that he did not feel equal to the occasion; he also failed to send an explanation for his absence.

During the evening Andrews was taken ill and retired to bed early. He had not yet fallen asleep when the curtains of his bed were suddenly drawn back, and he saw Lord Lyttleton standing there,

wearing the distinctive dressing-gown which he kept at his friend's house.

The surprised Andrews believed that Lyttleton had made a belated arrival, and probably intended some practical joke. So he called out to the figure, "You are up to some of your tricks. Go to bed, or I'll throw something at you". But the figure merely gazed at him seriously, and said, "It's all over with me, Andrews".

Andrews, who still believed that it was his friend who stood before him, reached down, picked up a slipper and threw it; whereupon the figure moved silently into the dressing-room. Having been a previous victim of Lyttleton's practical joking, Andrews got from his bed and followed the figure into the dressing-room. But when he tried both the door of the dressing-room and the door of his own bedroom, he found that both were bolted.

Mystified, but still suspecting nothing but a trick, he rang for the servants, and asked them where Lord Lyttleton was. They replied that so far as they knew, he was not in the house.

"Well," said Andrews, "if he does come, tell him that all the beds are occupied, and that he must seek a room in one of the inns at Dartford."

It was not until late on the following day that Andrews heard of his friend's death. He fell into a deep faint, and "was not his own man again for three years".

Alarm at Wellington Barracks

George Jones was nineteen, a private in the Coldstream Guards.
Like any other soldier in His Majesty's Army, even at the best of
times he did not find sentry-go at the Recruit House, as Wellington
Barracks was known in 1804, one of the more attractive of the
military duties he was called upon to perform. But there was no
getting out of it. Every man in the regiment had to take a turn at it
some time or other, though to some, among them George, it
seemed to come round more often than it did to others more
fortunate.

The trouble with George was that he missed the Welsh valley
which he had deserted at the same time that he had deserted Geronwy
Williams, who would so firmly claim that the brief, and to him
disappointing, incident that had happened "up the mountain" had
yet been long enough, so she insisted, to make a father of him. If
Geronwy had been less like her mother he would have "done right
by her" while hoping for the best; but he saw the force of his own
mother's remark when he had confided in her that Gwyneth
Williams for mother-in-law would make life hell for any man,
while the combination of Geronwy as wife would undoubtedly be
the death of him.

"If you wanted to go up the mountain," his mother had gone on,
"why didn't you take a nice sensible girl like Gladys Evans the
Butcher? She would have played fair by you, because she isn't like
Geronwy who knows that her chances of getting a husband while
her mother continues in the land of the living are very slim. If

anything had happened with Gladys you could have married her and had a good wife. Sometimes, George bach, I wonder why the good Lord has given me such innocents for children. This valley is no Garden of Eden, I tell you, even if all you young fellows imagine yourselves to be Adam. There are more serpents here than in a hundred Edens, and they don't walk on their bellies, but upright on their feet—and they're all female."

"Geronwy says she'll let the whole valley know I took her up the mountain against her will—dragged her up by the hair, she said —if I don't marry her. But you're right, mam, her mam would be the death of me. What shall I do?"

"If it was any other girl, I'd say defy her, stay and brazen it out," his mother told him. "But that won't work with Geronwy Williams in league with her mother. They'll have you in the church before you can say coal-mine. There's only one thing you can do, George— leave the valley while the going is good; and that means before first-light tomorrow.'

"Leave the valley, mam!" The very idea made him go cold all over. "But, mam, where shall I go?"

"Go to London, like David Rees and Alun Griffiths, and apply for fat George s pence," Mrs Jones advised briskly. "They've joined the Coldstream Guards, so you'd have friends there. It's a pity the Welch aren't in London, but you can't have everything. Once you're in the King's uniform, she can't touch you. But if you stay here, I'll guarantee she's Mrs George Jones within three months."

"I suppose you're right, mam," her son agreed. "Oh God! What's me dad going to say?"

"You leave him to me!" his mother promised. "Say nothing."

It all happened so suddenly that almost before he knew where he was he was in London and asking the way to the Recruit House, and before he could say *coal-mine*, he was donning the King's uniform, and pocketing the King's pence.

That had all taken place some eight months ago. He had settled down reasonably well, and was in the process of being transformed into a fair specimen of a fighting-man. He was happiest when taking orders—which was mostly all that was required of him— and both he and his NCOs appreciated the fact that he was unlikely for reasons of intellectual quality to rise above the rank of private.

To begin with he had found London a bewildering place. There were so many people, and the press of carriages in all the main thoroughfares made a clatter which would have sent the people of the valley mad. He was also disappointed when he found there were

no mountains one might go up, until David and Alun showed him that mountains were not necessary. But even so, there were times when he longed for the peace and quiet of the valley, a longing accentuated by a letter he received from his mother three or four months after his arrival at the Recruit House, telling him in effect that his flight had been unnecessary, since time had proved that Geronwy Williams had suffered no effect, either good or ill, from going up the mountain with him.

He was thinking about the valley now, and musing on the immoral designings of females, as he stood at ease in his box at half-past one in the morning of 3 January, 1804. All was quiet, and the quietness was made more acute by the thick carpet of snow which blanketed the streets and dwellings of London.

It was piled in long low ridges along the edges of the parade ground, the result of hours of shovelling by his fellow privates. He supposed that there was some advantage in being on guard at times like this, since while his companions had laboured, he had been snugly asleep in his bunk; though it would have been good to have a shovel in one's hands again.

Peering surreptitiously round the edge of his box to make certain that no snooping NCO or orderly officer was making his rounds, George cradled his rifle in the crotch of his left arm and banged his gloved hands together. It was a cold night, though not so cold as he had known it in the valley.

As he tried to increase the feeling in his numbed fingers, he stared across the square at the trees in the park. Under the silver light of the lately risen moon they looked like sugar-coated pyramids. "Pretty, they are," he muttered half-aloud. "Mam would like to see them."

The sound of heels being clicked dully two hundred yards on his left brought him to his duty. Shouldering his rifle, he stepped smartly out of his hut, jerked himself round so that he faced his left, and counting to himself, with right arm swinging in the approved fashion, he set off at measured pace to meet the figure he could plainly see approaching him with the same gait.

It was David Rees, who, as he drew nearer, called softly to George, "Hellish quiet, ain't it, bach?"

"As quiet as the valley," George agreed. "The trees in the park are pretty."

The two soldiers came together face to face, halted with muffled thuds of their feet, and slowly began to turn about.

"Saw your Polly tonight," David said between closed teeth, as he

performed his motions. "She asked where you were. Said you'd missed a treat tonight. Where were you?"

"Cleaning the colonel's copper scuttles, worse luck!" George explained. "That was the greatest mistake I made."

"What was?"

"Tell you next time," George said over his shoulder, for they were now standing back to back. "Was Polly peevish I wasn't there?"

"You're right. She said tell you to be there tomorrow or she'll look around. You're seldom there, she said, when the time's most right."

Though they spoke no word aloud, both men stepped smartly off, making back to their boxes with unhurried tread.

"I'll be there!" George told himself. Somehow he would have to arrange it that the colonel's lady called for someone else to clean her scuttles the next time she thought it necessary.

The short walk had done a little towards restoring his circulation, and he settled back into his box, the valley forgotten, what he had missed put out of his mind by the anticipatory warmth of his meeting with Polly tomorrow. The pleasure he was experiencing, however, was not so all-embracing as to prevent him from ruminating on the dictatorial propensities of womankind. For in her way, Poll was little different from Geronwy Williams, or Gladys Evans, or Blodwen Richards, when it came to the point. Nevertheless, of the half-dozen or so girls whom he had known in the way that he had known Polly, she was the one with whom he felt most safe; safe enough to marry, later on perhaps—if he could get out of cleaning copper scuttles at unpropitious moments.

Once more the quietness all around made itself known to him. Once more he looked across at the trees in St James's Park, and remarked to himself how pretty they were. Odd though it might seem, he found himself sighing with contentment.

Suddenly, however, his peace with the world was shattered, the pretty trees in the park sent scurrying from his thoughts, and all his limbs were seized with a cramping coldness that had nothing to do with the snow or the frost. Had some emergency arisen now, he could not have dealt with it, for he was clamped to the spot, unable to move even those muscles which would have allowed him to cry for help, while his eyes were rooted to a spot on the ground before him from which the cause of his terror slowly rose.

From the hard and gravelled surface of the parade-ground, at a spot where no manhole cover was, not four feet away from him, with slightly swaying motion, ascended a figure of a woman. In

the moonlight George could clearly discern the pattern of her gown; it was of cream satin with broad red stripes, and between the stripes were vertical rows of red spots. When she had emerged to the height of her waist, a curiously phosphorescent mist gradually began to form about her, and as more of her appeared, until at last the hem of her gown swept the ground, so it enveloped her, and yet did not envelop her, but swirled about her in a kind of eddying frame.

Her very appearance, as George was later to confess, would have been enough to throw him off balance; but there was one specific feature of her that was the real cause of his terror.

She had no head!

The stump of her neck, jagged and torn and raw, rose up out of a lace ruffled collar. It swayed a little towards him two or three times, as if, had there been a head, its owner were addressing herself to him.

Completely paralysed though he was, George knew that he ought to challenge the apparition, but when he tried to speak he could force no sound from tongue or lips.

For fully two minutes, he afterwards deposed, the apparition stood there facing him. Then slowly it turned about and began to walk with slow stately stride across the parade-ground towards the park. When it was some fifty yards from him, it disappeared from his sight.

Only when it had gone did George regain the power of movement. So well had his drill sergeants done their work, however, that without any outward panic he stepped out of the box, and marched to the half-way point between his box and that of David Rees. There he paused.

"David! David!" he called quietly. "Come here, quick!"

"Don't be a damn fool!" he heard David call back. "Do you want us both in the guard-house?"

"David, please come here!" George called again. "I'm not fooling. I've seen something."

"I'll knock the daylight out of you," David replied, "if you are fooling." But he had detected an unwonted urgency in George's voice, and swung out of the box and marched smartly to him.

When George had told him what had happened, David replied that it must have been a trick of the moonlight on the snow.

"It wasn't, I tell you!" George insisted. "It was a woman, and she had no head. She stood there for fully two minutes, before she turned and walked off across the square. If it had been a trick of the

moonlight it wouldn't have lasted so long. What do you think I ought to do?"

"You'll have to tell the orderly officer and the sergeant of the guard who are just coming up behind you,"his friend told him.

"What do you think you two men are doing?"the sergeant asked sharply when he came up. "Don't you realize that you both risk a charge for leaving your post while on guard duty?"

"Jones says he's just seen a ghost, sir."

"That's likely!"snapped the disbelieving sergeant.

"Well," said George. "It can't have been a living person, because it had no head."

"There are no ghosts in the Recruit House,"affirmed the sergeant. "I'll deal with you when you're relieved. Come to me in the guard-house as soon as you've handed in your weapon."

"Sergeant!"George replied smartly.

"Get back to your posts, both of you."

As the sergeant and orderly officer walked away, the sergeant quite forgetting that the Ensign's name was ap Rice, said, "Bloody Welsh! They're as bad as the Scots when it comes to seeing things."

"I would suggest that you might be mistaken,"replied the recently-joined young Ensign diffidently.

"I beg pardon, sir," the sergeant apologized. "But your country-men are . . ."

"Shall we say more sensitive than you very practical Englishmen? the Ensign suggested.

"By all means, sir,"agreed the sergeant, silently telling himself that this young gentleman would go far. "Perhaps you would care to question Jones when he comes off duty."

"No, sergeant. I'll leave that to you. But perhaps I might be present."

When half an hour later, in response to the sergeant's invitation to give a full account of what he thought he had seen, George did so exactly, and refused to be persuaded that the whole incident could be rationally explained. His stubbornness puzzled the sergeant. If the Ensign had not been present, he would undoubtedly have put George on extra duties, but since he was anxious to show Mr ap Rice that Englishmen are not the irrational beings he and his countrymen were he dismissed George with a warning.

"Well what do you think?"the Ensign asked when George had gone.

"A trick of the moonlight, sir,"the sergeant said.

"You don't think the man was lying?"

"No, sir, I don't. But no more do I believe in ghosts."

"Don't you, sergeant? Don't you?" Smiling, the Ensign left the guardroom.

After a moment's cogitation, the sergeant drew the incidence-book towards him, and wrote, "Private Jones, G., reported that while on sentry duty on No. 3 point, at about half after one in the morning, he saw the ghost of a headless woman on the parade ground".

When the adjutant inspected the book the following morning and read the sergeant's laconic entry, he smiled. One could always trust the Welsh to be diverting, he told himself.

The incident might have been quite forgotten had not another sentry, three nights later, on guard at No. 3 point, been found by the orderly officer and sergeant of the guard in a dead faint in his box. When he came to, he told much the same story as George had told.

At his later interrogation, it was suggested to him that he had allowed George's story play too much on his imagination. On the face of it this seemed unlikely, because the man was a guardsman with some years' service, during which he had proved himself to be an eminently practical soldier. In any case, he told his interrogators, he had not heard George's story.

This turned out to be quite true, because when George had had some sleep, and came to think over what had happened, in the cold light of day it seemed too fantastic. So he had decided to keep quiet about it, and made David Rees promise to do the same.

The Englishman was then recalled, and was instructed on pain of court martial on a charge of disobeying a lawful order to keep absolutely mum.

When, however, the following week yet another veteran guardsman reported an identical experience, it became virtually impossible for the story not to get around the regiment, with somewhat unsteadying results.

Nor was this all. The headless lady was soon found not to be the only ghost haunting the environments of Recruit House. Another sentry, one Richard Donkin, while on duty behind the Armoury House, had an unsettling experience which he reported not only to his superiors, but to all who would listen to him.

The matter had now reached such a pitch that the Colonel realized that unless something were done the effect on the regiment could be extremely detrimental.

"Somehow we must show these stories to have no basis in fact whatsoever," he wrote to the Secretary for War. "I therefore intend,

subject to no veto emanating from you, sir, to ask Sir Richard Ford, one of the Westminster magistrates, to undertake an inquiry, and to take from all those who claim to have had these experiences statements under oath, with all the consequences for the committal of perjury attached thereto."

So Sir Richard Ford set up his court of inquiry in the barracks, and took statements from all concerned, beginning with George. The one point which immediately struck him on comparing the various statements was the similarity of the facts set out by the witnesses. The apparition rose from the ground, the aura of light was bright enough for the pattern of the gown to be seen even on a moonless night, and every man deposed that the figure was headless. Then, too, it always turned away, and began to walk towards the canal which (at that time) ran through St James's Park.

Now Sir Richard was an old inhabitant of Westminster, and going back over the history of the Foot Guards he recalled that some twenty years before there had been some scandal attaching to the Coldstreams; something to do with murder. On looking up the records, he discovered that his memory was sound. A sergeant in the Guards had killed his wife, and in an attempt to make it difficult to identify the body, had hacked off the head before throwing the remainder of the corpse in the canal in the park, from which it was eventually recovered. His gruesome attempt to escape the consequences of his crime failed, because five witnesses came forward who were able to show that the gown—of cream satin with red stripes and red spots between the stripes—in which the body was clothed when taken from the canal, was the same that the sergeant's former wife had once possessed.

This, contrary to the hopes of the colonel, provided a basis of possibility for the headless lady, though it did not explain why she had not decided to "walk" before, for there was no record of her having been seen by anyone before she appeared to George Jones. With Richard Donkin's ghost, Sir Richard Ford had less success.

Donkin's signed statement, which he made to the magistrate, reads thus:

"At about twelve o'clock at night, I was on sentry duty behind the Armoury House, when I heard a loud noise coming from an empty house near my post.

"At the same time I heard a voice cry out, 'Bring a light! Bring me a light!' The last word was uttered in so feeble and changeable a tone of voice that I concluded that some person was ill, and consequently offered them my assistance. I could, however, obtain no

answer to my proposal, although I repeated it several times, and as often the voice used the same terms.

"I endeavoured to see the person who called out, but in vain. On a sudden the violent noise was renewed, which appeared to me to resemble sashes of windows lifted hastily up and down, but that they were moved in quick succession and in different parts of the house, nearly at the same time, so it seems to me impossible that one person could accomplish the whole business.

"I heard several of my regiment say they have heard similar noises and proceedings, but I have never heard the calls accounted for. I would not have reported this occurrence had it not been for the incidents relating to the headless lady."

The house was identified and searched. It had been empty for a number of years, but except for deterioration natural to being so long unoccupied, nothing was found which would account for the sounds of the opening and closing of windows. The records were also searched, but nothing came to light to suggest a possible reason, whether rational or irrational, for the ghostly voice, or the other sounds.

With regard to the headless lady, to restore confidence among the men the sentry points at the Recruit House were re-sited, so that no box stood near to the spot where she always appeared. This reorganization soon proved to have been unnecessary, however, for a clergyman, having asked permission to spend the night at former No. 3 point, and having passed the whole of his watch reciting prayers for the souls of the faithful departed, she was never seen again.

The Ghost of Garpsdal

Iceland is a country famous for ghosts and supernatural manifestations of all kinds. One of its most impressive stories concerns a minister of the Church, and has been set down and witnessed by another.

In the year 1807 there was living at a house called Garpsdal a young minister, Mr Saemund, and his wife and child. Mr Saemund was a man of some fortune, and Garpsdal was by way of being a small estate, something between manor-house and farmstead. There were sheep and cows in the Saemund pastures, Saemund boats on the sea-shore close by, servants and farm-workers "living in" at Garpsdal. It was a comfortable and peaceful household, which made the disturbances of Autumn, 1807, all the more strange.

It all began one September night when three of Mr Saemund's servants were sleeping in the room they shared. Outside a harvest moon shone on quiet fields, a few white still forms that were recumbent sheep, and a silver sea beyond. Suddenly, a shattering noise broke the silence—the door of the servants' bedroom cracked and splintered as though an axe had been driven through it. The three started up—Thorsteinn Gudmundsson, the eldest, reaching for his staff, which always lay beside him at night—Magnus Jonsson, the young shepherd, rubbing his eyes, while the boy Thorstein ran behind him for shelter.

"Stand by to fight him, lads!" shouted Gudmundsson.

But no one entered. When they unlatched the broken door, there was no one on the landing outside, nor had anyone else

234

in the house been disturbed. Baffled, they all went back to bed.

Next day another alarming thing occurred. Mr Saemund was sitting in his garden-house, making notes for a sermon; it was a fine, warm day. His peace was broken by the sound of loud, furious hammering and the splintering of wood. He looked up; there was nothing to be seen, and he concluded that the noise was coming from the direction of the seashore. He put down his notebook and hurried through the home-meadow and out by the gate that led to the shore. All the way he could hear the steady sounds of chopping, hammering and breaking. He arrived on the beach, and stopped in consternation. His finest fishing-boat, the *Sigrid*, lay ruined on the sand—her timbers shattered, her mast broken, her sails torn off and flung into the sea. Deliberate violence of the most savage kind had destroyed her. But whose violence? As far as the eye could see, the beach was deserted. Other boats lay quiet and empty. Nobody could have run away in the short time since the sounds had ceased—which had been about the time Mr Saemund passed through the meadow-gate to the shore. No bobbing head revealed a fugitive swimming out to sea. There was nothing to account for the *Sigrid*'s wanton destruction.

Mr Saemund afterwards said that at this moment it did not occur to him that there might be a supernatural explanation. Somebody had done the damage and got away. How they had done so was another matter.

He was in church, marrying two of his parishioners, when the next outrage occurred. Nobody saw it, for most of his household were also at the ceremony. When they returned, they found the doors of four sheep-houses chopped to matchwood. "Aha!" said the minister, "this time the villain has been clever; he has picked a time when we were all away. Magnus, you must keep a sharp watch on the place tonight." He knew Magnus Jonsson for a smart, intelligent youth who would not be slow to strike down and capture the enemy.

But the stranger Magnus encountered that evening was not at all of the kind he expected. His dog, Glam, had rounded up the sheep and got them into the sheep-houses, and Magnus was going from one sheep-house to another making sure that the broken doors, which he had temporarily boarded up, were secure. He returned to the first one, and stopped in his tracks. All the ewes but one were huddled in a corner, as if in fear; the exception lay on its side on the ground, kicking and struggling as if held by an invisible attacker. Beside it, but not touching it, stood a young woman. Magnus's

impression was of a tallish, thin figure, fair hair dressed in two long braids, after the fashion of unmarried girls, and a blue or grey dress over which was a large apron. The face he could not describe except to say that it was "sharpish".

"What are you doing here?" he asked. "And what have you done to my ewe? She's dying!"

"I have not touched her," replied the woman. "I came to ask you to sell me a ewe for roasting, and thought I would choose one for myself. But since the creature is dying you may as well give her to me."

"We'll see what my master has to say about that!" replied Magnus angrily, and called out (though he knew his master was nowhere near), "Mr Saemund, come quickly! we've got a thief here!"

"He will not hear you," said the stranger with a cold smile. "The sheep is mine; see, it is almost dead."

At that moment there arrived on the scene an old woman servant, Gudrun Jonsdottir, who had lived at Garpsdal all her life. She was known for something of a Wise Woman, and had a wonderful way with animals.

"Come here, Gudrun!" called Magnus. "Here's one of my ewes been hurt by this woman here—see what you can do with it!"

Old Gudrun bustled in and knelt down creakily by the writhing animal, ignoring the woman who still stood motionless by it.

"Why, the poor thing—it's in a convulsion!" she exclaimed. "What has given it such a turn? There, there, be easy, lamb, be easy." And she handled, stroked, and patted it as if it had been a sick child. Magnus watched in astonishment as its struggles lessened and its panting breaths grew slower. After a moment or two it began to try to get up, and Gudrun gently helped it to its feet. It trotted quietly to join its sisters in the corner, while Magnus stared and Gudrun smiled contentedly.

"Gudrun can cure all the sick ones, you see," she said. "But what brought the poor thing into such a case?"

"Why, *she* did!" Magnus pointed to the strange woman—— she stood immovable, her face expressionless. "Get out, will you?" he said to her. "I'll set the dogs on you if you don't."

He moved to the door and opened it. As he did so, a beam in the ceiling broke as if a rending blow had been delivered to it, and the broken pieces of timber were flung with violent impetus in Magnus's face, by no visible agency. He threw up his hands to protect his eyes from the flying splinters; when he lowered them, the strange woman had vanished, though he had not felt her pass him. A moment

later, Mr Saemund's horses, which were stabled in the yard outside, began to whinny, neigh, and kick their stalls as if badly frightened. Magnus went out to them, but they were in too frenzied a state to approach; even Gudrun's soothing words had no effect.

Two days later a fearful outbreak of smashing and breaking occurred all over Garpsdal; panels were ruined, doors broken in, upstairs and downstairs the havoc was wrought. Half-crazed, Mr Saemund collected the servants and told them to stay in the hall while his great Bible was fetched. Then, as the bangs and crashes rang through the house, he held a short service of exorcism, and opened the house door, commanding the evil spirit to leave. Suddenly Magnus cried out: "There she goes!"

"Where? Where? Did you see her leave the house?

"No, she has gone into the sitting-room."

None of the others had seen this, but to Magnus's eyes the figure of the girl from the sheep-house had been clear. He ran into the sitting-room, Mr Saemund and some of the braver servants behind him. There she stood by the window, her dress now a clear grey and her hair lighter than it had looked before. Magnus pointed her out to his master.

"I see nobody!" said Mr Saemund in a puzzled tone. As he spoke, a pane of glass in the window shattered into small pieces.

"She has gone through the window!" cried Magnus; but could not explain how she could have done so—he merely knew that her figure had disintegrated and that he had seen something flit like a bird through the gaping hole in the glass.

That night, and for a week after, the sitting-room resounded with bangs and thumps, making it impossible to talk quietly or read without disturbance. Mr Saemund repeated the service of exorcism more elaborately, but without effect. Poor Magnus, the only one to have seen the spirit who was causing all the disturbances, came under some suspicion from his fellow-servants, who thought that he was in some way responsible and was playing some kind of trick on them. Magnus indignantly denied this, and Mr Saemund absolved him of blame, having stood beside him in the hall and sitting-room when the damage was being done.

On 28 September the troubles reached their height. That evening Magnus and two women servants were out in the barn; Mr Saemund and his wife were in the sitting-room. The evening had been fairly quiet after the noise of the previous week; but about eight o'clock a great blow was struck on the sitting-room ceiling, bringing down some plaster on to the carpet. At the same moment, the wooden

partition between the sitting-room and the weaving-shop was broken down. As the minister's wife rushed to her husband for protection, three windows smashed simultaneously—one above the bed where Mr Saemund occasionally slept after working late on sermons or parish duties, another above his writing-desk, and a third in front of the cupboard door. Glass littered the floor and papers blew wildly about—then, through one broken window came flying a piece of wood that seemed to be part of a table, and through another came a garden spade. Mr Saemund and his wife rushed out of the room, into a hall full of terrified servants.

"Come on—into the loft!" cried one, and others followed him like driven sheep. Magnus and Gudrun, however, stayed with their master and mistress; and as Gudrun moved to Mrs Saemund's side, a great tub of washing, which had been standing in the kitchen, came hurtling at Gudrun's head, knocking the old woman over and submerging her with dirty linen. It was hardly noticed in the confusion—for now everything that was at all loose was flying about in the air, amid the screams and cries of the servants. The minister opened a cloak-room door, intending to take refuge, but a sledge-hammer came whirling out at him from the interior, hitting him sharply on the side and the hip. He fled back to the sitting-room, and the others followed him and huddled there in a terrified group, with nightmare around them. Everything was dancing—ornaments, books, chairs—and a volley of deal splinters from the broken partition rained into faces and stuck like burrs in hair and clothes. Mrs Saemund fainted with terror, and several of the women were in hysterics.

"Come," said Mr Saemund, "I am taking my family to shelter away from here, and those of you who wish must come with us. My neighbour at Muli Farm will take us in, I know." And picking up his unconscious wife he carried her out of the dreadful room, while Gudrun followed with the baby, who—after the way of babies—had slept peacefully through all the din.

That night Garpsdal was deserted, and its dwellers slept at Muli, an exhausted terror-haunted sleep. But next day Mr Saemund returned, declaring that he would get the better of this demon, and that it should not drive him away from his home. He found Garpsdal in a fearful state of disorder, but quiet; and gradually the servants returned to it, though Mrs Saemund and the baby remained at Muli

For some weeks there was peace, though there were those who. declared that the ghost had not finished with Garpsdal. The men worked hard; glass was replaced, new doors and panels fitted, until

the house began to look almost like its old self. Then, one morning, the troubles began again.

It was Sunday, and the household was almost ready to go to church. Everyone, from the small boot-boy upwards, was dressed in sober Sunday best, and Garpsdal was a place of peaceful bustle. Mr Saemund, sermon-notes in hand, paused at the front door as one of the maids called him back.

"Sir, sir, it's started again! It's hammering in the pantry!"

His mouth grimly set, the minister shut the door and hurried towards the kitchens. His staff followed him, cowed and whispering. As they neared the pantry the familiar, dreaded sounds grew louder. Mr Saemund flung open the door.

"There she is!" cried Magnus. The girl was standing with her back to them, pulling at the pantry shelves with her bare hands. She seemed to use little effort, yet the strong wood broke at her touch and the shelves and their contents crashed to the ground. There was a terrifying, slow, wanton destructiveness about her method that struck Magnus with horror.

"I cannot see her," said Mr Saemund. "Speak to her, Magnus."

Magnus stepped forward. He noticed for the first time that the figure was by no means transparent—he could not see the portion of the shelves before which she was standing. But yet he knew her for no human being.

"Stop, in God's name!" he called out to her.

She lowered her arms, which had been reaching to the upper shelf, and turned round. For the first time he had a clear and close view of her face. The sharpness that he had noted before was the sharpness of bone, and the eyes were cold because they were quite hollow; the cold smile was a lipless one. It was the face of a skull that confronted Magnus. With a cry of horror, he stepped back and fell on his knees, praying.

"You do well to pray, Magnus," said Mr Saemund. "On your knees, the rest of you, while I wrestle with this fearful thing." Though he could not see the ghost, he sensed vividly its malevolent presence.

"This is a duel between you and me, Spirit," he said. "I have bidden you away before with bell, book and candle, according to the rites of the Church. Now I say to you in my own person—get back to the Hell you came from, and leave this Christian house! You have done your worst to it, and you may assault the bodies of those who live in it, but our souls you cannot touch, for they are God's and not the Devil's. Look to yourself, Spirit, for the Church too can curse! Begone, I say—begone!"

Magnus raised his head from his hands to see how Mr Saemund's words affected the visitant. He could hardly believe what he saw.

"She's going, sir—fading through the wall!"

He ran to the window. "Yes, there she is, outside in the byre-lane. I'm going to chase her away!"

Mr Saemund tried to pull him back, but Magnus was out of the room and out of the house before anyone could stop him. Gudrun, who had a particular fondness for the boy, hobbled out after him, calling that he was a foolhardy lad. As she reached the lane, she saw Magnus stop in his tracks as a shower of mud and dirt rose up from the road to envelop him. He shook himself and ran on—only to be stopped again by the impact of a huge stone which struck him full in the chest. He fell, and Gudrun, hurrying to his side, received a violent blow on the arm. So badly hurt was the old woman that for three weeks afterwards she kept to her bed.

Here the hauntings might have ended, but for the folly of Magnus's cousin, the shepherd Einar Jonsson, a brave and hard-headed young man who had not shared in the general terror. For the most part of the time he had been out in the fields or the sheep-houses, tending his flock, and so had not witnessed the doing of the damage, or heard much of the noise. One night, after a Christmas revel, Einar and some of his mates were discussing the ghost.

"I don't believe she existed at all," said Einar. "You were always making up stories, Magnus, even as a lad."

"I *did* see her," replied Magnus. "I wish I had not; I shall never forget it."

"I tell you what—I'll command her to appear to me—then I shall see for myself. She seems a forthcoming lass—she won't refuse a personable man like me!" Einar was laughing, and laughed more at the protests of Magnus and the others that he would be committing the wildest and wickedest folly if he did any such thing. The subject was changed, the cup passed round again, and before long the party retired to bed.

Einar slept in his hut near the sheep-houses, for some of his ewes were due to lamb, and he had to be within sound of them. He lay down on his pallet the worse—or the better—for wine, and thought of his joking threat. *Should* he summon the ghost—and tomorrow tell the others some fantastic story of the result? Perhaps then they would realize how credulous they had been to believe Magnus's story at all.

He sat up, clapped his hands three times, and called out: "Ghost of Garpsdal, I command you to appear to me!

It was the anxious bleating of the sheep that brought lanterns bobbing through the yard to the sheep-hut, an hour or so after midnight. Within the hut Magnus and the others could hear a noise as of something frantically throwing itself from side to side, and strange muffled cries. They opened the door. Within was a wild thing in torn clothing, bleeding from self-inflicted wounds, and raving incoherently as it repeatedly dashed its head against the walls. Two hours before it had been the gay, daring Einar Jonsson.

It seemed for some time as though Einar's brain would be permanently affected; but slowly he regained his senses, though he was never to be the same man again, and had aged ten years in looks during his illness. When asked what had happened in the hut, he could only say: "The girl appeared over my head and attacked me." No questioning could extract more than this. When he was as recovered as he was ever likely to be, Einar left Garpsdal and went to work on a farm many miles away.

Only one more piece of evil was worked on the Garpsdal household; during Einar's illness Mr Saemund rode over to Muli Farm one day, and spent the night there. When next morning he went to collect his horse from the stable, he found it dead from no apparent cause, its body black and swollen. She who had been baulked of a sheep had claimed a horse.

Seeing that the evil influence could even reach to Muli, Mr Saemund brought his family back to Garpsdal. Every night and morning special prayers against daemonic power were held; with effect, for the hauntings ceased. Some months later, on 28 May, 1808, Mr Saemund solemnly recounted to his friend Gisli Olafsson, another minister, and to two other witnesses, everything that had happened since the outbreak began; and his wife and servants confirmed his story.

Magnus lived to be an old man—he was still alive in 1862—but there is no evidence that he ever again saw the Ghost of Garpsdal.

Mischief Among the Dead

A poltergeist, said the late Harry Price, is an "alleged ghost", with "certain unpleasant characteristics". The ordinary ghost, though often inconsiderate, clumsy, noisy and frightening, is generally considered to be inoffensive, and even friendly and well disposed to the living persons who occupy its place of haunting.

But the poltergeist has none of these supposed feelings of friendship to those of us on this side of the grave. Its reported activities would suggest that it is animated by a destructiveness and spite which seems to be without purpose. It is a vindictive agency which has a nuisance value the ordinary ghost does not have. A poltergeist is said to infest, rather than haunt a place.

Poltergeists have been reported in many places, among them, not surprisingly, churchyards.

They are not to be confused with the many harmless ghosts reported to haunt countless churchyards—such as the pathetic child victims of Mary Cotton, hanged in 1873 for the murder of her four children, and suspected on good evidence of having murdered twelve more, at West Auckland, Durham.

These children haunted the churchyard and rectory where their bodies had been buried, exhumed and dissected. One disconsolate little ghost girl, clad in her pathetic burial shroud, they said, followed the terrified village postman home one evening, and then went into the room where his child lay asleep. This poor little ghost was finally consoled and sent back on her eternal journey by an old woman who lived in a haunted house and was used to ghosts, and who said after-

wards: "It was lonely and cold in the dark churchyard. I did my best to comfort it. It won't trouble you again."

She was right. That little ghost was not seen again. In a previous century the kindly old soul who was not afraid of it would no doubt have been burnt alive as a witch in league with the devil.

Poltergeists cause a different sort of trouble to those sad phantoms whose sudden appearance among the gravestones is calculated to make the bravest heart quail. In certain churchyards they have been known to get into family vaults and play havoc with the coffins.

The following occurrence was reported from the village of Stanton in Suffolk in the year 1815:

"On opening the vault some years since, several *leaden* coffins with wooded cases that had been fixed on biers were found displaced, to the great astonishment of many inhabitants of the village. The coffins were placed as before and properly closed; when some time ago, another of the family dying, they were a second time found displaced, and two years after they were not only found all off the biers, but one coffin, as heavy as to require eight men to raise it, was found on the fourth step that leads into the vault. Whence arose this operation in which it is certain no one had a hand?"

There was a suggestion that the displacement of the coffins might have been caused by underground water, but there was no sign of this on the different occasions when the vault was opened, and it would be surely impossible for lead coffins to be displaced by even a sudden inrush of water.

The classic case of this, and certainly the best authenticated, comes from Barbados in the West Indies. The events took place in the little churchyard attached to Christ Church which is near the lighthouse on the southernmost point of the island, about a half-hour's drive out of Bridgetown.

The vault was a hundred feet above sea level and hewn into the solid rock. It had a stone floor and walls, and was sealed with a great slab of blue Devonshire marble, so heavy that it took several men to lift it.

The vault had belonged to several old Barbados families. Originally it had been built for the Walronds. Then it passed to the Elliotts, who married into the Walrond family. These families were members of the King's Council, rulers of the island, plantation and slave owners, people of wealth and position.

In the year 1724 the Honourable James Elliott, a member of Barbados Council, died at the age of thirty-four, and his sorrowful widow, Elizabeth, daughter of Thomas Walrond, put her husband's

remains in her family vault, upon the tombstone of which she caused an inscription to be carved, saying he was "brave, hospitable and courteous, of great integrity in his actions, and conspicuous for his judgement, and vivacity in conversation". He was "snatched away from us on the 14th of May" in that year, "and died lamented by all who knew him".

It is not recorded what other coffins the vault contained in 1724, but it fell into disuse for the better part of a century. In July, 1807, an application was made to the Rector of Christ Church to permit the remains of Mrs Thomasina Goddard, who was a relative of the Elliotts, to be buried in the vault. Permission was granted.

Workmen accordingly broke the seals which were found to be intact. Negro slaves moved aside the massive marble slab to open the tomb, and it was discovered to everyone's surprise that the vault was empty. There was no sign of the remains of any of the Elliotts or of the Walronds. The burial, however, was proceeded with and Mrs Goddard was laid to rest in the tomb on 31 July, 1807.

The vault then came into the hands of the Chases, a wealthy, influential family in the island, plantation and slave-owners as were all Europeans of substance in the West Indies in those days. The Chase family coat-of-arms was carved upon a tablet over the entrance of the vault and can be seen there today.

The first Chase to be buried there was Mary Anna Maria, the infant daughter of the Honourable Thomas Chase, who died in February, 1808. The child was put in a lead coffin and brought to the vault, which, when it was opened, was found to be in order, the wooden coffin of Mrs Goddard being in its proper place.

On 6 July, 1812, the vault was opened again to receive the body of another daughter of Thomas Chase—Dorcas Chase. This time the burial party found the vault in a state of confusion. The lead coffin containing the body of the infant Anna Maria was found standing nearly upright, head downwards on the opposite side of the vault to which it had been originally placed. The large wood coffin of Mrs Goddard had also been moved out of its place.

The surprised burial party put the coffins in their right places, laid the lead coffin of Dorcas Chase upon the floor of the vault, replaced the massive slab of marble across the mouth of the vault where it was cemented in the presence of the rector and other persons and sealed with the mason's seal.

The tomb was apparently opened again that year for the burial of the Honourable Thomas Chase, upon which occasion no disorder was reported in the vault. The vault was not opened again until

25 September, 1816 for the burial of an infant, Samuel Brewster Ames, when it was observed that the lead coffins were in a state of disorder. Once again the vault was tidied up and resealed.

During that year there had been one of the many revolts among the slaves who had become so numerous in the West Indies that their white masters had difficulty in keeping them under. Among the white people murdered by the slaves was Samuel Brewster, a relative of the Chase family, and when the vault at Christ Church was opened to receive his body they found the place once more in a state of great confusion, the heavy lead coffins being toppled from their places and apparently hurled across the floor of the vault.

On 9 July, 1819, the body of Miss Thomasina Clarke was brought to the vault for burial, and once more the same confusion was found. The Rector, Dr T. H. Orderson, D.D., was greatly concerned. He noticed particularly that the disorder was confined to the lead coffins. Coffins of wood had not been moved.

Negroes were brought in to tidy up the mess. It was observed that the wood coffin of Mrs Goddard, buried there in 1807, had fallen to pieces. This was "tied up in a small bundle", as Dr Orderson put in his report, "and placed between Miss Clarke's coffin and the wall."

So disturbed were the good rector and the Chase family at the strange and apparently unnatural happenings in the vault that they brought the matter before Lord Combermere, the Governor of Barbados.

Combermere had served in the Peninsular War, when he had commanded the cavalry under Wellington and had fought with some distinction at Salamanca. He was an honest-to-goodness soldier and he decided to make a practical test of these strange stories. No doubt he thought the Negroes were up to some of their black devilry, but he had to be sure that it was not just a case of tomb-breaking. He took the matter into his own hands and went to the churchyard himself with his ADC, the Hon. Major Finch.

Under their supervision and in the presence of Dr Orderson the coffins were replaced and Major Finch made a drawing of their exact positions, which has been preserved. Fine sand was then sprinkled over the floor of the vault, the heavy marble slab was cemented in position and the masons and the officials put various secret seals and marks in the soft cement.

The original intention of Lord Combermere was to wait until another death in the Chase family would occasion the re-opening

of the vault. Nine months went by, but the Chases did not oblige with a death. Then Combermere decided to open the vault.

There was a meeting on 18 April, 1820, at Eldridge's Plantation, which was next to the church. According to one report the meeting was brought about by a story that a great noise had been heard coming from the interior of the vault. Others said that his lordship had merely become impatient, and indeed curiosity was burning hotly in the minds of all those who knew about the strange happenings inside the Chase vault.

The Governor had with him on the momentous morning of 18 April the Hon. Nathan Lucas (who later made a careful and factual report of the affair), Major Finch, the Rector (Dr Orderson), and two other gentlemen who had an interest in the matter—Robert Bowcher Clarke and Rowland Cotton.

First of all a careful examination was made of the various seals and secret marks made at the entrance of the vault on the previous July. All these were found to be intact. Despite the careful scrutiny which was made, there was no sign that anyone had tampered with the entrance of the tomb. Combermere and his companions satisfied themselves that it was impossible for anyone to have entered the vault. "Not a blade of grass or stone was touched", wrote Nathan Lucas. "Indeed collusion or deception was impossible."

It was noon and the negro slaves of the adjoining plantation were coming in from their whip-driven labour in the fields. Eight or ten of them were taken into the graveyard to undertake the heavy labour of opening the vault.

The place was found to be in the uttermost confusion—the great lead coffins, some of which would take a half a dozen men to handle, had been hurled across the vault and tumbled against the stone wall, some upside down, one standing on its head. But the wooden coffins were in their original positions. The tied-up bundle of Mrs Goddard's coffin had not been moved. Major Finch made a drawing of the positions of the coffins, which remains part of the documentation of this interesting case.

The vault was then thoroughly examined. There were no imprints or marks of any kind in the sand which had been sprinkled on the floor when the vault was closed and sealed the previous July. Lucas himself examined every part of the walls and the arch of the vault. Every square inch of the walls was struck by a mason in his presence and found to be solid rock. There was no water in the vault, or marks where it had been.

Someone suggested that it had been caused by an earthquake,

but an earthquake which would topple immense lead coffins from their places and hurl them about the vault would have been a very severe one and it would have levelled every building in the neighbourhood, if not in the whole island. This theory was discounted, as was the suggestion that it had been caused by flooding. The rock vault was tinder dry on 18 April, 1820, and was in a level churchyard where there could not possibly be a flow of water. In any case, it would require the force of a hurricane wave to throw immense lead coffins around. Water would certainly have made the wooden coffins float, and yet these had not been moved.

Nathan Lucas confessed himself at a loss to account for the strange thing which he had witnessed in company with other persons of unimpeachable integrity, who were equally puzzled.

"Thieves certainly had no hand in it," Lucas wrote, "and as for the negroes having anything to do with it, their superstitious fear of the dead and everything belonging to them precluded any idea of the kind. All I know is that it happened, and that I was an eye-witness of the fact."

Lord Combermere's investigation at the Chase vault, and the conclusions drawn from it, caused a great stir in Barbados where an official report on the matter was published.

At the request of the Chase family, all the coffins were taken from the vault and buried in separate graves, and the vault was abandoned. The Governor ordered that it be left permanently open, and thus it has remained ever since.

Although the affair caused a great stir in the island neighbourhood at the time, no mention of it was made in the newspapers of the day, nor was any comment made about it in the contemporary burial register at Christ Church, the entries of which were made by Dr Orderson. The story has been told many times and has several sources, though none so documented and reliable as that of Nathan Lucas.

A similar occurrence was reported to have taken place in the cemetery of Arensburg on the island of Oesel in the Baltic. This was in the year 1844. The details of this coffin disturbance were almost identical to those of the Barbados incidents, and there is some doubt that they ever took place.

The subject of coffin disturbance took a Gothic turn in a story emanating from Lincolnshire in the mid-eighteenth century, which though undocumented and improbable to a degree is worth the telling.

A squire's lady fell out with her husband's brother who lived

with them, and for years they lived in a state of bitter hatred and quarrelsomeness which continued without respite or forgiveness until the day of their respective deaths. The squire's lady died first and was put in the family vault. On his deathbed the brother-in-law begged not to be buried in the same tomb "with that accursed woman", for their mutual hatred was such that it would endure into the other world. His request was not taken seriously and he was accordingly put into the family vault. Thereupon a mighty uproar was heard within the sealed vault. So great was the noise of human and material conflict issuing from within the tomb that it was forthwith opened. The great coffins had not only been hurled about the vault, but were even thrown together in positions suggesting they were in mortal combat. When they were replaced and the vault closed, the same thing happened again. The wise old squire who had survived his quarrelsome relatives and was living at last in peace in the manor-house, solved the problem by building a dividing wall inside the vault with the coffins of his wife and brother on either side of it. Whereafter peace and quiet was restored in the embattled graveyard.

A pretty story, but not to be taken as seriously as the Barbados coffin mystery, which was so thoroughly investigated and tested at the time. These events cannot be dismissed as having been caused by earthquakes or flooding. The reader may prefer one of several explanations, but the poltergeist theory is the only one which seems to fit the facts.

The negroes believed that an evil spirit called a Jumbie caused the disturbances among the coffins, and this is still believed today among the natives. Jumbies apparently originated from Zombies, the walking dead. They are mischief-making spirits who wander about at night causing the kind of pointless disturbances which took place in the Chase vault.

The Whiskered Sailor of Portsmouth

Not many years after the *Victory* had sailed from Portsmouth, bearing Nelson towards Trafalgar and death, a certain Mr Hamilton arrived in that town. He was on his way to join a ship, in which he was to proceed abroad. As his chaise rolled through the narrow, twisting streets, he saw, with some dismay, that Portsmouth was fuller than he had ever seen it.

It was at all times a bustling town, with its sailors home on leave and waiting to join their ships, the wives and families who were lodging with them, and the townspeople to whom the Fleet meant daily bread and butter. Blue jackets, shiny hard hats, and the gay scarves and vests beloved of sailors were everywhere. On the arms of their pigtailed wearers hung ladies as bright as parakeets in the finery of the Regency. Muslin dresses outlined their figures; their white-stockinged feet twinkled in black sandals, their high-dressed curls sprouted coloured feathers. Jewish clothes-dealers lurked outside slop-shops heaped with gaudy garments, while above their heads swung the sinister black doll that was the sign of their trade. Here and there a tar overcome with Portsmouth ale was being removed from the gutter by officers of the Watch, and outside every inn an uproarious group was drinking and commenting, not always printably, on passers-by.

Today, Mr Hamilton noticed unusual figures in the crowds. Well-dressed folk who could only be Hampshire gentry, and others who were patently farmers in from the country districts, were almost as numerous as the sailors. Mr Hamilton, who did not rejoice in

the company of large numbers of his fellow-men, turned his mouth down in disapproval.

His face lengthened still further when, after disembarking from the chaise at the door of the George, his usual hostelry, he inquired for a room and was told there was none available.

"Everything taken, sir. I've even had to put two gentlemen in the loft over the stables."

"But this is ridiculous!" exclaimed Mr Hamilton impatiently. "You've always had a room for me before. Well, I shall take myself somewhere else."

"You'll be lucky if you do, sir," returned the landlord. "It's the same all over the town, not a bed to be had."

"Why, what's the matter with the place?"

"The matter? Why, just about everything. There's a county election on, and all the folk have come crowding in from round about. Then there's this pesky wind, that won't let the Fleet sail."

"But my ship leaves tomorrow!" said Mr Hamilton.

"I'll be surprised if it does, sir. Not a vessel's left Portsmouth since last Friday, and the place is choc-a-bloc with tars and passengers bound for foreign ports."

Mr Hamilton sighed. "Then can you recommend me to any place at all where I might get a bed for as long as I have to stay here?"

"Sorry, sir—no idea. Your best plan would be to hire a horse and get out to Cosham or Bedhampton—you might get a room out there."

Mr Hamilton thanked him, without any great enthusiasm for the suggestion, and turned away, after arranging that his valise and a heavy carpet-bag might be left at the George until he was ready to sail. Then he set out to wander the Portsmouth streets. Traipse out to Bedhampton? Ridiculous. As like as not there'd be nothing there but some dark hole of a room in a one-eyed country inn with a piggery under the window. A man with profound confidence in his own exemption from the misfortunes to which others were liable, Mr Hamilton felt sure that somewhere in Portsmouth he could find a respectable lodging.

It was a fine day, with a sharp breeze blowing, which, if the enemy of the Fleet, was still refreshing to a man who had just endured a coach journey from London. He briskly negotiated knots of strollers who swarmed across his path like shoals of fish, skirted the unofficial public meetings that were taking place wherever a reasonably open space presented itself, beneath banners bearing the

legend: "Bloggs for Prosperity!" or alternatively "Snooks for King George and Old England!"

Once, while threading his way through a particularly close press of people, Mr Hamilton was conscious of a groping tug in the region of his waistcoat. Spinning round, he found himself looking down at a small, bright-eyed, extremely dirty young woman resplendent in an orange dress with green flounces. So close were they pressed together that she could barely withdraw the hand that had been seeking his fob-watch and purse of guineas. Mr Hamilton raked her with a cold naval eye, and she vanished as though the earth had swallowed her, beneath the arm of a bulky farmhand at her side. Mr Hamilton walked on, shaking his head. There were some shady characters in Portsmouth.

The landlord of the George had not erred on the side of pessimism. Every inn Mr Hamilton tried was full to overflowing. At one he was graciously invited to share a bed with two other men; an offer which he hurriedly declined. At another, he was approached by a furtive-looking person of Lascar features who offered to conduct him to a "prime billet" kept by a "decent woman". Hastily pulling his sleeve away from the filthy hand that clutched it, Mr Hamilton moved sharply away and began to traverse yet another street. Suddenly a brilliant thought struck him—he would go down to the dockyard and request a berth in the ship in which he was to sail. Why had he not thought of such a thing earlier? Quickening his step, he made his way back to the swarming environs of the dockyard, and accosted the sentry at the gate.

"*Euryalus*, sir? She's not come round from the Downs yet."

Mr Hamilton muttered an imprecation. "Well, when do you expect her?"

"Not today, unless the wind changes."

Further inquiries revealed that such ships as lay in port were filled to capacity with officers who had got there first; no quarters for Mr Hamilton could be found.

He returned to his wanderings, by now in a very bad humour. He was hot, tired, and footsore. The sun was going down and an autumn dusk was spreading. Time pressed, for any honest citizen who tramped the Portsmouth streets after dark ran the risk of anything from minor robbery to murder. By this time Mr Hamilton felt he was wandering in a maze, as he recognized places and objects he had passed before. There was the very same dead cat he had noticed in the gutter as his chaise drove into the town; and here was the milliner's window containing a very fetching rose-pink bonnet

that he had considered buying for his wife. He determined to find a new direction, and struck off north-east of the town, where the streets were quieter.

His enterprise was almost immediately rewarded. Turning a corner, he found himself in a short street of which the principal feature was an inn, announcing itself to be the *Admiral Collingwood* and bearing an unflattering likeness of that gentleman on its swinging sign. With the boldness of despair, Mr Hamilton charged the door and found himself in a reasonably clean hall-way, with a tap-room opening off it and a door which he imagined led to the kitchens at the end. A smart double rap brought immediate response in the shape of the landlady.

"Yes? What were you wanting?"

She was sharp-featured, even vinegary, with steely grey eyes and a rat-trap of a mouth. But at least she was not sluttish; and after a day in Portsmouth Mr Hamilton was a connoisseur of sluts. He asked her if she had a room to let.

"Why, yes, Captain, if you've no objection to a double-bedded one."

"I don't wish to share a room, if you mean that."

She shrugged bony shoulders. "Take it or leave it, Captain."

Mr Hamilton thought of the falling dusk, and the hardness of the streets, and the guineas in his purse.

"I'll take it—if you'll let me pay to keep the other bed empty."

The landlady eyed him suspiciously. "Pay double for one bed? Got some prize-money to spend, eh, Captain?"

"My money's my concern, and I am not a captain. You heard my offer."

"Very well. It's all the same to me, if you're that fond of your own company, so long as the bed's paid for. I'll show you the room."

She stumped up the stairs in front of him to a door on the first landing. "Here it is, and there's not a finer in Portsmouth."

Mr Hamilton rather doubted this, but had to concede that the room was large, airy and clean so far as he could see, though the bed-curtains were shabby and the furniture sparse and poor. However, beggars could not be choosers. He paid her the five shillings she demanded as a surety of his good faith, and ordered a meal—for by now he was extremely hungry and thirsty. After a refreshing wash (it was an agreeable surprise to find the basin uncracked and the ewer full) he descended, and found his meal set out in a small private room. Anything in the way of food would have been welcome to him, and he enjoyed every mouthful of his supper—a

brace of roast pigeons, a dish of sweetbreads, and the best part of an apple pie, washed down with draughts of excellent beer. Having smoked a pipe or two, to allow the food to digest, and read a copy of the local paper which was lying in the bar, he decided to make an early night of it.

The bright moonlight which streamed in through the windows made the room less shabby and more attractive altogether; the bed in particular looked inviting, and examination revealed the mattress to be free from lumps. Mr Hamilton undressed; gazed from the window for a few moments at the garden outside, in which a few tired small trees and rambling plants surrounded a plot of earth which had been recently dug. Perhaps they were going to grow vegetables there, he reflected sleepily; or possibly the digging was done by cats. He hoped the cats would not make their presence obvious later. As it was, things were pretty quiet. The noise in the tap-room had died down before he came upstairs, and in any case was hardly audible from this room. He locked the door—one could not be too careful—got into bed, and was asleep in a moment.

It seemed hours later that a noise woke him. He looked at his watch on the bedside chair, and found that he had only been asleep a little over an hour. Cursing, he subsided and turned over, preparing himself for sleep again. Then he hastily sat up. In turning, he brought himself to face the other bed; and the other bed, to his astonishment and indignation, was occupied.

The brilliant moon showed him the occupant clearly. He was a young man, obviously a sailor, naked to the waist but wearing full-bottomed trousers and what seemed to be the type of red spotted handkerchief known as a "Belcher" about his head. He half sat, half lay, on top of the bedclothes, and seemed to be in a deep sleep.

Mr Hamilton was furious. He thought of the sum he had promised the landlady to ensure privacy, and of the money he had already paid her. How dared she cheat him like this? Well, he would soon put a stop to it. He swung his legs out of bed—and then paused. The night was cold—too cold to spend in altercation with a powerfully built young tar, particularly when one was only clad in a shirt oneself. The man seemed quiet enough—he was not even snoring. With luck, he would lie there till morning, and Mr Hamilton would enjoy a peaceful night. He got back into bed, and though ruffled soon fell asleep again.

It was broad daylight when he awoke, and the moonlight had been replaced by equally brilliant sunlight. The sleeping sailor still

lay in the same position, as if he had never stirred all night. Mr Hamilton looked curiously at the handsome, composed face—really rather distinguished, for a common seaman—and reflected that the Polls and Sues of Portsmouth must admire beyond expression the fine pair of black side-whiskers that sprouted from the jaw. He bent nearer to examine the handkerchief round the man's head —and saw, with a slight start, that what he had taken for a red-and-white spotted band was really a white bandage heavily soaked with blood, a smear of which had trickled down the man's left cheek and marked the pillow.

Before he had had time to reflect on this, another thought struck him. How had the man got in at all? He remembered clearly locking the door before going to bed—and in fact it was still firmly locked, as he found when he tried it. The door was in the centre of one side of the room, nearly half-way between the two bed-heads; and as Mr Hamilton stood by it, a bed-curtain hid the stranger from his view. He turned back, determined to shake the man awake and demand an explanation. Then he stopped short, his mouth open in amazement. The man had vanished! Scarcely an instant before he had been there—now he was gone. Silently and with the speed of light he must have slipped out.

Mr Hamilton began a frantic reconnaissance of the room. There must, of course, be another door. He felt round the walls. There was no panelling, only shabby and peeling wallpaper beneath which the outline of a hidden door would have been perfectly obvious. No tall cupboard or press was in the room. The window-curtains were too skimpy to hide even a small child, and there was no one under either bed.

Mr Hamilton was baffled, to say the least of it. He dressed, unlocked the door, and went downstairs. It appeared that he was the first person stirring, but there soon appeared a slipshod, dirty maid-of-all-work, armed with coals to lay the tap-room fire. Mr Hamilton inquired of her whether she had seen his companion anywhere in the house.

"Sailor? I ain't seen no sailors. They don't come in not as early as this."

"But this man spent the night here—you must have seen him! Look, the front door is still bolted. Have you let him out at the back?"

The maid looked at Mr Hamilton as if she doubted his sanity.

"I dunno nothing of it, I tell yer," she said, gathering up her bucket and departing.

Mr Hamilton paced an imaginary deck until the arrival of the landlady on the scene. He had been preparing a little speech for her.

"Good morning, madam."

"Morning to you, sir."

"May I have my bill, please? I am leaving immediately."

"Your bill? Why, won't you be requiring breakfast? You can have it as soon as you like."

"I shall certainly not take breakfast, nor anything else in this house, madam, after your unpardonable breach of faith in respect of my sleeping arrangements."

"Here—what are you talking about? What do you mean?"

"What do I mean? I paid for the sole occupation of the room."

"Well," she flashed back, "and you had it, didn't you? And though I say it, there ain't a more comfortable room in all Portsmouth. Why, I might have let that spare bed five times over last night, and just because of your fancy I didn't do it. Call yourself a gentleman, trying to bilk an honest woman!"

Mr Hamilton took a deep breath. The lady had sharp, untended nails, and he imagined them preparing for an attack on his cheeks. He laid a guinea on the bar.

"Far from trying to bilk you, madam, I am quite prepared to pay you the money you asked. I suffered no actual inconvenience from the presence of my fellow-lodger—only, having agreed to pay double for the indulgence of my fancy, as you call it, I did expect the conditions to be kept on your side."

"Why, and so they were!" she retorted.

"If you say so of course I must take your word for it. I suppose, then, that one of your servants introduced the man into my room without your knowledge."

"*What* man? There was nobody in your room, unless you let him in yourself. You had the key, hadn't you? Why, I heard you lock the door, as I was going to bed."

"Yes, that's true," conceded Mr Hamilton. "But be that as it may, there was a man—a sailor—in my room last night; though I know no more how he got in or out than I do where he got his broken head or his remarkable whiskers."

Mr Hamilton delivered this parting shot from the door, and glanced back to see how his opponent had taken it. To his surprise, her face had lost its angry flush and had turned very pale. For a moment she struggled to speak, and then managed to breathe out one word.

"Whiskers!" she gasped.

"Yes, whiskers. I never saw such a splendid pair in my life."

"And a broken head—oh, come back, sir, for heaven's sake come back, and tell me truly what you saw last night!"

"Why, no one, madam, but this sailor. I suppose he took refuge in my room from some drunken party, to sleep off the effects of the liquor."

"What was he like? You must tell me!"

Mr Hamilton described the man, his dress, and the bandaged head; after which the landlady threw herself into a chair, flung her apron over her head, and sat rocking herself to and fro in an agony of distress.

"God have mercy on me!" she cried. "It's all true, then, and the house is ruined for ever!"

Mr Hamilton, concerned, sat down beside her. "Pray compose yourself, madam. There is some strange story here—won't you tell me what it is, and satisfy my mind?"

After a burst of sobbing, and a restorative draught from one of her own brandy-bottles, the landlady became quiet enough to give her explanation.

"Truly, sir, it was not murder!"

"Murder!"

"Three nights before you came, it happened. This party of young sailors was drinking here quietly enough, when in come some marines as had been at the bottle elsewhere. One of these gin-shops, I shouldn't wonder—nasty places, as I wouldn't lower myself to keep. Well, a quarrel broke out between the two lots, and the noise brought me running from the kitchen. You understand, sir, I could do little, being a widow with no man behind me, but I did what I could to quiet them. When I saw it was no use I drew away for fear of being hurt myself. Then as I watched from behind the hatch, there I saw one of the marines throw a pewter pot into the party of sailors, and I saw it hit the tallest of them on the head. He fell straight to the ground senseless, and oh! the blood! Blood everywhere. Well, I feared the worst for him, poor lad, and indeed I was right to do so, for though they carried him upstairs and placed him on the bed, in a few minutes he was dead."

"But why did you not call the watch?" demanded Mr Hamilton.

"Because of bringing a bad name upon the house, sir. Some of his mates were for making trouble and said that the marine who threw the pot should hang, but others persuaded them out of it, and some went away as quick as they could. At last I agreed to let the marines bring him down and bury him in the garden at the back."

Mr Hamilton remembered his vision of excavatory cats, and shuddered slightly. Then he said:

"I can't understand why this man was not sought after to rejoin his ship."

"He had just been discharged, his mates said, and no one would inquire after him. So I thought it was all hushed up. But now I see it was of no use, sir, and a punishment on me for trying to hide a bad deed. I shall never dare to put anybody into your room again, for it was there they laid him. They took off his jacket and waistcoat, and tied up his wound with a handkerchief, but they never could stop the bleeding till—all was over. And as sure as you stand there a living man, he's come back to trouble us, for if he'd sat to you for his picture you could not have described him better than you have done."

Mr Hamilton thanked the landlady courteously for her story, and promised that he would not add to her troubles by spreading it about in Portsmouth. Then, having strangely little appetite for breakfast, he bade farewell to her and walked down to the Point, where he found that his ship was expected hourly. That afternoon she appeared and he immediately went on board. The next morning he set sail for the Mediterranean, and did not set foot again in Portsmouth for eighteen years.

After all this time, he was once more on his way to the Dockyard; this time to take up a shore appointment there. He was sharing a chaise with Captain Hastings, R.N., and Mrs Hastings, who noticed, as they approached the centre of the town, that Mr Hamilton's face became increasingly grave. Mrs Hastings, a lively, inquisitive lady, demanded the reason.

"I was thinking of events called up by the sight of that lane we have just passed," he replied. "I have never told any living soul of it before, but to old friends like you, and after such a lapse of time, I think I may now repeat it." And when they reached their lodgings, he recounted to them the whole strange story.

Nothing would satisfy Mrs Hastings but that next day they should go and reconnoitre the haunted inn. They walked through the busy streets to the turn of the lane; but no *Admiral Collingwood* could they see. A building something like what Mr Hamilton remembered of it certainly stood there, but it now housed a greengrocer's shop, and behind it rose the pinnacles of a Methodist chapel which had certainly not been there before. They called at the shop, bought some apples, and led the conversation round to the vanished inn; but could learn nothing from the shopkeeper except that it

had been converted into a shop some five years before. Then, at Mrs Hastings's insistence, they strolled round to the Chapel which backed on to the building, and accosted a lady helper who happened to be arranging flowers in the choir. The most cunning of questions, involving such matters as burials and consecrations, failed to extract any information from her; and they were obliged to leave the scene without knowing whether any skeleton had been turned up when the place was built. Mrs Hastings would have pursued the matter, but Mr Hamilton felt it inadvisable to push it any farther.

It remained long in Mrs Hastings' mind. One day she told it to her friend Mrs Hughes, grandmother of the author of *Tom Brown's Schooldays*; and Mrs Hughes in turn told it to the Reverend R. H. Barham, author of *The Ingoldsby Legends*. Mr Barham wrote it down at her dictation, but, sad to say, never retold it in one of his immortal poems; and the Whiskered Sailor of Portsmouth lies in a nameless grave, forgotten by all but a few who have read Mr Hamilton's story.

The Reverend John Jones
and the Ghostly Horseman

At the beginning of the last century, the Reverend John Jones was minister of Bala, in Merionethshire. He was a clergyman of high principle and unblemished character, and was famed throughout the whole Principality for the zeal and fervour with which he preached the Gospel.

Because of his gift of oratory, he was much in demand at religious meetings, and having appreciated that his eloquence had been bestowed upon him by the Almighty so that he might use it as an instrument to bring souls to salvation, he never refused a request to speak, no matter how far he would have to travel from his own parish. In the summer of 1820 he had received such an invitation to attend a religious meeting at Machynlleth, in the neighbouring county of Montgomery.

He left his house in Bala about two o'clock in the afternoon, travelling on horseback and alone. It was a hot day, and when he reached the village of Llanwchllyn he stopped at the inn to water his horse and refresh himself with a stoup of ale. As he sat on the bench outside the inn, tasting his ale and watching his beast drink deeply at the trough, he noticed a man reclining in the shade of a tree. By the man's side was a sickle sheathed in straw, and from this, and from the man's appearance, Mr Jones judged that he was an itinerant reaper in search of employment.

When the minister had finished his ale, he put down the mug on

the bench beside him, and took from his pocket his heavy silver watch, flicked open the front and saw that if he were to reach Machynlleth in time he must delay no longer. As he put his watch back into his pocket he happened to glance across at the man, and saw that he was now sitting up and was watching him.

Mr Jones remounted his horse, and set off. The next part of his journey lay through a wild and desolate region, almost completely uninhabited.

When he had ridden for about an hour, and was on the point of emerging from a wood at the top of a long and steep slope, he saw a man coming towards him on foot. As the man drew nearer, Mr Jones recognized him as the man who had been resting near the inn in Llanwchllyn. On coming up, the man touched his hat, and said, "Good day to you, Minister, is it possible that you can tell me what hour it is?"

"Why certainly," the parson replied, feeling in his pocket for his watch. "It is a few minutes past a quarter after four."

"I am obliged to you, sir," the man said, touching his hat again. "Good journey to you."

"And good day to you, my good man," replied Mr Jones, and urged his horse on once more.

The track down the hill was bordered on both sides by tall hedge-rows, and at the foot of the hill was a gate which gave access to a field through which the next part of the track ran. When he was about half-way down the hill, Jones's attention was attracted by something moving on the other side of the hedge on his left, and going in the same direction as himself.

At first he thought it must be an animal of one kind or another, but when he came to a place in the hedge where the bushes were lower than the rest and not so thick, he saw that it was a man bent double and that over his shoulder he carried a sickle sheathed in straw.

Made curious by the man's strange behaviour, the parson watched him for some time wondering what he could be about. But when he saw the man stop, kneel on one knee and begin to unsheathe his sickle, he felt a shudder of fear pass through him. For he recalled that the man had seen his watch, which was a valuable one, and now seemed to be preparing to attack him as he reached the gate, in order to rob him of it, since, while Jones watched, he had run on to the gate and was crouched down behind a bush beside it.

Though he was at this time in his early thirties, and was sturdy and strong, the minister was totally unarmed, and would be at a grave

disadvantage in warding off any attack from a man armed with a sharp sickle. He reined in his horse, and looked about him in all directions, hoping to see someone he could tell his fears to and for whose help he might plead. But there was not a person in sight.

His fear mounting as each minute passed, he considered that discretion would be the better part of valour, and had actually half-turned his horse, intending to make his way home again, when he realized that his craven alarm was about to make him temporarily forsake the Lord. What he was doing, and from the same motives, was what Peter had done when he had denied Jesus thrice before cock-crow.

The meeting which he was on his way to attend was a very important one. Many would attend it seeking the Lord, and he had been asked especially to speak to them so that his inspired words might show them the way. If he did not go, he told himself, how many might be lost that day who but for his cowardice would have been saved. As long as there existed the faintest possibility of his getting there, he must go on.

Right though this decision might be, however, it did not change the situation in which he found himself. Only a few hundred yards away from him was an armed man waiting to spring on him while he was at a disadvantage. For in order to continue he must pause at the gate, open it, pass through and close it behind him.

What could he do to make the attack fail? Should he put his heels to his horse, urge her at the gate, hoping that she would leap over it? But she was aged and docile, and in the four or five years that he had owned her she had never once been put into a gallop, and certainly had never leapt over anything, let alone a five-barred gate. If only the gate had been open!

He then looked about him, wondering whether he could leave the track and make his way across the fields. But this was not possible either. Where the hedges were not too high, they were too thick with brambles for the horse to pass through; and even where, on his right, there were open gaps in the hedges, these gaps were protected by sheer rocky banks which only a beast far more nimble than his mount could hope to negotiate with success.

He could not go back, and ever again be at peace with his conscience; an alternative route was denied him; and to go forward he must risk a personal encounter with his potential armed assailant, the outcome of which, unless a miracle happened, must certainly mean his injury, if not his death.

Once again he pulled himself together. For a minister of God he

was exhibiting an unforgivable lack of trust and confidence in Divine protection.

"I am a weak and sinful man, O Lord!" he groaned. "Please show me what I must do!"

For several moments he bowed his head in silent prayer. As he confessed later: "For all my self-abasement, I prayed rather in despair than in a spirit of humble trust and confidence. Yet, when I had said my Amen, my prayers seemed to have had a soothing effect on my mind, so that, refreshed and invigorated, I proceeded anew to consider the difficulties of my position."

Aged and slow though his mare might be, by this time she had grown impatient at the delay, and of her own accord began to move off down the slope. Jones had allowed the reins to fall on her neck while he had been pondering what to do, and her unexpected movement made him clutch at them. He pulled on them to check her, but as he did so his eyes fell upon an object close to him, and he saw to his utter astonishment that he was no longer alone.

There by his side was another horseman. He was dressed in a black suit and hat, which contrasted sharply with the whiteness of his mount. Jones's surprise at seeing him there was so intense that for several moments he was unable to speak.

"He had appeared," the minister recounted, "as suddenly as if he had sprung from the earth. He must have been riding behind me and overtaken me. And yet I had not heard the slightest sound. It was mysterious and inexplicable!"

Now his situation was completely changed, for no assailant, however desperate, would attempt to attack two opponents. Over-joyed by his release from his perilous position, Jones soon overcame his feelings of wonder, and he began to speak to his companion.

"Have you seen a man since you came out of the wood?" he asked.

Having waited for some seconds for an answer and not receiving one, he went on: "Hiding down there by the gate is a man with a sickle. He has designs upon my silver watch, and possibly upon the few coins I have on me. Did you see him?"

Still the man did not reply, and becoming embarrassed the minister said: "I cannot tell you how happy your coming has made me. I have desperately been considering what to do. I am on my way to Machynlleth to address an evangelist meeting there. I had thought of turning back, may the good God forgive me, but then I thought of the souls I might save from damnation with my humble words, and knew I must go on. But I could see no way of avoiding an

encounter with the villain yonder. Now that you have come, I have no longer any fear. Shall we go on?"

He turned and looked at his companion, and realized that the man had been giving him only the slightest attention, but was gazing intently in the direction of the gate at the bottom of the hill. His embarrassment increased, particularly as the horseman seemed deliberately disdaining to reply to him. So he decided to keep his peace, and looked in the direction of the gate.

And now he received yet another surprise. For as he watched he saw the reaper come out of his hiding place and begin to run across the field to the left, re-sheathing his sickle as he went.

"There he goes!" he pointed excitedly. "Perhaps you thought I had been imagining the man. But now you can see him."

His companion nodded, but still did not speak.

Almost overwhelmed with relief at the passing of the danger, Jones urged his mare forward, and the horseman rode by his side towards the gate. The relief had made the minister even more garrulous, and as they went he continued to address the man in black, though he was both surprised and not a little hurt by the traveller's continued and, as it seemed to him, mysterious silence.

As they reached the gate the figure of the reaper was disappearing over the brow of a neighbouring hill.

"He has gone!" the minister sighed. Then to the horseman, "Can it be doubted for a moment that my prayer for help was heard, and that you were sent for my deliverance by the Lord!"

It was at this point that the minister realized that, having from his appearance judged the horseman to be English, he had spoken in the English tongue ever since he had been in his company. He is a Welshman, he told himself, who does not or will not speak English, and he repeated his last question in Welsh.

To his joy the man at once replied, with a single word, *Amen.*

As he rode forward to examine the fastening of the gate, Jones continued to ply his companion with questions in the Welsh.

"Have you come far, sir? Are you going far? I am going to a religious gathering at Machynlleth; are you going in that direction? If you are, perhaps you will give me the honour and extreme pleasure of your company? Or is your destination Llangollen; or are you perhaps going south? It is deserted countryside hereabouts ..."

While he was speaking, he was pulling at the latch of the gate with his stick. It was proving a difficult operation, and for a moment he thought he would have to dismount; but at last the latch came up and the gate swung slowly into the field.

Jones pulled his horse to one side, and as he turned towards where he expected to find the horseman waiting he said, "Do you go on . . ."

He did not finish the sentence, for the horseman had disappeared.

Dumbfounded, the minister looked up the slope, the whole of which he could see. The horseman was not in sight, and yet if he had returned by the way he had come he could not have had time to reach the wood.

"What could have become of him?" I asked myself, the minister recorded in an account of his experiences which were later included in a memoir published in a number of the Welsh quarterly periodical *The Essayist*, in commemoration of his recent death in 1853. "He could not have gone through the gate, nor have made his horse leap the high hedges which on both sides shut in the road.

"Where was he? Had I been dreaming? Was it an apparition, a spectre which had been riding by my side for the last ten minutes? Could it be possible that I had seen no man or horse at all, and that the vision was but a creature of my imagination?

"I tried hard to convince myself that this was the case, but in vain; for unless someone had been with me, why had the reaper re-sheathed his murderous-looking weapon and fled? Surely, no; this mysterious horseman was no creation of my brain. I had seen him; who could he have been?

"I asked myself this question again and again; and then a feeling of profound awe began to creep over my soul. I remembered the singular way of his first appearance—his long silence—and then again the single word to which he had given utterance; I called to mind that this reply had been elicited from him by my mentioning in our own tongue the name of the Lord, and that this was the single occasion on which I had done so.

"What could I then believe?—but one thing, and that was that my prayer had indeed been heard, and that help had been given me from on high at a time of great danger.

"Full of this thought I dismounted, and throwing myself on my knees I offered up a prayer of thankfulness to Him who had heard my cry, and found help for me in time of need.

"I then mounted my horse and continued my journey. But through the long years that have elapsed since that memorable summer's day I have never for a moment wavered in my belief that in the mysterious horseman I had a special interference of Providence, by which means I was delivered from a position of extreme danger."

"Steer Nor'West"

Captain John S. Clarke, master of the schooner *Julia Hallock*, trading between New York and Cuba, put down his glass, and looking his companion straight in the eyes said firmly: "I'm telling you in all seriousness, sir, that though I've never had personal experience of one myself, I am utterly convinced of the existence of apparitions which can give warning of future events."

Mr Robert Owen, formerly United States minister to Naples and now enjoying a well-earned retirement in Cuba's sunshine, returned the gaze and shook his head.

"You surprise me, sir," he remarked. "You are a tough old sea-dog, if you will forgive the expression, an eminently practical and rational man, huh?"

"Right, sir."

"Then how can you, in this year of Our Lord eighteen hundred and fifty-nine, possibly believe in spirits? The idea that they exist and are capable of manifesting themselves to human beings goes against every concept of rational thinking. For consider, sir, the predicament we should be in if it were true. Let me try to put it concretely. Supposing you had been happily married for some time and your dear wife died. In your bereavement you would at first ridicule every suggestion that you should find a replacement for your dear departed. However, as time passed, you discovered that the loneliness of your single state was more than you could bear and presently you realized that a certain lady of your acquaintance was of such character that you felt you could make a happy life together.

"The more you thought about it, the more you became certain of the feasibility of the idea, and one day you plucked up courage and asked her to become Mrs John S. Clarke, and she consented. Once the nuptials were performed, they would have to be consummated. Right?"

"Right," agreed Captain Clarke.

"But supposing, when you took your new spouse in your arms, you recalled that your former spouse was a spirit, capable of watching every move you made, even if she did not actually manifest herself to you? You get my meaning?"

"Perfectly, sir," said the Captain. "But that is not the point. In my view there are certain spirits to whom the gift of revealing themselves to those left behind is given."

"You mean only some spirits have special gifts, so to speak, bestowed upon them? But, sir, the Good Book tells us, that however class-ridden we may be in this life, in the life hereafter all are equal."

"I was thinking," replied the Captain, "of the generally accepted principle of spirit-lore that, for example, the spirits of suicides or the victims of murder are deprived of eternal rest, and roam the world earth-bound, because of the sin they have committed in taking their own lives, or because of the violence with which they have been deprived of life."

"I have heard of that conception, sir, but again I must reject it for the simple reason that it, too, goes against all the teaching of Holy Writ. Would the Almighty in His great mercy further punish those who had been so unfortunate as to be incapable of tolerating life here below to such a degree that they robbed themselves of His most precious gift, or, in the case of those murdered, had this precious gift taken from them—would God, I say, further deprive these unhappy people of the delights of Paradise? Surely, if anyone were to receive special treatment in Heaven, it would be these unfortunates."

"I can follow your arguments, sir, and I must admit that the logic of them does not escape me," Captain Clarke replied. "At the same time, however, I find myself very much in the position of an eminent French lady I once read of.

"As I recall, her name was Madame du Deffand. Perhaps you have heard of her, sir?"

"Certainly," replied the former Minister. "The Marquise Marie-Anne de Vichy-Chamrond du Deffand. She was a great *salonière* and renowned for her letters. She had a great if cynical wit, and her later fame rested on an outstanding talent for the analysis of character.

She was a great friend of Voltaire, Montesquieu, Fontenelle, D'Alembert and her other great contemporaries. In her later life she formed a close, but entirely moral relationship with the eminent English writer, Horace Walpole. I have read the published volume of her correspondence."

"I did not know she was so famous a lady," Captain Clarke admitted. "But if she was all you say, then her comment gives much greater force to my argument."

"And that comment was?"

"A gentleman asked her one day, 'Do you believe in ghosts, Madame?' to which she replied, 'No, sir, but I am afraid of them.'"

Mr Owen laughed.

"Without meaning to make fun of you in any way, sir," he said, "I think you have not fully appreciated Madame du Deffand's incapacity for foregoing the coining of an epigram whenever the opportunity was afforded her."

"That's as may be, sir," retorted the Captain. "But on the other hand, I submit that while apparitions have not yet been scientifically accounted for, the many authenticated ghost-stories told for many centuries, and very widely believed, in my view, sir, forbid any thinking person from declaring that there is nothing in it when haunted houses and the return of disembodied spirits are being discussed. I mean no offence, Mr Owen."

"I take none, sir."

"I have travelled widely about the world, sir," the Captain went on, "and I have found a belief in ghosts to be as widely distributed as the Religious Idea itself. Even in the remotest islands of distant seas, and among the most unlettered savages, religion has been found and as invariably the belief in ghosts."

"The unlettered are always more susceptible to suggestion, Captain, than those who have been trained to think," Owen said. "With savages, whatever their religion is, it is more than nine-tenths superstition—and so is the belief in ghosts."

"Maybe, sir, maybe. But it is also true that there cannot be smoke without fire. I am convinced that if I were capable of discoursing on the philosophy of religion and of the supernatural, I could show that a belief in religion, even in the Christian religion—did not an angel or spirit release Peter from Herod's prison?—I would go so far as to say, necessitates a belief in ghosts. I can't do that, because I haven't the learning; but can I tell you a story that I had at first hand, which, more than anything else, has confirmed my belief in apparitions?"

"Certainly you may," Owen replied. "I shall listen attentively.

*   *   *   *   *

In 1836 and 1837 (Captain Clarke began) I sailed in the same ship with a certain Robert Bruce, who was first mate. Bruce was an Englishman, a Devon man, despite his name. He had been born in the last years of the last century at Torquay when that now famous watering-place was just a village, consisting of a few straggling cottages on a shingly beach. Like his father before him, he was reared to the seafaring life, and by the time he was thirty had become the first mate of a ship sailing between Liverpool and St John's, New Brunswick.

I joined the *Evening Star* as second mate, and this threw us a good deal together. It is some time since I heard of him; indeed, I don't know if he is still alive. I did hear of him for some years after I left the *Star*, the last news being that he was master of the brig *Comet*, and back on his old Liverpool to New Brunswick run.

Robert Bruce was as truthful and straightforward a man as ever I met in my life. We were as intimate as brothers; and two men can't be together, shut up for nearly two years in the same ship, without getting to know whether they can trust one another's word or not.

He always spoke of the circumstances of the incident I am about to relate in terms of reverence, as of an occurrence that seemed to bring him nearer to God and to another world than anything that had ever happened to him in his life before. I'd stake my life upon it, that he was speaking the truth, the whole truth and nothing but the truth, in the very extraordinary account which I shall now deliver to you.

Robert Bruce was such a good seaman that he became a first mate by the time he was thirty. At the time of the incident, the ship he was in was on her way from Liverpool to New Brunswick. They had been about six weeks at sea, and were near the banks of Newfoundland.

After sunset one day, the captain and his first mate, Robert Bruce, after having taken an observation, went below to calculate their day's work. For some reason or other, Bruce's calculations did not answer to his expectations, and he became so absorbed in the problem before him that he did not notice that the Captain had quitted the cabin.

Presently he found that he had made a simple error in his reckonings, and as soon as he had finished the calculations he called out,

supposedly to the captain, but without looking round, "I make the latitude so and so, and the longitude so and so. Can that be right? What do you make them?"

When he received no reply, he repeated the question, and this time glanced over his shoulder, and seeing a man, whom he took to be the captain, bent over the latter's writing table, he expected an answer. But when there was still no reply, he got up and began to cross to the captain's table.

As he did so, the figure at the table raised its head, and to his utter astonishment Robert Bruce saw that it was not the captain, but an utter stranger!

Like his great namesake, Bruce was no coward, but as he met that fixed gaze looking silently at him, and became conscious that it was not the face of anyone that he had ever seen before, he was overcome with apprehension. Instead of stopping to question the apparent intruder, he rushed up on deck in such evident alarm that he alarmed the captain whom he found back on the bridge.

"Why, Mr Bruce," exclaimed the master, "whatever is the matter? You look as if you'd seen a ghost."

The discovery of the captain on the bridge astonished the mate even more.

"I did not see you leave the cabin, sir," he exclaimed. "How long have you been here?"

"Oh, five or ten minutes, Mr Bruce. Why do you ask?"

"Then who is it, sir, sitting at your desk?"

"Sitting at my desk?" the captain said sharply, in his turn becoming more astonished by the all-too-apparent trepidation of his customarily cool-headed senior officer. "Mr Bruce, have you taken leave of your senses?"

"No, sir, I assure you. There is someone sitting at your desk in the cabin. Who is it, sir?"

"No one I know of," the master told him. "You must be suffering from hallucinations, Mr Mate."

"But I tell you I'm not, sir. I plainly saw a stranger sitting at your desk."

"But there's no stranger aboard the ship, Mr Bruce. We've been six weeks at sea, so how could a stranger come aboard? You must have seen the steward there, or the second mate; who else would go down without orders?"

"Sir, I know the steward and the second mate as well as I know you," Bruce retorted. "I swear it was neither of them. It was someone I had never seen before, sitting in your armchair, writing on

your slate. I did not know you had left the cabin, and when I had finished my calculations I asked you what you had made yours. When no one replied, I turned round and saw you sitting at your desk, still writing, so I began to cross the cabin, and when I was about halfway across you looked up, only it wasn't you, but this complete stranger. Sir, I can't be mistaken, because he looked me full in the face, and if ever I saw a man plainly and distinctly in this world, I saw him."

The captain now realized that Bruce was absolutely convinced of the truth of what he was saying.

"But who can it be?" he said, half to himself.

"God knows, sir, I don't," Bruce replied. "All I know is, I saw a man, and I had never seen him before in all my life."

Sure that Bruce was allowing his imagination to run away with him, the captain said sternly: "You must be crazy, Mr Mate. I repeat, how could a stranger come aboard when we're six weeks at sea without our knowing!"

"I realize that, sir," Bruce replied. "Yet I am prepared to swear on the Bible that I saw a stranger sitting in your arm-chair.

The captain regarded the mate for some seconds in silence, then with a shrug of his shoulders he said: "All right, Mr Bruce. Go down and ask him to be good enough to step up here on the bridge and we'll ask him how he came aboard and what it is he wants."

The mate hesitated, and this the captain knew to be unlike him.

"Come now, Mr Mate!" he said. "I've given you an order which I wish to be obeyed."

"The truth is, sir," Bruce replied with a good deal of embarrassment, "I'd rather not go down alone."

Now the captain's anger was rising swiftly.

"Mr Bruce, pray go down at once, and don't make a fool of yourself before the crew," he said quietly, yet sternly, for he had noticed that one or two sailors engaged on their duties nearby, as well as the helmsman, were regarding the mate in some alarm.

"I hope, sir," Bruce replied obstinately, "that you've always found me willing to do my duty, but could you not come down with me, sir?"

Not wishing to provoke more of a scene before the crew, and beginning to realize that his thoroughly reliable first mate was the last man to make such a fuss without good cause, with a grunt he left the bridge followed by Bruce.

When they reached the cabin they found it empty, as the captain had suspected they would.

"Well, Mr Bruce," he exclaimed, "didn't I tell you you had been dreaming?"

"It is all very well, sir, to say so; but if I didn't see that man writing on your slate, may I never see my home again."

"Ah! Writing on the slate!" the captain said. "If he was writing on the slate, the writing should still be there; provided of course that *he* was ever here and ever wrote."

As he said this, the captain strode across the cabin to his desk, and picked up the slate.

"Good God!" he exclaimed. "There's something here, sure enough. Is that your writing, Mr Bruce?"

The mate took the slate, and there in plain, legible characters were the words, "Steer to the nor'west".

"Is this your idea of a joke, Mr Bruce?" the captain thundered.

"On my word as a man and a sailor, sir," the puzzled Bruce replied, "it would not be my idea of a joke either. I have told you the exact truth, sir. I know no more of this writing than you do, sir."

The captain sat down at his desk, and was silent for several minutes, while Bruce stood by more apprehensive than ever. At last the master turned over the slate, and pushing it towards the mate said: "Write the words, *Steer to the nor'west*".

When Bruce had obeyed, the captain closely compared the two specimens of handwriting, for some moments. Then he said: "Mr Bruce, be good enough to tell the second mate to come here immediately."

When Bruce returned with the second mate, without any explanation the captain said to the younger man: "Please write on Mr Bruce's slate the words *Steer to the nor'west*."

With a slightly puzzled air, as though he believed the captain might be becoming somewhat eccentric, the second mate complied. Once more the captain compared the two examples of handwriting, and now bewilderment began to crease his forehead.

Dismissing the second mate, he turned to Bruce, saying: "Someone must have written these words, and I intend to find out who it is, who is trying to make fools of us. Every man who can write shall come here and write the words. In that way we shall soon find out who the ruffian is. We'll begin with the steward. Call him up, Mr Bruce. God help the man who thinks he can play this dangerous kind of joke with me."

So the steward came and wrote the words, and the handwriting on the captain's slate was clearly not his. He was followed by the nine men of the crew able to write, and within a comparatively short

time, the captain realized that he still had not solved the mystery.

"Sir," Bruce suggested. "Could anyone have stowed away before we left Liverpool?"

"I don't see how, Mr Bruce, without his being discovered long before now," the Captain said. "But we will find out. The ship must be searched. Order up all hands, Mr Mate."

By this time, something of the incident had circulated among the crew, who believed that a stranger had come aboard in some mysterious manner and had to be found. They did not need the captain's order to search every nook and cranny of the ship, and went about their task thoroughly and with eager curiosity. Two hours later, Bruce had to report to the captain that no strange person had been found, nor was there any sign at all that a stowaway had been on board.

"I must admit I am strangely puzzled, Mr Bruce," the captain confessed. "What can it mean? That's what I would like to know. What can it mean, if it does mean anything?"

"I can't say, sir, I'm sure," Bruce replied. "I saw the man write; you see the writing. It must mean something."

The captain paced the cabin, while Bruce stood patiently by until a decision had been made.

"Do you believe in ghosts?" the captain asked him presently.

"Why, no, sir," Bruce told him. "Though I have met some who do."

"Neither do I believe in ghosts or apparitions or call them what you will," said the captain, "but do you know what, Mr Bruce?"

"No, sir."

"We have the wind free, and I have a great mind to keep her away and see what will come of it. Just by way of experiment, Mr Mate, if you understand. What would you say to that?"

"In your place, sir, I surely would," Bruce agreed. "At the worst, we shall only lose a few hours."

"I'm glad to have that answer, Mr Bruce. Well, be it so. Go and give the course Nor'west; and, Mr Bruce, have a good look-out aloft, and let it be a hand you can depend on thoroughly. I am sorry that I should have ever doubted your word, Mr Mate."

"I would have done the same, sir, situated similarly." Bruce smiled his gratitude for the apology.

So the necessary orders were given, and about three o'clock on the following afternoon the look-out reported an iceberg nearly ahead.

As the captain and the mate trained their glasses in the direction given by the look-out, the latter's excited voice informed them

that he could now see what looked like a vessel of some sort close to it.

"Can it be true?" the captain said quietly to the mate. "Do you imagine, Mr Bruce, that Providence has sent us this way to assist an unfortunate ship that has run foul of an iceberg?"

"If that man sitting at your desk, sir, was Providence, or sent by Providence," Bruce replied, "then I should say yes."

On coming nearer to the iceberg, both men could begin to make out a vessel, somewhat dismantled, apparently frozen in the ice, and from the movement on her decks it seemed that she still had a good many human beings on board. And so it turned out.

As soon as they had communicated their distress, the captain sent out boats to the stranded vessel, to bring those still living on board his ship. She proved to be a schooner from Quebec bound for Liverpool, with between fifty and sixty passengers aboard. She had run into pack ice and had finally been frozen in fast. She had been in this situation, which was now most critical, for several weeks. She was stove in, her decks swept—in fact, she was a wreck. All her provisions and almost all her water had gone, and her crew and passengers had given up all thoughts of being rescued. It was no wonder that their gratitude for their unexpected deliverance was proportionately great.

All were physically in a weak condition, but the crew of the rescue ship quickly devised all kinds of tackle, and with great tenderness for the hardened, rough men they were, they lost no time in transferring the victims from the wreck to the warmth and shelter of their own vessel.

As Mr Bruce stood at the side of his ship supervising the taking on of the guests, one of them, more vigorous than most, hauled himself up the ladder which had been lowered over the side. But even he was almost exhausted when he reached the deck, and Bruce hurried forward to support him.

It was when the man lifted up his head to thank the mate that the latter almost started back, letting the man fall. His consternation now equalled the bewilderment he had experienced when he had seen the man sitting in the captain's arm-chair. For the face that he now gazed into was the face of the stranger whom he had seen writing on the captain's slate, "Steer to the nor'west".

At first he tried to persuade himself it must be his fancy playing him tricks, but the more he examined the man the more sure he felt he was right. It was not only the face; the man's build and even his dress corresponded exactly.

As soon as the exhausted crew and starving passengers had been cared for, and the ship was back on course again, Bruce went to his captain and asked him to go down to the privacy of the cabin with him, as he had something of importance to tell him.

When they reached the cabin, the captain exclaimed with a laugh, "Not another ghost, I hope, Mr Mate!"

"On the contrary, sir," the mate replied. "It seems that it was not a ghost which I saw this morning, for I swear that man is alive and now aboard this ship."

The captain strode to his chair and sat down in it heavily before he said with a feigned tone of weariness: 'I beg you, Mr Bruce, let us have no more mysteries. Explain what you mean. Who is alive?'

"Why, sir, Bruce told him, "it is a mystery, but the same one. One of the passengers we have just saved is, I am convinced, the very man I saw writing on your slate yesterday. Indeed, I'd swear to it in any court of justice."

"Upon my word!" the captain exclaimed. "This gets more and more singular. But since you proved right on that other occasion, I cannot reject what you say now. Have the goodness to show me this man."

So going below, they found the man talking to the captain of the wrecked ship. On their coming up, both the captain and the passenger expressed their gratitude for having been saved in the warmest terms.

"It was a terrible fate you have preserved us from," the passenger said. "For I cannot conceive a worse way to die than by slow death from exposure and starvation."

"Sir," replied the captain, "we have only done our duty, and I am sure your captain would have done the same for us had our roles been reversed. Gentlemen, I wonder if I may trespass upon your indulgence, and ask you to step up into my cabin for a few moments?

Both men gave their ready agreement, and when they were in the cabin with the door closed, and the captain had put generous tots of rum before them, he said: "I hope, sir, you will not think that my mate and me are trifling with you if I ask you to write a few words on my slate."

Plainly surprised by this somewhat strange request, the passenger laughed, and taking the slate and pencil he asked: "How can I refuse to do anything you request, no matter how strange the request may seem at this moment? What shall I write, sir?"

"A few words are all I want," the captain told him. "Suppose you write, *Steer to the nor'west?*"

Still smiling, the passenger complied, and when he had done handed the slate back to the captain. In silence, though inwardly excited, the captain took the slate to his desk and getting the slate on which the words had been so mysteriously written the day before out of the drawer in which he had carefully placed it, put the two side by side on his desk.

After but a quick glance, he let out an exclamation and called Mr Bruce to his side.

"I knew it, sir," the mate said, his voice trembling a little.

Turning to the passenger, the captain handed him the two slates.

"Would you," he asked, "say that both of these specimens are in your handwriting?"

"You know one of them is," the passenger replied, "for you saw me write it. And . . . and this I could also swear to, though I know I did not write it. Sir, what is the meaning of this? Who wrote the other?"

"Ah, that, sir, is more than I can tell you. My mate here, Mr Bruce, told me that he saw you sitting writing it at this very desk shortly after dusk yesterday evening."

On hearing this, the captain of the wreck and the passenger exchanged what seemed to be glances of intelligence and surprise, and then the captain asked, "Did you dream that you wrote on this slate, Mr . . . ?"

"Not that I remember," replied the passenger.

"You speak of dreaming," said Bruce. "May I ask what this gentleman was doing say about half after five yesterday evening?"

"Mr Mate," said the captain, "the whole thing is quite mysterious, and I had intended to speak to you about it as soon as we got a little quiet.

"This gentleman, here, was so exhausted by yesterday afternoon as to be at the end of his tether. We had already lost three passengers, and I hoped, though I feared it, that we should not add a fourth to that number. In mid-afternoon, however, he fell into a deep sleep, and he slept so for two hours and more. In fact, he awoke shortly after six o'clock.

"I was by his side when he came to again, and on seeing me he said, "Captain, we shall be rescued, and that very soon; by sunset tomorrow at the latest." I thought at first that he was still light-headed, as he had been some time before he slept, but then I realized that he was quite rational, so I asked him his reason for making such a statement.

"He then told me that he had dreamed he had been on board a

vessel, and that she was coming to our rescue. He described the vessel's appearance and outward rig, and to our utter astonishment, when your ship hove in sight, she corresponded exactly to his description.

"To be honest, I had not put much faith in what he had said, yet still I hoped there might be something in it, for drowning men you know, captain, will catch at straws. As it has turned out, I cannot doubt it was all arranged in some incomprehensible way by an overruling Providence, so that we might be saved."

After a pause, the other captain said: "Well, gentlemen, there cannot be a doubt that the writing on the slate, let it have come there as it may, saved all your lives. I was steering at the time considerably south of west, and altered my course to the nor'west, and had a look-out aloft to see what might come of it. But you say, sir, you did not dream of writing on a slate?"

"No, sir, I have no recollection whatever of doing so. I got the impression that the ship I saw in my dream was coming to rescue us, but how that impression came I cannot tell. There is another very strange thing about it," he added. "Everything here on board seems to me quite familiar, yet I am certain I was never in your vessel before. It is all a puzzle to me. But what did your mate see?

Bruce then told them the story exactly as I have told it out here, Mr Owen, and I must say, as I said earlier, sir, that knowing Bruce as I did, and knowing that he would not lie even to save his life, I fully agree with their conclusion—that it was certainly a special interposition of Providence which saved them from what seemed a certain death.

"It is certainly a most impressive relation, Captain Clarke," replied Owen. "You almost have me converted, but when you began our discussion you spoke of ghosts. This man was still alive."

"But it was his spirit or ghost that Bruce clearly saw," Clarke insisted.

"But was it, was it, Captain?" Owen asked. "I would be the first to admit that your friend Bruce did see the likeness of the passenger sitting in the captain's arm-chair; but in that case, if the man was alive, as indeed he was, it might have been that somehow he projected his plea to be saved so strongly that in some quite incomprehensible fashion his thoughts went out across the ocean to the nearest vessel ... To be quite frank, Captain, I can't explain it, any more than you can."

"But you still don't believe in ghosts, sir?" Captain Clarke asked.

"To misquote Madame du Deffand, Captain, 'No, but I own they do exist'."

The Haunted House at Hydesville

The hamlet of Hydesville, New York State, was in 1848 a very humble place. It was a cluster of small wooden houses, in one of which lived a farmer named John Fox, his wife, and their two little girls—Margaretta, aged about thirteen, and Catherine, about nine. There were other children out in the world, and one had died in infancy.

The Foxes were a highly respectable family, devout Methodists, and until March, 1848, had led a very normal life. They believed, no doubt, in the Devil, but John Fox was not deterred from taking the little house by rumours that it was "queer". Rapping noises had been heard in it, which had gained it a certain reputation for unpleasantness. After three months of living in it, the Foxes began to hear these raps themselves. Sometimes there was merely a light knocking, but at other times the sounds were louder, and gave the impression of furniture being moved. Margaretta and Katie were very frightened—they insisted on their bed being moved into the bedroom of their parents—but when it was placed there both beds were rocked and shaken by the heavy rain of knockings that broke out.

"I'll find the cause of this, if I have to take the house to pieces," said John to his wife. And they searched every nook and cranny— renewing their efforts when they noticed that the sounds were much stronger at night than by day. But no concealed trickster could be found. Then, on the night of 31 March, there was a new development. The noises had been getting louder and louder, and

on the night of 30 March the family had had very little sleep. On the 31st they therefore went to bed early—Mrs Fox "almost sick with tiredness". Hardly had they lain down when the noises began. The elder Foxes groaned; but little Katie, emboldened by the presence of her parents, called out to the unseen presence—whom she obviously imagined as a cloven-hoofed Devil—"Mr. Splitfoot, do as I do!" and she clapped her hands several times. The sound instantly echoed her with a similar number of raps. When she stopped, it stopped. Then Margaretta said: "Now, do just as I do—count one, two, three, four," clapping as she spoke. The rappings echoed her. Then Katie thought of an explanation. "Oh, Mother, I know what it is. Tomorrow is April-Fool day, and it's somebody trying to fool us."

Mrs Fox thought of a test. She asked the unseen rapper to rap out her children's ages, successively. Instantly it obliged, leaving a pause before recording the age of her three-year-old child who had died.

"Is this a human being that answers my questions so correctly? she asked. There was no answer. "Is it a spirit? If it is, make two raps. Two raps smartly followed. Then Mrs Fox's questions elicited the information that the rapper was the spirit of a man who had at the age of thirty-one been murdered in the house, and that his remains were buried in the cellar. He added some details about his family, and said that his murderer would never be brought to justice.

"Will you continue to rap if I call my neighbours?" asked Mrs Fox. The raps indicated that the entity was willing. Accordingly, Mr Fox called in several neighbours, who came to scoff and remained to marvel. One of them, a Mr Duesler, interrogated the spirit, by whom he was told that the murder had taken place in a bedroom about five years before—that it had been committed with a butcher's knife—that the body had been taken on the night after the murder down the cellar stairs and buried ten feet below ground. The victim had been murdered for five hundred dollars, he said.

The awe-struck circle who heard this strange story called in other friends and neighbours, until the house was full. But Mrs Fox, alarmed, took her children away, leaving her husband on guard, while more and more curious neighbours piled in to listen to the noises. They were simple, superstitious people, the folk of Hydesville; the spirit's story was widely believed. It was decided to try to prove it by digging for the remains, and John Fox led a working party to the cellar.

But alas! Although they dug and dug until they came to water

and had to stop, nothing came to light. Sceptical glances were cast at the Fox family. Both husband and wife made affidavits, to protect their own reputation. The neighbours, behaving with great good sense, formed themselves into a committee of investigation, recording and collating the facts, and even having the evidence printed within a month. *A Report of the Mysterious Noises Heard in the House of Mr John D. Fox* was published at Canandaigua, New York.

In the summer, when the ground was dry, digging operations began again. This time they were not quite fruitless. There was evidence of *something* having been buried—a plank, some traces of charcoal and quicklime, and some strands of hair and pieces of bone, which a doctor thought came from a human skull. But nothing more evidential was found.

Then another piece of testimony was produced. Four years before, the house had been occupied by a Mr and Mrs Bell, whose hired help had been a girl called Lucretia Pulver. She now came forward and told her story. One day, she said, a travelling pedlar had come to the door—a man of about thirty, wearing a black frock-coat and light-coloured trousers. Lucretia heard him talking to Mrs Bell about his family, and Mrs Bell told her he was an old acquaintance. Soon after he arrived Lucretia was surprised to be dismissed by Mrs Bell, who gave the excuse that she could not afford to keep her. Before going, Lucretia told the pedlar that she would like to buy some things from him, but had no money with her; and he agreed to call at her house with them the next morning. But next morning came without a sign of him, nor did Lucretia ever see him again. Three days afterwards, she was astonished to be asked to return to the Bells' home. A job was a job, however, and she went back to work for them. She noticed, without thinking much of it, that Mrs Bell was re-making some coats, which she said were too large to fit Mr Bell; and that several articles from the pedlar's pack were lying about the house. One evening Mrs Bell sent Lucretia down to the cellar to shut the outer door. In crossing the floor, the girl fell near the centre of it, and landed on uneven, loose earth. Her scream brought Mrs Bell, who laughed at her servant's fright, and said rats must have been busy in the ground. Soon afterwards Mr Bell went to work to fill in the "rat-holes".

There were other strange things about the house—rappings, and the footsteps of somebody who seemed to be walking about but was never seen. Mrs Pulver called and reproached Mrs Bell for letting her daughter be terrorized. Mr and Mrs Bell were not any too comfortable themselves, and after some weeks they left.

After them, a family called Weekman moved in. They too heard the noises and footsteps, and doors opened of themselves. Then a Mrs Lafe, who shared the house, saw a strange man in the bedroom next to the kitchen. She had been in the kitchen for a long time, and had seen nobody pass her. The stranger, she said, was a man in a black frock coat, a black cap, and light pantaloons. "I know of no one like him," she added.

Lucretia's story immediately drew suspicion on Mr Bell, who was by now living at Lyon, New York. Affronted at the rumours, he sent a statement of his personal integrity signed by forty-four people; there was no evidence against him, and the rumours ceased.

But, whoever might be his murderer, the ghost became more active than ever. Poor Mrs Fox's dark hair turned white in a week. As the hauntings were more noticeable when Margaretta and Katie were at home, they were sent away—Margaretta to a brother, David Fox, and Katie to her sister at Rochester, Mrs Fish. The noises followed them. Mrs Fish, a music-teacher, was unable to continue her work. In vain the family prayed with their Methodist friends for divine help and relief. Where the girls went, the spirit went too. Other people, including Leah Fish, began to develop gifts of what was later to be called mediumship, and spirit messages began to be received from other departed people than the original communicator. Hydesville had, in fact, become the birthplace of modern Spiritualism. But that is another story.

It is sad to record that the fame which came to the two Fox sisters, as they grew up, eventually brought ruin to Margaretta, who towards the end of her life became an alcoholic. She confessed publicly that the famous rappings had all been trickery, produced by herself and her sister by means of cracking their toe-joints. But although on her death-bed Margaretta was unable to move hand or foot, a woman doctor who attended her distinctly heard strange, unaccountable knockings.

Many years passed, and the famous haunting of Hydesville was forgotten by all but a few. Both sisters were dead, and the truth or untruth of Margaretta's confession died with them. Or so it seemed, until a news item appeared in the *Boston Journal* for 23 November, 1904.

Some children had been playing in the cellar of an old house at Hydesville—known as "Spook House" from local tales of what had happened there. Suddenly one of the walls had crumbled and fallen, partly burying one child. The rest, terrified, ran for help. Mr William Hyde, the house's owner, came to the rescue and brought other

men with him. When they rescued the child from the heap of stones and rubble in which it lay, they found that the collapsed wall was a false one, and had a space between it and the original cellar foundation. In it lay—the headless skeleton of a man, and beside it a pedlar's tin box.

The discovery completely exonerated the Fox sisters of trickery, and corroborated the statement of Lucretia Pulver and the doctor's diagnosis of the bone fragments as being those of a skull. Bell—for the murderer can have been no other—must have cut off his victim's head, attempted to burn it, and then clumsily buried it in quicklime, under the loose earth which Lucretia had noticed. Then, after Lucretia's tumble, he had reburied it and the rest of the body under the false wall.

So, after fifty-six years, the story told by the pedlar's wandering ghost was proved true in every detail; and, as he had prophesied, his murderer was never brought to justice.

The Guardian Ghost

In 1850 there lived in the village of Ringstead, in Northampton-shire, a butcher with the somewhat outlandish name of Weekly Ball. He was in his later forties, married with several children. Broad-shouldered and thick-set, with the florid complexion of the chronic drinker and misshapen with an incipient paunch, even on sight he was not, one would have thought, physically attractive. Add to his uncomeliness a generally known ill-temper, and he was the last person a young girl would be likely to risk her reputation for.

But the female psychological structure is for ever providing surprises and even some shocks; and there was one girl at least who provided both for the worldly-wise inhabitants of Ringstead. Perhaps if her father had still been alive he would have made her see sense or so impressed her with his paternal authority that she would have forgone the consummation of her attraction to the butcher, though even this is problematical, since her nature was derived entirely from her father. Her mother was a faded, retiring woman, worn out before her time by the strain of her late husband's conjugal demands and the shame of his infidelities, and she had neither the personality nor the urge to attempt to curb her husband's traits so blatantly obvious in his daughter.

On the other hand, it would be unfair to attach too great blame to Mrs Atley for her daughter's amatory non-conformism. Lydia Atley was in service at the hall. When Weekly Ball first impinged on her consciousness, she had already been a member of the squire's household for six years, and at eighteen she had graduated from

maid-of-all-work to second housemaid. She shared a room with the third housemaid, and since her duties kept her occupied from half-past five in the morning until after dinner, except for one afternoon a week and one Sunday in three, she had little opportunity for visiting her mother. Mrs Atley, therefore, was not in a position to bring any great degree of influence to bear on her daughter's development into womanhood, even had she had any great inclination in that direction.

Lydia was a comely girl. Her hair was raven black, which often, as the light caught it, shone with a rich green sheen. Her face was oval, a shape accentuated by the highly set, faintly prominent cheek bones and tapering chin. In the nun's coif, with downcast mien, she would have given the appearance of genuine asceticism, an effect which would have been immediately dispelled when she raised her head and revealed a full moist mouth and large dark eyes which smiled even when she was out of humour. As for the rest of her, it was only too evident, despite the swinging fullness of her mid-Victorian print and her starched apron, that her bosom was ripely firm and her hips roundly supple.

She was not quite eighteen when Weekly Ball first set eyes on her. It had been a chance occurrence. One of his roundsmen had been laid up, and the other had been delayed by an accident to his trap, and it was three o'clock in the afternoon when he realized that the saddle of mutton for the squire's dinner was still hanging from its hook at the back of the shop.

Calling to his happy-go-lucky but submissive wife to keep a look-out for any customer who might come along, he saddled his mare, wrapped up the mutton in a cloth, and mounting with it before him as though he were riding pillion to it, he trotted up to the hall. It was his first visit to the hall for several years. Orders were either given to the roundsman, or a servant with business in the village would call at the shop with them. Regularly on the first of each month the squire's lady would draw up in her carriage, he would go out to her with the account already drawn up, she would scrutinize it, and, always satisfied, since she had "a poor head for figures" and the squire was generous, she would tell her companion to count out into Weekly Ball's hand the sum due. And it was to Weekly Ball's credit that though he could have done so with impunity, he never once attempted nor was tempted to overcharge the hall.

Dismounting at the kitchen door, he knocked. The face of Mrs Knowls, the cook, appeared at the window.

"Come in, Mr Ball," he heard her call faintly to him through the glass.

The kitchen was a large and spacious room. Down the centre stood a vast white scrubbed deal table, and along one of the long walls stretched a dresser on which countless plates and moulds and pans were set out. Practically the whole of the opposite wall was taken up by an immense kitchen range, with ovens on either side.

On one half of the table, on wire trays, lay batches of newly baked scones and cakes. They were still steaming from the oven, and the smell of them filled the kitchen with a heady aroma.

"I was just beginning to be anxious, Mr Ball," Mrs Knowls said. "I thought the impossible had happened at last and you had forgotten. You're only just in time, you know."

The butcher explained, with apologies, the reason for the late delivery, but while he was addressing the cook his gaze was held by one of the two girls who were cleaning numerous brass fire-irons at the far end of the table. They were there by the kindness of the cook, who appreciated their complaints that they could not do their work properly in their own pantry which, having no fire, was today as cold as a tomb.

"Well, no harm's done now you've come," the cook said. "Would you take a glass of elderberry wine, Mr Ball?"

"That's civil of you, Mrs Knowls," he accepted. "Thank you kindly."

"It will keep out the cold, Mr Ball. It's a long time since it's been as cold as this so early in October. Lydia, put the poker in the coals, there's a good girl."

The girl, who had attracted the butcher's attention, left the table and went to the grate, her movement supple and subtly suggestive, at least to a man of Ball's sensitivity to such things. The cook was fetching the wine from the larder, and going over to the range and pretending to warm himself Ball said quietly to the girl, "I don't think I've seen you before. Are you from the village or hereabouts?"

"Yes, Mr Ball. Tom Atley's girl."

"Then I know your mother. She's a customer of mine."

"If spending a few pence weekly makes her that, I suppose she is," the girl agreed pertly.

"How is it I haven't seen you in the village then?"

"Because I don't come down much. My mother lives this side, and I don't get much time off."

"When do you get time off?"

"One afternoon a week. Wednesdays mostly."

"Then you'll be off tomorrow. I'm planning to pick my pippins tomorrow before the hard frost gets them. You know my orchard. If you stop by, I'll give you a basket for your mother."

The girl looked him straight in the eyes, her own eyes shining with amusement and excitement. Mrs Knowls's footsteps could be heard crossing the flagstones of the larder.

"Will you come?" Ball whispered urgently.

With a slight toss of the head and a broad smile, the girl said, "You work fast, Mr Ball . . . Yes, I'll come!"

"Lydie!" the girl at the table exclaimed, but could say no more as Mrs Knowls emerged into the kitchen weighed down by a large unopened flagon of elderberry wine.

"Sorry to have kept you waiting, Mr Ball," the cook said. "I thought—in fact, I'm sure—I had a flagon opened, but like as not Tom Fletcher's finished it off. I'll have a word with him. He'll never make a butler if he can't keep off the liquor."

"You shouldn't make such good wine, Mrs Knowls," Ball remarked with buoyant gallantry.

"Tom Fletcher would drink anything. Besides, I made the wine for all the servants' hall, not just for him," the cook said.

She went to the dresser and took down a pewter tankard from its hook. Having dusted it with her apron, she uncorked the flagon and filled the tankard two-thirds full with blood-red elderberry wine.

"Is that poker ready, Lydia?" she asked.

The girl drew the poker from the fire.

"It's got the glowingest red tip you ever saw, Mrs Knowls," she said, smiling at Ball.

"Bring it here, then, quick. Come along girl, before it goes dull. You know what to do with it? Plunge it straight into the tankard, but be sure it doesn't touch the glass at the bottom."

With a firm, unhesitating movement, the girl followed the cook's instructions. Even when the contact of the red-hot iron with the liquid made a sudden sizzling and sent up a cloud of steam, she did not flinch. The watching butcher noted every action she made, and became aware of an inner tension rising in him.

The girl withdrew the poker from the tankard, and passing so near to him that he caught the special aroma of her, put the iron back on its hook.

"There you are, then, Mr Ball," the cook said. "Mulled elderberry wine will keep the dampness out of any bones."

Ball took up the tankard, and with a graceful bow for one so

sturdily built, said, "Your good health, Mrs Knowls . . . ladies!" He took a draught and smacked his lips. "Finer than any other I've ever tasted, Mrs Knowls!" he complimented her. "No wonder Tom Fletcher can't keep away from it."

"Thank you, Mr Ball," the cook beamed with pleasure. "It is my speciality."

As he slowly quaffed from the tankard, though he addressed his inconsequential gossip to the cook, he kept his eyes on the girl who had returned to her work with renewed vigour. From time to time she glanced up at him, her eyes still shining, a faint smile playing about her lips.

When he could no longer reasonably prolong his visit, he took his leave.

Within a short time of his going, the girls, having finished their chore, went up to the room they shared at the top of the house. As they went, they did not speak, but as soon as they were in their room the younger girl burst out, "Lydie, you're not serious about going to old Ball's orchard, are you?"

"Of course I am!" Lydia Atley replied firmly, throwing herself down on her bed. "Why not? My mam could do with some apples."

"It's more than apples he'll be giving you, if you don't watch out. My dad says he's as las . . . lascivious as a young ram."

"Betsy!" Lydia Atley exclaimed in mock horror. "How could you bring yourself to say such a thing. A girl of your age."

"I'm nearly as old as you are, Lydie," the girl protested, "and when you've got six brothers like I have, you have to be as simple as Silly Tommy Hodge not to know what's what."

"Tommy Hodge isn't all that simple by what Mabel Penrose says," Lydia replied.

"Don't change the subject!" the younger girl snapped. "Promise me you won't go."

"I'll certainly promise no such thing!"

"Then let me go with you."

"How can you when your afternoon's Thursday?"

"I'll slip out."

"And get caught and lose your place!" Lydia swung her legs off the bed and began to unpin her apron. "Don't worry about me, Betsy dear. I can look after myself."

"*You'll* get caught, like you thought Ben Ridgeway had caught you a couple of months since."

"I've learned a thing or two since then."

"So you think! Besides, how can you ever think of letting an old man like Weekly Ball even lay a finger on you?"

"He's not old . . . not all that old." Lydia's voice changed, and she seemed to be musing to herself. "I know he's not handsome; anything but. But there's something about him. Like and like, I reckon." She stood up, and unbuttoning her dress shrugged it off her shoulders and let it fall about her feet. "Anyhow, I'm tired of wasting my time with fumbling boys who've got no idea what a girl wants. Weekly Ball will know, I'll be bound."

"Please, Lydie, for the last time!" Betsy pleaded.

"Sorry, Betsy dear!" her friend told her. "If you were made like me, you'd know."

So, Lydia Atley met Weekly Ball in his orchard the next afternoon. It was the first of many meetings, not only on Wednesday afternoons, but in the dark winter evenings and the gloaming of summer ones. From time to time, Betsy would try to remonstrate, but to no avail, and presently she became engrossed in her own affair with Lydia's late boy, Ben Ridgeway, the nineteen-year-old-son of the head groom.

But then there came a time when Betsy noticed that a change had come over her friend. She no longer chattered, no longer smiled and joked; instead she went about her work in a kind of automatic daze.

Betsy said nothing, though she was sure she knew the reason for the change. She had no desire to taunt her friend; she could only feel pity for her. If the same thing should overtake her, at least Ben Ridgeway could marry her—not that it was likely to happen, because she was keeping Ben at his proper distance, the better to keep him attached—but Weekly Ball was married already, with a slatternly wife and a brood of seven, soon to be eight, to prove it. So she kept her counsel, knowing that if Lydia wanted to tell her what was in her mind she would in her own good time.

So it happened a night or two later, when Betsy went to their room and found Lydia already in bed and sobbing her heart out. Betsy tried to cheer her friend up, still hesitating to reveal that she had guessed. Eventually, when Lydia's sobs only increased the more comfort she received, Betsy did blurt out, "You're in the family way, aren't you?"

Lydia at once stopped weeping and sat up, exclaiming, "How did you know?"

Betsy smiled, "I guessed. It wasn't difficult. It's about the only thing that would lower your spirits."

"He promised me it wouldn't happen. He said he'd see to that. But it has, Betsy. There's no doubt of it."

"Have you told him?"

"No."

"But whyever not? I know he can't marry you, but he's well off. He can afford to help you."

"He won't like it. Not a little bit. He's mean and he's selfish, and ever since he became a churchwarden he's been scared someone will find out about him and me."

"Well, then, I don't know what you're worrying about. Tell him if he won't help you, you'll ask the squire to. Squire'll soon put him in his place. Promise me you'll tell him. Even if he says no, and you don't tell squire, you won't be any worse off than if you keep it to yourself. Anyhow, you won't be able to keep it to yourself much longer, and as soon as it shows the missus won't keep you on. Promise, now."

"You're right, Betsy dear. Sensible as always," Lydia replied. "I promise."

Next evening, Betsy was in bed with the candle still burning, waiting for her friend, when Lydia came quietly in. She could see at once from the change in Lydia's spirits that she had kept her promise.

"What did he say?" she asked.

"He didn't like it," Lydia told her, "but he's promised to give me some money so that I can go away. We've got it all planned. I'm going to give in my notice tomorrow, and next week he'll give me the money."

"What excuse are you going to give for your notice, Lydie?" the practical Betsy asked.

"I'm needed to look after a sick aunt in Northampton, I'll go there and take a room, and he'll come and visit me. He has a friend, a butcher there, who'll give me a job when the baby's come."

So Lydia Atley gave a week's notice, and the night after she left the hall she kept a rendezvous with Weekly Ball at their customary meeting-place—a hut in the butcher's orchard.

It so happened that one of the villagers, Robert Hickens, was taking a short cut down a little-frequented track that ran beside the orchard. He later deposed that as he was passing the hut he heard a woman's voice which he recognized to be Lydia Atley's, saying: "I don't believe you mean to give me any money at all. I've a feeling you mean to kill me, Weekly Ball." Asked why he had said nothing when Lydia Atley disappeared from the village, an embarrassed

Hickens mumbled that he had always been of the opinion that it is best to keep out of other people's business.

After that night, Lydia Atley was never seen alive again. When her mother was asked where her daughter was, she replied that Lydia had left the cottage that evening, her few possessions packed in a wicker basket, saying that she was going to Northampton. She was tired of country life, she had said, and wanted to live in a town. Since this came from her mother, everyone was prepared to accept it as the explanation of Lydia's disappearance from the village.

All might have been put out of mind had not Betsy, in the early weeks of the following spring, allowed herself to be lured to the secluded spot near the butcher's orchard by Ben Ridgeway. There, after a while, Ben began to press his attentions, but as usual, when in Betsy's view he started to be too importunate, she told him that she was not prepared to grant him any further favours until they were married.

"But we're going to be married in June!" Ben exclaimed. "That's only two months away, so why plague ourselves by waiting?"

"Something could happen," Betsy replied firmly.

"But we'd be married before it began to show!" the young man pointed out. "Supposing I say I can't wait? It's not just the birds and the sheep, and the cattle and foxes that get extra lively in the spring, Bet."

"I'm beginning to know that!" Betsy retorted.

Ben changed his approach. Stroking her hair, he said quietly, "Look, my dear, when you've said 'No' before, I've always stopped haven't I? But I needn't have; I'm a good sight stronger than you. Then why do you think I stopped? I've done that to show you I love you."

"I know that, Ben."

"Do you think I'd ask you now if I didn't love you?"

Betsy sighed, and when she did not reply he increased the ardour of his caresses, pleading in whispers that made him sound as if he were moaning with pain, as indeed he was. And suddenly Betsy became aware that she was beginning to suffer, too, and that her resolve was weakening. "It can't matter much now, like he says," she found she was telling herself. "He does love me, and I love him, and we are getting wed in June." Then she had no strength, no desire, to resist him any more; and he knew she had stopped resisting.

All the weeks of longing pent up seemed to burst the banks of his respect for the chasteness of the girl whose arms were about his neck, and whose breath brushed his cheek in encouraging searing waves.

Suddenly, however, his excitement was cut off in mid-course. Taken by surprise by the strength of Betsy's unexpected action, he saw her sit up, and heard her crying out, "Lydie! Lydie!" Then she jumped to her feet and began to run down the track, still calling her friend's name.

He scrambled to his feet, perplexed, and began to hurry after her, but before he came up with her she had stopped, and having looked round as though searching for something or someone, she turned and ran towards him, and when she threw herself into the protection of his arms he found her trembling from head to foot.

"What's up, old girl?" he asked, holding her tightly to him.

"I saw her," the girl wept. "I saw her, Ben! Lydie Atley! She was looking down at me and moving her finger backwards and forwards as though to warn me. When I sat up, she turned away and began to walk down the path; then, just as I was catching her up, she disappeared. Where has she gone?

"You were seeing things, sweetheart!" the young man tried to comfort her. "I didn't see anyone."

"But I saw her! I tell you I saw her! She was warning me I was doing wrong."

"If she'd been walking down the path, I would have seen her, too," Ben Ridgeway insisted, "and I tell you there was no one. Besides, if she'd been there, she would have stopped when you called her. She was your best friend, wasn't she?"

"I tell you I saw her?" the girl persisted. "I'm scared, Ben, please take me back to the hall."

It took several days for Betsy to recover from the experience. She had implored Ben to say nothing to anyone about what had happened, and he had agreed, attributing the whole incident to the inscrutable ways of womenfolk. However, when they met a week later, she saw at once that he was more than ordinarily serious.

"What is it, dear?" she asked.

"There's a tale going round the village," he said. "Vicky Easton's putting it out. She and Charlie Baynes were in the glebe meadow last night, when Vicky cried out and said there was Lydia Atley watching them. I went and had a quiet word with Charlie, and he told me they were going to do what we were doing when it happened. You haven't said anything to anyone, and Vicky's heard, have you, Bet?"

"I haven't told a soul," she assured him.

He scratched his head, puzzled. "Well, I don't know," he said. "Charlie says keep it quiet, because he didn't see anything, like me.

But Vicky says Lydia was standing there, wagging her finger at them, like you said." He laughed and shook his head. "Poor old Charlie's fed up, too," he grinned, "because that was the end of that, and Vicky says he'll have to wait now until they're wed."

"And so will you, Ben Ridgeway!" Betsy told him firmly.

In May another story was heard in the village of yet another couple in similar circumstances being interrupted by Lydia Atley. Again the man had seen nothing, but the girl had watched the figure walk as far as the churchyard gate, look in for a time and then, on turning away, had disappeared.

By this time there was no point in Betsy and Ben Ridgeway keeping silent, and when yet a fourth couple added their story, it would have been strange indeed if the people of Ringstead had not begun to attribute the otherwise unseen Lydia's appearances to supernatural causes. Though Robert Hickens still kept his counsel, soon everyone was certain that the girl had met an untimely end; and in the secret conversations of the village, the butcher Weekly Ball was being named as Lydia's murderer.

There was no evidence, however. Only Betsy knew of the liaison between Lydia and Ball, and uncorroborated evidence was not enough, while the absence of a body made a direct accusation impossible.

If Ball knew of the stories which were circulating in the village, he gave no sign of it. Stories of his promiscuity continued to make the rounds, but every Sunday he bore his staff before the Rector, who had chosen him for his warden, at Matins and Evensong.

So fifteen years went by, during which time the legend of Lydia was kept green by her occasional appearances to couples who were in train to cool the intolerable heat of their blood. She appeared only in the light evenings of spring and summer, and sometimes on a Sunday afternoon in winter. But for her obvious preference for the daylight, Ringstead might have become the most chaste village in England.

Then one day in the spring of 1865, Daniel Hobson was hedging and ditching in the lane that ran by Weekly Ball's orchard. The previous winter, a nearby stream had overflowed its course and had tumbled into the ditch which skirted one side of the lane. It had never happened before, and when the ditch had carried the water into the churchyard, so that two or three vaults near the gate had been flooded, the rector had consulted the squire, and the latter had given instructions that next hedging-and-ditching time the ditch was to be dug out and deepened, so that if the stream overflowed again the ditch would contain the surplus.

The task of doing this had been allotted to Daniel Hobson, and it was while he was engaged upon it, not far from the hut in Weekly Ball's orchard, that he uncovered the skeleton of a woman. In the natural order of things, an inquest was ordered, and at it Dr James, who was also the coroner, informed the jury that the skeleton was that of a young woman, not yet fully mature, and that the lower jaw had two teeth missing.

Betsy was not the only acquaintance of Lydia Atley who knew that she had had two teeth missing. Several members of the jury did also, and despite all attempts of the coroner to deter them by pointing out that the evidence was too slight, they found the skeleton to be that of Lydia Atley, that she had been murdered and that the man who had murdered her was Weekly Ball, the butcher. Nothing Dr James could say to them could make them bring in the open verdict he advised, or withdraw the name of Weekly Ball, and he had no alternative but to register their findings officially, and automatically inform the authorities.

The sheriff's officers were equally required to make an investigation, and to every lawyer's surprise they decided that the evidence, though circumstantial, warranted the arrest of the butcher on a charge of murder. So he was committed by the magistrates, the squire and the rector, to the next Northampton assizes.

Weekly Ball took the matter seriously enough to engage one of the most astute lawyers in the county town, who in turn engaged the services of one of the best pleaders on the circuit.

Both these lawyers comforted their client with their opinion: "You have no cause for fear, Mr Ball. The Grand Jury are bound to throw out the indictment."

To these gentlemen's surprise, and to the surprise of many others, however, the Grand Jury returned a True Bill, and it was just as well that Weekly Ball had spared no expense for his defence. After a hearing lasting two days, at which Betsy Ridgeway, now a matron with five children who proved that their father had eventually assuaged his particular thirst, and Robert Hickens, were the principal witnesses, the butcher was acquitted. The chief factor in his acquittal was the discovery by his counsel that not far from the spot where the skeleton had been found there had formerly been a traditional gipsy burial ground, and he successfully argued that there was nothing to prove that the bones turned up by Daniel Hobson were not those of a gipsy girl who had died of natural causes and been buried there by her tribe.

The people of Ringstead, convinced of the rightness of their own

convictions, could not accept this verdict. Though they might not be able to avenge the life of the girl with the life of the butcher, they could refuse to have him any longer among them. Weekly Ball recognized the power of their opinion, and wisely sold up and left the county.

As for Lydia Atley, the burial of her bones in the consecrated ground of the churchyard with the full honours of the church was not sufficient to calm her spirit. For several years thereafter she prevented, by materialization at the crucial moment, the conception of many a potential inhabitant of Ringstead on the wrong side of the blanket.

But as the years went by, her appearances became fewer and fewer. The last time she was seen was in 1874, when, with poetic justice, she interrupted the midsummer-eve celebrations of Isaac Ridgeway, Betsy's eldest.

Charles Kean's Ghost Story: "Nurse Black"

Charles Kean and his wife Ellen were the leading lights of the English stage in the 1850s—London's most eminent actor-managers. Both were enthusiastic antiquarians, and it must have been gratifying to them when an authentic ghost-story occurred in their own family circle. For years after the actual happening, the Keans would tell it, with great dramatic effect, and every assurance to their listeners of its absolute truth.

Mrs Kean's sister, Ann Tree, had married John Kemble Chapman, ex-theatre manager and a well-known London publisher. Their family was large—eleven children—and finding London unhealthy for the younger ones they decided to move out to the country.

The house they chose was in Cheshunt, Hertfordshire. Owned by Sir Henry Meux, it was let to them furnished. The number of rooms was ample, even for their many children and servants—for a comfortable household in those days included a staff of at least eight. There were good grounds, extensive lawns, and stout trees for the more adventurous children to climb. Altogether Mrs Chapman, surveying her new home, was very pleased with it.

Like her sister, she appreciated picturesque antiquity, and of this there was plenty. The house was about two hundred years old, built some time in the early seventeenth century. Ancient oak beams supported its ceilings, the fireplaces in the best rooms were carved with elaborate and fantastic designs. Not only was there a fine, broad, central staircase, but two others, spiral and break-neck, for

the use of servants. The original diamond-paned windows remained, some scratched with the initials of previous owners; and a wealth of sound panelling kept the house snug and draught-free. A complete nursery suite was available for the children and their staff, a head nurse and two assistants, and the children were delighted to discover above it a range of attic rooms, in which they could play games, dress up and revel noisily to their hearts' content.

As with many fortunate country dwellers, John Chapman found himself inundated with friends in need of a weekend rest and the benefit of country air. Both he and his wife were social, hospitable characters, and it was well known among their London friends that they could always be counted on for hospitality and cheerful entertainment. Particularly so, as John Chapman spent several nights a week in London, in order to attend to his business, and liked his wife to have the pleasure of lively company as often as possible, to off-set the evenings she spent with no one to talk to but her elder children. Rooms were always kept ready for guests, and Ann Chapman never complained when they arrived unexpectedly. She was a practical, well-balanced woman, capable and sensible; and John frequently congratulated himself that he had not married a specimen of the feeble and helpless femininity so much in fashion at that time.

Ann did not employ a housekeeper, preferring to see to household details herself. Always, when guests were expected, she supervised the preparations, and undertook a last-minute inspection of the rooms to be occupied. The best of these, reserved for her husband's more important business acquaintances, was known as the Oak Bedroom—so called from its richly-carved oak panelling, and from the large four-poster bed, also made of oak, with hanging curtains embroidered with a design of oak-leaves and acorns. The room was dark and possibly a little forbidding, but was certainly impressive, and Ann insisted that it should always be kept in perfect order.

One autumn evening, as dusk was coming on, she went up to the Oak Bedroom with a pile of aired linen. John was bringing home an author friend, whose work he wanted to discuss in the peace of his own home rather than in the bustle of a Fleet Street office. The maid responsible for the linen stores was new, and Ann did not trust her to make the bed up as it should be made.

The lock on the Oak Bedroom door was old and strained, and Ann had some difficulty in turning the handle, cumbered as she was with an armful of sheets and pillow-cases. Once in the room, she put down her bundle and looked round for a candle to light. In this

dark room it was hardly possible to make the bed as neatly as it should be made.

But as she stretched out her hand for the match-holder, she stopped short. She was not alone in the room. By the far window stood a woman. Ann took in at a glance that she was young and slender, with long dark hair down her back. She was dressed in what seemed to be a white shawl or wrapper over a silk petticoat—Ann particularly noticed how the fading light from the window caught the shine of the silk. The girl was leaning forward eagerly, looking through the window, as if at someone in the garden below.

Almost without conscious thought, Ann remembered that the servants were all at tea and the children in the nursery. It could not be any of them. There remained the possibility that a stranger had somehow got into the house and wandered upstairs; but, without knowing why, Ann dismissed this idea at once. She felt, as she afterwards put it, that she was seeing something she ought not to have seen—something that ought not to have been there—and with a sudden shudder of horror, she covered her eyes with her hands. When she uncovered them, the figure had vanished.

By this time her skin was cold with panic. But she was not the kind of woman to let fear stop her from carrying out a task. With shaking hands, she unfolded the linen, stripped back the bed coverings, and made up the bed ready for the night, turning in corners and smoothing down pillows as though nothing out of the ordinary had happened.

She said nothing to anyone about her experience, even to her husband when he came home that night. Next morning she looked up anxiously as their guest entered the breakfast-room, wondering what he might have to say—or even whether he might sharply ask for a carriage to take him back to London at once. But he seemed calm and cheerful, and congratulated his hostess on the comfort of his bed and the peace of his room. Ann told herself that she had suffered from an optical illusion. Of course there had been no figure there. How could there have been?

It was all the more of a shock to her when, some days later, a young nursery-maid, Kitty Brocket, came to her shaking and crying, with a tale of having seen something awful. It was difficult to get sense out of the girl, but with patient questioning Ann got her to say what the trouble was. She had been going down the lobby in the kitchen quarters, taking the nursery rubbish to the back door, when she had seen a face at the small window which gave on to the yard outside. Kitty found it difficult to explain in what way the face

frightened her; but Ann gathered from her confused account that it was the face of an old woman, hideously ugly, with some kind of old-fashioned cap on the hair and an expression of awful malignance.

Ann had no wish to encourage the girl's fears. It must have been a gipsy, she said—there were plenty in that part of the country. In that case, Kitty pointed out, how could she have got into the yard at all? There was no way into it except through the kitchen, and Cook would never have let a gipsy past her. Ann had to admit that this was true. To satisfy Kitty, she went down with her, and together they looked through the small window where the face had been seen. The yard was empty. Flagstones, a pair of clothes-props, and a pump were all that was to be seen in it. They visited Cook, who confirmed that she had had no callers that morning, and would never have let such people in. Ann hastily agreed with her that young girls were very fanciful—Kitty must have been deceived by some trick of the light.

Two nights later, another tale was brought to Ann. The house-parlour-maid had been disturbed in the night by loud noises, like someone beating with an iron bar on the pump in the yard, which her bedroom overlooked. The children's nurse confirmed that she had heard the same sound on the previous night, when she had gone down to the kitchen to heat some milk.

The next story came from the nursery. Little Maria, who was not usually a nervous or imaginative child, complained that when she had been lying awake a very ugly lady had looked at her round the edge of the nursery door. Her mother assured her that it was a dream. If only she could have believed herself that it had been!

All this week John Chapman had spent in London. Ann was more than relieved to think that he would be home for the weekend on Friday night. The strain was beginning to tell on her of keeping a cheerful face in front of the family and the servants, for fear of spreading panic. Superstitious country girls were only too ready to entertain tales of haunting, and Ann might very well find herself faced with a staff determined to give notice in a body. Besides, there might be some reasonable explanation for the manifestations. In a final attempt to clear up the mystery, she called the servants together and told them, as casually as possible, that gipsies were rumoured to be in the neighbourhood and that it would be as well to search the house thoroughly, in case one had concealed himself somewhere in order to carry out a robbery. Dutifully, if apprehensively, they dispersed—opening every cupboard, tapping every panel, exploring every outhouse and the darkest corners of the

cellars. But no trace was found of any gipsy—not greatly to Ann's surprise.

When John Chapman arrived home she was waiting, prepared to tell him everything that had happened. But he was not alone; a Mr Hall, a member of the publishing firm, had returned with him for the weekend. Ann welcomed the visitor, and after making sure that he would be happily occupied in her husband's study, went upstairs to prepare the Oak Bedroom.

In the bustle of her husband's homecoming her preoccupation with the "hauntings" had temporarily been banished. She thought of nothing beyond sheets and warming-pans as she tripped up the broad staircase, and when she heard footsteps behind her turned to see who it might be.

But there was nothing, nobody; only an empty staircase, and the shadowy hallway below.

Panic seized her, as she hurried downstairs again, and took refuge in the cheerful, noisy day nursery until it was time to go down to supper. The meal proceeded pleasantly enough, and the gentlemen retired to the study with port and cigars, while Ann occupied herself with her needlework. A few moments later there was a tap at the door. The house-parlour-maid, a middle-aged woman called Mrs Tewin, entered, pale-faced and shaken out of her usual calm. She, too, had a story of footsteps—footsteps which had followed her all the way upstairs to the Oak Bedroom, and into it. When she stopped by the fireplace, and put down the warming-pan she was carrying, the steps also stopped. Mrs Tewin, who had been the first person to hear the strange knockings some nights before, was thoroughly frightened, and wished to give her notice.

Ann soothed her, and told her to reconsider her decision in the morning, when she had slept on it, and Mrs Tewin, fortified by a little brandy-and-water, took herself nervously to bed.

That night, Ann told her husband everything. Many men would have laughed and told her not to be ridiculous. But John Chapman came of a theatrical family, and like all in the world of the theatre he was prepared to believe in the supernatural. To Ann's great relief, he promised to arrange his work so that he could stay at home during the following week, and investigate the mystery for himself.

He was not disappointed. Within the next few days the footsteps were heard again, by several of the servants and two of the elder children—soft, steady, infinitely menacing. They were heard not only on the staircase and in the Oak Bedroom, but in other parts

of the house. Lying in bed one night, Ann heard them coming up to the door—she leapt out of bed, threw open the door—to find the landing completely empty. The next night John saw her putting something under her pillow as they were retiring to bed. He asked what it might be, and Ann silently produced a loaded pistol. Her husband was horrified, and pointed out that though she showed a brave spirit in arming herself against the intrusions, she would make no impression upon a ghostly visitant with a bullet, and might very well shoot some harmless passer-by of flesh and blood. Ann saw the sense of this, but insisted on keeping the pistol within reach.

By now she had ceased to pretend in front of the servants that nothing unexplainable was happening. A spirit of dread had crept through the house, and the servants took to moving about the house in droves, like wild animals herding together against a common enemy. The children caught the infection of fear, especially the two older girls, Patty and Maria; and the younger children began to be nervous and fretful, particularly after the ugly old woman was seen again in the dark night nursery. As the servants sat at dinner one day the latch of the door lifted, and the door slowly opened—to admit Nobody—and then quietly closed itself again, at which one of the maids fainted and the girl Kitty Brocket went into violent hysterics.

John Chapman, hearing of this, determined to share the servants' dinner next day in case the phenomenon repeated itself. Exactly the same thing occurred, and though he ran at once to the door and examined it, there was nothing to explain the silent opening and shutting.

That afternoon he was reluctantly obliged to return to town, first making his wife promise that she would have one of the maids to share her bedroom. Willingly enough, she chose Mrs Tewin, who was to sleep in a single bed in the corner of the Chapmans' bedroom.

About one o'clock in the morning Ann was roused by agonized muttering from the other bed: "Wake me! Wake me!" Mrs Tewin was saying, her eyes tight shut and her face working with agitation. Ann leapt from her own bed and shook the woman awake. Mrs Tewin thanked her earnestly for rousing her from a dreadful dream she had had, in which she was conscious of having been asleep, but quite unable to wake herself.

She had dreamt, she said, that she was in the Oak Bedroom, in bed. By the window a young woman was standing, pale and dishevelled, with long dark hair, and dressed in an old-fashioned

white robe. She had her back against the wall and was staring across the room at another woman, who stood over on the fireplace side of the bed. The sight of this woman, said Mrs Tewin, filled her with indescribable fear—not merely because of her extreme ugliness but because of a dreadful malignancy in her expression. Mrs Tewin noticed that she too was dressed in old-fashioned clothes, with a frilled cap on her scanty grey hair.

"What have you done with the child, Emily? What have you done with the child?" she asked the young woman, in a mocking tone.

"Oh, I did *not* kill it!" replied the girl. "He was preserved, and grew up, and joined the —— Regiment, and went to India."

Then the young woman drew nearer to the bed and spoke to the sleeper directly. "I have never spoken to mortal before," she said, "but I will tell you all. My name is Miss Black, and this old woman is Nurse Black. Black is not her name, but we call her so because she has been so long in the family."

Here the old woman interrupted the speaker by coming up and laying her hand on the dreaming Mrs Tewin's shoulder, saying something which she could not afterwards remember—for, feeling a burning pain in her shoulder where the phantom hand touched her, she had been aroused enough to know that she was dreaming, and had called out to her mistress to waken her.

Next morning Ann lost no time in making inquiries in Cheshunt for anything that might be known about the house and its history. At last, an old inhabitant was able to tell her that seventy or eighty years before, about 1775, the house had been tenanted by a Mrs Ravenhall, who had a niece named Miss Black living with her. Nothing else was recalled about them.

It says much for Ann Chapman's courage that she voluntarily spent a night alone in the Oak Bedroom, after hearing this. Again she saw the young woman in white—this time standing in one corner of the room, weeping and wringing her hands, and looking down mournfully at the floorboards. Next day a carpenter was called in to take up the boards; but whatever had lain underneath them had been taken away.

As time went by, the disturbances began to grow less, and finally died away altogether, to the relief of the Chapmans. But one more strange thing was to happen. Some years after the manifestations, John Chapman was compelled by reasons of business to leave Cheshunt and remove his family back to London. A few days before they were due to leave Ann awoke one morning to see standing at

the foot of her bed a dark-faced man in a workman's clothes, with a fustian jacket and a red scarf round his neck. As she looked at him, he vanished. John Chapman lay beside her asleep, and saw nothing, and she did not tell him of the incident.

A few days later it was found that the supply of coals had run out, and that more were needed to keep the family warm until the removal. John Chapman said that he would order them that day on his way to London. Next morning, Ann congratulated him on having remembered the commission; but he replied, with surprise, that it had entirely slipped his memory. None of the servants had ordered the coals, and Ann, thoroughly puzzled, decided to go into the village and make inquiries herself. The coal-merchant told her that he had indeed sent the coals, in response to an order given by a dark man, wearing a fustian jacket and a red scarf, whom he did not know but took for a new servant of the Chapmans.

It was with immense relief that John and Ann drove away finally from the haunted house of Cheshunt, and not until they arrived at their new home did John tell his wife that he had heard of several previous tenants who had been driven out by the uneasy spirits of the unhappy young mother and the evil Nurse Black.

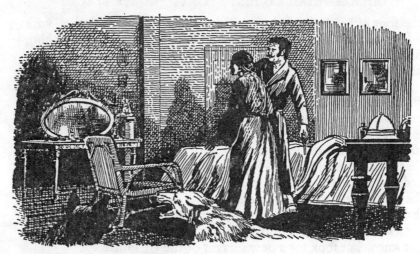

Ghosts of the Mutiny

The Indian Mutiny, that great revolt of the Bengal native army in 1857, was a bloody and treacherous business undertaken by violent men, and involving the brutal murder of many harmless civilians. So many women and children were horribly slaughtered that the reputation of Herod pales beside that of some of the mutineers.

It is not surprising—especially in a country noted for legends and mysticism—that supernatural echoes of the Mutiny were heard for long after it was over. Nearly all involved violent haunting. Such was the case of the Haunted Palace, visited about 1890 by a government official, Mr Gerard, and his wife. The Gerards had reached the town of Hissar, where, on behalf of the Government, they exchanged hospitality with the Europeans living there.

Their visit coincided with Christmas. On Christmas Day they were invited to dinner by Colonel Robinson, an officer holding a staff appointment. The party was small—the Gerards, Colonel and Mrs Robinson, their elder and younger sons, and the Civil Surgeon of the station. The Palace, where the Robinsons lived, had once been the residence of the Rajahs of Hissar; but after the Mutiny the then Rajah was removed and the Palace taken over by the British Government.

Mr and Mrs Gerard were struck by the strange approach to the Robinson's apartments, which were in the upper part of the Palace. The huge doors on the ground-floor level were boarded up and had obviously not been used for a very long time. An iron staircase like a fire-escape, attached to the outside wall, led up to a long,

high hall, running along the front of the building, and containing many high windows. Parallel with this was a similar room, used by the Robinsons as a dining room. Next to this came the drawing-room, and at the far end of it a door led into the bedroom, and another from the bedroom into the bathroom.

Dinner was a pleasant, informal affair, and Mrs Gerard remarked to her host that they must have an excellent cook. She was surprised when he replied that this treasure was shortly leaving them, in spite of raised wages and other inducements. A new one, he sighed, would have to be recruited from somewhere outside the district.

This struck Mrs Gerard as very odd, and she inquired why a local servant would not do. "Because nobody for miles around would take service here," answered Colonel Robinson. "We were told so when we came, but we didn't believe it." Mrs Gerard expressed great surprise that such a pleasant couple could not keep their servants. The Colonel, smiling, told her that it was not their employers the servants did not like—it was the Palace. "It's haunted, you see," he explained.

Mrs Gerard raised her eyebrows, and replied that it was just like superstitious native servants to believe such nonsense. *She* didn't believe in such things, and she hoped Colonel Robinson did not, either. He raised his eyebrows and smiled at her; and Mrs Gerard, slightly annoyed, called across the table to Mrs Robinson that the Colonel was teasing her with a stupid ghost-story.

Mrs Robinson, who had been chatting away gaily enough to the Surgeon, immediately stopped, and looked nervously at her little boy, who, at the mention of ghost-stories, had become all eyes and attention.

"It's true enough, unfortunately," she said, "but I'll tell you about it later, if you don't mind."

Mrs Gerard instantly turned to Colonel Robinson and apologized for mistaking his intention. "It would not be the first time I've been disbelieved!" he told her.

After dinner, Mrs Robinson and Mrs Gerard, the only ladies of the party, moved into the drawing-room, while the gentlemen remained to smoke and drink their port. Mrs Robinson's small son was taken to bed by his ayah, though he would obviously have preferred to stay and listen to whatever fascinating story his mother was going to tell. As soon as the ladies were seated by the drawing-room fire, Mrs Robinson offered to tell her guest the truth about the manifestations that made it impossible for her to keep servants; and Mrs Gerard, sipping her coffee, listened attentively.

The Robinsons had moved to Hissar fifteen years before. They were pleased with the appointment, but less pleased to find that no arrangements had been made about quarters for them. At last they decided to move into part of the old Palace, now shut up and deserted. It was well-built and weather-tight, and only wanted thoroughly cleaning and airing. The Robinsons could make themselves a splendid flat from the four large parallel rooms, and the smaller ones would easily adapt into bedroom and bathroom.

So far so good. The cleaning and refurbishing of their apartments proceeded, and they were able to move in very speedily. But, they were told, they would never keep servants—the place was badly haunted—"wicked things had been done there"—and nobody who knew the Palace would work in it. Like most Europeans of their day and age, Colonel and Mrs Robinson were not prepared to take this seriously. They imagined that somebody wanted them to stay away from the Palace—perhaps somebody who wanted to use it as a headquarters for some nefarious undertaking. So they laughed, and moved in.

Rumour proved all too true. No native of Hissar would agree to join their staff; and the old servants they had brought with them soon left, with feeble excuses. Undefeated, and still healthily sceptical, the Robinsons recruited servants from other districts, and paid them well. The household at the old Palace settled down into a well-organized routine, and the Robinsons were very content with their dwelling. "You see, dear, it's all nonsense about this haunting," said the Colonel to his wife.

Then came an unpleasant surprise. One night Mrs Robinson had gone to bed as usual, and was just hovering between waking and sleep when she heard what she thought to be her husband fumbling about with her bunch of keys at the locked wardrobe. She remembered, sleepily, that she had put her keys and watch under her pillow before going to bed, as she always did—her husband must have got up and removed them while she was dozing. Hardly bothering to open her eyes, she called to ask him what he was doing.

There was no answer; the rattling noise continued. Mrs Robinson roused herself and sat up—to see her husband, not at the wardrobe, but beside her in bed, staring at her. He, too, had heard the noise, and had thought it was his wife, rattling her keys. To prove that he had been wrong, she put her hand under the pillow, and withdrew the keys. The Robinsons stared blankly at each other.

Meanwhile, the sound grew louder. It seemed to them now more

like the rattling of chains than of keys. Nor did they hear it alone—their two great dogs, who always slept in their room, had stirred, risen, and were now growling in their corner. The noise was certainly alarming, for to the rattling was now added a dragging sound, like metal trailing on stone, and a heavy, ominous thudding like gigantic footsteps.

"What on earth can it be?" said Colonel Robinson. "Someone's playing tricks—that's it. I told you they wanted to keep us out of this place. Well, I'm getting up to find out."

Slipping out of bed, he turned up the lamp, put on his dressing-gown and placed his loaded revolver in the pocket of it. His wife began to reach for her dressing-gown.

"I must come with you! Don't leave me alone in here, George!"

Gently he pushed her back, telling her that if there was going to be a physical struggle, and perhaps shooting, she would be better out of it. She remained sitting on the edge of the bed, trembling violently, and watching her husband as he took up his hurricane-lamp and opened the door, calling the dogs to come with him. But there was no need. As soon as the door was opened they rushed past him and out of the room, growling deeply. Then Mrs Robinson was alone in the room.

It seemed to her that she had been there for hours, though in fact it was not more than a few minutes, when a remarkable thing happened—the strange sounds stopped, suddenly, after drawing so near and growing so loud that Mrs Robinson felt she would be deafened by them. There was absolute silence, and she felt this to be as frightening as the previous noises.

Then, through the open door, came the dogs; not the bold creatures that had rushed out ahead of the Colonel, but beaten, crawling things, dragging themselves along, their eyes rolling and their bodies shaking with fear. Mrs Robinson had never seen them look like this before. They appeared to have had a terrible shock, which had sent them almost out of their minds. She approached them and tried to comfort them; but they crawled out of her reach and hid under the bed, where they crouched, whining. Then Colonel Robinson returned.

"Whatever has happened?" asked his wife. "What have you seen?"

"These two poor dogs have seen something," he replied, "but I haven't. I can't understand it. As I walked from room to room the sounds seemed to come nearer and nearer——"

"Just as they did in here," she put in.

"—until when I came to the dining-room they stopped, all in a

moment. Before I got to it I met the dogs coming back—as you see them now, poor things. I don't know what all this means, Mary, but I intend to find out."

And he lost no time in calling up the servants to make a thorough search of the Palace. All night the Robinsons and the staff tramped up and down with lanterns, through great empty rooms, up and down winding staircases, into cellars and dungeons. Not one trace of the night's activity rewarded them—not a single footprint in the dust. Eventually they gave up the search and went, exhausted, to bed.

When they woke next morning, hardly believing in the strange events of the night, a dreadful confirmation met their eyes. Under their bed lay the two beautiful dogs, cold and dead. They had died of sheer fright.

The Robinsons' distress was great. They had hardly taken in the tragedy when the first of their servants gave notice. After him came another, and another—all with excuses involving sick parents or family troubles. By the end of the day not one was left.

Now that the Robinsons were alone in the Palace, the noises of the night returned with a regularity that amounted to persecution. Always they were the same—beginning softly, with a light metallic rattling, and increasing to a dreadful clashing and tramping. It seemed to occur always on a festival or holiday, whether native or English. The Robinsons became partly resigned to it, though they never ceased to cling to each other in apprehension when the terrible crescendo began. One night, Mrs Robinson, who had been lying with the bedclothes over her head, trying to shut out the sound, suddenly sat up and clutched her husband's arm.

"Elephants!" she exclaimed. "George, it's elephants!"

Her husband stared. "How on earth can it be elephants? Where?"

"How do I know where? Phantom ones, I suppose. But it *is* elephants, dragging chains and tramping. Can't you hear it?"

He listened, and finally agreed.

It was not long before Mrs Robinson's guess was confirmed. A native who was not too frightened to talk to them told them the dreadful legend of the man who had been Rajah of Hissar at the time of the Mutiny. An inhumanly cruel man, in the tradition of the terrible Indian rulers of the eighteenth century, he had elephants specially trained to destroy people. If any of his many wives angered him, he would have them shut into the underground dungeons of the Palace; then the elephants were admitted to them, and either trampled them to death or caught them up and dashed out their brains against the dungeon walls.

When the Mutiny broke out, the Rajah prepared to treat the hated British as he had treated his own people. As the rebellious troops swept in from Delhi, many Europeans fled. But those who were unable to escape were seven men and their wives, with fifteen small children and two Eurasian native servants.

Desperate, they risked the Rajah's evil reputation and begged him for help. He would give it, he said; they should be safe. Let them only take refuge with him in the Palace and nobody should touch them. Thankfully they came, the pathetic little band, babies in arms, small children led by the hand, expectant mothers and anxious husbands. They were brought up to the apartments later used by the Robinsons, and shut into the room at the end—the Robinsons' future bathroom. Then the Rajah's soldiers burst in and hacked them to pieces, leaving not a single one alive.

The British relief troops, when they arrived, found the room ankle-deep in blood, corpses heaped on top of one another, the walls sticky with brains and blood; and—almost worst of all—sixteen of the corpses were headless, and the heads, in a graded line, were placed mockingly on the mantelpiece of the room to be used by the Robinsons as a drawing-room.

Mrs Robinson ended her story. Her guest, who had been listening in appalled silence, looked up at the mantelpiece, now cheerful with flowers and family photographs.

"And do you still hear the sounds now?" she asked.

"No. It seemed as though, having got us on our own and nearly frightening us to death, they had served their purpose. But none of the servants will believe that, of course."

"I wonder why it was only the elephants you heard, and not—the other sounds?"

"We don't know. But I thank God we were spared those."

Mrs Gerard remembered the great barred doors that had led to the basement—and the dungeons—glanced up again at the mantelpiece, and shuddered deeply. The door opened, and she looked towards it in fear; but it was only the gentlemen who entered, rosy and good-tempered from their port.

*   *   *   *   *

Another strange story of the Mutiny concerned Mrs Torrens, widow of General Torrens. In 1856 she was living at Southsea, Hampshire. Her daughter had married a Captain Hayes and gone out to India with him. Mrs Torrens naturally regretted that she was so far away, but knew her to be happy and had no fears for her future.

One night, however, her attitude was abruptly changed. She dreamed, vividly, that she was in India, in the town where her daughter's husband was stationed. There seemed to be something like a revolution in progress. Dark-faced natives were surging in the streets, shouting and waving guns and other weapons—some of which, Mrs Torrens noticed with horror, had blood on them.

As is the way of dreams, she was not particularly surprised that nobody seemed to notice her presence or to offer to molest her in any way. Nor did it seem strange to her that she knew by instinct how to get to Captain Hayes's barracks, though the situation had never been described to her. In a few minutes she was there. The building was encircled by a mass of yelling natives, all apparently bent on murdering those within. And yet Mrs Torrens passed unharmed through them, entered the building, and found herself guided to the quarters of Captain Hayes.

To her intense horror, she found the Captain and her daughter had already been attacked by the insurgents, and were struggling wildly in the grasp of five or six savage-looking Sepoys. Now came the most terrible part of her dream. She found herself quite helpless to move, to call out, or to make any sort of impression on the attackers or the attacked. She could only stand there, paralysed by her dream-state, and watch the indescribably horrible death of her daughter and son-in-law. So ghastly was it that she awoke, trembling and in a cold sweat.

So dreadfully vivid had been the dream that she could not feel the usual relief of a sleeper waking from nightmare. The terrible impression remained with her, and prompted her to sit down and write to her daughter, urging her to come home at once. Posts in those days were slow, and it was some weeks before the reply came. To her disappointment, it was to say that Mrs Hayes felt she could not leave her husband in India on such slight grounds; but she took her mother's warning seriously enough to promise to send her children to England. Before very long they arrived, and Mrs Torrens's mind was relieved on their account, at least, although she had not seen them in her dream.

1857 came, and with it the outbreak of the Indian Mutiny. When Captain Hayes and his young wife were reported to have been brutally murdered, Mrs Torrens's distress held no quality of shock, for she already knew too well the manner of their death. The supernatural warning had been true in every particular.

* * * * *

Presumably the dream of Mrs Torrens had been sent to her by the forces responsible with kindly intentions. An equally good spirit operated in the case of a Captain's wife whose fate was happier than that of Mrs Hayes. She had been warned, at her husband's quarters in Meerut, of the approach of the mutineers, and was packing, ready for flight. Suddenly the door of her bedroom flew open, and there entered a terrible figure—a huge, wild-faced Sepoy, waving a blood-stained axe. Mrs X, like Mrs Torrens in her dream, was rooted to the spot; but with fear, not with the helpless immobility of the dreamer. She managed to pray, however, for the habit of prayer was strong in her and she knew that she stood more in need of help now than ever before.

Time was suspended as they faced each other—the giant Sepoy, a dreadful genie-figure drunk with blood-lust, and the small Englishwoman, half-dressed, her pathetic possessions strewn at her feet. Then an extraordinary thing happened. The floor-board beneath her shook and creaked, as though somebody tremendously heavy had stepped in front of her, and she felt something brush against the front of her skirt. The Sepoy's grinning face changed. If it were possible for a brown face to turn pale, his paled in an instant, and his eyes widened with horror. For a moment he faced his ghostly antagonist; then turned and fled from the room.

Mrs X fell on her knees and prayed once more. But this time it was a prayer of deep thankfulness.

The Artist's Ghost Story

Charles Dickens was fascinated by ghost stories, and never lost the chance of telling one in print. In the magazine *All the Year Round*, which he edited, he published one told to him by an acquaintance. Some time later he received another version of it, much fuller and more circumstantial, from a Mr Heaphy, an artist, saying that this was the true story and he was prepared to vouch personally for all its details. Dickens questioned him closely, and was satisfied with his answers. He reprinted it, as told by Mr Heaphy, and described it as "so very extraordinary, so very far beyond the version I have published, that all other like stories turn pale before it".

This is the story Mr Heaphy told:

I am an artist. One morning, a few years ago, I was at work in my studio when a military acquaintance of mine dropped in for a chat. I was not sorry to be interrupted, and pressed him to stay to luncheon, which he did willingly. While we were still sitting over our sherry, a young model arrived for a sitting which I had booked with her; but I was in no mood for work, and told her to go away and come back the following day—I would, of course, recompense her for loss of time. She left, but in a few moments was back, to ask hesitantly whether I could possibly manage to pay her at least a part of her money then and there, as she was rather short that day. Of course, I was only too pleased to do this, and she went away happily. My friend and I resumed our chat, but again there was an interruption. This time my visitors were strangers.

They introduced themselves as a Mr and Mrs Kirkbeck, of

Yorkshire, and were an agreeable and obviously well-to-do middle-aged couple. I inquired how they had found me, and they answered that they had heard of me previously but had forgotten my address, which had just been given to them by my model, whom they had met in the street. They had seen a portrait of mine, and admired it—would I be prepared to come to their country home, and paint themselves and their family? Naturally, I was delighted at the chance of such a commission—they made no objection to the fairly steep price I named, and asked if they could look round the studio and choose the style of picture they would prefer. My military friend, something of a wag, took it upon himself to show them round and dilate on my artistic merits in a way that I would have been ashamed to do myself—but the Kirkbecks, simple souls, listened reverently and seemed deeply impressed. The commission was mine. All that remained was to settle the date of my visit to them, and we found a mutually convenient one in the first week of September. Mr Kirkbeck then gave me his card, and he and his wife left the studio, followed soon after by my friend.

Left alone, I looked at Mr Kirkbeck's card, and was surprised and disappointed to find that it contained only his name—no address. I looked in the Court Guide, of which I happened to have a copy, but the name did not appear in that. Well, I thought, the Kirkbecks would no doubt realize soon enough what had happened, and get in touch with me. I put the card in my desk and forgot the whole affair for the time being.

When September came, I had heard nothing more from the Kirkbecks, and left London to carry out a series of painting engagements in the north of England. Towards the end of the month, I was dining at a country-house on the edge of Yorkshire and Lincolnshire—not, I must add, with people I already knew, but because the friend with whom I was staying had been invited, and had asked if I might go with him. Out of the chatter over dinner a name came to my ears—that of Kirkbeck. I enquired whether anyone of that name lived locally. No, was the reply—but the Kirkbecks did live at the town of A, at the other end of the county.

Naturally, I followed up this coincidence by writing to Mr Kirkbeck explaining what had happened. I was pleased to get an almost immediate reply, saying that he was very glad to have heard from me after his ridiculous mistake in neglecting to give me his address, and suggesting that I should call on my way south. Accordingly, I arranged to go to see him the following Saturday, stay the weekend, return to London to attend to business, and come back

to Lincolnshire a fortnight later to carry out my commission.

On the Saturday morning I boarded the York–London train, from which I proposed to change at Retford junction. It was a wet, foggy, thoroughly nasty October day, hardly worth looking out at. I was quite glad at the prospect of company when at Doncaster a lady joined me in the carriage, which had so far been empty except for myself. I was sitting next to the door, with my back to the engine, and this seat I offered her; but she graciously refused it, and took the corner opposite, remarking that she liked to feel the air on her face. Then she began to settle herself comfortably in her seat— spreading her cloak beneath her, arranging her skirts, and putting back her veil over her hat. Now that her face was revealed, I could see that she was about twenty-two. Her hair was auburn, and in sharp contrast to it her eyes and rather thick eyebrows were almost black. Her eyes were large, expressive and beautiful, and her mouth generous and firm. Her complexion was of that healthy, transparent pallor which sets off so well such dark eyes. Altogether, although she was not strictly a beauty according to the taste of our times, her face pleased me more than if she had been.

When she had settled herself to her satisfaction, she borrowed my Bradshaw, and asked me to help her to look up the London–York trains. From this, we passed to more general topics, and I was surprised to find that we were soon talking with the ease of old friends. There was in her manner something that one does not usually find when chatting to a perfect stranger, though there was nothing in the least forward about it; and she even seemed to know things about me that I could not possibly have told her. It was all very odd, but a most agreeable way of passing a long, dull, journey.

When I prepared to get out at Retford, and rose to say goodbye, she offered me her hand, and I shook it. "I dare say we shall meet again," she said, and I replied, with truth, "I hope we shall, indeed". And so we parted.

I arrived safely at the Kirkbeck's house, unpacked, dressed for dinner, and went down to the drawing-room some time before seven, at which hour the butler had told me we should dine. The lamps were not lit, but a good blazing fire threw its cheerful light into every corner of the room, and illuminated the figure of a lady who was standing by the mantelpiece, warming a very handsome foot on the edge of the fender. I noticed that she was dressed in black, but did not at first see her face, which was turned away from me. Imagine my astonishment when she turned to face me, and I saw that she was none other than my lady of the railway-carriage! She

showed no surprise herself, but smiled and said, "I told you we should meet again".

I was completely without words. I had left her in the London ·train, and had seen it start when I got out of it. The only way in which she could have reached this place was by going on to Peterborough, and then returning by a branch line, a circuit of about ninety miles. When I did recover my voice, I said I wished I had come by the same conveyance as she had done.

"That would have been rather difficult," she answered.

At this moment the servant came with the lamps, and said that Mr Kirkbeck would be down in a few minutes. The lady strolled to an occasional table and, picking up a book of engravings, handed it to me, open at a portrait of Lady A., and asked me to look at it and tell her whether I thought it like her. I was looking at it when Mr and Mrs Kirkbeck appeared, and I was requested to take Mrs Kirkbeck in to dinner. She took my arm, but I hesitated a moment to allow Mr Kirkbeck to precede us with the lady in black. Mrs Kirkbeck, however, did not seem to understand what I meant, and we passed on at once.

The dinner-party consisted only of us four—Mr and Mrs Kirkbeck at the top and bottom of the table, the lady and I on each side. I, feeling my position as guest, addressed myself mostly, if not entirely, to my host and hostess, and I cannot remember that I or anyone else addressed the lady opposite to me. Remembering a slight want of attention to her in the drawing-room, I concluded that she must be the governess. I noticed, however, that she made a splendid diner—she seemed to enjoy both the roast beef and the tart that followed, and to drink her claret with a connoisseur's appreciation. Probably the journey had given her an appetite.

Dinner over, the ladies retired. Mr Kirkbeck and I remained over port for a few minutes, and then joined the ladies in the drawing-room. By this time a large party had collected. Brothers and sisters-in-law were introduced to me, and several children, together with Miss Hardwick, their governess. So my mysterious lady was not the governess, after all. Once more I found myself talking to her, and she led the conversation round to portrait-painting, and asked me if I thought I could paint her portrait. I replied that I thought I could, if I had the chance. She then asked me to look at her carefully.

"Do you think you could remember my face?"

"I'm sure I could never forget it," I answered.

"Well, of course, I would have expected you to say that—but do you seriously think you could paint me from memory?"

I could try, I said, but I would much prefer sittings. She replied firmly that that would be impossible; she could not promise me even one sitting. Before I could argue further, she declared that she was rather tired, shook me by the hand, and left me. I need hardly say that it was some time before I slept that night, so many were the problems she had presented me with. But at last I told myself that it would all wait until breakfast-time, when no doubt some of my puzzlement would be resolved.

However, breakfast came, but no lady in black appeared. We went to church, we returned to luncheon, and so the day passed, but still no lady—and what was even more curious, no reference to her. She must be some relative, I thought, who had gone away early in the morning to visit another member of the family. But at least I was entitled to find out. When the servant came in to draw my curtains the next morning, I asked him the name of the lady who had dined with us on Saturday evening.

"A lady, sir?" he replied. "No lady, only Mrs Kirkbeck, sir."

"Yes—the lady who sat opposite me, dressed in black?"

"Perhaps Miss Hardwick, sir?"

"No, she came down afterwards. Come, come, you must remember—the lady dressed in black who was in the drawing-room when I came down to dinner on Saturday."

The man looked at me as if I were mad, and said:

"I never see any lady, sir."

I decided to ask my hosts to solve the mystery for me. You may imagine my feelings when they assured me, most positively, that no fourth person had dined at the table on Saturday evening. They remembered it clearly, as they had discussed whether they should ask Miss Hardwick to take the fourth place, but had decided against it. They could not even think of anyone they knew answering to my description of the lady.

Weeks passed. I re-visited the Kirkbecks, and returned to London. One afternoon, near Christmas, I was sitting at my table, writing a letter, with my back towards the folding-doors of my waiting-room. Suddenly I became aware that someone had come through the doors, and was standing behind me. I turned—it was my lady of the railway-carriage, my lady in black.

I suppose my face must have given away my astonishment, for she apologized for entering so quietly, and disturbing me. Her manner had subtly changed since we had last met—it was not exactly grave,

but somehow more mature and composed than it had been. She asked whether I had made any attempt at a portrait of her, and I said I had not. She was sorry about that, she said, for she wanted one for her father. Then she produced an engraving—not the one she had shown me at the Kirkbeck's, but a different one—which she thought would help me because of its likeness to her. Then she laid her hand on my arm very earnestly, saying:

"I really would be most thankful and grateful if you would do this for me—and believe me, *much depends on it*."

I snatched up my pencil and a sketch-book, and by the dim light that remained in the room began to make a rapid sketch of her. But when she saw what I was doing, she turned away, and instead of helping me by standing still, began to wander about the room looking at pictures. In this difficult way I made two hurried but rather expressive sketches of her, and shut my book, for I could see she was preparing to leave. This time she took my hand in hers, and held it firmly instead of shaking it. "Goodbye," she said; and I remembered she had not said this to me before. I saw her out, and on the other side of the folding doors it seemed to me that she faded into the darkness like a shadow. But I took this to be something thrown up by my imagination.

I rang for my maid, and asked why she had not announced the visitor properly. She was not aware there had been one, she replied; anyone who had been in must have come in when she left the street door open about half an hour before, while she had slipped out to the shops.

Shortly after Christmas I set out on my travels again, and by a long train of accidents and delays found myself at Lichfield, with no train to Stafford, my destination, that evening. It was a most annoying situation, and I had no choice but to accept it and put up at the Swan Hotel for the night. I particularly dislike passing an evening at an hotel in a country town. I never take dinner at such places, preferring to go without rather than eat the sort of meal they give one—books are never available, the local newspapers are uninteresting, and I have always read *The Times* from cover to cover during my journey. So when forced to stay at such places I usually occupy myself with writing letters.

This was the first time I had been in Lichfield; but I remembered, while waiting for tea to be brought, that I had twice recently been on the point of visiting it, once for a commission, and another time to get material for a picture. "How strange!" I thought to myself. "Here I am at Lichfield by accident, when I have twice been pre-

vented from coming here on purpose." I remembered that I had an acquaintance in Lichfield, and thought I might as well ask him to come round and pass an hour or two with me. Accordingly, I rang for a waitress, and asked her if, as I recollected, Mr Lute lived in the Cathedral close. He did, she replied, and she would see that a note was taken round to him. I wrote my note, despatched it, and sat down to wait for my friend.

About twenty minutes later there was shown in to me—not my friend, but a gentleman in late middle age, carrying my note in his hand. He imagined, he said, that I had sent it in error, as he did not know my name.

"I am so sorry," I said. "There is obviously another Mr Lute living in Lichfield."

"No," he replied. "I am the only one of that name."

"Well, this is very strange. My friend must have given me the right address, for I've written to him there. He was—how can I describe him?—a fair young man—he came into an estate after his uncle had been killed hunting with the Quorn—and he married a Miss Fairbairn about two years ago."

"Yes, indeed, I know who you mean," replied the stranger, "you're speaking of Mr Clyme. He did live in the Close, but left it recently."

I was completely taken aback. My friend's name *was* Clyme—how could I possibly have thought it was Lute and how could I have unconsciously guessed that a Mr Lute *did* live in the Close? I began to stammer out some of this to my visitor, who interrupted me quietly.

"There's no need to apologize. As it happens, you are the very person I most want to see."

"I am——?"

"Yes, because you are a painter, and I want you to paint a portrait of my daughter. Will you come to my house with me, and do so?"

I hardly knew what to answer, but he pressed me so hard to come with him, and offered to put me up at his house, that I decided without much reluctance to leave the unappetizing Swan and accept his invitation. I packed, cancelled my reservation for the night, and accompanied Mr Lute to the Cathedral Close.

On our arrival at his house we were greeted by his daughter Maria, a fair-haired, distinctly handsome girl of about fifteen. She had a self-possessed, composed manner older than her years, such as is often seen in girls who have been left motherless or otherwise thrown upon their own resources. Her father introduced us (saying

nothing of the reason for my being there) and asked her to prepare a room for me; he then went upstairs. His daughter left me to give directions to the servants, then returned, to tell me that I should not be seeing her father again that evening, as he was unwell and had retired for the night. I could either sit with her in the drawing-room, or in the housekeeper's room, where there was a fire and I could have a smoke and a drink. The doctor would be in soon to see her father, and no doubt he would join me in a little refreshment.

As she seemed to be recommending this course, I followed her suggestion with some little private amusement. She joined me by the fire and chatted away, intelligently and with a remarkable command of language for her age. She was obviously inquisitive about my reason for coming to stay with them; and I told her that it was to paint her portrait.

At this she became silent and thoughtful. Then she spoke, in a different tone.

"It is not my portrait that Father wishes you to paint, but my sister's."

"Then I shall look forward to meeting her," I said.

"You cannot do that; my sister is dead—she died some months ago. My father has never recovered from the shock of her death, and his one wish is to have a portrait of her—something he does not possess. I think, if he could have one, his health would improve—for as you see, he is not . . ."

Here she hesitated, stammered, and burst into tears. When she could speak, she continued:

"It is no use hiding anything from you. Papa is insane—he has been so ever since dear Caroline died. He says he is always *seeing* Caroline. The doctor cannot tell how much worse he may be getting, but we have to keep everything dangerous out of his reach—knives and scissors, and such things. I hope he will be well enough to talk to you tomorrow."

I asked whether they had any likeness of the dead girl for me to work from—any photograph, or sketch. No, nothing, Maria replied. Could she describe her sister clearly? She thought she could—and there was a print somewhere that was very much like her.

It was not much to go on, and I did not expect any portrait I might produce under these conditions to be particularly good. I *had* painted portraits before merely from descriptions, but always from very detailed ones; and even so the results were not what I would call satisfactory.

The doctor came to attend to Mr Lute, but I did not see him, and retired early, seeing how much my little hostess had to attend to. Next morning I was glad to hear that Mr Lute was decidedly better, and that he hoped nothing would prevent my attempting the portrait. Directly after breakfast I set to work, on a foundation of such description as Maria could give me. I tried again and again, but without a hope of success, it seemed. The features were separately like Caroline's, Maria said, but the expression was not. I worked on for the best part of the day with no better result. The different studies I made were taken up to Mr Lute, but always the same answer came down—no resemblance. I was fairly worn out by the end of the day—a fact not unnoticed by kindly little Maria, who said earnestly how grateful she was to me for the trouble I was taking, and how sorry she was that her powers of description were so poor. And it was *so* provoking—she had a print, a lady's portrait, that was so like Caroline—but it was missing from her book—she had not seen it for three weeks or so. I asked if she could tell me who the print was of, as I might be able to get one in London. She answered, Lady Mary A. Immediately she said this a number of things began to make fantastic sense in my mind. I ran upstairs and came down with my sketch-book, in which were the two pencil sketches of my lady in black, and the print she had given me, glued in. Silently, I placed them before Maria Lute. She looked at me for a moment, then at the sketches and the print; then, turning her eyes full on me, with fear in them, asked: "Where did you get these? Let me take them to Father, instantly."

She was away ten minutes or more. When she returned, her father was with her. He seemed a different creature from the man I had seen the night before. Without preamble, he said:

"I was right all the time. It *was* you I saw with her, and these sketches are from her, and from no one else. I value them more than all my possessions, except this dear child," and he put an arm round Maria's shoulders. Maria, delighted but deeply puzzled, declared that the print in my sketch-book must be the one taken from her book about three weeks before—and as proof she pointed out the gum marks at the back, which exactly matched those left on the blank leaf.

I immediately began an oil painting based on the sketches, Mr Lute sitting by me hour after hour, chatting away sensibly and cheerfully. He avoided direct reference to what Maria had termed his delusions; but next day, after he had been to church for the first time since his bereavement, he asked me to go for a walk with

him, and approached the subject directly. His extraordinary statement is best told in his own words.

"Your writing to me from the inn at Lichfield was one of the most inexplicable things imaginable. As soon as I set eyes on you, I knew you. When Maria and the doctor and others have thought me raving mad, it was only because I saw things that they did not. And I saw my dear Caroline. Since her death, I know, with a certainty nothing will ever disturb, that at different times I have been in her actual, visible presence. I saw her once, distinctly, in a railway carriage, speaking to a person opposite her, whose face I could not see. Then I saw her at a dinner-table, with others, of whom *you* were one. (This time, I learnt afterwards, I was thought to be in one of my longest and most violent paroxysms, for I saw her continuously with you, and in a large group of people, for some hours.) Then again I saw her, standing by your side, while you were either writing or drawing. I did not see you again until we met face to face in the inn parlour."

I have often visited Mr Lute since the day when he told me this strange story. His health is perfect, and he seems entirely to have recovered from the grief of his bereavement. The portrait now hangs in his bedroom, with the print and the two sketches by the side, and written beneath is:"C.L., 13th September 1858, aged 22."

Phantoms of the East

India, with its long history of violence, mystery and bloodshed, must have a million ghosts. Many of them are the sad spirits of English men, women and children who were murdered during the Mutiny of 1857. Towns which had once held military cantonments still had their ghosts many years afterwards, and in the country around many a bungalow is haunted by the restless ghost of a woman who had been murdered and mutilated while trying to escape from the inflamed mutineers. Some servicemen on learning the horrible fate of their families committed suicide in despair, thus adding to India's already prolific hauntings.

In Lansdowne, a small cantonment town in the foothills of Garhwal, a ghostly rider on a pale grey horse, wearing a white mess dress uniform, was sometimes seen riding slowly in the moonlight, head well down, along a bridle path under overhanging trees. He had been seen and followed many times, but no one had ever succeeded in getting near enough to him to see his face. Even the most venturesome of the young officers who had followed him on horse-back found that however fast they rode, the ghostly rider rode faster. Swift and silent he galloped ahead, always keeping his distance, until eventually he would dissolve and vanish into nothing.

Many a traveller coming into Lansdowne had reported seeing him and believed that he had appeared in order to warn them of danger either from marauders who would have robbed them, or from choosing unwise camping sites which might be inhabited by snakes. He would lead them to a more congenial spot and then vanish.

No one had ever seen his face, until one night in 1937. The native sergeant commanding the quarter-guard of a Frontier Force battalion was informed by the sentry that an officer had arrived to take Grand Rounds. He was not the field officer of the week, but he had answered the sentry's challenge correctly and the sergeant thought that he must have been instructed to take the Grand Rounds in place of the field officer of the week. Everything went off quite normally, and the time was noted in the log—Grand Rounds taken at 2.20 a.m.

The field officer had been ill, but no one knew until the next night when he saw the entry in the log. He questioned the native sergeant who told him that he had turned out to an officer wearing white dress uniform with a pale face and side whiskers. According to the sentry he had ridden up on a grey horse and had not said a word except to answer the sentry's challenge with the usual "Grand Rounds".

The Lansdowne ghost appeared every ten years, but he had not taken Grand Rounds before. It was said that he was an officer who shot himself in 1858, a year after his wife and children were murdered by the mutineers.

The way in which they had met their deaths was discovered from another source. One of the officers then stationed at Lansdowne had lived for a while in one of the old pre-Mutiny bungalows, a few of which were still inhabited, though most of them were derelict, empty and neglected, overgrown by creepers and left to the bats and the cobras.

This officer related how one hot June night he had been awakened by an irregular flickering light which played on the wall of his bedroom, and which looked as though it was reflecting a big fire burning outside. He could hear no sound of a fire, and when he got up to look he found that there was no fire. He could see nothing to account for the reflected flames which continued to crawl across the wall for about ten minutes before they died away.

This happened for three nights and on the fourth night the flames appeared to be stronger than ever. He could get no sleep in that airless, oppressive and eerie room, so he went on to the balcony to have a smoke. As he stood there he saw two shadowy figures moving across the parched grass of the lawn. He went down to see who they were, but they vanished. He did notice, however, that they were armed and that their dress was strange to him.

On making inquiries he found that there had been another bungalow in the big garden beside his own, and that on a June

night in 1857, when the Bengal Native Cavalry then occupied the lines, two of the troopers came to give the signal for the beginning of the Mutiny there. They had been instructed to murder the adjutant in his bed, and afterwards to set fire to some of the surrounding bungalows. One of those bungalows had been the funeral pyre of the wife and two children of a certain officer who after a year's solitary brooding had committed suicide. He was believed to be the Lansdowne ghost.

India is a country of Black Magic where spells, charms and curses often bring disaster and sometimes death to the unfortunate person involved. Kattadiyas make charms which can harm enemies. They have the power to charm anyone, and it is believed that with the help of the devil they can kill. Much money can be made by a Kattadiya. Then there is the Light Teller, who can tell the victim of a charm what is wrong and how to counteract the charm and break it. The spirits evoked at practices of Black Magic are accountable for some of the worst kinds of hauntings, for they are evil and malignant, and dangerous to the mind as well as the body.

Just such an evil spirit attached itself to the wife of General Beresford of the Indian Army, who while out driving one day in the late 1870s with her husband became distressed at the sight of an ayah, dressed in rather grubby white robes, acting in a dangerous manner. She was walking rapidly and kept crossing the road in front of their horses, keeping so close to the carriage that Mrs Beresford entreated her husband to be careful or they would run over the foolish ayah.

"What ayah?" growled the General. "I don't see any ayah."

"But she's right in front of you in the middle of the road. For God's sake, Henry, stop. I am sure you have run her down."

The General could still see nothing, and had felt no sign of an impact, but his wife appeared to be so upset that he pulled up and, throwing the reins to her, jumped down into the road to look. As he expected, there was no sign of an ayah, and he told his wife she must be dreaming.

But Mrs Beresford was still convinced that she had seen the ayah, and when her husband remounted the box, she got down herself to make quite sure, for she was certain that she had seen the ayah as plainly as she had seen her husband. But the road was empty and there was no one under the wheels of the carriage. Puzzled, she took her place once more beside the General and they continued on their way without further mishap. She had to agree with the General

that the ayah must have been a delusion brought on by the heat and fatigue.

But from that day poor Mrs Beresford was haunted by the tall white swathed figure of the ayah, who would suddenly appear in all parts of the house. Grinning evilly, it would glide noiselessly past her, leaving Mrs Beresford frightened and full of foreboding. But no one else saw it; nor did any other member of the household experience any of the horror and anguish which beset Mrs Beresford every time the apparition appeared to her.

She began to doubt her sanity and was fearful of the consequences, for the ayah's appearances were constant and usually when she was alone. But sometimes the fiendish-looking thing in the dirty white robes appeared to her when she was with her husband, but he never saw the apparition, and was disturbed by the sight of her state of fear, as with pale face and staring eyes she pointed a trembling anger at the non-existent apparition.

Something would have to be done, for he could see that his wife's health was deteriorating and she was becoming a nervous wreck. He contacted a doctor friend of his and explained her hallucinations, as he called them. His friend asked if the dear lady had not perhaps been attending spiritualist meetings, but the General assured him that his wife was not the type of woman to participate in such things, for she abhorred anything which was not quite "nice".

"In that case," said the doctor, "perhaps you should get leave of absence and take your wife home for a spell. It seems to me that her mental condition necessitates a complete change of environment."

"But we have only just got back from the Old Country. I can't ask for more leave already."

"Well, all I can suggest is that she should see a doctor who specializes in nervous complaints."

But Mrs Beresford would not hear of going to such a doctor. She had another, rather more pleasant, idea. She said that if only her daughter could be with her to keep her company, then she would be all right.

The General at first would not hear of it, for their daughter was still at school in England, and, being only sixteen, had to complete her education. But nothing else would satisfy Mrs Beresford, and eventually the General had to agree. Barbara would be sent for.

Mrs Beresford threw herself both physically and mentally into making preparations for her daughter's arrival, and though the terrible ayah still appeared to her, she managed enough strength of will not to let it upset her quite so much as it had done previously.

Perhaps she was getting used to its fiendish grin, and as it had never attempted to harm her physically her confidence increased, and by the time Barbara came she seemed a little better. Her daughter was with her a lot, and whenever the ayah appeared Mrs Beresford was able to ignore it to a certain extent.

At first she had wondered if Barbara might also see the fearsome ayah, but like her father the girl was unaware of its appearance. Barbara put down her mother's occasional nervous reactions, when her face paled slightly and her eyes held fear, to a neurotic state. She was having another of her hallucinations.

Then one night Mrs Beresford was awakened from sleep by the feel of a bony hand on her shoulder. Its touch was icy, and it seemed to bite into her warm flesh as the hideous, spine-chilling touch gripped her and shook her. Mrs Beresford screamed, for she knew that the bony hand which held her was that of the ayah, and as she opened her eyes she could see its shape bending over her. She was petrified. Her husband, sleeping in the bed next to her, jumped up in alarm and lit the lamp.

"What in the name of thunder is going on?" he asked his almost hysterical wife.

The ayah had vanished as the lamp was lit and between frightened sobs his wife told him what had happened, and how the awful apparition had gripped her shoulder. But the General dismissed the idea as ridiculous, saying that if his wife was going to start this sort of thing in the middle of the night he would have to sleep alone. He was not going to have his nights disturbed by such fancies.

By this time the servants and Barbara had arrived on the scene, and Mrs Beresford, though still frightened, told them that she had had a nightmare, and she was sorry to have disturbed everybody.

It was not until they had all gone back to bed that she was conscious of the pain in her shoulder. Just before the General turned out the lamp, she slipped her nightdress down from her shoulder and there she saw five distinct red marks, small and narrow, the marks of fingernails. Mrs Beresford dared not ask her husband to light the lamp again, and so she lay there sleepless and afraid until the light of morning seeped through the shutters. Not till then did she sleep, and then only fitfully until it was time to get up, by which time the marks on her shoulder had disappeared, and she had no proof to show of her story of the terrible ayah's attack.

But she was convinced that the ayah would come again, with the result that she was unable to sleep, and her restlessness disturbed her husband's nights as well. The General took refuge in another room

and Mrs Beresford begged her daughter to sleep in the room with her. Barbara said she would do so if her mother would see a doctor about her nervous condition.

And so together they went to see a different doctor, one who had spent all his life in India and knew and understood the country. He listened to Mrs Beresford's story with both interest and understanding, and encouraged her to tell him everything. For the first time she was able to talk about it freely with an understanding person who did not even suggest that she was suffering from some kind of mental affliction. The ayah was something real and frightening, and the doctor seemed to understand that. She wished that she had gone to him before. The consultation impressed Barbara too, especially when he told them that he had other patients who had complained of similar persecutions.

"In this part of India," he said, "Black Magic is practised extensively and some strange cult may have evoked an evil entity. It is not unusual for such spirits to attach themselves to someone who has the misfortune to contact them. This ayah seems to have attached itself to you, Mrs Beresford."

"But what must I do?"

"If it appears again, you must speak to it. No matter how frightened you are, you must ask its purpose in the name of God. I believe that is the only way you will be rid of it. It has worked in other cases."

Mrs Beresford went away much relieved at having at last found someone who understood, and who assured her that she was not going mad after all. The fact that the apparition was still to be dealt with seemed of secondary importance now. But if she had known all, she would not have thought of it as secondary, for the doctor had neglected to tell her that spirits like the evil ayah could seriously injure their victims, and were quite capable of actually killing them.

However, Barbara was not now so disbelieving of her mother's story, nor was she so complacent about it. The thought that her mother's fearsome apparition was real and not just a figment of her nervous state was to her something much more frightening and distressing, and as the day wore on Barbara began to get afraid of the coming night. She would much rather have slept in her own room, but she did not want to be thought a coward by her parents. She noticed that her father had not offered to go back to sharing his wife's room, making the excuse that he had a busy time ahead and needed a good night's rest. So there was nothing for it. Barbara had to sleep in her mother's room, and the next two nights she was

miserable and nervous and slept very little. But the terrible ayah did not come.

On the third night Barbara slept from sheer exhaustion, and was suddenly and frighteningly awakened by a suppressed scream of terror from the other bed and the sound of struggling.

She sat up quickly, her eyes fixed on her mother's bed, and there in the feeble light of a flickering candle she saw it—the fearsome ayah with the horrible, grinning, ugly face, just as her mother had described it. It was bending over her mother and its long bony fingers had her by the throat. Frantically Mrs Beresford was trying to pull the hands away, but the ayah was tall and strong, and she was intent on killing her victim.

For a moment Barbara was paralysed with fear, and then she screamed at the top of her voice, knowing that the rest of the household would hear and come to their assistance.

The ayah released Mrs Beresford and turned its glaring, venomous eyes on Barbara, who felt herself engulfed in a feeling of hatred. She wanted to get out of bed and run as far away as possible, but she could not move a muscle.

Then Mrs Beresford, with an effort of will which took every particle of her remaining strength, managed to speak in a croaking voice which she hardly recognized as her own.

"In the name of God," she moaned, "go away! Leave me alone!"

As she spoke the long bony hands were lifting her bodily from the bed, and then she lost consciousness.

Barbara gazed in fascinated horror as the fearful apparition lifted the inert body of her mother, who was by no means a small woman, as though she had been a child. The ayah lifted Mrs Beresford right up and then flung her on to the floor, as though in disgust, and then, as the door of the bedroom burst open to admit the General, it vanished into nothingness, leaving behind a coldness which in the hot and humid night struck the General as remarkable as he bent over his unconscious wife.

While smelling salts were administered to Mrs Beresford, Barbara told her father what had happened. The doctor was contacted and he arrived early the next morning to find Mrs Beresford suffering from shock and somewhat bruised, but otherwise unhurt. He told the General that if his wife had been unable to speak to the evil spirit it would probably have killed her.

"But what I can't understand," said the General, still incredulous of the whole thing, "is why did the wretched thing attach itself to my wife in the first place? I was the one who ran it down. I

never saw the damned thing of course. Still can't believe it myself."

"These things are difficult to explain, but I assure you, General, they do exist. It may have chosen your wife because she was obviously more vulnerable. On the other hand, it may have done so in order to punish you the more by attacking the one you love."

"And what if it turns up again?" asked the General, now somewhat subdued.

"I don't think it will. I have never heard of one returning after being spoken to. Most people are too terrified to speak to ghosts, of course. But if they do, it usually makes all the difference."

The doctor was right. The fearsome ayah was never heard of again.

The Fur-Trader's Corpse
and The Gold-Miners' Vengeance

What power has a body after death? Many people will ridicule the
idea that a corpse is anything more than an agglomeration of dead
matter. So how can it have any power? Indeed this is what reason
tells us.

But when considering some well-authenticated stories of very
strange happenings it is as well perhaps to suspend judgment
about what happens when death intervenes.

Here are two quite remarkable stories—the first one an eerie
experience which befell a party of fur-traders who were transporting
a body across the ice in the haunted Arctic wastes of North-West
Canada; the second a truly gruesome tale of ghostly horror from the
pioneer days of Australia.

There are many tales in legend and folk-lore of the body of a
dead person exercising a supernatural power. It is an accepted thing
in some primitive societies that a life of some kind lingers in the
corpse. Many stories have been told which suggest there may be
something in this.

In the wild places of the world strange things can happen, things
which are beyond reason. The tellers of both of these stories went to
some lengths to establish that the facts they told were true and that
these happenings really did take place.

Who knows what truth lies behind these strange events? The
reader can only use his own judgment and form his own conclusion.

The Arctic story concerned the body of a hardy fur-trader named Peers who managed the Hudson Bay Company's post at Fort McPherson, which is on the Peel River, a tributary of the Mackenzie River. This is in the farthest north, less than a hundred miles from the Arctic Ocean.

Peers was an Anglo-Irishman who went to the Far North in the 1840s. For two or three years he was at the Hudson Bay Company's Mackenzie District headquarters at Fort Simpson. He was then moved to Fort Norman, and finally to Fort McPherson, the company's most northerly station, five hundred miles nearer the Pole than Fort Simpson.

Peers was good at his job, well thought of by his friends, and popular among the Eskimos in the Peel River Preserve.

In 1849 he married one of those hardy women who went north with their menfolk to endure the rigours of the Arctic in the pioneer days when there were few modern comforts to soften the severity of that terrible climate. They had two children.

But Peers was not happy at Fort McPherson, though there is some evidence that his wife was, for she stayed on there after his death and remarried. The true story of Peers's unhappiness in this place was never revealed. It might have been a very human one—to do with his marriage, the fact that his wife was practically the only woman in this isolated outpost beyond the Arctic Circle, and may well have been sought by other men.

Although only thirty-three years old, Peers began to have premonitions of death and his mind dwelt rather morbidly upon his place of burial. He expressed the wish very strongly that he did not want to be buried at Fort McPherson, where he had not been happy. Nor did he wish to be buried at Fort Norman.

He died suddenly and unexpectedly on 15 March, 1853, and was buried, at least temporarily, at Fort McPherson.

The man who succeeded him as manager of the post was Alexander Mackenzie, and in 1855 Mackenzie married Peers's widow.

Peers's body was still lying in the permafrost of his temporary grave on the banks of the Peel River. With the temperature always well below freezing point, the body was in a state of perfect preservation, the flesh as fresh as on the day Peers died.

Finally in 1859 at the request of his widow, now Mrs Mackenzie, it was decided to transfer Peers's body to Fort Simpson and re-inter him there. Whether during the six years when he lay in this place where he did not wish to be buried, his restless spirit was troubling his good lady who had now married his successor, we do

not know. But both Mrs Mckenzie and her husband were determined that the body had to go, and there is good reason to suppose that the late Augustus Peers, wherever he was, was eager for his refrigerated remains to make the arduous journey five hundred miles along the frozen floes of the great Mackenzie River to Fort Simpson.

So they exhumed Peers, finding him not unexpectedly looking exactly the same as when he was buried six years previously. It was decided to send the body south to Fort Simpson by dog-sledge during the winter months.

The body was placed in a new and large coffin, lashed on a sledge and the party set off in the early months of 1860, the coffin drawn by a team of three dogs. On the second sledge was bedding and provisions.

Despite the unwieldiness of the coffin, the first part of the journey was accomplished without incident. Above Fort Norman the body had to be removed from the coffin and secured in its grave wrappings on to the sledge, as the route lay across great masses of tumbled ice on the Mackenzie River, and to have carried the body in the cumbersome coffin would have been impossible.

On 15 March, the seventh anniversary of Peers's death, the party were encamping for the night by the river-bank. It was a fine day, unusually warm for the time of the year. The flesh of the body on the sledge began to thaw out, and the hungry dogs for the first time scented it. To them it was fresh meat—and it was feeding time. This explains why the journey was made during the winter. Temperatures well above freezing are usual in the summer months in the Far North, and the body would swiftly decompose during the long and difficult journey south. There was a furious and ravenous barking around the silent corpse while the party were preparing camp—the time when the dogs were always waiting impatiently to be fed.

As the party turned to investigate the disturbance, they all distinctly heard the word "Marche!" shouted in a loud voice. The dogs immediately quietened.

Not one of the party had spoken and there was no other living soul within hundreds of miles of them.

One member of the party who had known Peers said that it sounded exactly and uncannily like his voice.

"Marche is a French word universally used in the North-West to make dogs move or to drive them away. The familiar "Mush" now used is a corruption of the word, and is apparently the way the Indians and Eskimos pronounced it.

Three days later the call "Marche" was heard loudly once more while they were making camp. This time the temperature was well below freezing and there was no question of the dogs scenting the body again. But the party were attracted by the mysterious calls, and decided for some reason to move the body train from the place where they had left it to one nearer the camp.

In the morning they found tracks of a wolverine at the spot where they had originally left the body train. The wolverine would undoubtedly have torn the body to pieces.

On 21 March, 1860, the remains of Augustus Richard Peers finally arrived at Fort Simpson safely and intact and were buried in the graveyard there two days later.

The party were much concerned about their experience during this strange journey, and each of their accounts agreed with the other. They all heard the mysterious voice, coming on both occasions from the direction of the sledge on which the body lay, and at a time when no living person was anywhere near it. The voice sounded just like that of the dead man.

Roderick Macfarlane, who led the party, was convinced that, owing to the strong feeling Peers had about where his body should be buried, his spirit watched over that tortuous winter journey along the frozen Mackenzie River, that it knew the hungry dogs had scented his body on that unusually warm March evening, and knew also of the presence of the wolverine, a vicious and destructive animal which would certainly have made havoc of his remains.

*   *   *   *   *

The story of the life and death of George Woodfall is one of the strangest to come from the continent of Australia. The details were pieced together from Woodfall's own statement, and the accounts of the men who found his body in the strangest and apparently most unnatural circumstances.

George Woodfall was an Englishman of good family who emigrated to Australia about 1850 to seek his fortune, after losing all his money in the Old Country.

In February, 1851, a Californian gold-miner named Hargraves discovered gold at Summerhill Creek, which is a hundred miles or so to the north-west of Sydney. Woodfall was among the first of the immigrants in the great gold rush that followed when rich finds were also made in Victoria.

Woodfall joined up with two men—Harper and Freeth—rough characters both. Harper had come out years previously on a convict

ship. But neither he nor Freeth were really bad characters. Living the pioneer life brings out the best as well as the worst in men.

Gold prospecting, however, is more likely to bring out the worst. Certainly it brought thousands of undesirables to Australia, to the great concern of the authorities.

No one, certainly not Woodfall, pretended that Harper and Freeth were blackguards of the deepest dye, and they did not deserve the treatment meted out to them by Woodfall—an educated man and an English gentleman.

Neither Harper nor Freeth could write their own names, yet they were good mates to Woodfall, welcoming him when he arrived at the diggings, and sharing, as Woodfall admitted, fair and square in everything.

The three teamed up together and struck gold. Between them they did well enough, travelling about in the mountains, prospecting, carrying with them their loads of gold dust and nuggets, already worth a considerable fortune. Indeed they had enough each to make themselves comfortable for life. But prospectors are never satisfied. Gold creates in them a fever which cannot be satisfied. They want more and more of it.

They were talking about going to Sydney and cashing up when they discovered a wondrous cave in what looked like a gold-bearing mountain, from which leaped a spectacular waterfall. The cave was difficult to get into. They found the entrance after some arduous climbing. It was a vertical shaft in the face of the mountain, and to descend it they had to drive wooden stakes into the soft rock.

When they got down they found a vast, cathedral-like cavern which reverberated to the distant thunder of the mighty waterfall. Their torches illuminated great stalactites and stalagmites, and glittered on multi-coloured prisms of rock. Most exciting of all to them, they saw quartz in the great pillars which supported the roof of the cave.

But this splendid and awe-inspiring place yielded little in the way of gold. The quartz, though exquisite in appearance, was poor in gold.

To get it they had to break into a rock formation which was like one of those great exquisitely carved altar-pieces in a cathedral. Behind this, they found a smaller cave.

After searching in vain for gold in this strange and splendid place, they decided to pass the night in the small cave, before resuming their journey to Sydney.

The talk that night was of their plans for the return to civilization

They each calculated the value of their gold, and came to the conclusion that they hadn't done too badly. Each said it would be the soft life for them in the future. They had had enough of roughing it, and wanted to enjoy the sweets of civilization, which their gold would enable them to do.

As the talk drifted to yarns about Sydney and the wild times of the old days, George Woodfall fell unusually quiet. His thoughts ran on very different lines to those of his companions. For them their share of the gold was enough, but not for him. He had come to Australia to rebuild his fortune, and he would not be satisfied with the kind of money that these simple diggers considered riches. The total amount of their gold represented a respectable sum of money. With that for his capital, Woodfall was convinced he could really make money.

But there was little chance of robbing his two companions and making away with the gold. He would be a marked man. That sort of thing would not be forgiven or forgotten.

There was only one solution—to kill them.

Harper and Freeth soon fell into a heavy sleep. Woodfall lay awake planning their murder. It would have to be done very swiftly, and before the fire they had lit in the cave burnt out.

Woodfall waited until the fire was low and then he struck silently and suddenly with his razor-sharp knife. First Freeth, who was closer to him. He got him with one blow right through the heart.

But though Freeth was dispatched so quickly and suddenly, Harper was instantly awake, that sixth sense which men often acquire while living in the wilds suddenly alerted.

Harper stumbled to his feet and launched himself straight at Woodfall. But Harper was still half-asleep, and Woodfall had not much difficult in dealing with him. He grasped him by the throat and tore at his gullet. They fell over, fighting madly. Woodfall's knife was dropped in the desperate struggle, but he retained his hold on Harper's throat, and Harper went down in a state of semi-consciousness.

Woodfall turned and picked up his knife, then came for his comrade once more to finish him off. Harper struggled up into a sitting position, his face livid, eyes protruding, mouth open and gasping. He was unable to speak, for he had been all but strangled by Woodfall. He looked up desperately at Woodfall, and put his hands together, praying for mercy.

But this Woodfall did not give. He had gone too far anyway. He plunged his knife deep into Harper's chest. Harper died with a

harsh and terrible cry which echoed and re-echoed through the great vaults of the cathedral-like cave nearby.

Woodfall decided to leave the place at once, even though it was night-time. He collected the gold from his companions' packs, but the sight of his comrades lying there slain so treacherously by his own hand was too much for his conscience, and he decided to bury them. It would be the best way of hiding the crime, anyway.

But he found digging in the hard soil extremely difficult. It was more a case of hewing than digging. After he had dug a shallow pit, he gave up the idea of burying them. After all, it was unlikely that anyone would ever discover this cave in this lovely and remote spot. And if they did there would be nothing to connect him with the bodies of Freeth and Harper.

So he laid their bodies in the shallow pit he had excavated, and covered them with some loose stones. And thus he left them and went to Sydney.

The date was 20 September. The year 1852 or 1853.

No one knew him at Sydney, which in those days was a city with a population of 100,000, compared with two million today. It was a large enough place for George Woodfall to remain comparatively unknown. He told everyone he had lately arrived from England with a modest amount of capital he wished to invest.

When the occasion arose Woodfall took a chance, in the same way as he had taken a chance in the cave when he robbed and murdered his two comrades. He invested nearly all of his capital in the Benambra Mine. A week later the shares rocketed and he was a very rich man.

Woodfall was so pleased with his success that he forgot his crime and enjoyed himself. He bought a fine house on Pott's Point, where he entertained at first lavishly and not wisely.

September came around again, and one evening about the middle of the month he was sitting alone by the open window of his house gazing across the dark waters of Port Jackson to the harbour lights at the Heads, when he fell into a fit of bitter remorse over what he had done. He would have given all his wealth to have washed the blood from his hands. In that mood he had a strong impulse to rush to the police and confess his crime.

Momentarily the mood passed and he turned away from the window with the reflection that dead men could surely tell no tales.

As he turned into the room, he heard a voice distinctly say: "It is time. Let us begin."

Thinking at first that burglars were about, he got out his revolver and made a search. But there were no intruders around his house— no intruders from this world, that is.

Woodfall put out the lights and prepared to go to bed. He picked up the candle and started for the door.

He had hardly taken a step, he says, when suddenly something like a heavy body fell with a thud at his feet. As he stumbled back in alarm he began to hear sounds—sounds that had haunted him for months, but now they burst terrifyingly upon his ears.

There was the waterfall reverberating in the background, and then, splitting his eardrums, came Harper's last terrible cry as he died with Woodfall's knife deep in his chest. There were other noises, too, terrifying, indescribable, unspeakable noises which shook and echoed around the house.

He sank into a chair, covering his ears with his hands to try and shut out the spectral sounds, but was unable to do so. He was back in the cave now, in that awful night, in a living nightmare that appalled his senses.

At any moment he expected his servants to be aroused by the terrible, frightening noises which rose every now and then in a crescendo to Harper's unforgettable scream of death.

But no one in the house stirred, and he soon became aware that he was the only one who could hear these sounds—this devil's concert, as Woodfall called it.

When this thought was brought home to him, the sounds suddenly ceased. Then, as plain as if he was standing next to him, he heard Harper's voice.

"You are growing forgetful, George. In a week's time it will be September the twentieth. We are here to remind you."

George Woodfall was now in a state of the uttermost terror. He was convinced of the presence not only of Harper but of Freeth in the room. But it was Harper who spoke, Harper whose death cry was a living echo in his brain.

"Your time has not come yet, George, but before it does we will teach you to remember. We will expect you in the cave on the twentieth. Don't forget to come. That is the only way you will escape us."

"Yes, I will come," muttered Woodfall, and then his consciousness ceased.

A dream? A waking nightmare prompted by his tormenting conscience?

At all events Woodfall went to the cave and there he spent, he

said, "a night of such agonizing horror that I wondered afterwards how I came to retain either life or reason after it".

What took place in that cave can only be imagined. But it is not likely that Woodfall could have brought himself to touch the bodies of the two men he had murdered and placed in that shallow pit. This is an important point, in view of what happened later.

Every year now he made this terrible pilgrimage to the cave, and spent a whole night in a kind of hellish communion with his victims, whose bodies lay rotting in the shallow pit. Each year they became more decayed, more skeletal, and yet in some unnatural way more alive.

But only by going there each year did they give him peace. After the fourth year, he tried not going. But there was no evading his grim pilgrimage. Harper and Freeth came and haunted him at Pott's Point—came after him and drove him to the cave for his grim annual ritual.

This experience had one beneficial effect upon Woodfall. It changed his whole life. He gave up all forms of gaiety and enjoyment, and tried to make amends by good deeds. He gave to charity. He went to church regularly, and became one of Sydney's most respected citizens.

No one dreamed he was a murderer, for he kept his terrible secret locked up inside him. For some reason, he could not confess to what he had done. He was quite unable to. If he did, would Harper and Freeth leave him alone in peace at last?

And after twenty miserable, haunted years, and after nineteen visits to the unspeakable cave, he finally decided to make his confession.

One night he wrote it out, and finished it by saying that he would make one more pilgrimage to the cave, because this, he felt, he must do. Then he would return and give himself up.

And so he went on his last pilgrimage, but he never returned.

Sydney mourned an upright and benevolent citizen, whose disappearance was both a sensation and a mystery. No foul play was suspected. His affairs were found to be in perfect order. He was greatly missed, and later they put up a monument to him.

The mystery remained unsolved for five years.

In the late 1870s two men, William Rowley, an engineer who had planned and made many canals in New South Wales, and the Rev. Charles Power, of St Chrysostom Church, Redfern, Sydney, were spending one of those energetic holidays typical of the nineteenth century, camping and travelling in the wilds of the Blue

mountains, and living off the land by eating such meat as could be shot by Rowley's gun. The Rev. Power employed his energies more suitably catching butterflies for his large Australasian collection.

Both of them knew George Woodfall by reputation and by sight.

It was on 20 September when they came upon the mountain from which leaped the spectacular waterfall. Here they camped for the night, enchanted by the wildly beautiful scenery, fascinated by the waterfall, and totally unaware that the day marked the anniversary of a certain grim event.

After supper, while they were yarning over their pipes by the camp fire, there was a great thunderstorm, during which, by some strange trick of the eyesight perhaps, a blood-red glare settled over the waterfall, so that it appeared to them like a torrent of blood.

They regarded it as a strange natural phenomenon, but when the storm passed off the red glare was still above the waterfall and right in the midst of the water, it seemed, a man appeared.

They started forward, stumbling in the darkness, then stopped, transfixed to the spot, for they saw that the man had a face that was long dead, with the flesh shrunken and dried and in some places rotted away. It was a mere skeleton, a thing, they thought, from the outer darkness. It seemed suspended there in a blaze of crimson light, alternately beckoning to them and then writhing in anguish.

It took them an hour and a half to climb to the spot where they had seen the ghost, and another hour to reach the summit where the waterfall leaped down the chasm. The precipice was sheer and the mountain towered above them in the night.

Climbing higher, they saw a fallen ironbark tree which had been blazed with an axe and an arrow pointing directly downwards.

Close by they found the entrance to the cave, now overgrown with shrubs. Rowley cut a sapling and beat away the undergrowth, revealing the mouth of the cave which led vertically downwards.

The wooden stakes made by Woodfall and his two companions twenty-five years previously were still there and just as secure. Lighting their bull's-eye lantern, Rowley and Power descended.

Some minutes later they stood in wonder and astonishment in the great cathedral-like cavern. The huge rock formation made like an altar-piece particularly impressed and interested Power, and while he was admiring it Rowley went through past the broken quartz rock into the smaller cave beyond.

His exclamation of horror brought Power hurrying after him.

"What's the matter?" asked the clergyman.

"Come, let's go back," said Rowley, obviously shaken. "This is no place for us."

"For heaven's sake—what is it?" demanded Power.

Rowley illuminated the scene with the bull's-eye lantern.

In front of them was the shallow open grave. The earth which had been dug up to make it and piled at the side had been hardened almost to stone by the endless drip of water from above. Even the tools with which the grave had been dug were still lying there.

But what took their horrified attention was the skeleton of a man, bush shirt and trousers rotted to tatters, half sitting at the side of the grave, peering into it, grinning in a way in which only a skull can grin.

In the grave itself lay two more bodies, one on top of the other. The topmost was a skeleton similar to the one sitting at the grave-side. Underneath it was the body of a man in the last stages of decay, though he had not been dead for anything like the time which the other two had been.

There was something weirdly familiar about him to the two horrified men who peered down into the grave, and when Rowley reached down with his sapling and brushed aside the upmost skeleton, they could see that the man underneath was the man who had appeared to them above the waterfall just after the thunderstorm.

Both men were mystified as well as appalled by their discovery. There was something weird, unnatural, about the whole thing—in the very attitudes of the two corpses in the pit, quite apart from the apparition by the blood-red waterfall.

The fact that two of the bodies had obviously been dead for many years longer than the third puzzled Rowley and Power. And how was it possible that the man who had plainly been the last to die was found lying *underneath* a man who had died many years before him?

To the Reverend Charles Power there was something devilish about the whole thing—something that smelt of the very pit of hell.

They looked around the cave and found an old coat, fast falling to pieces with age, but which was obviously well tailored and of good cloth. It had the label of Schuylen, one of Sydney's best tailors. In the coat they found a flat metal box containing the inscription: "George Woodfall, Pott's Point, Sydney", and they had the answer to the mystery, for inside was his confession of how he had killed Harper and Freeth for their gold, and then been made to return to this place every year by some hideous force he was unable to resist.

The answer to the mystery? It was only part of the answer.

In his confession Woodfall said he would go to the cave for the last and twentieth time after writing his confession, and then give himself up. But he did not return from the cave. How then was he killed?

Originally he had laid the bodies of Harper and Freeth in the grave. There they lay for nineteen years and more, and thus he found them on each wretched visit he made to this place of hideous memory. On the twentieth pilgrimage, after he had made his confession, *did he arrive there to find them sitting on the edge of the grave awaiting him, knowing that he had finally delivered himself into their power?*

Rowley and Power buried the three bodies in the cave, and Power read the burial service over them.

The clergyman never understood why Woodfall, having finally confessed to his crime, was then delivered into the power of the spirits of darkness. But he firmly believed that his and Rowley's footsteps had been guided to the cave to find Woodfall's confession, and to give the three bodies a Christian burial, so that their long-tormented spirits should rest in peace at last.

Over their remains he and Rowley piled a cairn of gold-bearing quartz.

The Coach Calls for George Mace

The village of Watton lies almost at the centre of the triangle formed by Thetford, Wymondham and Swaffham, in Norfolk. Today it has fewer than four thousand inhabitants; a century ago it had more than a thousand less, and one of them was George Mace.

By day Mace worked as stockman for a farmer at Ovington, a couple of miles or so north and slightly east of Watton. By night, he was the leader of one of the most successful gangs of poachers ever to operate in the county.

The country over which George worked under the stars has changed remarkably little compared with the changes which have generally overtaken the rural countryside of Britain. Here and there, there has been some ribbon development and the villages have tended to sprawl a bit. But there are still wide-open spaces devoted to the production of barley, wheat and oats, broken up by woods, coppices and spinneys, just as there were in George's days.

At the time of which we are writing, George was in his middle thirties. For a Norfolk countryman born and bred, he had an unusually lively mind. About five foot ten tall, he had the broad shoulders, fair hair and pale blue eyes of his Saxon forebears, and in his customary gait could still be observed traces of the Saxon lope. His ruddy, weather-beaten features had been given a handsome turn, too. When the older people talked of him, sooner or later they would hint at the story which had followed his mother from Breckles, where, before she had married her late husband, she had been in service at the hall; according to which she was already pregnant

when Jos Mace had led her to the altar, that the Squire of Breckles had given Jos a marriage gift that was noticeably larger than was customary, and that he had once ridden over to the Watton cottage not long after the birth of Flo Mace's first-born, George. Certainly, none of her other children, whom she had produced annually until the day Jos drank too deeply at Swaffham market, fell into the Wissey on his way home and remembered too late that he could not swim. When they had fished him out of the mill-race by Hilborough and had filled in his grave in Watton churchyard, Flo decided that she had had sufficient connubial bliss to last her the rest of her life, and had settled down to bringing up the departed Jos's brood and George—if we are inclined to give credence to the local tradition.

George had been eight when Jos had so suddenly removed himself from the family circle, and he had immediately gone to work for the farmer at Ovington who had employed his father. In spring and early summer his duties were to keep the birds from attacking the seeds after sowing and the young shoots after sprouting, by wielding a noisy rattle. At harvest time he took his place with the sheavers, following the scythe-men; in autumn and winter he helped the stockmen.

It was during this apprenticeship to the land, and particularly during the long spring and summer days of bird-scaring, that he laid the foundations of his vast store of the lore of the countryside. He began leaving the cottage at night, after his brothers and sister were asleep, and though he invariably went out empty-handed, just as invariably he returned shortly before dawn with a rabbit or a hare, a pheasant or a brace of partridge stuffed inside his shirt. His mother, anxious to raise him well, never failed to scold him, just as she never forgot to wink as she took the booty from him, with silent but heartfelt thanks that today the stew-pot and her children's bellies would not be empty.

By the time there was down on his chin, George had impressed his employer with the way he had with animals, and his employer's youngest daughter with his knowledge of the ways of men. The stockmen of the neighbourhood respected his advice, and the more generally knowledgeable nodded sagely and murmured something about "a chip off the old block", and were not referring to Jos. But there also comes a time when recognition of professional skill cannot be invoked to overlook the visible results of personal concupiscence. Two small Georges had already been born to as many mothers, when the maternal grandfather of the third little George, egged on by

his wife, arrived at Flo's cottage to declare that her George, at not quite eighteen, was nevertheless old enough to shoulder his respon-sibilities.

George, however, thought otherwise, though he did not say so. He was too young yet to be tied down; he had not yet had time to discover which of the wenches in the neighbourhood would suit him best.

However, he said, "Name the day, gaffer; that's all you've to do," and the man, relieved, had turned to Flo and said, "In that case, Mrs Mace, you'd best put your head together with my missus."

When they were alone, Flo had burst out laughing.

Surprised, George had asked, "Why're you laughing, mam? Aren't you going to scold me?"

"What? For something you can't help. It's born in you. Besides, I know you well enough, my boy, to know that you've no intention of marrying the girl."

Taken somewhat aback by this unexpected understanding, George laughed too.

"You're right, mam," he said. "I haven't—at least not until . . ."

"It'll be best if you get away for a bit," Flo said. "If you stay around here, one night we shall find our thatch alight. Out of sight, out of mind. Where do you plan to go?"

"In the army," George told her, "then I shan't have to worry where my next meal's to come from, or about a roof over my head. Besides, I'll get about a bit, see other men, go to other places. You never know, I may even get to India."

"Well, mind you come back, son."

"I'll promise you that. But are you sure you'll be all right if I go? There's my pittance from old Thrower, and there won't be so many rabbits for the pot. I don't know what's wrong with those boys, but neither Frank nor Bert have got it in them to be good poachers. I've done my best with 'em, but it's no good."

"Don't worry about me, son. We'll be all right," his mother assured him. "You might even get a commission. They do sometimes award commissions on the field."

"I doubt it, mam. You've got to have more education than I've got, and more breeding, to be an officer."

"More education maybe," Flo Mace agreed cryptically. "But you can read and write and figure. When will you go?"

"The end of the week. I'll walk over to Norwich and see the recruiting sergeant there. You'd best see Nan's mam tomorrow."

"You can leave that to me. I'm glad you'll be here a few days

yet. But take care, George, don't whisper a word in front of the young ones."

Well, George joined the army on the following Sunday, and did not return to Watton for fifteen years. He saw India and he came through the shambles of the Crimea; he did not become an officer, but he did rise to be sergeant.

By the time he came home again, the youth of eighteen now a man of thirty-three, he found little changed. There were differences, naturally. Except for his youngest sister, who was in service to the widow of a late Canon of Norwich, and looked set fair to be an old maid, all his brothers and sisters were married and in their own cottages; the mothers of the three little Georges had also taken husbands, and the little Georges were all beginning to have down on their chins; the two eldest were even shaving once a week.

He had come from London by the Great Eastern Railway's line to Thetford, and there he had caught the carrier to Swaffham. The ancient man did not recognize him, which was no wonder, for the still developing youth had matured into a broad-shouldered man.

A mile or so from the village he had stopped the cart, and, thanking the old man, had got down. Hitching his pack on to his shoulder, he had watched the cart trundle away, then he had struck out across the fields. It felt strange to be among the old familiar sights again; but they were all there, and the air smelt as it always did, free and bold and strong, different from the air in any other place he had been in on this side and the other side of the world.

The strangeness had begun to come over him as soon as the carrier's cart had emerged from Thetford and turned into the Watton road, and as the familiar sights had begun to multiply the strangeness had turned to embarrassment. It was on account of his embarrassment that he had stopped the cart and got down.

As he trudged his way through the fields, the sun set, but it would not be dark yet for another hour. He had a mile or so still to go, so sitting down under the lee of a hay-rick he took his almost empty bundle of food from his pack and ate a little. And as he looked about him, presently two rabbits sped across the field to their warren on the edge of the spinney nearby.

He smiled to himself. He knew the place well.

Feeling in his pockets, he found a length of cord, and crossing to the spinney he carefully selected a twig, cut it and shaped it with his knife, fashioned a loop in the cord, and attaching the running end to the twig, which he stuck firmly into the ground above the entrance to the burrow he had chosen, he arranged the loop round

the edge of the hole. This any poacher could have done; but what he did next, few could do.

Stretching himself flat on the ground so that he lay above the burrow with his head above the hole, he made intermittent, small, special sounds with his lips. Five minutes, perhaps, he waited, then below his face, and only inches from it, appeared the twitching muzzle of a rabbit. He made his sound a little more loudly, and suddenly a furry body was writhing violently, attempting to free itself from the loop about its neck, which drew tighter with every movement it made.

With a grunt of satisfaction, he put down a hand and seized the struggling animal by the nape of its neck. Pulling up the twig, he stood up, took hold of the rabbit by its hind legs with his left hand and brought down the outer edge of his rigid right hand on the back of its head. It quivered once, and was still. Again George Mace grunted with satisfaction.

Re-setting the snare, he repeated his ritual, and within another five minutes the still warm body of a second rabbit lay beside the first. Gathering two large dock leaves, he made masks of them, which he fitted over the rabbits' snouts, tying them in place with strands of long coarse grass. This done, he put the rabbits into his pack, certain that any blood that might trickle from their nostrils would not soil anything with which they came into contact.

By the time he had done this the dusk was rapidly changing into night. He still had a short walk before he reached home, but before he came to the village it would be dark—as he had planned.

A light was burning in the kitchen window of the cottage. When he peered through it, he saw his mother sitting by the hearth, her hands busy with some sewing. Momentarily he was shocked to see that the jet black hair he remembered was now mostly white, until he recalled that his mother, too, had aged and must be now in her middle-fifties.

Moving quietly to the cottage door, he felt silently for the latch. His finger closed on it, and patiently he lifted it. When he felt it free of the catch, he pushed open the door and placed himself in the doorway.

For a moment his mother did not see what had happened. Then some little movement he made distracted her attention from her needle, and she looked up. During all of five seconds, she gazed at him; then with a cry, she sprang up, scattering her sewing, and flung herself into his arms.

"George!" she cried. "You've come home!"

"Yes, mam, I've come home," he said.

"Come to the light and let me look at you!" She looked at him hard and long. "Yes . . . yes . . ."she said at last. Then moving again into his arms, she asked, "Will you stay long, son?"

"I'm home for good, mam," he told her.

"For good?"she asked, disbelieving.

"For good," he repeated.

"You'll be hungry,"she said, at once practical, "and I've little in the larder. I'll go and ask Mrs Utting if she can lend us a piece of bacon."

"No need, mam," he laughed, and pulled the rabbits from his pack.

She laughed, shaking her head as she took them, and remembered to wink.

As they ate together when the food was cooked, she asked, "What will you do, George?"

"Look round for a farmer who wants a stockman."

"Maybe Farmer Thrower will take you back. Then you could live here with me."

"I'll do that, mam, in any case. But I'll go and see Thrower first thing in the morning.

The farmer was doubtful at first. For fifteen years George had had no dealings with stock. Eventually, however, at George's suggestion, he took him on a month's trial.

At the end of a week he told George he could stay as long as he liked.

George Mace's return was a nine-days' wonder in the village. There were some, whose memories were long, who warned certain parents, "Lock up your daughters now George Mace is back!" But as time went by he proved them wrong. Not a girl in the village received his special attentions, though there were some who tried to attract them; each Saturday afternoon he walked the ten miles to Swaffham; on Sunday night he walked the ten miles back. What he did in between made him and the village happy.

There were even more who said that he would not be staying long. After the excitements of all that soldiering, Watton would be too quiet for him. He proved them almost as wrong; but not quite.

It would have been strange if he had settled down entirely to the slow tempo of the countryside. To begin with, however, he welcomed the change, and so great was his interest in animals that he became absorbed in his job. What excitement he felt he needed he tried to find in poaching, and for a time he did achieve it in pitting

his wits against those of the gamekeepers. But he did not like killing for killing's sake, and now that there were only two of them at the cottage it was difficult to dispose of his catches. Admittedly some could be passed on to trusted neighbours, but in these days, when a man could be transported for fourteen years for stealing a rabbit or two, should the poacher be caught and the landowner invoke the letter of the law, it was too dangerous to be too prodigal with illicit gifts.

There was one other point, too. George was a born leader, as his attainment of non-commissioned rank had proved. Had he lived on the coast of Kent or Sussex or Cornwall he would have undoubtedly made a great reputation as a leader of smugglers. Here in the depths of the Norfolk countryside such an outlet was denied him. Or so he thought, until without warning one or two of the landowners decided to intensify their war with the poachers.

Within a space of four weeks, two men from Watton, one from Soham Toney and one from Ashill, fell into gamekeepers' traps, and on being brought before the magistrates, who were also the squires, instead of being dealt with summarily, were committed to Norwich assizes, where they were sentenced to transportation for periods ranging between twelve and thirty years.

Such a thing had never happened before within living memory. A fine of a shilling or two, or if the offender were young, a sound birching, had always been deemed sufficient punishment. The good people of Norfolk were scandalized; but they were also cowed; and one result was that the children of a number of families now often went hungry.

The landowners were led by the new squire of Holme Hale. He was a youngish man who had started out as a lawyer in London, and was not making much of a go of it, when he unexpectedly inherited his uncle's estate. He was an unpleasant character, in any case; but he added to this an ignorance of the Norfolk countryside and its people, while deceiving himself that they were like any other rogues. Somehow he managed to persuade one or two of his neighbours to join him in his anti-poaching campaign, and then when the men were brought before the Swaffham bench he dragooned his fellow magistrates into a committal to assizes.

This declaration of war was a godsend to George Mace. He accepted it as a personal challenge. When the two Watton men were caught he was sorry, but not wholly sympathetic, because he believed that if they had been poachers worth their salt they would have avoided any trap. But when the two others were also seized, he realized that

the standard of poaching efficiency was inferior to the efficiency of the gamekeepers, and that this could lead, in a very short time, to a discontinuance of the art altogether. In his view, this would have been a calamity of the first order; first, because the poacher is an integral part of the English country lore; second, because it would mean victory for the squires, and particularly for the hateful squire of Holme Hale. This he perceived as his duty not to permit.

After some thought, he decided to band the poachers of Watton's immediate environs into a gang under his leadership. He would raise their standard of performance by tuition, and then they would operate on a military basis. If all went as he was certain it would they could have the gamekeepers with their backs to the wall in no time.

Personally, all he asked of the plan was the success of his gang's operations. He realized, however, that this would not satisfy his men, who would come in, not for the excitement or the satisfaction of defeating the enemy, but for the tangible rewards. But on the scale he planned, these rewards would be too large for local distribution, so he worked on a scheme for supplying the hotels of the district with cheap game, the proceeds from which would be evenly shared among the gang.

Within six months he was ready to begin operations. Under him he had a dozen men, who, though still not the expert he was himself, were, nevertheless, the cream of the poachers of East Anglia. From them he demanded and received unquestioning obedience.

For a time the gamekeepers were bewildered, until they learned, as they were bound to since the trees and the grass in the countryside have tongues, of the existence of the Mace gang. But knowledge without evidence is not sufficient to allow justice to be seen to be done.

To acquire evidence, they countered by forming an organization of their own. But still they had no success, for George conducted his operations with a strategy and tactics which would have gladdened the heart of old Wellington, had he still been alive to learn of it. He had his intelligence corps and his agents who planted false information, and by this combination he let loose his men in one section of the region while the gamekeepers waited miles away to pounce on poachers who were supposed to walk into their traps, but never did.

For a little over a year George and his gang operated with immense success. He lost not a single man, and every one of them was richer by five shillings a week from the proceeds of the sale of their booty after they had filled the bellies of their families and their neighbours.

George was well pleased, though he was wise enough not to underestimate his opponents; and it was in this frame of mind that in October, 1867, he planned his fiftieth operation. The territory chosen was to be five square miles due south of Watton, in the triangle of Thompson–Tottington–Breckles. Working in groups of three—two to operate, one to keep look-out—they were to begin on the Thompson–Tottington line and converge on Breckles, where at half-past three in the morning they were to meet at a hut which stood in a spinney edging one side of the drive leading up to Breckles Hall. George would fulfil his usual role of scout-out-ahead and liaison between the groups, for though his agents had filtered the information that the gang proposed working the Holme Hale estate, the property of the man who was primarily responsible for it all, he judged it wiser to avoid whatever independently working gamekeepers there might be in his area.

As the men had now come to expect, the operation went without a hitch, and shortly after three o'clock the groups began to arrive at the Breckles hut. While waiting, they laid out their haul, which was a particularly good one, and chatted in whispers about the experiences of the night.

Sometimes George would already be waiting at the rendezvous when the first group arrived. At others, he would come a quarter of an hour before time. Sometimes, though not often, he would arrive after all the rest.

As half-past three approached, and he had not come, a silence fell upon the men. He always had a good word for them, and did not stint his praise if the bag was a good one. And the simple countrymen, whose admiration for their leader was boundless, derived a great personal satisfaction from his approval.

"George is late tonight," one of the men murmured as the clock on the Breckles coach-house chimed the half-hour.

"He'll come!" he was assured.

Ten minutes later, he said again, "George has never been as late as this."

"He'll come, I tell you!" insisted his companion.

But as the minutes sped by and still Mace did not appear they began to be apprehensive.

"Something must have happened to him!" exclaimed the man who had spoken first, his voice unsteady with rising fear.

"Not to George," he was told, but this time with less conviction.

When four o'clock had struck, and there was still no sign of him, all the men were alarmed, and some were becoming angry. There

were some who condemned the leader for exposing them to such risks; the hut was far too close to the house, they said.

"If we're to get home before light," one of them grumbled, "we can't wait much longer."

"We'll give him until the clock chimes the quarter," said Jim Harris, whom George had appointed his lieutenant. "If he hasn't come then, we'll hide the bag in Boulter's spinney. He'll have a good reason for not coming, you may be bound."

They crouched on their haunches, leaning their backs against the wall of the hut, straining their eyes at the grey darkness of the spinney, and their ears for the least sound which would tell them someone was approaching. They crouched in silence, stifling their individual emotions, tensed and puzzled.

The clock chimed the quarter.

"Right," said Jim Harris. "You, Dick, and you, Bert, you'll come with me to Boulter's spinney. The rest of you make your ways home separately."

But before any of them could move, sounds reached them which froze them where they squatted.

"A coach!" exclaimed Dick Utting. "At this time of night!"

"George said the squire's away in London," Jim Harris whispered. "This'll be him coming home. No one move till it's gone."

But fascinated by the sounds, no one obeyed him, and all edged their way to the end of the hut, from where they could see the drive.

Presently the coach came into view. Its lamps were brighter than usual and appeared in some strange way to envelop with their light the whole of the equipage.

As Jim Harris watched it come rolling up the drive, and heard the clop of the horses' hooves on the gravel and the scrunch of the wheels, he felt the skin of his scalp tightening and a river of ice course down his spine. For there was something truly strange about the coach—though the reins were clearly being held, there was no coachman sitting on the box!

Nor, apparently, was Jim the only one who had noted this lack of a driver, for from several tight throats about him came exclamations of "My God!"

There was not one of them who would not have jumped to his feet and fled had he been able. But although the desire filled them, limbs would not respond.

And all the time the coach was coming nearer, until presently it drew level with the hut.

Then they saw the reins pulled taut. They saw the horses halt.

Then, after a pause, they saw the door of the coach open and the steps let down.

Again there was a pause, then the steps were put up and the door closed.

But not one of the twelve had seen anyone step down.

The coach swayed a little, as though someone were re-mounting the box. The reins were shaken, and the horses moved forward.

But no sooner had they done so than the coach vanished!

The silence which followed was broken only by the expletives of men and the noise they made as they crashed their way through the spinney intent only upon escape.

Two or three hours later, one of the grooms who lived in the lodge cottage walked up the drive towards the Hall to begin another day's work in the stables. As he came to the hut, he saw lying in the driveway, at the very spot where the poachers had seen the coach stop, the still body of a man. He ran to it, and turned it over, thinking it must be one of his companions who had come home the evening before the worse for drink. But he did not recognize the man; and he was not drunk, but quite dead. Whoever he was, he had died peacefully, for his parted lips were curved in a happy smile. There was something familiar about the features, nevertheless, and for a time the groom was puzzled. But he had worked at Breckles all his life, and at last it came to him.

"The old squire!" he exclaimed, and rising to his feet began to hurry towards the Hall shouting as he went.

Later in the day the body was identified as that of George Mace of Watton, whose mother thirty-five years ago had been a housemaid at the Hall. From the heap of rabbits, hare and other game found behind the hut, it was clear that the poacher had had an otherwise successful night.

Dr Jessop, the local chronicler, who records these events in his book *Frivola*, has written: "There was nothing to show what had killed him. There were no marks of violence on the body nor any signs of sudden illness. His time had come, and he had been fetched away by a Power which even the boldest poacher cannot hope to defy."

Flo Mace's verdict was different. Through her weeping she murmured, "He went home at last!"

Shades of Murder

What causes a haunting we shall never know this side of the grave. The number of people whose deaths have been intermingled with tragedy, sadness or intolerable pain and anguish is infinitely greater than the number of reported hauntings. It is well known that some people see ghosts where others do not, and it may be that in places like Belsen and the battlefields of the First World War there is a haunting on a scale and on a plane of which mortals are not aware; for if hauntings do take place at all, and there is good evidence that they do, then the pattern must make sense, and there must be reasons why some hauntings come through to us and others do not, why relatively unimportant events cause a haunting and quite appalling tragedies apparently do not. And why do the romantic kind of hauntings seem to outnumber the other sort?

For centuries it has been believed that a haunting can be caused by a young life being cruelly and suddenly terminated. This creates an angry and vengeful spirit.

This belief was common among the priests of the early civilizations, who marked the burial of their monarchs by slaughtering young human victims and immuring them in the royal tomb. The idea was to create young and virile spirits to guard and protect the King on his journey into eternity. This rite was practised by many early peoples, including the Bronze Age Shang Dynasty, the Mycenaean Greeks, the Sumerians and the Aztecs, and was a world-wide part of religious practice. It has come down with the passing millenia into comparatively modern times when young victims

were bricked up live into the foundation walls of buildings, their pathetic skeletons being discovered even today.

The theory of truncated lives creating angry ghosts seems to be borne out by the number of hauntings connected with crime, particularly murder. Murder has been a mere drop in the ocean of human suffering, if one does not term as murder the quasi-official slaughter which has gone on under various oligarchies since time began.

The numbers of children and young people who have been murder victims will never be told, for many murders have not been discovered, and murderers of course have been known to escape justice, even though they were tried for their crime.

Such a case was that of the murder of Jane Clouson in the parish of Kidbrooke, London, in 1871. Jane was a servant in the house of a Greenwich printer named Ebeneezer Pook. She was seventeen and a pretty girl and was seduced by Pook's young son, Edmund, who was twenty. It was more than just an isolated seduction. They had quite an affair, lasting several months, with the result that Jane became pregnant.

Mr and Mrs Pook found out what had been going on under their respectable, God-fearing roof, and sacked Jane on the spot, though they later denied that this was why she was dismissed. Jane, not unreasonably, turned to Edmund for support, for he had made the girl all sorts of false promises in order to secure her favours. But Edmund was neither willing nor able to support her and certainly had no thought of marrying her. His brother had already brought down the parental wrath by marrying beneath his station and he had no intention of provoking his formidable father in the same way. But Jane was insistent that he should do the right thing by her in one way or another, and the poor child was indeed desperate in the hard, Victorian world, with no parents to turn to.

Edmund, full of promises he did not intend to keep, arranged to meet her at Blackheath on the evening of 26 April, 1871. Early the following morning she was found battered nearly to death in Kidbrooke Lane, a haunt of lovers in those days. She died in Guys Hospital without recovering consciousness. Edmund was tried for her murder, but as the Judge ruled that all the statements Jane had made before her death which incriminated him were hearsay and inadmissible as evidence, he was found not guilty and discharged.

The verdict caused an uproar and there were disturbances in Greenwich. There were disturbances also in the astral plane apparently.

But it was not until Edmund had been found not guilty and been released that Jane's ghost returned to the scene of the crime and began to haunt Kidbrooke Lane. It should be remembered that this part of London, S.W.3, has been entirely rebuilt since the 'seventies, and the Kidbrooke Lane which Jane haunted no longer exists, having been completely built over. Then it was a stretch of open country between Kidbrooke and Eltham which was largely under cultivation.

Kidbrooke Lane was, as mentioned, a popular resort for the courting couples of the neighbourhood. It was narrow, shaded by trees and tall hedges and crossed by a small stream named Kid. The lane ran through cornfields and farmland and offered plenty of sheltered privacy for dalliance.

On the night of the murder it had been patrolled at regular intervals by P.C. Gunn. Jane was murdered about 8.30 and left lying by the side of the lane past which the constable patrolled twice during the night without seeing her. Towards dawn she partly recovered consciousness and crawled into the centre of the lane as the constable came by the third time, moaning "Oh, my head! My head!" Her face and head had been terribly battered with a lathing hammer later found. This was a long-handled tool with an axe opposite the hammer head and made a very vicious weapon. Lovers in the lane that night had heard her screams, but no one troubled to investigate.

Jane's spectral screams were heard again and again by courting couples in Kidbrooke Lane and her ghost was seen more than once by the patrolling policemen. She appeared in a white dress, her face running with blood.

Her dreadful cries were heard for some years until Kidbrooke Lane finally disappeared, as all the open land between Eltham and Shooters Hill Road was gradually built on. Rochester Way was built right across the old lane which was completely swallowed up in bricks and mortar. Only then did Jane's reproachful ghost desert the now unrecognizable place where her wretched lover battered her to death.

The only champion Jane had on this earth was a man named Newton Crosland, who wrote a deliberately libellous pamphlet after Edmund Pooke's acquittal. He was taken to court, but Edmund got only nominal damages, for Crosland's counsel, the redoubtable Sergeant Parry, put up a formidable case for justification on the grounds that Pook was guilty of Jane's murder, and would have been convicted but for the Judge's ruling about the hearsay evidence.

But a man cannot be tried twice for the same murder—at least not in this world. It would be satisfying to think that in his encounter with Jane in the next world he got his deserts. The Pook Case did not enjoy the fame of the story of Maria Marten and the Red Barn. Here was another wronged girl murdered, but this time it was the murderer who paid the penalty and who remained earthbound to haunt the place of his misdeeds.

Compared with Jane Clouson, Maria Marten was a rather more tarnished maiden when William Corder foully murdered her in the now immortal Red Barn. She had already had an illegitimate child by Corder's elder brother Thomas, and another by a man named Matthews. She was the belle of the Suffolk village of Polstead, and was certainly free with her favours. The countryfolk of Suffolk had a reputation for immorality during the nineteenth century, as was observed during the Peasenhall Case (1902). Whether it was deserved or not is another matter.

William and Maria had an illegitimate child which died a mysterious death, and Maria's ageing father pressed William, now relatively well off following the deaths of his father and brother, to make his erring daughter into a respectable woman. The reluctant Corder eventually appeared to agree, conditional upon the would-be bride going away secretly with him. She got no farther than the Red Barn, where he gave her both barrels and buried her beneath the earthen floor.

William Corder was not a clever murderer and he incriminated himself by writing letters about Maria which aroused the suspicion of her family—particularly her mother-in-law, old Marten's young wife, who dreamed twice, she declared, that Corder had shot Maria and buried her under the floor of the Red Barn.

The floor was dug and Mrs Anne Marten's remarkable dream prophecy turned out to be true. Corder meanwhile had married a school-teacher he met through a matrimonial advertisement in the *Sunday Times* in the year 1827, and was living in London. The case against him was overwhelming and he was publicly hanged outside the gates of Bury St Edmunds gaol on 11 August, 1828. All the workmen in the town went on strike that morning in order to go to the hanging.

The remarkable dreams of Anne Marten which had led to Corder's undoing were given a more natural explanation by the villagers of Polstead who knew the participants of this famous drama and who believed that Maria was hated by her stepmother, who it was, they said, who put the idea into William's head to lure

Maria into the Red Barn and kill her and bury her there. William agreed and promised to send Anne Marten money regularly as a sweetener to keep her quiet about what she knew. But he stopped sending her the money after a while and so she betrayed him—merely for the sake of a few pounds. At his trial he could not accuse her of being his accomplice, for his defence was a denial of the deed.

Another rather more picturesque theory told in Polstead after the murder was that William Corder was having an affair with Anne Marten, a young and attractive woman, just a year or two older than Maria. According to this theory, Anne planned the murder of her step-daughter to get her out of the way so that she could run off with William Corder.

Both of these theories support the view held by many people in Polstead at the time that Anne Marten invented the dreams in order to avenge herself on Corder for letting her down.

A haunting was fully expected as a consequence of this foul deed. Just after the discovery of Maria's body a false alarm about the raising of her ghost came about in the following manner.

Morbid sightseers gathered at the Red Barn, though perhaps in less numbers than they would have done today, for in the 1820s there were the full horrors of a public hanging and a dissection for those so inclined. One man arrived at the Red Barn and finding it empty went inside and looked into the empty grave, from which Maria's remains had been recently dug. Some singularly morbid impulse made him lie down in the grave. Just then a lady and gentleman, prompted by the same species of curiosity, entered the barn, and the man got up hurriedly from the trench. The transfixed couple thought, in the semi-darkness, that it was Maria's ghost rising from her uneasy grave. The lady screamed and fainted on the spot.

But apparently Maria's ghost did not walk, despite the fact that her poor remains were buried and dug up three times. The haunting arose from the manner in which her murderer's body was disposed of after his hanging.

After he had cut down the corpse, the hangman secured the remarkable price of a guinea an inch for pieces of the rope from the tumultuous crowd which thronged the scaffold. The rope was supposed to have acquired magical properties after the hanging.

The corpse was then taken to the Shirehall, Bury St Edmunds, for the dissection, an astonishing public performance on the part of the authorities of the day The body was cut open from throat to abdomen and the skin folded back to display what was beneath. The remains were laid upon a table and then 5,000 people were

admitted to view this gruesome exhibition of human butchery, shuffling past in a gaping endless stream the whole day long. At six p.m. the room was closed in the faces of thousands more hard-stomached wretches clamouring to see the sight.

Inside the hall two artists, with the assistance of a fourteen-year-old boy who held the bloodstained corpse, made various death masks of the hanged man. These, which are still preserved, bear little resemblance to William Corder, for hanging not only stretches the neck but completely distorts the features.

The following day Corder's body was taken to the West Suffolk General Hospital and completely dissected for the learning and information of the medical students there, who at least had some legitimate interest in such a proceeding. Corder's skeleton has been kept at the hospital and is used to this day for the teaching of anatomy—it being complete with the significant exception of the skull.

Several surgeons got busy on the grisly remains. Part of the scalp was dried and preserved and still exists. A book giving an account of the trial was bound in Corder's tanned skin, and this still graces the shelves at Moyse's Hall Museum, Bury St Edmunds.

The spirit of the guilty man might not have been too much disturbed at his body being used in this manner, but it is what happened to the skull which caused the haunting.

This was stolen from the skeleton in the hospital by a Dr Kilner, who substituted for it a spare skull he happened to possess. Dr Kilner took Corder's skull home, and for some reason best known to himself polished it and mounted it in an ebony box. This was about fifty years after the hanging.

Thereafter there was no peace in the good doctor's house. Skulls, as has been observed in many a strange story of haunting, seem to have an extraordinary power to create unaccountable mischief and disturbance. This is thought to be because the seat of the mind and thoughts is considered to be of great importance by the spirit which has left it.

Corder's ghost, it appeared, was considerably annoyed at Dr Kilner's action and proceeded to haunt him in the most nerve-racking manner. Candles blew out, doors slammed, a strange man in ancient clothes msyteriously appeared and just as mysteriously vanished.

The doctor soon found the haunting by the man whose skull he had tampered with merely to satisfy a personal whim rather more than he could bear, even though he did not believe in ghosts. Every-

where he went he heard footsteps behind him and heavy breathing over his shoulder. At night the doors of the house were opened and slammed violently, and his terrified household heard frantic hammering and sounds of sobbing issuing from the drawing-room where the skull was kept in its ebony box.

Dr Kilner, despite his disbelief in ghosts, knew very well by this time that his theft of Corder's skull was the cause of all the trouble, which soon held his whole household in the grip of terror. It looked as though he would have to get rid of the thing. It was out of the question to return it to its proper place in the hospital. It was highly polished and looked almost like tortoiseshell, quite different from the rest of Corder's skeleton. Too many questions would be asked.

In vain he hoped that Corder's disturbed ghost would settle down. One night he was awoken by one of the spectral noises and went on to the landing with a candle to see the door of the drawing-room being turned by a ghostly white hand. As the door was opened by the phantom hand, Kilner was stunned by a tremendous explosion like the report of a gun.

He ran downstairs and into the drawing-room where he was met by a gust of icy wind. The box which had contained the skull was lying in fragments on the floor. The skull itself was undamaged and was upon one of the shelves of the cabinet.

After that Kilner lost no time in getting rid of his ill-acquired trophy. He gave it to a friend of his, Mr F. C. Hopkins, a retired official of the Commissioners of Prisons who had bought old Bury St Edmunds gaol where Corder had been hanged, and was living in the governor's house.

Somewhat reluctantly, the retired prison official accepted the unwelcome gift and took it home wrapped in a silk handkerchief. On the way home he fell and sprained his ankle, and the skull rolled, grinning evilly, in front of a lady who fainted on the spot.

This was only the beginning of disasters for Hopkins too. Illness, family troubles, financial misfortunes, quickly overtook him.

He did the wisest thing and took the unwanted relic to a country graveyard where he bribed a grave-digger to give it a Christian burial.

Thus Corder's skull got its ardently desired peace, and thereafter, we are told, both the Hopkins and the Kilners flourished.

It will be seen that these hauntings resulting from murder do not run to pattern. In the case of William Corder, he returned from the shades fifty years after his crime and expiation, not because he was a troubled, uneasy spirit, but because he was, presumably, annoyed

at the use to which his precious skull had been put. This is a widely observed characteristic of ghosts. They are very touchy about the skulls belonging to their mortal and long-discarded remains, and a skull can create a most remarkable haunting.

Jane Clouson's ghost hovered in Kidbrooke Lane in reproachful protest because her murderer never paid for his crime. The victims of Landru, however, the French mass-murderer, are said to haunt the Forest of Rambouillet, which is not far from his infamous Villa Ermitage where he used to lure women and murder them for their few paltry possessions. Landru was condemned and executed on 25 February, 1922.

Perhaps it was the sheer quantity of Landru's victims which caused the restless spirits of Rambouillet. He was condemned for the murder of eleven women, though he is believed to have killed many more. The French police at one time put the figure as high as three hundred. The eerie wailings and sobbings of the Forest of Rambouillet have been heard by a number of people.

For several years after the execution of Landru, bodies of murdered people were found in the forest, and the mystery of these deaths has never been solved.

Local legend has it that Landru himself—who went to the guillotine protesting his innocence to the last in face of incontrovertible evidence—returned to the scene of his former crimes as an evil spirit and entered into the bodies of innocent people and made them commit these murders. This at least would explain why the murders remain a mystery, for motiveless crimes are the most difficult to solve.

The celebrated Dick Turpin was in reality a coarse and vicious thug, despite the rather more romantic legends which have gathered around his name. He beat up and tortured his victims with pitiless brutality.

Once he fractured the skull of an old farmer and then poured boiling water over his head, while taking it in turns with his companions to rape the maid. On another occasion, when he met with an old woman's refusal to reveal the whereabouts of her valuables, he exclaimed: "God damn your blood, you old bitch! If you won't tell us, I'll set your arse on the grate." And he and his thugs sat the poor old lady in the fire until she finally had to tell where her money was.

Turpin was hanged at York in 1739, jumping off the ladder in order to secure for himself a quick end. Despite his brutalities, he was a very popular criminal of his day, and was hanged amid the

ecstatic plaudits of the mob. But he doesn't seem to be having it so good in the other world, for his tormented ghost has been seen riding on horseback at Loughton in Essex with the ghost of the old woman he had tortured in the fire, clinging to his back.

Jack the Ripper caused the greatest murder sensation of the nineteenth century, and his horrific deeds of death naturally attracted people of a psychic turn of mind. The year was 1888.

Stories of hauntings naturally followed these memorable murders. A headless woman was seen night after night sitting on a wall in Hanbury Street, Spitalfields, near the spot where 47-year-old Anne Chapman was murdered and savagely mutilated by Jack the Ripper, who had cut her head right off and then tied it in place with a handkerchief.

Millers Court, where the Ripper killed his last known victim, Mary Kelly, echoed with her ghostly screams for long afterwards.

Some people suggested that Jack the Ripper's crimes were connected with witchcraft, and that his murders were a species of black magic. He certainly seemed to employ some strange ritual in the way he arranged not only the belongings of the women he murdered, but also the organs he took out of their bodies. This was particularly noticed in the case of Mary Kelly, the only murder he committed in the comparative safety of a room. It was thought by some people that in this murder he was obsessed by ideas of human sacrifice and obscene magical rites.

Be that as it may, he was never caught and the psychologists, rather than the occultists, have a more plausible explanation of his actions.

Black Shuck—the Dog of Death

The moon rose, red and round, over the wild, wet levels of Wicken Fen. There the swamps and pools, reed-beds and waterways are still much as they were nine hundred years ago when Hereward the Wake threw back the Norman knights and men-at-arms in the reeds on Aldreth Causeway. There was until recent years an inn on the river bank which bore the enchanting name of "Five Miles From Anywhere—No Hurry".

A rough crew of turf-diggers, sedge-cutters, and dyke-dydlers sat by the turf fire in the sanded, red-curtained parlour. I said casually: "Well, who's coming home by the bank?" The short cut by the bank would save a mile on the road home.

"That owd Shuck Dog run there o' nights, master," said Jake Barton, spitting into the white ash of the turf fire. "Do ye goo, he'll hev ye as sure as harvest. I 'ouldn't walk that owd bank, not if I had to goo to Hanover."

"Ne me yet nayther," chimed in two or three. "Yew recollect what happened to one young woman. She up and died arter that owd Dog runned her!"

"Well, I'm going," says I. "Are you coming, Fred? Your way lies my way, and it'll save you half a mile."

Fred shied like a horse.

"No, sir! No, sir! Yew 'on't ketch me on that there bank at night. I 'ouldn't goo theer not for the King o' England! Ah! Yew may hev your gret owd duck gun but if we'd got machine guns, I 'ouldn't goo. An' ef yew goo, the owd Dog'll heve ye, sure as harvest."

I have known Fred since boyhood. He was my constant companion on shooting days in the Fen. He could jump a dyke like a greyhound, walk any man off his legs, drink a quart, fight anyone. That night he was scared—and admitted it.

"What are you scared of, Fred? Do you think we'll find a dead monk in the water like the one Jake thought he saw that night he was netting the dyke for fish?" I asked.

"No, I ain't skeered of no monkses. That's the Dog. He run that bank o' nights, big as a calf, Master Wentworth, black as tar, wi' eyes like bike lamps! Do[1] he see you, you'll up and die! There ain't a man what can see that owd Dog and live. Do he does, he'll goo scatty."

"But my father shot on the bank scores of nights after duck, Fred. He said the best flight was by the old black mill."

"I dessay, but he niver seed the Dog. Do he'd ha' been a dead 'un."

Fred told me that a few years before his sister, who went to meet her sweetheart by moonlight tryst at the black draining mill, had seen the Dog.

"The Dog, sir, cum along that bank quiet as death. Jest padded along head down, gret olde ars flappin'. That worn't more'n twenty yards off when that raised that's head and glouted (glared) at her— eyes red as blood. My heart! She shruk[2] like an owd owl and runned along that there bank like a hare. Run, sir! Nuthin' could ha' ketched her. I reckon if we'd ha' sent her to Newmarket she'd ha' won the Town Plate for us! She come bustin' along that bank like a race-hoss, right slap into her young man. He collared hold of her and she went off in a dead faint!"

"Did her young man see anything, Fred?

"Nit nothin'!"

"Well, she's still alive, Fred. The Dog didn't kill her. It won't kill us either."

"Ha! Take more'n an owd Dog to kill her. She's as tough as hog leather. But that wholly laid her up for a week and she've bin a 'clan-janderin' about it ever since."

So Fred did not walk with me by Spinney Bank that night. The presence of a double eight-bore and the promise of a quart of beer failed to shake the prestige of the Dog. And when I told him next day that I had walked home alone that night by the bank he answered: "More fule yew! But then, happen the owd Dog don't hut the gentry!"

[1] Do—if.
[2] Shruk—shrieked.

This legend of a ghostly dog persists all over East Anglia. A very dear friend, the late Lady Walsingham, about whom there was "no nonsense, my dear", believed in it implicitly. She had seen it!

One night at Leiston in Suffolk, on the coast, where the Dog is known as "The Galleytrot", she and the then Lady Rendlesham sat up in the churchyard to watch. At twelve precisely a slinking, sable shadow slipped among the gravestones like a wraith, leaped the low churchyard wall and slid down the dark lane towards the sandhills like an evil whisper. Neither of these self-possessed ladies drank, sat up late or had ever heard of Hannen Swaffer.

Now this Black Dog is the same mythological animal as Black Shuck, the enormous ghostly hound of the Norfolk coast who is said to pad along the cliff-top path between Cromer and Sheringham.

On the high coast road that goes dipping down through woods and over heathy commons where the sea-wind blows, between Cromer and Sheringham, there are villages whose inhabitants will not walk the windy miles of that lonely road at night if you were to offer them ten pounds and a cask of beer.

They are scared, these hardbitten Norfolk fishermen and ploughmen.

W. A. Dutt, in his book, *The Norfolk Broadland*, says:

"One of the most impressive phantoms, and one of the best known in Norfolk, is Old Shuck (from the Anglo-Saxon, Scucca or Sceocca, the early native word for Satan), a demon dog, as big as a fair-sized calf, that pads along noiselessly under the shadow of the hedgerows, tracking the steps of lonely wayfarers, and terrifying them with the wicked glare of his yellow eyes. To meet him means death within the year to the unhappy beholder. As Shuck sometimes leaves his head at home, though his eyes are always seen as big as saucers, he is, as Mr Rye says, 'an animal more avoided than respected'. One of his chief haunts is Neatishead Lane, near Barton Broad; but he also favours Coltishall Bridge, over which he always ambles without his head; and a very special promenade of his is from Beeston, near Sheringham, to Overstrand, after which his course is uncertain.

A curious variation of this ghostly hound is said to haunt an overgrown and little-used lane called Slough Hill in the parish of West Wratting on the Suffolk borders of Cambridgeshire. Police Constable A. Taylor, of The Tiled House, Panton Street, Cambridge, tells me that, in his youth, this lane, which is on the road from West Wratting to Balsham, was haunted by an extraordinary thing called

"The Shug Monkey". It was, he says, "a cross between a big rough-coated dog and a monkey with big shining eyes. Sometimes it would shuffle along on its hind legs and at other times it would whizz past on all-fours. You can guess that we children gave the place a wide berth after dark!"

He adds that Spanneys Gate into West Wratting Park was haunted by a White Lady.

Another believer in the Black Dog is Mrs Sophia Wilson, a native of Hempnall, near Norwich. Mrs Wilson writes to me:

"There is a stretch of road from Hempnall called 'Market Hole' and when I first lived at Hempnall sixty-one years ago, my husband told me that there was something to be seen and had been seen by different residents.

"Well, my dear husband passed on and I never really thought anything more about the incident until one night my son who was then about twenty-four came in from Norwich looking white and scared. I said, 'Whatever is the matter? Are you ill?' and he said, 'No. Coming down Market Hole I had a bad turn. I saw what appeared to be a big Dog about to cross in front of my bike and I thought I should be thrown off, but it just vanished. When I got off my bike and looked round, there was nothing to be seen, and I felt awful.' "

Another version of Black Shuck is said to haunt villages in the Waveney Valley round about Geldeston. It is known as "The Hateful Thing" or "The Churchyard or Hellbeast", and although usually seen in the form of a huge dog, it has been known to take the shape of a "Swooning Shadow", whatever that may be. It is a sign that some unusually horrible wickedness has just been committed or is about to be.

An old village woman claimed that she saw it when walking home at night from Gillingham to Geldeston. She tells the story in the following words:

"It was after I had been promised to Josh and before we were married that I saw the 'Hateful Thing'. It must have been close upon the time that we were to be married for I remember we had got as far as 'waisting' it.

"It was between eight and nine and we were in a lane near Geldeston when we met Mrs S., and she started to walk with us, when I heard something behind us, like the sound of a dog running. I thought it was some farmer's dog, and paid little attention to it, but it kept on just at the back of us, pit-pat-pit-pat-pit-pat! 'I wonder what that dog wants', I said to Mrs S. 'What dog do you mean?' she said, looking all round.

" 'Why, can't you hear it?' I said. 'It has been following us for the last five minutes or more! You can hear it, can't you, Josh?' I said. 'Nonsense, old mawther,' said Josh, 'just you lug hold of my arm and come along.' I was walking between Josh and Mrs S. and I lay hold of Mrs S's arm and she says, 'I can hear it now; it's in front of us; look, there it be!' and sure enough just in front of us was what looked like a big, black dog; but it wasn't a dog at all; it was the 'Hateful Thing' that had been seen hereabouts before and it betokened some great misfortune.

"It kept in front of us until it came to the churchyard, when it went right through the wall and we saw it no more."

She said that many people in the district had seen it and that its favourite haunt was the "Gelders", which was a local name for a clump of trees by the wayside on the Beccles Road. Mr Morley Adams adds:

"I found from conversation with other folk in the neighbourhood that her words were quite true; but apart from this woman, I found no one who had actually seen the beast, but they all knew someone who had. I gained the following further information about this weird wraith: At times it is seen as a large black dog, with eyes of fire and foaming mouth. If no fear is shown, he will walk just behind you, but his paws make no sound upon the ground. The person who sees him should not attempt to turn back or the beast will growl and snarl like a mad dog. He has been known to drag children along the road by their clothes, and dire disaster overtakes the individual who persists in running away from him.

"The people who are most likely to see the 'Hell-hound' are those born under the chime hours, or towards the small hours of a Friday night."

The same Dog runs in Essex along the lonely coast road from Peldon to Tolleshunt D'Arcy. William Fell, gamekeeper of D'Arcy, swore to me that he had seen it twice on Wigborough Hill.

The Black Dog is one with the Ghostly Hound of Dartmoor who haunts the moor and hunts terrified humans to their death in the quaking bogs. The Hound of the Baskervilles is a Dorsetshire version. All have their roots in the Hound of Odin, the mighty dog of war, whose legend came to Britain a thousand years ago when the long-ships grounded in the surf, the ravens flew at their mast-heads, there was battle and the clang of swords in the swirling mists, and "all around the shouts of war and the cries of sea-raiders beaching their ships".

In a letter dated 29 August, 1956, Mrs Barbara Carbonnell, who is deeply interested in folklore and church architecture in Devon, offered to send me various notes connected with the widespread legend of the Black Dog "together with some well-authenticated instances of its appearance in the County of Devon".

It will be noted that her hauntings all seem to occur in the vicinity of an "old straight road", precisely the same sort of road as the Peddar's Way in Norfolk and Suffolk. Mrs Carbonnell writes:

"These notes cover a period of roughly six to seven years. I began to interest myself in the legend of the Black Dog about 1923, and from then until 1931, followed every tale I heard, visiting the places concerned and talking to people of all classes, getting in touch with others who had left the neighbourhood and generally checking all information.

"About 1925, I became aware that there were a remarkable number of legends about it occurring on one particular stretch of road, and that this particular piece of road had the remains of a far earlier road forming part of its ditch.

"I had recently interested myself in the theory put forward by Alfred Watkins in his book *The Old Straight Track*, and it occurred to me to try if a straight line plotted on the map between the two points, Copplestone and Torrington, where legend said the Black Dog 'ran', would give me any clue as to where further legends of his appearance would emerge.

"It must be remembered that, in the first instance, I was only told by a man, at that time our gardener, that his father had several times seen 'the Black Dog of Torrington' that haunts the road by Stopgate, on the way to Copplestone, when, on his rounds as van man to a firm of millers, he came along that road at night. It was only after confirming this with the man himself, and learning from others that the dog had been seen near Stopgate, that I decided to 'plot' my line from Torrington to Copplestone (with extensions to the edges of the maps). I found instances of Black Dog hauntings in places through which the line passed, which otherwise it would not have occurred to me to visit.

"The whole distance, across country, from Copplestone westwards to the coast is no more than twenty-six to twenty-seven miles, and since I got no evidence of any 'Haunting' in the last five miles, the distance where such evidence did occur would be about twenty-one miles.

"In these twenty-one miles I was well rewarded by the stories I got from the country people, stories which had a certain similarity

but which were told me without any prompting from me. I was well known in that part of the country, and it was my habit to go off either alone or with my husband, and get into conversation with farm folk and villagers asking for old tales of the countryside. I did not deliberately start asking questions about the Black Dog. It was known that I was engaged in getting notes for Parish history, that I was engaged in transcribing Parish Registers, and that any 'old tale' about olden days would be well received. In this way ghost stories were bound to crop up, and this was how those of the Black Dog emerged.

"I have given the accounts of what I was told briefly, confining myself to what my informants said, using as far as possible their own wording from my notes written at the time.

"A van driver, who first told me of his experience at Stopgate, was a man then between sixty-five and seventy, a most respected and respectable man, a Plymouth Brother and strict teetotaller, who for nearly forty years had driven the miller's wagon between Copplestone Mills and Torrington.

"IIis work kept him out to all hours; two heavy horses and a load of sacks, doing that journey sometimes three times a week in all weathers, meant long hours, and often it was not before the early morning that he got back to Copplestone.

"When asked about the Black Dog, he was quite willing to tell me of his experiences. He seemed to consider it nothing unusual to see 'they sort of things', while admitting that he was 'scairt' the first time, hastily getting under the shelter of the van hood (his van was, of course, a heavy four-wheel one with a stretched canvas hood) when the Dog 'appeared' the first time. Rather than remain seated on the side of the shaft, as was his custom, he said that as the years went on and he became familiar with the Dog's appearance, he did not trouble to do so, often walking at the head of his team regardless of the 'gurt Hound' running beside him, 'so big as a calf' were his words.

" 'But', he added, 'I durstn't touch him, nor speak when he were by.'

"I found no legend of such haunting to the east of Copplestone, on extending the line in that direction; and taking into consideration the fact that all my informants spoke of it as the Black Dog of Torrington, and of its 'running between there and Copplestone', I made little search on that side, concentrating on the NW line, but probing beyond Torrington towards the coast, with some success.

"The results of these years of search are small, but certainly give

some idea of the strong hold such legends have and how the apparitions, as described to me, have a definite likeness.

"In the years when I was following up these clues, motor transport in the out-of-the-way parts of Devon was by no means so common as today. Though a number of farmers, even then, had cars, very few villagers had a motor-bus service connecting them; and even now, thirty years later, there is only a small proportion of the places named which have.

"There was, and still is, a very definite 'cliqueyness' about Devon villagers, which not even modern conditions has really broken down. Their own parish, their own church (even if they don't attend it very regularly), their own customs, and, very strongly, their own legends, are strictly their *own*, not to be confused with those of other villages, and in getting these stories I seldom found anyone willing to admit that the haunting known by them could have any connexion with that in any other neighbourhood.

"Numbers of people, living in and near Copplestone, spoke of the Black Dog of Torrington that comes to Copplestone Cross, but, except for the van driver, none of them spoke of seeing it, and, as will appear, his experience of the spectre was at a point some three to four miles farther west.

"At Down St Mary, a hilltop village, with an ancient Saxon church with tympanum, said to be pre-Domesday foundation, numbers of villagers spoke of hearing the Torrington Dog baying and 'rushing' up this lane on dark nights. It was said to be specially noisy as he 'tore by' the Smithy, and I was told that the old smith (dead before I began my search) had often seen it. From the top of the Lane, the Black Dog crossed the road and went rushing between the Church and Schoolhouse, 'knocking down the corner of the Schoolhouse' as he headed for the lane beyond. He reached the Schoolhouse always about midnight.

"When I asked how it was that the corner of the Schoolhouse showed no signs of damage, the old man who had told me this shook his head and replied:

" 'Well, there 'tis, he do knock'n down. I've a-heard the stones fall as he goes rorin' by, and I've heard the same from my father and grandfather time and again. It's true, right enough.'

"Another man told me how, when he was a lad, he and several others of the same age were going home after a choir supper at Christmas. Their way lay down the lane towards Copplestone and, as they passed the smithy, they all heard the Black Dog of Torrington coming up the lane. They ran into a field and saw a great dog

'as big as a calf', quite black, with shining eyes, pass the smithy and go towards the Schoolhouse. It was baying as it ran, and, as it passed the Schoolhouse, they heard a crash 'like stones falling in a quarry'. They did not venture out into the lane until they heard the sound of baying growing fainter and there was nothing to be seen. 'Us ran for it, to git back home,' he added.

"I heard this sort of story from others in the village.

"Following the lane from the Church at Down St Mary, the line goes through the farm called Thorne, and passes through the crossroads of Stopgate, Blackaditch (so called, though the modern signpost omits the second 'a') and Aller. It was along this stretch of road, which for some 32 miles has a deep ditch where the earlier road ran, that the Line conforms closely, and it was on this stretch that the van driver so frequently saw the spectre of the Black Dog of Torrington. From Aller Bridge the Line diverges from the main road through Holm (farm).

"In Wembworthy there were vague tales of 'something' that haunted the road by Smithen; there is nothing more definite, but the name Smithen is suggestive.

"At Wyke or Week Hill, St Giles-in-the-Wood, as at Hollocombe, the country folk were not inclined to speak of legends, and when, tentatively, the Black Dog of Torrington was mentioned, I noticed a secretive look (called in Devon 'looking sideways') as they shook their heads.

"The Line I had plotted ran here parallel with, and close alongside, a steep hill road to the SW of the village, called Wyke or Week Hill (spelt both ways locally), with a farm called Allens Week at the top. Having found the St Giles's search unrewarding, I should have given up hope of any tales hereabouts, but, on my return home, I remembered that the woman who kept the village shop in our village of Bow came from St Giles's, and that her father still lived there. Next day I went down to the shop. She had from time to time told me many trifles of local history, and was well aware of the interest such things had for me. I told her I had been to St. Giles's and asked: 'Did you ever hear of the Black Dog of Torrington?'

"As I spoke, two village women came through the door, and, to my surprise, Mrs Jewell, usually so friendly and forthcoming, snapped, 'No, never', and transferred her attention to the two who had come in, most pointedly bidding me good morning.

"Puzzled by her manner, I left the shop and went on down the village. Half an hour later, as I passed the shop again, Mrs Jewell came to the door, caught me by the arm and said:

" 'Come back, do. I've a lot to tell you,' and pulled me into her parlour behind the shop.

" 'What did you want to know about the Black Dog of Torrington?' she asked. I told her I wanted to hear any tales of it that I could and particularly if there were any stories of it having been see in St. Giles-in-the-Wood.

" 'It's always about there. Everyone knows of it,' was her reply, but she added: 'it's bad luck to speak of it there', and—hesitantly— 'I'm not sure if it's a good thing for me to tell you of it now, but I've seen it myself several times when I was a child living there, again when I was a young maid, and, once again, years later.'

" 'Where, in St Giles's, did you see the Black Dog?' I asked. Her answer came: 'On Week Hill. He's all about in St Giles's Parish. but mostly he runs on Week Hill. That's where I first saw the old thing.'

"In great detail she told me her experiences, sending her daughter-in-law into the shop, and speaking in a low tone, for she said, 'if doesn't do to talk loud about such things, and I wouldn't want people here to know what is seen in St. Giles'.

"This is what she told me:

"When about ten years old, roughly in the early 1870s, she was walking back with her father after Harvest Festival supper in the village round about 11 p.m. Their way lay up Week Hill, where they lived in a cottage near Allen's Week. 'It was a moonlight night and suddenly a sound of something panting came from behind us, and a great black dog"as big as a calf"with great shining eyes came alongside us. I caught at Father's hand and cried out. Father said, 'tis the Black Dog! Hold my hand, don't speak, walk along quiet and don't cry out.' "

"For the most part of a quarter of a mile the dog kept beside them. She described how huge it seemed, how its tongue hung out 'like a great piece of red flannel', and how when she and her father turned off the road to their cottage the dog kept on past the gate 'and then disappeared'. Her father told her he'd seen it 'many a time', and it didn't do any harm, but, she added, she was shaking with fright and could not sleep for thinking of it.

"She did not see the spectre again until she was about fourteen, when, with two other girls, she was returning from one of the farms. Again the Dog was on Week Hill; the girls were crossing a field path leading to it. All three saw it running with its nose to the ground and baying 'as loud as a pack of hounds'. On another occasion, just before she got to her home, it passed her, 'appearing

right in front of me and rushing by and gone in a flash as though it had never been there when I jumped out of its way.'

"Many years later, after she married, she and her father were driving home from Torrington market and between Great Torrington and Allen's Week, the Dog suddenly came from the ditch and made the pony shy and bolt. She assured me that even recently (this would be between 1925–30) the Dog has been seen in St Giles's, but that no one would be willing to speak of it.

"From a friend who, at that time, lived at Little Silver, a mile or so NE of Allen's Week I learned that the road near there was said by the country people to be 'haunted', but he was very vague as to what the haunting was.

"At Frithelstock, on the hill above the River Torridge, stand the ruins of a Priory adjoining the east end of the Parish Church. The Priory was built in the seventeenth century; there are several references to it in the Bishop's Registers (Exeter) and in the fourteenth century the Bishop found that the monks had badly fallen away from Christianity, had built themselves an altar to Diana, in the woods above the river, where they worshipped. Accordingly, he visited the Priory, forced the monks to destroy the Altar, 'and with their own hands, drag the stones away', removing all traces of it.

"The road on which the following incident occurred is a new road, cut out of the hillside along the bank of the River Torridge in the middle of the nineteenth century, the old road from Torrington to the west going up through the village of Frithelstock and passing between the Smithy and the Church and Priory.

"At the point where the incident recorded took place, the road, for half a mile, has sheer rock to a height of twenty feet on one side, with the river, bounded by a wall, immediately below, and at this point wide and swift flowing. My plotted Line extended from Torrington, across the Torridge in the Parish of Weare Gifford. The distance from the point on the road, as the crow flies, is one mile.

"The incident occurred on the road below Frithelstock Priory in January, 1932.

"In 1932, we were living two miles out of Bideford at a vicarage, where my married daughter and her husband were spending part of the latter's leave with us. He was in the Administration in Tanganyika Territory. One night in January, 1932, while staying with us, they went over to dine with a relative living at Winkleigh, and returned home soon after midnight.

"Their route to and from Winkleigh lay through Torrington from Bideford. I did not see them on their return, but at breakfast next

morning my daughter asked in a casual way did I know of any instances of the Black Dog legend occurring between Bideford and Winkleigh.

"My reply was to tell her a little of the instances I had at Stopgate, Down St Mary, and St Giles-in-the-Wood.

" 'Nothing on the Torrington–Bideford road?'

" 'No,' I replied.

" 'Well, listen to this,' she said, and told me the following.

"She and her husband, returning from Winkleigh, passed through Torrington soon after 11 p.m. It was not a dark night. Though sometimes cloudy, there was a small moon.

"As they drove along the road beside the Torridge below Frithelstock, there suddenly appeared in the headlights what she described as 'the most enormous black dog I've ever seen', so suddenly, and so near, that her husband who was driving braked so hard as to stall the engine, to avoid hitting it. They both saw the dog, and both felt sure the front of the car must hit it. When the car stopped, the dog was nowhere to be seen.

"I fetched my map, and she and her husband identified the spot where this had happened. There was nowhere the creature could have gone other than up the sheer cliff on one side or over the wall into the river on the other, and there was no sign of him on the straight piece of road ahead or behind. He had, in fact, completely disappeared.

"My daughter described the incident as 'most uncanny'. Asked by me how big the dog was, she replied, 'bigger than any dog I've ever seen, quite black.'

"My son-in-law, who had always been strongly sceptical of such legends, and who had often expressed belief that those things were always capable of a normal explanation, agreed with the facts she had told me: indeed, he stressed the way in which the creature seemed to appear without any sign of where it came from, and the equally sudden way in which it disappeared without a trace.

"Later, on checking my Torrington to Copplestone Line, I found that the place on the road where this happened lay one mile from the Line across the river Torridge.

"Mr Freeman, some time Rector of the Parish, then a man of nearly eighty, told me in 1923 that the legend of the Black Dog had been current in Thorverton in his day.

"There is (or was, forty years ago) an Inn standing at the corner of a lane on the outskirts of Lyme Regis called the Black Dog Inn, and lending its name to the lane where there was the legend that the

spectral Black Dog ran nightly, and at midnight 'knocked down the corner of the Inn'.

"Near Thelbridge there is an area called Black Dog, which thirty years ago was not even a hamlet, only an inn of this name, and a smithy there. It lies on a crossroad a mile or so south of Thelbridge.

"There is some legend of a Black Dog haunting in the neighbourhood of Tiverton, but the details I cannot give you. I was told of it by a man of the name of Blackmore, an exceedingly well-educated, superior type of man, who was gardener to a friend of mine who, in 1926, was living at West Hill, Ottery St Mary, Devon.

"He told me he and his father had both seen the Black Dog, that he knew many people in the Tiverton area who were quite certain that it appeared from time to time, adding that he knew of several other places where people he knew had seen it, but only in his own area had he had any experience of it."

Mrs Carbonnell's researches add more to the general knowledge of the Black Dog legends in Devon than any previous individual researches have contributed.

The Strange Haunting at Ballechin

The ghosts of Ballechin House, Perthshire, did not acquire anything like the fame of their spectral counterparts at Borley Rectory. Yet this Scottish haunting is in many ways a better one. It was perhaps more accurately observed and authenticated than the Borley haunt, and though it was enlivened by controversy, it is not tainted with the kind of suspicion which fell upon the great Borley haunting after the death of its sponsor, Harry Price.

The Ballechin haunting is relatively unknown, despite the fact that it has everything that a good haunting should have—house guests freezing with cold and fear in a lonely Highland mansion, ghostly nuns weeping by a frozen burn, spectral tattoos of a fearsome nature, the disembodied paws of a dog, to mention only a few of the unexplained phenomena which chilled the spines of the people who stayed at Ballechin.

The furious controversy which arose over the haunting and which raged in the stately columns of *The Times* during the year of Queen Victoria's Diamond Jubilee, was merely over the propriety of whether the matter should have been investigated by members of the Society for Psychical Research without the permission of the owners of the property.

This raises an interesting point as to whether the ownership of a house gives one any rights in respect to the ghosts which might be haunting it. This is not a matter which is ever likely to engage the attentions of a court of law, and need not detain us, for what

happened at Ballechin during those haunted 'eighties and 'nineties is much more interesting and exciting.

Ballechin House is in a splendid Highland setting, a few miles from Logierait, overlooking the valley of the River Tay before it is joined by the Tummel below Pitlochry. Not far away at Dunkeld is a famous distillery which produces spirits of a different order.

The Steuart family owned the estate since the sixteenth century. The Steuarts were the lineal descendants of King Robert II of Scotland. Ballechin House was built in 1806 to replace the ancient manor-house which was then demolished and which stood on a different site.

The Steuart who apparently caused the haunting was Robert, who was born in the year of the building of Ballechin House. In 1825, at the age of nineteen, he went to India and became an officer in the army of the East India Company. Twenty-five years later he retired with the rank of Major. He had inherited Ballechin in 1834 on the death of his father. When he arrived home from India in 1850 he found his house occupied by tenants, and he built himself a small house in the grounds, called Ballechin Cottage, where he lived until the tenancy expired, when he moved into the big house.

Major Steuart had a pronounced limp, presumably acquired during his service, active or otherwise, in India. He was unmarried, but kept a young housekeeper. He had two brothers and six sisters. One of these sisters, Isabella, became a nun, assuming the name of Frances Helen, later to become a key figure in the haunting. She died in her nunnery on 23 February, 1880.

Old Major Steuart, who died in 1876, was a great eccentric. In India he had made a study of the supernatural, and he firmly believed in transmigration and of spirit return after death. During the quarter of a century he lived at Ballechin he acquired a reputation in the district for being a very queer bird.

He filled the house with dogs, his favourite being a large black spaniel, whose body he proposed to occupy after his death. Why the old Major should have expressed preference for a dog's life in the other world we do not know, and there is no intention here to speculate upon the workings of his eccentric mind. But people who prefer the company of dogs to that of humans are not uncommon. Presumably the next stage is the desire to become a dog.

However, the "mad Major's" intention to enter the body of his black spaniel was taken seriously enough by his heirs and relatives, who upon his death promptly had all his dogs shot, thus forestalling, as they imagined, the Major's post-mortem intentions. Obviously his

spiritual society on a canine level, or indeed on any other level, was not desired by his relatives.

Under a will made in 1853 the Major left Ballechin to the children of his married sister Mary. There were five children of this marriage. The eldest son died in 1867 without issue, and the following year Major Steuart added a codicil which excluded the three younger children from any benefit under his will. This left John, the second son, who inherited Ballechin on his uncle's death in 1876, and who immediately changed his name to Steuart, in order presumably to maintain the family tradition, if not the direct family line.

This John Steuart was a Roman Catholic, as was his aunt Isabella, still secluded in her convent. The old Major had been a Protestant, and was buried in the churchyard at Logierait beside the grave of his previously mentioned 27-year-old housekeeper, Sarah, who had died suddenly and mysteriously in 1873.

Whether their lying side by side in Logierait churchyard paralleled in any sense their relationship during their life time at Ballechin House is a matter upon which there was much interesting speculation, though it was too delicate a matter to be touched upon by the Victorian ladies and gentlemen who investigated the old Major's post-mortem activities twenty years after his death.

But it was well noted that Sarah died in the main bedroom at Ballechin, which became the most haunted room in the house. The ghost of the old Major was often heard limping around the bed in which she breathed her last.

John Steuart enjoyed the amenities of Ballechin and the income that went with the estate for twenty-one years. He was a married man with several children. His eldest son went into the army, his youngest became a Jesuit priest. During John Steuart's lifetime Ballechin Cottage, the small house his uncle had built in the grounds when he returned from India in 1850, was used as a retreat for nuns. The Steuarts were a devout Catholic family.

It was during this time that the haunting started. Not long after the old Major's death, Mrs Steuart was doing her household accounts in the room which used to be the old man's study when suddenly the room began to smell overpoweringly of dogs. She remembered that this was how the place smelt at the old Major's death when they had all the dogs destroyed. As she sat at her little desk smelling the doggy aroma, she felt herself being pushed against by an invisible dog. It seemed that the execution of the Major's unfortunate dogs had not been sufficient to frustrate the intentions of their late master's disembodied spirit.

Ever since the Major's death Ballechin had been troubled by knockings and mysterious sounds, like explosions, and the sound of people quarrelling came suddenly from nowhere into the middle of a room in the most eerie fashion.

Servants would not stay. The strange goings on at Ballechin became the talk of the neighbourhood and it gained the reputation of being the most haunted house in Scotland.

In the late 1870s the governess of the Steuart children became alarmed at the queer noises in the house and left. Many other people complained of the noises. A Jesuit Priest, Father Hayden, who was staying in the house, said that the noises seemed to come from between his bed and the ceiling and sounded like continuous explosions of petards, so that he could not hear himself speak.

Father Hayden, who was at Ballechin for the purpose of giving spiritual ministrations to the nuns staying at Ballechin Cottage, complained to his host about the noises. John Steuart thought they were caused by the old Major, who was perhaps trying to attract Father Hayden's attention in order that prayers might be offered for the repose of his soul.

The good Jesuit priest was alarmed by other things, particularly by the sound of a large animal, such as a dog, throwing itself up against the bottom part of his door on the outside. There was no dog there to cause such a noise. Father Hayden also heard taps and knockings and something which sounded like a scream.

The Steuart family were very reticent about the haunting, and would have nothing to do with any investigation of it, but John Steuart himself is reported to have seen a procession of monks and nuns from a window, and there was corroboration from a totally independent source of Father Hayden's report of the curious noise overheard between the bed and the ceiling, from a married couple who later occupied the same room as he did.

Evidence that the haunting was assuming frightening proportions was seen in the fact that in 1883 a new wing was built at Ballechin House for the express purpose of providing rooms for the children of the family outside the haunted area.

This gave Ballechin House a total of twelve bedrooms, eight of them on the first floor in the main part of the house. On the ground floor was a spacious hall and three large reception rooms. In the basement, apart from the kitchens, and pantry, were a smoking-room and a large billiards-room. Servants were accommodated in the attics. One bathroom served the needs of the whole house, the front elevation of which was in Georgian style broken by a bold

central bow, which gave the house a certain character, if not distinction.

There seems little substance in reports that Ballechin was haunted before the death of Major Steuart in 1876. Its ghostly reputation was acquired in the two decades which followed the demise of the eccentric old psychic, whose peculiar beliefs seemed to spark off some unaccountable happenings.

John Steuart, after, it can safely be assumed, having led an exemplary life devoted to the interests of the Roman Church, was gathered to his fathers in the January of 1895 in sudden and tragic fashion, the event being preceded by a startling omen on the morning of his departure for London on some family business. He was talking to his agent in the study when their conversation was interrupted by three knocks so loud and violent that the two men had to interrupt their conversation. Later that day the master of Ballechin left for London to meet a sudden death in the busy streets where he was run over and killed by a cab.

The next Steuart of Ballechin was a Captain in the Army, who had had enough of the haunted family house on the lonely Scottish hillside and had no desire to live there. It had 4,400 acres of shooting and he had no difficulty in letting it for the 1896 grouse season to a wealthy family whose identity was cloaked behind the description of their being "of Spanish origin".

Captain Stewart did not tell his tenants that Ballechin was haunted. They took it for a year, paying the rent in advance, and hurriedly evacuated the house after seven weeks of nightly terror and intolerable uproar for which they could find no physical cause.

The daughter of the house, terrified at the sound of a man limping around her bed, called in her brother, who then slept on the sofa. The limping began again and he heard it as well and agreed that someone was limping around his sister's bed, but neither of them saw anything. This was the room and presumably the bed in which Sarah, Major Steuart's young housekeeper, had died in 1873. The brother later claimed to have seen the ghost twice—once in the shape of an indeterminate mist and once in the shape of a man who came in by the door and vanished in the wall.

One lady who was a guest at Ballechin during that haunted September of 1896 wrote of the alarm caused by the violent knockings, shrieks and groans heard every night. Guests were awakened by blows upon their doors so violent that they expected the panels to burst in. When they opened their doors there was no one there.

There was one room, she said, into which even the dogs could not be coaxed.

The tenants did not return to Ballechin House, thus forfeiting the greater part of the year's rent which they had paid in advance.

The haunting was the subject of an article in *The Times* of 8 June, 1897, which made light of the whole affair. This was followed by a letter from a Harold Sanders, who was the family butler at Ballechin House during the haunted tenancy of the previous autumn. Sanders described the fearful uproar which disturbed everyone in the house, including the servants, and eventually drove them away. Parties of gentlemen, he said, sat up at night, armed with sticks and revolvers, vowing vengeance upon the disturbers of their sleep.

This redoubtable haunting had already received the attention of that band of devoted ghost hunters, the Society for Psychical Research, which had been formed in the 1880s. Following the flight of the 1896 tenants, several members of the S.P.R. decided to rent the place and investigate the haunting themselves.

The 3rd Marquess of Bute, who had been interested in the haunting since 1892 when Father Hayden had told him of his strange experiences at Ballechin during the lifetime of John Steuart, was the leading light in this most interesting investigation. Bute was himself a Scot. His family name was Crichton-Stuart. He was deeply interested in psychic matters, but he was unable to undertake the investigation himself, so he delegated it to Colonel Lemesurier Taylor and Miss A. Goodrich-Freer, both well-known psychical researchers of the 'nineties. Colonel Taylor took the lease in his name and the Marquess footed all the expenses.

Colonel Taylor was well known for his investigations of haunted houses, both in England and in America, and when he took on the lease of Ballechin House, Captain Steuart's agents in Edinburgh, Messrs Speedy, merely expressed the hope that the new tenant would not make the haunting a subject for complaint, as the last tenant had done. Taylor gave this undertaking, saying he was well aware of what had happened during the previous tenancy.

Bute and his investigators planned to invite guests to Ballechin who had knowledge of psychic phenomena, or who were open-minded and objective on the subject. None of them knew the history of Ballechin.

A hostess was therefore necessary, Colonel Taylor being a widower and without a daughter. Bute asked Miss Freer to undertake these duties and to begin the investigation in the absence of Taylor, who was pre-occupied with a family bereavement at the beginning of 1897.

Miss Freer, after having engaged a staff of servants in Edinburgh, took up residence at Ballechin on 3 February, accompanied by her friend, Miss Constance Moore, a daughter of the Rev Daniel Moore, Prebendary of St. Paul's, and Chaplain to Queen Victoria.

Thick snow lay on the ground. The gloomy house looked forbidding. Inside, wrote Miss Freer in her Journal: "It felt like a vault, having been empty for months. None of the stores ordered had arrived. We had no linen, knives, plate, wine, food and very little fuel or oil." After dining off bread and milk and a tin of meat which they bought in Logierait, they went to bed. "The room was so cold that we had to cover our faces, and we had no bed linen."

The two friends slept from exhaustion, for they had had a busy and tiring day in Edinburgh, but they were awoken at three in the morning by loud clanging noises echoing through the house. At 4.30 they heard sounds of voices. None of these sounds could be accounted for in the morning.

The house was paralysingly cold and they spent some days thawing out the icy rooms, and trying to make the place comfortable. "It will soon be very pleasant," wrote Miss Freer optimistically, "and only needs living in, but it feels like a vault."

The next night they heard a phenomenon which was repeatedly experienced during the investigation—the sound of someone reading aloud in the manner of a priest "saying his office".

The devotion and determination of these Victorian psychic investigators is something to be marvelled at. Their energy and patience were inexhaustible. Not only was Lord Bute willing to pay a substantial sum of money to maintain a large house-party for the sole purpose of a ghost-hunt, but his assistants and collaborators freely gave their time and were prepared to face possible dangers and considerable discomfort in pursuit of what they considered to be psychic knowledge. The lady ghost-hunters of that romantic age were no less intrepid than the men, and showed a toughness and tenacity which gives the lie to the legend of the frailty of Victorian womanhood.

They took their experiments and investigations at Ballechin in deadly earnest. They kept records and times of the observed phenomena, listed as "visual", "tactile" and "audile". They tried to reproduce the various noises by normal means, nearly always without success. They continually changed bedrooms so that a variety of reports could be collated on the noises heard in the different rooms.

They had a staff of servants to minister to their needs. Below stairs the ghost-hunting of the various lady and gentleman guests

was the subject of some derision, except by those servants who had themselves been frightened by paranormal phenomena. In particular was the continual change-round of bedrooms the subject of ribald comment in the servants' quarters, with jokes of a predictable nature.

A detailed account of the investigation was collated into one of the most curious ghost books on record entitled *The Alleged Haunting of B—— House*. This was a joint report by Miss Freer and Lord Bute, and it followed an acrimonious dispute over the whole affair with the Steuart family, with the result that nearly all the proper names, including that of the house itself, were suppressed. This book, now something of a collector's piece, was published in 1899 by George Redway of London, and is the main source of information on the haunting.

Miss Freer herself saw apparitions of nuns on the snow near the frozen burn several times. On the first occasion it was a solitary nun weeping in a way Miss Freer described as "passionate and unrestrained". Other times there were two nuns, one on her knees weeping while the other was trying to reason with her in a low voice.

These nuns were naturally related to the time of John Steuart when Ballechin Cottage was used as a nuns' retreat, although the weeping nun was thought to be Major Steuart's sister, Isabella, who it will be remembered had entered a convent where she died in 1880.

Psychic experiments in automatic writing were made with an apparatus known as a Ouija board, and messages were reported from "intelligences" giving their names as Ishbel and Marghearad (Gaelic forms of Isabel and Margaret). In reply to questions as to what could be done which would be of use or interest, the writers were told to go at dusk and in silence to the glen near the burn— the place where Miss Freer had seen the weeping nun and her companion.

It seemed that the haunting was centred around three sets of circumstances. Firstly, the nuns. What sin or sadness caused Isabella to weep so desolately in the snow-covered glen? With this was obviously connected the sound of the priest chanting, and later the appearance of a spectral crucifix. Secondly, there was the mysterious death of Major Steuart's young housekeeper, Sarah, which apparently made him limp eternally around the bed upon which she died—not in the servants' quarters, but in the best bedroom in the house, and ever since haunted. Thirdly, there was the Major's beloved black spaniel, into whose body this strange old man wished

to enter after death, and which was shot remorselessly with all the other dogs in a vain attempt by the family to prevent this happening.

Animal ghosts have been reported before, but none is better attested than this case. It will be recalled that Mrs John Steuart felt the phantom dog brush up against her while in the Major's study shortly after the old man's death in 1876, and during the next twenty years a number of people reported the pattering of the feet of invisible dogs, sounds as of wagged tails striking on doors and wainscots, and frequently the noise was heard as of a dog blundering up against a door.

A Pomeranian aptly named Spooks shared with Miss Freer the most frightening and unnerving of all these canine experiences. The dog slept on Miss Freer's bed, and in the middle of the night of 4 May, 1897, Miss Freer was woken by the animal uttering terrified whimpers. Lighting her candle Miss Freer saw Spooks staring in terror at the table beside the bed. Following the animal's gaze, Miss Freer saw a pair of black paws, and nothing else, resting upon the table. "It gave me a sickening sensation," she said.

The party had servant trouble, of course. Some of the maids were terrified of the noises in the house and left. The cook didn't believe in ghosts, but thought the house "very queer" and the mysterious noises made her feel uncomfortable. She told Miss Freer that Ballechin was famous all over the countryside for being haunted, and that there was a story that a priest had been murdered by the wife of a former owner. This was supposed to have happened about the time of the Reformation.

Even the most sceptical of the maids shared in the strange experiences of the other inhabitants of the house. Lizzie, the kitchen-maid. who had been greatly lacking in respect for her betters in the way she ridiculed the ghost-hunting ladies from the south, had the frightening experience of having her bedclothes torn off her by invisible hands, after which she spent half the night screaming. Carter, the upper house-maid, woke up one dawn to see plainly standing beside her bed half of the figure of a woman in a grey shawl. The woman had no legs. Her body ended at the waist and was suspended in the air. The petrified maid hid shivering under the bedclothes till morning when she fled from Ballechin never to return.

When Miss Freer and Lord Bute published *The Alleged Haunting of B—— House*, they clothed their book in such a cloud of anonymity that it made no impact at all. Few people knew what "B——House" was, despite the curious slip on page 82 where Ballechin is acci-

dentally printed in full. The silly squabble in *The Times* had been long forgotten, and to call it an "alleged" haunting was to belittle the book, for it was obvious that its authors did not regard it as an alleged haunting.

Thus the Ballechin haunting never acquired anything like the fame of Borley, though it well deserved to. The similarities between the two hauntings are remarkable. In particular a former owner of each house was morbidly interested in ghosts and vowed that he would come back and haunt after his death. And in each case—if we are to believe the evidence—he did.

Ballechin House finally went out of the Steuarts' possession. In 1932 it was bought by a Mr R. Wemyss Honeyman, who still (1965) owns the estate. In later years the house was uninhabited— at least by denizens of this world. Its end came in 1963 when it was demolished.

The Amherst Mystery

A strolling player, in the world of the nineteenth-century theatre, might see and experience many strange things. But Walter Hubbell, "an actor by profession, being duly sworn before a Notary Public in New York" in the year 1888, gave testimony of having been concerned with some even stranger events than are usual in his profession.

In 1879, he told his hearers, he had been acting with a strolling company in Amherst, Nova Scotia. They were based there for some little time, their repertory was familiar and needed no further rehearsal; Mr Hubbell found himself with some leisure time to fill in. His was a lively, enquiring mind, with a keen curiosity about the fashionable cult of Spiritualism, which had swept over America. Everywhere mediums had sprung up, and Walter Hubbell had given himself much satisfaction proving some of their "phenomena" to be fraudulent. Now, in Amherst, he heard of a conspicuously haunted house, and determined to investigate it.

The house, at first sight, did not appear particularly ghostly. It was a pleasant detached cottage, with a pretty garden, in it lived the Teed family—Daniel Teed, a highly respectable and respected foreman in a shoe factory, his wife, as "good a woman as ever lived", according to her neighbours, their baby, little Willie, and Mrs Teed's two sisters, Jennie and Esther—both pretty girls, but Esther particularly attractive with her large dark-lashed grey eyes, tiny hands and feet, and frank, charming expression. John Teed, Daniel's brother, also lived in the somewhat crowded house.

The trouble had begun one night. Jennie, who shared a bed with Esther, had been suddenly awakened by her sister leaping out of bed with a scream, and a cry of: "A mouse! there's a mouse in bed with us!" Search revealed no trace of any mouse, and the sisters went back to sleep.

Next night, also in the girls' bedroom, violent rustling noises were heard in a green band-box which stood on the floor. After a few minutes, to the sisters' alarm, the band-box rose a foot in the air of its own volition, and went up and down several times. When it had returned to its normal position Esther screwed up her courage and opened it. But it was quite empty.

Next night an even more alarming thing happened. Esther, who had gone to bed feeling unwell, found herself to be swelling up, as if from some dreadful disease, until her body was almost twice its usual size. When her family rushed in, summoned by the cries of her and her sister, they were further alarmed by loud peals of thunder—or what sounded like thunder—which suddenly peeled out, under a bright evening sky without a cloud in it.

Esther's swelling subsided, but next day she was still unwell, and could only eat "a small piece of bread and butter, and a large green pickle". Four nights later, all the bed-clothes covering her and Jennie flew off as if ripped away by invisible hands, and came to rest in a corner of the room. Once more the Teeds rushed in to investigate, and found the uncovered body of Esther "fearfully swollen", even more so than before. Her sister replaced the bed-clothes, but they instantly flew off again, and the pillow struck John Teed a smart blow in the face. "I've had enough of this!" he declared, and left the room without waiting for further manifestations. But the rest of the family bravely remained, and seated themselves all round the bed, holding down the struggling bedclothes with the weight of their bodies. Again the mysterious peals of thunder sounded, in the midst of which Esther suddenly fell peacefully asleep, the bedclothes settled down, and the family tiptoed away.

The local doctor, Dr Carritte, was summoned next day to examine Esther. While he was doing so, the bolster beneath her head launched itself at him, struck him a violent blow on the head, and then soared back into place under Esther's. The doctor staggered to a chair, overcome with shock; and while he sat there, nerving himself to continue his examination of the girl, he heard a metallic scratching noise coming from the wall behind him. Turning to see what it was, he found on the wall the sentence:

"Esther Cox! You are mine to kill."

This was the first of many pieces of writing, all of a threatening character, which "came out of the air and fell at our feet", the family testified. While the mystified doctor was examining the writing on the wall, bits of plaster fell from the ceiling and began to whirl about the room, while the peals of thunder renewed themselves. Terrified, Dr Carritte left.

It says something for his courage that he returned next day. This time, as he bent over his patient, a hail of potatoes from an invisible source flew at him and sent him reeling across the room. More prepared for trouble than on the previous day, the intrepid doctor produced from his bag a bottle of sedative mixture and administered some to Esther (we are not told whether he took one himself). The medicine, however quietening its effects on the girl, had no influence on the manifestations—loud pounding noises were heard from the ceiling, and continued until the doctor had left the room.

Now the clergy began to take an interest in the case—which they somewhat oddly attributed not to the supernatural, but to electricity, a discovery of which America had become conscious—commercial electric lighting had been in use for about three years, and electric trams and street cars for about one. But general knowledge of the powers of electricity was not wide. The reverend gentlemen's curiosity seems to have been keen, for they visited the Teed house for months, and were only driven away when poor Esther fell ill with diphtheria. On recovering, she went to recuperate at the house of some friends in Sackville, New Brunswick. Her departure brought peace to the Teed home; nor did any haunting trouble the house at Sackville while she was in it. But once she was back in Amherst, the nuisance broke out again with redoubled force. "I'll burn your house down!" cried a voice—and a rain of lighted matches fell from the ceiling, to be promptly extinguished by the family, who by now were prepared for almost anything.

But having begun to play with fire, the ghost could not leave it alone. His next trick was to set Mrs Teed's ample skirts on fire. She was more frightened than hurt, and the subsequent fires started about the house did little actual damage. However, the heads of the Amherst fire-brigade heard of the incidents, and suspected that an arsonist—probably Esther—was at work. Threats were uttered against her—the righteous Dr Nathan Tupper suggested that she should be flogged, as a way of driving out the evil. Her brother-in-law promptly removed her for safety to the house of a Mr White. But the ghost (now known as Bob, by which name he signed some

of his communications) had got really expert at fire-raising, and continued his larks in Esther's absence. A piece of iron placed on the girl's lap "became too hot to be handled with comfort" and then flew away like a ponderous bird.

At this point the inquisitive and sceptical Walter Hubbell came on the scene. He spent days with the Teeds, and very much to his own surprise could not find any of the evidences of fraud he had expected. Was Esther, then, a genuine medium? "There's money in this!" thought the astute young man, reared as he was in show business. He decided to become impresario to Esther, exhibiting her on a platform while he delivered a lecture and "Bob" obliged with manifestations.

But his idea was doomed to failure. The exhibition took place, but the only objects to fly through the air were those hurled at Mr Hubbell by the spectators, and the only loud noises were their hisses and boos. Bob had failed to oblige, as is the way of ghosts when called on to perform tricks. Back to Amherst came poor Esther from her unsuccessful tour. Mr Hubbell, still determined to find out more about Bob, moved in with the patient Teeds, and had ample evidence of the reality of the hauntings. In Esther's absence from the house, his own umbrella and a large carving knife threw themselves at him furiously, and only his natural agility saved him from serious injury. As he was getting his breath back, a huge armchair moved ponderously out of its corner and charged at him like a bull. "To say that I was awed would indeed seem an inadequate expression of my feelings," commented Mr Hubbell with restraint.

The ghost's next trick was really unkind. Three times was little George Cox, Esther's brother, undressed in public by invisible hands, to his great distress. Then Bob returned to his favourite pastime of fire-raising. Walter Hubbell's own words are the best account of his reactions to this.

"This was my first experience with Bob, the demon, as a fire-fiend; and I say, candidly, that until I had had that experience I never fully realized what an awful calamity it was to have an invisible monster, somewhere within the atmosphere, going from place to place about the house, gathering up old newspapers into a bundle and hiding it in the basket of soiled linen or in a closet, then go and steal matches out of the match-box in the kitchen or some-body's pocket, as he did out of mine; and after kindling a fire in the bundle, tell Esther that he had started a fire, but would not tell where; or perhaps not tell her at all, in which case the first intimation we would have was the smell of the smoke pouring through the

house, and then the most intense excitement, everybody running with buckets of water. I say it was the most truly awful calamity that could possibly befall any family, infidel or Christian, that could be conceived in the mind of man or ghost. And how much more terrible did it seem in this little cottage, where all were strict members of church, prayed, sang hymns, and read the Bible. Poor Mrs Teed!"

One member alone of the family had never been the object of Bob's malice. This was the cat, a sedate character who had reacted with calm acceptance to all the terrifying things that had been happening in her home. One day Walter Hubbell, looking down at her plump form comfortably couched on the hearthrug, observed: "At least *she*'s never been tormented." At this, the cat was instantly lifted five feet high in the air, suspended for a moment, and then dropped on the shoulders of the screaming Esther. "I never saw any cat more frightened," said Walter Hubbell later. "She ran out into the front yard, where she remained for the balance of the day."

Now the versatile Bob turned his attention to music. The Reverend R. A. Temple, minister at the Teeds' church, called to hold a meeting of prayer and exorcism—his own recipe, using slips of paper inscribed with a verse from the Prophet Habakkuk: "For the vision is yet for an appointed time, but at the end it shall speak, and not lie." The ghost retaliated not by speaking, as requested, but by loud and raucous trumpet-playing. This it kept up until Mr Temple rushed from the house; and, pleased with its own performance, continued to play afterwards until the wretched Teeds were almost deafened. The proceedings concluded with a sort of firework display of lighted matches.

Things had gone too far. Daniel Teed was only the tenant of the cottage; its owner was a Mr Bliss, who heartily disliked the way his property was being treated. He insisted that Esther leave at once. It seemed hard to part her from her family, but on the whole, they agreed, it was the best thing to do. Esther removed to the house of a Mr Van Amburgh, and Bob's demonstrations instantly ceased.

Only once did he break out again. Esther was accused of setting fire to a barn, in which she happened to be when it broke into flames. Now that the hauntings were fading from the public memory, she was arrested for simple incendiarism, and sentenced to four months' imprisonment. But those who remembered all too vividly the works of Bob pleaded for her, and she was soon released.

Like so many other young girls who have been the centre of supernatural happenings, when she married, as she soon did, all

the horrors ceased. She became a normal young matron, and faded from history.

And what of Mr Hubbell? It is not recorded that he entirely gave up his hobby of psychic research, but he certainly did not bring to it his former sceptical attitude. It would be satisfying to know that one of his roles was that of the Ghost in *Hamlet*.

Glamis, the Haunted Castle

Glamis Castle, the Forfarshire seat of the Earls of Strathmore, home of the present Queen Mother and birthplace of Princess Margaret, has had for many years the reputation of being "the most haunted house in Britain". Its outward appearance certainly does much to further this claim, with its high cluster of ancient-looking towers and turrets, in stone that is grim and almost frowning, apparently grey with age and heavy with the weight of time. Inside, too, many of the gloomy rooms, long stone-flagged corridors and cold echoing vaults, with walls which are in places fifteen feet thick, all combine to give an overpowering air of massive antiquity and eeriness— though there are some very charming suites of rooms and pleasant apartments also.

Built on the basic traditional pattern of a strong central tower surrounded by a fortified courtyard, Glamis lies in a valley about twenty miles north of Dundee. It is overlooked by Hunter's Hill, traditionally the location of the assassination of King Malcolm II of Scotland in 1034. The castle itself was at one time reputed to be the place where Macbeth, Thane of Glamis, murdered King Duncan in 1040; and a sword and a shirt of mail, both supposedly belonging to Macbeth, are on view in one of the rooms.

But no part of the building can actually be dated much earlier than about the end of the fourteenth century, and in fact only the central tower itself can definitely be ascribed to that period. Later additions, in deliberately feudal styles of architecture, are responsible for much of the "atmosphere"; over the years and the centuries,

successive owners have pulled down, rebuilt or added on different parts of Glamis, until now it is difficult to tell where the real ends and the imitation begins. There was extensive reconstruction, for instance, in the seventeenth century; new wings and passages were added, wide stone fireplaces were constructed, and the Great Hall on the third floor was constructed. But since that time many of these alterations have in their turn been altered again, or replaced with others, so that now it is not even certain which parts are "genuine" seventeenth-century building, and which merely imitations of it.

The site itself, however, is an ancient one which had been fortified and held for many centuries by the early Kings of Scotland. It was given by Robert II (grandson of Robert the Bruce) to his son-in-law Sir John Lyon when he made him his Great Chamberlain in 1372. Sir John began extensive building there, though presumably a ruined castle already stood on the site, but he was not able to complete the work, being mortally wounded in a duel in 1383.

His son, who became the first Lord Glamis, lived to finish his father's work, and he died a natural death in 1445, being one of the few members of the family who succeeded in living-out the whole course of his life peacefully and quietly. But *his* son, the second Lord Glamis, more than made up for his father's respectability: he was a notorious drunkard and gambler, known to all as "The Wicked Laird" and, because of his thick whiskers and long hair, also as "Earl Beardie". There is a portrait of him at Abbotsford, and he it was —as we shall see—who in time became a traditional bogeyman for Scottish children, his name being corrupted to "Earl Patie" by the Forfarshire peasantry.

But with none of these persons or events can Glamis Castle really definitely be associated, however. Written historical records are inadequate until nearly a hundred years later, when John, sixth Lord of Glamis, was living there with his young wife Janet Douglas, who was famous throughout Scotland for her dark beauty. He was living there, that is, until he was discovered one morning lying on the stone floor of an inner apartment, having died suddenly while eating a meal alone. His wife was charged with having poisoned him, but the evidence against her being insufficient, her trial was abandoned.

Six years afterwards, however, she was again on trial for her life, charged this time with plotting to murder no less a person than James V of Scotland, and also with being a witch. Her servants were bribed to give false evidence, and her young son was tortured until he agreed to assist the prosecution by committing perjury against

his mother. The beautiful Janet Douglas was found guilty, and was burned to death on Castle Hill in Edinburgh in 1537 "without any substanciall ground", according to Henry VIII's representative in his report from Scotland to his King.

The son's estates were annexed, and he was imprisoned. But after three years he was released, and after the death of James V his estates and possessions were restored to him and he became the seventh Baron Glamis. His son, another John like his father, also like him continued the family tradition of being involved in violence and misfortune, meeting his death at an early age in a street brawl with a number of the Lindsays, the hereditary family enemies of the Lyons.

By the time Patrick Lyon succeeded to the estates in 1660, Glamis lay almost deserted, badly neglected and poorly furnished, and the family's standing and fortune was at its lowest ebb. But Patrick was a proud, determined and methodical man. By what one of his contemporaries described as "a course of self-denial"—by which he meant refraining from the sort of riotous living, drinking, brawling and heavy gambling which most of his ancestors had indulged in— in a period of thirty years he succeeded in restoring both the castle and his family's fortune.

A man of great integrity and honour, Patrick was made the first Earl of Strathmore and he became a Privy Councillor in 1682, loyally serving James II of England until that monarch fled from the country on the arrival of William of Orange in 1688. There is good reason to believe that Patrick was deeply implicated in Jacobite plotting for the restoration of the Old Pretender, but two years later he eventually took an oath of loyalty to William.

Perhaps as a precaution for his own safety during these times, Patrick ordered many structural alterations to Glamis, chiefly to create a number of secret chambers within its walls. But methodically he kept a "Book of Record" of all the work which he had done, and this was discovered and published by the Scottish Historical Society in 1890.

In it can be read such entries as: "June 24, 1684. Agried with the four masones in Glammiss the digging down from the floor of the litil pantry off the lobbis a closet designed within the charterhouse there." Another entry on 25 July of the same year indicates that the work was being made more elaborate: "I did add to the work before mentioned of a closet in my charterhouse, severall things of a considerable trouble, as the digging thorrow passages from the new work to the old, and thorrow that closet againe, so that I now

have the access off one floor from the east quarter of the house to the west syde."

Patrick died in 1695, and once again tragedies began to occur regularly in the Lyon family. Patrick's son, the next in succession, died fighting at Sherrifmuir in the abortive Jacobite rising of 1715. His brother Charles then became Earl of Strathmore, and he was a lrue upholder of the Lyon family addiction to gambling. He was killed at the gaming tables in a fight in 1728. According to local tegend he was losing heavily in this game and to try to end his constant succession of losses persisted in betting on, staking all his possessions one by one until eventually he lost Glamis Castle itself to his opponent, who was one of the hereditary family enemies, the Lindsays. Incensed at this final indignity, Charles leaped to his feet, drew his sword and accused his opponent of cheating. In the fight that followed, he was run-through and died.

But this is yet another legend. Records show that he was in fact killed by a man called James Carnegie of Finhaven. The fight may well have been caused by an accusation of cheating, but as the estates and the castle have remained in the hands of the Lyons, the story of their being lost one by one must be only a fiction.

In the eighteenth century Glamis had a widespread reputation as a haunted building, full of secret chambers containing terrible secrets. Sir Walter Scott arranged to spend a night there so that he could experience its atmosphere for himself, and perhaps use it in one of his historical novels. He wrote afterwards that he found it a deserted and barely-furnished place, with suits of medieval armour standing in lines along its corridors. He was given a room which had a four-poster bed with tartan hangings, and he wrote "I must own that when the door was shut I began to consider myself as too far from the living and somewhat too near the dead". But to his disappointment he neither saw nor heard any evidence of ghosts or hauntings.

Numerous other people since Scott claim to have done so, however, and are prepared to swear that they have seen the gigantic figure of the bearded "Earl Patie" roaming the corridors of the castle. He is perhaps looking for someone to play cards with, since the original legend concerning him naturally features gambling. It was described by a ghost-story writer at the beginning of this century like this:

"Many many years ago, when gentlemen got regularly drunk at dinner-time and had to be carried to bed by their servants, there reigned at Glamis one 'Patie', known to all as 'The Wild Lord of

Glamis'. He was notoriously good at all the vices, but his favourite was that of gambling, and he would play even with the servants and the stable hands. One dark and stormy November Sunday night he called for the cards and, drinking heavily, demanded that someone should play with him. But no one would, not even any of the servants, as it was of course the Sabbath.

"In desperation Patie at last sent for the family's Chaplain, and demanded a game of him. But the cleric refused, forbidding all in the castle to desecrate the Sabbath with such things as cards, which he described in forthright tones as 'the deevil's bricks'. Finally Patie swore a terrible oath, and went grumbling upstairs to his room, saying he would play with the Deevil himself then.

"He had not been long in his room when a loud knocking at the door of it was heard, followed by a deep voice calling out and asking if a gambling partner was still required. 'Yes,' roared Patie, 'Enter, whoever you are, in the foul fiend's name!' A tall dark stranger, muffled in a long black coat and with a huge black hat, strode in and sat down at once at a table, swinging the door to behind him with a bang.

"The terrified servants who had crept upstairs and along the corridor to listen could hear within the most violent oaths and curses from both the players as the game got faster and more furious. Patie lost game after game, until finally he had nothing left to play with, and offered to sign a bond for anything the stranger should wish, so long as the game could continue.

"Greatly daring, the old family butler put his eye to the keyhole, so that he might spy what was going on within the room. But no sooner had he done so than there was a blinding flash of light and he fell backwards, rolling in agony on the floor, with a bright yellow circle round his eye. The door flung open, and Patie strode out furiously cursing the servants for spying on him—but when he turned to re-enter the room to continue his game, he saw that his opponent had disappeared, taking with him the signed bond—which was, of course, for Patie's soul.

"Pale and afraid, Patie knew then that the other gambler had truly been the Devil himself. The game had broken-up, he said, when suddenly and without turning round to look at the door behind him, the fiend had called-out 'Smite that eye'—and no sooner had he done so than a flash of lightning had crackled across the room and hit the keyhole into which the unfortunate butler had been peering.

"Patie lived on for another five years after this incident, but after

his death every Sabbath night in November his ghost returned to the room to play again with his opponent the Devil, and try and win back his soul. Shouts and curses and strange noises could plainly be heard by any who were brave enough to stay and listen nearby, until at last, so great was the annual disturbance that the incumbent Lord of Glamis many years ago had the passage leading to the room bricked up, since when Patie and his gambling companion have been seen and heard no more."

* * * * *

If Glamis depended only on this folk-tale for its reputation of "most haunted house in Britain" it would never have achieved such status, for the legend of "Earl Patie" is little more than a traditional mock-horror bed-time story for Scottish children, intended presumably to deter them from excessive card-playing, particularly on the Sabbath—and perhaps also from keyhole peeping.

But guide-books to the place are emphatic and unanimous in their constant reference to other and more real terrors, connected with the castle—nearly all of which spring from rumours of a hidden chamber within its walls, reputed to contain a terrible Strathmore-family secret. This secret is traditionally known only to three people—the possessor of the castle, his heir, and his factor (steward). "Why the factor should be one of the three", says one popular guide-book, "is a question which has always excited the Caledonian mind."

"There is an impenetrable mystery at Glamis," asserts another, "and the legend of Earl Beardie will not account for all the things which have been seen and heard there. All that is known, beyond all possible doubt, is that the secret of Glamis—whatever it is—is revealed to the heir to the estates on the evening before his twenty-first birthday: and though successive heirs, when they were young men, have made light of the mystery, after they came of age and the secret has been revealed to them, they have obviously found it so truly dreadful that they have never thereafter talked about it."

The rumours have of course inspired many guesses, both at the location of the secret chamber and at what exactly it does contain. By some it is said to have been the scene of Patie's gambling with the Devil and that he is condemned to stay there at play until Judgment Day: others are sure that the beautiful Janet Douglas still lives on, because she was a witch, and is now confined there, hideously old of course but quite indestructible. Some say that the Lyon family are cursed with an immortal vampire who was born into the suc-

cession hundreds of years ago, and has to be kept hidden for ever; and others again, that the secret chamber actually contains a pile of mouldering skeletons, all that now remains of sixteen members of the Ogilvy family who once sought refuge in the castle in the seventeenth century, and were treacherously kept prisoner there by their host and eventually starved to death.

Wild though these rumours are and always have been, they are persistent enough and long-lasting enough to indicate that there really is (or was, in fairly recent times) a genuine secret concerning Glamis. According to Lord Halifax, the Earl of Strathmore whom he himself knew personally became, after his twenty-first birthday, "a changed man, silent and moody and never smiling. And his own son, when his turn came to be initiated into the family secret, absolutely refused to be enlightened because he could constantly see the effect of it on his father".

The resident Earl of Strathmore in 1870 is quoted as having said to his wife: "I have been into the secret chamber, and I have learned what the secret is—and if you wish to please me, never mention the matter to me again. I can only say that if you could guess the nature of the secret, you would go down on your knees and thank God it was not yours."

But it seems Lady Strathmore, her curiosity aroused, persisted in her inquiries and approached the other person who knew the secret, the Earl's factor—who was described by Lord Halifax as a shrewd, hard-headed Scotsman, not given to exaggeration or gossip. He replied that it was fortunate she did not know the secret, and then looking earnestly at her went on very gravely: "If your Ladyship did know it, I assure you you would not be a happy woman.'

By 1880 a contributor to *All the Year Round*, the magazine which had in its early days been edited by Charles Dickens, wrote that a workman who had "recently" been carrying out some structural alterations to Glamis had on one occasion inadvertently driven his crowbar through what he thought was solid brickwork, and had discovered a large cavity on the other side of it. There being no one about to supervise him, he had enlarged the hole and climbed through, finding himself in a secret corridor. He had gone along to the end of this, and found a locked door; then, frightened at his own boldness, he had returned and gone to the foreman of the work, telling him what he had done. The Earl, who was in London at the time, had been hastily summoned back to Glamis by the factor. The workman had been given a large sum of money, as an inducement to him and his family to emigrate to Australia, which

presumably he had done, as he had never been heard of since.

At that period many strange sights and noises were reported by good authority: the wife of a former Archbishop of York, when she stayed at Glamis, said that she had seen a huge bearded man dozing in a chair before the fire in her room, and as she watched him he had groaned softly and slowly faded away. A Provost of Perth had seen this same figure too, and that of a lady dressed all in white, gliding silently about the corridors in the middle of the night. There were "strange, weird and unearthly sounds", said another lady, who reported being awakened one night by the feel of a beard brushing her face; and others had been disturbed by nocturnal crashes and bangs, usually at about four o'clock in the morning.

That inveterate and itinerant Boswell of the minor aristocracy, Augustus Hare, had stayed at the castle: and he noted in his diary that the Earl seemed to have a look of perpetual sadness. He had also, said Hare, built on a whole extra wing of the castle for children and servants to sleep in, because so many frightening things happened in the older parts of it in the night.

In 1908 a writer in *Notes and Queries*—by no means given to publishing mere sensationalism or idle gossip—referred to the current story "that in the castle of Glamis there is a secret chamber, in which is confined a monster who is the rightful heir to the titles and property, but is so unpresentable that it is necessary to keep him perpetually out of sight". And in 1925 another writer referred to the castle and "its inviolable secret, which is no nearer solution to-day than it was hundreds of years ago".

That there has been a mystery connected with Glamis Castle and the Earls of Strathmore there can be little doubt: and many o those who made guesses at what it really was were not as far from the truth as might have been supposed. The subject has recently attracted the attention of the contemporary writer and historian Paul Bloomfield, and after lengthy and most careful research he has now produced what may probably be regarded as the definitive solution of it. He reveals a story of a family haunted, not by a ghost, but by a living being who in their own eyes at least had brought shame upon them. To help to conceal it they used the traditions and legends concerning Glamis which were ready at hand, and encouraged inquirers to believe them: before long the family secret had become inextricably confused with old rumours, and what was current and real had taken-on the guise of a centuries-old mystery.

The painstakingly precise piecing-together of the painful and now long-passed family secret by Paul Bloomfield reads at times

like a detective-story, and the interested reader who wishes to study it at length is referred to his *Red Blood and Royal* (1965). Briefly, the story is this:

Bloomfield discovered in an early edition of Cockayne's *Complete Peerage* that in October, 1821, the first-born son (and consequently the heir) of the then Earl of Strathmore was recorded as having died within a month of his birth. He was in fact born severely deformed, probably mongoloid, and it was not thought that he would live for very long. When in the following year another son, Thomas George, was born, he was therefore registered and regarded as the family heir.

On the death of his father, Thomas became the twelfth Earl of Strathmore: but it was then revealed to him that he had in fact an elder brother *who was still alive*, but who was kept out of sight because of his physical and mental deformities. Thomas himself died at the age of forty-three, in 1865, childless: and the title and the estates then passed to his younger brother Claude, who was already married and had five sons.

On and on lived the first-born son of the eleventh earl; year after year fed and looked-after and excluded both from public view and from the position of Lord of Glamis, which in truth he could neither have filled nor even understood. It is he, Bloomfield suggests, who was the occupant of the "secret chamber", and the constant and unnerving problem which he was to his family came in time to be believed as a "centuries-old mystery" rather than the result of a well-meaning miscalculation about his likely age of death.

He remained alive probably until he was over fifty years old, during which time the succession fell in turn upon three men, each of whom had to be told who the rightful heir really was, and what he was. When he did eventually die, which Bloomfield deduces to have been some time in the 1870s, the next heir could then "absolutely refuse" to be initiated into the family secret—because there was no longer any need for the "mystery" to be perpetuated. The myths and legends had served their purpose at Glamis.

The "crashes and bangs in the night" which many guests have reported? Probably the old-fashioned mechanism of the central clock, whose weights rise and fall noisily within the central tower. And the bearded figure of "Earl Patie", and the white lady? Well . . . there is no doubt that many people have seen ghosts in many places; and certainly Glamis Castle, both by tradition and by appearance, would be a fine place for them. . . .

The Horror at No. 50 Berkeley Square

In 1890, the Society for Psychical Research organized an inquiry among the citizens of London to try to discover how many of them had had experience of ghosts and hauntings. Questionnaires were sent to seventeen thousand selected at random. Of these 15,316 replied that they had not had any such experience, while 1,684 replied that they had. This figure represents some ten per cent, and is certainly high; at the same time, however, it is not disproportionate for a city so old as London and so rich in its history of violence, strange events and ancient buildings.

At that time, in the 1890s, when Berkeley Square was in the hey-day of its elegance, No. 50 was one of the most famous of all London's haunted houses. Sightseers from other parts of London, and even visitors from the country, seeking a thrill which would cost them nothing, found their way to the Square and stood before the house, imagining what it might be like to submit to the experience of an encounter with the Nameless Horror.

The house itself served to heighten the chill spasms of cold which coursed down the spines of even the least imaginative as they stood gazing at it. It had been empty for many years, and its Georgian façade was pocked with every evidence of general decay. Window-panes were broken, and those that were not were covered with grime. Through some less opaque than the rest, curtains could be seen hanging tipsily from cock-eyed rods, their tatters moved by interior currents of air. The paint of the window-frames clung precariously here and there in flakes; the brick-work was shadowed with the

dark grease-dirt of the capital's soot-laden atmosphere. The area, leading to the basement, was a rubbish dump for torn and discoloured scraps of paper, bottles and the carcase of a cat. Even the house-agents' To Let sign contributed to the general dilapidation, for it hung crazily from its tilting post.

All this was bad enough, but the elegance of the rest of the houses surrounding the dignified railed-in garden of the Square accentuated No. 50's eccentricity, and added to the awesomeness of its supernatural tenant. Its identification as the Nameless Horror was, in itself, enough to provoke a response in anyone who recognized the existence of the supernatural; and it was an apt name, for, on the evidence of those who at one time or another claimed to have been in its presence, it had no human shape, nor any recognizable animal form. It seems to have been a presence rather than a ghostly object, though the horror expressed in the eyes and features of those who had challenged it and lost, indicated that it did at times make itself visible.

Before the house achieved its evil reputation it had resembled any of the others in Berkeley Square. But this conformist period did not last long. Its strange non-conformity descended upon it after it had been vacated by a tenant of the late eighteenth century, a Mr Du Pré, of Wilton Park, and was attributed to the fact that Du Pré had confined in its attics an insane brother, whose madness made him so violent that no one could approach him. He even had to be fed through a slot in the door.

Whether this unhappy man's restless spirit was the Horror or not it is difficult to say. For the room which the Horror haunted was not in the attics, but a bedroom on the second floor.

Rumours naturally tend to enlarge the reputation of a house so haunted; and it was certainly rumour on which the author of an article in the now defunct society magazine *Mayfair* relied when he wrote in 1888: "The house in Berkeley Square contains at least one room of which the atmosphere is supernaturally fatal to mind and body alike ... The very party walls of the house, when touched, are found saturated with electric horror. It is uninhabited, save by an elderly man and woman, who act as care-takers; but even these have no access to the room. That is kept locked, the key being in the hands of a mysterious and seemingly nameless person, who comes to the house once every six months, locks up the elderly couple in the basement, and then unlocks the room and occupies himself in it for hours."

Rumour also provided alternatives to the Nameless Horror. One

was that the haunting was by a child in a Scots plaid who is said to have been frightened to death in her nursery and afterwards wandered about the house wringing her hands and sobbing. Another purported that the ghost was of a man who had gone mad in an upper room waiting for a message which never came. (This is close enough to be a variation of Mr Du Pré's mad brother.) Yet another stated that the spectre was a young girl who threw herself from a top-floor window to escape the sexual importunings of a satyr-guardian who was also her uncle. She rarely came into the house, but fluttered outside a window like a bird, tapping on the panes, begging for entrance. None of these ghosts, however, has ever been authenticated.

This is not true of the Nameless Horror, who was vouched for by no less a person than Lord Lyttleton, member of that family whose experiences of the supernatural give them a valid claim to the title of being "the most haunted family in England". Lord Lyttleton demanded to be allowed to spend the night in the room, and when permission was granted, armed himself with two blunderbusses loaded with buckshot and silver sixpences. The latter, taking the place of silver bullets, were to protect him against any machination of witchcraft and the Powers of Darkness. He reported next morning that something had come into the room and leapt through the air at him. Fortunately he had been able to fire one of his blunderbusses at it, and it had fallen like a plummeting pheasant and then suddenly disappeared. Asked to describe what it was that had entered the room, he could not.

Even the Horror is differently described in two newspaper reports of the early nineteenth century. One maintained that it was the ghost of a man with extremely horrible features, white and flaccid, pierced by an enormous round mouth. (This has affinities with Mr Du Pré's brother.) The other report described it as a strange creature with many legs or tentacles, and declared that it was no ghost but a reptile of darkness which periodically emerged from the sewers of Berkeley Square. If this were so, it is odd that it haunted no other house in the Square—only No. 50.

Besides the Lord Lyttleton already mentioned, there are two authenticated accounts of encounters with the Horror. One is of a gentleman who refused to be deterred by the reputed fate of earlier victims and insisted on passing the night in the Ghost Room; the other is of two seamen of her Majesty's Navy who emulated the gentleman in all ignorance, one of whom afterwards gave a full account of his experiences to the Metropolitan Police.

Sir Robert Warboys, seventh baronet, was the first to challenge the Horror. He was a young man, just turned thirty. His patrimony was such that he could afford to live in fine style, while his tastes, though lavish, were well controlled, so that there was never any possibility of his becoming bankrupt, as so many of his class contemporaries, often much wealthier than he, became within a few years of inheriting.

His seat was at Bracknell, in Berkshire. It was a large Queen Anne country-house, yet not so large that it was a drain on his resources. It was beautifully appointed and furnished, the mirror of the impeccable taste of the wife of the third baronet who had built the house. His servants and his tenants admired, loved and respected him.

His fortune and his establishment alone made him an extremely eligible bachelor in the eyes of those mothers of nubile daughters senior to him in rank, at least up to and including Viscountesses. His striking good looks, virile deportment and sporting prowess made him even more eligible in the eyes of the daughters themselves. Even those mothers and daughters who knew of the presence at Warboys Hall of a darkly handsome manservant, and who had heard faint whispers that the relationship between master and man was not quite an orthodox one, did not deter them, just as it did not deter the servants and tenants from respecting, loving and admiring their master or from being on terms of cordial friendship with his personal servant, for the young men comported themselves with the utmost discretion.

When Sir Robert visited London he stayed at White's or Boodle's. He was always in Town for the season, and made two or three other visits of a week or two's duration at other times of the year as the whim took him or necessity drew him. Though most of his fellow clubmen were aware of the reason for his disinclination towards matrimony, only the most unreasonably bigoted found it necessary to boycott his company on this account. In fact, the majority of those who came into contact with him, whether knowledgeable or ignorant, found him a pleasant companion. His prowess as an expert shot and a hard rider to hounds, together with his patronage of the race-courses and the prize-ring, far outweighed his alleged secret sporting with the valet. In short, he was regarded as an honourable gentleman, a pleasant acquaintance and a good master.

Sir Robert was also a practical man. Warboys Hall was an eminently practical place. It had been built in the middle of a field— since converted into an English park—on ground that had no

history beyond a brief and indirect mention in Domesday. The house had no holes and corners which might provoke the invention of legends, and its former owners had died peaceably in their beds. No apparitions, no mysterious tappings and nothing at all that could have a claim to the supernatural had any attachment to the mansion.

Brought up in such surroundings it was not surprising that there should be "no nonsense" about Sir Robert, and this being so that when the conversation in White's smoke-room turned, one day, upon the haunted houses of London, he should feel constrained to pooh-pooh the existence of ghosts. He did it in such a way, however, that the believers felt they must convince him of the mistakenness of his views.

They soon discovered that he was not easily swayed, and it was when they were trying to find some argument that might at least make him reconsider his stand, that the then owner of No. 50 Berkeley Square came into the room.

"Here's a man you can't refute!" exclaimed Lord Cholmondeley.

"Oh," said Sir Robert, "and why not?"

"Because he has a ghost in his house—50 Berkeley Square. You must have heard of it!"

"I fear not, my lord," Sir Robert confessed.

"Benson," Lord Cholmondeley called to the newcomer. "The very man we wanted to see. We're trying to convince Warboys, here, of the existence of ghosts, apparitions and the like. Tell him about yours. He must be convinced then."

Benson looked at the company seriously.

"I hope your lordship will not press me," he said. "We prefer not to talk about it."

"What! You have one of the most famous ghosts in all London living with you, and you prefer not to talk about it?" Lord Cholmondeley expostulated. "Come man!"

"Perhaps it's because Mr Benson doesn't really believe in it himself," Sir Robert remarked.

Again there was a brief silence as they all looked at Benson to see whether he would respond to the challenge.

"We believe in it," he said at last.

"Have you ever seen it?" asked Warboys, who seemed to be intrigued now by Benson's patent reluctance.

"No, we have not," he was told.

"Then you've heard it, perhaps?"

"No."

"Then why . . . ?"

"Because, Sir Robert, the records are too well authenticated to leave any room for doubt."

Lord Cholmondeley brought his hand down heavily against his thigh.

"Now you've gone so far, man, surely you can tell him in outline at all events," he said to Benson. "Warboys is the most sceptical fellow in this matter that I've ever encountered. You obviously believe in the supernatural, as all the rest of us do. You have a duty to convert him, if only for his own sake."

So Benson gave way to the pressure of the company, and once having begun overcame his reluctance and made a full recital of the Horror, much of which was new even to the well-informed among his audience.

When he had finished, Lord Cholmondeley turned to Sir Robert. "There, Warboys," he said. "Changed your mind now?"

Sir Robert shook his head.

"I'm afraid not, my lord," he said. "My whole reason rejects the concept of ghosts and apparitions. Those who claim to have seen them have allowed themselves to be swayed by irrational concepts and, since they are predisposed, have placed themselves outside the control of reason. In such a state imagination can easily run riot. No, my lord, I do not believe that any practical man who sets store by reason has ever seen a ghost. As proof, you have only to look at Mr Benson, there, to see that he is an utterly rational man, despite what he has told us. He has lived at 50 Berkeley Square some ten years, he has said, and neither he nor any of his family or household have seen or heard the Horror."

"But he told us," remarked another of the group, "that he has kept the room shut up all the time he has inhabited the house. That's why he has not seen it."

Sir Robert laughed.

"My dear fellow, if ghosts are as active as you say they are, it presupposes that they have personalities of some sort," he said. "This one in Berkeley Square by all accounts has a most unpleasant personality. We all know that unpleasant personalities are people who force their attentions upon those with whom they come into contact. I submit that your—er—Horror would demand an audience, and if It were deprived of an audience, as you say, sir, It has been these ten years, It would have made Itself known in other ways. Ergo, since It has not done so, It does not exist.

"This is pure surmise, Warboys," Cholmondeley suggested.

"No more surmise, my lord, than your contention that the Horror exists."

Before any other voice could be added to the argument, a young man who, so far, had not spoken was heard to say: "Sir Robert, you're a sporting sort of fellow. Why not volunteer to spend a night in Mr Benson's haunted room; then we should all know."

"I could not possibly permit it, Sir Dougall!" Benson exclaimed firmly before Warboys could reply.

"I don't see that you would have any responsibility, sir," the young Scots baronet maintained. "Sir Robert is fully adult. If he is prepared of his own free will, without the slightest coercion, to challenge your Horror, the responsibility is entirely his."

"But . . ." began Benson.

"Young Forster's right, you know, Benson," Lord Cholmondeley said. "I'm sure that not a single one of us here, including Warboys, would hold you in the slightest degree responsible. What do you say, Warboys?"

"Certainly not, my lord."

"What do you say to Forster's suggestion?"

"I'm willing to take up his gage, my lord," Warboys smiled. "And what's more, I'm prepared to wager a hundred guineas to fifty with anyone here that I shall emerge from the room in the morning entirely unscathed. I undertake to hand over the whole of my winnings to—well let's say, since I am myself an orphan, to the Foundling Hospital."

"Well said!" exclaimed Cholmondeley. "Now Benson . . ."

"I still don't like it, my lord," Benson replied.

"Supposing all of us here come to your house on the night arranged and share the responsibility with you?" a Colonel Raynes suggested.

"That's an excellent idea," Cholmondeley agreed.

"I'm quite prepared to take any means to safeguard myself that you care to name, Mr Benson," Warboys said.

Benson looked round the company and gave a short laugh.

"I'll agree that Sir Robert has not been coerced in the slightest degree," he smiled. "But I shall always maintain, gentlemen, that I have been submitted to the most strenuous coercion from all present."

"Then you agree, Benson?" the Colonel asked.

"On condition that Sir Robert arms himself and that he rings for assistance immediately he feels he needs it," Benson said. "Further, that all of us shall stay on watch all night."

"Well, Warboys?"

Sir Robert bowed. "Of course. But I am quite certain my weapon will be unused next morning and no bells will ring."

"Right," said Cholmondeley. "Forster, be good enough to ring for the secretary to bring the betting book."

"There, gentlemen," objected Benson, "I must ask you to humour me. In my opinion this is not a suitable wager to be recorded in this or any other betting book. By the same token, Sir Robert, I hope you will excuse me from not responding to your wager."

This was agreed, the gentlemen merely stating their stakes. When all had done so, Warboys stood to win three hundred and fifty guineas, or lose seven hundred.

So it was all arranged. The gentlemen present were to dine at 50 Berkeley Square at nine o'clock three evenings from now. Next day, Benson sent his wife and children, their governess and nurse down to the country. When Mrs Benson pressed him for the reason, her husband adamantly refused, asking her to bear with him and he might explain later.

When the company met at the appointed time, an impartial observer would have noticed at once that not one of the gentlemen present was in normal control of his nerves. They talked more loudly with a bonhomie which they would have considered far from *comme il faut* either in their own drawing-room or in the club smoking-room. One or two had clearly attempted to fortify themselves beforehand, but nevertheless accepted the before-dinner drink which Benson offered them.

They raised their glasses to Sir Robert.

"We trust," said Lord Cholmondeley, "that it won't be too scarifying an experience for you."

"I am obliged, my lord, gentlemen," Warboys replied smiling, but again the observant would have noticed that his smile was fainter than usual, an uncertain flicker around his lips.

"Are you still as sceptical as you were, Sir Robert?" Sir Dougall Forster asked him.

"I would like to say yes. Indeed, I will say yes," Warboys told him. "On the other hand, I must admit that I am not quite so inwardly calm as I should expect to be. But that is the result of your treatment of the affair, gentlemen. I suggest that I would have to be unusually insensitive not to be affected by the excitement you are so kindly trying to hide."

"Look here, Sir Robert," Benson said, "if you would like to withdraw, I am quite certain that none of us would hold you to your undertaking. Am I not right, gentlemen?"

"Certainly," Cholmondeley agreed. "None of us would think the worse of you, Warboys."

"Come, Sir Robert," Benson went on. "Withdraw, I beg you. Let's turn the dinner into a celebration of discretion's superiority over valour, eh?"

Warboys shook his head.

"I am sorry, sir," he said. "If I withdrew I would never again take any pride in my self-respect. Please do not press me, gentlemen. I have armed myself, as you required. My pistol is in its case in the hall. You may load it for me, before I retire."

"Very well," Benson said. "We will press you no further, Sir Robert. But I would request one thing of you. Indeed, I think that as your host, I dare insist upon it."

"And that is, sir?" Warboys asked.

"That you will give your solemn promise that should anything happen and you should feel you need assistance, you will not hesitate to ring. My butler has rewired the bell so that it will ring here."

He pointed to the wall above one of the drawing-room doors.

"That is the bell there," he said. "We can be with you in two minutes of your ringing. You will promise that for my peace of mind, will you not?"

Warboys nodded. "Yes, sir, I will do that. But I will ask you something in return. If I need assistance—which I am convinced I shall not—I will ring twice. If I ring once, ignore it, since I may do so from sheer nerves, for I will confess to you again, gentlemen, that I am experiencing an internal excitement which I did not at all expect to do. Do you agree, sir?"

"Yes, I agree," Benson told him.

At that moment the butler announced dinner. Though Benson suggested that for the duration of the meal they should make no reference to what was to come, most of them seemed to find it difficult, if not impossible, to keep their thoughts, at least, free. The result was that the conversation was cast in an entirely artificial mould, which increased every guest's discomfort. Benson had gone to great pains in devising the menu, and his cook had excelled herself in its preparation. It ought to have inspired wit and brilliant talk; instead there settled over the dining-table an atmosphere that one can imagine attending a wake of Irish mutes.

Benson, at all events, was relieved when the port had gone round the second time and he could suggest the adjournment to the drawing-room. Here Warboys declined coffee and presently announced that he would be glad if his host would show him his room.

"I suggest we all go up," Cholmondeley said.

So they all trooped up to the second floor and were shown into the room which was now open for the first time in ten years at least. They saw a dark room, furnished with heavy furniture. A large four-poster bed faced the two windows which overlooked Berkeley Square; it filled at least one-quarter of the floor-space. Much of the rest of the latter was taken up with heavy mahogany chests and presses, two or three chairs and various small tables. Two lamps burned on commodes one on either side of the bed.

Going to the bed, Benson turned to Warboys and said, "Here is the bell-pull, Sir Robert. It works with great ease."

He gave it a vigorous pull, and in the silence the faint ringing of the bell in the drawing-room on the floor below could be heard.

"As you saw," Benson went on, "since the drawing-room is on the first floor, we have only one flight of stairs to mount and we shall be with you."

"Let me remind you," said Warboys, "not to disturb yourselves if I only ring once."

"Right," Cholmondeley muttered. "Well, let us leave him to it, gentlemen. Good-night, Sir Robert."

Left to himself, Warboys removed his coat, cravat and shoes and lay down on the bed, outside the covers, for the fire, which now glowed in the grate, had warmed the room. Beside his right hand he placed the pistol cocked; beside his left hand he arranged the tasselled end of the bell-pull. He did not expect to sleep, so he propped himself up on the pillows and prepared to watch out the night.

When the gentlemen returned to the drawing-room, the ormulo clock on the mantelpiece indicated twenty minutes past eleven.

"What shall we do?" Lord Cholmondeley asked. "Shall we organize ourselves into watches or what?"

"There is little need for that, I think, my lord," Benson remarked. "I for one shall not sleep, and in any case, if we do drop off, the bell is loud enough to waken the soundest sleeper. Though I pray God we never hear it."

"Amen," said Cholmondeley. "I confess this is a wager I shall be happy to lose."

So the company settled themselves, and sank into a drowsy silence. The hands of the clock on the mantelpiece approached midnight, and presently its silver chimes sprinkled themselves on the breathing room. Half-way through, they were joined by the more, masculine bass of the grandfather clock on the landing, and the

last of these was still vibrating in the air when the bell above the drawing-room door pealed shortly.

The men sat up, their half-stupor shaken off, their gaze fixed upon the bell.

Benson had started for the door, but Lord Cholmondeley reminded him of their undertaking. "He must ring again, Benson."

The last word was stifled by a second violent peal, so violent that the bell seemed on the point of jerking off its spring.

Benson was first through the door, with the others hard on his heels. Taking the stairs two at a time, he was half-way up when a shot rang out. Seconds later he flung open the door of the room.

Sir Robert Warboys was sprawled half on the bed, his head near the floor, his legs agape on the covers. In his left hand he grasped the bell-pull which had come away from its spring; on the floor by his out-flung right hand lay his pistol.

Benson knelt on one knee, placed his hands beneath the shoulders and raised the body on to the bed. It was only now, as the light from one of the lamps fell on to the face, that the onlookers drew in their breath, and young Sir Dougall Forster let out a cry.

"My God!" he exclaimed. "For God's sake cover him!"

For Sir Robert's eyes stared at them and his lips, drawn tightly back over his teeth, revealed the latter tightly clenched as though he were suffering an epileptic fit. But it was the ineffable terror, the stark dread, in the dead eyes that almost unmanned them.

"Is he dead?" Lord Cholmondeley asked in almost a whisper.

"Quite dead," Benson replied.

"How? Did he shoot himself?"

"No, my lord, it is no suicide."

"For God's sake cover him!" Sir Dougall urged again.

Benson drew a cover about the lifeless body and over the face.

"Let us go down, gentlemen," he said. "It is my fault. I should never have permitted it. It was like this with the rest."

"But what can it have been that struck such terror into him? Colonel Raynes asked, speaking more to himself than to the company.

"God knows!" Benson replied. "No one has ever seen It and lived."

The death of Sir Robert Warboys preyed so much upon Benson's conscience that within a few months he decided to vacate 50 Berkeley Square. It was now that the house entered upon its long tenantless period. For more than forty years it stood, gradually becoming more and more derelict, and it was shortly before the end of this time that the two sailors came upon it.

The frigate *Penelope* returned to Portsmouth, from a year or more's cruise in the West Indies, at the beginning of Christmas week, 1887, and after making their vessel ship-shape, the crew were paid off and given two weeks' shore leave. Among the ship's company were two young seamen, who decided that rather than slake their various thirsts in the tap-rooms and stews of Pompey they would make for the greater excitement of the metropolis.

They reached London the day before Christmas Eve, planning to spend twenty-four hours in carousal before they parted to join their families in Halstead, in Essex, and Reading, respectively, for the festivities. Unfortunately their recent deprivations had been so protracted that they lost all count of time.

They also lost all count of their money. So when at last they realized it was Christmas Eve they discovered, too, that they had no money to get them home.

Earlier in the day it had begun to snow and though it was no longer doing so, it was freezing hard.

"I'm not walking home in this," Edward Blunden said. "It'll get colder during the night. Besides, it may be possible to get a lift in a carriage tomorrow, at least part of the way. What are you going to do, Bob?"

"I'm of the same mind as you, Ted," Robert Martin answered. "We'll find somewhere to lie up for the night and see what the Christmas spirit turns up for us tomorrow. Let's start looking for shelter before we freeze to death."

It was as Martin said this that they turned into Berkeley Square.

"Well, we shan't find anything hereabouts," said Blunden.

"You never know, Ted," Martin remarked. "We may see some skivvy in an area who'll take pity on two poor waifs and offer to share with them the warmth of her attic."

"And pigs may fly, Bob!" Blunden retorted. "Let's make for Euston. At least we'll have a roof over our heads there."

"Why tramp all the way to Euston when there's an empty house at hand?" Martin asked, coming to a stop before No. 50 Berkeley Square, whose TO LET sign reeled askew on its pole, insecurely tied to the area railings.

They backed to the edge of the pavement and looked up at the dark house.

"Can't be anyone living there," said Martin. "Look at those broken windows."

"You may be right at that," his companion agreed. "Do you think we can get in?"

"Let's try the area."

So they made their careful way down the weed-overgrown steps. The door to the basement was closed securely, but a nearby window was hanging loose from its hinges. Without a word, Martin climbed through, followed by Blunden.

Martin pulled a stub of tallow candle from a pocket and lit it. Surveying the shambles in what had been the kitchen where Mr Benson's cook had prepared the dinner on the evening of Sir Robert Warboy's death, the two seamen were for a time speechless. Then Blunden said in an involuntary whisper:"No one's lived here for years. Let's see what the rest of the place is like."

Cautiously, the flickering candle casting the fantastic shadows about them, they mounted the stairs to the main hall. The dining-room, which led from the hall, was empty. In a far corner a dark object scuttled, its shadow thrown on to the wall momentarily monstrous.

"Rat! remarked Martin.

"Looked more like a sheep," Blunden said. "Look, it's gnawed away all the boards in that corner. What a hole!"

"We shan't freeze, anyhow, Martin pointed out. "There's plenty of wood for a fire. Come on, let's see if there's anything more inviting upstairs."

As they mounted the main staircase, the stairs seemed to register their objections at being trodden upon after so long a period, in shrieks of pain that went billowing up the well of the stairway, until they died away in the high distance.

"Eerie," remarked Blunden laconically.

"You're right," his companion agreed."Have you got another stub of candle handy, Ted. This stub's nearly done."

"For God's sake, don't let it go out, Blunden pleaded, fumbling in his pocket and producing a length of candle. When this had been lit, they continued with their exploration of the house.

All the rooms they entered had the same dank atmosphere, the same air of forbidding dilapidation.

"The place hasn't been lived in for years," Martin remarked. 'I wonder why? Because this is what they call a desirable residential London square."

"Maybe the owners died leaving no one to follow," Blunden suggested.

"But whoever looked after things would have to try to get what he could for it. Besides, you saw the To Let board down there. Someone's obviously trying to sell it."

"Yes, that's right. But it stumps me.

"Me, too."

While they had been talking they had mounted to the second floor, and having looked into the room at the back of the house they came to that overlooking the square. As soon as they crossed the threshold, both together gave an exclamation of surprise.

"This is the place for us!" Martin almost shouted. "Carpets on the floor, chairs, even a bed!"

"I don't like it," Blunden replied. "Let's go, Bob."

"Are you out of your mind?" Martin exclaimed. "I'll go down and get some of those rotten floor-boards and we can light a fire. We'll be as snug as bugs."

"I'd rather go to Euston," Blunden persisted.

"In heaven's name why?"

"Well, look. The rest of the house is empty, but this room's fully furnished, Why?"

"That's as may be," Martin said. "But you can see for yourself that no one's been in this room for years, even if it is furnished. Perhaps who ever lived here didn't like this furniture and it's to be sold with the house. Or perhaps he was moving to a smaller place, and the furniture was too big for it. Look at the size of that bed! It'd take four with comfort. . . . Come on, Ted, be reasonable."

By degrees, Martin wore down his friend's resistance, and presently a fire was burning in the hearth, before which the two sailors gratefully warmed themselves, while they ate the scraps of food which they had carried in their packs for just such an emergency.

"I told you we'd be snug here," Martin remarked. "And we are! You're glad we stayed now, Ted?"

"I suppose so," Blunden replied, though obviously not fully at ease.

"Well, I'm for bed!" Martin declared, throwing an armful of wood on to the fire. "What about you?"

"You go to sleep if you want," Blunden said. "I'll sit here for a bit."

Martin looked at his companion, his bewilderment showing plainly on his face.

"What is the matter with you, Ted?" he asked.

"I don't know, honest, Bob," Blunden replied. "But this place has a funny feeling. It's still giving me the shivers a bit."

"I don't feel it. You're imagining things. Come and sleep a bit, like I said. You won't get far on the road to Reading in the morning if you stay up all night. Tell you what, we'll leave a candle burning, if that'll help."

So once again Blunden allowed his friend to persuade him, and with a candle stuck in a bed of its own tallow on top of one of the commodes at the side of the bed, they lay down, and were presently both asleep.

The next thing that Martin knew was being roughly wakened by Blunden.

"What's up?" he asked. But though Blunden's lips worked, no sound came from them. With an obvious effort he raised a trembling arm and pointed across the room to the door.

The fire was still flickering in the grate; the candle on the commode made one or two grotesque shadows dance on the opposite walls. But apart from these, the room appeared just as it was when Martin had last seen it.

Puzzled, Martin asked again, "What's up, Bob? What's the matter?"

At last Blunden found his speech.

"Listen!" he said in a harsh whisper.

Martin listened intently. At first he could hear nothing. Then a sound reached him. Curious padding footsteps were mounting the stairs. They came slowly, with a long pause between each; but after each pause the next sound was undeniably nearer to the landing. Then they were on the landing itself.

"It'll be someone like us," Martin said quietly. "Someone looking for shelter. A tramp, maybe, who's seen the light from the fire. Hey, you outside? he called out. "We're in here!"

Again they listened, and heard the slithering steps approaching the door. Then slowly the door began to open, and as it reached half-way suddenly "something" glided quickly through the opening into the room.

Blunden let out a yell, as together they leapt out of bed. For a second or two they looked at the intruder, then Blunden, spotting a curtain rail propped up by the wall near one of the windows, made a dash for it. It was a false move, for whatever it was placed itself between the bed and the door, effectively barring escape from the room.

The shadow from one of the bed-posts fell across it, half obscuring it, so that neither man could make out its exact form. All they could see were two outstretched hands which looked like talons.

It stood for a moment like that, then gradually it began to edge its way forward towards Blunden, who let out a shriek and raised the curtain-rod over his shoulder, prepared to strike.

At the sound of the sailor's yell, the Horror began to move more

quickly, its feet making scratching sounds on the well-worn carpet. In doing so it left the door unguarded, and seeing his opportunity Martin leapt across the room, and tumbling rather than leaping down the two long flights of stairs he reached the front-door.

He said afterwards that he could not remember pulling back the rusted bolts which securely closed the door, but soon he was running along the square calling for help. As he reached the corner of the side-street by which he and his companion had entered the square only two or three hours earlier, he collided full tilt into a policeman on his beat.

"For God's sake!" he implored. "Come quickly!" and then collapsed, half-fainting at the policeman's feet. As the policeman bent over him there came the sound of crashing glass, followed by a series of cries, then silence.

He raised Martin to his feet and demanded, "What've you been up to then?"

"For God's sake, come quickly!" Martin repeated. "My pal ... and seizing the policeman's arm he dragged him into the square and to No. 50.

Seeing the open front-door, the policeman exclaimed, "My God, you haven't been in there!"

"Yes. We were sheltering there, upstairs in the room with the bed," Martin told him. "My pal's being attacked up there. Please ..."

"He was being attacked, you mean," the policeman said half to himself as he flashed his dark-lantern down into the area.

Martin looked down the lantern's beam, and on the flag-stones of the area saw the motionless body of Blunden sprawled on its back. But it was not the grotesque attitude of the limbs of his friend which caused Martin to collapse fainting once more against the rails. The look of indescribable terror in Edward Blunden's staring eyes was to trouble him in nightmares for the rest of his life.

The Bird of Lincoln's Inn

In January, 1901, four years after the Diamond Jubilee celebrations which marked the sixtieth year of her reign, Queen Victoria died at the age of eighty-two at Osborne House in the Isle of Wight. There the following day her sixty-year-old son Edward heard himself at last proclaimed King of England. His Accession Speech to the Privy Council—which he composed himself and delivered without any reference to notes—announced his determination to be a constitutional sovereign in the strictest sense of the word, and during the next session of Parliament which he opened the following month he took only one additional title—"King of The British Dominions Beyond The Seas".

After descriptions of the great State funeral of Victoria, and news and comment about the accession of Edward, who though he had now succeeded to the throne had yet to be crowned, contemporary newspaper readers then for a few months at that time had a quiet and unexciting period, with little to inspire or alarm them, or even merely to hold their interest.

During the first weeks of May, 1901, readers of the London *Daily Mail*, for instance, were chiefly concerned, like nearly everyone else in England, with the dull and apparently interminable accounts of the war in one of the "King's Dominions Beyond The Seas", South Africa. By then it had dragged on for over two years: though of course it was invariably presented in the Press as increasingly successful. Bloemfontein, Johannesburg and Pretoria had all been captured; and after long sieges both Ladysmith and Mafeking had been re-

lieved, and the war was in fact as good as over. But though their defeat was obvious to English newspaper readers the obstinate Dutch settlers, or "Boers" as they were called, refused to recognize it. They continued determined guerilla-resistance under their newly-appointed Commander-in-Chief Louis Botha (who was eventually to become the first Prime Minister of the Union of South Africa).

"Botha's March—Boer Move East With Five Guns—Another Raid On Cape Colony" were the headlines to one report from the *Daily Mail*'s War Correspondent in South Africa at that time: a young man named Edgar Wallace, who in later years was to earn world-wide fame as a prolific writer of detective stories and thrillers. An article by him on "How The War Stands To-day" gave, said the introductory paragraphs for it written in London, "a most interesting statement as to the condition of the Army, of a very reassuring character. It will be read with gratification."

Elsewhere in the same paper's pages was a report of an interview with the young Member of Parliament for Oldham, Mr Winston Churchill, who had returned the year before from South Africa where he had been held captive for a short period by the enemy. He stated that any rumours that the Boers had deliberately allowed him to escape were completely false, and a story to this effect by the Chief of the Transvaal Secret Police "was a lie from beginning to end. Not only did the Boers make no arrangements for my escape", went on Mr Chirchill in the interview with the *Mail*'s Lobby Correspondent at the House of Commons, "but they made every effort to effect my recapture. The whole suggestion is just the kind of desperate lying which one has learned to expect on any side of any controversy connected with South Africa."

From the continent there was news of a different kind. "Paris, Wednesday. The ingenuity of Monsieur Lepine, the Paris Prefect of Police, has no limits. After the *cycling agents* he has now inaugurated the *automobile police*. Their function is to chase the "chauffeurs" who persist in exceeding the legal pace. Hitherto offending motor men were watched and pursued by the *cycling agents*, but in the chase between the bicycle and the motor-car the policeman was bound to get left. But it has been remarked that the policeman will exceed the regulation pace himself—and so who is going to look after him?"

The paper's Correspondence Column was constantly agitated by a lengthy controversy on a subject which aroused fierce passions—the question of whether or not women should smoke in public. "Why will not a salutary fashion set in", asked one liberal-

minded writer, "permitting all women who so desire to smoke openly and in public without the stigma of being declared 'fast', outrageous, or 'bad form'? The life lived nowadays is so fast that women, no less than men, frequently much more than men, require a mild narcotic."

Next day a stern answer came from another correspondent. "Any scientific medical man or woman," he proclaimed, "who has studied the subject of nicotine knows that it is not very hurtful to the male, but acts quite in a different manner on the female." Any claim to "scientific" objectivity that the writer may have had then disappeared. "And Heaven forbid," he went on magisterially, "that ladies should smoke in the streets; for we already have too many degenerate hoydens."

But by far the strangest item of "news" which appeared in the *Daily Mail* of this period was a story which has since become famous, and has frequently been told and retold, and often with a great deal of imaginative embellishment. It first appeared in print on Thursday, 16 May, 1901, under the headlines "A London Ghost— Inexplicable Happenings In Old Chambers".

"The following story", it began, "is contributed by a Correspondent of the *Daily Mail* on whom every reliance can be placed. It seems inexplicable, but perhaps a solution of the apparent mystery may suggest itself to some ingenious reader. It is very easy to laugh at a ghost story, but here is one which, laughable or not, actually happened on the night between Saturday, 11 May, and Sunday, 12 May" (that is, five days before the report appeared), "in a house in a square, in one of the Inns within a stone's throw of the Law Courts."

The writer then attempted to define his own position: "A personal explanation is inevitable in a thing of this sort", he said. "But I will make it as short as possible. I am not a believer in ghosts, neither am I a disbeliever. I am no spiritualist, nor am I a sceptic. I simply don't know. But I *am* curious."

He then went on to describe the situation into which his curiosity had led him. "A rather well-known man of letters, a personal friend, took chambers about eighteen months ago in the said Inn, of which he is not a member. It was an old house, early Georgian probably, and consisted mainly of sets of lawyers' chambers. His rooms—three sitting rooms and a bedroom—were the only rooms in the building inhabited at night, save for the caretaker who lived in the basement.

"The writing-man's rooms were on the third floor, and shut-off

from the rest of the house by a short staircase and a solid door. He paid an unusually low rent, and explained this by admitting that there must be something queer about the rooms, as there had been seven or eight tenants in two years. They had one and all left in a hurry, and the agents were anxious to let at almost any rent.

"My friend filled-up most of the wall space with books, read, wrote, and mused during most of the day and part of the night, and he admitted to me in his more confidential moments that 'things happened' there. He did not specify exactly what occurred, but after a time he became nervous and fidgety. Last month he left the chambers rather suddenly, declaring he could stand it no longer. He cleared away all his belongings, and once more the rooms were empty.

"With another friend who is of much the same temperament as myself, I arranged an all-night sitting in these rooms where 'things happened'. Two chairs and a table were absolutely the only furniture left in the place. We unlocked the front door a little before midnight on Saturday last, locked it behind us, and turned on the electric light. We were alone in the house.

"After mounting the stairs from the outer door, there was a smallish room through which we passed into the principal apartment. This had a fireplace on the north wall and two doors in the south wall, through one of which was the entrance from the stairs. The other door was that of another small room which had no means of communication, so that there was no connection between the two small rooms save through the large room.

"We searched the place thoroughly, closed and locked the windows, and pulled down the registers of the three fireplaces. There was absolutely no possibility of anyone being hidden anywhere in the rooms. There were no cupboards, no recesses, no dark corners and no sliding panels. Even a black beetle could not have escaped unnoticed.

"The walls were entirely naked, there were no blinds or curtains. On the floor of the two smaller rooms we spread powdered chalk, such as is used for polishing dancing floors. This was to trace anybody or anything that might come or go.

'We had been warned that nothing happened in a room in which folks were watching. The doors leading to the little rooms were closed, and we sat in the big room and waited. We were both very wide awake, entirely calm, self-possessed and sober, expectant and receptive, and in no way excited or nervous. It was then about a quarter past midnight.

"We talked in ordinary terms, told each other tales, exchanged experiences, for we had both travelled a good deal; and curiously enough discovered we had a mutual friend whom we had never mentioned before, although we had known each other for years. I only mention these trivialities in order to imply that so far as I am able to judge we were in quite an ordinary frame of mind. We did not deem it necessary to feel each other's pulses or take one another's temperatures, but I am convinced that having done so we should have found ourselves to be entirely normal.

"At seventeen minutes to one, the door opposite to us on the right leading to the little room to which there was no communication save through the room in which we were sitting, unlatched itself and opened slowly to its full width. The electric light was on in all the rooms. The click of the turning of the door handle was very audible. We waited expectantly. Nothing happened.

"At four minutes to one precisely, the same thing occurred to the door on the left. Both doors were now standing wide open. We had been silent for a few seconds, watching the doors. Then we spoke.

" 'This is unusual,' said I.

" 'Yes,' said the other man. 'Let's see if there's any resistance.'

"We both rose, crossed the room and, expecting something, found nothing. The doors closed in the usual way, without opposition or resistance.

" 'Draught of course,' was our comment, and we sat down again. But we knew there was no possibility of draught, because everything was tightly shut. While the two doors had stood open we had both noticed that there was no mark on the sprinkled chalk.

"We talked again, but there was a tension, a restraint, which we had not felt before. I cannot explain it, but it was there. Longish silences ensued, and I am sure we were both wide awake.

"At 1.32—my watch was on the table with a pencil and sli p o paper on which I noted the times—the right-hand door opened again, exactly as before. The latch clicked, the brass handle turned, and slowly the door swung back to its full width. There was no jar or recoil when it became fully open. The opening process lasted about eleven seconds. At 1.37 the left-hand door opened as before, and both doors stood wide. We did not rise, but looked on and waited.

"At 1.40 both doors closed simultaneously of their own accord, swinging slowly and gently to within about eight inches of the lock, when they slammed with a slight jar; and both latches clicked

loudly, the one a fraction of a second later than the other. Between 1.45 and 1.55 this happened twice again, but the opening and closing were in no case simultaneous. There were thus four unaided openings and three closings. (The first time we had closed them ourselves.)

"The last openings took place at 2.7 and 2.9, and we both noticed marks on the chalk in the two little rooms. We sprang up and went to the doorways.

"The marks were clearly defined birds' footprints in the middle of the floor, three in the left-hand room and five in the right-hand room. The marks were identical, and exactly $2\frac{3}{4}$ inches in size. We are neither of us ornithologists, but we compared them to the footprints of a bird about the size of a turkey. There were three toes and a short spur behind. The footprints converged diagonally towards the doors of the big room, and each one was clearly and sharply defined, with no blurring of outline or drag of any sort.

"This broke up our sitting. We raised our voices to normal pitch, measured the footprints and made a sketch of them, lighted our pipes and sat down in the big room. Nothing more happened: the doors remained open, and the footprints clearly visible. It was just half-past two.

"We waited till half-past three, discussing things we knew nothing about. Then we went home, locking the outer door behind us and dropping the key in an envelope into the letter-box of the house agent's office nearby. On the Embankment we were greeted by an exquisite opal and mother-of-pearl sunrise.

"I have stated here exactly what happened, in a bald matter-of-fact narrative. I explain nothing, I understand nothing. I am not convinced nor converted nor contentious. I have simply recorded facts. And the curious thing about it is that my curiosity has not been cured."

*   *   *   *   *

Not surprisingly the story when it was first printed excited considerable comment. The next day the *Daily Mail* reported that many letters had been received "from people anxious to investigate the story set forth at length yesterday". But the report continued, obviously with the intention of deterring crowds of would-be ghost-seekers: "On referring the matter to our correspondent we learn that, at any rate for the present, it is not possible either to repeat the experiment or to give publicity to the address of the chambers."

But more serious investigators also had their interest aroused.

Mr E. T. Bennett, the Secretary of the Incorporated Society for Psychical Research, was enthusiastic about the story and told a *Daily Mail* reporter that it was going to be considered at the next meeting of his Society's committee. "The worst of these stories", he said, "is that as a rule when investigation is proposed their authors cannot substantiate them, and the stories themselves will not bear any inquiry. This particular story, however, seems to be told with sincerity and in a commonsense manner that is unusual in such cases. Therefore it becomes really interesting. One of the objects of my Society is to carefully enquire into alleged phenomena apparently inexplicable by known laws of nature, commonly referred by spiritualists to the agency of extra-human intelligence. This seems to me to be such a case, and I shall certainly bring it before the members of the Society."

But the results of his Society's inquiries were not published in the *Daily Mail*. Nor is there much reference to them in the Society's minutes or annually-published *Proceedings*, from which it may be concluded that little concrete or conclusive information was discovered to substantiate the story. Occasional references in the *Proceedings* through the years suggest what conclusions were reached. The writer of the article was seen, at some unspecified time and place, by Mr Pidding of the Society for Psychical Research, and told him "he and his friend had no anticipation that night as to what they might discover"—a statement which conveys more by what it omits to mention than by what it actually says.

Five years after the alleged occurrence, in 1906, another reference in the *Proceedings* sounds, in passing, a note of doubt about "the value of the story of the bird in the *Daily Mail*"; and the last reference to it of all, in 1913, is even more sceptical: "If reliance is to be placed on the statement of the writer in the *Daily Mail* it is a point on which judgment may be reserved.

Yet the story itself, unlike many ghosts, refuses to disappear, and over the years it has gradually gained credence as something which really happened. At different times and by different writers it has been described as "A story than which there is none more strange, more eerie or more macabre"; "One of the major mysteries of the ghost-hunter's world"; "One of the most ghastly authenticated hauntings of all time"; and "The terrible true story of the Bird Elemental."

As most popular writers of ghost-stories use one another as sources rather than go to the trouble of checking back to primary accounts, their stories show little variation apart from a few im-

provements in what might be called the "mise-en-scène". In one well-known version the two men are described as "sitting at a green baize table in a room blindingly lit by electric light, while the floor and walls shone with a ghastly whiteness", and on the table were "a bottle of whisky, a syphon of soda, a packet of sandwiches and a pack of cards". In another, the occurrence was described as "inopinate and inexplicable" and before the marks appeared in the chalk on the floor the watchers allegedly heard "scribbling noises at the windows".

No one has yet explained the significance of an apparently-invisible turkey, the point of the whole story, or what conclusions are meant to be drawn from it. That it is as one writer described it "One of the major mysteries of the ghost-hunter's world" is certainly true, for the whole story certainly has numerous mysterious elements.

Perhaps the major one is why the writer of it was not identified to readers of the *Daily Mail*—particularly as it was in fact that paper's own News Editor, Ralph D. Blumenfeld; and the friend he claimed to have been with him was Max Pemberton, at that time Editor of *Cassell's Magazine*, later a director of Northcliffe newspapers, who was knighted in 1928. Two such responsible and experienced journalists could have done much to substantiate the story by putting their names to it. Yet Pemberton never even referred to it in any of his own writings, and Blumenfeld concealed his own connection for many years.

When he did finally admit authorship, well over twenty years afterwards, he was adamant that the story as he had written it was true in every detail. "I've heard a lot of ghost stories in my life," he said to a friend who questioned him about it. "And I've sent a lot of reporters out on assignments to haunted houses. I don't believe in ghosts one way or the other—but I do know that this thing happened. We both heard what we heard, felt what we felt, and saw what we saw—but don't ask me for an explanation."

He was willing too to be a little more specific about the actual location of the house, being prepared to say that it was "actually in Lincoln's Inn". But he could—or would—give no more details than that: and anyway, he said, it would be impossible to find as the house had been pulled down after the First World War, and another building had been erected on its site. "No hauntings have been noticed there in the new building", he added.

In re-telling the story, he claimed that he had taken a twenty-four-hour lease of the chambers at the time of the incident, in an attempt to discover what happened there. He had himself ordered

all the furniture to be taken out, and the rooms stripped quite bare in preparation for the experiment. Apparently he was overlooking the fact, when he said this, that in the original printed version of the story which he wrote at the time, the occupant of the chambers had supposedly left, clearing away all his belongings and leaving the rooms empty. . . .

What really happened "in a house in a square in one of the Inns within a stone's throw of the Law Courts"during the night between May 11th. and 12th., 1901, it is now impossible to tell, and no really serious evidence as to the veracity of Blumenfeld's story can ever be produced.

But as a tail-piece to this story of an invisible bird there is one little curious and minor coincidence. On the night of 11 May, 1901, in Cambridge, over fifty miles away from London, and knowing nothing of what was going on in Lincoln's Inn, a medium named Mrs Verrall was sitting in the dark doing what she called her "automatic writing"—holding a pencil on a sheet of paper and allowing it to be moved about by any "spirit" which wished to use this method of communication. As usual she felt the pencil moving rapidly; and as usual she went to bed without looking at what had been written.

The following morning, when she looked at the paper, she thought it meaningless; there was a very roughly scrawled drawing and underneath it some words in Latin. "I showed the script to my husband next day", she said. "We could make nothing of it, and were much amused at the drawing of what we often referred to in the next four days as 'the cokyoly bird.' It was certainly a very strange-looking creature, rather like a child's drawing of a turkey: and underneath it was carefully written "Calx pedibus inhaerens difficultatem superavit". Which, roughly translated, means "Chalk sticking to the feet has got over the difficulty".

She kept the paper, and dated it. Four days later she read in the *Daily Mail* the account of what had happened in the chambers near the Law Courts.

Writing about the incident twelve years later in a paper for the Psychical Research Society, she described it simply as "a minor demonstration of precognition"—for by that time none of her fellow-members of the Society was prepared to accept, without reservation, the still-anonymous account in the *Daily Mail*. "But at least it shows that I was told what was going to appear in the peper", said Mrs Verrall—and it was left at that.

The Ghosts of Versailles

Marie-Antoinette was a figure of romance and tragedy. Legends have gathered around her. Ever since her death on the scaffold on 16 October, 1793, her ghost has haunted Europe both figuratively and literally.

In 1816 her daughter, who never forgave France, saw her mother's last letter written in the condemned cell and kept secretly by Robespierre, who knew what its value would be. It was yellow, stained and blurred with tears. ("Never seek to avenge our deaths. ... Oh God, how heartbreaking it is to leave my poor dear Children for ever!") By then Marie-Antoinette was already back to haunt Versailles, where on a memorable day in October, 1789, a breathless page ran to her with a letter warning her that the Paris mob was upon Versailles.

This particular day, said by tradition to be 5 October, became the centre of the most famous and most widely accepted of the world's ghost stories. But long before two English maiden ladies paid their celebrated visit to the Petit Trianon in August, 1901, the story of the haunting of the place by Marie-Antoinette had been told at Versailles. It was said that on a certain day in August not only does Marie-Antoinette appear in the gardens of the Petit Trianon, but also her courtiers are there to re-live that afternoon in the unforgotten past—perhaps the very last day of the *ancien régime.*

1789 had been a year of disaster for Marie-Antoinette. Her eldest son died, and so did her brother. She was blamed for being respon-

sible for France's bankruptcy, which was the immediate cause of the Revolution. On 14 July in that memorable year, the revolutionaries of Paris captured the Bastille and razed it to the ground, and on 5 October the mob marched on Versailles, the royal family were removed to Paris, and the long idyll of Versailles was over for ever.

On that last afternoon before the days of terror when the mob arrived at Versailles, Marie-Antoinette had sat sketching in her own private garden called the Petit Trianon. It was a pleasant October afternoon. The leaves were on the ground. The Queen, depressed by her thoughts about the bad times in which she lived, and the disturbances which had even affected the sacred precincts of the royal palace itself, sought the company of a girl called Marion, who was the daughter of a gardener, and who had lived in the grounds all her life.

Marie-Antoinette then returned moodily to her sketching in her favourite grotto. A feeling of gloom, of terrible foreboding, came upon her, and again she called to Marion, but instead she was surprised to see in front of her a page from the palace, all breathless after running, a letter in his hand, fear in his eyes.

The letter was from the Minister at the palace telling her that the Paris mob was approaching Versailles, that the situation was urgent and that she should return to the palace with all speed. The Queen at first proposed to return to the palace by foot, walking by a short cut through the trees, but the page dissuaded her by impressing on her the danger of the approaching situation, and begged her to go to the château in the Trianon while he went for her carriage. The page ran to the château to order it to readiness. She followed him there more sedately.

This story was apparently told by the girl Marion to Julie Lavergne, who lived at Versailles from 1838 until 1844, and who included it in a volume of reminiscences of the *ancien régime* she compiled, entitled *Légendes de Trianon*. Marion had married a man named Charpentier who was appointed head-gardener at Versailles by Napoleon in 1805, a position he held for many years, and his son after him, and so Marion would have been accessible to Julie Lavergne when she was gathering material for her book at Versailles during the eighteen-thirties and forties. The story of that afternoon at the Petit Trianon on 5 October, 1789, is therefore considered to have a good foundation of truth.

In 1901 two English ladies walked right into this scene in the past. They were Miss Anne Moberly and Miss Eleanor Jourdain,

who were successive Principals of St Hugh's College, Oxford. They were women of education and some standing.

Anne Moberly was born in 1846. Her father was Headmaster of Winchester College and later Bishop of Salisbury. She lived in a cultured, donnish society. All her brothers were scholars, and though she received no formal education she eagerly acquired both culture and learning and developed a facile pen. After her father's death, she was in 1886 appointed Principal of St Hugh's and had in her charge the first Victorian girls who dared to invade the man's world and become undergraduates. The University made her an honorary M.A.

Eleanor Jourdain was born in 1863, the daughter of a Derbyshire vicar. A brilliant, ambitious girl, she went to Lady Margaret Hall, Oxford, and got an honours degree in Modern History. She was an M.A. of Oxford and a Doctor of the University of Paris, and she specialized in French literature. She became headmistress of a large girls' school at Watford, and upon the resignation of Miss Moberly in 1915 she was appointed to succeed her as Principal of St Hugh's. Since 1901 the two women had been close friends, for in that year Miss Jourdain had been appointed Vice-Principal to Miss Moberly.

In 1900 Miss Jourdain acquired a flat in Paris, which, in partnership with a Mlle Ménégoz, she ran as a small finishing school for her English pupils at her school at Watford. During the holidays she used this flat as a very useful *pied-à-terre* in Paris. Here Miss Jourdain was staying with Miss Moberly in the August of 1901, when the suggestion of Miss Jourdain becoming Vice-Principal of St Hugh's was under discussion.

On 10 August the two friends went on their famous trip to Versailles. Neither had been there before. Although both of them were teachers and lecturers, they professed that they did not have an intimate knowledge either of the French Revolution, or of the history of the palace of Versailles, or of the topography of its grounds, considerably altered since the days of Marie-Antoinette. Miss Jourdain confessed that in August, 1901, her ignorance of Versailles and its significance was extreme, and Miss Moberly said she had a limited knowledge of French history, though her brother had once written a poem on Marie-Antoinette which had won the Newdigate Prize in 1867. It was usual for people to feel very strongly about the fate of Marie-Antoinette in those days and certainly the Misses Jourdain and Moberly were no exceptions.

At Versailles they walked through the rooms and galleries of the great palace and then Miss Moberly suggested that they went to the

Petit Trianon in view presumably of her youthful feeling for Marie-Antoinette, for, although the Petit Trianon was constructed by Louis XV for the enjoyment of Madame du Barry and Madame de Pompadour, the place has always been associated with Marie-Antoinette

And so, armed with a Baedeker map, they set off. It was warm and cloudy, with a flower-sweet wind blowing across the gardens into their faces as they walked. They reached the Grand Trianon, and passing it on their left, continued in the direction of the Petit Trianon.

Their subsequent wanderings in the place have long been the subject of discussion, but the best, and indeed only, description of their famous adventure is their own, put down in two separate accounts, written by each of them, and published under the modest and appropriate title *An Adventure* by several famous publishing houses in a number of various editions. The edition used here is that published by Faber and Faber in 1931.

Beyond the Grand Trianon was a broad green drive which led, according to their map, to the Petit Trianon, but Miss Jourdain espied an attractive-looking path which had been cut into the rising ground, and at her suggestion they went along it. They passed some farm buildings, at a window of which Miss Moberly saw a woman shaking a white cloth.

According to Miss Jourdain's observation, these farm buildings were deserted and she noticed agricultural implements, among which was a plough, lying about. Miss Jourdain found the impression of this place "saddening", while her companion was surprised that the French-speaking Miss Jourdain did not ask the way from the woman at the window. But apparently Miss Jourdain did not see her.

They were now in the middle of their joint dream, their hallucination, their ghost world, call it what you will, and they walked forward with a strange and steadily deepening feeling of depression and unreality enveloping them. This feeling of melancholy and dejection, which was very intense and which they both shared, was one of the most interesting aspects of their strange adventure in the past, for they themselves had no reason to feel in this way.

They next encountered two men in greenish uniforms with three-cornered hats. They were obviously gardeners and were working with a wheel-barrow, and, says Miss Moberly, "a pointed spade". They asked them the way and the men directed them straight on.

It is worth noting at this point that gardeners at the Trianon in

1901 did not wear uniforms of that kind, and there had been no plough in the gardens since the days of Louis XVI. These and other strange facts the two ladies discovered later.

As they stood talking to the gardeners, who replied to them in a "casual and mechanical way", Miss Jourdain observed a cottage, detached and well built, in the doorway of which a woman and a girl were standing. Miss Jourdain paid particular attention to their unusual mode of dress. Both wore white kerchiefs tucked into the bodice. The dress of the girl reached down to her ankles, although she seemed to be no more than thirteen or fourteen. The woman was in the act of handing a jug to the girl. Their clothes were quite different to the style of 1901. Only Miss Jourdain saw this particular little tableau from the past.

They continued towards a wood, beneath which was a circular garden kiosk, rather like a small bandstand, in which a man was sitting. This man, seen by both women, wore a heavy black cloak and a slouch hat. His face somehow filled them both with fear and unease. He was marked by smallpox, his complexion dark and his expression, said Miss Jourdain, evil. Although he turned to look at them, his eyes were somehow unseeing. He looked through them.

This strange feeling of unreality and unnaturalness was felt acutely by both women. The scene itself had an eerie, lifeless, other-worldly appearance—"like a wood worked in tapestry", as Miss Moberly put it. "There were no effects of light and shade," she said, "and no wind stirred the trees. It was all intensely still." As for the man sitting in the kiosk, Miss Moberly found his appearance repulsive. His odious expression gave her a "moment of genuine alarm". She asked Miss Jourdain which was the way and, as neither of them wished to approach the dark-visaged man in the cloak, they were a little relieved to hear someone behind them, running towards them in breathless haste.

Turning, they found themselves face to face with a man who, though they heard him running up towards them, appeared suddenly and unaccountably beside them, as though he had passed through the nearby wall of rock.

"Distinctly a gentleman," wrote Miss Moberly. He was dark-eyed, handsome, with crisp, curling black hair beneath a large sombrero hat. His good-looking face was red with the exertion of running. He wore buckled shoes and a dark cloak thrown across him, the end outflung with the speed of his running.

"*Mesdames, mesdames,*" he exclaimed excitedly, "*il ne faut pas passer par là. Par ici—cherchez la maison!*"

427

Miss Moberly said that he might have said "madame", not "mesdames", and Miss Jourdain, the French scholar, said that he pronounced "faut" as though it was "fout". According to Miss Moberly he said a great deal more which she was unable to follow. But they gathered that he desired them to go to the right and not to the left.

He then ran on with what they described as a peculiar and curious smile. Where he went they did not know, and were not prepared to admit that he vanished. But suddenly he was just not there, although they could still hear the sound of his running, a sound which Moberly said was close by them.

And so they continued and walked over a small rustic bridge which crossed a little ravine. A tiny waterfall trickled from the bank above, so close to them that they could have touched it as they passed over the bridge. Across the bridge the path went under trees towards the English garden in front of the Petit Trianon, which Miss Moberly described as a "square, solidly built small country house".

On the terrace in front of the house Miss Moberly saw a lady in a shady white hat sitting sketching. The lady's light summer dress was arranged on her shoulders "in handkerchief fashion". It was long-waisted, full-skirted, though the skirt occurred to Miss Moberly to be rather short (by 1901 standards), and showed too much leg. She wore a pale green fichu. Miss Moberly thought her appearance was unusual and old-fashioned, although, she said, people were wearing fichu bodices that summer.

Miss Moberly said that the lady looked up as they passed by. She had a pretty face, though she was not young. "It did not attract me," said Miss Moberly, who said she felt annoyed at her being there, for she took her at first to be a tourist. She was of course describing the feelings she experienced at the time, when she did not suspect who the lady might have been. If she had known, her reaction would certainly have been very different.

Miss Jourdain did not see the sketching lady, in the same way that Miss Moberly did not see the woman and the girl in the cottage doorway. To her the place was deserted, but she remembered drawing her skirt away, as though someone were near her, and then wondering why she had done so.

They went on to the terrace, with Miss Moberly feeling that she was walking in a dream—"the stillness and oppressiveness were so unnatural". As they crossed the terrace she once more noticed the sketching lady, this time her back view. At the corner of the terrace they saw a second house, a door of which opened and a young man came out. He slammed the door behind him and then turned to

them saying he would show them the way into the house. He took them to an entrance in the front drive.

Miss Moberly said that this man had the "jaunty manner of a footman, but no livery", and he seemed to be mockingly amused at their appearance. The feeling of dreariness and depression was very marked at this point.

In the front entrance of the Petit Trianon they came upon a French wedding party, a very gay affair, in which the two English maiden ladies joined, and, although they did not disclose the extent of their gaiety upon this nuptial occasion, Miss Moberly said she found it very interesting, and that they "felt quite lively again".

Afterwards they took a carriage back to the Hôtel des Réservoirs in Versailles, where they had tea. They did not mention the events of the afternoon until a week later, when Miss Moberly said to Miss Jourdain: "Do you think that the Petit Trianon is haunted?" "Yes, I do," replied Miss Jourdain.

When they began to discuss their visit to the Petit Trianon, they both realized the strangeness of their experience. Why had not Miss Jourdain seen the lady who was sketching? It seemed inconceivable to both of them that she had not done so. Why did they both experience the same feeling of inexplicable depression beginning at exactly the same point in their walk—a fact which they both concealed from each other at the time? How to explain the mystery of the running man, who though he was out of their sight seemed to be running by their side?

Their strange adventure haunted them for years, and during that time they conducted intensive research in order to solve the mystery. First of all they deposited on record in the Bodleian Library their two independent accounts of what had happened, with the result that they were later able to establish a convincing case for the genuineness of their experience.

They found out that the woods, the bridge, the ravine, the cascade and the kiosk no longer existed, though they had been there in the days of Marie-Antoinette. The door in the Petit Trianon through which the young man had come had been blocked up for nearly a hundred years. Long-forgotten maps were discovered which bore out the accuracy of their description of Versailles as it was in Marie-Antoinette's days.

When they returned to the same place again, everything was different. They could find no trace of the paths they had taken. The Petit Trianon itself had a different aspect. The trees and the grass where the lady sat sketching had gone. It was all totally different

to the atmosphere of "silent mystery by which we had been so oppressed".

As a result of their researches, they came to the conclusion that the dark-visaged man at the kiosk was the Comte de Vaudreuil, a Creole who had suffered from smallpox and who was one of Marie-Antoinette's friends. The running man they placed as the messenger who had come to warn the Queen of the approach of the Paris mob. They had now read Julie Lavergne's *Légendes de Trianon*, and the story of this incident as told by the gardener's daughter, Marion—called Marianne by Lavergne. Marion would have been about fourteen in 1789, and Miss Moberly and Miss Jourdain thought that she was the girl seen in the cottage doorway by Miss Jourdain.

It was after they had had their Versailles adventure that they heard the legend about Marie-Antoinette and her ghostly retinue regularly haunting the Petit Trianon on a certain August day.

A number of people had seen these Versailles ghosts, and came forward to substantiate the story of Miss Moberly and Miss Jourdain, in particular a Versailles couple and their artist son who lived in a flat overlooking the grounds of the old palace, and who had seen Marie-Antoinette several times sitting at her sketching by the Petit Trianon. They too had observed the topographical details as they existed in 1789. They too had encountered a man in eighteenth-century costume with a three-cornered hat.

This was no ordinary ghost story, and neither Miss Jourdain nor Miss Moberly thought of it as such. They put forward an interesting explanation.

It will be remembered that the incidents which triggered off the haunting took place on 5 October, 1789, but the date of the adventure at Versailles was 10 August, 1901. The legend was that Marie-Antoinette always appeared at the Petit Trianon in August. It was on 10 August, 1792, that the Tuileries was sacked and the doomed royal family took refuge in the Hall of Assembly and later the Temple.

The Moberly-Jourdain theory was that when Marie-Antoinette sat in the Hall of Assembly during those agonizing hours, she cast her mind back to her last afternoon at Trianon, when the messenger arrived with the news of the approach of the Paris mob. So intense had been her emotion at recalling this scene, that it had been projected into the minds of people who in later times were in the spot where it had taken place. Miss Jourdain and Miss Moberly believed that they had entered into this act of Marie-Antoinette's memory through their being at the Petit Trianon on that particular day.

The intense bitterness and sadness of the Queen's thoughts would

explain the depression which fell upon Miss Moberly and Miss Jourdain as they entered into the "act of memory" one hundred and nine years later. It would explain also their fear of the Comte de Vaudreuil, for Marie-Antoinette considered him responsible for much of her suffering.

The "running" man who begged them not to walk through the gardens but to go to the house would have addressed them as "madame", not as "mesdames", as Miss Moberly thought he had done, for in the scene they were the Queen, and not themselves. It would also account for his pronunciation of the word "faut" as though it was "fout", which was apparently the Austrian way of speaking French, and Marie-Antoinette had surrounded herself with servants and courtiers from her own country.

Such was the theory of time-travelling telepathy which they put forward to account for their adventure at Versailles, and the years of research they spent confirmed in their minds that they were right.

Miss Moberly and Miss Jourdain hesitated to present their strange adventure as a ghost story. In their opinion no well-educated person would think it could be explained by calling it one. They had many critics, particularly among the intellectual ladies of their acquaintance, who received the story of the haunting at the Trianon with somewhat wounding scepticism and put forward ingenious explanations in attempts to discredit it.

But although they received short shrift from their own sex, their story was taken seriously by such prominent men as Professor C. E. M. Joad and J. W. Dunne, who regarded it as one of the best-established ghost stories on record.

A Bargain with a Ghost

Is it possible for ghosts to live amicably with humans? A psychic practitioner and palmist, well known internationally many years ago as Cheiro, claimed to have had this unique relationship in a haunted house he rented in the centre of London before the First World War.

He was Count Louis Hamon, and his pseudonym Cheiro was derived from the Greek "cheir", the hand. It was pronounced the same as Cairo.

Count Hamon's remarkable story solved a murder mystery of eighteenth-century London, and told a strange and sad love story which continued after life on the astral plane, though earthbound to a room in an old Georgian house in Central London.

Hamon in his account of the incident declined to identify the house for the curious reason that he believed he would be liable to be sued for heavy damages by its owners on account of "damage to the reputation of property" under an old English law. He stated that he had lodged documentary proof with the editor of the London Publishing Company. Any such documentation of this kind, however, was almost certainly lost in the 1940 Blitz on London which obliterated the records as well as the stocks of so many publishing houses in the city.

Hamon came across the house by chance and was greatly attracted by its air of old-world charm, standing back as it did from the busy thoroughfare which had grown up around it, and from which it was half hidden by trees.

The Count was a man who had travelled a great deal, and he had decided to settle down in London for a while. This, he thought, was just the house for him. Although there was no indication that the place was available either to be bought or rented, he went up to the front door, through a quaint overgrown garden where a little fountain splashed placidly as it had done for the past two centuries. He pulled the iron chain of an ancient bell.

The door was opened by an elderly man who was deaf and Hamon had some difficulty in making him understand that he was looking for a house, and had heard that this one might be to let. The old gentleman was telling him that he had made a mistake when his wife appeared in the hall.

She told a different story. The old house was full of strange noises, particularly knocks on the woodwork, and no servant would stay. Her husband was deaf and did not hear the noises. The house was getting more than they could manage and she had it in her mind to try and let it, as the noises had been getting on her nerves.

Her frankness about the noises impressed Count Hamon, who reckoned that he was not afraid of such things. The house intrigued and attracted him immensely with its unusually shaped rooms, its age-black oak beams and panelling, its Tudor fireplaces and mullion windows. He learned that the house was owned by the old man who had inherited it from an eccentric and aged uncle less than a year previously.

"Do you think the place is haunted?" asked Hamon.

The lady of the house would not commit herself. It was sufficient that she had warned the prospective tenant about the strange noises, which were certainly not her imagination, for every servant she had employed had heard them and had refused to stay.

"What about the eccentric uncle?" asked Hamon.

She could not tell him much about this mysterious character, except that he had lived there alone with an ancient butler and they inhabited only the front part of the house. The back rooms had been shut up and were never allowed to be used.

Despite this somewhat ominous introduction to the house of his dreams, Count Hamon took a lease upon it, and acquired the key two weeks later. He decided to have the place redecorated and restored to something like its ancient style, before he moved in.

As he walked around the empty silent house, planning the re-decoration, he came into one room which had a strange effect upon him and seemed to defeat any attempt to fit it into his plans for the

house. This room was in the oldest part of the building, was below the level of the hall on the half-landing leading down to the basement. The decorator who was doing the work was equally at a loss, and so Hamon decided to lock the room and leave it untouched.

The work proceeded smoothly, and as soon as two rooms were completed Hamon fitted them up for himself and his secretary, and moved in. He did not engage any servants and he arranged that they should have their meals out. His secretary was a Yorkshireman named Perkins, a stolid, down-to-earth man older than the Count.

Among the improvements Hamon had installed in the house was electric light, which had the effect of dispersing some of the more mysterious shadows in the place. On their first night he and Perkins got back from the evening meal about ten, made sure that all the doors and windows were properly fastened, extinguished all the lights and retired to their respective rooms.

Hamon read for a while, then switched off his light and settled down to go to sleep. The house was quiet, with the sound of the London traffic a distant lullaby. He lay there for a while, then suddenly sat up with a start.

Downstairs there was a distant noise of the opening and shutting of a door. This was followed by heavy footsteps sounding on the uncarpeted floors. The footsteps came upstairs and became louder and louder as they approached his door.

By now Louis Hamon was bolt upright in his bed, his heart hammering. He was afraid to switch on his light for fear the gleam under the door would attract the intruder, whoever he might be. He heard the staircase squeak on the loose tread he had particularly noted that evening as he came up to bed.

The footsteps stopped right outside his door. At first he was convinced that the intruder was human, despite the stories the old lady had told him. He got out of bed, picked up the heavy poker from the fire-grate and stood there waiting.

Instead of the door bursting open as he expected, there was a sudden, sharp rat-a-tat, tat, *tat-tat* on the door, the last two knocks coming with almost bone-breaking force on the centre panel of the door.

For some reason this knocking banished the thought from his mind that the intruder was human. He switched on his electric light and went over to the door, some awful fear clutching at his very bowels. But whatever it was, he was determined to face it. All his life he had dabbled in psychic matters, and he had learned to respect and to dread the unknown. But he knew that whatever

agency was here in this house, there was no escaping it, once that grim knocking had been made upon his door.

Pulling back the bolts, he opened the door wide. A dark and empty landing faced him.

He stood there breathing hard and staring into the darkness, words beginning to form on his trembling lips. As if to answer him before he had spoken, the reply came in a way which froze his very blood.

Upon the open door right beside his head came that awful knocking once more—as clear and sharp as though hammered out by knuckles made of bone without flesh.

He jumped back and slammed the door with a crash that echoed and re-echoed through the empty old house. Hastily shooting the bolt home, he returned to his bed and waited, quaking with fear.

But nothing more happened that night, and with the courage which daylight and the rebirth of another day in the city brings he scoffed at his fears of the night. After all, he was a psychic observer. There was really no need to be afraid of such things. Anyway, it was more likely that he imagined the whole thing, that it was perhaps a dream prompted by the stories the old lady had told him about this house.

If he had thought that his experience had been some kind of hallucination, this idea was banished from his mind by a talk he had with Perkins at breakfast-time. He too had heard the noises in the night—the footsteps and those nerve-racking rat-a-tats.

"I'm damned if I'll stop in this house another night, sir. I was scared, I don't mind confessing."

Hamon was surprised. Perkins was a man of affairs, level headed, honest, and had had considerable experience of the world.

"What are we going to do about it?" he asked.

Perkins suggested giving up the lease on the grounds that the house was not habitable, and getting the owners to return what money had been spent on it, under threat of legal proceedings if need be. But when Hamon explained to him that the lady concerned had warned him about the strange noises before he took the house, and that anyway he liked the place and had no intention of leaving it, Perkins agreed to stop.

The following night both men spent the hours of darkness seated in armchairs before the fire in Count Hamon's room. They had armed themselves with coffee and sandwiches and stout pokers besides, this latter precaution upon Perkins's insistence, for the

master of the house had little faith in pokers being of any defence against whatever was troubling the house at night.

Once more they heard the footsteps followed by the sharp rat-a-tat-tat upon the door. This was followed by the sound of a click—the unmistakable noise of an electric light being switched on.

"That's no ghost!" exclaimed Perkins, unbolting the door and pulling it open.

The landing was flooded with light. But there was no one there. They stood listening. The house was enveloped in the silence as of death. They could see that the lights were on in the hall. They had distinctly remembered turning them off. Both men descended the stairs, their pokers gripped firmly in their hands.

"Can't be a ghost with all these lights," muttered Perkins to reassure himself.

When they reached the hall every lamp was on. To their left the dining-room door was wide open and the room was in darkness. Beside the door they could plainly see the three brass switches controlling the three lights in the room, and as they watched the switches were turned on one by one before their eyes, filling the room with light.

They stepped inside, expecting that someone was playing a trick. But the dining-room, ablaze with light, was empty. It was not possible that anyone was concealed there, or that the lights could have been pulled on by means of wires or strings.

As they were making sure of this, a strange hollow laugh sounded so close to them that it could only have been made by someone in the room. And yet there was no one there. The laugh sounded again, more sinister, mocking them and terrifying them.

They turned and fled to Hamon's room, without bothering to turn the lights out. They were found all turned on, even down in the basement, when the workmen arrived in the morning, after Hamon and his secretary had spent the rest of the hours of darkness sitting shivering by the dying fire and wondering what strange and unpredictable force they were up against in this old house.

They were determined not to give in. Perkins produced a terrier the following night, on the principle that if there was anything human about the ghost, the dog would be certain to smell him out. Hamon was quite agreeable to the scheme for he knew from experience that dogs showed more terror than humans when encountering the supernatural.

Taking the dog with them, they made a tour of the house before

they retired, locking all the doors and windows and seeing that all the lights were switched off.

They arrived at the door of the small room on the half-landing leading down to the basement which the decorators had so far not touched and which Hamon kept locked.

He unlocked the door and went in, striking a match, as there was no electric light in there. Perkins came in after him, calling the dog to follow.

But the dog refused to go inside the room. He lay crouching outside, whining, his hair standing up on end in terror, like bristles. Hamon himself, with his extra-psychic perception, felt something of what the dog felt. It was an extremely uncomfortable feeling. Locking the room, they left it and went upstairs, followed by the dog still trembling and whining.

"Well, what do you think of that, Perkins?" asked Hamon.

Perkins did not reply, but poured two cups of coffee with an expression on his face which was a sufficient commentary on the situation.

The only footsteps they heard in the house that night were those of the policeman on the beat, who came knocking on their door in very unghostly fashion, wanting to know what was going on in the house. He had tried the back door, found it locked securely, and then he heard the sound of the bolts being drawn back and the door was opened before his eyes. He went inside to find the place ablaze with lights, but empty.

Count Hamon had some difficulty in assuring the policeman of his bona fides, the house being mostly unfurnished and still in the hands of the decorators. It was useless trying to explain what was really going on—even if he knew himself. The constable searched the house from top to bottom, including the small room on the half-landing into which the dog once more flatly refused to go, crouching down in terror, trembling from nose to tail.

The policeman ponderously made notes, said he would have to hand in a full report on the affair, and finally he left.

Hamon heard no more from the police, and the strange thing was that after that for some weeks he heard no more from the ghost. But he did not believe that the visit of a humble London bobby had deterred any supernatural agency there might have been in the house.

The decorations were completed and Count Hamon took up residence in the house officially. Among his early visitors was the dramatist Henry Hamilton, who had a strangely interesting story to tell him.

He told Hamon that he knew about the house being haunted, as some friends of his had once lived in it, and had had to leave because of the strange noises and knockings. He said that he himself had got in touch with the ghost in that very room and received a message from it. This he had written down and placed in a sealed envelope which he handed to his host, suggesting that he should also attempt to do the same thing and then compare the two messages.

Hamon promised to do so, though he heard no knocks for some weeks, until the night he had a party of friends to dinner. They sat around the fire in the drawing-room, having coffee and brandy after the meal.

Their conversation was suddenly interrupted by a series of sharp knocks on a crystal bowl. The knocks were so persistent that Hamon, believing that the ghost was trying to get through with some message, took out a pencil and writing pad and addressed the unknown entity telling it that he proposed to call out the letters of the alphabet, and for the ghost to make a knock on the crystal bowl when Hamon reached the requisite letter which would spell out a message.

This arrangement worked well enough and the message came through beginning: "My name is Karl Clint. I lived here about a hundred and twenty years ago." If they went to the empty room in the half-landing, the message said, they would hear more.

The party did so. They lit candles and sat around a small table, and the tapping message laboriously continued, the sounds much stronger than before, being made upon the wall above where the candle burned.

"I am Karl Clint. I own this house. I murdered Arthur Liddel in this room and buried him underneath."

The mortals asked the ghost if there was anything it wanted them to do about it. The reply was that there was nothing they could do. In answer to the question whether the spirit wanted any prayers said, the answer came very firmly in the negative.

Hamon asked if there was any way in which he could help, and the reply was that the ghost wanted to be left alone in his own house.

"Why can't people keep away?" he demanded.

At this point the ghost apparently became exasperated, for the candle was suddenly extinguished and there was a loud bang on the door. The company groped their way out, only too glad to escape from the haunted room.

When his friends had gone Hamon opened the sealed envelope which Henry Hamilton had given him and which he had kept

locked in his desk. The message which had been received by Hamilton was precisely the same, almost word for word, with the one Hamon had taken down from the ghost in the little room that night.

Hamon then began to make inquiries about the history of the house. He examined the old records of the parish and found that the original part of the old house—that is, the part at the back which included the room on the half landing—had been a farmhouse which was owned by a German named Karl Clint between the years 1740 and 1800. Hamon also found reference to the disappearance of a man named Arthur Liddel who had been associated with Clint and was last seen in his company. Some years later Karl Clint left the neighbourhood and since then the property changed hands many times, and was enlarged by the addition of what was now the front of the house. The farmland itself disappeared and was swallowed up in the expansion of London during the nineteenth century.

Count Hamon gradually built up his menage in the old house, engaging servants, opening up some of the old rooms and installing electric light everywhere, except in the one room which he kept locked.

With this gradual encroachment into the old part of the house, the noises began once more, and Hamon was awakened by the spectral rapping on his bedroom door. Two of his servants who heard the noises, immediately gave notice.

Hamon decided to hold a seance. He had a plan to get to the bottom of the haunting and to come to terms with the ghost if possible. He invited to the house a blind medium named Cecil Husk with whom he had worked before, and who seemed to have the power to make spirits materialize.

The seance was held in the dining room with the blind medium sitting in a circle of Hamon's friends before a table on which was a small lamp with a red shade. All the other lights in the house were extinguished.

Immediately the knocking started—on the ceiling, on the mirror, on the chandelier. Then began the tramp of heavy footsteps, which seemed to come from the unused room on the half-landing.

The footsteps stopped outside the door of the room, and then, says Hamon, a dark shadowy cloud formed inside the room by the door, which grew thicker, more dense and opaque and moved over towards him. Out of this cloud materialized the head and shoulders of a man—a face with a weary hunted look, lonely, and long dead. As the features developed more clearly they could see a

close-cropped beard and reddish hair, a teutonic-shaped head. It was the face of a man of about forty-five or fifty.

All the company, except the blind medium who sat before the red lamp deep in his trance, stared in fascination as the lips of the man from the past began to move in an attempt to speak. At first they just opened, and no sound came; and then after what seemed a tremendous effort, the sound of a voice materialized into the room, issuing from the lips, coming first in unintelligible whispers and guttural mutterings.

Only gradually did sense come out, and then suddenly the ghost demanded in a voice that everyone in the room could hear:

"Why are all these people in my house?"

Hamon replied that they were his friends, and they were all there to try to help him. Would he not tell them something about himself?

"I am Karl Clint. I lived here as far as I can make out a hundred and twenty years ago. But time makes no difference to me now. It is people who change. Why have you come to my house?"

"Because I liked your house," replied Hamon. "Perhaps I can help you by living here."

"No one can help me. I want only to be left in peace." The voice was filled with infinite sadness.

"But you are not at peace," Hamon said. "If you were, you would not frighten people as you do."

"I can't get away. Since the night I died, I am here all the time."

Hamon asked Clint to tell them about the murder of Arthur Liddel, and the ghost replied that during his lifetime he was living in this house with a woman named Charlotte whom he loved more than life itself. They were not married, and Liddel took a great fancy to Charlotte, and tried to tempt her to go away with him by offering her money. Liddel was better off than he, Clint, who was a hard-working farmer, and he thought he could buy Charlotte with his money.

"One night he went too far," said the ghost, "and I killed him as I would a mad dog."

Although he knew it was murder, he would not hesitate to do the same thing again if he and Liddel were living. He buried the body in a hole he dug in the floor in the room downstairs. He filled it with quicklime, and cemented it over. So far as he knew the body was still there.

Charlotte helped him to dispose of the body, he said, but she never got over the fear of being found out for the murder. She died

a few years later and was buried in the churchyard nearby.

After that Karl Clint returned to his native Germany, but he never knew a moment's happiness. Finally he committed suicide.

"And then—I can't tell you how it came about—but one day I seemed to wake up in the room downstairs and I have been here ever since."

He did not want to leave the house, he said. Why should he? It was the only place he called home—the only place he was ever happy in. It was where he lived with the one woman he ever loved. The only happiness he ever knew, he experienced here in this house. Why should he ever leave it? There was no place for him to go. No release for him, ever.

Besides, there was Charlotte. "She is here with me. We live the old happy days over and over—until Liddel comes. And then I kill him again—over and over again."

Hamon, very much moved by all this, wanted to know whether there was any way in which he could help this unfortunate being from the past. The fact that he had murdered did not make Hamon any the less desirous of helping him. It seemed that his punishment was very long and very grievous.

The ghost wanted only one thing—the room downstairs, where he lived his incomprehensible existence with the shadowy Charlotte. He wanted the room to remain untouched, and for no one ever to enter it after dark. He required only two chairs and a table there. The human occupants could then have the rest of the house to themselves, and the ghost would not trouble them again.

This Hamon promised. That night he placed two chairs and a table in the little room where had taken place that murder long forgotten by everyone except the wretch who had it on his eternal conscience. Hamon locked the door and put the key in his safe.

The ghost troubled him no more. There were no more knockings, no more disturbances. Behind the locked door of Karl Clint's room there was silence and, it seemed, peace. Whatever was going on between the ghostly lovers in that lightless room where they had had their happiness and had committed their crime, no sign or sound of it came to the world outside.

After some years Hamon decided to move to another house in a different part of London. But he did not feel that he could go without letting Karl Clint know what was happening, and at least thanking him for keeping his part of the bargain so faithfully.

So he had another seance. Clint soon materialized once more. Hamon told him what his intentions were, and duly thanked him

for keeping faith. Was there anything he could do to help him before other people moved into the house?

To his great surprise, declared Hamon, the ghost asked if he might move with him to his new house, for Hamon was the only person he had ever known who had shown sympathy and understanding.

There was nothing very much Hamon could do about it, and anyway he was not afraid of this particular ghost now. Clint told him that there was a portrait of Charlotte hidden in the panelling of his room, and would he take it with him and hang it in his new house?

Hamon found the picture and when he moved he hung it in his study.

He swears to the truth of this extraordinary ghost story, which he told in a book entitled *True Ghost Stories* and which was published many years ago by the Psychic Book Club.

The Ghostly Cavalry Charge
and The Spectres of Crécy

When, where, and why, does one see a ghost? Ninety-nine people out of a hundred probably never see one at all. Of those who do some clearly imagine that they have seen a ghost. Others may create a wishful vision and convince themselves that they have seen a ghost.

I confess that although I have been interested in ghost stories, local legends and folklore all my life and have sat up until the small hours in thirty to forty of the most haunted houses in Britain, I have only once seen what I am prepared to swear was a ghostly vision.

There was the night when I sat late working on the Bowes-Lyon family papers in the Charter Room of Glamis Castle "the most haunted house in Britain". Lord Strathmore was out to dinner. The butler had gone down to the village. Only the cook and a maid-servant were left in that great, grim, turreted castle of 120 rooms, the oldest inhabited castle in Scotland, the home of the Monster of Glamis, the place in which Macbeth was murdered, the house where Earl Beardie gambled with the devil—and has been seen since by more than one person sitting in a great armchair by the flickering fire. The house of the Tongueless Woman, of Jack the Runner, of the Grey Lady, of blood-stained floorboards and secret chambers. What other house could offer such a field of ghosts on a dark night in winter when the snow fell, wild geese bayed overhead—and the

lights suddenly went out. The whole place was plunged in darkness.

I groped my way to Duncan's Hall. I struck a match and saw a prison door yawning open in the wall and a grizzly bear standing guard over it—stuffed. I stumbled down to the Crypt where surely ghosts should walk and into Malcolm's Chamber where the king was murdered and bolted doors opened on their own account.

It was a chance in a million to see, hear or feel the presence of a ghost. Not a thing moved, rustled or showed during that hour of Stygian blackness. Then the lights went up. A snow-storm which had blacked out half Angus had failed to produce a glimmer of a ghost.

There was that night in Craster Tower on the bleak Northumbrian coast where Crasters have dwelt for more than eight hundred years and a Grey Lady walks. My wife and I slept in one room, our small daughter in another just across the landing. At two in the morning she came into our room to say that someone had opened the front door, walked upstairs, come into her bedroom and then crossed the landing and gone into the drawing room—"a woman all in grey".

I spent the next three nights in my daughter's bedroom. At two each morning I woke. I saw nothing, heard nothing and, although I tried hard to imagine it, I felt nothing. The Grey Lady was not for me.

I have met three men and a woman who swear that they have seen Black Shuck, the ghostly dog of East Anglia. I have walked the lonely paths by cliff and breck and fen where Black Shuck runs —and have never seen him. But I have heard the bittern boom on undrained, quaking fens and seen Wills o'the Wisp dance their corpse-candle dance over stinking swamps which beckon men to death. Black Shuck was not there.

I have slept in Blickling Hall, that magnificent Norfolk house, but saw no sign of Anne Boleyn, whose ghost visits her ancestral home, although the man in the next bedroom complained that he was woken twice in the night by uncanny noises. I have waited for the ghost of Thomas Wentworth, "the Great Earl" of Strafford, to walk headless down the staircase at Wentworth Woodhouse and saw not even a mouse. Nonetheless, a footman swore most solemnly that he had seen "Black Tom" walk downstairs with his head underneath his arm.

I have lived and slept many days and nights in a small and enchanting manor house, built in 1421 and the home for two and a half centuries of my father's family, but I saw no sign of the Strangling Ghost, although he terrified a blameless brigadier and frightened

a vulgar profiteer out of his wits when they both slept on successive nights in the bedroom called the Justice Room. The legend is that the Strangler only grips by the throat, as they sleep, those who deserve to be hanged from the kingpost beam where they dealt justice in the old days. Perhaps the brigadier was not so blameless after all. Certainly the wife of a dead and gone Royal Academician, who fled screaming from the room one night when her husband was in London, was, as we all knew, no better than she should have been and not half as good as she ought to have been. I saw nothing—which is my alibi.

True, I was once kicked down the oaken stairs at Holme Hall, high in the Derbyshire hills, by the ghost of Bradshaw the Regicide, who signed the death warrant of Charles I. My host swore that it was Bradshaw's ghost who launched the kick. I prefer to think that I slipped on the polished oak as a result of his '45 port.

The explanation, surely, of all these failures to see the appropriate ghost in so many authentic ghost-haunts is that one was not there at the exact moment of time when ghosts are due to appear according to whatever supernatural laws may govern them.

A highly competent scientist, who is also a ghost-hunter with a notable bag of apparitions to his credit, swears to me that ghosts only appear on the scenes they choose to haunt at certain fixed periods of time. These periods may, according to his theory, be annual, bi-annual, even centennial. On the other hand, whoever is lucky enough to see the ghost may be one of those rare people of extra-sensory perception to whom the supernatural is more or less an open book.

After all, when we consider that, today, it is possible to transmit pictures from the moon and to televise voices, noises, colours and events round the world in a matter of seconds, it is perhaps not unreasonable to suppose that events of the past and the people who took part in them, have been "photographed on the retina of time" to recur at stated intervals and be seen by the few.

This brings me to my own one authentic vision of the supernatural. I went to France in the First World War shortly before that war ended. Youth, and a bit of luck, saved me from the horrors of trench warfare. When we moved up to the Front Line the Germans were on the run. Dead lay in tens of thousands on the battlefields of Ypres, Mont Kemmel, Vimy Ridge, Messines, Bailleul and Warneton Ridge. Towns and villages had long been battered flat. Outerdem, Meteren, Neuve Eglise, Vlamartinghe, Poperinghe and the rest, in that grey land of the dead, were heaps of rubble.

Here, if anywhere, was surely the place where the dead should walk. I, as a young soldier, daily in charge of drafts of German prisoners, scantily guarded, relying for my escort parties largely on B.2 and C.3 types of infantrymen, had no time to think of ghosts. Each day was a kaleidoscope of dirt, danger, lice and hard slogging.

One afternoon I climbed into the upper floor of a half-ruined barn and gazed out over the grey, rolling sullen fields, pocked with shell-holes, writhing with barbed wire, stinking of the dead. Every tree was a tortured skeleton of itself. The cornfields behind the Line, where the tide of battle had surged back and then retreated, were yellow, sodden, beaten flat by rain, men, tanks and the dead. I thought for a brief moment that this land on which I now gazed had been torn and tortured by wars and armies from Alva to Wellington, from Waterloo to Sedan. That moment of thought raised no ghosts.

A month later the Armistice had been signed. We were in camp on a sodden hillside at Neuve Eglise, a bitter winter ahead.

The guns in Flanders were silent at last. In that final month of the grey winter of 1918 an eerie stillness dwelt on the battlefields of France and Belgium. Dead lay unburied in fields and sodden trenches. Guns and rifles, shells and Mills bombs lay rusting. Warneton Ridge was a wilderness of mud and crawling wire, shell-pocked and lonely as the wind. Mont Kemmel, "The Gibraltar of Northern France", alone with its dead and its torn trees, loomed above the grey plains that have been Europe's cockpit for centuries.

By day carrion crows croaked death-like from shattered trees, travesties of nature whose bare trunks were bullet-scarred and shell-splintered. Moated farms and straggling villages stood ruined, roofless, and gaping-walled—if they stood at all.

By night the winter moon looked on the twisted dead, the corn-fields and roofless farms with white dispassion. Frost mantled the trees and whitened the tents where No. 298 Prisoners-of-War Company crouched by the gaunt ruins of Neuve Eglise, the village which was blown to atoms in an hour.

No longer was the night horizon lit by the fantastic spears and flashes of gunfire, the ghostly aurora borealis of the front line, no longer pin-pointed by star-shells or shuddering with the thunder of guns.

In our tents and shacks outside the great barbed-wire cages which prisoned 450 Germans, newly-taken, we, the guards, shivered with cold. In their prison-tents the Germans slept like sardines for warmth's sake. We were new to our prisoners, who, a month before,

had been fighting us. The arctic cold smote English and German alike.

So when at the railhead to pick up post and rations I heard by chance words of a great country auberge—an old posting-inn of the eighteenth century—whose stables and ruined rooms were full of abandoned Queen stoves, that perfect little camp-cooker, I determined to impound the lot.

Next day, late in the afternoon, after a morning of sudden thaw, I took Corporal Barr, that minute but unquenchable fighting man, and set off along a rutted road to the east. Flooded fields lay on either side. Rotted crops stained the soil. The smell of dead men, cold and oily, that smell which strikes to the pit of the stomach like the smell of a dead snake, was heavy on the air.

Ahead, in the afternoon sun, the road gleamed with sudden splashes and shields of light where water lay. Two kilometres, near enough three, and we came to the standing archway of the auberge. The yellow walls of what had been a fine old Flemish inn stood windowless, gazing like dead eyes over the fields of the dead. Bullets had sieved its walls. Shells had shattered the roof where rafters and roof-tree stood stark as the ribs of a skeleton.

Under the great arch which had echoed to the clatter of coachwheels and rung with the guttural cries of Walloon and Flamande farmers, the courtyard, with its mighty midden, showed a foursquare array of stables, barns, cart-sheds and coach-houses. Doors sagged on broken hinges and sandbags filled empty windows.

Within were wooden bunks, the black ashes of long-cold fires, rusty dixies and mouldy webbing, mildewed bully and Maconochie tins—and Queen stoves!

We found at least a score—enough to warm our pitiful shacks and spare one or two for the prisoners. I told Corporal Barr to bring a party of prisoners next day and remove the lot.

That dour and unimpressionable little man with the square, short body, the beetling black eyebrows and steady eyes—a soldier among the best of them—said "Aye". He was being loquacious.

Then we started back. It was, maybe, three to three-thirty and far from dark. In the sunset the sky had cleared to a wide band of apple-green fading into pink. Overhead, high clouds caught a sudden ethereal sheen of crimson and flamingo. The heavens were alight above the stricken earth. On our left, fields lay waterlogged and gleaming—lake beyond miniature lake.

On the right a low upland swept up to a torn, fantastic wood of larch and birch. The thin trees were twisted into grotesque shapes by

shell blast. It was a Hans Andersen wood of Arthur Rackham trees through whose sun-reddened trunks we could see cloud-masses lit with a Cuyp-like glow.

Suddenly, as we splashed through the sunset pools of that deserted road, German cavalry swept out of the wood. Crouching low over their horses' withers, lance-tops gleaming, red pennons flying, they charged out of that spectral wood—a dozen or more German Uhlans in those queer high-topped hats which they had worn in the dead days of 1914. I saw horses, men, lances, and flickering pennons clear and sharp in the level sun.

And up the slope to meet them galloped French dragoons—brass cuirasses flashing, sabres upswung, heavy horse-tail plumes dancing from huge brass helmets. Fierce-moustached and red-faced, they charged on heavy Flemish chargers to meet that flying posse of grey-faced men who swept down with slender lances on flying horses—the hurricane meeting the winter wind.

Then the vision passed. There was no clash of mounted men—no melée of shivering lance and down-smashing sabre, no sickening unhorsing of men or uprearing of chargers—only empty upland and a thin and ghostly wood, silver in the setting sun. The earth was empty. I felt suddenly cold.

I am no spiritualist, but to the truth of this vision I will swear.

I glanced at Corporal Barr. He looked white and uneasy.

"Did you see anything?" I asked.

"Aye—something mighty queer," said that non-committal little Glasgow baker. "Ssst! look! Wha's that?" he gasped. His rifle bolt clicked back, a cartridge snapped in the breech and the butt leapt to his shoulder. In a gap in the hedge on the left two baleful eyes glared at us from a dim, crouching shape. At the click of the rifle bolt it sprang to its feet—a wolf in shape and size—and loped into a sudden burst of speed.

Two rifles cracked almost as one as the grey beast splashed through the shallow floods. Bullets spurted up sudden fountains as it raced away. Not one touched it. Yet the day before I had killed a running hare with my .303 and Barr could pick a crow off a tree at a hundred yards.

The beast raced belly-low into the sunset, leaving a trail of flying water. Bullet after bullet cracked after it, missed by yards. We were both off our shooting.

No wolf was that half-starved ghoul of a beast, but one of the lost, masterless Alsatian sheepdogs of the dead farmers, pariahs of the battlefield who ravished the flesh of the staring dead.

We reached camp, shaken and oddly shy of talking too much.

Next day, at Neuve Eglise, that skeleton of a village on the spine of the Ravelsberg, I drank a glass or two of vin rouge at the estaminet of the one and only Marie, a kilometre up the road from the Armentières Road *douane*.

I asked her of the wood and the auberge. And Marie, forty-five and peasant-wise, said: "Ah! M'sieu, that wood is sad. It is on the frontier. A wood of dead men. In the wars of Napoleon, in the war of 1870—in this war in 1914—always the cavalry of France and Germany have met and fought by that wood. If you will go beyond the auberge half a kilometre only, you will find a *petite eglise*. There you will see the graves of the cavalry of all these wars. It is true, I tell you."

I went. In the tiny churchyard were the graves. And the headstones told the brief and bloody tales of gallant horsemen in frontier skirmishes which had played prelude to three mighty wars. And since I love a horse and revere a good rider, whether he is a Uhlan or a Gascon under Murat, a turbaned Mahratta or a red-coated fox-hunter, I stood in homage for a frightened minute.

Now that is a true tale. Twenty-six years later I told it in the Second World War to a few men. A Sheffield steel man, Colonel Shepheard, listened intently. I finished on a faint note of defiance— "believe it or not".

"I do believe it,"he said steadily."I saw something of the same sort in the last war!" And he told me this astounding story in a calm, matter-of-fact voice.

During the 1914–18 War, as a staff colonel, he was travelling in a car from Hazebrouck to Wimereux. He had with him a French captain as interpreter and aide. The car passed through various villages, none of outstanding note. He took an idle interest in the flat, poplar-lined fields, the white-washed farms and grubby villages.

At Wimereux they dined and slept. And the colonel dreamed.

"I dreamed, he told me,"that I was travelling the same road again in the same car through the same villages. But with a difference. As we approached one village the car slowed down and stopped. On either side of the road were flat fields.

"Suddenly out of the earth on each side of the road rose up the hooded, cloaked figures of silent men—rank beyond rank. There were thousands of them—all cloaked and hooded like monks. They rose slowly, and every man stared fixedly at me. It was a queer, wistful, sad stare, like a dumb question or a dumb warning.

"Their cloaks were grey, almost luminous, with a fine, silvery

bloom on them like moths' wings. I seemed to touch one and it came off on my fingers in a soft dust.

"I can't remember if I got out of the car or just sat and touched the man nearest me. But they stared and stared endlessly, pitifully, with a sadness which went right to my heart.

"Then, slowly, they all sank back into the ground—rank after rank of hooded men sinking into the earth, their eyes fixed on me to the last!"

He shook his shoulders with a half-shiver, half-shudder. I waited.

"Next morning at breakfast," he went on, "I told my French aide of my dream. He listened and suddenly became excited."

"'You know the name of that village near where your car stopped?' he asked.

" 'No,' I said, 'What was it?'

" 'Crécy!' he said.

"So," said ex-staff Colonel Shepheard, "I had seen in my dream the cloaked and hooded thousands of the archers who died on Crécy field in August, 1346. That," he added simply, "is why I believe your yarn."

And, to cap this tale and that of the ghostly cavalry skirmish at Bailleul, there is the tale of Major S. E. G. Ponder, the Oriental traveller and novelist, who lives at Torquay.

Major Ponder, a Regular gunner, served in the 1914–18 War in a Heavy Battery of the Royal Artillery under a Major Apultree, a red-faced, choleric officer with a sultry blue eye, a scalding flow of language and the kindest heart imaginable. He was, says Ponder, the last man on earth to see a ghost.

On a night in autumn, 1916, on the Aisne, a captain whom he prefers to call "A" and a subaltern whom he calls "B" were ordered to go up the Hessian trench to the most advanced O.P. in order that Captain A should show Lieutenant B the field of fire.

"It was," said Major Ponder, "a macabre O.P., for the parapet and parados were built mainly of the bodies of dead Germans! For some reason the dead did not seem to decompose on the Somme—something in the soil. They simply looked like alabaster—very odd.

"Well, the Boche put down an extra-heavy barrage that night and neither A nor B showed up. I wasn't particularly worried about them as there were several deep dug-outs they could get into.

"Next morning, about six, I was having a mug of tea in the mess— a half-buried Nissen hut—when Apultree appeared in the door. He was dead white and shaking like a leaf.

" 'Good Lord, what's the matter,' I said.

" 'I've seen B,' he said queerly.

" 'He's back all right, then?' I said.

" 'No, he's dead!'

" 'What on earth do you mean?' I said.

" 'He suddenly appeared in the door of my dug-out,' said Apultree, 'and I said, "Ah! so you're back to report all right!" '

" 'No,' he said, 'I'm not back to report, sir, only to tell you I was killed last night.'

"And," added Ponder quietly, "he was too. Shell splinter in at the back of his ear and right through his head. Apultree had seen him all right—no doubt about that. I believe every word he said."

The Mystery of Borley

A great deal, far too much in fact, has been written about Borley Rectory. Here was a good haunting which was exploited in the most cynical fashion until it became history's most profitable ghost story. When Borley Rectory was discovered by Harry Price and Fleet Street in 1929, apparently there weren't enough ghosts for these incorrigible publicity hounds, so others had to be invented. Thus poltergeist phenomena were engineered which has caused the cynics to dismiss the whole haunt as the biggest ghost hoax of all time.

The answer is perhaps not as simple as that. The existence of ghosts is not disproved by the discovery of unscrupulous invention of man-made phenomena. Whatever be the truth about Borley Rectory, it remains one of the century's most interesting ghost stories.

Borley is a hamlet in Essex, a few miles from Sudbury. It has an early English church, and according to an unsubstantiated legend, a monastery once stood upon the site of the Rectory. Seven miles away at Bures was a nunnery. The legend goes that in the thirteenth century a young novice at Bures fell in love with a monk at Borley monastery and they eloped. Their fleeing coach was pursued and overtaken by the ecclesiastical authorities and the pair of lovers were brought back to suffer death. The monk was beheaded—some say hanged—and his would-be bride was bricked up alive in her own convent. Since then Borley has been haunted by the headless monk and the nun as well as the phantom coach.

This story has been told locally for generations, despite the fact that the probability is that there was never a monastery at Borley, though it is thought there was a Benedictine priory there.

But the nun herself is not so easy to disprove. She has been seen by a number of witnesses. Dressed in black, with bowed head, she walked in the Rectory garden, her hands clasped in prayer.

Another explanation for the nun's ghost came out of a series of seances during which the story was told of a French nun named Marie Lairre, who came from her convent at Le Havre in the seventeenth century and married Henry Waldegrave, who lived in a house on the site of Borley Rectory, where he strangled her on 17 May, 1667, and buried her body underneath the cellar floor.

The Waldegraves were an influential Roman Catholic family who were patrons of Borley church and owned Borley Manor for some three hundred years. Their splendid tomb can be seen in the church, and there was a legend that their coffins in the crypt under Borley church had been tumbled about much in the same way as those at Christ Church, Barbados.

The Waldegraves fled from England with James II and his court in 1688 during the struggle for the Protestant succession when the Catholic branch of the Stuarts—the Jacobites—was banished for ever. There is a story that one of the Waldegraves, Arabella, became a nun in France, then renounced her vows and returned to England as an agent for the Stuart pretenders. She came to Borley and there she was murdered and has since haunted the place.

Thus we have three stories in explanation of the Borley nun, each one strongly romantic. But the Marie Lairre story appears to be better established, if one can accept the various contacts which have been made with the ghost by means of seances, planchette and wall writings. Marie Lairre's alleged remains were found under the old cellar floor at the Rectory and were given a Christian burial at Liston churchyard in 1945. Masses have been said for her soul at Arundel and Oxford.

Another branch of the Waldegrave family held the patronage of Borley during the eighteenth century, but it was not a sufficiently important living for it to be of any consequence until the end of the century. In the first part of the nineteenth century the living was held by the Herringham family.

Finally came the Bulls, a family of parsons and landowners who acquired Borley in the middle of the century. The Rev. Henry D. E. Bull (born in 1833) became record of Borley in 1862 and the following year he built the famous Rectory.

It was an ugly, rambling, red-bricked building, to which in 1875–76 he added a wing in order to house his innumerable family —he had fourteen children: some reports say seventeen—as well as his large staff of domestics. The rectory had some twenty-five rooms, extensive cellars, about three acres of garden, a cottage and other buildings. It cost about £3,000 to build.

Bull was a sporting parson who wore canonicals only for Sunday morning service. The rest of the time he was in tweeds and usually with a shot-gun. He would even pot at rooks from the Rectory drawing-room on Sundays after church. It didn't look as though the Victorian Sunday hung very heavily at Borley.

The new rector acquired, along with his tasteless house, a well-established ghost, for the nun had been seen for centuries. She walked regularly in the rectory garden.

Henry Bull, far from being put off by his spectral tenant, was fascinated. He did her the honour of erecting a summer-house in his garden opposite the Nun's Walk, which was a long path which skirted the lawn, in order to watch her. There are no records of her walking at night, but always during daylight, particularly at dawn and at dusk.

Henry's son, Harry, also followed the family tradition and was ordained. He became curate to his father, and the two of them would spend hours in the summer-house sitting there, smoking their pipes and watching for the nun which they claimed to have seen a number of times.

It must not be thought that the Bull family were morbidly obsessed with the occult. The opposite impression is created by those who later gave their recollections of those Victorian days at Borley Rectory, where Henry Bull's great tribe of offspring was frequently joined by those of his brothers and sisters whose marriages were equally fruitful.

The Bull family were rich and they entertained well in their great rambling Rectory where the ghosts were all part of the entertainment. The staff, however, were not all amused by the apparitions. In 1886 a nursemaid (later to become Mrs E. Byford) left her post at the Rectory after hearing the ghostly noises. "I only stayed a month," she said in 1929, "the place was so weird."

Not only was the nun seen a number of times by various members of the family and their guests, but also the phantom coach and four would come clattering down the narrow lane beside the Rectory, waking the household and bringing white faces and round eyes to the many bedroom windows to see the celebrated sight, though

some claimed they got so used to it that they slept right through it.

As early as 1886 poltergeist activity was reported within the Rectory—stones thrown about, visitors' boots being found unaccountably on top of the wardrobes, tooth glasses sailing across the room. The poltergeists did not, as some people aver, have to await the arrival of Harry Price in 1929. They were, it seems, active at Borley when Price was a mere five years old and could hardly have been held responsible for them.

The Rev. Henry Bull died in his sixtieth year in 1892 and his son succeeded him as rector of Borley. Life continued at the Rectory with the same massive family parties and ghost hunts. Old Henry Bull apparently now joined the company of Borley apparitions and was seen by his son and members of his family, rather, one must think, to their concern, or were they so used to ghosts at Borley that it didn't worry them?

On the evening of 28 July, 1900, the four Misses Bull were returning to the Rectory from a garden party. It was getting dusk and as they were crossing the lawn they all of them saw the nun, dressed in black, head bowed, hands clasped in prayer. Miss Ethel Bull saw the nun on several occasions, and she also saw other apparitions, notably a strange man who stood beside her bed, and once or twice, she said, she felt someone sitting on the side of her bed.

The Rev. Harry Bull, who married in 1911, and not unnaturally took a great interest in ghosts, joined his father in the shades in 1927 and the sixty-five years of the Bull incumbencies at Borley ended. Throughout the whole of Harry Bull's incumbency the Borley ghosts continued their haunt—the nun, the headless monk, and the phantom coach clattering along the road from Sudbury.

Harry Bull died on 9 June, 1927, and Borley Rectory remained empty of human habitation until 2 October, 1928, when the new rector of Borley, the Rev. Guy Eric Smith, and his wife moved in. The Smiths, who had lived in India, came to Borley ignorant of its ghostly reputation.

The Rectory was a shock to them. The great, rabbit-warren of a place was without gas, electricity or main water. The water supply, which had to be pumped from a well, was totally inadequate. Apart from the bad sanitation, the place was in a dilapidated state, with broken pipes and leaking roofs. Grimly cold, the huge house was impossible to heat. In all, a great contrast to the warm gaiety of the place at the height of the Bull days.

In this dark, cold, oppressive Rectory the Smiths found them-

selves not only up against Victorian housing and sanitation at its worst, but also in the middle of a rather formidable haunt.

Thoroughly alarmed and worried about their parishioners' fear of even entering the haunted Rectory, they wrote to the Editor of the *Daily Mirror* in June, 1929, asking him if he could put them in touch with a psychical research society and telling him of the extraordinary things which were happening in the Rectory—strange lights seen in empty, locked rooms, bells ringing unaccountably, slow dragging footsteps heard in empty rooms. The nun had been seen again, and the phantom coach had swept through the hedge on to the lawn and then vanished.

The *Daily Mirror* put the Smiths in touch with Harry Price, who was already well known for his investigations into psychic phenomena. Price went to Borley Rectory on 12 June. The place was already headline news.

With the arrival of Harry Price the poltergeist phenomena increased in the most marked fashion. Small missiles flew about the Rectory, keys leaped unaccountably from keyholes, ornaments hurled themselves down the stairs.

It seems clear that at this point at least Harry Price had his own reasons for keeping the haunt going, by fair means or otherwise. During one of these noisy and dangerous sessions with the alleged poltergeists, Charles Sutton, a reporter on the *Daily Mail*, was hit on the head by a large pebble. He says he was suspicious of Price and felt his pockets which he found full of brick ends and pebbles. His editor wouldn't unmask Price, on the lawyer's advice, owing to the risk of libel, as there was no other witness, and so the story couldn't be told until after Price's death.

Sutton wasn't the only one who suspected Price of creating additional phenomena in order to boost the Borley sensations. It was obvious that the Rev. and Mrs Smith were suspicious, though they were too polite to say so. After they left the Rectory, they said they had done so because of its broken-down condition, and that they did not believe that the house was haunted by anything else but rats and local superstition. Mrs Smith said later that after the arrival of Harry Price she and her husband were astonished at the sudden onset of phenomena. It is worth noting incidentally that Price was an accomplished conjuror.

A seance was held at the Rectory by Price, in which several people took part—the Smiths, two sisters of the late Rev. Harry Bull and a reporter from the *Daily Mirror*. After unsuccessful attempts, Price later reported, they finally got through to the spirit

whose footsteps were heard in the Rectory, and the spirit declared itself to be that of Harry Bull. Various private matters were addressed to the spirit by the Misses Bull, and the result of the attempted communication does not seem to have been very successful.

During the Smiths' incumbency at Borley a skull mysteriously appeared in the library cupboard. It was a small skull in perfect condition and said to belong to a young woman.

But according to some villagers the skull was a possession of the Rev. Henry Bull. During the 'nineties, they said, the skull was buried in the churchyard, but such a commotion broke out in the Rectory —knockings and screaming and crashing, and bedclothes being pulled off the beds while their occupants were sleeping—that the thing was hastily dug up and restored to its place in the library. Screaming skulls of course are a fairly common form of haunting.

If the Smiths' incumbency of Borley aroused many questions in people's minds about the haunting, what followed during the next incumbency was strange and remarkable indeed.

The Smiths left the Rectory in July, 1929, finally leaving Borley for Norfolk in April of the following year. The Rectory remained empty for seventeen months, and then in October, 1930, the Rev. Lionel A. Foyster, with his young wife Marianne, and baby daughter Adelaide, moved in. Foyster was a cousin of the Misses Bull, daughters of the Rev. Henry Bull, who were patrons of the living.

Immediately upon their arrival the haunting began at an even greater intensity. The phenomena were now mainly poltergeist. Objects were moved, bottles, stones and other missiles were thrown about the Rectory, doors were mysteriously locked and unlocked, bells rang unaccountably, furniture was overturned, messages appeared on the walls. Apart from this there were footsteps, strange odours, apparitions, as well as a tremendous noise.

The Borley ghosts seemed somehow attracted towards Mrs Foyster, a young and vital woman, and the phenomena which took place were observed not only by her husband, but by several independent witnesses, some of them people of standing.

Strange footsteps were heard about the house on the day that the Foysters moved into the Rectory, and a voice was heard calling "Marianne, dear". No one was ever able to trace the voice, or anyone who could have made the sound of the footsteps. For a short period Harry Bull made a spectral appearance in his old Rectory, being seen on the staircase in a dressing-gown carrying a scroll of paper.

After a lull in this ghostly activity, the poltergeists then got to work, particularly in the kitchen, where jugs and crockery were

moved about, often disappearing for days. Bells jangled although all the wires had been disconnected. Hymn-books suddenly appeared in the oven, and articles of all description began to hurl themselves about the Rectory, propelled apparently by no human agency. During this poltergeistic bombardment, Mrs Foyster was hit and hurt several times.

Foyster himself made a diary of these phenomenal happenings. At a later stage Price, seeing what enormous interest there was in what was happening at Borley Rectory, turned the whole thing into a very profitable publicity stunt.

The truth of this strange story of ghosts and humans will probably never be known. It cannot be said that Harry Price, who died in 1948, emerges with much credit from the affair.

In 1931 a series of messages addressed to "Marianne" appeared on the walls of the Rectory. They were all appeals directed presumably to Mrs Foyster—"Marianne, please get help", "Marianne, lights, Mass, prayers". They were written in a childish hand, and seemed to have a Roman Catholic flavour, and the impression was created of some poor soul in the nether world wanting the prayers, the Mass and incense of those in this world. These messages were investigated by a number of interested people, and several theories were put forward to explain them. One of these was that Mrs Foyster was a poltergeist-focus, and this of course could explain a great number of things.

The Foysters left Borley in October, 1935, as Mr Foyster had to give up the living owing to his persistent ill-health. The ecclesiastical authorities, owing to Borley Rectory's somewhat infamous reputation, decided to sell the place and provide other accommodation for the Borley incumbents.

It was not an easy place to sell. Price offered to rent it for a year, and he entered into a tenancy beginning in May, 1937, He didn't intend to live there. He wanted to carry on his psychic experiments. To this end he advertised in *The Times* for investigators who were prepared to go to Borley and make scientific observations of the phenomena.

A number of ladies and gentlemen of integrity and sincerity joined in Harry Price's great ghost-hunt, which attracted enormous attention and was featured both in the Press and on the BBC. Among those camping out in the cold spooky rooms of the near-derelict Rectory was the famous Professor C. E. M. Joad, who is reported to have seen pencil markings appear on a wall.

The spectacular activity of the Foyster period ceased with the

departure of Marianne and her invalid husband. During the Price tenancy very little occurred which could not have been contrived by Price himself, and indeed he is gravely suspected by a number of his associates of artificially creating phenomena.

In 1937 seances were held in the Rectory to try and get in touch with the departed spirits which were troubling the place, and it was from these sessions that Miss Helen Glanville, using a planchette, obtained the story of Marie Lairre, who was murdered by her husband, Henry Waldegrave, in 1667 and her body buried unceremoniously beneath the cellar floor of the old demolished house which once stood on the Rectory site. Marie Lairre's trouble was the fact that she had been buried in unconsecrated ground without any Masses or prayers said for her soul, a matter of grave and eternal importance for a woman who had been a nun in the seventeenth century.

Many other messages were received in various ways from the several restless spirits of Borley, the total effect of which seemed to confuse the issue. One message received in March, 1938, said that the Rectory was to be burnt down that night.

Actually the place was burnt down eleven months later. One supposes that spirits travelling in the infinite pathways of eternity may be forgiven being a year out in their calculations. But destroyed by fire Borley Rectory was, and it happened on the midnight of 27 February, 1939.

There was nothing supernatural about the fire. The Rectory had been bought by Captain W. E. Gregson, in December, 1938, who renamed it Borley Priory, and who was experiencing the usual Borley phenomena of strange noises, furniture tossed about, and waves of incense in some of the rooms. On the night of the fire, while the new owner was sorting out some books, a pile of volumes fell, knocked over a paraffin-lamp and within seconds the room was in flames. Unable to cope with the formidable conflagration which rapidly spread, the alarmed Captain ran to the nearest phone and alerted the Sudbury Fire Brigade. By the time the engines arrived the Rectory was a mass of flames and the roof had fallen in.

The watching crowds saw figures moving in the flames as Borley burnt itself out. The local constable saw two figures, a man and a woman, dressed in cloaks, leaving the Rectory at the height of the fire. He asked Gregson who they might be, but Gregson told him that there was no one on the premises but himself. The constable was certain he had seen them leave the burning building and cross the courtyard.

The villagers also saw these two unearthly strangers leave the Rectory, walking out of the very heart of the flames. They wore cloaks, the villagers said. One was a young girl, the other a "formless figure".

And so Borley was burnt to a shell. The walls and chimneys stood. Inside was blackened, twisted desolation. But it was by no means the end of the story.

The sceptical said that Harry Price saw to that. He certainly kept the story going, and to a large extent kept a monopoly on the Borley news by making his observers sign an agreement not to divulge anything they had seen or heard except to him. He was working on his first book on Borley, which was published in 1940, and which became a best-seller. The interest in Borley continued unabated. At least it took people's minds off the darkest days of the war.

The Borley ghosts apparently had not been driven away by the fire. Mysterious figures were seen among the ruins and at the windows of rooms which now had no floors.

Interest in Borley was enormous. It was considered by many to be the most authenticated haunting in the world. Price's many critics had to keep silent about what they knew or suspected, owing to the law of libel.

During the war Borley was the centre of many a ghost hunt, and a spooky visit there was a popular diversion for occult-minded servicemen of various nationalities. Harry Price, of course, was as busy as ever, propagating the legend, lecturing, broadcasting, writing another book about it.

The gutted building, however, was in a dangerous state. It had been greatly damaged by gales and it was finally decided to pull the ruins down.

Seances were still being held at which contact was claimed to have been made with the mysterious nun, Marie Lairre, and at one of these Marie Lairre revealed the place where her bones were to be found. In August, 1943, Price supervised digging in the cellar of the ruined Rectory and some human bones were found which were claimed to be the remains of Marie Lairre. In 1945 these remains were given a Christian burial in Liston churchyard by the Rev. A. C. Henning, and it has since been assumed that her unquiet spirit is finally at rest.

But what of the other Borley spirits? According to reports, the Borley site has continued to be haunted. The haunting has survived the death of Harry Price (in 1948), which event was immediately

followed by a series of accusations against him by people who no longer had the libel law to fear and who said the whole haunt was a hoax.

There is little doubt that Price faked some of the Borley phenomena, but it still remains one of the most interesting ghost stories of all time. When the dust of controversy dies down, it will no doubt emerge as one of the strangest and most formidable haunts on record.

The Ghostly Trapper of Labrador

In 1959 Lord Beaverbrook suggested that I might like to go on a tour of exploration throughout the "barrens", muskegs, trackless forests and scattered outposts of Newfoundland and thence into the far north of Labrador where no English or American writer had been before. The suggestion was that I should write a book covering the long history of Newfoundland, Britain's oldest colony, of which Labrador is a political part, together with a survey of the economic resources and future of those vast and bitter lands where winter reigns for most of the year, the silence can be felt and men are scarce.

It is the land of the giant, shambling moose, of herds of caribou moving like prehistoric shadows against blue-green lichened rocks, of the bear and the wolf and the dancing spearpoints of the Midnight Sun.

There followed an intensive tour of Newfoundland, by plane, truck, canoe, log raft and on my flat feet.

It is odd, but true, that the hairy-chested, iron-fisted men of the frozen north hate walking. Trappers and hunters walk. The rest go on wheels where wheels can go.

Once on a three-mile walk out of St John's, Newfoundland, with Brigadier Michael Wardell, Beaverbrook's right-hand man in the Maritime Provinces of Canada, we were passed by a Cadillac. The driver turned and looked at us curiously.

We reached the point of our three-mile stroll, Signal Hill, where Marconi received the first transatlantic wireless message from

Poldhu in Cornwall in 1903. We stood on the hill where history had been made, gazing out across the Atlantic for a few minutes. Then we turned and started striding back on our Sunday morning constitutional. A mile along the road the Cadillac drew up alongside.

"Say, you guys wanna lift?"

"No, thanks," we replied.

"Gee, you wakkin' all the way back?"

"Sure," I said. "We like walking."

"Jesus, you must be Limeys." And he drove off.

Not, you see, the sort of country, one would have thought, to believe in ghosts. They believe in newsprint, iron ore, pulp mills, salmon and the dollar.

Yet, a week later, a world away out of this world, they told me what is surely the strangest modern ghost tale of this century, whilst we were sitting round the stove in an Atwell Arctic hut, on the bleak shore of Wabush Lake, in the wilderness of Labrador. Three days later I heard an echo of the same tale from Ashuanipi Joe, my Red Indian guide, away up at Mile 274, in the heart of the birdless forest. Wolf and bear country. A week later I heard it from Magistrate Corbett at Goose Bay.

Finally, when we got back to St John's, the 400-year-old capital of Newfoundland, Mr Leo English, the Curator of the Museum, an erudite, scholarly man, confirmed the story.

We were a pioneering party on that day of autumn sun and lonely wind, on the edge of Wabush Lake. Five of us: Mr W. J. Keogh, Minister of Mines, Fred Gover, Secretary of Mines, my friend Gordon Pushie, Director of Economic Development for Newfoundland, my wife, and myself—guests of the Premier of Newfoundland, the Rt Hon Joseph Smallwood.

A land of bleak, unending, grey-green wilderness—of long lakes and utter silences. This is Labrador. Arctic winds blowing over an earth that even in the brief, hot summer is frozen, hard as iron, to a hundred feet or more below the surface.

This is the land where "Smoker" and his white ghost team run. Irving Penny, a trapper, can tell the tale.

One day of blinding snow, Irving was driving his ten-dog team over the bleak Partridge Hills, hauling a heavy komatik (sledge) through slushy snow. The sou'-east wind blinded him. His eyelids almost stuck together. He "mushed" on, cursing, hoping for a snow-bank to burrow into for the night.

Suddenly he heard, faintly, in the blizzard, the sound of another

dog-team. The heavy figure of a man, dressed all in white furs, loomed out of the swirling snow. He was driving a team of fourteen pure-white huskies, pushing on into the teeth of the blizzard with utter confidence. Irving yelled at him. The man did not even turn his head. Irving followed him.

Half an hour later the winter huts of the fishermen of Frenchmen's Island loomed up in the swirling snow-mist. The white team ahead passed the first house, disappeared behind the second one. Irving, pretty well done in, pulled up at the first house, rapped on the door.

The fisherman who opened the door welcomed him in. Every man's front door is open to you in Newfoundland and Labrador, where they still speak, not with the nasal twang of North America, but with the soft West Country accent of their Bristol ancestors. They use the antique words and phrases of Somerset moors and marshes, the rolling hills of Gloucestershire.

Irving put up his team for the night, and when he had settled down in front of the fire, said to his host: "Who was the feller in white who came in, in front of me?"

"No one came in—not a soul," his host replied.

So Penny told him his tale of the all-white trapper with the all-white team who had guided him to safety. The fisherman laughed shortly.

"That was 'Smoker'. He brought you here. He always turns up when it blows a blizzard. Saving his soul—*and* it needed it."

The story began in 1910, when a trapper named Esau Gillingham, a Newfoundlander, crossed over the Straits of Belle Isle into Labrador, and put down a few lines of traps. They did not pay too well. But Esau soon got to know every fisherman, Red Indian, Eskimo and trapper along the coast from Battle Harbour and Black Bear River in the south way up to Nain in the Fraser River country. Some say that he even travelled as far north as Cape Chidley, where the ice-flows of Ungava Bay meet the cold tides of the Atlantic Arctic.

In those lonely settlements life was, and still is, as hard as nails. If you cannot shoot, fish, or trap, you starve. The coastal steamers, few and far between, and the Grenfell Mission are—or were, before the coming of aircraft—the sole links with the outer world. We were lucky. We had ex-Canadian Premier Mackenzie-King's own big plane with the two finest bush pilots in the north, plus a little red Beaver float-plane to hop from lake to lake. But when Esau Gillingham hit the north in 1910, Bleriot was a futurist nightmare buzzing like a bee from France to England.

Hard living demands hard liquor. Rum, in those northern winters, is a godsend. But rum supplies were few, far, and precious. So Esau set up a secret still in a forest of black spruce and there, until his death, he brewed a hellish concoction from spruce cones, sugar, and yeast. Sheer deadly moonshine. The Labrador trappers called it "smoke". Hence Esau's nickname.

Moonshining paid better than trapping. So in summer Smoker sailed his boat from cove to cove selling his poison. In winter he travelled with a big keg of it strapped to his komatik. The stuff did its worst.

Some who drank it went mad. Others beat their wives, smashed up their miserable homes. Some died of exposure when they collapsed dead drunk in the snow. So the Mounties took a hand. They caught up with Smoker, smashed his keg, and clapped him into gaol in St. John's. Twelve months of hard labour and penitence. When he came out he swore: "They'll never see me inside there again."

Back to Labrador went Smoker—with a plan. For months he trapped—with one object only. He wanted white skins. One by one he caught three dozen ermine, a couple of white fox, and made himself an all-over suit of pure white skins. At the same time he collected every white huskie he could beg, borrow, or steal. He built a white komatik and lashed a white-painted keg to it. Then he started up business in "smoke" once again.

Year after year the white team with the white-clad figure cracking his whip yelling them on, "mushed" from settlement to settlement, from log cabin to Eskimo igloo. Poison was abroad in the land once more. Time and again the Mounties tried to catch him. But the white figure with the white team melted into the white silences.

Then an informer split on him. "Smoker's still is in a spruce-belt near Brazil's Pinch", he told them.

The police rounded up Smoker. They took him to a wood.

"We know your still's in there," the sergeant said. "Now lead us to it. We'll shove you in gaol for the rest of your life, if you don't."

"My still's in there, O.K.," Smoker replied. "Go right in, boys, and find it." A policeman started to walk towards the trees. Smoker grabbed him, said quietly: "Son!—there's fifty bear-traps scattered around that still. Mind where you put your feet."

Since a bear-trap can break a man's leg, the police thought better of it. They had to let Smoker go, for lack of evidence. They never caught him again.

Things went from bad to worse. More of his customers went mad.

One or two went blind. Then Smoker kidnapped a woman, strapped her to his komatik, and took her off to his log hut, out in the forest where the timber wolf slinks like a grey ghost, and the black bear dwells. Weeks later he sent her home. She was raving. Apart from this ravishment he had three Eskimo wives. Meanwhile, not a white dog was safe on the coast. Smoker stole them all.

In the end he took to drinking his own rot-gut. He killed an Indian, strangling him with his bare hands, in berserk rage. What few mothers there were on that cold coast of winds and loneliness, terrified their children with the threat that "Smoker'll get you if you're naughty".

Finally, he went back to Newfoundland. There, in 1940, he fell off a fish-platform, near the Gander River—one of those spindly "flakes" on which they dry the cod—and broke his back. Three days later he died in agony, repentant. With his last breath he gasped:

"Lordy, Lordy, God! I don't want to go to Hell. Let me drive my dogs along the coast to the end of Time. I'll make up for all the bad I've done."

So if you turn up in Labrador one day when the snow drives like the white breath of death, and the Hamilton Falls, higher by far than Niagara, shout their hoarse thunder over the lonely wastes—remember Smoker. He may show you the way to go home.

The Sceptic's Tale

All right! I will allow you your triumph, all you believers in ghosts. I will make my admission right away. I used to be a sceptic about ghosts, but I am a sceptic no longer. I hardly could be, not since I went to Cullen. I know *you* won't scoff. Scientists may. Let them. I am a journalist. I work with facts. And the fact is that, at Cullen House, Banffshire, on the night of 8 August, 1964, I heard the footsteps and felt the presence of a man who died in 1770.

By a strange irony, it was my total disbelief in ghosts that led me to have this experience. It all began when I went to interview Tom. Tom is a clairvoyant. When he told me about his work, it was hard for me to understand; when he added that he could detect and identify ghosts, my disbelief must have been very apparent. He asked me point-blank whether I believed in the supernatural. I shot back a blunt "No".

"Come with me to Scotland," Tom replied. "And I will prove to you that ghosts exist."

Who could resist such a challenge? Not I—especially when Tom told me that Cullen House is one of the most romantic and splendid of Scotland's castles and that its owner, Lady Seafield, is the most generous of hostesses. So I accepted—on two conditions. Tom was not to tell me the ghost story. And he was not to say which part of Cullen was haunted. That way, my imagination would have no chance to act up.

We flew to Aberdeen on 8 August: Tom, myself, and Alan, a Fleet Street columnist who had long wanted to see Tom "at work"

467

with ghosts, and thought he might get a story. Alan was, if anything, even more sceptical than I. As we drove through the rich farmlands Tom told us ghost stories about the castles we passed. Green Ladies, Curses, Warnings of Death ... we heard the lot. In the bright sunshine they sounded preposterously melodramatic. If we had known that in some fifteen hours' time we were to be gripped by the same forces at which we laughed ... But how could we? It was inconceivable.

However, when we arrived at Cullen even Alan had to agree that it was, at least, the perfect setting for a ghost-story. Long before we reached the village great thunderheads had built up in the sky; by the time we turned in at the gates everything was still. We caught a glimpse of the sea, heaving beneath a smooth, oily swell; then we were in the drowned gloom of a wood, the bare trunks of the trees twisting their way upwards as if to the surface of water. A turning suddenly brought us right into the courtyard of the house, a huge, fortress-like pile of granite blocks, heraldic beasts, gargoyles, coats-of-arms, all crowned by a jumble of towers, turrets, mossy slates and sly little windows, rearing up against a background of inky sky. When the engine was switched off a tremendous quietness fell about the place, broken only by thunder muttering round the distant hills, and the roar of the burn, foaming over the rocks at the base of the crag on which the castle is perched.

It was all gloriously appropriate, the Gothic castle of fiction come to life. But the interior gave quite another impression; all was light, white, beauty and taste. Paintings and tapestry, china and glass; huge rooms, airy windows; everything had clearly been modernized in the eighteenth century and again, discreetly, in modern times. No ghost, said Alan and I to each other, smugly, would stand a chance in such a civilized setting.

Tom's room was on one of the main bedroom corridors; when Alan and I were led on and up I thought we would find that we were in deliberately spooky rooms; I expected slit windows, four-posters, black oak furniture. But although we were in the oldest part of the house, and somewhat isolated from the others, no one could call our rooms atmospheric. Alan's—the Pulpit Room—was at the head of the spiral staircase; small and white, with plain, "good" furniture. Mine—the Church Room—was around the corner. It was three times the size of Alan's but no more ghostly, with its modern twin beds, enormous windows and thick carpeting; the archers' turrets in the corners had even been converted into walk-in cupboards. Opposite the door was a bathroom; the passage con-

tinued only a few yards before stopping at a low little door in the wall. I mention these details to show that there was absolutely nothing to stimulate the imagination.

There were a number of people staying in the house. All knew Cullen well; all knew why we three were there. Yet no one referred to the ghost. I never had the impression that the subject was being avoided; rather that it was not of sufficient interest to be mentioned. By tea-time I doubted whether Tom's challenge would be met. And when, at dinner, I asked a cousin of Lady Seafield's whether Alan and I were in the haunted part of the house and received a direct and faintly amused negative, I was sure nothing would happen.

We went to bed around 11.30. The thunder had long since ceased; now the moon glimmered through a light sea-mist that coiled past the windows. When I leaned out, the air felt cool and fresh, and I could hear the slight noises of night-birds. When I closed the curtains and shut my door the whole tower was lapped in utter silence. I was glad. I was dog-tired from our 6 a.m. start, and expected to go to sleep almost at once.

But I did not. The more I tried to relax the more tense I became. The bed was exceedingly comfortable; there was nothing to keep me awake. And yet I felt exactly as I used to feel when on night patrol in the army; all my animal senses were tuned up to their fullest extent. I could not imagine why, until I realized that the atmosphere in the room was changing. Very slowly, so slowly as to be almost imperceptible, I felt a growing thickness, an increasing oppression, as if the afternoon's thunderstorm was gathering again in the room. As it grew stronger I felt the symptoms of fever; my body alternated between heat and icy shivers; I had difficulty in breathing evenly; my heart pounded; I felt a vague illogical distress.

It was a ridiculous situation. Here was I, a man of thirty-six, who did not believe in the supernatural, sleeping in the part of the house I had been assured was not haunted, with another man only a few yards away—but acting like a child afraid of the dark, staring now at the faintly moonlit windows, now at the long cheval glass glimmering in the corner. And listening. Straining my ears. But for what? Nothing. . . .

I must have lain there for an hour and a half before I heard the footsteps. For a second my heart bounded. But the sounds were so faint and far away that I thought, after listening for so long, that my hearing was playing tricks with me. Then it was unmistakable. They were footsteps. And they were coming up the stairs. The foot-

falls were uneven; every now and then they stumbled. But they were not in the least furtive; I could distinctly hear the scrape of leather on stone. I felt no fear—until I thought of something that made my flesh crawl. I heard feet on stone. *But the stairs were thickly carpeted.*

One cannot remember degrees of emotion, but I think my fear at that moment was the worst fear I have ever felt; worse than fear in the army, worse than fear at sea—and that can be bad. I had never known that one could be literally "scared stiff". Now I did. I was rigid. I felt I must have light, but I had to make a vast muscular effort, as well as that of will, to switch on the bed-side lamp. In fictional ghost-stories light usually defeats the supernatural. I can only tell you that in this case it made no difference whatsoever. In the second before switching on the lamp I thought: "I shall see familiar objects; ordinary, everyday things; my clothes on the chair; my shaving gear; luggage; books. And they will dispel this terror". They did not.

I remember, too, thinking that I only had to get up, open the door, and see who it was. I am not ashamed to admit that I simply could not do this.

The footsteps stumbled round the corner of the passage and stopped outside my door. My bed was only four or five feet from the door; I propped myself up on one elbow and stared at the handle, terrified that it might turn. A cold sweat trickled down my chest. For a second the handle seemed to tremble, and I felt my scalp tighten and the hair on my neck rise like a dog's hackles. Then the footsteps retreated. I do not know where they went. I think my fear was so intense that it confused my mind for a moment. In any case, they died away.

I am sure no one will be surprised to hear that I did not sleep much for the rest of that night. I hoped that the atmosphere of the room would die down after the footsteps ceased, and return to normal; but it remained hot and turbulent until dawn. I did, of course, doze off. But I awoke several times, with a violent start, as if someone was in the room.

True ghost-stories never seem to parallel fiction. In a story the haunted guest enters the breakfast-room haggard or furious, and either receives or demands an explanation. End of story. I did no such thing, for the simple reason that in daylight I felt a fool. I did ask Alan, casually, whether he had gone downstairs for anything in the night, but he said no. I also asked whether he had slept well; he said he had. As for telling Tom anything . . . it was unthinkable.

Someone *could* have come upstairs; the room *could* have been hot. I had proof of nothing.

That night there was a large dinner-party, and we did not get to bed until the small hours. I did not look forward to returning to the Church Room, but I was, by now, very tired and consequently, I suppose, more relaxed. I did not hear the footsteps again, but the atmosphere was as thick and as ominous as the previous night and, as before, I slept fitfully. However, this I put down to nervous expectancy.

The following morning Tom took us to meet the Ritchies, Lady Seafield's factor and his wife. Mrs Ritchie is an expert on the history of Cullen House and has, in fact, written the visitors' guide-book. I asked her how my room and Alan's received their names. She was in the middle of a fascinating account of clandestine services held on our staircase during Jacobite days when she looked at me with a quizzical expression and said: "And might I ask why you're so interested in those rooms?"

"Because we are sleeping in them," I told her.

Mrs Ritchie gasped. "Have you been all right?" she asked.

I suspected the truth in that moment, but I was still hesitant as I told my tale. When I finished, and before anyone else could say anything, Alan broke in.

"But this is fantastic," he exclaimed. "I haven't heard the footsteps, but I have felt exactly the same atmosphere as you describe. In fact," he admitted. "I have spent two of the most disturbed and frightening nights of my life."

Tom exploded with laughter. "Wonderful!" he crowed. "I asked for you to be put in those rooms, but I never really thought you would hear the ghost."

Alan and I turned to Mrs Ritchie.

"Why, yes," she said. "That is the haunted part of the house."

Then she told us the story.

Soon after Bonnie Prince Charlie's final defeat, Cullen was inherited by James, 6th Earl of Findlater (the title has since died out) and 3rd Earl of Seafield. James was known as "the Mad Earl". One gathers he was not permanently insane, but periodically he would be seized by some kind of fit, during which he became violent. As he always knew when a seizure was coming on he would lock himself into the library and drop the key out of the window. When he had recovered, his factor, who was also his closest friend, would let him out.

One day—3 November, 1770, to be precise—the factor returned

too soon. When the Earl came round he found that he had murdered his friend. Horror-stricken, the distracted man rushed from the room, stumbled up the tower staircase just outside, and went into the attics—the attics that lie past our rooms. There he cut his throat.

So much for the story? What of the hauntings? Mrs Ritchie herself had had no experiences, beyond "uncomfortable feelings" in the library. However, both she and Tom promised us all the corroborative evidence we needed back at the house.

Walking back through the soft sea mist Alan and I discovered that our experiences tallied exactly. But we were still not prepared to concede the point to the triumphant Tom, until we had heard what Lady Seafield and her relatives had to say. And we would both sleep in my room that night.

Most of our resolution to hold out was immediately shattered. When Tom told our hostess and fellow-guests of our experiences no one looked in the least surprised, least of all Lady Seafield, who looked up from carving ham and said in her usual quiet way: "I am so sorry. Would you like other rooms? She might have been apologizing for uncomfortable beds.

Over lunch almost everyone had a tale to tell. Lord Strathspey, Lady Seafield's cousin, a bluff soldier with an immensely distinguished record, admitted: "I wouldn't sleep in those rooms for a thousand pounds. My wife and I usually stay in the room below, and any number of times I've heard the most frightful racket coming from up there when I know the rooms are empty. Footsteps on the stairs and someone tramping about." He went on to tell us that only two months before another relative was so disturbed in the Church Room that he had rushed downstairs at 3 a.m. and refused ever to sleep there again.

Lady Seafield's son told us that as a child, long before he had heard the ghost story, he had always been "terrified" of the library; after lunch, Lady Seafield herself said that although she had never actually seen the ghost she had "felt his presence" many, many times, especially when she was a child.

"I knew nothing about the ghost," she said. "But I always hated the library and that staircase. My fear became so bad that my mother, who was also worried by strange stories told her by other guests, had the whole area exorcized. She didn't tell me, of course, but I can remember her sending me and a cousin up to the library afterwards and, for the first time, we weren't frightened".

Apparently, however, the exorcism was effective for only about

thirty years. In 1943 Mrs Yeats, now a guide, then a maid in the house, nearly witnessed a re-enactment of the tragedy. One afternoon, when the family was away, she went into the library to dust. To her astonishment she saw an old gentleman sitting in one of the big armchairs.

"I can see him as vividly today as when I first saw him," she told us. "I got the impression he was a kindly person. He was smiling and watching someone who was seated at the desk. I never looked to see who that person was, but I noticed him out of the corner of my eye. The atmosphere in the room was very strained; although the old gentleman was smiling he looked ill at ease, almost fearful.

Imagining that the two men were staying in the house Mrs Yeats apologized and retired. In a bedroom only a few yards away she found the head housemaid, who told her categorically that there was no one staying in the house. Mrs Yeats insisted that she come and see the two men. The other woman agreed; but when they re-entered the library the room was empty.

Tom thinks (and most people agree with him) that Mrs Yeats—the last person in the world to imagine such a thing—saw the ghost of the murdered factor. The shadowy figure at the desk would have been the Mad Earl.

Alan and I had only one more task ahead of us—to visit the attics. Before it got dark we went through the little door beyond my room, up a steep, narrow, spiral stair, and found ourselves right under the slates. The outer room was unremarkable; there were a few pictures and some odds and ends of furniture stacked neatly around the walls. Nor, at first glance, was there anything remarkable about the inner room—until we saw the huge irregular stain, a great blotch, roughly a yard square. It looked just as though someone had spilt oil on the rough pine floor. Later, in London, I asked a doctor what an old bloodstain on soft wood would look like. Without a moment's hesitation he said "Oil".

After such a sensational day Alan and I were so convinced that our last night at Cullen would be anticlimactic that we decided not to share my room after all. However, no sooner was I alone than the atmosphere closed in with such speed and force as to seem positively menacing, and I was plucking up courage to summon my neighbour when a sheepish Alan appeared to ask whether he could move in after all. The Pulpit Room, he said, was insupportable.

Around 2 a.m. I heard the footsteps approaching, exactly as on the first night. As they reached the door I switched on the light. Alan awoke with a start, just in time to hear the footsteps retreating.

As before, we were both awakened constantly, once by a tremendous crash from somewhere overhead. At 5 a.m., when Tom came to call us, we capitulated.

On the plane back to London we talked of nothing else. *How* can one hear the footsteps of a man who died nearly two hundred years ago? *Why* should one feel, even share, his emotional instability and despair?

Tom could not tell us; he only had a theory.

"Just because we die it doesn't mean that we change our way of life in a hurry," he said. "The Earl is tied to Cullen; he comes back with the same agitation and agony of mind in his present existence, whatever that is, that he had when he was alive".

We listened, and nodded, and said that he was probably right. After all, who were we to disagree? We were sceptics no longer.

Brighton Ghosts

Brighton has more character, more history and more architectural beauty than any seaside town in Britain. Among its manifold attractions is the fact that it is renowned for its ghosts—if one can list ghosts as attractions.

Although there are no really ancient buildings in Brighton, it nevertheless has some unique features which are not to be found elsewhere. There is, for instance the Lanes, a network of narrow alley-ways and twittens situated right in the centre of the town, and which represent the old paths which once separated the various gardens or parcels of land.

In the Lanes are to be found all manner of quaint little shops selling antiques, bric-à-brac, second-hand books, old silverware and china. Victoriana and Brightoniana. Antiquarians and seekers of the unusual find the Lanes a happy hunting ground. The late Queen Mary was frequently to be seen in the narrow, drowsy passageways of this oasis in busy Brighton.

Though the district has been largely rebuilt within the last century or so, there are many very old houses, and some of the buildings were built into part of the ancient Priory of St Bartholomew, the old walls of which with their characteristic flint buttresses can be seen in the cellars of some of these quaint houses. Beneath others are to be found ancient pillars, gothic arches, and the massive oak timberings of medieval times.

Various ghosts are reported to have been seen in the Lanes, the most persistent and most famous of which is the grey nun who haunts

the alley-ways at twilight. This nun is distinguishable from all other nuns by the fact that if you peer underneath the dark cavity of her hood, you will find that there is no face there at all. Such human inquisitiveness causes the nun to glide quickly towards the Old Friends Meeting House where she walks through an archway which has been bricked up for more than a century.

Her story is linked with the Chapel and Priory of St Bartholomew which was built shortly after 1120 and destroyed, together with the whole town, during a naval attack upon Brighthelmstone by the French fleet in 1514. During the twelfth century the Priory, which was only a small one and dependent on the Priory of St Pancras, Lewes, was guarded by a detachment of soldiers against the depredations of the bands of robbers who roamed the Sussex countryside.

The girl—no one knows her name—was a novice in a religious institution not far away, beautiful of course by tradition, and she fell in love with one of the soldiers who guarded St Bartholomew's. The two eloped and were chased by soldiers. The novice and her lover, who put up a valiant fight, were finally overcome and brought back to face the rough justice of the time—the traditional punishment of being bricked up alive together within the walls of St Bartholomew's.

This is a familiar story. There are countless legends of eloping nuns being walled up alive with their lovers; but it must be remembered that countless girls in those days were forced into convents without their having any desire to pursue the way of life prescribed by these institutions, and the savage punishment of being walled up alive for the crime, not so much of unchastity, but of getting married, was not uncommon in those days. Though a dreadful death, it was convenient for the ecclesiastical authorities, for it did not actually involve them in the shedding of blood; and as the wretches slowly starved to death, the good Abbot and his monks could pray for their souls on the other side of the brickwork.

This unfortunate nun has for the last eight hundred years haunted the scene of her miserable incarceration and death. But why the nun only? Why has not the soldier joined his mistress in the haunting? The reason is that by tradition the nun had committed the far greater sin, and has probably damned her immortal soul for all eternity, poor thing.

Brighton really came into its own when the Prince Regent, later George IV, settled there and built his fantastic Pavilion. He was followed by his Court and society, for whom the many rows of splendid Regency houses, now the glory of Brighton, were built.

Prinny himself is said to haunt the underground passageway which connects the Royal Pavilion with the Dome, though not many have seen him. Martha Gunn, the famous bathing woman, is said to haunt the Pavilion kitchens which she frequented during her lifetime.

Queen Victoria quickly abandoned Brighton as a royal residence as it was far too vulgar and public for her tastes. She sold her uncle's Pavilion, ghosts and all, to the town for £50,000, which has turned out to be an excellent investment, for, restored in all its splendour. this unique building is now one of the showplaces of England.

Despite Victoria's frown, Brighton greatly prospered during her long reign, for the curious but probably human reason that it was one of the few places in her realm where Victorianism did not take a firm foothold. Brighton always remained raffish and gay.

But many aspects of the grinding puritanism which was one of the characteristics of nineteenth-century life took root in Brighton, as was only to be expected. The harsh poor laws and the unfeeling treatment of unmarried mothers caused untold suffering and unhappiness all over the country. In consequence of this, a particularly interesting haunting resulted in Finsbury Road, which is in early-Victorian Brighton, on the slopes of the steep hill which rises on the eastern side of the Old Steyne valley. The building concerned had once been a workhouse, and then later became a Church Army Home for Fallen Women.

In 1952 this building was taken over by Mr and Mrs B. B. Funnell, who own a furniture-making business, Bevan Funnell Limited. Mr Funnell at the time was a member of Hove Borough Council, and became Mayor of Hove in 1960. He was also a Special Constable, and both he and his wife are practical, matter-of-fact business people. The truth of their story is indisputable, and there is no question of their imagining the strange and ghostly things they experienced in this building.

As soon as they took over the place and moved in with their staff and equipment, strange things began to happen. Although the building was locked up carefully every night, as all business premises are, the constable on the beat continually found the doors all unlocked and Mr Funnell had to return to lock up again. So frequently did this happen that Mr Funnell and the police were convinced that intruders were getting into the place, although there was no evidence that this was so, and nothing had been stolen.

The matter was investigated by Brighton CID, who went there one night with Mr Funnell to find the place unlocked, after all the

doors had been previously locked most carefully in the presence of several persons when the staff left earlier that evening.

Upon entering the building both Mr Funnell and the police officers heard footsteps plainly on the upper floor. It was the sound of people running about and talking.

The police, confident of arresting these troublesome intruders at last, ran up the stairs. The noises and the footsteps were coming from a large room in the upper storey. The police officers flung the door of the room open.

Instantly the sounds ceased as if they had been cut off by a switch. There was no human being in that room, and the whole building was now wrapped in utter silence. Puzzled, the police made a thorough search of the building, but found no one and could find no cause for the strange and quite unmistakable sounds of people talking and walking about which both they and Mr Funnell had heard very plainly.

Baffled, the police left. Someone, they said, must be playing some kind of trick.

But trick or no, the noises continued and increased, and soon began to be heard in the daytime. The staff became a little un-nerved by the ghostly footsteps tramping about on the floor above them. They often went up to the floor above to try and locate the sounds, or surprise the intruders, but, like the police, whenever they opened the door of this haunted room they were greeted by an unnerving silence.

Once one of the workmen saw a ghostly woman in black standing in the workshop. At first he thought it was a customer, and turned to Mr Funnell to comment to him upon the fact, but when he looked again at the woman she had vanished. A thorough search failed to find any such woman in the building.

The Funnels and their staff were now convinced that they were in a haunted building and they began to make inquiries about its history and found out that it had been a workhouse and then a Home for Fallen Women. Unmarried females unfortunate enough to have children were treated harshly in Victorian times, and institu-tions for their "rehabilitation and salvation" were run practically on penal lines.

This Finsbury Road building was a gloomy place and it had seen much tragedy and unhappiness. "You could feel the misery in the very walls," Mrs Funnell said.

In the centre of the building was a small room they used as an office. Across the passage was a cloakroom and lavatory.

One day in this passage they were assailed by a strong perfume. This was no ordinary perfume and it was smelt by everybody. Mrs Funnell described it as a perfume such as she had never smelt before. It was a heavy, musky smell, almost like incense. But it was by no means an ecclesiastical smell. It was peculiarly feminine and sensuous—a woman's scent, quite unforgettable.

Sometimes this extraordinary perfume would seem to blow in waves through the building. They could discover no reason, no origin for it. Nothing that was used in the workshop could produce such a smell.

Spectral smells of this kind are not uncommon. They were noted at Borley Rectory (in pre-Price days) and also at Hinton Ampner.

One day a heavy knitted cardigan in black wool appeared mysteriously in the cloakroom. It was hanging on a peg and was deeply impregnated with this strange perfume. No one owned it. It had been left there by no one. A day or two later it vanished as mysteriously as it had come, and was never seen again.

The pet dog belonging to Mr and Mrs Funnell was on one occasion found shut in one of the upstairs rooms by a heavy sliding door which could not have been accidentally closed by the dog itself. There was no one on the premises who could have closed the door.

It is true that that little mystery as well as the problem of the black knitted cardigan impregnated with the mysterious perfume, could have had a natural explanation; and in fact the Funnells suspected for a long time that they were being subjected to tricks played upon them by a person or persons who had some interest in getting them to leave the building.

But even supposing this were so, some of the things that happened completely baffled explanation.

The eerie business of Mrs Funnell's typewriter set all their nerves on edge. This typewriter was in the little office across the corridor from the cloakroom. Mrs Funnell at that time did all the office work connected with the firm's business and was the only one on the premises who used the typewriter. Upon a number of occasions this typewriter would be heard typing fast and furiously when no one was in the room. When the door was opened the noise of typing instantly stopped. No one was ever able to explain this mystery.

As was to be expected, the Funnells had plenty of trouble with their staff over the haunting. Many were frankly scared off straight away. Others laughed at the idea of ghosts being there, but soon

changed their minds. Others stuck it out of loyalty to the firm, or a reluctance to believe in such supernatural nonsense—in particular one woman who at first was plump, jolly and looked the picture of health. After a while the atmosphere in the factory at Finsbury Road played upon her nerves and health to such an extent that she was a changed person. She lost weight, became worried and unhappy. It was as though the weird feeling of misery which was in the very walls of the building had in some way become transferred to her.

In 1953, a year after the Funnells took the building, some local spiritualists held a seance there in an attempt to get in touch with the troubled spirits, often a way by which a haunting can be ended.

Mrs Funnell attended this seance, during which the ghost was apparently contacted by the medium, a man, who asked it why it was troubled. The reply came through in a girl's voice, speaking in an uneducated Sussex accent.

"Matron is cruel to me. I am desperately unhappy. I've tried to be good, but I can't." She sounded a miserable, weeping thing, said Mrs Funnell.

The Funnels were sceptical about this seance. After all, it was well known that the place had been a home for unmarried mothers in Victorian times, and it was easy to imagine that it had been a house of desperate unhappiness and harsh, even pitiless, discipline.

Nevertheless, a strange thing happened immediately after the seance had finished. As soon as the spiritualists had left, there was a tremendous noise of people running about the building, of doors banging, people calling, of pounding footsteps.

And then suddenly there was silence.

This silence lasted uninterruptedly until the Sunday before the Christmas of 1954, when Mr Funnell went to the office in the building by himself to catch up with a rush of work. By now the ghosts had been almost forgotten, and the strange, unaccountable events of the past couple of years had completely gone out of his mind which at that moment was concerned only with the urgency of coping with the rush of Christmas business.

He went into the little office where his wife's typewriter had been heard unaccountably typing in her absence. It was a bright sunny morning and there were no shadows or reflections in the little room which was half-flooded with December sunshine as he opened the door.

He got the shock of his life.

As he entered the room he heard something drop, and he turned

to look at the sloping desk which ran along the wall to the corner of the room. In this corner, which was perfectly light and without any shadows, he saw a dark grey shape upon the desk. The shape was half-hooded and in some strange way incomplete. It was a shape without a great deal of form, though it seemed to have density and substance. It would appear that when Mr Funnell came into the room it was in the act of materialization, and it was materializing on the desk, resting upon it.

Mr Funnell said that this thing seemed to emanate a strange and deadly power, which filled him with an overwhelming fear. The effect upon him was devastating. He fled.

When he arrived home he was ashen, and his wife said that he looked almost like one dead himself.

Mr Funnell was so shaken by his experience that he told the story to the Vicar of his Church, who arranged an exorcism. What took place at the exorcism was not revealed, but the exorcist, a Sussex man, claimed to have been able to make contact easily with this troubled spirit and was able to give it such comfort as was necessary to prevent its further activities in Finsbury Place.

Whether one can believe this or not, the Funnells were not troubled any more by this particular ghost. They presently left the building which was pulled down, flats being erected in its place. But strange noises are still reported from the part of the flats approximating the position where the little office and cloakroom were.

The feeling of malignancy, directed towards him, as opposed to his own natural fear, which was reported by Mr Funnell, raises interesting questions. He described it specifically as a feeling of hate towards him. Some would say it was an evil spirit"from the bottomless pit of hell"and this would explain the sensation he felt. On the other hand the exorcist apparently did not come into contact with any malignant spirit of this kind. There may have been more than one spirit there, of course. Judging by the uproar sometimes heard in the place there must have been a whole flock of ghosts disturbing the building.

There are some who think that the dead are envious of the living, hating them because they possess flesh and blood they no longer have, and desires and lusts they can no longer satisfy. This is a very old idea and is embodied in the primeval Cult of the Dead, which held that the young in particular resent death and return to the place of their demise in order to torment and terrify the living.

Equally terrifying and somewhat more grisly was the experience

some years ago of a Brighton antiquarian. He had heard that there was a hoard of old books in the basement of a junk shop near the junction of Upper Rock Gardens and Edward Street, a part of Brighton which was built in the early years of the nineteenth century.

He found the books stored in what had been the old kitchen and which was now disused—a musty, desolate place which did not boast an electric light. His attention was particularly drawn to an alcove in which was a great stone sink shaped like an ancient sarcophagus. Above the alcove was an archway of small, blood-red bricks set in a curious zig-zag pattern. The place had a strange, eerie atmosphere, and had it not been for the very promising collection of old books which were stored there he would not have cared to stay. It was getting towards evening, and the owner of the junk shop said that he never remained in the place after dark, and gave him the keys, telling him to look through the books at his leisure and lock the place up when he went.

Arming himself with a couple of candles, a flask of coffee and some sandwiches, the antiquarian settled down in the gloomy basement and began to browse through the fascinating books he found there, oblivious at first of the silence which was deep, oppressive and unearthly.

After a while a feeling of macabre chill began to creep over him. The place had an atmosphere of evil as well as coldness which made him feel afraid and uneasy. Suddenly the books lost all interest for him and he could not shake off the feeling that he was not alone in that silent, candle-lit basement kitchen, with its great coffin-like sink, and that someone—or indeed something—was there also, watching him.

He stood up suddenly and looked towards the archway, and to his terror he saw a naked woman standing beside that dreadful sink. The woman was fat, almost shapeless, and his terror was caused by the fact that she had the face of someone long dead, with eyeless sockets and cheeks falling in with decay. But her limbs, he said, were swollen and blotched. It was an appalling and ghastly sight.

The spectre seemed to hover there beside the great sink, the eyeless sockets appearing to be fixed upon him.

"Who are you? What do you want?" stammered the terrified antiquarian.

If he expected a reply—and ghosts sometimes do reply, though it is said they have to be spoken to first before they can speak themselves—he was disappointed. The ghost just stood there, or rather hovered, before his eyes.

He had a book in his hand and he suddenly flung it at the apparition. It went straight through her and hit the archway behind. Then slowly the thing disappeared.

Gathering his belongings, the antiquarian left in a hurry, no longer interested in the fascinating old books.

He had arranged to leave the keys with a woman who lived in the upper part of the tall old house.

"Good gracious me, sir!" she exclaimed when he knocked on her door. "Have you been down there in that dungeon? You look as pale as a ghost. Me—I wouldn't go down there for all the money in the world. The old boy had no right to let you—not after dark."

The antiquarian asked what it was down there that was so frightening, not revealing what he himself had seen, and the woman told him that the basement had been haunted for the past half-century or so, and that she herself had once met the ghost on the old cellar stairs, and the thing had gone right through her, leaving her in a state of shivers for weeks afterwards and bringing back her rheumatism and arthritis in the most painful fashion.

It transpired that about sixty years previously a man had murdered his wife in that kitchen and had dismembered her body in that great old sink, with the object of burying the remains underneath the stone floor of the kitchen. Fortunately the law caught up with him before he could complete his odious work.

A Mayoress of Brighton, as well as a Mayoress of Hove, was involved with a Brighton ghost. This was Mrs Anne Johnson, wife of Major A. J. M. Johnson, T.D., who was Mayor of Brighton in 1960–61. Shortly after the last war Mrs Johnson was living in a flat in Prestonville Road.

Every night as she got into bed she noticed a curious sensation that somebody else was sitting on the end of the bed, although no one else was in the room. After a while, the invisible presence vanished. She got used to her nightly unseen visitor, although she did not stay in that particular flat for long. After she had vacated the place, a retired member of the Brighton Police Force told her that it was at that flat and in that very room that a man had murdered his wife. Mrs Johnson is not a psychic type of woman and has never had such experiences either before or since.

A curious haunting took place at the turn of the century in Whitchurch House, one of those large detached residences which face Brighton's Preston Park on the main road coming into the

town, and it was told many years later by a woman who had been a housemaid there at the time, now a Mrs M. E. Holland of Woodingdean, Brighton.

Whitchurch House stood in its own grounds and had its own stables and coachhouse. Leading off the dining-room was a small room called the den, which had french windows opening on to the lawn. Mrs Holland's duties included cleaning the den, which she did at six-thirty every morning.

At this hour precisely every morning these french windows slowly opened and slowly shut again. At first Mrs Holland thought it was the wind, or that it was a trick by one of the other maids. But there was no wind and there were no other maids about.

What was really strange was the fact that when the doors opened they were securely locked and bolted, and so they were after they had closed again.

This happened regularly every morning at half-past six. The puzzled Mrs Holland regarded the phenomenon with great curiosity. She tried to stop them while they were being opened in this peculiar manner, but was unable to, for they were being moved by an irresistible force. Once she opened the doors herself before half-past six, but they immediately shut themselves and waited until the appointed time.

On each occasion when the doors opened themselves in this mysterious way, cold air came into the den, regardless of whether it was cold outside or not.

Becoming frightened, Mrs Holland told the master of the house, who at first laughed at her, but then got up early one morning and witnessed the phenomenon himself. Visibly shaken, he sold up and left the house immediately, leaving the mystery unsolved.

This is the kind of ghost story which surely no one could possibly have invented.

INDEX

Acknowledgements

The editor and publishers express their acknowledgements to Geoffrey Bles, Ltd., and the Executors of the late Lord Halifax for permission to condense from *Lord Halifax's Ghost Book*, and to Rider and Co. for permission to condense from *Ghosts with a Purpose* by Elliott O'Donnell.